3RD EDITION

business law

Pearson Education Australia
Unit 4, Level 3
14 Aquatic Drive
Frenchs Forest NSW 2086

www.pearsoned.com.au

Senior Acquisitions Editor: Joy Whitton
Project Editor: Sandra Goodall
Editorial Coordinator: Maria Lynch
Copy Editor: Kathryn Lamberton
Proofreader: Annie Chandler
Indexing by Jonathan Jermey
Cover design by Mazart Designs
Typeset by Midland Typesetters, Australia

Printed in China (EPC)

3 4 5 11 10 09 08

National Library of Australia
Cataloguing-in-Publication Data

Gibson, Andrew, 1947 - .
Business law.

3rd ed.
Includes index.
ISBN 9780733981012 (pbk).

ISBN 0 7339 8101 1 (pbk).

1. Business law – Australia. 2. Commercial law – Australia.
I. Fraser, Douglas, 1947– . II. Title.

346.9407

PEARSON
Prentice
Hall

An imprint of Pearson Education Australia (a division of Pearson Australia Group Pty Ltd)

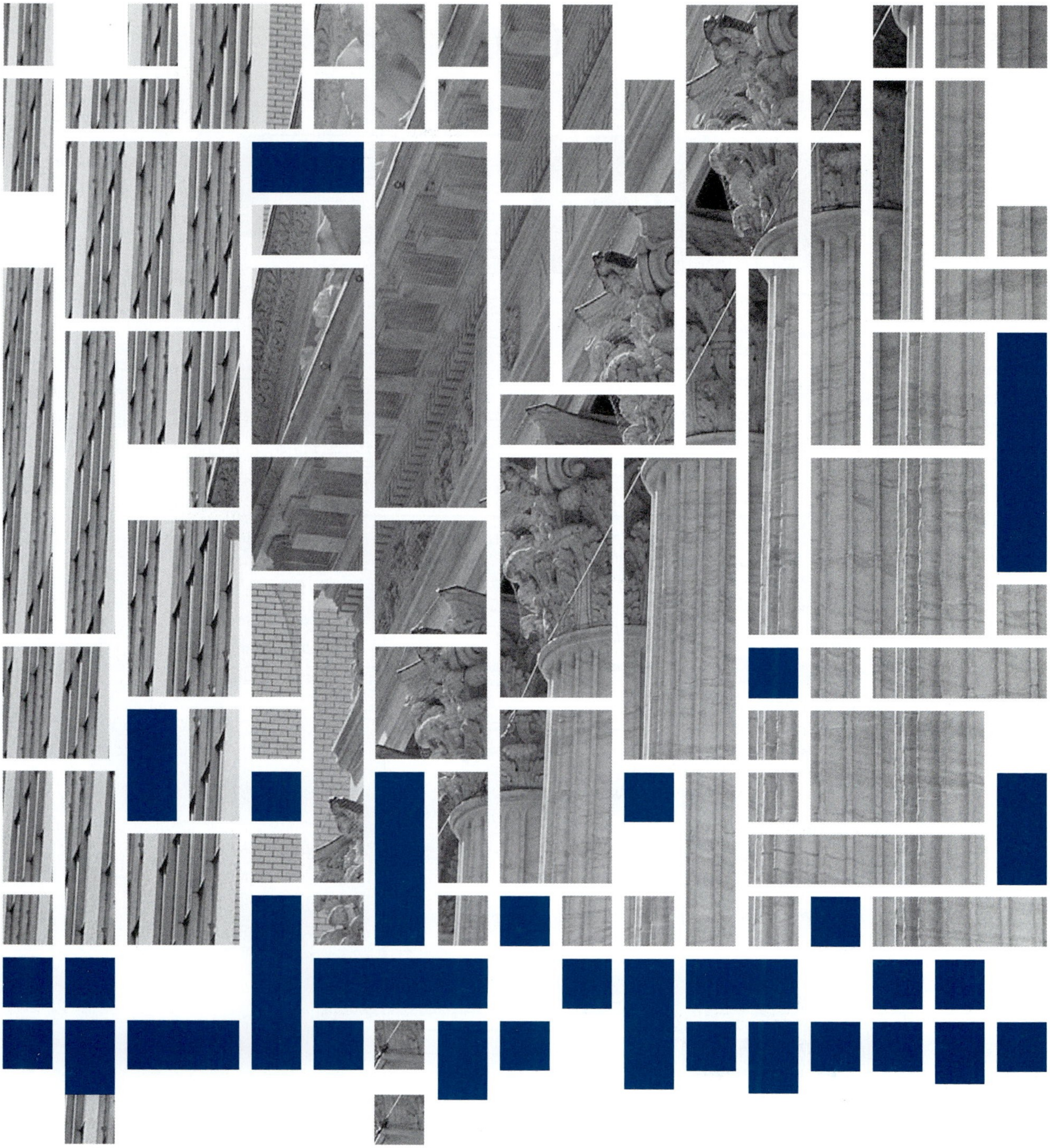

3RD EDITION

business law

Andy Gibson and Douglas Fraser

PEARSON

Education Australia

How to Use This Book

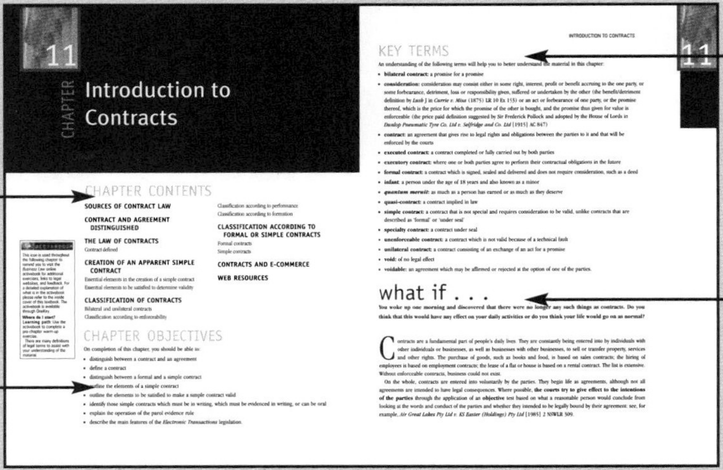

Chapter contents provide a snapshot of the chapter

Chapter objectives establish learning goals and create a framework for later chapter review

Key terms introduce terms which may be unfamiliar to you and which have specialised meanings

A '**what if . . .**' real-life scenario opens each chapter. These are designed to help you discover the relevance of the chapter content to your life situation

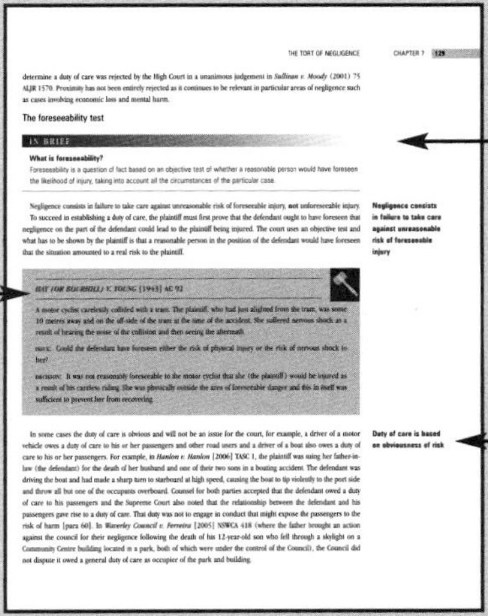

In brief boxes summarise key points relevant to the particular area of law under discussion

Cases have been integrated into the text and have been broken up into a number of parts, to make them as user-friendly as possible

Margin notes highlight particular important points, thereby ensuring they are easily and quickly found

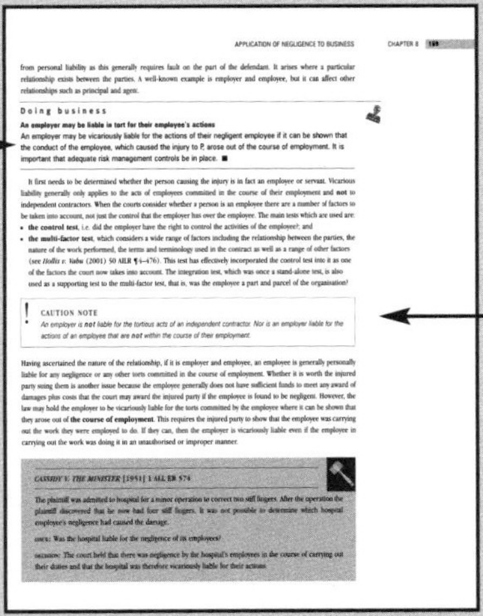

Doing business boxes are intended to put a particular topic into a business context and show how to avoid or minimise legal problems

Caution notes alert you to areas of the law that might contain difficult concepts to understand or to a possible misapplication or misperception of the law

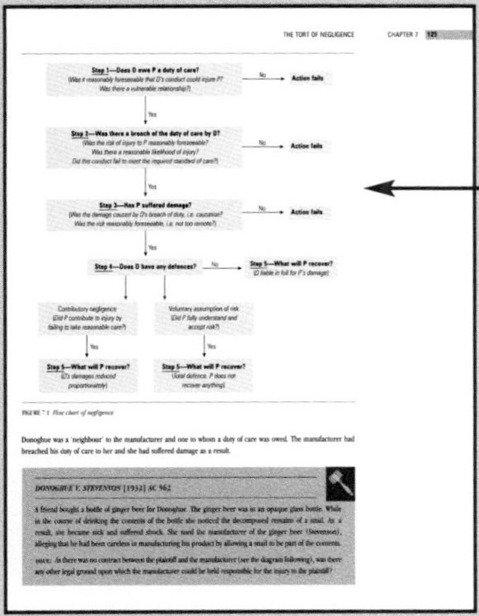

THE TORT OF NEGLIGENCE CHAPTER 7 125

Step 1—Does D owe P a duty of care?
(Was it reasonably foreseeable that D's conduct could injure P? Was there a vulnerable relationship?)
No → **Action fails**
Yes ↓

Step 2—Was there a breach of the duty of care by D?
(Was the risk of injury to P reasonably foreseeable? Was there a reasonable likelihood of injury? Did the conduct fail to meet the required standard of care?)
No → **Action fails**
Yes ↓

Step 3—Has P suffered damage?
(Was the damage caused by D's breach of duty, i.e. causation? Was the risk reasonably foreseeable, i.e. not too remote?)
No → **Action fails**
Yes ↓

Step 4—Does D have any defences?
No → **Step 5—What will P recover?** *(D liable in full for P's damage)*

Contributory negligence *(Did P contribute to injury by failing to take reasonable care?)*
Yes ↓
Step 5—What will P recover? *(D's damages reduced proportionately)*

Voluntary assumption of risk *(Did P fully understand and accept risk?)*
Yes ↓
Step 5—What will P recover? *(total defence. P does not recover anything)*

FIGURE 7.1 *Flow chart of negligence*

Donoghue was a 'neighbour' to the manufacturer and one to whom a duty of care was owed. The manufacturer had breached his duty of care to her and she had suffered damage as a result.

DONOGHUE V. STEVENSON [1932] AC 562

A friend bought a bottle of ginger beer for Donoghue. The ginger beer was in an opaque glass bottle. While in the course of drinking the contents of the bottle she noticed the decomposed remains of a snail. As a result, she became sick and suffered shock. She sued the manufacturer of the ginger beer (Stevenson), alleging that he had been careless in manufacturing his product by allowing a snail to be part of the contents.

ISSUE: *As there was no contract between the plaintiff and the manufacturer (see the diagram following), was there any other legal ground upon which the manufacturer could be held responsible for the injury to the plaintiff?*

Contains numerous **flow charts** and **diagrams** and adopts the **'plain English'** approach. These features, together with the section on **how to study law**, should help you achieve the learning outcomes for what is a complex and challenging subject

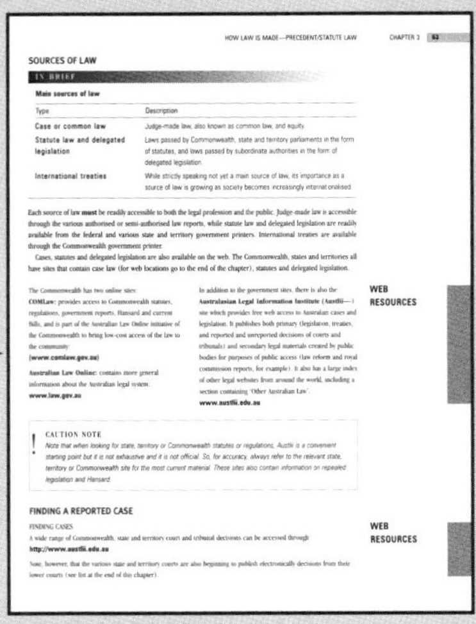

HOW LAW IS MADE—PRECEDENT/STATUTE LAW CHAPTER 3 63

SOURCES OF LAW

IN BRIEF

Main sources of law

Type	Description
Case or common law	Judge-made law, also known as common law, and equity.
Statute law and delegated legislation	Laws passed by Commonwealth, state and territory parliaments in the form of statutes, and laws passed by subordinate authorities in the form of delegated legislation.
International treaties	While strictly speaking not yet a main source of law, its importance as a source of law is growing as society becomes increasingly internationalised.

Each source of law **must** be readily accessible to both the legal profession and the public. Judge-made law is accessible through the various authorised or semi-authorised law reports, while statute law and delegated legislation are readily available from the federal and various state and territory government printers. International treaties are available through the Commonwealth government printer.

Cases, statutes and delegated legislation are also available on the web. The Commonwealth, states and territories all have sites that contain case law (for web locations go to the end of the chapter), statutes and delegated legislation.

WEB RESOURCES

The Commonwealth has two online sites:
COMLaw: provides access to Commonwealth statutes, regulations, government reports, Hansard and current Bills, and is part of the Australian Law Online initiative of the Commonwealth to bring low-cost access of the law to the community
(www.comlaw.gov.au)
Australian Law Online: contains more general information about the Australian legal system.
www.law.gov.au

In addition to the government sites, there is also the **Australasian Legal Information Institute (Austlii—)** site which provides free web access to Australian cases and legislation. It publishes both primary (legislation, treaties, and reported and unreported decisions of courts and tribunals) and secondary legal materials created by public bodies for purposes of public access (law reform and royal commission reports, for example). It also has a large index of other legal websites from around the world, including a section containing 'Other Australian Law'.
www.austlii.edu.au

! CAUTION NOTE
Note that when looking for state, territory or Commonwealth statutes or regulations, Austlii is a convenient starting point but it is not exhaustive and it is not official. So, for accuracy, always refer to the relevant state, territory or Commonwealth site for the most current material. These sites also contain information on repealed legislation and Hansard.

FINDING A REPORTED CASE

WEB RESOURCES

FINDING CASES
A wide range of Commonwealth, state and territory court and tribunal decisions can be accessed through:
http://www.austlii.edu.au

Note, however, that the various state and territory courts are also beginning to publish electronically decisions from their lower courts (see list at the end of this chapter).

References to **appropriate websites** for you to go to for further information on a particular topic can be found throughout, as well as at the end of, many chapters

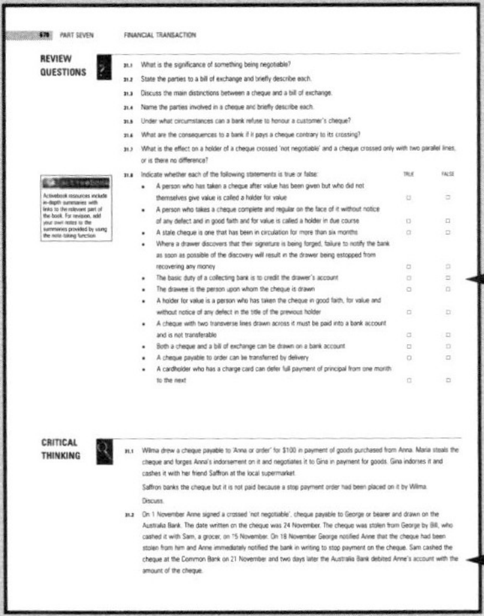

678 PART SEVEN FINANCIAL TRANSACTION

REVIEW QUESTIONS

31.1 What is the significance of something being negotiable?
31.2 State the parties to a bill of exchange and briefly describe each.
31.3 Discuss the main distinctions between a cheque and a bill of exchange.
31.4 Name the parties involved in a cheque and briefly describe each.
31.5 Under what circumstances can a bank refuse to honour a customer's cheque?
31.6 What are the consequences to a bank if it pays a cheque contrary to its crossing?
31.7 What is the effect on a holder of a cheque crossed 'not negotiable' and a cheque crossed only with two parallel lines, or is there no difference?
31.8 Indicate whether each of the following statements is true or false:

	TRUE	FALSE
• A person who has taken a cheque after value has been given but who did not themselves give value is called a holder for value	□	□
• A person who takes a cheque complete and regular on the face of it without notice of any defect and in good faith and for value is called a holder in due course	□	□
• A stale cheque is one that has been in circulation for more than six months	□	□
• Where a drawer discovers that their signature is being forged, failure to notify the bank as soon as possible of the discovery will result in the drawer being estopped from recovering any money	□	□
• The basic duty of a collecting bank is to credit the drawer's account	□	□
• The drawee is the person upon whom the cheque is drawn	□	□
• A holder for value is a person who has taken the cheque in good faith, for value and without notice of any defect in the title of the previous holder	□	□
• A cheque with two transverse lines drawn across it must be paid into a bank account and is not transferable	□	□
• Both a cheque and a bill of exchange can be drawn on a bank account	□	□
• A cheque payable to order can be transferred by delivery	□	□
• A cardholder who has a charge card can defer full payment of principal from one month to the next	□	□

activebook
Activebook resources include in-depth summaries with links to the relevant part of the book. For revision, add your own notes to the summaries provided by using the note-taking function

CRITICAL THINKING

31.1 Wilma drew a cheque payable to 'Anna or order' for $100 in payment of goods purchased from Anna. Maria steals the cheque and forges Anna's indorsement on it and negotiates it to Gina in payment for goods. Gina indorses it and cashes it with her friend Saffron at the local supermarket.
Saffron banks the cheque but it is not paid because a stop payment order had been placed on it by Wilma.
Discuss.

31.2 On 1 November Anne signed a crossed 'not negotiable', cheque payable to George or bearer and drawn on the Australia Bank. The date written on the cheque was 24 November. The cheque was stolen from George by Bill, who cashed it with Sam, a grocer, on 15 November. On 18 November George notified Anne that the cheque had been stolen from him and Anne immediately notified the bank in writing to stop payment on the cheque. Sam cashed the cheque at the Common Bank on 21 November and two days later the Australia Bank debited Anne's account with the amount of the cheque.

Chapter **Review questions** assist your understanding of key concepts and issues as they arise and also serve as a quick revision tool

Critical thinking questions are included at the end of each chapter to encourage discussion and debate among students

The **Activebook** is a new feature. It is an interactive online book that contains chapter summaries, examples of legal documents and forms, case extracts, and statute extracts. It includes interactive quizzes and questions that check your understanding of concepts, and provides feedback and model answers. You can also make your own notes against key parts of the text

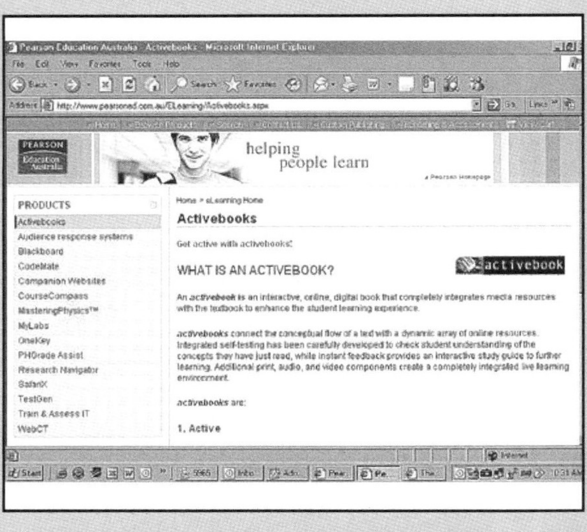

CONTENTS

Brief Contents

CONTENTS

Detailed Contents

PREFACE

Preface

The third edition of *Business Law* continues to provide students of commercial or business law with an accessible and student-friendly, but authoritative and comprehensive textbook. *Business Law* provides extensive coverage of business law topics and considers the legal environment in which businesses must operate. Care has been taken to ensure that the text represents current law in **all** states and territories. *Business Law* will satisfy the requirements of most business or commercial law subjects throughout Australia.

The third edition has retained the distinctive layout of the first two editions. The learning aids such as **In brief**, **Doing business** and **Caution note**, the **'boxed' cases**, **margin notes** and **flowcharts** continue to feature strongly throughout the text.

A number of changes have been made to the third edition. Briefly, these are:

- the placement of **Key terms** at the beginning of each chapter to try to assist students to better understand what they read;
- the placing of the chapter on insurance in Part Three following the chapters on tort law. As the text notes in Chapter 6, Introduction to the Law of Tort, on page 113, 'The law of tort is an area of the law that often only becomes relevant to people and businesses after the happening of a loss-making event.' The purpose of insurance is to minimise the effect of a loss-making event and so it seemed more appropriate to have the chapter on insurance following on from the chapters on the law of tort;
- topic coverage has been increased in a number of areas to reflect changing needs in student understanding of how the law interfaces and interacts with business. For example, coverage has been expanded on specialist courts, the developments taking place in the legal system with eCourts, the growth of facilitative processes such as alternative dispute resolution, the use of the web as a source for case law and legislation, the effects of the evolution of the civil liability reforms to the law of negligence, and the introduction of the uniform defamation laws. The previous chapter on white collar crime and business ethics has been expanded and split into two chapters, Chapter 4 dealing with criminal law in a business setting and Chapter 5 discussing ethics and morals in the context of business law situations.

THE LEGAL ENVIRONMENT OF BUSINESS

Business Law presents topics that are traditionally part of business law courses.

Part One—Legal Framework contains three chapters that introduce the student to the legal framework of business. Chapter 1 discusses what law is, the major sources and categories of law and how the legal system developed in Australia. Chapter 2 examines the court system within which the legal system operates, the growth in specialist courts, the impact of eCourts on the legal system and the growth in alternative forms of dispute resolution. Chapter 3 considers how the law is made.

Part Two—Business Crime and Ethics While the majority of the legal concepts covered by this book deal with business and commerce in the context of civil law, the criminal law also has considerable impact. Chapter 4 discusses these criminal law aspects of business relationships. It considers white collar crime as well as examples of criminal offences created by the various statutes referred to in the book. Chapter 5 briefly discusses business ethics and morals and emphasises the idea 'just because it is legal, that does not make it right'. The concepts of ethics and morals are considered in the context of the law with reference to several ethical theories.

Part Three—Civil Liability and Insuring against Risk begins by looking at the question of tortious liability, that is the liability of an individual or business for any injury or damage that they may have caused to an innocent party and considers the impact that the civil liability changes may have on the laws of negligence. To assist students' understanding of tort law, and negligence in particular, the law of tort is considered over four chapters. Chapter 6 explains the general principles of tort law. Chapter 7 examines perhaps the most important of the torts—negligence and the changes that the civil liability legislation introduced in most Australian jurisdictions might have on negligence. Chapter 8 then explores some of the areas of tort absorbed by negligence, as well as some of the categories of negligence and again considers the impact that the civil liability legislation might have on occupier's liability and recreational providers. Chapter 9 rounds off the discussion of tort law by considering some of the other areas of tort law apart from negligence, such as nuisance, trespass, the new uniform defamation laws and the economic torts, that are relevant to business. Chapter 10 considers how to minimise the effects of the law of tort, and risk, on business by considering the ways in which assets can be protected against damage or loss through insurance.

Part Four—Law of Contracts contains 10 chapters that cover the basics of the common law of contracts. Without contracts, business and the community as we know them today would not exist.

Part Five—Consumer Law contains five chapters. The primary focus of this section is on consumer rights and protection. Chapter 21 examines the sale of goods and Chapter 22 discusses the terms implied into contracts by statute law. It examines their interpretation and their application to contracts involving both consumers and 'non' consumers (businesses). Chapter 23 looks at consumer protection legislation and Chapter 24 explores consumer credit and privacy. Chapter 25 examines the growing importance of electronic commerce.

Part Six—Business Organisations and the Law begins with a chapter on agency. The three following chapters discuss the common forms of business ownership that exist in Australia today—corporations (companies) and partnerships—with the third chapter examining which business entity is most suited to a particular business. Chapter 30 examines the impact of the restrictive trade practices provisions of the *Trade Practices Act 1974* (Cth) on businesses.

Part Seven—Financial Transactions Chapter 31 looks at the different methods that are used to pay for goods or services, that is by bill of exchange, cheque or credit/debit card. The purpose and operation of the *Financial Transaction Reports Act 1988* (Cth) is also examined.

Part Eight—Debt Recovery examines what happens to those people or businesses who cannot pay their debts. The chapter looks briefly at the process of debt recovery in the lower courts before examining bankruptcy in detail. It then describes liquidation, administration and receivership of companies.

Part Nine—Types of Property covers two types of property. Chapter 33 begins by looking at the distinction between real property (or realty) and personal property and goes on to took at interests in land and how ownership and possession may be obtained as well as the mortgaging and leasing of land. Chapter 34 looks at a completely different kind of 'property' right called intellectual property, such as patents, designs, copyrights and trademarks.

Part Ten—Employment covers aspects of the work environment, including the new WorkChoices legislation, and the employment relationship.

BUSINESS APPLICATION

Many business law textbooks take a legalistic approach to presenting legal topics to business students. A common comment from students in business courses is: 'Why are we studying law? We aren't going to be lawyers. If we need legal help or advice, we will go and see a lawyer.' While this statement is partly true, the reality is that an awareness of one's legal rights and a general knowledge of the law is important in business today. This book recognises that what is important to students studying commercial or business law is the application of court decisions, statutes and government regulation to business and their daily lives.

There are a number of features that have been incorporated into* Business Law *that will demonstrate the application of law and government regulation to the business environment.

There are many features in the book that are designed for your benefit. These features are tools to help make your learning more effective and to help you to see the relevance of the book's content to your life and work. We strongly suggest you spend some time reading **How to Use This Book**, on pages iv and v, to get the most out of your text and the new interactive online Activebook version.

We would be grateful for any comments or suggestions from teachers or students concerning *Business Law*. Your feedback will improve future editions.

This book is up to date as at 30 July 2006 although it should be noted that changes to the law that take place after the 30 July may be found on the Pearson Education companion website to assist users to keep up to date. You can contact us at these email addresses (and yes, you will get a reply as we do appreciate the input):

andygibson100@hotmail.com.au
dfraser1@ozemail.com.au

Andy Gibson
Douglas Fraser
September 2006

KEY

Key to Case Report Abbreviations

Some of the more commonly encountered case reports and references that can be found in Commercial Law are mentioned below. However, this is not an exhaustive list of all the case reports and references. Where the case reports are from another country or are a reference or journal, details appear in brackets after the report's name.

ABC	Australian Bankruptcy Cases
AC	Appeal Cases 1891 to present (England)
ACL	Australian Current Law (a reference guide)
ACLC	Australian Company Law Cases
ACLD	Australian Company Law Digest
ALJ	Australian Law Journal (articles only)
ALJR	Australian Law Journal Reports
ALR	Australian Law Reports
ASLR	Australian Securities Law Reporter
ATPR	Australian Trade Practices Reporter
All ER	All England Reports (England)
App Cas	Law Reports, Appeal Cases (England)
ATR	Australian Torts Reports
BCLC	Butterworths Company Law Cases
CB	Common Bench Reports (England)
CLR	Commonwealth Law Reports
Ch	Law Reports, Chancery Division 1891 to present (England)
DLR	Dominion Law Reports (Canada)
ER	English Reports (England)
Ex/Exch	Exchequer Reports (England)
FLC	Family Law Reports
FLR	Federal Law Reports
HL	House of Lords (England)

ILJ	Insurance Law Journal (articles)
IPR	Intellectual Property Reports
KB/QB	King's Bench/Queen's Bench Reports 1891 to present (England)
LIJ	Law Institute Journal of Victoria (articles)
LQR	Law Quarterly Reviews (articles)
LR(NSW)	Law Reports (New South Wales)
LSB	Law Society Bulletin (South Australia) (articles)
LSJ	Law Society Journal (New South Wales)
LTR	Law Times Reports (England)
Lloyd's Rep	Lloyd's Reports (England)
MLR	Modern Law Review (articles)
NSWLR	New South Wales Law Reports
NSWR	New South Wales Reports
NTR	Northern Territory Reports
NZLR	New Zealand Law Reports
QdR	Queensland Reports
QSCR	Queensland Supreme Court Reports
QSR	Queensland State Reports
QWN	Queensland Weekly Notes
SALR	South Australian Law Reports
SASR	South Australian State Reports
SCR(NSW)	Supreme Court Reports (New South Wales)
SCR(NSW)Eq	Supreme Court Reports, Equity (New South Wales)
SR(NSW)	State Reports (New South Wales)
TLR	Times Law Reports (England)
TPC	Trade Practices Cases
TasLR	Tasmanian Law Reports
VLR	Victorian Law Reports
VR	Victorian Reports
WALR	Western Australian Law Reports
WAR	Western Australian Reports
WLR	Weekly Law Reports (England)
WN(NSW)	Weekly Notes (New South Wales)
WR	Weekly Reporter (England)

TABLE OF Cases

Page numbers in **bold** indicate boxed discussions of cases

TABLE OF Statutes

UNITED KINGDOM

COMMONWEALTH

AUSTRALIAN CAPITAL TERRITORY

NEW SOUTH WALES

NORTHERN TERRITORY

QUEENSLAND

SOUTH AUSTRALIA

TASMANIA

VICTORIA

WESTERN AUSTRALIA

UNITED STATES

STUDY SKILLS

Study Skills

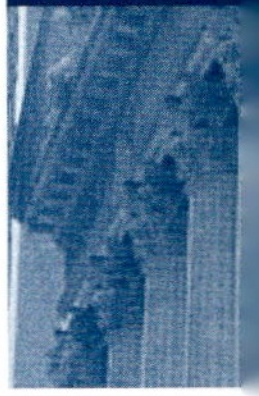

To get the most out of studying Business or Commercial Law, and to get the best possible marks for submission of tutorial problems, tutorial participation and exams, take the time to read the following information carefully.

A useful website is **Web Wombat** which provides a gateway to access some interesting sites if you are looking for information on how to conduct legal research <http://www.webwombat.com.au/law>.

STUDY TECHNIQUES

Develop a good study pattern

1. **Good study methods ensure good results.** However, in developing those good study methods it is worth remembering that some people work better early in the morning while others work better at night, some prefer absolute quiet while others like to have some background noise. So choose a study method that suits you best.
2. **Develop a study plan and stick to it.** Success is developed through the technique of self-discipline. If you are to be successful in this subject you must be prepared to do some reading every week, attempt all the tutorial questions and attempt as many other questions as you can.
3. **Learn to understand.** The best way to learn a topic is through understanding the material. Some memorising is unavoidable, but try not to 'rote' learn, i.e. try not to memorise the text.
4. **Learn over time.** Learning is most effective when it is done over a period of time, particularly in the case law. An understanding of a topic, and ultimately the course, is by layers, beginning with the basics first.
5. **Don't cram for the exam.** Business or Commercial Law is not a course that you can really 'cram' for, as lots of students who have done poorly can testify to. If you leave everything until the last minute you will not get a good grasp of the material. This means that when you come to do the exam there will be a lack of understanding of the subject material. This in turn affects confidence, breeds anxiety and reduces efficiency for the exam and ultimately the final result.
6. **Work in small groups.** It is rare for one person to know all the material so well that they can say they will get 100 per cent. However, it is surprising how much you do know and with two or three other students, you will discover that learning can be fun. Even more surprising is that you will do well in the subject too.

Goals

7. **Set a goal, aim high, but be realistic.** Goals need to be achievable, not impossible.
8. **The two most important goals are**, in order of priority:

- understanding the material that is set down in the subject outline; and
- passing the assessment that is set down for the subject. This means completing tutorial exercises, participating in tutorials and reading the exam paper carefully so that you are clear about what it is that the examiner is asking. It never ceases to amaze how many people do not read the exam questions carefully, or in their hurry to complete the exam and get out of the room, do not answer all the questions.

Read the subject outline

9. Read the subject or course outline carefully. It provides important information on:
   - what topics will be covered during the semester;
   - how those topics will be taught (e.g., by lecture, tutorial, workshop). The preparation for a lecture is basically about receiving information (passive learning), while tutorials and workshops are about active learning (participatory learning);
   - what the learning outcomes will be (often called 'learning objectives'). These tell you want you need to know, or have to learn or achieve by the end of the semester;
   - what the assessment criteria is (e.g., submission of tutorial questions, tutorial participation, an essay, a practical exercise, an exam) and under what sort of conditions (e.g., submission of an essay by a certain date, an open-book or closed-book exam under supervised conditions over a set period of time);
   - what the weighting of the assessment is (i.e. how many marks will be allocated for each piece of assessment and on what basis). There is little value in spending a disproportionate amount of time on an assessment item worth only a few marks, so balance your time accordingly, particularly in an exam; and
   - plagiarism (taking someone else's work and calling it your own) and collaboration of work is unacceptable, so ensure that any work that has to be submitted is your own work and not that of others.
10. From reading the subject outline it is then possible to work out what is an approporiate study pattern and plan for you.

Preparation

11. Read each topic carefully **before** a class. This way more time can be spent listening and considering what is being said. There are a number of advantages, including:
    - an opportunity to be more selective in what needs to be written down;
    - being able to listen. It is difficult to listen and write at the same time; and
    - filling in gaps in understanding. Questions may arise during the course of reading that can be answered in class.
12. If there are tutorials in the subject, make sure you have attempted all questions beforehand in full (pretend that the tutorial questions are what you are going to get in the exam). Tutorials offer the best chance to go back over the answers that you have prepared beforehand and discover whether you have understood the topic or not.

Be an 'active' learner

13. For the best understanding of a topic, use an 'active' learning approach. This is best achieved through working in small groups and repeated acquaintance with the material. It is also about going into tutorials well prepared.
14. 'Active' learning is about doing and includes:
    - **summarising the material**—pick out main points, develop connections and form a structure;
    - **answering questions**—the more questions you attempt, the faster you can discover whether you understand a topic or not;
    - **looking for options**—there are generally two sides to every problem. In 99.9 per cent of cases that go to court, each side thinks they have a chance of winning. Would there be any point in bringing (or defending) an action otherwise? While a problem may at first glance appear to be clear cut, go back and review the facts carefully at least a couple of times and look at it from both sides; and

- **working in groups**—working in small groups is a good way to learn. There is an incentive to do the work because you don't want to let your friends down. Also, in discussing a topic with others, gaps can be revealed and rectified. It is also a more informal and less stressful environment than a classroom.

15. 'Passive' learning is all about reading and assenting. While some passive learning is necessary, attempt to answer questions on each topic to the best of your ability to check understanding and that you are on 'the right track'. It is amazing how many students go into tutorials unprepared, expecting to pick up what they don't know by some process of osmosis and then do well in the exam. Unfortunately, experience shows that this is not the way to do well.

Reading hints

16. There is a lot of reading in most Business or Commercial Law, but you can get through it (and have a life) if you do the following:
    - **Begin with an overview**—when studying a topic, gain an overview first. Identify the basics and reflect on what you already know about the topic. It is what you don't know about a topic that you have to learn. Why waste time trying to re-learn what you already know?
    - **Initially 'skim' read**—to help save time when reading, try to develop the habit of 'skim' reading. When you come to material that is relevant to the topic you are studying, slow down and read it carefully.
    - **Read actively**—note key paragraphs and phrases, make margin notes in your text and summarise the material. Use headings, sub-headings and key words. Often material can be turned into a flow chart.
    - **Spread your reading time over a number of periods**—this allows you to reflect on what you have read and helps in understanding the topic.
    - When reading a statute understand the importance of:
      - joining words such as 'and', which joins two parts of a sentence together, and 'or', which splits a sentence into two or more parts or indicates alternatives that apply. Section 52(1) of the *Trade Practices Act 1974* (Cth) is an example of the difference a word can make in a sentence:

        'A corporation shall not, in trade or commerce, engage in conduct that is misleading **or** deceptive **or** is likely to mislead **or** deceive.'

        If you replace the word 'or' with the word 'and', what effect does that have on the section?
      - words which are directive, such as 'shall', and words which are discretionary, such as 'may'. What is the effect of each in a section of an Act?
      - words such as 'includes' which are generally used by the draftsperson before examples are given to tell the reader that the examples are not exhaustive.

ASSESSMENT

17. Assessment can take a variety of forms including:
    - **Multiple-choice items**—a question or incomplete statement followed by four or five options from which you choose the best or most appropriate answer. For example:

      'Law made by Parliament is known as:

      a common law
      b statute law
      c equity law
      d merchant law.'
    - **Written short answers**—these are questions that generally have pre-determined answers and can be answered in a few words, a sentence or at most a paragraph, e.g., 'Define a cheque'.
    - **Project**—this involves an in-depth investigation of a selected topic over a considerable period of time. It will result in the participant carrying out research and the completion of a project report. For example:

      'Are labels on products in supermarkets misleading or deceptive to consumers? Are they breaching the law?'

This would require research into product labelling and an examination of labelling law.

- **Essay**—this is an open-ended form of assessment and involves general discussion of a legal topic. Depending on the context in which the question is being asked, i.e. tutorial question or exam time, it may require research. For example:

  'All contracts are agreements, but not all agreements are contracts. Discuss.'

- **Practical exercise or problem questions**—these involve solving a problem and are used extensively in tutorials and exams. For example:

  'It was a very hot Gold Coast day and Sam, who was 17, and his mates were diving into the water from the footbridge at MacIntosh Island to keep cool. There were large signs at each end of the bridge, and in the middle, prohibiting jumping from the bridge into the water. The council was aware that the currents in the area made the water shallow in spots and unsafe for people diving from the bridge. Also, people swimming in the area near the bridge could not be seen by people jumping from the bridge.

  Around mid-afternoon, Sam was attempting to dive close to a friend and he failed to see another swimmer, who was pushing a board in front of him, come out from under the bridge. Sam hit the board and broke his neck.

  Discuss.'

  NOTE that the question asks you to 'discuss'. This means your answer must be in essay form. Dot points would not be satisfactory and you would lose marks because you had not done what the examiner had asked you to do.

- **personal interview**—lecturers may decide to elicit information through asking a student questions on a face-to-face basis.

ESSAYS

18. If you are writing an essay:

- you will generally be given a topic which focuses on a particular area in the subject and you will be expected to research the topic in some depth, present a detailed analysis of the topic and demonstrate an understanding of it. Where the question is a quote, you will need to decide whether the quote is an integral part of the essay question. If it is, you will be expected to present an argued case as to why you agree or disagree with the quote; or
- you will be expected to formulate a question which focuses on a particular area of law within the subject. Again, you will be required to research the topic, present a detailed analysis of it and demonstrate an understanding of the area.

19. Where you need to formulate a question (a research essay), unless you already have a question in mind, you will need to read widely to begin with. This will help you with an overview of the subject area and begin to focus your mind on possible areas that you might be interested in investigating further with a view to developing a research essay question from. As you gain an understanding of an area, you will begin to find specific areas within the general area that you might be interested in researching further. At this point you need to refer to more specific sources such as specialist texts and journal articles, cases and statutes.

20. Note carefully the following points in relation to essay writing as it applies to all law essays:

- **Begin with a draft plan.** It is easier to make amendments on a draft. It also gives you time to reflect on what you have written and to add any other ideas or arguments that may come to mind.
- When writing the essay, the **introduction** should:
  - introduce the topic of the essay;
  - provide definitions;
  - provide background information on the topic for the reader;
  - address the essay question;
  - set out the structure of the essay; and
  - move from the general to the specific.

On average, an introduction will be a half to three-quarters of a page and three or four paragraphs. Remember that an introduction should not contain any conclusions. Any conclusions should go at the end of an essay, not at the beginning in the introduction!

- The **body** of the essay should:
  - contain a discussion of the key areas of the topic;
  - provide a logical flow from one paragraph to the next; and
  - contain in each paragraph an introductory sentence setting out what is to be discussed in the paragraph, sentences which develop the introductory sentence through reasons, examples, facts, quotes etc. and a concluding sentence which will provide a link to the next paragraph.
- The **conclusion** should be reasonably short and not contain any new material. It can:
  - summarise the key areas of the body; and/or
  - be a final comment on the topic; and/or
  - comment generally on the current situation.

21. Try to keep to the following guidelines:

- **Write simply, clearly and concisely, i.e. work on the K.I.S.S. principle** or, in other words, keep it simple.
- **Avoid the use of technical terms and complicated concepts** unless you understand what they mean. Terms and phrases out of context tell the reader you don't understand the topic and it will cost you marks.
- Make sure that the arguments in your answer are in a logical and well organised order. Look at whether there is a case to be made for both sides.
- Your opinion is important but provide legal support for it from a relevant legal principle, a decided case or relevant piece of legislation. **A case or statute is primary source material** and is preferable to secondary source material, e.g., a text.
- Keep referring back to the question.
- Remember to acknowledge sources, i.e. **DO NOT PLAGIARISE**.
- Collaborate in the preparation of the essay **BUT** make sure that what you submit is your own work.
- **Check the spelling and grammar** as poor spelling and grammar can destroy a good essay. The reader can only go on what is written down, not what is in your head and if the reader cannot understand what it is you are trying to say because of poor spelling and/or grammar, you will lose marks.

22. If you are using quotes:

- **one to three lines** is part of the body of the essay and enclosed with quotation marks and the source; and
- **four or more lines** should be **indented**, no quotation marks are required but the source must be included.

ANALYSIS OF A LEGAL PROBLEM

23. Some legal problems that you encounter are clear cut, however, others are not. Problem questions are examples of situations where it is often possible for each side to interpret the facts and consequences differently to the other side.

24. Problem questions are often simplified fact situations based on case law, sometimes involving more than one area of the law or more than one principle in a specific area of law.

25. Writing the answer. In attempting to answer problem-type questions, there is no one set approach that must be used. However, there are some useful tips that you should remember. When you begin writing an answer, remember that you are writing for the reader, and all that the reader will have to go on is what you give them. They generally can't ask you a question to clarify a point because you are not there. This is particularly true if you are doing an exam. They can only award marks for what you have written, i.e. what is in front of them, so try to ensure that you have done the following:

- **Identify the relevant facts or issues**, i.e. what are the parties arguing about? Get a clear view of the order of events, and how they fit together. You can do a flow chart of the events if it helps. Once you understand the problem, then you can isolate the areas where a dispute of law, given the fact, is likely to occur.
- **Identify the relevant area of law.** Is it a question concerning application of common law principles, e.g., contract law, tort law, criminal law, etc. or statute law? In the case of the former, this means knowing what each of these areas of law is about, but only in the context of the course.
- **If a broad area of law applies (e.g., tort law), can it be narrowed down (i.e. what particular area of tort law?)?** Tort law covers a number of different actions including negligence, trespass, nuisance and defamation to mention but a few. These actions may in turn have a number of sub-categories, e.g., with trespass, is it trespass to the person (and in turn, assault, battery or false imprisonment?) or to goods or to property? A decision has to be made on which action seems most suitable and why. This requires an understanding of what each action is about (i.e. to what sort of fact situation does it apply to?) because a person who is defamed is not going to be able to bring an action in trespass to right the wrong against them. Wrong action, no remedy.
- **Having identified the area of law, consider what elements have to be established to succeed in an action based on that area of law.** For example, in the case of tort law and negligence, for the plaintiff (the person bringing the action in a civil case and here the party suffering the 'harm') to succeed you would need to establish each of the following elements, and in the following order:
  - that the defendant (the person who caused the 'injury' to the plaintiff) owed a duty of care to the plaintiff not to 'harm' them;
  - that the defendant breached their duty of care to the plaintiff; and
  - that the plaintiff suffered damage as a result of the breach of duty.

  You would then need to consider whether the defendant had any defences that they could rely on to defeat the plaintiff's claim, e.g., had the plaintiff accepted the risk or contributed to the injury? And you would be doing this on the basis of considering both the common law and statute because much of the law of negligence is now regulated by statute—in this case the *Civil Liability Act 2003* (Qld). After you had done all this, you might then be in a position to say whether, in your opinion, the plaintiff could succeed in their case, i.e. recover damages or monetary compensation for the 'harm' they suffered. Go back and look at Sam jumping off the bridge and getting hurt. Can he sue anyone?
- Memorising material is useful, e.g., certainly memorise the elements that are necessary to establish a negligence action, but **apply what you have memorised to answering a problem for good marks**. Memorising and understanding are not one and the same thing;
- If using **legislation** to support an answer, **make sure that the legislation is relevant**, e.g., Queensland legislation only applies within Queensland, NSW legislation only applies within NSW, Victorian legislation only applies within Victoria and so on. In other words, state and territory legislation only applies intrastate. Note that Commonwealth legislation has national application and applies across state borders. Also, make sure the legislation is **current**, i.e. it is up to date. Use the legislation website of the relevant state to check. Do **NOT** rely on Austlii to provide you with current legislation. Out of date legislation is useless and in real life, unlike the case of answering a legal problem where you would lose marks, could result in getting you into serious financial trouble, either with a client or with a statutory authority responsible for enforcing the legislation.
- When using **cases**, two points to keep in mind are:
  - what jurisdiction does the case come from?; and
  - what level is the court situated in the hierarchy?

  This is not important if it is a High Court case. However, if it isn't, those questions become important because of the issue of precedent, i.e. whether the case is one which must be followed (binding precedent) or one which may be followed (persuasive value), becomes important.

- **Apply the law to the facts in issue.** Here is where the benefit of a concise statement of the facts in issue becomes important because it is here where a decision must be made on the similarities or differences between the facts and the law. Explain why the law applies to the facts. It is not enough to state the law and then the relevant facts without explaining if and why the law applies to those facts. It is your ability to analyse that is important to the reader and where the bulk of your marks will come from.
- **Reach a conclusion**. This is where you give your overall opinion linking facts and law together. The degree of certainty is up to the writer and is to some extent dependent on the facts given in the problem. Where you cannot be certain of the outcome because, for example, not all the facts are given, it might be wiser to begin your conclusion by stating that 'In my opinion . . .'

26. Note that there is often no right or wrong answer in a problem question. Don't be concerned if you arrive at a different conclusion to that arrived at by your friends. Assessment is principally based on recognition of central issues and your discussion of the relevant principles of law to those issues and it is rare for the writer of a problem question to provide all the facts required to make a decision (space just doesn't permit it and you might need a day to read the question!). So you can make assumptions, but be realistic and make them in the context of the facts presented in the problem.

A POSSIBLE APPROACH TO ANSWERING A PROBLEM QUESTION

The approach below needs to be converted into essay form to be satisfactory for assessment purposes.

Question 1

Ian was a teacher at Ashmore High School. Nikki, 17 years of age, was a student in Ian's Legal Studies class. Frank, Nikki's father, asked Ian to give Nikki some extra tuition in Legal Studies after school and promised to pay Ian $1000 for his efforts. Ian agreed and proceeded to tutor Nikki until the exams. When Ian approached Frank for the money he was told that he had a duty to teach Nikki and ensure that she reached the necessary standard to pass the examination.

Can Ian force Frank to pay the $1000? Discuss.

What are the issues?

1. Refusal of Frank to pay the $1000 for the extra tuition given outside school hours.
2. Agreement reached between the parties.
3. Frank's argument that he didn't have to pay because Ian had a duty to bring Nikki up to the required standard.

What law applies?

Contract law.

What are the relevant legal principles?

Consideration, and in particular:

1. Performance of an existing public duty.
2. Performance of an existing contractual duty owed to the offeree.

Relevant cases (if any)

1. *Collins v. Godfrey* (1831) 109 ER 1040—a promise to pay for a man's appearance in court under *subpoena* was considered not to amount to good consideration because the offeree was under an existing legal duty to appear in court anyway.
2. *Glasbrook Bros v. Glamorgan City Council* [1924] AC 270—the police performed a task that they considered in excess of requirements and were successful in establishing that a contract existed because they performed a duty that was above and beyond their public duty to perform.

Application of the law to the facts

1. The question that arises here is whether Ian, when providing the extra tuition to Nikki in order to bring her up to the required standard, was performing an existing public duty or performance of a duty that was above and beyond that normally required of a school teacher.
2. Two arguments can be put forward:
   - A duty of a teacher is to ensure that their students reach the required standard set by the education authorities. Whatever means that are necessary to obtain this standard are acceptable. Extra tuition for those students unlikely to reach the required standard by the time of the exam would be compulsory for the teacher. Thus, any agreement to undertake extra tuition for financial gain would see a teacher doing no more than they were already required to do under their contract of employment, i.e. teach, and therefore would be unenforceable. If this was the case, then there would be a lack of consideration.
   - It could be argued that a teacher's duty is to teach students according to an established syllabus and within the rules and regulations of the relevant education authorities.

Conclusion

It is suggested that the second argument would be more likely to succeed. In the case of the first argument, taken to its logical conclusion, it would mean that teachers who failed to provide the extra tuition for students deemed unlikely to reach the required standard by the time of the exam would be in breach of their duty. This is clearly not the case. It is considered that the duty of a teacher is to teach to the syllabus, within the time limits specified and under any guidelines laid down by the education authorities and the school. An agreement to undertake extra tuition for particular students would therefore amount to an extra duty over and above that already owed in much the same way as occurred by the police in *Glasbrook Bros v. Glamorgan City Council* [1924] ACT 270 where the court found that the police had performed in excess of requirements. It would therefore be enforceable, the consideration being the additional duty performed by Ian.

EXAMINATIONS

To reduce the stress of examinations and to give yourself the best chance of success, try to take the following steps (these steps, incidentally, come directly from the best students over the years):

1. **Preparation** for the exam **starts in week 1** of the semester when you learn about the assessment for the course, and start reading and taking notes. Law is best learnt by building up knowledge over the whole semester. By the time of the exam, you will have a good general coverage of the whole subject.
2. **Do not rewrite the text. Summarise each topic area.** Flow charts for various areas can help when it comes to remembering concepts.
3. Once you have organised your course materials, try to do the following:
   - if you are not already with a friend/s, start now. Check your summaries and then your understanding of the material by testing each other;
   - do all the tutorial problems again and any past exam papers **under exam conditions**. **Find out how good you really are**; and
   - **summarise your summaries**.
4. In the exam, the following steps are critical:
   - **Read the instructions carefully on the front of the exam** (you would be amazed how many people don't) as you need to know:
     - how much reading time there is and what you can do in that reading time, e.g., write down information, highlight etc.;
     - how many parts to the exam there are and whether you are expected to answer every part, e.g., are there alternatives?;

  - whether you are expected to answer every question or only a certain number of questions from each part; and
  - work out the mark breakdown so time can be allocated for each question. To get the best possible mark, you have to complete the whole paper. The best way to ensure that the paper is finished within the time allowed is to work out how much time you have for each question, leaving a few minutes at the end to check the paper over. Then be ruthless and stick to it.
- **Read each question carefully**, and make sure you understand what the examiner wants. Identify the legal issues or areas of law that the questions appear to be concerned with.
- **Do the questions you are most comfortable with first.** This builds up your confidence and with it your ability to answer the questions that you are not so confident in **but make sure you carefully number each question correctly**.
- If you are allowed, in reading time list the main points for each question.
- **If you look like running out of time, switch to point form.** Again, remember, you only get marked on what you write as this reflects what you know.
- **Use the full exam time.** The only time you leave early is when you know you have achieved a mark of 100 per cent. Keep going back over what you have written because it is surprising how often you will find extra points that can be added to an answer to make it better.
- **Have some time left at the end of the exam for reviewing.** That one extra point at the end of the exam could be the difference between a pass and a credit and distinction, etc.

5. When reading a problem question:
   - **Read it carefully and**:
     - identify the parties;
     - consider who has done what to whom;
     - refer back to the question and see what it is that you have been asked to do, e.g., advise, discuss, contrast, suggest remedies etc.;
     - consider what large area of law might apply, e.g., is it contract, tort, business structures, consumer protection, consumer credit etc.? Remember it is possible for a question to contain more than one issue;
     - can you narrow the large area of law down further to a particular area?
     - what are the elements of these areas? and
     - read the facts again so you can apply the elements to the facts.
   - **Determine how long your answer should be by looking at the mark allocation.** Five marks is probably no more than .75 to a page, 10 marks about 1.5 to 2 pages, 15 marks about 2.5 to 3 pages and so on.
   - **The marks allocated to a question will also often provide a guide as to how many issues the question may contain**, e.g., a question worth 5 marks will generally only contain a single issue, a question worth 10 mark questions will generally contain two issues, and so on.
6. **Some things NOT to do for an exam, including:**
   - **If the exam is open book, DO NOT use your texts or notes until you have exhausted your memory.** Open book exams are a real trap for students for a number of reasons:
     - students think they don't have to work during the semester because they can take their materials in to the exam with them and look up the answers. If you don't understand the material, how do you know where to look for it to help write the answers?
     - looking up material for answers is very time consuming. Even with good indexing, there is a real chance that you will not finish the exam in the time allocated because of the time spent looking up information; and

- the examiner can expect better answers. You have access to materials such as cases, statutes and text materials that you would not have access to in a closed book exam.

- **If the exam is open book, DO NOT quote large chunks of text or statute** without showing how it applies to the facts. It is surprising how many students think that marks are allocated on quantity rather than quality.
- **DO NOT fail to relate the law to the facts of the problem.** Show how the relevant principles of law fit the facts of the problem.
- **DO NOT give personal opinion without supporting it with relevant law.**
- **DO NOT tell the examiner there is not enough information to answer the question.** You are being asked to provide advice on the information given. If you feel additional information is needed, state what it is and why you need it and incorporate it into your answer.
- **DO NOT tell the examiner there was not enough time.** You are trying to blame the examiner for failing to organise yourself better.

PART ONE

LEGAL FRAMEWORK

CHAPTER 1

Introduction to the Australian Legal System

CHAPTER CONTENTS

activebook

This icon is used throughout the following chapter to remind you to visit the *Business Law* online activebook for additional exercises, links to legal websites, and feedback. For a detailed explanation of what is in the activebook please refer to the inside cover of this textbook. The activebook is available through OneKey.

Where do I start?

Learning path: Use the activebook to complete a pre-chapter warm-up exercise.

There are many definitions of legal terms to assist with your understanding of the material.

CHAPTER OBJECTIVES

On completion of this chapter, you should be able to:

- explain what law is, and identify the major sources and categories of law
- recognise what are 'rules' and what is 'law'
- explain the distinction between 'law' and 'justice'
- explain the role of ethics in law
- explain the classification of laws
- explain the distinction between civil law and criminal law
- describe the effects of international law on the Australian legal system
- explain the main sources of law in the Australian legal system
- outline the historical development of the legal system in England, and subsequently Australia
- outline briefly the impact that Mabo has had on the Australian legal system
- explain how Commonwealth and state powers are divided under the Commonwealth Constitution
- explain what is meant by the separation of powers.

KEY TERMS

An understanding of the following terms will help you to better understand the material in this chapter:

- **common law:** that part of the law of England which developed from the common custom of the country as administered by the common law courts. It can also mean judge-made law as distinct from statute law
- **equity:** fairness and justice. Originally operated alongside the common law and intended as a supplement to it, but now incorporated into a single system
- **injunction:** a discretionary order or decree issued by a court in its equitable jurisdiction by which a party to an action is required to do, or refrain from doing, a particular thing. Injunctions are either restrictive (preventive) or mandatory (compulsory) and interlocutory (interim) or perpetual
- **jurisprudence:** the science or theory of law
- **law merchant:** that part of the common law relating to mercantile matters
- **mercantile law:** that branch of the law dealing with commercial transactions. It usually encompasses partnership, companies, agency, bills of exchange, sale of goods, insurance, carriers and bankruptcy
- **plaintiff:** one who brings a civil action against another
- **specific performance:** an equitable remedy compelling a person to carry out their contractual obligations where damages would be an inadequate remedy for the breach of an agreement. It is not obtainable for contracts of personal service
- **statute:** an Act of Parliament; a law passed by the legislature
- **writ:** a document in the name of the Queen issued by a court or an officer of the Crown commanding the person to whom it is addressed to do or stop doing a particular act.

what if . . .

You were part of a group of explorers colonising a new land. Would you:

- **use the legal system that you grew up with?**
- **establish a new legal system?**
- **have no legal system at all?**

Law is basically a device to regulate the economic and social behaviour of society and its purpose is to preserve the economic and social welfare of our society by introducing an element of control into the day-to-day activities of its citizens, and its businesses. If human beings lived in complete isolation, and did not carry on any economic activity or recognise any superior authority, there would be no need for laws to exist as there would be nothing to regulate and nothing to control. However, the reality is otherwise. A society's citizens don't live in complete isolation and economic activity is carried on. They share a common government. Inevitably they will come into contact with one another and conflict will arise because they will have different needs and desires. The law, as a regulatory device, provides the mechanism for society to function by priorising these needs and desires through tools such as legislation (Acts and regulations of Parliament) and, in the case of a common law system such as ours, case law (decisions of the courts).

In our society, the law as a regulatory tool not only prescribes what people **cannot** do, it also informs people of what they **can** do and what they **must** do. For example, you **cannot** commit a crime, but you **can** own property, and you **must** pay taxes. In addition, the law also plays a number of other roles such as guaranteeing our freedoms, permitting free enterprise, and providing a means to settle disputes peacefully.

How do business and the law interface? News stories about business and the law in Australia have appeared frequently in the media over the years, but often the stories are only newsworthy because they are extraordinary or controversial, for example:

- billion dollar mergers of multinational corporations, such as BHP and Billiton in 2001, resulting in the world's largest diversified resources company;
- the privatisation of Telstra by the Commonwealth government;
- criminal investigations of insider trading in the securities industry, such as the trial and conviction of the late high-profile stockbroker Rene Rivkin in 2003;
- corporate collapses, such as the Bond Group and Qintex in 1989, the insurance company HIH and One.Tel in 2001, and the Westpoint Group in 2005; and
- corporate fraud involving high-profile Australians such as Alan Bond (the Bond Group), Christopher Skase (Qintex), Ray Williams (HIH) and Jodie Rich (One.Tel).

Such stories raise a number of interesting legal issues, but they also create the impression in the minds of many people that business law is largely removed from their everyday lives. However, this is far from the truth. Business laws shape every stage of commercial enterprise and because people are constantly engaged in business transactions, business law is relevant to all members of society. For example, the principles of contract law enable both individuals and businesses to rely upon agreements:

- of employment;
- to purchase raw materials;
- for the purchase and sale of goods or services;
- for the purchase of a home or a business;
- to insure property; and
- for the appointment of an agent

by providing a remedy to persons injured by another's failure to perform an agreement.

To understand how contract law operates, and for that matter the law in general, it is in the interests of everyone to have some understanding of the nature and sources of law, to be aware of what actions society as represented by government will take, why those actions have been taken and how they will affect business. In the case of Australian law, it is principally based on English common law, which in turn has been influenced by other legal systems, such as the French civil system.

The main sources of law in this country, which regulate both business and the community in general, are found in:

- the laws made by the Commonwealth, state and territory parliaments and under the auspices of:
  - the Commonwealth Constitution; and
  - state and territory constitutions;

- case law, which is found in: – the decisions of federal and state courts; and
- so much of the common law or statute law of England that has not been repealed.

The Commonwealth Constitution is the fundamental law of Australia, binding everybody including the Commonwealth Parliament and the parliament in each state and territory. Any action, including legislative action, must be in accord with the Constitution or it will be invalid. It establishes the basic framework of the Commonwealth government and gives it limited powers to govern the conduct of business and business relationships. For example, the *Corporations Act 2001* (Cth) regulates companies. The securities laws regulate the sale and trading of shares issued by companies. The *Trade Practices Act 1974* (Cth) provides a code of conduct for the business community by discouraging unfair trading practices between businesses and encouraging fair-trading practices between businesses and the consumer.

The states also have powers under their respective constitutions and the Commonwealth Constitution expressly guarantees the continuing existence of the states and their constitutional powers. Subject to a few exceptions, such as the ability to impose customs and excise duties (s. 90) and raise defence forces (s. 114), the Commonwealth Constitution does not restrict the areas about which the states can make laws. As a result, the state parliaments can pass laws on a wider range of subjects than the Commonwealth Parliament, and for this reason areas such as education, criminal law and business have been the domain of the states. For example, the fair trading, consumer credit and sale of goods legislation are all areas of state legislation that are used to regulate business activity.

The federal and state courts hear civil and criminal cases and the decisions they arrive at add to the laws that regulate the conduct of persons (both natural and legal) in both a business sense and in their interaction in the community. This is called 'case law' and is discussed further in Chapter 3.

> This chapter provides an introduction to the history and sources of law in Australia, the Doctrine of Reception and the growing importance of native title, Commonwealth and state powers, and the separation of powers.

WHAT IS 'LAW'?

Over the centuries writers have made numerous unsuccessful attempts to produce a universally acceptable definition of 'law'. Each writer has their own view, in large part due to the fact that any definition of 'law' will be shaped by the writer's moral, political, religious and ethical views, and influenced by the society in which they live. Yet, in spite of this lack of agreement on a precise definition of 'law', it is still possible to identify two common themes:

- control by humans; and
- human conduct, regulated by a superior authority or power—usually the state.

Given that it is difficult to provide a precise definition of 'law', a useful general definition is that it is:

> *a set of rules, developed over a long period of time regulating people's interactions with each other and which sets standards of conduct between individuals and other individuals, and individuals and the government and which are enforceable through sanction.*

In the case of Australia, 'the law' consists of rules and principles of conduct that are enacted by governments, embedded in constitutions and statutes, and embodied in decisions of the courts.

SOURCES OF THE LAW

Two main sources of law in Australia can be identified (see Figure 1.1).

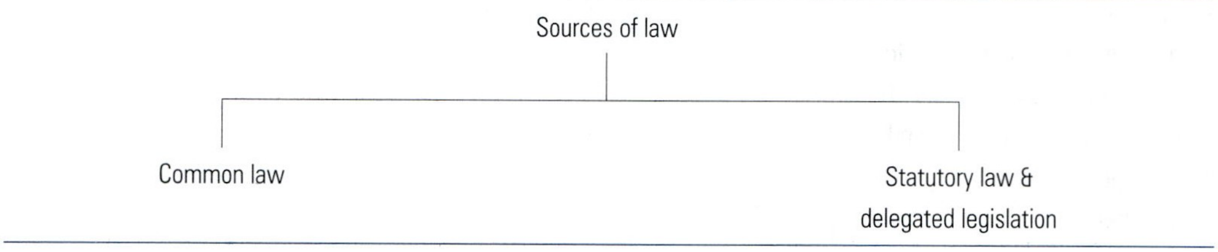

FIGURE 1.1 *Sources of law*

Common law

These are laws created through the **reported decisions of judges** in the higher courts. (See Chapter 3 for more detail.)

Common law is created through decisions of courts

It is also known as:

- case law;
- precedent; or
- unenacted law.

The term 'common law' usually includes the principles of equity (or equity law) which are discussed below.

Statute law

Statute law is created by Parliament

These are laws (see Chapter 3 for more detail) established by the people through:

- their federal or state parliamentary representatives (in the form of **statute law** or **legislation**) and also known as **enacted law**; or
- other government bodies (in the form of by-laws, orders, rules and regulations, and known as **delegated legislation**).

ARE 'RULES' ALWAYS 'LAW'?

While it is generally true to say that the 'law' is a set of rules, it doesn't automatically follow that all 'rules' are (or will be) 'law'. There are numerous examples of rules governing daily behaviour that are not laws and, as a general rule, will not become laws. There are rules controlling sport, games, social behaviour, family behaviour, schools and colleges. The list is endless.

IN BRIEF

When does a 'rule' become 'law'?

To determine when a rule becomes law, consideration should be given to:

- where the rule comes from;
- how a person will be dealt with when the rule is broken;
- how the person will be punished; and
- by whom.

'JUSTICE' AND THE 'LAW'

A concept that is closely identified with law is **justice** which means 'that which is right or fair'. Unfortunately, 'justice' can also be a difficult term to define. As Lord *Denning*, one of England's greatest judges, suggested:

> *It is not a product of intellect but of spirit. The nearest we can go to defining justice is to say that it is what right-minded members of the community—those who have the right spirit within them—believe to be fair.*

There is 'social justice', 'moral justice' and 'legal justice'. They may or may not all coincide. It will depend on the situation and the context in which the term is used. For example, the fine for parking in a 'No Parking' zone is the same whether you are rich or poor. This may be considered legally and morally just, as everyone is seen to be equal in the eyes of the law. However, it can be inequitable or unfair as the person who is rich can more easily afford to pay the fine than the person who is poor.

Law attempts to represent what society believes is right or fair. Justice in our society means that everyone is entitled to be treated fairly under our legal system. However, it is unrealistic to suggest that our legal system can be absolutely foolproof and just. It isn't. As society evolves, it is to be hoped that the legal system will also evolve and that existing injustices will gradually disappear and be replaced by fairness.

Australian society has developed a reasonably fair system of rights and duties. Where someone has their rights infringed, they may seek relief through the law. This may take the form of a civil action where they may seek a remedy in, for example, the form of monetary compensation (or damages) from the other party. Or it may be by way of a complaint to the police resulting in a criminal prosecution against the other party and, for example, their jailing by the courts. It may even possibly be an action in both civil and criminal law.

LAW AND ETHICS

Despite the law's importance as a source of rules of conduct, society would still not function effectively without individuals developing some form of moral standards and beliefs, what might be called ethical considerations. Ethics is concerned with what is right and what ought to be, not accepting what is. The purpose of law is to govern the conduct of all members of society, both natural and legal (i.e. in the case of the latter, partnerships and companies), while ethics provides guidance for individuals with respect to ascertaining the soundness of rules and their impact upon relationships.

> **activebook**
> To help you to remember and understand the topics covered so far, and for links to legal websites, refer to your online activebook. Model answers provide feedback to problems and exercises.

While law and ethics derive from different authorities and for different reasons, they are often related, particularly in an area such as business law where businesses have often used legal standards as the sole reason for justifying particular courses of action.

To determine appropriate business conduct for decisions that are not guided by a legal standard, businesses have begun to adopt business codes of ethics or conduct to guide employees when considering ethical issues during the decision-making process. Part IVB of the *Trade Practices Act 1974* (Cth), Part IV of the *Fair Trading Act 1987* (WA) and Part 3 of the *Fair Trading Act 1992* (ACT) all provide for legal recognition of industry codes of conduct, designed by and agreed to by an industry, and which regulate the conduct of participants in that industry towards other participants in the industry, and to consumers in the industry. Adherence to such rules may be mandatory, for example, the Franchising Code of Conduct, or voluntarily establishing best standard practices and binding only those who have agreed to be bound, such as the Code of Banking Practice.

Some of the legal rules that will be covered in the study of Business Law which have ethical characteristics include:

- the assumption that both parties will exercise good faith when entering into a contract;
- web issues such as privacy and cyber-squatting;
- intellectual property considerations involving copyright, patents, designs, trade marks, use of confidential information and passing-off;
- the restrictive trade practices and consumer protection provisions of the *Trade Practices Act 1974* (Cth);
- the regulation of directors under the *Corporations Act 2001* (Cth);
- the statutory embodiment of the principle of *uberrimae fidei* (i.e. each party will exercise the utmost good faith towards the other party when entering into the contract) under the *Insurance Contracts Act 1984* (Cth); and
- aspects of employment and industrial law which impose obligations on employers in relation to anti-discrimination, occupational health and safety, minimum wages and conditions, and insolvency, while employees are expected to exercise a duty of fidelity.

The principles of business law discussed in this text provide an opportunity to examine not only legal issues, but also ethical issues. In some cases, the rule of law provides an ethical minimum to which a business must adhere. In other cases, a decision may have been arrived at on the basis of compliance with a legal principle and can be the basis for ethical inquiry. Other laws that may be encountered as you read through the text are based on moral judgements and they also can be subject to ethical analysis as to validity. (See Chapter 5.)

WHAT IS RULE OF LAW?

The rule of law was formulated in its modern form in the late 19th century by an eminent Oxford academic lawyer, Professor Dicey, and is at the heart of our present legal system. It is based on the idea that laws should conform to a minimum standard of fairness in both content and procedure. He suggested that the rule of law involves three propositions:

- No person must be punished except for a breach of the law. This means that a person should be able to know whether what they may want to do is lawful or unlawful. It also recognises the law as the highest authority in society.
- All persons are equal before the law irrespective of status or position.
- The rights or freedoms of citizens are enforceable in the courts.

CLASSIFICATION OF LAWS

IN BRIEF

Major legal systems in the world

Legal systems	Characteristics
Civil Law	Derived from Roman law, it is a complete code of written laws whose primary source of law is legislation. It is inquisitorial in form and forms the basis of the legal systems of most Western European countries, Japan and the former colonies of France, Spain and Portugal in Latin America, the near East, Indonesia, Thailand, Vietnam and parts of Africa.
Common Law	Derived from case law (or precedent) and statute, it is accusatorial in form with an emphasis on remedies. It forms the basis of English law and can be found in the United States, as well as Commonwealth nations including Canada, Singapore, Malaysia, New Zealand, parts of Africa, India and Pakistan.
Sino-Soviet	Based on the philosophy of Karl Marx (i.e. the eradication of capitalism and the elimination of private ownership), its emphasis on codes means it is really only a variant of the civil law, but with an emphasis on public law. It applies to more than 30 per cent of the world's population.
Hindu	Hindu law is based on the doctrine of proper behaviour. It is followed by Hindus, who make up 20 per cent of the world's population, regardless of their nationality or where they live.
Islamic	The Islamic legal system is derived from the Koran. It coexists with other laws and also applies to approximately 20 per cent of the world's population.
Talmudic	The Talmudic legal system is derived from the Old Testament and is the law of Jewish people, wherever they may be.

As a broad generalisation, it is possible to classify the legal systems of the world into three main families of law: civil law, common law and socialist law. However, it should not be assumed that this grouping is an exhaustive listing. What can be said is that most other legal systems in the world possess characteristics which can be identified with one or more of these systems and so they mark a convenient starting point when considering a modern classification of legal systems.

Legal systems may be classified into three main families: civil law, common law, socialist law

One further point is that the civil law system and the common law system are arguably converging. Common law systems are finding it increasingly difficult to rely on judge-made law and as a result are turning to codification of their laws, while the civil law systems are beginning to acknowledge the existence and use of precedent (a reference to the use of previously decided cases to assist in deciding a similar case today). In the not too distant future, the distinctions between the two may be sufficiently blurred to the point where they are effectively one and the same system.

The common law system

The Australian legal system is what is known as a common law system where legal principles are developed by judges through case law. This is a system that was inherited from England and similar systems can be found in former British colonies such as the United States, Canada, New Zealand, Malaysia and Singapore.

In Australia, two basic areas of law can be identified: civil law and criminal law (see Figure 1.2).

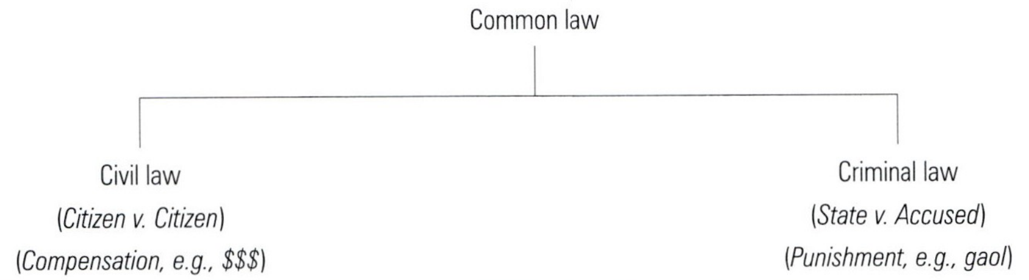

FIGURE 1.2 *A basic classification under common law*

Civil law

The term 'civil law' can have one of two meanings, depending on the way in which the words are used. It can mean:

- a reference to a legal system, e.g., the legal system used in Europe; **or**
- a reference to an area of law within the common law system.

The distinction is important. In the case of the former, the civil law system is a complete legal system with its origins in Roman law and the Napoleonic Codes. The law is set out in codified legislation and there is little reliance on case law (or judge-made law). It is a legal system which is generally non-adversarial or inquisitorial. Where the term **'civil law'** is used in the common law system, it refers to an action brought by one individual against another where the **mode of procedure is accusatorial and the emphasis is on remedies**. Business law is primarily about civil disputes, which result in remedies for the winning party and liabilities for the losing one.

Civil law—an action by one individual against another

Criminal law

In criminal cases the action is brought by the Crown on behalf of the state (not the police, as they enforce the law) against a person for the commission of an act which the state considers to be a crime and which should be punishable by a penalty. (See also Chapter 4.)

Criminal law—an action brought by the Crown against an individual

International and municipal (or domestic) law

In addition to the basic classification of civil law and criminal law under the common law system, another major classification is international law and municipal or domestic law.

There are also numerous sub-classifications that can be made to specific parts of the legal system, such as contract law, the law of torts, criminal law, property law, environmental law and company law, to mention just a few.

International law

International law regulates conduct between nations

States could not enjoy the benefits of trade and commerce, exchange of ideas, or even normal routine communication without some system of international law. **International law is that body of law concerned with regulating for the most part the conduct between nation states.**

While international law is principally concerned with relations between states,(known as **public international law**), there are also laws that apply to individuals engaged in international transactions referred to as **private international law** or conflict of laws).

Two main sources of international law that can affect business are:

- **Customary rules** of international law. Until the mid-19th century, most of the established rules of international law had been derived from international custom and from established practices between nations, e.g., the concept of *terra nullius*. Australian courts have recognised that these customary rules are deemed to be part of the law of the land, subject to the qualification that they must not be inconsistent with any statute or rule of common law.
- **Treaties and conventions** (agreements) which since the mid-19th century have begun to replace traditional customary rules. Two reasons can be suggested:
  - customary rules take a long time to respond to changing international circumstances; and
  - recognition of the growing inability of existing customs to meet the demands of the growing interdependence of states through technological, communication and transport developments in the latter part of the 20th century.

Since Federation, Australia has ratified over 900 international treaties and conventions. Three of the main trade agreements have been:

- **GATT**—the General Agreement on Tariffs and Trade is a multilateral treaty which aims to encourage free trade in goods and services.
- **The Vienna Sales Convention**—a multilateral treaty which sets out standards of conduct for sales agreements between traders of signatory countries.
- **APEC**—the Asia Pacific Economic Cooperation is a regional treaty of which Australia is a member and which provides special trading advantages to its member states.

International treaties and conventions are not part of municipal or domestic law unless they are given express legislative approval by the Commonwealth government as they fall under its exclusive powers under the Commonwealth Constitution. However, the High Court has taken the view that ratification can create legitimate expectations that an administrative decision-maker would conform with a convention even though it may not have been incorporated into domestic law. For example, in *Minister for Immigration v. Ah Hin Teoh* (1995) ALJR 423, *Mason* CJ and *Deane* J said that ratification of a treaty is 'a positive statement by the [Commonwealth] government to the world and the Australian people that the government and its agencies will act in accordance with the treaty'. At the end of the day this could have the effect of making domestic policies invalid.

Municipal (or domestic) law

Municipal or domestic laws are a state's internal law

Municipal or domestic laws come from statute or case law. They regulate the **relations or conduct between individuals** (or natural persons), and **organisations** (legal persons) that come **within the state's borders**. This does not mean that the individual or organisation must be a citizen of the state making the law. For example, if you visit the United States, you are subject to the municipal or domestic laws of that country, not the municipal or domestic laws of Australia. Similarly, a visitor from the United States to Australia is subject to the municipal or domestic laws of Australia, not the municipal or domestic laws of the United States.

Doing business

Who is a 'person' in law?

All rules of law are concerned with the activities of persons. For the purposes of the law, the reference to a 'person' includes not only a reference to human beings but also extends to entities (or organisations) who can have rights and obligations in much the same way as natural persons. Two examples of entities are the Crown and companies. ■

MAJOR AND MINOR TYPES OF LAWS

Australian law has its origin in English law

The legal system of each state in Australia can trace its origins back to England. It is possible to identify three major and three minor types of laws in the English legal system (see Figures 1.3 and 1.4). While each is quite different, together they form a system of laws, and it is this legal system that Australia has inherited.

ORIGINS OF MAJOR SOURCES OF ENGLISH LAW

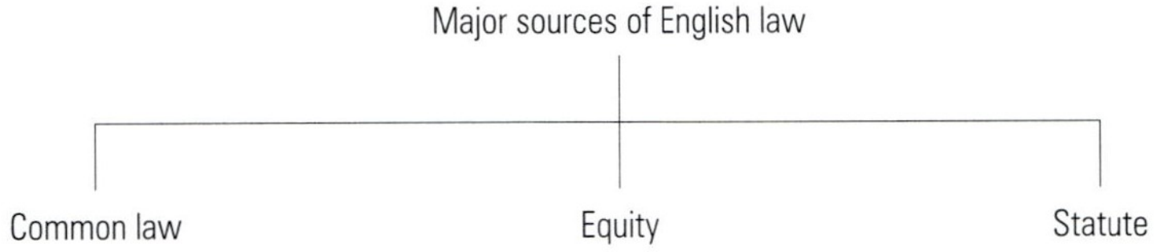

FIGURE 1.3 *Major types of laws found in England*

Before the Norman Conquest

The English legal system has a great diversity of sources. It dates back to the time of the country's early inhabitants and their folk laws and customs. Prior to the Norman conquest in 1066, the customs and ideals of the various invaders had been grafted into the local system of laws where they had settled. This **'customary' law** was administered in local courts, or moots, and interpreted according to local custom, each court or moot having its own territorial jurisdiction. At that time, the geographic diversity of the population, almost non-existent communications and an uneducated population all worked against a unified legal system. During this period two important sources of English law came into existence:

- **Diplomata**—charters containing grants of land, which were to become important in the development of **property law**.
- **Dooms**—laws handed down by the King which later were to form the basis of **criminal and tort law**.

The growth of common law

In 1066, William, Duke of Normandy, later known as William the Conqueror, landed in England and claimed the English throne. To gain support for his claim, William promised not to change the law of England as he found it.

In order to consolidate his position, William appointed a number of judges (Justices in Eyre) and sent them out to hold courts around the country. They were told to:

- administer a uniform system of law in the name of the King throughout the country;
- report to the King any potential threats from any nobleman or group of noblemen; and
- assess the wealth of the country so that taxes could be levied on the owners of land. In those days, wealth was measured in land holdings (for more information on the Domesday Book see: **http://www.nationalarchives.gov.uk/museum/item.asp?item_id=1**).

Common law developed from common application of law to the whole of England

By the reign of Henry II (1154–1189), the practice of sending the royal justices throughout the country 'on circuit' began to result in a fairly uniform body of law developing around the country—the common law. The judges were assisted in finding an agreement among themselves by keeping records known as plea rolls. They set out not only the facts of each case and the judgement, but often the reasoning behind the judgement, in much the same way as our modern law reports do.

The Provisions of the Assize of Northampton in 1176 divided the country into six circuits. The *Curia Regis* (the King's Council) was given the responsibility for guiding and supervising the royal courts, and the royal justices were given power to hear most civil and criminal matters. In 1178 Henry II decreed that five of his royal justices were to remain in London at the royal court and hear the pleas of the common people, thus establishing the Court of Common Pleas.

Henry II also established an elaborate system of auditing royal accounts known as the pipe rolls. In the event of a dispute over payment of royal levies, a group of men from the King's Council would meet at the Exchequer and try to resolve the matter. This was to become the Court of Exchequer.

During the reign of Henry II, writs (orders to answer charges before the King) also came into wide use. They were purchased from the King's Clerks of Chancery and stated the complaint, ordering the named person to right the wrong or show the King's justices why they should not. The issuing of new writs to cover new wrongs meant that the common law was fairly flexible at this time, because it could easily adapt to meet changing conditions.

When the Provisions of Oxford were passed in 1258, the common law lost much of its flexibility. If the facts in issue did not fit the standard form of the writ, the action could fail.

The development of equity

Equity emphasises fairness and justice

As a result of the growing inflexibility and rigidity of the common law after the Provisions of Oxford, many petitioners turned to the King to hear their pleas. As the 'fountain of justice' in the realm, these petitioners believed that the only way that they were going to get justice for their cases was for the King to personally hear them. This belief was reinforced by the King's approach to dealing with the hardships and injustices resulting from the application of the common law on the basis of fairness and justice. Once the King had made a decision on a particular set of facts, future litigants could petition him whenever similar circumstances arose (an early example of precedent).

From the reign of Henry II the office of the Chancellor increased in importance. One of the roles of the Chancellor was 'keeper of the King's conscience'. Since a frequent complaint was that the petitioner had been deprived of justice by some unconscionable act, the Chancellor as 'keeper of the King's conscience' was expected to advise the King as to what ought to be done to ensure that these petitioners received just and equitable treatment.

By the 14th century Court of Chancery were set up. They administered a new body of law, known as **equity law** and they took account of new developments and provided a wider range of remedies than the common law courts. There was now in effect an additional jurisdiction alongside the common law, and in the course of time two distinct bodies of judge-made law were created—common law and equity.

For several centuries England had two parallel court systems, sometimes offering alternative remedies in the same cases, sometimes coming into conflict and competing for the same litigants. In 1620, James I decided that **in the event of a conflict between equity and common law, equity would prevail**.

In the event of a conflict with common law, equity prevails

The *Judicature Act of 1873* combined the two legal systems and created one Supreme Court of Judicature. The Act did not abolish the distinction between common law and equity; it simply directed the courts of common law to take into consideration the rules of equity. Where the two systems came into conflict, equity would continue to prevail over the common law and this is the position in Australia today.

Common law damages available 'as of right' while equitable remedies only available when damages not an adequate remedy

Equity law does not apply to all civil disputes, and it has no application in criminal law. Where equity might apply—for example, where the injured party (the plaintiff) does not want damages because there will not be adequate compensation (which is the main remedy under common law and available 'as of right')—an equitable remedy has to be specifically asked for by a party in court. The equitable remedy sought will mostly be one of two main types:

- an **injunction**: a court order that directs a person to stop doing something that could harm the interests of another. It can be granted as a temporary order (an interlocutory injunction) before the court makes a final order in the matter or as a final injunction; or

- **specific performance:** a court order directing a person to carry out an obligation that he or she has accepted to do, usually in a contract, e.g., to complete a sale of land.

IN BRIEF

Differences between common law and equity

Common Law	Equity
1. Is a comprehensive system.	1. Not a comprehensive system, e.g., never had a criminal jurisdiction.
2. Remedies are not discretionary.	2. Remedies are discretionary.
3. Common law rights are enforceable at any time, subject to the operation of a state or territory's Statute of Limitations.	3. Remedies must be applied for promptly or they may not be enforceable.
4. Common law rights are valid against the whole world.	4. Equitable rights are valid only against those persons specified by the court.

Statute law

The first attempt to limit the theoretically absolute power of the King (the concept of 'Divine Right') was the forced signing of the Magna Carta by King John in 1215 (to view the Magna Carta see **<http://www.britannia.com/history/magna2.html>**). This led to Parliament starting to make statutes as we know them today, though the process was different. Legislation was made initially by the King after the meeting with Parliament was over. However, by the reign of Henry VI (1422–1461), laws were being framed and discussed by the two Houses into which Parliament was divided—the House of Tenants-in-Chief and Ecclesiastics (which was later to become the House of Lords) and the House of Elected Knights and Citizens (the House of Commons).

Since about the middle of the 19th century, the great majority of English law has come from Parliament in the form of statutes. The Crown does not play a significant role in the law-making processes of Parliament.

The laws created by Parliament are the highest ranking in the land, overruling **all** other laws. While statute law assumes the existence of common law, in the event of common law and statute law clashing, the latter will generally prevail. Common law principles will be maintained only to the point where they conflict with statute law.

In the event of a conflict, statute law overrules all other laws

ORIGINS OF MINOR SOURCES OF ENGLISH LAW

It should not be assumed that the three major types of law above are the only sources of English law. There are a number of other sources of English law that have played a role in the development of the English legal system and two of these which have had an impact on the development of business law are law merchant and Roman law.

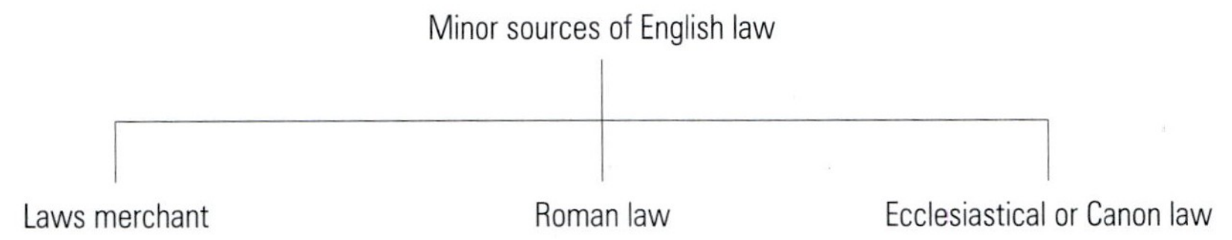

FIGURE 1.4 *Minor sources of English law*

Law merchant

As trade and commerce grew in the 15th and 16th centuries, English traders began to expand their business activities into Europe. This resulted in them coming into contact with the merchant law of Europe which had its origins in Roman law. By the 18th century, the common law courts had begun to hear merchants' disputes. As a result, many of the principles governing merchants' transactions became part of the common law.

Roman law

Roman law, known as civil law in Europe, never really gained a strong foothold in England, even though England was part of the Roman Empire. Fragments of Roman law can be found, for example, as part of ecclesiastical or canon law, and in business law as a result of English merchants trading in Europe.

ORIGINS OF AUSTRALIAN LAW

Colonies established by England were classified as being one of two types:

- Territory that was acquired by **treaty or military victory**. In such cases the territory was administered according to the original laws of the inhabitants until they were replaced by the laws of the colonising power.
- Territory that was *terra nullius*. As early as 1608, the principle was established that Englishmen took English law with them when they entered a 'new' territory. *Terra nullius* could also be applied to territories where the inhabitants had not created an organised society with a recognisable legal system. This concept was also known as the **Doctrine of Reception**.

If Australia had been gained by conquest or ceded by treaty, the existing laws in force in Australia at that time would have applied until superseded by the laws of England. However, while the English government had given orders to the early governors to negotiate treaties with the local inhabitants, by the mid-19th century the legal view was that Australia at that time was not owned by any group or state. As no recognised legal system was seen to exist, the common law of England applied from the moment of colonisation. The thousands of years of Aboriginal occupation were not considered sufficient to give any land rights to the occupants at common law, because the type of society that the Aboriginals existed in was one that was totally alien to the authorities: *Cooper v. Stuart* (1889) 14 App Cas 286.

Mabo* gave judicial recognition that Australia was not *terra nullius

It wasn't until *Milirrpum v. Nabalco Pty Ltd* (1971) 17 FLR 141, an action brought on behalf of several Arnhem native land holders against the mining operations of Nabalco (which failed because the court felt bound by the decision in *Cooper v. Stuart*), that evidence established that the Aboriginals had a set of sophisticated social customs and rules which could be recognised as a system of law.

The High Court decisions in *Mabo v. Queensland (No. 2)* (1992) 175 CLR 1 (the *Mabo* case) and in *The Wik People v. Queensland*; *The Thayorre People v. Queensland* (1996) 187 CLR 1 (the *Wik* case), and the passing of the *Native Title Act 1993* (Cth), marked a watershed for Indigenous peoples in Australia. The decisions recognised that Australia was not *terra nullius* at the time of settlement and that Indigenous peoples had rights to native title under the common law.

MABO V. QUEENSLAND (NO. 2) (1992) 175 CLR 1

The claim, brought by the Meriam people, who occupied a group of islands known as the Murray Islands in the Torres Strait between Queensland and New Guinea, was that they could trace their occupancy back to before white settlement. The Murray Islands were annexed to Queensland in 1879 and became subject to Queensland law from that date. However, based on evidence of continuous land ownership, three of the Murray Islanders claimed that any land rights that the state might claim to have would be subject to the rights of the Murray Islanders, based on local custom and traditional title.

ISSUE: Was Australia territory that was acquired by treaty or conquest, or territory that was *terra nullius*? What was the status of the colony at settlement? If the Australian colonies were said to have been acquired by settlement based on *terra nullius* and the Aboriginals were not an organised society, then the laws of England applied. If the colony was acquired by conquest, the laws of the original inhabitants would be recognised, subject to the right of the English Parliament to override local laws.

DECISION: The High Court agreed that the Murray Islanders were entitled to possession, occupation, use and enjoyment of their lands. By a six-to-one majority, the Court agreed that the Australian common law 'recognises a form of native title which, in the cases where it has not been extinguished, reflects the entitlement of the indigenous inhabitants, in accordance with their laws or customs, to their traditional lands . . .' (p. 1).

COMMENT: Native title was not defined by the High Court, but could be said to be the term used to describe the common law rights and interests of any particular group of Aboriginal and Torres Strait Islander peoples in land according to their laws, traditions and customs. Native title is a pre-existing right that evolved over thousands of years and is not a grant or right created by governments.

Doctrine of Reception laid to rest

For the first time, the common law rights in land of Australia's Indigenous people were recognised and it was proclaimed that native title must be treated equally before the law with other titles that flow from the Crown. The Doctrine of Reception or the principle of *terra nullius* was effectively laid to rest by the High Court. (See also pp. 714–715.)

Does Mabo have implications other than for native title?

Whether the decision in *Mabo* extended beyond the question of Aboriginal land rights to recognition of Aboriginal customary law in criminal cases was explored in the case of *Walker v. State of New South Wales* (1995) 69 ALJR 111. The Chief Justice of the High Court, *Mason* CJ, rejected the proposition that criminal legislation did not apply to persons of Aboriginal descent on the basis that all people should stand equal before the law. He went on to find that even if the customary criminal law had survived English settlement, it had been extinguished by the criminal legislation passed by the states and territories.

WALKER V. NEW SOUTH WALES (1994) 182 CLR 45

Walker, an Aboriginal, was charged with a criminal offence under New South Wales law.

ISSUES: Did the *Mabo* decision establish that Australian governments lacked the power to pass laws affecting Aboriginal people?

If a state could pass laws affecting the Aboriginal people, were they effective before they consented to them?

DECISION: The High Court held that the New South Wales Parliament has power to make laws for the peace, welfare and good government of New South Wales in all cases. The *Mabo* decision did not suggest that Australian parliaments lacked legislative competence to regulate or affect the rights of the Aboriginal people or that these laws are subject to their acceptance or consent.

COMMENT: It was also argued that the effect of the *Mabo* decision was that Aboriginal customary criminal law survived British settlement, in the same way that the customary law relating to land tenure of the Meriam people existed. However, the court did not accept this proposition as it ran contrary to the principle that all people stand equal before the law. *Mabo* is not authority for the proposition that criminal laws of general application do not apply to Aboriginal people. English criminal law did not, and Australian criminal law does not, accommodate an alternative body of law operating alongside it.

From penal colony to Federation (1788–1900)

Table 1.1 Statutory developments between 1788 and 1900

New South Wales Act 1823 (Imp) (The *Third Charter of Justice*)
Australian Courts Act 1828 (Imp)
Australian Constitution Act 1850 (Imp)
New South Wales Constitution Act 1855 (Imp)
Colonial Laws Validity Act 1865 (Imp)

Between 1788 and 1823 both the colonists and the convicts were subject to the complete control of the English Parliament, effectively being under martial law. All the laws of England were brought by Governor Phillip and his settlers to a territory that was considered to be *terra nullius*, so the Doctrine of Reception applied.

It was not until 35 years after the first British settlement in Australia that the general law of England applied to the colony. Until then it had not been practical to apply a legal system identical to England's legal system. Two reasons can be suggested:

- the colony was initially established as a penal colony, consisting mainly of convicts and their guards; and
- the early free settlers (those who came of their own free will) did not have the necessary expertise or numbers to set up a system identical to that in England.

New South Wales Act 1823 (Imp) (The *Third Charter of Justice*)

In response to pressure from free settlers and former convicts for a legal system and limited self-government, the English Parliament passed the *Third Charter of Justice* which led to the *New South Wales Act 1823* (Imp). This Act:

- established the Supreme Court of New South Wales, with a chief justice (who had to certify any laws passed by the legislature as being consistent with the laws of England) and three judges. The court had a civil and criminal jurisdiction based on the English legal system; and
- established a Legislative Council, whose first task was to make laws in the colony consistent with those of England. The Governor was obliged to consult with the Council and the English Parliament still had the right to disallow any law passed by the legislature.

The first stage of change from martial law to self-government and ultimately independence was limited in its operation because nearly two-thirds of the population had been convicts or were still serving their sentences. The Governor's sole right to initiate legislation and override the wishes of the Legislative Council was seen by the English Parliament as a safeguard to ensure they retained control of the colony.

Australian Courts Act 1828 (Imp)

In 1828 the English Parliament passed the *Australian Courts Act*, which gave limited self-government to the colony. This Act:

- required the Governor to consult with the Legislative Council. Provision was made for the legislature to decide, in doubtful cases, how English law was to apply to New South Wales and Van Diemen's Land; and
- provided that English statutes passed after 1828 only applied to Australia if there were particular provisions contained in them to that effect. English law still applied to the settlements of Western Australia (established in 1829) and South Australia (established in 1834).

It marked the beginning of the evolution of Australian law by providing that all laws then in force in England should be applied in Australia as far as was reasonably consistent with local conditions.

The *New South Wales Act* and the *Australian Courts Act* together gave New South Wales not only a style of government based on the English model, but also a similar legal system.

English law	NSW statutes
pre-1828	1828–today

FIGURE 1.5 *Sources of New South Wales law*

Australian Constitution Act 1850 (Imp)

The *Australian Constitution Act* enabled the colonies to take the next step towards independence. This Act:

- gave the Legislative Councils of the colonies the power to create local legislatures, which in turn had the power to regulate the right to vote, grant membership of the councils and make laws for the 'peace, welfare and good government of the respective colonies';
- provided a basic format for the drawing up of constitutions for New South Wales, Victoria, South Australia and Tasmania; and
- effected the separation of the Port Phillip District (Victoria) from New South Wales.

The Legislative Councils in New South Wales, Victoria, South Australia and Tasmania drew up constitutions on the format of the 1850 Act. While there are some differences between the constitutional paths each chose, a common feature was that each had a bi-cameral (two-house) legislature.

New South Wales Constitution Act 1855 (Imp)

The Legislative Council had been expanded to 24 elected members and 12 members appointed by the Governor in 1842, but its law-making power was still limited to legislating in a manner consistent with English law. However, in response to demands from the colonists for greater self-rule, the English Parliament passed the *New South Wales Constitution Act* in 1855.

This Act:

- established a **Constitution** for New South Wales; and
- provided for a **bi-cameral legislature**, i.e. a parliament consisting of two Houses—a **Legislative Assembly** (the Lower House) and a **Legislative Council** (the Upper House), with the Governor as the sovereign's representative. It was empowered to make laws for 'the peace, order and good government of New South Wales'. This meant that it had the power to raise taxes and duties, but it was not clear whether the Parliament could amend its own Constitution or pass laws that were inconsistent with the English Parliament.

The colonies' separation from New South Wales

After their separation from New South Wales, Tasmania (1854), Victoria (1855) (see Figure 1.7) and Queensland (1859) became independent colonies and achieved self-government with their own constitutions. Again, this was a result of English Acts of Parliament. These colonies inherited English law to 1828, and New South Wales law between 1828 and the date of their self-government.

South Australia (1856) and Western Australia (1890) achieved self-government without inheriting any New South Wales law as they had not been part of that colony.

English law	Western Australia statutes
pre-1890	1890–today

FIGURE 1.6 *Sources of Western Australian law*

The *Colonial Laws Validity Act 1865* (Imp)

The *Colonial Laws Validity Act 1865* established:

- the right of the colonies to amend their own constitutions; and

- that the colonies could enact legislation without necessarily applying English domestic law to Australian law, provided that no English statute directly applied to the colony in question. Where an English statute contained express provisions that it had to be followed by colonial governments, it was said to have paramount force.

From Federation to today

Table 1.2 Statutory developments since 1900

Commonwealth of Australia Constitution Act 1900 (Imp)
Constitution Act 1902 (NSW)
The Constitution Act Amendment Act 1921
Statute of Westminster 1931 (Imp)
Statute of Westminster Adoption Act 1942 (Cth)
Privy Council (Limitation of Appeals) Act 1968 (Cth)
Imperial Acts Application Act 1969 (NSW)
Privy Council (Appeals from the High Court) Act 1975 (Cth)
Australia Act 1986 (Cth) and the *Australia (Request and Consent) Act 1985* (Cth)

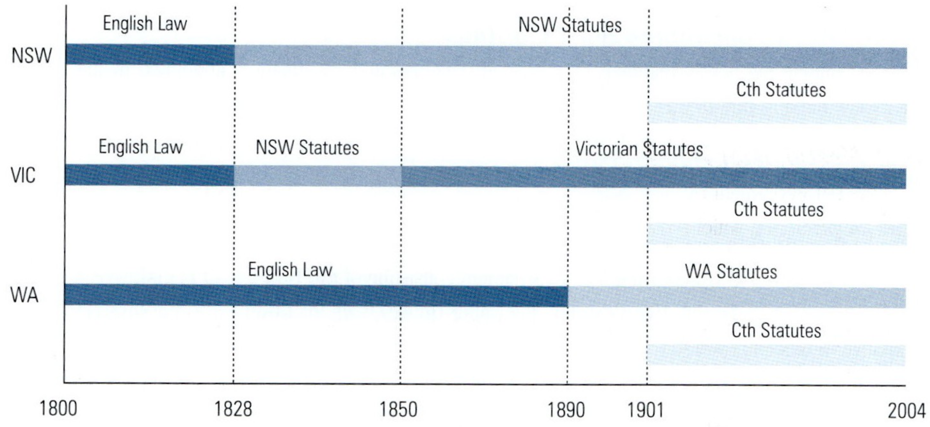

FIGURE 1.7 *Sources of NSW, Victorian and Western Australian law today*

Commonwealth of Australia Constitution Act 1900 (Imp)

The *Commonwealth of Australia Constitution Act* was enacted on 1 January 1901, transforming the six former colonies into states and creating a federal system of government. This is a system where the powers are divided by the Constitution between the Commonwealth and the states. Attached as a schedule to the Act was the **Commonwealth Constitution**.

Under this federal system, specific powers were granted exclusively to the federal or Commonwealth Parliament under the Constitution. Any remaining powers remained with the states. The Commonwealth Parliament was based on the Westminster system of government. It was a bi-cameral parliament consisting of the House of Representatives (the Lower House) and the Senate (the Upper House). The Act also established the High Court of Australia, although at this stage its decisions could still be appealed to the Privy Council in London.

Federation made Australia a dominion

The effect of Federation was to make Australia a **dominion**. This meant it was a self-governing country, although the *Colonial Laws Validity Act* still gave the English Parliament the power to pass any laws that it felt were necessary to protect the interests of the British Empire.

One of the effects of Federation was to add an additional source of law to the states' legal systems. It also effectively added a third level of government to Australia, so there now is:

- a federal or Commonwealth government;
- state governments; and
- local governments i.e., councils and shires.

Constitution Act 1902 (NSW)

In 1902 the *Constitution Act* was passed, establishing a constitution for New South Wales with the power to legislate for the peace, order and good government of the state.

The Constitution Act Amendment Act 1921 (Qld)

Queensland is the only state with a uni-cameral parliament

The Queensland Parliament began life as a bi-cameral parliament but today is a uni-cameral parliament, comprising only one House, the Legislative Assembly (Lower House). It is the only uni-cameral state parliament in Australia (the Australian Capital Territory and the Northern Territory are also uni-cameral parliaments). The Queensland Legislative Council (the Upper House) was abolished in 1922 by *The Constitution Act Amendment Act 1921*.

Statute of Westminster 1931 (Imp)

The *Statute of Westminster 1931* marked the beginning of the final stages in the evolutionary process of Australian independence. The Commonwealth Parliament gained the right to repeal or amend applicable laws passed by the English Parliament; and it was stated that future statutes passed by that Parliament had no force in the dominions unless requested by the dominion Parliament. However, the Act did not come into force until it was ratified by the Parliament of each dominion, which in Australia's case was not until 1942.

Statute of Westminster Adoption Act 1942 (Cth)

The Commonwealth Parliament did not ratify the *Statute of Westminster* until 1942 when it passed the *Statute of Westminster Adoption Act*, which it made retrospective to 3 September 1939 (the date of the outbreak of the Second World War) and removed the final limitation on self-government. This meant that the Commonwealth could amend or repeal any English law. It also marked the end of the application of the *Colonial Laws Validity Act*, giving the Commonwealth power to pass extra-territorial legislation (these are laws that apply outside the limits of the territory controlled by Parliament).

Privy Council (Limitation of Appeals) Act 1968 (Cth)

In 1968 the Commonwealth Parliament passed the *Privy Council (Limitation of Appeals) Act* abolishing appeals to the Privy Council from the High Court on matters involving federal law. However, it was still possible for a litigant to appeal from a state Supreme Court or the High Court on matters of state law.

Imperial Acts Application Act 1969 (NSW)

The *Imperial Acts Application Act* repealed a large number of English statutes that still applied in New South Wales although some statutes, such as the Magna Carta, were preserved.

Privy Council (Appeals from the High Court) Act 1975 (Cth)

In 1975 the Commonwealth Parliament removed the right of appeal from the High Court to the Privy Council. However, it was still possible for litigants to appeal from a state Supreme Court to the Privy Council on questions of state law.

Australia Act 1986 (Cth) and the *Australia (Request and Consent) Act 1985* (Cth)

These Acts repealed the *Colonial Laws Validity Act 1865* and abolished what was known as the repugnancy rule, whereby a state law which was inconsistent with an English law was invalid. Since 1986 no statutes passed by the English Parliament have had any effect on the Commonwealth or the states.

The legislation also abolished the right of appeal to the Privy Council from the state Supreme Courts. This broke the last direct link with the English legal system and completed the process of constitutional development.

To achieve Australia's status as an independent and sovereign nation, the six states first had to pass uniform legislation (the *Australia Acts (Request) Act 1985*) requesting the Commonwealth Parliament to enact the *Australia Act 1986*. The *Australia Act 1986* in turn requested approval of the *Australia Act 1986* by the English Parliament. This then requested and consented to the *Australia (Request and Consent) Act 1985* (Cth) passed by the Commonwealth Parliament.

Doing business

There are three potential sources of regulatory laws in Australia that business **must** be aware of: Commonwealth, state and territory, and local government. ■

COMMONWEALTH AND STATE POWERS

Exclusive powers of Cth prevail over state powers

(The Commonwealth Constitution is available online at: **http://www.aph.gov.au/senate/general/constitution/**)

When reading the Commonwealth Constitution today it should be remembered that it reflects the colonial interests of the 1890s. As a result, the only exclusive powers (i.e. powers controlled only by the Commonwealth, such as defence, customs and excise) are those few given to it by agreement of the colonial (state) politicians (see Figure 1.8).

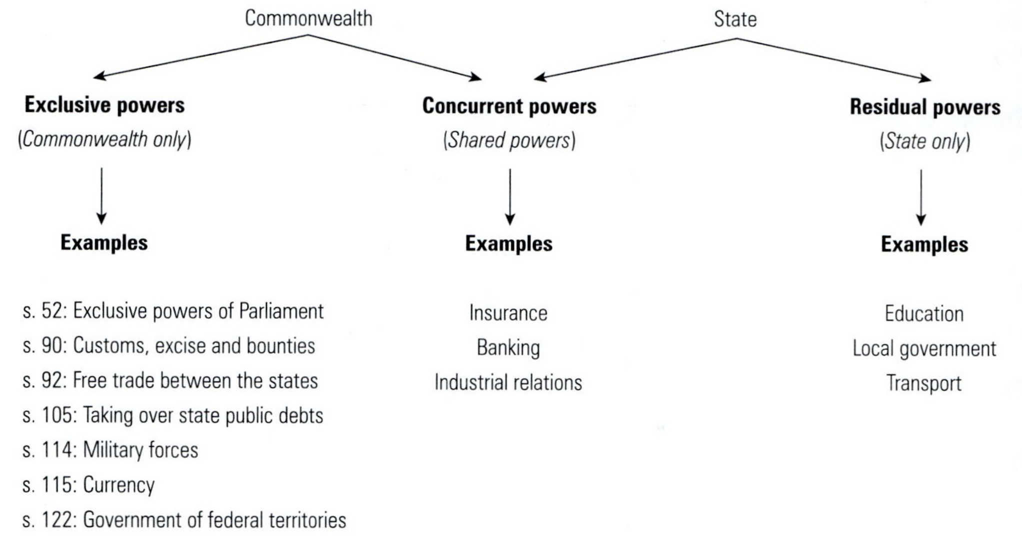

FIGURE 1.8 *Exclusive, concurrent and residual powers*

Where there is any inconsistency between laws made under the exclusive powers of the Commonwealth Constitution by the Commonwealth and any state laws, s. 109 of the Commonwealth Constitution provides that the state law, to the extent of the inconsistency, shall be **invalid**.

Bulk of Cth powers are held concurrently with states under s. 51

The bulk of the Commonwealth's powers are **concurrently** held (i.e. shared) with the states, of which the **most important is s. 51** (see Figure 1.9). This means that both the Commonwealth and the states have the power to legislate in these areas. However, political reality and s. 109 may in practice make it difficult for a state to legislate in an area where the Commonwealth has already passed legislation.

If nothing at all is said in the Commonwealth Constitution about an area, authority to legislate in that area remains with the states and is said to be a **residual** power; for example, local government, education and transport. If the

Commonwealth attempted to pass a law in respect of a matter not within the powers conferred upon it by the Constitution, the law would be *ultra vires* and, therefore, invalid.

Residual powers are those that are not exclusive or concurrent powers

WALLIS V. DOWNARD-PICKFORD (NORTH QUEENSLAND) PTY LTD (1994) 68 ALJR 395

Goods belonging to Wallis suffered $1663 damage while being transported across Queensland by a removalist company. The company admitted liability but only offered to pay $200, the maximum required under the now repealed Queensland *Carriage of Goods by Land (Carrier's Liabilities) Act 1967*.

ISSUE: Was the state Act with its limit on the amount of damages recoverable invalid under s. 109 of the Constitution because it clashed with the Commonwealth's *Trade Practices Act 1974* where there was no limit?

DECISION: The High Court held that the Queensland Act, which validly attempted to limit contractual liability for breach of warranty, was inconsistent with the Commonwealth Act. While both Acts were proper exercises of legislative power, there was an inconsistency as the state Act limited the amount of damages to $200. Therefore, s. 109 of the Constitution made the state Act invalid and the removalist company was liable for the full loss, i.e. $1663.

The Constitution

PART V.—POWERS OF THE PARLIAMENT.

Part V. Powers of the Parliament.

51. The Parliament shall, subject to this Constitution, have power[11] to make laws for the peace, order, and good government of the Commonwealth with respect to:— Legislative powers of the Parliament.

(i.) Trade and commerce with other countries, and among the States:

(ii.) Taxation; but so as not to discriminate between States or parts of States:

(iii.) Bounties on the production or export of goods, but so that such bounties shall be uniform throughout the Commonwealth:

(iv.) Borrowing money on the public credit of the Commonwealth:

(v.) Postal, telegraphic, telephonic, and other like services:

(vi.) The naval and military defence of the Commonwealth and of the several States, and the control of the forces to execute and maintain the laws of the Commonwealth:

(vii.) Lighthouses, lightships, beacons and buoys:

(viii.) Astronomical and meteorological observations:

(ix.) Quarantine:

(x.) Fisheries in Australian waters beyond territorial limits:

(xi.) Census and statistics:

(xii.) Currency, coinage, and legal tender:

(xiii.) Banking, other than State banking; also State banking extending beyond the limits of the State concerned, the incorporation of banks, and the issue of paper money:

(xiv.) Insurance, other than State insurance; also State insurance extending beyond the limits of the State concerned:

FIGURE 1.9 *(continues)*

(xv.) Weights and measures:

(xvi.) Bills of exchange and promissory notes:

(xvii.) Bankruptcy and insolvency:

(xviii.) Copyrights, patents of inventions and designs, and trade marks:

(xix.) Naturalization and aliens:

(xx.) Foreign corporations, and trading or financial corporations formed within the limits of the Commonwealth:

(xxi.) Marriage:

(xxii.) Divorce and matrimonial causes; and in relation thereto, parental rights, and the custody and guardianship of infants:

(xxiii.) Invalid and old-age pensions:

(xxiiiA.) The provision of maternity allowances, widows' pensions, child endowment, unemployment, pharmaceutical, sickness and hospital benefits, medical and dental services (but not so as to authorize any form of civil conscription), benefits to students and family allowances: Inserted by No. 81, 1946, s. 2.

(xxiv.) The service and execution throughout the Commonwealth of the civil and criminal process and the judgments of the courts of the States:

(xxv.) The recognition throughout the Commonwealth of the laws, the public Acts and records, and the judicial proceedings of the States:

Altered by No. 55, 1967, s. 2. (xxvi.) The people of any race~~, other than the aboriginal race in any State,~~ for whom it is deemed necessary to make special laws:

(xxvii.) Immigration and emigration:

(xxviii.) The influx of criminals:

(xxix.) External affairs:

(xxx.) The relations of the Commonwealth with the islands of the Pacific:

(xxxi.) The acquisition of property on just terms from any State or person for any purpose in respect of which the Parliament has power to make laws:

(xxxii.) The control of railways with respect to transport for the naval and military purposes of the Commonwealth:

(xxxiii.) The acquisition, with the consent of a State, of any railways of the State on terms arranged between the Commonwealth and the State:

(xxxiv.) Railway construction and extension in any State with the consent of that State:

(xxxv.) Conciliation and arbitration for the prevention and settlement of industrial disputes extending beyond the limits of any one State:

(xxxvi.) Matters in respect of which this Constitution makes provision until the Parliament otherwise provides:

(xxxvii.) Matters referred to the Parliament of the Commonwealth by the Parliament or Parliaments of any State or States,[12] but so that the law shall extend only to States by whose Parliaments the matter is referred, or which afterwards adopt the law:

(xxxviii.) The exercise within the Commonwealth, at the request or with the concurrence of the Parliaments of all the States directly concerned, of any power which can at the establishment of this Constitution be exercised only by the Parliament of the United Kingdom or by the Federal Council of Australasia:

(xxxix.) Matters incidental to the execution of any power vested by this Constitution in the Parliament or in either House thereof, or in the Government of the Commonwealth, or in the Federal Judicature, or in any department or officer of the Commonwealth.

FIGURE 1.9 *Extract from s. 51, Australian Constitution*

The High Court has, since inception, adopted a number of tests to settle the question of what happens in the event of a conflict between the provisions of state and Commonwealth laws. The 'covering the field' test is used most frequently. This involves consideration of:

- whether the Commonwealth law was intended to be supplementary to or cumulative upon state law, in which case both laws could coexist; or
- whether it was intended to exclusively govern the particular conduct or matter, in which case the state law would be inconsistent and therefore invalid.

Much of the expansion of federal power in recent years has taken place through High Court interpretation of the Constitution. A good example of the expansion of federal power in the area of business law has been the *Trade Practices Act 1974* (Cth) which extends beyond regulation of unfair trading practices of businesses to consumer protection. A careful examination of the Constitution would reveal that there is no power to regulate trade practices or consumer protection as such. Instead, the Commonwealth has relied on a number of specific powers in the Constitution, of which the most important is the corporations power (s. 51(xx)). However, the Act also catches the activities of individuals. Commonwealth power includes trade or commerce with other countries (s. 51(i)), within a territory (or between territories or a state and a territory) (s. 122), or supply of goods or services to the Commonwealth (s. 52). Individuals may also be caught under the postal and telecommunications power (s. 51(v)) as Part V Div. 1 (Unfair Practices) and Div. 1A (Product Safety and Product Information) are based on this head of power.

However, federal power could be expanded by a state or states handing over any powers they have to the Commonwealth. One example was the Victorian government handing over its industrial relations powers to the Commonwealth in 1998. Alternatively, Commonwealth powers could be expanded through the use of s. 128 of the Constitution, which allows the Constitution to be changed by referendum.

Changing the Constitution

Changing the Constitution is difficult

The Commonwealth Constitution can only be formally (amended) changed if the following requirements set out under s. 128 of the Constitution are satisfied:

- the proposed amendment is passed by an absolute majority of members in both the House of Representatives and the Senate;
- the proposal is put to a vote of the Australian voters (**a referendum**) within two to six months of the absolute majority vote;
- the proposal is approved by a majority of the voters and there is a majority approval in a majority of the states. In other words, more than 50 per cent of the voters nationwide must say 'Yes' and a majority of voters in at least four states must say 'Yes'; and
- the Governor-General gives Royal Assent to the amendment.

Since Federation there have been 43 proposals to change the Constitution, but only eight have been successful. Such has been the conservatism of the Australian voter! This was again demonstrated by the referendum in November 1999 when the attempt to introduce a preamble to the Constitution and make Australia a republic were soundly rejected by the electorate. In reality, the expansion of federal power has been more a result of the interpretation of the Constitution by the High Court.

The powers of the territories

The Northern Territory and the Australian Capital Territory both have a form of self-government but they have not achieved state status. They both have an elected Legislative Assembly (they are uni-cameral parliaments) which may pass laws unless they are blocked (vetoed) or modified by the House of Representatives or Senate of the Commonwealth Parliament. For example, the Northern Territory had its voluntary euthanasia legislation blocked in 1997 and its Native Title legislation blocked in 1999.

SEPARATION OF POWERS

One of the features of the Australian Constitution is that it provides for the separation between the legislative, executive and judicial powers of the Commonwealth (see Figure 1.10).

The doctrine of separation of powers, formulated by French philosopher and jurist Montesquieu in 1748, has been enshrined in the Commonwealth Constitution (but **not** in state constitutions):

- Section 1 vests **legislative power** in a federal Parliament, consisting of the Queen, the House of Representatives and the Senate.
- Section 61 vests **executive power** in the Queen and is exercisable by the Governor-General at Commonwealth level and by Governors at state level. The body that advises the Governor-General is the federal Executive Council (s.62). As a matter of convention the Governor-General will generally act as advised by the Prime Minister.
- Section 71 vests **judicial power** in the High Court and such other federal courts as the parliament creates.

The functions of the three branches are:

- The **legislative** function—the enactment or making of the law through the Commonwealth or state parliaments.
- The **executive** function—the formulation of policy and its administration through the Cabinet (or the Ministers within the Cabinet) of the elected Commonwealth or state government.
- The **judicial** function—the interpretation, application and enforcement of the law through the court systems of the Commonwealth and the states.

Under the doctrine of separation of powers, the **legislature** (Parliament) is the **supreme law-maker**. The judicature is meant to give effect to the laws.

In reality, there is little or no separation between the executive and legislative functions in Australia

In theory, the doctrine of the separation of powers means that no one person or body shall exercise more than one power. However, in reality, there is no separation between the executive and the legislative functions of federal government. Executive power generally rests with those ministers in government who form the Cabinet. The Prime Minister and the executive ministers are also elected members of Parliament, which is the arm that exercises the legislative function. By contrast, the separation between the Judicature on the one hand and the Parliament and the Executive on the other is strict: *A-G for Australia & Kirby v. R and the Boilermakers Society* [1957] AC 288.

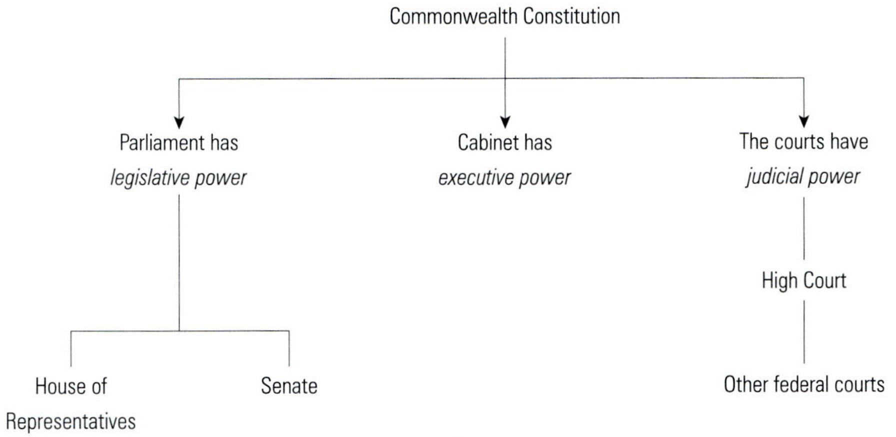

FIGURE 1.10 *Doctrine of separation of powers*

WEB RESOURCES

The amount of material available on the web for topics in this chapter continues to grow at a phenomenal rate. As a result, no attempt has been made to try to include all the sites. What follows are some of the better sites that we have been able to discover and many have gateways to further sites. No doubt new and better sites will continue to spring up and as we become aware of them we will list them on the Pearson web pages.

AUSTRALIA'S LEGAL SYSTEM

Australian Law Online: This is a very useful site prepared by the Commonwealth government that looks at a variety of topics relevant to this text and this chapter including: the Law in Australia, the parliamentary system, an overview of the Constitution and the process of law-making. Click on the topic Legal system on that page and go to About our Legal System:
http://www.law.gov.au/

Parliament of Australia: a very comprehensive Commonwealth government site which provides detailed information on the House of Representatives, the Senate, legislation, committees and the workings of Parliament:
http://www.aph.gov.au/index.htm

Parliamentary papers: a useful site for finding information on Bills and their purpose, background and main provisions:
http://www.aph.gov.au/library/pubs/index.htm

About the courts: Where do our laws come from? A Queensland site which provides a good web page summary on where Australia's laws come from:
http://www.justice.qld.gov.au/education/courts/ourlaws.htm

Queensland online reference guide: a guide to information about Queensland and its government, Cabinet and Parliament:
http://www.qld.gov.au/you_and_your_government/index.html

Victorian government: the general gateway into Victoria. If you go to the Government and Politics site you will find quite extensive information about each of those topics:
http://www.vic.gov.au/VictoriaOnline

Tasmania: a useful site containing information on Tasmania's parliamentary system can be found at:
http://www.parliament.tas.gov.au/

New South Wales: an excellent gateway not only to NSW government agencies but also to business (see other related links):
http://www.nsw.gov.au/

For specific information on the New South Wales Parliament:
http://www.parliament.nsw.gov.au/

South Australia: general information on the South Australian government and its government departments:
http://www.sa.gov.au/

For specific information on the South Australian parliamentary system, and linkages to other Australian governments as well as to South Australian departments:
http://www.parliament.sa.gov.au/

Western Australia: a general gateway to government and government departments in Western Australia:
http://www.wa.gov.au/

For specific information on government and the parliamentary system:
http://www.wa.gov.au/government.html

Northern Territory: contains information on the Northern Territory government and its various departments:
http://www.nt.gov.au/

For information specifically on the Northern Territory Parliament:
http://www.nt.gov.au/lant/parliament/parliament.shtml

Australian Capital Territory: for information on the Australian Capital Territory government and its departments:
http://www.act.gov.au/

For information specifically related to the Australian Capital Territory Legislative Assembly:
http://www.parliament.act.gov.au/

REVIEW QUESTIONS ?

activebook

Activebook resources include in-depth summaries with links to the relevant part of the book. For revision, add your own notes to the summaries provided by using the note-taking function.

1.1 If you were asked to provide a definition of 'law', how would you define it?

1.2 Are there any benefits for a business in adopting an ethical code of practice? Discuss.

1.3 Explain the role that law fulfils in society. What happens when that role breaks down?

1.4 Are the three propositions of the 'rule of law' formulated by Professor Dicey in the 19th century still valid today? Discuss.

1.5 Indicate whether each of the following statements is true or false:

	TRUE	FALSE
▪ Common law emphasises rights, civil law emphasises remedies	☐	☐
▪ International treaties and conventions automatically become part of domestic law	☐	☐
▪ Laws made by parliaments are called statute law	☐	☐
▪ Common law is a code-based legal system	☐	☐
▪ Laws made by courts are called statute laws	☐	☐
▪ Common law and equity are administered in different courts	☐	☐
▪ Roman law, canon law and merchant law are major sources of English law	☐	☐
▪ The Provisions of Oxford 1258 made the common law much more flexible	☐	☐
▪ Equity emphasises fairness and justice	☐	☐
▪ The main remedy for an action based in the common law is damages	☐	☐
▪ Equitable remedies are only allowed at the discretion of the court and when damages are not an adequate remedy	☐	☐
▪ Specific performance is a court order directing a person to do something	☐	☐
▪ Common law and equity are administered in separate courts	☐	☐
▪ The *Colonial Laws Validity Act 1865* (Imp) gave the colonies the right to amend their own constitutions	☐	☐
▪ The *Statute of Westminster 1931* (Imp) made Australia a federation	☐	☐
▪ The effect of the decision in the *Mabo* case was to lay to rest the idea that Australia was *terra nullius*	☐	☐
▪ Separation of powers is a reference to the division of powers between the Commonwealth and the states	☐	☐
▪ When a Commonwealth Act clashes with a State Act, the State Act must be followed	☐	☐
▪ The highest court of appeal from decisions of state courts in Australia is the Privy Council	☐	☐

1.6 Explain the differences between international law and domestic law, if any.

1.7 Why did common law become so rigid and inflexible?

1.8 In what ways does equity law differ from common law?

1.9 What are the main differences between common law and statute law?

1.10 In the event of a conflict between common law and statute law, which prevails? Explain why.

1.11 Explain why it was important to define the status of a colony upon settlement?

1.12 What major changes were brought about by:

- *The Australian Courts Act 1828* (Imp)?
- *The Australian Colonies Government Act 1850* (Imp)?
- *The Colonial Laws Validity Act 1865* (Imp)?
- *The Commonwealth of Australia Constitution Act 1900* (Imp)?
- *The Statute of Westminster 1931* (Imp)?

1.13 Briefly explain what effect, if any, that High Court decisions such as *Mabo* and *Wik* have had on the Doctrine of Reception and the Australian legal system.

1.14 Explain what is meant by each of the following terms:

- Exclusive powers
- Concurrent powers
- Separation of powers
- *Terra nullius*
- Native title.

1.15 List the three functions of government referred to in the doctrine of separation of powers and consider whether you think that the distinction today is in fact artificial.

1.16 Are judicial appointments to the Bench of the High Court consistent with the doctrine of separation of powers? Discuss.

CRITICAL THINKING

1.1 With three tiers of government and a population of a little under 20 million people, is Australia over-governed and over-taxed?

1.2 Will Australia ever become a republic? Consider the debates that took place in 1999 and whether they are more or less valid today.

CHAPTER 2 Legal Systems

CHAPTER CONTENTS

activebook

This icon is used throughout the following chapter to remind you to visit the *Business Law* online activebook for additional exercises, links to legal websites, and feedback. For a detailed explanation of what is in the activebook please refer to the inside cover of this textbook. The activebook is available through OneKey.

Where do I start?
Learning path: Use the activebook to complete a pre-chapter warm-up exercise.
There are many definitions of legal terms to assist with your understanding of the material.

CHAPTER OBJECTIVES

On completion of this chapter, you should be able to:

- explain the role of the police and the courts in the legal system
- describe the court system at state and federal levels
- state the jurisdictional limits for each court in your state
- draw up the court hierarchy of your state
- explain the features of a court hierarchy
- explain the role of the ombudsman
- identify and describe alternative ways of settling disputes
- explain the roles of the parties to a legal action
- describe some of the duties performed by barristers and solicitors
- explain the main role of the jury in the court system.

KEY TERMS

An understanding of the following terms will help you to better understand the material in this chapter:

- **appeal:** any proceeding taken by a litigant from a lower court to a higher court
- **appellant:** one who appeals
- **bailiff:** a court officer employed to serve writs, make arrests and executions on the property of judgement debtors
- **barrister:** a legally qualified person who practises before the Bar, generally in intermediate and superior courts
- **class action or group proceeding:** an action brought by one or a few on behalf of a larger group who have a common cause
- **complainant:** the plaintiff in a legal or equitable pleading
- **defendant:** the person against whom a civil action is being brought; the person being sued
- **in camera:** the public and the media are not allowed into the court
- **indictable offence:** the more serious crimes and generally heard before a judge and jury in the intermediate and superior courts
- **judgement:** the final order of a court entered upon the completion of an action
- **jurisdiction:** the power and authority conferred upon a court, either by statute or constitutionally
- **jury:** a body of sworn men and women summoned to decide questions of fact in a court of law
- **plaintiff:** the party commencing a civil action in a court of first instance
- **QC:** Queen's Counsel
- **R:** stands for **Rex** or **Reg**, depending on whether there was a King or Queen on the throne in England at the time the matter came to court and means that the Crown was a party to the case (often found in criminal law cases)
- **respondent:** a person against whom an appeal is brought
- **SC:** Senior Counsel; this term replaces that of Queen's Counsel and is a term given to a barrister of eminence in the profession
- **summary offence:** a minor criminal offence, dealt with in a lower court.

what if . . .

You were arrested and charged by the police for murder on the basis that you fitted the description of a person seen leaving the scene of the crime with a gun. The police do not believe anything you say and have no interest in pursuing the investigation any further because they are convinced you did it. At the time, you were home alone asleep in bed and no-one knew where you were. Would it matter to you that murder was a criminal offence and not a civil law matter under the common law or doesn't it matter?

There are two major court systems in Australia:

- the federal court system; and
- the court system of the six states and two territories.

Each of these systems has jurisdiction to hear different types of cases, and because of the importance of the legal framework to the business environment, it is necessary to understand how each system operates in the event that a dispute leads to litigation.

The process of bringing and maintaining, or defending, a lawsuit (called litigation) is both time consuming and costly owing to the complex procedural rules employed within our court systems. As a rule of thumb, the higher the court in a court hierarchy, the greater will be the legal costs.

The legal system in Australia is adversarial in nature, and while using a solicitor or barrister is not compulsory, most parties will inevitably use them when they are involved in litigation. The solicitor will be used in pre-trial matters while the barrister will represent them in court.

In response to the expense and difficulty of bringing a lawsuit, several forms of alternative dispute resolution have been developed, which are being used more and more often to resolve commercial disputes.

> This chapter discusses the various court systems, the jurisdiction of the courts to hear cases, alternative methods to the courts to resolve disputes, the functions of some of the judicial and quasi-judicial tribunals and the ombudsman, the role of court personnel, and the litigation process.

WHAT IS THE ROLE OF THE POLICE AND THE COURTS?

The role of the police

In theory, everybody in the community is responsible for apprehending law-breakers. However, in practice this is a function that is usually better left to the police force. The police force plays no direct role (although they certainly play an indirect role) in the creation of new laws. Nor are they concerned with the punishment of wrongdoers.

IN BRIEF

The role of the police

The main function of the police is to enforce the laws created by other authorities. They serve the law itself, and are independent of the government.

Police enforce the law and are community guardians of the peace

The police are the **community guardians of the peace** (the armed forces are the guardians of the state). Their duties include:

- the prevention of crime;

- the apprehension of offenders against the criminal law;
- the protection of life and property;
- the enforcement of the law; and
- the safety of the public.

In order to achieve these ends, each of the states and the Commonwealth have their own police force which is under their exclusive control.

A considerable amount of police time, and some will say it is too much time, is involved in work in and for the courts. Some of their court work includes:

- acting as Crown prosecutors in the lower or inferior courts (Magistrate's and Local Courts);
- appearing as witnesses of fact in criminal and traffic cases;
- acting as enforcers of court judgements; and
- responsibility for the initiation and conduct of the majority of prosecutions for summary offences (minor offences, such as shoplifting) and the less serious indictable offences (such as assault). Offences which are more serious, such as armed robbery and murder, are brought in the intermediate and superior courts.

The role of the courts

The role of the courts is **administration of the law**. They have a **criminal** and a **civil jurisdiction**. Jurisdiction means the cases or matters that a court can hear, and is established by the statute which creates the court. The more serious the case or matter, the higher within the court hierarchy will be the court that will hear it.

The courts administer the law

Criminal jurisdiction

A crime is an act or conduct by a person that is against the interests of the community as set down by statute and established by case law, and which can result in criminal proceedings being brought against that person. The court where the case will be heard is determined by the seriousness of the offence. For example, shoplifting is a crime but in the eyes of the community it is not considered a serious crime. In most Australian jurisdictions it is usually considered a summary offence, i.e. a minor offence, and is heard in an inferior court such as the Magistrate's or Local Court. On the other hand, murder is considered by the community to be the most serious of crimes (an indictable offence) and is heard in the highest state or territory court, i.e. the Supreme Court.

Criminal jurisdiction—state brings an action against the accused

While the courts are responsible for sentencing a person convicted of a crime, the **penal services**—prison, probation and parole—**are responsible for the convicted person's punishment and rehabilitation**.

Civil jurisdiction

A **civil case** is brought before the courts (i.e. within their civil jurisdiction) when **an individual or organisation commences an action against another individual or organisation**. The court in which the case will be heard will be determined by the amount of money involved and this is set by Regulation, i.e. the executive arm of government will set the amount (see Chapter 3).

Civil case—individual or organisation versus individual or organisation

ORIGINS OF THE COURTS

Until Federation, each colony had its own court system. While the states maintained their court systems after Federation, Chapter III of the Commonwealth Constitution gave the Commonwealth the power (s. 71) to establish a federal court system in addition to the High Court of Australia. The High Court plays a dual role as it forms part of the federal and state court hierarchies, hearing appeals from the courts of the states, as well as deciding cases affecting the Commonwealth Constitution.

Each state has its own tiered system of courts (see Figure 2.1) with jurisdiction over most matters within state boundaries, as well as limited federal jurisdiction, for example, in the area of taxation. This tiered system of courts forms what is known as a court hierarchy, and is similar for all states and the Commonwealth, though the names of the courts do vary.

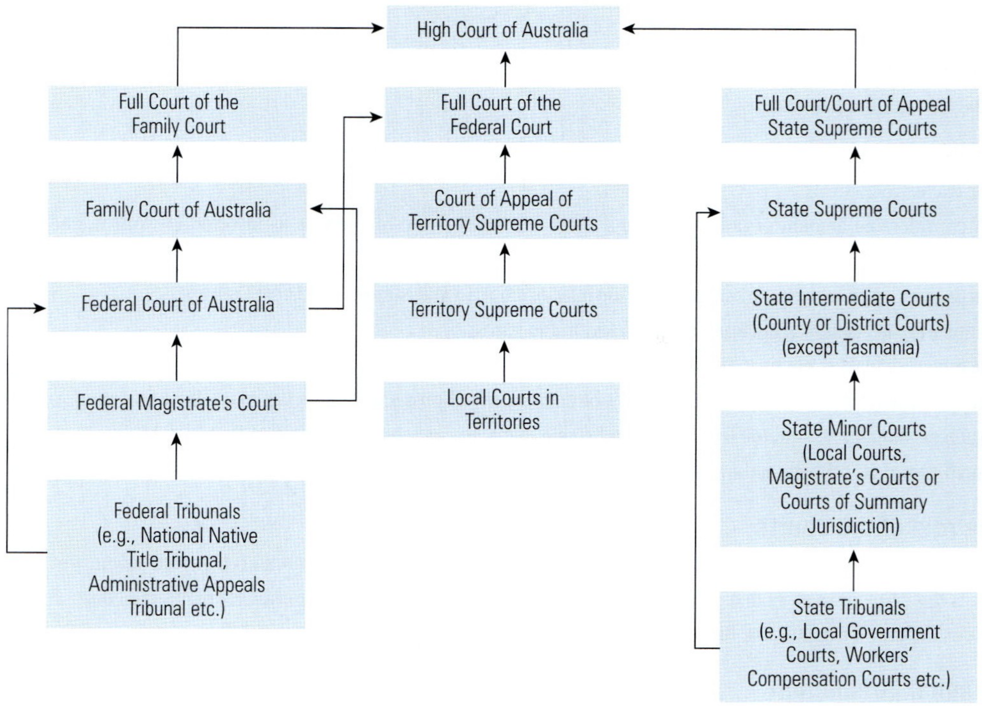

FIGURE 2.1 *The court system*

activebook

To help you to remember and understand the topics covered so far, and for links to legal websites, refer to your online activebook. Model answers provide feedback to problems and exercises.

ORIGINAL AND APPELLATE JURISDICTION

Where a matter is brought to court for the first time, the court that hears the case because it is within its jurisdiction is called a **court of first instance** and is said to have an **original jurisdiction**. If the decision in the case goes on appeal to a higher court, the court that hears that appeal is known as an **appeal or appellate court**, and it is said to have an **appellate jurisdiction**.

> **!** CAUTION NOTE
>
> *It should be noted that the majority of disputes that go to court will be argued before a judge, or judge and jury, on issues of* ***fact*** *rather than issues of law. It is therefore important for businesses to ensure that they keep good records of all their important transactions and any disputes they may have with customers.*

THE STATE COURT HIERARCHY

WEB RESOURCES

For further information on the relevant court system and court, click on the court and tribunals link at the following sites:

Australian Capital Territory:
http://www.courts.act.gov.au/

New South Wales:
http://www.lawlink.nsw.gov.au/

Northern Territory:
http://www.nt.gov.au/justice/

Queensland:
http://www.courts.qld.gov.au/

South Australia:
http://www.courts.sa.gov.au/

Tasmania:
http://www.courts.tas.gov.au/

Victoria:
http://www.courts.vic.gov.au/

Western Australia:
http://www.justice.wa.gov.au/

Because of problems with one-level legal systems, most countries have adopted a hierarchical or tiered court system. Australia is no different. Both the states and the Commonwealth have adopted **hierarchical** court systems. Under this system, the position of a court in a hierarchy indicates the types of cases that it will hear, as well as providing an appeal process for a decision from a lower court to a higher court (see Figure 2.1). As a general rule, the procedures in the lower courts are not as complex as those in the superior courts. While copies of their decisions are not kept in law reports, some jurisdictions are beginning to keep electronic records of some lower court decisions, for example, those of the Federal Magistrate's Court of Australia, Local Court of NSW, County Courts of Victoria, District Court of Queensland, and the Magistrate's Court of Tasmania (for anti-discrimination matters and Coroner's Court decisions).

Inferior (Magistrate's or local) courts

Inferior courts are at the base of a court hierarchy

Inferior or local courts are located at the bottom of the court hierarchy. They are the most numerous of the courts and deal with relatively minor matters which make up around 90 per cent of the matters that come into the court system (see Figure 2.2). They are generally presided over by persons called magistrates (see p. 55) although some states still allow justices of the peace to preside over their courts (see p. 55). Different names are given to these courts in the various states, and in some states the civil and criminal jurisdictions are conducted by separate courts (see Table 2.1).

The aim of these courts is to settle disputes locally, quickly and cheaply where possible. There is less emphasis on formality than is found in the higher courts, though they are still expected to follow procedural rules and the laws of evidence.

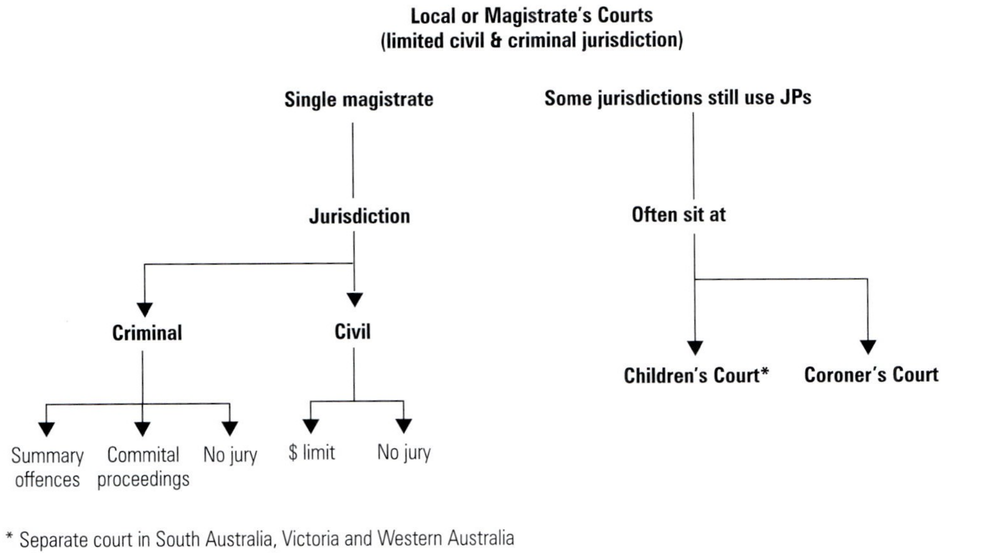

FIGURE 2.2 *Inferior courts*

Criminal jurisdiction of inferior courts

Criminal jurisdiction—summary offences, minor indictable matters and committals

The criminal jurisdiction of local courts includes:

- **All summary offences** (now called 'simple offences' in Western Australia). These are the **less serious crimes** such as failure to pay traffic fines, drink driving, firearm offences, drunk and disorderly behaviour, shoplifting. These matters are disposed of by the magistrate in a summary manner by fine, imprisonment or both.
- **Indictable offences.** These are generally heard in intermediate or superior courts before a judge and jury as they are **more serious criminal offences**. However, provision is made by statute in most states for some less

Table 2.1 Courts—states and territories

	Inferior	*Intermediate*	*Superior*	*Appeal*
Australian Capital Territory	Magistrate's	Nil	Supreme	Court of Appeal
New South Wales	Local	District	Supreme	Court of Appeal
Northern Territory	Magistrate's	Nil	Supreme	Court of Appeal Court of Criminal Appeal
Queensland	Magistrate's	District	Supreme	Court of Appeal
South Australia	Magistrate's	District	Supreme	Full Court
Tasmania	Civil Division Court of Petty Sessions (criminal)	Nil	Supreme	Full Court
Victoria	Magistrate's	District	Supreme	Court of Appeal
Western Australia	Magistrate's Children's Drugs Family Violence Local (civil) Court of Petty Sessions (criminal)	District	Supreme	Court of Criminal Appeal Full Bench (civil)

Note: All state and territory court systems lead to the High Court of Australia.

serious indictable offences to be heard summarily in the local court, generally with the consent of the accused (in Western Australia, these are known as 'either way' offences). For example, stealing and breaking and entering may be heard in the local court, but there is a restriction placed on the jurisdiction of the local court to hear a matter if the value of the property stolen exceeds a statutory dollar amount. For example, in New South Wales (and the same is true of all states) the value of the property stolen cannot exceed $5000. If it does, the matter cannot be heard summarily in the Local Court.

- **Committal proceedings** are a preliminary hearing before a magistrate of the more serious indictable offences such as murder, manslaughter, armed robbery, rape, fraud and the like. Here the police must produce enough evidence to satisfy the magistrate that the accused has a *prima facie* ('on the face of it') case to answer in a higher court. If the magistrate is of the opinion that there is enough evidence for a jury to convict the accused of the offence charged, the person will be remanded for trial at a later date in a higher court before a judge and jury, otherwise the matter will be dismissed.

Civil jurisdiction of inferior courts

Civil jurisdiction restricted to minor matters

The civil jurisdiction of inferior courts is restricted to the hearing of relatively minor matters such as debt claims, minor contractual matters and motor accident claims. All states set a maximum monetary limit for damages claims, which is being continually revised upward and differs in every state (see Table 2.2). The courts also hear matters outside those involving claims for damages arising from state and federal legislation, for example, minor family law matters under the *Family Law Act 1975* (Cth) although the establishment of the Federal Magistrate's Court has meant that they hear fewer federal matters than previously was the case.

Local or Magistrate's Courts only have original jurisdiction

As the inferior courts are found at the bottom of the court hierarchy, they only have **original jurisdiction**. However, in most states they have a limited ability to review and deal with objections to some administrative decisions of tribunals.

Table 2.2 Civil jurisdiction limits

State/Territory	*Lower courts*	*Intermediate courts*	*Superior courts*
Australian Capital Territory	Magistrate's Court Maximum: to $50 000	No court	Supreme Court Over $50 000
New South Wales	Local Court Small claims: to $10 000 Other: to $60 000	District Court Maximum: $60 000–$750 000 All motor vehicle accidents: no limit	Supreme Court Over $750 000
Northern Territory	Local Court Maximum: to $100 000 Small claims: to $10 000*	No court	Supreme Court Over $100 000
Queensland	Magistrate's Court Small claims: to $7500* Minor Debts Court: to $7500 Other: $7500–$50 000 CTTT – $25 000	District Court Maximum: $50 000–$250 000	Supreme Court Over $250 000
South Australia	Magistrate's Court Personal injury: to $80 000 for motor vehicle accidents Other: $6000 to $40 000 Small claims: to $6000	District Court Personal injury & property: $80 000–$150 000 Other: over $40 000	Supreme Court Personal injury & property: over $150 000
Tasmania	Magistrate's Court Maximum: to $20 000 Minor civil claims: to $5000	No court	Supreme Court Over $20 000
Victoria	Magistrate's Court Arbitration: to $5000* Maximum: to $100 000 VCAT: unlimited	County Court All personal injury claims Other: $100 000–$200 000	Supreme Court Over $200 000
Western Australia	Magistrate's Court Civil matters: to $50 000 Minor cases: to $7500 Consumer/trader claims: to $50 000 Minor case consumer trader claims: to $7500	District Court Maximum: $500 000 Unlimited for personal injury Unlimited for claims for damages from motor vehicle accidents	Supreme Court Over $250 000

*If the amount claimed by a plaintiff is less than $5000 in Victoria, the matter goes to arbitration before a Magistrate but without the formal rules of evidence applying. If the amount is less than $10 000 in New South Wales or $5000 in the Northern Territory, the matter will be heard in the Small Claims Division of the Local Court. In Queensland and Western Australia, the matter will be heard in the Magistrate's Court. These amounts are subject to change and can be checked from the respective states' Department of Justice website.

Inferior courts as Coroner's Courts

An inferior court may also function as a **Coroner's Court**. In such a case, its administrative machinery and jurisdiction is generally established under a separate statute, though the court still consists of a magistrate who is now acting as the coroner. The Coroner's Court investigates **unexplained deaths** and has the power, if satisfied that there is a *prima facie* case, to recommend a person for trial in a higher court.

Inferior courts as Children's Courts

Inferior courts may also act as **Children's Courts** (known as Juvenile Courts in the Northern Territory and Youth Courts in South Australia). The court is established under separate legislation. It hears all summary and indictable offences (except particularly serious crimes such as murder, which are heard in the Supreme Court after a committal proceeding), by persons under the age of 18 at the time the offence was committed or under the age of 18 when appearing in court. In the interests of the child, proceedings are usually held *in camera* (the public and the media are not allowed into the court) and legal formalities are kept to a minimum.

A number of jurisdictions have established a specialist court to deal with matters involving minors. For example:

- **Victoria**. A separate Children's Court has been established as a specialist court with two divisions to deal with matters relating to children and young people. The Family Division hears applications relating to the protection and care of children and young persons at risk, and applications for intervention orders while the Criminal Division hears matters relating to criminal offending by children and young persons.
- **Western Australia**. The Children's Court deals with all complaints of offences alleged to have been committed by young people between the ages of 10 and 17 years (inclusive). If the young person charged has turned 18 after the date of the alleged offence, then the person still appears before the Children's Court. It also deals with cases of abuse or neglect of children and can make an order that a child become a ward of the state.
- **South Australia**. The Youth Court is divided into three administrative branches: the Court Registry, the Family Conference Team, and the Care and Protection Unit. The registry deals with all matters referred into and out of the Youth Court. The court hears trials and guilty pleas in criminal cases for youths under the age of 18 years, child protection applications and applications for adoption of children. The Family Conference Team conducts family conferences for young offenders. The Care and Protection Unit conducts family care meetings.

Small Claims Division

Most states have added a Small Claims Division to the jurisdiction of the inferior courts to try to resolve disputes between consumers and traders (only Tasmania and South Australia will allow disputes between private individuals) in a manner that is intended to be:

- quicker
- cheaper
- non-legalistic and
- often fairer

than would be the case under the traditional system. See page 44 for further information.

Intermediate (District or County) courts

States with no intermediate court

Tasmania and the territories do not have intermediate courts

Because their populations are too small to support such a court and its staff,

- Tasmania
- the Northern Territory and
- the Australian Capital Territory

have no intermediate court between the inferior courts and the superior courts. Appeals from the local courts go directly to their respective Supreme Court in civil matters.

States with intermediate courts

Intermediate courts form the middle level of the court hierarchy and are presided over by a judge, who is referred to as 'Your Honour'. In practice and procedure there are few differences between these courts and the superior courts, although they are known by different names in the various states:

- County Courts in Victoria; and
- District Courts in New South Wales, Queensland, South Australia and Western Australia.

Original civil jurisdiction generally set by money limit

The **original civil jurisdiction** of these courts is usually determined by a monetary jurisdictional limit (see Table 2.2) and, as a general rule, the case will be heard before a judge alone (the judge decides both questions of law and fact). Where a jury is used, it will be a jury of four or six people.

In their **criminal jurisdiction**, intermediate courts deal with the bulk of indictable offences except for capital offences such as murder, treason and sedition (in Western Australia the District Court deals with serious criminal offences for which the maximum penalty is 20 years' imprisonment). The case will be heard before a judge (who decides all questions of law) and a jury of 12 (who decide all questions of fact) although in Western Australia an accused may choose to have a trial by judge alone. If the accused is found guilty by the jury, then the judge is responsible for sentencing them.

Intermediate courts have limited appellate jurisdiction

These courts also have limited **appellate jurisdiction**. They can hear appeals from inferior courts and some tribunals (although it should be noted that there is no appeal on civil matters from the Magistrate's Court in Victoria). These are known as *de novo* appeals because the judge re-hears the matter and can overturn any finding of fact or point of law decided in the lower court, as well as being able to substitute its own decision (see Figure. 2.3).

Intermediate courts 'sit' regularly in the capital cities and the larger country centres.

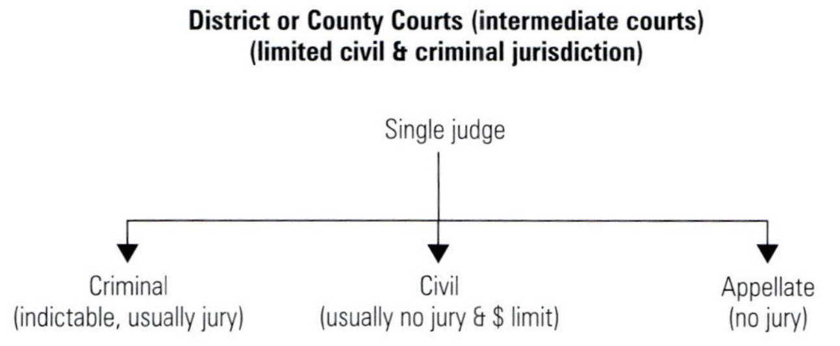

FIGURE 2.3 *Intermediate courts (not Tasmania, ACT or NT)*

Superior (Supreme) courts

Supreme courts have unlimited original civil jurisdiction

The highest court within a state or territory is the **Supreme Court**. It has unlimited **original jurisdiction** (there is no upper monetary limit—see Table 2.2) and can, in theory, hear any matter at all. However, in practice, it only hears the most serious matters or cases involving difficult points of law (see Figure 2.4). Most sittings are in capital cities, but the court does go 'on circuit' to country centres.

Courts of record create precedent

Unlike the lower courts, the superior courts in each state are '**courts of record**'. This means that the decisions are recorded in the form of **law reports**. These are available for future reference as precedents for judges in both superior courts and other courts, as well as for other interested parties such as barristers and solicitors. See, for example, the law reports on the Austlii site at: **http://www.austlii.edu.au**.

In its criminal jurisdiction a judge will sit with a jury of 12. Most civil cases are heard by a judge alone; however, where there is a jury, a judge will usually sit with a jury of four, although a jury of six or 12 will be empanelled in rare cases.

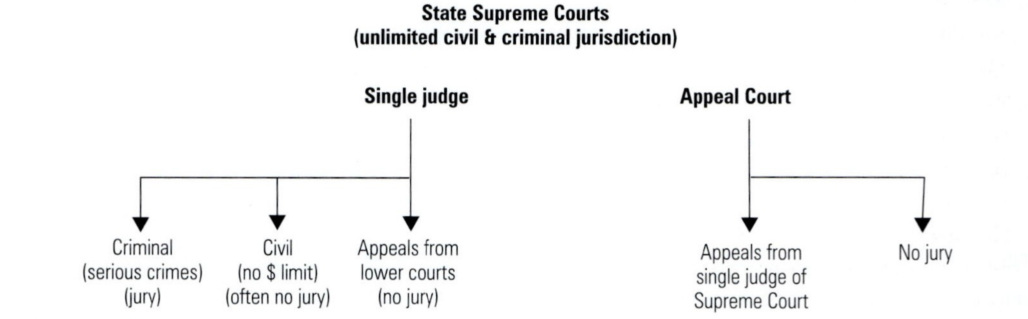

FIGURE 2.4 *Superior courts*

Supreme Court has appellate jurisdiction

In each state the Supreme Court also exercises an appellate jurisdiction. Three states and both territories have established **Courts of Appeal**:

- New South Wales
- Queensland
- Victoria
- Australian Capital Territory and Northern Territory (appeals from the Magistrate's Courts are heard by a single judge).

In the remaining states there is a right of appeal from a single judge to a full court of the Supreme Court. In each jurisdiction, an appeal is normally heard before three judges, although a full bench of five or more judges will hear matters involving important points of law. Appeals in the Australian Capital Territory go to the Federal Court.

Specialist courts

In addition to the state and territory courts noted above, there has been a large growth in other specialist courts (and tribunals) designed in part to:

- relieve the workload of the inferior (and intermediate) courts;
- establish courts with specialist expertise to deal with growing community concern with issues such as drugs and family violence; and
- deal with high volume specialist areas such as workers' compensation.

While of considerable practical importance, many of these courts have little to do with commercial law but are included here to show the growth in specialist courts that has taken place in recent years. These courts include:

- **Family Court.** In Western Australia, a state Family Court has been established with state and federal jurisdiction in matters of family law to deal with divorce, property of marriage, residence, contact and other matters relating to children, maintenance and adoptions.
- **Family Violence Court.** Western Australia established a Family Violence Court in 1999 to deal exclusively with family violence matters.
- **Family Matters Court.** In the Northern Territory a Family Matters Court has been established to deal with, and make orders in respect of, welfare or guardianship of children considered to be in need of care.
- **Drug Courts.** New South Wales, South Australia and Western Australia have established Drug Courts to deal with offenders who are dependent on drugs. Drug usage and dependence is becoming a serious issue in business for employers. These courts assist drug-dependent offenders to overcome both their drug dependence and their criminal offending. In New South Wales, the Drug Court deals with adults, while the Youth Drug and Alcohol Court deals with young offenders.
- **Compensation or Work Health Court.** New South Wales (Compensation Court) and the Northern Territory (Work Health Court) have established specialist courts to resolve workers' compensation matters.

- **Land and Environment Court.** This New South Wales court has jurisdiction over the fields of planning, building, pollution, heritage, valuation and land tenure. The court consists of judges, who have the status of Supreme Court judges, and assessors, who have experience in planning and development. Appeals from decisions of the assessors are heard by a judge of the court as a re-hearing. There is a right of appeal to the Court of Appeal on most matters.
- **Environment, Resources and Development Court.** This South Australian court has jurisdiction to deal with disputes over the development and management of land use, the natural and built environment, natural resources and pollution.
- **Liquor Licensing Court.** Western Australia has established a Liquor Licensing Court to hear and determine references from the Director of Liquor Licensing, applications to review decisions of the Director of Liquor Licensing and disciplinary complaints against licensees.
- **Industrial Relations Courts.** These courts are currently concerned with various aspects of workplace relations. The extent of their role in the future will depend on what happens with the changes proposed to the *Workplace Relations Act 1996* (Cth) by the *Workplace Relations Amendment (WorkChoices) Act 2005* (Cth) as this legislation proposes a single national system of employment and industrial relations (see Chapter 35).

eCourts

The courts are turning to e-technology for efficiency

The courts are increasingly turning to e-technology to try and provide lawyers and the public with timely and cost effective access to courts, as well as reducing litigation costs. This is being reflected in changes that are taking place to the civil procedure rules of the courts. For example:

- **New South Wales.** Section 56(1) of the *Civil Procedure Act 2005* (NSW) provides that the 'overriding purpose' of the Act and rules of court, in their application to civil proceedings, 'is to facilitate the just, quick and cheap resolution of the real issues in the proceedings' and to that end there is an obligation on both the court and the parties to give effect to that purpose. To help achieve that purpose the courts have established an electronic case management system (ECM) under s. 14B of the *Electronic Transactions Act 2000* (NSW). The *Uniform Civil Procedure Rules 2005* (NSW) allow extensive electronic case management, including filing of pleadings, defining of issues, provision of essential particulars, making of admissions, filing of list documents, delivery or exchange of experts' reports and the holding of conferences of experts, provision of copies of documents in electronic form, administration and answering of interrogatories, service and filing of affidavits, giving of evidence, the use of telephone or video conferencing, the provision of evidence in support of an application for adjournment or amendment, and the filing of written submissions.

  The Supreme Court has established a new ecmCourt which will operate entirely by electronic communications between legal practitioners and a judge, via CourtLinkNSW. Formal applications and directions given in the course of the management of a case before trial, where oral evidence is not taken, can be conducted between the practitioner's office and the judge's chambers without the need to attend court. The ecmCourt will operate in the same way as a traditional court.
- **Northern Territory.** Video conferencing is available in the Darwin Supreme Court and Magistrate's Court, as well as at a number of locations in the territory.
- **Queensland.** Queensland courts have introduced a package of eCourt services. It currently permits eSearching, allowing litigators and the public to search active civil court files 24 hours a day, seven days a week free; eListing to help lawyers bid for trial dates online rather than go to court to request the dates, thus doing away with callovers; eChambers, which streamlines chambers-style applications and hearings, and enables parties to post submissions, draft orders and other documents onto a secure online bulletin board that is only accessible by the court and the other parties involved in the case; and eCourtroom, which promotes the use of evidence management and litigation support technology during disclosure and trials, as well as removing the need for lawyers to attend court for simple disputes.
- **South Australia.** The Magistrate's Court Electronic Lodgement service allows lodgement of general claims, minor civil action claims and pre-lodgement notices.

- **Tasmania.** There is an online service for the downloading of some Magistrate's Court documents.
- **Victoria.** The Magistrate's Court lodgement services allow lodgement of complaint forms, default order requests, warrants to seize property and summons for oral examination. The County Court has an eFiling system (known as ICMS or Integrated Courts Management System), which allows legal practitioners or litigants to electronically lodge and process court documents relating to civil cases, and Court Connect, a search facility of the Court's Case and List Management System (CLMS) for civil matters and listing details for matters within the criminal jurisdiction where a future listing exists.
- **Western Australia.** In this state there is provision for electronic trials in both the District and Supreme Courts, with the court and the parties deciding before the matter receives a hearing date if the hearing is to be conducted using electronic technology.

WEB RESOURCES

FEDERAL COURTS

For further information on the relevant court, click on the court link at the following sites:

Federal Magistrate's Court:
http://www.fmc.gov.au/

Federal Court:
http://www.fedcourt.gov.au/

Family Court:
http://www.familycourt.gov.au/

High Court:
http://www.hcourt.gov.au/

In addition to the state court hierarchy, provision existed under Chapter III, s. 71 of the Constitution for a federal court hierarchy. However, it was not until the mid-1970s, and the establishment of the Federal Court of Australia and the Family Court of Australia, that a distinctive federal court hierarchy began to appear in the Australian legal system. Today there are four federal courts: the High Court, Federal Court, Family Court and the Federal Magistrate's Court.

The High Court, Federal Court and Family Court have both original and appellate jurisdiction and are all courts of record. In their original jurisdiction, the judge decides both questions of law and facts—there is no provision for juries in the federal courts.

Federal Magistrate's Court

Federal Magistrate's Court hears minor matters concerning consumer protection under the *TPA*, bankruptcy and family law

The Federal Magistrate's Court was established to reduce the workload of the Federal Court and the Family Court. Under the *Federal Magistrates Act 1999* (Cth) it has:

- concurrent jurisdiction with the Federal Court in relation to all matters arising under the *Bankruptcy Act 1966* and parts of the *Trade Practices Act 1974* relating to unfair practices and product safety and information (up to $200 000);
- power to hear applications under the *Administrative Decisions (Judicial Review) Act 1977*;
- power to hear appeals from the Administrative Appeals Tribunal, although they still have to be instituted in the Federal Court, but the Federal Court can transfer those down to the Federal Magistrate's Service;
- power to hear matters arising under the Human Rights and Equal Opportunity Commission; and
- jurisdiction in family law matters, including the power to deal with all divorce applications.

Family Court

The *Family Law Act 1975* (Cth) introduced what are essentially no-fault divorce laws and established the **Family Court of Australia** in 1976 to deal exclusively with:

- divorce
- custody of children
- contact with children
- division of property
- maintenance of a spouse
- counselling
- mediation.

While of considerable practical importance, this court has little to do with commercial law. For more information on the operation of the Family Court see: **http://www.familycourt.gov.au**

Federal Court of Australia

Federal Court—jurisdiction over all other Commonwealth matters

The Federal Court of Australia was established under the *Federal Court of Australia Act 1976* (Cth) and comprises a Chief Justice and 30 other judges. Its jurisdiction extends to traditional Commonwealth matters such as:

- trade practices (Chapters 23 & 30);
- intellectual property (Chapter 34);
- bankruptcy (Chapter 32);
- federal taxation;
- immigration and social services; and
- review of federal administrative decisions.

Most matters coming before the Federal Court are heard before a single judge. These decisions can be appealed to the **Full Court** of the Federal Court, comprising three judges. It can hear appeals from:

- single judges of the Supreme Court of a territory in both their civil and criminal jurisdictions;
- single judges of the Federal Court; and
- appeals from state Supreme Courts exercising federal jurisdiction in such matters as income tax, bankruptcy, trade marks and patents.

Special leave of the **High Court** is necessary to appeal from a decision of the Federal Court.

The High Court

http://www.hcourt.gov.au/

High Court—both a Federal Court and final Court of Appeal in state system

The High Court of Australia was established in 1901 under s. 71 of the Constitution with three aims:

- to exercise a defined **original jurisdiction**; for example, to hear cases involving indictable offences against the laws of the Commonwealth, where the Commonwealth itself is suing or being sued, or where there is a dispute between two or more states, or matters involving residents of two or more states;
- to serve as the **final court of appeal** within the Australian legal system. It can hear appeals from state Supreme Courts and the Federal Court;
- to **guard** and **interpret** the Australian **Constitution**.

Under s. 75 of the Constitution, the court has original jurisdiction in cases that affect foreign affairs, constitutional issues and matters concerning the legislative power of Federal Parliament. In its original jurisdiction, the High Court is usually presided over by a single judge. However, in those cases concerning the Commonwealth Constitution the court is usually composed of five judges and is referred to as the Full High Court.

Special leave must be given by the High Court for an appeal

The bulk of the High Court's work is in its appellate jurisdiction. It is now the final court of appeal in Australia and its appellate jurisdiction is found in s. 73 of the Constitution, which provides that the court can hear and determine appeals from:

- a justice/s exercising the original jurisdiction of the court;
- any other federal court, or court exercising federal jurisdiction; and
- any state Supreme Court.

An appeal from a state Supreme Court does **not** lie '**as of right**'. Because of the increasing number of cases being appealed to the High Court, **special leave to appeal is needed**. The High Court will hear the application and decide whether or not to hear the case. Special leave to appeal will generally only be granted where the case involves some important issue of law, or in a criminal case, if there appears to be a serious miscarriage of justice. (See the High Court Bulletin published online at: **http://www.austlii.edu.au**). Appeals are usually heard before three justices although important cases may be heard before a Full Bench or Full Court.

The High Court consists of a Chief Justice and six other justices. It is now permanently situated in Canberra, although it can still sit in other places around Australia.

High Court not bound by its own previous decisions

While the High Court is a 'court of record', it does **not** consider itself bound by its own previous decisions. However, it will only overrule a previous decision with the greatest caution and then only in a clear-cut case, for example, *Commonwealth Trading Bank of Australia v. Sydney Wide Stores Pty Ltd* (1981) 148 CLR 304 (see Chapter 31, p. 662).

Appeals to the Privy Council have been effectively abolished

ABOLITION OF APPEALS TO THE PRIVY COUNCIL

Appeals to the Privy Council on federal matters were abolished with the passing of the *Privy Council (Limitation of Appeals) Act 1968* (Cth), making the High Court the final court of appeal on federal matters. The passage of the *Privy Council (Appeals from the High Court) Act 1975* (Cth) further restricted appeals from the High Court but it was not until the passage of the *Australia Act 1986* (Cth) abolishing the right of appeal from the state Supreme Courts to the Privy Council, that the last link with the Privy Council was removed.

FEATURES OF A COURT HIERARCHY

The hierarchy of courts serves a threefold purpose:

- it provides a **system of appeals** through which dissatisfied litigants may appeal from a decision of a lower court to a higher court to have the matter reconsidered;
- it allows different forms of **hearing** according to the gravity of the case—the more important or more serious cases will get the best legal advice, while minor matters will be quickly, cheaply and conveniently dealt with; and
- it is instrumental in the building up of **precedent** (see Chapter 3).

Right of appeal

In theory, if either party is dissatisfied with the outcome of their case, they may apply to a higher court (perhaps all the way to the High Court, depending on the choice of the party appealing, the nature of the case, whether they can afford it, and, most importantly, whether the High Court gives leave) for reconsideration of the decision. In practice, however, this right is limited because of the expense involved in mounting an appeal to a higher court. The higher you go up a court hierarchy the more expensive it becomes. As well as this limitation, there are jurisdictional and other arbitral limits imposed to prevent waste of time and public money on relatively minor legal problems. For example, there is normally no appeal against the finding of facts by a court; an appeal to a higher court is usually based on a point of law.

Right of appeal can be against direction or severity

The right of appeal is still very wide. It is an important part of our system to safeguard against injustice. The appeal may be against either of two elements in the decision: its direction or its severity. It is not unknown for the prosecution in a criminal case to appeal against the leniency of the decision.

ALTERNATIVE METHODS TO COURTS

IN BRIEF

Alternative methods of dispute settlement

In an attempt to overcome some of the traditional problems associated with the court system, for example, lack of accessability, delays, costs, ignorance and intimidation, government, business and the community have turned to alternative methods of dispute resolution:

- tribunals
- ombudsmen
- alternative dispute resolution (see Figure 2.5).

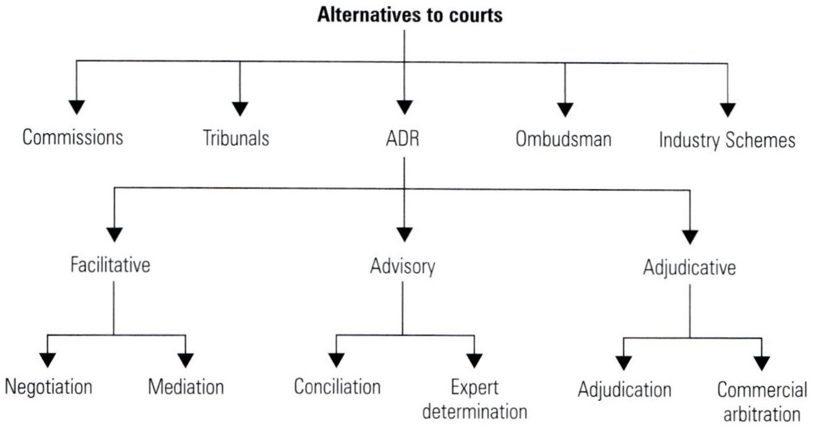

FIGURE 2.5 *Some alternatives to going to court*

Growth in alternative dispute settlement methods in response to failings of legal system

A basic legal principle of modern society is that no person must suffer punishment or pay damages for any conduct not expressly forbidden by law. This principle is reinforced by the fact that the legal rights of both individuals and corporate bodies should be determined by the courts. However, community pressure has forced governments, both state and federal, to provide the means whereby both citizens and entities can obtain easier access to decision-making bodies.

This has been achieved through judicial or quasi-judicial powers or by authority being given to officials who stand more or less in connection with the government of the day, and who may also be subject to government influence. Examples of such decision-making bodies that are outside the court system but which exercise jurisdictions and perform functions similar to those of courts of law include licensing courts, fair rent courts and arbitration courts.

Transport regulation boards and town planning appeal tribunals are examples of special administrative tribunals that not only resolve disputes between people by the application of legal rules, but make or recommend decisions that are in accord with government policy, and are said to perform 'quasi-judicial' functions.

Over the last few years there has been a rapid growth in alternative methods of dispute resolution outside formal court proceedings. This has arisen because of a number of major criticisms of the traditional court system by lawyers, governments and other concerned groups about the delays, costs, ignorance and intimidation within the traditional court system. Alternative methods of dispute resolution can provide expedient, private and efficient methods of resolution of commercial disputes where the disputing parties generally feel satisfied with the result as these methods are not accusatorial and there is not a winning party and a losing party.

Mediation, conciliation and arbitration procedures are being introduced into court and tribunal procedures. For example:

- In Victoria the *Magistrates' Court Act 1989* s. 102 provides that the magistrate must refer claims under $10 000 to arbitration. The *Commercial Arbitration Act 1984* (Vic) does not apply to this type of arbitration. Section 88 of the *Victorian Civil and Administrative Tribunal Act 1998* provides that the Victorian Civil and Administrative Tribunal, or the principal registrar, may refer a proceeding to mediation.
- In New South Wales the *Local Courts (Civil Procedure) Rules 2005* (NSW) provides for compulsory mediation for claims up to $10 000 in the Local courts, while the *Civil Procedure Act 2005* (NSW) provides for compulsory arbitration in certain matters in the District and Supreme Court. Mediation is also available in the majority of civil cases even after a case has started.
- Industrial disputes under both Commonwealth and state legislation are subject to conciliation and arbitration.

- The Small Claims or Consumer Claims Tribunals of all states and the territories work on the principle of mediation and arbitration. Under these tribunals a referee will attempt to mediate a dispute between a consumer and a trader and will only make an order if the parties fail to compromise.
- Community Justice Centres rely on mediators to resolve disputes between neighbours, families, etc. Here, the mediators encourage the parties to solve the matter for themselves. If they can't get a resolution to the dispute, they can suggest further steps the parties may take to try to resolve the matter, but they cannot make any orders.

Facilitative processes

Negotiation

Negotiation: a facilitative process that involves voluntary and confidential discussion between the parties

Negotiation is a **facilitative process** that involves **voluntary and confidential discussion between the parties**, either with or without a third party, to try to mutually resolve a dispute. The outcome generally remains confidential between the parties. This usually will not have the same force of law as an award.

Mediation

See **http://www.vcat.vic.gov.au** and the mediation site for a VCAT video on mediation.

Mediation: a facilitative process that involves a voluntary confidential negotiation process with a mediator

Mediation is also a **facilitative process** for resolving disputes. Like negotiation, it is a **voluntary confidential negotiation process**, but an independent and neutral third party (the **mediator**) will assist the parties to try and find a way to resolve their dispute. If an outcome is reached, it can be kept confidential between the parties.

It is particularly useful in complex matters where the parties may have ongoing contact and/or the dispute involves multiple parties because the parties, with the assistance of the mediator, may find a solution that is satisfactory to all parties. The mediator **cannot** impose a decision upon the parties.

Mediation can be implemented prior to, or at the same time as, other forms of dispute resolution such as arbitration or court proceedings. Mediation is being increasingly used in commercial, non-commercial and non-criminal matters by the courts to try to reach settlement quickly and cheaply. It is also used by the Telecommunications Industry Ombudsman to try to resolve telecommunications disputes.

If mediation fails, the parties may then turn to arbitration or the courts to have the matter in dispute settled.

Advisory processes

Conciliation

Conciliation: an advisory process similar to mediation but the conciliator plays a more active role in getting an outcome

While the terms mediation and conciliation are used interchangeably, they are different processes because of the role played by the independent third party. The parties to a dispute, again with the assistance of a neutral third party (the **conciliator**), identify the dispute, develop options, determine what alternatives are available, and try to reach an agreement. The conciliator may exercise an **advisory role** on the content of the dispute, and suggest options and possible solutions. Their role is generally more directive than a mediator, but the role is not a determinative one.

Expert determination

Expert determination: an advisory process using an independent expert to assist the parties on some disputed issue of fact or law

Expert determination, or independent expert appraisal, is a process that provides for an **independent expert** to be appointed by the parties to give a determination on some disputed point of fact or law. The process is **advisory** and is generally effective in settling disputes that are simple in content, for example, what is an accepted trade or industry practice, or technical in nature.

The independent expert adopts such procedures that are suitable for obtaining the information from the parties, giving each party a reasonable opportunity to put their case and deal with that of the opposing party. The independent expert is not an arbitrator of the matter/s in dispute and the parties will decide beforehand whether the determination is to be final and binding on them. If it isn't, it may form the basis for negotiating a settlement, or at least clarifying the issue.

Determinative processes

Adjudication

Adjudication: a determinative process involving the appointment of an adjudicator who can force a respondent to make a payment

New South Wales (*Building and Construction Security of Payment Act 1999* (NSW), *Contractors Debts Act 1997* (NSW)), Queensland (*Building and Construction Industry Payments Act 2004* (Qld)), Victoria (*Building and Construction Industry Security of Payment Act 2002*) and Western Australia (*Construction Contracts Act 2004*) have established 'adjudication' processes to ensure payment for work, goods or services under contracts in the construction industry. An independent person (an **adjudicator**) is appointed under the relevant Acts Authorised Nominating Authority or chosen by the parties. Adjudication is carried out on the basis of the documents that the parties submit, although the adjudicator can call a conference, and they will then make a determination as to the amount of money (if any) that the respondent must pay the claimant, when it is to be paid, and whether any interest should be paid.

Queensland also has an adjudication process in place under the *Body Corporate Community Management Act 1997* to assist lot owners in body corporates to resolve disputes (provision is also made under the Act for mediation and conciliation).

Commercial arbitration

Commercial arbitration: a determinative process using an arbitrator chosen by the parties to settle a dispute by making an award

Commercial arbitration has long been used as a means of **settling commercial disputes**. All the states and territories have enacted essentially uniform domestic Commercial Arbitration Acts while the Commonwealth has enacted the *International Arbitration Act 1974* (Cth). It is a **formal dispute resolution process** which involves the hearing of a dispute by an independent third party (an **arbitrator**). The arbitrator will be of the party's choosing and will be someone who is familiar with the professional or technical background of the matters in dispute. Typically, on appointment, the arbitrator will call a preliminary conference with the parties to agree on how the arbitration will be conducted. This will help ensure that the outcome will be acceptable to all parties.

Providing that the arbitration is conducted according to the principles of natural justice, that is that all parties are treated equally and fairly, the manner in which the arbitration will be conducted may be varied by the parties to suit the circumstances. For example, in the case of a small matter, the parties and the arbitrator may agree that the matter be dealt with just by the submission of documents, which would significantly reduce each party's costs. Where the matter is more complex, there may be the submission of formal claims and the lodging of defences, and evidence may be submitted by each party and be subject to cross-examination, so that the whole process is more in the form of a judicial-style hearing.

At the end of the hearing the arbitrator will make an **award**. Unless the parties have expressed a contrary intention when agreeing to arbitration, the award will be **final and binding** on the parties, hence the reason why arbitration is referred to as a **determinative process**. The award can be enforced in the same manner as a court judgement.

Doing business

Use of arbitration clauses

While the parties to a commercial contract will often assume that a dispute between them will never arise, commercial reality shows otherwise. It is good commercial practice to consider including an 'arbitration clause' in a commercial contract because it has the following advantages over going to court:

- **quick** (the courts have long waiting lists for commercial matters);
- **private** (the courts are public forums, although confidentiality can be obtained on settlements);
- **confidentiality** (the public are not admitted and the arbitration is held in private);
- cheap (legal costs in a court case are significantly higher than in arbitration);
- **the arbitrator will have a professional or technical background of the matters in dispute** (judges will not generally have a similar professional or technical background to an arbitrator); and
- like a court judgement, awards can be **final and enforceable**.

Note that an agreement to submit a dispute to arbitration can be made by the parties after a dispute has arisen. ■

While commercial arbitration is an expedient, efficient and private alternative to the courts, a decision on legal issues arising from the dispute (or the arbitration, e.g., the denial of natural justice) can still be appealed to the courts. The Rules of Court of all Australian jurisdictions also allow a judge to refer questions of fact out to arbitration.

Commercial arbitration is generally chosen by the parties because not only can the matter be dealt with more quickly, in private and without the formality of the courts but an arbitrator can be chosen with the necessary professional or technical background to the matters in dispute.

JUDICIAL AND QUASI-JUDICIAL TRIBUNALS

Tribunals are quasi-judicial bodies

In addition to these alternative methods of dispute settlement, there has also been a growth at state and federal level of permanent and non-permanent tribunals. As society has grown more complex, so has the range and complexity of legal issues. As a result, there has been a spectacular growth in specialisation within the legal system, and the response of parliaments, both state and federal, has been to legislate to set up a number of specialist tribunals to deal with specific problems. They are not courts in the strict sense, though they do perform many of the functions and powers associated with courts, hence the use of the term 'quasi-judicial'.

IN BRIEF

Reasons for the growth of judicial and quasi-judicial tribunals

For much the same reasons for the development of alternative dispute resolution procedures, the main aim of the development of tribunals has been to provide people with a:

- cheap
- quick
- fair

dispute settlement process in accordance with community needs, keeping formalities to a minimum.

It is possible to identify a number of differences between tribunals and traditional courts:

- The jurisdiction of a tribunal is usually limited to a particular and narrow area and the 'chairperson' is usually a specialist in that area.
- Courts are presided over by lawyers who are judges while tribunals can often be presided over by non-legal experts.
- The atmosphere, procedures and rules of conduct in a tribunal are generally less formal and strict, making them far less intimidating to a potential litigant.
- Legal representation is often prohibited or restricted in an attempt to try to contain the costs of bringing an action.
- Appeals are restricted. In many tribunals, the decision of the tribunal is final unless the losing party can show there has been an error of law.
- Tribunals can take into account factors that would not necessarily carry a great deal of weight in a court because of the law of evidence.

While a tribunal hearing is similar to a court hearing, formalities are kept to a minimum. As a result of different procedures and rules of evidence, tribunals do not make law that is to be followed and applied by other courts or judicial bodies. They do not create precedent.

Tribunals are subject to review by the courts

Tribunals are subject to a degree of control by the courts. All tribunal procedures are reviewable by a superior court to ensure that justice has been properly administered, that is that there has been no denial of natural justice and that the tribunal has correctly followed the procedures set down for it. This means that both sides **must** be given the opportunity of being heard. If one side elects to say nothing, they cannot complain later. Similarly, the tribunal (or court) must reach its decision in good faith and, as a general rule, must publish its reasons for arriving at a decision.

Tribunals created under federal legislation are subject to review in the Federal Court, while tribunals created under state legislation are subject to control of the Supreme Courts. Both federal and state tribunals are reviewable through the use of the writ of *certiorari*, which allows any person who believes that a tribunal (or even a lower court) has acted beyond its powers or not complied with the principles of natural justice to apply to a superior court to have that decision reviewed.

Some federal tribunals

Administrative Appeals Tribunal (AAT)

http://www.aat.gov.au

The Administrative Appeals Tribunal was established in 1975 to review the decisions of Commonwealth government departments, including ministers and officials, and statutory bodies. The tribunal does not have a general power to review any decision made under Commonwealth legislation. It can only review a decision if an Act or regulation specifically provides that the decision is subject to review by the tribunal and to date it has power to review decisions made under more than 400 separate Acts and regulations. Some of the better known areas over which the tribunal has jurisdiction include taxation, social security, customs, corporations, freedom of information, veteran's entitlements, immigration and citizenship.

The tribunal's function is to determine whether a particular decision is the correct or, in the case of a discretionary area, the best decision based on the facts. To assist it in determining this, it has access to government files.

Any person who is affected by an administrative decision can appeal to the AAT, seeking a review of that decision. Once the tribunal has heard all the evidence, it then has the power to affirm, vary or set aside the original decision.

The Australian Competition and Consumer Commission (ACCC)

http://www.accc.gov.au

The main functions of the Australian Competition and Consumer Commission are:

- **administration and enforcement** of the restrictive trade practices and consumer law provisions of the *Trade Practices Act 1974* (Cth);
- **granting of authorisations** of certain restrictive trade practices that would ordinarily be prohibited but which give the public a benefit that, to the satisfaction of the Commission, outweighs the adverse effect on competition; and
- **providing assistance to the public** by engaging in research, education of the public and the business community, and by providing consumer guidance.

The commission has the power to prosecute breaches of the Act, and to authorise anti-competitive behaviour that would otherwise be illegal on public benefit grounds.

It has a full-time chairperson and a number of full-time members appointed by the Commonwealth government.

The Australian Competition Tribunal

The Australian Competition Tribunal provides an appellate jurisdiction for authorisations under the competitive conduct rules of Part IV of the *Trade Practices Act*. It also re-hears Australian Competition and Consumer Commission decisions to refuse, or to grant, authorisation for agreements or practices that might be anti-competitive, involve exclusive dealing, or be a breach of the merger provisions of the *Trade Practices Act*. The tribunal has no staff or physical resources of its own and is managed by the Federal Court with registry services and administrative support provided by the staff of the Federal Court.

Some state tribunals

New South Wales Consumer, Trader and Tenancy Tribunal

http://www.fairtrading.nsw.gov.au/corporate/cttt.html

New South Wales has rationalised the number of independent tribunals that deal with disputes between consumers and traders. The *Consumer, Trader and Tenancy Tribunal Act 2001* (NSW) has established a Consumer, Trader and Tenancy Tribunal.

The tribunal is intended to provide informal, timely and inexpensive methods of dispute settlement. To achieve this, the law requires the tribunal to use its best efforts to help both parties reach an agreement through conciliation **before** it will hear the case and make a decision. If the parties can't reach an agreement, the dispute will then be heard by the tribunal. Nothing said in the conciliation process can be repeated in the hearing unless both parties consent.

If the parties can reach an agreement, they should write down what they have agreed to, sign it and present it to the tribunal for a formal order. If the parties can't reach an agreement, the tribunal will hear the application and make a decision. In normal circumstances, legal representation before the tribunal will not be permitted. It is an offence to wilfully contravene or fail to comply with a non-money order or decision of the tribunal.

The tribunal has eight separate divisions:

- The **General Division** deals with general disputes about goods and services between consumers and traders (under the *Consumer Claims Act 1998* (NSW)), and traders and suppliers, up to $25 000.
- The **Commercial Division** deals with consumer credit contracts (as defined in the *Consumer Credit (New South Wales) Act 1995* (NSW)), Travel Compensation Fund claims appeals, Retirement Village Industry Code of Practice breaches, and disputes over commissions being charged by property, stock and business agents.
- The **Home Building Division** deals with disputes between owners and builders or other contractors. It will deal with disputes between contractors and their suppliers or subcontractors as well as appeals involving residential building insurance up to $500 000. Because of the amounts involved, lawyers are more likely to be involved in this area.
- The **Motor Vehicle Division** deals with consumer disputes involving motor vehicles.
- The **Residential Parks Division** deals with matters relating to residential parks, that is land on which caravans and/or moveable dwellings are placed.
- The **Retirement Villages Division** deals with disputes between retirement village administration and one or more residents.
- The **Strata and Community Schemes Division** deals with strata scheme management and community schemes management. Before the tribunal will hear a matter, the parties must first try mediation, and if this is unsuccessful, the parties can apply to have the matter adjudicated. If the parties are not happy with the adjudicator's decision, only then can they lodge an appeal to have the matter heard before the tribunal.
- The **Tenancy Division** deals only with tenancy matters arising under residential leases. The tribunal can make orders up to $20 000 in the case of rental bonds and $10 000 for all other disputes.

Orders are final and binding unless the chairperson decides that the matter be re-heard, and a re-hearing is not automatically granted. The amount involved for a re-hearing must be between $500 and $25 000 if money is claimed or in dispute unless it involves a residential park, retirement village or residential tenancy. An applicant has 14 days in which to lodge an application for a re-hearing and they must establish on the balance of probabilities that the first decision was either not fair and equitable, against the weight of the evidence, or was based on not all the evidence being available at the time of hearing and that a re-hearing would achieve a different result (s. 68). Only one re-hearing is allowed after any completed proceedings.

The tribunal may make new orders at the re-hearing. If a party believes that the tribunal has made an error of law, they may appeal to the Supreme Court.

The Victorian Civil and Administrative Tribunal (VCAT)

http://www.vcat.vic.gov.au/

The Victorian Civil and Administrative Tribunal was established in 1998 by the *Victorian Civil and Administrative Tribunal Act 1998* (Vic) and given extensive jurisdiction. Some of the disputes it deals with include:

- consumer matters relating to supply or purchase of goods or services;
- credit;
- discrimination;

- domestic building works;
- guardianship and administration;
- residential tenancies;
- retail tenancies; and
- legal profession disputes up to $25 000 and issues of professional misconduct (since December 2005).

The VCAT also deals with disputes between people and government including:

- planning and land valuation;
- licences to carry on businesses (including travel agents, motor car traders and others);
- state taxation;
- Transport Accident Commission decisions; and
- freedom of information issues.

Anyone can apply to the VCAT to resolve a dispute arising from the supply or possible supply, or purchase or possible purchase, of goods and services regardless of whether the goods or services are for private or business use, including traders, companies, businesses, consumers and individuals. Services must be supplied in trade or commerce and may include some claims relating to interests in real estate. There is no limit on the amount of a claim.

Before applying to the VCAT, the parties should have tried to settle the dispute. It is also possible to request a court to transfer a case to the VCAT. If the court is satisfied that the case is primarily a consumer and trader dispute and it would be more appropriate for the VCAT to deal with it, it will be transferred.

Once an application is made to the tribunal, a mediation, directions hearing or compulsory conference may take place depending on the case, for example, in a civil claims hearing, a compulsory conference must be first held for cases over $10 000. Where a hearing is held, all parties have the opportunity to call or give evidence, ask questions of witnesses and make submissions.

Parties can put their case directly to the VCAT themselves or, in some circumstances, the VCAT can allow the use of a lawyer or professional advocate, although in nearly all cases of $10 000 or less, the parties will have to present their own case. In limited circumstances, where the amount involves more than $10 000, the parties may be allowed to have a legal representative or professional advocate.

At the end of a hearing, the tribunal makes a decision. If any party believes the tribunal made an error on a point of law, they can lodge an appeal with the Supreme Court.

Queensland Commercial and Consumer Tribunal (CCT)

http://www.tribunals.qld.gov.au

The Commercial and Consumer Tribunal of Queensland was established by the *Commercial and Consumer Tribunal Act 2003* (Qld) under the Department of Tourism, Fair Trading and Wine Industry Development to deal with a broad range of matters including:

- reviewing decisions of the Board of Architects of Queensland;
- determining building disputes (up to $50 000 in the case of minor commercial building disputes and major commercial building disputes by consent) and applications for review of Queensland Building Services Authority decisions;
- reviewing decisions on liquor licensing matters;
- determining disputes between residential park owners and home owners (where internal dispute resolution and, if necessary, mediation, had failed);
- reviewing decisions of the Plumbers and Drainers Board of Queensland;
- reviewing decisions of the Board of Professional Engineers of Queensland;
- conducting disciplinary proceedings against licensees and registered employees, reviewing administrative decisions of the Chief Executive and deciding claims over $5000 against the Claim Fund in relation to property agents and motor dealers;

- dealing with disputes between retirement village administrators and residents (but only after attempts to settle the dispute internally had failed, when application could be made to the tribunal to have the matter referred to mediation and, if that were not successful, to the tribunal for a hearing);
- resolving consumer and industry-related disputes;
- reviewing decisions on gaming machine allocations; and
- hearing appeals against decisions to refuse or revoke licences or penalties imposed by stewards in all three racing codes.

Proceedings may be started by an individual; however, provision is made under the Act to allow application by a group of individuals if permitted under an empowering Act. (The purpose of the establishment of the tribunal was to consolidate a number of tribunals into one body, and the Acts that established the jurisdiction of those tribunals now apply to the CCT.) The parties must represent themselves whenever possible. However, representation may be allowed for:

- mediation, if the mediation allows it;
- tribunals, if the tribunal allows it; or
- a particular type of matter, e.g., debt recovery, disciplinary proceedings.

The parties generally pay their own costs.

A tribunal decision can only be appealed with the District Court's leave, and only on an error of law or a jurisdictional point.

Dispute Settlement Centre of Victoria

Access through **http://www.justice.vic.gov.au/**

Under the auspices of the Victorian Department of Justice, the Dispute Settlement Centre of Victoria provides informal, impartial, accessible, low-cost dispute resolution services to individuals and small and large groups across a wide range of disputes, including those involving trees, fences, noise and behaviour of people, workplace and business disputes, and planning and environmental disputes. It will generally only charge a fee to cover expenses if it is assisting a large organisation to resolve a complex internal dispute; otherwise its services are free. All contact with the centre is confidential and anything said during mediation, or documents prepared for a mediation, are not admissible in any court or legal proceeding under the *Evidence Act 1958* (Vic.).

The Dispute Settlement Centre provides a dispute advisory and referral service, mediation and community education. Mediators do not give advice or make decisions about the dispute. They manage the process while the parties determine the content.

New South Wales Administrative Decisions Tribunal

http://www.lawlink.nsw.gov.au/adt

The Administrative Decisions Tribunal commenced operation in 1998. It centralised the work of several tribunals and courts to provide people with a convenient and accessible service for review of administrative decisions and hearing of certain general complaints, for example, discrimination, professional misconduct.

The tribunal consists of a General Division, five specialist divisions (Community Services Division, Equal Opportunity Division, Legal Services Division, Retail Leases Division and a Revenue Division) and an Appeal Panel. Its main role is to review administrative decisions of New South Wales government agencies including:

- freedom of information decisions;
- certain decisions regarding adoption, community and disability services;
- discrimination complaints;
- certain types of professional misconduct cases; and
- retail lease claims.

! CAUTION NOTE

*Decisions of tribunals are generally only subject to judicial review if natural justice has **not** been followed.*

OMBUDSMAN

The term 'ombudsman' means 'agent or representative of the people' and the person occupying this role is the link between the people and the bureaucracy of a government or large commercial organisation such as banking, insurance, private health and telecommunications. They are sometimes referred to as 'ombuds'. They investigate complaints about administrative actions and decisions made by government departments, statutory bodies, local authorities and the commercial areas noted above.

Unless the ombudsman considers that it would be reasonable to hear the matter first, a person who has a problem with a government department or statutory body should first try to exhaust all the normal avenues in an effort to resolve the matter. If this fails, they may then approach the ombudsman.

Ombuds can only make recommendations, not take action

A complaint must be made in writing. If the ombudsman considers that it falls within their jurisdiction, a copy of the complaint will be sent to the relevant authority for comment. This may resolve the matter, but where it doesn't, the ombudsman will investigate the validity of the complaint. On completion of the investigation, the ombudsman makes a recommendation as to whether or not the complaint is justified and the opinion will be forwarded to the appropriate authority. If, in the opinion of the ombudsman, the complaint is valid, recommendations are made to the appropriate authority for rectification.

If these recommendations are not acted upon, then the ombudsman may make these recommendations, in the case of the Commonwealth, to the Governor-in-Council and both Houses of Parliament, or in the case of the states or territories, to the Governor and to both Houses of Parliament (except in Queensland where there is no Upper House). The ombudsman has **no power to order rectification of a wrong** where it involves a government department or statutory body.

Apart from the independent Office of the Commonwealth Ombudsman (the Commonwealth Ombudsman is also the Defence Force Ombudsman, the Immigration Ombudsman, the Postal Industry Ombudsman and the Taxation Ombudsman) and the independent Offices of the State Ombudsmen, two industry examples of where an ombudsman is used are:

- **The Telecommunications Industry Ombudsman**
  http://www.tio.com.au/
  The Telecommunications Industry Ombudsman has power to investigate telecommunication service complaints, including complaints about services, response to faults, billing and interference with privacy. Unlike his or her government counterparts, the Telecommunications Industry Ombudsman can not only investigate a complaint but can also attempt to resolve it by mediation. If that fails, the ombudsman can order the provider to pay compensation up to a maximum of $10 000 or to compensate or take some other form of action up to a limit of $50 000. If the complainant accepts the decision of the ombudsman, they cannot take any other course of action.
- **The Banking and Financial Services Ombudsman**
  http://www.abio.org.au
  The Banking and Financial Services Ombudsman provides an alternative dispute resolution scheme for bank customers and small businesses who have unresolved disputes of up to $150 000 with a member bank or affiliate.

THE ADVERSARY SYSTEM

Dispute resolution through the courts in Australia is adversarial

In Australia, the basic method of dispute resolution is still the **adversary system** of justice. This means that there are two opposing sides in a dispute who will argue their case in a court presided over by a neutral third party in the form of a magistrate or judge and one side will win and one side will lose (Figure 2.6). Subject to the rules of evidence, the

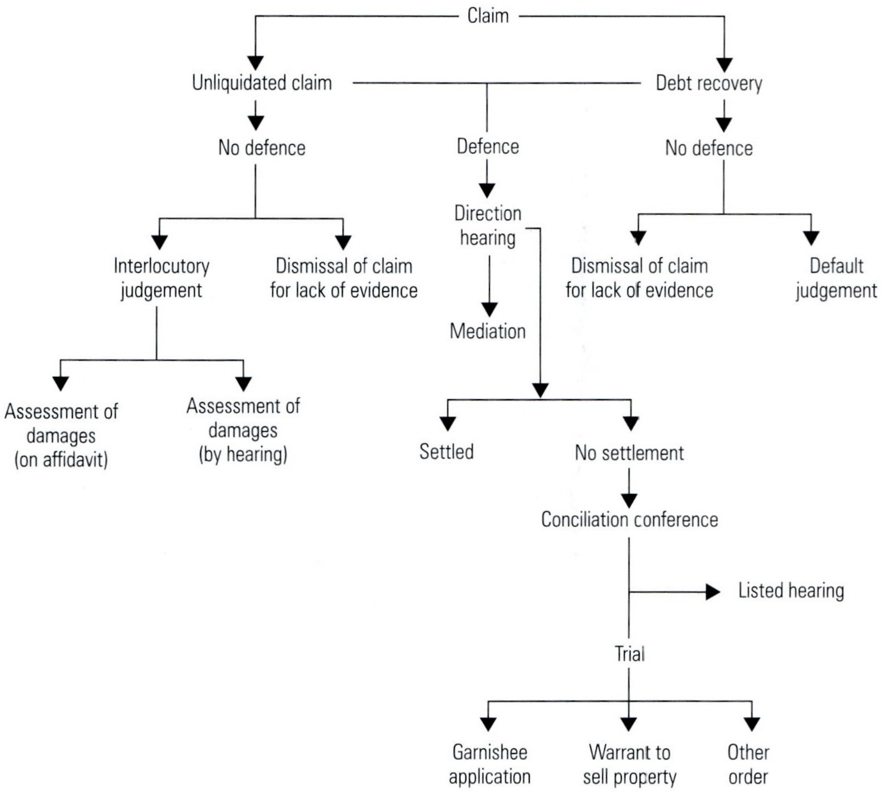

FIGURE 2.6 *Litigation process in a civil court*

parties have control over the witnesses they wish to call and the evidence they wish to produce. The truth of the evidence is tested by both sides asking questions (examination and cross-examination) and, at the end of the day, there will be a winner and a loser:

- in a civil case the side that wins is the side that can prove that their case is the more believable 'on the balance of probabilities'; and
- in a criminal case it is whether the Crown can prove 'beyond reasonable doubt' that the accused committed the crime they were charged with.

The main groups of participants in the adversary system are:

- the parties;
- the barristers and solicitors who will act on behalf of the parties;
- the judiciary who will preside over the court; and
- the jury (if there is one).

The course of an action through the litigation process in a **civil action** is similar in all jurisdictions. The plaintiff starts the action by making a claim against another person or organisation.

THE PARTIES

Civil action

In a civil law action the action is brought by one person (natural or legal), known as the **plaintiff**, against another, known as the **defendant** (Figure 2.7):

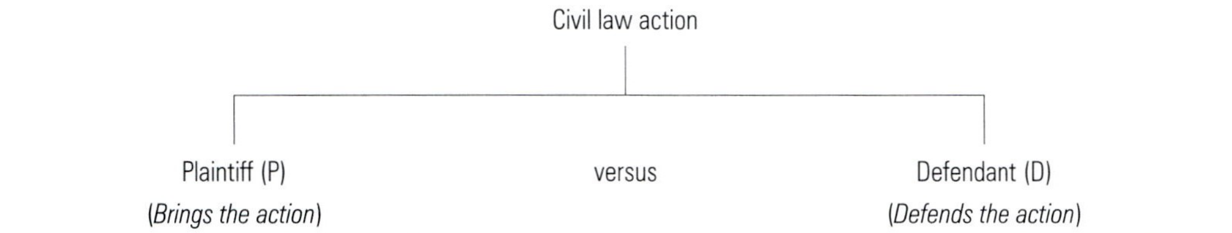

FIGURE 2.7 *Parties in a civil action at first instance (the first time in court)*

The burden (or onus) of proof is on the plaintiff to prove their case on the **balance of probabilities** (standard of proof). They will be seeking a remedy from the court in the form of monetary damages and/or a court order directing the other party do (specific performance) or refrain from doing (injunction) some particular act or acts.

The onus is on the plaintiff in a civil case to prove their case on the balance of probabilities

If the losing party is unhappy with the court's decision, they may decide to try to lodge an appeal with a higher court. Note that the plaintiff may no longer appear as the first-named party and the terms by which the parties are referred to may have changed from plaintiff and defendant to appellant and respondent (Figure 2.8):

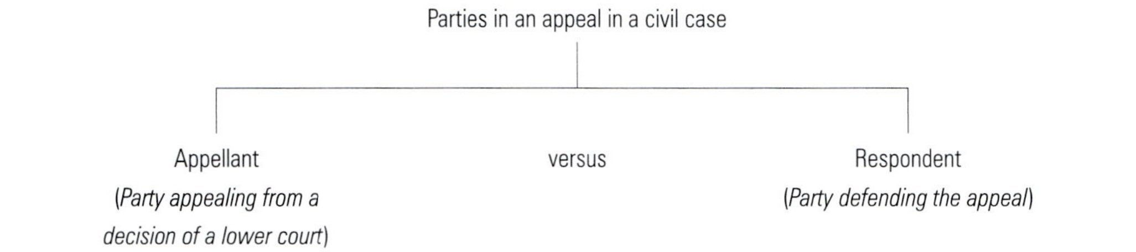

FIGURE 2.8 *Names of parties in an appeal case*

IN BRIEF

Possible remedies for a plaintiff in a civil action

Remedy	Characteristics
Damages	The main remedy of the common law courts is monetary compensation.
Specific performance	A discretionary remedy in equity, it is an order to make the defendant do a particular thing or act.
Injunction	A discretionary remedy in equity, it is an order restraining the defendant from doing a particular thing or act.

Criminal action

In a criminal action, the Crown is bringing an action against an accused person (Figure 2.9):

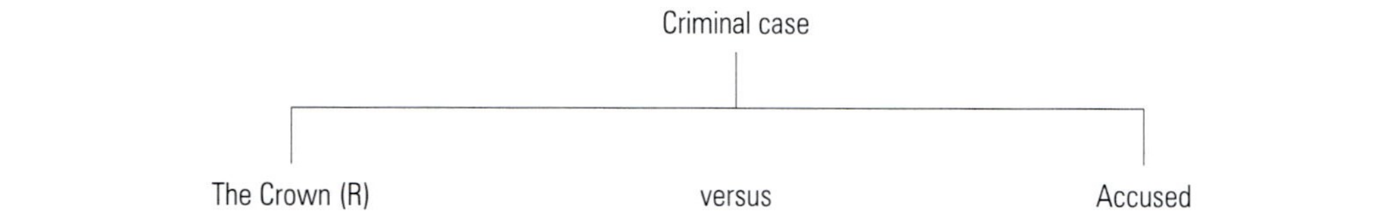

FIGURE 2.9 *Parties in a criminal case*

The onus is on the Crown in a criminal case to prove the guilt of the accused beyond reasonable doubt

The **onus is on the Crown**, through the actions of a prosecutor, to establish a case against the accused **beyond reasonable doubt**, a much higher burden of proof than is the case in a civil action. This generally requires the prosecutor to establish two things: first, that the accused had the intention, or *mens rea*, to commit the crime—such as the intention to shoplift or the intention to kill, and secondly, that the accused carried out the act or conduct (the *actus reus*)—such as the shoplifting or the killing. If the accused is found guilty, the court will then apply what it considers to be the **appropriate penalty** for the offence based on guidelines set down in the relevant criminal code or statute, for example, fine, jail or a bond.

There are a number of statutory offences, called crimes of **strict liability**, where intention is not necessary for an offence to occur, such as some breaches of the *Corporations Act 2001* (Cth). For example, s. 952E provides that it is an offence for a financial services licensee to give a defective disclosure document or statement to another person, whether or not they know it was defective; s. 952G makes it an offence for a financial services licensee to provide disclosure material to an authorised representative if the disclosure document or statement is defective, irrespective of whether it was known to be defective or not; and s. 1041E provides that it is an offence to make false or misleading statements that induce persons to apply for or acquire financial products, or have the effect of increasing, reducing, maintaining or stabilising the price for trading in financial products on a financial market irrespective of whether the person making the statement knew it was false or not.

Business activities are increasingly attracting criminal penalties. Fines for companies, and fines and possible imprisonment for directors and executives, are becoming common in all Australian jurisdictions, for example, at state and territory level for breaches of state and territory occupational health and safety laws and environmental legislation. At federal level, breaches of the restrictive trade practices sections in Part IV of the *Trade Practices Act 1974* (Cth) carry fines of up to $10m for corporations and up to $500 000 for individuals, while breaches of the consumer protection provisions in Part V can result in either civil or criminal proceedings (criminal proceedings for breach of the consumer protection sections are brought by the Australian Competition and Consumer Commission under Part VC). Under the *Corporations Act 2001* (Cth), companies can be fined up to $1.1m for insider trading, while individuals can be fined up to $200 000 or sent to jail, for example, well-known stockbroker Rene Rivkin was convicted of insider trading and sentenced to nine months periodic detention and fined $30 000 in 2003.

THE LEGAL PROFESSION

In Australia, the legal profession consists of solicitors and barristers

In Australia, while it is not compulsory to use a solicitor in the pre-trial process or a barrister in court, nearly all litigants will have recourse to a solicitor and usually a barrister as well, if the matter goes to court.

The term 'lawyer' is often used by the layperson to refer to both barristers and solicitors and is an expression commonly used in the United States, but this can be misleading. There is either a legal separation or an unofficial separation of the legal profession in all states and the territories:

- **Victoria, Tasmania, South Australia, Western Australia, the Australian Capital Territory and the Northern Territory**—qualified persons are admitted to practise as both barristers and solicitors. In practice, an independent bar exists in all states and the territories as some people choose to practise only as barristers.
- **New South Wales and Queensland**—as a matter of law, a qualified person can practise as either a barrister or a solicitor, but not as both. The two branches are mutually exclusive, though it is still possible to change from one branch to the other.

While it is common for a solicitor to undertake court appearances for clients, especially in the inferior courts, it is unusual for solicitors to undertake court appearances on behalf of their clients in higher courts. Both barristers and solicitors have the right to represent their clients as advocates before any state court. However, solicitors and clients still prefer to employ a barrister in higher courts because of the barrister's experience in court-room work.

Duties of a solicitor

Solicitor's work is mainly non-litigious

Although solicitors do represent their clients in court, the majority of their work is **non-litigious** in nature; that is, it does not involve appearances in court. Examples of solicitors' work include:

- conveyancing and drafting (drawing up documents);
- the preparation of wills and administration of estates;
- family law problems;
- taxation problems; and
- preparation of various legal documents relating to topics such as the drawing up of contracts, the formation or dissolution of businesses, and the preparation of documents and all other relevant matters prior to trial in which a barrister is employed on behalf of the client (called a brief).

Duties of a barrister

Barrister's work is opinions and court appearances

While it is possible in some states for the public to go straight to a barrister, the tendency for a person seeking legal advice is to go to a solicitor first. As a result, barristers are still almost completely dependent on instructing solicitors for work.

Barristers have two main functions:

- They give '**opinions**' to clients on the facts presented to them, setting out the relevant law and indicating the likely outcome of any action. This gives the client the opportunity to decide what course of action to take on the matter in dispute.
- A barrister may be '**briefed**' as 'counsel' for a client in either a civil or criminal case, and be required to appear in court to represent and plead or argue a case for their client.

THE JUDICIARY

Justices of the Peace

Justices of the Peace hold honorary positions. They usually have no legal training or experience, though many states have now introduced special law courses for them.

Bulk of JP's work is witnessing documents and issuing warrants

The bulk of their duties today are **witnessing documents** for members of the public and **issuing warrants** to enable the police to arrest offenders or search premises. In the case of a warrant, a Justice of the Peace has to be satisfied that there is 'good cause' before authorising its issue.

In South Australia, Queensland and Western Australia, Justices of the Peace are also entitled to preside in a Magistrate's Court.

Magistrates

Magistrates preside over inferior courts

Magistrates preside over inferior courts. They are full-time salaried public servants (hence the expression 'stipendiary' magistrate) and are selected from among the clerks of court, barristers, solicitors, government and academic lawyers.

Judges

Judges are appointed to intermediate and superior courts

Judges are generally appointed from members of the Bar. However, in recent years solicitors have been appointed to the benches of both intermediate and superior courts.

The **duties** of a judge are:

- to ensure that the rules of evidence are followed;
- to ensure that each party is fairly treated according to the law;
- to instruct the jury on matters of law;
- to decide on points of law and make a ruling on their relevance in a matter before the court;
- to sum up the arguments impartially, and explain to the jury (when used) the law regarding the particular action;
- where a case is heard before a judge alone, to determine questions of fact and law before arriving at a decision;
- to ensure that the burden of proof has been discharged;
- in a criminal case, to pass sentence if the jury returns a guilty verdict. In a civil case, to assess damages;
- to discharge the jury, if a jury has been used; and
- to hear appeals.

THE JURY

Juries only decide questions of fact

A jury is a body of men and women summoned and sworn under oath to **determine questions of fact** fairly and objectively in a judicial proceeding. Juries are the exclusive judges of fact, and when necessary they will also assess compensation or damages.

Criminal trials

Everyone accused of an indictable offence has the right to a trial by a judge and jury of 12 persons in an intermediate or superior court. In South Australia, an accused has the option of a trial by a judge alone. However, all states make provision for less serious indictable offences to be tried in an inferior court, if both the accused and the Crown consent.

Civil trials

The use of juries in civil cases has largely been abolished in most jurisdictions unless required in the interests of justice, with the judge deciding both questions of fact and law. Where a civil case is heard with a jury it will usually consist of four, five or six members in an intermediate court and 12 in a Supreme Court. Only a majority verdict is required. If the plaintiff wants to have a matter heard before a jury, most jurisdictions now provide that before the case starts the plaintiff has to pay into the court the costs of having a jury.

Doing business

Cost–benefit analysis of suing

The cost of bringing a lawsuit can be very expensive. No guarantee can be given that you will win and, in the event that you should lose, you may find that the other side will ask the court that you be ordered to pay their legal costs as well as your own.

The choice of whether to sue or defend an action should be analysed like any other business decision that you make. This means doing a cost–benefit analysis of the action. If you are the plaintiff, the analysis will help determine whether it is worth suing. For the defendant, it will help determine whether to settle out of court.

The following are some of the factors that should be taken into account:

- the probability of winning or losing (remember, no one can guarantee a win);
- the amount of money at stake if you win or lose (can you afford it?);
- legal costs (your legal representatives can provide an estimate);
- loss of time (cost your time and, if any, staff time);
- short- and long-term effects on the relationships of the parties (in an adversarial situation, there is no win–win position, only a win–lose);
- short- and long-term effects on the reputations of the parties (what will be the cost of lost reputation?);
- the aggravation and stress associated with the action;
- given the propensity of the legal system for error, ask yourself if you can afford an appeal; and
- other factors peculiar to the parties and the action. ■

REPRESENTATIVE OR CLASS ACTIONS

Class actions allow individuals or businesses with similar claims to combine in the one legal action against the same person or organisation

Class actions, or grouped or representative proceedings, allow individuals or businesses with similar, or substantially similar, claims to combine together in the one legal action against the same person or organisation.

A class action enables those who would be deterred from seeking compensation because of factors such as:

- time;
- the relatively small size of their claim; and
- legal costs, for example, where the defendant has sufficient financial resources to take the fight all the way through the court system

to gain access to the law.

All Australian jurisdictions, including the Commonwealth, allow representative actions in accordance with the general Rules of Court. Representative proceedings in the state and territory Supreme Courts are commonly known as the 'same interest' procedure (in Victoria 'group proceedings') and essentially provide that, where numerous persons have the same interest in any proceeding, the proceeding may be started or continued by or against one or more of the group on behalf of all of the group or part of it. For example, the New South Wales Uniform Civil Procedure Rules 2005 is a fairly typical example of the law found in all jurisdictions in that it permits representative actions, although Victoria and the Federal Court have specific 'opt-out' provisions. This is a limited form of class action available in common law jurisdictions where a person sues in their own name on behalf of other specified persons who have 'opted in'.

In recent times, there has been a significant growth in class actions brought in Australia, and against a very diverse range of defendants. Examples of actions include:

- product liability claims involving, e.g., breast implants, knee implants, heart pacemakers, tobacco, aircraft fuel, faulty home alarms, and foodstuffs;
- actions against major public utilities, e.g., suppliers of Sydney's drinking water, financial institutions for breaches of credit legislation, government agencies; and
- shareholder litigation in respect of misleading and deceptive conduct by companies to their shareholders in takeovers, prospectuses and in releases to the Australian Stock Exchange.

Commonwealth laws

Federal Court of Australia Act 1976 (Cth)

Under Part IVA of the *Federal Court of Australia Act 1976* (Cth) and Part 4A of the *Supreme Court Act 1986* (Vic.), groups of seven or more persons with common legal claims have the power to bring representative proceedings. It was argued in *Bright v. Femcare Ltd* [1999] FCA 1377 (6 October), a representative action case involving breaches of ss. 52, 53(c) and 75AD of the *Trade Practices Act 1974* (Cth), that Part IVA was unconstitutional because it was beyond the legislative competence of the Commonwealth Parliament. However, *Lehane* J in the Federal Court found that the Commonwealth Parliament did have the power to enact Part IVA. The constitutional validity of Part 4A of the *Supreme Court Act 1986* (Vic.) was then unsuccessfully challenged by Mobil on similar grounds to those raised in *Bright v. Femcare* in *Mobil Oil Australia Pty Ltd v. Victoria* [2002] HCA 27 with the High Court unanimously upholding its constitutional validity.

If the Federal Court has jurisdiction, a representative action may be brought under Part IVA of the *Federal Court of Australia Act 1976* (Cth). The applicant must:

- have a personal cause of action against a defendant;
- be able to describe or identify at least seven others who have a cause of action against the defendant;
- specify the nature of the claims made on their behalf;
- specify the nature of relief being sought; and
- specify the questions of law or fact common to the claim of the group members.

The applicant does not have to name or identify the number of group members involved in the action.

The Federal Court (and the Victorian Supreme Court) is an 'opt-out' proceeding. This means that the consent of each member of the group is not required to commence proceedings. If a member of the group wishes to leave the proceedings they can 'opt out' but they must do so before the date fixed by the court. If the defendant is unsuccessful in its defence, it will be liable for the loss and damage suffered by each member of the group that has not opted out. Alternatively, a defendant may seek to limit its potential exposure to liability by applying for an order that the group be 'closed', that is by asking the Federal Court to fix a date by which unidentified members of the group must identify themselves.

A class action may be discontinued by the court in certain circumstances. For example, if the court considers that it would be more cost effective if each member of the class conducted a separate proceeding, or that a class action did not provide an efficient and effective means of dealing with the claims of all the class members, or that no reasonable cause of action is disclosed.

Where a class action is successful, the defendant will be ordered to pay the costs of each and every member of the class. Where the claim fails, generally the only party who can be required to pay the defendant's costs is the party who is named as the representative of the class, however, in *Cook v. Pasminco Ltd (No. 2)* [2000] FCA 1819 the plaintiff's solicitors were ordered to pay the defendant's costs because the court found that they had failed to give any proper consideration of whether the claim had any chance of success.

Trade Practices Act 1974 (Cth)

Section 87 of the *Trade Practices Act 1974* (Cth) allows the Federal Court to make ancillary orders on behalf of a person who may not necessarily have been a party to the trade practices proceedings where a breach of Part V (consumer protection) is involved.

Three well-publicised class actions in Australia were:

- **Esso**—as a result of the 1998 explosion at the Esso Gas Refinery in Sale, Victoria, Esso, the Energy Networks Corporation and a number of gas companies were sued for negligence and breaches of the *Trade Practices Act 1974* (Cth) and the *Fair Trading Act 1985* (Vic.) by a Victorian law firm on behalf of four classes of gas users—householders, workers that were stood down, restaurants and industrial gas users. In that case (*Johnson Tiles Pty Ltd v. Esso Australia Ltd (No. 3)* [2003] VSC 244) the Victorian Supreme Court held that businesses that had suffered property damage or economic loss flowing from property damage were able to recover their losses but that other claimants, such as domestic gas users and stood-down workers, were not able to recover their losses.
- **McDonald's**—as a result of the 1999 'Monopoly McMatch & Win' promotion, it was alleged that people with winning tickets had been refused their prizes. The Federal Court subsequently decided in favour of McDonald's in *Hurley v. McDonald's Australia Limited* [2001] FCA 209.
- **Phillip Morris (Australia) Ltd**—six named applicants brought representative proceedings in their own names claiming that they, and the persons in their class, had contracted lung cancer as a result of the marketing, advertising and promotion of the respondent tobacco companies' cigarettes in *Phillip Morris (Australia) Ltd v. Nixon* [1999] FCA 1281. As the claims arose out of a series of events and over a period of time, the court struck out the plaintiff's claim on the basis that claims involving a multiplicity of issues should be brought on an individual basis.
- **GIO Shareholders**—between August and November 1998 GIO (now AG Australia Holdings Limited), its directors and Grant Samuel & Associates made statements to GIO shareholders during the defence of a hostile takeover that they should reject a takeover offer of $5.35 per share. Six months later the company revealed losses of $2 billion and the shareholders received only $2.75 per share. The shareholders brought a claim that the statements made by the former board and Grant Samuel & Associates were misleading, deceptive and/or negligent. In a bitterly contested case, the Federal Court approved a $97 million settlement to over 22 000 shareholders in *King v. AG Australia Holdings Ltd (formerly GIO Australia Holdings Ltd)* [2003] FCA 1420.

WEB RESOURCES

GENERAL

Lawlink NSW: the site of the New South Wales Attorney General's Department. It contains a wealth of information on a wide range of legal topics for projects and research. It is an excellent gateway for information on NSW courts and tribunals:
http://www.lawlink.nsw.gov.au/

Australian Law Online: a very useful site prepared by the Commonwealth government that looks at a variety of topics relevant to this text. For material on this chapter go to the topic headed 'Australian Legal System' and click on courts:
http://www.law.gov.au/

Complaint line: a good gateway site for anyone who has a consumer complaint and is not sure where to go:
http://www.complaintline.com.au/

Legalonline: the Victorian government's legal information website that provides a good coverage of business law topics, as well as information on the legal system:
http://www.legalonline.vic.gov.au

Ombudsman: for a link to the various government Ombudsmen sites:
http://www.complaintline.com.au/government_department.html#anchor704982

Web Wombat: a useful gateway to access a large number of courts around the country (and around the world for that matter) as well as some interesting sites if you are looking for information on how to conduct legal research:
http://www.webwombat.com.au/law

JURIES

Jury information: information on the selection and role of jurors can be accessed from a number of sites including:

NSW:
http://www.lawlink.nsw.gov.au/ots.nsf/pages/jury2

Queensland:
http://www.justice.qld.gov.au/courts/jurors.htm

Tasmania:
http://www.courts.tas.gov.au/supreme/users/jury/jury_contents.htm

Victoria:
http://www.legalonline.vic.gov.au

Go to Legal system and click on 'jurors'.

WA:
http://www.justice.wa.gov.au/portal/server.pt
Click on 'jurors' under Courts, Tribunals and Boards.

? REVIEW QUESTIONS

2.1 What is the difference between a court of first instance and an appellate court?

2.2 Describe the purpose of committal proceedings being conducted in the inferior courts.

2.3 What is the original jurisdictional limit of inferior courts in civil matters? Can it be exceeded?

2.4 Distinguish between a summary offence and an indictable offence. Under what circumstances can an indictable offence be heard in an inferior court?

2.5 Explain why an inferior court has no appellate jurisdiction.

2.6 Explain why an accused person may prefer to have an indictable matter dealt with summarily in an inferior court rather than in an intermediate court.

2.7 Explain the meaning of the expression 'in camera'. Is there any justification for a matter to be heard in camera?

2.8 The High Court has three important functions. Identify them.

2.9 How does the original jurisdiction of the High Court differ from that of the state superior courts?

2.10 Upon what grounds does the High Court rely for appellate jurisdiction in both state and federal matters?

2.11 Is the High Court a state or a federal court? Explain your answer.

2.12 List the reasons that have led to the rapid growth in administrative tribunals and alternative methods of dispute resolution.

2.13 In what ways do the procedures of the tribunals differ from those of the traditional courts?

2.14 What is the importance of a court hierarchy in the legal system?

2.15 Is the burden of proof the same in a civil trial as in a criminal trial?

2.16 Who has the burden of proof in a civil case?

2.17 Distinguish between the terms 'barrister' and 'solicitor'.

2.18 Discuss the role of the judge in a jury trial. How does it differ when there is no jury?

2.19 Indicate whether each of the following statements is true or false:

	TRUE	FALSE
▪ Police are community guardians of the peace	☐	☐
▪ The County Court of Victoria is bound by a decision of the NSW Supreme Court	☐	☐
▪ The role of the jury is to decide matters of fact	☐	☐

activebook

Activebook resources include in-depth summaries with links to the relevant part of the book. For revision, add your own notes to the summaries provided by using the note-taking function.

	TRUE	FALSE
▪ A person who appeals against a previous court decision is the respondent	☐	☐
▪ The number of jurors in a criminal trial is normally six	☐	☐
▪ Inferior courts are courts of record	☐	☐
▪ The High Court only has appellate jurisdiction	☐	☐
▪ The standard of proof in a civil case is beyond reasonable doubt	☐	☐
▪ The onus of proof in a criminal case is on the accused to prove their innocence	☐	☐
▪ Judges can be chosen from the ranks of barristers or solicitors	☐	☐
▪ The jury decide questions of law while the judge decides all questions of fact	☐	☐
▪ An appellant is a person starting an action while a respondent is defending it	☐	☐

CRITICAL THINKING

2.1 How successful has the appointment of ombuds been in the country? Discuss.

2.2 In commercial matters, is the common law adversarial system the best way of settling disputes? Discuss.

2.3 Is there still a role for the jury in today's legal system? Discuss.

CHAPTER

How Law is Made— Precedent/Statute Law

CHAPTER CONTENTS

CHAPTER OBJECTIVES

On completion of this chapter, you should be able to:

- Precedent:
- – describe the doctrine of precedent
- – have an understanding of the practices followed by the courts in relation to judicial precedent
- – describe and explain the importance of the court system in relation to precedent
- – describe and explain the meaning of *ratio decidendi* and *obiter dicta*
- Statute law:
- – list the steps by which Parliament creates a statute
- – identify the methods used by the courts for their interpretation of statutes
- – apply the common law rules of statutory interpretation
- – explain the more important maxims used by the courts to assist them in statutory interpretation, in particular, *noscitur a sociis* and *ejusdem generis*
- – explain the purpose of delegated legislation.

activebook

This icon is used throughout the following chapter to remind you to visit the *Business Law* online Activebook for additional exercises, links to legal websites, and feedback. For a detailed explanation of what is in the Activebook please refer to the inside cover of this textbook. The Activebook is available through OneKey.

Where do I start?
Learning path: Use the Activebook to complete a pre-chapter warm-up exercise.

There are many definitions of legal terms to assist with your understanding of the material.

3

KEY TERMS

An understanding of the following terms will help you to better understand the material in this chapter:

- **appellant:** the party appealing a decision. They may be either the plaintiff or the defendant from when the case went to trial the first time
- **delegated legislation:** regulations and by-laws passed by a subordinate authority, such as a municipal council or a government undertaking like the railways, in reliance of some regulation-making powers conferred by an Act of Parliament upon it
- ***ejusdem generis*:** of the same kind of nature. In cases of statutory interpretation where particular words are followed by general words, then the general words will be limited to the same kind as the particular words
- ***noscitur a sociis*:** the meaning of a word can be gathered from the context
- ***obiter dictum*:** a saying by the way. An observation by a judge on a matter of law which is not essential to the decision before them, and which is therefore not part of the binding precedent established by the case
- **preamble:** that part of a statute set out in the beginning giving the reasons for the Act
- **precedent (also known as *stare decisis*):** a judgement or decision of a court of law cited as an authority for deciding a similar set of facts in later cases. Precedent may be binding if it is from a court in the same hierarchy and on a higher level. Persuasive precedents are non-binding on courts if they are outside their court hierarchy or from a court on a lower level
- ***ratio decidendi*:** the reason for a decision, which makes binding precedent for the future
- **respondent:** a person against whom an appeal is brought. They may be either the plaintiff or the defendant from when the case went to trial the first time
- ***stare decisis*:** to stand by that which has been decided. A case decision serves as a legal precedent in the deciding of a subsequent similar case
- **statute:** an Act of Parliament; a law passed by the legislature.

what if . . .

You were asked to explain the meaning of the following section after a friend came to you and said that they wanted to trade in their unregistered motorbike at a Sunday morning car market:

> **'It shall be an offence to sell a defective vehicle in a public place during the week.'**

There are two main sources of law in our legal system: case law (or judge-made law) and statute law. An understanding of the main principles underlying each source is important when trying to understand how the law and business interact.

This chapter looks first at case law and the terminology that is commonly used when studying law—*ratio decidendi* and *obiter dictum*—and then examines some of the more important features of precedent. A good understanding of court hierarchies discussed in Chapter 2 will make this chapter easier to understand. The chapter then examines statute law. This is an area of law of considerable importance to business, and knowledge of the basic principles of how to read and interpret a statute are useful tools to have.

SOURCES OF LAW

IN BRIEF

Main sources of law

Type	Description
Case or common law	Judge-made law, also known as common law, and equity.
Statute law and delegated legislation	Laws passed by Commonwealth, state and territory parliaments in the form of statutes, and laws passed by subordinate authorities in the form of delegated legislation.
International treaties	While strictly speaking not yet a main source of law, its importance as a source of law is growing as society becomes increasingly internationalised.

Each source of law **must** be readily accessible to both the legal profession and the public. Judge-made law is accessible through the various authorised or semi-authorised law reports, while statute law and delegated legislation are readily available from the federal and various state and territory government printers. International treaties are available through the Commonwealth government printer.

Cases, statutes and delegated legislation are also available on the web. The Commonwealth, states and territories all have sites that contain case law (for web locations go to the end of the chapter), statutes and delegated legislation.

WEB RESOURCES

The Commonwealth has two online sites:

COMLaw: provides access to Commonwealth statutes, regulations, government reports, Hansard and current Bills, and is part of the Australian Law Online initiative of the Commonwealth to bring low-cost access of the law to the community:

http://www.comlaw.gov.au

Australian Law Online: contains more general information about the Australian legal system:

http://www.law.gov.au

In addition to the government sites, there is also the **Australasian Legal Information Institute (Austlii—)** site which provides free web access to Australian cases and legislation. It publishes both primary (legislation, treaties, and reported and unreported decisions of courts and tribunals) and secondary legal materials created by public bodies for purposes of public access (law reform and royal commission reports, for example). It also has a large index of other legal websites from around the world, including a section containing 'Other Australian Law'.

http://www.austlii.edu.au

! CAUTION NOTE

Note that when looking for state, territory or Commonwealth statutes or regulations, Austlii is a convenient starting point but it is not exhaustive and it is not official. So, for accuracy, always refer to the relevant state, territory or Commonwealth site for the most current material. These sites also contain information on repealed legislation and Hansard.

FINDING A REPORTED CASE

WEB RESOURCE

FINDING CASES

A wide range of Commonwealth, state and territory court and tribunal decisions can be accessed through:

http://www.austlii.edu.au

Note, however, that the various state and territory courts are also beginning to publish electronically decisions from their lower courts (see list at the end of this chapter).

Cases are found by their citation

Before considering questions of *res judicata*, *ratio decidendi* and *obiter dictum*, it is first necessary to be able to find the case. Reference for a case is known as its citation and refers to the method used to indicate where to find a particular case. Different types of citation are used for traditional law reports and for electronic reports.

Traditional law reports

When trying to find a case in a **set of traditional law reports** using a case citation, two factors should be kept in mind:

- In every country where judge-made law is in use, **each report** will have its own **abbreviation**. (A guide to the meaning of some of the more commonly used law report abbreviations can be found at the beginning of this book on pp. xvii–xviii.
- The date will appear either in **round** or **square brackets**:
  - When the reference to the year is **not** essential to find the volume (i.e. the law reports are numbered by volume from inception), then the date is placed in **round brackets** (if there is a date). For example, a typical citation would appear as shown in Figure 3.1.

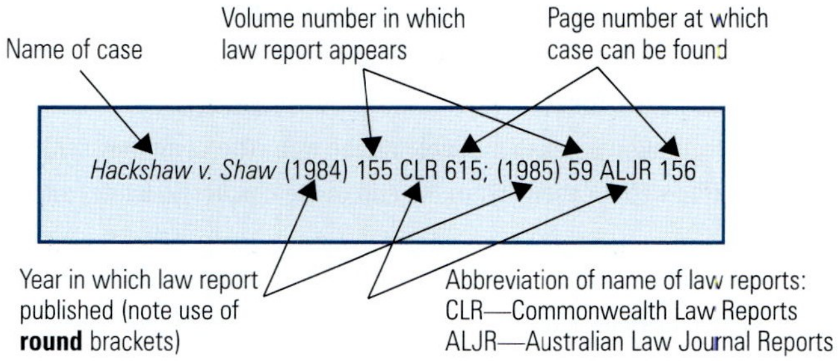

FIGURE 3.1 *Citation using round brackets*

In *Hackshaw v. Shaw*, there are two citations as the case has been reported in two different sets of law reports. The use of round brackets around the year means that the case can be found by simply going to the volume number of the relevant law reports. In this case, by going to volume 155 of the 1984 *Commonwealth Law Reports* and turning to page 615. The case can also be found in volume 59 of the 1985 *Australian Law Journal Reports* at page 156. The difference in dates between the two law reports for the same case merely reflects different dates when the case was published by the respective law reports. In neither case does the practitioner actually need to know the year of publication to find the case.

  - The use of square brackets tells the practitioner that the law reports are numbered by year only, rather than year and volume number (see Figure 3.2).

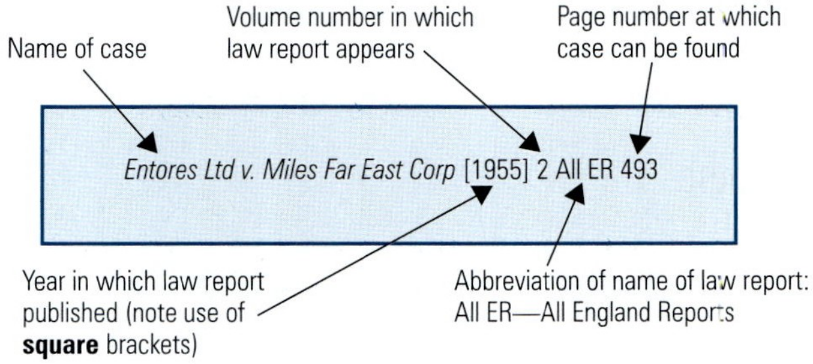

FIGURE 3.2 *Citation using square brackets*

This tells the practitioner that to find the case it is necessary to go to volume 2 of the 1955 All England Reports at page 493. The square brackets tell the practitioner that in this particular set of law reports, the **year is vital** in finding the case. As the name suggests, these are reports of decisions of an English Court.

– There is a trend by some law publishers to ignore the convention of square and round brackets and just use round brackets for all dates.

Electronic versions of judgements

In addition to the citations used for traditional law reports, there are also **electronic 'online' citations**. These are described as **report neutral** or **medium neutral** citations. The name of the case and year of publication are still retained (the year being in square brackets), but the volume and page numbers are replaced by the initials of the court making the decision and the judgement number (see Figure 3.3).

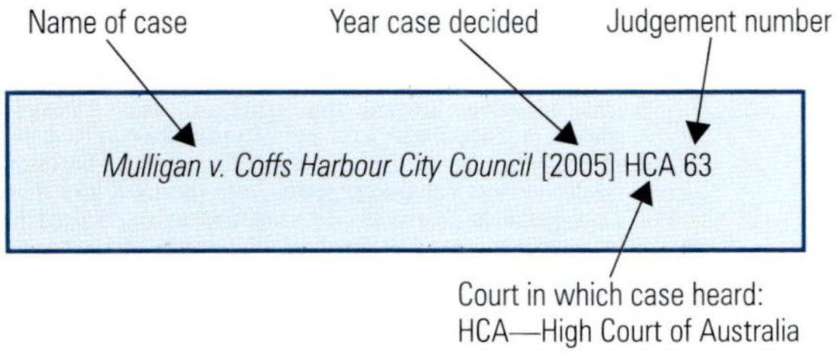

FIGURE 3.3 *Report neutral or medium neutral citation used for electronic versions of law judgements*

Each judgement is divided into numbered paragraphs. A citation from a law report contains the page number, for example, *Entores Ltd v. Miles Far East Corp.* [1955] 2 All ER 493 at 495. In the case of an electronic judgement, the relevant individual paragraph is cited, for example, *Mulligan v. Coffs Harbour City Council* [2005] HCA 63 at [10].

Advantages of electronic databases include:

- availability of cases much sooner than is the case with law reports (which have to be published);
- the recording of reported (i.e. cases which appear in law reports) and unreported decisions across a wider ranger of courts than just the traditional superior courts, providing greater access to a much wider range of court decisions than was previously possible;
- greater access to the law by the community; and
- low or no-cost access to legal materials.

For more details on finding cases electronically see: **http://www.auslii.edu.au**

Throughout the text, references to cases have been made, followed by the citation. You will notice that while many of the cases have the traditional citation (see Figures 3.1 and 3.2), in some instances you will see cases cited by the report neutral or medium neutral citation system, which will mean that they have been sourced from an electronic database (usually Austlii) (see Figure 3.3) and may not have been available in law reports at the time of writing. After the publication of a case in the law reports, it is usual to cite the law report rather than the report neutral or medium neutral online version.

Where the case can be found in the law reports

AUSTRALIAN LAW JOURNAL REPORTS 1985

Court where the case was heard

Vol 59 HIGH COURT OF AUSTRALIA 156

Parties

HACKSHAW v. SHAW

Judges who heard the appeal and the dates of the hearing

Canberra, February 21, December 11, 1984. } Before Gibbs C.J., Murphy, Wilson, Deane and Dawson JJ.

Catchwords

Negligence — Duty of care — Of occupiers of premises — Relationship to general duty of care arising from proximity and foreseeability — Whether single duty — Whether dual duties — Duty of care to trespasser — General duty based on additional relationship arising from dangerous activity of occupier — Relevance of fact of trespass to general duty — Trespasser on farm — Use of firearm by farmer to immobilise motor car — Trespasser shot.

Trespass to the person — Battery — Whether intent or negligence necessary — Onus of proof thereof.

Summary of facts by the Reporter of the case

The appellant, a girl aged sixteen years, travelled along a country road at night in the front passenger seat of a car driven by a young man. As the car approached the gate of a farm the driver turned the lights off and drove some distance into the farm to a petrol tank kept by the owner and occupier of the farm, the respondent, for his fuel supply. The driver began to pump petrol from the tank into the car. The appellant and the driver were trespassing on the farm. The farmer did not live on the farm. For at least a year past he had been troubled by thefts of his petrol, and the police had told him that he would have to get a description of the car used in the thefts before they could do anything. On this night he was waiting concealed nearby, as he had been at night for a week past, with the purpose of immobilising the car and that way discovering the identity of the thief. When the driver began to put petrol in his tank, the respondent fired a rifle shot at the engine and at the same time called to the driver to go away and leave the car. The appellant lay down on the front seat. When the driver ran around in front of the car, the respondent fired a second shot at the car to frighten the driver. It penetrated the front car door and struck the appellant in the arm.

The appellant sued the respondent for damages for negligence. The jury found that the respondent did not know or believe that any person other than the driver was or might be in the car, but that the respondent should have known or believed that some other person might be in the car. It also found that the respondent was negligent in firing the shot that hit the appellant, and that the appellant had been guilty of contributory negligence. There was no allegation that the respondent intended to shoot the appellant, and the jury found that the shooting was not reckless. Judgment was entered for the appellant, but it was set aside and judgment was entered for the respondent on appeal to the Full Court of the Supreme Court of Victoria.

Summary of the decision by the Reporter

Held (by Gibbs C.J., Murphy, Wilson and Deane JJ., with Dawson J. dissenting), that the respondent was under a duty of care to the appellant, the finding of negligence on the respondent's part established a breach of that duty, and the judgment for the appellant on her negligence claim must be restored.

Per Gibbs C.J. and Wilson J. The respondent in discharging his firearm placed himself in a relationship to the appellant additional to that of occupier and trespasser, with the consequence that he came under a general duty of care to the appellant in respect of the reasonably foreseeable consequences of his acts. While in determining whether there was a breach of this duty the fact that the appellant was a trespasser was a relevant fact, the relationship of occupier and trespasser did not displace the general duty of care arising. The presence of the appellant was reasonably foreseeable by the respondent.

Cases referred to by judges in course of their judgements

Munnings v. Hydro-Electric Commission (1971) 125 C.L.R. 1; *Public Transport Commission (N.S.W.) v. Perry* (1977) 137 C.L.R. 107: and *Commissioner for Railways v. Anderson* (1961) 105 C.L.R. 42, applied. *Voli v. Inglewood Shire Council* (1963) 110 C.L.R. 74, considered. *Commissioner for Railways v. Quinlan* [1964] A.C. 1054, not followed.

FIGURE 3.4 *A case report headnote. Hackshaw v. Shaw (1985) 59 ALJR 156. Reproduced with the express permission of © The Law Book Company Limited, a part of Thomson Legal & Regulatory Group Asia Pacific Limited, http://www.thomson.com.au.*

CASE LAW (PRECEDENT)

IN BRIEF

Res judicata, ratio decidendi* and *obiter dictum

Term	Description
Res judicata	The final order of the court binding the immediate parties to the decision.
Ratio decidendi	The legal reasoning upon which the decision in a case was based. Only the *ratio* is capable of creating a binding precedent.
Obiter dictum	Anything else said about the law in the course of a judgement that does not form part of the matters at issue. It can only create a persuasive precedent.

Res judicata

***Res judicata* applies only to the immediate parties**

The doctrine of *res judicata* applies only to the immediate parties to the case. It assumes that:

- there are two opposing parties;
- there is a definite issue; and
- the court has so decided the issue acting within its jurisdiction.

It means that the decision and final order of the court binds the parties to the proceedings. It is the judgement in the strictest sense. Other parties in similar disputes in the future are not so bound.

Ratio decidendi and obiter dictum

***Ratio decidendi*—reason for the decision**

In addition to its *res judicata* face, the legal reasoning upon which the decision in that case was based may be used by judges in future cases when confronted with similar facts. This is the *ratio decidendi* (the reason for deciding) (see below under precedent).

***Obiter dicta*—sayings by the way**

Anything else said about the law in the course of a judgement that does not form part of the matters at issue is called *obiter dicta* (sayings by the way). It has no binding power, although it can exercise an extremely strong influence in a lower court, and even in a court of equivalent standing, depending on the court and the judge.

***HEDLEY BYRNE & CO. LTD V. HELLER & PARTNERS LTD* [1964] AC 465**

The appellants were advertising agents and the respondents were merchant bankers. The appellants had a client called Easipower Ltd who was a customer of the respondents. The appellants had placed substantial forward orders for advertising and they asked their bank to ask Easipower's bankers what the credit worthiness of Easipower was. The respondents replied that they considered Easipower financially stable, though at the top of the letter they sent to the appellant's bank they stipulated that the statement was made '*without responsibility on the part of the bank or its officials*'. Relying on the reference, the appellants placed orders for advertising time and space for Easipower. The appellants assumed responsibility for payment of this time and space. Easipower subsequently went into liquidation, and the appellants lost over $34 000 on advertising contracts.

ISSUE: Did the exclusion clause protect the bank from liability?

DECISION: The respondents were not liable to pay any damages to the appellants (the decision) because the clause inserted by the respondents to take no responsibility for any advice that they may have given was adequate to exclude the assumption by them of a legal duty of care, and thus an action in negligence (the *ratio decidendi*).

COMMENT: The case is probably better known for what the judges in the House of Lords said about liability for negligent misstatements than the actual decision itself. They were unanimous in saying that the bank would have been liable for their negligent misstatements if they had not put such a clause in their reference. This was *obiter dictum* because it did not go to the matter at issue, i.e. the effectiveness of the clause.

This has, in fact, turned out to be a most persuasive piece of *obiter dictum* by the House of Lords. It had been thought that a negligent misstatement, whether spoken or written, could not give rise to an action for financial loss, unless there was a contract that may have existed between the parties. Later decisions have extended this statement of *obiter* in both English and Australian courts (see, for example, Chapter 8 and the discussion on negligent misstatements on pp. 164–166).

Unfortunately it is not always easy to identify the *ratio decidendi* of a case. For example:

- the judges may have different reasons for arriving at the same conclusion;
- their reasons may be unclear; and
- they may have reached a correct decision but for quite the wrong reasons.

There are numerous possibilities and the reality is that identification of the *ratio decidendi* in a case requires long practice in the analysis of reported cases.

IN BRIEF

Guidelines to identifying the ratio of a case

- Summarise the key facts of the case.
- What is/are the issue/s?
- What was the court's decision?
- What were the reasons the court gave for its decision?

activebook

To help you to remember and understand the topics covered so far, and for links to legal websites, refer to your online Activebook. Model answers provide feedback to problems and exercises.

Even when you have established what the *ratio decidendi* of a case is, it is still not an easy task to determine with any accuracy how this will be applied in future cases. It must be kept in mind at all times that you are talking in terms of general principles. In coming to a particular conclusion, a judge may have stated the general proposition of law upon which reliance was placed either widely or narrowly.

LEGAL CASES AS PRECEDENT

One of the features in building up both common law and equity was the doctrine of precedent. A precedent has been defined as 'a judgement or decision of a court of law cited as an authority for the legal principle embodied in its decision'. In its simplest form, 'following a precedent' means that a question should be resolved in a certain way today because a similar question was so decided yesterday. This process of following an established procedure is known as *stare decisis*, which literally means 'to stand by a decision'.

Precedent attempts to ensure fairness and equality

The doctrine of precedence seeks to ensure that people will be treated equally and fairly over a long period. This gives everyone the opportunity to conduct their affairs in the knowledge that certain rules and procedures operate to make it possible to predict, with a fair degree of certainty, what the likely outcome will be in the event of a dispute.

In order for precedent to operate there has to be in existence a court hierarchy where the lower courts will be bound by the decisions of higher courts in that hierarchy (see Chapter 2). In order to determine the importance of a decision, factors that have to be considered include:

- Where does a particular court fit in a hierarchy?
- Who was the judge (or judges)?
- Even if a decision comes from a higher court in the same hierarchy, it is only the *ratio decidendi* which can create a binding precedent. Anything else said in a judgement about the law is at best only capable of being of persuasive value.

IN BRIEF

Some advantages and disadvantages of precedents

Advantages	Disadvantages
Promotes consistency	Precedent may not be relevant to today's circumstances but has to be followed
Coherence	Slow to respond to community changes
Certainty	May require an Act of Parliament to change
Efficiency	
Justice—equality and fairness	

Rules of precedent

IN BRIEF

Courts of record and the operation of the doctrine of precedent

Court	Binding precedent	Persuasive precedent
High Court	All state and federal courts	On High Court
Full Court of Federal Court	Single judge of Federal Court and Full Court of Federal Court	High Court and courts in other hierarchies
Single judge of Federal Court	Single judge of Federal Court	Courts in other hierarchies
Courts of Appeal (NSW, Vic., Qld), Full Bench and Full Court of Supreme Court	Single judge of Supreme Court District (County in Vic.) Court and Inferior Court in same hierarchy	High Court and courts in other hierarchies
Supreme Court	District (County in Vic.) Court Inferior Court in same hierarchy	High Court and courts in other hierarchies
Privy Council	None in Australia	All Australian courts
House of Lords	None in Australia	All Australian courts

Courts of record

Only superior courts of record can create binding precedent

Only the more important courts in a hierarchy (the Superior Courts which **formally record in writing** their court reports) have their decisions followed in later cases by other courts. Known as courts of record, any judgement of any superior court that is accurately reported is entitled to consideration. However, the great majority of recorded cases will not create precedents. They will be decided by the application of existing legal rules.

Binding precedent

Binding precedent only binds courts in same hierarchy

In the case of a binding precedent (the *ratio decidendi* of an earlier case decision) each court is bound by the decisions of courts of the same level or higher than it in the same hierarchy of courts, whether or not it believes a decision is correct. To determine whether a court is part of the same hierarchy, consider whether it is linked by a right of appeal.

For example, the District Court in New South Wales is bound to follow a previous decision of the New South Wales Supreme Court where the facts of the two cases are similar because both courts are in the same jurisdiction. This saves the parties the time and expense of appeals, for the decision will be 'correct' in the light of the decision in the higher court. However, it is not bound to follow a previous decision of the Queensland Supreme Court even though the facts of the two cases may be similar because the Queensland decision is from a different jurisdiction.

Where there has been a clear error and the court is convinced that the previous decision was wrong, judicial preference is to permit the Court of Appeal, the Full Court or the Full Bench of the Supreme Court (depending on which state the matter is being heard in), or even the High Court if the matter goes that far, to correct the error.

Persuasive precedent

Persuasive precedent can only influence courts

A persuasive precedent can only influence a decision. Examples of persuasive precedents are judicial statements which are *obiter* from a court of binding status within the same hierarchy, or decisions of equivalent or higher standing courts from other hierarchies cited in argument in a local case being heard. For example, the House of Lords decision in *Hedley Byrne & Co. Ltd v. Heller & Partners Ltd* above might be quoted in a New South Wales case or a decision of the Victorian Supreme Court may be quoted in the Queensland Supreme Court. In either case, the decision quoted does **not** have to be followed because it is from a different jurisdiction.

How persuasive a decision in a case is depends to a large extent on how much importance the court attaches to two factors:

- **the judge**—the more eminent the judge, the more influential their decision is likely to be, e.g., *Dixon* and *Denning* judgements would be considered carefully by a court if they were raised in argument by counsel for either side; and
- **the court**—the higher the court, the greater its influence.

High Court precedent is binding on state courts but only persuasive on itself

In some cases a decision can be **both** a binding and a persuasive precedent. A High Court decision is of binding force on other Australian courts, but since the High Court has always been prepared to overrule one of its own earlier decisions if it thought the decision was wrong, the precedent is only of persuasive value on the High Court.

Some judicial techniques

The *ratio decidendi* will stand as binding or persuasive authority, but may be diminished or lost

The *ratio decidendi* of a case will stand as either binding **or** persuasive authority, though as a result of later cases its authority may be diminished or even lost. When a precedent is cited (quoted) by a barrister, the court **must** consider it when deciding the issues before it.

If a judge fails to follow a binding precedent, the case may be appealed by the losing party (the appellant) and the decision of the judge reversed because the judge has made an error of law. If the case is not appealed, for example, because the losing party can't afford the costs, then the decision will stand for the immediate parties but may be overruled in a later case by the appropriate court in the same hierarchy.

IN BRIEF

What can happen when a case is cited in argument by counsel

Outcome	Description
Adopted	The case is said to be followed or applied by the court.
Affirmed	The court agrees with the earlier decision.
Reversed	Changed by the appeal in a higher court being upheld.
Overruled	An appellate court decides a similar matter, in a later case, on the basis of a different legal principle. In this event, the *ratio decidendi* of the later case decided in the higher court is followed, and the earlier decision is no longer considered to be good law.
Distinguished	The court finds some material difference between the facts of the two cases, thus allowing the court to qualify or avoid an earlier precedent without the need to overrule it.
Disapproved	If a court cannot overrule a case, it may state by way of *obiter dictum* that the earlier case is no longer good law.

STATUTE LAW

The second major source of law within the Australian legal system is statute law. This is law made by Parliament and any subordinate bodies to whom Parliament has delegated power to legislate, for example, local councils.

Statute law consists of laws made by Parliament and subordinate bodies

Statutes assume the existence of common law, and in many cases they reaffirm common law principles, for example, the sale of goods legislation of each state and the *Bills of Exchange Act 1909* (Cth).

It is also possible for a statute to change the common law because the common law principle with which it is concerned no longer meets current social conditions. For example, the common law principle of freedom to contract has been modified by industrial relations legislation in all states. This prohibits both employers and employees from excluding the provisions of the legislation in relation to wages and holidays.

Where statute law and common law conflict, statute law will prevail to the extent of the conflict. No development of the common law can ever have this effect, although it should be noted that with every generalisation an exception to the rule can be found. In employment law, where an award is not as favourable as the relevant contract of employment, the contract of employment will prevail.

Statute law generally prevails where it conflicts with common law

IN BRIEF

Some key points about statutes

A number of key points about statutes can be identified including:

- They are law made by Parliament and those subordinate bodies to whom Parliament delegated power to legislate.
- They are the supreme law in Australia.
- In the event of conflict with common law, statute law will prevail.
- They assume the existence of common law and often re-affirm common law principles.
- They may modify or replace the common law.
- They can often react faster to, and better reflect, current community needs than the common law.
- They can be made retrospective (i.e. to apply to transactions before the legislation was enacted).

How is statute law made?

Sources of legislation

A proposal for new legislation could come from a variety of sources including:

- a suggestion from a member of Parliament from either side of the political arena, though this is relatively rare today because of the way in which Parliament works;
- a decision of the Cabinet of the government in power (the most common source nowadays);
- a decision made by a political party at one of its conferences;
- a result of pressure from the Opposition; or
- a government department, or recommendations and pressure from industry and other interested organisations.

This list is far from exhaustive.

From idea to Act

Proposals for most new legislation come from the party in power. This means that new legislation is first submitted to Cabinet by the minister or ministers concerned, usually after prolonged departmental discussion, including interdepartmental conferences if more than one department is affected or involved (see Figure 3.5).

After approval or amendment by Cabinet, the proposals are submitted to the Office of Parliamentary Counsel, which drafts all Bills coming before Parliament. A Bill is the draft of the proposed law. After final drafting by this office (and this is never easy, because both Acts and regulations are becoming increasingly technical in their nature despite a trend towards plain English), the Bill goes to the Legislation Committee of Cabinet for approval. It is then ready for Parliament.

When a Bill is introduced into Parliament, it is frequently accompanied by an explanatory memorandum making its objects clear to the members of both Houses. The fact that a Bill is brought before Parliament does not mean that it is now a part of the law or that it will necessarily become so. Before the Bill can be considered part of the law of the land, it must go through three reading stages.

For a Bill to become an Act it must be passed by both Houses (except Queensland)

As it is usual for Parliament in Australia to consist of two Houses (bicameral legislatures consisting of an upper and a lower House), the Bill must be considered three times by each House (except in Queensland, which only has a lower House). If a Bill is brought before a Parliament that has two Houses, it must be passed by both Houses before it can become an Act of Parliament.

All Bills, other than those proposing to alter the Constitution, are passed by a simple majority of the members present and voting.

The practice and procedure of each House of Parliament—the federal Parliament and the parliaments of each of the states—are contained in a set of rules, passed by each House respectively, known as Standing Orders.

Most Bills are introduced into the Lower House

Most Bills are introduced in the lower House of Parliament (the House of Representatives at Commonwealth level and the Legislative Assembly at state level). They pass through the following stages (using the federal Parliament as an example, but remember that Queensland and the territories have no upper House of Parliament):

1. **Notice**—notice is given on one day for the presentation of a Bill on a subsequent day. Notice is not required for Appropriation and Supply Bills or Bills dealing with taxation matters.
2. **Presentation and 'first reading'**—this is a formality, for the whole Bill is not actually read. The Minister presents the Bill to the House and its title is read by the Clerk of the House.
3. **Second reading**—immediately after the first reading, it is usual for the Minister to move that the Bill be now read a second time. The Minister then outlines its purpose in general terms. At the end of the second reading speech, the debate is adjourned on a motion usually put forward by an Opposition member. This enables the members to study the provisions of the Bill, and the debate, when resumed, is on the broad principles involved. If the House agrees, the whole Bill with amendments (if any) is read through a second time at the end of the debate. However, the Opposition may oppose the Bill in this second reading and vote against it.

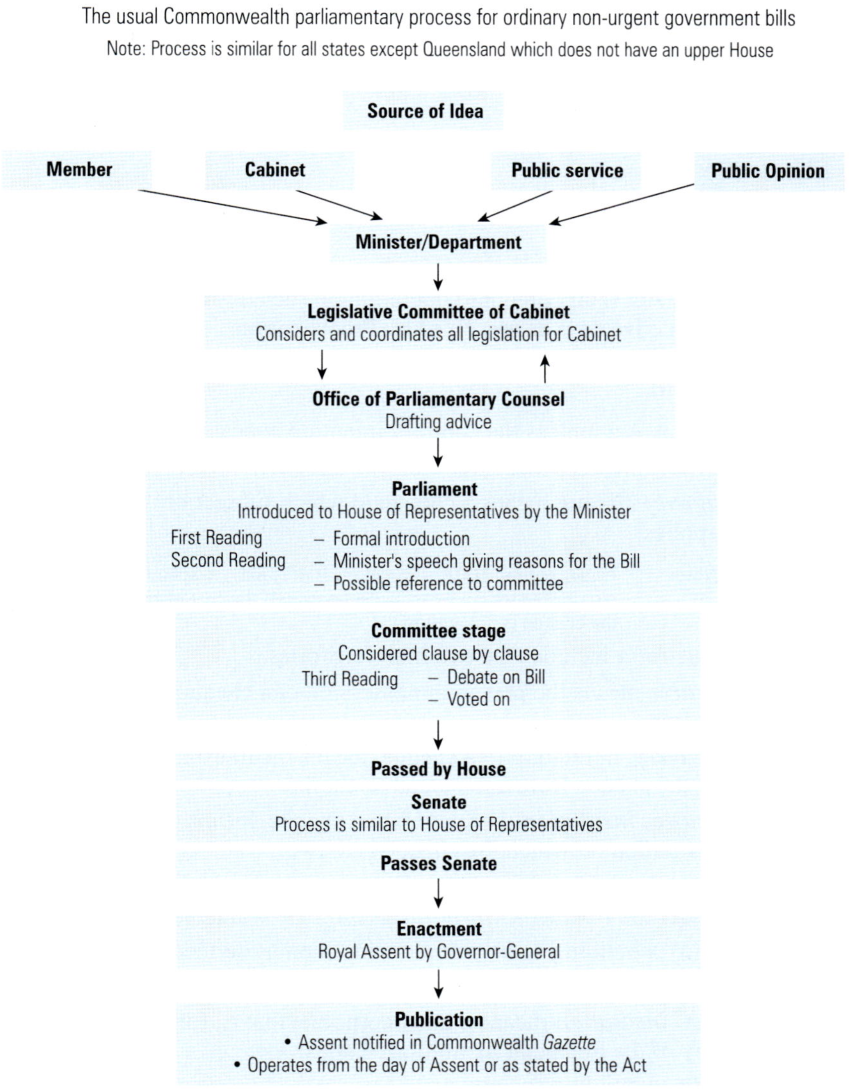

FIGURE 3.5 *How statute law is made*

4. **Committee**—when the Bill passes its second reading, the House then resolves into the committee of the whole, or it may dispense with the committee stage and go straight to the third reading. The committee consists of the whole House without the Speaker. In committee, the Bill may be examined in close detail, clause by clause, or it may be taken as a whole. Amendments to clauses may be moved and a vote may be taken on each clause and on the suggested amendments.
5. **Report, recommittal and adoption**—the Bill is then reported to the House with or without amendments and a motion is moved for the adoption of the report.
6. **Third reading**—the motion for the third reading is moved by the Minister. Although this motion can be debated, it is usual for it to be passed without further discussion.
7. **Transmission to the Senate**—when the Bill has passed all stages in the Lower House, it is transmitted to the Senate, where it must pass a similar sequence of stages. If the Bill is amended in the Senate, the amendments are referred back to the Lower House for its agreement.

Long title — **An Act relating to cheques and certain other negotiable instruments**

Part I—Preliminary

1 Short title [*see* Note 1]

Short title — This Act may be cited as the *Cheques Act 1986*.

2 Commencement [*see* Note 1]

This Act shall come into operation on such day as is, or on such respective days as are, fixed by Proclamation.

Section number — **3 Interpretation**

(1) In this Act, unless the contrary intention appears:

action includes a counter-claim and set-off.

Definitions — ***agency cheque*** means a cheque to which subsection 100(2) applies.

Note: Under section 100A, subsection 100(2) may, in specified circumstances, apply to a cheque even if the customer's signature on the cheque is not authorised.

Australia includes the external Territories.

bearer means the person in possession of a cheque payable to bearer.

delivery, in relation to a cheque, means the transfer of possession of the cheque from one person to another.

drawee institution, in relation to a cheque, means the financial institution on which the cheque is drawn.

FCA institution means a body that is a registered corporation under the *Financial Corporations Act 1974* and that is:

(a) a building society or a credit union as defined in that Act; or

(b) prescribed for the purposes of this definition.

FIC institution means a body corporate that is, for the purposes of any of the Financial Institutions Codes:

(a) a building society; or

(b) a credit union; or

(c) a special services provider.

financial institution means:

(a) the Reserve Bank of Australia; or

(b) a bank within the meaning of the *Banking Act 1959*; or

(c) an FIC institution . . .

119 Regulations

The Governor-General may make regulations, not inconsistent with this Act, prescribing matters:

(a) required or permitted by this Act to be prescribed; or

(b) necessary or convenient to be prescribed for carrying out or giving effect to this Act.

FIGURE 3.6 *Extract from an Act of Parliament*

8. **Presentation for Royal Assent**—once the Bill has passed both Houses, it is sent to the Governor-General (the Governor in the states) for Royal Assent. Under s. 57 of the Commonwealth Constitution, a Bill must be passed by both Houses in complete agreement before it can be presented to the Governor-General; the states have a similar requirement.

The Bill is now an **Act of Parliament** (enacted law) and becomes effective after 28 days. In the case of the Commonwealth, this is after the date of the Royal Assent, unless another date is stipulated in the Bill itself. The date of commencement of the Act will also be announced by the government in the respective state or in the Commonwealth *Government Gazette*.

If there is disagreement between the two Houses at the federal level, Standing Orders provide for conferences at which each House, represented by a small number of members known as managers, resolve these disagreements. These managers of the two Houses then meet to try to agree on the changes that should be made to the Bill. If, for example, the Senate twice rejects or fails to pass a Bill, or passes it with amendments to which the House of Representatives will not agree, and if there is an interval of three months between rejections, the Governor-General may dissolve both Houses simultaneously and call for elections to the House of Representatives and the Senate. If the deadlock continues after the election, the Governor-General may call a joint sitting of members of both Houses who then vote together on the proposed law. If it is then passed by an absolute majority of all members, it is taken as having passed both Houses and presented for Royal Assent. Double dissolutions have taken place three times at federal level—1914, 1915 and 1974—but a joint sitting followed only in 1974.

An Act is valid forever unless repealed

Once an Act of Parliament comes into existence, it remains law until it is repealed by a later Act of Parliament. The key elements that make up an Act are set out below in Figure 3.6 from the *Cheques Act 1986*.

Most Acts of Parliament set out the law on a particular matter in broad terms. They also contain a section stating that detailed rules necessary to give effect to the legislation can be found in the relevant regulations. For example, in the case of the Cheques Act (see Figure 3.6), s. 119 provides that the Governor-General (remember that this means the Executive or Cabinet) may make regulations that are not inconsistent with the Cheques Act, which are required or necessary for giving effect to the Act, for example, reg. 2A of the *Cheques Regulations 1987* (Cth) sets out the prescribed corporations for the purposes of the definition of 'FCA institutions' under s. 3(1) of the Cheques Act (see Figure 3.7).

CHEQUES REGULATIONS 1987 - REG 2A

2A FCA institutions

For paragraph (b) of the definition of FCA institution in subsection 3 (1) of the Act, the following registered corporations are prescribed:

(a) Elders Rural Finance Limited;

(b) Primac Elders Limited;

(c) Wesfarmers Dalgety Limited;

(d) Wesfarmers Limited;

(e) Westralian Farmers Co-operative Limited.

FIGURE 3.7 *Extract from Cheques Regulations*

Methods of statutory interpretation

With the increasing complexity of legislation, doubts about the meaning of a word or phrase may arise because the extent to which the words apply to particular facts is unclear. There may be doubt either because of ambiguities or even about the extent of operation in the Act itself. Such doubts create problems in applying any set of written rules.

Courts interpret statutes, not make them

The courts are not only concerned with finding out what has happened (a factual question), but they also play an important part in the interpretation of statutes (a legal question). To assist in interpreting statutes, the courts' principal sources of guidance are:

- Acts Interpretation Acts;
- extrinsic materials;
- common law rules of statutory interpretation; and
- precedent.

The first two sources are statutory rules, while the last two sources are the rules developed by the courts as part of the common law.

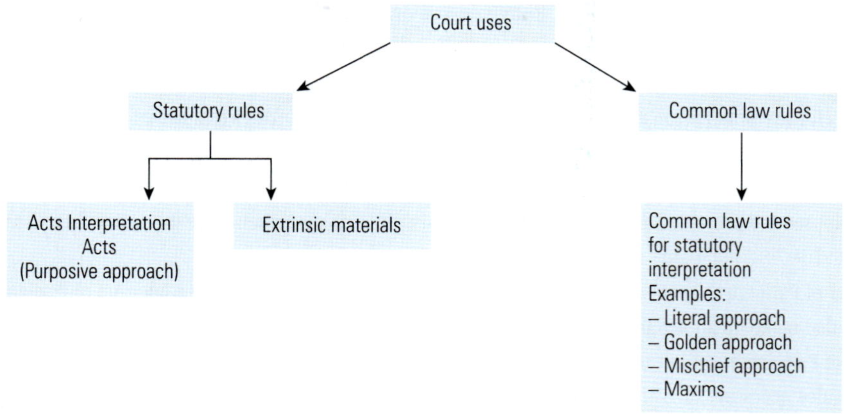

FIGURE 3.8 *Methods of statutory interpretation available to the court*

Interpretation Acts: a purposive approach and extrinsic materials

Purposive approach—focuses on purpose or aim of the legislation

The Interpretation Acts form part of the legislation of all states and the Commonwealth. By the 1980s the majority of parliaments had introduced amendments directing the courts to interpret legislation in such a way that it reflected the apparent **purpose or intention of the legislators** (a 'purposive' construction). Courts in most jurisdictions have been directed to follow this approach by their Parliament. This is an extension to one of the common law rules to statutory interpretation looked at below—the mischief approach (see Figure 3.8)—but rather than looking at the problem, the court looks at the purpose or aim of the legislation. It requires the courts to interpret the words in the legislation in such a way as to help the legislation achieve its purpose, rather than relying on, for example, a literalist approach which may leave the words ineffective and defeat the purpose of the legislation. The Commonwealth and the states and territories have all incorporated similar provisions in their Interpretation Acts, directing the courts to have regard to the objects and purposes of an Act when interpreting its provisions. Thus s. 15AA(1) of the *Acts Interpretation Act 1901* (Cth) provides:

> *In the interpretation of a provision of an Act, a construction that would promote the purpose or objects underlying the Act (whether that purpose or object is expressly stated in the Act or not) shall be preferred to a construction that would not promote that purpose or object.*

To give effect to the purpose of the legislation, *McHugh* JA in *Bermingham v. Corrective Services Commission of New South Wales* (1988) 15 NSWLR 292 at 302 suggested that a court may read words into a legislative provision if it was satisfied that Parliament had inadvertently failed to deal with the matter required to be dealt with to achieve the purpose of the Act (thus the similarity with the common law 'mischief' approach below) if three conditions were satisfied to the satisfaction of the court:

- it knows the mischief with which the Act was dealing;
- it is satisfied that Parliament inadvertently overlooked an eventuality which had to be dealt with if the purpose of the Act was to be achieved; and
- it can state with certainty the words that Parliament would have used to overcome the omission if its attention had been drawn to the defect.

However, if the words of the Act are clear, effect must be given to them notwithstanding that the end result may be absurd.

This legislation (Table 3.1) enables the courts to use extrinsic (external) material in the interpretation of provisions of Acts. For example:

- parliamentary debates;
- headings, margin notes and end notes of the legislation under scrutiny;
- reports of Royal Commissions, Law Reform Commissions and committees of inquiry that have been tabled in either House;
- treaties or other international agreements referred to in the Act;
- any explanatory memorandum attached to the Bill;
- any document declared by the Act to be relevant; and
- anything recorded in the official reports of the proceedings of Parliament.

Table 3.1 Acts Interpretation Acts: purposive reading and extrinsic materials

Jurisdiction	Act	Purposive reading	Extrinsic materials
Commonwealth	*Acts Interpretation Act 1901*	s. 15AA	s. 15AB
Australian Capital Territory	*Legislation Act 2001*	s. 139	s. 142
New South Wales	*Interpretation Act 1987*	s. 33	s. 34
Northern Territory	*Interpretation Act 1998*	s. 62A	s. 62B
Queensland	*Acts Interpretation Act 1954*	s. 14A	s. 14B
South Australia	*Acts Interpretation Act 1915*	s. 22	s. 19
Tasmania	*Acts Interpretation Act 1931*	s. 8A	s. 8B
Victoria	*Interpretation of Legislation Act 1984*	s. 35	s. 36
Western Australia	*Interpretation Act 1984*	s. 18	s. 19

RE WARAMUNGU LAND CLAIM; EX PARTE ATTORNEY GENERAL (NT) (2000) 77 ALR 27

The *Aboriginal Land Rights (Northern Territory) Act 1976* allowed Aboriginal Land Councils to make claims over certain areas of land but excluded roads over which the public had a right of way (ss. 11, 12). The Waramungu Aboriginal Land Council made a claim over land under the Act which contained a stock route. A stock route is where sheep and cattle can be moved from place to place by stockmen and feed along the way. The legislation did not mention stock routes and in the Minister's second reading speech, he referred only to the 'roads over which the public has a right of way' and named the roads he was referring to.

ISSUE: Could the Northern Territory government reject the claim, arguing that a stock route fell within the meaning of ss. 11 and 12?

DECISION: The Land Council argument that the court should take into account the Minister's second reading speech was appropriate in order to determine the correct interpretation of the Act. As a result, the references to roads in ss. 11 and 12 were intended to describe the general roadway system and not intended to pick up the network of stock routes. The land claim could not be rejected on the basis of those sections.

Unless a contrary intention appears in a statute, either express or implied, the statute is read in the light of the Acts Interpretation legislation.

In some cases, statutes will contain a direction to administrators and the courts that they are to interpret the legislation in a certain way and this is found at the beginning of the statute in an objects section. For example, s. 3 of both the Commonwealth (1982) and Victorian (1983) Freedom of Information Acts sets out the basic underlying principles of freedom of information. They do this by:

- setting out the objects of the law, which is basically to extend as far as possible the right of the community to access information in the possession of the government (s. 3(1)); and then
- directing both the administrators and the courts that the statute be interpreted so as to ensure that the object of s. 3(1) be met (s. 3(2)).

Definitions sections are used to clarify words

Some statutes carry their own definitions of terms. These are often terms that recur throughout the various sections of the statute and that the drafter feels needs clarification. They are set out in a definition section at the beginning of the statute.

Common law rules of statutory interpretation

In addition to these statutory aids, the courts also have resort to the common law rules of statutory interpretation and precedent. Approaches to interpretation used by the courts (which in turn create precedents) may be summarised under three main headings as follows.

The literal or plain meaning approach

Literal rule—courts give literal effect to the words

The courts assume that the meaning and intention of the legislature is clear in the statute to be interpreted, and that the courts need to do no more than give effect to those words. A disadvantage of this approach is that words can often have more than one meaning, so the courts have to decide which approach should apply and this can sometimes lead to a result the legislature may not have intended.

The whole Act is read and understood before a detailed examination of a section, or of particular words in a section, is begun. Words and sections must be read in the context of the whole Act, rather than in isolation, for their meaning to be clearly ascertained.

***FISHER V. BELL* [1961] 1 QB 394**

Bell, a shopkeeper, had displayed a flick knife in his shop window with a price tag on it. He was charged by Constable Fisher under an English Act which among other things stated that: 'Any person who sells, lends or gives a flick knife to any other person commits an offence'.

ISSUE: Does placing the flick knife in the window with a price tag attached amount to a 'sale' or an offer to sell?

DECISION: According to a literal interpretation of the words, Bell had not committed an offence because the display of goods in a shop window only amounted to an invitation to treat.

COMMENT: If hardship results from applying the literal meaning of the Act, it is up to Parliament to correct that hardship by applying an amending Act, which is what they did in this case. It is not a problem for the courts, as their task is to interpret legislation, not make it.

Golden rule—only used where a literal interpretation would lead to an absurd, unjust or repugnant result

The golden rule approach

This takes the plain meaning of the words used in the statute and adheres to that meaning unless it is at variance with the legislators' intention discovered from the reading of the statute as a whole or unless that plain meaning leads to:

- an absurdity
- an injustice or
- repugnancy.

The rule is only a gloss of the literal or plain meaning rule. Where the words in an Act are at variance with the legislators' intention or can lead to an absurdity, injustice or repugnancy, the court will attempt to choose a meaning that will avoid such a result.

***LEE V. KNAPP* [1967] 2 QB 442**

Lee was involved in a motor vehicle accident and stopped only for a moment after the accident and then, seeing no one was injured, drove off. He was charged with an offence under s. 77(1) of the *Road Traffic Act 1960* (UK):

'If in any case, owing to the presence of a motor vehicle on a road, an accident occurs whereby . . . damage is caused to a vehicle . . . other than that motor vehicle the driver of the motor car shall stop . . .'

ISSUE: Could it be argued that the requirement to 'stop' after an accident was satisfied if a driver halted momentarily?

DECISION: The phrase means the driver of the motor vehicle shall stop and remain where he or she has stopped for as long as is necessary for anybody who has a right to do so to personally get any information which they may require.

COMMENT: To apply the literal rule here would have produced an absurd result because the driver could momentarily stop their car after an accident and then drive away, leaving the victim or bystanders with no time to get any relevant information about the driver or the car.

This means that the court will determine the purpose of the Act. In such a case the judge is treading a thin line that separates legislative from judicial functions.

The mischief approach

Mischief rule—courts look at overall intention of legislation

Where a literal interpretation is not possible—for example, because words or phrases are ambiguous, vague or uncertain—the courts will:

- look at the law before the statute was passed;

***SMITH V. HUGHES* [1960] 1 WLR 830**

The *Street Offences Act 1959* (UK) prohibited soliciting by prostitutes 'in a street'. To try to get around the operation of the Act, prostitutes began to try to attract business by standing at their windows or on their balconies and calling out to passers-by.

ISSUE: Did the Act extend to include the activities of prostitutes who attempted to attract business from windows or balconies or did it only catch the activities of prostitutes who were actually soliciting on the street?

DECISION: That the words 'in a street' extended to include the activities of prostitutes from windows or balconies, as the 'mischief' that the *Street Offences Act* was directed at was to allow people to use the streets without being solicited.

- look to the overall intention of the legislation as discovered from reading the Act as a whole; and
- ask: What mischief is it that this statute is intended to remedy? What was its social purpose?

Where a statute provides a number of specific examples, matters not stated are not covered.

By going outside the text of the statute to determine the Act's function, the mischief or purpose approaches are significantly different to the literal and golden rule approaches in looking at the problem.

Maxims

Maxims are aids to construction, not rules of law

Maxims are not rules of law but rather are **aids to construction**. While the drafter tries to define words in such a manner that every possible interpretation is covered, no definition can be exclusive or perfectly describe a class of people, things or acts. There are a number of maxims (guides or aids) that are available to assist the courts in determining the meaning of a word or phrase. Two of the more important are:

- *noscitur a sociis*; and
- *ejusdem generis.*

Noscitur a sociis

***Noscitur a socciis*—the meaning of a word or phrase is derived from its context**

Noscitur a socciis ('it is known from its associates') is used where a word is ambiguous or unclear in a group of specific words. Its meaning is limited to the same class or type of things as the specific words.

***PRIOR V. SHERWOOD* (1906) 3 CLR 1054**

In an attempt to control bookmaking, the authorities passed legislation which prohibited bookmaking in any 'house, office, room or place'. In an attempt to avoid the legislation, the accused conducted his bookmaking activities in a lane at the back of his house.

ISSUE: Did a prohibition on bookmaking in any 'house, office, room or place' extend to include a public lane?

DECISION: Although the word 'place' has a potentially wide application and could therefore include a public lane, the court preferred to restrict its application to mean an enclosed place which is like a house, room or office.

Ejusdem generis

***Ejusdem generis*—broad, general word is limited to the same class as the more specific words preceding it**

Ejusdem generis means of the same kind, class, or nature and is known as the class rule. This rule is used to find a viable meaning for a broad general word, such as 'building', when that word follows a group of more specific words—for example, 'any house, flat, villa, unit **or other building**'. In this case we can say that the principle of *ejusdem generis* applies. The word 'building' is limited to the same class as that which precedes it—here, places where people live. All the specific words preceding a general word **must** form a class. Thus a reference to 'any plant, root, fruit or vegetable production growing in any garden' does not extend to trees since there is no class here.

The class rule cannot be used to find the meaning of a word that is of a specific nature, nor can it be used unless there are two or more specific words before the general word. Thus, in the case of the phrase 'any flat or other building', the class rule does not apply; flat on its own does not form a class.

Word problems

It is useful to be aware of the problems that can arise in statutory interpretation involving the use of particular words. In particular situations, the courts will resort to the following rules:

- words will generally be given their normal dictionary meaning (in this case *The Macquarie Dictionary* is used as it provides definitions of words used in an Australian context);

- technical words are generally given their technical meaning;
- words are interpreted according to their current meaning;
- if a word is used more than once, it should be given the same meaning unless a contrary intention exists in the Act; and
- a statute should not be given retrospective effect unless expressly provided for in the statute.

In addition, there are a number of commonly encountered words that a reader should be aware of, including 'means' v. 'includes' and 'and' v. 'or'.

'Means' v. 'includes'

Definitions of words and expressions in legislation will often commence with either 'means' or 'includes'.

'Means' is used when the draftsperson wants the defined words to have an **exact meaning**. Section 4(1) of the *Trade Practices Act 1974* (Cth) sets out definitions of various terms found within the Act. It states that '"Commission" means the Australian Competition and Consumer Commission ...' Thus, Commission in this legislation refers to the ACCC and no other commission.

'Includes' is not an exhaustive definition. It **expands or clarifies the ordinary meaning of the defined word by giving examples**. In s. 4(1) of the *Trade Practices Act*, '"supply"', when used as a verb, 'includes . . . sale, exchange, lease, hire or hire-purchase . . .' The draftsperson has attempted to enlarge the ordinary meaning of 'supply' through the use of the word 'includes' and the examples.

'And' v. 'or'

'And' is used when the draftsperson wants the words or phrases to be read together. It is a **joining word**. **'Or'**, on the other hand, is used to **split words or phrases** and the importance of the distinction between the two words is well illustrated in s. 52 of the *Trade Practices Act*. Section 52(1) states: 'A corporation shall not, in trade or commerce, engage in conduct that is misleading or deceptive.'

By using the word 'or', the draftsperson has given the section much wider impact. It can catch 'conduct' that is misleading **or** 'conduct' that is deceptive. If the word 'and' had been used instead, s. 52 would have been very restricted in its operation. For a corporation to be caught, its conduct would have had to have been both misleading and deceptive. It is possible for conduct to be misleading but not deceptive and vice versa, but unless the conduct was both misleading and deceptive, there would not have been a breach of s. 52.

International treaties can be part of domestic law

International treaties are not automatically part of domestic or municipal law

International treaties and conventions are not part of municipal or domestic law unless they are given express legislative approval. This generally has to be given by the Commonwealth Parliament in the form of an enabling Act, because the negotiation, signature, and ratification of international treaties and conventions are matters that fall within the ambit of the Commonwealth Constitution under the external affairs power: s. 51(xxix). However, it should also be noted that the High Court has taken the view that ratification can create legitimate expectations that an administrative decision-maker would conform with a convention even though it may not have been incorporated into domestic law. For example, in *Minister for Immigration v. Ah Hin Teoh* (1995) 69 ALJR 423 *Mason* CJ and *Deane* J said that ratification of a treaty is 'a positive statement by [the government] to the world and the Australian people that [the government] and its agencies will act in accordance with [the treaty]'.

What is delegated or subordinate legislation?

Delegated legislation is made by subordinate authorities

As society becomes increasingly complex, state, territory and Commonwealth legislation has increased significantly. At the same time, there has been a corresponding increase in delegated or subordinate legislation, because parliamentarians do not have the time to deal with all those matters requiring regulation by law, nor do they always have the necessary technical expertise for detailed rule-making. The problem has been overcome by the passage of statutes that delegate power to subordinate authorities, such as:

- government departments, for example, departments of Education and Health;
- local government (councils and shires); and
- statutory authorities, for example, transit authorities, electricity and hydro-electricity authorities, gas and fuel authorities

to make the necessary rules. The most common of these rules are by-laws, regulations and orders-in-council.

Draft regulations are prepared by an officer of the government department or authority concerned. The procedures laid down in the enabling Act determine what is required to make them valid. The regulations generally only need the assent of an authorised Minister or officer or the assent of a duly constituted governing body (they do **not** require the approval of Parliament). Once approved, regulations are usually published in the *Government Gazette*, though again the form of publication may be determined by directions contained in the enabling Act. While regulations do not require the approval of Parliament, they must be 'tabled' (or presented) before each House of Parliament. For example, in the case of the Commonwealth, regulations must be tabled within 15 sitting days of notification, and either House may disallow a regulation. The requirement of tabling regulations within 15 sitting days may amount in practice to some months as Parliament generally only sits for eight days in a month and there are lengthy summer and winter recesses. When a regulation is disallowed, it will then cease to have effect, although before its disallowance it would have been effective.

Delegated legislation is not an original source of law

As delegated or subordinate legislation is not an original source of law (it acquires its effectiveness from an Act of Parliament), its validity can be challenged in the courts through administrative law. Any authority given by Parliament must be exercised within that power. If the regulations are not within the scope of the enabling Act, or if all the terms of the enabling Act have not been complied with, the regulations may be challenged as being *ultra vires* (which literally means 'beyond the power') and unenforceable.

IN BRIEF

Some advantages and disadvantages of delegated legislation

Advantages	Disadvantages
Saves parliament time, allowing it to concentrate on broad policy issues	Parliament, as the main law-making body, is abdicating its responsibility to make laws
Allows expert bodies with the necessary technical expertise to make better laws	Over-regulation of society
Allows the passing of local laws to meet local needs, e.g., local councils to pass laws for their community	Lack of adequate checks and balances even though Parliament has the power to overrule or disallow delegated legislation
Allows administrative bodies to regulate their own affairs, enabling them to operate more efficiently	Finding out about new laws

Given the fact that ignorance of the law is no excuse, there is increasing cause for concern that we are becoming over-regulated and that society's rights and freedoms are being eroded.

Both the Commonwealth and the states have special committees to review delegated legislation. For example, in the Commonwealth Parliament it is the responsibility of the Senate Standing Committee on Regulations and Ordinances. The task of the committees is to ensure that the delegated legislation is in accordance with the enabling Act and not an attempt at a major change to the law. Regulations and ordinances are also reviewed regularly to ensure that they remain up to date and meet the needs of the community. For example, in Victoria regulations have a maximum life expectancy of 10 years.

! CAUTION NOTE
Validity of regulations can be challenged under administrative law.

WEB RESOURCES

While the range of judgements of courts and tribunals published on the Austlii site is very broad, Commonwealth, state and territory court sites also electronically publish decisions of superior courts and, in some cases, lower courts and tribunals which are not found on the Austlii site:

Australian Capital Territory: contains selected Magistrate's Court judgements
http://www.courts.act.gov.au/

New South Wales:
http://www.lawlink.nsw.gov.au/ (all also on **austlii.edu.au**)

Northern Territory: contains judgements of Magistrate's Court
http://www.nt.gov.au/justice/

Queensland: contains District Court judgements
http://www.courts.qld.gov.au/

South Australia: contains judgements from the Environmental Resources & Development Court
http://www.courts.sa.gov.au/

Tasmania: contains Magistrate's decisions
http://www.courts.tas.gov.au/

Victoria: contains judgements of County Court
http://www.courts.vic.gov.au/

Western Australia: access to all WA courts through the Department of the Attorney-General portal. Judgements of the District Court are now available
http://www.justice.wa.gov.au/

? REVIEW QUESTIONS

3.1 What is the doctrine of *res judicata*?

3.2 Explain the importance of *ratio decidendi* and *obiter dictum* in a case.

3.3 What are some of the advantages and disadvantages of the system of judicial precedent?

3.4 What are the rules of judicial precedent?

3.5 Explain the difference between binding and persuasive precedent.

3.6 Would the Supreme Court of New South Wales have to follow an earlier decision of the Supreme Court of Queensland if the facts of both cases were the same? Explain your answer.

3.7 Is there any value in a two House Parliament or should the Commonwealth and states consider the Queensland system as more appropriate for the new millennium?

3.8 Can the principles of *ejusdem generis* be applied to the following:
a 'theatres and other places of entertainment'?
b 'meat, fish, poultry and other provisions'?
c 'bottle, tin, glass, carton, package, paper, food or other refuse'?
d 'car, truck, motorcycle or other form of motor-powered vehicle'?

3.9 What purpose does the legislature hope to achieve through the use of extrinsic materials in the interpretation of legislation? What is wrong with the courts' traditional methods of interpretation? Discuss.

3.10 Consider the following section from an Act and then answer the questions that follow:
It shall be an offence to sell an offensive weapon including a rifle, shotgun or revolver in a public place.
Is it an offence if:

activebook

Activebook resources include in-depth summaries with links to the relevant part of the book. For revision, add your own notes to the summaries provided by using the note-taking function.

a A sold his flick knife to B while they were looking at magazines in a newsagency.

b C gave D his airgun when C visited his home.

c E auctioned F's grandfather's World War I rifle to G.

d H, an infant, who lived on a farm, swapped his .22 rifle with I at the market for a Remington so that he could shoot wild pigs.

3.11 Apart from the examples of authorities that rely on delegated legislation given in the text, can you name any other bodies that use delegated legislation?

3.12 Is society over-regulated? Discuss. (You will find it useful in answering this question to look at the range of by-laws on your local council or shire's books. You could also look at the by-laws passed by those bodies managing major sporting venues such as the Sydney Cricket Ground, Melbourne Cricket Ground, the Gabba and so on.)

3.13 Indicate whether each of the following statements is true or false:

	TRUE	FALSE
▪ The law made by Parliament and any subordinate bodies is called statute law	☐	☐
▪ Where common law and statute law conflict, statute law prevails	☐	☐
▪ The draft of a proposed statute law is called delegated legislation	☐	☐
▪ The maxim *noscitur a sociis* refers to the rule used to find a viable meaning for a broad general word	☐	☐
▪ There is really no difference between the mischief approach and the purpose approach adopted by the courts in questions of statutory interpretation	☐	☐
▪ A persuasive precedent is one which the lower courts in a court hierarchy must follow	☐	☐
▪ A High Court decision can be both persuasive and binding	☐	☐
▪ The doctrine of *res judicata* is really only another name for the *ratio decidendi* of a case	☐	☐
▪ Where a higher court believes that a lower court has made an error of law, it may overrule the earlier decision	☐	☐
▪ *Obiter dictum* can never be a binding precedent	☐	☐
▪ Maxims are rules of statutory construction	☐	☐
▪ On the Commonwealth's signing of an international treaty, it automatically becomes part of domestic law	☐	☐
▪ Delegated legislation cannot be subject to review in the courts	☐	☐
▪ There is no process for review of delegated legislation by Parliament	☐	☐

CRITICAL THINKING

3.1 Why do you think there have been so few double dissolutions of Parliament, for example, at Commonwealth level? Discuss.

3.2 Has the Westminster system of Parliament outlived its usefulness? Is it time for a new form of government? Discuss.

BUSINESS CRIME AND ETHICS

PART TWO

CHAPTER 4
Criminal Law in a Business Context

CHAPTER CONTENTS

activebook

This icon is used throughout the following chapter to remind you to visit the *Business Law* online activebook for additional exercises, links to legal websites, and feedback. For a detailed explanation of what is in the activebook please refer to the inside cover of this textbook. The activebook is available through OneKey.

Where do I start?
Learning path: Use the activebook to complete a pre-chapter warm-up exercise.

There are many definitions of legal terms to assist with your understanding of the material.

CHAPTER OBJECTIVES

On completion of this chapter, you should be able to:

- explain the sources of criminal law
- explain the main classification of offences in criminal law
- explain the two elements that must be present in the commission of a crime for a conviction
- describe the level of proof that is required for the Crown to obtain a conviction
- explain what white collar crime is
- describe different types of white collar crime
- describe examples of statutory criminal law relating to business situations.

KEY TERMS

An understanding of the following terms will help you to better understand the material in this chapter:

- ***actus reas***: a guilty act, and in combination with *mens rea*, produces criminal liability
- **arrest:** the taking into custody of a person by the police
- **bail:** the procedure by which an accused person charged with a criminal offence is released from police custody on the understanding that they will return to court at a future date
- **felony:** serious crime and an indictable offence (e.g. murder), in contrast to misdemeanour
- **fraud:** an intentionally dishonest act or omission done with the design of gaining material advantage over another
- **indictable offence:** an offence that can be prosecuted on indictment. It is a more serious offence and generally tried by judge and jury
- **indictment:** is a written accusation that a person has committed a certain crime
- ***mens rea***: guilty mind
- **misdemeanour:** less serious crime and generally a summary offence
- **summary offence:** less serious (or minor) offence where questions of law and fact are dealt with 'summarily' by a magistrate (no jury)
- **summons:** an order to appear voluntarily at a certain court at a particular time and place to either give evidence, produce documents or answer a charge, in contrast to arrest
- **theft (or laraceny):** stealing (i.e. taking without the consent of the owner)
- **warrant:** an official court document issued by a justice of the peace or judge directing a police officer to arrest a named person and present them to the court to face the charge/s set out in the warrant.

what if . . .

Henry Smith, the managing director of Oxford Pty Ltd, purchased on credit $25 000 worth of equipment from you on behalf of Oxford Pty Ltd. Henry knew that Oxford Pty Ltd had been in severe financial difficulties for several months and the company had a serious cash flow problem. Two weeks after incurring the debt with you, the company goes into liquidation and the liquidator advises creditors that the company will only be able to pay 10 cents for each dollar owed. Henry Smith continues to live in a big house and drive an expensive flash car.

A crime is an offence against the state. It is the task of the police to apprehend those who commit crimes and prosecute them in a court of law. In minor cases heard in the Magistrate's or Local Court, this will usually be the role of a police prosecutor, while in more serious cases heard in the District (County in Victoria) or Supreme Courts, a state Crown prosecutor will manage the case on behalf of the state or territory. If the accused is found guilty, depending on the seriousness of the crime, they will be punished by either imprisonment or some lesser penalty, such as a fine.

There is often an overlap between criminal acts and civil wrongs. The commission of a crime will generally involve some type of offence against an individual and/or their property and will also attract civil liability, generally in the form of a tort.

This chapter provides an overview of criminal law procedure and examples of statutory crimes in a business situation. It begins by looking at the sources of criminal law, and then examines the main classifications of criminal law. It examines the two elements that generally must be present for the actions of a person to constitute a crime as well as the standard of proof required in order for the Crown to obtain a conviction. The topic then considers some of the offences that are commonly referred to as white collar crime. And finally, it briefly considers criminal penalties for statutory offences established by several major Acts of Parliament referred to in a number of chapters of this book.

SOURCES OF THE CRIMINAL LAW

The complexity of criminal law in Australia means that this chapter will only focus on broad principles rather than on a detailed examination of the relevant principles on a state by state basis. Each state and territory has its own criminal legislation. Queensland (*Criminal Code 1997*), Western Australia (*Criminal Code Act 1913*), Tasmania (*Criminal Code Act 1924*) and the Northern Territory (*Criminal Code Act 1983*) have codified their criminal law so that the common law has no relevance. Codification makes the laws easier to find and, it can be argued, more responsive to changes in community values than the common law. In the remaining states and territories there is significant legislative coverage of the criminal law, but the common law is still relevant.

It should also be noted that the Criminal Codes and Crimes Acts do not necessarily cover every criminal offence. At federal level, for example, sections in both the *Corporations Act 2001* and Part V of the *Trade Practices Act 1974* provide for criminal penalties where the relevant Acts are breached. At state or territory level, breach of environment protection legislation is a criminal offence and conviction can carry a substantial fine.

DIFFERENCES BETWEEN CRIMINAL LAW AND CIVIL LAW

The basis of criminal law is normally contained in the mental element (*mens rea*) to commit a crime **and** the carrying out of the act (*actus reus*) by the accused. But note the following:

- not all conduct requires intention to amount to an offence. For example, crimes of strict liability, such as some breaches of the *Corporations Act 2001* (Cth) (e.g., breaches of s. 1041E (false or misleading statements);
- in some cases, the same conduct can give rise to civil or criminal liability (e.g., assault or fraud can be both crimes and torts); and
- an increasing number of aspects of business conduct that do not fall within the criminal law can carry criminal penalties (e.g., breaches of occupational health and safety legislation, environmental legislation, the *Trade Practices Act 1974* (Cth) and the *Corporations Act 2001* (Cth)).

IN BRIEF

Contrast between criminal and civil law

Feature	Criminal	Civil
Who brings action?	State (usually) because criminal act is against community	Individual (victim) because individual suffers a personal loss
Who enforces judgement of the court?	State	Individual
Standard of proof	Beyond reasonable doubt	Balance of probabilities
Guilty mind (*mens rea*) required?	Yes (usually)	No
Onus of proof	Accused is presumed innocent till state proves guilt	Plaintiff (person bringing the action) must establish their case
Punishment or remedy?	Punishment	Remedy
	Prison	Damages—Money
	Fine	Compensation
	Community service	Injunction
	Loss of licence etc.	Specific performance

CLASSIFICATION OF OFFENCES

Most offences fall into one of three broad classifications:

- wrongs against morality, such as murder and manslaughter, assault;
- threats to the peace and good order of the community, such as property crimes like robbery; and
- statutory offences against laws directed at maintaining minimum standards of health, safety and consumer protection within the community.

These are in turn classified as either indictable or summary offences.

Indictable offences

Indictable offences—most serious offences

Indictable offences are the more serious offences and include crimes such as murder, manslaughter, rape, robbery, burglary and theft. They are **triable by way of indictment**. The offence is first dealt with by a preliminary hearing in the Magistrate's or Local Court to determine whether there is enough police evidence to warrant sending the accused for trial in a higher court before a judge and jury. Guilt or innocence is determined by the jury at the higher court.

Summary offences

Summary offences—less serious offences

The **less serious offences**, such as common assault, being drunk and disorderly, and various breaches of statutory regulations, are **triable summarily**. This means that they are dealt with by a magistrate rather than a judge and jury.

Indictable offences dealt with summarily

In the case of certain offences, magistrates have been given statutory powers to deal with an indictable offence summarily. These are usually cases involving loss or damage to property up to a certain monetary value and, as a general rule, the accused must consent to the summary hearing. There are advantages for the accused in having a matter dealt with summarily including:

- the matter will be dealt with quickly;

- it is much cheaper to have a matter dealt with in the Magistrate's or Local Court than in a higher court; and
- the prospect of a lower penalty if convicted because the penalties a magistrate can impose are much lower than in a higher court.

The magistrate must also be satisfied that there are no serious issues involved and that an appropriate sentence can be imposed on the accused in the event of conviction. In all cases, the magistrate can direct the accused to stand trial in the relevant higher court.

CRIMINAL PROCEDURE

Commencement of proceedings

Criminal proceedings commence either by:

- **arrest**, where a police officer makes an arrest and the person is subsequently charged and brought before a court as soon as reasonably practicable. The arrest can be by warrant where a justice of the peace or judge directs a police officer to arrest a named person and bring them before the court on the charge set out in the warrant or without a warrant where the person is caught committing an offence; or
- **summons**, which is an order to a person to appear at a certain court at a particular date and time to answer a particular charge.

A person held in police custody may be released on bail on the condition that they will appear in court at a specified time and place to answer the charge made against them.

Committal

Committal proceedings determine if police evidence is sufficient for a trial before a judge and jury

In the case of an indictable offence, a committal hearing (or preliminary proceedings) takes place in the Magistrate's Court to **determine whether there is sufficient police evidence against the defendant for the matter to be sent to trial before a judge and jury**. If the magistrate decides there is a *prima facie* case, the seriousness of the offence will determine whether the case is heard in an intermediate or superior court (Supreme Court). If the magistrate finds that there is not enough evidence, the charges against the defendant are dismissed.

Trial

The trial of an indictable offence will normally take place in a District/County Court or Supreme Court, depending on the seriousness of the matter to be heard. Jurisdiction is determined by the Act that created the court.

There are a number of stages that can be identified:

- the arraignment—the charges;
- the plea of the accused—guilty or not guilty;
- the empanelling of the jury—who will decide all questions of fact;
- the opening of the Crown case—at the end of which the defence counsel may make a submission that the accused has no case to answer which, if successful, will result in the accused being discharged; and
- if the judge concludes there is a case to answer, the defence will present its evidence; there will be the judge's summing up (a summary of the evidence presented and directions on points of law) followed by the jury's verdict; and if the jury finds the accused guilty, the sentence.

Where the matter is dealt with in the Magistrate's Court, it is called a summary hearing, with the magistrate determining both questions of law and fact. There is no jury.

ELEMENTS

IN BRIEF

Elements

In order to establish the guilt of a person, it is generally necessary for the Crown to prove:

- a wrongful act (*actus reus*); and
- a guilty mind (*mens rea*).

Certain statutory offences of a minor or regulatory nature involving strict liability do not require the element of 'intent'.

Guilt requires a wrongful act and a guilty mind

For a person to be found guilty of a crime, two elements **must** be present at the same time:

- a wrongful act (the *actus reus*); **and**
- a guilty mind which may involve intention (*mens rea*), foresight, knowledge or awareness.

It will sometimes happen that, while the consequences of a person's actions will have serious results and cause harm to others, for example, because of their reckless conduct, this will not amount to criminal liability. Their actions might be negligent, based on the standard of care to be applied using the reasonable person test, but to amount to criminal liability the accused must be guilty of 'gross negligence', which is based on a much higher standard of care.

Statutory offences often do not require a guilty mind

If the source of the offence is statutory, such as workplace health and the like, there might not be any reference to the question of *mens rea*. The doing of the act will be sufficient and it is often the case that the accused will be punished for an act over which they had no control because it was carried out by an employee. The prosecution needs only establish that the act was done and that the accused was the responsible party under the Act (which is not always the person who did the act). The reason for the breach is irrelevant. Because of the onerous nature of this type of legislation, these laws tend to be strictly construed by the courts. For example, in the case of the Garibaldi metwurst contamination in South Australia in 1994–95, there were some 150 cases of food poisoning, including one death. The directors and the financial controller could not be charged under the *Food Act 1985* (SA) because the investigations took longer than six months and the six-month time limit during which such an action had to be brought had elapsed.

STANDARD OF PROOF

IN BRIEF

Standard of proof in criminal matters

The standard of proof required of the Crown in criminal matters is that the case must be proved '**beyond reasonable doubt**'. However, in cases of a minor regulatory nature where the offence is one of strict liability, once the prosecution has established the offence on the facts, the onus shifts to the defendant to establish 'on the balance of probabilities' that their actions fell within one of the statutory defences.

A person charged with a crime is presumed innocent until proved guilty

A person charged with a crime is presumed innocent until proven guilty. The burden, or onus of proving guilt, is on the Crown and not the police. The Crown has to establish beyond reasonable doubt that the accused did what they have been charged with or they must be acquitted. This can be contrasted with the lower standard of proof required in civil cases, such as negligence or breach of contract. Here the plaintiff only has to establish on the balance of probabilities that the defendant has a case to answer to be successful.

WHITE COLLAR CRIME

White collar crime may be described as a crime **committed by a person inside a business or government organisation**, where the person takes advantage of their professional or clerical position in order to carry out the crime. Typical white collar crimes are embezzlement, bribery, insider trading and computer-related crimes.

Because of the complexities of modern business, white collar crime is very difficult to detect; in fact, the victims may not even realise they are victims. The perpetrator may also effectively be beyond apprehension, due to the 'paper trail' used to distance the perpetrator from the crime.

Examples of common white collar crimes

Embezzlement/misappropriation

Embezzlement is the fraudulent conversion of property by a person to whom the property has been entrusted. Embezzlement usually involves the falsification of accounting and other records to hide the misappropriation of funds or other property. It should be noted that in the case of embezzlement, the property has been directly or indirectly entrusted to the person who takes the property for their own use. In the case of robbery, the property is taken by someone who has not been entrusted with it.

Recently a former Commonwealth Bank employee appeared in court for allegedly transferring $10.5 million from clients' accounts into his own before losing most of it at a Sydney casino.

Bribery

Bribery occurs when one person gives another person money, property, favours or anything else of value in return for some advantage or preferential treatment.

A variation of bribery is a secret commission. A secret commission arises where a person who is the agent or representative of another person takes a commission from a third party without disclosing that commission to their principal. Both Commonwealth and state legislation prohibit secret commissions.

At the time of writing, the Cole Commission is conducting an inquiry into bribes paid to the regime of Saddam Hussain by WB Ltd for the supply of wheat to Iraq under the United Nations Oil for Food program.

Theft/robbery

Theft involves taking the property of someone else without their permission. In a white collar crime situation it can range from an employee taking stationery for their own use to cash received from the sale of goods and services.

Recently two people, including a former company director, appeared in a Perth court over the alleged theft of $1 million from Southern Wine Corporation.

Insider trading

Insider trading involves the use of price-sensitive information which is not publicly available and which has been obtained as a result of a connection with a company. The price-sensitive information relates to matters which would be likely to affect the price of the shares or other securities of the company.

The prohibition is based on the idea that in a free market there should be equality of access to information. A person with inside information must not trade in those securities either personally or by using someone else, or communicate the information to others.

A noted Sydney stock broker and investment advisor, Rene Rivkin, was convicted and gaoled for insider trading.

As to the ethical issues involved with insider trading, see page 105.

Industrial espionage/sabotage

Industrial espionage involves obtaining access to confidential information such as secret formulae, client lists, marketing plans and financial information such as costing and pricing methods.

It could also involve an employee selling confidential information about other employees or clients.

Industrial sabotage involves doing something to disrupt the efficient operations of a competitor's business such as infecting the competitor's computer network with a virus.

Money laundering

Money laundering is the expression used to describe the process whereby criminals convert the proceeds from crimes such as drug dealings into legitimate funds or property, thereby enabling the criminal to openly use the 'laundered' funds or property.

One of the main reasons for the Financial Transaction Reports Act was to assist in identifying transactions which may involve money laundering.

Environmental vandalism

In the context of white collar crime, environmental vandalism relates to actions taken to dispose of waste products contrary to environmental laws and procedures. The aim is to avoid the financial and time cost involved in disposing of the waste legitimately. Common examples are disposing of liquid waste directly into sewers, drains or watercourses and discharging gases and vapours into the atmosphere.

It is quite common to hear reports of watercourses being polluted by illegal discharge of industrial waste. Recently Sydney Harbour was closed to fishing because of heavy metal contaminants.

Computer-related crimes

Computer related white collar crimes are not new crimes, they are new ways of perpetrating old crimes. Computer technology readily lends itself to traditional white collar crimes like embezzlement. The computer facilitates access to personal accounts such as bank accounts and the unauthorised transfer of funds from those accounts.

The computer also makes it easier to access, copy and alter records and confidential information and to carry out industrial espionage and sabotage.

Examples of computer crimes which are becoming more prevalent are identity theft and obtaining access to the bank accounts of other persons using automatic teller machines.

STATUTORY CRIMINAL LIABILITY IN BUSINESS SITUATIONS

While most people connected with a business operation, either as the owner, employee or customer, will be well aware that there may be civil liability such as damages for breach of contract or negligence, they are probably less conscious of the possibility of criminal liability over and above the civil liability.

Examples of this often unrecognised criminal liability are set out below. This list of examples is not intended to be comprehensive, but is merely indicative of penalties which may be imposed for breaches of a variety of pieces of legislation referred to in this book.

> **activebook**
> To help you to remember and understand the topics covered so far, and for links to legal websites, refer to your online activebook. Model answers provide feedback to problems and exercises.

Trade Practices Act 1974 (Cth)

Consumer protection provisions

A breach of a consumer protection provision of the Trade Practices Act may result in damages, compensation for any loss (s. 82) and injunction to prevent further breaches (s. 80), or a fine (s. 79). While damages and injunctions are civil remedies, a fine is a criminal remedy and may be imposed for any breach of the consumer protection provisions except s. 52, misleading and deceptive conduct. There is no criminal liability for breaches of misleading and deceptive conduct because it is recognised that the breach may occur unintentionally. The fine which may be imposed under the other provisions may be up to $1.1 million for a corporation and $220 000 for an individual. A list summarising the offences relating to unfair practices is set out in Table 4.1.

Restrictive trade practices provisions

The restrictive trade practices provisions of the Trade Practices Act prohibit activities such as:

- abuse of monopoly power;
- price fixing;
- boycotts;

- resale price maintenance; and
- agreements to restrict competition.

Table 4.1 Summary of offences relating to unfair practices

Practice	*Section of* Trade Practices Act
False representations as to goods (various specific examples)	75AZC
False representations as to services	75AZC
False representations as to land	75AZD
Misleading statements about home-operated businesses	75AZM
False representations as to employment	75AZE
Cash price to be stated (cannot advertise part only of the consideration)	75AZF
Offering gifts or prizes without intending to supply	75AZG
Misleading conduct to which industrial property convention applies	75AZH
Misleading conduct regarding services	75AZI
Bait advertising	75AZJ
Referral selling	75AZK
Accepting payment without intending to supply	75AZL
Coercion or harassment at place of residence	75AZN
Pyramid selling	75AZO
Unsolicited credit cards	75AZP
Inertia selling (unsolicited goods)	75AZQ
Product safety and product information	75AZS, 75AZT, 75AZU

The Federal Court of Australia can impose fines (s. 76) for breaches of the restrictive practices provisions. In respect of a body corporate, the maximum penalty is a fine of up to $10 million. Individuals can be fined up to $500 000 (s. 76).

The Australian Competition and Consumers Commission is primarily responsible for the administration of the Trade Practices Act. For further information on the ACCC see: **http://www.accc.gov.au**

Privacy Act 1988 (Cth)

The Privacy Act imposes controls on the use of credit reporting information as well as other information acquired in respect of individuals. Failure to comply with the controls can result in fines of up to $150 000 for a company and $30 000 for an individual.

The Office of the Federal Privacy Commissioner is primarily responsible for the administration of the Privacy Act. For further information see: **http://www.privacy.gov.au**

Financial Transactions Reports Act 1988 (Cth)

The principal object of the Financial Transactions Reports Act is to assist the administration and enforcement of taxation laws; its secondary function is to authorise the collection, analysis and distribution of information regarding cash transactions to Commonwealth and state law enforcement authorities. These procedures may be particularly useful in detecting criminal activities and money laundering.

The Act imposes fines and/or prison terms for various types of non-compliance. Examples are:

- Section 28: failure to provide information—a natural person, $13 200 and/or two years' imprisonment; corporation, $66 000;
- Section 29: false or misleading information—a natural person, $33 000 and/or five years' imprisonment; corporation, $165 000; and

- Section 24: opening a bank account in a false name—a natural person, $13 200 and/or two years' imprisonment; corporation, $66 000.

Any person who leaves Australia can be requested to make a declaration regarding the taking of currency out of Australia. The person may also be searched and any luggage or other goods examined. Any undeclared currency found may be seized and the person fined $6000 and/or given 12 months' imprisonment.

The Australian Transaction Reports and Analysis Centre (AUSTRAC) is primarily responsible for the administration of the Financial Transactions Reports Act. For further information on AUSTRAC see: **http://www.austrac.gov.au**

Occupational health and safety legislation

The aim of occupational health and safety legislation is to create safe workplaces. To this end, the legislation imposes an obligation on all persons involved in a workplace, from the employer and the employee to the supplier of goods and equipment and the visitor, to ensure that the workplace is safe and that safety equipment is not made inoperable. Failure to comply with the Act can give rise to substantial fines for companies and individuals in addition to any liability for injuries caused by negligence.

In addition to claims for compensation for loss or injury, a breach of occupational health and safety legislation may result in fines and/or imprisonment.

Examples of the penalties are set out in Table 4.2.

Table 4.2 Occupational health and safety legislation penalties

Commonwealth		**Penalties**
Corporation		$242 000
Individual		$9 900
New South Wales		
Corporation	First offence	$550 000
	Second or subsequent offence	$825 000
Individual	First offence	$55 000
	Second or subsequent offence	$82 500 and/or 2 years
South Australia		
Corporation		$200 000
Individual		$100 000
Employee		$10 000
Tasmania		
Corporation		$150 000
Individual		$50 000
Victoria		
Corporation		$900 000
Individual		$180 000
Western Australia		
Corporation		$100 000
Where breach results in death or serious harm		$200 000
Employee		$10 000

Where the breach involves the reckless endangering of persons, an individual may be imprisoned for up to five years in addition to a fine of up to $180 000.

The website for the National Occupational Health and Safety Commission is useful for more information: **http://www.nohsc.gov.au**

Bankruptcy Act 1966 (Cth)

The *Bankruptcy Act 1966* (Cth), s. 263, makes it an offence for a bankrupt to fraudulently conceal property with the intent to defraud creditors. The prescribed penalty is imprisonment for three years.

Section 263 also provides that it is an offence where 'a person disposes of, removes, retains or conceals property that has been seized as part of the property of a bankrupt, knowing it to have been so seized or with intent to defeat the seizure of such property'. The penalty is imprisonment for one year.

Sections 265, 266, 269 and 271 of the Act concern irregular conduct by the bankrupt in respect of their assets and dealings. For example, a bankrupt must:

- disclose all their property to the trustee;
- disclose any disposition of property made within the two years immediately preceding the date of bankruptcy;
- comply with all directions of the trustee;
- if aware that a person has lodged a false proof of debt, inform the trustee about it; and
- provide a proper explanation of any loss or depreciation of any assets that has occurred within the previous two-year period.

The penalty for non-compliance is imprisonment for one year. However, a three-year gaol penalty is prescribed for a bankrupt who deceives or defrauds creditors in order to gain their consent on any matter connected with the bankrupt's trade dealing, property or business affairs.

Sections 265, 268, 270 and 272 provide penalties ranging from one to three years' imprisonment for a debtor and/or bankrupt who seeks to evade or delay creditors by fraudulent actions or who leaves Australia without the consent in writing of the trustee.

CRIMINAL LIABILITY INVOLVING COMPANIES

Company liable

People are not usually criminally liable for their actions unless they intended to do something wrong (i.e. have a guilty mind). While a company may be recognised by the law as being a 'person', it certainly does not have the characteristics of a natural person—it does not have a mind. For a company to be directly liable for a crime, the court must attribute fault to the company. The *Criminal Code Act 1995* (Cth) makes companies criminally liable if:

- a physical element of a statutory offence is committed by an employee, agent or officer of a company acting within that person's actual or apparent scope of employment or authority; and
- if intention, knowledge or recklessness is an element of the offence, that state of mind will be attributed to the company if:
  - the company's board or senior management tacitly or impliedly permitted or authorised the offence; or
  - a corporate culture existed which encouraged or tolerated the offence; or
  - the company failed to create or maintain a corporate culture or code which required compliance with the law.

Management of a company

Individuals connected with the management of a company may be liable for breaches of duties imposed by the *Corporations Act 2001* (Cth). Examples of breaches of duties which may result in criminal liability involving a fine of up to $220 000 and/or five years' imprisonment include:

- failure to act in good faith in the best interests of the company and for a proper purpose (s. 181);
- make improper use of position (s. 182);

- make improper use of information (s. 183); and
- failure to prevent insolvent trading (s. 588G).

If an individual engages in insider trading, the court may impose a fine of up to $200 000 and/or five years' imprisonment.

The Australian Securities and Investments Commission is primarily responsible for the administration of the Corporations Act. For further information see: **http://www.asic.gov.au**

CYBERCRIME

The *Cybercrime Act 2001* (Cth) amended the *Criminal Code 1995* (Cth) to create criminal offences for such actions as:

- unauthorised access, modification or impairment with intent to commit a serious offence;
- unauthorised modification of data;
- unauthorised impairment of electronic communication; and
- maximum penalties range from two years to 10 years' imprisonment.

CIVIL PENALTY

Civil penalties are a special type of statutory penalty. Although a pecuniary penalty (fine) would normally be imposed as a result of a criminal offence, the court proceedings for a civil penalty are civil proceedings in that rules of evidence and procedure are civil not criminal. This means that proof of the breach is on the balance of probabilities not beyond reasonable doubt. Using the civil standard of proof makes it much easier to establish the breach. It is therefore referred to as a civil penalty even though it is intended as punishment. The use of civil penalties is expanding.

Following are examples of legislation under which civil penalties are imposed.

Consumer Credit Code

If a credit provider contravenes a 'key requirement' of the Code, the court may make an order requiring the credit provider to pay an amount of money as a civil penalty.

If a credit provider becomes aware that it has contravened a particular key requirement in respect of a large number of credit contracts, it may apply for a civil penalty upon itself. It may do this in order to place a limit on its liability and to prevent individual borrowers applying for individual civil penalties, thereby keeping the legal proceedings restricted to one court action. The maximum civil penalty for all contraventions of the particular 'key requirement' throughout Australia is not to exceed $500 000 in total.

Where a borrower or a guarantor under a credit contract applies for a civil penalty, the maximum civil penalty shall not exceed an amount equal to all the interest charges payable under the contract. The amount of the civil penalty may be set off against any amount due to the credit provider under the credit contract.

Corporations Act 2001 (Cth)

A civil penalty may be imposed where an officer of a company has failed to comply with the Act relating to the management of the company. Civil penalties allow the court to prohibit the person from managing a company and/or to impose a pecuniary penalty of up to $200 000. This pecuniary penalty will not apply unless the contravention:

- materially prejudices the interests of the corporation or its members; or
- materially prejudices the corporation's ability to pay its creditors; or
- is serious.

The penalty is a civil debt payable to the Australian Securities and Investments Commission.

Examples of sections for which a civil penalty may be imposed include:

- act in good faith in the best interests of the company and for a proper purpose (s. 181);
- not make improper use of position (s. 182);
- not make improper use of information (s. 183);

- failure to prevent insolvent trading (s. 588G); and
- insider trading (s. 1043A).

Spam Act 2003 (Cth)

The *Spam Act 2003* (Cth) and *Spam (Consequential Amendments) Act 2003* (Cth) make it illegal to send most types of commercial electronic messages without the recipient's consent. The Act is aimed primarily at emails; however, it also applies to mobile text messages and faxes. Voice messages are not covered by the Act. The Act also makes it unlawful to supply, acquire or use software designed to collect electronic addresses from the Internet and to supply, acquire or use address lists generated by that software. The Act imposes civil penalties of up to $1.1 million. The only prosecution to date under the Spam Act has been *Australian Communications and Media Authority v. Clarity1 Pty Ltd* [2006] FCA 410, where the ACMA successfully prosecuted Clarity1 Pty Ltd and their managing director for sending out at least 50 million unsolicited commercial e-mails in breach of the Spam Act.

WEB RESOURCES

Australian Competition and Consumer Commission (ACCC):
http://www.accc.gov.au

Australian Securities and Investment Commission (ASIC):
http://www.asic.gov.au

Australian Transaction Reports and Analysis Centre (AUSTRAC):
http://www.austrac.gov.au

REVIEW QUESTIONS

4.1 What is an indictable offence and in what courts is it usually tried?

4.2 In respect of a criminal prosecution, who has the burden of proof and what is the standard of proof?

4.3 In criminal law, what is meant by the requirements that there must be a wrongful act and a guilty mind?

4.4 What is the difference between embezzlement and theft?

4.5 What is meant by the expression 'white collar crime'?

4.6 How do court proceedings for a civil penalty differ from normal criminal proceedings?

4.7 Can a company be charged with a crime? Discuss.

4.8 What is the difference between criminal law and civil law? Discuss.

CRITICAL THINKING

4.1 Some four months after the closure of his account, and knowing that there were no funds in it, B thought that he would try his card in his bank's automatic teller machine (ATM) for fun when he was going past it with some friends. He inserted the card in the ATM, keyed in his personal identification number (PIN) and the sum of $200. To his amazement the ATM paid him this amount because the machine was temporarily not online to the bank's central computer and had been programmed to pay up to $200 to any person who had a card and correctly programmed in their pin numbers. When offline the machine was incapable of determining whether the card holder had an account that remained current and, if so, whether the account was in credit.

Has B committed an offence?

4.2 If G, a shop manager, was short of cash during the week, she would take money from the till and replace it with a valid cheque the following morning. One Friday evening, just before closing time, she took $100 from her employer's till, intending to repay it on Monday morning with a valid cheque. However, G was dismissed on Saturday when she failed to arrive at work on time. She had been given numerous warnings by her employer that she would be dismissed if she continued to arrive at work late.

Has G committed any offence? Discuss.

activebook

Activebook resources include in-depth summaries with links to the relevant part of the book. For revision, add your own notes to the summaries provided by using the note-taking function.

CHAPTER 5

Ethics and Business Practice

CHAPTER CONTENTS

activebook

This icon is used throughout the following chapter to remind you to visit the *Business Law* online activebook for additional exercises, links to legal websites, and feedback. For a detailed explanation of what is in the activebook please refer to the inside cover of this textbook. The activebook is available through OneKey.

Where do I start?
Learning path: Use the activebook to complete a pre-chapter warm-up exercise.

There are many definitions of legal terms to assist with your understanding of the material.

5

CHAPTER OBJECTIVES

On completion of this chapter you should be able to:

- describe the connection between ethics and business
- understand the relationship of law and morality
- explain morals and ethics
- outline the major theories of ethics
- understand how ethics might operate in a business context
- outline some of the issues confronting ethics in corporations.

KEY TERMS

An understanding of the following terms will help you better understand the material in this chapter:

- **categorical imperative:** a standard of morality—'imperative', because it establishes principles; 'categorical', because the principles are unconditional with no exceptions
- **consequentialism:** concerned with the consequences. It is an approach to morals that evaluates behaviour according to the consequences of that behaviour
- **deontological ethics:** requires a person to do the right thing regardless of the consequences
- **ethical considerations:** involves going beyond self-interest in reaching a decision
- **ethical investing:** investment in companies that operate ethically, provide social benefits and are sensitive to the environment
- **ethical judgement:** one which can be seen to apply to everyone in similar circumstances and not only to a particular individual
- **ethical opinions:** concerned with behaviour and with establishing ways in which people should behave
- **ethics:** relates to morals, the treatment of moral questions and acting in a morally correct, honourable way
- **morals:** concerned with the distinction between right and wrong
- **organisational integrity:** based on the self-regulation of an organisation in accordance with a formal set of guiding principles
- **relativism:** provides that moral values are relative to a particular environment
- **utilitarianism:** a form of consequentialism ethics, which holds that an act is right as long as it produces the greatest good for the greatest number
- **virtue ethics:** stresses the type of moral qualities that put us in a position to act morally
- **virtues:** personal qualities that provide the basis for an individual to lead a good and noble life.

what if . . .

You owned shares in a company and you needed money to pay some outstanding debts so you sold the shares. A week after you sold the shares the company announces a huge profit and the shares immediately increase in value by 25 per cent. You later find out that the person who purchased your shares was the spouse of a senior executive of the company.

This chapter provides an overview of ethics and how they may apply to numerous business situations, which may or may not give rise to liability in law. It briefly examines the connection between ethics and the law. The chapter then considers some terms used in connection with the study and classification of ethical issues. And it very briefly considers business practices which, though not necessarily illegal, are highly questionable on the basis of morality and ethics.

ETHICS AND BUSINESS

Acting ethically involves acting in a morally correct and socially responsible way

Acting ethically involves acting in a morally correct and honourable way. The attitudes that 'making profits is all that matters' and 'as long as it is legal it is all right' are gradually being forced aside by a more ethical approach. While ethical business conduct may impose a cost on business, that cost may be offset by an increase in public confidence.

The Australian banking industry has been subjected to much public criticism for the change from the 'local bank' to an impersonal, profit-oriented corporate giant. The public criticism has focused on the withdrawal of services as a result of staff cuts, branch closures and the imposition of a fee for virtually every service. While the banking industry may argue that better services are simply being provided in a new way, many former bank customers have turned to other financial institutions and some communities have even started their own community bank.

Inquiries into the collapse of HIH Insurance and One.Tel in Australia have exposed how self-interest and greed exacerbated these failures and complimented incompetence and lack of effective scrutiny by executives and senior officers. It is often said by proponents of a *laissez faire* approach that business is quite able to regulate itself and what is good for business is good for everyone. This argument suffers when a market leader like HIH fails so spectacularly and catastrophically. The impact of that failure was not limited to shareholders and unsecured creditors, it also affected employees, policy holders and claimants under policies. It resulted in a restructuring of the insurance industry and was a major cause of an insurance crisis, particularly in public liability insurance.

Community attitudes and standards are changing. The community is now very aware of business matters and their consequences, particularly those consequences which impact on individual members of the community. If business does not adopt acceptable ethical standards Parliament is likely to impose standards. In Australia, partly motivated by corporate collapses, the Commonwealth Parliament has amended the *Corporations Act 2001*, setting new standards for the independence of auditors (see Pt 2M.4, Div. 3—Auditor independence).

THE LAW AND MORALITY

Laws are relative to their society

In terms of ethical relativism, it should be noted that laws are relative to their time and their society. What is appropriate at one period in time may not be appropriate to another; likewise, the law should reflect the attitudes of the society in which it exists and, therefore, what is acceptable in one society may not be acceptable in another. And social attitudes may change over time resulting in a corresponding change in the law.

In Chapter 1 we considered four concepts:

- what is 'law'?
- 'justice' and the 'law'
- the rule of law
- the development of equity.

Let us now consider these concepts again but in a moral or ethical context.

What is 'law'?

What is meant by 'law' will be determined by the individual's moral, political, religious and ethical views, and influenced by the society in which they live. A general definition of 'law', as quoted in Chapter 1, is:

> ***a set of rules**, developed over a long period of time **regulating people's interactions** with each other and which **sets standards of conduct** between individuals and other individuals, and individuals and the government and which **are enforceable through sanction**.*

So let's analyse each of the parts of this definition:

Law—a set of rules

1. **A set of rules.** The rules specify what may be done or what may not be done, regardless of whether the rules are just or unjust. If you break the rules and you get caught you will be subject to the specified penalty (sanction).

   Morally, the rules should be just, but from a strict legal sense that is not absolutely necessary. There are totalitarian dictatorships around the world which are not based on justice in any normal sense but their laws (rules) must be obeyed, or else.
2. **Regulating people's interactions.** The members of a society, such as the citizens of a country, the residents of a city or even the occupiers of a house, need to know what they can and cannot do. If there is no clearly understood system regulating the members' conduct there will be chaos.

   While the law regulates the interaction between people, it cannot anticipate all eventualities. Circumstances not covered specifically by the law will need to be resolved on an ethical basis.
3. **Setting standards of conduct.** Although the law sets rules of conduct, the purpose of the rule may go beyond the specific rules set out in the law. The purpose of the law may be to give a guide to conduct that is unacceptable and the rules may primarily be aimed at demonstrating that society is serious about eliminating the unacceptable conduct. An example of this is anti-discrimination legislation which is stated in fairly general terms and applied very widely, the underlying purpose being to eventually eliminate discrimination in all its forms.

   From an ethical point of view, the law may set the minimum standard which society expects or will tolerate.
4. **Enforceable through sanction.** The law will impose a penalty or other sanction to punish and deter non-compliance.

   Since ethics is a matter for the individual, it cannot be enforced through sanction unless the ethical standards have become part of the law or the rules of an organisation such as a professional body.

'Justice' and the 'law'

Justice—right and fair

A concept that is closely identified with law is **justice**, which means 'that which is right or fair'. Unfortunately, 'justice' can also be a difficult term to define. As previously stated in Chapter 1, Lord *Denning*, one of England's greatest judges, suggested:

> *It is not a product of intellect but of spirit. The nearest we can go to defining justice is to say that it is what right-minded members of the community—those who have the right spirit within them—believe to be fair.*

In Chapter 1 we distinguished between 'social justice', 'moral justice' and 'legal justice' and saw that they may or may not all coincide. It will depend on the situation and the context in which the term is used. Restating the example in Chapter 1, the fine for parking in a 'No Parking' zone is the same whether you are rich or poor. This may be considered legally and morally just, as everyone is seen to be equal in the eyes of the law. However, it can be inequitable or unfair as the person who is rich can more easily afford to pay the fine than the person who is poor.

The rule of law

Laws should conform to a minimum standard of fairness in both content and procedure

The rule of law is based on the idea that laws should conform to a minimum standard of fairness in both content and procedure. Professor Dicey, an Oxford academic lawyer who formulated the concept in the late 19th century, suggested that the rule of law involves three propositions:

- No person must be punished except for a breach of the law. This means that a person should be able to know whether or not what they want to do is lawful or unlawful. It also recognises the law as the highest authority in society.

- All persons are equal before the law irrespective of status or position.
- The rights or freedoms of citizens are enforceable in the courts.

The rights and freedoms of individuals are enforceable by the courts, not arbitrarily determined administratively. An individual may be the perpetrator of the most heinous crime, but by giving that individual their day in a proper court of law, we are all assured of our moral and legal rights. For example, several people were captured in Afghanistan by the army of the United States of America during the invasion of Afghanistan as part of the 'War on Terror'. These people were transferred to the marine base at Guantanamo Bay in Cuba. Although many have since been released, after several years some have still not been dealt with according to the normal legal proceedings that we take for granted. To arbitrarily say they are terrorists and then take away their normal rights is a contradiction of the rule of law and the concept of justice. As Kant argued, we should not devise principles for acting from which we are exempt; we must be prepared to have the actions we carry out against others used against ourselves.

The development of equity

Legal rules based on natural justice and fairness

As we saw in Chapter 1, the concept of equity law arose as a result of the growing inflexibility and rigidity of the common law. Petitioners believed that the only way that they were going to get justice for their cases was for the King to personally hear them. The King eventually delegated this role to the Chancellor, who became the 'keeper of the King's conscience'. The Chancellor was expected to advise the King as to what ought to be done to ensure that these petitioners received just and equitable treatment. In other words, the strict rules of the common law might be modified in appropriate circumstances in order to achieve what was the right result. This may be seen as a form of consequentialism ethics.

Letter of the law and spirit of the law

The strict wording of a law (the letter of the law) may allow an individual to do something which is not really in accordance with the intentions (spirit) of the law. The distinction between the letter and the spirit of the law is largely a moral or ethical problem: 'I have found a loophole which I may be able to use to avoid the restrictions of the law; however, in the circumstances, should I take advantage of it?'

MORALS AND ETHICS

Morals are concerned with the distinction between right and wrong

Morals are concerned with the distinction between right and wrong. Ethics relate to morals, the treatment of moral questions and acting in a morally correct and honourable way. Ethical considerations involve going beyond self-interest in reaching a decision. An ethical judgement is one which can be seen to apply to everyone in similar circumstances and not only to a particular individual.

Ethical opinions are concerned with behaviour and with establishing ways in which people should behave. Ethical opinions must be reasoned, they must not be mere personal preferences. Self-interest is not an ethical reason for acting; appearing to be ethical to enhance the interests of a business is not ethical business conduct.

The public at large, the government and the company's shareholders, all have an interest in the behaviour of businesses. A business might adopt an ethical approach for two reasons:

1. **The market will ultimately punish unethical behaviour.** The James Hardie Industries Group was the subject of severe adverse comment regarding its decision to move its head office and major assets 'offshore'. It was argued by claimants for compensation for lung cancer and other diseases allegedly caused by exposure to the Groups's products that the move was to defeat their claims. There was a backlash by both the community and government bodies against the Group and its products.
2. **Governments may legislate to protect consumers and to control trading.** Notable examples of this are the *Trade Practices Act 1974* (Cth), which prohibits 'unfair practices', i.e. unfair activities businesses might engage in against consumers. The Act also prohibits certain anti-competitive conduct. Other examples of such legislative intervention are:
   - the Consumer Credit Code;
   - residential and retail tenancies legislation; and

- recent amendments to the *Corporations Act 2001* (Cth) in regard to the provision of 'financial services' and auditing and financial reporting requirements for companies, particularly listed public companies.

THEORIES OF ETHICS

Consequentialism and utilitarianism

Consequentialism evaluates behaviour according to its consequences

'Consequentialism' means concerned with the consequences. It is an approach to morals which evaluates behaviour according to the consequences of that behaviour. The behaviour will be morally right or wrong, depending on whether or not it produces a specified type of consequence.

A form of consequentialism, known as utilitarianism, was developed by the 16th-century philosopher, Jeremy Bentham. He argued that ethically right behaviour was to perform the action which resulted in a greater number of utilities than could be achieved by any other action. Bentham thought of utilities as actions which produced either pleasure or pain: the action which produced a greater amount of pleasure than pain was the action which should be performed. Bentham was not being hedonistic when he used the words 'pleasure' and 'pain'; he could have used expressions like 'for the general good' and 'to the general detriment'.

To apply this to a modern business context, if a business meets the aims of most of the people affected by its decisions without disproportionately rejecting the aims of others, the actions of the business will comply with utilitarianism ethics.

Deontological ethics

Deontological ethics requires a person to do the right thing regardless of the consequences

Deontological ethics requires a person to do the right thing regardless of the consequences. It is at odds with consequentialism ethics in that it considers that the consequences can never be an appropriate justification for the act. The end does not in itself justify the means.

The 16th-century German philosopher, Immanuel Kant, was a proponent of deontological ethics. Kant argued that morality required one to do one's duty regardless of the consequences. He also argued that one's duty is determined by reference to consistency and rationality and not by reference to consequences. Knowing what to do in a situation will be determined by a set of principles established by deductive reasoning, independent of the specific circumstances, and possibly even before the specific circumstances are known. Kant held that actions must be guided by principles which apply irrespective of the consequences of the actions and that an action can only be morally right if that action was performed as a duty, not in expectation of a reward.

Kant's categorial imperative is a standard of morality

Kant proposed a standard of morality which he referred to as the 'categorical imperative'; categorical, because it is unconditional with no exceptions, and imperative, because it involves principles. In other words, a principle must be obeyed without exception. Kant put forward several principles as the basis of the categorical imperative. An interpretation of a couple of principles which are representative of the categorical imperative are:

- When considering a course of action, examine the motive or rationale for carrying out that action. Once the rationale has been determined, examine the rationale to decide if it could be a universal law, that is, can everyone, everywhere act upon it.
- We should never use other people as objects to further our own ends.
- We should not devise principles for acting from which we are exempt; we must be prepared to have the actions we carry out against others used against ourselves.

The 20th-century philosopher, William Ross, updated Kant's concept of duties and set out some duties of his own which may apply to business situations as well as to personal situations:

- duties that result from an act for which the actor is responsible;
- duties of gratitude which arise from the actions of others;
- duties of justice;
- duties of beneficence;
- duties of self-improvement; and
- duties not to injure others.

Virtue ethics

Virtues are personal qualities that provide the basis for an individual to lead a good and noble life. Virtue ethics stresses the type of moral qualities that put us in a position to act morally. It rejects the idea of dealing with moral problems by applying the correct maxim; instead, it focuses on a person's response to a moral problem as that of a moral person.

Virtue ethics stresses personal moral qualities

Relativism

Relativism suggests that moral values are relative to a particular environment. It argues that moral values can differ from one culture to another, from one society to another, from one time to another, and even from one individual to another.

Relativism moral values are relative to a particular environment

ETHICS IN A BUSINESS CONTEXT

Following are examples of common business situations that raise ethical issues.

Insider trading

Insider trading is an example of white collar crime (see p. 92). It is mentioned as an unethical business practice because many do not see anything wrong with the concept of insider trading. This fact draws attention to the difficulty in establishing ethical business practices. Some people cannot see or understand the concept.

Insider trading—taking advantage of private information not publicly available

Insider trading is not an example of taking advantage of a fair business opportunity. It is stealing. One party has information which is not known to the other party. The information is obtained solely because of their connection with the company. Knowing the price of the shares will increase when the information is made public they quickly act to buy the shares of a person who does not have the information and does not have the means of obtaining it. The value of the shares does increase after the information is made public. The buying party has stolen the increase in value from the selling party. That is why the practice is unethical and why the Parliament has made it illegal.

Note: It is also the answer to our 'What if . . .' challenge at the beginning of this chapter.

Giving and receiving gifts

Depending on the circumstances and the nature of the gift, there may be nothing wrong with the giving and receiving of gifts. However, the old adage 'there's no such thing as a free lunch' must be remembered. Is the gift a favour which one day will be called in? While the gift may be small and, on its own, a minor matter, is it actually one of many gifts? The answers to questions like these indicate whether the gift is ethical or not.

Conflict between commercial interests and social utility

While corporations such as banks, health funds, telecommunications suppliers and the media are business organisations which must look after their business interests, they also provide a social utility. They provide a special community need which should be considered in all their decisions.

Conflict of interest

A conflict of interest will arise when an individual is in a position where they cannot fairly and properly act in the interests of one party without prejudicing the rights and interests of another party for whom they also act.

For instance, a solicitor would be in a conflict of interest situation if he/she acted for the seller and purchaser of a house. As solicitor for the seller, they may wish not to disclose something, but as solicitor for the purchaser they would be expected to discover that same thing. How can the solicitor act fairly and properly for both seller and purchaser?

Unconscionable contracts

An agreement may comply with all the legal requirements for the court to recognise it as a contract but it may nonetheless be grossly unfair and against good conscience (see pp. 334–335). One of the parties may be taking excessive advantage of the misfortune or weakness of the other party. They may have included terms in the contract which impose an excessive burden on the other party.

Unconscionable contracts are grossly unfair and against good conscience

While it could be argued that a contract is an agreement and the other party did not have to agree to the terms, that argument is not always in keeping with the realities of some commercial relationships. The relative bargaining positions of the parties may be very different. One of the parties may be virtually unable to negotiate anything, and the extent of their negotiating position may be 'take it or leave it', as is often the case where standard form contracts are involved.

Misuse of limited liability of a company

Under the Doctrine of Separate Legal Entity, a company is recognised as a legal person, separate and distinct from its shareholders. This means that the rights and obligations of a company belong to the company not to the shareholders. Those obligations include the debts incurred by the company.

While the Doctrine of Separate Legal Entity and limited liability were established to encourage the entrepreneur and to safeguard the entrepreneur against the loss of personal as well as business assets, the doctrine has often been abused with the result that creditors and employees have lost considerable amounts of money while the principals of the company have effectively lost nothing.

Tax evasion/tax havens

No one likes to pay tax and there is never total agreement with the way taxes are spent. However, the community—and individuals within the community—expect certain services, and if they are not provided to the expected standard, objections will be made. Those services obviously require funding and that funding comes mainly from taxes.

Everyone pays tax in some form, even if it is only the Goods and Services Tax (GST). Everyone therefore makes some contribution. While everyone endeavours to reduce their tax burden, some try to eliminate it totally by the use of various tax-avoidance schemes and overseas tax havens. Many methods of tax avoidance are both ethically wrong and illegal.

Ethics is not about self serving, it is about doing the right thing despite the personal costs.

activebook

To help you to remember and understand the topics covered so far, and for links to legal websites, refer to your online activebook. Model answers provide feedback to problems and exercises.

CORPORATIONS AND ETHICS

Business ethics is about how we conduct our business affairs; it is about individuals and the institutions with which they deal; it is about expectations and requirements, including the social and economic requirements of society.

A corporation (company) is a legal entity, that is, upon registration it is given the legal status of a person, separate and distinct from the shareholders and the directors. The law recognises the corporation as a person even though it does not exist in a physical sense. But can such a non-natural person have ethical responsibilities, given that the legal entity has no character or conscience in the normal sense? Should ethics be part of the framework of corporations and, if yes, how? Should ethical standards be imposed on a market economy in which corporations work?

Company directors have a fiduciary duty to act in the interests of their company and the best interests of the shareholders. Does that entitle them to ignore ethically suspect practices which benefit shareholders? Should the role of the company director diminish their moral responsibility for the actions of their company or employer? Does individual conscience, character and choice have a place in a corporate situation?

Institutionalised wrongdoing

Unethical behaviour and illegal actions are often the result of social forces within an organisation which bring pressure on an individual to do wrong. In the process the individual themselves may be changed. In a corporate situation, it may be difficult to identify an individual who was responsible for a wrongful act, but if they were identified, they would probably be a person who looks and acts like everyone else.

Corporations sometimes become committed to certain courses of action and the individuals who advocated the course of action will often be reluctant or unwilling to change it, even though ethical problems become apparent as the action progresses. There could be many reasons for this, not the least of which is the belief that to stop the action would be an admission that they were wrong. A further problem in large organisations is that the action can develop 'a life of its own'. The action may be an ongoing process which is handed from one individual to another as the various individuals move through the organisation's hierarchy. The individuals simply 'go with the flow' and either do not question the situation or do not consider it to be their problem because it was implemented by someone else.

Individuals within the organisation may become aware that certain conduct is a serious breach of occupational health and safety guidelines and represents a major health risk, or the corporation may be manufacturing a product with a hidden defect, which has the potential to cause serious injury. The individual may report the problem to the decision makers and, having done so, they may feel they have fulfilled their responsibilities. The decision to halt ongoing processes because of potential future harm requires making a decision to take action, while maintaining the status quo requires no action. Therefore the decision to stop the process often requires clear and overwhelming evidence of the danger before the decision can be made.

If the potential danger occurs and someone is seriously injured, the organisation may go into damage control and endeavour to cover up knowledge of the warnings and, depending on the nature of the injury, they may totally deny that there is any responsibility on the part of the organisation. The rationale for this is that, if the decision maker admits that an injury has occurred, then they may be accused of culpability for knowingly allowing the event to happen. This often results in denials that the harmful consequences are genuine or that they were actually caused by the corporation's processes. Once the cover-up has commenced, it is like a lie—one lie leads to another lie, which in turn leads to a further lie, and so on and so on. Likewise, further concealment becomes necessary, evidence of any previous injuries needs to be destroyed and individuals in the organisation who might discover the previous harm are hindered or threatened.

Organisational integrity

Many executives are quick to deny that the corporation should bear responsibility for the wrongful actions of an individual. They will describe the wrongful act as an isolated incident perpetrated by an individual without the knowledge or consent of the corporation. However, unethical business practices usually involve the cooperation of others and reflect the values, beliefs and behaviour patterns of the corporation's operating culture.

Organsiational integrity is based on self-regulation in accordance with a formal set of guiding principles. An integrity program identifies ethics as a motivational force in the organisation. Ethical values will be involved in the establishment of organisational systems, the decision-making process and the search for business opportunities. Integrity programs often comprise a code of conduct, training in compliance with the legal obligations of the organisation, systems for the reporting and investigation of possible breaches, as well as a system of controls and audits to ensure that the integrity program is being complied with.

Corporate codes of conduct

Code of conduct—method of conducting business based on ethical factors

In the United States of America, President George W. Bush put forward a 10 Point Plan for corporate responsibility. The plan was a response to the Enron and WorldCom corporate collapses. The plan has been voluntarily adopted by some corporations. It has also been influential in the New York Stock Exchange and NASDAQ revising their requirements for the listing of corporations. The *Sarbanes-Oxley Act of 2002*, passed by the United States Congress, has given legislative support to the plan. The 10 Point Plan is as follows:

1. Each investor should have quarterly access to the information needed to judge a firm's financial performance, condition and risks.
2. Each investor should have prompt access to critical information.
3. CEOs should personally vouch for the veracity, timeliness and fairness of their companies' public disclosures, including their financial statements.
4. CEOs or other officers should not be allowed to profit from erroneous financial statements.
5. CEOs or other officers who clearly abuse their power should lose their right to serve in any corporate leadership positions.
6. Corporate leaders should be required to tell the public promptly whenever they buy or sell company stock for personal gain.

7. Investors should have complete confidence in the independence and integrity of companies' auditors.
8. An independent regulatory board should ensure that the accounting profession is held to the highest ethical standards.
9. The authors of accounting standards must be responsive to the needs of investors.
10. Firms' accounting systems should be compared with best practices, not simply against minimum standards.

The 10 Point Plan together with support material may be viewed on the White House Corporate Responsibility page at: **http://www.whitehouse.gov/infocus/corporateresponsibility**.

Some companies have recognised the value of adopting an ethical approach to their business dealings and have implemented a Code of Ethical Conduct. A good example of such a code of conduct is the Corporate Code of Conduct and Business Ethics adopted by Ruralco Holdings Limited (ABN 40 009 660 870) of Girraween NSW. A listing of the individual topics covered by the Ruralco code follows. The introduction setting out Ruralco's aim in establishing the code has been reproduced in full as it gives a very good outline of this company's commendable effort in establishing high ethical standards. The full code may be read at: **http://www.crt.ruralco.com.au/code_cond.htm** (© Ruralco Holdings Limited ABN#: 40 009 660 879 Corporate Code of Conduct and Business Ethics).

1. Introduction

Ruralco's vision to be Australia's largest, most innovative and successful group of independent businesses servicing rural Australia requires the Company to adopt best practice business standards. Ruralco is committed to maintaining ethical standards in the conduct of its business activities. It expects and requires all its officers and employees to have a personal commitment to meeting these standards. These standards go beyond mere compliance with laws and regulations. They also embrace the core values which are essential to Ruralco's continued success to the Company.

2. Purpose of this Code: Ruralco's Business Ethics

- *2.1 Openness, Honesty and Integrity*
- *2.2 Mutual Respect*
- *2.3 Fairness*
- *2.4 Ethical Conduct*
- *2.5 Compliance with Laws.*

3. Business Conduct

- *3.1 Compliance with Laws and Regulations*
  - *(a) Trading in shares*
  - *(b) Privacy*
  - *(c) Intellectual property*
  - *(d) Use of unlicensed software*
- *3.2 Personal and Professional Conduct*
  - *(a) Financial integrity*
  - *(b) Giving gifts*
  - *(c) Accepting gifts*
  - *(d) Business agreements and contracts*
  - *(e) Confidentiality*
  - *(f) Smoking and the use of drugs and alcohol*
  - *(g) Gathering information on Ruralco's competitors*
  - *(h) Conflict of interest*
  - *(i) Use of Company's resources*
  - *(j) Private employment and honorary voluntary positions*

3.3 Relationships with others
4. Whistleblowing
5. More Information

ETHICAL INVESTING

Ethical investment—investment which considers ethical/moral factors as well as purely financial factors

At one time, investment 'in the stock exchange' was seen as the exclusive field of the high finance operators. That has changed with superannuation funds controlling huge amounts of money contributed by individuals who have little or no knowledge of the stock exchange and how it works. Many individuals who ordinarily would never have thought of investing in company shares have done just that as a result of the public floats of previously government-owned institutions such as the Commonwealth Bank, Qantas, Telstra and the TAB. This introduction to shareholding has widened interest in this form of investment and it has also encouraged socially responsible investment in that many investors are now expressing concern over the activities of the companies in which they are directly investing, or indirectly investing in, through financial institutions such as banks and superannuation funds.

Ethical investing is investment in companies that operate ethically, provide social benefits and are sensitive to the environment. In addition to the usual considerations such as adequate returns and security, the socially responsible investor considers whether or not the investment is ethical. This means judging a company or institution primarily on its products and/or services as well as socially responsible governance practices. The usual guidelines for determining which company to invest in, or not invest in, include considerations as to whether the company is associated with, or linked to, factors such as:

Positive factors

- environmental protection
- pollution control
- conservation of resources
- health and safety of the workplace and the community
- ethical employment policies.

Negative factors

- armaments
- oppressive regimes
- environmentally damaging practices
- unethical employment practices
- animal exploitation
- tobacco or alcohol
- gambling
- pornography.

ETHICAL PROFESSIONAL ADVICE

High-flying entrepreneurs such as Alan Bond and Christopher Skase may have provided the conceptual idea and driving force for their schemes but they did not have the specialist professional expertise to make them happen; for that, they turned to professional advisers such as lawyers and accountants. When such high-flyers eventually fail and are exposed, their reputations may be destroyed but their professional advisers step back into the shadows and are overlooked.

In a similar vein, there have been recent examples of some large corporations like tobacco companies and chemical and mining companies stretching the legal system to the limit to avoid culpability for their activities. Courts have formal processes and procedures aimed at enabling the litigating parties to obtain relevant information and documents held by the other party. One such process relates to the 'discovery' of documents. In *McCabe v. British American Tobacco Australia Services Ltd* [2002] VSC 73 the Supreme Court of Victoria found that the legal advisers for the tobacco company had subverted the court's discovery process by advising the tobacco company to destroy documents so that they would no longer be available for the court proceedings. Although the Supreme Court's finding was overturned on appeal, as was noted at the beginning of this chapter, 'just because it is legal doesn't make it right'.

WEB RESOURCES

A fine example of a code of conduct:
http://www.crt.ruralco.com.au/code_cond

White House Corporate Responsibility 10 Point Plan:
www.whitehouse.gov/infocus/corporateresponsibility

REVIEW QUESTIONS

5.1 List examples of legal rules that have ethical characteristics.

5.2 What are the business benefits of ethical considerations?

5.3 What has been the effect of a lapse of ethical standards by businesses?

5.4 What should be the ethical duties of businesses?

5.5 What is socially responsible investing?

5.6 What is not socially responsible investing?

CRITICAL THINKING

Consider the following statement in the context of business dealings: 'It may not be right but it isn't illegal'.

i Is the fact that something is not illegal sufficient to make it acceptable?

ii If a business was to conduct its operations in an ethical manner, what criteria or benchmarks would be used to determine what is an appropriate ethical standard in a particular situation?

iii List some situations you have experienced or heard of in which a business has engaged in conduct which may have been legal but was not morally correct (unethical). Give reasons as to why you believe the conduct was not morally correct (unethical).

CIVIL LIABILITY AND INSURING AGAINST RISK

PART THREE

CHAPTER

Introduction to the Law of Tort

CHAPTER CONTENTS

activebook

This icon is used throughout the following chapter to remind you to visit the *Business Law* online activebook for additional exercises, links to legal websites, and feedback. For a detailed explanation of what is in the activebook please refer to the inside cover of this textbook. The activebook is available through OneKey.

Where do I start?

Learning path: Use the activebook to complete a pre-chapter warm-up exercise.

There are many definitions of legal terms to assist with your understanding of the material.

CHAPTER OBJECTIVES

On completion of this chapter, you should be able to:

- explain the nature of a tort
- recognise the importance of time in bringing a tort action
- explain the general principles of tortious liability
- explain the difference between a tort and a crime
- explain the difference between a tort and a contract
- distinguish between a direct and indirect tort.

KEY TERMS

An understanding of the following terms will help you to better understand the material in this chapter:

- **act of God:** a natural event or occurrence which cannot be foreseen and which happens
- **defamation:** a tortious action encompassing both words spoken (slander) or recorded (libel) which tend to injure a person's reputation
- **negligence:** a tort, actionable at the suit of a person suffering damage as the result of the defendant's breach of duty to take care to refrain from doing those acts which a reasonable person could reasonably foresee as being likely to injure them
- **nuisance:** a tortious action encompassing both those actions that interfere with the enjoyment of a right that all members of the community are entitled to (public nuisance), and those actions that result in a wrongful disturbance or interference with a person's use or enjoyment of land (private nuisance)
- **tort feasor:** one who commits a tort
- **tortious:** wrongful
- **trespass:** a tort involving the wrongful interference with the person or property of another and including: (a) trespass to the person—assault, battery and false imprisonment; (b) trespass to land; and (c) trespass to goods.

what if . . .

You were walking around a supermarket when you slipped on some olive oil that had been spilt on the floor by another shopper just in front of you when the bottle slipped through her fingers and broke on the floor, causing you to fall and injure your back before you could get out of the way. Could you seek compensation from anyone? Would it make any difference if the shopper had deliberately dropped the bottle?

The law of tort is an area of the law that often only becomes relevant to people and businesses **after** the happening of a loss-making event. As a result, an understanding of the law of tort on both business and non-business activities is very important.

The range of interests which the law of tort protects is very wide and includes:

- Liability for breach of duty to take reasonable care which raises, *prima facie*, the question of **negligence**—today the most important area of tort (see Chapter 7).
- Liability arising out of **occupation** or **possession of property**, which includes negligence and private nuisance (see Chapters 8 and 9).
- Direct interferences with person and property, which fall within the area of **trespass** (see Chapter 9).
- Liability for misrepresentations which affect a person's reputation and standing in the community. These fall under the area of **defamation** (see Chapter 9).
- Interests in economic relations, which are concerned with protection from interference with contractual relationships, and the right to fair and honest commercial dealings with other persons. These fall within one of the areas of inducing **breach of contract**, **conspiracy** or **intimidation** (see Chapter 9).
- A fraudulent misrepresentation which does not form part of a contract. This may amount to the tort of **deceit** (see Chapter 9).
- **Breach of statutory duty**, generally involving motor traffic and workplace health and safety issues (see Chapter 8).

This chapter begins by considering what a tort is and the basis on which it operates, that is, through compensation for the injured party. It then looks at the function of the law of tort, the principles on which the law of tort rests and the rights protected by the law of tort. It then considers how the law of tort differs from the law of contract and the criminal law.

GENERAL PRINCIPLES OF TORTIOUS LIABILITY

IN BRIEF

What is a tort?

A tort is 'a **civil wrong** other than a claim for breach of contract' and for which a right of civil action for damages may arise. It is an act or omission of the defendant that creates an infringement of an interest of the plaintiff that the law will recognise and which involves the plaintiff proving on the balance of probabilities that their version of the facts is the more believable.

It was noted in Chapter 1 (see p. 12) that from the 12th century on, an action in the royal courts was usually commenced by a royal writ issued by the King's Clerks of the Chancery. The purpose of the writ was to inform the defendant about the facts upon which the plaintiff's grievance was based and the remedy they sought. Today, a plaintiff will start proceedings by writ of summons for all actions in tort.

RANGE OF REMEDIES IN THE LAW OF TORT

Tort law is concerned with remedies

The modern law of tort operates on the basis of **remedies** to persons for the harm suffered to them by the conduct of others. It does not necessarily follow that this will automatically take the form of monetary compensation, because the damage suffered by the injured party may take many forms apart from physical injury. For example, it may be physical damage to property, damage to financial interests or injury to reputation. In these sorts of cases the injured party may only be seeking an injunction to stop the offending party from causing further damage.

Nor does it automatically follow that because a person suffers loss or damage, they should be entitled to compensation. There must be some reason for shifting the loss from the sufferer to the wrongdoer and a plaintiff will not necessarily always have a case for compensation by proving damage to their person, property or relationships at the hands of the defendant. For example, there may be a statutory restriction on what a plaintiff may recover, such as the civil liability legislation that all Australian jurisdictions have passed. For some harms that a plaintiff may suffer, there is no legal remedy. For example:

- The harm may be considered too trivial to warrant the attention of the courts.
- The harm may have been caused by accident without wilfulness or negligence being present.
- There may be a complete defence available to the defendant.
- There might be a question of national security involved.

COMPENSATION OUTSIDE TORT LAW

Statutory compensation may be available to P

It should not be assumed that the only compensation available to an injured person will come from a remedy in the law of torts. Other forms of compensation which provide alternative protection to suing in tort, and do not depend upon proof that a tort has been committed, exist in statutory schemes (relief may also be available for a tort victim in the social security system) such as:

- workers' compensation schemes which exist in all Australian jurisdictions;
- criminal injuries compensation schemes which also exist in all Australian jurisdictions; and
- motor accident compensation schemes which exist in the Northern Territory, Tasmania and Victoria.

The existence of statutory compensation schemes for injured parties highlights deficiencies within the law of torts for a plaintiff including:

- the difficulty with being able to prove a tort, i.e. proving fault on the part of a defendant;
- an insolvent or uninsured defendant, making recovery of damages difficult or impossible even if a tort is proved;
- reduction of damages because of the plaintiff's contributory negligence;
- the cost of litigation;
- the delay in obtaining compensation, placing pressure on a tort victim to settle the action before going to court, thereby increasing the chances of under-compensation; and
- the difficulties in assessing accurately the plaintiff's actual loss, e.g., assessing whether the plaintiff's injuries will worsen in the future.

activebook

To help you to remember and understand the topics covered so far, and for links to legal websites, refer to your online activebook. Model answers provide feedback to problems and exercises.

TIME LIMITS FOR TORT ACTIONS

! CAUTION NOTE

*Injured parties **MUST** be aware that there are time limits set by relevant state or territory limitation legislation within which an action must be brought, or they may become statute barred, that is, lose the right to bring their case and recover compensation!*

Statutes of Limitation establish time within which an action must be brought

If an injured party feels that they should be entitled to compensation they must take legal action within a certain time or the defendant may be able to raise the defence that the action has become statute barred. The onus is on the defendant to show that the plaintiff's claim falls outside the extension guidelines of the legislation. However, the limitation legislation in all jurisdictions gives the courts a discretion to extend the limitation period if the court considers the plaintiff has a reasonable chance of success **and** it is just and reasonable in the circumstances.

Where the defendant is successful in raising the defence of statutory limitation, the effect on the injured party is that they will not be able to win the case. The defendant will raise this defence at the commencement of proceedings, that is, at the start of the case.

There is considerable uniformity in all Australian state and territory jurisdictions as to present-day limitation periods on actions in tort (see Table 6.1).

The date on which the time commences to run, that is, the date the injured party must commence their action, will depend on whether the tort is actionable *per se* (without proof of damage) or not:

- in torts actionable *per se*, time commences to run from the date of the act committing the tort; and

Table 6.1 Statutes of limitation of the states and territories

State	*Statute*	*Personal injury Negligence/ nuisance/trespass*	*Defamation*	*Other torts*
Australian Capital Territory	*Limitation Act 1985*	3 years	1 year	6 years
New South Wales	*Limitation Act 1969*	3 years	1 year	6 years
Northern Territory	*Limitation Act 1981*	3 years	–	3 years
Queensland	*Limitation of Actions Act 1974*	3 years	1 year	6 years
South Australia	*Limitation of Actions Act 1936*	3 years	1 year	6 years
Tasmania*	*Limitation Act 1974*	3 years	–	6 years
Victoria	*Limitation of Actions Act 1958*	3 years	1 year	6 years
Western Australia	*Limitations Act 2005*	3 years	1 year	6 years

*In Tasmania, one year for defamation (*Defamation Act 2005*)

- in torts such as negligence, where proof of damage is required as part of the cause of action, time will generally commence to run from the date when the damage occurs. However, in cases of latent injury or damage the courts have been given a statutory discretionary power to extend the limitation period, while in the cases of negligently constructed houses or buildings the courts have taken the approach that the damage does not occur until the defect becomes discoverable by due diligence (the ACT has statutorily limited this period to 15 years—s. 40, *Limitation Act 1985*).

WILSON V. HORNE [1999] AUST. TORTS REPORTS ¶81-504

Between the ages of five and 12, the plaintiff had been subjected to sexual assaults by the defendant. At the age of 25 she developed a stress disorder when she began to recall the assaults.

ISSUE: Could she bring an action under trespass or negligence? In the case of negligence, when did the negligence occur—at the time of the assaults, or at the time she developed her mental disorder?

DECISION: The Full Court of the Tasmanian Supreme Court held she could not bring an action for trespass as this was statute barred by the passage of time. She suffered the assaults some 13 to 20 years earlier and a trespass action had to have been commenced within six years of the assault occurring.

She could bring an action for negligence. Damage is a necessary prerequisite for a cause of action in negligence and the court found that this occurred when the stress disorder developed, so she was not statute-barred by the *Limitation Act*.

LIABILITY

It is the function of the law of tort to determine when the law will, and when it will not, provide a remedy for damages suffered to a plaintiff. Where a plaintiff has suffered damage in accordance with the rules of liability, providing that the rules are correctly stated, then they can be said to be the victim of a tort and entitled to seek a remedy for the infringement or breach of their interest. It is this pursuit of remedies by a plaintiff which is the very essence of tort law.

It should be noted, however, that a person who has suffered damage may still have redress without being the victim of a tort—for example, under the law of contract. The law of tort is not the only area of law capable of correcting breaches of obligation.

ELEMENTS OF THE LAW OF TORT

Tort is mainly concerned with accidental injury to person or property

Much of the law of tort is concerned with **accidental injury to person** (i.e. physical or mental) **or property** and, subject to certain qualifications and exceptions, the general approach of the law of tort to this problem rests on two principles:

- an **act or omission** by the defendant interfering with some right or interest of the plaintiff which causes damage; and
- the interference must give rise to a cause of action for **damages** which should as nearly as possible be equal to the plaintiff's loss.

What rights are protected by the law of tort?

Two types of right are protected under the law of tort and they can be classified as absolute rights and qualified rights (see Table 6.2).

Table 6.2 Rights protected by the law of tort

Absolute rights	*Qualified rights*
Direct interferences with the person or property of the plaintiff, e.g., trespass	*Indirect interferences* with the person or property of the plaintiff, e.g., negligence, nuisance
Actionable *per se* (without proof of damage)	Plaintiff must suffer some damage

DISTINGUISHING BETWEEN TORT AND CRIMINAL LAW

While tort and criminal law both had their origins in revenge and deterrence, and even today there are still overlaps between tortious and criminal conduct, there are important differences between the two forms of liability (see Table 6.3). The essential difference between a tortious action and a criminal prosecution is one of purpose. In a tortious action, the parties are concerned with the resolution of a private dispute which may result in the award of some appropriate remedy, for example, damages or an order for the return of property. In criminal proceedings the prosecutor is a representative of the public and concerned with punishment and the repression of crime.

Table 6.3 Criminal and tort law distinguished

	Criminal law	*Tort law*
The standard of proof	Crown must prove its case beyond reasonable doubt	Plaintiff must prove their case on balance of probabilities
Sanctions and remedies	Punishes offender for their offence	Exists to compensate victims
Consent	Whether the victim consents to the accused's actions is irrelevant	The injured party can consent to the defendant's actions
Role of the Crown	A convicted person can be pardoned	The Crown has no authority to pardon a tort short of legislating

DISTINGUISHING BETWEEN TORT AND CONTRACT LAW

Both the commission of a tort and the breach of a contract can result in a civil action which will result in similar remedies for a plaintiff—compensation. And in some cases the two actions are indistinguishable. For example, in cases of concurrent liability, to date only involving negligence, where the contractual duty is one of reasonable care, liability can arise in both tort and contract in relation to the same conduct by the defendant. For example, where a doctor negligently treats their patient:

- they may have broken an implied term in their contract with that patient to take reasonable care; and
- liability may arise in tort because they have broken their duty of care in regard to their patient.

However, for the breach of contract to amount to the tort of negligence, it will have to be shown that a duty of care exists and that the plaintiff has suffered actual damage as a result of the breach.

Should the action then be brought in tort or contract? In those jurisdictions which have enacted legislation reforming the laws of negligence, that is all but the Northern Territory, harm resulting from negligence is now subject to a single legal regime regardless of whether the claim is brought in contract or tort. In the Northern Territory, if there is a common law duty of care imposed upon one of the parties already, then, as a matter of law, there is no concurrent and co-extensive contractual duty of care. If the duty already exists by virtue of tort law, then it can't be presumed that the parties intended to also imply a term into the contract to give it business efficacy. Thus the action should be brought in tort: see *Hawkins v. Clayton* (1988) 164 CLR 539.

Despite situations where tortious and contractual duties overlap, it is possible to identify two major differences between the two areas of law—promises and agreement (see Table 6.4).

Table 6.4 Contract law and tort law distinguished

	Contract law	*Tort law*
Promises	Concerned with having the promises of others performed	Interests covered are wider, covering both person and property
Agreement	While contractual duty mainly comes from agreement of the parties, it can be imposed by law	Tortious duty is imposed independently of the consent of the parties, though rights and duties may be varied contractually

DIRECT AND INDIRECT TORTS

Torts can be divided into three groups:

- intentional (or direct) torts;
- unintentional (or indirect torts); and
- miscellaneous torts.

Intentional torts are based on action in trespass

Intentional torts are based on an action known as **trespass**. Their history can be traced back to the mid-13th century when the law began to replace the customary laws of self-redress and vengeance with criminal prosecution for the accused and an award of damages for the plaintiff. An intentional tort is one where a defendant intentionally carries out a wrongful act that directly causes harm to the plaintiff, hence the alternative title of direct torts. Business-related **direct** torts include:

- trespass: to the person (assault, battery, false imprisonment), to land, to goods;
- indirect intentional torts of action on the case and deceit;
- defamation (libel and slander); and
- the economic torts (intimidation, interference with contractual relations, conspiracy, unfair competition, passing off, misrepresentation and injurious falsehood).

Unintentional torts, e.g., negligence, are based on action on the case

Unintentional torts are based on a legal action known as **action on the case**. The best known unintentional tort today is negligence. Negligence, as an action in its own right, is a relatively recent development in the law of torts. It can be traced back in its modern form to the English case of *Donoghue v. Stevenson* in 1932 (see Chapter 7 for a more detailed explanation). Prior to 1932, plaintiffs had to rely on the concept of a legal duty of care in the form of 'the common custom of the realm'. To be liable on the case, a person who had undertaken to do something for another would have to do it so badly that their conduct was considered wrongful. The wrongful conduct that caused the damage had to be indirect. If the wrongful conduct was by direct force, then it was trespass.

Of the **miscellaneous torts**, that is, those which are neither intentional nor unintentional, the one most relevant to business is nuisance.

WEB RESOURCES

FindLaw Australia: a very useful site for finding information on tort law (and most other areas as well). Type in torts to the search engine on the site: **http://www.findlaw.com.au**

The Ipp Report: to see the final report of the Law of Negligence review which culminated in the states and territories introducing civil liability legislation see: **http://revofneg.treasury.gov.au/content/review2.asp**

A PDF copy is available at:

http://revofneg.treasury.gov.au/content/Report/PDF/lawnegfull.pdf

REVIEW QUESTIONS

6.1 What is a tort?

6.2 Explain the difference between a direct and an indirect tort.

6.3 Explain the major differences between an action based in tort law and an action based in contract law.

6.4 As an injured plaintiff, would you prefer to bring an action against the person who caused the injury in tort law or in criminal law? Explain why.

6.5 Indicate whether each of the following statements is true or false:

	TRUE	FALSE
▪ A tort is a civil wrong rather than a criminal wrong	☐	☐
▪ The law of torts is concerned with compensation	☐	☐
▪ In the case of a negligence action, it must be commenced within six years or else it will be statute barred	☐	☐
▪ The law of torts is the only area of law capable of correcting breaches of obligation	☐	☐
▪ The law of torts is concerned with absolute and qualified rights	☐	☐
▪ The standard of proof is the same for both criminal law and tort law	☐	☐
▪ Tortious duty can only be imposed by agreement	☐	☐
▪ Negligence is an intentional tort	☐	☐
▪ Intentional torts are based on action on the case	☐	☐
▪ Trespass is a direct tort and actionable *per se*	☐	☐

activebook

Activebook resources include in-depth summaries with links to the relevant part of the book. For revision, add your own notes to the summaries provided by using the note-taking function.

CRITICAL THINKING

6.1 Given the huge increase in premiums for public liability insurance coverage that has occurred since 2002, and which appears to be likely to continue to increase, forcing insurance coverage beyond the reach of many, have lawyers gone too far in seeking compensation for anyone who is injured? Should a no-fault accident compensation scheme be introduced into the country similar to that in New Zealand or do you think that the civil liability legislation passed by the states and territories following the Ipp Report is enough? Discuss.

CHAPTER 7 The Tort of Negligence

CHAPTER CONTENTS

activebook

This icon is used throughout the following chapter to remind you to visit the *Business Law* online activebook for additional exercises, links to legal websites, and feedback. For a detailed explanation of what is in the activebook please refer to the inside cover of this textbook. The activebook is available through OneKey.

Where do I start?
Learning path: Use the activebook to complete a pre-chapter warm-up exercise.

There are many definitions of legal terms to assist with your understanding of the material.

CHAPTER OBJECTIVES

On completion of this chapter, you should be able to:

- explain what negligence is
- identify the elements necessary to establish negligence
- explain when the defendant owes a duty of care to the plaintiff and the tests that the courts use to determine whether a duty of care exists
- explain when the defendant breaches their duty of care
- explain whether the plaintiff has suffered recoverable damage
- explain what defences a defendant can raise to a negligence claim.

KEY TERMS

An understanding of the following terms will help you better understand the material in this chapter:

- **contributory negligence:** the defence in an action at common law for damages for injuries arising from negligence which the plaintiff's own negligence directly caused or contributed to their own injuries
- **negligence:** a tort, actionable at the suit of a person suffering damage as the result of the defendant's breach of duty to take care to refrain from doing those acts which a reasonable person could reasonably foresee as being likely to injure them
- ***res ipsa loquitor*:** the thing speaks for itself. This maxim describes the legal position where the circumstances of an accident are such that there is little doubt that the accident would have happened only because of the defendant's negligence, and that in the absence of further evidence the defendant would be held liable.

what if . . .

You were walking along the footpath when you tripped over a broken piece of concrete outside a shop and fell, breaking your arm and injuring your back. Would you be able to sue the owner of the shop or the council for your injuries?

Since the modern version of negligence was established in 1932 in the decision of *Donoghue v. Stevenson* [1932] AC 562 (see p. 125), negligence has become by far the most important area of tort law. It is capable of almost infinite expansion and adaptation. The liability of a manufacturer of ginger beer in opaque bottles has been extended to include among other things defective products and defective structures, factory accidents and road accidents, negligent misstatements and personal injuries caused by third parties. It has impacted extensively on both business and the community generally.

The response of business and the community to the threat of negligence-based litigation has been to take out insurance against that risk, in particular, public liability insurance (see Chapter 10 for further information on insurance). This provides financial protection against claims arising from personal injury or property damage caused to third parties by the negligent actions of the insured. To obtain such protection, an insured enters into a policy of insurance with an insurer (an 'insurance contract') whereby the insurer agrees to indemnify the insured for loss suffered as a result of the occurrence of a specified event upon the payment of a premium. However, the last few years have seen massive increases in the cost of premiums for policy holders to obtain financial protection, leading to an insurance crisis for both business and the community.

In response to public concerns about the cost and availability of third party liability insurance, in July 2002 the Commonwealth and state attorneys-general commissioned a review by Justice *Ipp* into the law of negligence, including its interaction with the *Trade Practices Act 1974* (Cth) (the 'Review of the Law of Negligence Inquiry'), culminating in the 'Ipp Review' in October 2002. Following its release, state and territory jurisdictions adopted a rather *ad hoc* legislative approach towards the recommendations of the review, with some jurisdictions going further than others in providing statutory direction for the courts when considering cases involving issues of negligence. Whether the reforms make any difference to the personal injuries environment and result in a fall in premiums is problematical and they may result in being described as nothing more than window-dressing. However, there appears to be evidence to suggest that there has been a substantial decline in civil filings in personal injury matters, at least in Victoria and New South Wales, according to the Productivity Commission Review of Government Services report released in January 2006.

The *Ipp* Report recommendations

In its final report of 2 October 2002 the Ipp Review made a number of recommendations including:

- a national approach in the form of a single statute;
- application to any claim for damages for harm resulting from negligence, regardless of whether the claim is brought in tort, contract, under statute or otherwise;
- establishing a standard of care for medical practitioners (including a duty to inform) and professionals generally;
- not permitting not-for-profit organisations to be exempt for negligently caused personal injury or death;
- providing protection for recreational service providers from liability for personal injury or death suffered by a voluntary participant in a recreational activity as a result of the materialisation of an obvious risk, or failing to give a warning or give notice of obvious risks;
- amendments to the *Trade Practices Act 1974* (Cth) relating to any negligently caused injury or death brought under Part IVA or Part V;
- amendments to the limitation period (to be three years from the date of discoverability) and the long-stop period (12 years after the events on which the claim is based), suspension of the limitation period for minors and incapacitated persons, and changes to the limitation principles where an action is brought by the personal representative of a deceased person; and
- contributions between tort feasors.

In summary, the effect of the changes that have taken place to date have been:

- codification, and in some cases variation, of certain common law rules of negligence in relation to foreseeability, standard of care, causation and remoteness of damage, contributory negligence, assumption of risk and mental harm as they affect claims for damages for harm suffered by a person due to the fault of another;
- establishment of restrictions for damages for harm suffered by a person due to the fault of another as a result of engaging in sporting and other recreational activities;
- introduction of a new public policy defence and a statutory protection for public and other authorities that carry out public functions. Unlike other jurisdictions, Tasmania has extended the removal of the duty of care obligation for public or other authorities where dangerous recreational activities are involved;
- replacing the concept of joint and several liability with proportionate liability as the basis for assessment of claims for damages for pure economic loss;
- providing protection from personal civil liability for good samaritans and volunteers; and
- permitting a person to give an apology without it amounting to an admission of liability.

A number of points should be noted about the legislative reforms that have taken place to date. First, the reforms do not represent a complete codification of the laws of negligence. They focus on a number of specific aspects identified by the Ipp Review as being in need of either restatement or reform. Second, the legislative reforms occurring in Australian jurisdictions are not uniform, and while the aim was to produce a consistent national approach to tort reform in accord with Ipp recommendation 1, as will be seen below, this has not occurred. Third, the full effect of the reforms to the laws of negligence will not be known for some time because it takes time for a matter to finally reach the courts. But what is clear is that many of the decisions prior to the reforms will still have application to the new statutory-based negligence action. Finally, cases currently coming before the appeal courts often involve questions of negligence based on pre-reform laws of negligence because the case at first instance pre-dated the reforms.

> This chapter discusses what has to be established in order for a plaintiff (P) to succeed in a negligence action against a defendant (D), both under the common law and in light of the reforms that have taken place with respect to the law of negligence. The following chapter looks at a number of torts that have been absorbed by negligence, as well as a number of categories of negligence, and the impact that the legislative reforms may have on these categories. In negligence, a person is only liable for harm that is the **foreseeable consequence** of their actions.

NEGLIGENCE AND HARM

When people hear the word '**negligence**' they generally take it to mean carelessness or thoughtlessness. However, this is not completely accurate even though the area of torts it falls under, that is, unintentional torts, may suggest otherwise. Careless acts do **not** necessarily amount to negligence and therefore lead to an action under the tort of negligence. A person is only liable for harm that is the **foreseeable consequence** of their actions, that is, their failure to exercise reasonable care and skill.

In negligence, a person is only liable for harm that is the *foreseeable consequence* of their actions

In *Lochgelly Iron and Coal v. M'Mullan* [1934] AC 1, Lord *Wright* said:

> *In strict legal analysis, negligence means more than needless or careless conduct, whether in omission or commission. It properly connotes the complex concept of duty, breach and damage thereby suffered by the person to whom the duty was owing.*

The states and the Australian Capital Territory have all adopted Ipp recommendation 2 that harm resulting from negligence should be subject to a single legal regime regardless of whether the claim is brought in contract, tort, under a statute, or under any other cause of action. This has the effect of overcoming the problem of the same event potentially being able to give rise to several different causes of action. For example, a patient injured by the carelessness of their doctor might sue the doctor in negligence and contract. The action in negligence would be based on the doctor's breach of their duty of care towards the patient, while in contract it would be based on breach of an implied contractual duty of care. If the reforms were only to apply to negligence, then it would be possible for the plaintiff to avoid them by choosing to bring the action in contract. However, the reforms generally apply to all claims for damages for failure to exercise reasonable care or skill, whether they are brought in tort, a claim for a breach of a non-delegable duty of care, in contract as a breach of a contractual duty of care, or as an action for breach of a statutory duty or warranty of reasonable care (Vic: s. 44, *Wrongs Act 1958*; NSW: ss. 3A, 3C, *Civil Liability Act 2002*; Qld: Sch. 2, *Civil Liability Act 2003*; SA: s. 51, *Civil Liability Act 1936*; WA: s. 5A, *Civil Liability Act 2002*; Tas: s. 10, *Civil Liability Act 2002*; ACT: s. 41, *Civil Law (Wrongs) Act 2002*).

The Northern Territory is yet to legislate on this issue

'Harm' is broadly defined and includes personal injury or death, damage to property or economic loss (Vic: s. 43; SA: s. 3; ACT: s. 40), although New South Wales, Queensland, Western Australia and Tasmania have extended this definition to include **any** civil claim for damages for harm (NSW: s. 3B; Qld: s. 4; WA: s. 3; Tas: s. 9).

IN BRIEF

A definition of negligence

Negligence is the omission to do something which a reasonable person would do, or doing something which a prudent and reasonable person would not do. It is the failure to exercise reasonable care and skill.

ELEMENTS OF NEGLIGENCE

The elements of an action based in negligence, whether at common law or under the civil liability legislation, are the same in title but not necessarily the same in content. They are:

Negligence consists of three elements: duty, breach, and damage

- **A duty of care**—this is a duty owed by one person (the **defendant**) to another (the **plaintiff**) and based on the relationship between them, i.e. foreseeable risk of injury and established to the satisfaction of the judge. **The common law position did not change under the civil liability reforms.**
- **A breach of the duty of care**—the plaintiff then has to establish whether the standard of care the defendant has exhibited has been breached. At common law this required consideration of two factors—the degree of foreseeable risk created by the defendant's conduct and the reasonableness or otherwise of the defendant's response—and was based on an objective standard of the reasonable person and how they would have responded to the foreseeable risk based on the facts of the case. Under the civil liability reforms to the laws of negligence, the reasonable person in the circumstances test has been replaced with a three-limb test (where all three elements

have to be satisfied—foreseeability, a risk that is not insignificant and that a reasonable person in D's position would have taken precautions). In addition, all jurisdictions have adopted a common set of general principles that a court **must** take into account in determining whether a reasonable person would have taken precautions against a risk of harm. In addition, some jurisdictions have also set out a number of 'other principles' that a court **should** take into account in determining liability.

- **Damage**—if there has been a breach of the duty of care by a failure to conform with the standard of care that a reasonable person would exercise, did the plaintiff suffer actual damage or loss and was that damage caused or contributed to by the defendant's breach (**causation**) and also a foreseeable consequence of that breach (the issue of **remoteness**)? Under the civil liability reforms, the onus is on the plaintiff to establish on the balance of probabilities any fact relevant to the issue of causation. All jurisdictions bar South Australia have also drawn a distinction between 'factual causation' and 'scope of liability' in an attempt to simplify the current tests used by the courts in relation to causation.

IN BRIEF

What has to be established?

The injured party (P) must establish on the **balance of probabilities** (it is a civil action) under both the common law and the civil liability reforms to the laws of negligence that have taken place that:

- the defendant owed them a duty of care;
- the defendant breached that duty of care to them; and
- they suffered actual loss or damage recognised by the law.

A typical negligence action can look as shown in Figure 7.1.

Step 1: Does the defendant owe a duty of care to the plaintiff?

P must establish duty of care owed by D—a *question of law* for the judge to decide

The onus is on the plaintiff to first **establish** that a duty of care was owed by the defendant. The decision as to whether or not it exists is **one of law for the judge**, taking into account the particular facts of the individual case.

The circumstances in which a duty to take reasonable care will arise were first described by Lord *Atkin* in *Donoghue v. Stevenson* [1932] AC 562 in terms of the 'neighbour principle':

> *The rule that you are to love your neighbour becomes in law, you must not injure your neighbour; and the lawyer's question, Who is my neighbour? receives a restricted reply. You must take reasonable care to avoid acts or omissions which you can reasonably foresee would be likely to injure your neighbour. Who in law, is my neighbour? The answer seems to be—persons who are so closely and directly affected by my act that I ought reasonably to have them in contemplation as being so affected when I am directing my mind to the acts or omissions which are called in question (at 580).*

The existence of a duty of care has historically been determined by reference to the test of **reasonable foreseeability of injury or damage** resulting from the defendant's act.

While there is no set formula to establish when this duty of care may arise, Lord *Atkin* suggested in *Donoghue v. Stevenson*:

- you must take reasonable care to avoid acts or omissions which you can reasonably foresee would be likely to injure your neighbour; and
- your neighbour is any person who is so closely and directly affected by what you do that you ought reasonably to have them in contemplation as being so affected when you are directing your mind to the acts or omissions which are called into question.

In *Donoghue v. Stevenson* it was reasonably foreseeable then that if the manufacturer failed to take care in the preparation of the ginger beer, so that a snail was included in it, the ultimate consumer could suffer injury. Therefore

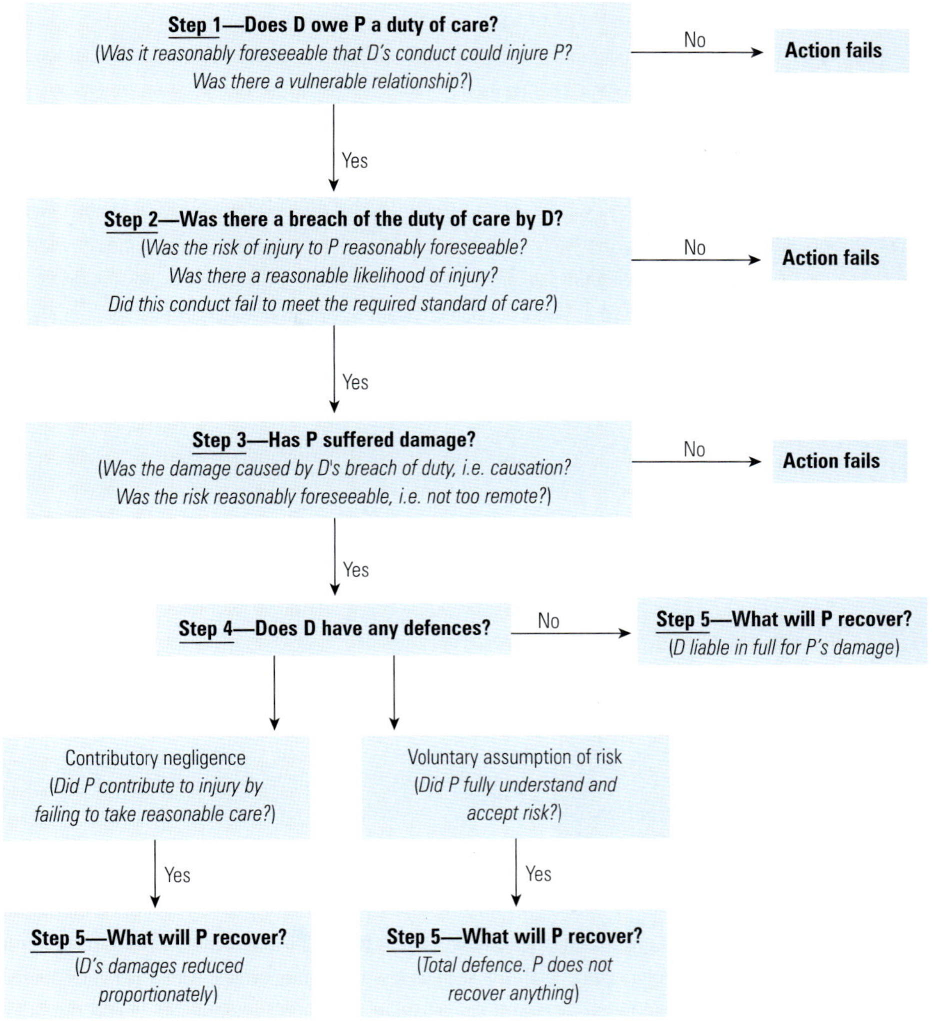

FIGURE 7.1 *Flow chart of negligence*

Donoghue was a 'neighbour' to the manufacturer and one to whom a duty of care was owed. The manufacturer had breached his duty of care to her and she had suffered damage as a result.

DONOGHUE V. STEVENSON [1932] AC 562

A friend bought a bottle of ginger beer for Donoghue. The ginger beer was in an opaque glass bottle. While in the course of drinking the contents of the bottle she noticed the decomposed remains of a snail. As a result, she became sick and suffered shock. She sued the manufacturer of the ginger beer (Stevenson), alleging that he had been careless in manufacturing his product by allowing a snail to be part of the contents.

ISSUE: As there was no contract between the plaintiff and the manufacturer (see the diagram following), was there any other legal ground upon which the manufacturer could be held responsible for the injury to the plaintiff?

DECISION: By a majority decision, the House of Lords held that the plaintiff was entitled to recover damages against the manufacturer in negligence. Any person who manufactures products in such a way that there is no reasonable possibility of intermediate examination before they reach the ultimate consumer, and who knows that the absence of reasonable care on their part will result in an injury to the consumer's life or property, owes a duty to the consumer to take reasonable care.

COMMENT: At the point in time this case was heard, i.e. 1932, this was the only possible legal avenue open to Donoghue. She didn't buy the drink, her friend did. This meant that she could not sue in contract, because there wasn't one. Nor could she rely on the sale of goods legislation, because she did not buy the drink. See the diagram below. Nor were there any remedies available, as there would be today, against the supplier or manufacturer, for example, under consumer protection legislation such as the *Trade Practices Act* (see Chapter 23).

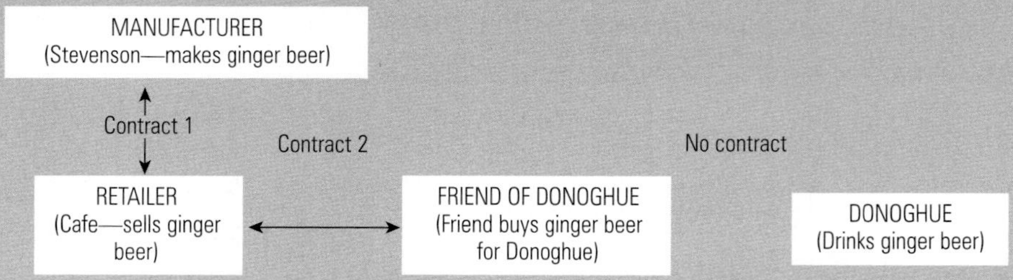

CASE REFLECTION: Would this principle only apply to situations where the goods are packaged and sealed? What other types of situation might it also apply to?

Failure to act generally will not create a duty situation

At common law there will generally be **no** breach of duty where physical harm or loss arises as a result of a **failure to act** as the liability for an omission involves the imposition of a duty to take positive action. The courts prefer to only impose an obligation to take care when acting, as this is seen as less of an interference with a person's liberty. Thus there is no duty to effect a rescue, and this is so even if the defendant has the means available to effect a rescue. For example, in *Council of the Shire of Sutherland v. Heyman* [1985] HCA 41; (1985) 157 CLR 424, *Brennan* J stated: 'A man on the beach is not legally bound to plunge into the sea when he can foresee that a swimmer might drown' [para 9]. However, this rule is subject to a number of exceptions, usually arising from reliance or dependence by the plaintiff on the defendant where a duty of care may arise to take positive action, for example, a driver may be held liable for causing damage through failing to indicate he/she was turning.

GOLDMAN V. HARGRAVE [1967] 1 AC 645

A tree on Goldman's farm was struck by lightning and caught fire. Goldman had the tree cut down and left the stump to burn itself out. Three days later the wind freshened and the fire revived, and because of the dry state of the land, the fire spread to his neighbour's land.

ISSUE: Was leaving the stump to burn itself out a reasonable step to take to ensure that the fire wouldn't flare up again, given the dry conditions? Was Goldman under a positive duty to take reasonable steps to reduce the risk?

DECISION: Goldman was liable for the spread of the fire to Hargrave's land. The existence of a duty must be based upon knowledge of the hazard, the ability to foresee the consequences of not checking or removing it, and the ability to abate it. Where the hazard could have been removed with little effort and no expenditure, Goldman should have ensured the fire was completely out.

COMMENT: In this case, nuisance was pleaded as an alternative action to negligence. The facts here are such that there is little material distinction between liability in nuisance and liability in negligence. In many cases the tort of nuisance overlaps the tort of negligence (see Chapter 9, pp. 202–205).

Other common law examples of situations where liability for an omission have arisen and positive action has been required include:

- **Doctor and patient**—a doctor is under a duty to warn a patient of the inherent risks in proposed procedures (*Rogers v. Whitaker* (1992) 175 CLR 479).
- **School authority and students**—school authorities are under a duty to take reasonable care of students while they are under the school's control (see *Mason* J, in *Commonwealth of Australia v. Introvigne* (1982) 150 CLR 258 at 269).
- **Local councils** entrusted with statutory powers to protect public safety (*Parrammatta City Council v. Lutz* (1988) 12 NSWLR 293 and *Pyrenees Shire Council v. Day* (1998) 192 CLR 330).
- **Statutory authorities** in the exercise of their statutory powers (*Crimmins v. Stevedoring Industry Finance Committee* (1999) 167 ALR 1).

The civil liability reforms provide some protection for professionals and public authorities

However, the majority of jurisdictions (WA and ACT aside, and the Northern Territory which is yet to introduce its changes to the laws of negligence) have introduced a new test for standard of care of professionals. A 'professional' is defined as a person practising a profession and includes doctors. The standard to be applied by the court in determining whether such a defendant has acted with due care is determined by reference to what could be reasonably expected of a person professing that skill (and not a greater level of skill) and the relevant circumstances as at the date of the alleged negligence and not a later date. A professional can avoid liability if it can be established that the professional acted in a manner that was widely accepted in Australia by peer professional opinion as competent professional practice, although such opinion cannot be relied upon if the court considers it unreasonable or there is a duty to warn of risk. In both cases the common law will continue to apply (Vic: Pt X, Div. 5, *Wrongs Act 1958*; NSW: Pt 1A, Div. 6, *Civil Liability Act 2002*; Qld: Chp't 2, Pt 1, Div. 5, *Civil Liability Act 2003*; SA: Chp't 2, Div. 4, *Civil Liability Act 1936*; WA: —; Tas: Pt 6, Div. 6, *Civil Liability Act 2002*; ACT: —).

Victoria (Pt XII), New South Wales (Pt 5), Queensland (Chp't 2, Pt 3, Div. 1), Western Australia (Pt 1C, *Civil Liability Act 2002*), Tasmania (Pt 9) and the Australian Capital Territory (Chap 8, *Civil Law (Wrongs) Act 2003*) have all modified the common law position by incorporating a number of general principles to be employed in determining whether a public or other authority owes a duty of care or has breached a duty of care. The principles that apply in determining the duty question for a public authority include the financial and other resources that are reasonably available to the authority for the purpose of exercising those functions (their general allocation not being open to challenge), the broad range of an authority's activities, evidence of compliance with general procedures and any applicable standards. For the purposes of an action against a public or other authority, there is not an absolute duty on an authority to do, or not do, a particular thing unless the act or omission of the authority was so unreasonable that no public authority with the same functions could properly consider the act or omission to be a reasonable exercise of its functions. 'Public or other authority' includes the Crown, a local government or any public authority.

Special protection is also given to road authorities for failure to carry out roadwork, unless the authority had actual knowledge of the particular risk which resulted in the harm. The South Australian provision is the broadest of all jurisdictions because it provides that a road authority is not liable in tort for a failure to maintain, repair or renew a road or to take other action to avoid or reduce the risk of harm that results from a failure to maintain, repair or renew a road. However, the section has only a two-year life before it will be reviewed (s. 42).

Doing business

If you make an attempt at an act, be careful

If you have already made **some attempt** at an act, there is a **duty** upon you to take reasonable care, particularly if previous actions may create a situation of reliance. ■

It seems that if you have already made **some attempt** at an act, there is a **duty** upon you to take reasonable care. However, the duty does not extend to that of an insurer. It only attaches where a person knows, or ought to know, by exercising reasonable care, of the existence of the danger. For example, previous actions may create a reliance situation.

MERCER V. SOUTH EASTERN AND CHATHAM RAILWAY COMPANIES' MANAGING COMMITTEE [1922] 2 KB 549

The defendant railway company normally closed the gates of a level crossing when a train was approaching. On one occasion the gates were accidentally left open and the plaintiff, who regularly used the crossing, was hit by a train as he was crossing.

ISSUE: Did the practice of closing the gates only when a train was approaching create a duty of care towards users of the crossing?

DECISION: The company's practice of closing the gates created reliance on the part of the plaintiff and a positive obligation on the defendants to ensure that the gates were closed when a train approached.

Tests for duty of care

Since the modern tort of negligence evolved in 1932, the courts have struggled to come up with a satisfactory test that can be used to determine whether a duty of care exists or not. The approach to the question of the existence of a duty of care today is determined by application of the 'foreseeability' test and whether there was a vulnerable or dependency relationship between the defendant and the plaintiff (see Figure 7.2). The test of proximity as a general criterion to

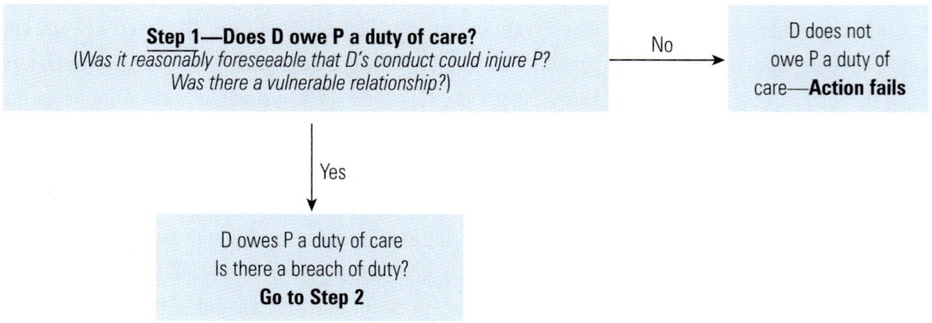

FIGURE 7.2 *Step 1 in establishing a negligence action—duty of care*

determine a duty of care was rejected by the High Court in a unanimous judgement in *Sullivan v. Moody* (2001) 75 ALJR 1570. Proximity has not been entirely rejected as it continues to be relevant in particular areas of negligence such as cases involving economic loss and mental harm.

The foreseeability test

IN BRIEF

What is foreseeability?

Foreseeability is a question of fact based on an objective test of whether a reasonable person would have foreseen the likelihood of injury, taking into account all the circumstances of the particular case.

Negligence consists in failure to take care against unreasonable risk of foreseeable injury

Negligence consists in failure to take care against unreasonable risk of foreseeable injury, **not** unforeseeable injury. To succeed in establishing a duty of care, the plaintiff must first prove that the defendant ought to have foreseen that negligence on the part of the defendant could lead to the plaintiff being injured. The court uses an objective test and what has to be shown by the plaintiff is that a reasonable person in the position of the defendant would have foreseen that the situation amounted to a real risk to the plaintiff.

***HAY (OR BOURHILL) V. YOUNG* [1943] AC 92**

A motor cyclist carelessly collided with a tram. The plaintiff, who had just alighted from the tram, was some 10 metres away and on the off-side of the tram at the time of the accident. She suffered nervous shock as a result of hearing the noise of the collision and then seeing the aftermath.

ISSUE: Could the defendant have foreseen either the risk of physical injury or the risk of nervous shock to her?

DECISION: It was not reasonably foreseeable to the motor cyclist that she (the plaintiff) would be injured as a result of his careless riding. She was physically outside the area of foreseeable danger and this in itself was sufficient to prevent her from recovering.

Duty of care is based on obviousness of risk

In some cases the duty of care is obvious and will not be an issue for the court, for example, a driver of a motor vehicle owes a duty of care to his or her passengers and other road users and a driver of a boat also owes a duty of care to his or her passengers. For example, in *Hanlon v. Hanlon* [2006] TASC 1, the plaintiff was suing her father-in-law (the defendant) for the death of her husband and one of their two sons in a boating accident. The defendant was driving the boat and had made a sharp turn to starboard at high speed, causing the boat to tip violently to the port side and throw all but one of the occupants overboard. Counsel for both parties accepted that the defendant owed a duty of care to his passengers and the Supreme Court also noted that the relationship between the defendant and his passengers gave rise to a duty of care. That duty was not to engage in conduct that might expose the passengers to the risk of harm [para 60]. In *Waverley Council v. Ferreira* [2005] NSWCA 418 (where the father brought an action against the council for their negligence following the death of his 12-year-old son who fell through a skylight on a Community Centre building located in a park, both of which were under the control of the Council), the Council did not dispute it owed a general duty of care as occupier of the park and building.

Was there a vulnerable relationship?

While the first question to establish a duty of care is whether the loss suffered by the plaintiff was reasonably foreseeable, a second question must be asked and it goes to the vulnerability of the plaintiff and control of the defendant. This requires consideration of three factors:

- Was the defendant in a controlling position through resources, knowledge or legal duty and aware of their position?
- Was the plaintiff reliant on the defendant?
- Was the defendant in such a position that required them to be protective of the plaintiff?

Duty of care and recreational activities

> **activebook**
> To help you to remember and understand the topics covered so far, and for links to legal websites, refer to your online activebook. Model answers provide feedback to problems and exercises.

Negligence is still a fault-based system (*Perre v. Apand Pty Ltd* (1999) 73 ALJR 1190 per *McHugh* J at 1214) and as a matter of law, there is a point at which those who indulge in pleasurable but risky pastimes must take personal responsibility for what they do. That point is reached when the risks are so well known and obvious that it can be reasonably assumed that the individuals concerned will take reasonable care for their own safety. Since the High Court handed down its decision in *Agar v. Hyde* (2000) 201 CLR 552, decisions by courts in other Australian jurisdictions have adopted a similar approach in shifting the acceptance of responsibility on to participants who wish to voluntarily participate in recreational activities where there are known potential risks of serious injury. For example, the scope of the duty of care was limited in the following cases:

- bodysurfing—*Prast v. Town of Cottesloe* (2000) 22 WAR 474 (bodysurfer dumped by a wave that rendered him tetraplegic);
- walking in a forest reserve—*Secretary to the Department of Natural Resources and Energy v. Harper* [2000] 1 VR 133 (walker injured by a tree falling in high wind while visiting a forest reserve);
- playing baseball—*Insurance Exchange v. Dooley* [2000] NSW CA 159 (16 August 2000) (fielder obstructed runner contrary to the rules of baseball and they collided and the fielder was injured); and
- playing indoor cricket—*Woods v. Multi-Sport Holdings Pty Ltd* (2002) 208 CLR 460 (cricketer suffered an eye injury while playing indoor cricket).

Whether a duty of care exists or not is a question of law. But it is a question that can only be answered by reference to the facts of each individual case. It is necessary to consider all the circumstances that may have a bearing on the relationship between the parties in order to determine whether, as a question of law, a duty of care exists. This includes:

- consideration of the risk of the particular injury which occurred;
- the relationship of the defendant to that risk; and
- the nature of the damage that the plaintiff suffered.

The factual question is to what extent, if any, is the risk of serious injury from participation in the recreational activity obvious? Is there a hidden danger which the defendant should be aware (for example, as in the diving cases) or is the danger obvious and inherent in the recreational activity being undertaken (for example, as in *Prast v. Town of Cottesloe* [2000] 22 WAR 474 where the plaintiff was bodysurfing in the ocean)? The legal question concerns the effect of the obviousness of the risk on the obligation to take reasonable steps to avoid foreseeable risk of injury. The relevant question is whether the defendant, with his or her state of knowledge, acted as a reasonably prudent person should have done once it is determined that a risk of injury exists. 'Was the defendant's failure to eliminate the risk demonstrative of a want of reasonable care for the plaintiff?' per *McHugh* J in *Tame v. New South Wales* (2002) 76 ALJR 1348 at 1364–5.

A participant in a recreational activity not only owes a duty of care to other participants to operate within the rules, but also a duty to take reasonable care for their own safety where they are voluntarily participating in 'high risk' recreational activities. Failure to exercise reasonable care in the former case may result in liability to an injured participant while in the latter case voluntary acceptance of the risk may act as a 'bar' to an action for damages.

In the case of sport, do the sport's rule makers owe a duty of care to participants to ensure that the rules do not unnecessarily place the players at risk?

***AGAR V. HYDE; AGAR V. WORSLEY* [2000] HCA 41**

Two amateur rugby union players broke their necks when scrums collapsed on top of them during the course of play. They alleged that, among other claims, the International Rugby Union Board, which was responsible for drawing up the rules of the game, was negligent in the way they had drawn up the rules relating to scrums.

ISSUE: Was a duty of care owed by the rugby union rule-making body to players?

DECISION: The High Court held that as amateur players who were aware of the risks inherent in playing rugby, the plaintiffs had to bear the consequences of their actions.

COMMENT: In the course of his judgement, *Gleeson* CJ at para 16 said of sport:

People who pursue recreational activities regarded as sports often do so in hazardous circumstances; the element of danger may add to the enjoyment of the activity. Accepting risk, sometimes to a high degree, is part of many sports. A great deal of public and private effort, and funding, is devoted to providing facilities for people to engage in individual or team sport. This reflects a view, not merely of the importance of individual autonomy, but also of the public benefit of sport. Sporting activities of a kind that sometimes result in physical injury are not only permitted; they are encouraged.

Where the risk is obvious, the plaintiff has to be prepared to accept the consequences of his or her actions, whether it be in sport or any type of recreational activity.

Who is the reasonable person?

Reasonable person is someone of normal intelligence

The reasonable person is someone of normal intelligence, credited with such perception of the surrounding circumstances and such knowledge of other pertinent matters as a reasonable person would possess. If a person professes to have a particular skill—for example, driving a car—he or she is required to show the skill normally possessed by persons claiming such a skill. The law requires the person to show such (reasonable) skill as any ordinary member of the profession or calling to which they belong would normally show.

Doing business

If there is knowledge of risk of injury, greater care should be taken

If an employer has a greater than average experience of a particular risk, greater precautions may have to be taken than would normally be the case. Did the defendant, with their state of knowledge, act as a reasonably prudent person should have done once it was determined that a risk of injury existed? Was the defendant's failure to eliminate the risk demonstrative of a want of reasonable care for the plaintiff? Similarly, if a business deals with infants, the standard to be applied is not the same as that of an adult but of a child of like age, intelligence and experience, thus requiring the business to take greater care. ■

In addition to infants, perhaps the aged, whose mental and physical faculties are impaired, are also a category apart.

It is this requirement of reasonableness which has substantially contributed to the flexibility inherent in the negligence action. It permits social judgements by the courts relevant to the times to be made within the law-making process.

Step 2: Has the defendant breached their duty of care

***Standard of care* is objective and a question of fact**

Once the plaintiff has established to the satisfaction of the court that the defendant owed him or her a duty of care (a question of law for the judge to decide), the plaintiff then has to establish that the defendant has breached that duty of care. Under the civil liability reforms (the 'reforms') to the laws of negligence, there is a degree of uniformity between the jurisdictions when assessing what is an appropriate standard of care.

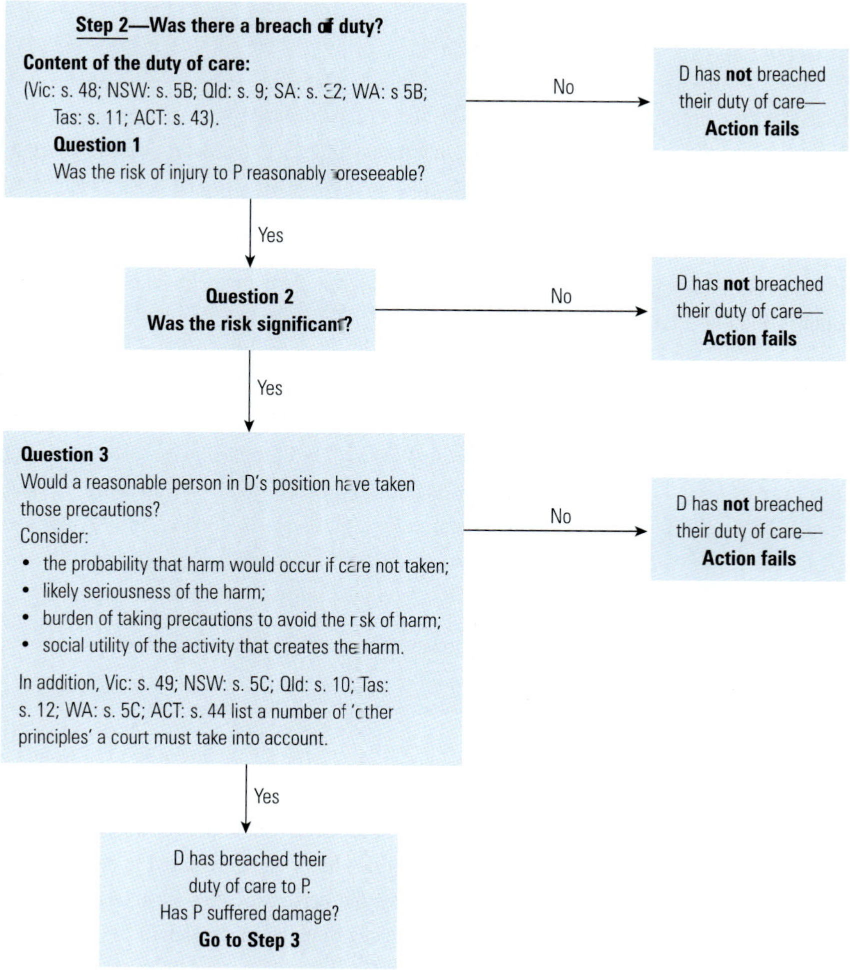

Note: References are to the following Acts: *Wrongs Act 1958*; NSW: *Civil Liability Act 2002*; Qld: *Civil Liability Act 2003*; SA: *Civil Liability Act 1936*; WA: *Civil Liability Act 2002*; Tas: *Civil Liability Act 2002*; ACT: *Civil Law (Wrongs) Act 2002*. The Northern Territory is still under the common law rules.

FIGURE 7.3 *Step 2 in establishing a negligence action—breach of duty*

At common law, the court is required to identify what a reasonable person in the position of the defendant would have done by way of response to the reasonably foreseeable risk (see *Graham Barclay Oysters Pty Ltd v. Ryan* (2002) 211 CLR 540). This question is similar to the first limb of the duty question under the reforms which provide that a person is **not** negligent in failing to take precautions against a risk of harm unless:

Two part test: first part goes to foreseeability of risk

- **there was foreseeable risk** (that is, it is a risk which the person knew or ought to have known based on what a 'reasonable person' would have known if they were in the position of the defendant); **and**
- **the risk was not insignificant** ('insignificant' risks include risks that are far-fetched or fanciful while risks that are 'not insignificant' are all other risks); **and**
- **in the circumstances, a reasonable person in the position of the defendant would have taken precautions** (Vic: s. 48(1); NSW: s. 5B(1); Qld: s. 9(1); SA: s. 32(1); WA: s. 5B(1); Tas: s. 11(1); ACT: s. 43(1)).

Second part goes to precautions a reasonable person might have taken

In deciding whether a reasonable person would have taken precautions against a risk of personal injury, **the court should consider** (not must consider) a number of factors, among other relevant things, in determining whether a reasonable person would have taken precautions against a risk of harm (or what measures a defendant could reasonably be expected to have taken to avoid the harm) including:

If probability of risk of injury is small, D may be able to disregard it

- **The probability that the harm would have occurred if care had been taken** (to be considered objectively). In *Boulton v. Stone* [1951] AC 850, the House of Lords found that a defendant may be justified in disregarding a foreseeable risk of injury where there was only a remote chance of being hit by a cricket ball while walking past the ground and one that a reasonable person would discount.

The greater the risk, the greater the demand for precautions

- **The likely seriousness of the harm** (to be considered objectively by reference to the particular circumstances of the case). In *Paris v. Stepney Borough Council* [1951] AC 367, the House of Lords held that where an employer knew that an employee had only one good eye and failed to provide safety goggles, while the risk of injury to the good eye was small, the consequences of injury were serious and so the employer was in breach of his duty of care to the employee when he was blinded in the good eye, i.e. he became completely blind.

If cost of removal of risk is low, D should remove it

- **The burden of taking precautions to avoid the risk of harm.** This requires the court to balance the risk against the measures necessary to eliminate the risk and includes consideration of cost. In *Woods v. Multi-Sport Holdings* (2002) 208 CLR 460, the High Court held that it was open for the trial judge to find that the defendant had not breached their duty of care by failing to provide an indoor cricketer with a helmet when such protective gear had yet to be designed or manufactured, and the rules of the game did not allow for the use of such helmets.

Is the activity of value to the community?

- **The social utility of the activity** that caused the harm. This refers to the idea that some activities are more worth taking risks for than others, e.g., playing sports has health benefits for the individual and for the community in terms of a healthier population, but sports also carry a higher risk of injury to a participant than to someone who does not play sport, so the benefits have to be weighed against the costs and a decision made accordingly (Vic: s. 48(2); NSW: s. 5B(2); Qld: s. 9(2); SA: s. 32(2); WA: s. 5B(2); Tas: s. 11(2); ACT: s. 43(2)).

These factors, in substance, are a reiteration of *Mason* J's remarks in *Wyong Shire Council v. Shirt* (1980) 146 CLR 40 at 47–8. However, they do **not** all have to be satisfied in order to establish breach. *Ipp* J in *Waverley Council v. Ferreira* [2005] NSWCA 418 at para 51 suggests that what they provide is a framework for deciding what precautions the reasonable person would have taken to avoid harm and this involves weighing up the first two factors against the last two factors (subject to each being applicable in the particular circumstances of the case. In *Ferreira*'s case below, for example, the court did not feel that social utility was an issue.)

WAVERLEY COUNCIL V. FERREIRA [2005] NSWCA 418

(While it is a New South Wales Court of Appeal decision and hence only of persuasive value in other Australian jurisdictions which have implemented civil liability reforms in the area of negligence, the case still provides a useful illustration of how courts in other jurisdictions may go about determining the issue of foreseeability and what sort of reasonable steps should be taken, if any, against a particular risk.)

A 12-year-old boy died when he fell through an unprotected skylight in a community centre situated in a park under the control and management of the local council. The park was designed to attract children and was equipped with swings and other playground equipment. The centre had erected a wire mesh fence around the building, but at the rear of the building the fence was attached to the building and surrounded by undergrowth. The undergrowth plus the wire mesh of the fence made it quite easy for children to climb on to the roof of the building. The Council was aware that children did climb on to the roof. The boy's father brought a claim for damages against the Council for mental harm as a result of the death of his son (under s. 32(1) of the Civil Liability Act).

ISSUE: While the Council accepted it owed a duty of care, did it breach its duty by failing to remove the fence and undergrowth and place a protective grille over the skylight (in this case, within the terms set out in s. 5B of the NSW Act)?

DECISION: The court found that the risk was foreseeable in terms of s. 5B(1)(a). It was established as a matter of fact that the defendant Council knew, or should have known, that children frequently climbed on to the roof of the building. It should then have been reasonably foreseeable to the Council that a child who climbed on to the roof might seriously injure themselves if they fell to the ground. In the circumstances, the risk was not insignificant (s. 5B(1)(b)) and a reasonable person in such a case would have taken precautions to avoid, or at least minimise, the risk (s. 5B(1)(c)).

COMMENT: In deciding whether a reasonable person would have taken precautions against a risk of harm (the s. 5B(2) criteria), the court found:

- there was a reasonable possibility of harm occurring if the fence and undergrowth were not removed and children were not prevented from using the fence to access the roof. Similarly, as the Council knew that children played on the roof, there was a reasonable possibility of a child falling through a skylight if a grille was not placed over it (satisfying s. 5B(2)(a)); **and**
- the likely seriousness of the harm should the risk occur (i.e. the consequences of falling of the roof) was serious injury or death (satisfying s. 5B(2)(b));
- the fence served no practical purpose and there was no reason to keep the undergrowth, and the cost for the Council of making reasonable inspections of the roof and skylights (and installing grilles) was small (satisfying s. 5B(2)(c)); **and**
- the social utility of the activity that creates the risk of harm was found not to be relevant in this case (s. 5B(2)(d)).

Weighing up the first two factors (ss. 5B(2)(a) and (b)) against the third (s. 5B(2)(c)), the court held that a reasonable council would have taken the precaution of removing the fence and undergrowth and installing grilles.

Some jurisdictions have set out a number of 'other principles' that a court should take into account in determining liability including:

- **the burden of taking precautions** to avoid a risk of harm, such as the burden of taking precautions to avoid similar risks of harm for which the person may be responsible (see, for example, in *Telstra Corporation Ltd v. Bisley* [2005] NSWCA 128, the Court of Appeal held that the primary judge was not in error in finding that Telstra could have taken appropriate precautions when they removed the cover over a pit without facing undue or disproportionate cost);
- **the fact that a risk of harm could have been avoided** by doing something in a different way does not of itself give rise to liability. The onus is on the plaintiff to prove that the method used was unreasonable in all the circumstances and that an alternative method existed that the defendant should have used; and
- **the subsequent taking of action** that would (had the action been taken earlier) have avoided a risk of harm does not of itself give rise to an admission of liability in connection with the risk (Vic: s. 49; NSW: s. 5C; Qld: s. 10; SA: s. —; WA: s. —; Tas: s. 12; ACT: s. 44).

What standard of care is expected of the reasonable person?

The reasonable person is equipped with the same skills and expertise as a person exercising a particular trade or profession. This means that it is generally not acceptable to argue that inexperience should be a valid excuse for failure to attain a standard of care that would ordinarily be expected of a person in that position.

Is the standard of care flexible?

Standard of care is flexible

The standard of care will **vary** from situation to situation and is flexible.

In an ordinary action in negligence where the plaintiff is a passenger who has been injured in a motor vehicle driven by the defendant, the relationship of proximity is simply that of driver and passenger. Normally the standard of care required is the degree of care of an experienced and competent driver.

COOK V. COOK (1986) 162 CLR 376

The appellant, to the knowledge of the respondent, had never held a driver's licence or a learner's permit. She was invited by the respondent to drive the respondent's husband's car for practice, while the respondent rode as a passenger. The appellant, while attempting to drive between a parked car and a fence, accelerated and hit a concrete pole, injuring the respondent.

ISSUE: What standard of care should apply in the case of a learner driver?

DECISION: The High Court held that the standard of care was that of the inexperienced driver. However, the learner driver's conduct in accelerating rather than braking, or even slowing down to avoid a parked car, fell below even the standard of an inexperienced driver.

COMMENTS: If there are special and exceptional circumstances that can transform the relationship between the parties outside the usual category, then an adjustment of the ordinary standard of care is justified. As the plaintiff encouraged the defendant's driving, and by her actions she undertook to supervise it, that special element of the relationship (i.e. the inexperience and incompetence) took it out of the ordinary standard of care and adjusted it to the standard of the ordinary inexperienced driver.

CASE REFLECTION: If an accounting firm assigned an inexperienced trainee accountant to prepare the books of account and tax return for a client, would the firm have to satisfy the standard of care of the average fully qualified accountant or the standard of care of an inexperienced trainee accountant? Why?

The reasonable person in the case of a child is a child of similar age and experience

In relation to children, the reasonable person test gives way to the standard of a **child of similar age and experience**. Children are assumed to be less capable than adults in taking care of themselves. Therefore, those who are placed in a position of responsibility for children, directly or indirectly, must make their safety the foremost concern and carry a more onerous duty of care. In *Waverley Council v. Ferreira* above, the court rejected the argument of the Council that it was entitled to expect a child having the capacity to climb on to a roof to take sufficient care for his own safety and not put his weight on a skylight. In the court of first instance, the judge had noted that 12-year-old boys will climb on to roofs without any real appreciation of the danger. They do not perceive danger in the same way an adult perceives danger.

MCHALE V. WATSON (1966) 115 CLR 199

A 12-year-old-boy threw a dart at a tree. The dart bounced off the tree and struck a 9-year-old girl in the eye.

ISSUE: Should the reasonable person be applied in the context of the age of a 12-year-old?

DECISION: The High Court held that the standard of care to be applied was that of a 'child of the relevant age'—in this case, a 12-year-old.

COMMENT: While *McTiernan* J thought that an adult would have realised the risk of the dart glancing off the tree and hurting a bystander, the boy was judged by a lower standard.

At common law

At common law the onus is on the plaintiff to satisfy the judge that a duty of care is owed by the defendant. **The standard of care is objective** and the **standard** required is that of the **reasonable person** standing in the place of the defendant. Thus, failing to adopt the usual practice in similar circumstances that others would adopt may be evidence of failing to observe the standard of care which a reasonable person would follow. This is a question of **fact** in each case and focuses on the conduct of the defendant and the risks created by their conduct.

In the case of children, the standard is that of a child of similar age and experience. As such, it is a standard that will vary from case to case and which hasn't changed under the civil liability reforms to the laws of negligence.

In considering the question of the standard of care the court asks two questions:

- *Was the risk of injury to the plaintiff reasonably foreseeable?* This is a **question of law**. The issues the court considers are similar to those looked at when trying to determine whether the defendant owed a duty of care. If the answer is 'yes', i.e. that the risk in question was foreseeable, the court then considers the second question.
- *Was there a reasonable likelihood of the injury occasioned by it?* In *Wyong Shire Council v. Shirt* (1980) 146 CLR 40 the High Court suggested that a person cannot be held liable for failure to take precautions against a risk that could be described as 'far-fetched or fanciful', even if it was foreseeable, and the High Court has since approved that approach on a number of occasions, including as recently as late 2005 in *Vairy v. Wyong Shire Council* [2005] HCA 62 and *Mulligan v. Coffs Harbour City Council* [2005] HCA 63. The former case involved a swimmer diving from a rock platform into the ocean, and the latter, a swimmer diving thigh deep into a tidal creek where he had dived successfully on a number of occasions before he was injured, but in both cases the High Court emphasised the proposition that people ought to take reasonable care for their own safety and was not prepared to accept that the councils were in breach of their duty.

  Mason J in the *Wyong* case at 47–8 suggested it was necessary to take into account four factors in deciding what precautions the reasonable person would have taken to avoid the harm that had occurred and, hence, what precautions the defendant could reasonably be expected to have taken, and these factors have been largely incorporated into the civil liability reforms, including:
  - the probability that the harm would have occurred if care had been taken. Where the risk is small and the circumstances are such that a reasonable person would think it right to neglect it, the defendant **may** be justified in disregarding such a foreseeable risk of injury;
  - the likely seriousness of the harm. The greater the risk, the greater the demand for precautions on the part of the defendant;
  - the burden of taking precautions to avoid the risk of harm. If the cost of eliminating a risk is low and will cause little or no inconvenience, a defendant's failure to take such steps will not be justifiable. However, where the cost of eliminating the risk is not economically justifiable, a different outcome may result, although the social utility of the defendant's conduct is really a policy issue for the judge to decide. The judge may have to balance the risk to the plaintiff against the overall benefit to the community; and
  - the social utility of the activity that caused the harm. If the activity is of value to the community, e.g., by improving the general health and wellbeing of the community through improved fitness by the playing of sport, and the risk of serious injury is not high, the defendant may be justified in continuing the activity.

Once it is determined that a risk of injury exists, the question then is: *Was the defendant's failure to eliminate the risk demonstrative of a want of reasonable care for the plaintiff?* per *McHugh* J in *Tame v. New South Wales* (2002) 76 ALJR 1348 at 1364–5.

Doing business

Take steps to reduce the reasonable likelihood of injury

Whether dealing under the common law or the civil liability reforms, the onus is on P to show that it was reasonably practicable for D to take precautions against the risk, and once P has done so, the burden of proof switches to D to establish that it was unreasonable in the circumstances to take such precautions. Risk management principles suggest that constant monitoring of:

- the probability of risk;
- the seriousness of the consequences if something were to occur; and
- the opportunities for, and cost of, eliminating the risk

are all serious concerns of a responsible business manager if liability for the business is to be minimised. ■

Step 3: Has the plaintiff suffered damage?

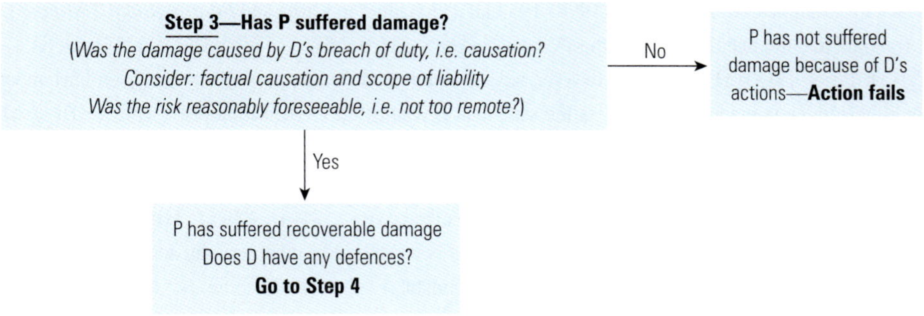

FIGURE 7.4 *Step 3 in establishing a negligence action—damage*

P must show some loss or damage

Under both the common law and the civil liability reforms, the plaintiff must show that some **loss** or **damage** was suffered as a result of the defendant's breach of duty (see Figure 7.4). Damage may be:

- economic (e.g., lost or missed sales);
- to property (e.g., damage caused by faulty plumbing or electrical wiring); or
- to the person (e.g., a broken arm or leg as a result of a motor vehicle accident) as long as there is actual damage.

This raises two more questions for the plaintiff to prove:

- that the loss or damage to the plaintiff was 'directly caused' by the defendant's breach of their duty of care (**causation**); and
- that the loss or damage to the plaintiff was 'not too remote' from the breach (**remoteness of damage**).

Civil liability reforms to causation

***Causation*—consists of factual causation and scope of liability**

The reforms set out a number of general principles concerning causation and whether negligence caused the particular harm, with the onus of proof on the plaintiff based on the balance of probabilities (Vic: Pt X, Div. 3; NSW: Pt 1A, Div. 3; Qld: Chp't 2, Pt 1, Div. 2; SA: Pt 6, Div. 2; WA: Pt 1A, Div. 3; Tas: Pt 6, Div. 3; ACT: Chp't 4, Pt 4.3). While the provision in part codifies the existing law, it also goes further by drawing a distinction between 'factual causation' and 'scope of liability' in an attempt to simplify the current tests used by the courts in relation to causation.

A decision as to whether a breach of duty on the part of the defendant caused particular harm comprises two elements:

- **factual causation**—that is, if the defendant had acted carefully, would the plaintiff have suffered this particular loss. Did the defendant cause the harm?; and
- that it is appropriate for the scope of the negligent person's liability to extend to the harm so caused (**scope of liability**)—should the defendant be held responsible for the harm? This effectively absorbs the issue of remoteness

(Vic: s. 51(1); NSW: s. 5D(1); Qld: s. 11(1); SA: s. 34(1); WA: s. 5C(1); Tas: s. 13(1); ACT: s. 45(1)).

In the case of exceptional circumstances (some jurisdictions use the expression 'appropriate case'), where a breach of duty is established but does not satisfy the requirement of 'factual causation', the court is required to consider, among other relevant things, whether or not and why responsibility for the harm should be imposed on the defendant (Vic: s. 51(2); NSW: s. 5D(2); Qld: s. 11(2); SA: —; WA: s. 5C(2); Tas: s. 13(2); ACT: —).

If it is relevant to deciding factual causation to determine what the person who suffered harm would have done if the negligent person had not been negligent, the matter is decided subjectively, that is, what the injured person would have done, in the light of all relevant circumstances as distinct from the objective test of the conduct of a reasonable person (see for example *Chappell v. Hart* (1998) 195 CLR 232 (failure to warn) and *Bonnington v. Wardlaw* [1956] AC 613 (plaintiff had not been provided with safety gear) (Vic: s. 51(3); NSW: s. 5D(3); Qld: s. 11(3)(a); SA: —; WA: s. 5C(3)(a); Tas: s. 13(3)(a); ACT: —). However, any statement made by the person who has been hurt about what they would have done is inadmissible, unless the statement is against the person's interest (NSW: s. 5D(3)(b); Qld: s. 11(3)(b); SA: —; WA: s. 5C(3)(b); Tas: s. 13(3)(b); ACT: —).

In deciding the scope of liability, the court has to consider among other things whether or not, and why, responsibility for the harm should be imposed on the defendant (Vic: s. 51(4); NSW: s. 5D(2); Qld: s. 11(4); SA: s. 34(3); WA: s. 5C(4); Tas: s. 13(4); ACT: s. 45(3)). This is a value judgement and the section does little to help determine when it is appropriate to extend liability to a defendant.

In deciding liability for breach, the plaintiff must establish on the balance of probabilities any fact relevant to the issue of causation (Vic: s. 52; NSW: s. 5E; Qld: s. 12; SA: s. 35; WA: s. 5D; Tas: s. 14; ACT: s. 46). This reverses the current position where the onus has been on the defendant once it has been established that the plaintiff was owed a duty of care and the defendant had breached that duty, and that the plaintiff had suffered a foreseeable injury.

If there are a number of possible defendants and it is not possible to assign responsibility for causing harm to any one of them, the courts may assign responsibility under existing common law principles to all the defendants, but in doing so it must consider the position of each defendant individually and state the reasons for bringing the defendant within the scope of liability (SA: s. 34(2); ACT: s. 45(2)).

Causation at common law

In negligence, causation determines not only the extent of the damages recoverable, but also whether the action succeeds at all. There is no cause of action unless the plaintiff proves that the damage suffered was **caused** by the defendant's breach of duty.

The general test used by the courts, though it is not always appropriate (e.g., if there is more than one cause), is the '**but for**' test. Here the assumption is that the defendant's fault is a cause of the plaintiff's harm. Therefore, the harm would not have occurred to the plaintiff 'but for' the defendant's actions. If the harm would have happened in any event, then the defendant's negligence is not the effective cause of the plaintiff's damage.

ALEXANDER V. CAMBRIDGE CREDIT CORPORATION LTD (IN REC.) **(1987) 9 NSWLR 310**

The receiver of Cambridge Credit alleged that the auditors had negligently certified the company's accounts as being a true and fair view of its financial position in 1971. If the auditors had not been negligent, the company's debenture holders would have been alerted to the true financial position of the company and would have acted to appoint a receiver immediately. The auditors argued that Cambridge's losses had been caused by three factors—government policies, the collapse of the land boom and the company's own business decisions.

ISSUE: Did the company suffer the loss because of the auditor's report or because of other factors?

DECISION: The auditors were not negligent because no causal connection could be established between their breach in 1971 and the loss suffered by the company by reason of its collapse, or that the company had even relied on the audit report.

COMMENT: The trial judge found that, but for the negligence of the auditors, the true financial position of the company would have been revealed in 1971 and it would have been able to avoid the losses it subsequently incurred. He saw the negligent audit as the direct cause of the collapse of the company. The Appeal Court saw the other factors as intervening between the negligent audit and the collapse, so in its view there was no direct cause.

CASE REFLECTION: If a person jumped off a pedestrian overpass bridge and, just before the person hit the ground, the person was struck by a car travelling along the highway, would the car driver be responsible for the person's injuries?

In *Chappel v. Hart* (1998) 72 ALJR 1344 the High Court approved its earlier decision in *March v. Stramare (E & MH) Pty Ltd* (1991) 171 CLR 506 where the High Court specifically rejected the 'but for' test as the exclusive test of factual causation. *McHugh* J at 1350 explained how the issue of causation must now be approached:

> *Before the defendant will be held responsible for the plaintiff's injury, the plaintiff must prove that the defendant's conduct materially contributed to the plaintiff suffering that injury. In the absence of a statute or undertaking to the contrary, therefore, it would seem logical to hold a person causally liable for a wrongful act or omission only when it increased the risk of injury to another person. If a wrongful act or omission results in an increased risk of injury to the plaintiff and that risk eventuates, the defendant's conduct has materially contributed to the injury that the plaintiff suffers whether or not other factors also contributed to that injury occurring. If, however, the defendant's conduct does not increase the risk of injury to the plaintiff, the defendant cannot be said to have materially contributed to the injury suffered by the plaintiff. That being so, whether the claim is in contract or tort, the fact that the risk eventuated at a particular time or place by reason of the conduct of the defendant does not itself materially contribute to the plaintiff's injury unless the fact of that particular time or place increased the risk of injury occurring.*

The issue of causation was raised in *Cook v. Australian Capital Territory Racing Club Incorporated and the Australian Jockey Club* [2001] ACTSC 106 where the court applied the 'common sense' test referred to in *March v. Stramare* (1991) 171 CLR 506 and *Chappel v. Hart* (1998) 195 CLR 232 in order to determine whether the heart attack of a jockey had been caused by dehydration from excessive use of the sauna. In *Cook*'s case, a former leading professional jockey suffered a heart attack while weight reducing in a sauna that was provided for jockeys at the Canberra race course. The court had to consider whether the sauna and the dehydration associated with its use was the major cause of the heart attack and came to the conclusion that it was.

In *Kenny & Good Pty Ltd v. MGICA (1992) Ltd* (1999) 73 ALJR 901 the High Court held that the facts satisfied both the 'but for' test and the tests in *Chappel v. Hart*.

KENNY & GOOD PTY LTD V. MGICA (1992) LTD (1999) 73 ALJR 901

As a result of a valuation by a real estate valuer (the defendant), a bank advanced a loan to the owner secured by a mortgage over the property. The bank insured the mortgage over the property with a mortgage insurer (the plaintiff). When the owner defaulted on the loan, the bank sold the property under its power of sale but it wasn't enough to cover the loan and so they claimed on their mortgage insurance policy.

ISSUE: Was the real estate valuer negligent? Was there some causal connection between the breach of duty of care and the damage suffered?

DECISION: The High Court found that on the facts the 'but for' test was satisfied. The facts also satisfied the tests in *Chappel v. Hart* because the negligence of the valuer was directly responsible for the making of the insurance contract by the plaintiff. If the valuation had been a correct one, there would have been no loss suffered by the plaintiff as it would not have given the mortgage insurance at all.

Remoteness at common law

***Remoteness*—would a reasonable person foresee such a happening?**

The consequences of negligent conduct can continue indefinitely and the 'remoteness of damage' question allows the court to consider whether, and to what extent, a defendant should have to answer for the consequences of their negligent conduct. This is now part of scope of liability under the civil liability reforms.

The question to consider is whether the defendant could have reasonably foreseen the loss that occurred. Where the possibility of damage as a result of a careless act by the defendant is considered to be too remote, damages cannot be recovered. This is a **question of law** to be determined by the judge and the test used is that of **foreseeability**—could a reasonable person foresee such a happening? There has to be a real risk, one which would occur to the mind of a reasonable person in the defendant's position and which would not be ignored as being far-fetched.

OVERSEAS TANKSHIP (UK) LTD V. MORTS DOCK & ENGINEERING CO. [1961] AC 388 (ALSO KNOWN AS *THE WAGON MOUND NO. 1*)

The defendants carelessly discharged oil from their ship, *The Wagon Mound*, into Sydney Harbour. The wind and tide carried the oil beneath the plaintiff's wharf where welding operations were being carried on by the plaintiff's employees. After being advised that they could safely weld, the plaintiff's employees continued their work. Some 55 to 60 hours after the original discharge, molten metal set some waste floating in the oil on fire. The flames quickly developed into a large fire which severely damaged the wharf. The oil also inhibited the use of the plaintiff's slipways.

ISSUE: Was damage to the wharf by fire from the welding operations reasonably foreseeable?

DECISION: While it was found as a matter of fact that damage to the wharf by the fouling of the plaintiff's slipways was foreseeable, damage by fire was not reasonably foreseeable. Thus, the defendants were not liable because the fire was not a foreseeable consequence of their negligence.

CASE REFLECTION: Could it be argued that the fire would not have occurred but for the continuation of the welding operations? If the welding operations were stopped due to safety reasons associated with the oil, could the wharf owner have claimed compensation for loss of production?

In *Overseas Tankship (UK) Ltd v. Miller Steamship Co. Pty (The Wagon Mound No. 2)* [1967] AC 617 (PC) the plaintiff owner of a ship damaged by the fire started by the discharge of the oil from *The Wagon Mound* catching fire due to the welding operations succeeded in an action against the owners of *The Wagon Mound.* According to the Privy Council, the plaintiff shipowner was able to prove that the damage in question was reasonably foreseeable and therefore not too remote.

Step 4: What defences will a defendant raise?

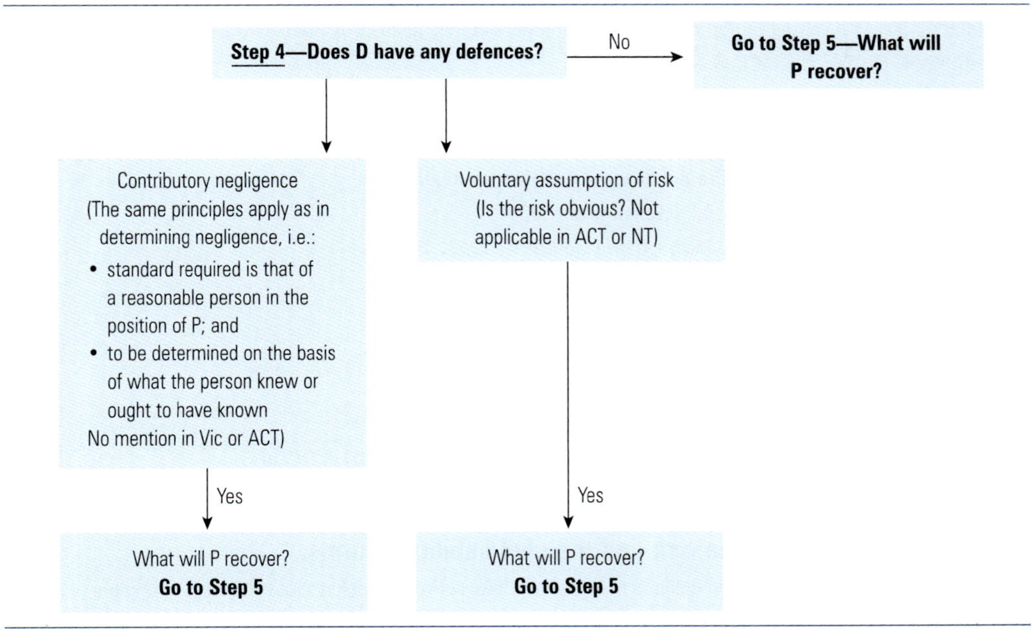

FIGURE 7.5 *Step 4 in establishing a negligence action—defences*

In addition to the defences of contributory negligence and voluntary assumption of the risk, in very exceptional cases the following defences could be raised:

- self-defence
- act of God
- a defence based on statutory authority
- mistake.

Contributory negligence under the civil liability reforms

Apart from the Northern Territory, all the states and the Australian Capital Territory have incorporated principles into their civil law reforms that are applicable in determining contributory negligence. South Australia and Western Australia aside, all jurisdictions have also altered the common law by specifically allowing the court, where it thinks it just and equitable, to reduce a plaintiff's claim by 100 per cent, thereby defeating the plaintiff's claim (Vic: s. 63; NSW: s. 5S; Qld: s. 24; SA: —; WA: —; Tas: s. 4(1), *Wrongs Act 1954*; ACT: s. 47). This overcomes the High Court ruling in

Wynbergen v. Hoyts Corporation Pty Ltd (1997) 149 ALR 25 and *Astley v. Austrust Ltd* (1999) 73 ALJR 403 (a case involving the apportionment legislation of South Australia held that apportionment for contributory negligence only applied in a tort action).

***Contributory negligence*—the principles applicable are the same as for determining negligence**

The principles that are applicable in determining whether a person has been negligent also apply in determining whether the person who has suffered harm has been contributorily negligent (Vic: s. 62(1); NSW: s. 5R(1); Qld: s. 23(1); SA: s. 44(1); WA: s. 5K(1); Tas: s. 23(1); ACT: —). As for the common law, contributory negligence must be pleaded and proved by the defendant.

To determine whether a plaintiff has been contributorily negligent, the standard of care is based on a reasonable person in the position of the plaintiff and the matter will be decided on the basis of what the person knew or ought to have known at the time (Vic: s. 62(2); NSW: s. 5R(2); Qld: s. 23(2); SA: —; WA: s. 5K(2); Tas: s. 23(2)). If the plaintiff is an infant, the standard of care is that of an infant—see, for example, *Waverley Council v. Ferreira* [2005] NSWCA 418 above on page 133.

There is a presumption of contributory negligence if the person who suffers harm was intoxicated or if the person who suffers injury was relying on the care and skill of a person they knew to be intoxicated (NSW: s. 50; Qld: s. 47; SA: s. 46; WA: s. 5L; Tas: s. 5; ACT: ss. 92, 95, 96).

Apportionment of damages are based on what is fair and reasonable between the parties (see Table 7.1).

Table 7.1 Legislation governing the defence of contributory negligence

Victoria	ss. 62, 63 *Wrongs Act 1958*
New South Wales	ss. 5R, 5S, *Civil Liability Act 2002*
Queensland	ss. 23, 24, 47, *Civil Liability Act 2003*
South Australia	ss. 44, 45, *Wrongs Act 1936*
Western Australia	ss. 5K, 5L, *Civil Liability Act 2002, Div. 5*
Tasmania	ss. 4(1), 5, 23(1), *Civil Liability Act 2002*
Australian Capital Territory	ss. 47, 92, 95, 96, *Civil Law (Wrongs) Act 2002*
Northern Territory	s. 16, *Law Reform (Miscellaneous Provisions) Act 1956*

Voluntary assumption of the risk and the civil liability reforms

In essence, the civil liability reforms to the laws of negligence have revived the defence of voluntary assumption of risk to a negligence action in general, that is, it is no longer going to be limited to just sporting situations. Using it as a complete defence in other areas was very difficult because it had to be established that the plaintiff had a precise knowledge of the risk, a full and free understanding and appreciation of the particular risk, and voluntarily accepted that risk.

***Voluntary assumption of risk*—is the risk an obvious one?**

The Northern Territory aside, all the states and the Australian Capital Territory jurisdictions have amended the common law defence of voluntary assumption of risk (*volenti non fit injuria*) in a limited way. A distinction is drawn between 'obvious' risk and 'inherent' risk. An 'obvious' risk is a risk that, in the circumstances, would have been obvious to a reasonable person in the position of the defendant and includes risks that are patent or matters of common knowledge, risks that may have a low probability of occurring and risks that are not prominent, conspicuous or physically observable. It involves a blend of subjective and objective elements (Vic: s. 53; NSW: s. 5F; Qld: s. 13; SA: s. 36; WA: s. 5F; Tas: s. 15; ACT: —).

Where the defence is raised and the risk of harm is an obvious one, the plaintiff is presumed to have been aware of the risk, unless the plaintiff can prove on the balance of probabilities that he or she was not aware of the risk. For the purposes of the defence, a person is said to be aware of a risk if the person is aware of the type or kind of risk. It is not necessary to know its precise nature, extent or manner of occurrence. To raise the defence, the defendant must establish that the risk was such that a reasonable person in the position of the plaintiff would have taken steps to avoid it (Vic: ss. 54(1), 56; NSW: s. 5G; Qld: s. 14; SA: s. 37; WA: s. 5N; Tas: s. 16; ACT: —).

A defendant does not owe a duty of care to a plaintiff to warn of an obvious risk unless the plaintiff has asked for advice about the risk. The defendant is required by statute to warn the plaintiff of the risk if the risk is a risk of injury or death to the plaintiff from the provision of a health care service (in Victoria and South Australia this includes a diagnostic, therapeutic or any other service directed or aimed at maintaining or restoring health: s. 3A) by the defendant (Vic: s. 54(2); NSW: s. 5H; Qld: s. 15; SA: s. 38; WA: s. 50; Tas: s. 17; ACT: —).

The civil liability reforms in all jurisdictions, except Tasmania and the Australian Capital Territory (ACT: Sch. 3 only refers to inherent risks in the context of equine activities) which have preserved the common law position, have codified the common law position insofar as a person is not liable in negligence for harm suffered by another person as a result of materialisation of an inherent risk. However, this does not exclude liability in connection with a duty to warn of a risk. An 'inherent risk' is a risk of something occurring which cannot be avoided by the exercise of reasonable care and skill (Vic: s. 55; NSW: s. 5I; Qld: s. 16; SA: s. 39; WA: s. 5P; Tas: —).

Apologies or expressions of regret

Making an apology is no longer treated as a clear admission of fault. An individual can generally now express regret in connection with any matter alleged to have been caused by them without it being construed as an admission of fault or liability (Vic: s. 14J; NSW: s. 69; Qld: ss. 70–72; SA: s. 39; WA: s. 5AH; Tas: s. 7; ACT: s. 12; NT: s. 13).

Step 5: What will the plaintiff recover?

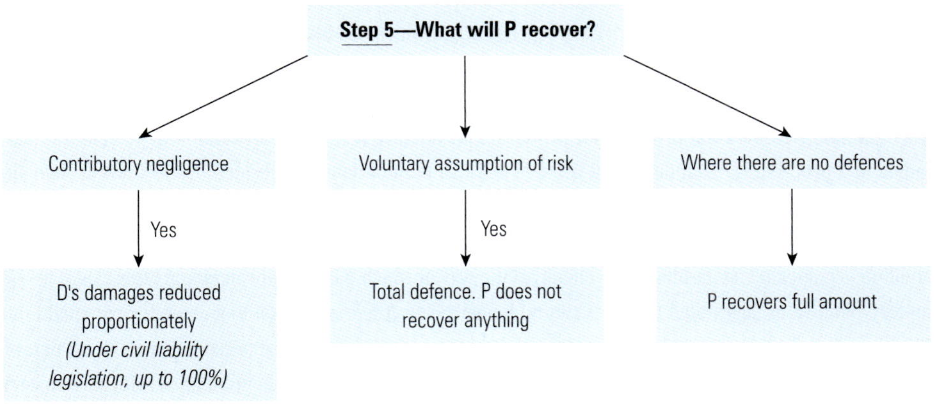

FIGURE 7.6 *Step 5 in establishing a negligence action—damages*

Generally in a tort action the plaintiff will be seeking monetary compensation for the damage they have suffered. This could be damage to the person or property damage (see Figure 7.6).

Measure of damage is concerned with the question of the **amount** the defendant must pay for the damage that has been inflicted on the plaintiff and for which liability has been established. The exact amount the defendant will have to pay will be determined by whether they have any defences that they can raise against the plaintiff's claim.

Measure of damages is concerned with a $$ amount

As part of their civil liability reforms, all jurisdictions have introduced legislation to try to contain compensation payouts by the courts for personal injury in the belief that this will lead to a slowdown in premium increases for third party and public liability insurance:

- **Commonwealth**—the *Taxation Laws Amendment (Structured Settlements and Structural Orders) Act 2002* removes tax disincentives for agreeing to or awarding structured settlements. The *Trade Practices Amendment (Personal Injuries and Death) Act 2006* amends the Trade Practices Act to prevent individuals, and the Australian Competition and Consumer Commission in a representative capacity, from bringing actions for damages for personal injuries or death resulting from contraventions of Division 1 of Part V of the Act (dealing with unfair practices). The amendments do not apply to actions for damages resulting from contraventions of Division 1 of Part V relating to smoking or other use of tobacco products.

- **Victoria**—the *Wrongs and Other Acts (Public Liability Insurance Reform) Act 2002*, incorporated into the *Wrongs Act 1958*, limits the amounts that may be recovered as damages for death or personal injury caused by the fault of a person and giving courts the power to order structured settlements as an alternative to lump sum payouts for future economic loss.

  The *Wrongs and Limitation of Actions Acts (Insurance Reform) Act 2003* amended the *Wrongs Act 1958* by, among other things, providing for thresholds in relation to the recovery of damages for non-economic loss, limiting the damages that may be awarded for gratuitous attendant care services, and providing for proportionate liability in proceedings for economic loss.
- **New South Wales**—the *Civil Liability Act 2002* introduced procedures for personal injuries damages claims for personal injury or death including caps and thresholds on personal injury damages, limits on legal costs in small personal injury damages claims, and restrictions on bringing or defending claims without reasonable prospects of success.

  The *Civil Liability Amendment (Personal Responsibility) Act 2002*, imported into the *Civil Liability Act 2002*, gave the courts power to order structured settlements as an alternative to lump sum payouts for future economic loss. Provision was also made for proportionate liability by providing if that there was more than one defendant in a proceeding, each defendant was liable to an amount of damages decided by the court as being just and equitable having regard to the extent of the defendant's responsibility for the harm.
- **Queensland**—the *Personal Injuries Proceedings Act 2002*, which has been incorporated into the *Civil Liability Act 2003*, introduced pre-litigation procedures for personal injuries damages claims. The *Civil Liability Act 2003* subsequently gave the courts power to give the parties a reasonable opportunity to negotiate a structured settlement.

  The *Civil Liability Act 2003* provided for proportionate liability. It also provided that if there is more than one defendant in a proceeding, each defendant is liable to an amount of damages decided by the court as being just and equitable having regard the extent of the defendant's responsibility for the harm. While the liability of each defendant is initially several only, provision is made for liability to be joint and several in certain circumstances. In addition, significant changes have been made to the way in which damages for personal injuries are assessed. Exemplary, punitive or aggravated damages can no longer be awarded in relation to a claim for personal injury damages unless the act was an unlawful intentional act done with intent to cause personal injury or an unlawful sexual act. A defendant will now be able to suggest specified action a plaintiff should take to mitigate damages. Assessment of personal injury damages will be calculated according to a scale running from 0 to 100 against which awards for general damages for personal injuries will be assessed.
- **South Australia**—the *Wrongs (Liability and Damages for Personal Injury) Amendment Act 2002*, which has been incorporated into the *Civil Liability Act 1936*, deals with damages for personal injury and applies in relation to a claim for personal injury arising from a motor vehicle accident or an accident caused wholly or in part by negligence or some other unintentional tort on the part of a defendant or by a breach of a contractual duty. Liability for damages may be excluded if the court is satisfied beyond reasonable doubt that the accident occurred while the plaintiff was engaged in conduct constituting an indictable offence, and is satisfied on the balance of probabilities that the plaintiff's conduct contributed materially to the risk unless in either case the circumstances of the case were exceptional or were harsh and unjust. The Act also attempts to reduce unreasonable delay in resolution of a claim by a personal representative of a deceased person.
- **Western Australia**—the *Civil Liability Act 2002* initially placed restrictions on the courts' capacity to award damages for death or injury of a person caused by the fault of another person for non-pecuniary and pecuniary loss, and permitted structured settlements.

  The *Civil Liability Amendment Act 2003* amended the *Civil Liability Act 2002* by replacing the concept of joint and several liability with proportionate liability as the basis for assessment of claims for damages for pure economic loss. Joint and several liability still remains the basis for assessment of damages for claims in respect to personal injury and death.

- **Tasmania**—the *Civil Liability Act 2002* places restrictions on the level of damages that may be awarded in cases where the use of recreational drugs by the injured party has contributed to their injury or on the right of the injured party to claim damages if they are injured while engaging in serious criminal activities. It also gave courts the power to order structured settlements as an alternative to lump sum payouts for future economic loss. A structured settlement is one where payment of an award for personal injury damages is made in the form of periodic payments rather than a lump sum settlement.

  The *Civil Liability Amendment Act 2003*, which was incorporated into the *Civil Liability Act 2002*, established thresholds applying to assessment of general damages for personal injury or death.
- **Australian Capital Territory**—the *Civil Law (Wrongs) Act 2002* provides that a judgement or decision against a person for damage caused by a wrong does not prevent an injured party from bringing an action against someone else who is also liable. Provision is also made for the first person who is liable for damage caused by a wrong to be able to recover contribution, that the courts considers just and equitable, from a contributor who is also liable for the same damage. Guidance is provided to the court in assessing damages for a person's death, loss of earnings, loss of capacity to perform domestic services and tariffs for damages for non-economic loss. A claims procedure must be followed by both the claimant and respondent and the respondent must attempt to resolve a claim within the period prescribed by regulation or, if no period is prescribed, within six months after receiving a complying notice of claim. The Act sets out the obligations of the parties in relation to documents and information so that liability can be assessed and quantum determined in relation to damages. Provision is made for pre-court procedures for personal injury claims, including defining the role, and limiting the number, of witnesses who may give expert medical evidence. The court has also been given power to make structured settlements. Schedule 3 also limits liability for injury or death of a participant while participating in an equine activity.
- **Northern Territory**—the *Personal Injuries (Liabilities and Damages) Act 2003* provides a number of reforms including placing a cap on damages and a threshold for personal injury damages claims for non-pecuniary loss, as well as permitting structured settlements.

  The *Personal Injuries (Civil Claims) Act 2003* aims to improve the efficiency of processes for the resolution of claims for damages for personal injuries and to assist the affordability of those claims.

WHAT HAS TO BE PROVED?

In view of the distinction between law and fact, it may be useful to summarise the provinces of law and fact in negligence (see Table 7.2).

Joint tortfeasors—two or more persons have caused P's injury

Where **two or more** persons have caused injury to the plaintiff, the requirement that there be proof of negligence of one of them can create difficulties, unless they were **joint tortfeasors**. This rule has been relaxed in two instances:

- In head-on collisions, in the absence of explanation as to which of the drivers was at fault, both are considered to be at fault.
- Where two or more persons caused injury to the plaintiff and there is no proof, except that the injury was caused by one of them alone, the burden is placed on them both, with each required to show that they were not responsible.

Table 7.2 What are matters of fact and matters of law?

Matters of fact	*Matters of law*
Resolving conflicts in the evidence	All questions of duty
Evaluating the conduct of the parties	The standard of care
Did the defendant cause the damage and what was its extent?	Questions of remoteness

Res ipsa loquitur ('the facts speak for themselves')

***Res ipsa loquitur*—the facts speak for themselves**

There is a rule of evidence that allows the plaintiff to treat the actual facts of the case as evidence of the defendant's negligence—the facts speak for themselves, or *res ipsa loquitur.* This rule can be used when the plaintiff would be faced with difficulty in furnishing direct evidence of negligence because they were under the control and management of the defendant at the time the injury took place. The defendant will lose their case unless it can be proved that the accident resulted from a specific cause which does not suggest negligence on the defendant's part but, on the contrary, points to its absence.

In order that the rule should operate, three conditions must be satisfied:

- The plaintiff's injury was one that **ordinarily would not happen** if proper care had been taken.

GEE V. METROPOLITAN RAILWAY CO. [1873] LR 8 QB 161

A train door fell open shortly after the train had left a station, resulting in the plaintiff falling out of the train and being severely injured. The plaintiff pleaded *res ipsa loquitur* applied since accidents of this sort do not usually occur if proper care is taken and this was something within the exclusive control of the railway company. The plaintiff was in no position to show that there had been some careless act and so it was left to the railway company to show they had taken all reasonable care.

ISSUE: Could the railway company show that they had taken all reasonable care?

DECISION: That as the railway company were unable to show that they had taken all reasonable care, they were held to have been negligent.

- The plaintiff was injured by something within the **exclusive control** of the defendant.
- There is an **absence of explanation** and no room for inference.

MUMMERY V. IRVINGS PTY LTD (1956) 96 CLR 99

The plaintiff entered a timber shed of the defendant to buy some timber. As he was walking over to the foreman, who was using a circular saw cutting some timber, he was hit in the face by a flying piece of wood and badly injured. The plaintiff pleaded *res ipsa loquitur.* The defendant did not provide any evidence.

ISSUE: Did *res ipsa loquitur* apply?

DECISION: The High Court held that the plea of *res ipsa loquitur* failed. The physical cause of the accident was the wood flying from the saw but there was no evidence to show that the occurrence was due to the negligence of the employer's foreman.

WEB RESOURCES

The Ipp Report is available on the web (note it is a large file) at:
http://revofneg.treasury.gov.au/content/review2.asp

A PDF copy is available at:
http://revofneg.treasury.gov.au/content/Report/PDF/lawnegfull.pdf

REVIEW QUESTIONS

7.1 In order to succeed in an action in negligence, what must a plaintiff establish?

7.2 In determining the existence of a duty of care, discuss the main features of the tests used by courts.

7.3 In the tort of negligence, the reasonable person plays an important part in determining foreseeability and whether there has been a breach of the standard of care. Who is the reasonable person?

7.4 Why did Donoghue sue in tort and not contract in *Donoghue v. Stevenson*? Discuss.

7.5 When will a duty of care arise?

7.6 In assessing whether a breach of duty of care has occurred, reference is made to the standard of the reasonable person. Discuss how the reasonable person standard is regarded in law and the factors the courts take into account when judging the standard of care under common law and the civil liability reforms.

7.7 A Sydney tramway passenger was injured in a collision with another tram which occurred after the driver collapsed at the controls. The plaintiff argued that the collision could have been avoided if the tramway authority had fitted the tram with a system known as 'dead man's handle', a system in use on Sydney's trains. This would have stopped the tram and avoided the accident. The device had been rejected by the tramway authorities because it was felt that it could cause the drivers to become tired, irritated and inefficient. There was no evidence of any similar device in use on two-man trams anywhere in the world.

Will the plaintiff succeed in his claim? Explain your reasoning.

> **activebook**
> Activebook resources include in-depth summaries with links to the relevant part of the book. For revision, add your own notes to the summaries provided by using the note-taking function.

7.8 A bush fire brigade had a vehicle specially modified to handle a large jack used in certain emergency situations. The vehicle was being used on another call when an urgent call came through for the use of the special jack at a serious accident close to the fire brigade headquarters. The officer-in-charge ordered that the jack be placed in the back of the only other vehicle at the fire station. On the way to the accident scene, the driver braked suddenly at an intersection and the jack shifted, injuring one fireman.

Can the injured fireman successfully sue his employer on the basis of the negligence of the officer-in-charge placing the jack in a vehicle not specially built to carry it? Explain your reasoning.

7.9 The 'but for' test is important in determining causation. However, it has limitations. Discuss what these limitations are and whether the court uses any other tests in determining causation. Consider the question both from a common law perspective and from the perspective of the civil liability reforms.

7.10 Having established duty, breach and damage, is the defendant liable for all the damage suffered? Discuss.

7.11 Indicate whether each of the following statements is true or false:

Statement	TRUE	FALSE
▪ An action in negligence must be commenced within three years from the date when the tort was committed	☐	☐
▪ To establish a duty of care, foreseeability and proximity must be present	☐	☐
▪ The question whether a duty of care is owed is a question of fact	☐	☐
▪ The standard of care is a fixed and inflexible standard	☐	☐
▪ The reasonable person test, in the case of children, gives way to the standard of a child of similar age and experience	☐	☐
▪ A plaintiff who has voluntarily assumed the risk will not recover any damages in a negligence action	☐	☐
▪ Contributory negligence is a complete defence in negligence	☐	☐
▪ When determining any fact relevant to the issue of causation, under civil liability legislation, the onus is on the defendant	☐	☐
▪ A person cannot claim for injury as a result of something which was an obvious risk	☐	☐
▪ Under civil liability legislation, 'harm' only includes personal injury	☐	☐

	TRUE	FALSE
▪ Under civil liability legislation, a person is not negligent in failing to take precautions against a risk of harm unless there was foreseeable risk, or the risk was not insignificant, or a reasonable person in the position of the person would have taken precautions	☐	☐

7.12 In a negligence action, some issues are questions of fact while others are questions of law. Briefly explain what is meant by the terms 'questions of fact' and 'questions of law' and then indicate what issues are questions of fact and questions of law in a negligence action.

7.13 Explain what is meant by the expression 'standard of care' in negligence.

7.14 The plaintiff, in order to succeed in an action in negligence, must show that he or she suffered some damage as a result of the defendant's breach of duty. Explain what is meant by the expression 'damage'.

7.15 Frank, a football lover, frequently attended games at his local ground. On one occasion the football was kicked into the stand where he was sitting, hitting him on the head and knocking him out of his seat, causing him to break his arm.

Can Frank sue either the local council or the football club, or both, in negligence for the broken arm that he received? Discuss.

7.16 It was late at night and very wet and, rather than wait for a taxi to take her home, Anna was only too happy to accept a lift from Michael. He smelt strongly of alcohol and had trouble keeping the vehicle on the road. Anna decided to continue the journey as it was raining very heavily. Shortly afterwards, Michael lost control of the vehicle and hit a tree, leaving the occupants in the vehicle seriously injured.

Will Anna be able to successfully sue Michael in negligence? What does she need to establish in order to succeed in such an action?

CRITICAL THINKING

7.1 Have the recommendations of the Ipp Review on negligence, adopted by the states and territories, resulted in a reduction in public liability insurance premiums and personal injury actions? Discuss.

CHAPTER 8

Applications of Negligence to Business

CHAPTER CONTENTS

CHAPTER OBJECTIVES

On completion of this chapter, you should be able to:

- Identify and discuss the application of the tort of negligence at common law and the civil liability reforms to the following:
  - occupier's liability
  - strict liability
  - product liability
  - defective structures
  - negligent misstatements
  - employer or vicarious liability
  - breach of statutory duty
  - motor vehicle accidents

activebook

This icon is used throughout the following chapter to remind you to visit the *Business Law* online activebook for additional exercises, links to legal websites, and feedback. For a detailed explanation of what is in the activebook please refer to the inside cover of this textbook. The activebook is available through OneKey.

Where do I start?

Learning path: Use the activebook to complete a pre-chapter warm-up exercise.

There are many definitions of legal terms to assist with your understanding of the material.

- Explain how a bailment may be created
- Describe the duties of a bailor and bailee
- Explain and discuss the relationship between bailment and the tort of negligence.

KEY TERMS

An understanding of the following terms will help you to better understand the material in this chapter:

- **non-delegable duty:** a duty that cannot be passed on or delegated to another person to try and avoid responsibility or liability
- **negligent misstatement:** a statement of fact, advice or opinion made in business that is relied upon by another but which is inaccurate or misleading
- **occupier's liability:** the liability of those people who have control over their land or premises to anyone who comes onto their property to ensure that they are not exposed to danger and risk of injury
- **strict liability:** liability without fault
- **vicarious liability:** where the actions of one person render another person liable. For example, the actions of an employee in the course of their employment may make their employer tortiously liable.

what if . . .

You were a volunteer lifesaver and when you went to rescue a swimmer who was drowning, in the course of bringing them into shore you were both 'dumped' by a large wave, causing you to lose your hold on him, resulting in him breaking his neck and becoming a quadriplegic. Would you be legally responsible for his injuries? If you weren't, would the club be liable?

One of the features of the development of the modern law of negligence since 1932 has been its ability to absorb other areas of tort law concerned with liability for wrongful conduct. This chapter focuses on a number of areas of activity which have a great deal of significance for people in business, and consumers. As in Chapter 7, the common law and statutory changes to the laws of negligence are considered separately at this point because the cases currently coming before the courts are still being decided on common law principles of negligence. It will probably be 2006 before reported cases considering the civil liability reforms start to filter out of the court system.

This chapter discusses two torts that used to be areas of the law in their own right but have been absorbed by negligence—occupier's liability and non-delegable duties. For convenience they are dealt with in this chapter rather than Chapter 7. The chapter then goes on to consider a number of situations which have given rise to a duty of care, including product liability, defective structures, negligent misstatements, employer liability or vicarious liability, breach of statutory duty, motor vehicle accidents, volunteers and good samaritans.

OCCUPIER'S LIABILITY

Doing business

Occupiers of premises owe a duty of care to entrants

Occupiers because of their **control** over their premises **owe a duty of care**, which in some cases is non-delegable, to **anyone** (even trespassers) who comes on to their property to ensure that they are not exposed to danger and risk of injury. Where the risk is obvious, far-fetched or fanciful the duty is minimal but care still needs to be exercised. ■

Civil liability reforms generally

The importance to the community of recreational activities and the need to provide protection to recreational providers against negligence claims for obvious risks has been recognised in all jurisdictions. Unfortunately, the approach as to how this protection will apply is not uniform. Some jurisdictions have dealt with the issue by directly incorporating protection for recreational providers into their legislative reforms of the laws of negligence; others have approached the problem as part of their consumer protection legislation by allowing recreational providers to contract out of, or at least limit, their liability. South Australia has adopted a Code of Practice. The Australian Capital Territory has adopted a more general approach to the issue of occupier's liability, although interestingly it has felt the need to give special protection to equine activities. What seems clear is that the common law position with respect to occupiers will not change to any great extent in the post-reform era.

At both common law and since the civil liability reforms, occupiers of premises, who are not necessarily the owners, owe a duty of care to people coming onto their premises to ensure the premises are not dangerous. This form of liability, which can be non-delegable in certain circumstances, arises because of the **occupier's control** over their premises, and includes anyone who enters the premises, including guests, those who enter by express or implied permission—such as visitors and salespeople—and even those who are uninvited, such as trespassers.

HACKSHAW V. SHAW (1984) 155 CLR 614; (1985) 59 ALJR 156

A farmer who had been robbed of petrol at night on a number of occasions decided to try to catch the thief himself. He lay in wait for the thief and when he saw a trespasser drive up, leave his car and move towards the petrol, he fired a number of shots into the vehicle to try and immobilise it. Unfortunately he shot the thief's girlfriend, who was crouching in the front seat.

ISSUE: As it was night when the farmer fired into the car and he could not tell whether there were any other occupants in the vehicle, was there a foreseeable risk of injury to any person who may have been in the car during the shooting?

DECISION: The High Court held by a majority that the defendant was liable to the plaintiff for negligence. As it was night and visibility was poor, the possibility that another person might have been in the car ought to have been foreseen by the farmer and he should have taken appropriate steps to check before shooting into the vehicle.

COMMENT: An occupier must take reasonable care to avoid a reasonably foreseeable risk of injury to a visitor, even to a trespasser.

An occupier *must* take reasonable care

The rules that once applied to occupiers have now been incorporated into the general duty of care of the law of negligence. This means that an occupier must take reasonable care, though what is reasonable will vary according to the circumstances.

***AUSTRALIAN SAFEWAY STORES PTY LTD V. ZALUZNA* (1986) 162 CLR 479**

The respondent was injured when she slipped on the wet floor of the appellant's supermarket. It had been a rainy day and persons entering the store had made the floor wet.

ISSUE: Should the duty of an occupier towards an invitee be treated according to the ordinary common law duty to take reasonable care to avoid foreseeable risk of injury?

DECISION: The duty which an occupier of land owed to an invitee should properly be seen as the ordinary common law duty to take reasonable care. This would vary with the circumstances of the plaintiff's entry upon the premises, but the measure of the discharge of the duty is what a reasonable person would do by way of response to the foreseeable risk.

COMMENT: The High Court took this case as an opportunity to remove the restrictive rules of occupier and visitor, which varied according to the class of visitor, i.e. invitee, licensee, trespasser, and replace them with the general duty of care of the law of negligence.

CASE REFLECTION: If the rain had stopped, would there be a duty on the supermarket owner to take steps to dry the floor?

IN BRIEF

Establishing occupier's liability

To establish a case of occupier's liability, a plaintiff must establish that:

- the defendant has occupation or control of the land or structure;
- the hazard was in the nature of a 'trap' and not obvious; and
- the defendant was negligent in not putting some protection in place or giving a warning.

It is not enough to establish that a person has been injured on the premises. It has to be established that the defendant was responsible for the injury, or ought to have known that there was a real risk of injury and unreasonably had done nothing about removing it.

Who is an occupier?

Onus on P to establish D has occupation or control of land/structure

In order to succeed in an action against an occupier, the plaintiff must **establish** that the defendant has **occupation or control** of the land or structure, which is a question of fact. Ownership on its own is not enough.

Control and physical presence on the defendant's part are the primary considerations, though it is not necessary for a person to have entire control over the premises.

***AC BILLINGS & SONS LTD V. RODEM* [1958] AC 240**

The defendant contractors blocked the usual approach to the building on which they were working and advised people that entrance to the building should be made through an adjoining property. The plaintiff was injured when she fell through a hole on the adjoining property while using the right of way at night.

ISSUE: Was there a duty on the contractor to ensure that there was safe access to and from the site?

DECISION: Although the contractor had no right to interfere with the adjacent property, there was a duty to provide a reasonably safe approach. Therefore he could be liable to a person seeking to enter or leave the building if, as here, the person is forced into the danger on an adjoining property. Occupation may be exercised jointly with persons in actual possession of the premises. Where control is shared, each is under a duty of care towards persons who may come lawfully on to the property to the extent of their degree of control.

What are premises?

Premises include a wide range of fixed and moveable structures, such as plant and machinery, as well as moveables such as ships, railway carriages and even ladders. South Australia (*Civil Liability Act 1936*, s. 19), Western Australia (*Occupier's Liability Act 1985*, s. 2), Victoria (*Wrongs Act 1958*, s. 14A(b)) and the Australian Capital Territory (*Civil Law (Wrongs) Act 2002*, s. 2, Dictionary) have all enacted legislation on fixed or moveable structures.

The role of negligence

An occupier of premises having control over both the premises and the entry of persons on to the premises owes a duty of care to ensure that these entrants do not suffer injury on the premises. **Where the risk is obvious, the duty will be minimal**.

Where the risk is obvious, the duty will be minimal

***PHILLIPS V. DALY* [1989] AUST. TORTS REPORTS ¶80-234**

The defendants occupied a hotel which had a carpark separated from the building by two logs. The logs were about 6 metres long, 40 centimetres high and 30 centimetres wide, painted white and with obvious protuberances. The plaintiff, having parked her car, climbed over the logs instead of walking around them and lost her balance. She fell and was injured.

ISSUE: Were the defendants in breach of their duty of care towards an invitee even though the risk was obvious?

DECISION: The defendants were not in breach of their duty. It was daylight and the risk was obvious. There was nothing hidden or unusual about it, though it should be noted that now an occupier is liable in respect of dangers *per se*, that is, whether they be hidden, unusual or obvious. There is a duty if the danger is foreseeable.

COMMENT: The court would have been conscious of the fact that to hold the defendants liable where the danger was obvious could place them in the position of an insurer.

The test at common law for determining what the occupier must do to discharge their duty of care was spelt out by *Mason* J in the High Court in *The Council of the Shire of Wyong v. Shirt* (1980) 146 CLR 40, where he suggested that two questions had to be considered:

Test—is the risk real and what would a reasonable person do about it?

- Would a reasonable person in the defendant's position have foreseen that the conduct involved a real risk of injury to the plaintiff? If the risk is real, and it doesn't matter if it is remote or unlikely to happen, then:
- What would a reasonable person do in response to the risk?

This requires consideration of a number of factors, some of which include:

- the magnitude of the risk;

- the cost of removal of the risk;
- its degree of probability;
- whether the risk is ordinary; and
- whether it is obvious.

As was noted in Chapter 7, these factors have been largely incorporated into the civil liability reforms.

Occupier's liability generally

Over the last few years there has been an increase in the issue of occupier's liability of sporting clubs, associations and their officials. Officials owe a duty of care to participants. The duty of an official to a participant rests on the legal concept of contractual duty of care. When a contractual duty is performed negligently and damage results, tort action for recovery of damages is possible (see, for example, *Renehan v. Leeuwin Ocean Adventure Foundation Ltd* [2006] NTSC 4, where the plaintiff, a trainee on board the *Leeuwin*, fell when climbing the mast of the sail-training ship. The trial judge in the Northern Territory Supreme Court, *Mildren* J, considered that breach of an implied term in contract was coextensive in content and concurrent in operation with the duty which arises in negligence to take reasonable care for the plaintiff's safety. He found that there was a duty on the part of the *Leeuwin* to ensure that instructors would take reasonable care for the safety of novice crew and that they breached that duty by failing to put in place a system that would reduce what was an obvious risk and that the plaintiff suffered damage as a consequence. As a result, the *Leeuwin* had been both negligent and in breach of an implied term in their contract with the plaintiff to exercise reasonable care. However, it should be noted that where the risk of injury to the participants is obvious, the courts are becoming increasingly reluctant to find a breach of the duty of care.

While the following cases were decided before the reforms to the laws of negligence, the outcomes would have been no different if they had been brought after the reforms had been put in place:

- **Inadequate sporting surfaces:** *Wagga Wagga City Council v. Mark Sutton* [2000] NSWCA 34 (25 February 2000) (footballer injured during football match when he put his foot in a hole on the playing surface, onus on occupier council to take reasonable care to ensure the ground was in a safe condition for play) and *Nowak v. Waverley Municipal Council* [1984] Aust. Torts Reports ¶80–200 (the plaintiff, a rugby league player, tripped over a protruding sprinkler on a football ground and broke his leg. In an action against the defendant council, which was responsible for ground maintenance, while it was established that the plaintiff was aware of the existence of the sprinkler, there was still an obligation on the council to take positive measures to make the ground safe to play on). However, note that the court was not as sympathetic towards a golfer in *Buttita v. Strathfield Municipal Council* [2001] NSW CA 365 (8 October 2001) (where a golfer was injured when he slipped on the edge of a golf green which was slippery after rain). The court held that the wet slope was not a hidden hazard but an 'occupational' hazard commonly encountered in playing golf in wet weather and one for which the occupier was therefore not liable in negligence. Nor was the court sympathetic to the plaintiff in *Town of Mosman Park v. Tait* [2005] WASCA 124 (where the plaintiff had suffered an ankle injury when she stepped into a hole while participating in a T-ball training session). While it was accepted that the council owed a duty of care as occupier to the users of the field, the court held that they had not breached their duty of care. The court found that while the hole was a potential danger to the plaintiff and the risk was a significant one because of its size and depth, the maintenance and inspection regime of the council to inspect the grounds on an approximately weekly basis during the course of mowing was an adequate response to the risk posed by the inevitable appearance, from time to time, of irregularities in the grass surface. The duty of the council was in relation to dangers of which it knew or ought to have known: see also *Jones v. Bartlett* (2000) 205 CLR 166 at par. 102; *Graham Barclay Oysters Pty Ltd v. Ryan* (2002) 211 CLR 540.
- **Negligent conduct of operations:** *Canterbury Municipal Council v. Taylor* [2002] NSWCA 24 (a local council owned and operated a velodrome with an inner field on which they allowed touch football to be played.

A touch footballer stepped back on to the track while cyclists were using it and he was struck and later died. The court found that the council brought itself under a duty of care to both the touch footballers and the cyclists to take reasonable care to avoid injury to both groups of users); *Langham v. Connells Point Rovers Soccer Club Inc* [2005] NSWCA 461 (the plaintiff tripped over a low-strung rope the same colour as the ground strung across the entranceway to a park where soccer was being played). At first instance, the judge had found there was no breach of duty on the part of the club. However, on appeal the Court of Appeal found that stringing a rope the same colour as the ground across an entranceway involved the creation of a concealed hazard of an unusual kind (distinguishing the case from the driveway and pedestrian cases such as *Ghantous v. Hawkesbury City Council* (2002) 206 CLR 512 where the High Court suggested that a pedestrian could be expected to keep a proper lookout for what he or she would expect to see, allowing for some inadvertence), and which persons in the position of the plaintiff would not have anticipated or expected. There was therefore a foreseeable risk of harm which required the respondent club to warn people of the presence of the rope barrier. While the probability of someone tripping over such a rope might be low, the magnitude of the risk of a person in the plaintiff's position failing to see the rope and tripping over it and causing significant injury was high. There should have been some warning of the presence of the rope.

- **Lack of proper signage warning of a risk:** where the defendant is aware of the risk and it is significant, but for little cost and effort could be reduced by signage and the defendant does nothing, then liability may follow: *Canterbury Municipal Council v. Taylor* (above). However, compare *Prast v. Town of Cottesloe* [2000] WAR 474 (appellant rendered tetraplegic after being dumped when body-surfing, see page 130); *Department of Natural Resources & Energy v. Harper* [2000] 1 VR 133 (the respondent, a visitor to a forest in a National Park, was injured by a tree falling during a high wind); *Woods v. Multi-Sport Holdings Pty Ltd* [2002] HCA 9 (cricketer hit in eye while playing indoor cricket). The High Court decided 3–2 that the occupier did not owe a duty of care. The two dissenting judges found that the occupier should have had warning signs; *Vairy v. Wyong Shire Council* [2005] HCA 62; *Mulligan v. Coffs Harbour City Council* [2005] HCA 63 where the two appeals were heard together by the High Court (both cases involved plaintiffs who had dived into shallow water, suffering catastrophic injuries). In *Vairy*'s case the High Court decided 3–2 that the council did not have an obligation to erect warning signs as adults participating in sporting or recreational activities are assumed to know the risks of diving from rock platforms into water of unknown depth and should be expected to owe a duty of care to themselves where the risk was obvious. In *Mulligan*'s case, the High Court unanimously held that there was no duty on the council to erect warning signs as the danger of diving into water of variable depth existed at most beaches and waterways and it was difficult to see how warning signs would change anything. Swimmers were expected to exercise commonsense when swimming in water of variable depth and poor visability
- Whether the person coming onto another's premises is expected to act reasonably.

MODBURY TRIANGLE SHOPPING CENTRE PTY LTD V. ANZIL [2001] AUST. TORTS REPORTS ¶81-585

The plaintiff, an employee of a tenant in the shopping centre, was severely injured when he was assaulted by three unknown men. The assault took place at 10.30 p.m. in the shopping centre carpark as he was on his way home. Four lighting towers in the carpark had been turned off at 10.00 p.m.

ISSUE: Was the failure to leave the lights on negligent, because the risk of injury from such assaults in a badly lit carpark was foreseeable?

DECISION: The High Court by a majority held that there was no defect in or on the premises. The shopping centre had no control over the behaviour of the plaintiff's attackers and there was no evidence of reliance by the plaintiff on the lighting in the carpark to ensure his safety when going to or from his parked car. Thus, there was no breach of the shopping centre's duty of care.

COMMENT: The shopping centre was not under a duty to take reasonable care to protect those lawfully on its land against criminal acts of third parties in the absence of a knowledge of risks from criminal acts by third parties. The standard of care of the occupier will depend on the circumstances of each case and is clearly a stringent one. This may be particularly true of cases where the premises are open to the public for recreational purposes (see 'Public authorities' below) or are accessible by children, where a greater measure of protection will be required.

Legislation in Victoria (*Wrongs Act 1958*, s. 14B(3), (4)), South Australia (*Civil Liability Act 1936*, s. 20(2)), Western Australia (*Occupier's Liability Act 1985*, s. 5(1), (4)) and the Australian Capital Territory (*Civil Law (Wrongs) Act 2002*, s. 168) also suggests matters that should be taken into consideration in trying to determine whether an occupier has discharged his or her duty of care.

Causation is also an important issue. The onus is on the plaintiff to establish that the defendant has not taken reasonable care. For example, an area where problems arise is in spillage cases. Where a substance has been spilled in premises through which a large number of people pass, such as a supermarket, it is the duty of the occupier to have a reasonable system of cleaning and inspection in place. The plaintiff must be able to prove what a reasonable system is and also establish that if a reasonable system had been employed the spillage would have been cleaned up before they slipped and fell on it. The plaintiff will also need to establish how long the spillage had been present before the accident.

Occupier's liability, recreational providers and statutory reforms

The Australian Capital Territory

Unlike other jurisdictions that have legislated in the area of recreational providers, the Australian Capital Territory (the 'ACT') has opted for a more general approach to the issue of occupier's liability by setting out a number of rules in relation to occupier's liability and partially codifying the common law rules about the standard of care an occupier must show to people entering on the premises in relation to any dangers to them (s. 168, *Civil Law (Wrongs) Act 2002*). The ACT has also added, as Schedule 3 of the *Civil Law (Wrongs) Act 2002*, protection for those involved in providing equine (horse) activities.

An occupier of premises owes a duty to take all care that is reasonable in the circumstances to ensure that anyone on the premises does not suffer injury or damage because of the state of the premises or things done or omitted to be done about the state of the premises (s. 168(1)).

In deciding whether the duty of care has been discharged by the occupier, the court must take into consideration a number of factors including (s. 168(2)):

- the gravity and likelihood of the probable injury;
- the circumstances of the entry on to the premises;
- the nature of the premises;
- the knowledge of the occupier about the likelihood of people or property being on the premises;
- the age of the person entering the premises;
- the ability of the person entering the premises to appreciate the danger; and
- the burden on the occupier to make the premises safe as compared to the risk of the danger to the person.

In relation to equine activities, Schedule 3 attempts to balance the rights of participants with the obligations of providers of equine activities and is modelled on legislation used in the United States. 'Equine' means a horse, donkey, mule or hinny, while an 'equine activity' is very broadly defined and includes most equine activities. It is not limited to competitive activities but includes among other things teaching, agisting, riding and even shoeing an equine. However, the schedule does not extend to cover the horseracing industry, nor does it prevent or limit liability for any actions under the *Trade Practices Act 1974* (Cth), the *Fair Trading Act 1992* (ACT) or workers' compensation claims. Also, the schedule does not protect providers of equine activities against harm or injury to spectators at an equine activity unless they are in an unauthorised area and in immediate proximity to the equine activity.

It should not be assumed that the schedule provides complete protection to a defendant against liability. Under the schedule an equine activity sponsor, professional or anyone else involved in an equine activity is only liable for an injury or death of a participant resulting from the inherent risks of equine activities in particular circumstances, for example, if the defendant provided equipment or tack and knew that it was faulty or intentionally injured the participant.

The definition in the schedule of 'inherent risks of equine activities' preserves the common law position that a person is not liable in negligence for harm suffered to a participant as a result of the materialisation of an inherent risk, which in this case is a risk arising from an equine activity. Inherent risks of equine activities include the propensity of an equine to behave in unpredictable ways that could result in injury or death to people on or around them, hazards, collisions and the propensity of a participant to act negligently that may contribute to the injury to the participant or others, for example failing to maintain control of the equine.

activebook

To help you to remember and understand the topics covered so far, and for links to legal websites, refer to your online activebook. Model answers provide feedback to problems and exercises.

Recreational providers

Where the approach has been through statutory reform of the laws of negligence, a defendant is considered not to be liable for harm suffered by a plaintiff as a result of the materialisation of an **obvious risk** of a **dangerous recreational activity** engaged in by the plaintiff, whether or not the plaintiff was aware of the risk. An 'obvious risk' is a risk that would have been obvious to a reasonable person in the position of the plaintiff and combines subjective and objective elements. It includes risks that are patent or are a matter of common knowledge, risks of low probability, as well as risks that could be considered to be not prominent, conspicuous or physically observable (NSW: s. 5F, K, L, *Civil Liability Act 2002*; Qld: s. 13, *Civil Liability Act 2003*; WA: s. 5F, H, *Civil Liability Act 2002*; Tas: s. 20, *Civil Liability Act 2002*). 'Recreational activity' includes any sport (whether it is an organised activity or not), any pursuit or activity engaged in for enjoyment, relaxation or leisure, or any pursuit or activity engaged in at a place (such as a beach, park or other public open space) where people ordinarily engage in sport or in any pursuit or activity for enjoyment, relaxation or leisure (NSW: s. 5K; WA: s. 5E) while a 'dangerous recreational activity' is an activity engaged in for enjoyment, relaxation or leisure that involves a significant risk of physical harm to a person (Qld: s. 18; WA: s. 5E; Tas: s. 19).

In New South Wales and Western Australia, a defendant does not owe a duty of care in relation to recreational activities where a plaintiff has been given a risk warning. A 'risk warning' is an oral or written warning given to people before they engage in a recreational activity organised by a defendant that is reasonably likely to result in them being warned of the risk. It is not necessary that the defendant establish that the person received or understood the warning or was capable of receiving or understanding it. The warning can be of a general nature that includes the particular risk (NSW: s. 5M; WA: s. 5I).

A defendant will not be able to rely on a risk warning unless it is given by or on behalf of the defendant or on behalf of the occupier where the recreational activity is being held, if it is established on the balance of probabilities that:

- the harm resulted from breach of an Act that established procedures or practices for personal safety;
- if the warning was contradicted by any other representations as to risk made by or on behalf of the defendant to the plaintiff; or
- if the plaintiff was required to engage in the recreational activity by the defendant (NSW: s. 5M; WA: s. 5I).

A recreational service provider may include in a contract with a person an express or implied term (that is, a waiver) which excludes, restricts or modifies liability for harm resulting from the failure to exercise reasonable care and skill in the supply of recreational services, notwithstanding any other written or unwritten law. However, a recreational supplier will not be able to rely on a waiver to avoid specific statutory safety standards. 'Recreation services' means services supplied to a person for the purpose of, in connection with or incidental to participation in any recreational activity. The effect of the section is to make it possible for both participants and spectators, or anyone else associated with a sporting activity for that matter, to accept responsibility for any harm that they may sustain while participating in or watching a recreational activity by waiving their contractual rights that the services will be provided with reasonable care and skill (NSW: s. 5N; WA: s. 5J).

The common law position as to the effectiveness of a waiver given to or on behalf of a child remains essentially unchanged. In Western Australia, risk warnings to parents or to competent adults who are responsible for children aged 16 to 18 years extend to those children. However, if the person is under the age of 18 years and suffers from a physical or mental disability and does not understand the risk warning, the risk warning will not operate (WA: s. 5I(16)).

Consumer protection approach

The consumer protection approach is dealt with below under the heading of 'What is the position of those who pay to enter?' As noted above, some jurisdictions have allowed recreational providers to avoid the problem of liability by allowing them to incorporate an exclusion clause, waiver or disclaimer in a contract with a participant who wished to participate in a recreational activity. See also Chapter 18 (pp. 370–380).

Code of Practice

In South Australia, the *Recreational Services (Limitation of Liability) Act 2002* permits a provider of recreational services to apply to the Minister for registration of a Code of Practice governing the provision of recreational services and setting out the measures that the provider will take to ensure a reasonable level of protection for consumers. A provider of recreational services may apply to the Minister to register an undertaking to comply with a code that is already registered. Provided that the registered provider gives the notice required by the regulations, the effect of registration is to modify the duty of care owed by a provider to a consumer, so that the duty of care is governed by the registered code. Thus, the provider will only be liable in damages if the consumer can establish that a failure to comply with the registered code caused or contributed to the injury.

What is the position of those who pay to enter?

For contractual entrants, D need only show reasonable care taken for primary purpose of contract

If a person can establish entry by contractual right, then the nature of the duty owed will turn on the express or implied terms of the contract of entry. Where there is no express term excluding the occupier from liability, there is an implied warranty in the contract which establishes that the premises are as safe for entry as a reasonable person can make them. Thus, the person who has paid the price of entry can bring an action in tort or contract if they are subsequently injured on the premises through no fault of their own (see, for example, *Renehan v. Leeuwin Ocean Adventure Foundation Ltd* [2006] NTSC 4 on p. 154).

The occupier can even be held liable for the actions of third parties on the premises if they lead to injury to contractual entrants—for example, in the entertainment area. The duty is non-delegable and is incapable of being discharged even by the employment of an independent contractor. If the contract confers only a right to remain on premises, the higher duty is not owed, for example, a restaurant customer.

Prior to the civil liability reforms, in some jurisdictions the occupier was given power by statute to exclude liability to entrants on the premises. Legislation in South Australia (*Civil Liability Act 1936*, s. 20(4)) and Western Australia (*Occupier's Liability Act 1985*, s. 7(1) excluded liability of entrants by contract but did not extend to cover non-parties to the contract. In the absence of statutory provision, voluntary assumption of the risk may have been available as a defence to the occupier where there was an express agreement with the entrant excluding the occupier's liability.

Since the insurance crisis, the Commonwealth, Victoria and the Northern Territory have all passed legislation enabling a recreational service provider to seek a waiver from participants, of the service provider's contractual obligations to provide services with due care and skill, for injury or death as long as an express warning orally or in writing was given to the participant (Cth: s. 68B, *Trade Practices Act 1974* enabling recreational and sporting providers to contract out of implied warranties in consumer transactions under s. 74; Vic: s. 32N, *Fair Trading Act 1999*; NT: s. 68A, the *Consumer Affairs and Fair Trading Amendment Act 2003*).

Public authorities

One of the largest, if not the largest, groups of occupiers in Australia are the public authorities. The extent of their liability can be found in two decisions of the High Court set out below. Where the danger is unnatural or hidden, a public authority will owe a duty of care to warn persons, using the area as intended by the public authority, of foreseeable risks.

Where the danger is unnatural or hidden, a public authority owes a duty of care to warn persons using the area of foreseeable risks

NAGLE V. ROTTNEST ISLAND AUTHORITY (1993) 177 CLR 423

A person was injured on property controlled by the Authority after diving off a rock ledge at a swimming area and striking a submerged rock. The Authority had promoted the site as a place where it was safe to swim and had not installed any signs warning would-be swimmers of the dangers.

ISSUE: By failing to install a warning sign, had the public authority breached its duty of care to swimmers using the site?

DECISION: The High Court found that the public authority was aware of the **hidden danger** and so owed swimmers a duty of care. It breached its duty of care by failing to install a warning sign advising swimmers against the risks of diving into the water from the ledge.

Where the danger is **obvious**, as in *Phillips v. Daly* (p. 153), or in *Vairy v. Wyong Shire Council* [2005] HCA 62; *Mulligan v. Coffs Harbour City Council* [2005] HCA 63 (p. 155), an occupier, and the courts, will generally assume that most entrants will take reasonable care for their own safety.

ROMEO V. CONSERVATION COMMISSION OF THE NORTHERN TERRITORY (1998) 72 ALJR 208

Romeo and her friends were visiting the Darwin Casuarina Coastal Reserve, which was managed by the Northen Territory Conservation Commission. They were attending a gathering at the carpark in the reserve and, around midnight, after spending the evening drinking, Romeo crossed over the fence that had been erected to stop people going too near the edge of the cliff, crossed through some vegetation and fell over the edge. She sustained severe injuries and was paralysed.

ISSUE: Did the Authority owe a duty of care to warn against obvious dangers?

DECISION: The High Court held that there was no breach of the Authority's duty of care to Romeo for failing to provide precautions. In this case Romeo was both affected by alcohol and inattentive to what was an obvious danger.

COMMENT: *Kirby* J suggested that in the case of public authorities, the courts have begun to address more closely the limited resources available to them for the execution of the functions and responsibilities committed to them by statute. Other relevant factors in considering occupier liability, at least in the case of public authorities, would be the age, capacity, sobriety and the possible inadvertence of the entrant as well as consideration of the preservation of the aesthetics of a natural environment and the cost of improvement of safety. *Brennan* CJ was of the view that to hold the Authority liable in such circumstances would place them in the position of an insurer.

DOING BUSINESS

Liability of public authorities for provision of public facilities

Where members of the public are encouraged to visit sites, such as parklands, which are under the care, management and control of public authorities, and which have provision of facilities such as carparks, lookouts and picnic spots, a duty of care may well exist. Liability will depend on whether the danger is hidden (Nagle) or obvious (Romeo). Public authorities and their insurers should ensure that they have in place risk management programs that regularly assess the standard of precautions which are in place. ■

All state jurisdictions (South Australia has only restricted liability for road authorities: s. 42) and the Australian Capital Territory have, in their civil liability reforms to the laws of negligence, set out a number of general principles to be employed in determining whether a public authority owes or has breached a duty of care. As for negligence generally, these apply to any claim for damages resulting from negligence, regardless of whether the claim is brought in tort, in contract, under statute or otherwise (Vic: s. 80; NSW: s. 39). 'Public authority' includes the Crown, a local council or any public authority established by or under an Act for a public purpose.

In addition to the general principles set out in the civil liability legislation for determining the duty question, a court must also take into account:

- the financial and other resources that are reasonably available to the authority for the purpose of exercising those functions, their general allocation not being open to challenge;
- the broad range of an authority's activities; and
- evidence of compliance with general procedures and any applicable standards (Vic: s. 83; NSW: s. 42; Qld: s. 35; WA: s. 5W; Tas: s. 38; ACT: s. 110).

A public authority is not liable for an alleged breach of statutory duty in connection with the exercise of, or a failure to exercise, a function of an authority where the function of the authority is conferred on it specifically in its capacity as a public authority, and where the relevant provision does not impose an absolute duty on the authority to do or not do a particular thing. However, a public authority will be liable if the act or omission was so unreasonable that no authority could properly consider the act or omission to be a reasonable exercise of its functions (Vic: ss. 84, 85; NSW: s. 43; Qld: s. 36; WA: s. 5U; Tas: s. 40; ACT: s. 111).

Victoria and the Northern Territory aside, other jurisdictions have provided special protection to protect road authorities against tort action for failure to carry out road works (NSW: s. 45(1); SA: s. 42 but note that this protection only runs for two years, s. 42(3); Qld: s. 37; WA: s. 5Z; Tas: s. 42; ACT: s. 113).

Tasmania is the only jurisdiction to extend the removal of the duty of care obligation for public or other authorities where dangerous recreational activities are involved. No duty of care is owed for a recreational activity where a defendant has given the plaintiff a risk warning. A defendant is not entitled to rely on a risk warning where, for example, the warning contradicted any representation as to risk made by the defendant to the plaintiff (Tas: s. 39).

Where a non-delegable duty is owed, there is a more onerous duty on D: the duty to *ensure* that all reasonable care is taken

Non-delegable duties and strict liability

In addition to the duty to take reasonable care there is in a limited number of situations a more onerous duty, the duty to **ensure that all reasonable care is taken**. The High Court has recognised that a non-delegable duty of care includes employer–employee, landlord–tenant, hospital–patient and teacher–pupil relationships and the rule in *Rylands v. Fletcher*.

Where a person who had control of premises brought a dangerous substance onto the premises, or carried on a dangerous activity, or allowed another to do one of those activities, and it escaped and caused damage to another's property, they would have been liable under the rule in *Rylands v. Fletcher* [1866] LR 1 Ex 265. They will now be liable in negligence.

BURNIE PORT AUTHORITY V. GENERAL JONES PTY LTD (1994) 68 ALJR 331

General Jones occupied part of a building owned by the Burnie Port Authority. The Port Authority employed independent contractors to carry out renovations. In the course of installing additional refrigeration, which involved considerable welding, the insulation materials caught fire. The ensuing fire damaged goods owned by General Jones, who then sued the Port Authority on the basis of negligence and the *Rylands v. Fletcher* rule.

ISSUE: Did the defendant owe the plaintiff a non-delegable duty of care in respect of its property? Did the defendant ensure that all reasonable care was taken by the contractors?

DECISION: The High Court held that the rule in *Rylands v. Fletcher* (i.e. strict liability for anyone who brings on to their land something not naturally found there and which does damage if it escapes) was no longer part of Australian law and is now absorbed into the general law of negligence. A person taking advantage of the control of premises to introduce a dangerous substance, to carry on a dangerous activity, or to allow another to do one of those things, owes a non-delegable duty of care to avoid a reasonably foreseeable risk of injury or damage to the person or property of another.

COMMENT: This non-delegable duty of care is a duty to ensure that all reasonable care is taken. The defendant could not escape his obligations to the plaintiff by hiring competent and experienced staff. There was a duty on the defendant to ensure that they took reasonable care.

In each case where a non-delegable duty of care exists there is a higher standard of care required by the person owing it with respect not only to what they do but also to ensure that, where tasks are delegated, they are carried out with reasonable care and skill.

NORTHERN SANDBLASTING PTY LTD V. HARRIS (1997) 71 ALJR 1428

The landlord (Northern Sandblasting) bought the house in 1984. In November 1986 it asked Briggs, their usual electrical contractor, to make some electrical repairs to a refrigerator and stove at the house. Mr and Mrs Harris entered into possession of the property in December 1986. The electricity was already connected when they moved in. On 2 June 1987 they had reported that the stove was not working and so the landlord asked Briggs if he could repair it. On 4 June their daughter went to turn off a sprinkler. The lawn was wet and she did not have anything on her feet. On touching the tap she was electrocuted and suffered severe brain damage as a result of faulty workmanship by Briggs.

ISSUE: Did the landlord owe a non-delegable duty of care to the child living with her parents to ensure that reasonable care was taken by the electrician in carrying out the repairs?

DECISION: The High Court held that the landlord did owe a non-delegable duty of care to ensure that reasonable care was taken in the repair of the stove.

COMMENT: In this case, the non-delegable duty of care was marked by a special dependence and vulnerability as it involved a child. The fact that the landlord was not allowed by law to carry out the repair did not allow him to escape his duty. A non-delegable duty can be performed by someone else. It just cannot be discharged by using someone else.

The High Court's decision in *Northern Sandblasting Pty Ltd v. Harris* created a lot of uncertainty and confusion about the responsibility of landlords for defects on residential premises and the extent of their liability if a tenant or some other person was injured on them. In *Jones v. Bartlett* [2000] HCA 56 the High Court attempted to rein in the decision in *Northern Sandblasting Pty Ltd v. Harris* by suggesting that the duty of a landlord is simply to take reasonable care to put and keep premises in a safe state of repair and to avoid foreseeable risks of injury to tenants.

JONES V. BARTLETT [2000] HCA 56

The plaintiff, Marc Jones, moved into a house that his parents rented from the defendant landlord, Graham Bartlett. Jones injured himself by carelessly putting his knee through an internal glass door, which did not meet the standard for plate glass as set out in the Australian Standard at the time of the accident.

ISSUE: Was the landlord under a duty to inspect the house or have it professionally inspected before letting it? It was argued that if the landlord had done so, he would have been advised that the sheet of glass in the internal door did not meet Australian Standards.

DECISION: By a six to one majority the Court decided that the landlord did not owe a duty of care to Jones. There was nothing about the premises that alerted, or should have alerted, the owners or their agent to any unusual dangers. The duty of a landlord is simply to take reasonable care to put and keep premises in a safe state of repair. It was not defective in any relevant sense.

Victoria and New South Wales have treated the issue of a breach of a non-delegable duty as one of vicarious liability and imposed a strict liability. This means that where there is a breach of a non-delegable duty, there is an absolute duty on the defendant to ensure that reasonable care is taken by the person carrying out the work or task delegated or entrusted to them by the defendant. The duty cannot be discharged by the taking of reasonable care by the defendant and is really not an issue of negligence although a breach of duty will be created by negligence (Vic: s. 61; NSW: s. 5Q; Tas: s. 3C).

Doing business

Non-delegable duties carry no error for mistake

Where a non-delegable duty of care exists, there is a higher standard of care required by the person owing the non-delegable duty of care in respect not only to what they do but also to ensure that where tasks are delegated, they are carried out with reasonable care and skill. A non-delegable duty can be performed by someone else **but** it cannot be discharged by using someone else. ■

CATEGORIES OF NEGLIGENCE

Product liability (defective products)

As far as manufacturers are concerned, the same duty is owed in respect of all products. The principle of *Donoghue v. Stevenson* can only be applied where the defect is hidden and unknown to the consumer, otherwise the directness of cause and effect is lost. It amounts to a guarantor's liability.

Manufacturer's liability can be found in both common law and statute

GRANT V. AUSTRALIAN KNITTING MILLS [1936] AC 85

The appellant, a doctor, contracted dermatitis as a result of wearing woollen underwear that contained chemicals which, it was found, had been left in them due to the lack of care of the manufacturer. The respondents produced evidence that they had manufactured nearly five million pairs of underpants without a complaint and argued that no one could say that they were not a reasonably careful manufacturer.

ISSUE: Did the manufacturer owe a duty of care to the appellant?

DECISION: The Privy Council held that the appellant could recover in both contract (for breach of an implied term under the *Sale of Goods Act*) and tort for negligence. Even though he may have had an opportunity to inspect the garments before wearing them, the chemicals were a hidden and latent defect that could not be reasonably detected. Therefore, the respondent owed the appellant a duty of care.

COMMENT: Today, manufacturers also face the possibility of liability. Part VA of the *Trade Practices Act 1974* (Cth), as well as the various state consumer protection laws, have greatly increased the consumer's rights against third parties.

CASE REFLECTION: If the consumer had a unique allergy to the particular chemicals, could the manufacturer use that as a defence to a claim for compensation by the consumer for the manufacturer's negligence?

If a person consumes or uses a thing that they know to be dangerous or faulty, they cannot complain if something then goes wrong because they have deliberately chosen to take that risk.

However, the difficulties facing a consumer in bringing an action against a manufacturer in negligence, for example, because of the difficulty in proof of fault, have been strengthened by consumer protection legislation such as Part VA of the *Trade Practices Act 1974* (Cth) entitled Liability of Manufacturers and Importers of Defective Goods (see Chapter 23). This has had the effect of providing a person who is injured or who suffers property damage as a result of a defective product having a right to compensation from a manufacturer or importer without the need to prove fault. If the defective goods damaged the person or property of the consumer, the manufacturer is strictly liable.

Doing business

Product liability

- Where there is a possibility for an intermediate examination or inspection of the goods, if the examination is done negligently, the intermediary may be liable. In each case, however, it is a question of whether intermediate examination was contemplated.
- Where there is a distributor, if a product is dangerous *per se*, then there is a duty to give adequate warning for taking precautions. While this does not amount to strict liability, the duty of care is in proportion to the risk involved. The greater the danger, the greater the care required.
- Sellers and repairers are under similar duties to distributors and manufacturers.
- The enactment of Part VA of the *Trade Practices Act 1974* (Cth) has created a statutory product liability for compensation of a plaintiff by the manufacturer without proof of negligence for loss caused by defective goods. ■

Defective structures

Liability in negligence can extend to defective structures

Where the builder, architect or engineer knows or is careless or not skillful in the design or construction of a structure so that the structure itself is defective, they may be liable if the plaintiff suffers damage as a result of the defect.

BRYAN V. MALONEY (1995) 69 ALJR 375

In 1979 Bryan, a builder, built a house. Shortly after completion the house was sold and then resold again in 1986 to a Mrs Maloney. Because the house was constructed with inadequate footings, serious damage became apparent some six months after Mrs Maloney bought the house. She sued Bryan for negligence.

ISSUE: Does the builder's liability in negligence extend to later owners even if the Statute of Limitations appears to have expired?

DECISION: The High Court held that on the basis of causal proximity, the builder owed a duty of care to the owner of the house at the time of the damage becoming apparent.

It was foreseeable by a builder that the negligent construction of the house with inadequate footings was likely to result in economic loss to the owner of the house at the time when the inadequacy of the footings was first noticed. A builder was in a better position to avoid the financial risks posed by latent defects in the structure of a house than subsequent owners would be. Thus, Mrs Maloney was entitled to recover damages assessed on the basis of the decrease in the value of her house by the faulty workmanship.

COMMENT: The right to sue a builder from the time the defect becomes apparent is limited to New South Wales, Queensland, Western Australia and Tasmania. In Victoria, South Australia, the Northern Territory and the Australian Capital Territory, legislation requires the occupant to make a claim within 10 years of the issue of an occupancy certificate.

The High Court also left open the question whether manufacturers should owe a duty of care to consumers of their products as regards the quality of their products.

Negligent misstatements and the common law

The courts have often imposed a duty to avoid making careless statements that can harm a person. Thus, in *Clayton v. Woodman* [1961] 3 All ER 269, the court held that the architects were under a duty of care to the plaintiff for those careless misstatements causing damage to property or persons as they came within the principle of *Donoghue v. Stevenson*. In *Barnes v. Commonwealth* (1937) 37 SR(NSW) 511 and *Furniss v. Fitchett* [1958] NZLR 396, nervous shock was caused by verbal communication. In the latter case the court held that the doctor owed his patient at common law a duty to take reasonable care to ensure that no expression of his opinion as to her mental stability or condition should come to her knowledge. In certain circumstances a doctor may be able to foresee that a statement they make would be capable of causing physical harm, whereas a person with no medical knowledge might never be expected to foresee such a result.

***Negligent misrepresentation*— duty on D to avoid making careless statements which cause harm**

The whole matter of economic loss caused through careless statements was reconsidered by the House of Lords in *Hedley Byrne & Co. Ltd v. Heller & Partners Ltd* [1964] AC 465. The court came to the conclusion that a negligent misstatement, whether spoken or written, could give rise to an action for financial loss, apart from any contract that existed between the parties. However, it was equally clear that an action would not lie unless it could be established that the maker of the statement owed a duty of care to the recipient, though it was not necessary for the plaintiff to be personally known to the defendant.

The principles formulated by the court in *Hedley Byrne* represented an extension of the general principle formulated by Lord *Atkin* in *Donoghue v. Stevenson*. It had long been accepted that no action would lie for a pecuniary loss suffered as a result of acting upon an innocent misrepresentation unless it constituted a term of the contract, although it may have been made negligently, as the defendant owed no duty of care to the plaintiff.

The High Court approach, however, differed from that of the English courts. In *Mutual Life & Citizens' Assurance Co. Ltd v. Evatt* (1968) 122 CLR 556 (see below), the High Court held that the defendant was liable for their negligent misstatements. A duty of care extended not only to professional advisers but also to persons who give advice in 'serious circumstances'. The Privy Council, on appeal, rejected this view.

MUTUAL LIFE & CITIZENS' ASSURANCE CO. LTD V. EVATT [1971] AC 793

MLC Assurance Co. Ltd and HG Palmer (Consolidated) were subsidiaries of MLC Ltd. A policyholder of MLC Assurance sought advice on the investment potential of HG Palmer and was told that it would continue to be financially stable and safe to invest in. When HG Palmer went into liquidation, the policyholder lost his investment and as a result sued MLC Assurance and MLC Ltd.

ISSUE: Did a 'special relationship' exist such that it could be said that MLC were giving investors advice in serious circumstances? Did MLC have or profess to have 'special skill' for the provision of financial advice?

DECISION: The policyholder's appeal failed because MLC Assurance was not in the business of giving advice on investments. It did not claim to have the necessary skill and competence to give such advice or to exercise the necessary care to give reliable advice.

COMMENT: While the view of the High Court was rejected by a majority of the Privy Council, the importance of the High Court decision and the test formulated by *Barwick* CJ now lies in its application in *Shaddock's* case (see below).

In *L. Shaddock & Associates Pty Ltd v. Parramatta City Council (No. 1)* (1981) 150 CLR 225 the High Court held that a duty of care covered both the giving of information and advice.

Duty extends to both supply of information and advice

L. SHADDOCK & ASSOCIATES PTY LTD V. PARRAMATTA CITY COUNCIL (NO. 1) (1981) 150 CLR 225

The defendant Council received an inquiry from the solicitors for the plaintiff developers as to whether land which the plaintiff proposed to buy was affected by any Council road widening proposals. The Council was under no legal obligation to answer such questions, but it always had. The Council failed to disclose that there was a proposal. Replies to similar inquiries had disclosed the proposal. Relying on the Council's answer, the plaintiff purchased the property, only to discover that the proposal would lower the value of the property and prevent the proposed redevelopment. Unlike *Hedley Byrne* and *Evatt*, the plaintiff had not sought expert opinion. Instead, he had sought factual information.

ISSUE: Did the Council owe a duty of care for the giving of information or did it only apply to the giving of advice?

DECISION: The High Court held that liability for the giving of information was not limited to commercial business activities. The duty extended to those supplying advice or information to others whom they knew would rely on it in circumstances which were reasonable for them to do so. In this case the Council, a public body, had in its possession information which was largely inaccessible through other channels and which was of importance to those seeking it. Thus, the Council owed a duty to take reasonable care to ensure that it supplied the correct information.

CASE REFLECTION: Would a company that obtains comprehensive legal advice about a prospectus it intends to issue inviting people to invest in its shares be able to claim compensation from the legal firm when the issue fails because of legal defects in the prospectus?

There must be assumption of responsibility by D *and reasonable* reliance by P

In *San Sebastian Pty Ltd v. The Minister Responsible for Administering Environmental Planning and Assessment Act* (1986) 162 CLR 340, the majority of the High Court attempted to bring the principles underlying the existence of a duty (in the case of negligent misstatements causing economic loss) closer to the ordinary general principles of negligence.

SAN SEBASTIAN PTY LTD V. THE MINISTER RESPONSIBLE FOR ADMINISTERING ENVIRONMENTAL PLANNING AND ASSESSMENT ACT (1986) 162 CLR 340

Plans for redevelopment of an inner city area as office space were publicly exhibited by a planning authority. The plaintiff development company purchased land in reliance of the plans which were ultimately abandoned some four years later. The developer could not develop the land as they had hoped and were forced to sell it at a loss.

ISSUE: Could a public exhibition of plans for a redevelopment by a planning authority amount to a representation? Did the documents contain any expression, either express or implied, that they could be relied upon by the developers?

DECISION: The High Court found that there had been no representation by the authority that the plans were final and correct or an invitation to the developer to act on the plans. There was no causal link between the actions of the planning authority and the financial loss suffered by the developer.

COMMENT: The special skill and competence of a person making a statement are still important considerations in the duty question. However, the majority of the High Court in this case identified assumption of responsibility by the defendant and reasonable reliance by the plaintiff as important features in these types of cases.

An inadequate response can amount to a negligent misrepresentation if P has relied upon it

In *Pyrenees Shire Council v. Day* (1998) 192 CLR 330, the council was in breach of its duty of care to the new tenants and the neighbours. The council had been told that the chimney was defective, but took no steps under its powers to alert the occupiers or to enforce compliance to the notice. They were aware of the risk of harm and the damage that could arise from the risk was foreseeable. As a result the High Court held that the council was liable for their inadequate response.

Doing business

The importance of care in the making of statements

There seems to be no reason, other than policy considerations, why liability should be confined to instances of negligent responses to a plaintiff's request for information or advice. A defendant volunteering information or advice could be liable for negligent misstatements if they have, or profess to have, skill and competence in the area which is the subject of the communication **and** proof of actual reliance by the plaintiff can be shown. They may warrant the correctness of what they say or assume responsibility for its correctness. They may also invite the recipient to act on the basis of the information or advice, or intend to induce the recipient to act in a particular way where they may have an interest in the recipient so acting. ■

Auditors

Does the maker of a statement owe a duty of care to persons other than the person to whom the statement was communicated? In the case of auditors who prepare audits for the companies commissioning them, are they liable to third parties who rely on the information for investment purposes? A restrictive approach has been adopted by the High Court in *Esanda Finance Corporation Ltd v. Peat Marwick Hungerfords (Reg)* (1997) 71 ALJR 448 to reliance by third parties in such cases.

ESANDA FINANCE CORPORATION LTD V. PEAT MARWICK HUNGERFORDS (REG) (1997) 71 ALJR 448

Esanda lent money to a company, Excel, relying on accounts prepared by Peat Marwick Hungerfords. The accounts overstated the company's loans and it subsequently defaulted on the loan. As a result, Esanda suffered a loss on the loan. It then sought to recover those losses from the auditors, arguing that the auditors owed them a duty of care in regard to the preparation of the audit report.

ISSUE: How far does the duty of care extend in relation to third parties?

DECISION: There was no cause of action in negligence against the auditors. In cases of negligent misrepresentation, an intention to induce reliance is only one of the various means to show that the plaintiff's reliance upon the statement was reasonable. Reliance on the audit report on its own was not enough.

CASE REFLECTION: If the company being audited had told the auditors, prior to the commencement of the audit, that the report would be referred to a lender in support of the loan application, would the auditors be likely to be liable to the lender for the negligent audit? Explain your answer.

Will the civil liability reforms make any difference to an auditor's liability?

This means that a duty will not be imposed upon the maker of a particular statement where it is used for a different purpose. Thus, while company directors owe a duty of care to persons who subscribe for shares by way of a prospectus, their duty does not extend to subsequent purchasers of the shares. A similar conclusion would arise in the case of auditors where their advice is tendered for a particular transaction; however, liability could be incurred where the auditor is aware that the client will use the accounts to induce a third party to invest. In the latter case, the auditor can reasonably foresee that the accounts will be used as a direct inducement to a third-party investor.

Developments in other jurisdictions and policy considerations will play an important role in the development of the law in relation to auditor liability. They are often one of the few parties remaining solvent after a corporate collapse (along with lawyers) and have become the subject of a considerable amount of litigation over audited accounts in recent years. In an attempt to limit liability, New South Wales (*Professional Standards Act 1994*) and Western Australia (*Professional Standards Act 1997*) have capped accountants to a maximum liability. For example, in New South Wales, where the fee charged was less than or equal to $50 000 it is $500 000 and where the fee is more than $50 000 it is 10 times the fee up to a maximum of $50 million.

Other areas

It should not be assumed that the area of negligent misstatements is limited to financial advice causing pecuniary or economic loss. In *Rentokil Pty Ltd v. Channon* [1990] Aust. Torts Reports ¶81-019, a plaintiff recovered damages for the loss caused by negligent misstatements in a written report that a house was free of termites prior to his purchase. The house was so badly termite infested that it had to be demolished.

Negligent misstatements and civil liability reforms

Where matters currently stand with respect to negligent misrepresentation under the civil liability reform packages of the states and territories (the Northern Territory aside) is unclear. A number of jurisdictions have introduced as part of their civil liability reforms a statutory standard of care for professionals and, in those jurisdictions, the approach is relatively uniform (Vic: Pt. 10, Div. 5; NSW: Pt. 1A, Div. 6; Qld: Ch. 2, Div. 5; Tas: Pt. 6, Div. 6).

A 'professional' is defined as a person practising a profession. The standard to be applied by the court in determining whether a defendant has acted with due care is basically determined by reference to:

- what could be reasonably expected of a person professing that skill (and not a greater level of skill); and
- the relevant circumstances as at the date of the alleged negligence and not a later date.

A professional can avoid liability if it is established that the professional acted in a manner that was widely accepted in Australia by peer professional opinion as competent professional practice. However, if the court determines that the opinion is unreasonable or there is a duty to warn of risk, then the professional will not escape liability.

Remedies

Apart from recovering damages in the tort of negligence based where the plaintiff is returned to the position they would have expected to be in had the misstatement not been made, the plaintiff is also entitled to consequential loss arising from the misstatement. The plaintiff may also be able to seek a remedy under the tort of deceit.

The negligent misstatements may also amount to false or misleading conduct in breach of ss. 52 and 74 of the *Trade Practices Act 1974* (Cth) as well as the relevant state and territory Fair Trading legislation. If these causes of action are proved, the court may rescind the contract (s. 87 TPA) and award damages (s. 82 TPA).

IN BRIEF

Prerequisites to recovery for negligent misstatements

For a plaintiff to recover damages for a negligent misstatement, P must establish:

- **A duty of care.** This is established through a relationship of proximity between the parties. This may be circumstantial, e.g., a professional relationship, or causal. Policy considerations, such as the public interest, may also be important.
- **A breach of duty.** P must establish that:
  - D made a representation or statement; and
  - D knew, or ought to have known, it was being requested for a serious purpose; and
  - the representation and statement by D would be acted upon; and
  - if the statement was inaccurate they could suffer loss. [No distinction is made between provision of information and provision of advice. Even predictions and omissions may be caught.]
- **Damage.** P must establish that there is a connection between D's omission and the damage they have suffered—the causative element. This means establishing that they have relied to their detriment on D's information or advice.

***Vicarious liability*—** **a person can be held liable for the acts or omissions of another**

Employer liability or vicarious liability

It is possible at law for a person to be held responsible for the acts or omissions of another, even though they may not have been personally at fault. This is known as vicarious liability and is **always strict liability**. It must be distinguished from personal liability as this generally requires fault on the part of the defendant. It arises where a particular relationship exists between the parties. A well-known example is employer and employee, but it can affect other relationships such as principal and agent.

Doing business

An employer may be liable in tort for their employee's actions

An employer may be vicariously liable for the actions of their negligent employee if it can be shown that the conduct of the employee, which caused the injury to P, arose out of the course of employment. It is important that adequate risk management controls be in place. ■

It first needs to be determined whether the person causing the injury is in fact an employee or servant. Vicarious liability generally only applies to the acts of employees committed in the course of their employment and **not** to independent contractors. When the courts consider whether a person is an employee there are a number of factors to be taken into account, not just the control that the employer has over the employee. The main tests which are used are:

- **the control test**, i.e. did the employer have the right to control the activities of the employee?; and
- **the multi-factor test**, which considers a wide range of factors including the relationship between the parties, the nature of the work performed, the terms and terminology used in the contract as well as a range of other factors (see *Hollis v. Vabu* (2001) 50 AILR ¶4–476). This test has effectively incorporated the control test into it as one of the factors the court now takes into account. The integration test, which was once a stand-alone test, is also used as a supporting test to the multi-factor test, that is, was the employee a part and parcel of the organisation?

! CAUTION NOTE

An employer is ***not*** *liable for the tortious acts of an independent contractor. Nor is an employer liable for the actions of an employee that are* ***not*** *within the course of their employment.*

Having ascertained the nature of the relationship, if it is employer and employee, an employee is generally personally liable for any negligence or any other torts committed in the course of employment. Whether it is worth the injured party suing them is another issue because the employee generally does not have sufficient funds to meet any award of damages plus costs that the court may award the injured party if the employee is found to be negligent. However, the law may hold the employer to be vicariously liable for the torts committed by the employee where it can be shown that they arose out of **the course of employment**. This requires the injured party to show that the employee was carrying out the work they were employed to do. If they can, then the employer is vicariously liable even if the employee in carrying out the work was doing it in an unauthorised or improper manner.

CASSIDY V. THE MINISTER [1951] 1 ALL ER 574

The plaintiff was admitted to hospital for a minor operation to correct two stiff fingers. After the operation the plaintiff discovered that he now had four stiff fingers. It was not possible to determine which hospital employee's negligence had caused the damage.

ISSUE: Was the hospital liable for the negligence of its employees?

DECISION: The court held that there was negligence by the hospital's employees in the course of carrying out their duties and that the hospital was therefore vicariously liable for their actions.

COMMENT: The reason that the employer is held responsible arises as a consequence of the employment relationship and it has the effect of making the employer an insurer of the employee. In other words, the employer must be prepared to take the good (the profits) with the bad (negligent employees).

The action of the employee **must** be connected with their contract of employment or, as noted above, the law will not hold the employer vicariously liable for a tort committed by an employee.

DEATONS PTY LTD V. FLEW **(1949) 79 CLR 370**

Deatons operated a hotel. Flew, a customer at the hotel, acted offensively to one of their employees, a barmaid, who asked him to go away. An argument developed and the barmaid threw a glass of beer and then the glass into Flew's face. The customer brought an action against her employer for damages.

ISSUE: Was the barmaid acting within the scope of her employment at the time of the incident?

DECISION: The High Court held that the barmaid's actions were outside the scope of her employment. She was employed to serve drinks to customers. Accordingly, Deatons was not liable to Flew for damages.

COMMENT: Even if the assault is an excessive mode of performing the employee's duty to the employer, the employer will generally be vicariously liable for the consequences.

It is not always easy to determine who is the negligent employee. Where the employer is found to be vicariously liable and the employee can be identified, in certain limited cases it might be possible for the employer to seek indemnity from the employee. The employer can argue that the employee is in breach of a term of their contract of service by failing to act competently.

LISTER V. ROMFORD ICE AND COLD STORAGE CO. LTD **[1957] AC 555**

Lister was employed by Romford Ice as a truck driver. His father was employed by the same company and worked with his son. One day while reversing his truck into a loading bay the son lost sight of his father, who was directing him, and accidentally ran over him. The father then brought an action against the employer and succeeded on the basis that Romford Ice's employee, the younger Lister, was negligent. The company's insurance company then exercised its right of subrogation by bringing an action against the son. It stepped into the shoes of the company and claimed that the son had been in breach of his duty to drive the truck carefully. As a result of his failure to exercise due care and skill, he had caused his employer to suffer damage.

ISSUE: Should the son have to indemnify the employer (i.e. the insurance company) for the loss that they had suffered?

DECISION: The son had been negligent in the manner in which he drove the truck. He owed a duty of care to exercise his skills as a truck driver with due care and competence, and he had broken his duty of care by running over his father. He was therefore in breach of his employment contract.

In South Australia (*Civil Liability Act 1936*, s. 59(3)) and the Northern Territory (*Law Reform (Miscellaneous Provisions) Act 1956*, s. 22A(3)) an employer is bound to indemnify an employee except where it can be established that there has been serious and wilful misconduct on the part of the employee.

It may also be possible for the employer to claim an indemnity from the employee as a 'joint tortfeasor' under the law of contribution, but only if the employer can establish they were not guilty of any personal fault. In New South Wales (*Employees Liability Act 1991*), South Australia (*Civil Liability Act 1936*, s. 59(1)(a)) and the Northern Territory (*Law Reform (Miscellaneous Provisions) Act 1956*, s. 22A) an employer is again bound to indemnify an employee except where the employee's liability was due to serious and wilful misconduct.

Breach of statutory duty

Breach of statutory duty involves a strict statutory standard of care

Breach of statutory duty is a separate and distinct action from negligence. A breach of statutory duty can arise without negligence because a strict statutory standard of care may be imposed. However, private liability may arise simultaneously where the breach of statutory duty constitutes evidence of negligence.

Most actions for breach of statutory duty involve motor traffic and workplace injuries. The standard of care is going to be determined by the words of the statute and the breach must be the cause of the plaintiff's injuries, which were of the kind that the statute sought to prevent.

Motor vehicle accidents

In the event of personal injury arising from a motor vehicle accident, some states have retained common law actions ('fault-based' schemes); others have replaced them with a 'no fault' scheme; still others use a combination of the two (see Table 8.1).

Table 8.1 Statutory compensation schemes for motor vehicle accidents

Jurisdiction	*Scheme*
Australian Capital Territory *Road Transport (General) Act 1999*	**No-fault scheme** If the driver is injured, they must be able to demonstrate that another driver was at fault
New South Wales *Motor Accidents Act 1988* *Motor Accidents Compensation Act 1999*	**Fault-based scheme** Necessary for the accident to be caused by the fault of the owner or driver of the motor vehicle Right to weekly benefits for medical, hospital and rehabilitation costs and income support where the injury is caused by the fault of another Right to sue for damages for personal injury and death where the damages exceed $65 000 Statutory maximum amounts set for damages in respect of non-economic loss, home care services and nervous shock No right to sue for claims under $17 500
Northern Territory *Motor Accidents (Compensation) Act 1979*	**No-fault scheme**
Queensland *Motor Accident Insurance Act 1994*	**Fault-based scheme**

continues

Table 8.1 Statutory compensation schemes for motor vehicle accidents *continued*

Jurisdiction	*Scheme*
South Australia *Motor Vehicles Act 1959*, Part IV	**Fault-based scheme** Claims over $10 000 may be sought in a negligence action The injured party has a restricted right to sue in negligence. Statutory limit on what may be recovered in certain instances (*Civil Liability Act 1936*, s. 35a)
Tasmania *Motor Accidents (Liabilities and Compensation) Act 1973*	**No-fault scheme**
Victoria *Transport Accident Act 1986*	**Partial no-fault** The Transport Accident Commission handles all claims for compensation for anyone injured or killed in a transport accident People who are seriously injured in a transport accident and can prove fault may sue for additional compensation Breach of statutory duty involves a strict statutory standard of care
Western Australia *Motor Vehicle (Third Party Insurance) Act 1943*	**Fault-based scheme** Claims under $10 000 are handled by the State Government Insurance Commission

Other civil liability reforms

Volunteers

All jurisdictions have recognised the importance of the role of volunteers in the community and moved to provide reasonably uniform protection for them against civil liability.

The *Commonwealth Volunteers Protection Act 2002* provides protection for Commonwealth volunteers from civil liability. An individual does not incur civil liability for anything that the individual has done in good faith in doing work for the Commonwealth or a Commonwealth authority if it is work done by the individual on a voluntary basis and organised by the Commonwealth or the Commonwealth authority (s. 6(1)). In such cases, the Commonwealth or Commonwealth authority incurs liability (s. 7) although the volunteer may be required to assist in defence of any action (Cth: s. 8). A volunteer is not covered by this Act if liability is covered by a scheme of compulsory third-party motor vehicle insurance, liability arises from a defamation action, their ability to carry out the work properly was significantly impaired by a recreational drug, or the individual was acting, and knew or ought to have known that they were acting, contrary to instructions or outside the scope of the activities authorised by the Commonwealth or the Commonwealth authority (Cth: s. 6(2), (3), (4)).

State and territory legislation protects a volunteer from liability for any act or omission done in good faith while doing community work organised by a community organisation or as an office-holder of a community organisation (Vic: s. 37, *Wrongs and Other Acts (Public Liability Insurance Reform) Act 2002*; NSW: s. 61, *Civil Liability Act 2002*; Qld: s. 39, *Civil Liability Act 2003*; SA: s. 4, *Volunteer Protection Act 2001* and the ACT: s. 8(1), *Civil Law (Wrongs) Act 2002* both require the act of the volunteer be voluntary **and** without recklessness; WA: s. 6(1), *Volunteers (Protection from Liability) Act 2002*; Tas: s. 47(1), *Civil Liability Act 2002*; NT: s. 7(1), *Personal Injuries (Liabilities and Damages) Act 2003*). Instead, liability attaches to the community organisation for which the volunteer works (Vic: s. 39; SA: s. 5(1); WA: s. 7(1); Tas: s. 48(1); ACT: s. 9(1); NT: s. 7(3)) and the injured party cannot sue the volunteer personally unless one of the exceptions below applies. An indemnity against the liability of a community organisation by a volunteer is of no effect (Vic: s. 40; WA: s. 8; Tas: s. 49; NT: s. 7(5)).

'Community work' is broadly defined and means any work that is **not** done for financial gain and includes work that is done for a sport, recreation, tourism or amusement (Vic: s. 36; NSW: s. 60(1)—although this section does not cover leisure or recreational activities; Qld: s. 38(1); SA: s. 3; WA: s. 3; Tas: s. 44; ACT: s. 7(1); NT: s. 7(7)). A 'volunteer' is a person who provides a service in relation to community work on a voluntary basis (Vic: s. 35(1); NSW: s. 60(1); Qld: s. 38(1); SA: s. 3; WA: s. 3; Tas: s. 44; ACT: s. 6; NT: s. 7(7)). A volunteer is permitted reimbursement of reasonable expenses incurred while doing the voluntary work (Vic: s. 35(2); NSW: s. 60(2)(b); Qld: s. 38(2); SA: s. 3; WA: s. 4; Tas: s. 45; ACT: s. 6; NT: s. 7(7)). 'Community organisation' includes an incorporated association and a body corporate (Vic: s. 34); NSW: s. 60(1); Qld: s. 38(1); SA: s. 3; WA: s. 3; Tas: s. 44; ACT: s. 6; NT: s. 7(7)).

The range of exceptions where a volunteer may be able to be sued varies somewhat from jurisdiction to jurisdiction. However, some examples of exceptions include knowledge of the volunteer that they were acting outside the scope of the activities authorised by the community organisation, that they were acting contrary to instructions, or the volunteer was affected by alcohol or drugs when doing the work and failed to provide the service in a proper manner (Vic: s. 37; NSW: ss. 59, 62–65; Qld: ss. 40–44; SA: s. 4; WA: s. 6(2); Tas: s. 47; ACT: s. 8; NT: s. 7(2)).

Enhancement of public safety

Queensland has gone further than other jurisdictions in providing protection that enhances public safety in the *Civil Liability Act 2003*. Division 7 deals with enhancement of public safety by offering protection to a person performing duties for a prescribed entity, or a prescribed entity, who is providing first aid, or other aid or assistance, to a person in distress in circumstances which could be described as an emergency (ss. 26(1), 27(1)). The act or omission must be done in good faith and without reckless disregard for the safety of the person in distress (s. 26(1)(c)).

A 'person in distress' is described as a person who is ill or injured, apparently ill or injured, or at risk of injury (s. 25). The definition of a 'prescribed entity' is contained in Schedule 1 of the *Civil Liability Regulations 2003* and includes bodies such as Surf Life Saving Queensland, St John Ambulance, the rural fire brigade and the Queensland Ambulance Service.

Good samaritans

Most jurisdictions have recognised the importance of the role that good samaritans play in the community and the need to protect them from civil liability. Protection is now provided for good samaritans from liability for an act done, or an omission made honestly and without recklessness, in assisting or giving advice about the assistance to be given to a person who is injured or at risk of being injured, or in need of emergency medical assistance (Vic: s. 31B, *Wrongs Act 1958*; NSW: ss. 56, 57, *Civil Liability Act 2002*; NT: s. 8, *Personal Injuries (Liabilities and Damages) Act 2003*; SA: s. 74 *Civil Liability Act 1936*; WA: s. 5AD, *Civil Liability Act 2002*; ACT: s. 5(1), *Civil Law (Wrongs) Act 2002*). Protection from civil liability will not apply if the good samaritan was intoxicated while giving the assistance or advice, or caused the injury or risk of injury in the first place (Vic: s. 31B(4); NSW: s. 58; SA: s. 74(4); WA: s. 5AE; ACT: s. 5(2); NT: s. 8(3)).

Professionals

Victoria, New South Wales, Queensland and Tasmania have adopted the Ipp recommendations in providing protection for professionals against civil liability claims by introducing a new test for standard of care by professionals. A 'professional' is a person practising a profession and includes doctors. The standard to be applied by the court in determining whether such a person has acted with due care is determined by:

- reference to what could be reasonably expected of a person professing that skill (and not a greater level of skill); **and**
- the relevant circumstances as at the date of the alleged negligence and not a later date (Vic: ss. 57, 58, *Wrongs Act 1958;* NSW: s. 50, *Civil Liability Act 2002;* Qld: s. 21 *Civil Liability Act 2003;* Tas: s. 21, *Civil Liability Act 2002*).

A professional can avoid liability if it is established that the professional acted in a manner that was widely accepted in Australia by peer professional opinion as competent professional practice unless the court determines that the opinion is unreasonable, in which case the court must give reasons in writing, or there is a duty to warn of risk, in which case the common law will continue to apply (Vic: ss. 59, 60; NSW: s. 5P; Qld: s. 22; Tas: s. 22).

BAILMENT

> **!** CAUTION NOTE
>
> *Bailment involves temporary transfer of possession.*

The duty of a bailee in relation to goods which they hold in their possession on behalf of a bailor involves duty of care. A bailee must take reasonable care of the goods that they have been entrusted with unless there is a contract of bailment in existence between the parties, in which case there may be a higher or lower duty of care, depending on the terms the parties have agreed to.

What is a bailment?

A bailment comes into existence whenever **possession of goods is transferred** from one party (the bailor) **possession of goods →** to another (the bailee) **on the understanding that the goods will be returned to the bailor** or disposed of as directed by the bailor upon completion of the purpose for which they were loaned. The bailor is not transferring ownership.

IN BRIEF

Conditions to be satisfied for a bailment to come into existence

- The bailor must retain title and ownership.
- The bailee must only have temporary possession and control of the goods.
- The ultimate possession of the property must revert back to the bailor in identical form, unless the goods are ordered to be transferred to a third party.

How does a bailment arise?

A bailment situation generally arises in one of two ways:

- where the owner surrenders the goods to another for the purpose of having some services performed on them, such as leaving clothes with a drycleaner, leaving a car at a garage for a service or a watch with a jeweller for repairs. The person receiving the goods is expected to be skilled and experienced in their profession and to return the goods upon completion of the service; or
- when a person borrows or rents goods from the owner (e.g., an equipment-hire business), in order to use them for their own purposes, such as hiring a cement mixer, borrowing a neighbour's tools or lawnmower, renting a car for a trip or even buying a car on hire-purchase.

In either form of bailment contract, there is a voluntary delivery or transfer of possession of the goods by the owner to another party that creates the bailment relationship.

Bailment and sale

A *sale* involves transfer of ownership but not necessarily possession

A bailment is different from a sale. A sale effects a change of ownership and may or may not change possession, depending on what the parties have agreed to. For example, a company with liquidity problems may sell some of its equipment and then lease it back from the purchaser without the equipment ever leaving its premises. A bailment, on the other hand, has no effect on ownership, merely possession.

Bailment or licence?

Bailment must be distinguished from a licence to use land or other premises for the purpose of leaving or depositing goods because of the lower standard of duty of care placed on a licensor. In a bailment situation, possession of goods passes from one person to another. This is not necessary in the case of a licence. This becomes a crucial issue where it must be determined whether a bailee's duty of care was owed when the goods have been lost or damaged. Whether possession has changed hands depends in each case on who has control over the goods, and this is a question of fact.

A licence may not involve transfer of possession

***TINSLEY V. DUDLEY* [1951] 1 ALL ER 252**

Tinsley left his motor bike in an unattended, closed yard adjoining and forming part of the hotel premises of the licensee, Dudley. When Tinsley left the hotel he found that his motor bike had been stolen.

ISSUE: Was Dudley a bailor or licensor?

DECISION: There was no delivery of possession to Dudley, either actual or constructive. Therefore he was not liable for the loss as he was only a licensor.

The outcome in *Tinsley v. Dudley* can be contrasted with the decision in *Ultzen v. Nicols* [1894] 1 QB 92 and the difficulty for the courts in determining whether the relationship between the parties is going to be one of bailor and bailee or licensor and licensee.

***ULTZEN V. NICOLS* [1894] 1 QB 92**

On entering the defendant's restaurant, a waiter took the plaintiff's coat and hung it up behind the plaintiff. When the plaintiff had finished his meal, he went to collect his coat and found it missing.

ISSUE: Was there a bailment of the coat or merely a taking of the coat by the waiter as part of the service provided by the restaurant but without any intention of taking charge of it?

DECISION: There was evidence on which the jury was justified in finding that there was a bailment of the coat. The action of the waiter, who relieved the plaintiff of his coat and selected the place where to put it, suggested that there was an intention of taking charge of it.

COMMENT: The issue of the bailment has to be determined first. If the court came to the conclusion that the defendant was merely a licensor and there was no delivery of possession, as in *Tinsley*'s case above, there would be no need to address the issue of negligence.

How can bailments be classified?

A bailment can arise out of a contract or possession

A bailment can arise at law in one of two ways:

- by **virtue of a contract between the parties**. Here the contract will override the general principles of common law, subject, of course, to any statutory limitations; or
- by **virtue of a relationship of possession**. It is here that the general principles of bailment law are important.

The rights and remedies that flow from each creation are different:

- **Sub-bailment of the goods. Here the bailee delivers the goods to a third person (the sub-bailee) for a limited time or particular purpose**. By taking possession of the goods, the sub-bailee comes to owe the duties of a bailee not only to the sub-bailor who delivered the goods, but also to the head bailor, even though there is no privity and no contract between them.

MORRIS V. CW MARTIN & SONS LTD [1965] 2 ALL ER 725

Morris sent a mink stole to a furrier for cleaning. With the consent of Morris, the furrier sent the fur on to CW Martin & Sons, who were expert fur cleaners. The fur was stolen by an employee of CW Martin & Sons while it was still in their possession.

ISSUE: Did a bailment relationship exist between Morris and CW Martin & Sons, even though he had not entered into a contract with them?

DECISION: The relationship of bailor and bailee existed between Morris and CW Martin & Sons.

- **Gratuitous bailee**. The bailment may be for the benefit of the bailor or the bailee, or even for the benefit of both parties, but no money is involved—for example, deposit of goods in a bank safety deposit box for which there is no charge, borrowing a car for a trip or lending a car to a person to see if they would like to buy it. Here there is a lesser duty than where the bailment is for reward.

GRAHAM V. VOIGHT [1989] AUST. TORTS REPORTS ¶80–296

Before leaving his lodgings, a tenant left nine stamp albums valued at $30 000 with his former landlady. She failed to redeliver them.

ISSUE: Did she owe a duty of care as a gratuitous bailee to forward the stamp albums on to the former tenant?

DECISION: The Supreme Court of the Australian Capital Territory held she had a duty of care as a gratuitous bailee to take reasonable care of the stamp albums bailed to her and she was in breach of that duty when she failed to deliver them after being requested to do so by the owner.

- **Involuntary bailment**. A person who receives unsolicited goods—for example, through the post—becomes an involuntary bailee, as does a person who finds goods. Where a person is an involuntary bailee, their duty is probably no higher than to take reasonable care of the goods.
- **Bailment by finding**. A person finding goods is not a true bailee because the goods have not been bailed to them for a particular purpose. However, if a finder does take possession of goods, and they are negligent and damage or lose them, they may be liable for the damage caused.

DUTIES OF THE BAILEE

The duties imposed upon a bailee, independently of any contract that may exist between the parties, include:

Duty to take care of the goods by a bailee

Bailees are expected to take reasonable care of the goods in their possession

All bailees are expected to take reasonable care according to the circumstances. This is a variable standard and factors that could be taken into account in determining the standard of care include:

- whether the bailment is gratuitous or for reward;
- the expertise of the bailee;

- the nature of the goods bailed; and
- whether it is for the benefit of one party or both.

Doing business

Whether the bailment is for reward or gratuitous, all bailees owe a duty of care to the bailor

The bailee must take reasonable care of the goods bailed to them and this is to be judged according to the circumstances of the bailment. The distinction between a gratuitous bailee and a bailee for reward, in relation to the standard of care in a negligence action, has largely disappeared. The position is that a bailee must exercise the degree of care which an ordinary reasonable person would take in all the circumstances, whether the bailment is gratuitous or for reward. ■

A bailee can restrict their exposure to risk through the use of an exemption clause

There is nothing to stop a bailee from attempting to exclude or limit their liability for negligence through the use of an exemption clause (refer to Chapter 18). However, it should be kept in mind that statutory restrictions on the operation of such clauses are becoming increasingly more extensive (e.g., state and territories legislation such as the Fair Trading legislation of the states and territories, Part 2B of the *Fair Trading Act 1999* (Vic.), the *Consumer Transactions Act 1972* (SA), as well as Commonwealth legislation in the form of s. 74 of the *Trade Practices Act 1974*).

The onus of proof

While a bailee for reward is not an insurer of the goods, they will be liable for loss or damage to the goods if they cannot show that they have taken reasonable care for their safekeeping. The onus is on the bailee to disprove negligence (i.e. that the loss or damage to the goods occurred without any negligence on the part of the bailee).

***PITT SON & BADGERY LTD V. PROULEFCO SA* (1984) 153 CLR 644**

The plaintiff had purchased bales of wool from the defendant wool broker. The bales were stored by the wool broker in an old timber wool store, which was poorly fenced, unlit, unattended and there was no fire sprinkler system. The wool store was burnt to the ground.

ISSUE: Was the wool broker a bailee?

DECISION: The High Court held that the wool broker was a bailee of the wool and therefore had the duties of a bailee for reward. By failing to maintain adequate fencing to prevent entry into the wool store, the bailee failed to discharge the onus of proving that it had taken reasonable precautions to prevent the destruction of the plaintiff's wool. The wool broker was therefore liable for breach of his duty to take reasonable care of the wool when an arsonist broke in and set fire to the store.

Duty to retain possession

While the general principle is that a bailee is under an obligation to retain possession of the goods bailed, a sub-bailment can be created by implication as in a case such as *Morris v. CW Martin & Sons Ltd* on page 176.

Duty not to use or misuse the goods

The nature of the bailment, and the terms of the contract where there is one, will set out what the bailee can and can't do with the goods bailed. Unauthorised use can result in the bailor suing in the tort of conversion or trespass, allow the bailor to sue for breach of contract or convert a fixed term bailment into a bailment revocable at will.

Duty to return the goods

The bailee's duty is to return the goods at the end of the bailment, subject to any agreement to the contrary.

DUTIES OF THE BAILOR

There are two duties imposed by the common law upon a bailor:

A duty of care to the bailee as regards danger and safety of goods

A bailor must make known any hidden dangers

A bailor, whether the bailment is gratuitous or for reward, will be liable in damages to a bailee who suffers loss or damage resulting from the dangerous character of the goods if no warning has been given to the bailee. Once a warning has been given, if the bailee still accepts possession, then any right of action for any loss or damage the bailee may suffer is lost.

***PIVOVAROFF V. CHERNABAEFF* (1980) 21 SASR 1**

A market gardener lent an onion sorting machine to a neighbouring onion grower. When the machine had been bought it had had a guard but this had been removed by the bailor. When telling the neighbour how to use the machine, he warned him to keep children well away from it because it was dangerous. The neighbour operated the machine with the help of a 13-year-old boy. During the course of operations, the boy got his hand caught in the machine and it was badly mutilated.

ISSUE: Could the boy bring an action against the bailor?

DECISION: The Full Court of South Australia held that the bailor had a duty to warn the bailee of the dangers associated with operating the machine without the guard, and he had adequately done so.

COMMENT: The bailee was liable in negligence for the injuries that the boy suffered.

A duty not to interfere with the bailee's possession

If the bailment is for a fixed term, the bailor cannot retake possession unless the bailee is in breach of a duty not to use or misuse the goods. If the bailment is at will, however, the bailor may retake the goods.

WEB RESOURCE

Transport Accident Commission: A useful site for students seeking information on the *Victorian Transport Accident Act* and compensation:

http://www.tac.vic.gov.au/WEB

REVIEW QUESTIONS

8.1 Indicate whether each of the following statements is true or false:

	TRUE	FALSE
■ Occupiers of a property owe no duty of care to entrants	☐	☐
■ Strict liability as a separate action no longer exists and now forms part of the law of negligence	☐	☐
■ Vicarious liability can make a person liable for the wrongful acts of another if certain criteria are satisfied	☐	☐
■ To succeed in an action based on a negligent misrepresentation, the plaintiff will need to show reliance on the defendant's statements	☐	☐
■ Under a fault-based scheme for recovery of damages from a motor vehicle accident, it is not necessary to establish fault	☐	☐

	TRUE	FALSE
■ A person who suffers injury as a result of a defective product may take action under either tort law in negligence or consumer protection legislation	□	□
■ Breach of statutory duty is a distinct and separate action from negligence	□	□
■ In order to succeed in an action in occupier's liability, the plaintiff must establish that the defendant has control over the premises	□	□
■ The essential characteristic of bailment is the passing of property to the bailee	□	□
■ The bailee owes the same duty of care to the bailor irrespective of the type of bailment	□	□

8.2 Discuss the standard of care required of an occupier in the 21st century.

8.3 What needs to be established by a plaintiff in order to succeed in an action against an occupier for injuries received on the premises of the occupier?

8.4 Jonas was employed by Rapid Couriers as a courier. His father was employed by the same company and worked with his son. One day while making a delivery, the son lost sight of his father, who was directing him, and accidentally ran over him. Discuss.

8.5 Palsgraf was standing near some elevated scales on the railway platform waiting for a train to pull in. Further down the platform a man carrying a small parcel was attempting to get on a train which had begun to pull out from the platform. Two railway guards endeavoured to push the man on to the train and in doing so caused him to drop his package. The package, containing fireworks, fell between the platform and the train and exploded. The vibrations from the explosion caused the scales to fall on Palsgraf, injuring her.

Has Palsgraf a remedy in negligence against the railways? Discuss.

8.6 Norris had decided for some time that he wanted to purchase a motel. After looking at several different areas, he settled on Port Stephens in New South Wales as offering him both the potential for a business and the lifestyle he was seeking. He rang a number of real estate agents, inquiring whether they had any motels listed for sale. He finally found a motel and general business listed with an estate agent called Evatt. Evatt told Norris that once he got going in this business it would be a gold mine. Norris sought an accountant's advice and then proceeded to buy the business. Within six months of buying the motel and general business Norris was broke because there were neither the tourist numbers nor local population to sustain the business.

Can Norris sue the estate agent for his statements about the business? Will he succeed? Explain your answers.

8.7 Discuss the development of the law of negligent misstatements. What would you consider to be the central issue that has to be established for a successful negligent misstatement action?

8.8 In what type of bailment does the bailee owe a greater duty of care: a gratuitous bailment or a bailment for reward?

8.9 Under what circumstances does a bailor owe a duty of care to a bailee?

8.10 Houghland, a passenger in one of McAnn's buses, had his suitcase stored in a luggage compartment of the bus for a trip from Brisbane to Cairns. The suitcase was lost during the course of the trip north.

i Has a bailment been created?

ii If so, what sort of bailment is it?

iii Can Houghland recover damages for the cost of the lost suitcase?

activebook

Activebook resources include in-depth summaries with links to the relevant part of the book. For revision, add your own notes to the summaries provided by using the note-taking function.

CRITICAL THINKING

8.1 Under what circumstances do you think an employer should be vicariously liable for the actions of an employee? Has the law gone too far?

8.2 Is it time that all Australian jurisdictions provided protection for auditors from unlimited liability in the carrying out of their auditing duties or is the current law satisfactory? Discuss.

CHAPTER 9 Other Business Related Torts

CHAPTER CONTENTS

activebook

This icon is used throughout the following chapter to remind you to visit the *Business Law* online activebook for additional exercises, links to legal websites, and feedback. For a detailed explanation of what is in the activebook please refer to the inside cover of this textbook. The activebook is available through OneKey.

Where do I start?
Learning path: Use the activebook to complete a pre-chapter warm-up exercise.

There are many definitions of legal terms to assist with your understanding of the material.

CHAPTER OBJECTIVES

On completion of this chapter, you should be able to:

- identify and explain the key elements of trespass:
  - trespass against the person
  - trespass against land
  - trespass against goods
  - nervous shock
- identify and explain the key elements of defamation
- identify and explain the main types of economic torts
- identify and explain the key elements of nuisance
  - public nuisance
  - private nuisance.

KEY TERMS

An understanding of the following terms will help you to better understand the material in this chapter:

- **assault:** direct interference with the person (the body) of the plaintiff and actionable *per se* (without proof of damage)
- **battery:** the striking of another
- **chattels:** any property other than freehold land; articles of personal property
- **conversion:** that tort which is committed by a person who retains another's property without permission and with the intention of depriving them of the use and possession of it
- **defamation:** a tortious action encompassing both words spoken (slander) or recorded (libel) which tend to injure a person's reputation
- **detinue:** the common law action available to a person claiming the specific return of goods wrongfully retained by another, or their value
- **imputation:** meaning
- **libel:** defamation in some permanent form such as writing, film. etc., and actionable without proof of special damages
- **nuisance:** a tortious action encompassing both those actions that interfere with the enjoyment of a right that all members of the community are entitled to (public nuisance), and those actions that result in a wrongful disturbance or interference with a person's use or enjoyment of land (private nuisance)
- **slander:** defamation of a non-permanent form such as words and gestures. It is actionable only on proof of special damage
- **trespass:** a tort involving the wrongful interference with the person or property of another and including: (a) trespass to the person—assault, battery and false imprisonment; (b) trespass to land; and (c) trespass to goods.

what if . . .

You lend your car to a friend to help him get to university while his is being repaired after breaking down. He promises to return the car as soon as his is fixed. After his car is repaired, despite repeated requests by you for him to return your car, he fails to do so. What do you think can be done in this case?

The last two chapters looked at the best known and most litigated area of tort law: the tort of negligence. However, negligence is not the only area of tort law relevant to business. There are also:

- the trespassory torts (trespass to the person, to land, to goods and nervous shock) which are intended to protect the physical and property rights of individuals from infringement by others;
- the tort of defamation which is intended to protect the reputation of a person or business in the community;
- the economic torts, including intimidation, interference with contractual relations, conspiracy by the use of unlawful means, passing off, injurious falsehood and deceit, which are available to protect business interests; and
- a miscellaneous tort, the tort of nuisance (private, public and statutory). Linked to the use and enjoyment of land, it is concerned with indirect harm and has growing importance today as an environmental tort.

This chapter looks at two other groups of torts that are also important to business:

- the intentional torts including trespass, defamation and what are described as economic or business torts; and
- a miscellaneous tort—nuisance.

INTENTIONAL TORTS

Trespass

Trespass is **a direct and intentional interference** with the **person or property** ('property' here meaning goods or land) of another and is actionable *per se* (**without proof of damage**). Where the injury is intentional but indirect, for example, the defendant sets a trap that causes injury to the plaintiff, there can't be an action in trespass (the plaintiff would have to sue on what is known as an 'action on the case').

Trespass can be classified as shown in Figure 9.1.

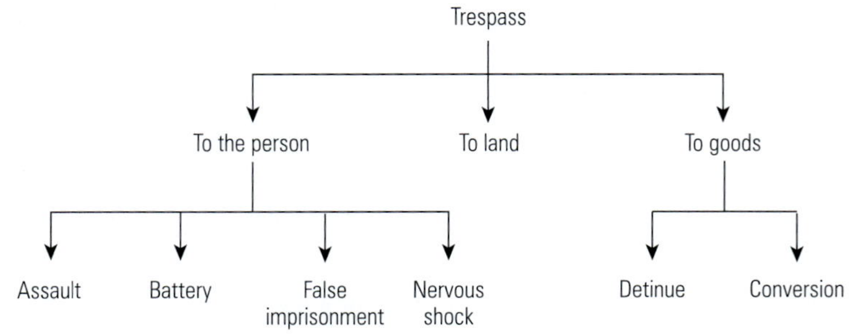

FIGURE 9.1 *Types of action under trespass*

Trespass to the person

Trespass to the person*—direct and intentional interference to the person and actionable *per se

This is **a direct interference with the person** (or body) of the plaintiff and is **actionable** *per se* (see Figure 9.2). The interference may be intentional or negligent, the onus being on the defendant to prove the absence of both on the defendant's part. The plaintiff does not have to prove any actual damage.

Assault and battery are **crimes** as well as **torts**. In three jurisdictions (see Table 9.1), assault and battery have been merged under the single name of assault under their criminal codes and this acts as a bar to further civil proceedings for the same action (except Tasmania). However, the magistrate has the power to award damages to a successful plaintiff as well as power to impose a criminal conviction.

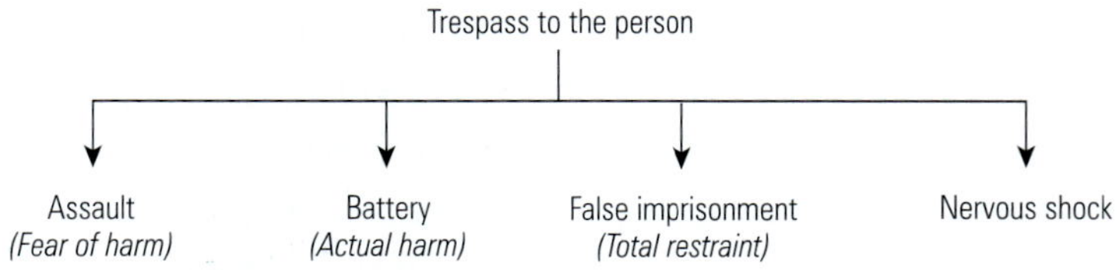

FIGURE 9.2 *Types of action under trespass to the person*

Table 9.1 States where assault and battery are crimes

Queensland	*Criminal Code 1899*
Western Australia	*Criminal Code Act Compilation Act 1913*
Tasmania	*Criminal Code Act 1924*

Assault

IN BRIEF

Assault

A person commits an assault if:

- there is an intentional act by the defendant; **and**
- the plaintiff reasonably believes they are in imminent danger of harmful or offensive contact.

Assault—would a reasonable person have been put in fear of their safety?

Whether an assault has taken place involves an **objective test** of the reasonable person—would a reasonable person be put in fear of their safety in similar circumstances? **Words on their own can amount to assault if the defendant has the ability to carry out the threat immediately and the plaintiff's fear of imminent contact is reasonable.** For example, threatening telephone calls could amount to assault. However, words can also have the effect of removing the threat of imminent direct physical contact.

Damages are usually awarded to a successful plaintiff, though in the absence of damage they are usually only nominal. An injunction may be awarded to restrain a future anticipated assault.

Battery

IN BRIEF

Battery

A person commits a battery when:

- a defendant intentionally or negligently does an act which
- brings about an immediate or direct harmful or offensive contact to the plaintiff.

Battery requires directness and is a question of fact

A plaintiff can't complain where contact is a normal part of everyday life—for example, brushing against another person in a crowded passageway.

Battery is not measured in degrees of force. The least touch is 'force' and substantial damages may be awarded where an affront to personal dignity is involved—for example, the wrongful taking of fingerprints, or kissing or spitting on another person. It may not even be necessary for the defendant to touch the plaintiff—for example, removing a chair from beneath the plaintiff as they were about to sit down, causing them to fall and injure themselves, would amount to battery.

Normally an assault would precede a battery, but it is possible to have a battery on its own—for example, hitting a person from behind with no warning.

Those who participate in contact sport, such as rugby league or Australian rules football, are taken to have consented to the infliction of some form of physical force which is within the rules, or to commonly encountered infringements of the rules. However, participants do **not** consent to those actions that are outside the rules and are dangerous. In such a case, the player would be liable for damages for the personal injuries caused to the injured player by the battery, although such actions are very rare.

A club can also be vicariously liable for a player's battery arising from a deliberate breach of the rules which led to the injury of an opposing player. For example, a coach who instructs his or her players to 'stop' members of the opposing team in an illegitimate way could find their club held vicariously liable for the actions of their coach and players if members of the opposing team were injured. For example, in *Canterbury Bankstown Rugby League Football Club v. Rogers* [1993] Aust. Torts Reports ¶81–182, the plaintiff and defendant were professional rugby league footballers. The defendant alleged that, while attempting to execute a 'smother tackle', his shoulder had accidentally struck the plaintiff breaking the plaintiff's jaw. The plaintiff alleged he had been intentionally struck in the head by the defendant. Both the New South Wales Supreme Court and Court of Appeal held that the defendant's club could be vicariously liable for the defendant's actions.

Damages (including exemplary damages which are awarded by the court where it wishes to punish the defendant for his or her actions) are normally awarded by the court but the amount the plaintiff will recover will depend upon the extent of the damage that they have suffered.

False imprisonment

IN BRIEF

False imprisonment

False imprisonment occurs where a person **intentionally** and **directly** places a **total restraint** upon the liberty of another.

***False imprisonment* requires a total intentional restraint**

For false imprisonment to occur, the restraint must be total and without lawful justification, depriving the plaintiff of their liberty. The imprisonment must follow directly from the defendant's act and, unlike battery, it need have no physical effect upon the plaintiff's person.

An entire, though temporary, restraint is also false imprisonment. But note that **the restraint must be total** or the plaintiff will be unsuccessful in their action.

***BALMAIN NEW FERRY CO. LTD V. ROBERTSON* (1906) 4 CLR 379**

The ferry company operated a service between Balmain and Sydney. Entry to the ferry was through a set of turnstiles, operated by inserting a penny in a slot in the machine. Above the turnstiles was a sign stating: '*A fare of one penny must be paid on entering or leaving the wharf. No exception will be made to this rule whether the passenger has travelled by ferry or not.*' Robertson paid his penny to gain admission and finding that he had just missed the ferry, he attempted to leave without paying another penny. He was stopped and forced to pay by the attendants.

ISSUE: Given that Robertson had used the ferry numerous times before, could he argue that the conduct of the defendant's employees amounted to false imprisonment?

DECISION: The High Court held that there was no false imprisonment as Robertson had not been totally restrained. There was nothing stopping Robertson from getting on the next ferry and travelling to the other side of the harbour and getting off there.

If a reasonable escape route is available, there can be no false imprisonment, but this will depend on the circumstances in each case.

Submission to restraint, as a result of threats, is false imprisonment. It appears that it is unnecessary to know that you are being restrained. Nor does the action of restraining the plaintiff need to be the action of the defendant. For example, you could be locked in your room while asleep by a servant or employee of the defendant and this could amount to false imprisonment. Once restraint is proved, it is up to the defendant to prove that the restraint was lawful.

The remedies available to the plaintiff include the *writ of habeas corpus* (an order directed to the person wrongfully holding another to produce that person before the court to determine if they are being wrongfully held) and damages.

Nervous shock

IN BRIEF

Nervous shock

Nervous shock occurs where a person wilfully does an act that is intended to cause physical injury to another, and that does in fact cause a reasonably foreseeable physical harm to them.

The test of liability in intentional shock is on the intention of the defendant's conduct. Does the defendant intend to cause a nervous shock? This means that **the truth or falsity of the defendant's statement or actions is not relevant**.

Test—did D intend to cause nervous shock?

***WILKINSON V. DOWNTOWN* [1897] 2 QB 57**

Downtown wished to play a practical joke on the plaintiff so he told her that her husband had been seriously injured. As a result, the plaintiff laid out money for a taxi to bring her husband home and she also suffered nervous shock and became very ill.

ISSUE: Can a person who has wilfully done an act intended to cause physical harm to another, and which in fact does cause physical harm, be held responsible for their actions?

DECISION: Downtown's conduct was intended to upset the plaintiff, and did in fact succeed in upsetting the plaintiff. The harm she suffered was reasonably foreseeable, and the effect was not too remote, as the connection between the cause and effect was both close and complete.

COMMENT: There are two points to note about this decision. First, the decision is probably limited to the case of words causing shock. All that is required is conduct which is foreseeably likely to bring about the harm suffered.

Second, the High Court accepted the *Wilkinson v. Downtown* principle in *Bunyan v. Jordan* (1936) 57 CLR 1. In that case the defendant had, while in the hearing of the plaintiff who knew he had a gun, for the purpose of putting emotional pressure on his sons, threatened suicide. Shortly after making the statement the plaintiff heard a shot and as a result suffered nervous shock. The defendant had no intention of committing suicide, wanting only to scare people. As a result, the High Court held that there was no reasonable foreseeability of a person in the plaintiff's circumstances suffering nervous shock and so liability could not exist under the *Wilkinson v. Downtown* principle.

Trespass to land

IN BRIEF

Trespass to land

There must be a direct **and** voluntary physical interference with another person's lawful possession of land. Motive is irrelevant.

Three areas are covered by this tort:

- **intentional or negligent entry** upon land without permission;
- **remaining** after permission to stay has expired, and using a right of entry for a purpose other than for which it was granted; and
- **leaving** things on land without permission, for example, dumping rubbish.

P must be in or entitled to possession of land and D must cause a direct invasion of P's land

Only a person in **exclusive possession of land**, or immediately entitled to exclusive possession at the time of the interference, can maintain an action for trespass. As well, the act of the defendant must cause a **direct invasion** of the plaintiff's land. For example, throwing a stone on to the plaintiff's land would constitute a trespass. Actual entry itself need not be that of the defendant, but **there must be some entry**.

While the subject matter of this form of trespass is land, it includes:

- **things attached** to the land and capable of being separately possessed, such as buildings, rooms in buildings, plants and crops;
- the **air space** above the land to a reasonable height (e.g., an advertising sign overhanging another's property would constitute a trespass—*Kelsen v. Imperial Tobaccos* [1957] 2 All ER 343, but flying over the plaintiff's land for the purposes of photographing it does not (although it might create a private nuisance)—*Bernstein v. Skyviews & General* [1978] QB 479; and
- the area **beneath** the surface (e.g., a tunnel dug under another's land could amount to a trespass).

A person can lawfully enter land with the express or implied consent of the person in possession or entitled to possession but they must leave within a reasonable time of being asked or they will become a trespasser: *Halliday v. Nevill* (1984) 155 CLR 1 at 7–8 (see, for example, *Candy v. Thompson & Ors* [2005] QSC 111 below on p. 187).

Remedies available to the plaintiff will take the form of damages and/or an injunction. If the defendant has possession of the land and the plaintiff wishes to recover it, then it will be necessary to bring an action in ejectment for recovery of the land. This may be combined with an action for damages.

Torts to goods (or chattels)

Goods or chattels may be owned or possessed. It is possible for the owner to be in possession of the goods, but equally it is possible for ownership to be in one person and possession in another. Hence, it is important to ascertain whether the person in possession is in fact the owner for the purposes of passing title. Ownership of goods arises through title, while possession is a state of fact and not necessarily a right (see Figure 9.3).

In the case of torts to goods, three possible classifications can be identified::

- **trespass** based on a **wrong**;
- **detinue** based on **possession** in the defendant; while
- **conversion** based on a **right to possession**.

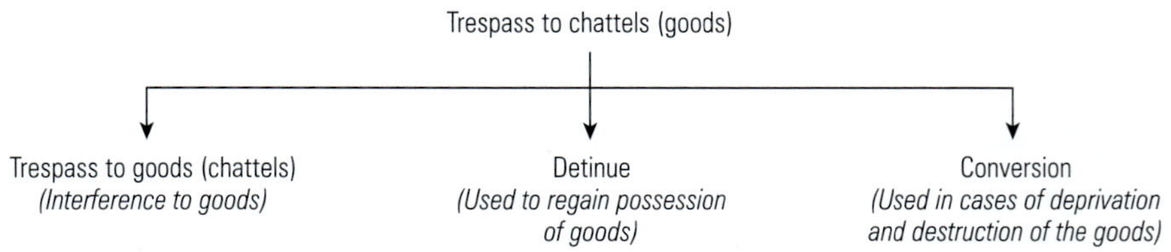

FIGURE 9.3 *Three major torts arising under trespass to goods*

Trespass to goods

IN BRIEF

Trespass to chattels

Trespass to chattels is based on a **wrong**. It occurs where there is:

- a direct and intentional or negligent act of **interference**
- with chattels in the plaintiff's **actual possession** without lawful justification.

P *must* be in actual or constructive possession of the goods at the time of D's act

The plaintiff **must be in actual or constructive possession** of the chattels (goods) at the time of the defendant's act. An exception to the rule of possession can arise where there is a bailment, that is, where there has been a transfer of possession of a chattel from one person to another for a limited period of time (see pp. 174–178).

It is not necessary for the plaintiff to establish ownership. Trespass to goods is established in the same way as trespass to land. That is, **there must be intention and physical control** which, like the other trespasses, is actionable *per se*. This means that trespass to goods may occur without the goods even being taken away.

Chattels are any tangible property that is not land or attached to land. It includes cheques, gases and animals. Chattels may be owned or possessed, and trespass protects the person in possession against acts interfering with their possession. This is in contrast to conversion and detinue described below, which protect the rights of the plaintiff against acts of the defendant which are intended to deprive the plaintiff's right to possession.

CANDY V. THOMPSON [2005] QSC 111

Mr Candy, the registered owner of a property at Hervey Bay in Queensland, had found a joey (baby kangaroo) on the road. He obtained an interim permit from the Queensland Parks and Wildlife Service (QPWS) to look after it at his Hervey Bay property until it could be released back into its natural habitat. When the permit expired, Mr Candy did not apply to extend it, although he knew he needed a permit to keep the kangaroo. The kangaroo continued to live at the Hervey Bay property where it was looked after by Mr Candy and his daughter. The QPWS eventually decided to remove the kangaroo from the Candy household and to release it back into the wild.

When the QPWS came to collect the kangaroo, they walked up the driveway to the house and spoke with Mr Candy. They then entered the house to remove the kangaroo and, despite some threats and remonstrations by Mr Candy, he assisted them to remove the kangaroo. His daughter, however, told the defendants to go away and get out of her room.

ISSUE: Did the QPWS (through Thomson) trespass on the plaintiff's land or in his house? In removing the kangaroo, did the defendants commit a trespass to goods?

DECISION: It was held that there would have been an implied consent for the defendants to walk up the path or driveway to the house entrance for the purpose of lawful communication with, or delivery to, any person in the house (based on the High Court decision in *Halliday v. Nevill* (1984) 155 CLR 1 at 7–8).

It was also held that the entry into the house did not constitute a trespass as from the facts it was clear that Mr Candy had invited the QPWS officers in and he did not withdraw his permission. His daughter's remonstrations to get out of her room did not revoke that licence as he was the registered proprietor of the land and entitled to exclusive possession of it.

Mr Candy had the kangaroo in his possession unlawfully as he was not authorised under the *Nature Conservation Act 1992* (Qld) to keep it once his permit had expired. The defendants were authorised persons who could take the kangaroo. Thus, there could be no trespass to goods as the kangaroo was not in his lawful possession.

COMMENT: If Mr Candy had had a permit to keep the kangaroo it might have produced a different result. The kangaroo would then have been lawfully in his possession.

The usual remedy is damages. It is assessed on the basis of whether the goods have been removed or not. In the case of the former the damages would be the full value of the goods, while in the case of the latter the damages would be the actual loss suffered.

Conversion

Conversion involves an unreasonable refusal to return P's chattel by a person in possession of it

Conversion occurs when a person deals with another's goods in a manner that is inconsistent with the **plaintiff's right to immediate possession**. The lawful owner is deprived of the immediate use and possession of their chattels—for example, stealing the goods of another, receiving stolen goods as a purchaser, wrongfully collecting the proceeds of a cheque, destroying the plaintiff's chattel, delivery by a carrier or bailee of a chattel which is the subject matter of a contract of carriage or bailment to the wrong person. If the owner has surrendered the right to immediate possession, for example, by a bailment, then the owner is not entitled to bring conversion.

Conversion is available where the plaintiff is out of possession at the time of the defendant's act and is principally (not exclusively, as conversion may protect those in possession or entitled to immediate possession such as bailees and bailors, mortgagees and mortgagors, and finders [as to finders see, for example, *Armory v. Delamirie* on p. 707]) concerned with protecting owners, while trespass to chattels, where the requirement is the actual possession of the chattels, is essentially concerned with the protection of the possessor of the chattels.

IN BRIEF

Making a claim in conversion

A person **lawfully entitled** to property in or possession of chattels, but who may be out of possession at the time of the defendant's act, can maintain an action for conversion against anyone doing an act that involves:

- a right to **immediate possession**; **and**
- an **intentional denial** by the actions of the defendant to that right.

They can only claim the value of the chattels.

For an act to amount to conversion, the plaintiff must be entitled to property or possession in the chattel and there must be on the part of the defendant:

- an intentional act of dealing with the chattels on the part of the defendant (unlike trespass, mere negligence is not enough); and
- a physical dealing with the goods, i.e. selling the goods without effecting delivery would not be sufficient to amount to conversion. There must be both the sale and the delivery for it to be conversion.

Damages are the usual remedy for conversion. The amount of damages that will be awarded is assessed on the value of the goods and, upon payment, ownership of the goods passes to the defendant.

Detinue

Detinue involves an unreasonable refusal to return P's chattel when demanded

Detinue is based on a demand by the plaintiff for the immediate return of goods and a subsequent refusal by the defendant. It is wider than conversion because **it lies against a person who no longer has possession at the time of the demand**.

IN BRIEF

Making a claim in detinue

If P wants return of specific goods, they will claim in detinue and must prove that:

- they are entitled to **immediate possession** of the goods;
- a specific demand was made for their **return**, nominating a place/s for their return; **and**
- the defendant **unreasonably refused** to return them after the plaintiff demanded their return at a specific time and place.

Where the defendant is in possession of the plaintiff's goods at the time of the plaintiff's demand, the defendant commits both conversion and detinue, because at this point of time the two torts are identical. It is where the defendant is no longer in possession that there is a difference between the two actions.

Where the defendant is still in possession of the goods, the plaintiff can seek return of the goods or damages for their detention, or be awarded the value of the goods and damages for their detention.

Defences to intentional torts

Defences to intentional torts include:

- **consent** (for example, in a contact sport it is assumed that the parties voluntarily accept the risk of injury which occurs within the rules during the course of play);
- **self-defence** (a person is allowed to use reasonable force to defend themselves against attack by another);
- **necessity; protection of property** (as long as only reasonable force is used);
- **statutory authority** (such as the legal duty to arrest);
- **necessity; authority of law** (for example, a policeman preventing a breach of the peace, or a gas, electricity or water meter reader carrying out their duties);
- **abatement of a nuisance** (for example, entry onto another's land to extinguish a fire);
- **licence** (that is, with the consent of the person in possession of the land); and
- **defence of property rights**—however, the defendant's actions must be reasonable, not involve excessive use of force and be proportionate to the risk. In *Hackshaw v. Shaw* (1984) 155 CLR 614; (1985) 59 ALJR 156 (for the facts see p. 151) the defence of property rights was not available to the farmer because the High Court considered that the use of a firearm was excessive force in those circumstances. There was a disproportionately high risk of killing or seriously injuring someone over what was a relatively minor matter.

DEFAMATION

This was an area of law that had become very complex until the adoption of the uniform defamation laws in 2006 by the states and territories. Two reasons can be suggested for this. First, at a national level, there were the approaches adopted by the states and territories towards the question of defamation. The common law had been replaced or amended by statute in an ad hoc manner with the result that whether there was an 'actionable defamation' would often depend on the jurisdiction in which the material was published. Secondly, there was, and still is, the issue of technology. Radio, television and the Internet don't recognise national or international boundaries, raising issues such as choice of law, jurisdiction, forum and reciprocal enforcement. While these reforms will go some way towards solving the problems associated with state and territory boundaries, they will not solve the type of problems associated when a person in Australia is defamed by someone in another country, such as *Dow Jones & Company Inc. v. Gutnick* [2002] HCA 56 where the matter involves material downloaded in Victoria from a website in the USA.

activebook

To help you to remember and understand the topics covered so far, and for links to legal websites, refer to your online activebook. Model answers provide feedback to problems and exercises.

DOW JONES & COMPANY INC. V. GUTNICK [2002] HCA 56

Dow Jones, the publisher of *Barron's Magazine*, published an article Mr Gutnick considered to be defamatory. A small number of print copies of *Barron's Magazine* were sold in Victoria. The article was also published in Barron's Online, a website operated by Dow Jones on a webserver in New Jersey. A number of online subscribers downloaded and read the article in Victoria. Gutnick commenced defamation proceedings in the Victorian Supreme Court but sued only in respect of publication in Victoria.

ISSUES: Did the Victorian Supreme Court have jurisdiction to hear the case? Did US or Australian law apply?

DECISION: The Victorian Supreme Court had determined that the case could be heard in Victoria. Dow Jones was denied leave to appeal by the Victorian Court of Appeal and subsequently sought and was granted leave to appeal to the High Court. The High Court unanimously held that the principles, which apply to determine the applicable law in Internet defamation cases, are the same as those that apply in relation to other types of media defamation cases, i.e. the court will apply the law of the place in which the cause of action arose, which in this case was Victoria. Thus, the Victorian Supreme Court had jurisdiction to hear the case and apply Victorian law.

COMMENT: The High Court confirmed the rule that the place in which each cause of action arises is the place of the reader. This means that in the case of an Internet publication, for the purposes of Australian law, a new cause of action will arise each time a new person accesses and reads defamatory material on a website.

The High Court decision has created a potential problem for Internet publishers and the issue of jurisdiction will continue to be a hotly contested argument for some time to come. Internet providers will need to determine which laws to consider when assessing whether they are likely to be successfully sued in relation to material published on a website, as most websites can be accessed from anywhere in the world. However, in the US where many of the major Internet publishers are located, a decision by the fourth circuit Court of Appeals following the decision of the High Court was that two Connecticut-based newspapers could not be sued in Virginia for articles posted on their websites, because these articles were not 'intentionally aimed at' a particular audience, in this case at a Virginia audience.

The common law continues to operate alongside the defamation laws

In developing the model provisions (Vic: *Defamation Act 2005*; NSW: *Defamation Act 2005*; Qld: *Defamation Act 2006*; SA: *Defamation Act 2005*; WA: *Defamation Act 2006*; Tas: *Defamation Act 2005*; ACT: *Defamation Act 2006*; NT: *Defamation Act 2006*), the focus has been on the substantive areas of defamation law where uniformity is important. The general law will continue to apply, except to the extent that the Acts provide otherwise. Most importantly, the common law test for determining what is defamatory is preserved by the legislation (s. 6(1)).

While one of the main objects of the defamation legislation is the introduction of uniform defamation laws, the legislation also attempts (s. 3):

- not to place unreasonable limits on freedom of expression;
- to provide effective and fair remedies for those people whose reputations are harmed by publication of defamatory material; and
- resolution of disputes quickly and in a non-litigious way by way of the publisher making an offer to make amends without the plaintiff needing to resort to litigation.

Litigation may follow a failure to make amends

If the matter is not able to be resolved by an offer to make amends, then litigation may follow. Provision is made in the Acts for a plaintiff or defendant to elect to have defamation proceedings tried before a jury (s. 21(1)). However, if there is to be a prolonged examination of records or the trial involves scientific, technical or other issues that a jury might find difficult to consider, then the matter must be heard before a judge alone (s. 21(3)). Where a jury is used, it can decide whether the defendant has published defamatory material and whether any defences can be established but only the **judge** can determine the amount of damages (s. 22(3)).

Only the judge can decide the amount of damages

The legislation provides that a person only has a single cause of action in relation to the publication of defamatory matter, regardless of whether it has one or more defamatory imputations contained in it. This means that a plaintiff will no longer have to prove 'special damages' or actual loss where the defamatory material is in a transient form, that is, slander (s. 8).

If a matter is published wholly within a particular Australian jurisdiction, the substantive law that is applicable in that area must be applied in that jurisdiction (s. 11(1)). If there are multiple publications in more than one Australian jurisdiction, the jurisdiction with which the harm occasioned by a publication has its closest connection must be applied (s. 11(2)).

What does defamation mean?

The legislation does not seek to define the term 'defamation' and, as noted above, operates by reference to the common law (s. 6). Defamation can be defined as a false statement about a person that is likely to damage their reputation in the community.

At common law defamation involved two torts:

- **libel**—defamation in a permanent form, e.g., film, book, letter, and actionable *per se* (without proof of damage) with damage to reputation being presumed; and
- **slander**—defamation in a temporary or non-permanent form, e.g., speech or a gesture, with the onus on P to prove actual loss if they are to recover damages, but that distinction has now been abolished (s. 7).

Defamation is concerned with a person's reputation

Basically there are three kinds of defamatory statement:

- those which lower a plaintiff's reputation in the community;
- those which are likely to injure a plaintiff's reputation in their trade or profession; and
- those where other persons are likely to be induced to shun, avoid, ridicule or despise the plaintiff.

Under the legislation, there is now a single cause of action for multiple defamatory imputations in the same matter. This reflects the position at common law by making it clear that it is the publication of defamatory matter that is the basis for a civil action for defamation (s. 8).

Who can sue and be sued?

Only the living and excluded corporations can sue

Only the living can sue. **The dead cannot be defamed**; and because defamation is personal to the deceased, their estate is unable to sue on their behalf even if it can prove temporal loss arising from the statement (s. 10).

The legislation restricts the ability of corporations to be able to sue for defamation. The legislation has essentially adopted the NSW position that only a company (called an 'excluded corporation'):

- which was not formed for financial gain for its members (or corporators); or
- employs less than 10 employees and is not related to another corporation, and
- the corporation is not a public body, can sue (s. 9).

Defamation may be brought not only against the original publisher, but also against anyone who takes part in the publication or re-publication of the material. In addition, re-publication by someone other than the original writer may result in an action against the original writer as well as the re-publisher.

An action must be brought within one year of publication (Sch. 5).

The Defamation Acts encourage alternative dispute resolution as an alternative to the courts

Resolution of disputes without litigation

The legislation seeks to encourage alternative dispute resolution by establishing a voluntary offer of amends settlement process between a publisher and an aggrieved person **before** litigation and basically reflects what was Part 2A of the

Defamation Act 1974 (NSW). While this process is designed to encourage speedy resolution of defamation complaints, the parties remain free to use other settlement processes that already exist under legislation governing civil procedure and the rules of the courts (s. 12).

An apology does not constitute an admission of fault or liability

A publisher may make an offer to make amends (s. 13(1)). Such an apology, however, does not constitute any admission of fault or liability by the publisher (ss. 13(4), 20(1)) and cannot be used in any civil proceedings as evidence of fault or liability of the publisher (s. 19).

To be effective, the apology must be made within 28 days of the publisher being given a 'concerns notice' (s. 14(1)(a)) or a defence has been served on the publisher by the aggrieved person (s. 14(1)(b)). The concerns notice sets out the details of the defamatory imputations (or meanings) as the aggrieved person sees them (s. 14(2)) .

If the 'content of offer' is to be effective each of the following factors must be satisfied (s. 15):

- it must be in writing; **and**
- be readily identifiable as an offer to make amends under Pt 3, Div. 1; **and**
- if the offer is limited to particular defamatory imputations, it must state that the offer is limited and identify the particular imputations; **and**
- it must include an offer to publish a reasonable correction; **and**
- if material containing the matter has been given to someone else by the publisher, the publisher must include in the offer that they will take reasonable steps to tell the other person the matter is or may be defamatory; **and**
- it must include an offer to pay the expenses reasonably incurred by the aggrieved person before the offer was made, and any expenses incurred by the aggrieved person in considering the offer; **and**
- may include an offer to publish an apology, or pay compensation for any economic or non-economic loss.

An offer to make amends may be withdrawn (it must be in writing) before acceptance (s. 16(1)). However, there is nothing to prevent a publisher making a renewed offer, even in the same terms as the original offer (s. 16(2), (3)), but it must be made within 14 days of the withdrawal of the original offer (s. 16(5)), and if it is, the effect in either case will be that the renewed offer will be treated as a new offer (s. 16(4)).

If the publisher carries out the terms of an offer to make amends that is accepted, the aggrieved person cannot continue or enforce an action for defamation (s. 17(1)). A court may order the publisher to still pay expenses incurred by the aggrieved person as a result of accepting the offer and any costs that form part of those expenses (s. 17(2)).

If a reasonable offer to make amends is not accepted, it is a defence to an action for defamation if the publisher (s. 18(1)):

- made the offer as soon as practicable after becoming aware that the matter was, or might have been, defamatory; **and**
- at any time before trial was ready and willing to carry out the terms of the offer; **and**
- in all the circumstances the offer was reasonable.

In determining whether an offer to make amends is reasonable, the court **must** have regard to any correction or apology published before any trial, including the extent to which the correction or apology is brought to the attention of the audience of the matter in question, taking into account the prominence given to it compared to the prominence given to the defamatory material when published and the period that has elapsed between publication of the offending material and publication of the apology (s. 18(2)).

What is required to succeed in a defamation action?

Statement must be defamatory in its ordinary and natural sense

Where there has been a failure to resolve the matter by way of an offer to make amends, the plaintiff may elect to proceed to litigation. As noted above, this can be with or without a jury (unless there is prolonged examination of records or technical, scientific or other issues that might be beyond a jury to understand) (s. 21). Having made the election to go to trial, the plaintiff will have to establish that the material is defamatory, did refer to or identify the plaintiff and was published. However, the legislation does make important changes to the defences available to a defendant.

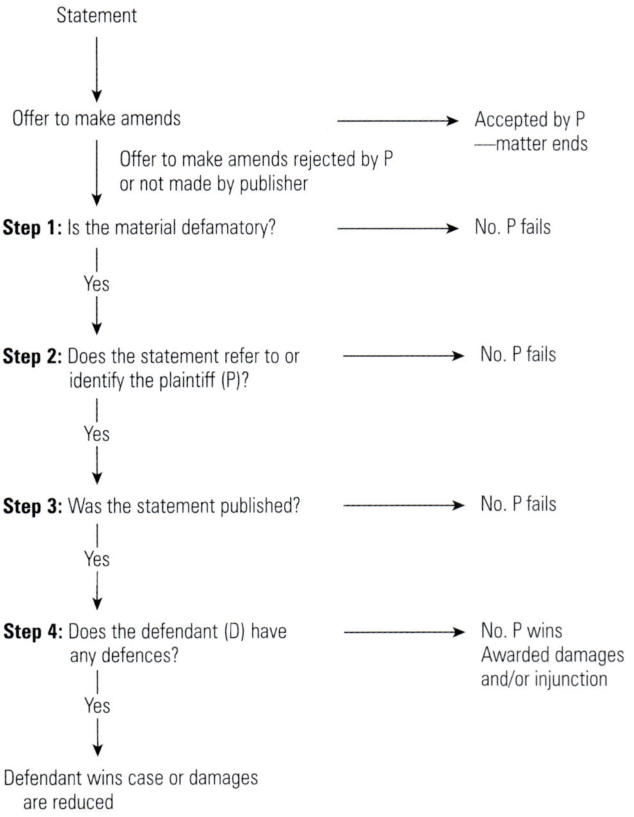

FIGURE 9.4 *Elements that a plaintiff must establish to succeed*

Step 1: Is the material defamatory?

Did the statement of the defendant in its **ordinary and natural sense** defame the plaintiff? The statement must be read as a whole and involves two stages:

- first, the **judge** must be convinced that the statement was capable of being defamatory according to its 'ordinary and natural meaning'.

MIRROR NEWSPAPERS LTD V. HARRISON (1982) 56 ALJR 807

The front page of the newspaper contained a statement that a number of people had been arrested and charged over the assault of a Member of Parliament. The report went into some detail about the affair, stating that the arrests were only made after 'intense investigation' had been undertaken by a 'special squad of detectives'. Harrison was one of the people arrested.

ISSUE: Was the newspaper story defamatory according to its ordinary and natural meaning as it implied Harrison was guilty of the offence?

DECISION: The High Court found that the statement was not defamatory. The statement was not capable of bearing the implication that Harrison was guilty of a criminal offence or that he was directly or even indirectly involved. It merely reported that Harrison had been arrested and charged with assault.

CASE REFLECTION: Could the newspaper article have been defamatory if it included editorial comment regarding the incident and the people involved?

- secondly, if the statement is capable of being defamatory, it is for **the jury** to say whether in the circumstances it was defamatory.

MOROSI V. BROADCASTING STATION 2GB PTY LTD **[1980] 2 NSWLR 418**

A radio announcer at 2GB had repeated a statement made by another person about the conduct of Ms Morosi, who was a staff member of the Deputy Prime Minister, Dr Cairns. The original statement had suggested that the personal conduct of Ms Morosi was questionable; and the radio announcer had then gone on to say that the statement was untrue. Ms Morosi claimed the remarks were defamatory and sued the station. The station argued that the broadcast was not capable of being defamatory as it was defending Ms Morosi and was encouraging the public to question the truthfulness of the media.

ISSUE: Could the jury find that the statement was defamatory in the circumstances, even though the radio station had said, immediately after the making of the statement, that it was untrue?

DECISION: The words were capable of being defamatory when looking at the broadcast as a whole. The jury at first instance had applied the standard of a reasonable, intelligent listener and found that the statement was defamatory in the circumstances. The subsequent statement that the comments were untrue did not outweigh the impact of the original comments.

CASE REFLECTION: Might the announcer have avoided the defamation if the broadcast commenced with a comment regarding the truthfulness of the media and then repeated the statement as an example of media dishonesty?

Whether the statement lowered the plaintiff in the estimation of right-thinking members of the community—and that can be as few as one or two people who knew the plaintiff—is determined by using the standard of the reasonable person which may vary according to community standards.

Step 2: Does the statement refer to or identify the plaintiff?

It is not necessary that the statement actually includes the name of the plaintiff, or was even intended to defame anyone.

E HULTON & CO. V. JONES **[1910] AC 20**

A fictitious article in a newspaper referred to a person named Artemus Jones, a churchwarden of Peckham, as conducting an amorous liaison with a woman who was not his wife, while on holiday in Dieppe. Unfortunately for the newspaper, there was a real Artemus Jones, a barrister who was not a churchwarden and who did not live at Peckham. A number of people still thought that the article referred to him.

ISSUE: Would people reasonably believe that the article, even though it was fictitious, was based on Jones the barrister rather than Jones the churchwarden?

DECISION: The court held that the real Artemus Jones was entitled to recover damages as people reasonably believed that the article referred to him.

CASE REFLECTION: Does the fact that the article was entirely fictitious and written without intention to defame anyone reduce the impact of the statement on the character and career of the real Artemus Jones?

It is enough if it can be **reasonably concluded** by those who know the plaintiff that the statement is about the plaintiff. This is a question for the judge to decide. If it is, the jury decides whether in fact it does so.

It only has to be *reasonably* concluded that statement refers to P

Reference to members of a class of people is not actionable by individual members of that class unless it can be proved that the statement is capable of referring to all the individual members of the class. In *Random House Pty Ltd v. Abbott* [1999] Aust. Torts Reports ¶81–533 the appellants had published a book that suggested that one of the unidentified wives of two Liberal Party federal ministers had, before her marriage, slept with both men in order to get them to change their political allegiances. The Federal Court of Appeal held this to be defamatory of both wives.

Step 3: Was the statement published?

'Published', in cases of defamation, means that the statement must have been made known to a **third party** who was **capable of understanding** the defamatory meaning. This may be words, signs, gestures or some other form of communication.

Statement must be made known to a third party

A person who republishes defamatory material becomes a new publisher, as was seen above in the *Morosi* case.

If the third party did not understand what was being said—for example, because the statement was made in a foreign language—then no action could lie.

Step 4: Does the defendant have any defences?

The scope of defences under general law has not been limited by the uniform defamation laws (s. 24).

Justification (s. 25)

The defence of justification (or truth) is available to a defendant if it can be shown that the allegation is **substantially true**. This reflects the common law position that 'truth alone' is a complete defence to an action in defamation. This means that a person who has had something truthful published about them is not entitled to receive compensation, even though they might feel that they have been defamed.

Justification or truth requires a heavy onus on the defendant to prove the defamatory statement was true

The defence of justification is difficult to establish because the defendant has the difficult task of proving to the satisfaction of the court that the allegedly defamatory statement was, in fact, true. A defendant is much more likely to invoke other defences such as fair comment or honest opinion where the truth of the publication is not a central issue. Furthermore, at common law, a defendant who genuinely, but incorrectly, believed the statement was true did not have a defence.

Contextual truth (s. 26)

Contextual truth prevents a plaintiff from taking minor matters out of context in what is a substantially true publication

It is a defence for the defendant if he or she can prove that the defamatory matter carried, in addition to the defamatory imputations (or meanings) of which the plaintiff complained, one or more other imputations (called 'contextual imputations') that were substantially true and that the defamatory imputations did not do any further harm to the reputation of the plaintiff because of the substantial truth of the contextual imputations. The purpose of the defence is basically to prevent plaintiffs from taking relatively minor imputations out of their context within a substantially true publication.

Absolute privilege (s. 27)

Absolute privilege recognises society's interest in the importance of free speech

This defence allows people to say exactly what they like without fear of legal proceedings. It accepts the defamatory nature of the statement but defends it on the grounds that the interests of the community are seen as more important than the reputation of the individual in the community. The legislation sets out two instances where absolute privilege applies:

- statements made during sittings in Parliament, in parliamentary papers and government or statutory inquiries; and
- judicial proceedings and their reports.

Schedule 1 sets out further additional publications to which absolute privilege applies.

Reports, if published, must be published in good faith if they are not to be actionable in defamation. Good faith suggests the absence of improper motivation and a normal mode of publication.

Publication of public documents (s. 28)

This defence provides that it is a defence to the publication of defamatory material if the defendant proves that the matter was contained in a public document (or a fair copy of a public document), or a fair summary of (or an extract from) a public document. 'Public document' is broadly defined in s. 28(4) to cover a wide range of material including parliamentary reports, civil judgements and other publicly available material, including the documents referred to in Schedule 2 of the Acts.

Fair reporting of matters of public concern (s. 29)

It is a defence in the publication of defamatory matter if the defendant proves that that matter was contained in a fair report of any proceedings of public concern. The onus is on the defendant to establish that:

- the matter was (or was contained in) an earlier published report of proceedings of public concern; **and**
- the matter was (or was contained in) a fair copy, summary or extract from an earlier published report; **and**
- the defendant had no knowledge that would reasonably make them aware that the earlier published report was not fair.

The term 'proceedings of public concern' is broadly defined in s. 29(4) and extended in Schedule 3 to cover a wide range of proceedings including those of parliamentary committees, commissions of inquiry, law reform bodies, local councils, and a range of corporate, professional, sport and recreation bodies.

Qualified privilege (s. 30)

Qualified privilege provides protection where there is a moral or legal duty to make what might otherwise be defamatory statements

At common law, **qualified privilege** permitted a certain degree of protection but not complete immunity. The privilege was qualified because it could be negatived by other factors, such as malice (and this is still the case under the legislation: s. 30(4)). It can be used as a defence where (s. 30(1)):

- the recipient of the statement has an interest or an apparent interest in the subject of the information; **and**
- the material published was in the course of providing the recipient with information relating to that subject; **and**
- the conduct of the person publishing the material is reasonable in the circumstances.

In determining what is 'reasonable in the circumstances', a court may take into account:

- the extent to which the matter published is of public interest; **and**
- the extent to which the matter published relates to the performance of the public functions or activities of the person; **and**
- the seriousness of any defamatory imputation carried by the matter published; **and**
- the extent to which the matter published distinguishes between suspicions, allegations and proven facts; **and**
- whether it was in the public interest in the circumstances for the matter published to be published expeditiously; **and**
- the nature of the business environment in which the defendant operates; **and**
- the sources of the information in the matter published and the integrity of those sources; **and**

- whether the matter published contained the substance of the person's side of the story and, if not, whether a reasonable attempt was made by the defendant to obtain and publish a response from the person; **and**
- any other steps taken to verify the information in the matter published; **and**
- any other circumstances that the court considers relevant.

> **!** CAUTION NOTE
> ***Absolute privilege is a complete defence*** *but* ***qualified privilege is limited****, with D having to establish that comments were reasonable and not recklessly indifferent or motivated by malice!*

Honest opinion (s. 31)

Section 31 provides for a number of defences relating to the publication of matter that expresses an opinion that is honestly held by its maker rather than a statement of fact. The section identifies three situations:

Honest opinion refers to the expression of an opinion that is honestly held rather than a statement of fact

- where the opinion was that of the defendant (s. 31(1));
- where the opinion was that of the defendant's employee or agent (s. 31(2)); or
- where the opinion was that of a third party (s. 31(3)).

In each case, the opinion must relate to a matter of public interest and it must be based on proper material. 'Proper material' is defined in the legislation to mean material that is substantially true, was published on an occasion of absolute or qualified privilege, or was published on an occasion that attracted the protection of the defence of publication of public documents (s. 28) or the defence of fair reporting of proceedings of public concern (s. 29).

Innocent dissemination (s. 32)

The defence of innocent dissemination essentially codifies the common law. It is a defence to the publication of defamatory matter if the defendant proves that:

- the defendant published the matter in the capacity, or as an employee or agent, of a subordinate distributor, e.g., a bookseller or librarian (s. 32(3));
- the defendant neither knew (nor ought reasonably to have known) that the matter was defamatory; and
- the defendant's ignorance was not due to the defendant's own negligence.

This section is particularly important for Internet providers and other disseminators of electronic information as these providers will now be treated as subordinate distributors, unless a service provider was, in fact, the author or originator of the defamatory material, or had the power to exercise editorial control over the matter.

Triviality (s. 33)

It is a defence for a defendant if he or she can show that the circumstances of the publication were such that the plaintiff was unlikely to suffer any harm.

Remedies

The normal remedy for defamation is damages. Juries will no longer be able to award damages. The amount of damages that may be awarded will be determined by the court and the damages to be awarded must bear a rational relationship to the harm that the plaintiff suffers (s. 34).

The main remedy for defamation is damages

Damages for non-economic loss are to be limited to $250 000 (adjusted annually). In *Sleeman v. Nationwide News Ltd* [2004] NSWSC 954, a journalist from the *Sydney Morning Herald* was awarded $400 000 in damages after a jury found that an article in *The Australian* newspaper conveyed the impression that he was a dishonest journalist. Today, the most that the journalist could be awarded would be $250 000, unless the court is satisfied that the circumstances are such as to warrant an award of aggravated damages (s. 35). In awarding damages, the state of mind of the defendant is generally not relevant except to the extent that the malice or other state of mind affects the harm sustained by the plaintiff (s. 36). Exemplary or punitive damages cannot be awarded (s. 37).

In assessing damages, evidence is admissible by the defendant as to why the amount to be awarded to the plaintiff should not be reduced, including (s. 38):

- the defendant has made an apology to the plaintiff;
- the defendant has published a correction; or
- the plaintiff has already recovered damages, received compensation, or brought proceedings in relation to a similar matter.

ECONOMIC TORTS

This group of torts is concerned with intentional interference with an economic interest and protection against economic loss to a plaintiff. However, they are not concerned with cut-throat competition. A person generally owes no duty to another to prevent economic loss even though the first person may intend to cause economic loss to the other. Where the law has allowed an action in tort to lie, and these torts rely on the intention of the defendant, are:

- where the defendant has been dishonest or acted out of improper motive: the torts of deceit, injurious falsehood and conspiracy by the use of lawful means;
- where the defendant has inflicted loss through unlawful means: the torts of intimidation, use of unlawful means and conspiracy through unlawful means; and
- wilful violation of a right: the torts of inducement of breach of contract and passing off.

IN BRIEF

Torts available for protection of economic interests

There are a number of specific torts, often referred to as economic torts, which are available to protect business interests:

- Intimidation
- Interference with contractual relations
- Conspiracy by the use of lawful or unlawful means
- Passing off
- Injurious falsehood
- Deceit (Misrepresentation).

Intimidation

***Intimidation*—D must intend to harm P and loss must occur**

The tort of intimidation, which is part of the tort of intentional interference with trade or business, was identified by Lord *Devlin* in *Rookes v. Barnard* [1964] AC 1129. He suggested it may arise in one of two ways:

- threats of an **unlawful act** by the defendant so that the plaintiff acts to their own loss; or
- threats of an **unlawful act** by the defendant against another person to intentionally force them to do harm to the plaintiff.

ROOKES V. BARNARD [1964] AC 1129

Rookes resigned from his union after a dispute. Union members then threatened Rookes' employer with an unlawful strike if he did not dismiss him. As a result of the threat, the employer lawfully dismissed him. Agreements between the employer, the union and the employees' individual contracts of employment provided for 100 per cent union membership, and also that there should be neither strike nor lock-out.

ISSUE: Did the threat by unionists to withhold their labour constitute a threat to break their contracts? Were their actions intimidatory?

DECISION: To coerce a person to do or abstain from doing something that they would otherwise have every right to do, by unlawful means amounted to the tort of intimidation.

An unlawful act would include a tort or a breach of contract.

The defendant must intend to harm the plaintiff if there is to be a cause of action and loss must be proved as a result of the conduct induced by the threat. As the defendant must intend to harm the plaintiff, intimidation may be both a tort and a crime.

Damages may be awarded by the court for any loss that may be reasonably inferred, as well as exemplary (punitive) damages and the court, in its equitable jurisdiction, may make an order of a negative or mandatory injunction.

Interference with contractual relations

***Interference with contractual relations*—D knowingly encourages another to break their contract with P**

A defendant who **knowingly induces** a contracting party to break a valid existing contract is liable to the other party to the contract in tort. There must be:

- a valid existing contract;
- awareness by the defendant of the contractual relationship;

LUMLEY V. WAGNER (1852) 42 ER 687

Wagner, a well-known opera star, had been engaged by the plaintiff (Lumley) to sing at the Queen's Theatre, London. Before the start of the opera season, she entered into a contract with Gye to sing at another venue even though Gye was aware of the first contract.

ISSUE: Did Gye's actions amount to an interference with contractual relations and bring about a breach of contract?

DECISION: Gye's actions in inducing Wagner to break her contract with Lumley amounted to a direct and malicious interference with contractual relations and that an action in tort based on interference with contractual relations lay against Gye.

- intention by the defendant to cause or induce the breach of contract (although there may be no need for the plaintiff to establish this point if it can be shown as an inevitable inference that some degree of interference with trade or business must follow from the unlawful conduct of the defendant, e.g., *Ansett (Operations) Pty Ltd v. Australian Federation of Air Pilots* [1991] 1 VR 637;
- wrongful or unlawful interference by the defendant;

***MERKUR ISLAND SHIPPING CORPORATION V. LAUGHTON* [1983] 1 ALL ER 334**

The defendant trade unionists had a dispute with the plaintiff shipowners. The shipowners had entered into a contract with a charter party in relation to one of their ships. The vessel was then subchartered and the subcharterers then entered into a contract with a tugboat company to move the ship. The union convinced the seamen on the tugboat to break their contracts of employment and refuse to move the ship. As a result, both the charter and subcharter could not be performed and the plaintiffs suffered a loss because of the industrial action.

ISSUE: Were the union's actions in inducing the seamen on the tugboat to break their contracts of employment sufficient to amount to an indirect interference to produce a breach of contract?

DECISION: The plaintiffs had a cause of action in tort against the union as they had used unlawful means to bring about indirectly an interference with the main contract. The unlawful means in this case was the inducing of the seamen on the tugboat to break their contracts of employment.

- a breach of contract as a result of the wrongful or unlawful interference; and
- damage to the plaintiff.

Damages may be awarded for any loss that may be reasonably inferred, as well as exemplary (punitive) damages and the court, in its equitable jurisdiction, may make an order of a negative or mandatory injunction. Remedies may also be available under the 'secondary boycott' provisions of Part IV of the *Trade Practices Act 1974* (Cth) and the Fair Trading legislation of the states and territories.

Conspiracy by the use of lawful or unlawful means

***Conspiracy*—unlawful act or means to injure P**

The tort of conspiracy, which may also be a crime, may arise if it can be established that there is:

- an agreement between two or more persons;
- using lawful or unlawful means with the **intention to injure** the plaintiff's business or other economic interests; **and**
- the act is carried out and the purpose achieved.

There **must** be an intention to injure the plaintiff. Where lawful means are used, intention to injure the plaintiff must be predominant. In the case of unlawful means, mere intention is sufficient.

A plaintiff must show that actual damage was suffered.

Passing off

***Passing off*—misrepresentation by D that their goods or services are connected with P**

Passing off involves a recognition by a defendant of the quality of the plaintiff's goods and a misrepresentation by the defendant that their goods are connected with the plaintiff, a so-called intellectual property right. Examples of passing off include use of another's trademark and the use of another's name to induce people to believe that the businesses are connected. Actual damage is not required.

Factors that **must** be present in order to succeed in a claim include:

- a misrepresentation by the defendant that their goods or services are connected with the plaintiff;
- that the misrepresentation or passing off by the defendant was made in the course of trade; **and**
- that the misrepresentation or passing off was intended to deceive potential purchasers.

It is not necessary to show that anyone was actually deceived but mere uncertainty or confusion is not enough. **There must be a likelihood that people would be misled or deceived.** A plaintiff will be more likely to succeed where they have, for example:

- a name that is descriptive and formulated in a distinctive way, such as 'Taco Bell' (*Taco Co. of Australia Inc. v. Taco Bell Pty Ltd* (1982) 43 ALR 177);
- a name specifically associated with a product of a particular region such as 'champagne' which is associated exclusively with the Champagne region of France (*J. Bollinger v. Costa Brava Wine Co. (No. 2)* [1961] 1 WLR 277); or
- a name specifically associated with a product of a particular composition.

A successful plaintiff may recover damages (for commercial loss, loss of goodwill, damage to reputation) or elect to claim an equitable remedy of account to recover any profits made by the defendant. The plaintiff may also seek an injunction to stop the defendant continuing to carry on business.

Injurious falsehood

Injurious falsehood is an economic tort that may be used by a business to sue other businesses or individuals who make false, misleading or critical statements about the plaintiff's goods or services. For a plaintiff to succeed they must show:

- they had an established reputation;
- the statement by the defendant was made with intent to harm the plaintiff's reputation; and
- they suffered, or are reasonably likely to suffer, loss as a result.

Injurious falsehood—used by a business to sue other businesses or individuals who make false, misleading or critical statements about P's goods or services

Because of the difficulty of proof, it is easier for businesses to rely on ss. 52 and 53 of the *Trade Practices Act 1974* (Cth) (see Chapter 23).

Deceit (Misrepresentation)

Common law: Often representations will be made during contractual negotiations which will induce the other party to enter into a contractual relationship (see p. 324). If these representations are untrue, they are called misrepresentations and there are a number of legal remedies available to an injured party to choose from. Choosing one does not exclude the others.

If the misrepresentation is innocent (i.e. not negligent) or not fraudulent, for example, where a person gave information in the honest and reasonable belief that it was correct, then **no** remedy will lie in tort. However, if a fiduciary, confidential or special relationship exists, then an action may lie in the tortious area of negligent misrepresentation (see p. 327).

In the case of a fraudulent misrepresentation where there has been an intentional deceit by one party (see p. 325), the fraudulent conduct forms the basis of the tort of deceit. The effect on the contract is to make it voidable at the option of the injured party. This gives the injured party the choice of carrying on with the contract if they wish, but suing for damages in tort. However, they must make their decision to go on with the contract or rescind within a reasonable time of discovering the fraud.

Statutory remedies: The failure of the common law to provide adequate remedies for misrepresentation, in particular innocent misrepresentation, led South Australia and the Australian Capital Territory to statutorily expand the remedies that were available with the passage of the *Misrepresentation Act 1972* (SA) and the *Civil Law (Wrongs) Act 2002* (ACT), see Chapter 15. These laws provide that where a contract has been induced by an innocent misrepresentation, damages and rescission may be available (see also pp. 324–330).

Both the South Australian and Australian Capital Territory legislation provide for criminal penalties where misrepresentations are made in the course of trade or commerce for the purpose of inducing a person to enter into a contract. Liability can extend to an employer where the person making the misrepresentations is acting in the course of their employment.

The Fair Trading legislation of the states and territories and the *Trade Practices Act 1974* (Cth) have also significantly altered the law relating to misrepresentations.

> **!** CAUTION NOTE
> *In the case of fraudulent misrepresentation, the remedy lies in tort as the tort of deceit,* ***not*** *contract.*

MISCELLANEOUS TORTS

Nuisance

After intentional torts, the tort of nuisance is the next oldest in the area of the law of torts. This is not surprising as it reflects the importance of property and its use and enjoyment in a feudal, essentially agricultural, society. Hence its connection to land.

IN BRIEF

The tort of nuisance is concerned with land

The tort of nuisance may be either public or private. It consists of an **unreasonable interference** with the **use and enjoyment of land** and is concerned with **indirect harm**.

If an interference created by a defendant constitutes a nuisance, the defendant will be liable for the nuisance, whether or not they failed to take reasonable care. Types of nuisance are private, public or statutory (see Figure 9.5).

Public nuisance

The origins of public nuisance can be found in the criminal law. It is an unlawful act or a failure to discharge a legal duty generally related to land which interferes with the enjoyment of a right available to the general public and may result in the offender being prosecuted.

There are numerous statutes that confer wide powers on local authorities and other government bodies for the control and abatement of public nuisances, for example, smoke, fumes, noise, etc. In exceptional circumstances where a plaintiff has suffered financial damage or loss, they may bring a civil action against the offender.

What has to be proved in a private right of action?

A plaintiff must establish:

- first that the 'nuisance' was **substantial and unreasonable** and materially affected the reasonable comfort and convenience of life of a class of the population of which the plaintiff was a member, e.g., a shop owner. This is a question of fact in each case; **and**
- secondly that they have suffered **particular damage** over and above that suffered by the public because of the nuisance—e.g., loss of custom, physical injury or loss of business profits. 'Particular damage' is not limited to 'special damage' in the sense of actual financial loss.

The damage suffered by the plaintiff must not be too remote and the test for remoteness is the same as the one for negligence—reasonable foreseeability.

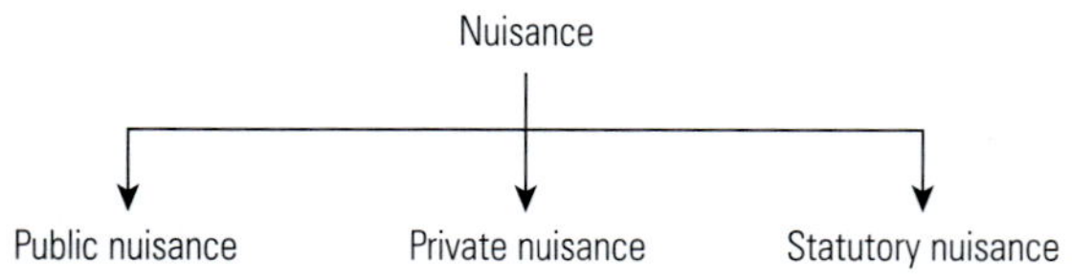

FIGURE 9.5 *Types of nuisance*

Often, both public nuisance and negligence may be available. Where this is the case, it is to the plaintiff's advantage to bring the action in public nuisance because once it is proved that the defendant caused it, the burden of proof moves to the defendant to provide an excuse. In negligence, the burden of proof remains on the plaintiff throughout.

Remedies

The remedy for a public nuisance is by indictment, information or injunction at the initiative of the Attorney-General, and in certain cases by summary process. If special damages are caused to a plaintiff, they may be able to maintain an action for damages, abatement or an injunction.

Private nuisance

Private nuisance involves a substantial and unreasonable interference with someone's enjoyment of their interest in land. It does not have to be committed from land. It can be committed from the highway or even from the air space above the land. What it must do is interfere with the enjoyment of the land by the person in occupation, who may be the owner or a tenant. It is relied upon when the interference is indirect or where the invading 'thing' is intangible, for example, noise or offensive smells.

IN BRIEF

Private nuisance distinguished from public nuisance

A private nuisance can be distinguished from a public nuisance in the following ways:

- it is not a crime;
- it can be committed against an individual or a class of the population; **and**
- it must be committed against land.

What has to be proved?

***Private nuisance*—an indirect interference by D of P's use or enjoyment of their land**

Only the person in **occupation** of the affected land (who could be the owner or a lessee) can sue. To succeed, the plaintiff needs to establish:

- First, that there has been an **indirect**, substantial and **unreasonable interference** with the use or enjoyment of land by the defendant.

  Factors for consideration of what is 'unreasonable interference' include:
  - duration
  - locality
  - gravity of the harm
  - motive
  - alternatives.
- Second, that they have suffered actual **damage**.

Damage can be physical or indirect

Damage can be in the form of physical damage to the land, buildings or goods (chattels) through vibrations, flooding, fire, the roots or branches of trees, and the like; or an interference with the enjoyment of the land through noise, smell, dust, or even reasonable fear of one's health or safety.

***ROBINSON V. KILVERT* (1889) 41 CH D 88**

Kilvert manufactured paper boxes that required hot and dry air. He heated his premises which raised the temperature in the premises of Robinson above him where Robinson stored sensitive paper. It was damaged because of the increased temperatures.

ISSUE: Were Kilvert's activities an indirect, substantial and unreasonable interference with Robinson's enjoyment of his premises?

DECISION: Robinson was not entitled to succeed since there would have been no damage but for the exceptional sensitivity of his trade.

Who may be sued?

The two main defendants who could be sued are:

- the person who caused the nuisance or authorised it (thus an employee can make their employer vicariously liable for the nuisance they created if the employee was acting in the course of the employment at the relevant time); and/or
- the occupier of the land from which the nuisance came. However, the occupier must have had knowledge or means of knowledge of the nuisance and failed to take reasonable steps to bring it to an end, though with ample time to do so.

The creator of the nuisance need not be in occupation of land and, in fact, the nuisance does not even have to be committed from private land, for example, in *Bernstein v. Skyviews* [1978] QB 479 (where the nuisance was created from the air space above the plaintiff's land).

***SEDLEIGH-DENFIELD V. O'CALLAGHAN* [1940] AC 880**

A local council, without the permission of O'Callaghan as occupier, laid a pipeline in a ditch on their land to carry off rainwater. In order to prevent leaves and other rubbish blocking the opening, a grating was placed over it, but the work was badly done. As a result, during a heavy rainstorm some three years later, the grating became blocked and the adjoining premises were flooded.

ISSUE: Was O'Callaghan, as the occupier, liable for the nuisance created by the council?

DECISION: O'Callaghan was responsible because he had acquired knowledge of the risk of flooding through a servant, who was in charge of cleaning the ditch, and they had used the pipe to get rid of water from their property without taking any steps to make it safe over a three-year period.

COMMENT: Once the occupier knows, or ought to know, of a nuisance created by a third party, there is a duty of care to remove it. Failure to do so can make the occupier liable through inaction for failing to remove it once he or she has knowledge of it ('continuing it') or using it for the defendant's own purpose ('adopting it').

Doing business

Responsibility of an occupier may be wider than you think

The effect of the decision in *Sedleigh-Denfield*'s case is that an occupier could also be responsible for nuisances created by independent contractors, by employees, and even by third parties. The occupier may even attract liability for an activity on their land which results in offensive conduct taking place outside it, for example, a fête, the races or even an outdoor concert. ■

Defences

Defences include:

- consent;
- statutory authority (for example, public authorities);
- taking of reasonable precautions (the duration of the nuisance is short-lived and the defendant has taken all reasonable precautions, for example, in the demolition or renovation of a building); and
- contributory negligence.

It is not a defence for a defendant to argue that the plaintiff has 'come to the nuisance', for example, by moving near to a private airport or race track, that the activities benefit the public, or that the benefit to the public outweighs the detriment to the plaintiff.

Remedies

The usual remedy is an injunction to stop the defendant from continuing the nuisance if it can be shown that the nuisance is likely to be a continuing one. Damages are only available once damage has occurred.

An alternative remedy to going to court may be the remedy of abatement where the plaintiff puts an end to the nuisance—for example, by cutting the branches of a tree overhanging the plaintiff's property or cutting the roots of an encroaching tree. However, where the plaintiff takes this course of action, the offending branches or roots must be returned on demand to the defendant.

Statutory torts

Tort of breach of statutory duty: in certain situations, a plaintiff may have an action in the tort of breach of statutory duty, for example, where there is a breach of industrial safety provisions. The requirements are similar to, but not the same as, those of the tort of negligence. The essential elements are:

- the statutory duty in question must have been intended to confer a civil remedy in tort;
- the statutory duty must be owed by the defendant and the defendant must be in breach of that duty. Liability is strict, so there is no need to establish fault on the defendant's part;
- the plaintiff must be a person for whom the benefit of the Act was passed and the harm must be of the kind that the Act was intended to protect the plaintiff from; and
- the damage suffered by the plaintiff must be caused by the breach and related to personal injury or damage to property.

New torts

Tort of invasion of privacy: it is often assumed that the only tort still undergoing expansion and refinement is the tort of negligence. However, this is not the case. For example, in *ABC v. Lenah Game Meats Pty Ltd* (2001) 208 CLR 199, the High Court held that there was no authority preventing the tort of invasion of privacy and in 2003, the District Court in Queensland in *Grosse v. Purvis* [2003] QDC 151 used the High Court decision as authority to award the plaintiff $178 000 damages against the defendant for his harassment and stalking of her. *Skoien* J suggested that a **tort of invasion of privacy** could exist if a plaintiff could establish that the offensive behaviour of the defendant caused the plaintiff to suffer anguish and post-traumatic stress disorder. The plaintiff has to show:

- a deliberate act by the defendant;
- which intrudes on the privacy or seclusion of the plaintiff;
- which would be considered highly offensive to a reasonable person; and
- which causes the plaintiff mental, psychological or emotional harm or distress, or which hinders the plaintiff in their lawful activities.

Statutory nuisance is concerned with the expanding area of environmental, zoning, health and safety Acts, delegated legislation and regulations that are emanating from Commonwealth, state and territory governments, local councils and shires, as well as government departments.

REVIEW QUESTIONS

?

9.1 Indicate whether each of the following statements is true or false:

Statement	TRUE	FALSE
Trespass actions are actions *per se*	☐	☐
Trespass to the person involves a direct interference with the person of the plaintiff	☐	☐
A person who borrows a friend's textbook without permission and then refuses to return it commits the tort of detinue	☐	☐
Trespass to land can arise if rubbish is left on land without permission	☐	☐
False imprisonment involves a total restraint of the plaintiff by the defendant to move about	☐	☐
Trespass to goods can occur without the goods being taken away	☐	☐

9.2 To point an unloaded gun at a person could constitute an assault if the person did not know it was unloaded, but if they knew it was unloaded, then there could be no assault. Discuss.

activebook

Activebook resources include in-depth summaries with links to the relevant part of the book. For revision, add your own notes to the summaries provided by using the note-taking function.

9.3 Joe owned a milk bar just around the corner from a very busy highway. However, because he was around the corner, most people didn't know about his shop and so they didn't stop. To try to make more people aware that he was there, Joe erected a large sign which, while it was visible from the highway, also projected over the land owned by Pat on the corner. Pat objected to the sign and threatened legal action.

What sort of action could Pat bring? What would Pat need to establish and do you think such an action would be successful? Explain your answers.

9.4 Bert had bought an old house in a country town as a weekender. The land surrounding the house was overgrown with tall grass and shrubs. Bert realised that this could be a fire hazard in a hot summer and so decided to trim the shrubs and burn the grass and rubbish. He was careful to clear a wide path around the edge of his property to ensure that the fire could not spread to adjoining properties and he arranged to have the local bushfire brigade on standby in case anything went wrong. He selected a cool day with little or no wind for his burning off. Because the town had not had rain for some considerable time, the ground was far drier than Bert imagined and the fire quickly took hold. It engulfed the old house and then swept on to neighbouring properties, destroying several adjoining houses before the local fire brigade was able to get it under control and eventually put it out.

The neighbours wish to know whether they have any legal rights that they can enforce against Bert. Advise them, and in your answer suggest any defences that Bert may raise.

9.5 Explain the meaning of defamation.

9.6 Explain the difference between absolute and qualified privilege as defences to a defamation action.

9.7 Explain why it is necessary that, in a defamation action, publication to a third person is required. Why can't you have a defamation action involving only two persons?

9.8 Consider whether each of the following statements is defamatory, explaining your reasoning:

i Brett said to Pete, 'You are a thief. You stole my textbooks from my locker.'

ii Paul, a Member of Parliament, in a speech in Parliament stated: 'Sophia was a well-known crime figure who liked nothing better than being seen with members of the opposition.' This, in fact, wasn't true.

iii In the editorial of a national newspaper, on the basis of Paul's speech in Parliament, Wayne had written, 'Opposition members seen with well-known crime figure'.

9.9 Indicate whether each of the following statements is true or false:

Statement	TRUE	FALSE
Where a statement is made in Parliament, absolute privilege is a complete defence to a defamation action	☐	☐
For a plaintiff to succeed in a defamation action, they have to show that the statement has been made known to a third person	☐	☐

▪ A person who repeats or republishes defamatory material is as liable as the original publisher	☐	☐
▪ Conspiracy is both a crime and a tort	☐	☐
▪ To knowingly induce another party to break a contract is a tort	☐	☐
▪ The tort of passing off involves the threat of unlawful force to the detriment of the plaintiff	☐	☐
▪ A private nuisance is a crime as well as a civil wrong	☐	☐
▪ Anybody who is affected by the actions of a person can sue in private nuisance	☐	☐

9.10 Distinguish between a public and a private nuisance.

9.11 State what has to be established in order for a plaintiff to succeed in an action in private nuisance.

9.12 What defences can a defendant raise against an action brought against them for private nuisance?

9.13 Erica lived next door to Philip, who had planted a row of gum trees down his and Erica's boundary. As the trees grew, their branches began to hang over into Erica's yard. This caused loss of light into her backyard and covered it with dead leaves and branches.

Advise Erica whether there is anything that she can do, giving reasons for your advice.

CRITICAL THINKING

9.1 What reasons can you put forward for the need for a uniform defamation law?

9.2 How important are the economic torts to business? Discuss.

CHAPTER

Insurance

CHAPTER CONTENTS

activebook

This icon is used throughout the following chapter to remind you to visit the *Business Law* online activebook for additional exercises, links to legal websites, and feedback. For a detailed explanation of what is in the activebook please refer to the inside cover of this textbook. The activebook is available through OneKey.

Where do I start?

Learning path: Use the activebook to complete a pre-chapter warm-up exercise.

There are many definitions of legal terms to assist with your understanding of the material.

CHAPTER OBJECTIVES

On completion of this chapter, you should be able to:

- identify and briefly explain the main features of insurable interest
- identify and briefly explain the main features of indemnity
- identify and briefly explain the main features of utmost good faith
- identify and briefly explain the main features of subrogation
- explain how the *Insurance Contracts Act 1984* (Cth) has affected each of the above common law principles
- describe the duties and liabilities of insurance agents and brokers
- list and describe the common forms of insurance applicable to a business organisation
- explain the difference between general insurance and life assurance policies.

KEY TERMS

An understanding of the following terms will help you to better understand the material in this chapter:

- **act of God:** a natural event or occurrence that cannot be foreseen and that happens independently of human intervention, such as an earthquake or storm
- **assurance:** a term used interchangeably with insurance. Refers to contracts where the event or risk covered is a certainty, for example, death
- **broker:** a mercantile agent for the purchase and sale of goods, stocks and shares, insurance policies, etc.
- **brokerage:** the commission payable to a broker
- **commission:** the sum paid to an agent, usually expressed as a percentage of the price or premium or the sum insured
- ***contra proferentum*:** the doctrine that the construction least favourable to the party putting forward an argument or document should be used against him or her
- **cover note:** an interim contract of insurance pending the acceptance or decline of a full contract of insurance
- **indemnity:** protection against loss, usually provided by way of contract of insurance
- **insurable interest:** the pecuniary interest that the insured has in the subject matter of the insurance. It signifies the benefit the insured will gain from the preservation of the subject matter insured or the detriment they will suffer from its loss
- **insurance:** a contract whereby a person called the insurer agrees in consideration of money paid to them (the premium), by another person called the assured, to indemnify the latter against loss resulting on the occurrence of a specified event. It refers to terms based upon a risk or contingency
- **insured:** the person covered by an insurance policy
- **insurer:** the person who contracts, for a premium, to indemnify another against losses. Also called an assurer
- ***pluvius*:** characterised by or due to the action of rain, for example, insurance against rain
- **premium:** the price payable for a contract of insurance
- **subrogation:** the substitution of one person or thing for another so that the same rights and duties which were possessed by the original person are transferred to the substituted one. For example, an insurer is generally subrogated to the rights of the insured on paying their claim
- ***uberrimae fidei:*** in the utmost good faith.

what if . . .

You purchased a new car but you had a bad driving record and knew you would have difficulty obtaining insurance. You decide to insure the car in the name of another member of your family, such as one of your parents, because they have a good driving record and a high no claim bonus. You have an accident and you make a claim under your parent's name. If the insurance company suspected that your parent did not own the car, they would probably refuse to honour the policy. What would be the insurance law reasons which would support their action?

A business cannot operate without incurring risk and sometimes subsequent loss. That loss may arise from a natural disaster such as a fire, earthquake or storm. On the other hand, a loss can be incurred because of a legal action brought against the business, for example, for breach of contract or out of the law of tort of negligence. To minimise the risk of loss, good advice to any businessperson will always be to ensure that their premises and equipment, or any goods that they purchase, are insured to full market value. From inception until termination, uncertainty as to the firm's business direction is one of the major concerns of the owner/s and manager/s. Thus risk is an important factor in the day-to-day running of a business and it can pose problems in a number of ways. Some of these are:

- Risk of loss of the firm's assets and earning power through damage or destruction of its plant and equipment by fire, flood, wind or other perils.
- Risk of loss of goods the firm may purchase or sell through damage or destruction of its plant or warehouse, or in transit.
- Risk of loss from unintentional acts that cause loss to others (e.g. a negligent act of an employee, a defective product), resulting in legal liability.
- In the case of a manufacturer, there is product risk.
- For all firms there is market risk.
- All firms also face social risk such as strikes, laws which hinder business operations, and political decisions which have the effect of restricting business activity.
- All firms face financial risk.
- In many businesses there is one person (e.g. an owner, a partner, a manager) upon whom the success of the business is dependent. For these businesses the risk of death of that person is important.

Insurance is a means for persons and businesses to protect and compensate themselves against the risk of loss. Insurance is vital to personal, business and estate planning. However, the cost of public liability/public risk insurance premiums has risen dramatically in Australia in the last few years for a number of reasons, including larger compensation payouts by the courts and, perhaps one of the most important, the collapse of the Australian insurance group HIH in 2001 which, through its competitiveness, had kept premiums artificially low.

As a result of a perceived crisis in public liability/public risk insurance, all of the states and the Australian Capital Territory passed legislation modifying the application of the law of negligence, tightening up aspects of the making of claims and associated court proceedings. The aim of these statutory changes is to reduce claims and thereby reduce premiums. For details of the statutory changes you should refer to Chapters 7 and 8.

This chapter examines the concepts underlying insurance, the making of the insurance contract, construction of the policy, the law regarding agents and brokers, and some common types of business insurance.

RISK

Risk can be said to fall into two categories. It will be either:

- **speculative:** there is uncertainty that could result in either a gain or a loss, such as a business venture; or
- **pure:** should the risk occur it will result in loss—for example, loss of property by fire, flood or storm, or the death or disability of a key employee caused by an accident.

Risk is either speculative (uncertain) or pure (there will be loss if it occurs)

The distinction is important because **as a general rule it is only possible to obtain insurance coverage in the case of pure risk**. The risk is not created by the parties but exists because of the potential for loss beyond the control of the parties. The insured benefits from the protection purchased, the insurer benefits from the receipt of the premium.

Spreading the risk

Insurance is concerned with spreading risk

Insurance is concerned with the spreading of risk in order to protect persons or property against loss resulting from expected or unexpected events which are beyond the control of the parties. The primary objective of insurance is to gain the cooperation of a large number of people with a common interest to share the particular risk against which insurance is desired. It is essential that 'large' numbers of persons be involved because it has the effect of making the individual's share of any loss relatively small.

Before agreeing to compensate or indemnify someone from loss, an insurance company will first want to have some idea of the risk associated with what they are being asked to insure. With this information it is then possible to calculate a sum to be paid by the insured person as a premium to safely cover the possible liabilities of the company.

WHAT IS AN INSURANCE CONTRACT?

A contract of insurance, found in a document called a policy, is one whereby:

- an insurer (the person who is prepared to cover the whole or a portion of the loss and who is either an insurance company or an underwriter);
- in consideration of the payment of a sum of money (the premium);
- agrees to indemnify the insured/assured (the person taking out the insurance);
- against some risk such as fire, accident or theft, or to pay a fixed sum on the happening of a certain event, such as death.

IN BRIEF

Is there a difference between insurance and assurance?

Contract of insurance: the insured is indemnified against unforeseeable loss or damage which may or may not occur, e.g. damage to property by fire or loss by burglary.

Contract of assurance (or a contingency contract): the assured or their representatives will receive a sum of money on the occurrence of an event which must occur at some time, although the time of the occurrence, such as the death or personal injury of the assured, is uncertain.

Insurance is an aleatory contract

An insurance contract can be distinguished from an ordinary business agreement. Generally, in a business agreement the seller believes that the price they are being paid for their goods or services is about equal to their value, while the buyer believes that the goods or services are about equal to their price. However, in the case of an insurance contract the insured knows that they are paying a sum (the premium) far less than the insurer is going to have to pay if the event insured against occurs. This is known as an **aleatory contract**, where the conditions are an essential part of the bargain and performance is limited to those risks.

FIGURE 10.1 *Parties to an insurance contract*

PARTIES TO AN INSURANCE CONTRACT

Two parties—the insured (who takes out the coverage) and the insurer (the company who takes on the risk)

In an insurance contract, the party taking out the insurance coverage is known as the 'insured' or 'assured', depending on the type of coverage being sought though the distinction is of little importance today; the other party is insurer (see Figure 10.1).

Two classes of person make up the category of insurer:

- insurance **companies:** they are limited by their constitutions as to the kinds of insurance that they can enter into; and
- **underwriters**: they are not bound to particular kinds of insurance because they are not limited by a constitution. They 'underwrite' or assume the risk themselves, but frequently will insure the risk at a lower premium elsewhere. Perhaps the best known underwriters are Lloyds of London.

SOURCES OF INSURANCE LAW

Sources of insurance law are statute and common law

While the basic principles of insurance can be found in the common law, a considerable body of Commonwealth, state and territory legislation has been enacted in this area, replacing and modifying common law principles.

Commonwealth legislation

Includes the *Marine Insurance Act 1909*, the *Life Insurance Act 1945* and *1995*, the *Insurance Act 1973*, the *Insurance Contracts Act 1984*, the *Insurance and Superannuation Commissioner Act 1987*, *Australian Securities and Investment Commission Act 1997* and the *Corporations Act 2001* (which was amended by the *Financial Services Reform Act 2001*).

The states and territories

There is provision for compulsory workers' compensation and third-party insurance and marine insurance, while New South Wales has retained the *Insurance Act 1902*. The state government insurance offices have generally been made subject to the Commonwealth *Insurance Contracts Act*.

GENERAL INSURANCE CODE OF PRACTICE

General insurers regulated by General Insurance Code of Practice

(Available online at: **http://www.ica.com.au/codepractice/**)

All insurers offering general insurance products to consumers must subscribe to the General Insurance Code of Practice, which came into force in August 2000 and is reviewed every three years. The code aims to ensure:

- that consumers are fully informed about insurance products and documentation;
- improved standards of service; and
- that consumers have a fair complaints and dispute resolution system.

The code is administered by the Australian Securities and Investments Commission (ASIC) as part of its expanded consumer role. ASIC however does not have the power to mandate industry codes. Industry must first decide whether it wants to develop a code and then decide whether to have ASIC approve the code.

The Life Insurance Code of Practice was superseded by the *Financial Services Reform Act 2001* (Cth) and is now administered by ASIC.

ADMINISTRATION

(For further information see **http://www.apra.gov.au**)

The Australian Prudential Regulation Authority (APRA), established in July 1998, is responsible for overseeing the management and financial practices of insurance and reinsurance companies, most members of the superannuation industry and financial institutions, while ASIC is responsible for regulating investment products and financial advisers.

INDUSTRY COMPLAINTS RESOLUTION

General insurers

(For information on the Insurance Ombudsman Service see **http://www.iecltd.com.au**)

Complaints about general insurance are heard by the Insurance Ombudsman Service

Insurance policyholders (but not large corporations) who have complaints about general insurance with an insurance company may use the services of the **Insurance Ombudsman Service (IOS)**. The service operates on a two-tier level with:

- consumer consultants at the first tier; and
- a panel, referee or adjudicator at the second tier.

The role of the consumer consultant at the first tier is to respond to enquiries and encourage resolution of complaints through conciliation between the applicant and the insurance company utilising the insurer's Internal Dispute Resolution (IDR) process. If the insurer's IDR process fails to resolve the matter, the matter can be referred to the second tier of the service. At this level binding determinations can be made by an adjudicator for amounts up to $5000 and by a panel or referee for amounts up to $150 000 where the claim does not exceed $290 000. A panel or referee may also make recommendations for an amount greater than $150 000 but not exceeding $290 000 where the claim does not exceed $290 000.

Consumers who are natural persons and who are making a claim of up to $3000 in relation to motor vehicle property damage against an insured or against a person to whom the insurance extends may also use the service.

If an applicant is dissatisfied with the decision of an adjudicator, referee or panel, they still retain their rights to legal action through the court system.

Life insurers

(For information on life insurance complaints see **http://www.fics.asn.au**)

If the case involves a complaint against a life insurer and is less than $250 000 (if it is more than this, you must go through the court), or is a complaint about an income protection policy of less than $6000 per month, the policyholder may apply to the **Financial Industry Complaints Service (FICS)**, which is an External Dispute Resolution (EDR) scheme. ASIC issue Australian Financial Services Licences to providers of financial services, of which life insurance companies are such providers, and a condition of this licence is that the licensed holder must be a member of an approved EDR scheme if they are dealing with retail clients, and FICS is an approved scheme.

Complaints about life insurance are heard by the Financial Industry Complaints Service

Under FICS, the insured must first attempt to redress the matter with the insurer. A case manager will be appointed by FICS and will attempt to resolve the matter by conciliation. If no resolution is reached, the matter can be referred to a panel or adjudicator (if the amount is less than $30 000 and not of a complex nature) for formal determination, which is then binding on the insurance company. The scheme is free to consumers and is funded by the life insurers on a 'user pays' basis. The policyholder does not have to accept a determination and can take further legal action.

Brokers

(For information on insurance broker complaints see **http://www.ibdltd.com.au/html/**)

Complaints about brokers are heard by Insurance Brokers Disputes Limited

Insurance Brokers' Dispute Limited (IBD) is a free consumer service designed to handle complaints between insurance brokers (most insurance broking firms subscribe to the IBD) and their clients. Like general and life insurers, insurance brokers must participate in an ASIC approved External Dispute Resolution scheme. Brokers are required to have an Internal Dispute Resolution scheme and the policyholder must first try to resolve the dispute at this level. Failing this, the complaint can go to the IBD's general manager. If the dispute is still not resolved to the satisfaction of either party, then it will be referred to an IBD referee.

The referee, who is legally qualified, will issue a decision which is binding on IBD members, although not binding on consumers, who can take further legal action if they are not satisfied with the referee's decision.

The referee can handle general insurance disputes up to $10 000 and life insurance disputes up to $50 000 that relate to a broker's acts after they joined the scheme. The referee can also order corrective advertising, name the broker in their annual report and recommend to the IBD cancellation or suspension of the broker's registration. As with insurers, there is no right of appeal for brokers.

CONCEPTS UNDERLYING INSURANCE LAW

IN BRIEF

Four key concepts underlie insurance law

Concept	Description
Insurable interest	Stated in economic terms so that as long as the insured has suffered a pecuniary or economic loss through the damage to or destruction of the subject matter they will be able to claim on their policy.
Indemnity	The aim of all forms of insurance contract, except contracts of life and some accident insurance as they are contracts of contingency, is to put the insured back to the position they occupied before the occurrence of the loss.
Utmost good faith	Insurance contracts are all contracts of the 'utmost good faith' because the parties are not in an equal bargaining position with respect to knowledge of the possible risk involved.
Subrogation	Subrogation applies to contracts of indemnity and entitles the insurer to 'step into the shoes' of the insured after payment of the loss and have all their rights, including the right to sue a third party if they caused the loss.

Insurable interest

At common law, the insured in every contract of general insurance had to have something called 'insurable interest' present. It was a right in law or equity and had to be present at the time that the loss was incurred. See, for example, *Macaura v. Northern Assurance Co. Ltd.*

***MACAURA V. NORTHERN ASSURANCE CO. LTD* [1925] AC 619**

Macaura owned a tree plantation. The plantation was covered by an insurance policy. He subsequently sold the plantation to a company of which he was the only shareholder, though the purchase money remained owing to him. After the sale, Macaura continued to insure the plantation in his own name. A fire broke out and destroyed the plantation. When Macaura attempted to claim on the policy, the company refused to pay.

ISSUE: Did Macaura have an insurable interest at the time of the loss?

DECISION: The insurance company did not have to pay. The plantation company was a legal entity in its own right, separate to its shareholders and while it was the owner of the plantation and had an insurable interest, it had no policy. Macaura, on the other hand, had a policy, but because he had assigned the plantation to the company he had no insurable interest.

Sections 16 and 17 of the *Insurance Contracts Act* have removed the common law rule requiring the insured to have an insurable interest at the time of taking out the policy. An insurance contract is no longer void if the insured did not have an insurable interest in the subject matter of the contract at the time the contract was entered into (s. 16).

Insurable interest is stated in economic terms

As long as the insured has suffered a pecuniary or economic loss through damage to or destruction of the subject matter they will be able to claim on their policy (s. 17). The effect of these sections on a case such as *Macaura v. Northern Assurance* is that Macaura would have succeeded in his claim. This is because, under the *Insurance Contracts Act*, the insured is entitled to recover any loss they have suffered provided that it is covered by the insurance contract, irrespective of whether or not they have an insurable interest at the time of loss. In the case of **general insurance, insurable interest is now stated in economic terms as pecuniary or financial loss**.

Doing business

Important to disclose changes to risk

Most insurance contracts carry a clause requiring written disclosure of changes in risk to the insurer. Failure to comply will amount to a breach of a term and may entitle the insurer to avoid payment in the event of a claim. Where no notice has been included in the policy, it will automatically operate on renewal, since renewal usually constitutes a new contract and failure to disclose would amount to a breach of the utmost good faith. ■

Change of insurable interest

If the nature of the insured's interest changes, this does not affect the validity of the contract unless something to the contrary is clearly stated in the contents of the policy. Often a policy will provide for notice to be given to the insurer where this occurs.

Where no notice is provided for, the principle of good faith and the duty of disclosure will operate on the renewal of a policy, since a renewal usually constitutes the creation of a new contract. This means that all material facts arising between the date of the original contract and the date of renewal should be disclosed before renewal of the policy.

> **!** CAUTION NOTE
> *Unless otherwise provided, a change in insurable interest does not affect a contract until renewal.*

Examples of insurable interest in general insurance

Insurable interest exists if a person is liable to pay money in the event of a loss

An insurable interest exists if a person is liable to pay money in the event of a loss. They are said to have a pecuniary interest because their interest can be measured in monetary terms. This applies to:

- the purchase of goods if they are at the purchaser's risk;
- mortgagees and mortgagors;
- landlords and tenants;
- common carriers; and
- a creditor against a debtor's insolvency.

An engagement binding in honour is not enough to support an insurable interest, nor will an unsecured creditor have an insurable interest in a debtor's property, though the creditor may insure against the debtor's insolvency.

However, persons who are not parties to a contract of general insurance may be entitled to claim their loss from the insurer provided that there is an express or implied intention in the contract that they are to be covered and that they relied on that intention (s. 48).

Can you have insurable interest in life assurance?

As is the case with general insurance, life assurance policies to which the *Insurance Contracts Act* applies are no longer subject to the common law rules that an insured must have insurable interest in the life insured at the time the policy was entered into.

Like policies of general insurance, a policy of life assurance or a contract that provides for the payment of money on the death of person by sickness or accident is no longer void by reason only that the insured did not have an insurable interest in the subject matter of the contract at the time of its making.

Indemnity (return to a pre-loss position)

Indemnity—aims to return the insured to their pre-loss position

The aim of all forms of insurance contract, except contracts of life and some accident insurance because they are contracts of contingency, is to put the insured back to the position they occupied before the occurrence of the loss. This is known as **indemnity and it aims to enable the insured to purchase protection against loss, to the extent of their insurable interest**. It is not intended that the insured make a profit out of their loss.

How much the insured is entitled to claim will depend on the amount of coverage that they have specified in the policy. If the owner of a house has insured the house for $100 000 against fire and a fire breaks out destroying the premises, they will recover up to a maximum of $100 000 as that is the value of the policy.

The value of the insured property is taken at the date of loss when determining how much can be recovered. This may not be the same as the replacement value of the house unless regular adjustments are made to the policy at renewal time to allow for inflation.

Over-insurance

Indemnity is usually settled by payment of a sum of money that the parties have agreed to in the policy. For example, fire and burglary policies are generally construed as contracts of strict indemnity.

If a property is insured for $100 000 and it is destroyed, the insured will not necessarily recover the full amount. The insured is only entitled to the cost of replacement. If the building only costs $80 000 to replace and it is insured for $100 000, the insured has over-insured by $20 000 and only the lesser sum will be paid.

Contracts of life assurance and personal accident assurance are, of course, exceptions to the indemnity principle. Because there is no possibility of placing a value upon human life, if the insured can afford the premiums then they can insure themselves for whatever value they feel they are worth.

> **!** CAUTION NOTE
>
> *Over-insurance—the insured is only entitled to recover to the extent of their loss unless the contract is non-indemnity such as life assurance.*

Double indemnity

If the insured has taken out two or more policies in relation to the same risk—a double indemnity—and the total of the policies exceeds the loss sustained, a choice exists as to which insurer to claim from. However, the insured cannot recover more than the loss: s. 76.

If one insurer does not provide full indemnity, the insured can claim the balance from the other insurer or insurers. The insurer who has indemnified the insured, on the other hand, can claim contribution from the other insurer or insurers so that the loss is shared equally between them.

Valued policies

For some business people it may be worth considering a valued policy as it provides an exception to the indemnity principle. Here the parties agree in advance on the value that the insured property should have in the event of loss or damage. If the property is subsequently lost or damaged, the insured recovers the agreed amount, regardless of the actual value of the property at the time of the loss or damage.

> **!** CAUTION NOTE
> *Valued policies—exception to indemnity principle as parties agree in advance on value of property.*

The doctrine of utmost good faith (*uberrimae fidei*)

Insurance contracts are contracts of the 'utmost good faith'

Unlike contracts for the sale of goods or provision of services, **insurance contracts are contracts of the 'utmost good faith'**, or *uberrimae fidei*. This is because the parties are not in an equal position with respect to knowledge of the possible risk involved. The person with the greatest knowledge of the risk involved is the proponent. It follows that they should have to disclose all those facts that could influence the insurance company as to whether or not it will accept the risk.

Under the *Insurance Contracts Act* **both parties are required to act in good faith towards each other** (s. 13). Neither party will be able to rely on any provision of the contract where this has not occurred.

How long does the duty of disclosure last?

Duty of disclosure lasts up until the contract is formed

The duty to disclose all material facts lasts right up until when the contract is formed (ss. 21, 25), which is usually when the insurer accepts the proposal. Any new material fact that arises after the proposal has been completed, but before it has been accepted, must also be disclosed. Even a change of circumstances which renders a previously correct answer incorrect must be notified to the insurer if it is material. However, failure to disclose any increase in risk may be of limited value for an insurer unless they include a clause to protect themselves and which can operate as a condition subsequent: s. 54.

Under the *Insurance Contracts Act* the insurer must inform the insured in writing of the nature and effect of the duty of disclosure prior to their entry into the contract: s. 22. On the other hand, the Act requires the insured to disclose any matters that they know to be relevant to the insurer's decision to accept the risk and its terms: s. 21.

As a renewal usually creates a new contract, all material facts arising between the date of the original contract and the date of the renewal should be disclosed before renewal as they could affect the risk: s. 11(9).

> **!** CAUTION NOTE
> ***Renewal creates a new contract*** *and disclosure of any new risks that may have arisen since taking out the last contract must be disclosed.*

What is the extent of the insured's duty to disclose?

The duty of disclosure on the part of the insured is found in s. 21 of the *Insurance Contracts Act*. Section 21A modifies the insured's obligation of disclosure in respect of certain types of insurance contract, referred to as 'eligible contracts of insurance', for example, contracts of general insurance **for cars and home buildings and contents**. The insurer must identify the information it needs to assess the risk by asking specific questions in respect to its decision to insure. If the insurer does not get all the information it needs from these questions, it is deemed to have waived its duty of disclosure.

The insurer has two courses of action open to them:

- they can request the insured to answer specific questions regarding the risk (s. 21A(3)); or
- they can expressly request the insured to disclose 'exceptional circumstances' known to the insured, or that a reasonable person in the circumstances could be expected to know. The 'exceptional circumstances' must be relevant to the insurer's decision whether to accept the risk, and if so, on what terms (s. 21A(4)).

It must be noted that these provisions are a form of consumer protection and only apply to certain types of insurance, that is, motor vehicles, home buildings and home contents. In respect to other forms of insurance, what should be disclosed is dependent on the following considerations.

General insurance

The insured must disclose matters that they know are material to the insurer: s. 21(1). If the insured claims to be unaware that a fact was material, the test that the courts will apply is a combination of the common law 'reasonable insured' test and matters the insured knows, or which a reasonable person in the circumstances could be expected to know.

LINDSAY V. CIC INSURANCE LTD (1989) 16 NSWLR 673

The real estate agent of the insured had taken out fire insurance over a building that he managed for Lindsay. The premises were being used as a brothel. This was known by both Lindsay and the agent but was not passed on to the insurance broker who arranged the insurance, or to the insurer.

ISSUE: Can an insured be liable for the non-disclosure of their agent, even if the agent commits this breach without their knowledge?

DECISION: *Rogers* CJ in the Commercial Division of the New South Wales Supreme Court held that matters that are required to be disclosed are those matters which are known to the insured (s. 21(1)(b)) or his relevant agent (s. 21(1)) which go to the question of risk. Use by a tenant of part of the premises as a brothel was a matter that had to be disclosed to an insurer against fire because it increased the threat of arson, fights and threats. The effect of the non-disclosure was to entitle the insurer to reduce their liability on the claim to nil: s. 28(3).

The courts have the right to allow the insured to recover up to the full sum insured if the non-disclosure is minimal or insignificant and avoidance would be harsh and unfair on the insured: s. 31(2).

IN BRIEF

Facts considered material

Facts which could be considered to be material include:

- the name and occupation of the applicant;
- the health of the applicant;
- the previous insurance loss history of the applicant;
- whether the applicant has a criminal record;
- whether the applicant has had or is having financial problems;
- whether the subject matter is in greater danger than would normally be expected (e.g., taking out fire insurance on premises where an arsonist has made several attempts to destroy the property);
- if the risk to be insured against appears to be speculative;
- if the applicant has had a poor insurance record (e.g., a driver seeking comprehensive car insurance with a poor driving record and who has been refused insurance with other companies); and
- if the insurer's liability is likely to be greater than would normally be expected (for example, the cost of replacing a secondhand Rolls-Royce might be higher than the original cost).

Matters that are not material

The onus of establishing non-disclosure of a fact and its materiality lies upon the insurer and the standard of proof is the balance of probabilities. Gossip or rumours need not be disclosed because they are not 'facts'. Section 21(2) provides that the insured is not obliged to disclose matters:

- that reduce the risk;
- that are common knowledge to the insurer;
- that the insurer knew or should have known; and
- where there has been a waiver of disclosure by the insurer.

If non-disclosure is established and is considered to be fraudulent, the insurer will be able to avoid the contract (ss. 28(2), 29(2)).

activebook

To help you to remember and understand the topics covered so far, and for links to legal websites, refer to your online activebook. Model answers provide feedback to problems and exercises.

Liability of co-insureds

Even a failure by one co-insured to disclose a material fact may result in the innocent co-insured losing their rights under a policy: s. 28(3).

ADVANCE (NSW) INSURANCE AGENCIES PTY LTD V. MATTHEWS (1989) 166 CLR 606

Mr and Mrs Matthews took out a household contents insurance policy after their house had been burgled. They obtained a proposal form from the insurer and completed it at home. On the proposal form they answered 'no' to the following questions:

1 Had any previous claim been rejected?

2 Were there any other facts relating to the risks to be insured, or about the persons making the application, which should be disclosed to the insurer to enable them to make a true assessment of the application prior to acceptance?

3 Had they ever had a loss involving a claim of over $1000?

Two weeks after the policy had been issued, the Matthews' premises were damaged by fire, and goods were stolen from their premises. When they claimed on their policy, investigations by the insurance company revealed that:

- Mr Matthews had been a partner in a business that suffered damage by fire in 1980 and that a claim to the then insurer had been rejected. This had led to litigation which was eventually settled.
- That when the Matthews had been burgled, the loss of contents had cost them less than $1000 but the replacement cost had been over $1000.

As a result, Advance Insurance rejected the Matthews' claim on the grounds of non-disclosure and mis-representation.

ISSUE: Does failure by one co-insured to disclose a material fact mean that the innocent co-insured lose their rights under a policy?

DECISION: The High Court held that s. 21 imposed a duty on each person who becomes insured to disclose all material matters to the insurer. Thus, even if only one of the co-insureds were responsible for a fraudulent non-disclosure, the insurance company would be able to avoid the contract under s. 28(3). If the insurer can show that they would never have entered the contract in the first place, they may be able to reduce their liability to nil.

Doing business

Even a co-insured must tell the truth

Advance (NSW) Insurance Agencies Pty Ltd v. Matthews (1989) illustrates the importance of co-insureds disclosing all matters which are material to the question of risk. A failure by one co-insured to disclose a material fact may result in the innocent co-insured losing their rights under a policy. See also page 229 for further discussion on joint and composite policies of insurance. ■

Misstatement of the insured's age for life assurance

Misstatement of age does not void the policy

Special provisions apply where the non-disclosure is related to the insured's age. The **policy cannot be avoided**: s. 30. Where the true age is understated, the insurer may reduce the sum insured on a proportionate basis. If the true age has been overstated, the insurer must either increase the sum insured on a proportionate basis or reduce the premiums payable and repay the overpaid premiums (with interest).

Effect of the duty of disclosure

Under the *Insurance Contracts Act* the insurer has to inform the insured in writing of the general nature and effect of the duty of disclosure before or within 14 days of entering into a contract of insurance. Failure to do so will mean the insurer will be unable to exercise any rights under the Act in respect of non-disclosure, unless the non-disclosure is fraudulent.

Common knowledge

Common knowledge to insurer need not be disclosed

Where facts are common knowledge to the insurer, or they have learnt them from some other source, they need not be disclosed. The onus is on the insured to establish that the fact not disclosed was present in the mind of the insurer at the time the risk was accepted: s. 21(2).

Waiver of information

Disclosure will not be required where it has been waived by the insurer: s. 21(2)(d). If a question in the proposal form is not answered by the insured, or the answer given is 'obviously incomplete or irrelevant', the insurer will be deemed to have waived the requirement of an answer if it does not follow up the question: s. 21(3). It will not amount to misrepresentation: s. 27.

The material date as to when full disclosure should be made is the moment when a binding contract is concluded. If the insured has not disclosed all the relevant facts, the insurer has the option of rescinding the contract on learning the true position. The onus of proving non-disclosure is on the insurer.

Misrepresentation and onus of proof

The insurance contract can be invalidated by either mistake or misrepresentation. The first question to ask is whether the untrue statement made on the proposal form is part of the contract—has there been a misrepresentation? If there has, is it innocent or fraudulent?

The time to consider the truth of answers is at the time of making the contract. In order to determine whether a statement is accurate, look to the surrounding circumstances and construe the statement with reference to the facts of the case. If the statement is accurate when applied to the surrounding circumstances to which it was supposed to apply, then the insured will have done all that they can be expected to do.

Statements of fact and opinion

The *Insurance Contracts Act* protects the insured who provides a wrong statement made from reasonable belief against a claim of misrepresentation: s. 26(1).

Ambiguous questions

If a question on a proposal form is capable of two meanings (i.e. ambiguous), the approach taken by the court is to consider whether the answer given by the insured is true, based on a fair and reasonable construction of the question: s. 23. If they feel it is true on a reasonable construction of the question, the insurer will not be able to rely on misrepresentation as a ground to avoid the policy.

What is the effect of basis clauses?

Effectiveness of basis clause limited by *Insurance Contracts Act*

A basis clause is considered by an insurer as a condition precedent to liability under the contract and appears at the end of the proposal form. If any answers in the proposal form prepared by the insured were untrue, at common law the insurer could avoid the contract. However, the *Insurance Contracts Act* limits the effectiveness of basis clauses.

State legislation, such as s. 25 of the *Instruments Act 1958* (Vic.) or s. 18A of the *Insurance Act 1902* (NSW), also prevents avoidance of a policy of general insurance unless the incorrect statement in the proposal is fraudulent or material to the risk.

IN BRIEF

Effectiveness of basis clauses limited by *Insurance Contracts Act*

Section 13—parties will not be able to rely on provisions in a contract except in utmost good faith.

Section 22—the insurer must inform the insured of the duty of disclosure.

Section 23—the meaning of a question shall be determined by reference to the meaning that would be put upon it by a reasonable person in the circumstances.

Section 26—an untrue statement made on the basis of a reasonably held belief will not be a misrepresentation.

Onus of proof

Onus of proof lies on insurer to prove insured failed to disclose all material facts

The onus of proving that the insured has failed to disclose all the material facts, or has made a misrepresentation, rests with the insurers. That is, did the person making the statement know, or could a reasonable person in the circumstances be expected to know, that the statement would be relevant to the decision by the insurer whether to accept the risk, and if so, on what terms? (s. 26(2)). The test is similar to the test of non-disclosure under s. 21 (see p. 217).

Remedies for non-disclosure and misrepresentation

Insurers

Insurers who have acted unconscionably in the events leading up to the formation of an insurance contract could find that they have infringed Part V of the *Trade Practices Act 1974* (Cth) or the equivalent state or territory Fair Trading legislation.

Where there is an innocent misrepresentation by the insured

Where the insured has made an innocent misrepresentation in an application for general insurance, the insurer will generally not be able to avoid the contract. Their liability may be reduced to place them in the position they would have occupied had the misrepresentation not been made: ss. 28(1), 28(3). However, if the insurer can show they would never have entered into the contract at all had they known the true state of affairs, their liability could be reduced to nil: s. 28(3). This would have the same effect as avoidance.

***ORB HOLDINGS PTY LTD V. LOMBARD GENERAL INSURANCE* [1995] 2 QD R 51**

The insured had taken out a policy with Lombard for the coverage of a shopping arcade, which had been described in the proposal as being of a 'brick/iron' construction. In fact, two of the walls were brick but the other two were made of wood with an iron roof.

ISSUE: Where a misrepresentation is made innocently, can an insurer avoid the contract?

DECISION: The Queensland Court of Appeal held that as the evidence in the particular circumstances showed that the insurer would have declined to insure the building if it had known that two of the walls were made of timber, under s. 28(3) its liability under the contract was reduced to nil.

Where there is a fraudulent misrepresentation by the insured

Where there is a fraudulent misrepresentation, the insurer may avoid the contract (s. 28(2)), or at least reduce its liability in respect of a claim to the amount that it would have had if the misrepresentation had not been made (s. 28(3)). The court has power to disregard any avoidance of a contract by an insurer when it would be harsh and unfair not to do so, and allow the insured to recover an amount that is just and equitable in the circumstances: s. 31.

***PLASTEEL WINDOWS AUSTRALIA PTY LTD V. C E HEATH UNDERWRITING AGENCIES PTY LTD* (1990) 19 NSWLR 400**

An insurance broking firm in completing a proposal form for professional indemnity insurance with the respondent underwriters had answered 'No' to the question: 'Is it the practice of your firm to sign proposals on behalf of your clients?' The directors of the broking firm knew that the firm did sign proposals on behalf of clients.

ISSUE: Did the answer amount to a fraudulent misrepresentation? Was there a fraudulent non-disclosure of the firm's practice?

DECISION: In the circumstances, the New South Wales Supreme Court held that the broking firm's answer was a fraudulent misrepresentation since the directors of the broking firm knew of the firm's practice on behalf of their clients and they knew that this was relevant to the question of risk. Furthermore, the non-disclosure of the firm's practice in this respect was fraudulent. As a result, the respondent underwriters were able to avoid the policy under s. 28(2). The court also refused to 'disregard the avoidance' under s. 31 since the underwriters had been prejudiced by the fraudulent misrepresentation and non-disclosure.

! CAUTION NOTE

Fraudulent misrepresentation allows insurer to avoid the contract while innocent misrepresentation generally only allows a reduction in liability.

The doctrine of subrogation

Subrogation—places insurer in 'shoes' of insured

Subrogation is founded upon equitable principles and puts the insurer into 'the shoes' of the insured, but **only after payment** for the loss. Thus, it **only applies to contracts of indemnity** such as fire and motor vehicle insurance. It does not ordinarily apply to accident policies because today such policies are generally not indemnity policies (*Insurance Commissioner of Western Australia v. Kightly* [2005] WASCA 154 at para 29), unless they compensate

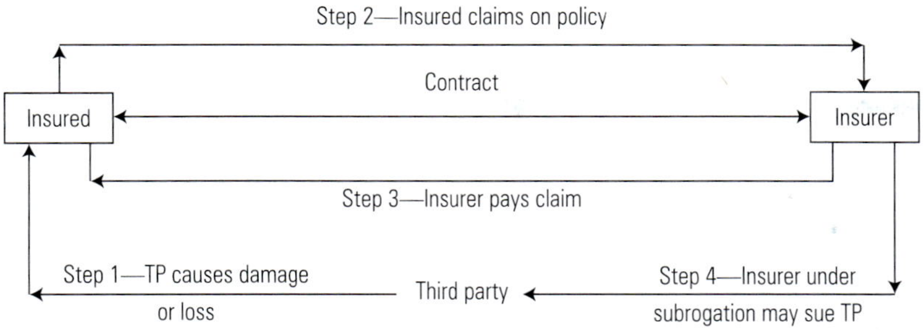

FIGURE 10.2 *Subrogation*

the insured for actual financial loss suffered as a consequence of an injury caused by accident. However, whether a contract is or is not one of indemnity will, at the end of the day, be detrrmined by the exact nature of the agreement between the parties, rather than what the parties have called the policy.

The effect of subrogation is that it gives the insurer all the rights of the insured against any third party who may have been responsible for the damage that gave rise to the claim. This prevents the insured from making a profit on the loss by also bringing an action against a negligent third party.

The insured must be careful not to do any act that may harm the insurer's right of subrogation—for example, by making an admission of liability to another driver in the event of a car accident.

The *Insurance Contracts Act* preserves the basic principle of subrogation (see Figure 10.2), but its application is limited in two areas:

- rights against a third party where there is a family or other relationship with the third party; and
- where the third party uses the insured's vehicle with the insured's consent (s. 65).

If the third party's conduct leading to the loss occurs either in the course of or arises out of their employment by the insured or is serious or wilful misconduct, then the insurer can take action to recover the loss: s. 65(2)(b). See, for example, *Lister v. Romford Ice and Cold Storage Co. Ltd.*

LISTER V. ROMFORD ICE AND COLD STORAGE CO. LTD [1957] AC 555

Lister was employed by Romford Ice as a truckdriver. His father was employed by the same company and worked with his son. One day while reversing his truck into a loading bay the son lost sight of his father, who was directing him, and accidentally ran over him. The father then brought an action against the employer and succeeded on the basis that Romford Ice's employee, the younger Lister, was negligent. The company's insurance company then exercised its right of subrogation by bringing an action against the son. It stepped into the shoes of the company and claimed that the son had been in breach of his duty to drive the truck carefully. As a result of his failure to exercise due care and skill, he had caused his employer to suffer damage. The son should therefore have to indemnify the employer (i.e. the insurance company) for the loss that they had suffered.

ISSUE: Can the insurer recover its loss against the son?

DECISION: The son had been negligent in the manner in which he drove the truck. He owed a duty of care to exercise his skills as a truck driver with due care and competence, and he had broken his duty of care by running over his father. He was therefore in breach of his employment contract.

COMMENT: The effects of this decision have been restricted at common law by legislation in New South Wales, South Australia and the Northern Territory.

Where the insurer exercises rights of subrogation, the insured will be entitled to any monies recovered by the insurer (less recovery costs) up to the maximum of their loss. Any surplus can be retained by the insurer: s. 67.

Doing business

Keep your mouth shut or risk losing your cover

Subrogation puts the insurer into 'the shoes' of the insured after payment of the loss. It gives them all the rights of the insured against any third party. These rights can be prejudiced by the insured admitting liability to an injured third party and it is not unusual to find indemnity policies containing a term to the effect that such an admission of liability may affect the policy. The moral of the story is to speak first with the insurer before admitting anything. ■

MAKING THE CONTRACT OF INSURANCE

The steps that would normally be followed in obtaining a contract of insurance after making inquiries with an insurance company or insurance broker are as follows.

The cover note (short-term cover)

Cover note—only provides interim coverage for a short period

The purpose of a cover note is to **provide temporary cover** for the proponent while the insurance company considers the proposal and decides whether to accept or reject it. It is a contract in its own right (s. 11) and it usually incorporates the conditions of the company's policy. It will not be issued for life assurance.

Most cover notes are of one month's duration. The insurers can indicate that they have rejected the proposal at any time within that period by notifying the proposer, or they may let the cover note expire without notifying the proposer. In either case, the insurer remains liable for what may occur until the cover note expires.

The insurer can cancel a cover note at any time: s. 60(4). However, an insurer must give three days' written notice if cancellation is to be effective: s. 59.

The proposal form (the offer)

Proposal form sets out details insurer needs to know for determining risk

The insurer will send the person seeking the coverage (the proponent or proposer) a proposal form to complete. This will usually contain certain questions common to all forms of insurance, including:

- the description of the proposed assured;
- the history of the proposed insured;
- what it is that is to be insured; and
- a description of anything that could make the risk greater than usual.

The offer does not come from the insurer. It is made by the person seeking to protect themselves by insurance against loss. If their offer is accepted, they become the insured (assured in a contract of life assurance), while the insurance company is known as the insurer.

As the normal rules of contract apply, an offer can be revoked any time before acceptance. Likewise, a counter-offer or conditional acceptance will cause the offer to lapse although the counter-offer may in turn be accepted, for example, by conduct.

BATTY V. PEARL **[1937] 1 AC 12**

X signed a proposal form in the life of her mother at a premium of 10p. per week. The sum assured was left blank on the proposal form when it was signed but was later filled in at £250, the agreed sum. However, the policy was issued for £1000. X paid the premium of 10p. per week for more than eight years before the company discovered the mistake.

ISSUE: Was the insurance company bound by its mistake?

DECISION: The company had made a counter-offer when it inserted £1000 on the policy, that is, £1000 for the 10p. per week instead of £250 for 10p. per week. This meant that X was free to accept or reject the counter-offer. By her conduct of paying the 10p. per week for the last eight years, she had clearly accepted the counter-offer. Therefore a valid contract existed for the sum of £1000 at a weekly premium of 10p. per week.

Disclosure requirements

All facts relevant to the risk must be disclosed

The proponent must disclose all material facts that could affect the risk: s. 21 (see Figure 10.3). If the proposal is a joint policy, the policy of disclosure applies to each of the co-insureds. If one of the co-insureds fraudulently completes their part of the proposal form, the insurer can avoid the contract (see *Advance (NSW) Insurance Agencies Pty Ltd v. Matthews* at page 219): s. 28(a).

It does not matter whether there is a question on the proposal form or not. In most proposal forms there is a specific question (often the last question on the proposal form) related to duty of disclosure. For example, a person who knows they are in financial difficulty should disclose this fact to the insurer when taking out a large fire insurance policy on their business. This will be the case even if there is no specific question on this point because it will be material to the insurer accepting the policy.

If the insurer rejects the proposal, the applicant can ask for written reasons for its decision to reject.

YOUR DUTY OF DISCLOSURE

Before you enter into a contract of general insurance with ABC Insurance, you have a duty, by law, to disclose to ABC Insurance every matter that you know, or could be reasonably expected to know, is relevant to the decision of ABC Insurance whether to accept the risk of the insurance and, if so, on what terms.

You have the same duty to disclose those matters to ABC Insurance every time you renew, vary or reinstate your contract of general insurance.

Matters which ABC Insurance consider to be relevant include:

- matters which you know, or could be reasonably expected to know:
  - will lead to the making of a claim under the contract; or
  - are more likely than normal to lead to the making of a claim under the contract;
- matters such as trading or credit difficulties;
- matters involving the criminal history of the insured.

You do not have to disclose anything:

- which reduces the risk to be undertaken;
- that is common knowledge;
- that ABC Insurance knows, or in the ordinary course of business, should know; or
- as to which compliance with your duty has been waived by the insurer.

FIGURE 10.3 *Duty of disclosure*

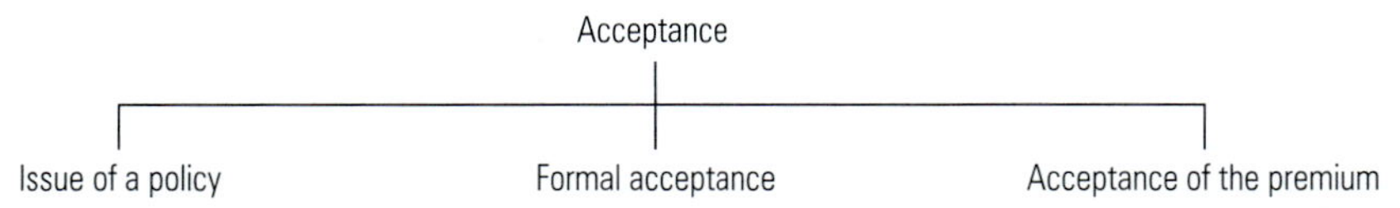

FIGURE 10.4 *Methods of acceptance of proposal*

Acceptance of the proposal

Acceptance must be in accordance with the terms of the offer. The introduction of any new terms would amount to a counter-offer (see *Batty v. Pearl*, page 224).

Issue of a policy

The policy is the dominant document

Where acceptance of the proposal is by way of the issue of a policy, the contract is usually to be found in both documents (see Figure 10.4). The proposal is usually stated to be the basis for the contract, and the policy incorporates it. The policy is the dominant document, and it must be agreed by the parties that the proposal is incorporated into it, otherwise the whole of the terms of the contract will be contained in the policy alone. In the event of any inconsistency between the proposal and policy, the policy will prevail.

Formal acceptance

Where a condition has to be fulfilled to bring the contract into existence, for example, payment of the premium, the contract does not come into existence until that condition has been satisfied.

Acceptance of the premium (consideration for the contract)

Consideration is the premium in return for the coverage

The consideration for a contract of insurance is the premium. It may be paid in a lump sum or at stated periods. Where the risk had changed at the time of payment of the premium the effect may be that the contract will lapse.

Where the insurers have accepted the premium, it seems that they have accepted the proposal even if no policy has been issued. Where this occurs, the insurers are liable if the insured suffers any loss under the policy. Once the insurer has accepted the proposal, a contract is completed and the duty of disclosure ceases.

CANNING V. FARQUHAR **(1886) 16 QBD 727**

Canning applied for life assurance and was told by the insurance company that no insurance contract could take place until the first premium was paid. Before the premium was paid, Canning fell over a cliff and died. The company refused to accept the premium from Canning's agent.

ISSUE: Had the policy lapsed because of the change in risk between the time of the original proposal and the payment of the premium?

DECISION: The company was under no obligation to pay the sum insured because the risk had substantially changed between the time of the original proposal and the tendering of the premium.

Date of the contract

Knowledge of the date of the contract is important for two reasons:

- it determines when the risk commences and ends; and
- if a material misrepresentation is made, the insurer is entitled to avoid the policy even after the happening of the event insured against.

The question is judged at the time of the making of the contract, so that which is true in the proposal may have become untrue at the time the policy was issued and the contract made (see *Canning v. Farquhar* above). Generally, the material time is when the proposal is made.

***LOOKER V. LAW UNION AND ROCK INSURANCE CO. LTD* [1928] 1 KB 554**

Looker stated in his proposal form for life assurance that he was free from any disease or ailment. In fact, at the time of acceptance of his proposal he was suffering from pneumonia, and shortly after the company accepted his proposal, he died.

ISSUE: Was the insurer liable on the policy?

DECISION: The insurance company was not liable on the policy, as the proposer was under an obligation to inform the insurers of any material change occurring before the contract was made in relation to the risk undertaken by them.

Renewal of the policy

Renewal notice is the offer by the insurer

Before expiration of the policy, the insurer will send the insured a renewal notice, usually 28 days prior to the policy lapsing. The renewal notice is an offer by the insurer to the insured, with acceptance taking place generally on payment of the premium. Life policies are normally treated as ongoing contracts and not subject to renewals.

Generally, an increase in the risk insured against during the life of the policy will result in the insurer's obligation ceasing as 'the risk insured against', as defined in the policy, has altered. However, where this is not the case, any change in risk will have to be notified to the insurer on renewal because it is the creation of a new contract.

Return of premium

The insured is entitled to a return of their premium if they can establish that there was a total failure of consideration in the sense that the risk was never attached.

***STRICKLAND V. TURNER* (1852) 7 EX 208: (1852) 155 ER 199**

Strickland and an insurance company entered into a contract of life assurance of the life of Turner, but, unknown to either Strickland or the company, Turner was already dead.

ISSUE: Was Strickland entitled to a refund of his premium?

DECISION: The court held that the contract was void in that there had been a total failure of consideration. The purpose of the contract was not in existence at the time of making the contract, and so Strickland would be entitled to a return of the premium.

IN BRIEF

Steps in obtaining a contract of insurance

Steps	Description
Cover note	Interim insurance that covers the insured for a short length of time, usually one month
Proposal	Contains a set of questions that will allow the insurer to determine the risk, and the answers the proponent gives will allow the insurer to determine the amount of the premium. The proponent must disclose all material facts that could affect the risk.
Issue of the policy	Acceptance of the risk by the insurer. The date of the contract will determine when coverage against the risk commences.
Renewal notice	Usually sent 28 days before the policy is due to expire with acceptance taking place on payment of the premium.

CONSTRUCTION OF THE INSURANCE POLICY

Doing business

Claims should be made promptly

Check the policy carefully with respect to notification of claims. Many policies require that the insured notify the insurer within a reasonable time, with appropriate documentation establishing loss, or they may have their claim reduced if the insurer is prejudiced by a delay in notification. ■

Who makes the claim?

The insured must make their claim promptly to avoid prejudicing the insurer's rights against a third party

Normally the insured makes a formal claim in accordance with the terms of the policy. This should normally be as soon as possible.

Sometimes a policy states that the insurer should be notified within a specified time. However, legislation in Victoria (*Instruments Act 1958*, s. 27), New South Wales (*Insurance Act 1902*, s. 18) and the Commonwealth (*Insurance Contracts Act 1984*, s. 54) prevents the insurer from refusing to pay a claim on the basis of late notification. However, the insured's claim may be reduced if the insurer's claims have been prejudiced by a delay in notification (e.g., a delay may affect the insurer's rights against a third party under the doctrine of subrogation).

The High Court delivered its judgement dismissing the appeal from the majority decision of the Queensland Court of Appeal in *FAI General Insurance Co. Limited v. Australian Hospital Care Pty Limited* [2001] HCA 38. The case concerned the operation of s. 54(1) of the *Insurance Contracts Act* and the failure by an insured to notify its insurer within the policy period of circumstances which might have led to a claim. The High Court held that s. 54 prevents an insurer denying a claim on the basis that an insured omitted to give notice of circumstances during the policy period even where the claim is made after the policy has expired.

***FAI GENERAL INSURANCE CO. LIMITED V. AUSTRALIAN HOSPITAL CARE PTY LIMITED* [2001] HCA 38**

A patient contracted septicaemia and septic shock while receiving treatment in the insured's private hospital. After his recovery, his lawyers wrote to the hospital indicating that the patient was considering suing the hospital and requesting access to certain medical records. The hospital refused to provide the records.

Before the hospital's insurance policy expired, the hospital's medical experts investigated the matter and concluded that there was no basis for a claim by the patient. They subsequently met with the patient's solicitor, advised him of their findings and formed the view that there would not be a malpractice action. The hospital did not notify its insurers of the matter with whom they had a 'claims made and notified policy'.

At the end of the policy period the hospital changed insurers, so that when the patient's claim did arrive, their current insurer declined cover on the basis that the claim arose prior to the inception date of the policy which was an exclusion in the policy. The hospital settled with the patient without admission of liability.

ISSUE: Could s. 54(1) cure a failure by an insured (with a claims made and notified policy) to notify of circumstances (during the policy period) of which it was aware might subsequently give rise to a claim? The insured (respondent) in the case had not given notice of the relevant circumstance.

DECISION: The High Court adopted a broad interpretation of s. 54(1) and held that insurers under claims made and notified policies which contain an occurrences notified clause will have to pay for claims arising out of circumstances discovered by the insured in the period of the policy, whether the insurer was notified or not.

Doing business

Will payment for loss be enough?

Businesses should check their policy to see what has been agreed to in respect of loss, for example, market value, warranty of value, subject to average, reinstatement or replacement to ensure that it adequately meets their business requirements. They should then ensure that it has been adjusted for inflation each year so that they are not underinsured. ■

Fraudulent conduct of another co-insured

Where two or more parties are insured under the same contract of insurance in respect of the same subject matter, for example, where a business premises or house are insured, whether the innocent co-insured can still recover under the insurance policy because of the fraudulent conduct of the other co-insured will depend on whether the policy of insurance is a **joint** or **composite** policy of insurance.

Under a **joint policy, the property insured is in effect treated as one** (see *MMI General Insurance Ltd v. Baktoo*) below.

Joint policy—co-insured are treated as one

MMI GENERAL INSURANCE LTD V. BAKTOO (2000) 48 NSWLR 605

Mr and Mrs Baktoo conducted, in partnership, a restaurant and retail shop. Separate from the business was a small residence. The couple insured the restaurant and home with MMI. The business premises were damaged by fire deliberately started by Mr Baktoo, but Mrs Baktoo played no part in the arson.

ISSUE: Could Mrs Baktoo recover under the insurance policy since she was a co-insured and had played no part in the arson?

DECISION: The New South Wales Court of Appeal held that Mrs Baktoo could not recover since the interests of the co-insured were joint and their interests are treated as one. The fraud of Mr Baktoo defeated a claim by an innocent co-insured.

Composite policy—co-insureds are treated separately

In the case of a **composite policy, the interests of the co-insured are separate**, that is, the insured is treated as having undertaken separate and distinct obligations to each of the co-insureds, so that the fraudulent conduct of one party will not prevent the innocent co-insured from recovering (see *Gilmor v. AMP General Insurance Co. Ltd* below).

GILMORE V. AMP GENERAL INSURANCE CO. LTD **(1996) 67 SASR 387**

A firm of solicitors had taken out a professional indemnity insurance policy for the firm, which stated that the partners were severally insured. Two former clients of the firm brought an action against the firm in respect of the dishonest conduct of one of the partners. The other partners sought indemnity under their policy and the insurer refused the claim because of the fraud of one of the partners.

ISSUE: Were the innocent partners entitled to rely on the policy notwithstanding the fraud of the other partner?

DECISION: The Supreme Court of South Australia held that as the policy was clearly a composite policy, the dishonest conduct of one partner did not prevent the innocent partners from recovering indemnity from the insurer in respect to their liability to the two clients.

Measurement of loss

Generally under an indemnity policy insured can only recover amount of loss

Generally, in the case of an indemnity contract, the insured will only be able to recover the actual amount of the loss. The insured cannot benefit from the destruction of the subject matter unless it is an agreed value policy (see p. 216).

Market value

In the case of subject matter insured at market value, **value is assessed at the time of loss or destruction** (i.e. its second-hand or resale value). It is therefore important for the insured to check the policy carefully in order to determine what has been agreed to in the case of loss.

Warranty of value

Contracts which contain 'warranty of value' and 'subject to average' clauses mean that **an insured will recover less than the amount of their loss**. They are inserted by insurers to protect themselves against underinsurance.

In the case of breach of a warranty of value in a policy, the insurer is only able to reduce the amount of a claim by the amount that fairly represents the extent to which its interests are prejudiced. This is usually the proportion of premium lost because of the under-valuation.

Subject to average

'Subject to average' clause protects the insurer against under insurance by insured

Where a contract of insurance has included in it a 'subject to average' clause, the **insured bears a *pro rata* proportion of any loss**. Notification in writing must be given to the insured of the nature and effect of an averaging clause before or at the time the contract is entered into if the insurer is to rely on it: s. 44(1). The clause is calculated as follows:

$$\frac{\text{Sum insured (SI)}}{\text{Full value of subject matter (FV)}} \times \text{Amount of loss (AL)} = \text{Amount payable (AP)}$$

Application of averaging in a commercial situation

For example, a person insures stock in their shop for $100 000 and the policy is 'subject to average'. The stock is damaged in a fire and the damage is assessed at $25 000 by an assessor who also values the stock at $200 000. The amount the insured will receive will be calculated as follows:

$$\frac{100\,000\ \text{(SI)}}{200\,000\ \text{(FV)}} \times 25\,000\ \text{(AL)} = \$12\,500 \text{ payable to the insured}$$

Section 44 of the *Insurance Contracts Act 1984* provides some relief for homeowners who find it difficult to accurately assess the true value of their property. It provides that an averaging clause will not be effective where the sum insured is 80 per cent or more of the value of the insured property if the property is to be used primarily and principally as the place of residence of the insured.

Application of averaging in the case of a residence below the 80 per cent

Where a house is valued at $150 000 but is only insured for $100 000, then the sum insured is less than 80 per cent of the full value. If a fire causes $60 000 worth of damage, and the contract contained an average clause, then the amount recoverable by the insured would be calculated as follows:

Step 1 $\dfrac{\$100\ 000\ (\text{SI})}{80\%\ \text{of}\ \$150\ 000\ (\text{FV})} \times \$60\ 000\ (\text{AL})$

Step 2 $\dfrac{\$100\ 000}{\$120\ 000} \times \$60\ 000$

Step 3 $\dfrac{5}{6} \times \$60\ 000$ = $50 000 payable to the insured

Where the residence is valued above the 80 per cent

If the house is valued at $200 000 and is insured for $180 000, and a fire causes $20 000 damage, even if the contract contained an averaging clause, the amount recovered would be the full $20 000. The clause would not apply because the insurer has insured their property within 20 per cent of full value (here it is to 90 per cent of full value).

Reinstatement or replacement

Some policies will contain a clause that damaged or stolen property may be 'replaced or repaired'. The implementation of this will vary between insurers, with some companies allowing the insured to decide and others making the decision on the insured's behalf.

Cancellation

Cancellation has to be made in accordance with the provisions of the Act or it will be void (s. 63), and written reasons must be given if requested by the insured: s. 75.

Cancellation must be in accordance with the Act

IN BRIEF

Circumstances where a policy may be cancelled

A policy may be cancelled by the insurer where the insured has:

- failed to comply with the duty of utmost good faith;
- failed to comply with the duty of disclosure;
- made a misrepresentation;
- made a fraudulent claim; or
- breached a term of the contract: s. 60.

AGENTS AND BROKERS

The Financial Services Reform Act 2001 (Cth) regulates all sections of the financial services industry including the insurance industry. Significant aspects of the Act are the requirements for licensing of financial services providers and the disclosure of a wide range of information regarding the financial product. The Act applies to all persons who provide a financial service whether as principals or as authorised representatives and includes general and life insurance brokers.

Insurance agent or insurance broker?

Agents act for particular insurers while brokers are independent

Most contracts of insurance are arranged through intermediaries who can be employees of insurance companies, agents or brokers. The difference between an insurance agent and an insurance broker is that:

- an insurance agent acts on behalf of a particular insurer; while
- an insurance broker acts as an independent adviser, not 'tied' to any one insurer.

Duties of an agent or broker

The duties of an agent or broker are determined by the express and implied terms that make up the agency agreement (see Chapter 26). These duties include:

- **Following the principal's instructions** The primary duty of an agent or broker is to exercise care and skill in following the principal's instructions. For example, where a broker receives payment from an insured in relation to renewal of an insurance contract and fails to renew it, the broker can be sued for breach of that duty by the principal.
- **Acting in person.**
- **Acting in good faith.**
- **Exercising reasonable care, skill and diligence** in performing the terms of the contract. An agent or broker who incorrectly completes a proposal form after having been supplied with the correct information, or who is aware of material facts and fails to disclose them, may be sued by the insured:
  - for breach of contract; as well as
  - being liable in negligence for breach of their duty to exercise reasonable care and skill.
- **Keeping proper accounts.**
- **Maintaining confidentiality of information.**
- **Accepting only the agreed or customary remuneration and nothing else**.

Liability of insurer for agents and employees

Insurer generally responsible for conduct of their agents and employees

The *Corporations Act 2001* (Ch. 7) now makes the insurer, as a financial services licensee, responsible for the actions of their agents and employees even where the agent or employee was not acting within the scope of their authority or employment: ss. 917A, 917B. For example, where an agent incorrectly completes the proposal, the insurer will be bound if it is reasonable for the insured to rely upon the agent completing the form.

Furthermore, any notice in the proposal form that a third party completes the form as the proponent's agent and not the insurer's agent is void. The insurer will be liable in respect of any loss suffered by the insured as a result of the conduct of their agent or employee.

Premiums paid to an agent or broker

Section 985B(1) of the *Corporations Act 2001* provides that if a contract of insurance is **arranged** by a financial services licensee (e.g., an agent or broker), the payment of funds by an insured (e.g., an insurance premium) to the licensee will constitute a discharge of the liability of the insured to the insurer. If the premium is not passed on to the insurer by the licensee, the insurer's only action is against the broker or agent, **not** the insured.

Section 985B(2) provides that payment to a financial services licensee, that is, the agent or broker, of money such as a premium in respect of a contract of insurance to be arranged or effected by the licensee with the insurer, is a discharge of the insured's liability to pay the premium to the insurer.

***MANUFACTURERS MUTUAL INSURANCE LTD V. JOHN H BOARDMAN INSURANCE BROKERS* (1994) 68 ALJR 385**

Metrot took out insurance coverage through John H Boardman Insurance Brokers. The broker obtained insurance through MMI. Before expiry of the policy, a renewal notice was sent to the insured's broker. The insured instructed the broker to renew the policy and he paid the broker the renewal premium. The broker failed to inform MMI of the renewal, and did not forward the cheque in payment of the premium. The premises were damaged by an earthquake and the insured lodged a claim with MMI which was rejected on the basis that the policy had lapsed.

ISSUE: Was the insured's payment to the broker capable of amounting to a renewal of the policy under s. 14(2) of the *Insurance (Agents and Brokers) Act 1984* (Cth)?

DECISION: The High Court held that the Act leaves the relationship between the broker and insurer to be determined by the common law and until the contract of insurance exists, there can be no liability. Therefore, s. 14 does not operate until there is a contract in existence. At common law an insurance broker is an agent for the insured, not the insurance company. Therefore the payment of the premium to the broker would not constitute acceptance of the offer of insurance. The contract would not come into existence until the broker informs the insurer.

TYPES OF INSURANCE CONTRACT

Fire insurance

A fire policy is a contract of indemnity. That means the loss or damage is assessed after the event has occurred. It is generally based on the replacement value of the property at the time of the loss. If there is particularly valuable equipment on the premises, the proponent should consider a separate or specific policy for that item.

A fire policy includes not only fire but also 'explosion, lightning or thunderbolt'. However, the policies of the various insurers are not identical in all details and should always be read carefully by a proponent to see exactly what is covered. Some policies include the cost of temporary accommodation where an insured's dwelling house has been destroyed by fire, the cost of site clearance and architect's fees, the cost of repairing electrical appliances damaged by fire, etc.

An averaging formula can only be applied where it is expressly provided for in the contract and its nature and effect is drawn to the attention of the insured before the contract is entered into: *Insurance Contracts Act 1984* (Cth) s. 44 (see p. 231).

IN BRIEF

Typical types of fire policy available for a business

Type of policy	Description
Specific	A policy for a defined property for a certain sum, e.g., a dwelling for $45 000.
Floating	A policy covering several different locations, e.g., stock at a warehouse, in retail stores or in transit.
General	A policy covering several different kinds of assets, dwellings and contents, buildings, machinery and stock.

Declaration	A policy that provides for variation in the value of stock held over a period of time. The initial premium is paid on the likely maximum value and is adjusted from time to time when the actual value is declared. Such premiums are usually 'subject to average'.
Replacement and greater reinstatement	This kind of policy is necessary where the replacement cost of a building will be greater than the original cost or its present market value.
Special	Special policies are designed to protect special interests, e.g., to cover livestock against death due to fire or lightning. Policies can also be obtained to protect the insured against loss of profits resulting from a fire.
Concurrent	More than one insurer covers the same items in the same place at the same time, with the proportion of the total amount shared between them, e.g., stock worth $120 000 is covered by three different insurers, each with a $40 000 policy. In a mixed fire policy, the proportion of the total amount that each insurer is covering is not specified and may vary between them.

OTHER KINDS OF GENERAL (INDEMNITY) INSURANCE

While most people are aware of the benefits of taking out fire insurance, there are a number of other kinds of indemnity policies which are applicable to a business organisation, as shown below.

IN BRIEF

Examples of policies of general insurance

Type of policy	Description
Policies concerning property	Businesses are able to insure against burglary, riot or civil commotion, water discharged from pipes or water systems, storm and tempest and impact by vehicles. Plate glass policies cover accidental damage to all kinds of glass in shops, factories and dwellings.
Motor vehicle insurance	There are two main types of motor vehicle insurance: **Comprehensive motor vehicle insurance**—covers the loss of or damage to the vehicle of the insured, as well as liability for damage to property of third parties. Under a comprehensive policy, the driver of the vehicle will be indemnified for personal injury. **Third-party property motor vehicle insurance**—a motorist is covered for liability for property damage to third parties only. Loss or damage suffered by the insured to their own property as the result of an accident due to their fault must be borne by them.
Public liability insurance	Owners of property (including body corporates/owners corporation), as well as tenants, may be made liable for damages to a third party should they suffer personal injury or property damage when they come onto the property.
Professional indemnity insurance	Protection for professional people, such as accountants, doctors, solicitors, architects, engineers and the like, against possible claims arising from negligence or breach of contract in the performance of their professional duties.
Legal expenses insurance	This indemnifies the insured against legal costs and should be taken out by people who don't qualify for legal aid because of their income.

Type of policy	Description
Product liability insurance	This form of insurance provides protection for an insured against claims for personal injury or property damage by third parties arising out of the use of the insured's products.
Policies concerned with loss of income	***Pluvius***—used by sporting bodies and event organisers to cover against possible loss of income due to rain. **Superannuation**—compulsory for employers to provide superannuation for their employees and is based on life policies. **Consequential loss policies**—the insurer indemnifies the insured for economic loss as a result of the disruption to the business following damage caused by an insured peril, such as loss of profits caused by loss of stock through fire. **Fidelity guarantee insurance**—protection for an insured against theft or dishonesty by employees. **Credit insurance**—a creditor can insure against the possibility of a debtor failing to pay a particular debt, or even all of their debts, e.g., by credit providers for personal loans and credit card finance. **Cash in transit insurance**—the insured is provided with protection against the loss of money by theft or otherwise when the money is in transit between specified locations, e.g., the delivery of a payroll from a bank to the place of business or the takings of the business to the bank.

Life assurance

A life assurance policy is not a contract of indemnity. It is intended to assure payment of the sum fixed by the policy at the date on which the specified event occurs. This event may be either the death of the insured or their attaining the age stated in the policy. For this reason, some life policies are more correctly termed policies of assurance or contingency assurance.

IN BRIEF

Typical life assurance policies

Type of policy	Description
'Whole of life' policies	The sum payable falls due on the death of the assured. The aim of this policy is to provide for the dependants of the assured. Such policies acquire a surrender value after being in operation for a specified period of time. They are acceptable as security for loans during the lifetime of the assured. They are popular policies for businesses and are known as 'key executive' or 'key employee' policies. They are purchased by a business on the life of an owner or key employee. They offset the loss of that person's services and provide the business with the cash flow necessary to carry on while it is in the process of reorganising after the loss of the key executive.
Endowment policies	The sum assured is payable when the insured reaches a stated age or, if death occurs, before the stated age. The whole of the sum payable under the policy plus bonuses is paid to the estate of the deceased insured.

Type of policy	Description
Annuity policies	The assured pays a fixed sum in consideration of receiving fixed periodic income payments which may be arranged to commence immediately or at a future date, e.g., when the insured attains the age of 60 years.
Term insurance	This type of insurance provides 'protection' only. Most term insurance is issued on five, 10, 15 or 20 year plans and renewable annually. The younger the proponent, the greater the possibility of obtaining term insurance.

Personal accident insurance

The cause of death or injury must be a result of an accident, which can generally be defined as 'bodily injury caused by violent, accidental, external and visible means'. The insurer agrees to pay a specified sum in the event of injury or death.

IN BRIEF

Types of personal accident insurance

Type of policy	Description
Individual personal accident policies	These are policies taken by persons outside the scope of workers' compensation insurance, such as self-employed business people or independent contractors.
Workers' compensation	It is compulsory for an employer to insure their workers against personal injury in all jurisdictions. Coverage only occurs to a worker injured while working within the scope of their employment (see Chapter 35).
Third-party compulsory motor	This covers the legal liability of the motorist in a vehicle in respect of personal injuries to members of the public, including passengers in the vehicle. The cover is compulsory. Renewal of registration of a motor vehicle is not granted unless there is evidence of third-party compulsory insurance having been obtained.

Hospital benefits and social service schemes

The main purpose of hospital benefits and social service schemes is to recompense people for all or part of the expenses they incur for medical and other treatment. A variety of schemes have been initiated since the early 1970s by federal governments in this area (e.g., Medicare).

WEB RESOURCES

Australian Law Online: A useful site for finding current legal news in Australia on a wide range of topics including changes to insurance law contract law through the 'Topics' gateway under 'Consumer protection':
http://www.law.gov.au

Australian Legal Information Institute: Perhaps the best general law site on the web for students looking for information about Australian law and the *Insurance Contracts Act 1984* (Cth):
http://www.austlii.edu.au/databases.html

Codes of practice—financial services industry: For information on ASIC's policy on approving codes of practice and how compliance is monitored (use the 'search' tool and type in 'codes of practice'):
http:www.asic.gov.au/

Private Health Insurance Ombudsman: For information on the private health insurance ombudsman and functions that include the ability to resolve disputes about private health insurance:
http://www.health.gov.au/privatehealth/consumers/phio.htm

REVIEW QUESTIONS

10.1 Indicate whether each of the following statements is true or false:

Statement	TRUE	FALSE
In an insurance contract, unlike a gambling contract, the risk is created by the parties and is speculative	☐	☐
The consideration in a contract of insurance is called the premium	☐	☐
All contracts of insurance are contracts of indemnity	☐	☐
The party taking a contract of insurance is known as the insurer	☐	☐
The basic source of insurance law today is found in state legislation	☐	☐
Under the *Insurance Contracts Act 1984* (Cth), an insured must have an insurable interest at the time of the loss in order to be able to claim in the case of general insurance	☐	☐
Insurable interest today is stated in economic terms as pecuniary or financial loss	☐	☐
Double indemnity is where the insured takes out two or more policies in the same risk	☐	☐
In a life assurance policy an insured must have an insurable interest in the life of the assured at the time of entering into the policy	☐	☐
Most contracts of insurance are contracts of the utmost good faith	☐	☐
The duty to disclose all material facts ceases once the proposal form has been completed and sent to the insurance company by the insured	☐	☐
The test of what is material is the 'reasonable insured' test	☐	☐
Gossip and rumours may be considered material and should be disclosed by the proposer to the insurer	☐	☐
Misstatement of the insured's age can allow the insurer to avoid a policy	☐	☐
If a question in a proposal form is ambiguous, the question will be construed against the insured	☐	☐
Subrogation applies to all contracts of insurance and has the effect of putting the insurer into 'the shoes' of the insured	☐	☐
A cover note provides temporary cover for the insured and once in place cannot be revoked by the insurer. It must expire	☐	☐
A person wishing to take out insurance will normally have to first fill in a proposal form. When they send it in to the insurance company, they will become the offeror	☐	☐
As a general rule, it is the insurer who notifies the insured of a claim	☐	☐
The duties of an agent or broker are regulated in principal by common law and the *Insurance (Agents and Brokers) Act 1984* (Cth)	☐	☐
In the case of an indemnity contract, the insured can only ever recover the actual amount of the loss	☐	☐
Where a 'subject to average' clause is included in an indemnity contract, the insurer bears a pro rata proportion of the loss	☐	☐
An insurance broker acts on behalf of a particular insurer	☐	☐
Every insurance intermediary is considered to be the insured's agent in relation to any matter relating to insurance	☐	☐
Insurers are liable for the actions of their agents or brokers if they are acting within the scope of their authority or employment	☐	☐
Fire insurance is a contract of indemnity	☐	☐

10.2 Indemnity is the basis of all forms of insurance contracts. Discuss.

10.3 Are there any exceptions to the indemnity principle? Explain why and give an example.

10.4 What is insurable interest? Discuss how the *Insurance Contracts Act* modified the common law principle of insurable interest and give some examples.

activebook

Activebook resources include in-depth summaries with links to the relevant part of the book. For revision, add your own notes to the summaries provided by using the note-taking function.

10.5 Explain how a gambling contract and a contract of insurance are distinguishable.

10.6 Discuss the purpose of a cover note in a contract of general insurance.

10.7 What is the effect, if any, of a basis clause in a contract of general insurance since the passing of the *Insurance Contracts Act 1984*?

10.8 Discuss the extent of the insured's duty to disclose under a contract of insurance, including in your answer which test is used to determine what is material.

10.9 Explain what an 'averaging clause' is. Include in your answer an explanation of why it is only found in general insurance.

10.10 Explain the difference between an insurance agent and an insurance broker.

10.11 Discuss the duties and liabilities of insurance brokers and agents.

10.12 List the insurance policies applicable to:

a employers;

b a supermarket being run in partnership as a small family business; and

c motor vehicle owners.

10.13 Brett, a university student studying accounting, is totally dependent on his father for financial support. He is not eligible for AUSTUDY because the family income is too great. Brett insured the life of his father for $500 000, payable upon his death. During the second year of his course his father died and when he claimed on the insurance policy, the insurance company refused to pay claiming:

- Brett misstated his father's age as being 49 when in fact it was 45.
- Unknown to anyone in the family, Brett's father had contracted the HIV virus after a blood transfusion. This fact only became known after an autopsy had been completed into his death.

Discuss whether the insurer can reject Brett's claim, indicating in your answer the type of policy that Brett is most likely to have taken out.

CRITICAL THINKING

10.1 The directors of Twenty-First Maylux Pty Ltd were a husband and wife who ran a gift shop. Insurance was taken out on the gift shop in the name of the company, through an insurance broker with Cover-All Insurance Ltd. While the proposal form did not contain any questions as to prior convictions, the husband had previously entered into insurance contracts where the proposals had contained questions about prior criminal convictions. The husband had a criminal record for drug offences.

A fire occurred on the premises and the directors claimed on their insurance policy with Cover-All Insurance. What defence will the insurance company raise and do you think it will be successful?

10.2 Brown has just bought a printing business at Ultimo. He has come to you, as the family accountant, for advice on whether to take out insurance. Ultimately, he will seek more detailed advice from an insurance broker, but at this stage he is interested in obtaining some general information about insurance and some of the different types of policy that you think he should consider for his new business venture. He has provided you with the following information:

- He has a wife and two children (a girl aged nine and a boy aged seven).
- He is renting a house at Sylvania Waters, as his previous house at Oyster Bay was burnt to the ground in a 1994 bushfire.
- He is leasing a factory at Hurstbridge.
- He is leasing a number of vehicles for the business.
- He owns a 2000 Holden Statesman car valued at $45 000 but which cost him $55 000 when he bought it.
- He is employing 15 staff.

- He has plant and equipment valued at $750 000 and trading stock valued at $250 000 in the printing offices at Ultimo.
- He is owed $250 000 by debtors.
- He owes creditors $25 000.
- One of his employees has been involved in two accidents in the last two weeks. One occurred while he was driving a company vehicle to deliver stock to a client and the other occurred when the same employee accidentally dropped a box of printing paper on a customer who was walking through the printery.

Advise Brown on the following matters:

1 The reasons for and against him taking out insurance.
2 What types of insurance you would advise him to consider taking out (explaining why).
3 What information he should disclose to the insurance company, if any, if he decides to take out insurance (explaining why).
4 What terms you think he should be aware of in insurance law that would help him better understand what insurance is and how it operates.

LAW OF CONTRACTS

PART FOUR

CHAPTER 11

Introduction to Contracts

CHAPTER CONTENTS

activebook

This icon is used throughout the following chapter to remind you to visit the *Business Law* online activebook for additional exercises, links to legal websites, and feedback. For a detailed explanation of what is in the activebook please refer to the inside cover of this textbook. The activebook is available through OneKey.

Where do I start?
Learning path: Use the activebook to complete a pre-chapter warm-up exercise.

There are many definitions of legal terms to assist with your understanding of the material.

CHAPTER OBJECTIVES

On completion of this chapter, you should be able to:

- distinguish between a contract and an agreement
- define a contract
- distinguish between a formal and a simple contract
- outline the elements of a simple contract
- outline the elements to be satisfied to make a simple contract valid
- identify those simple contracts which must be in writing, which must be evidenced in writing, or can be oral
- explain the operation of the parol evidence rule
- describe the main features of the *Electronic Transactions* legislation.

KEY TERMS

An understanding of the following terms will help you to better understand the material in this chapter:

- **bilateral contract:** a promise for a promise
- **consideration:** consideration may consist either in some right, interest, profit or benefit accruing to the one party, or some forbearance, detriment, loss or responsibility given, suffered or undertaken by the other (the benefit/detriment definition by *Lush* J in *Currie v. Misa* (1875) LR 10 Ex 153) or an act or forbearance of one party, or the promise thereof, which is the price for which the promise of the other is bought, and the promise thus given for value is enforceable (the price paid definition suggested by Sir Frederick Pollock and adopted by the House of Lords in *Dunlop Pneumatic Tyre Co. Ltd v. Selfridge and Co. Ltd* [1915] AC 847)
- **contract:** an agreement that gives rise to legal rights and obligations between the parties to it and that will be enforced by the courts
- **executed contract:** a contract completed or fully carried out by both parties
- **executory contract:** where one or both parties agree to perform their contractual obligations in the future
- **formal contract:** a contract which is signed, sealed and delivered and does not require consideration, such as a deed
- **infant**: a person under the age of 18 years and also known as a minor
- ***quantum meruit***: as much as a person has earned or as much as they deserve
- **quasi-contract:** a contract implied in law
- **simple contract:** a contract that is not special and requires consideration to be valid, unlike contracts that are described as 'formal' or 'under seal'
- **specialty contract:** a contract under seal
- **unenforceable contract:** a contract which is not valid because of a technical fault
- **unilateral contract:** a contract consisting of an exchange of an act for a promise
- **void:** of no legal effect
- **voidable:** an agreement which may be affirmed or rejected at the option of one of the parties.

what if . . .

You woke up one morning and discovered that there were no longer any such things as contracts. Do you think that this would have any effect on your daily activities or do you think your life would go on as normal?

Contracts are a fundamental part of people's daily lives. They are constantly being entered into by individuals with other individuals or businesses, as well as businesses with other businesses, to sell or transfer property, services and other rights. The purchase of goods, such as books and food, is based on sales contracts; the hiring of employees is based on employment contracts; the lease of a flat or house is based on a rental contract. The list is extensive. Without enforceable contracts, business could not exist.

On the whole, contracts are entered into voluntarily by the parties. They begin life as agreements, although not all agreements are intended to have legal consequences. Where possible, **the courts try to give effect to the intentions of the parties** through the application of an **objective** test based on what a reasonable person would conclude from looking at the words and conduct of the parties and whether they intended to be legally bound by their agreement: see, for example, *Air Great Lakes Pty Ltd v. KS Easter (Holdings) Pty Ltd* [1985] 2 NSWLR 309.

The following chapters examine the main principles governing the formation of a contract, its content, the methods by which a contract can be discharged or breached, and the remedies available to an injured party where a breach occurs.

> This chapter is an introduction to the study of contract law. It begins by looking at the distinction between a contract and an agreement, defines a contract, considers the elements necessary for the creation of a simple valid contract, the effect of a missing element, the various classifications of contracts that are used, the difference between a formal and a simple contract, and finally, the impact of e-commerce on contracts.

SOURCES OF CONTRACT LAW

Australian contract law is primarily derived from two sources. First, there is the common law. Much of contract law, and the right of freedom to contract, that applies in Australia is embodied in common law principles that were developed in the English common law courts, that is, case law decisions. As a result, many of the references contained in the following chapters on contract law will be to decisions of the English courts where these principles originated from, and which were adopted with approval by Australian courts.

Secondly, legislation such as the *Statute of Frauds 1677* (Imp) and much later Commonwealth, state and territory legislation amending or supplementing the common law rules of contract law developed by the courts, such as the *Trade Practices Act 1974* (Cth) and equivalent state and territory *Fair Trading Acts*.

Thus the study of contract law involves an examination of common law principles and the extent to which they have been affected by legislation. An examination of s. 52 of the *Trade Practices Act 1974* (Cth) prohibiting misleading or deceptive conduct, and the equivalent section in associated state and territory *Fair Trading Acts*, reveals just how extensive its impact is on contract law, impacting on almost all contract topics ranging from intention to discharge.

CONTRACT AND AGREEMENT DISTINGUISHED

A contract is a legally enforceable agreement

The terms 'contract' and 'agreement' are often used to mean the same thing. In fact, one of the traditional definitions of a contract is that it is a legally enforceable agreement.

Doing business

An agreement is not necessarily a contract

While every contract involves an element of agreement, do not assume that every agreement will result in a contract recognisable by law, because:

- the parties may not intend to create legal relations (e.g., many public competitions, going out with a friend on a social occasion); and
- one or more of the principles governing contractual relations may not have been satisfied (e.g., the purpose of the agreement is illegal, there is a lack of consideration). ■

Sometimes a contract exists irrespective of the wishes of the parties (e.g., compulsory third-party insurance). This can hardly be seen as an 'agreement', because neither you nor the insurance company has any choice about either the contents of the contract or even about whether you wish to make a contract.

THE LAW OF CONTRACTS

An agreement *must* contain a promise *and* be intended to be legally enforceable

To have any legal significance, the **agreement** must contain a **promise** and must have been intended by the parties to be **legally enforceable** in a court of law. It is the performance of this promise and its legal consequences which are fundamental to modern society and which form the basis of the study of contract law.

While contract law still recognises the principle of 'freedom to contract', since the 1960s the Commonwealth and state parliaments have increasingly limited this principle, to prevent abuse in the bargaining process between the consumer and the supplier, through the use of legislation, such as:

- the *Trade Practices Act 1974* (Cth), particularly s. 52 (see Chapter 23);
- the *Contracts Review Act 1980* (NSW) (see pp. 337, 349, 378);
- the *Frustrated Contracts Acts* of Victoria (1959), New South Wales (1978) and South Australia (1988) (see p. 398);
- state and territory consumer protection and Fair Trading legislation (see Chapter 23); and
- credit legislation (see Chapter 24).

These have all eroded the principle of 'freedom to contract'.

Contract defined

An agreement is concerned with promises

The agreement must contain a promise and, in legal terms, a promise is seen as a commitment or undertaking by a person that something will or will not happen in the future. **The person who makes the promise is called the promisor**, and **the person to whom the promise is made is the promisee**. People make promises every day—to meet someone, to lend some money, to obey certain rules.

IN BRIEF

Contract defined

A contract can be defined as an agreement containing promises made between two or more parties with the intention of creating certain legal rights and obligations and enforceable in a court of law.

Failure to perform a contractual promise incurs a legal liability

What distinguishes contractual from non-contractual promises are the consequences of failure to perform. A promisor who fails to perform a non-contractual promise has no legal liability. For example, the person who arranges to meet a friend at the movies and doesn't turn up is not going to be sued by the friend. On the other hand, if the promise is contractual (e.g., the promise to supply building materials to a building site for a builder to complete a house), the promisee is generally entitled to treat the promisor's non-performance as a breach and seek a remedy through the courts.

CREATION OF AN APPARENT SIMPLE CONTRACT

Essential elements in the creation of a simple contract

In order to create a contract (**NOTE:** at this stage there is no question whether the contract is valid or not), three elements **must** be present and they can be formulated as three questions (see Figures 11.1 and 11.2):

- Was there an **intention** to contract?—the parties must intend that their promises create legally enforceable obligations (see Chapter 12).

If there was:

- Was there an **agreement** between the parties?—an offer by one party and an acceptance by the other (see Chapter 13).

If there was:

- Was there **consideration**?—something of value passing from one party to another in return for a promise to do something, unless the agreement is made under seal, in which case consideration is not necessary (see Chapter 14).

With these three elements present, an **apparent** contract can be said to exist.

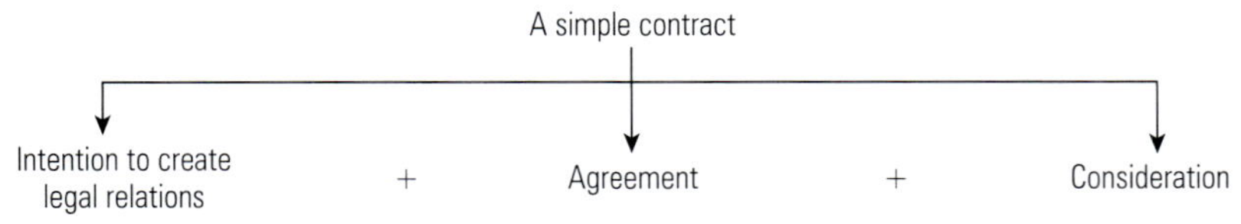

FIGURE 11.1 *Elements essential in a simple contract*

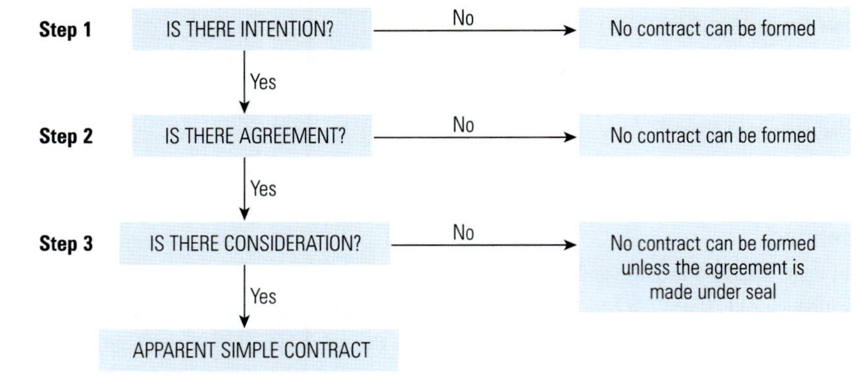

FIGURE 11.2 *Steps to an apparent simple contract*

Essential elements to be satisfied to determine validity

If the following elements are satisfied, again formulated as questions, then the apparent simple contract that was created above is valid (see Figures 11.3 and 11.4):

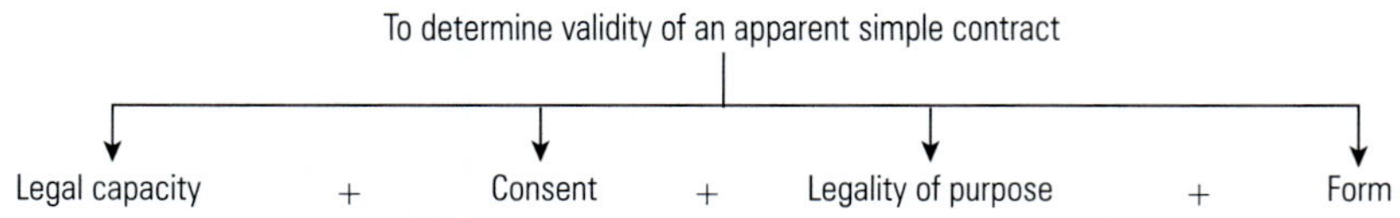

FIGURE 11.3 *Testing for validity*

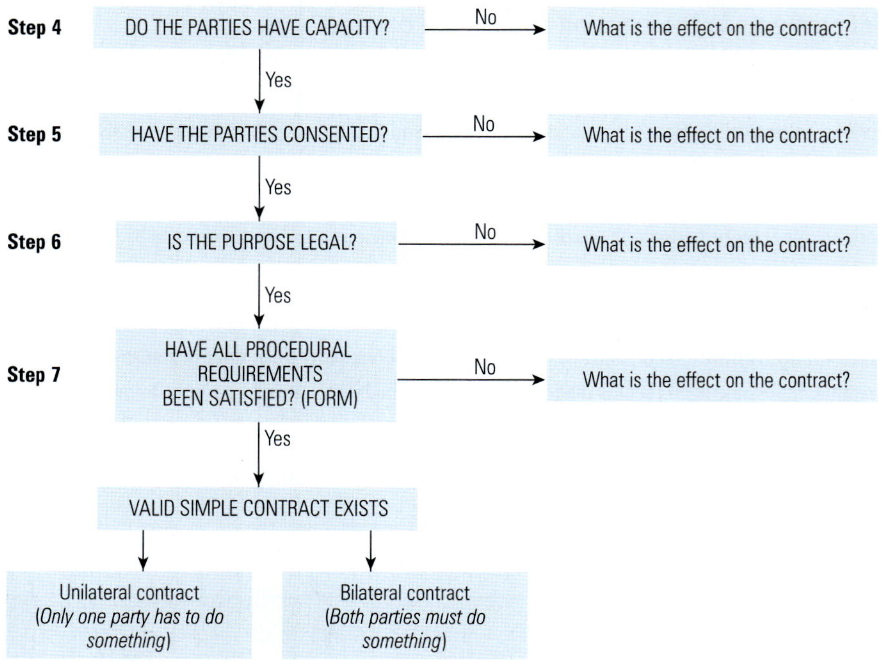

FIGURE 11.4 *Steps in determining validity*

- Did the parties have **legal capacity**?—the parties must be legally capable of entering into a contractual relationship (see Chapter 15).
- Did the parties have **consent**?—the contract must be a genuine expression of the intentions of the parties (see Chapter 16).
- Was there **legality of purpose**?—the objects or the purpose of the contract must be legal (see Chapter 17).
- Was there any particular **form** the contract needed to be in?—are there any statutory requirements which must be satisfied? (see below).

CLASSIFICATION OF CONTRACTS

Contracts may be classified in a variety of different ways. Each differs somewhat in formation, enforcement, performance and discharge.

IN BRIEF

Classification of contracts

Classification	Type of contract	Commentary
By promise	Bilateral	A contract entered into by way of exchange of promises; 'a promise for a promise'.
	Unilateral	A contract in which the offeror's offer can only be accepted by the performance of an act by the offeree; 'a promise for an act'.
Enforceability	Valid	All the elements are satisfied and enforceable by either party.
	Voidable	Only the injured party can enforce the contract or rescind.
	Void	No legal rights or obligations, so neither party can enforce it.
	Unenforceable	Lacking a procedural requirement to make it enforceable.
	Illegal	The purpose of the contract is contrary to statute or common law.
Performance	Executed	Performed at the time of making.
	Executory	Both parties still have obligations to perform.
Formation	Expressly	The contract is created by express words, i.e. by writing, orally or a combination.
	Impliedly	Created by conduct or actions of the parties.
	Quasi-contracts	An agreement imposed by law.
	Formal	A contract that requires a special form or method of creation but does not require consideration to be valid.
	Simple	A contract that does not require a special form but must have consideration present.

Bilateral and unilateral contracts

Contracts are either bilateral or unilateral, depending on what the offeree must do to accept the offeror's offer.

Bilateral contract

Bilateral contract: *both* parties have to perform their promises

The contract is bilateral if the offeror's promise is met by the offeree's specified counter-promise of acceptance. In other words, a bilateral contract is 'a promise for a promise' and it is the exchange of promises that creates the enforceable contract. There is no need for an act of performance to create a bilateral contract. For example, you promise to pay me $7500 for my car and I promise to sell it to you.

Unilateral contract

Unilateral contract: the offeree still has to perform their part of the bargain

A contract is unilateral if the offeror's offer can only be accepted by performance of the specified act by the offeree. There is no contract until the offeree performs the requested act as they have the option of whether to perform or not. It is a 'promise for an act'. For example, you give me $7500 and I promise to give you my car after the weekend.

Occasionally, it can be difficult to determine from the language of the offeror's promise whether it is an offer to create a bilateral or a unilateral contract. It appears that in questions of doubt, the courts are more likely to infer that a bilateral contract was intended.

The importance of the distinction

Where a contract is made which contemplates a unilateral contract, the terms of the offer will indicate that the offeror does not contemplate acceptance until performance of the act that has been called for has been completed. For example, in a reward case this would be the finding of the missing item. If the offeree abandons their effort half-way through, they would not be in breach of contract. Nor would they be entitled to payment for their efforts because they have not complied with the conditions for payment of the reward.

Problems can arise if the offeror of a unilateral contract attempts to revoke an offer after the offeree has begun performance. While there are no problems if the offeror withdraws their offer before the offeree begins performance, there may be difficulties where the offeree has begun or substantially completed performance. Part performance of the act called for may be regarded as sufficient consideration for the offeror not to revoke their promise.

Doing business

Note the difference between a bilateral and unilateral contract

The parties to a unilateral contract have different obligations from the parties to a bilateral contract. It is for this reason that the parties should understand whether the language of the offer is creating a unilateral or bilateral contract:

- A **bilateral contract** is created by an exchange of promises. A contract is created at the moment the offeree accepts the offer. If either party does not perform their part of the bargain, the contract is breached and the injured party can sue for damages.
- A **unilateral contract** is created by a promise for an act. In this case, the offeree is under no obligation to perform, and no contract exists until the offeree performs the requested act. Note that if the offeree does not perform, there is no breach of contract. However, if the offeree has commenced or completed the work requested to be performed, they may be able to sue the offeror if the offeror fails to pay. ■

Classification according to enforceability

Valid

A valid contract is one that the law will enforce. The parties intend to enter into a legal relationship and have agreed upon the terms, thus creating legal rights and obligations which the parties can enforce against each other.

Voidable

The contract remains valid and binding unless and until it is repudiated. Only the injured party can avoid the contract or compel the other party to go through with it. Repudiation must take place within a reasonable time or the right to repudiate may be lost. This might happen if you are induced by fraud to enter into a contract for, say, the purchase of shares. In this situation, you can either go ahead with the purchase or avoid it at your (not the seller's) option.

Void

There are no legal rights or obligations from the outset (void *ab initio*), which means that a person who enters into a void agreement cannot enforce it or be forced to comply with it. Nor could they pass on good title to a third party because they would have no title to give. For example, if A has his car stolen by B, who then sells it to C, the contract between B and C is void. B has no title to give to C. If C subsequently sells the car to D, then D gets the same title to the car that C had, that is, no title. A could then force D to give back the car or its value. D would have to then seek compensation from C, and C would have to try to find B to get back the value of the car.

Unenforceable

While the contract appears to be valid, **no legal action can be brought on it**, perhaps because some procedural requirement is lacking. For example, the contract may be of a type that needs to be evidenced in writing, or needs stamp duty. Correction of the defect will render the contract enforceable. This topic is dealt with in more detail below at page 251.

Illegal

When the purpose of the contract contravenes a statute or the common law, it will be illegal and **generally treated as being void**; for example, something of a criminal nature, such as robbing a bank with a friend. This is discussed in more detail in Chapter 17 when dealing with the topic of 'Legality'.

Classification according to performance

Executed contracts

The object of the contract is performed and completed at the time of making. For example, if I wash your car for $10 and you pay me as soon as I finish, the agreement has been fulfilled and the contract expires.

Executory contracts

One of the parties promises to do, or refrain from doing, something in the future. For example, I agree to wash your car next week for $10. Here, both promises are yet to be performed.

> **activebook**
>
> To help you to remember and understand the topics covered so far, and for links to legal websites, refer to your online activebook. Model answers provide feedback to problems and exercises.

Classification according to formation

Express contracts

This is a contract which is either wholly in writing, evidenced in writing, oral or partly written and partly oral. All the terms are agreed upon by the parties. For example, a contract for the lease of a house or unit is created by a written contract between the parties.

Implied contracts

The contract is implied from the circumstances surrounding the acts or conduct of the parties, for example, when catching a taxi it is implied that the fare will be paid and that the taxi driver will get you to your destination.

Quasi-contracts

The contract is the result of an agreement imposed by law, for example, third party car insurance, irrespective of whether there is agreement between the parties.

CLASSIFICATION ACCORDING TO FORMAL OR SIMPLE CONTRACTS

Another classification of contracts is into formal and simple contracts (see Figure 9.5). Of the two, the simple contract is the one most often encountered in commercial transactions today.

Formal contracts

A formal contract is a contract that must be written in a special way (i.e. form) and as a result has no need for consideration. It gets its **validity from its form alone**. There are two types of contract:

Formal contracts may not be the result of agreement or require consideration

- **Contracts of record**

  They can arise against the wish of one of the parties, so that they are independent of agreement.

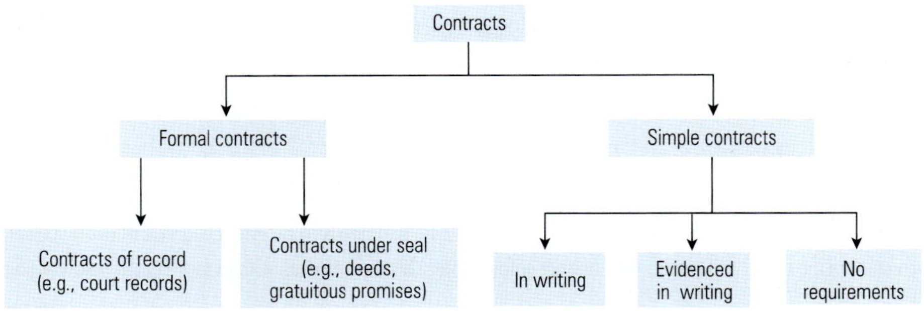

FIGURE 11.5 *Classification of contracts as formal or simple*

- **Contracts under seal**

  A contract by deed is a promise in writing, signed by the party or parties to the contract, witnessed by at least one witness not a party to the contract, sealed or expressed to be a deed, and delivered (or with at least an intention to deliver) without any other condition attached.

Where a deed is delivered subject to conditions and does not come into operation until the fulfilment of these conditions, it is called an escrow.

The time limit within which an action for a contract under seal can be brought before it becomes statute barred varies between states, but it is much longer than for an action on a simple contract (see Table 11.1).

Table 11.1 Time within which a legal action may be taken in contract

Limitations Acts	*Formal contracts*	*Simple contracts*
New South Wales, Queensland, Tasmania, and the Australian Capital Territory	12 years	6 years
Northern Territory	12 years	3 years
Victoria and South Australia	15 years	6 years
Western Australia	12 years	6 years

Simple contracts

Simple contracts *must* have consideration

If a contract is not under seal or a contract of record, then **valuable consideration must be present for it to be valid**.

Subject to statutory requirements, simple contracts can be created expressly, impliedly or by quasi-contract. Evidence of a simple contract is often by way of receipt, for example, from the supermarket or service station, which contains on its face the date and time of purchase, the items and the price, as well as the total price paid by the purchaser as evidence of acceptance of the items.

Doing business

If the contract is important, put it in writing

It is preferable to reduce contracts to writing and have them signed by the parties wherever possible if the contract has any importance to them. Written evidence provides greater certainty as to what they agreed to than is the case with verbal contracts, where much of the evidence will be based on the recollections of the parties. This can lead to expensive litigation as the parties argue over what they really agreed to. ■

If the parties have taken the time to reduce the agreement to writing, the courts will assume that it is a complete record of the contract. They are generally reluctant to admit evidence of acts or words of the parties prior to the execution of the document if this has the effect of adding to, varying or contradicting the written agreement. This is known as the **parol evidence rule** (see p. 360).

Parol evidence rule—contracts wholly in writing are presumed to be complete

Contracts void unless in writing

Certain simple contracts, to be valid and enforceable, are required by statute to be wholly in writing. If they are not, they are void. For example:

Contracts required by statute to be wholly in writing are *void* if they are not *in writing*

- Bills of exchange and promissory notes (*Bills of Exchange Act 1909* (Cth)).
- Cheques and payment orders (*Cheques Act 1986* (Cth)).
- Hire-purchase contracts (NT: 1961; Qld: 1959; Tas: 1959; Vic: *Hire-Purchase Act 1959*; WA: 1959).
- Real estate contracts (ACT: *Real Property Act 1925*; NSW: *Conveyancing Act 1919*; NT: *Real Property Act (SA) 1886;* Qld: *Property Law Act 1974*; SA: *Law of Property Act 1936*; Tas: *Conveyancing and Law of Property Act 1884*; Vic: *Property Law Act 1958* and *Instruments Act 1958;* WA: *Property Law Act 1969*).

Contracts that must be evidenced in writing

There is a second class of contracts that must be evidenced in writing. The absence of **writing** does not affect their validity, but it makes them unenforceable in a court of law. This is a requirement of proof which dates back to the *Statute of Frauds 1677* (Imp). There are only two main areas of application of the *Statute of Frauds* today in Australia—ss. 4 and 17. In all states, s. 17 has been repealed, but it has been re-enacted in some states and territories in their sale of goods legislation.

Contracts that must be evidenced in writing by statute are *unenforceable* if they are not in writing

Statute of Frauds (s. 4)

The provisions of s. 4 can be found in one form or another in Victoria, Tasmania and the Northern Territory. The Imperial Act is only partly followed in Western Australia. In those states which have adopted s. 4, only five classes of contract will be affected:

- special promises by executors or administrators to answer for damages out of their own money;
- contracts of guarantee—whereby one person promises to pay the debt of another in the event of default;
- an agreement made in consideration of marriage;
- contracts for the sale or disposition of land or any interest in land; and
- agreements not to be performed within the space of one year from the time they are made, or not to be performed within one year. The test is whether the agreement can be performed within a year, **not** whether the agreement is actually performed within a year.

Statute of Frauds (s. 17)

Only Western Australia (*Sale of Goods Act 1895*, s. 4) and Tasmania (*Sale of Goods Act 1896*, s. 9) have re-enacted s. 17 of the *Statute of Frauds* as part of their sale of goods legislation. Thus, contracts for the sale of goods costing $20 or more will be unenforceable unless one of the following three requirements is met:

- The buyer has accepted part of the goods so sold and actually received the same.
- The buyer has given something in earnest to bind the contract or has given something in part-payment to bind the contract.
- Some note or memorandum in writing of the contract is made and signed by the party to be charged or by their authorised agent. For example, an auctioneer is the agent of the seller and, after the sale, also an agent of the buyer.

The note or memorandum

A note or memorandum can take any documentary form—a letter, docket, invoice or even an entry in an auctioneer's book—and it does not even have to be contained in one document. It must show:

- the names of the parties;
- the subject matter;

COHEN V. ROCHE [1927] 1 KB 169

Cohen went to an auction conducted by Roche and successfully bid £60 for eight antique chairs. Roche entered the purchase price in his book, recorded Cohen's name alongside as well as the price of £60. Roche did not sign the book, but on each page was pasted a leaf from his printed catalogue which contained his name and address. Cohen subsequently refused to pay for the chairs, arguing that as the sale exceeded £10 the contract was unenforceable as there was no note or memorandum.

ISSUE: Once the sale was completed on the fall of the hammer, was the auctioneer acting as the agent for the buyer or was he still the agent for the seller?

DECISION: The entries made by Roche in the book showed that he recognised his printed name as his signature, and that as it was recorded after the sale, he was acting as an agent for the buyer and thus there was a valid contract in existence.

- the consideration; and
- the signature of the party to be proceeded against or their authorised agent.

In the absence of a note or memorandum, the contract is unenforceable. Money paid or property transferred cannot be recovered.

CONTRACTS AND E-COMMERCE

(E-commerce information: details on e-commerce are available from the National Office for the Information Economy (NOIE) <http://www.noie.gov.au>; **Department of the Treasury:** a very useful site for information on e-commerce generally <http://www.ecomerce.trasury.gov.au/default.htm>.) Business is steadily adapting to electronic commerce as contracts have never required any special form or method of communication at common law. The use of electronic means to complete business transactions rather than the traditional method of doing business face-to-face and the exchange of paper-based documents is becoming commonplace. The *Electronic Transactions Act 1999* (Cth) provides a legal framework to support and encourage businesses and consumers to use electronic commerce by providing that the law shall treat electronic and paper-based commerce equally as well as providing a template for the uniform state and territory legislation now in place across Australia (Victoria, New South Wales, South Australia, Tasmania and Northern Territory in 2000, Queensland and the ACT in 2001, Western Australia in 2003).

Main features of the *Electronic Transactions Acts* include:

- a transaction is not invalid because it took place wholly or partly electronically (Cth: s. 8);
- a requirement to give information in writing can be satisfied if the person gives the information by means of an electronic communication (Cth: s. 9);
- a requirement to provide a signature can be satisfied in relation to an electronic communication if a method is used to identify the person, their approval is obtained, and the method was as reliable as was appropriate for the purposes for which the information was communicated (Cth: s. 10);
- a requirement to produce a document in hard copy can be satisfied by producing the document in electronic form (Cth: s. 11);
- a requirement to record information in writing, to retain a document in hard copy, or to retain information the subject of an electronic communication can be satisfied by recording or retaining the information in electronic form (Cth: s. 12);
- in relation to the time and place of dispatch and receipt of electronic communications, unless the parties agree otherwise, the following rules apply:

- time of dispatch of the electronic communication occurs when it enters an information system designated by the addressee as the system for the receipt of electronic communications or, if no system is designated, when it comes to the attention of the addressee; and
- the time of receipt of the electronic communication is the time when the electronic communication enters the addressee's information system or, if no system is designated, when the electronic communication comes to the attention of the addressee (Cth: s. 14).

The formation of an e-contract is no different to the formation of a conventional contract. The first requirement is that there must be an intention to create legal relations, and a person accessing an online supplier with intention to buy a product or service is generally assumed to be intending to contract (see Chapter 12). The second requirement that must be present is that there is agreement between the parties (see Chapter 13), generally with the buyer making the offer by clicking on the 'Buy', 'I agree' or 'I accept' button or icon and the offer being sent when the buyer clicks on the 'send' button. Acceptance occurs when the supplier communicates an acceptance and this is received by the buyer. It is not caught by the postal acceptance rule which assumes that an offer is accepted on posting. The final requirement for creation of a simple contract, not its validity, is that consideration be present (see Chapter 14). Consideration includes a promise for a promise and this can be done electronically. Assuming these three elements are all present, then a simple contract comes into existence.

It is then necessary, as it is with as conventional contract, to determine whether the simple contract that has been created electronically is valid. The fourth requirement that has to be satisfied is the question of the legal capacity of the parties to enter into a contract (see Chapter 15). Parties who are considered to have limited legal capacity include minors, the intoxicated, the mentally ill, and corporations. The problem with legal capacity is that the contract is electronic and the parties may never meet, and may even be in different countries. If the buyer is a minor and the goods or services are for necessaries, then the contract will be binding but in other cases involving the issue of capacity, the situation is more problematic. The fifth requirement for a valid contract is the issue of consent, that is, there must be real agreement between the parties, and unless it is present, there can be no contract (see Chapter 16). An issue that can arise in dealing with a supplier on the Internet often involves unconscionability where the supplier attempts to impose harsh terms and conditions on the buyer. Finally, the e-contract must be legal, that is, not contravene any state, territory or Commonwealth law (see Chapter 17).

If each of the requirements is satisfied, so that it can be said that a valid e-contract has been created between the parties, the question that remains is: 'What have the parties to an e-contract agreed to?' This is an issue about contractual terms (see Chapter 18). Often clicking the 'Buy', 'I agree' or 'I accept' button will result in the terms set out in the website being incorporated into the contract. But this raises two problems in contract law. The first is the problem of implied terms, that is, what terms have been implied into the e-contract? The second problem is whether notice of the terms was given before are after the contract was formed. For example, if the e-contract contains an exclusion clause, notice of such a clause after the contract has been formed is ineffective. Notice must be brought to the attention of the buyer before the contract is made.

activebook

Activebook resources include in-depth summaries with links to the relevant part of the book. For revision, add your own notes to the summaries provided by using the note-taking function.

WEB RESOURCE

Australian Law Online: This is a very useful site prepared by the Commonwealth government that looks at a variety of topics relevant to this text. For material on this chapter go to the topic headed Legal system and click on courts: **http://www.law.gov.au/**

REVIEW QUESTIONS

11.1 Indicate whether each of the following statements is true or false:

	TRUE	FALSE
▪ For the creation of an apparent simple contract, intention, agreement and consideration must be shown to be present	☑	☐
▪ A valid contract is one which can be enforced by both parties	☐	☑
▪ A unilateral contract is one where both parties still have to perform their obligations	☐	☑
▪ A formal contract derives its validity from its form alone and does not require consideration to be present	☑	☐
▪ An executed contract is performed and completed at the time of making	☐	☑
▪ Contracts required to be wholly in writing by statute are void if they are not wholly in writing	☑	☐
▪ Under a void contract there are no legal rights or obligations	☑	☐
▪ Bills of exchange and cheques are required by statute to be wholly in writing	☑	☐
▪ To determine the validity of an apparent simple contract it is necessary to consider the questions of capacity, consent, legality and form	☑	☐
▪ The person to whom a promise is made is known as the promisee	☐	☑
▪ If a contract is void, it means it has no legal effect from the beginning	☑	☐
▪ Consideration must be present in every contract	☐	☑

11.2 List the elements that are necessary for the creation of a valid simple contract.

11.3 Explain the difference between a formal and a simple contract.

11.4 In the purchase of a motor car, or for that matter anything of value, why is it important to check that the seller has a valid title to the goods? Discuss.

CRITICAL THINKING

11.1 Why is it necessary today for some contracts to be wholly in writing and some contracts to be evidenced in writing? What purpose does it achieve? Discuss.

11.2 What sort of problems may arise in contract law for users of e-commerce? Discuss.

CHAPTER

Step 1: Intention to Create Legal Relations

CHAPTER CONTENTS

STEP 1: IS THERE INTENTION TO CONTRACT?

Social, domestic, and voluntary agreements

Business or commercial agreements

CHAPTER OBJECTIVES

On completion of this chapter, you should be able to:

- distinguish between social, domestic or voluntary, and business or commercial relationships
- explain how the courts use an objective test of a reasonable person to determine intention.

KEY TERMS

An understanding of the following terms will help you to better understand the material in this chapter:

- **domestic agreements:** ones made between family members and relatives
- **objective test:** would the words or conduct of the parties lead a reasonable person to believe, on the balance of probabilities, that legal relations were intended, i.e. they intended to create a contract?
- **social agreements:** ones made between friends or acquaintances
- **voluntary agreements:** where the parties may volunteer their services.

activebook

This icon is used throughout the following chapter to remind you to visit the *Business Law* online activebook for additional exercises, links to legal websites, and feedback. For a detailed explanation of what is in the activebook please refer to the inside cover of this textbook. The activebook is available through OneKey.

Where do I start?

Learning path: Use the activebook to complete a pre-chapter warm-up exercise.

There are many definitions of legal terms to assist with your understanding of the material.

what if . . .

You had satisfied all the legal requirements for a contract except that you never intended to enforce the agreement in court and you assumed that the other party never intended to enforce it either. Should you be forced to go ahead with the agreement on the basis that a contract exists?

Contracts are voluntary agreements between the parties. The first step that must be taken in establishing whether a simple contract exists or not is to establish whether the parties clearly intend that the agreement they are entering into is meant to create legal relations. This is generally not a problem in the case of business or commercial arrangements unless the parties don't want contractual relations to flow from their agreement. If a problem is going to arise, it is usually in relation to social or domestic arrangements between the parties.

> This chapter discusses the two main classifications of agreement—those which are presumed not to intend to create legal relations: the social, domestic or voluntary agreements; and those which are presumed to create legal relations: the business or commercial agreement.

STEP 1—IS THERE INTENTION TO CONTRACT?

In the first step it must be established that there is a clear intention by the parties that the agreement containing their promises is intended to be enforceable in law. If not, there can be no contract.

The parties must intend that their agreement is to have legal force

It rarely happens that the parties make any direct reference to the question of intention to contract within the contract itself. However, for a contract to be enforceable, the parties **must** intend that their promises create legally enforceable obligations and that these are ascertained from all the circumstances. In *Ermogenous v. Greek Orthodox Community of South Australia Incorporated* (2001) 209 CLR 95, *Gaudron, McHugh, Hayne and Callinan* JJ said, at para [25]:

> *Because the inquiry about this last aspect may take account of the subject matter of the agreement, the status of the parties to it, their relationship to one another, and other surrounding circumstances, not only is there obvious difficulty in formulating rules intended to prescribe the kinds of cases in which an intention to create contractual relations should, or should not, be found to exist, it would be wrong to do so. Because the search for the 'intention to create contractual relations' requires an objective assessment of the state of affairs between the parties (as distinct from the identification of any uncommunicated subjective reservation or intention that either may harbour) the circumstances which might properly be taken into account in deciding whether there was the relevant intention are so varied as to preclude the formation of any prescriptive rules. Although the word 'intention' is used in this context, it is used in the same sense as it is used in other contractual contexts. It describes what it is that would objectively be conveyed by what was said or done, having regard to the circumstances in which those statements and actions happened. It is not a search for the uncommunicated subjective motives or intentions of the parties.*

In *Ermogenous*, the High Court held that an agreement under which a church employed an Archbishop constituted an enforceable contract. In arriving at that conclusion, the Court made it clear that each case has to be considered individually. It rejected the traditional analysis applied in determining intention in the context of 'presumptions', that is, in the case of social, domestic or charitable agreements there was a presumption that the parties did not intend to create legal relations, while in the case of commercial or business arrangements, that the parties did intend to create legal relations, and that intention comes from what would objectively be conveyed by what was said or done, having regard to all the circumstances. Presumptions should not be applied too strongly. They are merely useful tools to identify who should bear the onus of proof.

This intention, express or implied, is usually a non-issue where it is clear that the arrangement is commercial in nature, for example, a business signing a contract with a supplier. Looked at objectively, generally the only conclusion that can be drawn in such circumstances is that the parties intended to create legal relations. However, it should be noted that it is possible for the parties:

- to agree that their agreement is binding 'in honour only', e.g., in *Rose & Frank Company v. JR Crompton & Bros Ltd* (1925) AC 445 the parties included a term which stated that the arrangement was not entered into as a formal or legal agreement but only as a record of intention; or
- not to be contractually promissory, e.g., in *Kleinwort Benson Ltd v. Malaysia Mining Corporation Berhad* (1989) 1 WLR 379 it was held that a letter of comfort did not show any intent to attract liability and in *Coogee Esplanade Surf Motel Pty Ltd v. Commonwealth* (1983) 50 ALR 363 it was also held that a letter of intent did not intend to create a contract.

The courts use an objective test to try to determine the intention of the parties. That is, what inferences would a reasonable person draw from the words or conduct of the parties. If a reasonable person would assume that there was no intention by the parties to be bound, then there is no contract. However, not carrying out the intention as the other party understands it may result in a breach of state or federal consumer protection legislation—for example, ss. 51A, 52 or 53 of the *Trade Practices Act 1974* (Cth).

IN BRIEF

Intention to create legal relations

Type of agreement	Assumption
Social, domestic and voluntary agreements	Parties **do not** intend to create legal relations. Onus on P to rebut and show contract was intended.
Business or commercial agreements	Parties **do** intend to create legal relations. Onus on D to rebut and show legal relations were not intended.

Social, domestic and voluntary agreements

Three types of agreement can be identified:

- **social** agreements—ones made between friends or acquaintances;
- **domestic** agreements—ones made between family members and relatives; and
- **voluntary** agreements—where the parties may volunteer their services.

The courts assume that the parties **do not** intend to create legal relations, even though the 'agreements' contain promises made by the parties.

Social/domestic/voluntary—assume parties *do not* intend legal relations

This assumption is **rebuttable** and the **onus is on the plaintiff** to produce evidence to show that a contract was intended. Thus, for example, in the case of a domestic agreement made while husband and wife still live together, it is assumed that the parties do not intend to create legal relations in relation to any promises they may make to each other.

***BALFOUR V. BALFOUR* [1912] 2 KB 571**

The defendant was a civil servant stationed in Ceylon. While on leave in England with his wife, it became obvious that she would be unable to return to Ceylon because of her failing health. He promised to pay her £30 a month as maintenance while they were forced to live apart. He subsequently wrote to her from Ceylon suggesting that they continue to remain apart, and he refused to continue his payments. She sued for breach of this agreement.

ISSUE: At the time of making the agreement, did the parties intend the arrangement to be anything more than a domestic agreement which would lapse once they were reunited?

DECISION: The arrangement was a domestic arrangement 'because the parties did not intend that they should be attended by legal consequences'. At the time the agreement was made the courts did not consider that the marriage had broken down.

COMMENT: Because of the *Family Law Act 1975* (Cth) Mrs Balfour wouldn't rely on contract law today and, as a result, a different result would probably occur.

CASE REFLECTION: As long as the parties have voluntarily agreed, why should a social/domestic agreement be treated differently to a business or commercial agreement?

However, if the husband and wife enter into an agreement while they are separated, it is easier for the plaintiff to rebut the assumption that no legal relations are intended.

MERRITT V. MERRITT [1970] 2 ALL ER 760

The defendant left his wife to live with another woman. The parties reached an agreement whereby the husband was to transfer his interest in the jointly-owned matrimonial home to his wife. When the husband refused to honour the agreement, she sued for breach of contract.

ISSUE: Can the presumption that no legal relations are intended be rebutted where the parties are not living together at the time an agreement is reached between them?

DECISION: The court held that the wife should succeed as the presumption against an intention to create legal relations does not apply when the parties are separated.

COMMENT: At the time the agreement was reached the parties had separated; while in *Balfour v. Balfour*, although the parties were separated by distance, the marriage had not yet broken down at the time the agreement was reached.

Look at the seriousness of the consequences to P

If the **consequences** of the promise are serious, the court may be prepared to say that there was an intention to create legal relations.

WAKELING V. RIPLEY (1951) 51 SR (NSW)183

The defendant was a wealthy old man who lived in a large house in Sydney. The plaintiffs, his sister and her husband, lived in England. The defendant wrote to the plaintiffs asking them to move to Sydney. He promised to provide them with a home and leave them all his property on his death. On the basis of his promise, they sold their home in England and the husband resigned his job. After the plaintiffs had lived with the defendant for over a year he quarrelled with them, sold the house and changed his will. The plaintiffs sued for breach of contract.

ISSUE: Where the consequences for the plaintiff of the defendant going back on their word are sufficiently serious, is this enough to rebut the presumption that the parties do not intend to create legal relations?

DECISION: There was ample evidence to indicate that the parties did intend to enter into a binding and enforceable contract as 'the consequences for the plaintiffs were so serious . . . '

COMMENT: The court looked at the seriousness of the consequences for the plaintiff where the defendant broke his promise. Another approach would be for the court to apply equitable principles, such as *estoppel*, to prevent the defendant going back on his promise (see Chapter 14), to provide relief.

Each case has to be looked at on its own facts. For example, agreements to participate in competitions and lotteries often appear on their face to be nothing more than friendly arrangements between the parties. However, in the event of a win, it would normally be assumed that the parties would have contemplated sharing the winnings.

***TREVEY V. GRUBB* (1982) 44 ALR 20**

A three-person syndicate won $218 000 in the lottery. The ticket was in the name of the defendant, who refused to share the prize with the plaintiff.

ISSUE: Was it just a friendly arrangement so that it could be said that there was never any intention on the part of the parties to enter into legal relations or share the prize?

DECISION: While this was a social arrangement, the nature of the agreement between the parties was such that they must have contemplated that it would be enforced in the event of them winning. Thus, there was a contract and the plaintiff was entitled to a share of the winnings in proportion to her contribution. In this case, the defendant was obliged to give 25 per cent of the winnings to the plaintiff to correspond with the 25 per cent she contributed to the regular entry fee.

COMMENT: The outcome was the same as that in the earlier English case of *Simpkins v. Pays* (1955) 1 WLR 975 where the defendant, her granddaughter and the plaintiff had regularly entered a competition that was run in a Sunday newspaper. The entries were in the defendant's name but they shared any costs. There was an agreement that any prizes would be shared and eventually one of the entries was successful. However, the defendant refused to share the prize with the plaintiff and in that case the court held that the nature of the agreement between the parties was such that they must have contemplated that it would be enforced in the event of them winning.

activebook

To help you to remember and understand the topics covered so far, and for links to legal websites, refer to your online activebook. Model answers provide feedback to problems and exercises.

Voluntary agreements

Doing business

Volunteer workers may not be covered for workers' compensation

Before a person volunteers their services, they should inquire whether they are entitled to workers' compensation. If they are injured 'on the job' and there is no contract of employment, they will not be eligible for workers' compensation. ■

Voluntary agreements—parties do not normally intend legal relations

Situations where the parties do not normally intend to create legal relations also extend to voluntary agreements such as participation with charitable or other voluntary organisations. In these types of cases the parties have entered into an agreement **but** it is clear from the surrounding circumstances that at the time of entering into the agreement, a contract was not intended. What did the parties intend? Did the parties intend to create an employment contract or a voluntary arrangement? For example, if the person is volunteering their services for nominal or no payment, the presumption is that no contract of employment was intended.

TEEN RANCH PTY LTD V. BROWN **(1995) 38 AILR ¶5-036**

Brown was a volunteer worker at a non-profit Christian youth centre. He received accommodation, food and the use of the camp facilities and was expected to obey camp rules but he received no wages. While working at the camp he was injured and he claimed workers' compensation.

ISSUE: Was there a contract of employment in existence between Brown and Teen Ranch that would in turn entitle him to be covered by workers' compensation?

DECISION: The New South Wales Court of Appeal held there was no evidence of intention to create legal relations by the parties and so no contract of employment could be said to exist. Brown's work was voluntary.

COMMENT: Even if there was intention present, the fact that Brown's labour was voluntary would suggest that there was no consideration present to support a contract (see Chapter 14).

Business or commercial agreements

Business/ commercial—assume that parties *did intend* legal relations

In business and commercial agreements the courts assume that there is an intention to create legal contractual relations.

EDWARDS V. SKYWAYS LTD **[1964] 1 WLR 349**

During an industrial dispute between an airline company and the British Airline Pilots Association, the defendant's representatives agreed to make *ex gratia* payments to the pilots' pension funds if the pilots were declared redundant. An *ex gratia* payment was made without admission of liability. When a pilot was declared redundant, the company refused to pay the *ex gratia* payment.

ISSUE: Was there a legally enforceable right to payment? Were legal relations intended by the agreement?

DECISION: As the subject of the agreement was commercial in nature, the presumption was that the parties intended to create legal relations. The onus was on the company to show that legal relations were not intended and there was no evidence to show, e.g., by the use of clear words, that the transaction was intended to be binding in honour only. There was, therefore, an enforceable contract and the pilot was entitled to the *ex gratia* payment.

However, the assumption is **rebuttable** by the use of clear words, for example by the use of an honour clause—and this will be accepted by a court.

ROSE AND FRANK CO. V. CROMPTON AND BROS LTD **[1925] AC 445**

A business agreement drawn up between a British and an American firm had all the signs of being a legally binding agreement but it contained the following clause:

> This arrangement is not entered into, nor is this memorandum written, as a formal or legal agreement, and shall not be subject to legal jurisdiction in the law courts . . . but it is only a definite expression and

> record of the purpose and intention of the parties concerned to which they each honourably pledge themselves . . .

The British firm ended its relations without notice and the American firm brought an action for breach of contract.

ISSUE: Was the effect of the clause such as to clearly show that the parties did not intend to create legal relations?

DECISION: That the clause in the agreement clearly indicated that the parties did not intend legal relations, and thus the agreement was not legally binding.

A contract may also be deprived of legal effect by express provision; for example, many lottery competitions contain an express term that they are binding in honour only. However, while a carefully worded clause can deprive a contract of legal effect, it cannot exclude the jurisdiction of the courts.

JONES V. VERNON'S POOLS LTD [1938] 2 ALL ER 626

A dispute arose between Jones and Vernon's Pools in relation to a winning entry that Jones alleged he had posted. He claimed that the company had lost his winning ticket and the company relied on the following clause:

> It is a basic condition of the sending-in and acceptance of this coupon that it is intended and agreed that the conduct of pools . . . shall not be attended by or give rise to any legal relationships, rights, duties or consequences whatsoever or be legally enforceable or the subject of litigation, but all such arrangements, agreements and transactions are binding in honour only.

ISSUE: Could the exemption clause prevent Jones from claiming his prize?

DECISION: The clause was effective to prevent any action being taken against Vernon's Pools, and the transaction was 'binding in honour only' since it clearly stated that any dealings between the parties were not intended to have legal effect.

COMMENT: The parties had conceded that a contract existed between them and the question that the courts had to consider was the effectiveness of the exclusion clause (see Chapter 18). Such clauses are common in lottery competitions.

CASE REFLECTION: If the parties agree not to create a legal relationship, does that mean the 'agreement' is outside the law and the parties can do what they like? Why?

While the parties to an agreement can expressly declare that they do not intend to create legal relations, they cannot make a binding contract and expressly exclude the jurisdiction of the courts. This would be contrary to public policy. For example, the following clause would be contrary to public policy:

> *In respect of any matter arising out of this agreement or any breach thereof the parties hereby acknowledge that the jurisdiction of the court is to be excluded.*

Where advertisements are concerned, it is presumed that they are not intended to create legal relations. However, each case should be looked at on its facts to see whether intention is present. Thus, the use of expressions such as 'one per customer' or 'rain check' by an advertiser in a newspaper advertisement or brochure is making it clear to the world at large that if they run out of a product they will get more in at the advertised price for the customer.

Advertisements are generally taken to mean legal relations are *not* intended

CARLILL V. CARBOLIC SMOKE BALL CO. [1893] 1 QB 256

The Carbolic Smoke Ball Company published an advertisement in a number of newspapers claiming that anyone who used their 'smoke balls' according to their instructions would not catch influenza. If they did, the firm would pay them $200. As a sign of good faith, the firm lodged $2000 with their bankers. Mrs Carlill used the smoke balls as directed, and contracted influenza. The company refused to pay the $200.

ISSUE: Was the advertisement nothing more than an advertising 'puff' and therefore lacked an intention to create legal relations?

DECISION: The court rejected this argument. The $2000 deposited at the bank clearly evidenced an intention to pay anyone who performed the conditions of the offer and who claimed the money.

COMMENT: This was only one of the issues that was raised in this case. Other issues included whether an advertisement could amount to an offer or only an invitation to treat, whether it could be made to the world at large (see p. 272), and whether there was consideration.

CASE REFLECTION: Was it reasonable for Mrs Carlill to believe that the advertisement was an indication of the company's' intention to pay, or should she have seen it as an obvious exaggeration (advertising puff) that should not be taken seriously? How would you distinguish between a serious claim and an exaggeration?

Doing business

Ensure that advertisements accurately reflect the intention of the advertiser

In the case of advertisements, it is presumed that intention to create legal relations is not intended but advertisers should make it clear in the advertisement if restrictions are to apply to avoid a breach of federal or state consumer protection legislation, e.g., in the advertisement use wording such as subject to seat or room availability. Similarly, the use of expressions such as 'one per customer' or 'rain check' make it clear to the world at large that the advertiser intends the customer to get the product at the advertised price if they run out. ■

REVIEW QUESTIONS

activebook

Activebook resources include in-depth summaries with links to the relevant part of the book. For revision, add your own notes to the summaries provided by using the note-taking function.

12.1 Indicate whether each of the following statements is true or false:

	TRUE	FALSE
▪ The law presumes that in social agreements the parties intend to create legal relations	☐	☑
▪ Domestic agreements can never be binding	☐	☑
▪ A clause excluding the jurisdiction of the courts is not valid	☑	☐
▪ A subjective test is used to determine the states of mind of the parties	☐	☐
▪ In commercial agreements, the courts presume that the parties did intend to create legal relations	☐	☐
▪ An honour clause can be used by the parties in a commercial agreement to rebut the presumption that the parties intend to create legal relations	☐	☐
▪ The onus is on the defendant to rebut the presumption that the parties did not intend to create legal relations in a business arrangement	☐	☐
▪ If the consequences are serious, the courts are prepared to find that intention may be present in a social arrangement	☐	☐

12.2 Discuss the presumption that the court applies in relation to social or domestic arrangements and compare it with that applied in business or commercial arrangements.

12.3 Peter and Mary were engaged to be married. Prior to the marriage, Peter agreed to make Mary a dress allowance of $1000 a year, to be paid in quarterly instalments of $250. Peter paid the allowance for the first three years of their marriage, and then he stopped payment. After Mary had separated from Peter, she sued to recover $4000 arrears of the agreed dress allowance. Do you think she is entitled to recover the money?

12.4 Brad always had a weekly Lotto ticket. One Saturday his numbers came up, and he claimed that he had won a prize. The defendants refused to pay him, claiming that they had never received his coupon. Brad claimed that a binding contract existed between himself and the defendant. The defendant relied on the following clause in the Lotto coupon:

> It is a basic condition of the sending in and acceptance of this coupon that it is intended and agreed that the conduct of Lotto and everything done in connection therewith and all arrangements relating thereto (whether mentioned in these rules or to be implied) and this coupon and any agreement transaction entered into or payment made by or under it shall not be attended by or give rise to any legal relationship, rights, duties or consequences whatsoever or be legally enforceable or the subject of litigation, but all such arrangements, agreements and transactions are binding in honour only.

Do you think Brad will be successful in claiming his winnings?

12.5 David was unemployed and suffered from a number of disabilities. To try to get him back into the workforce, Sam arranged for David to paint his (Sam's) house. The arrangement was to initially be on a trial basis in order to determine whether David was going to be capable of doing the job. Under the arrangement, Sam agreed to pay David $5 per hour as a starting rate and then, if he proved that he could complete the task, they would discuss the rate of payment again. As David was climbing a ladder to start the painting, he fell off it and was injured.

Is there a contract of employment in existence so that David would be entitled to claim workers' compensation? Discuss.

CRITICAL THINKING

12.1 Most social agreements have little significance to the parties. Explain why.

12.2 Should volunteer workers be covered by workers' compensation? Discuss.

CHAPTER 13 Step 2: Agreement between the Parties

CHAPTER CONTENTS

activebook

This icon is used throughout the following chapter to remind you to visit the *Business Law* online activebook for additional exercises, links to legal websites, and feedback. For a detailed explanation of what is in the activebook please refer to the inside cover of this textbook. The activebook is available through OneKey.

Where do I start?
Learning path: Use the activebook to complete a pre-chapter warm-up exercise.

There are many definitions of legal terms to assist with your understanding of the material.

CHAPTER OBJECTIVES

On completion of this chapter, you should be able to:

- explain what an agreement is in a legal sense
- outline and explain the rules relating to offer
- distinguish between an offer and an invitation to treat
- explain the ways in which an offer may be terminated
- outline and explain the rules relating to acceptance
- explain the operation of the postal rule.

KEY TERMS

An understanding of the following terms will help you to better understand the material in this chapter:

- **condition precedent:** delays the vesting of the right until the happening of the event
- **condition subsequent:** destroys the right upon the happening of an event
- **offeree:** the one to whom an offer is made
- **offeror:** the one who makes the offer.

what if . . .

You had been looking to buy a DVD/VCR for some time and were to receive in the mail a letter from Alex stating that:

> ***I have heard that you are looking for a Japanese DVD/VCR. I have one for sale for $750. If I do not hear from you within seven days I will assume that you accept my offer and I will bring it around to your house and collect the $750.***

Do you think doing nothing should amount to an acceptance under these circumstances and result in a binding contract?

Once it has been established that the parties intended to create legal relations, then the second step is to determine whether the parties have reached an agreement. For the purposes of the law, there must be an exact correlation between the two sides of the agreement—a *consensus ad idem* if you like. That is, the parties must have exactly the same thing in mind. This requires that there be an offer by one party (**offeror**) to be bound on certain terms and an unqualified acceptance to that offer communicated by the other party (**offeree**) to the offeror. Even in business there can be problems associated with the question of agreement. For example, exactly what is being offered and on what terms, has acceptance taken place, and if it has, at what point in time did it occur?

> This chapter considers the requirements, or rules, that have to be kept in mind if there is to be a valid offer and a valid acceptance that will give rise to contractual rights and obligations.

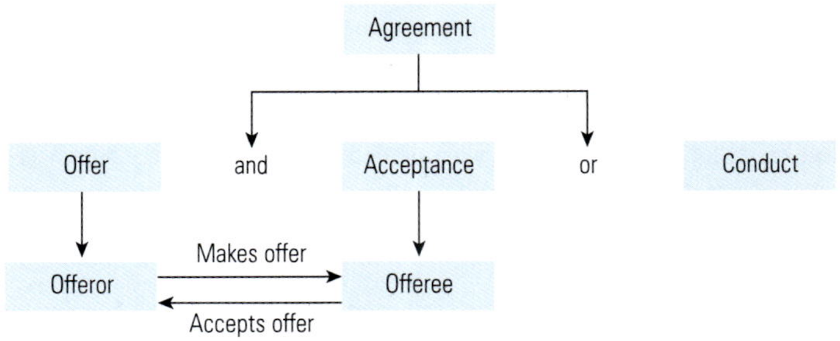

FIGURE 13.1 *Composition of agreement*

STEP 2—IS THERE AGREEMENT BETWEEN THE PARTIES?

Agreement

Traditionally, the courts have said that an agreement is reached when the conduct of the parties can be characterised in terms of an 'offer' by one party and an 'acceptance' by another. This technique is certainly important in determining the time and place of the agreement. It is also useful in determining the contents of the agreement. However, the 'offer–acceptance' approach may not always work. In some cases the courts have been prepared to take a 'global approach' by examining the acts and conduct of the parties to determine whether the parties have reached an agreement (see *McHugh* JA in *Integrated Computer Services Pty Ltd v. Digital Equipment Corp (Aust.) Pty Ltd* (1988) 5 BPR 11,110 at p. 11,117).

It is worth noting four things in relation to the nature of an agreement (see Figure 13.1):

1 Agreement is the manifestation by two or more persons of the **substance** of a contract. It is unusual for the parties to have discussed and agreed to every term of the agreement. In some cases, if the negotiations have been going on for some time, this may be true. However, in many commercial transactions there will only be broad agreement on the substance of the contract, with the details to be worked out later. It is the act of assent which gives rise to the agreement.

   In business today, many agreements are entered into on the basis of standard form documentation, the terms of which are often not negotiated between the parties, for example, consumer credit and insurance contracts. Not only is there a problem with ascertaining whether 'agreement' has been reached but, in some business transactions, whose terms will prevail.

> **!** CAUTION NOTE
>
> *Agreement does not have to go into detail as long as it can be said that a reasonable person would believe that an offer has been made or that the parties had reached an agreement.*

2 In deciding whether an agreement has been reached, it will be impossible to determine what was in the minds of the parties at the relevant time. Because intention is a state of mind, and a court cannot have direct access to the true, subjective state of mind of a party to an agreement, the courts rely on the 'objective test of a reasonable person'. What conclusions would a reasonable person reach when looking at the words and conduct of the parties? If a reasonable person believed that an offer had been made or that the parties had reached an agreement based on their conduct, then they will be bound, notwithstanding the possibility of there being no real 'meeting of the minds'.

3 The term 'agreement' presupposes that the parties are in an equal bargaining position. However, the reality is that in many consumer and commercial transactions, the inequality of bargaining power means that many contracts are not arrived at by 'real' agreement. The weaker party either accepts the terms or goes without. It is only where the pressure used by the stronger party is unconscionable that the courts may be prepared to set aside the contract (see Chapter 16).

4 Even if the agreement is considered to be non-contractual, it may still result in a breach of state or federal consumer protection legislation, for example, as misleading or deceptive conduct and a breach of ss. 51A, 52 or as false representations and a breach of s. 53 of the *Trade Practices Act 1974* (Cth) (see Chapter 23).

Agreement arising from conduct

Agreement can arise from conduct

While offer and acceptance are usually clearly expressed in an agreement, it is still possible for an agreement to arise by way of implication as a result of the conduct of the parties.

CLARKE V. EARL OF DUNRAVEN AND MOUNT-EARL **[1897] AC 59**

During a yacht club regatta, one of the competing yachts fouled a competitor and sank it. All the competitors had agreed to abide by the club rules, one of which provided that a competitor should pay all damages caused by their fouling another competing yacht.

ISSUE: Was there an agreement between the competitors?

DECISION: The rules 'indicate a liability on the part of the one to the other, to create a contractual obligation to discharge that liability'.

COMMENT: This is a difficult case to understand in traditional terms of offer and acceptance because it is an example of a multipartite transaction. That is, there were a number of parties and no clear offer to one party and acceptance by the other. The questions to consider here are then, 'Who made the offer? Who accepted?' While mere participation will generally not of itself provide the basis of a contract between the participants and the organisers, here there was evidence of intention to enter into a contract from the conduct of the parties having to sign undertakings to be bound by the club rules as a condition of entry.

RULES RELATING TO OFFER

IN BRIEF

Rules as to offer

1 There must be an intention or willingness to be bound or it may be an invitation to treat.
2 It must be a firm promise or it may be a request for information.
3 It must be communicated to the offeree.
4 It may be made to one person, a group or to the world at large.
5 It may be kept open if supported by consideration.
6 All terms must be brought to the notice of the offeree and followed exactly.
7 It may be terminated.

An offer is a clear expression of the terms under which a person is prepared to enter into a contract with another person and be bound by their acceptance on those terms. In other words, the offer creates in the offeree the ability to subsequently create a contract if they unconditionally accept the offeror's terms.

What makes a statement an offer depends on what the parties had in mind (the intention of the parties) at the time. In many disputes this will be impossible to determine so the courts will rely on the 'objective test of a reasonable person'. That is, would a reasonable person have thought that the offer was made with the intention of the person making it being bound as soon as it was accepted by the person to whom it was addressed?

What the parties want to call the statement is not conclusive as it may only be indicating a willingness to negotiate or an indication of the price that a person may be prepared to sell at (see, for example, *Harvey v. Facey* below on p. 271). If it is clear in the circumstances that a party intends their words or conduct to constitute an offer, then the courts will be prepared to construe it as such. An example of where an advertisement was considered to be an offer rather than an invitation to treat was the case of *Carlill v. Carbolic Smoke Ball Co.* (see p. 262). Similarly, the use of words such as 'rain check' or phrases such as 'until stocks run out' or 'one per customer' suggest something more than just an invitation to treat. The use of such words suggests that the offeror intended the offer to be promissory rather than a calling for offers.

!

CAUTION NOTE

Look carefully at the words or conduct of the offeror to determine if they are promissory or not in order to see whether they could amount to an offer. Is there an intention or willingness to be bound?

An offer may be made in **writing**, **orally** or by **conduct**. Whatever the method chosen, it is vital to the formation of a contract that the offeror indicates an intention or a willingness to be bound by the offer, otherwise it will be seen as an invitation to commence negotiations, or the soliciting of an offer.

Doing business

Put the offer in writing if it is important

If the proposed contract is important, then put the offer in writing for the purposes of certainty and reducing potential exposure to expensive litigation. The terms of the offer must be clear enough for the offeree to be able to decide whether to accept or reject the offer and should include at least the following:

- identification of the parties;
- identification of the subject-matter, and quantity if it is goods;
- consideration to be paid (how, when and where);
- time of performance; and
- method of performance. ■

Offer or invitation to treat?

Invitation to treat—an offer to consider offers

An offer must be distinguished from an invitation to treat. An invitation to treat is not an offer, but rather is an offer to consider offers. Instances generally considered to be invitations to treat include:

- auctions (see below);
- the advertisement of tenders (see below);
- catalogues;
- price lists;
- goods placed in shop windows and on shop shelves;

PHARMACEUTICAL SOCIETY OF GREAT BRITAIN V. BOOTS CASH CHEMISTS (SOUTHERN) LTD **[1953] 1 QB 401**

The defendant ran a self-service chemist shop, which was a novelty in those days. Pharmaceutical stock, including drugs, were on shelves in the shop. Customers would select their needs from the shelves and take them to the cash register. A registered pharmacist was at the cash register. The defendant was prosecuted under the *Pharmacy Poisons Act 1933* (UK), which stated that the sale of drugs was prohibited unless '. . . under the supervision of a registered pharmacist'.

ISSUE: Were the goods on the shelves with the prices marked on them an offer which the customers accepted when they took the goods off the shelves? If they were, the contract of sale was formed at this point and was thus unsupervised within the meaning of the Act.

DECISION: The display of goods on shelves, even with prices marked, was an invitation to treat. The offer took place when the customer selected the goods from the shelves and took them to the pharmacist at the cash register. The pharmacist could then accept or reject the offer. If the pharmacist accepted the money offered by the customer and entered the price in the cash register, a contract was formed at this point. Thus, the sale was under supervision and not a breach of the Act.

COMMENT: The decision recognises commercial reality. To have decided otherwise would have created an almost unworkable situation for customers who, for example, took goods off the shelves and then changed their minds and replaced them. If the goods on the shelves were offers, taking them off the shelves constituted acceptance. Returning them could amount to breach of contract.

CASE REFLECTION: What problems would it cause for businesses if all advertisements were considered offers?

- if the document contains a proviso that states the agreement is 'subject to contract', 'not valid until signed' or some similar requirement; and
- advertisement of goods or services in newspapers.

PARTRIDGE V. CRITTENDEN [1968] 2 ALL ER 421

Partridge advertised live wild birds for sale in a periodical bird magazine as 'Quality British ABCR . . . Bramblefinch cocks, Bramblefinch hens, 25/- each'. The advertisement appeared in the classified advertisements section of the magazine. Partridge was charged with offering live wild birds for sale.

ISSUE: Was the advertisement in the newspaper an invitation to treat or an offer?

DECISION: The advertisement was only an invitation to treat because nowhere was there any indication of an expression of intention to be bound. The case was dismissed.

COMMENT: An example in which an advertisement was considered to be an offer rather than an invitation to treat is the case of *Carlill v. Carbolic Smoke Ball Co.* (see p. 262).

Doing business

Care must be taken in the use of language by an offeror when promoting their products or services. ■

An offeror must take care that the language they use in circulars, catalogues, advertisements or other instances that have traditionally been considered to be invitations to treat, and therefore not capable of acceptance, is not misleading, deceptive or false. If the statements are misleading, deceptive or false they may be caught under Part V of the *Trade Practices Act 1974* (Cth) or the state and territory Fair Trading Acts and be subject to civil and criminal penalties.

A statement is not an offer if it expressly provides that the person making it must perform some further act before they are bound—for example, signing it. The offer must be unconditional or else it will be an invitation to treat.

Automatic vending machines, such as drink, confectionary and ticket dispensing machines, are not considered to be invitations to treat.

> **activebook**
> To help you to remember and understand the topics covered so far, and for links to legal websites, refer to your online activebook. Model answers provide feedback to problems and exercises.

Auctions

The advertisement of an auction is not an offer to hold it but an invitation to treat.

There are two methods by which a public sale of property by auction can take place as indicated in Figure 13.2.

HARRISON V. NICKERSON [1873] LR 8 QB 286

An auctioneer advertised an auction in a newspaper. Harris saw the advertisement and travelled to the sale only to find that the items on which he was interested in bidding had been withdrawn.

ISSUE: Was the advertisement to hold the auction a declaration of intention to hold the sale or an offer that was accepted by attending?

DECISION: The advertisement of the auction was not a guarantee that it would be held but simply a declaration of intention or an invitation to treat and so there was no contract.

Auction with a 'reserve price'

Auction with reserve—invitation to treat

Where there is a 'reserve price' (the seller has placed a minimum price on what the goods are to sell for), the auctioneer calling for bids is presenting an invitation to those present to make an offer. The person who makes the bid is making an offer to buy and it is then up to the auctioneer, who at this point is acting as an agent for the seller, to accept or reject the bid. The bidder can also withdraw any offer they have made up until the hammer falls. Acceptance occurs on the 'fall' of the auctioneer's hammer and the auctioneer then becomes the agent for the buyer.

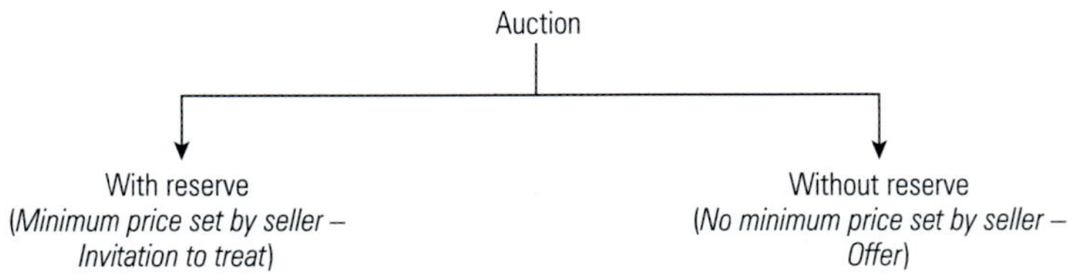

FIGURE 13.2 *Methods of auction*

Auction with no 'reserve price'

Auction without reserve—may be an offer

Where the auction is held 'without reserve' (there is no minimum price on what the goods are to sell for) the position is not so clear. One view is that the auctioneer has made a definite offer in the advertisement and is now the offeror. A person making a bid in reliance of the offer is accepting that offer, so failure to sell to the successful bidder could result in them bringing a personal action against the auctioneer.

Tenders

An announcement that goods are to be sold by tender is usually an attempt by the vendor (the seller) to **ascertain** whether an acceptable offer can be obtained for the goods and is an invitation to treat.

CAUTION NOTE

Whether a tender is an offer or conditional offer will depend on the exact wording used—does it specify exact needs (offer) or what may be required (conditional offer)?

If a company invites tenders for the supply of a definite quantity of goods (or services to be performed) over a given period of time and a tender is made in response to that call for tenders, then that tender is an offer. Whether acceptance results in a binding contract depends on the language of the original tender to offer, and here there are two possible outcomes:

- The company may have stated its exact needs—for example, it may have advertised for 1 000 000 tonnes of rolled steel to be delivered in 100 000 tonne monthly lots commencing from 1 January 2006. Acceptance of this type of tender would create a contract as the company has advertised what it **will** require.
- The company may have advertised only what it **may** require—for example, 1 000 000 tonnes of rolled steel to be delivered when and if demanded during 2006. Acceptance of this tender would create what is called a 'standing offer'. There is no binding contract until a specific requisition for the steel pursuant to the tender has been made. In this situation, the offeror can revoke their standing offer at any time and they would not be liable for any further deliveries, though they would obviously be bound by any requisitions made prior to the revocation.

Doing business

Avoiding problems with tenders

It is normal practice by those calling for tenders to expressly reserve the right not to accept any tender. However, it is also quite common that a tender is accepted which does not comply with the terms of the advertisement calling for tenders. To avoid problems of deceptive or misleading conduct arising under either s. 51A or 52 of the *Trade Practices Act 1974* (Cth) or the equivalent section in state or territory Fair Trading Acts, make it clear that you are reserving the right to accept non-complying tenders. ■

Offer or request for information?

Request for information does *not* destroy offer

It is necessary to distinguish a counter-offer from a mere **request for further information**, because the latter does not destroy the offer.

If there is not a firm promise, there is not a rejection of the original offer by the counter-offer.

HARVEY V. FACEY [1893] 1 AC 552

The plaintiffs telegraphed to the defendants: 'Will you sell Bumper Hall Pen? Telegraph lowest cash price'. The defendants replied by telegram: 'Lowest cash price for Bumper Hall Pen, $1800'. The plaintiffs treated this telegram as an offer and replied: 'We agree to buy Bumper Hall Pen for the sum of $1800 asked by you'. The defendants refused to sell the property.

ISSUE: Was the second telegram an offer which was accepted by the third telegram, thus creating a contract?

DECISION: The second telegram was merely an indication of the minimum price if the defendants ultimately decided to sell, and the third telegram was not, therefore, an acceptance but an offer to buy. That offer was not accepted and so there was no contract.

CASE REFLECTION: Businesses often engage in lengthy negotiations before actually entering into a contract. Could those lengthy negotiations make it difficult to determine what the terms of an offer are or even when it is accepted? Why?

There must be communication of the offer

The offer *must* be communicated

An offer is not effective until it is brought to the notice of the person to whom it is directed. Knowledge of the offer by the offeree is paramount. If the facts show that a person has acted in ignorance of an offer, or that they did not do the act with the intention of accepting the offer, there will be no acceptance and therefore no contract (see *R v. Clarke* below on p. 277).

Can an offer only be made to an individual?

An offer can be made to an individual, a group or the world at large

An offer may be made to:

- a particular person, in which case only that person can accept or reject it;
- a group of people, in which case any person within that group may accept or reject it; or
- the whole world (frequently by way of advertisement) where any person who is aware of the offer may accept it by complying with the terms of the offer.

CARLILL V. CARBOLIC SMOKE BALL CO. [1893] 1 QB 256

The facts of this case are discussed in Chapter 12 (p. 262).

ISSUE: Another issue that arose in *Carlill*'s case was whether an advertisement can contain an offer to the world at large.

DECISION: An advertisement can be an offer to the world at large if it was published in newspapers or magazines that had worldwide circulation. The special setting aside of the $2000 by the company indicated their intention to pay anyone who met the conditions set out in the advertisement. Mrs Carlill had accepted that offer by her performance of the conditions contained in the advertisement.

COMMENT: *Carlill*'s case is also an example of a unilateral contract. There is only one promisor and acceptance is by performance. This can be compared with a bilateral contract where there are mutual promises between the two parties.

CASE REFLECTION: How can a business that makes an offer protect itself if demand for its products or services exceeds supply?

Can an option to keep an offer open be enforceable?

The purpose of an option is usually to give the offeree time to consider whether they in fact wish to buy the item under consideration, or to give them time to raise the necessary finance. An option will arise if the offeror promises to keep the offer open for a **specified period**. However, it will be unenforceable unless it is supported by the offeree's **consideration** (usually money in the form of a deposit). Once consideration is given, the option is legally binding, making it effectively a mini-contract.

GOLDSBOROUGH MORT & CO. LTD V. QUINN (1910) 10 CLR 674

Quinn granted the plaintiff company the following option:

> I Quinn, in consideration of the sum of 50 cents paid to me hereby grant to Goldsborough Mort & Co. Ltd the right to purchase the whole of my freehold . . . lands . . . within one week from this date at a price of $4.40 per hectare . . .

Before the end of the week and before the plaintiff had accepted, Quinn told the company that he was withdrawing his offer. However, the company still went ahead and formally accepted the offer within the option time and sued for specific performance.

ISSUE: Could Quinn withdraw his option before the promised time period had elapsed where it was supported by consideration?

DECISION: The High Court held that the option, having been given for value (the payment of 50 cents) was enforceable and non-revocable. The company's acceptance was good and a binding contract was made which was enforced through an order of specific performance (the defendant was directed by the court to honour the option).

COMMENT: Usually the plaintiff in such cases will seek an equitable remedy in specific performance to force the defendant to carry out their promise rather than seek common law damages which may not be as beneficial.

CASE REFLECTION: Why should the giving of even nominal consideration be so important in the formation of a contract?

Doing business

Options and return of the consideration

The use of an option supported by consideration by an offeree can prevent the offeror from revoking their offer for a specified period. The offeror has also agreed not to sell the item to anyone other than the offeree within that period. However, the offeror should specify in the option contract whether the offeree will recover their consideration if the option is not exercised. ■

Must all the terms be brought to the offeree's notice?

All terms must be brought to the offeree's notice

Where an offer contains terms, all the terms must be brought to the notice of the offeree. Where all the terms of the offer are not brought to the notice of the offeree, a dispute may arise as to whether the parties have, in fact, ever reached an agreement. This is always a question of fact.

Terms must be followed exactly

Conditions *must* be exactly followed

Any terms or conditions specified by the offeror must be met by the offeree in accepting the offer, such as 'reply by fax only'. The key word is 'only' as it suggests that the offeror has a particular reason in mind for wanting a reply in this fashion. These terms or conditions must be exactly followed if there is to be a valid acceptance.

TERMINATION OF OFFER

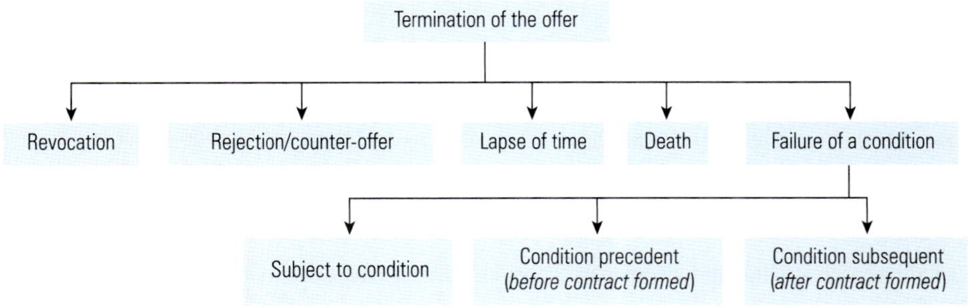

FIGURE 13.3 *Methods of termination*

Once an offer is terminated—and this **must** be done before acceptance takes place (except in the case of a condition subsequent: see p. 276) to be effective—the offer can only be revived by the offeror (see Figure 13.3).

Revocation (withdrawal)

For revocation to be effective, the offeree must be made aware that the offer has been withdrawn before acceptance can take place. Generally, there is no required method or special form of language required for revocation to be effective.

What has to be established is that:

- notice of revocation has been sent to the offeree; **and**
- the offeree has been made aware of the revocation.

DICKINSON V. DODDS **[1876] 2 CHD 463**

Dodds offered to sell to Dickinson some houses for £800. In his offer to Dickinson, Dodd's letter stated that the offer was 'to be left over until Friday, 9 a.m.'. On Thursday morning Dodds sold the house to a third party and Dickinson discovered this from a fourth party on Thursday evening. Before 9 a.m. on Friday Dickinson attempted to accept Dodds' offer by giving him a formal acceptance.

ISSUE: Must revocation of an offer be by the offeror only or can it be through a reliable third party?

DECISION: No acceptance had taken place. The offeree had become aware of the revocation of the offer from a reliable source and therefore the offer had been validly revoked.

If the offeree is **not aware** of the revocation of the offer before acceptance, a binding contract will come into existence between the parties.

BYRNE & CO. V. LEON VAN TIENHOVEN & CO. **[1880] 5 CPD 344**

On 1 October, Van Tienhoven & Co. posted a letter of offer of goods for sale from Cardiff in the UK to Byrne & Co. in New York. Byrne & Co. received the letter on 11 October and accepted it by telegram on the same day, and posted a letter of confirmation of the telegram on 15 October. In the meantime, Van Tienhoven & Co. had posted a letter withdrawing the offer on 8 October, which did not reach Byrne & Co. until 20 October.

ISSUE: Was the withdrawal of the offer by Van Tienhoven & Co. effective?

DECISION: The court held that the letter of withdrawal was ineffective as the contract was completed on 11 October with the sending of the telegram.

COMMENT: Up to the time the offer was accepted it could be revoked. However, once acceptance took place, a binding contract became effective unless the offeror was prepared to accept the repudiation.

The offeror can still withdraw the offer even when they said that the offer would remain open for a specified period, provided that the offer was **not** given under seal or supported by consideration (see *Goldsborough Mort & Co. Ltd v. Quinn* (1910) 10 CLR 674).

Rejection or counter-offer

An offer may be terminated expressly by the offeree through their words or conduct. It may also be terminated impliedly by a counter-offer which also amounts to a rejection.

Rejection by words, conduct or counter-offer terminates offer

It is necessary to distinguish between a qualified acceptance and a request for information. While a qualified acceptance amounts to a counter-offer, **a request for information generally does not cause the offer to lapse**.

HYDE V. WRENCH [1840] 3 BEAV. 334

The defendant offered to sell his estate to the plaintiff for £1200. The plaintiff rejected this offer. The defendant then offered to sell for £1000 and the plaintiff offered £950. The defendant decided not to sell at £950, and the plaintiff then tried to accept the offer of £1000.

ISSUE: Does a counter-offer amount to a permanent rejection of the original offer (unless revived by the original offeror)?

DECISION: The plaintiff's actions showed that he intended to reject both the defendant's offers, and this meant that he was no longer able to revive them by changing his mind and making a subsequent acceptance.

COMMENT: The only way that an offer can be revived once it has been rejected is if the original offeror wishes to revive it. Remember that the parties change places when a counter-offer is made. The offeree rejects the original offer and replaces it with a new one of their own, now making them the offeror. The original offeror has had their offer rejected and they are now considering whether to accept the new offer. They are now in the position of being an offeree.

CASE REFLECTION: Why should an offer lapse just because the offeree makes a counter-offer?

Lapse of time

An offer lapses:

Where no time is specified, offer lapses within a reasonable time

- where the offeror specifies a time during which the offer will remain open, it remains open only for that time; or
- where no time limit is specified, the offer remains open for a reasonable time.

What 'reasonable' means depends on the circumstances of each particular case, but includes the language used by the parties and the subject matter. Thus, an offer will be short-lived in the case of perishable goods, whereas in the case of land, providing that there is nothing in the offer to indicate a degree of urgency, the offer will remain open for a longer time.

If a person accepts an offer after it has lapsed, while the acceptance itself will not give rise to a binding contract, there is no reason why the original offeror couldn't treat it as an offer and accept it.

RAMSGATE VICTORIA HOTEL CO. LTD V. MONTEFIORE [1866] LR 1 EXCH 109

Montefiore applied for shares on 8 June but he was not told until 23 November that his offer had been accepted, that shares had been allotted to him, and that the balance owing on the shares was now due. Montefiore refused to pay and the company threatened to sue, alleging breach of contract.

ISSUE: Has the offer lapsed through passage of time?

DECISION: The offer to purchase shares had not been accepted within a reasonable time and the offer had therefore lapsed. Thus, there was no contract.

Lapse by death of either party

The effect of death on the offer will depend upon a number of factors, such as:

- the nature of the contract; for example—was it a contract of a personal nature?
  and
- the knowledge of the other party.

For example, if the offer were for a famous artist to paint your portrait for $10 000, the death of either you or the artist must terminate the offer because of the personal nature of the contract. In other cases the position is not quite so clear cut.

Notice terminates the offer, but where the offeree is unaware of the death of the offeror, it is possible that a valid acceptance can still bind the offeror's estate if the offer doesn't involve the personal involvement of the deceased offeror. In the case of the offeree dying, the general rule is that the offer is not meant to be made to a dead person but the wording of the offer may be such that it can be accepted by the offeree's estate.

CARTER V. HYDE (1923) 33 CLR 115

Carter gave Hyde a three-month option to buy certain premises. Hyde died before the three months had expired and his executors exercised the option.

ISSUE: Did the offer lapse on Hyde's death? Was it of a personal nature or could it be accepted by, for example, his executors?

DECISION: The High Court held that the option was not intended for the personal benefit of Hyde, but could be exercised by his executors for the benefit of the estate. Carter was therefore bound.

CAUTION NOTE

Death will only terminate a contract where it is for personal services.

Lapse by failure of a condition

If an offer is made subject to a condition and this condition is not fulfilled, then the offer will lapse. For example, a clause or term in the offer stating 'reply by fax' indicates a degree of urgency, and so acceptance by mail would not comply with the stipulation, thus causing the offer to lapse.

A **condition precedent** is a clause or term in the agreement stating that the **agreement** does not become a contract until the happening of a specified event. For example, a 'subject to finance' clause in an agreement, if not fulfilled, causes the offer to lapse.

A **condition subsequent** clause in a **contract** causes the contract to terminate as the parties have stated that the occurrence of a particular event will give the parties that right, the essential difference between the two conditions is that in the latter the contract is already in operation.

! CAUTION NOTE

Condition precedent must be satisfied for agreement to become contract, while condition subsequent terminates contract.

RULES RELATING TO ACCEPTANCE

IN BRIEF

Rules as to acceptance

The contract:

1 must be made in reliance of the offer;
2 must be strictly in accordance with the terms of the offer;
3 must be communicated to the offeror;
4 cannot be a cross-offer;
5 can only be accepted by the party to whom the offer was made;
6 must be absolute and unqualified; and
7 cannot be revoked without assent of offeror.

Acceptance converts promise by offeror into agreement

An acceptance converts the promise or promises of the offeror into an agreement. Before acceptance, neither party is bound to the agreement; after acceptance, both parties are. The acceptance contains two elements:

- a willingness to take exactly what is offered; **and**
- an agreement to pay the 'price' required.

The offeree becomes the acceptor when acceptance of the offer is signified by either the offeree's promise to perform (i.e. a promise to do or refrain from doing an act) creating a bilateral contract, or performance of the act requested by the offer creating a unilateral contract (see, for example, *Carlill*'s case on p. 262).

Acceptance may be made:

- in writing
- orally
- a combination of orally and in writing or
- by conduct.

However, it must conform with the manner indicated by the offeror. Again, the courts use an objective test to determine whether an acceptance has taken place.

Acceptance must be made in reliance of the offer

Offeree *must* intend to respond to offer

The offeree must **intend** to accept the offer otherwise there can be no agreement between the parties.

***R v. Clarke* (1927) 40 CLR 227**

Clarke had been arrested on a murder charge. He gave information which led to the arrest and conviction of the real murderers and as a result was subsequently released. When he claimed the reward of £1000 being offered by the government for information leading to the arrest and conviction of the murderers, the government refused to pay him.

ISSUE: Did Clarke give the information in reliance of the offer of the reward or to clear his name?

DECISION: The High Court held that Clarke was not entitled to recover the reward, because, while he was aware of it, he had no intention of claiming the reward at the time he complied with the offer. He was intent only on saving himself from the charge.

QUESTION: Think back to *Carlill*'s case earlier and consider what would have happened if Mrs Carlill had bought the smoke balls without knowledge of the advertisement but after she began using them she became aware of the advertisement and then subsequently contracted influenza. Would she have succeeded or does the decision in *R v. Clarke* suggest otherwise?

CASE REFLECTION: If it was not necessary for the offeree to be aware of the existence of an offer and to act in response to that offer, what could be the consequence?

Acceptance must be made strictly in accordance with the terms of the offer

Acceptance *must* be strictly in accordance with terms of offer

Where the offeror specifies a special method of acceptance, it must be followed exactly. Where no method is indicated, the custom of the trade or what is reasonable in the circumstances will be good acceptance. Thus, an offer by fax suggests the need for a prompt reply, so any method equally as fast or faster will be effective.

Acceptance must be communicated to the offeror

Acceptance *must* be communicated by some positive act by the offeree

As a general rule, acceptance **must** be communicated, either by words or conduct, otherwise the offeror will not know whether they are bound by their offer or not. In other words, some positive act on the part of the offeree indicating an intention to accept is required. However, the **offeror** may dispense with the requirement of communication as in *Carlill v. Carbolic Smoke Ball Co.* (see p. 262).

Mental acceptance on the part of the **offeree** is **insufficient** to create a contract, just as the imposition of an acceptance by the offeror on the offeree is insufficient.

FELTHOUSE V. BINDLEY (1862) 142 ER 1037

Felthouse wrote to his nephew offering to buy his horse, adding, 'If I hear no more about him I shall consider the horse mine at £40'. His nephew intended to sell the horse to his uncle, but did not reply to the letter. He told Bindley, who was auctioning his farm, not to include the horse in the auction as it was already sold. Bindley sold the horse by mistake and Felthouse tried to sue Bindley for conversion of his property.

ISSUE: Could the offer be accepted by the offeror stating that silence by the offeree will be deemed to be consent?

DECISION: The nephew's acceptance had not been communicated to the uncle. The horse did not therefore belong to him.

COMMENT: To have decided otherwise would have meant that an offeree was under an obligation to take positive steps to reject an offer if they did not wish to be bound. However, what would be the position if the offeree had wished to enforce the contract and followed the offeror's instructions and remained silent?

Doing business

When silence can amount to acceptance

While silence is generally not considered acceptance, even if the offeror states that it is, there are situations where silence can amount to acceptance:

- Where the offeree has indicated that silence does mean assent; e.g., 'If you don't hear from me by Friday, consider the goods mine'.
- Where the offeree has signed an agreement indicating continuing acceptance of delivery until further notification, e.g., monthly deliveries from book and record club memberships.
- Where there has been a long history of prior dealings between the parties. ■

The offeree or their authorised agent **must** communicate acceptance of the offer.

POWELL V. LEE (1908) 90 LT 284

Powell applied for the position of headmaster of a school and the board of the school passed a resolution appointing him. The board did not immediately notify Powell of its decision but a member of the board privately told him that the board had accepted his offer of employment. Subsequently the board rescinded its decision and appointed another person.

ISSUE: Was the communication by a board member authorised?

DECISION: There was no contract. Powell's offer had not been accepted as the resolution was not communicated by anyone with authority.

Cross-offers do not give rise to a contract

Cross-offers do not amount to agreement

The fact that the offers are identical is irrelevant. Contract law demands an acceptance, and with cross-offers there is no acceptance.

TINN V. HOFFMAN & CO. (1873) 29 LT 271

The parties wrote to one another on the same day, the plaintiff offering to buy 800 tons of iron at 69 shillings per ton and the defendant offering to sell 800 tons at 69 shillings per ton. The plaintiff sought to enforce the 'contract'.

ISSUE: Could an acceptance result if two identical offers cross in the post, each party being unaware of the other's offer?

DECISION: There was no contract. When a contract is made between two parties, there is a promise by one in consideration of the promise made by the other; there are two assenting minds and there is an exchange of promises. Where the promises or offers made on each side are made in ignorance of each other, neither of them can be construed as an acceptance of the other.

Who may accept the offer?

Only person/s to whom the offer is addressed can accept

Only the person/s to whom the offer was addressed can accept the offer. If someone else tries to accept the offer, that 'acceptance' is probably only at best an offer itself, which the original offeror, who is now the offeree, can accept or reject as they wish.

Acceptance must be absolute and unconditional

Acceptance *must* be absolute and unconditional

If acceptance is not absolute or unconditional, that is, it does not follow the conditions—if any—stated by the offeror, it will amount to a counter-offer (see also Rejection above).

A conditional assent is not an acceptance. For example, if a document contains a clause to the effect that it is 'subject to a formal contract to be drawn up by our solicitors', a contract does not come into existence until a formal document has been drawn up and accepted by the parties. The first document is merely a proposal to enter into a contract, a tentative agreement that may be disregarded by either party.

MASTERS V. CAMERON (1954) 91 CLR 353

The parties signed a memorandum drawn up by the vendor's agent which contained a clause to the effect that 'This agreement is made subject to the preparation of a formal contract of sale which shall be acceptable to my solicitors on the above terms and conditions . . .' The purchaser (Masters) wanted to withdraw from the agreement and the question arose as to who was going to be entitled to the deposit. If the contract was enforceable it went to Cameron and if it wasn't it went to Masters.

ISSUES: The High Court identified three possibilities:

1 Had the parties reached finality in arranging all the terms of their bargain and intended to be immediately bound, but at the same time proposed to have the terms stated in detail at a later date? or
2 Had the parties agreed upon all the terms and intended no departure from or addition to that which their terms imply, but made performance of one or more of the terms conditional upon the execution of a formal document? or
3 Is it the intention of the parties not to make a bargain until they execute a formal contract?

DECISION: The High Court held that the agreement was not in its final form as it had to be acceptable to Cameron's solicitors. They could have altered the contract if they had wished to. Whether they did was immaterial. So there was not an enforceable contract.

COMMENT: A fourth possible meaning of preliminary agreements is one where the parties are content to be bound immediately on the terms they have agreed to but they expect to make a further contract in substitution for the first contract, which the parties agree will contain additional terms.

It was clear that the parties in *Masters v. Cameron* did not intend to make a concluded bargain until after they had the solicitor's approval. Whether the parties have reached final agreement on the terms of their bargain is a question of fact in each case.

Instantaneous communications

Instantaneous communication—acceptance effective when received

Where the **communication of acceptance is instantaneous**, or almost so, **the contract is formed when the acceptance is received**. This means that in cases of agreements being communicated by means of telephone, teleprinter, fax or email, the contract is formed when and where the offeror hears or receives the offeree's acceptance.

The Electronic Transactions Acts provide that an electronic communication is taken to have been sent by the sender when it first enters an information system outside the control of the originator. A person is not bound by an electronic communication unless the communication was sent by, or with the authority of, that person (*Electronic Transactions Act 1999* (Cth): s. 15(1)) (see also pp. 252–253, 534–535).

ENTORES LTD V. MILES FAR EAST CORP. [1955] 2 QB 327

The plaintiffs in London were negotiating by telex with the Holland agents of the defendant, a New York corporation. The plaintiffs made an offer to the defendant's agents to buy goods from them, and this offer was accepted by a communication received on the plaintiff's telex in London.

ISSUE: Was the contract made in London?

DECISION: The court held that with instantaneous communications, the parties were in the same position as if they had negotiated in each other's presence. The contract was complete when the offeror received the acceptance in London and so English law applied to the contract.

COMMENT: The actual time the acceptance is received by the offeror is a difficult question to answer. If a fax or other form of instantaneous communication is used during regular business hours, then while consideration needs to be given to the intention of parties and normal business practice, it would seem to be sensible to treat acceptance as occurring on receipt on the offeror's fax machine. An exception may occur where a fax is received by staff who have no authority to bind their principal.

Rules as to contracts by post

Doing business

Avoiding problems with the postal rule

Where the parties contemplate the use of the post as a mode of delivery but wish to avoid the operation of the postal rule, that is, so that acceptance does not occur on posting by the offeree, the offeror may include a term in the offer to the effect that 'acceptance is only effective on receipt of notification of acceptance'. ■

Under postal rule, acceptance effective on posting

Where the parties contemplate the use of the post as a medium of exchange of promises, the rules as to the time of acceptance change. Thus:

- An offer made by letter is not effective until received by the offeree.
- Acceptance is effective as soon as it is posted.

ADAMS V. LINDSELL (1818) 106 ER 250

An offer to sell goods was posted on 2 September requesting a reply by return of post. However, the letter was incorrectly addressed and did not reach the offeree until 5 September. He accepted by post on the same day but the letter did not reach the offeror until 9 September. Since the offeror had not heard anything by 7 September, the date on which a reply could have been expected if the letter had been correctly addressed, the goods were sold to a third party on 8 September. The offeree sued for breach of contract.

ISSUE: When was the contract concluded—on posting or on receipt?

DECISION: Acceptance took place on 5 September when the letter of acceptance was posted. The offeror's mistake was held against him in this instance.

- If revocation of the offer is to be effective, it must be received by the offeree before they post their letter of acceptance (see, for example, *Byrne & Co. v. Leon Van Tienhoven & Co.* [1880] 5 CPD 344 above on p. 274).

CAUTION NOTE

In cases of contracts by post, read the letter of offer carefully to see whether it excludes the operation of the postal rule.

It does not make any difference if the letter is lost, delayed or destroyed on the way to the offeror provided that the parties contemplated the post as a means of communication. The courts have decided that the offeror has indicated a willingness to accept such risks by using the post as their agent. The offeror has the opportunity to specify, in the offer, any other form of communication to reduce these risks.

What commonly occurs in business is that an offer is usually expressed so as to exclude the operation of the postal rule by requiring actual communication of the acceptance. For example, 'Acceptance shall only be effective on receipt at this office'.

If the delay is the fault of the offeree, for example, by misaddressing it or failing to post it, then acceptance would occur on receipt (if the letter arrived at all!).

It should be noted that the Australian Postal Regulations enable a person who has posted a letter to recover it, provided that the reasons for recovery are satisfactory and the person puts the claim in writing.

The national Consumer Credit Code 1996 is a statutory modification to the general postal rule. Section 173(1)(b) provides that a document sent by post that is related to consumer credit will be considered to be given on the date when it would have been delivered in the ordinary course of post.

Withdrawal of acceptance by post

Once the offeree has accepted the offer, the agreement is binding on the parties unless they agree to release each other.

REVIEW QUESTIONS

13.1 Indicate whether each of the following statements is true or false:

	TRUE	FALSE
▪ In every agreement, there must be an offer and an acceptance	☐	☐
▪ The offeror is the person making the offer	☐	☐
▪ An offer may be made to the world at large	☐	☐
▪ Auctions 'without reserve' are offers	☐	☐
▪ A mere request for information does not destroy the offer	☐	☐
▪ An invitation to treat is an offer to consider offers	☐	☐

▪ In a unilateral contract there is only one promisor and acceptance is by performance	☐	☐
▪ If the terms of an offer are not followed exactly by an offeree, a contract will not come into existence	☐	☐
▪ Where a company has stated its exact needs in a tender, the tender will amount to an offer	☐	☐
▪ Agreement can only arise where there has been a response to an offer	☐	☐
▪ The acceptor is the person accepting the offer	☐	☐
▪ Under the postal rule, an offer is not communicated until it is received by the offeree	☐	☐
▪ Where no time is specified, an offer only remains open for a reasonable time	☐	☐
▪ If the contract is to be of a personal nature, the death of either party before acceptance will cause the offer to lapse	☐	☐
▪ A condition precedent is a term which causes a contract to terminate	☐	☐
▪ If the offeror waives communication of acceptance, then no agreement can take place	☐	☐
▪ Acceptance of the offer must be made strictly in accordance with the terms of the offer	☐	☐
▪ Only the offeree or their authorised agent can communicate acceptance of the offer	☐	☐

activebook

Activebook resources include in-depth summaries with links to the relevant part of the book. For revision, add your own notes to the summaries provided by using the note-taking function.

13.2 Why is it necessary to distinguish between an offer and an invitation to treat?

13.3 Under what circumstances will an apparent invitation to treat situation become an offer?

13.4 Andrew offered to purchase Rob's house and gave Rob six weeks for a definite answer. Rob, on the basis of this offer, bought another house. Before the six weeks expired, but after Rob had bought the second house, Andrew withdrew his offer.

Is Andrew entitled to do this?

13.5 Hardy sent out a circular to all his clients which read: 'We are instructed to offer for sale by tender the stock in trade of ABLE Imports . . . which will be sold at a discount in one lot . . . The tenders will be received and opened at our offices.' Spence submitted the highest tender but Hardie refused to sell the goods to him.

Has a contract been concluded between the parties?

13.6 A contract to purchase a car contains the following clause: 'If you are not completely satisfied with the car, return it in good condition within seven (7) days and we will give you your money back'. Is this clause a condition precedent or a condition subsequent? Explain your answer.

13.7 On 7 March, Brendan sent a letter by express courier to Sydney offering to buy flour from Steven. At the foot of the letter he added, 'Please write and return by express courier whether you accept my offer'. The letter was delivered to Steven on 8 March, and he wrote accepting the offer. However, instead of giving the letter to the express courier, Steven sent it by post. An express courier letter would have arrived back in Melbourne on 9 March, but the letter of acceptance did not arrive until 12 March. On 15 March, Brendan replied to Steven's letter saying that he had bought his requirements of flour elsewhere. Steven claimed that there had been a breach of contract.

Advise Brendan as to his legal position.

13.8 Could an offer sent by fax be accepted by letter if the offeror had not specified a particular method of acceptance? Give reasons.

13.9 An insurance company advertised an invitation to the public to subscribe for shares. Grant applied for 100 shares through the mail. The shares were duly allotted to him, and a letter of allotment was posted. However, the letter got lost in the mail and was never received by Grant. Nothing further was heard from the company for several years until a demand for payment of $400, a call on the shares. Grant claimed that he was never a shareholder and refused to pay.

Advise Grant.

CRITICAL THINKING

13.1 How can businesses that make offers protect themselves from the risk of loss associated with the rules of offer and acceptance by post?

13.2 What problems can you envisage occurring where businesses use printed standard order forms in the course of negotiations? See, for example, *Butler Machine Tool Co. Ltd v. Ex-Cell O Corp (England) Ltd* [1979] 1 WLR 401.

14

CHAPTER

Step 3: Consideration

CHAPTER CONTENTS

> **activebook**
>
> This icon is used throughout the following chapter to remind you to visit the *Business Law* online activebook for additional exercises, links to legal websites, and feedback. For a detailed explanation of what is in the activebook please refer to the inside cover of this textbook. The activebook is available through OneKey.
>
> **Where do I start?**
> **Learning path**: Use the activebook to complete a pre-chapter warm-up exercise.
>
> There are many definitions of legal terms to assist with your understanding of the material.

CHAPTER OBJECTIVES

On completion of this chapter, you should be able to:

- define consideration
- identify when consideration is present
- explain and apply the legal principles relating to consideration
- explain the distinction between past, present and future consideration
- explain the concept of promissory estoppel.

KEY TERMS

An understanding of the following terms will help you to better understand the material in this chapter:

- **consideration:** consideration may consist either in some right, interest, profit or benefit accruing to the one party, or some forbearance, detriment, loss or responsibility given, suffered or undertaken by the other (the benefit/detriment definition by *Lush* J in *Currie v. Misa* (1875) LR 10 Ex 153) or an act or forbearance of one party, or the promise thereof, which is the price for which the promise of the other is bought, and the promise thus given for value is enforceable (the price paid definition suggested by Sir Frederick Pollock and adopted by the House of Lords in *Dunlop Pneumatic Tyre Co. Ltd v. Selfridge and Co. Ltd* [1915] AC 847)

- **deed:** an instrument that has been signed, sealed and delivered and which does not require consideration to be valid
- **formal contract:** a contract that is signed, sealed and delivered and does not require consideration, such as a deed
- **simple contract:** a contract that is not special and requires consideration to be valid unlike contracts which are described as 'formal' or 'under seal'.

what if . . .

You are promised a raise by your employer for working hard for the last 12 months and then subsequently the employer changes their mind and refuses to pay. Are you legally able to enforce the promise by the employer?

In the case of '**formal**' contracts such as deeds, there is **no need for consideration**; the contract is valid because of its form. But in the case of all other contracts, called '**simple**' contracts, **valuable consideration is required** for the 'agreement' to become a contract. This is the third step in determining whether a simple contract exists.

This chapter considers the rules relating to consideration and the effect that promissory estoppel has had on contract.

STEP 3—IS CONSIDERATION PRESENT?

In the case of a simple contract, the third question to ask (Step 3) is, 'Is consideration present?'. Consideration is what each contracting party bargains for and gives in exchange for the return promise or performance of the other party. Or, to put it another way, simple contracts must contain a bargain—only bargain promises or promises that are given because they are paid for are enforceable.

The aim in defining consideration is to enable a distinction to be drawn between promises which are gratuitous—that is which are freely given (such as gifts)—and those which are onerous or 'paid for' by the incurring of some obligation.

CONSIDERATION DEFINED

Consideration is the price you pay to buy the other person's promise and it is this concept of 'price paid' which was adopted by Sir Frederick Pollock and accepted by the House of Lords in *Dunlop Pneumatic Tyre Co. Ltd v. Selfridge & Co. Ltd* [1915] AC 847:

> *An act or forbearance of one party, or the promise thereof, is the price for which the promise of the other is bought; and the promise thus given for value is enforceable.*

The **promisor** is the person **undertaking** the promise, while the **promisee** is the person who is receiving, or the recipient of the promise (see Figure 14.1).

Consideration **must** be present in every simple contract and is an integral part of the bargain which forms the basis of most contracts. It may be:

- something the promisee gives to the promisor;
- the carrying out of some act; or
- perhaps not doing something that the promisee had a legal right to do.

Once this condition is met, a bargain will exist. However, it does not have to involve money, although it **must** be something of value.

The question of the presence of consideration rarely causes a problem at the formation stage of a commercial relationship because one party has agreed to sell goods or services to another. As a matter of fact there will be mutual consideration present. However, problems may arise if the parties subsequently wish to change the arrangement. This is because the change may result in a new contract and this will raise questions about the consideration to support it.

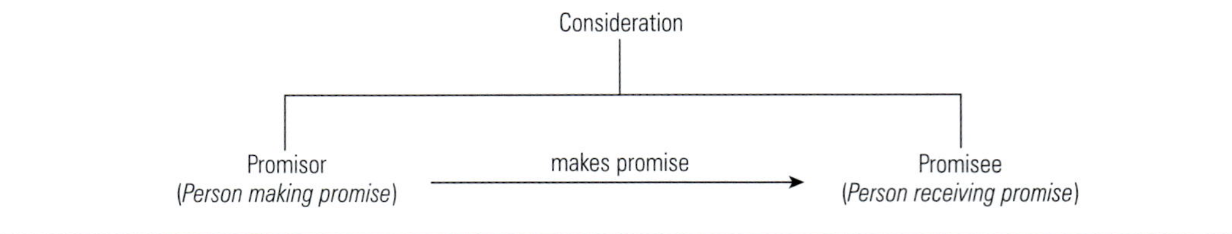

FIGURE 14.1 *Parties involved in consideration*

RULES FOR CONSIDERATION

IN BRIEF

Rules for consideration

1 Consideration is essential in every simple contract;
2 should be present or future but not past;
3 must move from the promisee;
4 must have some value, although the court is not concerned with its adequacy;
5 must be something more than the promise of an existing obligation;
6 must be possible of performance;
7 must be definite;
8 must be legal; and
9 must be referable to the other party's promise.

Consideration is essential to the validity of every simple contract

Gratuitous promises are unenforceable

If A promises to give B $100, B cannot enforce the contract as there is no act or promise in return. This is known as a gratuitous promise and is unenforceable unless under seal. Consideration is an essential element in every simple contract (see Figure 14.2).

Consideration must not be past

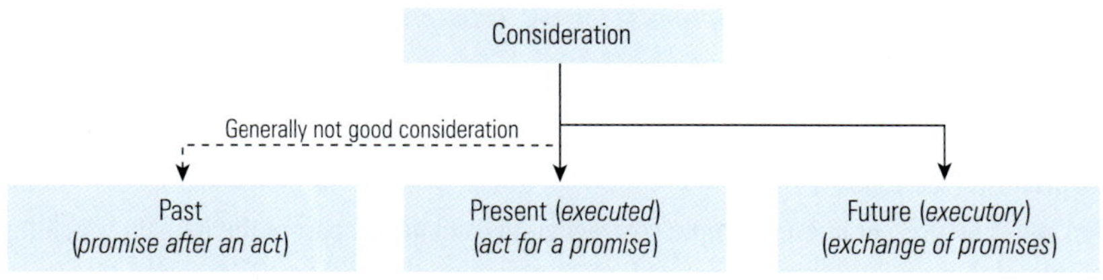

FIGURE 14 2 *Types of consideration*

Present (executed) consideration

Here an **act is done in return for a promise**. For example, in a 'reward' situation where the offeree finds the lost article and returns it for the reward, liability—that is, the payment of the reward—is outstanding on the offeror's part only. This would be an example of a unilateral contract (see pp. 247–248).

Present consideration—act done in return for a promise

Future (executory) consideration

Here the **parties exchange promises**, each promise being consideration for the other. In this type of situation consideration is intended to be performed in the future. For example, a sale of goods with payment on delivery would be an example of a bilateral contract (see pp. 247–248). Here performance of the agreement remains in the future, yet a contract has been made.

Future consideration—parties exchange promises

Past consideration

If a **promise is given after an act** has been performed, this will be considered past consideration and is generally not enforceable (see Figure 14.2). The act must be done in reliance of the promise.

Past consideration—promises *after* the act are generally not enforceable

ROSCORLA V. THOMAS [1842] 3 QB 234

Roscorla purchased a horse from Thomas. After the sale was completed, Thomas promised him that the horse was in good condition and not vicious. In fact the horse was vicious.

ISSUE: Was there consideration to support the promise that the horse was not vicious?

DECISION: The seller's promise was not binding. It was made after the sale had been completed and the buyer had given nothing in return for it. The buyer couldn't rely on the prior sale to support the new promise as it was past consideration.

COMMENT: A promise made after the contract has been concluded must be supported by new consideration or executed under seal.

CASE REFLECTION: Would the decision have been the same if the promise regarding the temperament of the horse had been made before the parties reached agreement? Explain your answer.

The rule that past consideration is no consideration frequently means that a promise, apparently made seriously, generally cannot be enforced by the promisee if it relates to past acts. Of course, if the promise also pertains to the future, then that part of the promise will be enforceable.

ANDERSON V. GLASS [1869] 5 WW & A'B(L) 152

Glass promised an employee higher wages, not only for the future but also for a past period when he was being paid a lower rate agreed to by the parties. Glass later refused to honour his promise.

ISSUE: Was the promise to pay the increased wages given before or after the act to be performed (the work)?

DECISION: The promise to pay increased wages with respect to the work already done was not binding because it was past consideration. The work had already been performed by Anderson and paid for by Glass, and as this was the only consideration Anderson could provide, his claim for the past period failed. The promise of future wages was enforceable because Anderson could provide consideration here.

However, a past act can be good consideration where a subsequent promise to pay a specific amount to the plaintiff can be directly connected to the defendant's original request to the plaintiff to perform some service. The performance of that service and the subsequent promise to make payment become part of the one transaction.

LAMPLEIGH V. BRAITHWAIT (1615) HOB 105; 80 ER 255

Braithwait killed a man and then sought Lampleigh's help to obtain a pardon for him from the King. Lampleigh had to travel to London in his efforts to obtain a pardon for Braithwait, and as a result incurred expenses. After obtaining a pardon for him, Braithwait promised to pay him £100 for his trouble. Braithwait failed to pay and Lampleigh sued on the promise.

ISSUE: Were Lampleigh's services originally performed at Braithwait's request?

DECISION: A contract existed, as the request for Lampleigh's services by Braithwait and the performance of those services, coupled with a subsequent promise to pay, were all part of the same transaction.

COMMENT: The previous request and the subsequent promise were treated as part of the same transaction. This is only sensible when it is considered that business is often conducted this way. For example, phone requests for goods or services often do not include a discussion about payment. But both parties assume that the goods or services will ultimately be paid for.

activebook

To help you to remember and understand the topics covered so far, and for links to legal websites, refer to your online activebook. Model answers provide feedback to problems and exercises.

IN BRIEF

When past consideration can be good consideration

Past consideration can be good consideration if it was provided at the request of the promisor and it can be shown that:

- the act was done at the promisor's request; **and**
- the parties understood that the act would be remunerated either by payment or the conferment of some other benefit; **and**
- the promise would have been enforceable if it had been promised in advance of the act in question.

Consideration must move from the promisee

The person who wants to enforce the promise *must* pay for the promise they receive

While consideration must move from the promisee, it need not move to the promisor. The person who wants to enforce a promise (the promisee) must pay for the promise they receive, though there is no need to pay for it in person, for example, payment could be through an agent appointed expressly for the purpose of making the payment.

DUNLOP PNEUMATIC TYRE CO. LTD V. SELFRIDGE & CO. LTD [1915] AC 847

Dunlop, a tyre manufacturer, sold its tyres to dealers who undertook to allow a 10 per cent discount from the plaintiff's list price when reselling the tyres to retailers. The dealer agreed that when he sold tyres to any retailer he would obtain from them a written undertaking that they would observe the plaintiff's prices.

Dew & Co., a dealer, entered into a contract with Dunlop. It sold tyres to Selfridge & Co., who undertook to abide by Dunlop's requirements. However, they later sold tyres below Dunlop's recommended price and Dunlop then brought an action against them for breach of the undertaking.

ISSUE: Could Dunlop enforce an agreement to which it was not a party?

DECISION: Only the parties to the contract could sue on the contract. Dunlop had not provided any consideration for Selfridge's promise and was not a party to the contract between Dew and Selfridge (see Figure 14.3 below).

COMMENT: In addition to the consideration rule, the case is also authority for the principle that only a person who is a party to a contract can sue on it. This is known as the privity rule (see Chapter 19).

Note also that the decision in *Dunlop*'s case precedes the *Trade Practices Act 1974* (Cth). If the same type of situation arose today, it would amount to a breach of s. 48 of the *Trade Practices Act 1974* (Cth). This section deals with resale price maintenance and what occurred in *Dunlop*'s case was an attempt by a manufacturer to impose a minimum price at which the tyres could be sold (see Chapter 30).

CASE REFLECTION: While only the parties to a contract have the legal rights and obligations, is it possible for someone else to get a benefit under the contract? If that benefit were not supplied, who would have the right to sue?

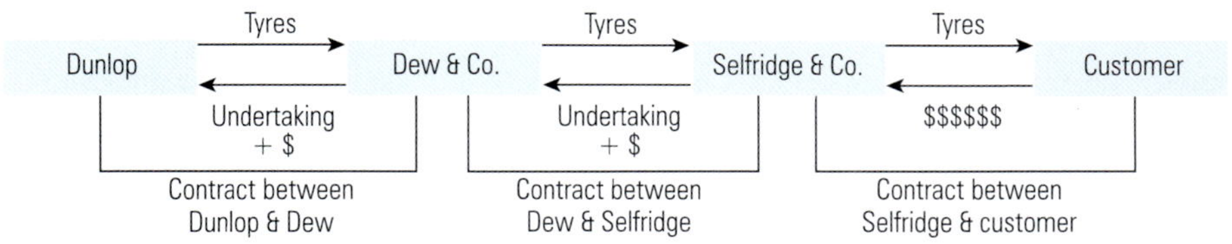

FIGURE 14.3 *Dunlop Pneumatic Tyres Co. Ltd v. Selfridge & Co. Ltd*

Where a promise is made to two or more people jointly (joint promisees), and only one of those persons provides consideration, the other party who has not provided the consideration can still enforce the promise.

COULLS V. BAGOT'S EXECUTOR AND TRUSTEE CO. LTD (1967) 119 CLR 460

A husband granted mining rights to a company to mine his land. In return a royalty was to be paid to himself and his wife. The wife provided no consideration for the agreement. When the husband died, the company stopped paying the royalties and the wife attempted to enforce the agreement.

ISSUE: Was the agreement between the company and husband alone, in which case royalty payments would cease on the husband's death, or was the wife a party to the contract and thus a joint promisee with her husband, in which case the royalty payments should continue to be paid to her?

DECISION: The High Court held that while consideration must move from the promisee, where the promise is made to promisees jointly, consideration need only move from one of them for the promise to be enforceable. Thus, she was entitled to the royalty payments.

COMMENT: The decision raises difficult questions of construction. It may not always be easy to tell whether a person who intended to take a benefit under a contract is a joint promisee with the person who provided the consideration, unless there is some express assurance to that effect. For example, the person providing the consideration may not make it clear to the person receiving it that the third party is to receive the benefit.

Consideration must have value but need not be adequate

Consideration *must* have some value

Consideration must be valuable, though it is left to the parties to decide at the time of making the agreement what is adequate.

CHAPPELL & CO. LTD V. NESTLÉ CO. LTD **[1960] AC 87**

To promote the sales of their chocolate bars, Nestlé offered a record for one shilling and sixpence plus three wrappers from sixpenny bars of chocolate. Chappell & Co. brought proceedings for infringement of copyright and Nestlé offered to pay a statutory royalty based on the one shilling and sixpence. They did not include the value of the wrappers.

ISSUE: While the wrappers of themselves were of no value (as they were thrown away), should they be included as part of the basis for determining the royalty to be paid using the purchase price of a bar as a benchmark? If a person wanted a record, they had to buy three sixpenny bars of chocolate.

DECISION: The wrappers formed part of the consideration because the one shilling and sixpence alone was not enough to obtain a record. As a result, Nestlé had to pay a royalty based on three shillings.

COMMENT: The case clearly illustrates the court's reluctance to become involved in the question of the adequacy of value. As long as there is something of value, the court will be satisfied. However, the court will not accept the proposition that a smaller sum of money can amount to good consideration to discharge a debt involving a larger sum (see e.g., *Foakes v. Beer* on p. 293).

CASE REFLECTION: Can the value of the benefit a person receives always be accurately measured in 'market value' terms? How would you assess the value of something having 'sentimental value'?

The question of adequacy will not concern the courts, for this would involve them in the task of examining every contract and trying to determine whether the price is reasonable—an impossible job, because the parties may have a very good reason for establishing a particular contract price. For instance, one party may owe the other a favour, or they may be hoping to get further business.

Consideration must be sufficient

The question of sufficiency should be distinguished from the question of adequacy. As long as consideration exists and has some value, the courts will not be concerned about its adequacy. However, it must be sufficient, that is, it must have some legal value or it may be considered insufficient and no consideration at all. The problem of what is 'sufficient', or of a value recognised by the law as amounting to good consideration, is not always clear cut, particularly where the plaintiff is already under an existing legal duty to the defendant. A number of situations can be identified which can amount to insufficency, as follows.

Repeating an existing duty imposed by the law

No legal detriment in repeating an existing duty *owed by law*

The general rule is that a person cannot recover money they have been promised in return for performance of, or promise to perform, a duty imposed by the law because there would be no legal detriment. For example, the promise to attend court when you have been subpoenaed would be a promise without consideration as you have a legal duty to attend. However, if the performance was beyond what a person was legally required to do, then that would amount to good consideration.

GLASBROOK BROS LTD V. GLAMORGAN COUNTY COUNCIL **[1925] AC 270**

Industrial trouble at Glasbrook Bros coal mine resulted in the police being called in. The police felt that a mobile patrol would be sufficient to protect the premises, but the mine owners insisted on the police being billeted on the premises, with the mine owners to pay for this service at a special rate. The mine owners later refused to pay.

ISSUE: Were the police doing more, or no more, than they were legally required to do?

DECISION: The police had provided protection over and above what they considered effective and this was sufficient consideration to support the promise of payment by the mine owners.

COMMENT: The courts appear to be ready to find consideration where possible, particularly if the outcome would be inequitable for the plaintiff where they had acted in reliance of the defendant's promise.

Repeating an existing duty owed to the promisor

Repeating an existing duty owed to the promisor is insufficient consideration as there is no **detriment**.

No legal detriment in repeating an existing duty *owed to the promisor*

STILK V. MYRICK **[1809] 2 CAMP 317**

A number of seamen signed on in London for a voyage to the Baltic and back. During the course of the voyage two of them deserted, and because the captain was unable to find two replacements, he promised the remaining seamen the wages of the two deserted seamen if they would work the ship safely back to London. This was agreed to and the return journey was successfully completed but the owners refused to pay.

ISSUE: Was the captain's promise enforceable?

DECISION: The sailors had undertaken to do all they could under the normal conditions of the voyage to bring the ship safely to port. The desertion of the two seamen did not extend the remaining seamen's existing contractual duty, so there was no new consideration.

COMMENT: It is worth noting that this case is more about contract modification than contract formation. The case illustrates the difficulties that can arise with consideration where the parties wish to make changes to the contract once it has started.

Acts in excess of their duty would be **good consideration**. If sufficient seamen had deserted so as to make the return voyage dangerous to life, then the remaining seamen would have been discharged from their original contract and the promise of extra wages would have been enforceable because there would be new consideration to support a contract.

Acts beyond those agreed to by the parties would be enforceable

HARTLEY V. PONSONBY **(1871) 119 ER 1471**

Nearly half the crew deserted the ship in Port Phillip in 1852 and to encourage the remaining 19 sailors to complete the voyage back to Liverpool via Bombay, the captain promised them extra wages. Because the ship was so undermanned, it was unseaworthy. When they arrived back in London the owners refused to pay the crew the extra wages.

ISSUE: Did the crew provide more than was originally contractually required of them?

DECISION: Sailing the ship back to London in an unseaworthy condition was more than the original contract required. The promise of extra wages was supported by good consideration.

COMMENT: An alternative view would be that the original contracts were discharged by mutual consent and new contracts substituted for them.

If the promisor derives some additional benefit by avoiding problems that can be associated with a promisee not performing, then the court will be prepared to find that there is sufficient consideration to support a subsequent agreement.

WILLIAMS V. ROFFEY BROS & NICHOLLS (CONTRACTORS) LTD **[1990] 1 ALL ER 512**

The plaintiff, Williams, entered into a contract with the defendant to perform certain carpentry work for a fixed sum but experienced financial difficulties because he had underquoted the job. When he told the defendant he would not be able to fulfil his obligations, the defendant offered to pay him an extra sum to complete the work and have the project finished on time. The defendant ran the risk of having a penalty clause in his contract with a third party being imposed if the project was not finished on time. Williams continued to work but when the defendant failed to pay more of the contract price, he stopped work and claimed the balance owing under the original contract plus the additional payment.

ISSUE: Was the promise of the additional payment enforceable or was it unsupported by consideration as the plaintiff was already under an existing legal obligation?

DECISION: The defendant's promise was enforceable. There was commercial benefit for the defendant in having the work completed on time and this amounted to sufficient consideration.

COMMENT: The issue of *promissory estoppel* was not raised in relation to the promise to pay the extra amount (see below, pp. 296–298).

Performing an existing legal duty for a third party

Performance of an existing contractual duty for a third party is good consideration.

SCOTSON V. PEGG **(1861) 158 ER 121**

The plaintiffs had entered into a contract with a third party to deliver a cargo of coal to him or to his order. The third party sold the coal to the defendant and told the plaintiffs, in accordance with their contract, to deliver it to the defendants. The defendants then made an agreement with the plaintiffs that in consideration of the plaintiffs delivering the coal to them at their request, they promised that they would unload it at a specified rate. The defendant subsequently broke his promise and the plaintiffs sued for breach of contract.

ISSUE: Could the defendant successfully argue lack of consideration? The plaintiff was already bound by the contract with the third party to deliver the coal to the defendant, so what were they giving in return for the defendant's promise?

DECISION: The delivery of the coal was a benefit to the defendant and so there was consideration to support the promise.

This rule has perhaps been used most successfully in cases involving exemption clauses (see Chapter 18) which benefit third parties.

Promises to pay lesser amounts

Part-payment of a debt

Payment of a lesser sum will not usually discharge a debt

Where there is payment of a lesser sum in discharge of a debt, there is usually not sufficient consideration to support the discharge. The debtor is promising to do no more than they are already contractually bound to do. For example, if A owes B $500, the correct way of discharging the debt is to pay the entire $500 to B on the due date. However, if A comes up to B on that date and offers to pay only $450, and B accepts the amount and issues a receipt in full settlement of the total debt, B can later claim the remaining $50: the implied promise is unsupported by consideration.

FOAKES V. BEER **(1884) 9 APP CAS 605**

Beer had obtained a court judgement against Foakes where he agreed to settle the debt by the payment of £500 immediately and the balance by instalments. Beer agreed not to take any further action on the judgement. All judgements bear interest from the date of judgement and after Foakes had paid the final instalment, Beer sued for interest. Foakes relied on the agreement.

ISSUE: Could Beer recover the balance by arguing that Foakes was already legally obliged to pay the full amount?

DECISION: Beer was entitled to recover because the payment of the smaller sum (the debt and costs) was not consideration for the promise to take any further action on the judgement. Foake's promise to pay the judgement was a promise to do something that he was already obliged to do.

COMMENT: The difficulty with the decision was that it ignored commercial reality. It struck down what were essentially fair and reasonable commercial transactions on the basis that they were not supported by consideration and allowed the promisor (who would be Beer in this case) to go back on their promise. This left the promisee with only limited recourse until the development of the principle of promissory estoppel (see below, pp. 296–298).

CASE REFLECTION: If the parties agree to write off part of the debt, why isn't that enough to make a contract?

Doing business

Avoiding the rule in *Foakes v. Beer*

The debtor can avoid the rule in *Foakes v. Beer* if they can show that the creditor requested payment of a lesser sum:

- at an earlier date than originally promised;
- at a different place (e.g., Melbourne instead of Sydney);

- in a different currency (e.g., gold rather than legal tender). Payment by cheque is not sufficiently different from that which the debtor was already obliged to do to amount to good consideration;
- they performed some other act that they were not bound by the contract to perform;
- by the signing of a deed of release;
- by part-payment by a third party; or
- in reliance on the defence of promissory estoppel.

In each of these situations if a creditor accepts payment of a lesser sum in full and final settlement of their debt, they will be bound by their promise not to sue for the balance. ■

Part-payment by a third party

Part-payment by a third party can discharge a debt

The creditor cannot claim the balance from the debtor. This would be viewed as a fraud on the third party because they had been led to believe that part-payment of the debt would extinguish the debt.

HIRACHAND PUNAMCHAND V. TEMPLE **[1911] 2 KB 330**

The debtor's father wrote to the creditor and offered to pay a lesser sum in full discharge of his son's debt. He enclosed a draft for the lesser sum which the creditor cashed. The creditor subsequently brought an action against the debtor for the balance of the debt.

ISSUE: Did the offer of the smaller sum by the father (a third party) and the acceptance of it by the creditor operate as a discharge of the debt?

DECISION: The creditor could not maintain the action because to do so would in effect be a fraud on the third party. The third party had paid the smaller sum in the belief that its acceptance discharged the debtor's liability to the creditor.

Forbearance to sue

Forbearance to sue and compromise can be good consideration

Forbearance to sue can amount to good consideration. A promise not to enforce a valid claim is clearly good consideration for a promise given in return. It is good consideration, even if the promise is to forbear only for a limited period or to dispense with a doubtful, but reasonable, legal claim.

HERCULES MOTORS PTY LTD V. SCHUBERT **(1953) 53 SR(NSW) 301**

Schubert purchased a new car from Hercules Motors, and after a short time found the paintwork faulty. Hercules Motors acknowledged that something would have to be done, and it was agreed that Hercules Motors would repaint the car and restore it to 'as new' condition. It was also agreed that the work would be supervised by a paint company representative, who would determine if the work was satisfactory. His report was unfavourable.

ISSUE: Was the promise to restore the car to 'as new' condition to avoid being sued by Schubert capable of amounting to good consideration?

DECISION: There was a genuine dispute between the parties and that the agreement to repaint the car was a compromise of that dispute. The compromise was good consideration for a new contract.

Composition or arrangement between a debtor and creditor under the *Bankruptcy Act 1966* (Cth)

Part 4, Div 6, allows a debtor to pay a lesser sum to creditors. For example, Alan Bond successfully negotiated a composition arrangement with his creditors in 1995 of $3.6 million in settlement of debts of $160 million. Once the composition has been made, a creditor cannot go behind the agreement and claim the full amount owing to them as this would amount to a fraud on the other creditors.

Moral obligations

Moral obligation, as well as natural love and affection, will not convert a promise into good consideration.

EASTWOOD V. KENYON (1840) 11 AD & EI 438

The plaintiff, who was the girl's guardian, spent money on her education and for the benefit of her estate. After the girl became an adult she promised to repay the plaintiff. She then married the defendant, who also promised the plaintiff he would pay for the money spent on his wife and the estate. When the husband failed to pay, the plaintiff then sued on the husband's promise.

ISSUE: Was there sufficient consideration to support the husband's promise to repay the money?

DECISION: This was no more than a moral obligation and not something that amounted to sufficient consideration.

COMMENT: The court was not prepared to accept that moral obligation, or natural love and affection, was enough because to do so would mean that to give a promise would become legally binding as soon as a defendant voluntarily accepted an undertaking. Hence the requirement of some additional factor that the courts could place a value on, however artificial that value may be.

Consideration must be possible of performance

If the promise of one of the parties is a physical impossibility—for example, to walk from Melbourne to Sydney in a day—no real consideration would be present.

Consideration must be definite

The consideration must be **real and identifiable**, and not too vague or indefinite in nature. For example, in *White v. Bluett* (1853) 23 LJ Ex 36 the son's abstaining from what he had no right to do (cease complaining to his father that he had not enjoyed the same advantages as his brothers) was not good consideration.

Consideration must be legal

Where the consideration is illegal, a breach of public policy or the civil law, there will be no consideration.

Consideration must be referable to the other party's promise

If consideration is not referable to the other party's promise, then the courts will not be prepared to enforce it.

WIGAN V. ENGLISH AND SCOTTISH LAW LIFE ASSURANCE ASSOCIATION **[1909] 1 CH 291**

A debtor executed a mortgage of an insurance policy in favour of his creditor who knew nothing of the mortgage and had not forborne to sue on it. After the death of the debtor, Wigan learnt of the assignment and tried to claim the insurance money.

ISSUE: Had Wigan provided consideration for the promise?

DECISION: The claim failed because Wigan had given no consideration for it.

PROMISSORY ESTOPPEL

IN BRIEF

What is promissory estoppel?

Promissory estoppel will allow a promise to be enforced even though the promisee has not provided consideration for that promise. It operates where it would be inequitable, or unconscionable, for the promisor not to be held to their promise.

Promissory estoppel may be used as a defence or to initiate a cause of action if the promisee's position has been altered in reliance of the promise.

Promissory estoppel may provide relief to an innocent party

The rule that there must be consideration present in every simple contract if it is to be valid has sometimes allowed a person to break an agreement and leave the injured party with no remedy. The development of the principle of **promissory estoppel** (an equitable remedy) may provide relief to an innocent party.

The modern doctrine of promissory estoppel was established by *Denning* J (as he then was) in 1946. It was at first only a defence (a shield) for a defendant against a plaintiff going back on their promise. If the defendant could show that they had relied on the plaintiff's promise and changed their position accordingly, so that they would now suffer serious loss if the plaintiff was allowed to return to their original contractual position, they could plead the defence of promissory estoppel.

CENTRAL LONDON PROPERTY TRUST V. HIGH TREES HOUSE LTD **[1947] 1 KB 130**

In 1939 the plaintiff leased a block of flats to the defendant for £2500 on a 99-year lease. During the war many of the flats were vacant and the defendant was unable to pay the annual rental. After discussions between the parties, the plaintiff agreed to reduce the rent to £1250 for the duration of the war. The defendant then paid the reduced rental until the end of the war. The plaintiff subsequently claimed the rental arrears for the last two quarters of 1945.

ISSUE: Could the defendant argue that notwithstanding the contract between them, that he had relied on the plaintiff's promise to reduce the rent during the war years? If the plaintiff was now allowed to return to the original agreement and be allowed to enforce it for the war years, wouldn't this be unconscionable (unfair)?

DECISION: *Denning* J held that the plaintiff was entitled to recover the last two quarters of rental. Then, by way of *obiter* he suggested that the defendant did not have to pay the arrears from the time of the agreed reduction in 1940 up to the time when the flats were again fully let in 1945 despite the fact that the defendant had given no consideration for the plaintiff's promise not to demand the full entitlement. The plaintiff was prevented (i.e. *estopped*) from going back on his promise to reduce the rental as this would have been unfair on the defendant.

Promissory estoppel can be used as either a shield or a sword

The principle of promissory estoppel was confirmed by the High Court in Australia in *Legione v. Hateley* (1983) 152 CLR 406. In 1988 the High Court in *Waltons Stores (Interstate) Ltd v. Maher* (1988) 164 CLR 387 considered the whole question of the application of the doctrine of promissory estoppel and came to the conclusion that:

- The doctrine no longer operated only as a defence or shield for a promisee, but could be used to commence an action.

WALTONS STORES (INTERSTATE) LTD V. MAHER (1988) 164 CLR 387

Waltons Stores negotiated with Maher for the lease of commercial premises. Under the proposal Maher was to demolish an existing building on the site and erect a new building to be leased by Waltons. Waltons' solicitors sent a draft agreement to Maher's solicitor specifying that fitting out of the new building had to be ready for commencement of business by 15 January 1984. On 7 November Maher's solicitor spoke to Waltons' solicitor stating that final agreement would have to be reached in the next few days if rebuilding was to be completed on time. Waltons' solicitor then forwarded a fresh set of documents with a number of amendments incorporated into them by Maher and a covering letter stating that while he hadn't received formal instructions from his client, he believed that Waltons' approval would be forthcoming and that he would advise Maher the following day if Waltons did not agree to any of the amendments. Some days later Maher's solicitor, having heard nothing from Waltons' solicitor, returned the documents duly signed 'by way of exchange'.

Receipt of the documents was not acknowledged for nearly two months, because Waltons—who had been advised by their solicitors that as contracts had not been exchanged they were not bound to proceed with the arrangements—instructed their solicitors to 'go slow' while they reviewed their country retailing strategy. Maher meanwhile, in the belief that he had a contract, proceeded to obtain finance for the redevelopment of the site and demolished the existing building, a fact known to Waltons through its Nowra manager. Erection of the new building was commenced to ensure completion by the due date, but when it was 40 per cent completed Maher was advised by Waltons' solicitors that Waltons were not proceeding with the project. Because the building work was so far advanced, Maher then sued for specific performance.

ISSUE: Could the doctrine of promissory estoppel be applied to a pre-existing contractual relationship, i.e. used as a sword?

DECISION: The High Court found that no contracts had been formally concluded. However, by retaining the executed documents for two months and remaining silent when it was aware that Maher was acting on the assumption that the lease was proceeding, it was appropriate in the circumstances to apply the doctrine of promissory or equitable estoppel. It was unconscionable to allow Waltons, knowing that the Maher was exposing himself to financial detriment by acting on false assumptions, to adopt a course of inaction which would lead or encourage him to believe that he had an agreement to complete the contract.

- Estoppel could apply even in the absence of pre-contractual obligations because Maher was able to use promissory estoppel to enforce a non-contractual obligation.
- Promissory estoppel, as permitted by the court in *Waltons'* case, negates the requirement that consideration is required in simple contracts and that it must move from the party suing to the party being sued.

In order to establish a case for promissory estoppel, the following elements must be satisfied. First, there must be an assumption created in the mind of the plaintiff (the promisee) by the defendant (the promisor). For example, in *Waltons Stores* there was an implied promise that the transaction would be, or had been, completed. Second, the defendant must be responsible for the assumption, which must be clear and unambiguous. Third, the assumption must be one of fact or law. Fourth, there must be reliance on the assumption by the plaintiff, that is, the plaintiff must have acted or refrained from acting on the assumption, and the defendant intended the plaintiff to act on the assumption. Fifth, the plaintiff acted to their detriment on the basis of the defendant's promise. Finally, unconscionability would arise if the defendant were allowed to go back on their representation.

It is still not clear how far the doctrine of estoppel applies. Subsequent decisions have done little to clarify the concept of estoppel, the element of detriment and the relationship between detriment and the remedy that should follow. Reliance on estoppel was successful in:

- *Foran v. Wight* (1989) 88 ALR 413 where even though the purchasers failed to tender performance and were not ready to settle at the date of settlement, the vendor's failure to perform an essential term by the due date was sufficient to enable the purchasers to rescind for repudiation or anticipatory breach and recover their deposit.
- *Blazely v. Whiley* (1995) 5 Tas R 254 where the defendant had moved into the plaintiff's house, paying the plaintiff's mortgage plus rent in the belief that they would ultimately be able to purchase the property at less than market value, P was estopped from denying the agreement.
- *Giumelli v. Giumelli* (1999) 196 CLR 101 where P left school aged 15 to work on his parent's farm and became a partner in the family business at 17, working without salary and for pocket money and expenses. When his family failed to honour a promise to subdivide the farm and create a separate property for him, he was able to rely on promissory doctrine based on their not honouring their promise.

Cases where reliance on estoppel was unsuccessful include:

- *Austotel Pty Ltd v. Franklins Selfserve Pty Ltd* (1989) 16 NSWLR 582 involving negotiations for the grant of a lease in a shopping centre which was under construction as the secretary's statement was not clear enough or sufficiently unambiguous to found an estoppel.
- *Commonwealth of Australia v. Verwayen* (1990) 95 ALR 321 where the majority (*Mason* CJ, *Brennan* and *McHugh* JJ) rejected the estoppel submission on the basis that he had not commenced his action in reliance of the Commonwealth's assurance although Verwayen was successful on other grounds.
- *Official Receiver in Bankruptcy v. Tooheys Ltd* (1993) 29 NSWLR 641 where the claim to promissory estoppel had been induced by the fraudulent misrepresentations of the party claiming to rely on the estoppel.
- *Easts Van Villages v. Minister Administering the National Parks and Wildlife* [2001] NSWSC 559 where the plaintiff had relied on the defendant's promise regarding the termination of his lease of a caravan park in the future and bought some new cabins while still in occupation, as he received rent from the cabins he had not incurred any detriment.

Doing business

Avoiding the operation of the doctrine of promissory estoppel

Application of the doctrine is really only limited to a **suspension of the promisor's rights, not a termination of them**. The promisor can withdraw the promise if reasonable notice is given to that effect to the promisee, and it is possible for a return to the position that the promisee occupied before the suspension of the promisor's rights. ■

REVIEW QUESTIONS

?

14.1 Indicate whether each of the following statements is true or false:

	TRUE	FALSE
▪ Consideration must be present or future, it cannot be past	☐	☐
▪ Consideration must be present in every simple contract	☐	☐
▪ Consideration must have a value that is recognised by law	☐	☐
▪ A promise as part of a marketing campaign can still be good consideration	☐	☐
▪ Future consideration is also known as executed consideration	☐	☐

▪ Consideration must move from the promisee to the promisor, or someone nominated by them	☐	☐
▪ A moral consideration cannot amount to good consideration	☐	☐
▪ Part payment of a lesser sum before the due date of a debt is satisfaction for the whole amount	☐	☐
▪ Performance of an existing contractual duty will not amount to good consideration because the promisee is doing no more than they are already obligated to do	☐	☐

14.2 What is meant by the expression 'valuable consideration'?

14.3 Define the term 'consideration' and explain the distinction between executed, executory and past consideration.

14.4 Under what circumstances will past consideration be good consideration, if ever?

14.5 What is a 'formal' contract and how does it differ from a 'simple' contract? Discuss.

14.6 Explain why past consideration was good consideration in *Lampleigh v. Braithwait* but not in *Roscorla v. Thomas*.

14.7 Rory offered a reward of $1000 to whoever would give information that would lead to the conviction of the person or persons who broke into his house and stole all his wife's jewellery. Max was a police officer in the district where the offence occurred, and during the course of his investigation he was able to provide the information which led to the capture and conviction of the felon.

Advise Max whether he is eligible to recover the reward.

Would your answer be any different if Max was off-duty when he discovered the information?

14.8 A daughter promised to look after her elderly parents as long as they lived. In return for the daughter's promise, the father promised to transfer to her his interest in some of 'his' property.

Is such a promise enforceable? Discuss.

14.9 David, a developer, borrowed $100 000 from Rees for a development project that he was associated with. The terms of the agreement were that the money would be repaid within 120 days at 14 per cent interest. At the conclusion of the 120 days David told Rees that he would be unable to pay the full amount as the development hadn't sold as well as had been expected. He offered to pay $90 000 by cheque immediately in full settlement of the debt. Rees accepted.

Rees subsequently claimed the balance of $10 000, plus the interest. David argued that he shouldn't have to pay any more because he had paid Rees under one of the exceptions to the *Foakes v. Beer* principle (i.e. payment in a different kind) and that the doctrine of promissory estoppel operated to protect debtors such as himself from just this sort of problem.

Who is correct here—Rees or David? Discuss.

14.10 A standby letter of credit was accepted by Standard Chartered Bank after the signature of the applicant was verified by the Bank of China with that in an authorised signatures book. The signature was in fact a very good forgery. Upon default of the letter of credit, the Standard Chartered Bank claimed the amount payable from the Bank of China.

Will Standard Chartered Bank succeed in their claim on the basis that promissory estoppel should apply here? Explain what they would have to argue to succeed in their claim.

> **activebook**
> Activebook resources include in-depth summaries with links to the relevant part of the book. For revision, add your own notes to the summaries provided by using the note-taking function.

CRITICAL THINKING

14.1 Is the equitable principle of promissory estoppel likely to be applied widely and freely or only in special situations? Explain your answer.

14.2 What is the purpose of consideration in a simple contract? Discuss.

15

CHAPTER

Step 4: Capacity of the Parties

CHAPTER CONTENTS

activebook

This icon is used throughout the following chapter to remind you to visit the *Business Law* online activebook for additional exercises, links to legal websites, and feedback. For a detailed explanation of what is in the activebook please refer to the inside cover of this textbook. The activebook is available through OneKey.

Where do I start?

Learning path: Use the activebook to complete a pre-chapter warm-up exercise.

There are many definitions of legal terms to assist with your understanding of the material.

CHAPTER OBJECTIVES

On completion of this chapter, you should be able to:

- recognise the classes of persons who have limited contractual capacity and describe the effect that each has on a simple contract
- outline the common law rules regarding contracts entered into by infants and which can be valid, voidable or void
- summarise statutory changes to the common law made in NSW in relation to infants
- summarise statutory changes to the common law made in SA in relation to infants
- outline the common law rules with regard to capacity to contract with respect to corporations and bankrupts, the mentally ill and those under the influence of alcohol.

KEY TERMS

An understanding of the following terms will help you to better understand the material in this chapter:

- **bankrupt:** a person who is unable to meet their debts when they fall due
- **corporation (also known as a 'company'):** a legal entity created by the *Corporations Act 2001* (Cth)
- **infant:** a person under the age of 18 years and also known as a minor
- **void:** of no legal effect
- **voidable:** an agreement which may be affirmed or rejected at the option of one of the parties.

what if . . .

You enter into an agreement with another student who is 17 years of age for the sale of your university text books and believing them to be sold, you turn down a number of offers from other students to buy the texts. Subsequently, the person who agreed to buy them tells you they have changed their mind and it is now too late to sell them. Should you be able to force the student who agreed to buy them to go ahead with the agreement?

The last three chapters considered the creation of a simple contract. In this and the following two chapters we look at the validity of what has been created, beginning with the question of the capacity of the parties. Capacity, or perhaps more accurately described as incapacity, refers to the ability of the parties to a contract to fully understand its terms and obligations. However, under both common law and statute law there are certain types of people who are considered to be incapable, either partly or wholly, of doing so. Those classes of person are subject to varying degrees of incapacity, raising the question (Step 4) of whether they understand what they are entering into.

> This chapter considers those persons who lack contractual capacity to enter into binding contracts: infants, corporations, bankrupts, mentally unsound persons and intoxicated persons.

STEP 4—DETERMINING VALIDITY: DO THE PARTIES TO THE CONTRACT HAVE FULL CONTRACTUAL CAPACITY?

Only a **normal, sane, sober adult person** has full capacity to make a contract—which is usually called '**capacity to contract**'. This means that they have the ability to understand what it is that they are entering into. Under common law (and in some states, statute law) some classes of people are treated as not having the ability to understand fully what it is they are entering into (see Figure 15.1). This can affect the validity of any contracts that may involve them.

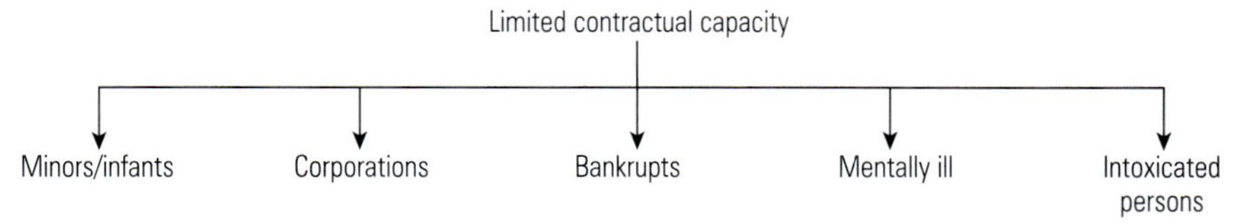

FIGURE 15.1 *Those persons with limited contractual capacity*

INFANTS (OR MINORS)

Infant/minor—a person under 18 years of age

Legislation in all states provides for full contractual capacity from the age of 18 years (see Table 15.1).

Victoria (*Supreme Court Act 1986*), New South Wales (*Minors (Property and Contracts) Act 1970*), and South Australia (*Minors Contracts (Miscellaneous Provisions) Act 1979*) have made alterations to the common law as it affects infants and these changes are dealt with in more detail later in this chapter (see pp. 306–309).

Table 15.1 Age of majority legislation

State	*Legislation*
Australian Capital Territory	*Age of Majority Act 1974*
New South Wales	*Minors (Property and Contracts) Act 1970*
Northern Territory	*Age of Majority Act 1981*
Queensland	*Age of Majority Act 1974*
South Australia	*Age of Majority (Reduction) Act 1971*
Tasmania	*Age of Majority Act 1973*
Victoria	*Age of Majority Act 1977*
Western Australia	*Age of Majority Act 1972*

The reason for the classification of contracts into valid, voidable or void (see Figure 15.2) is twofold:

- the inexperience of infants and their lack of judgement in business matters indicates that they should be protected from making foolish bargains; and
- the possible hardship that would result for adults who deal with infants if all contracts with minors were to be set aside must be, where practical, alleviated.

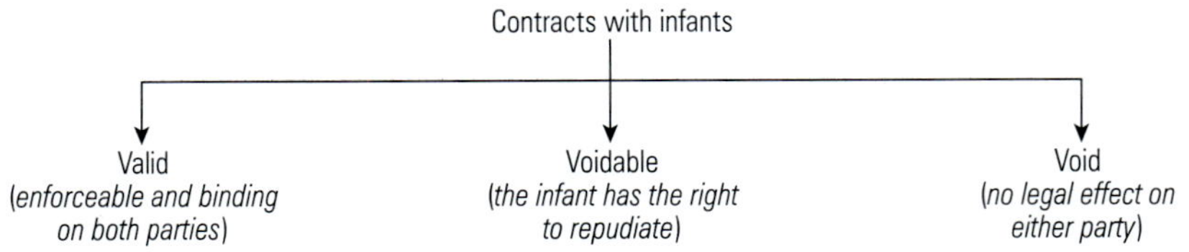

FIGURE 15.2 *Classification of contracts for an infant*

Valid contracts

If an infant pays cash for goods or services, they are bound. However, where they are still to pay for the goods or services, the general rule at common law is that a contract made by an infant is only valid and enforceable in two instances:

- contracts for necessaries; and
- beneficial contracts of service.

Necessaries

Necessaries can be goods or services but *must* be essential for reasonable comfort of infant

The word 'necessaries' includes articles and services essential for the reasonable comfort of the infant, as well as basic food, clothing and shelter. Goods supplied to the married infant's family, as well as goods supplied in contemplation of marriage, are also regarded as necessaries. This means that lifestyle and the infant's situation must be considered when trying to determine if the goods or services are capable of being necessaries or not.

IN BRIEF

When are goods necessaries?

To be successful, the plaintiff must be able to establish two issues:

- Are the unpaid goods or services capable of being necessaries? A question of law.
- Are the goods or services necessaries in the particular circumstances? A question of fact involving looking at whether the infant is already adequately supplied.

If it is established that the goods are necessaries, the infant only needs to pay a reasonable price for them.

The sale of goods legislation of the various states and territories defines necessaries as 'goods suitable to the condition in life of such infant and to his actual requirements at the time of sale or delivery'. In other words, the lifestyle and situation of the infant will determine what are necessaries.

To be successful, the plaintiff must be able to establish two issues:

Are the unpaid goods or services capable of being necessaries? A question of law

The court has to first be satisfied that, in the circumstances, the goods or services are capable of being a necessary and this is a question of law. The onus is on the plaintiff to prove that they are and if they fail, the case is dismissed.

***Onus on P* to prove that goods or services are of a type that may be necessary**

BOJCZUK V. GREGORCEWICZ [1961] SASR 128 (BEFORE THE AGE OF MAJORITY WAS REDUCED TO 18)

Gregorcewicz, an 18-year-old Polish girl, had a good job (by Polish standards) in Poland but still wished to emigrate to Australia. She asked a relative, Bojczuk, to forward her passage money, which she would repay. After coming to Australia and getting a job, she failed to repay the plaintiff.

ISSUE: Was the passage money capable of creating a contract for necessaries?

DECISION: The plaintiff had failed to prove that this was a contract for necessaries. The defendant already had a job that was satisfactory by Polish standards.

COMMENT: It was found as a matter of fact by the South Australian Supreme Court that the transaction was beneficial to the defendant but because the plaintiff failed to establish the preliminary question of law, the case was dismissed.

Once the court decides that the goods or services are capable of being necessaries, then it is necessary to consider the second point.

Are the goods or services necessaries in the particular circumstances? A question of fact

This means considering the actual requirements of the infant and deciding whether the infant was adequately supplied with these goods or services at the time of sale or delivery. It may be necessary here to consider the social standing of the infant, their occupation and other similar factors.

A trader who supplies goods to an infant on credit does so at considerable risk. If the infant is already well supplied with those articles, then the trader would be unable to enforce payment. Furthermore, if the trader had been unable to establish, for example, that the bike was a necessary in *Scarborough*'s case below, then not only would the infant not have been liable to pay (unless it was obtained by fraud), but there would be no obligation to return the bike either.

SCARBOROUGH V. STURZAKER **(1905) 1 TAS LR 117**

Sturzaker periodically rode his bike to work, a distance of some 15 kms. While still a minor, Sturzaker bought a new bike and traded in his old one as part payment before the delivery of the new one. He then attempted to avoid the contract.

ISSUE: In the particular circumstances that existed here, did Sturzaker need a bike?

DECISION: The Tasmanian Supreme Court held that the bike was a class of goods that could be classed as a necessary, and in this case it was in fact a necessary.

COMMENT: If the minor had not traded in his old bike, the new one could not have been considered as a necessary because he would have been sufficiently supplied with goods of that type.

Infant only has to pay a reasonable price

Even if the trader establishes that a contract with an infant is for the supply of goods or services that amount to necessaries, the contract can still be void if it contains harsh or onerous terms. The contract must, on balance, be favourable for the infant. If it is, the infant will only be bound to pay a **reasonable price** for the goods or services.

Doing business

Dealing with an infant in business

When dealing with an infant, a supplier of goods or services does so at considerable risk. If they hope to be able to enforce the contract, they must ensure that:

- the goods or services are capable of being, **and** are, necessaries;
- that the contract does not contain any harsh or onerous terms; and
- that the price is reasonable. ■

Beneficial contracts of service

Beneficial contracts of service are assumed to be binding

Beneficial contracts of service are the second exception to the non-enforceability of a contract entered into by an infant. These are contracts of employment, apprenticeship, training or education. In these type of cases the court will:

- examine the contract as a whole;
- weigh the onerous (harsh) terms against the beneficial terms; and
- decide whether the balance is in favour of the infant.

DE FRANCESCO V. BARNUM **(1890) 45 CH D 430**

Barnum entered into an apprenticeship agreement with De Francesco for a period of seven years to learn stage dancing, completing the apprenticeship when she turned 23. She agreed not to marry during the term of the apprenticeship and not to accept professional engagements without De Francesco's permission. De Francesco did not have to provide engagements or maintain her while she was unemployed, and he could terminate the agreement at any time if he thought she was unsuitable. When she was performing, he only paid her a minimum amount.

ISSUE: Taken as a whole, were the terms of the contract of employment so harsh as to be unreasonable?

DECISION: The contract was void. The onerous terms far outweighed the beneficial terms, for Barnum was at the absolute disposal of De Francesco.

A beneficial contract of service with a minor can contain unfavourable terms. The question is one of balance, looking at the contract as a whole.

HAMILTON V. LETHBRIDGE **(1912) 14 CLR 236**

The defendant, while still an infant, had entered into an article clerkship with the plaintiff. One of the terms in the agreement was that the defendant would not practise as a solicitor within 30 miles of Toowoomba, where the plaintiff had his practice. Another clause allowed the plaintiff to assign the articles to any other solicitor practising in Toowoomba or elsewhere in Queensland. A year after he had finished his articles, he commenced practise in Toowoomba and the plaintiff sought an injunction to stop him.

ISSUE: Could the defendant successfully argue that the clauses were so onerous that they outweighed the beneficial terms and that therefore the contract was not valid?

DECISION: The High Court was of the view that the covenant taken as a whole was enforceable, even though one of the clauses may have been onerous.

While benefit is the basis for the validity of this type of contract, this does not mean that any contract that the infant enters into and obtains benefits from will be enforced against the infant. Thus, a trading contract may result in financial benefit to the infant, but will not be binding.

MERCANTILE UNION GUARANTEE CORP. LTD V. BALL **[1937] 2 KB 498**

Ball, while still an infant, carried on business as a haulage contractor. He entered into a hire purchase agreement with a hire purchase company to buy a truck for use in his business. He fell behind in his repayments and was sued for the arrears.

ISSUE: Can an infant enter into a valid trading contract, even if it is clearly to their benefit?

DECISION: Because the contract was a trading contract, not a contract for the supply of necessaries or a beneficial contract of service, Ball could not be bound.

Cash transactions

If the infant pays cash for goods or services, they are bound irrespective of whether the contract is for necessaries or a beneficial contract of service. If no price has been agreed, the infant is only obliged to pay a reasonable price.

Contracts which are valid unless avoided

Rescission relieves the infant of any future liability

The class of contracts involved is limited to those through which the infant acquires an interest in some subject matter of a **permanent and continuous** nature and the contractual obligation remains until the infant decides to put an end to it. In the commercial area, these include purchase and lease of land, purchase of shares in a company and partnerships.

Obligations accrued up to rescission may remain enforceable

When an infant repudiates a voidable contract during infancy or within a **reasonable time** after becoming an adult (and this depends on the circumstances in each case), rights and liabilities that accrue after repudiation cease. The infant will remain liable for any obligations accrued up to the time of repudiation of the contract, unless there has been a total failure of consideration.

***CORPE V. OVERTON* (1833) 131 ALL ER 901**

A minor agreed to enter into a partnership agreement with an adult and paid $200 as an advance. He then repudiated the agreement before the partnership began to operate, and sued to recover his $200.

ISSUE: Has there been a total failure of consideration so that no contract can be said to have come into existence?

DECISION: He could recover the money, as he had repudiated the agreement before the partnership began to function and so there was a total failure of consideration.

Money already paid by an infant under a voidable contract is irrecoverable unless the consideration for which it was given has totally failed—that is, the infant has received no benefit from the contract whatsoever. However, no matter what the subject may be, the courts are reluctant to find that the infant has received no benefit.

***STEINBERG V. SCALA (LEEDS) LTD* [1923] 2 CH 452 (BEFORE THE AGE OF MAJORITY WAS REDUCED TO 18)**

Steinberg, a minor, applied for and was allotted shares in a company. She received no dividends and attended no meetings. Before she turned 21 she repudiated the contract and sought to recover the money she had paid.

ISSUE: Was there a total failure of consideration so that it could be said that Steinberg had accrued no benefit under the contract?

DECISION: Although she was allowed to have her name removed from the share register and she could rescind the contract, she could not recover the money paid. The allotment of shares had conferred a benefit on her. This meant that there was not a total failure of consideration.

COMMENT: The case illustrates the reluctance of the court to find that no benefit has accrued to an infant in a contract. The infant must establish that the consideration has completely failed in order to succeed.

Contracts which are not binding unless ratified

Non-necessaries and trading contracts can be ratified after attaining majority

This category catches purchases of non-necessaries and trading contracts. These are essentially the only other classes of contracts that an infant could enter into after taking into account the categories above. Here the contract cannot be enforced during infancy, nor after attaining majority unless the (now) adult elects to ratify it. But the contract is not void during infancy because the infant always had the ability to ratify it on attaining the age of 18.

The common law position has been modified by statute in most states. The statutory position is set out in Table 15.2. Tasmania has modified the common law in relation to guarantees and Queensland has retained the common law rules.

activebook

To help you to remember and understand the topics covered so far, and for links to legal websites, refer to your online activebook. Model answers provide feedback to problems and exercises.

Void contracts

In Victoria, the *Supreme Court Act 1986* makes the following contracts entered into by an infant void:

- contracts for the repayment of money lent or to be lent;
- contracts for payment of goods supplied or to be supplied, other than necessaries; and
- accounts stated (a debt).

Table 15.2 Statutory modifications to common law rules regarding ratification of contracts by infants and loan contracts with infants

State	*Legislation*	*Modification of the common law position*	
		Ratification of contracts	*Loan contracts*
ACT	*Mercantile Law Act 1962*	As for Queensland	As for Queensland
New South Wales	*Minors (Property and Contracts) Act 1970*	Contracts ratified after infant becomes 18 are enforceable	Loan contracts with infants enforceable against guarantors
Northern Territory	*Lord Tenterden's Act 1828* (Imp) 9 Geo IV c 14 (*Statute of Frauds*)	As for Queensland	As for Queensland
Queensland	*Money Lenders Act 1916*	Debts not enforceable unless ratified in writing and signed by the infant	All loans involving contracts are void
South Australia	*Minors Contracts (Miscellaneous Provisions) Act 1979*	Ratification must be in writing and made on or after the infant attains majority	As for New South Wales
Tasmania	*Minors Contracts Act 1988*	No ratification of contracts or debts after reaching majority	Contacts with infants are enforceable against guarantors
Victoria	*Supreme Court Act 1986*	No ratification of contracts or debts after reaching majority	All contracts involving loans, unpaid goods or accounts are void
Western Australia	*Lord Tenterden's Act 1828* (Imp) 9 Geo IV c 14 (*Statute of Frauds*)	As for Queensland	Common law applies

Torts by infants

Infants are generally liable for any torts that they may commit, although they are generally not liable for a tort connected with a contract.

Infants generally liable for any tort they commit unless connected with contract

JENNINGS V. RUNDALL **(1799) 101 ER 1419**

An infant hired a horse for riding, injuring it when he rode it too hard.

ISSUE: Was the tort so directly connected with the contract that the infant would not be liable in negligence?

DECISION: The infant was not liable in tort for negligence, for the act contemplated by the parties was riding, irrespective of how hard the horse was ridden.

COMMENT: If the infant had been expressly told not to ride the horse hard, then the infant could have been liable in tort. A similar result would occur if the act that caused the injury had not been contemplated by the contract. For example, if an infant hires a horse for riding and enters it in the local horse racing club's steeplechase and injures the horse as a result, the infant is liable in tort. The act complained of is outside the terms of the contract—that is, to ride the horse, not enter it in a local steeplechase.

New South Wales

In New South Wales the *Minors (Property and Contracts) Act 1970* has abolished this rule (s. 48) so that a person under the age of 18 years who is guilty of a tort is answerable for the tort whether or not:

- the tort is connected with a contract; or
- the cause of action for the tort is in substance a cause of action in contract.

The tort of deceit

Restitution is applicable if goods obtained by fraud are still in infant's possession

Infants are no more entitled than adults to keep goods obtained by fraud. The equitable doctrine of restitution may be applicable when the very same goods obtained by fraud are still in the possession of the infant.

If the infant no longer has the goods in their possession, the doctrine of restitution can no longer be applied. Nor does the doctrine of restitution apply where an infant obtains a loan of money by fraud, unless the actual notes or coins lent are still in the infant's possession and can be identified as such.

Statutory modifications in New South Wales and South Australia

New South Wales

NSW attempts to make infants liable in contract if they understand it is for their benefit

The New South Wales *Minors (Property and Contracts) Act 1970* reduced the age of full contractual capacity to 18 years of age. It attempts to make infants liable in contract, provided they have the ability to understand what they are getting themselves into, and that, at the time of contracting, it is for their benefit.

The Act bases the contractual liability of infants on the concept of a 'civil act'. Civil acts are defined in s. 6(1) as being 'any act relating to contractual or proprietary rights or obligations or to any chose in action' and include both contracts and dispositions of property. The test is whether the civil act is:

- for the '**benefit**' of the infant; and
- whether the infant **understands** the nature of the act.

'Benefit' is not defined anywhere in the Act, though it appears to be wider than the concept of necessaries considered earlier. Each case will depend upon its own facts at the time but taking into account factors such as:

- the age of the infant;
- the type of transaction;
- the station in life of the infant; and
- the fairness of the bargain.

An act is 'presumptively binding' where it is for the infant's benefit

An act is **presumptively binding** (the court presumes that the contract is valid if it falls into one of the categories listed below) where the act is for the benefit of the infant at the time of participation. The person wishing to enforce such a contract must establish that the contract falls within one of the following categories:

- The contract was for the infant's benefit: s. 19.
- A contract for the acquisition of property where the consideration paid or payable is not excessive at the date of the contract: s. 20.

***HOMESTAKE GOLD OF AUSTRALIA LTD V. PENINSULA GOLD PTY LTD* (1996) 14 ACLC 903**

In an attempt to prevent the compulsory acquisition of shares in a company subject to a takeover bid, shares were transferred to infants under a deed of arrangement signed by each infant's guardian. The plaintiffs then sought an order declaring that the transfers were voidable at their option.

ISSUE: Was the share transfer of 'benefit' to the infants as required by s. 19?

DECISION: The Supreme Court of New South Wales held that the share transfer was ineffective because the infants had not signed the deed of agreement (s. 16) and it was not of 'benefit' as required by s. 19.

- A contract for the disposal of property where the consideration received in part is not excessive: s. 20.
- A contract of investment in government securities.
- A contract with a consideration not exceeding $10 000 in the Local Court, $100 000 in the District Court or any amount in the Supreme Court if the court is satisfied is for the infant's benefit: s. 40.
- A contract for the disposal of property that was signed before an independent solicitor or the Public Trustee no more than seven days before the contract.
- Where the Supreme Court has granted the infant legal capacity.
- Where the infant makes a 'reasonable gift'.

Under NSW Act contracts are either valid or void

Under the New South Wales Act, the old distinctions between contracts of necessaries and beneficial contracts of service are no longer required, nor is the distinction between voidable contracts and 'void until ratified' contracts of any relevance. A contract is either valid or void.

The courts are given powers to ensure that equity exists between the parties in relation to all civil acts by infants. This includes returning the parties to their original positions where possible, and where this is not possible, at least making appropriate orders for restitution of benefits.

A guarantor to a contract involving an infant will be legally bound to the guarantee; however, the contract cannot be enforced against the infant.

Section 30 permits an infant to ratify (or affirm) a contract that was not presumptively binding, after they turn 18.

South Australia

SA Act not as extensive as NSW Act, leaving common law basically untouched

The South Australian *Minors Contracts (Miscellaneous Provisions) Act 1979* is not as extensive as the New South Wales Act. It basically leaves the common law untouched and only incorporates five specific recommendations of the Law Reform Commission of South Australia:

- Contracts entered into by infants that would be regarded at common law as voidable are regarded as unenforceable unless ratified in writing when the infant reaches full age: s. 4.
- Guarantors continue to remain liable as if the minor were of full legal capacity: s. 5.
- An infant can seek prior approval from the court to enter into a contract which the infant would not otherwise have legal capacity to enter into: s. 6.
- The court has a discretion to order restitution of some or all of the property to infants in certain circumstances: s. 7.
- The court may, upon application of the infant or their parent or guardian, appoint an agent to act on the infant's behalf for a particular transaction and make the infant liable: s. 8.

CORPORATIONS

Corporations are legal persons under the *Corporations Act 2001* (Cth)

Contracts can be made not only by 'natural persons', but also be made by 'artificial persons'. The latter are a creation of the law but are treated by the law as having the complete legal capacity of a natural person—for example, corporations.

Incorporation under the *Corporations Act 2001* (Cth) gives a company a **separate legal existence** from that of its members (see Chapter 27). It should be viewed as an independent person with its own rights and liabilities. As such, its contractual capacity is limited only by natural impossibility when it comes to entering into personal contracts because it is an artificial creation.

Where a company acts in excess of its powers under its 'replaceable rules'—that is, acts *ultra vires*—the other party may still enforce the contract under the *Corporations Act*. The doctrine of *ultra vires* was abolished in 1984, and s. 124 of the *Corporations Act* now provides that a 'a company has the legal capacity and powers of an individual'. This means that an act of a company is no longer invalid if it contravenes its Constitution (s. 125(1)).

BANKRUPTS

Bankrupts—limited contractual capacity under the *Bankruptcy Act 1966* (Cth)

As a general rule, bankrupts can still contract, but their contractual capacity is limited by the *Bankruptcy Act 1966* (Cth) (see Chapter 32). For example:

- If a bankrupt obtains $3000 or more in credit or goods or services, or trades under an assumed name, there must be disclosure of the fact that the bankrupt is undischarged.
- Property can only be acquired if it is for the benefit of the creditors.
- Company directorship or management roles are not permitted.

MENTALLY UNSOUND AND INTOXICATED PERSONS

Contracts with the mentally unsound or the intoxicated are usually regarded as being voidable at the option of that person unless they are for necessaries. The sale of goods legislation in all jurisdictions requires that mentally unsound and intoxicated persons who purchase goods which are necessaries must pay a reasonable price for them (see Table 15.3).

The fact that the selling party knows about the buyer's mental condition is irrelevant, because the latter is under an implied condition to pay for the goods anyway.

Mentally unsound and intoxicated persons—contracts other than for necessaries are voidable with onus on person wishing to repudiate

Where the goods are not necessaries, they may be able to repudiate the contract when they are again of sound mind or sober, if at the time of contracting:

- they were suffering from such a degree of mental instability or were so drunk that they were incapable of understanding the nature of the contract; and
- this was known, or ought to have been known, by the other party.

The **onus of proof** lies on the person wishing to repudiate the contract and must occur within a reasonable time of regaining sobriety or soundness of mind.

O'CONNOR V. HART [1985] 1 NZLR 159

An elderly farmer entered into a contract with Hart to sell him his land for a very low price. After the farmer died, his beneficiaries argued that the contract should be set aside.

ISSUE: Was the elderly farmer mentally unsound when he entered into the contract?

DECISION: The party seeking to avoid the contract on the grounds of mental unsoundness had to establish both the incapacity and that the other party was aware or should have been aware of this fact. The beneficiaries could not prove this and so the land sale was held to be valid.

Table 15.3 Relevant sections of sale of goods legislation

State	*Act*	*Section*
Australian Capital Territory	*Sale of Goods Act 1954*	s. 7
New South Wales	*Sale of Goods Act 1923*	s. 7
Northern Territory	*Sale of Goods Act 1972*	s. 7
Queensland	*Sale of Goods Act 1896*	s. 5
South Australia	*Sale of Goods Act 1895*	s. 2
Tasmania	*Sale of Goods Act 1896*	s. 7
Victoria	*Goods Act 1958*	s. 7
Western Australia	*Sale of Goods Act 1895*	s. 2

If a person **after** entering into a contract, then suffers mental illness or drunkenness, this will not affect the validity of the contract already entered into.

Contracts made during a lucid period are valid

MARRIED WOMEN

Married women have full legal capacity

Formerly, married women lacked full legal capacity on the basis that their legal personality and legal estate became one with the husband. The position today is that married women are in much the same position as a single man or woman, that is, they have for all practical intents and purposes full legal capacity.

Where the parties are living together, either as a married couple or not, the woman is able to pledge the man's credit for necessaries suitable to their style of living. This arises from the fact of cohabitation.

REVIEW QUESTIONS

15.1 Indicate whether each of the following statements is true or false:

Statement	TRUE	FALSE
An infant is a person under the age of 21 years	☐	☐
The onus of proof is on the plaintiff to establish that the goods or services provided to the infant are capable of being necessaries	☐	☐
For a beneficial contract of service to be valid, the benefits must outweigh any harsh conditions	☐	☐
If the court decides that the goods are necessaries, the infant only has to pay a 'fair and reasonable' price for them	☐	☐
Where voidable contracts with infants are concerned, infants can only recover money they have paid to the other party if they can establish that there has been a total failure of consideration	☐	☐
Under common law, trading contracts and contracts for non-necessaries are void unless they are ratified by the infant within a reasonable time of attaining the age of 18	☐	☐
The distinction between 'necessaries' and 'beneficial contracts of service' no longer applies in New South Wales	☐	☐
A person suffering from mental unsoundness or drunkenness is legally bound if they ratify a contract after regaining sanity or sobriety	☐	☐
Under New South Wales law, a contract with an infant is either valid or void	☐	☐
In all jurisdictions, sale of goods legislation requires that a mentally unsound or drunken person must pay a reasonable price for necessaries	☐	☐
A corporation can enter into contracts to perform personal services	☐	☐
Infants are generally liable for any torts they commit, irrespective of whether they are connected with a contract or not	☐	☐

activebook

Activebook resources include in-depth summaries with links to the relevant part of the book. For revision, add your own notes to the summaries provided by using the note-taking function.

	TRUE	FALSE
▪ If an infant has obtained goods by deceit, but they are no longer in the infant's possession, the doctrine of restitution cannot be applied	☐	☐

15.2 Discuss how a court decides whether goods or services purchased by an infant will result in a valid contract.

15.3 Janice, an infant, applied for and was allocated shares in a company; she received no dividends and attended no meetings. She is still to turn 18, and has received a call on the shares. As the company involved now seems to be doomed to failure, Janice wishes to know:

- whether she is bound to pay the balance of the price of the shares held by her; and
- whether she can recover the money already paid to the company.

Advise her. (Note that there is a subtle but very important difference between this question and *Steinberg v. Scala*.)

15.4 Ann, aged 14, signed a three-year contract with Ted in order to learn ballet dancing. The terms of the contract stated (a) that Ted would teach Ann ballet dancing to the best of his ability free of charge; (b) that during the three-year period, Ann could not accept stage engagements other than those under Ted; and (c) that Ted may employ Ann to perform on stage, but was not bound to do so. Ann accepted a stage engagement from Bill, as her income from Ted's employment was insufficient for her support.

Ted wishes to sue Ann for breach of contract. Advise him. (See *De Francesco v. Barnum*, p. 304) and compare carefully with the facts here.)

15.5 Sam, an infant, obtained a loan of money from Les by telling him that he was 19 when in fact he was only 16. Sam then defaulted on the repayments and Les, realising that no action could be brought on the contract, brought an action in tort for deceit.

Advise Sam whether Les is likely to succeed in his action.

15.6 Washington, an insane person of limited means, entered into a contract with Lincoln for the purchase of an antique axe and a cherry tree for $100. The price paid for both these items was fair and reasonable and, at the time the agreement was made, Washington seemed to be a normal person.

Washington refused to take delivery of either the axe or the cherry tree, or to pay for them. Lincoln wishes to know whether he can recover damages for breach of contract from Washington.

15.7 Bruce, while he was so drunk that he did not know what he was doing, bid successfully at an auction for the purchase of a house. It was clear to the auctioneer that Bruce did not know what he was doing. However, after Bruce sobered up he confirmed the contract with the auctioneer. He then subsequently refused to complete the contract.

Is Bruce bound?

CRITICAL THINKING

15.1 Should the age of majority be reduced to 16? Discuss.

15.2 Why should a corporation be viewed as an independent person with its own rights and liabilities when sole trading businesses and partnerships are considered to be synonymous with the owners? Discuss.

16

CHAPTER

Step 5: Genuine Consent

CHAPTER CONTENTS

activebook

This icon is used throughout the following chapter to remind you to visit the *Business Law* online activebook for additional exercises, links to legal websites, and feedback. For a detailed explanation of what is in the activebook please refer to the inside cover of this textbook. The activebook is available through OneKey.

Where do I start?

Learning path: Use the activebook to complete a pre-chapter warm-up exercise.

There are many definitions of legal terms to assist with your understanding of the material.

CHAPTER OBJECTIVES

On completion of this chapter, you should be able to:

- explain the effect of mistake on a contract
- define the different types of mistake, and illustrate with examples
- explain the effects of a common, mutual and unilateral mistake on the validity of a contract
- explain the effect of a mistake on a written document and the operation of the *non est factum* rule
- distinguish between fraudulent and innocent misrepresentation and explain their effects on a contract
- explain what is required to amount to negligent misrepresentation
- describe how the law relating to misrepresentation has been modified by statute
- explain the meaning of the terms 'duress' and 'undue influence' and their effects on a contract
- explain what constitutes unconscionable conduct at common law
- explain the effect of unconscionability legislation on unconscionable conduct.

16

KEY TERMS

An understanding of the following terms will help you to better understand the material in this chapter:

- **duress:** threats of, or use of, force that deprives the innocent party of exercising their free will
- **misrepresentation:** a false statement of fact, which may be intentionally or unintentionally made
- **representation:** a statement of fact
- **rescission:** to annul
- **unconscionable contract:** an unfair or unjust contract
- **undue influence:** improper use of power.

what if . . .

You decide to buy a car to replace the one that you currently own, which needs expensive repairs. Rather than buy the car from a registered motorcar dealer, you decide that you will try to save some money and buy privately. After weeks of searching you finally find a vehicle that meets your needs and budget. The seller has told you that he owns the car and in your haste to buy the vehicle, you fail to check on whether it has got 'clear title' through the Department of Transport. In fact, a check of ownership would have revealed that the seller had financed the car through a bank and that the loan was still outstanding. Having bought the car, you subsequently receive in the post a letter from the bank informing you that in the event you should not want to pay out the seller's loan, they will repossess the car from you. Do you own the car or don't you? What can you do?

A contract may still fail because there is no real consent to it by one or both of the parties. The basis of contract is agreement or consensus *ad idem* (meeting of the minds). If a party has entered into a contract based on mistake, misrepresentation, duress or undue influence or because of the unconscionable conduct by one party as a result of their superior bargaining position, then there is no genuine consent. Thus, the fifth question (Step 5) to be asked is, 'Is there genuine consent between the parties?' What have the parties agreed to?

The chapter considers whether one of the parties has entered into the contract as a result of mistake, misrepresentation, duress, undue influence or unconscionable conduct of the other party.

STEP 5—IS THERE GENUINE CONSENT?

MISTAKE

If one or other of the parties says that they have misunderstood the situation, or they have made a mistake, has an agreement been reached or not? As a general rule, if the parties appear to have reached an agreement, the law assumes that they have in fact reached agreement.

The law is reluctant to accept mistake as a ground for avoiding a contract, because it would provide an easy way out for a dissatisfied party, and would also seriously undermine the certainty and reliability essential to commercial transactions.

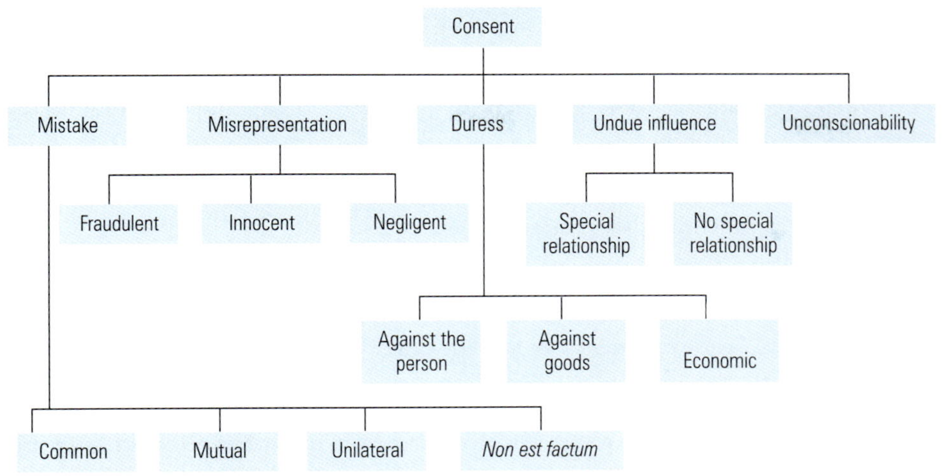

FIGURE 16.1 *Obstacles to genuine consent*

Where a mistake does operate, one outcome is to make the whole transaction null and void from the very beginning—that is, void *ab initio*. This would put the parties in the same position as if no contract had ever been made.

While the parties themselves may be unconcerned about being restored to their original positions, innocent third parties may not feel the same way. Suppose A sells a car to B under an 'apparent' contract. B then sells the car to C. If the original contract between A and B is now declared void for mistake, B has no title (ownership) to the car. B therefore cannot pass title on to C. The contract is void from the beginning and the title to the car will remain vested in A. C, who is a third party, would be required at common law to either return the car to A or pay A its value. C's right to sue B is generally limited because the guilty party usually disappears. It is because of this kind of injustice that the courts place such stringent limitations upon the operation of mistake.

In recent years there have been few reported cases on mistake. One reason may be the operation of ss. 51A and 52 of the *Trade Practices Act 1974* (Cth) or equivalent state and territory Fair Trading legislation which deal with 'misleading or deceptive conduct' (see p. 329).

Mistake of fact

Two principles are clear:

Only mistakes of fact can render a contract void

- Only **mistakes of fact** can render a contract **void**. If one of the parties makes a mistake of law (e.g., wrongly interpreting a statute), a mistake of judgement (e.g., buying clothes and then not liking the style or colour), or a mistake as to quality, then that party generally cannot rely on the mistake to avoid the contract. However, money paid under a **mistake of law** may be recoverable, if the money was paid by the payer under a mistaken belief that they were under a legal obligation to pay it or that the payee was legally entitled to payment of it.

***DAVID SECURITIES PTY LTD V. COMMONWEALTH BANK OF AUSTRALIA* (1992) 175 CLR 353**

The appellants entered into an agreement with the Commonwealth Bank in 1984 for a foreign currency loan. Part of the agreement provided that the appellants were to pay the bank in respect of its withholding tax liability on mortgage payments sent to the bank's branch overseas. The Full Court of the Federal Court held that the provision in the loan agreement for payment of the withholding tax was void under the *Income Tax Assessment Act 1936* (Cth).

ISSUE: Were the additional amounts paid in respect of the tax by the appellants recoverable since the money was paid under a mistake of law?

DECISION: The High Court held that payments made under mistake of law should be *prima facie* recoverable in the same way as payments made under a mistake of fact.

COMMENT: The case was sent back to the trial judge to see whether the appellants had paid the additional amounts under the contract because of their mistaken belief that the contractual arrangements that they had with the bank required them to, and whether the bank had changed its position in accepting the payments.

- There are very few mistakes of fact which provide grounds on which courts can invalidate a contract. As a result, a plaintiff may prefer to bring an action under s. 52 of the *Trade Practices Act 1974* (Cth) for 'misleading or deceptive conduct', under s. 51AA–AC for 'unconscionable conduct', or under s. 53 for 'false or misleading representations'.

IN BRIEF

Basic types of mistake of fact

Types of mistake	Description	Effect
Common mistake	**Agreement** but common error as to existence or identity of subject matter voidable at equity	Contract may be void at common law
Mutual mistake	A mistake made by both parties concerning a material fact that is important to the subject matter of the contract, so **no genuine agreement**	Contract void
Unilateral mistake	Only one party is mistaken about a material fact regarding the subject matter of the contract, so **no genuine agreement**	Contract may be void or voidable
Non est factum	Mistake as to the nature of the document, so **no genuine agreement**	Contract may be void or voidable

In the event of **common mistake**, there is a **genuine agreement** between the parties as they are both agreed on the same matters. The offer and acceptance have corresponded and the parties are of one mind. However, owing to **a common error as to some fundamental fact**, the agreement may have no legal effect. In the case of **mutual mistake, unilateral mistake and *non est factum* there is no genuine agreement**, as there is no real correspondence of offer and acceptance. These situations are now considered separately.

Common mistake

***Common mistake*—agreement but absence of existence or identity of subject matter**

In the case of a common mistake, the parties acknowledge the existence of an agreement (for that is admitted), but because of **a fundamental assumption as to the existence or identity of the subject matter**, they wish the court to set the agreement aside from the beginning. In other words, the parties are asking the court to treat the agreement as having no legal effect, and for any money or property that the parties have paid or conveyed to each other in reliance of that agreement to be recovered.

The courts have generally been reluctant to void contracts in which the common mistake involves accidental qualities or attributes of the subject matter.

LEAF V. INTERNATIONAL GALLERIES [1950] 2 KB 86

Leaf purchased a painting, mistakenly believed to have been painted by Constable, from International Galleries. When Leaf attempted to sell the painting five years later, he discovered the error and sought to rescind the contract for innocent misrepresentation and recover his purchase price.

ISSUE: Were the parties in agreement over the question of quality and subject matter?

DECISION: The claim in innocent misrepresentation failed because of a lapse of time. On an action based on mistake, there was no error in what was handed over. It was a specific picture. The parties were agreed in the same terms on the same subject matter, and that is sufficient to make a contract.

COMMENT: If the issue is about quality or attributes rather than existence, then mistake will probably not be available but note that the case was decided in 1950. Today, the buyer might argue negligent misrepresentation (the seller was an expert in his field and the buyer relied on his opinion) and breach of s. 52 of the *Trade Practices Act 1974* (Cth) (the seller's conduct amounted to misleading conduct).

CASE REFLECTION: Can the characteristics of the thing become part of the subject matter of the contract? Would it have made any difference if the buyer had said, 'I want a picture by Constable', as distinct from 'I want that picture?'

Common mistake must involve the existence or identity of the subject matter

A common mistake **must involve the existence or identity of the contract's subject matter**. The failure of such a contract to get off the ground is not due to the mistake, but to the absence of the thing upon which the contract is based.

PRITCHARD V. MERCHANT'S AND TRADESMAN'S MUTUAL LIFE ASSURANCE SOCIETY (1858) 140 ER 885

The beneficiary of a life insurance policy, which had lapsed because of non-payment of premiums, paid a renewal premium to revive the policy. However, neither party was aware that the insured had died prior to the payment being made.

ISSUE: Was the subject matter of the contract of a totally different nature to that which the parties thought?

DECISION: The beneficiary was not entitled to recover under the policy. While the premium was paid and accepted upon an implied understanding on both sides that the party insured was alive, both parties were labouring under a mistake. Thus, the transaction was void.

COMMENT: The beneficiary was entitled to recover his premium, however, as there was a total failure of consideration.

The High Court has denied that there is any hard and fast rule that the non-existence of the subject matter of a contract automatically renders that contract void. In each case it is a matter of construction.

McRAE V. COMMONWEALTH DISPOSALS COMMISSION (1951) 84 CLR 377

The Commission placed advertisements in newspapers calling for tenders for the purchase of an oil tanker, described in the advertisements as 'lying on Jourmaund Reef'. McRae successfully submitted a tender and the Commission accordingly gave a precise location by telephone and by letter. McRae then fitted out a ship and proceeded to the location given by the Commission and searched without success. In fact, never at any time was a tanker lying at or near the location given by the Commission, nor was there any such place as Jourmaund Reef.

ISSUE: If one of the parties makes an implied promise of the existence of the subject matter and the other party acts in reliance of that promise to their detriment, will the party making the promise be bound?

DECISION: By their advertisement to the public, the Commission impliedly promised that there was a tanker in existence, and on the strength of that promise, McRae had submitted a tender. The Commission could not now avoid its responsibilities.

COMMENT: As in *Leaf*'s case above, McRae today might have chosen also to sue for the negligent misstatements of the Commission (McRae could have argued that the Commission was the only party with the knowledge and that it was reasonable for McRae to rely on their knowledge) and possibly under s. 52 of the *Trade Practices Act* (the conduct of the Commission may have been misleading).

CASE REFLECTION: Could an argument be made for applying the principle of promissory estoppel in this case?

Where the contract is for the sale of specific goods which have perished at the time the contract is made, the sale of goods legislation of the various states and territories provides that '*where there is a contract for the sale of specific goods, and the goods, without the knowledge of the seller, have perished at the time when the contract was made, the contract is void*'. Thus, if A sells a car to B, and unknown to A the car has caught fire and burnt out an hour before the sale, the contract would be void and there would be no liabilities incurred on either side.

Equity may provide relief if mistake involves quality or attributes of subject matter

The decision in *McRae*'s case appears difficult to reconcile with the sale of goods legislation, unless the view is taken that this section does not apply at all if the goods never existed. In the example of the car above, the subject matter ceased to exist after the fire but before the sale. In *McRae*'s case the subject matter of the contract never existed. It seems that the court regards the existence of the goods as a condition precedent to liability in either party.

Equity may give relief where the mistake involves the quality or attributes of the subject matter. Here the court may treat the contract as voidable and order its rescission, but it is a discretionary remedy.

Mutual mistake

***Mutual mistake*—no real agreement as the parties are talking about different things**

In the case of mutual mistake, the parties are talking about **different** things. There is no real agreement between the parties.

Where mutual mistake has been pleaded, the courts apply an **objective test** of the reasonable person to the words or conduct of the parties to determine whether or not any agreement has been reached or whether or not the parties are at cross-purposes.

RAFFLES V. WICHELHAUS (1864) 159 ER 375

Wichelhaus had agreed to purchase a quantity of cotton from Raffles, to arrive 'ex Peerless from Bombay'. However, there were two ships of the same name sailing from Bombay, one in October which Wichelhaus had meant, the other in December which Raffles meant.

ISSUE: Do the offer and acceptance correspond?

DECISION: The contract was void *ab initio* because a reasonable person would have been unable to determine which ship the parties referred to.

CASE REFLECTION: If both parties were talking about the same type of merchandise, why was it important to know on which ship the goods were loaded?

Unilateral mistake

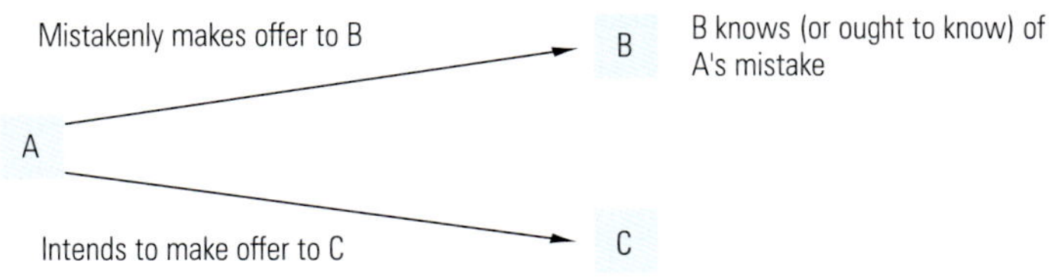

FIGURE 16.2 *Unilateral mistake*

Unilateral mistake— **only one party mistaken, so lack of agreement**

Like mutual mistake, there is a lack of agreement between the parties. However, here the **other party knows**, or ought to be reasonably aware, of the mistake and **does nothing to correct it**. Such cases usually involve a mistake as to the identity of the parties to the contract and while the majority of cases concern fraud, it should not be assumed that this is the only way unilateral mistake operates.

A mistake of this type can arise, for example, when A contracts with B, believing B to be C. It is A's intention to contract with C and C alone. B knows of A's intention at the time of acceptance; thus only A is mistaken (see Figure 16.2). In such a situation there is no correspondence between offer and acceptance, and the agreement can be avoided.

BOULTON V. JONES (1857) 157 ER 232

Jones normally dealt with Brocklehurst, who owed him money. However, unknown to Jones, Brocklehurst sold his business to Boulton. When Jones sent a written order for goods expressly addressed to Brocklehurst, Boulton struck out Brocklehurst's name and substituted his own and then completed the order. He didn't tell Jones of the change of ownership. When he asked for payment, Jones refused to pay, arguing he never intended to contract with Boulton.

ISSUE: Did Jones intend to contract only with Brocklehurst, or did he intend to contract with the business and whoever owned it?

DECISION: There was no contract because Jones had no intention of contracting with Boulton and Boulton knew this but assumed it did not matter.

Where parties meet face to face, presumption is contract intended to be concluded

Where the parties meet face to face

Where the parties meet face to face, it is assumed that a contract was concluded between the parties because the offer was accepted by the person to whom it was directed. The onus of rebutting the presumption lies on the party pleading the mistake of identity—the offeror in the above case—who must show that:

- A intended to deal with C and no one else—personal identity is vital;
- A never intended to deal with B and to this end A took reasonable precautions to check B's identity; and
- B knew that A never intended to deal with anyone but C.

CAUTION NOTE

*Where parties meet face to face and an innocent third party is involved, P **must** show identity is crucial to completion of contract or courts will treat contract as voidable, thereby generally giving third party title.*

Where the identity of a party to a contract is a matter crucial to the completion of that contract and this can be established, the courts will allow an action for unilateral mistake to succeed and treat the contract as void. However, if the intention is to deal with the offering party, whoever they might be, then the contract can only be treated as voidable. **The distinction becomes important when a third party becomes involved because until the injured party rescinds, the contract is valid and binding**. This means that if the swindler can sell the goods before the injured party rescinds and the third party is a purchaser for value and in good faith, they will get good title and the injured party will be left with the problem of finding the swindler if they want to get their money. The question of personal identity is vital.

PHILLIPS V. BROOKS [1919] 2 KB 243

A swindler entered a jewellery shop owned by Phillips and selected some items of jewellery. He offered to pay by cheque and said that he was Sir George Bullough and gave Phillips an address. Phillips checked the telephone directory and found Sir George Bullough at the address given. Phillips took the cheque and gave the swindler part of the jewellery. The swindler then pawned the jewellery to Brooks for cash. When the cheque was dishonoured, Phillips sought to recover the jewellery from Brooks.

ISSUE: Who did Phillips intend to contract with—the real Sir George Bullough or the person standing in front of him? Did Phillips take sufficient steps to check the identity of the person in front of him?

DECISION: Phillips had contracted to sell to the person who had physically entered the shop, whoever that might be. The contract was therefore voidable for fraudulent misrepresentation and not void for mistake. Thus, Brooks got good title to the jewellery because when he received the jewellery, Phillips had not rescinded the contract with the thief. The thief still had title and was able to pass this on to Brooks.

CASE REFLECTION: At what stage of the transaction did the purchaser supply a name? Was the name supplied for the purpose of entering into the contract or for some other purpose?

A similar outcome occurred in the case of *Lewis v. Averay* set out below. In both cases the court was of the view that the plaintiffs had not successfully rebutted the presumption that they intended to deal with the party in front of them, notwithstanding they had been fraudulently induced to believe that the person with whom they were contracting was someone else.

LEWIS V. AVERAY [1972] 1 QB 198

Lewis advertised his car for sale. A swindler rang him in response to the advertisement and, after taking the car for a drive, said he would like to buy it. He said he was 'Richard Greene', a well-known film actor. A price was agreed upon and the swindler wrote out a cheque and signed it 'R. A. Greene'. He wanted to take the car immediately but Lewis wanted proof of identity. The swindler then produced an admission pass from Pinewood Studios with the name 'Richard A. Greene' and a photograph of the swindler. Satisfied, Lewis let the swindler have the car. The cheque was subsequently dishonoured. In the meantime the swindler had sold the car to Averay, who bought it in good faith and for value.

ISSUE: Who did Lewis intend to contract with—the real R. A. Greene or the person standing in front of him? Did Lewis take sufficient steps to check the identity of the person in front of him?

DECISION: The contract between Lewis and the swindler was not void for mistake. Lewis intended to deal with the person before him (Greene), even though that person fraudulently pretended to be someone else. Therefore the contract was voidable because of the swindler's fraudulent misrepresentation, not void. The title to the car had passed to Averay before Lewis could rescind the contract with the swindler (i.e. after the bank notified him that the cheque was no good).

Doing business

ALWAYS check the identity of the party with whom you are dealing

The importance of unilateral mistake is that it makes the contract void *ab initio*. This means that a third party cannot get good title to the goods and the original owner can recover them. The remedy for the third party is against the swindler but this only occurs when the innocent party can establish that the identity of the other party is crucial to the completion of the contract. If payment is by cheque, it should be a bank cheque and if it isn't, do not part with possession and property in your goods until the cheque is cleared. ■

Where the parties deal through the post

Where the parties are dealing through the post, it is easier to establish that the innocent party intends to contract only with the party to whom they address the offer, and not with the swindler. The question is: Who did the plaintiff intend to deal with—a particular third party or the offering party even though they believed they were someone else?

Dealing through the post is easier to establish P only intended to contract with addressee

CUNDY V. LINDSAY [1878] 3 APP CAS 459

Blenkarn, a swindler, ordered goods from Lindsay, signing his letter in such a way that his name appeared to represent 'Blenkiron & Co.', a well-known firm. He gave an address close to theirs. Lindsay did not bother to check the address, but dispatched the goods to 37 Wood Street. Blenkarn immediately sold them to Cundy, who took them in good faith. Lindsay, upon discovering the fraud, brought an action for conversion to recover them from Cundy.

ISSUE: Who did Lindsay intend to deal with—the swindler or Blenkiron & Co.?

DECISION: The contract was void *ab initio* on the basis of unilateral mistake and so Cundy acquired no title. Lindsay knew nothing of Blenkarn, and Blenkarn knew this because he had induced it. Lindsay had only intended to deal with Blenkiron & Co.

Where the mistake is to a term

Unilateral mistake may involve existence or content of a term

While most cases of unilateral mistake involve questions of mistaken identity, not all such cases are of this type. The mistake may go to the existence or content of a term.

HARTOG V. COLIN & SHIELDS [1939] 3 ALL ER 566

An offer was accepted to sell 30 000 Argentine hare skins at a price based on weight per skin. The preliminary negotiations had proceeded on the clear understanding that the price was to be fixed in reference to each skin, not per pound, and expert evidence showed that trade custom was to fix the price by reference to a skin. The value of a skin was approximately one-third the value based on weight. When the seller discovered the error, he refused to supply the skins and the buyers sued for non-delivery of the goods at a fixed price based on weight.

ISSUE: Was the mistake known to the buyer?

DECISION: The buyer must have known of the mistake by the seller when the offer was made on a price based on weight and known that the seller intended to offer the skins at a price of so much per skin.

COMMENT: Whether the contract was void from the beginning because there was not a true acceptance of the seller's offer or voidable on equitable grounds is not clear; although, as there was no third party involved, it did not make a difference in the end.

However, it should be noted that the unmistaken party does not need to have actual knowledge of the mistake. It is enough if they ought to have known or strongly suspected that the plaintiff has made a mistake of a fundamental character.

Since *Taylor v. Johnson* there have been a number of views expressed about whether remaining silent with knowledge of the mistake is enough to warrant a court intervening to set the contract aside on the basis of unconscionability.

TAYLOR V. JOHNSON (1983) 151 CLR 422

Johnson granted an option to Taylor to purchase 10 acres (4 ha) of land for $15 000. When Taylor exercised the option, the parties entered into a written contract of sale for the land. In both the option and the contract, the sale price of the land was $15 000. Johnson subsequently refused to complete the sale on the ground that she had mistakenly believed that the sale price was $15 000 per acre rather than $15 000 in total.

ISSUE: Was there a unilateral mistake as to a fundamental term of a written contract, which would render the contract void at common law or voidable in equity if the unmistaken party has acted unconscionably?

DECISION: The High Court found that the evidence led to the inference that Taylor was aware that circumstances existed which suggested that Johnson was acting under a serious mistake or misapprehension about either the terms (i.e. the price) or the subject matter (i.e. its value) of the transaction. As Taylor had not materially altered his position and no third party rights were affected, Johnson was entitled in equity to an order rescinding the contract.

COMMENT: The decision focuses on the effect of the mistake and the conduct of Taylor. His actions were considered to be 'sharp business practice' and in this case amounted to unconscionable behaviour. He knew Johnson had made a serious mistake and was taking advantage of it.

Note also that the court did not find the contract void at common law on the basis of unilateral mistake. The High Court made it clear that where the unilateral mistake relates to the terms of a written contract, the mistaken party will not be able to rely on their own mistake to argue that the contract was void *ab initio*.

activebook

To help you to remember and understand the topics covered so far, and for links to legal websites, refer to your online activebook. Model answers provide feedback to problems and exercises.

Mistake and written documents (*non est factum*)

IN BRIEF

The defence of *non est factum*

To succeed in a plea of *non est factum*, the party raising the defence **must** establish that:

- the document is radically **different** from that which the signer expected; and
- failure to read and understand was **not due to carelessness or negligence**.

It sometimes happens that a person will sign a document and later discover that what they signed is fundamentally different to what they thought it was. In such a case the signing party would argue that the agreement was void because of *non est factum*. That is, that it is 'not my doing' or 'not my deed'.

Non est factum—it is later discovered that the signed document is radically different from what it was thought to be

To succeed in a plea of *non est factum*, two conditions must be met:

- the person must believe that the document that they signed is **radically different** to what that party believed it to be. The mistake must go to the fundamental nature of the document and not its contents; **and**
- there must be an **absence of carelessness or negligence** in the execution of the document.

FOSTER V. MACKINNON [1869] LR CP 704

Foster was entitled to receive payment on a bill of exchange for £6000. Mackinnon was an endorser of the bill and was *prima facie* liable on it. Evidence showed that Mackinnon was an old man of poor sight.

ISSUE: Did Mackinnon understand what it was that he was signing?

DECISION: Mackinnon was not liable on the bill, for he had not been negligent in signing. He had never intended to sign a bill of exchange. Therefore the apparent contract was void.

CASE REFLECTION: Would the principle involved in this case also apply to a person with no disability who applied for a loan then signed the loan contract without reading it? Explain your answer.

There is a heavy onus of proof on the person raising the defence, especially if a third party is involved. They have to establish that they acted carefully. It follows that if a party signs a document leaving blanks to be filled in by a third party, the plea of *non est factum* would be unavailable owing to the carelessness of the signer.

Signing without reading the document does not prevent the defence of *non est factum* from being raised. However, the classes of persons that can raise the defence are limited to two groups:

- those who are unable to read owing to blindness or illiteracy and who must rely on others for advice about what they are signing; and
- those who through no fault of their own are unable to understand the meaning of a particular document.

PETELIN V. CULLEN (1975) 132 CLR 355

Petelin, who spoke little English and could not read English, granted an option to Cullen, an agent, to purchase land owned by him (Petelin). After the option period expired, Cullen wrote to Petelin enclosing a cheque for $50 and a form to be signed by him acknowledging receipt of the money and granting a further extension of the option. Cullen urged Petelin to 'sign that you have received the $50', but no reference was made to the extension of the option. Petelin signed the document without reading it, thinking it was only a receipt. Cullen's principal subsequently tried to exercise the option but Petelin refused to sell the land.

ISSUE: Could Petelin show that what he had signed was radically different from what he thought he was signing without showing carelessness?

DECISION: The High Court held that the defence of *non est factum* could be successfully used. Petelin was able to show that he signed the document in the belief that it was radically different from what it was and that this belief was a direct result of Cullen's actions.

COMMENT: While it was normally necessary to establish that there was no carelessness or failure to take reasonable precautions in ascertaining the character of the document before signing it on the part of the innocent party, in this case the question of carelessness was not relevant. Petelin's belief that the document was merely a receipt had been caused by Cullen.

Even if the plea of *non est factum* is unsuccessful, there is generally an element of fraud or undue influence involved which would make the contract voidable. As long as there are no innocent third parties involved, the injured party will still be able to avoid the contract.

MISREPRESENTATION

IN BRIEF

Third parties, unilateral mistake and misrepresentation

Where **third parties** are involved, the plaintiff will not wish to press a claim in misrepresentation because the **right to rescission is lost and the contract is treated as voidable**. The difficulty for the plaintiff is highlighted in cases such as *Phillips v. Brooks* [1919] and *Lewis v. Averay* [1972]. Under mistake, the contract will be treated as void and hence it would be possible to recover the goods even from an innocent third party.

Where no third party is involved, P can plead either unilateral mistake or misrepresentation as the result will be the same

The apparent consent of the parties can be affected if it is subsequently found that one party has misrepresented the facts to the other. If the plaintiff party can establish a case for unilateral mistake, where that mistake has been induced by misrepresentation, they can either have the contract declared void *ab initio* for mistake, or disaffirmed for fraud. Where third parties are not involved, the result is the same in either case.

While each party should attempt to obtain all the information relevant to the contract, this is often impossible, and so it becomes necessary to rely on the representations, promises and conduct of the other party. It may happen that the other party may quite innocently misrepresent certain facts.

Representation

***Representation*—a statement of fact**

A representation is a **statement of fact**. The following are generally not considered to be representations: statements of law, statements as to future conduct or intention, statements of opinion, statements of a highly exaggerated nature, and silence or non-disclosure if it creates a false impression.

It is not necessary for the representation to be made directly to the representee as long as it is made with the intention that it should be acted upon by the representee, that is, it must produce a misunderstanding and be one of the reasons for inducing the contract. If the representee had knowledge of the untruth of a representation before the contract was entered into or signed, it is not possible to assert that the statement has misled them and any right to relief would be lost.

Types of misrepresentation

IN BRIEF

Types of misrepresentation

Type	Description	Remedy
Fraudulent	A false statement of fact made knowingly, or without belief in its truth, or recklessly, or carelessly as to whether it is true or false, with the intention to induce a person to enter into a contract, and which did induce the contract, causing the innocent party to suffer loss.	The remedy is not in contract but in the **tort of deceit**. Rescission and/or damages at the option of the injured party. May be remedy under Part V, *Trade Practices Act*.
Innocent	The maker of a statement of fact believes it to be true—there is a lack of intentional deceit.	No remedy in tort. **Right in equity** to rescind or resist an action for specific performance. Remedies under *Misrepresentation Acts* in SA and ACT, Part V, *Trade Practices Act*, and Fair Trading legislation.
Negligent	The maker of the statement innocently but carelessly makes a false statement, which the innocent party relies on and suffers loss.	Remedy in **tort of negligence** for damages; contract may be rescinded.

Fraudulent misrepresentation

Fraudulent misrepresentation— **intentional deceit**

Fraudulent misrepresentation is distinguished from innocent misrepresentation by the **intentional deceit** of one party by the other. The following elements **must** all be established in order to amount to a fraudulent misrepresentation:

- there must be a **false statement of fact**, not opinion, unless the person making the statement did not hold that opinion;
- the representation must be untrue;
- the person making the representation must know that it is false, or not believe in its truth, or be recklessly careless;
- the representation must be made with the intention that the other party acts in reliance on it;
- the statement must actually deceive the innocent party, i.e. be acted upon; and
- the innocent party must have suffered some loss.

***DERRY V. PEEK* (1889) 14 APP CAS 337**

The defendants, who were directors of a tramway company, had issued a prospectus stating that the company had a legal right to use steam to run its trams. At the time the prospectus was issued, the company had not received consent and the company never did in fact receive that consent. In reliance on the statement in the prospectus, the plaintiff subscribed for shares in the company from an original allottee on the open market.

The company was subsequently wound up and the plaintiff sued the directors alleging fraudulent misrepresentation.

ISSUE: While the representation was false, was there an intention by those issuing the prospectus to induce the plaintiff to enter into the contract?

DECISION: The prospectus was only issued for the purpose of obtaining members of the company on the original allotment of shares. As the plaintiff was not an original allottee, there was no intention on the part of the issuers to induce the plaintiff to enter into the contract.

Because a contract induced by fraud is **voidable** at the option of the deceived party, it remains binding until set aside. Thus, the position of the deceived party is as follows:

- Since fraud is a tort, in addition to any other remedy available to the deceived party, damages may be recoverable in an action for deceit. However, the deceived party must suffer actual damage.
- On discovering the fraud, the deceived party must elect either to affirm or rescind the contract. In the case of rescission, which is an equitable remedy, the deceived party must act promptly on discovery of the misrepresentation or the right to rescind may be lost. In the case of affirmation, the deceived party can insist that the representation be made good, if that is possible. Once a choice is made, it is irrevocable.

Affirmation does not prevent the deceived party from bringing an action for damages for deceit where the contract has been affirmed, for the action is one of tort.

! CAUTION NOTE

Fraudulent misrepresentation is a tortious action, not contractual, which impacts on a claim for damages.

Innocent misrepresentation

Innocent misrepresentation—lack of intentional deceit

An innocent misrepresentation is a misstatement of a material fact, made **without intention to mislead**, that is, in good faith, by one party and not known by them to be false, which induces the other party to enter into a contract. These are statements that are not terms of a contract and so there are no remedies for breach at common law unless:

- there has been a total failure of consideration; or
- the misrepresentation is a term in the contract.

Common law prevails to the exclusion of equity and the appropriate remedy will depend on whether the representation is a:

- **Condition**

  The representee has a choice:

  – the contract may be affirmed and be confined to damages; or

  – the contract may be treated as discharged and the representee may refuse to perform any obligations *and* sue the other party for a total failure to perform the contract.

- **Warranty**

  The only remedy is the recovery of damages. No order of rescission will be available in equity.

If the misrepresentation is not a term in the contract, the injured party's only remedies are going to be equitable.

WHITTINGTON V. SEAL-HAYNE (1900) 82 LT 49

The plaintiff leased premises from the defendant on the basis that the premises were in sanitary condition. The defendant genuinely believed that they were sanitary but they were found to be unsanitary after the plaintiff moved in.

ISSUE: Was the plaintiff entitled to rescission on the lease on the basis of an innocent misrepresentation?

DECISION: The plaintiff was entitled to rescind the lease and get a refund of rates that he had paid, as well as an indemnity on repairs that he had made.

COMMENT: The plaintiff was not entitled to recover lost profits on sales or for loss of the breeding season for his prize poultry as he would have had to establish fraud.

If the deceived party has not performed their part of the contract when the misrepresentation is discovered, they can refuse to do anything further and successfully resist an action for specific performance.

If the truth is discovered after performance of some or all of the contractual obligations of the deceived party, it may be no use repudiating. Here the deceived party will need the help of the court for an order of rescission to end the contract and restore the parties to the position they were in before the contract was formed, if that is possible.

Limits of rescission

Whether the misrepresentation is innocent or fraudulent, the right to rescind is lost in any of the following situations:

- if the injured party, with full knowledge of the facts and the misrepresentation, expressly or impliedly affirms the contract;
- if the parties cannot be substantially restored to their original positions;
- if a third party has acquired rights under the contract, in good faith and for value; or
- where land has been transferred or leased, and the transfer or lease has been executed.

Where the innocent misrepresentation is in the negotiations leading to a contract for the sale of goods, under sale of goods legislation rescission is available where a party is induced to enter into a contract for the sale of goods by an innocent misrepresentation.

Negligent misrepresentation

It was not until *Hedley Byrne & Co. Ltd v. Heller & Partners Ltd* [1964] AC 465 that the whole matter of economic loss caused through careless statements was reconsidered (see pp. 164–168 for further discussion on negligent misrepresentation). The House of Lords was unanimous that a negligent misrepresentation, whether spoken or written, could give rise to an action for financial loss, apart from any contract that may exist between the parties but, as the heading suggests, in the tort of negligence.

Subsequent decisions, **both** in the United Kingdom and in Australia, have extended the *Hedley Byrne* doctrine to include negligent pre-contractual statements between one contracting party and another which do not form part of the contract, as well as giving of information and advice. It is thus possible for a statement to be both a collateral contract or warranty (in relation to representations made in a pre-contractual context) and a negligent misstatement.

Statement may be both a collateral contract or warranty and a negligent misrepresentation

Because of the special nature of the tort, in order to succeed in an action for negligent misrepresentation, the plaintiff is going to have to establish that a '**special relationship**' exists between the parties.

ESSO PETROLEUM CO. LTD V. MARDON [1976] 2 ALL ER 9

Mardon, in reliance on the statements of Esso's expert that a service station would sell 900 000 litres of petrol a year, entered into a three-year lease with Esso. It turned out that sales were substantially less than that, i.e. some 355 000 litres. Mardon ended up being unable to pay for his petrol and as a consequence made a large loss. Esso sued for possession and monies owed on petrol supplied and Mardon counter-claimed for breach of warranty and negligent misrepresentation.

ISSUE: Was Mardon entitled to rely upon the skill and expertise of Esso?

DECISION: The statements of the expert were factual statements on a crucial matter made by someone who professed to and did have special knowledge and skill, which were intended to and did induce Mardon to enter into a lease. As such, they amounted to contractual warranties. Furthermore, the circumstances were such that the statements of the expert placed upon them a duty to exercise reasonable care to ensure that the representations were correct. That duty of care was held to exist both prior to and after the signing of the contract in relation to those representations. Accordingly, Esso was liable for the breach of duty of care for the negligent misrepresentations to Mardon concerning petrol sales, though the damages recoverable would be the same, whether assessed by reference to tortious or contractual liability.

COMMENT: The duty of care is an implied term of the contract but is imposed under the tort of negligence.

CASE REFLECTION: Could the statements made in this instance also constitute misleading and deceptive conduct under the *Trade Practices Act*?

IN BRIEF

Establishing negligent misrepresentation

To establish negligent misrepresentation, the following guidelines are useful:

- a **special relationship** must exist between the parties such that the person providing the advice or information must be aware that the party seeking the advice or information trusts them to exercise a **duty of care** in the giving of that information;
- the subject matter of the representation must be of a **serious or business nature**;
- the person providing the advice or information must realise that the recipient **intends to act upon** that advice or information;
- in the circumstances, it was reasonable for the recipient to rely on that advice or information; and
- the person receiving the advice must suffer damage, usually in the form of monetary loss.

Statutory modifications to the law relating to misrepresentations

The inability of the common law to satisfactorily deal with, in particular, innocent misrepresentations by awarding damages, coupled with the equitable remedy of rescission, so that the misled party is faced with an all or nothing choice, has resulted in limited statutory intervention at both federal and state levels.

Part V of *TPA* has directly impacted on the area of misrepresentation at an interstate level

Commonwealth legislation

The *Trade Practices Act 1974* materially affected the law in relation to innocent misrepresentations and negligent misstatements through the consumer protection provisions contained in Part V by **targeting conduct** rather than contractual situations and includes the following:

Misleading or deceptive conduct: s. 52(1)

This section prohibits corporations from engaging in conduct that is misleading or deceptive or is likely to mislead or deceive. It is a catch-all provision and capable of a much wider application than misrepresentation under the common law. It can catch misstatements of law, opinion, intention or even a case of silence if it misleads or deceives, or is likely to mislead or deceive anyone. Unlike the following sections where conduct is prohibited and breach is also a criminal offence, contravention only gives rise to civil remedies: s. 79.

Representations as to the future: s. 51A

This section provides that representations as to the future without reasonable grounds shall be taken to be misleading and widens the operation of the meaning of 'misleading' in s. 52. The onus of proof is on the person making the representation about a future matter to show that they had reasonable grounds for doing so.

False representations: s. 53

This section is narrowly defined, unlike s. 52, which is broadly defined. It covers a number of categories of prohibited representations in connection with the promotion, supply or possible supply of goods or services (e.g., a false representation that goods or services are of a particular standard when they are not).

False representations in relation to land: s. 53A

This section prohibits persons from making false representations in relation to land.

False representations in relation to employment: s. 53B

This section prohibits false representations in relation to jobs which do not exist or for self-improvement courses which are of little benefit to the job-seeker.

Misleading conduct regarding services: s. 55A

This section prohibits conduct that is liable to mislead the public as to the nature, characteristics, and suitability for their purpose or the quantity of any services.

Misleading statements about home-operated business: s. 59

This section prohibits the making of a statement that is false or misleading about the profitability or risk of any business activity that can be, or can be to a considerable extent, carried on at a person's place of residence.

Part VI deals with 'Enforcement and Remedies' and goes far beyond the limited remedy of rescission for innocent misrepresentation. It enables the courts to make a variety of orders not only to enforce actions against contraventions, but also to provide suitable relief for persons injured by such contraventions:

- Section 80 provides for an **injunction.**
- Section 82 confers a **private right to recover damages** in respect of loss or damage caused by the conduct of another person that was done in contravention of Part V.
- Section 87 provides the **court** with **power** to make a wide range of **discretionary ancillary orders**. These include declaring the relevant contract void *ab initio*, varying the transaction, ordering repair of the goods concerned, an order to supply specified services, and an order for the refund of money or the return of property concerned.

State legislation

Fair Trading Acts

Fair trading legislation catches intra-state conduct

As a result of the constitutional limitations placed upon the *Trade Practices Act*, the states and the territories between 1985 and 1990 introduced Fair Trading Acts mirrored on the *Trade Practices Act*. They catch the **intra-state conduct** of individuals and partnerships who make certain types of false or misleading statements.

Sale of Goods Act 1923 (NSW) and *Sale of Goods Act 1954* (ACT)

Sections 4(2A)(b) and 38(2) of the *Sale of Goods Act* (NSW) and s. 62(1) of the *Sale of Goods Act 1954* (ACT) expressly preserve the rules of equity relating to rescission for misrepresentation.

South Australian and Australian Capital Territory misrepresentation legislation

Section 7 of the *Misrepresentation Act 1972* (SA) and s. 174 of the *Civil Law (Wrongs) Act 2002* (ACT) both amend the common law. The only real difference between them is in the formulation of defences.

They provide that where a contract has been induced by misrepresentation then it shall give rise to an action for damages in the same way it would have had it been fraudulently made (i.e. there were no reasonable grounds for belief in the representation). The representor must have had a 'fair and reasonable' belief in the representation right up until the time of contracting.

VETTESE V. KEMP [2000] SASC 154

Shortly after the purchasers moved into their South Australian home, a retaining wall collapsed and required expensive repairs. The purchasers had relied on the agent's representation that council approval had been given for the wall when no such approval had been given.

ISSUE: Was there an actionable representation by the agent? Were the vendors vicariously liable for their agent's misrepresentation under s. 7(1) of the *Misrepresentation Act 1972* (SA)?

DECISION: The Full Court of the South Australian Supreme Court held that the purchasers were awarded damages against the vendors as they had been induced to enter into the contract by a misrepresentation made by the vendor's agent which was actionable under s. 7(1) of the Act.

COMMENT: The vendors were found to be vicariously liable for the representations of their agent. In addition, the agent was able to successfully rely on s. 7(2)(a) of the Act that he had reasonable grounds to believe, and did believe, that his representation as to council approval for the retaining wall was true.

The grounds upon which rescission may be obtained have been widened to include those situations where it is '**just and equitable**' in the opinion of the court to grant a remedy.

Fair Trading Act 1999 (Vic.)

Section 32OA of the *Fair Trading Act* has followed the South Australian misrepresentation legislation by providing for rescission of a contract for the sale of goods where an innocent misrepresentation has been made. For the section to operate, notice must be given to the seller within a reasonable time from the acceptance of the goods.

DURESS AND UNDUE INFLUENCE

Duress

***Duress*—use of threats of or violence to induce contract shows lack of agreement**

Duress is the use of violence or illegal threats against a person, their goods or economic interests to force them to enter into a contract against their will. Thus, there is a lack of voluntary agreement.

The duress does not have to be the sole reason for the coerced party entering into the contract. It only has to be one of the reasons and the effect on the contract is that it will be **voidable** at the option of the injured party.

BARTON V. ARMSTRONG (1973) 47 ALJR 781

Barton, who was in financial difficulty, had entered into a contract with Armstrong for the sale of shares. He subsequently wished to have the contract set aside and he argued that he had entered into the contract because of death threats made against him by Armstrong. Armstrong argued that this was not the only reason that Barton had sold the shares.

ISSUE: Was duress one of the factors that led to Barton entering into the contract with Armstrong?

DECISION: The New South Wales Court of Appeal held that the duress, while it was not the only reason for Barton entering into the contract, was a factor and so Barton could rescind the contract.

COMMENT: On appeal, the Privy Council in *Barton v. Armstrong*, [1976] AC104 decided that the onus was on Armstrong, the party who had made the threat, to show that it had no effect.

IN BRIEF

Types of duress

Type	Description	Remedy
To the person	Actual or threatened violence to one contracting party, or their immediate family or near relatives	Contract voidable at option of coerced party
To goods	Wrongful threats to seize, damage or destroy the goods of one contracting party	Contract voidable at option of coerced party
Economic duress	Economic pressure beyond normal acceptable commercial practice	Contract voidable at option of coerced party

To the person

***Duress to person—* actual or threatened violence against P**

Duress to the person is a relatively limited common law doctrine consisting of actual or **threatened violence** to one contracting party, or to their immediate family, by or on behalf of the other contracting party. The plaintiff has to establish:

- the duress operated to interfere with the free exercise of a coerced party's will; **and**
- the duress prevented the parties from meeting and negotiating on equal terms; **and**
- as a result of the duress, the mind of the coerced party did not go to the transaction.

Sections 53A(2) (false representations in relation to land) (see p. 493) and 60 (coercion or harassment at place of residence) (see p. 497) of the *Trade Practices Act 1974* (Cth) also affect this area of the law.

SEEAR V. COHEN (1881) 45 (NS) LTR 589

Seear induced Cohen to sign a promissory note by telling him that if he did not, criminal proceedings would be taken against his son for the misappropriation of a sum of money.

ISSUE: Was the threat of criminal proceedings a contributing reason for Cohen entering into the contract?

DECISION: The father was not liable on the promissory note, as the threat of criminal proceedings against his son amounted to duress.

COMMENT: In both *Barton*'s case (above) and this one, duress was not the only reason for the injured party to enter into a contract. What is important is that it was a contributing factor.

To goods

***Duress to goods*—extreme pressure leaving coerced party no alternative**

Duress to goods or property could occur where one party carries out or threatens to carry out the detention, seizure or damage to goods or property of another in order to induce them to enter into a contract.

In order to succeed, the coerced party would have to show that the coercing party used **extreme pressure**, thus leaving no real alternative on the coerced party but to submit (e.g., a threat to burn a person's business down and put them out of business if they did not agree to enter into a contract).

Economic duress

***Economic duress*—pressure beyond what is acceptable commercial practice**

This type of action is restricted to commercial activities and the illegitimate use of economic pressure to force a business into entering into a contract which they might not otherwise have entered into. The difficulty here is distinguishing between legitimate commercial pressure and economic duress.

To succeed in this action it would be necessary for the plaintiff to establish that:

- the pressure was one of the reasons which induced the coerced party into the contract; **and**
- the pressure was such that it was beyond what could be accepted as reasonable commercial practice, e.g., unlawful threats or unconscionable conduct. Overwhelming pressure, not amounting to unlawful threats or unconscionable conduct will not necessarily constitute economic duress.

It is unnecessary, however, for the plaintiff to prove that the illegitimate pressure was the sole reason for entering into the contract. It is sufficient if it is one of the reasons and if the plaintiff can establish that, then the onus shifts on to the person applying the pressure to show that they did not contribute to the plaintiff entering into the agreement.

***UNIVERSE TANKSHIPS INC. OF MONROVIA V. INTERNATIONAL TRANSPORT WORKERS FEDERATION* [1983] 1 AC 66**

The *Universe Sentinel* was owned by the plaintiff company. After unloading its cargo in Wales, the ship was subject to a ban by the defendants. The financial consequences of the ban were such that the plaintiffs agreed in writing to the defendant's demand to pay money into their welfare fund if they wanted the ship released. After the ship was released, the plaintiffs sought to have the contract declared void and to recover the monies that they had paid.

ISSUE: Was the fear of economic ruin beyond what the law would countenance as a legitimate commercial tactic?

DECISION: As the defendants did not dispute that their actions amounted to economic duress, the contract was void and the plaintiffs were entitled to their money back.

Undue influence

***Undue influence*—improper use of power**

Undue influence involves the improper use of a position of influence or power possessed by one person over another in order to induce the latter to act for the former's benefit. As a result, there is a lack of genuine consent to the agreement. Like duress, undue influence looks to the quality of the consent or assent of the weaker party. The action is based in equity and the usual remedy is rescission.

IN BRIEF

Types of undue influence

Type	Description	Remedy
No special relationship	Improper use of a position of influence or power, onus on P to prove D exercised influence	Contract voidable at option of weaker party
Special relationship	D stands in unequal relationship presumed to exist to P because of parental or confidential relationship, onus on D to prove that the transaction was voluntary and P understood the contract	Contract voidable at option of weaker party

Where a special relationship is presumed to exist

Here the defendant stands in an **unequal relationship** to the plaintiff in a relationship of influence or confidence. The onus of rebutting this presumption lies on the defendant, and they must prove that the transaction was a voluntary act and that the plaintiff understood the contract.

Where special relationship presumed to exist, D stands in unequal relationship to P and onus on D to rebut

Undue influence is presumed to exist in the following cases:

- parent and child;
- solicitor and client;
- trustee and beneficiary;
- religious adviser and devotee;
- doctor and patient;
- fiancé over fiancée (but not husband over wife); and
- guardian and ward.

Where no special relationship exists

Here the plaintiff must prove that the defendant **exerted influence** over them, and thus obtained a contract which they would not otherwise have made.

Where no special relationship presumed to exist, onus on P to prove influence by D

If undue influence can be established, then the **contract is voidable** at the option of the plaintiff. If the plaintiff is going to repudiate, then **repudiation must occur within a reasonable time**. As is the case with other voidable contracts, if an innocent third party gets involved, the injured party's right to repudiate may be lost.

Examples in this class would include taking advantage of a person who makes a gift of the whole or the bulk of their estate who:

- suffers from religious delusions; or
- believes in messages from the dead through a medium; or
- has little or no education.

When must the action commence?

The right of a person to have a transaction set aside on the grounds of undue influence should be promptly acted upon. If any unreasonable length of time is allowed to elapse, the right to rescission may be lost.

Action must commence within a reasonable time

***ALLCARD V. SKINNER* (1887) 36 CH D 145**

The plaintiff had joined a religious order as a novice and took the vows of chastity, obedience and poverty. As a result of her vows, the plaintiff had to give away her property. She left it to the sisterhood. The plaintiff ultimately left the sisterhood and some five years later asked for her money back.

ISSUE: What is a reasonable length of time in which to act?

DECISION: While there was a presumption of undue influence, this had not been rebutted. The fact that she waited five years to exercise her rights amounted to an affirmation of the contract.

CASE REFLECTION: Would the principle involved in this case be applicable to all voidable contracts?

UNCONSCIONABLE (UNFAIR) CONTRACTS

Unconscionable contracts can be set aside in equity if it can be shown D abused bargaining position

The general rule at common law is that the courts will not interfere with a contract which appears to be the result of unconscionable conduct by one of the parties. However, in its equitable jurisdiction the court will set aside a transaction as unconscionable where there has been an abuse by the defendant of their superior bargaining position in their dealings with the plaintiff. Unconscionable conduct involves questions of fact and degree and each case must be judged on its facts. If the facts show that the conduct of the defendant was such that in its factual setting fairness and good faith could properly be expected to be exercised and it can be shown they were not, then the conduct of the defendant may be described as unconscionable.

***COMMERCIAL BANK OF AUSTRALIA V. AMADIO* (1983) 151 CLR 447**

An elderly Italian couple, with little understanding of English or formal education, signed a mortgage over a block of shops to the Commercial Bank as security for payment of the debts of one of their son's companies. At the time of signing they were led to believe by the son that the guarantee was for $50 000 and limited to six months. They were also told by their son that the company was in a good financial situation when in fact it was in serious financial trouble. When the Amadios came to sign the mortgage the bank manager corrected the misunderstanding of the length of time the guarantee/mortgage was to run for, but did nothing else other than to get them to sign. When the son's company went into liquidation and the bank attempted to exercise its rights under the mortgage/guarantee, the Amadios attempted to have the contract set aside.

ISSUE: Was the conduct of the bank such that it could be regarded as unconscionable? That is, had the bank taken unfair advantage of its superior bargaining position for its own commercial gain?

DECISION: It was held by a majority of the High Court that a court in exercising its equitable jurisdiction could set aside a transaction if it was unconscionable, which in this case it was, for the bank to rely on the mortgage/guarantee. The bank was in a superior bargaining position to the Amadios as it knew the financial position of the son and also that the parents did not fully understand what it was that they were entering into. The parents were, in fact, in a position of special disadvantage because they did not understand the extent of their liability under the agreement. Nor did the parents understand the financial position of their son's company, which was being propped up by the bank. Essentially there was an abuse by the bank of its superior bargaining position in its dealings with the Amadios.

COMMENT: 'Unconscionable dealing looks to the conduct of the stronger party in attempting to enforce, or retain the benefit of, a dealing with a person under a special disability where it is not consistent with equity or good conscience to do so' per *Deane* J at page 474.

CASE REFLECTION: Would the conduct of the bank still be unconscionable if the Amadios had the benefit of independent legal advice?

IN BRIEF

What has to be established for a contract to be set aside as unconscionable?

For a contract to be set aside on the grounds that it was unconscionable, P must prove:

- they were in a position of 'special disadvantage' at the time of the contract;
- it must have substantially affected their ability to protect themselves;
- the defendant must have known, or should have known, of the plaintiff's disability and had taken advantage of it; and
- the actions of the defendant were unconscionable (i.e. unfair or unjust).

What amounts to a 'special disadvantage' is difficult to accurately define, but includes poverty, need, sickness, age, sex, drunkenness, illiteracy or lack of education, lack of assistance or explanation where assistance or explanation is necessary.

LOUTH V. DIPROSE **(1992) 110 ALR 1**

Diprose fell in love, and became infatuated, with Louth. She did not share similar feelings towards Diprose. In response to a crisis, which the court felt had been contrived by Louth saying she and her two children were going to be evicted from the house they occupied, Diprose made a gift of $60 000 to her to enable her to buy a house in her own name.

ISSUE: Was Diprose under a 'special disadvantage' which Louth had exploited to her advantage with the false crisis as to unconscientiously manipulate him or was this a case of an imprudent gift?

DECISION: The High Court held that Louth's conduct was considered to be unconscionable and the house was ordered to be transferred to Diprose. She had exploited his emotional dependence on her using the false crisis about the eviction to her advantage.

Statutory modifications to the common law

Commonwealth legislation

Consumers

Under Part IVA (ss. 51AA–51AC) of the *Trade Practices Act 1974* (Cth) which operates concurrently with the Fair Trading Acts of the states and territories, a person or corporation, acting in trade or commerce, is prohibited from engaging in conduct which is, in all the circumstances, unconscionable.

Section 51AA refers to conduct that is unconscionable within the meaning of the 'unwritten law' and applies the principles of the *Amadio* case to **business *versus* business disputes.**

OLEX FOCAS PTY LTD V. SKODAEXPORT CO. LTD **[1998] 3 VR 380**

The plaintiffs contracted to carry out construction work in India for the defendant. The defendant was required to pay to the plaintiffs certain advances and they were to be repaid by deductions from progress payments made by the defendant to the plaintiffs. As part of their contract, the defendant required bank guarantees as security from the plaintiffs to secure their performance of their contractual obligations.

Nearing completion of the contract, and after the greater part of the advances had been repaid, a dispute arose between the parties. The defendant then attempted to call in the balance of the guarantees outstanding without giving the plaintiffs any warning, with penalty.

ISSUE: Did the conduct of the defendant in calling up the guarantees without any warning amount to unconscionable conduct within the meaning of the general law and thus amount to a breach of s. 51AA?

DECISION: The Victorian Supreme Court held that the actions of the defendant were unconscionable and in breach of s. 51AA.

COMMENT: The court issued injunctions under s. 80. If the defendant had called up the guarantees to cover only the balance outstanding there would have been no issue of unconscionability.

Section 51AB is a more specific provision because it catches **'consumer' transactions** involving the supply of goods or services to a 'consumer' by a corporation or other person for 'personal, domestic or household use or consumption'. In trying to determine whether there has been unconscionable conduct, s. 51AB(2) lists a number of guidelines that the court may take into account including:

- the relative bargaining power of the company and the consumer;
- whether the conditions in the contract went further than was reasonably necessary to protect the company;
- whether undue influence, pressure or unfair tactics were used by the company or its agents during negotiations;
- whether the consumer understood the documents;
- whether the price and availability of the goods were more onerous than what could have been obtained elsewhere.

Unconscionable conduct in business transactions

Section 51AC is limited to business transactions up to $3 million

Section 51AC deals with unconscionable conduct in business transactions and mirrors the rights available to consumers under s. 51AB by providing that a corporation or a person must not engage in conduct that is unconscionable to a 'business consumer'. The section is primarily intended to protect small businesses that enter into commercial agreements with larger businesses and is limited to business transactions that do not exceed $3 million.

The checklist to assist the court in determining whether conduct is unconscionable is almost identical to the checklist in s. 51AB(2) above, though it should be noted that there are additional tests of unconscionability which are relevant to small business to which a court may have regard, including:

- the consistency of the supplier's conduct towards like business consumers in similar transactions: s. 51AC(3)(f);
- any industry code requirements: s. 51AC(3)(g), (h);
- non-disclosure by the supplier of any conduct that might affect the interests of the business consumer or any risks to the business consumer arising from the supplier's intended conduct: s. 51AC(3)(i);
- the extent to which the supplier was willing to negotiate the terms and conditions of any business contract for the supply of goods and services with the business consumer: s. 51AC(3)(j); and
- the extent to which the supplier and the business consumer acted in good faith: s. 51AC(3)(k).

Remedies for breach of Part IVA

The remedies for unconscionable conduct include an injunction (s. 80), damages (s. 82) and a wide range of ancillary orders under s. 87 including power to order the rewriting of a contract.

State legislation

The Fair Trading legislation of the states and territories contain provisions equivalent to Part IVA above which prohibit 'persons' or 'suppliers' from engaging in unconscionable conduct or trade.

The *Contracts Review Act 1980* (NSW) empowers the New South Wales Supreme Court to grant relief in respect of 'harsh, oppressive, unconscionable or unjust contracts' by refusing enforcement, declaring the contract void or varying it in whole or in part. Whatever approach the court adopts, it can take into account matters such as bargaining inequality and the use of unfair tactics, while having regard to the public interest and to all the circumstances of the case: s. 9(1).

NSW *Contracts Review Act 1980* gives relief for harsh, unconscionable or unjust contracts

***S H LOCK (AUST.) LTD V. KENNEDY* (1988) 12 NSWLR 482**

Kennedy orally agreed to guarantee a loan to her son-in-law's company up to a limit of $100 000. When she signed the written contract of guarantee it was unlimited.

ISSUE: Was the guarantee valid? If it was, to what limit?

DECISION: The New South Wales Court of Appeal held that the contract was valid but the guarantee was fixed at the orally agreed amount of $100 000.

Circumstances of the case would include:

- the relative bargaining strengths of the parties;
- whether the disgruntled party could negotiate changes;
- whether independent legal advice was sought or could be sought;
- what normal commercial practice was;
- the complexity of the language used;
- the age, health and mental capacity of the parties; and
- the education, literacy and economic circumstances of the parties.

Where the plaintiff was in a position to understand what they were doing because, for example, they had sought independent expert advice, then relief will probably not be available because of the difficulty in establishing that it was 'unjust' within the meaning of the Act.

***WEST V. AGC (ADVANCES) LTD* (1985) 5 NSWLR 610**

Against the advice of her accountant son and a barrister friend, West, a woman with limited business experience, gave a mortgage over her house to secure a loan from AGC, a finance company. The loan was for a business which employed her husband and which was having financial problems, and to pay out her existing home loan, which was in arrears. The business eventually failed and other guarantors of the loan had been made bankrupt, so AGC sought repayment of the loan from West through enforcement of the mortgage over the house.

ISSUE: How important was the obtaining of advice from her accountant son and a barrister friend?

DECISION: The New South Wales Court of Appeal held that in the circumstances the mortgage was not 'unjust' because she had entered into the agreement against the advice of her accountant son and her barrister friend.

COMMENT: The fact that a contract is unfair does not necessarily mean that it should be struck down under the Act. What is important is whether the contract is the product of unfair conduct by one of the parties in terms of what has been imposed or the means by which the contract was obtained.

Not all contracts are caught by the Act. The Crown and public corporations cannot seek relief (ss. 4 and 6), while contracts entered into for the purpose of trade, business or profession, other than a farming undertaking, and contracts of service under an award or agreement, are excluded (ss. 6(2) and 21) in addition to the *Contracts Review Act*, Part 9, s. 106 of the *Industrial Relations Act 1996* (NSW) gives the New South Wales Industrial Court the authority to alter or declare void any contract of employment that is 'unfair, harsh or unconscionable'.

Doing business

Steps to avoid claims of unconscionable conduct

For businesses to reduce problems of unconscionability arising in equity or statute law, they should ensure:

- there is equality of bargaining power;
- there is an opportunity to negotiate;
- that if one of the parties is at a 'special disadvantage', e.g., because of health, age, mental capacity, education, literacy, economic circumstances, they have time to consider the contract;
- independent legal advice is available if one of the parties is at a 'special disadvantage';
- the language of the agreement is in 'plain English' (easy to understand);
- pamphlets are produced in several languages explaining the contract; and
- normal commercial practice has been followed. ■

WEB RESOURCE

Australian Law Online: A useful site for finding current legal news in Australia on a wide range of topics including changes to contract law:
http://www.law.gov.au

REVIEW QUESTIONS

16.1 Explain the effect of the decision of the High Court in *David Securities Pty Ltd v. Commonwealth Bank of Australia* (1994) 175 CLR 353 on mistake.

16.2 The plaintiffs in London received an order from the Egyptian agent for 'Moroccan horsebeans described here as feveroles'. Not knowing what the term meant, the plaintiffs asked the defendants, who replied that feveroles were the same as horsebeans, which they were in a position to supply. The plaintiffs then ordered a quantity of horsebeans from the defendants and the goods so described in the written sale document that was drawn up were delivered to the plaintiffs, who in turn shipped them to Egypt. When they reached Egypt, the buyers refused to accept them since they were not feveroles.

Had the plaintiffs any cause of action against the defendants?

16.3 Ai Hong, a Chinese, had a very poor understanding of English. When Feng approached him with a document for his signature, Ai Hong was under the honest and mistaken belief that what he was to sign was only a letter of introduction to his agent. What he in fact signed was a lease of his shop premises to Feng; something which at no time did he intend or want to do. Feng is now suing for specific performance and damages for breach of contract.

Advise Ai Hong.

16.4 Indicate whether each of the following statements is true or false:

	TRUE	FALSE
▪ Only mistakes of law can render a contract void	☐	☐
▪ Where the parties misunderstand each other and are at cross-purposes, the contract may be void on the grounds of common mistake	☐	☐
▪ Where one of the parties is mistaken, and the other knows or ought to be, aware of this, the contract may be void on the grounds of unilateral mistake	☐	☐

- A common mistake must involve the existence or identity of the contract's subject matter ☐ ☐
- Where mutual mistake is pleaded, the courts apply an objective standard of the reasonable person ☐ ☐
- When pleading unilateral mistake, the presumption is that a contract was concluded and the onus is on the plaintiff to rebut this presumption ☐ ☐
- The carelessness of the signer in signing without reading the document prevents them from raising the defence of *non est factum* ☐ ☐
- When raising the plea of *non est factum*, the onus of proof lies on the person raising the plea ☐ ☐
- A claim in misrepresentation allows a plaintiff the right to rescind ☐ ☐
- A representation must be a statement of fact ☐ ☐
- Silence or nondisclosure by one of the parties does not normally affect the contract unless the contract is *uberrimae fidei* ☐ ☐
- Fraudulent misrepresentation is distinguished from innocent misrepresentation by the intentional deceit of the defendant ☐ ☐
- A contract induced by fraud is voidable at the option of the deceived party ☐ ☐
- Statutory modifications to law relating to misrepresentations arose because of the inadequacies of contract law ☐ ☐
- Duress involves the use of violence or threats of violence to induce a person to enter a contract ☐ ☐
- Undue influence occurs where a person uses their position of influence or power over another in order to get them to enter into a contract ☐ ☐
- Where no legally recognised special relationship exists between the parties, there is still a presumption of undue influence ☐ ☐
- An unconscionable conduct action is concerned with how the stronger party behaves towards the person with a special disability ☐ ☐

activebook

Activebook resources include in-depth summaries with links to the relevant part of the book. For revision, add your own notes to the summaries provided by using the note-taking function.

16.5 Explain why a plaintiff would prefer to base their case in unilateral mistake rather than fraudulent misrepresentation where a third party is involved.

16.6 Mark had been accustomed to dealing with Haddock, the owner of a shop, with whom he had a running account. He sent an order to Haddock's shop for the supply of some goods. The shop had that very day been sold to the foreman, Carey, who supplied the goods. Mark used the goods, and, when he learned of the change of ownership, refused to pay for them, claiming that he had intended to deal with Haddock personally as he had a set-off (i.e. he was owed money by Haddock) with him.

Is Mark liable for the price of the goods?

16.7 Explain the difference/s between innocent and fraudulent misrepresentation.

16.8 The vendor of a farm, which had never been used as a sheep station, stated to a prospective purchaser that in his judgement the property would be capable of carrying 2000 sheep. This proved to be untrue. The purchaser now wishes to avoid the contract.

What advice would you give the purchaser?

16.9 Leek owned a Jaguar car, which he advertised for sale. He eventually sold it to Lucy, who took it away, after giving Leek a cheque for $5000. The cheque was dishonoured when presented to the bank the following morning, and Leek immediately informed the police of the fraudulent transaction. Subsequently, Lucy sold the car through a firm of car dealers to Intergalactic Finance, who had no notice that Lucy had acquired the car fraudulently. You subsequently bought the car in good faith and without notice of the defect in title.

Do you have good title to it?

16.10 What does a plaintiff need to establish in order to succeed in an action involving a negligent misrepresentation? Discuss.

16.11 List three sections of the *Trade Practices Act 1974* (Cth) which deal with misrepresentations and misstatements.

16.12 Explain what is meant by the term 'duress' and distinguish it from undue influence.

16.13 Cases of undue influence fall into two classes. Briefly describe the main features of each class and give examples.

16.14 Explain how undue influence differs from unconscionable conduct.

16.15 Buttress gave a block of land that he owned to Johnson, unaware that he was giving it away forever. Buttress was illiterate, had only limited business experience and was of low intelligence. Johnson had been a close friend of the family for many years and Buttress had relied on him for advice, comfort and friendship.

When Buttress learned that he had given the land away forever, he tried to recover it. Do you think that he would be successful? Explain your answer.

16.16 In *Commercial Bank of Australia v. Amadio*, the High Court held that it was unconscionable for the bank to rely on the mortgage/guarantee. Explain what factors the court relied on to arrive at its decision.

CRITICAL THINKING

16.1 Have the statutory modifications to the common law in relation to consent in fact effectively replaced the common law? Discuss.

16.2 What has been the impact, if any, of s. 51AC of Part IVA of the *Trade Practices Act 1974* (Cth) in business transactions? Discuss.

CHAPTER

Step 6: Legality of Object & Step 7: Form

CHAPTER CONTENTS

CHAPTER OBJECTIVES

On completion of this chapter, you should be able to:

- distinguish between those contracts that are illegal and those that are void
- outline the ways in which a contract may be illegal under statute law
- discuss the validity of contracts established for illegal purposes in common law
- discuss the effect of a contract in restraint of trade and the circumstances where it will be legally enforceable
- identify those contracts which by statute must be evidenced in writing or wholly in writing.

activebook

This icon is used throughout the following chapter to remind you to visit the *Business Law* online activebook for additional exercises, links to legal websites, and feedback. For a detailed explanation of what is in the activebook please refer to the inside cover of this textbook. The activebook is available through OneKey.

Where do I start?
Learning path: Use the activebook to complete a pre-chapter warm-up exercise.

There are many definitions of legal terms to assist with your understanding of the material.

KEY TERMS

An understanding of the following terms will help you to better understand the material in this chapter:

- **clause:** a term in a contract
- **form:** in the sense that it is used in contract law, those statutory procedural requirements that need to be satisfied for some contracts to be enforceable
- **restraint of trade:** an agreement in which a party agrees to restrict or restrain their activities in the future to carry on their trade, profession or business with other persons who are not a party to the contract
- **void:** of no legal effect
- **voidable:** an agreement which may be affirmed or rejected at the option of one of the parties.

what if . . .

Since you left school you have worked in the courier industry and you know nothing else. You eventually established a courier business in Sydney that was very successful but a year ago, due to ill health, you were forced to sell it. The prospective buyer, who was aware of the reasons why you wanted to sell, wanted you to agree not to operate a similar business in Sydney for a period of three years. As you think that your health problems will prevent you from returning to work in any type of business and as the price that the purchaser is willing to pay is more than you thought the business was worth, and not wanting to risk the loss of the sale, you agree. A year later you have overcome your health problems and you are considering either establishing a new courier business or buying an existing one in Sydney. The purchaser of your old business has heard about your plans and threatened to take you to court for breach of contract if you go ahead and establish or purchase a new courier business. Notwithstanding that you had agreed to the restraint, should you be bound by such an agreement?

The sixth question (Step 6) to consider is: 'Is the purpose of the contract legal?' Unless evidence to the contrary can be shown, the courts presume that a contract is legal. That is, it is not against either public policy or the law.

If it can be shown that the intention of the parties in entering into a contract is to promote something illegal or contrary to public policy, or if the consideration for a promise (or even the promise itself) should involve doing something illegal or contrary to public policy, either by statute or at common law, then the contract will be either void or illegal.

> This chapter considers the legal position of the parties where the contract is illegal or void by statute, and illegal or void at common law. Because of the importance of restraint of trade to business, this is discussed in some detail. The chapter looks finally, albeit briefly, at the question of 'form,' i.e. are there any statutory procedural requirements that must be satisfied?

STEP 6—IS THE CONTRACT LEGAL?

The distinction between the different categories of contract is important, because the consequences that flow from each are quite different. Contracts can be illegal or void at both statute and common law (see Figure 17.1).

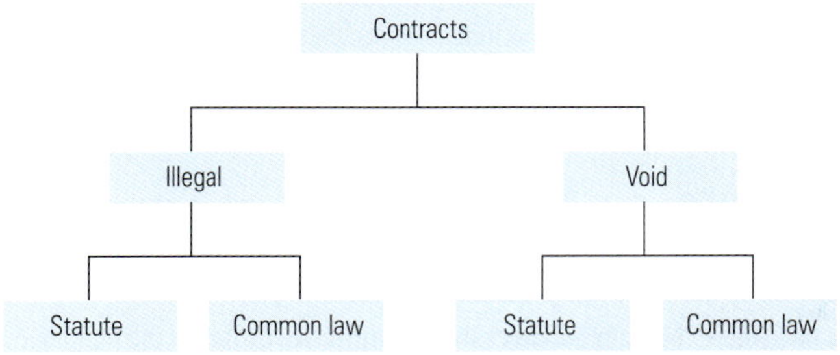

FIGURE 17.1 *Categories of contracts*

VOID AND ILLEGAL CONTRACTS DISTINGUISHED

Void contracts

An agreement rendered void at common law by statute, for example, a term in a contract that attempts to exclude the implied terms of the *Trade Practices Act 1974* (Cth), is void under s. 68 and will not be enforced by the courts. Any money paid or property transferred under such an agreement may be irrecoverable, though the court will do its best, taking into account all the circumstances, to restore the parties to their former positions where permitted.

Illegal contracts

Illegal as formed

A 'contract' deemed illegal when it is formed is **totally void**. Neither party has any rights or remedies under the transaction. However, because illegal contracts can carry penalties for violation, the consequences for the parties can be far more serious.

Any monies paid or property transferred under such a contract are generally irrecoverable, unless the complaining party can establish their case without disclosing the illegality. Where both parties are involved in the illegal purpose, the law takes the view that the defendant is in the stronger position.

Where a contract subsequently becomes illegal

Where a contract is not illegal at its creation, but subsequently becomes so, perhaps because of a statutory requirement or through the manner of its performance, no remedies are available to the guilty party. The innocent party is generally unaffected and can enforce their rights under the contract.

CONTRACTS AFFECTED BY STATUTE

Extent of invalidity

To determine extent of invalidity, look at the statute's terms

The extent to which Parliament may wish to ensure that neither party has any rights or remedies at all under the transaction, or go further and impose penalties for such an agreement, will depend on the construction of the statute's terms in each particular case.

Contracts void by statute

While many statutes declare the whole agreement null and void—for example, gaming or wagering contracts—there are also a lot of statutes which declare that only part of the agreement is void, and the remainder valid. For example, hire purchase legislation of all states declares void any attempt by an owner or retailer to limit their responsibility for the quality of their goods but does not make the contract void. As well, a term in a contract that attempts to exclude the implied terms of the *Trade Practices Act 1974* (Cth) is void (s. 68).

Subsequent transactions *may* be rendered void

Subsequent transactions directly related to the contract rendered void by statute, but not illegal, may themselves be rendered void if that is the intention of the statute. If the subsequent transaction is to get its validity from the earlier contract, which is now rendered void by statute, then that transaction will fail because the consideration for the later contract is the validity of the earlier one. As this no longer exists, there is a total failure of consideration.

If the contract is rendered void, but **not** illegal, any money paid under the contract is irrecoverable, irrespective of whether the party who has paid it can prove a total failure of consideration or not.

Contracts illegal by statute

There are a number of ways in which a contract may be affected by a statutory provision:

- The contract may be to do something which a **statute forbids**.
- The contract may be one where the statute **expressly or impliedly** prohibits the making of the agreement itself or the performance of the contract.

RE MAHMOUD V. ISPAHANI **[1921] 2 KB 716**

An Order made under the Defence of the Realm Regulations provided that no one could buy, sell or otherwise deal in linseed oil without being licensed. The defendant falsely told the plaintiff that he had the necessary licence, and then entered into an agreement with him for the supply of linseed oil. The defendant subsequently refused to take delivery and was sued by the plaintiff for non-acceptance.

ISSUE: Was the purpose of the statute to prohibit the making of the contract itself, thus making it unenforceable, or did the statute require the contract to be performed in a certain way?

DECISION: Because the contract was with an unlicensed purchaser, and this was expressly prohibited under the statute, the contract was illegal as formed, and thus void.

A statute may require that the contract must be performed in a certain way and will impose a penalty if it isn't. Failure to perform the contract in the prescribed manner may result in the contract being illegal as performed.

ANDERSON LTD V. DANIEL **[1924] 1 KB 138**

A statute required that any seller of artificial fertiliser had to provide the purchaser with an invoice stating the percentages of certain chemicals contained in fertiliser sold. A sale was made by the plaintiffs with an invoice which did not comply with the statutory requirements. The purchaser refused to pay, arguing that the contract was illegal and the debt was therefore unenforceable.

ISSUE: What was the reason behind the imposition of a fine? Was it for the protection of the public?

DECISION: The plaintiffs could not recover the contract price as the effect of the non-compliance was to render the contract illegal as performed. The purpose of the fine was to protect the public.

COMMENT: It should be noted in this case that the party seeking to enforce the contract was the party who was in breach of the statute. If it was an innocent party trying to enforce the contract, the court may be prepared to enforce it.

Yet in other cases, the statute may be regarded as primarily intended to raise revenue, imposing a fine upon the offending party, but not making the contract void:

- The contract, though lawful on its face, may be made in order to effect a purpose which a statute renders unlawful.
- The contract, although lawful according to its own terms, may be performed in a manner which a statute prohibits.

***ST JOHN SHIPPING CORPORATION V. JOSEPH RANK LTD* [1957] 1 QB 267**

The defendants chartered the plaintiff's ship. During the course of the voyage the ship had to put into port to load more fuel. As a result the ship was overloaded contrary to the *Merchant Shipping Act 1932*. When the ship arrived in England, the Master was successfully prosecuted for the offence. The defendants refused to pay part of the freight costs on the grounds that the plaintiffs had performed the contract in an illegal manner.

ISSUE: Was the Act intended to invalidate contracts or impose a penalty?

DECISION: The illegal loading was incidental to, rather than central to, the performance of the contract. Therefore the contract was valid as performed.

COMMENT: Of course, if both parties had intended to overload the ship, then the question of illegality would have been central to the contract and the defendants would not have had to pay their freight costs.

! CAUTION NOTE

Whether a statutory illegality makes a contract void depends on whether the statute makes the contract 'illegal as formed', and therefore unenforceable, or 'illegal as performed', so amounts owing may be enforceable and the guilty party may face a penalty.

THE COMMON LAW POSITION

Contracts illegal at common law

IN BRIEF

Contracts illegal at common law

The main classes of contracts illegal at common law are:

- contracts to commit a crime, tort or fraud against a third party;
- contracts that promote sexual immorality or prejudice the status of marriage;
- contracts which are to the prejudice of public safety or good relations with foreign countries;
- contracts which are prejudicial to, or delay, the administration of justice;
- contracts which promote public corruption;
- contracts which defraud the state of revenue; and
- contracts that involve a breach of duty.

Contract illegal at common law—contrary to public interest

This group of contracts are seen as violating the social or moral attitudes of the community and are prohibited as being contrary to 'public policy'. They often have penalties attached to them.

The main classes of illegal contract are:

Contracts to commit a crime, a tort or a fraud against a third party

The courts will not enforce a contract which has as its object the breaking of the law.

Contracts that are sexually immoral

Sexual morality may change over the course of time, as can be seen in the modern day live-in partner arrangement and community recognition of the rights of gay couples.

Contracts which are to the prejudice of public safety or of good relations with friendly countries

There are two types of agreement here—an agreement with an enemy alien and an agreement which could endanger friendly relations existing between two countries. In both cases, an agreement would be regarded as illegal.

Contracts prejudicial to the administration of justice

Any attempt to affect the administration of justice is illegal and void.

***PUBLIC SERVICE EMPLOYEES CREDIT UNION CO-OPERATIVE LTD V. CAMPION* (1984) 56 ACTR 39**

The defendant guaranteed repayment of a loan to his son from the plaintiff credit union if they would not report his son to the police for misappropriation of money from the credit union.

ISSUE: Was the guarantee void for illegality?

DECISION: The agreement was void for illegality as neither party could agree to prevent prosecution for an indictable offence.

COMMENT: If a person has a choice between a civil and a criminal remedy—for example, in a case of assault and battery—a compromise is both lawful and enforceable.

Contracts which tend to promote corruption in public life

'Lobbying' has to be distinguished from the type of agreement that involves the use of influence or pressure, unconnected with the merits of the claim, to an objective.

***PARKINSON V. COLLEGE OF AMBULANCE LTD* [1925] 2 KB 1**

The plaintiff 'donated' a substantial sum of money to the defendant organisation's funds in reliance of a promise that he would get a knighthood. The knighthood was not forthcoming, and so the plaintiff sued for the return of his money.

ISSUE: Was the promise of money in return for a knighthood against public policy and therefore illegal?

DECISION: The agreement was illegal. The parties were left in the same position as they were when the action was brought as they were both equally at fault and so Parkinson did not recover his 'donation'.

Contracts to defraud public authorities of revenue

A clear infringement of public policy can be found in agreements that intend to defraud the revenue of a country, whether at national, state or local level.

Contracts that involve a breach of duty

Contracts involving a breach of duty by an employee or agent are illegal.

Contracts void at common law

IN BRIEF

Contracts void at common law

Three types of contract are void, but not illegal, at common law:

- contracts which attempt to oust the jurisdiction of the courts;
- contracts prejudicial to the status of marriage; and
- contracts in restraint of trade.

Contracts void at common law—unenforceable as a matter of public policy

Three types of contract, or perhaps more accurately, clauses in two of the three types of contract above, are treated by the courts as void, but not illegal, at common law:

Clauses in contracts which attempt to oust the jurisdiction of the courts

If the parties try to create a legally binding contract without resorting to the courts, in the event of a dispute, the contract will be void. An arbitration agreement will be valid only if it is to operate as a condition preceding any recourse to the courts. This type of clause is common in commercial transactions.

Problems can arise where courts are asked to distinguish between contracts which attempt to oust the jurisdiction of the courts and contracts which are binding in honour only. In the latter, the parties expressly declare that they do not intend to create legal relations, for example in *Jones v. Vernon's Pools Ltd* (see p. 261).

Contracts prejudicial to the status of marriage

Contracts in restraint of marriage, marriage brokerage contracts and contracts made between married people providing for future separation are all void. On the other hand, contracts which restrict a person from marrying someone of a particular class, religion or nationality could all be valid.

Contracts in restraint of trade

It is more accurate to speak of a clause in a contract as being void than the contract as a whole. It is a general principle of common law, supported by statute, that an individual should be given a reasonable degree of freedom to engage in trade, undertake employment, or buy and sell goods, without undue restrictions. Anything contrary to this principle is regarded as contrary to public policy and in restraint of trade.

Restraint of trade

Individuals should be allowed a reasonable degree of freedom with regard to carrying on their trade, business or profession. This is in the interests of the public as well as the parties. The common law view of clauses in restraint of trade is that they tend to:

- injure the person involved by reducing their means of earning a livelihood;
- deprive the public of the services of persons in the capacities in which they may be most useful to the community as well as to themselves;
- discourage industry and enterprise and reduce the products of ingenuity and skill; and
- restrict competition.

activebook

To help you to remember and understand the topics covered so far, and for links to legal websites, refer to your online activebook. Model answers provide feedback to problems and exercises.

On the other hand, a person should be bound by their contracts. However, the fact remains that even today many contracts contain restrictive clauses. For example, in contracts of employment there is quite often a clause providing that upon termination of employment, the employee will not compete against the employer for a certain period. In the sale of a business, to protect the purchaser's goodwill, there will usually be a clause prohibiting the vendor from setting up a similar business within a reasonable distance and for a reasonable time near the purchaser. There is then a conflict between two principles. It wasn't until *Nordenfelt*'s case that the extent and duration of the restraint of trade was first considered to be valid.

NORDENFELT V. MAXIM NORDENFELT GUNS AND AMMUNITION COMPANY LTD [1894] AC 535

Nordenfelt sold his munitions manufacturing business which did business worldwide. He entered into a contract not to engage in the manufacture of guns, except for the company, anywhere in the world for the next 25 years. Two years later the company was amalgamated with another company, and the original contract in restraint of trade was expanded so that it read:

> '. . . or in any business competing or liable to compete in any way with that for the time being carried on by the company.'

Nordenfelt subsequently opened a new munitions manufacturing business in competition against the company he had sold his business to and they sought to enforce the restraint clauses.

ISSUE: Were the clauses reasonable or a restraint of trade and void?

DECISION: If the restraint was to be valid, it had to be reasonable in the interests of the parties and the interests of the public. The first clause was reasonable as it enabled the company to protect its interests. The second clause, while it was unrestricted as to space, was not unrestricted with regard to the nature of the business or the limited number of customers. It was also reasonable in the interests of the parties and not against the public interest.

CASE REFLECTION: Would the amount of consideration given for the restraint of trade have a bearing on the reasonableness of the extent and/or duration of the restraint of trade?

At common law, restraint clauses are *prima facie* void

The position at common law today is that while all clauses in restraint of trade are *prima facie* void (as they are contrary to public policy), if the person relying on the clause can show that the restraint is reasonable, the presumption of invalidity can be rebutted. They may also be affected by Part IV of the *Trade Practices Act 1974* (Cth) which deals with restrictive trade practices. If a clause is considered to amount to a restraint of trade, the court will try and delete the void term if the contract can still take effect with that term deleted.

IN BRIEF

Factors which determine whether a restraint is reasonable

Whether a restraint is **reasonable** in the interests of the **parties** and the **public** or not is determined at the date of the agreement after consideration of the following factors:

- the geographic extent of the restraint;
- the time period involved; and
- the type of business and the activity being restrained.

Where the sale of a business is concerned, note carefully the type of business, as the size of the area and the length of time will vary with the type of business.

Clauses in restraint of trade have been applied in the situations shown in Figure 17.2.

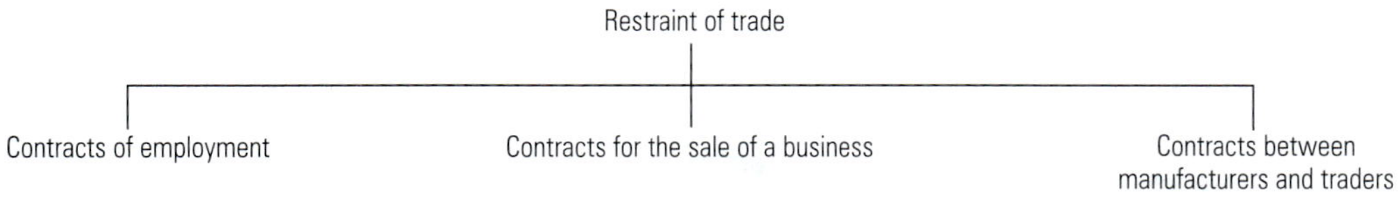

FIGURE 17.2 *Main categories of restraint of trade*

Restraint clauses in contracts of employment

Doing business

Making an employer–employee restraint valid

Because the parties in an employer–employee relationship are (usually) in an unequal bargaining position, restraint clauses in employee contracts will be struck down by the courts unless they:

- only protect intellectual property rights (such as trade secrets), customer connections or prevent an employee from working for a competitor during their current employment; and
- are of reasonable length in time. This is a question of fact in each case and will be determined by what is being protected; and
- are of reasonable geographical width. Again, this is a question of fact in each case and will be determined by what is being protected.

Care must be used or the Commonwealth or state/territory industrial relations legislation, or the *Contracts Review Act 1980* (NSW) if the applicant is in New South Wales, could be used to strike the clause down. ■

Employees often have access to confidential information, business contacts, trade secrets and the like. As a result, it is not unusual for employers to try to incorporate a restraint of trade clause (often called a covenant) into the contract of employment of their employee. Such a clause attempts to restrict the rights of these employees if they should ever work for a rival employer.

Restraint clauses cover confidential information and trade secrets

Restraint of trade clauses usually take two forms:

- restraints on confidential information or trade secrets learnt during employment; and
- protection of trade connections, such as customer lists.

These restraints form part of the employee's duty to the employer and generally do not appear expressly in the contract of employment between them.

In order for such a clause to be valid, it must be shown that the restraint is reasonable and there is some **proprietary interest** owned by the employer that requires protection.

The restraint *must* be reasonable and there *must* be a protectable interest

***FORSTER & SONS LTD V. SUGGETT* (1918) 35 TLR 87**

Suggett was employed as the works manager of a firm engaged in glass and glass bottle manufacturing. He was instructed in certain confidential techniques of glassmaking and he agreed that during the five years following the termination of his employment he would not engage in glass bottle manufacturing, or any other business connected with glassmaking, anywhere in the United Kingdom.

ISSUE: Is the restraint reasonable in the circumstances? Is there a proprietary interest that requires protection?

DECISION: In these circumstances the restraint was reasonable. The employer was entitled to protect and safeguard the confidential techniques he had developed. He could therefore legally restrain a former employee from using this information while employed by a rival firm.

Even then, it is still very difficult to convince the courts that the restriction placed on the employee by the employer is reasonable and not in restraint of trade. The reason for the court's attitude is that frequently there is an **inequality in the bargaining power between the employer and the employee**, with the employer dictating the terms on which the employee may accept the position. As a result, the courts will look at the relative bargaining power of the parties.

If the clause is merely an attempt to limit competition, the courts will usually find little difficulty in striking it down.

ATWOOD V. LAMONT [1920] 3 KB 571

Atwood carried on business in Melbourne as a tailor. He entered into a contract of employment with Lamont, which contained a clause providing that in the event of termination of the contract, Lamont would not carry on business as a tailor at any place within a 15 km radius of Melbourne. Lamont subsequently set up business in Geelong, outside the 15 km radius, but he had clients in Melbourne.

ISSUE: Was the geographic extent of the clause reasonable or merely an attempt to restrict competition?

DECISION: The clause was invalid because it was directed only to the prevention of competition.

The principles governing the operation of the restraint of trade doctrine have also been applied in the sporting world to the employment of sportspersons.

BUCKLEY V. TUTTY (1971) 125 CLR 353

Tutty had contracted to play football for the Balmain Rugby League Football Club. The terms of his contract with the club incorporated 'all the Rules, Regulations and By-laws of the NSW Rugby League'. This meant that a player could not transfer to any other club except with the consent of the Balmain Football Club. In the case of Tutty it refused to give its consent. In addition, the club could decide on the amount of transfer fee it wanted for a player that went on a transfer list.

ISSUE: Were the rules relating to the retention and transfer of players in restraint of trade? Did they satisfy the *Nordenfelt* criteria?

DECISION: The High Court found that the rules amounted to a restraint of trade because they prevented a player from transferring to another club, even after he had ceased to play for the club that retained him, and the transfer system had no rules which could impede a player from obtaining new employment.

Similar outcomes were achieved in *Hughes v. Western Australian Cricket Association (Inc.)* [1986] ATPR ¶40–736 and *Adamson v. New South Wales Rugby League Ltd* (1991) 31 FCR 242, although a challenge to a restraint in a contract of employment failed in *Buckenara v. Hawthorn Football Club Ltd* [1988] VR 39 because the duration of the restraint was found to last no longer than the contract.

Primary duty of employee is to employer during the time of employment

A restraint clause in a contract of employment which will be held to be valid in most instances is one which goes to the employee's present employment and provides that the employee shall not compete directly or indirectly while still in the service of that employer. The **primary duty of an employee is to the employer**. This situation must be distinguished from situations that relate to the position of employees after leaving their present employment. The question that has to be considered is whether a former employee should continue to owe a contractual duty to their former employer.

The case where the employee may want to be relieved from their contractual obligations but is prevented by a restraint clause is still subject to the tests discussed above. That is, for the clause to be valid it should be reasonable or fair, taking into account the interests of both parties.

***A. SCHROEDER MUSIC PUBLISHING CO. LTD V. MACAULEY* [1974] 1 WLR 1308**

Macauley, a 21-year-old unknown songwriter, entered into a five-year exclusive agreement with Schroeder Music Publishing Co. with an automatic option to extend, subject to the company's right to determine the agreement on a month's notice. Macauley had no similar right to terminate. The company held world copyright on all songs, paid minimal royalties and was under no obligation to promote or publish Macauley's work.

ISSUE: Had the publishing company used its superior bargaining position to gain an unfair advantage, such that there was not a genuine agreement between the parties?

DECISION: The contract was contrary to public policy because it was an unreasonable restraint of trade. The publishing company had used its superior bargaining power and as a result the bargain between the parties was unconscionable or not fair.

CASE REFLECTION: Could the clause still have been unreasonable if the company had published and actively promoted Macauley's work?

The options available to a person seeking relief under a contract of employment are not restricted to seeking relief under the common law. Statutory relief is available in the form of Part IVA (ss. 51AA, 51AB and 51AC) of the *Trade Practices Act 1974* (Cth) dealing with unconscionable conduct, in New South Wales in the *Contracts Review Act 1980* and the *Restraints of Trade Act 1976* and the Commonwealth, state and territory industrial relations legislation.

Restraints imposed on the vendor of a business

Sale of business—assumes parties in equal bargaining positions

In the sale of a business, where there is an element of goodwill, it is reasonable to expect that the purchaser will wish to stop the seller from opening a similar business to the one just sold, within a certain area and time period. Here the parties are dealing on a **'more' equal basis**, and as a result, the courts are generally prepared to uphold the validity of such clauses.

Each case has to be treated on its own merits and it will be a **question of fact as to whether the restraint is reasonable** in its protection of the purchaser's interest and not unreasonable in preventing the vendor from carrying on normal business activities.

***AMOCO AUSTRALIA PTY LTD V. ROCCA BROTHERS MOTOR ENGINEERING CO. PTY LTD* [1973] 1 ALR 385**

The Rocca Brothers owned some land in South Australia, and wished to build a service station on it. The family company leased its land to Amoco and subleased it back. A term in the sublease stated that they agreed only to sell Amoco products from that site for a period of 15 years, and that they would buy a minimum amount of petrol from Amoco each month during that period.

ISSUE: Was the length of time that they would buy Amoco products exclusively reasonable, given that nothing was said about profitability in the contract?

DECISION: The High Court held that the agreement went beyond what was reasonable to protect Amoco's interest, for it obliged the family company to carry on business on the site for a period of 15 years, notwithstanding that the business may lose its profitability.

It should be kept in mind that **the size of the area and the length of time will vary with the type of business**. Thus, a restraint imposed on the vendor of a milk bar will not be the same as the restraint imposed on the vendor of a BMW car dealership, although in both cases it still must be reasonable.

A restriction should not demand too much. Where a restrictive clause is held to be too wide, the likely outcome is that the clause will be void. The courts are very reluctant to narrow it to a reasonable scope.

While the courts will neither redraft nor narrow the operation of a restriction that is unreasonable, they will sever an unreasonable restriction from one that is reasonable. However, they must be two separate restrictions and the severed restriction must not affect the meaning of the reasonable restriction.

Trading agreements

It is not unusual to find a manufacturer or trader who will want to exclude competition from a market segment that they operate in order to maximise their profits. This may take the form of, for example, exclusive selling agreements or exclusive purchasing agreements. At common law the validity of such agreements will depend upon whether the agreement is a reasonable restraint first between the parties themselves, and, secondly, the public. However, finding that such an agreement is reasonable at common law does not automatically mean that the agreement will have force of law because such agreements are also subject to the provisions of Part IV of *Trade Practices Act 1974* (Cth), and in New South Wales the *Restraints of Trade Act 1976*, so it might still fail on grounds of public policy.

! CAUTION NOTE

Restraint must be reasonable in area and time, but note that size of area and length of time will vary with the type of business.

In New South Wales, the *Restraints of Trade Act 1976* has attempted to assist the courts in the severance of unreasonable restraints. The Act provides that a restraint of trade is valid only to the extent to which it is not contrary to public policy, whether it is expressed in severable terms or not: s. 4(1). Section 4(3) allows the court to order that a restraint clause be valid or invalid as the court thinks fit, providing it with the opportunity to modify what might otherwise be an unreasonable clause as it sees fit.

Many restraints of trade actions involving businesses rely on Part IV of the *Trade Practices Act 1974* (Cth), rather than the common law. The Act prohibits anti-competitive practices and the Act gives the court greater powers than are available under the common law (see Chapter 30).

STEP 7—FORM

The last question that needs to be considered (Step 7) is that of 'form'. 'Are there any statutory procedural requirements that need to be satisfied?' We saw in Chapter 11 that certain simple contracts were required by statute to be evidenced or wholly in writing, to be enforceable. However, to give continuity to the process of determining whether a valid simple contract exists or not, the question of form, that is, as Step 7, is raised here for convenience, though it is dealt with in more detail in Chapter 11 (pp. 249–250).

Form—are there any statutory requirements that need to be satisfied?

It should be kept in mind that the great majority of simple contracts that are entered into will not be subject to any statutory requirements to make them enforceable. They may be reduced to writing, but this will be done for the commercial convenience of the parties to try to introduce some certainty into the arrangements between them.

> **!** CAUTION NOTE
>
> *Always consider whether there are any statutory requirements that must be satisfied for the contract to be enforceable, e.g., does it have to be wholly in writing or evidenced in writing?*

? REVIEW QUESTIONS

17.1 Discuss the differences, if any, that exist between contracts void by statute and contracts illegal by statute.

17.2 John owns a pleasure boat which he uses to give paid trips out to the islands. Bill goes out on the boat to the islands, but upon his return refuses to pay, arguing that John has committed the following statutory breaches:

i The boat was licensed to carry 10 people, but 20 had gone on the trip. John was liable to pay a maximum $1000 fine if successfully prosecuted.

ii John had no Master's Certificate. He was liable to pay a maximum $500 fine.

iii John delivered cattle to a neighbouring island but the boat was only licensed to carry people.

Discuss each ground separately. What principles do these cases suggest you look at when examining the statute?

17.3 Brass hired a roulette table with all the ancillary equipment needed to play roulette from ACME HIRE. When they entered into the contract, neither was aware of the provisions of the *Gaming and Betting Act* that made the game unlawful but did not prohibit it. When Brass discovered the Act, he refused to pay the hire price.

Can ACME HIRE recover the hire charges?

17.4 Boron had fallen far behind in his rent to Helium. By the time Helium brought her action against Boron for arrears of rent, she was owed over $1000. In his defence, Boron argued that the action being brought against him must fail since the rent book issued to him did not contain all the information required under landlord and tenant legislation. The Act provided for a fine of $250 in the case of default.

Advise Helium as to the correctness, or otherwise, of Boron's argument.

17.5 A debtor made a composition with his creditors to pay them 10 cents in the dollar. He entered into a separate and secret contract with one of his creditors to pay them in full.

Is the separate contract to pay one creditor in full valid? Discuss.

> **activebook**
>
> Activebook resources include in-depth summaries with links to the relevant part of the book. For revision, add your own notes to the summaries provided by using the note-taking function.

17.6 Snell let a room to Naomi. Unknown to Snell, Naomi was a prostitute. When she fell behind in her rent, Snell was forced to sue for the arrears and Naomi raised the defence of illegality.

Can Snell recover the arrears?

17.7 Sam had been employed by a catering firm as an accountant. He was to receive a starting salary of $500 per week and an allowance of $150 per week for expenses. Both parties were aware that Sam's expenses were grossly overstated and would never exceed $50 per week, but the object was to minimise the amount of income tax that he would have to pay. Eventually Sam was summarily dismissed and he accordingly brought an action against his employer for two weeks' wages claimed to be in lieu of notice—$1000 but not the allowance.

Advise the employer as to whether he should pay the claim or not.

17.8 Explain why a restraint clause in a contract of employment is most likely to be struck down by the courts. In what circumstances will a restraint clause be likely to be considered valid in a contract of employment?

17.9 Samson was employed as a milkman by the Delilah Dairy. Part of Samson's contract of employment contained the following clause:

> The employee expressly agrees not at any time during one year after the Termination of his employment . . . either on his own account or as a representative or agent of any person or company, to serve or sell milk or dairy produce to . . . any person or company who at any time during the last two years of his employment shall have been a customer of the employer and served by the employee in the course of his employment.

Is the restraint between Samson and the Delilah Dairy valid?

17.10 Roberta was employed as a works manager with Littlewoods Recycling Works in Victoria. Her contract of employment contained a restraint of trade clause whereby she agreed that in the event of leaving Littlewoods she would not work in the recycling industry in either Victoria or New South Wales for five years from the time of leaving their employ.

Roberta has been approached by a rival firm in New South Wales who have offered to double her existing salary if she will go and work for them.

Roberta wishes to know whether the restraint clause in her contract of employment is valid. What advice would you give her?

17.11 Indicate whether each of the following statements is true or false:

	TRUE	FALSE
▪ An agreement rendered void by statute or common law is always void *ab initio*	☐	☐
▪ An agreement deemed illegal at its inception is totally void	☐	☐
▪ Where the purpose of the statute is to protect the public, and the statute expressly or impliedly prohibits the making of the agreement itself, the contract will be void	☐	☐
▪ Contracts which are prejudicial to the administration of justice are illegal at common law and thus void	☐	☐
▪ Contracts which are binding in honour only but attempt to oust the jurisdiction of the courts are valid	☐	☐
▪ Contracts in restraint of trade are regarded as *prima facie* void	☐	☐
▪ An employer can enforce a restraint of trade clause, in a contract of employment with an employee, which is not an attempt to limit competition	☐	☐
▪ The reason that restraints of trade in a sale of business are generally held to be valid is because the parties are dealing on a more equal basis	☐	☐
▪ If a restraint of trade clause in a contract of employment is harsh or unfair, the court may hold there was no genuine agreement between the parties and strike it down	☐	☐
▪ Many restraint of trade actions rely on Part IV of the *Trade Practices Act 1974* (Cth) because the courts have greater powers to vary or rectify a contract than under common law	☐	☐

17.12 Do the courts apply the same criteria in assessing whether a restraint clause in a contract of employment is valid as they do in a contract involving the sale of a business? Explain your reasoning.

17.13 Peter and Lee were dealers in imitation jewellery located near each other in Adelaide. Lee sold her business to Peter and agreed that she would not carry on nor be engaged in the sale, importation or manufacture of real or imitation jewellery anywhere in Australia for a period of two years. One year after selling the business Lee established a retail jewellery business in Cairns.

Can Peter enforce the covenant against Lee? Explain your reasoning.

CRITICAL THINKING

17.1 Explain what is meant by the expression 'gaming and wagering contracts'. Why should Parliament pass legislation to make them null and void? Can you name an exception to a gaming and wagering contract that would not be null and void?

17.2 In what ways has the law relating to restraint of trade at common law been affected by the provisions of the *Trade Practices Act 1974* (Cth)?

CHAPTER 18

Construction of the Contract

CHAPTER CONTENTS

activebook

This icon is used throughout the following chapter to remind you to visit the *Business Law* online activebook for additional exercises, links to legal websites, and feedback. For a detailed explanation of what is in the activebook please refer to the inside cover of this textbook. The activebook is available through OneKey.

Where do I start?
Learning path: Use the activebook to complete a pre-chapter warm-up exercise.

There are many definitions of legal terms to assist with your understanding of the material.

CHAPTER OBJECTIVES

On completion of this chapter, you should be able to:

- identify and explain the types of terms found in a contract
- distinguish between representations and terms
- recognise and explain the importance of collateral contracts
- distinguish between conditions and warranties
- outline when terms are implied into a contract and discuss their effects
- recognise an exclusion clause and discuss its effect on a contract.

KEY TERMS

An understanding of the following terms will help you to better understand the material in this chapter:

- **condition:** a stipulation going to the root of the contract which allows the injured party the right to rescind and/or claim damages. *See also* warranty
- **condition precedent:** delays the vesting of the right until the happening of the event
- **condition subsequent:** destroys the right upon the happening of an event
- **exclusion clause (also known as exemption or exception clauses):** a contractual term which attempts to limit or exclude the liability of persons inserting them into a contract
- **innominate term (also known as an intermediate term):** a contractual term, the remedy for the breach of which depends on the seriousness of the breach rather than upon the classification of the term as a condition or a warranty
- **parol:** oral, spoken
- **parol evidence rule:** the rule of evidence which states that additional oral evidence is not considered by the courts to either contradict, vary, add to or subtract from its terms when a contract is complete on its face
- **warranty:** a term of lesser importance to the main purpose of the contract and which, if breached, only allows the injured party to claim for damages. *See also* condition.

what if . . .

You own a business and to try to protect yourself from customers suing you, if they buy a defective product and are injured while using it, you include an exclusion clause in your contracts with them. However, when one of your customers is injured using one of your products and sues you in court, you discover that the clause that you drafted can be interpreted in a number of ways. The court decides that the exclusion clause is void and rules that you must pay damages to the customer. Is this fair considering that you drafted the clause and the meaning that the courts gave to the clause is not your meaning?

Assuming that a simple contract has been created (Steps 1 to 3 have been satisfied) and that there are no elements which affect its validity (Steps 4 to 7), it may be necessary to consider exactly what it is that the parties have agreed to include in the contract. In other words, what is the extent of the rights and obligations that the parties have entered into? The answer can only be found by deciding what are the terms of the contract (see Figure 18.1), and then what is their relative meaning and importance, but in the context of whether they have been qualified by the inclusion of an exclusion clause.

> This chapter is concerned with the content of the contract. That is, its terms, which may be express and/or implied, and whether the parties have qualified the operation of its terms by the use of an exclusion clause.

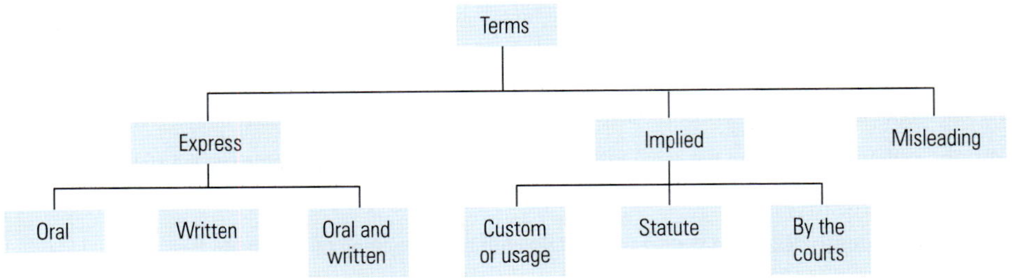

FIGURE 18.1 *Types of terms*

EXPRESS TERMS

IN BRIEF

The possibilities for a statement

In summary, the possibilities are that a statement could be:

- A **term**, in which case the statement will create contractual obligations between the parties, breach of which will result in the injured party being able to sue.
- A **collateral contract**, that is, a preliminary contract on which the main contract is entered into, breach of which will result in the injured party being able to sue.
- A **representation** which induces an offeree to enter into the contract but which is not part of the contract and so not actionable in contract law. However, if the representation is false, a remedy may lie under Part V of the *Trade Practices Act 1974* (Cth).
- A **sales puff** not intended to have any legal effect, in which case no remedy is available.

! CAUTION NOTE

Whether a statement is a representation or a term depends on the intention of the parties viewed through the eyes of a reasonable person taking into account a number of objective criteria.

Representations

Representations are not part of the contract though they may be actionable under statute law

These are statements of fact which **induce** an offeree to enter the contract but are **not part of the contract** and so are not actionable in contract law. If they are pre-contractually misleading or deceptive, then an action may lie under statute law (e.g., s. 52 of the *Trade Practices Act 1974* (Cth) or the equivalent section in the states' and territories' Fair Trading legislation), liability for negligent misrepresentation or promissory estoppel. A term, on the other hand, forms part of the contract and is legally binding.

The promissory nature of a statement and whether it is a representation or a term depends on the intention of the parties. The courts apply an objective test of a reasonable person, taking into account the conduct of the parties, and their words and behaviour to try to distinguish between the two.

Objective tests

In trying to ascertain the intentions of the parties from the particular facts before it, the courts will take into account the following matters:

- **How much time lapsed between the making of the statement and the final agreement?**
  The longer the lapse of time between the making of the statement and the final agreement, the more likely it is to be treated as an inducement and not intended to form part of the agreement.

Where an oral statement precedes a written contract, then the terms of the contract tend to be contained in the written document, and all oral statements tend to be pre-contractual.

- **Was the innocent party asked to check or verify the statement?**
  Here the statement is more likely to be an inducement (e.g., a mechanic's report on a car).
- **Was the statement made with the intention of preventing the other party from finding any defects, and did it succeed?**
  If a buyer, on the basis of the statement: 'The car is in excellent condition; you don't need to look it over', did not bother to look the car over, then the statement would most likely be an inducement or a misrepresentation.

HOPKINS V. TANQUERAY (1854) 15 CB 130

Tanqueray, the owner of a horse being inspected by Hopkins, a potential buyer, said to him that the horse was 'perfectly sound in every respect'. Hopkins did not bother to complete his inspection and bought the horse the next day at auction. Hopkins subsequently discovered that the horse was not sound and sued Tanqueray for breach of contract.

ISSUE: Was the representation by Tanqueray as to the condition of the horse a warranty?

DECISION: The statement made by the previous owner was an inducement or representation and not intended to form part of the contract.

CASE REFLECTION: Would the decision have been the same if the promise regarding the fitness of the horse had been made after the agreement but before delivery?

- **What importance did the parties attach to the statement?**
  If the parties place considerable importance on the statement, the courts will be more willing to treat it as a term and not as a mere representation. If a party does not rely on the statement, it will be a representation.

PYM V. CAMPBELL (1856) 6 E & B 370

An agreement for the sale of a patent was drawn up and signed. It was agreed at the time that the written agreement was not to be binding until the approval of a third party was obtained. The agreement of the third party was not given.

ISSUE: Was the approval of the third party necessary to make the contract effective?

DECISION: In an action on the written agreement it was established that the third party had not approved and therefore the agreement was not effective.

- **Did one of the parties have special skill or knowledge?**
  Where one of the parties has some special skill or knowledge not possessed by the other party with regard to the subject matter of the contract, then a statement is more likely to be treated as a term.

OSCAR CHESS V. WILLIAMS [1957] 1 ALL ER 325

Williams' mother had purchased a second-hand Morris Minor, believing it to be a 1948 model. In 1955 the car was traded in to a used-car dealer. The car's appearance and the papers supplied by Williams indicated it was a 1948 model. However, it was a 1939 model and the dealer sued Williams.

ISSUE: Was the statement as to age of the car a term of the contract, given that one of the parties had special knowledge or expertise as a car dealer?

DECISION: Of the three judges in the Court of Appeal, *Denning* and *Hodson* LJJ, held that the statement as to the age of the car was a mere representation which did not give rise to any liability for breach of contract. The plaintiff had special expertise as a motor vehicle dealer and should have taken steps to verify the age of the vehicle if he was in doubt about its true age. However, *Morris* LJ considered that the statement as to age was vitally important and therefore a term of the contract.

CASE REFLECTION: Would the decision have been likely to be the same if the purchaser had been an ordinary person and the seller was a car dealer?

The parol evidence rule

***Oral contract*— exactly what the parties said must be found as a matter of fact**

In the case of an **oral contract**, exactly what the parties said must be found as **a matter of fact**, and to this end the courts will admit as evidence all facts known to the parties, including both **actions and words** of the parties. Problems arise when the evidence is conflicting. Each party may have a different view of what was agreed to, and the meaning of what was said. This can raise difficult and costly problems of proof for the plaintiff.

Where the contract is completely in writing, the courts assume that all the terms agreed to by the parties are contained in the contract. However, problems may still arise in interpretation of particular terms that the court may need to resolve, for example, ambiguity.

***Written contract*— courts assume all terms are contained in the contract and are reluctant to admit further evidence**

In the case of a **written contract**, the court generally **will not admit evidence of acts or words of the parties prior to the execution** of the document if it has the effect of adding to, varying or contradicting the written agreement. This is because the courts assume that parties' intention is contained within the 'four corners' (the text) of the contract, known as the **parol evidence rule**. However, this rule is subject to a number of qualifications to try to avoid hardship or injustice. Oral evidence may be admitted:

- to prove a trade custom or usage;
- to show that the contract has not yet become effective;
- where the court is of the opinion that the written document contains only part of the agreement;

VAN DEN ESSCHERT V. CHAPPELL [1960] WAR 114

Before signing a contract for the purchase of a house, the purchaser asked the seller whether there were any white ants in the house. The seller told him there were none and the buyer immediately proceeded to sign the contract to buy the house. There was no reference in the written contract of the oral question relating to white ants. Later, the purchaser discovered that the house was riddled with white ants and sued the seller.

ISSUE: Could the buyer rely on the oral statement made by the seller immediately prior to entering into the contract that there were no white ants, even though it was not a written term in the contract?

DECISION: The Western Australian Full Court held that the specific request by the purchaser, and the seller's assurance that the house was free of white ants immediately before the purchaser signed the contract, was intended to form part of the agreement between the parties.

- to clarify any ambiguous language used in the contract; or
- where, due to a mistake of the parties, their agreement was not accurately expressed in the written contract.

Doing business

Where the agreement is written, ensure it contains all the terms

Remember that in the case of a written contract, the court generally will not admit evidence of acts or words of the parties prior to the execution of the document, if it has the effect of adding to, varying or contradicting the written agreement. While there are exceptions to this rule, to reduce exposure to litigation expenses, ensure that all the relevant terms are contained in the document and that there are no ambiguities. ■

COLLATERAL CONTRACTS

If a statement can be regarded as a collateral or a preliminary contract, so that the main contract would not have been entered into in the absence of the earlier statement, the courts may be prepared to enforce the promises made by the parties prior to the main contract.

***Collateral contract*—a preliminary contract on which the main contract is based**

DE LASSALLE V. GUILDFORD [1901] 2 KB 215

De Lassalle and Guildford entered into a lease of a house. Before signing the lease, de Lassalle had asked Guildford whether the drains were in order. In the last house he had been in they were blocked and he had been flooded out. He did not want it to happen again. Guildford told him that they were in good order, though there was no term in the contract to that effect. However, the drains were faulty and, as a result, de Lassalle was flooded out. The lease provided that the tenant was to keep them in good order.

ISSUE: Can de Lassalle rely on the statement by Guildford as to the condition of the drains?

DECISION: The defendant was in breach of an oral 'collateral' contract in respect of the condition of the drains. If Guildford had told de Lassalle that the drains were not in good order, he would never have entered into the lease.

In order to establish a collateral contract regarding a statement of fact it is necessary to show that the person making the statement not only intended it to be relied upon but also guaranteed its truth, and that there was reliance by the person alleging the existence of the collateral contract.

JJ SAVAGE AND SONS PTY LTD V. BLAKNEY (1970) 44 ALJR 123

Blakney entered into a contract with the defendants for the purchase of a boat. During the course of negotiations, Blakney sought the written advice of the defendants as to what would be a suitable engine for the boat. They commented on three types and recommended one in a letter which included the statement that the boat would have an 'estimated speed of 23 km/h'. The buyer accepted this recommendation but the contract specification and quotation contained no reference to speed. After the motor was fitted the boat failed to reach the speed estimated by the defendants.

ISSUE: Was the recommendation of the speed of the boat capable of being considered promissory and thus amount to a collateral contract?

DECISION: The High Court held that the representation in the letter was neither a term of the main contract nor a collateral promise. Although the statement as to the speed of the boat led to Blakney entering into the contract, it was not promissory, but rather an expression of opinion or representational.

COMMENT: The statement must be promissory, not representational, if it is to be actionable according to the High Court. However, if a statement is intended to induce and does induce, isn't it *prima facie* a term of the contract?

IN BRIEF

The significance of the collateral contract

Where a pre-contractual statement is not a term of the main contract, it may still have contractual effect as a collateral contract, thus providing the injured party with a remedy. Such a contract has an independent existence to the main contract and may be enforced by an action for breach of a promise. More importantly, the collateral contract is not caught by the parol evidence rule because it is oral.

Criteria for enforceability

Once a collateral contract is established, it is only valid and enforceable if the plaintiff can establish:

- that the statement relied on is promissory;
- that the collateral contract is consistent with the main contract, so that the provisions of the main contract are enforceable despite the collateral contract; and
- that the collateral contract is not supported by past consideration.

HOYT'S PTY LTD V. SPENCER (1919) 27 CLR 133

Spencer subleased premises to Hoyt's for a period of four years. The written sublease contained a proviso that Spencer could terminate the agreement at any time by giving four weeks' notice in writing to Hoyt's. Spencer subsequently terminated the sublease before the end of the four-year term. Hoyt's then claimed damages for breach of a verbal promise given by Spencer prior to the sublease being signed, that he would only terminate the lease if he himself had been served with a similar notice by the head lessor.

ISSUE: Was the collateral promise consistent with the main contract?

DECISION: The High Court was not prepared to infer a collateral contract. The verbal agreement and the proviso in the written sublease were inconsistent.

If the inconsistency comes from the operation of an exclusion clause in the main contract, the collateral promise will override the exclusion clause because it is the very thing that induces the injured party to contract.

MENDELSSOHN V. NORMAND LTD **[1970] 1 QB 177**

Mendelssohn had left his car at the garage of Normand Ltd. While the car was parked there it was broken into and some valuables were stolen from it. In the action that followed, Normand Ltd relied on a clause in their contract with Mendelssohn which protected them from liability in respect of 'loss or damage sustained by the vehicle, its accessories or contents howsoever caused'. The parking attendant who had parked the car had promised that he would lock the car, when in fact he didn't.

ISSUE: Could the carpark rely on the exclusion clause, notwithstanding the representation by their employee?

DECISION: The exclusion clause did not apply. The oral statement by the parking attendant was viewed as a collateral promise or contract that would be meaningless if the exclusion clause was to be allowed to prevail.

HOW IMPORTANT IS THE TERM?

Once it has been decided that a statement is a term, it then becomes necessary to determine what sort of term it is because the remedies available to an innocent party differ under each.

IN BRIEF

Features of terms

Term	Description	Effect
Condition	A vital or essential term	Non-performance may result in rescission and/or damages to P
Warranty	A term that is not essential to the main purpose of the contract	Damages only
Innominate term	Court focuses on seriousness of effects of breach of the contract	P can elect to affirm or rescind Damages available in either case
Condition precedent	A term that must be satisfied before a contract can come into existence	No enforceable contract will exist No remedy as no breach
Condition subsequent	A term in a contract which provides that the contract will terminate on the happening of a particular event	Terminates existing contract No remedy as no breach

activebook

To help you to remember and understand the topics covered so far, and for links to legal websites, refer to your online activebook. Model answers provide feedback to problems and exercises.

Condition or warranty?

Once the court decides that a statement is a term of a contract, it is then necessary to consider the statement's significance because the remedies available to the injured party differ. Not all of the obligations created by a contract are of equal importance and this is recognised by the law. Thus it is necessary to make a further distinction, between:

***Condition*—a vital term, breach of which allows P to rescind and/or seek damages**

A condition

This is a term that is vital to the contract. The parties consider it so important that its non-performance may be considered by the injured party as amounting to substantial failure to honour the contract at all and thus may be regarded as grounds for **setting the contract aside, and/or suing for damages**; and

***Warranty*—a term of lesser importance allowing P only to recover damages**

A warranty

The parties consider this type of term to be of lesser importance to the main purpose of the contract. If it is breached, the injured party must still perform their part of the contract but they have the right to **sue for damages** for any loss that they may suffer as a result of the breach.

Objective test

The parties rarely indicate whether a term is a condition or a warranty. And even if they do, the courts may not be prepared to accept what they say anyway. To try to decide on the importance of a term, the courts may:

- apply an objective test looking at the case as a whole and considering the importance of the broken stipulation as an inducement to the plaintiff to enter into the contract. **Is the stipulation essential to the contract**? If the answer is 'yes', then it is a condition; if 'no', then it is a warranty;

***ASSOCIATED NEWSPAPERS LTD V. BANCKS* (1951) 83 CLR 322**

Bancks, the creator of the cartoon character 'Ginger Meggs', contracted with the plaintiff newspaper company to provide them with a full page of his comic each Sunday to be published on the front page of their Sunday comic section. As a result of a newsprint shortage, the cartoon appeared on page three of the comic section instead of page one on three successive Sundays. Bancks treated this as a breach of contract.

ISSUE: Was the action by the newspaper a breach of a condition or a breach of a warranty of Banck's contract?

DECISION: The High Court held that the newspaper's undertaking to publish Banck's cartoon on the front page of the comic section was a condition of the contract. Banck's would not have entered into the contract unless he had been assured that there would be at least substantial performance of the promise by the newspaper.

or

- look at what effect the breach has on the contract. If the breach has had a serious effect, it could be treated as a condition.

***POUSSARD V. SPIERS & BOND* [1876] 1 QBD 410**

Poussard was engaged to play a leading part in an opera from the beginning of its run. Shortly before it was due to begin she fell ill and was unable to take part in the show until a week after the season had commenced. The producers, who had been forced to find a substitute, then refused her services.

ISSUE: Was Poussard's failure to attend the opening night sufficiently serious to entitle the producers to sack her?

DECISION: Poussard's promise to perform as from the first night amounted to a condition and her failure to attend entitled the producers to repudiate the contract.

If the breach does not have a serious effect on the contract then it will be treated by the courts as a warranty and the injured party will only be entitled to damages.

***BETTINI V. GYE* [1876] 1 QBD 183**

Bettini, an experienced opera singer, entered into a contract with Gye to perform in concerts for the whole opera season. He undertook to appear six days in advance for the purpose of rehearsals, but owing to illness only arrived two days in advance. Gye attempted to use the non-attendance as an excuse to terminate the contract.

ISSUE: Was the late arrival a sufficiently serious event to warrant terminating the contract? That is, was it a breach of a condition or a warranty?

DECISION: The undertaking by Bettini to attend rehearsals was subsidiary to the main purpose of the contract and would not prevent the singer from performing the rest of his contract. Thus, while Gye might claim compensation for any loss he had incurred, he was not entitled to repudiate the agreement.

CASE REFLECTION: Would the contractual guarantee regarding workmanship and materials, common with the sale of new goods, be a condition or a warranty? Why?

Intermediate or innominate terms

***Innominate term*— court focuses on seriousness of effects of breach**

It may happen that a term cannot be classified as a condition or a warranty until after a **breach of contract** has occurred. The courts have identified a further class of terms that lie between conditions and warranties, called intermediate or innominate terms.

The court focuses on **how serious the effects of the breach** are on the contract, rather than attempting to classify the term which has been broken as a condition or a warranty. Has the breach deprived the innocent party of **substantially the whole benefit** that they should have derived from the contract?

***HONG KONG FIR SHIPPING CO. LTD V. KAWASAKI KISEN KAISHA LTD* [1962] 2 QB 26**

The plaintiffs chartered the defendants' ship for a period of two years. The contract required them to provide a ship, which was 'in every way fitted for ordinary service' and the owners had promised to 'maintain her in a thoroughly efficient state in hull and machinery during service'. When the ship was delivered for charter, the engine room staff were incompetent and the machinery so run down it took 20 weeks to get the ship ready to sail. The defendants repudiated the contract and the plaintiffs sued for breach of contract.

ISSUE: Had the breach given rise to a situation which deprived the charterers of a substantial part of the benefit of the contract that they were entitled to expect from its performance?

DECISION: The defendants were not entitled to repudiate the agreement. While the ship-owners were clearly in breach of their obligations to provide a seaworthy vessel, this was not a condition of the contract of charter. Nor were the delays, taken in the context of the overall period of the charter, so great as to frustrate the commercial purpose of the charter. The defendants should have sought damages.

COMMENT: Nothing less than a serious breach of an innominate term entitles the innocent party to treat the contract as at an end.

Condition precedent

***Condition precedent*—a term that prevents an agreement turning into a contract**

The word 'condition' can also be used to refer to a term which unless and until it is satisfied **prevents a contract coming into existence**. However, care must be taken to decide what type of meaning is to be attached to the words 'condition precedent', because the High Court made it clear in *Perri v. Coolangatta Investments Pty Ltd* (1982) 149 CLR 537 that there are two possible options:

- Did the parties intend the term to be a condition precedent to the **formation or existence of a contract?** In this case, unless and until the condition is fulfilled, there are no enforceable rights between the parties.

PYM V. CAMPBELL (1856) 119 ER 903

The parties had negotiated for the sale of a portion of the proceeds of an invention of Pym's. The contract that the parties signed was on the express oral basis that the sale of the invention first had to be approved by a third party. Their approval was not given and so Campbell attempted to repudiate the contract.

ISSUE: Had a contract come into existence?

DECISION: Approval was a condition precedent to the contract coming into existence, and because it was not forthcoming, there was no contract.

- Was the term a condition precedent to the **performance of a party's obligations** under a contract? Here there is a contract, though the obligation of a party, or perhaps both parties, to perform depends on the fulfilment of the condition precedent. Non-fulfilment entitles them to terminate, for example, the purchase of a car subject to the seller obtaining a roadworthy certificate. In this case there is a binding contract, **but** performance depends on the fulfilment of the condition precedent.

Condition subsequent

***Condition subsequent*—a clause in a contract which can terminate the contract**

A condition subsequent is a **term in a contract** which can terminate it—for example, the death of one of the parties, the return of an item and exchange for another, or a refund if the item proves to be unsatisfactory.

HEAD V. TATTERSALL [1871] LR 7 EXCH 7

Head bought a horse from Tattersall. The contract provided that if the horse did not answer to its description, i.e. hunted with hounds, it could be returned within a set time period. The horse did not live up to its description and Head exercised his option to return the horse and recover his money.

ISSUE: Was the condition a valid term which Head could enforce?

DECISION: The court held that Head was entitled to the return of the purchase price. While a valid contract of sale had arisen, it was subject to the right to return the horse if it did not match its description and it was returned within the stipulated time.

IMPLIED TERMS

In addition to its express terms, a contract may contain a number of terms that the parties or the courts may 'read' into the contract and that are called 'implied terms'. In *BP Refinery (Westernport) Pty Ltd v. President, Councillors and Ratepayers of the Shire of Hastings* (1978) 52 ALJR 20 the Privy Council set down five conditions that had to be satisfied for a term to be implied into a contract. It must be:

***Implied terms*—terms that are read into a contract by the parties or the courts**

- reasonable and equitable;
- necessary to give business efficacy to the contract, so that no term will be implied if the contract is effective without it;
- so obvious that 'it goes without saying';
- capable of clear expression; and
- not in contradiction of any express term of the contract.

IN BRIEF

Types of implied terms

Term	Description
Custom or usage	Where there is an established custom or practice and it could be assumed that the parties must have contracted with that term in mind.
Statute	Certain statutes imply terms into certain contracts, e.g., Sale of Goods Acts; Part V, *Trade Practices Act 1974* (Cth).
By the courts	Terms may be implied by the courts to cure obvious omissions or to give the contract 'business efficacy'.
Uncertain	Where there have been prior dealings between the parties, or expert witness can fill in gaps, the courts may fill in the gaps to give the contract 'business efficacy'.
Meaningless	Terms for which the meaning can't be ascertained and which the court will sever if possible.

Terms implied by custom or usage

Where there is no express provision to the contrary in a contract, and the trade custom or usage relied on is so well-known that everyone in that business making a contract would be assumed to have included it as a term into the contract, then it may be implied by the courts.

***Terms implied by custom or trade usage*—terms the parties are already familiar with**

PELLY V. ROYAL EXCHANGE ASSURANCE **(1757) 97 ER 342**

Pelly had insured his ship and tackle during a voyage. On arrival, the tackle, according to the usage of shipmasters, was removed and put into a warehouse where it was accidentally lost as a result of fire. The insurers claimed that as the loss had occurred on shore, it was not covered by them because it was not within the scope of the voyage.

ISSUE: Was the putting of the ship's tackle in a warehouse such a normal practice that, if the parties had put their minds to it when making the contract, they would have included it as a term?

DECISION: The insurers' claim was rejected on the basis that the placing of the ship's tackle in a warehouse was normal practice, i.e. it was understood to be referred to in every policy.

Terms implied by statute

A number of statutes imply terms into a contract. When considering the operation of such terms, it is necessary to consider to what extent the parties may be able to modify or exclude them. Well-known examples are sale of goods, hire-purchase and Fair Trading legislation of the various states and territories and the Commonwealth *Trade Practices Act 1974*. For a fuller discussion of this legislation, see Chapters 22 and 23.

Terms implied by the courts

Terms implied by the courts**—where there is an oversight by the parties**

In some cases the intention of the parties is plain, but owing to an oversight on the part of the parties the contract may not give effect to what the parties wanted or understood. Where this is likely to occur, the judge may imply terms into the contract in order to overcome this omission and give effect to the intention of the parties—to give 'business efficacy' to the contract.

THE MOORCOCK **(1889) 14 PD 64**

The defendant wharf owner contracted with the plaintiff, a shipowner, to unload cargo at the defendant's wharf. Both parties were aware that the ship would go aground if moored to the wharf at low tide, but neither party expected the ship to suffer any damage as a result. As expected, the ship grounded at low tide while still being unloaded but she was damaged by a hard ledge beneath the mud. Nothing had been written into the contract between the parties to show how the situation would be resolved if the ship were damaged.

ISSUE: Was it reasonable to expect that the defendant's wharf would be safe for ships to dock at even at low tide?

DECISION: It was reasonable to expect that the defendant would take reasonable care to determine that the river bed would be safe to accommodate the ship during unloading. Without such an implicit undertaking, ships would not use the dock.

Uncertain terms

If there have already been dealings between the parties, or expert witnesses who can give evidence to fill in missing pieces in the contract in order to interpret the parties' intentions, the courts may be prepared to enforce the contract.

***Uncertain terms*—if the parties have had prior dealings, expert witnesses may fill in gaps**

HILLAS & CO. LTD V. ARCOS LTD (1932) 147 LT 503

Hillas had agreed to buy softwood timber over the season of 1930 with an option to purchase further timber in 1931. The option did not set out any particulars as to kind, size or manner of shipment. The 1930 shipment went well and Hillas attempted to exercise his option with Arcos in 1931. However, Arcos refused to deliver the timber, arguing that it was not meant to bind either party as the particulars had not been defined in the option.

ISSUE: Was the option enforceable, given that the particulars had not been spelt out between the parties?

DECISION: In view of the prior dealings between the parties, and the fact that reference could be made to what was normal business practice in the timber trade, the option was enforceable.

COMMENT: This case is a useful illustration of how reluctant the courts are to strike down a contract unless they have to.

CASE REFLECTION: Many companies issue invoices with 'Terms of Trade' printed on the back of the invoice. In many instances these 'terms of trade' are not mentioned or discussed prior to the issue of the invoice. Could the previous dealings rule imply these terms of trade into subsequent transactions?

If there are no past dealings and no expert witnesses to assist the court in trying to determine the intention of the parties, the court will have little alternative but to strike the contract down as **void for lack of certainty**.

SCAMMELL V. OUSTON [1941] 1 ALL ER 14

Ouston wanted to purchase a new truck on hire-purchase from Scammell. The written order for the truck included the statement 'on the understanding that the balance of purchase price can be had on hire-purchase terms over a period of two years'. The meaning of the phrase was never determined by the parties, and at the time there were a number of hire-purchase agreements available. Ouston subsequently refused to proceed with the agreement and was sued by Scammell for breach of contract.

ISSUE: Could any meaning be attributed to the phrase 'on the understanding that the balance of purchase price can be had on hire-purchase terms over a period of two years'?

DECISION: The reference to hire-purchase terms was so vague that no definite meaning could be attached to it. The contract was held void for uncertainty.

COMMENT: Note that this decision was handed down in 1941 and our understanding of the phrase today could result in a different outcome. Remember also that courts today try to uphold agreements where uncertainty is argued as a ground for avoiding the contract.

The court will imply a term by reference to the imputed intention of the parties only if it can be seen that such a term is necessary for the reasonable or effective operation of the contract.

MEANINGLESS TERMS

***Meaningless terms*—if the term has no meaning, courts will sever it if possible**

Terms may be worded in such a way that a reasonable person would be unable to determine their meaning. In such a case the validity of the contract will depend on whether these terms can be severed from the rest of the contract and **still leave it valid.** This is a matter of the construction of the whole contract and *Scammell v. Ouston* (p. 369) illustrates what happens when the courts cannot sever the term from the contract. However, where possible, the courts will sever the term to leave the parties with a valid enforceable contract.

FITZGERALD V. MASTERS (1956) 95 CLR 420

The parties entered into a contract for the sale of a farm. One of the clauses in the contract of sale provided that the 'usual conditions of sale in use or approved of by the Real Estate Institute of New South Wales relating to sales by private contract of lands held under the Crown Land Acts shall so far as they are inconsistent herewith be deemed to be embodied herein'. There was no such document in existence containing a set of conditions as to private sales and when the purchaser decided not to go through with the purchase, he relied on this clause to strike the contract down for uncertainty.

ISSUE: Can the offending clause be severed from the contract, thus saving the contract?

DECISION: The High Court held that the parties had meant to insert the word 'not' in front of the word 'inconsistent' and the parties did not intend that the contract of sale should be nullified unless effect could be given to the clause. As a result, the clause was severed from the contract.

EXCEPTION, EXEMPTION OR EXCLUSION CLAUSES OR TERMS

***Exemption clauses*—attempt to limit or exclude liability of person inserting them**

It is not unusual in business to find a party attempting to limit or exclude their liability in certain situations by including an exception, exemption or exclusion clause in the contract. Such clauses are frequently found in 'standard form' contracts. These are contracts that incorporate terms of a standard nature, often in fairly wide terms, applicable to all persons making a particular type of contract—for example, when making a booking contract with an airline, a bus company or the railway for a holiday, or parking your car at a carpark.

It is a question of some practical importance to know whether or not these terms or clauses form part of the contract. If they do, they bind the person entering into the contract, even if they don't understand them, or have not even read them. At common law, a party is bound to exercise reasonable care over the person or property of another that has been entrusted to them under a contract. Failure to exercise reasonable care may leave the entrusted person open to a claim for damages and it is this type of action that an exemption clause seeks to prevent. Its purpose is to relieve one of the contracting parties from liability that they would otherwise have.

The courts look at exclusion clauses very critically because there is often very little opportunity for a person to read the 'fine print' on the document they receive or sign. **The effectiveness of an exclusion clause is a matter of construction of the contract as a whole, taking into account the bargaining position of the parties.** Thus, in the case of a commercial contract, the courts will be prepared to assume that the parties were in an equal bargaining position and able to seek legal assistance, whereas in the case of a consumer contract, the parties may have been in unequal bargaining positions and the consumer might not have even had time to read the document.

Does the writing constitute a contractual document?

It has to be established at the outset that the particular document relied on as containing the exclusion clause is an essential part of the contract and not a mere acknowledgment of payment, such as a receipt.

Is the clause an integral part of the document?

***CHAPELTON V. BARRY URBAN DISTRICT COUNCIL* [1940] 1 KB 532**

Chapelton hired a deckchair from a pile owned by the Council, behind which was a notice stating: 'Hire of chairs 2d per session of three hours'. He took a chair, paid for it, and received a ticket which he put into his pocket after merely glancing at it. The chair subsequently collapsed and he was injured. A notice on the back of the ticket stated that 'The Council will not be liable for any accident or damage arising from the hire of chairs'. The council relied on the clause when sued by Chapelton.

ISSUE: Was the exclusion clause on the back of the ticket effective?

DECISION: The clause was not binding on Chapelton. The board by the chairs made no reference to an exclusion clause, and the ticket handed to him might reasonably be understood to be a mere receipt which the reasonable person would not expect to find conditions printed on.

If the document is found to be an integral part of the contract, much then depends upon whether it was signed by the acceptor or not.

Signed documents

If fraud or misrepresentation can be established, the person signing will not be bound.

***CURTIS V. CHEMICAL CLEANING & DYEING CO.* [1951] 1 KB 805**

Curtis delivered a wedding dress to a drycleaner and was asked to sign a receipt by the assistant. When she asked the purpose of the receipt, the assistant told her that it exempted the drycleaner from liability for damage to beads and sequins. The clause, in fact, exempted the cleaners from any liability whatsoever. The dress was returned stained, and the cleaners relied on the exemption clause in the signed receipt.

ISSUE: As the shop assistant had misrepresented the effect of the receipt, could the drycleaners rely on it?

DECISION: The company could not rely on the exemption clause as the assistant had misrepresented the effect of the document to Curtis, and she had relied on what the assistant had said.

CASE REFLECTION: If a person asks a relevant question when entering into a contract and gets what seems to be a reasonable reply, should the enquirer be legally obliged to verify the reply? What would be the practical effect of having to verify all replies to all reasonable inquiries?

However, in the absence of fraud or misrepresentation, the party signing is generally bound by all the terms in that document, whether they have read it or not.

L'ESTRANGE V. GRAUCOB LTD **[1934] 2 KB 394**

L'Estrange bought a vending machine from Graucob and signed a document headed 'Sales Agreement'. The document was an order form containing a number of clauses which L'Estrange failed to read. When the machine failed to work properly, he brought an action against Graucob alleging breach of fitness for purpose. Graucob relied upon a clause in the agreement which said: 'This agreement contains all the terms and conditions under which I agree to purchase the machine specified above and any express or implied condition, statement or warranty, statutory or otherwise, not stated herein is hereby excluded'.

ISSUE: Given that L'Estrange had signed the document, and there was no evidence of fraud or misrepresentation, was he bound?

DECISION: As there was no fraud or misrepresentation, he was bound, irrespective of whether he had read the document or not. The question of notice was irrelevant in such a case.

CASE REFLECTION: Is it reasonable to assume that a person who signs a legal document has always had the opportunity to read and comprehend it? Consider this question in the case of a standard term contract.

In both *L'Estrange v. Graucob Ltd* and *Curtis v. Chemical Cleaning & Dyeing Co.* there was an undoubted contract or the existence of a contract and the question was whether the party signing the document containing terms was bound by them. In each case the question was whether those terms formed part of the contract.

LE MANS GRAND PRIX CIRCUITS PTY LTD V. ILIADIS **[1998] 4 VR 661**

Iliadis had signed an agreement headed in red capital letters 'TO HELP WITH OUR ADVERTISING', which contained an exclusion clause stating that he would not take legal action against Le Mans if he were injured while go-kart racing on their premises. The document appeared to be for marketing purposes and no attempt was made to draw his attention to the exclusion clause, nor was he given time to read the document by Le Mans staff. While driving a go-kart Iliadis was injured and Le Mans relied on the exclusion clause to protect them from liability.

ISSUE: Was the exclusion clause effective as it had been signed and there was no evidence of fraud or misrepresentation?

DECISION: The Victorian Court of Appeal held that a person who signs a document containing an exclusion clause may not be bound if they have reasonable grounds for believing that the document was not contractual. In this case the document appeared to be for marketing purposes, there was no practical opportunity for a party to read the document before signing and the exclusion clause was not drawn to his attention.

In the New South Wales Court of Appeal decision of *Toll (FGCT) Pty Ltd v. Alphapharm Pty Ltd* [2003] NSWCA 75 it was held that it was no longer possible to assert that the signature of a party to a contract indicated a genuine consent to the terms. It is a strong indication of intention to be bound but it does not exclude consideration of facts and circumstances which may show otherwise. While the High Court overturned the Court of Appeal in *Toll (FGCT) Pty Ltd v. Alphapharm Pty Ltd* [2004] HCA 52, they did accept that there may be cases where it is material to ask whether a person who has signed a document was given reasonable notice of what was in it—for example, where mistake or misrepresentation is alleged or the signatory was not aware that the document they signed was contractual in nature.

Unsigned documents

Would the reasonable person have regarded the document as one that would contain contractual terms?

Where the document is unsigned, the question is whether the 'customer' knew of and consented to the exclusion clause. If they didn't, would a reasonable person have regarded the document as one that would contain contractual terms and not represent a mere receipt or acknowledgement?

Did consumer know of and consent to the clause?

CAUSER V. BROWNE **[1952] VLR 1**

Causer left a dress with Browne for dry-cleaning. During dry-cleaning it was stained. Causer claimed damages for breach of contract, and Browne relied upon provisions printed on a docket, handed to Causer when he left the dress for dry-cleaning, which read 'no responsibility is accepted for loss or injury to articles through any cause whatsoever'.

ISSUE: What would be reasonably understood as being the purpose of the docket? Did the drycleaners make the person who was receiving the docket aware that it might contain conditions?

DECISION: The docket handed to the husband did not constitute a contractual document. It would be reasonable to assume that it was only a docket for the customer to produce when collecting the goods, and not a document containing contractual terms exempting the defendants from liability for negligence.

Have reasonable steps been taken to give sufficient notice of the term?

Where the document is neither a receipt nor an acknowledgement—for example, tickets for rail, sea or air journeys—should the customer have constructive notice of onerous clauses in the document? Has the defendant taken reasonable steps to give sufficient notice of the term to this class of persons? This is a question of fact in each case.

Has reasonable notice been given?

THOMPSON V. L M & S RAILWAY CO. **[1930] 1 KB 41**

Thompson, who was illiterate, got her niece to purchase an excursion railway ticket for her. On the front of the ticket were the words 'Excursion. For conditions see back', and on the back was a notice stating that the ticket was issued subject to the conditions in the company's timetables. The timetables, which cost sixpence each, stated that persons travelling at excursion rates could not take action against the railway for any injuries, however caused. Thompson was injured while travelling on the train, and claimed damages against the company.

ISSUE: Had reasonable notice of the terms and conditions of travel been given by the railway company?

DECISION: It was reasonable to assume that a ticket, issued at a reduced rate, was likely to be subject to certain conditions. The only question was whether notice of these conditions had been given or not. It was thought that the reference on the back of the ticket was sufficient notification. The fact that Thompson was illiterate was irrelevant.

CASE REFLECTION: Should the court have taken into account that Thompson was illiterate? Do you think the decision was unreasonable?

If a condition is particularly onerous or unusual and would not be generally known to the customer, the party seeking to enforce the condition must show that it had been fairly and reasonably brought to the customer's attention.

This could be done in a variety of ways—for example, by displaying a large sign in a prominent position as is done in carparks. However, if there are unusual conditions, these must be brought to the customer's notice or they may be struck down as being unconscionable.

INTERFOTO PICTURE LIBRARY LTD V. STILETTO VISUAL PROGRAMMES LTD [1988] 2 WLR 615

Interfoto operated a photographic transparency library. At the defendants' request they forwarded transparencies with a delivery note requiring them to be returned by 19 March and advising the defendants that a holding fee of $10 per day plus tax would be charged for each transparency retained after 19 March. The defendants did not read the conditions and failed to return any of the transparencies until 2 April. Interfoto invoiced the defendants for $7566 holding fee from 19 March to 2 April.

ISSUE: Should notice have been given of the unusual nature of the clause by Interfoto?

DECISION: The condition was an unreasonable and extortionate clause that had not been brought to the attention of the defendants and therefore did not become part of the contract. The court ordered the defendants to pay an amount on *quantum meruit* for the retention of the transparencies beyond a reasonable period.

Can terms be introduced after the making of the contract?

Introduction of post-contractual terms is ineffective

Where the contract has been made, any subsequent introduction of an exclusion clause will be ineffective and the exclusion clause will not operate. These types of terms must be introduced while the contract is being formed so that the other contracting party has the opportunity of accepting or rejecting them (see Figure 18.2).

FIGURE 18.2 *Introduction of post-contractual terms*

OLLEY V. MARLBOROUGH COURT LTD [1949] 1 KB 532

A husband and wife arrived at a hotel as guests. After paying in advance and signing the register, they were shown to their rooms. On the wall of the room, this notice was fixed: 'The proprietors will not hold themselves responsible for articles lost or stolen unless handed to the office for safe custody'. Owing to the negligence of the maid, who left the bedroom door unlocked, the wife's furs were stolen. The hotel proprietors relied on the exemption clause.

ISSUE: Were the guests bound by the terms stated in their room? Were these terms incorporated in their contract for accommodation?

DECISION: The notice in the room was not incorporated into the contract. The rights of the guests could not be affected by subsequent notice, and the exemption clause did not apply.

CASE REFLECTION: Under what circumstances might the terms of a contract be altered or added to after the contract has been entered into?

Can terms be implied by custom or trade?

Had the guests in *Olley v. Marlborough Court Ltd* (above) been regular visitors to the hotel, they may have had sufficient opportunity to see and read the notice. Knowledge of the exclusion clause would then have been more readily inferred. The crucial test is whether reasonable notice of the term has been given.

Terms can be implied by *custom or trade usage*

***BALMAIN NEW FERRY CO. LTD V. ROBERTSON* (1906) 4 CLR 379**

The ferry company operated a service between Balmain and Sydney. Entry to the ferry was through a set of turnstiles, operated by inserting a penny in a slot in the machine. Above the turnstiles was a sign stating: '*A fare of one penny must be paid on entering or leaving the wharf. No exception will be made to this rule whether the passenger has travelled by ferry or not.*' Robertson paid his penny to gain admission and finding that he had just missed the ferry, he attempted to leave without paying another penny. He was stopped and forced to pay by the attendants. Subsequently he brought an action against the ferry company for assault and false imprisonment.

ISSUE: As Robertson had used the ferry numerous times before, could knowledge of the terms and conditions of travel be implied?

DECISION: The High Court held that as Robertson had travelled on the ferry numerous times before, he was aware of the conditions of travel and bound by them as he had reasonable notice of them.

CASE REFLECTION: If the purpose of the contract was the ferry trip, why should he have had to pay if he did not get onto the ferry? If Robertson had been able to foresee the problems he would have with the ferry company, do you think he could have successfully negotiated for those terms not to apply to him?

Interpretation of exclusion clauses

Assuming that the exclusion clause has been properly incorporated into the contract, three possible approaches to interpretation can be identified:

- **Strict construction against party relying on clause or term**

  Where the exclusion clause has been correctly incorporated into the contract, it will be strictly construed against the party who attempts to rely on it. This is known as the *contra proferentum* rule. The clause will be 'read down' by the court unless it specifies the type of liability to be covered and any ambiguity will be resolved in favour of the injured party.

Exclusion clauses are strictly construed against the party relying on them

WHITE V. JOHN WARWICK & CO. LTD **[1953] 1 WLR 1285**

White hired a bicycle from John Warwick & Co. The contract contained a clause stating that 'Nothing in this agreement shall render the owners liable for personal injuries to the riders of the machines hired'. White was injured while riding the bike. He sued John Warwick on two counts—in contract for breach of warranty on the basis that the bike was not fit for the purpose for which it was hired; and in tort for negligence in supplying a defective bicycle.

ISSUE: Did the exemption clause operate to protect the defendants in both contract and tort?

DECISION: The exemption clause only applied to protect the owners from their liability in contract, and not from their liability for negligence. Clear words needed to be used to exempt or limit liability for negligence as well. Any ambiguities will be strictly construed against the party relying on the clause.

Exclusion clauses do not apply outside the contract—the 'four corners' rule

- **The 'four corners' rule**

The 'four corners' rule of interpretation states that exclusion clauses do not apply to actions outside the contract. They will not apply to situations involving deliberate breach, or for conduct that is outside the objects of the contract.

THE COUNCIL OF THE CITY OF SYDNEY V. WEST **(1965) 114 CLR 481**

Before West parked his car at the defendant's carpark he was issued with a ticket that contained on the back of it the following clause:

> *The Council does not accept any responsibility for the loss or damage to any vehicle . . . however such loss . . . may arise or be caused.*

It also stated that:

> *This ticket must be presented for time stamping and payment before taking delivery of the car.*

A carpark attendant allowed a thief to drive West's car away after the thief claimed that he had lost his original ticket and presented another ticket on which was written a different registration number from that of West's car. West sued for breach of contract and in the tort of detinue.

ISSUE: Was the carpark attendant, in allowing a thief to take the car, acting outside the terms of the contract so that the exclusion clause did not operate?

DECISION: A majority of the High Court held that the validity of the exclusion was a matter of construction. In this case, the actions of the carpark attendant in releasing the car to the thief were outside the terms of the contract. It was not merely a negligent act but a delivery not authorised under the contract.

CASE REFLECTION: If there is any ambiguity or uncertainty in the wording of the exclusion clause, in whose favour should the court read that uncertainty? Why?

The effectiveness of an exclusion clause is a matter of construction

- **Interpretation according to the express agreement**

The High Court in the *Sydney City Council* case (above) held that the effectiveness of an exclusion clause is purely a question of construction of the contract as a whole in each case. Is the term or clause wide enough to exclude an action for the alleged breach?

It seems today that the courts are prepared to accept the validity of exclusion clauses, even where they have harsh consequences in:

- **commercial contracts**, because of the equality of bargaining positions that can exist between the parties;

PHOTO PRODUCTION LTD V. SECURICOR TRANSPORT LTD **[1980] AC 827**

Securicor contracted with Photo Production (the plaintiffs) to provide a night patrol service for the plaintiffs' factory. The main dangers that had been contemplated by the parties were theft and fire. One night while on patrol an employee of the defendants deliberately started a fire at the factory and the factory burnt down. The contract had an exemption clause which stated that Securicor were not to be liable for the injurious acts of their employees.

ISSUE: Will the exemption clause protect Securicor where there was a 'fundamental breach' of contract?

DECISION: The House of Lords held that legal liability of the parties should be determined in accordance with the express agreement contained in the contract. The company could not have foreseen such an act by its employee.

COMMENT: While Securicor were in breach of an implied condition to operate their security service with due and proper regard to the safety and security of their client's property, the clause was sufficiently precise to protect the defendant from liability.

However, the presumption of equality of bargaining positions in commercial contracts is a rule of construction based on the presumed intention of the contracting parties in each case.

DARLINGTON FUTURES LTD V. DELCO AUSTRALIA PTY LTD **(1986) 161 CLR 500**

Delco entered into a written contract with Darlington, a futures trader, to trade in the futures commodity market. Delco imposed certain trading limits on Darlington, but a Darlington employee acted beyond their authority and Delco lost $280 000. In the action that followed to recover the losses, Darlington attempted to rely on their exclusion clauses. Clause 6 provided that the client:

> *. . . acknowledges that the Agent will not be responsible for any loss arising in any way out of any trading activity undertaken on behalf of the Client whether pursuant to this agreement or not . . .*

Clause 7 provided that any liability on the Agent's part:

> *. . . arising out of or in connection with the relationship established by this agreement . . . shall not in any event (and whether or not such liability results from or involves negligence) exceed $100.*

ISSUE: Could Darlington successfully rely on the exclusion clauses?

DECISION: The High Court held that Clause 6 did not apply in this case because it only applied to trading activity by the broker acting within the investor's authority. On the other hand, Clause 7 successfully limited Darlington's liability to $100 per transaction arising out of or in connection with the relationship established by the agreement, even if, as here, it was unauthorised.

COMMENT: This decision followed the High Court's reasoning in *Sydney City Council* (p. 376) that exclusion clauses should be construed according to their natural and ordinary meaning in view of the contract as a whole, thereby giving due weight to the context in which the clause appears, including the nature and object of the contract and, where appropriate, construing the clause *contra proferentum* in case of ambiguity.

- **consumer contracts**—if there is no inequality between the bargaining positions of the parties, the courts may apply a similar standard to that in commercial contracts. However, where there is inequality of bargaining power, the courts may be less inclined to read the clause according to its plain and natural meaning if that is likely to produce a harsh result.

Deletion of unreasonable terms

Unreasonable terms will not be deleted at common law but may be deleted in equity as unconscionable

Where the court is faced with a wholly unreasonable term, the position of the common law appears to be that the court has no power to delete that term. An attempt has been made in New South Wales to remedy an unsatisfactory common law situation by the passing of the *Contracts Review Act 1980* which enables a court to reopen and rewrite an unfair contract. An extensive list of matters, which the court should regard in determining whether or not a contract is unfair, is found in the Act, and it is not just confined to exclusion clauses. A term may also be deleted if the court in its equitable jurisdiction decides that it is unconscionable.

Position of third parties

!

CAUTION NOTE

Third parties will not be protected because of doctrine of privity unless it is clear in the contract that they are to be covered.

Where the clause has been correctly incorporated into the contract, third parties will generally not be protected.

ADLER V. DICKSON [1955] 1 QB 158

Adler was a passenger aboard the *Himalaya*, which was berthed at Trieste. While Adler was boarding the ship the gangway slipped. He fell to the wharf and suffered serious injuries. Adler brought an action against the captain and boatswain of the ship. The company relied on the following term in the ticket: '*The company will not be responsible for and shall be exempt from all liability in respect of any injury to the person of any passenger*'.

ISSUE: Was the term sufficiently wide to protect the servants of the company?

DECISION: The exemption clause was not sufficiently wide to exempt the servants of the company from liability as they were not parties to the agreement between the company and Adler.

COMMENT: This arises because of a lack of express intention by the contracting parties to cover servants or independent contractors. Because of the strict application of the doctrine of privity of contract, where there is a lack of express intention, third parties are not treated as being a party to the contract.

For a third party to avoid the operation of the privity rule (see p. 384) and gain the protection of an exclusion clause (remember that a third party is not a party to the contract), they have to satisfy the four conditions set down by Lord *Reid* in *Scruttons v. Midlands Silicones Ltd* [1962] AC 446:

- the contract makes it clear that it was intended to benefit third parties;
- it was clear that the defendant was contracting for itself and third parties;
- the defendant had the authority of the third party to make the contract on their behalf. As this is an agency relationship, ratification can take place after the contract has been made (see pp. 548–549); and
- consideration has moved from the third party. The performance of an existing duty is good consideration if it is owed to a third party.

Statutes that affect exclusion clauses

Statutory intervention to cover shortfall in common law in protecting consumers

Both Commonwealth and state legislatures have intervened in the area of exclusion clauses. For example:

- Section 176, *Civil Law (Wrongs) Act 2002* (ACT) and s. 8, *Misrepresentation Act 1972* (SA) restricts the rights to exclude liability for pre-contractual misrepresentations.
- Under the *Trade Practices Act 1974*, if the exclusion clause is likely to deceive or mislead the consumer, then it would breach s. 52 of the Act. Sections 68 and 68A, *Trade Practices Act 1974* (Cth) prohibit the exclusion of implied conditions and warranties in consumer transactions. Manufacturers are also caught under Div. 2A of Part V of the Act as s. 74K renders void any exclusion clause or term that is inconsistent with Div. 2A. See Chapter 23.
- Section 64, *Sale of Goods Act 1923* (NSW) as amended by the *Commercial Transactions (Miscellaneous Provisions) Act 1972* (NSW) and the *Contracts Review Act 1980* (NSW) attempts to redress an inequality of bargaining power.
- Section 5, *Hire Purchase Act 1959* (Vic.) makes it impossible for an owner to exclude him or herself from liability in respect of new goods bought on hire-purchase. Section 32LA of the *Fair Trading Act 1999* (Vic.) prohibits a term that attempts to exclude, restrict or modify the application of Part 2A dealing with implied conditions and warranties in certain contracts of supply of goods or services. Section 32LA provides that any provision in a contract that attempts to exclude, restrict or modify liability or damages is void, while s. 32MA deals with limitation of liability generally.
- Under the sale of goods legislation of the states, the exclusion of the implied conditions that the goods:
  - are of merchantable quality,
  - are fit for their particular purpose, or
  - match the description and/or sample

  are prohibited and the exclusion clause is void. See Chapter 22.

While the above statutory changes have provided some protection to consumers from the operation of exclusion clauses, it should not be assumed that this will always be the case. For example, a number of Australian jurisdictions have provided statutory protection to recreational and sporting providers of recreational services against actions brought by consumers who have suffered personal injury:

- Section 68B, *Trade Practices Act 1974* (Cth), enables recreational and sporting providers of recreational services to contract out of implied warranties in consumer transactions under s. 74 (supply of services to a consumer).
- Section 32N, *Fair Trading Act 1999* (Vic.); s. 5N, *Civil Liability Act 2002* (NSW), s. 5J, *Civil Liability Act 2002* (WA); Sch.3 (limited to equine activities), *Civil Liability (Wrongs) Act 2002* (ACT); and s. 68A, *Consumer Affairs and Fair Trading Act 1990* (NT allow recreational and service providers to seek a waiver from participants which excludes, restricts or modifies liability for harm resulting from the failure to exercise reasonable care and skill in the supply of recreational services. Generally, the common law position as to the effectiveness of a waiver given to or on behalf of a child remains unchanged.

Summary of exclusion clauses

To summarise the functions of exemption clauses and the methods of control adopted by the courts:

- The clause must be included in the contract itself. Introduction after the contract is made is ineffective.
- **Signed documents**
  - As a general rule, an exemption clause in a signed document is effective unless fraud, misrepresentation or a statutory defence can be established.
- **Unsigned documents**
  - Did the 'customer' know of and consent to the clause? If they did not, would a reasonable person have expected to find such a clause in that type of document?
  - Have reasonable steps been taken to give sufficient notice of the term?
  - If the terms have not been brought to the notice of the 'customer', can they be implied by trade usage or custom trade?
- **Assuming the clause has been properly incorporated**
  - The courts interpret exemption clauses strictly against the party relying on them by placing an extremely literal and strict interpretation on them.
  - Exclusion clauses do not apply to actions outside the contract—the 'four corners' rule.
  - Generally a third party is not protected by an exemption clause unless there is express intention by the contracting parties to cover third parties.
  - The effectiveness of exclusion clauses is a matter of construction. In the case of commercial agreements, the parties are in a more equal bargaining position than consumers and so the courts are more likely to accept the validity of the clause.
  - If an exemption clause excludes liability for all terms in a contract, there is really nothing left in the contract. As the entire contract has been excluded, it is contrary to the principles of protection as conferred by the law.

Statutory protection

There is some statutory protection available to **consumers** in the form of Part V of the *Trade Practices Act 1974* (Cth); the *Misrepresentation Act 1972* (SA); s. 176, *Civil Law (Wrongs) Act 2002* (ACT); s. 17, the *Contracts Review Act 1980* (NSW); the sale of goods and fair trading legislation of the states and territories; and s. 5 of the *Hire Purchase Act 1958* (Vic.).

REVIEW QUESTIONS

?

18.1 Indicate whether each of the following statements is true or false:

Statement	TRUE	FALSE
▪ The promissory nature of a statement and whether it is a term depends on the intention of the parties	☐	☐
▪ If the innocent party is asked to verify the statement, it is more likely to be an inducement	☐	☐
▪ If one of the parties had a special skill or knowledge with regard to the subject matter of the contract, then a statement is probably a term	☐	☐
▪ In the case of a written contract, the courts assume that the intention of the parties is contained within the 'four corners' of the contract	☐	☐
▪ Breach of condition only allows the injured party to sue for damages	☐	☐
▪ An intermediate or innominate term is neither a condition nor a warranty	☐	☐
▪ If the stated terms fail to clearly indicate the intentions of the parties, the contract will be void for lack of certainty	☐	☐
▪ A condition subsequent terminates a contract	☐	☐
▪ Terms may be read in or implied from previous dealings between the parties	☐	☐
▪ A condition precedent may involve suspension of the contract until the event specified in the agreement takes place	☐	☐

▪ Breach of warranty allows the injured party to rescind and/or recover damages	□	□
▪ A term which provides that on the occurrence of an event the contract will terminate is known as a condition subsequent	□	□
▪ Liability for negligent acts may be excluded by the incorporation of an exclusion clause into the contract	□	□
▪ An exclusion clause will be effective after the formation of the contract	□	□
▪ Exclusion clauses are construed strictly against the party relying on them	□	□
▪ If the parties have had previous dealings, knowledge of the operation of an exclusion clause is more easily presumed	□	□
▪ If a person signs a document containing an exclusion clause, and there is no evidence of fraud or misrepresentation, they will be bound irrespective of whether they have read the document or not	□	□
▪ Exclusion clauses do not apply to actions outside the contract	□	□
▪ The effectiveness of an exclusion clause is a question of construction of the contract as a whole	□	□
▪ Because of the doctrine of privity of contract, unless there is an express intention, third parties are not treated as being a party to the contract and cannot obtain the protection of an exclusion clause	□	□
▪ There is no remedy at common law to delete an unreasonable term	□	□

activebook

Activebook resources include in-depth summaries with links to the relevant part of the book. For revision, add your own notes to the summaries provided by using the note-taking function.

18.2 Explain the importance of the distinction between a condition and a warranty.

18.3 How do the courts determine what is and what is not a term? What factors do the courts use to assist them in making a decision?

18.4 Explain what the 'parol evidence rule' is?

18.5 What is a collateral contract? What must be satisfied before the courts will infer a collateral contract?

18.6 Drum's cow was offered for sale at auction. One of the clauses contained in the auction catalogue stated that 'no animal is . . . sold with a warranty unless specifically mentioned at the time of offering, and no warranty so given shall have any legal effect or force unless the terms thereof appear on the purchaser's account'. Bidding was slow because of the cow's poor appearance. In a bid to get things moving, he said, 'there is nothing wrong with her . . . I will guarantee her in every respect'. Harp, on hearing this, successfully bid for the cow only to find when he got her home that she had TB. She died shortly thereafter.

Will the warranty in the catalogue protect Drum if Harp brings an action against him for compensation?

18.7 In order for a party to rely upon an exclusion clause, what must they show?

18.8 In the case of a signed contract, can the party signing avoid the operation of an exclusion clause?

18.9 Jones drove her car into Smith's Parking's new automatic carpark for the first time. There was a sign outside the carpark that listed the various charges and stated that owners parked at their own risk. When she drove up to the ticket machine, Jones was issued with a ticket. She then drove into the garage, where her car was mechanically parked. Jones was injured when she returned later to collect her car, and she claimed damages from the garage. The carpark attempted to rely on a condition exempting it from liability. On each ticket, in small print, were the words 'Issued subject to conditions . . . displayed on the premises'. On a pillar opposite the ticket machine were eight conditions, the second of which exempted the car park from liability for any injury to a customer on the premises. Jones would have needed to have parked her car in the garage and walked around to the pillar to have read the conditions.

Could the carpark successfully rely on the exemption clause to protect them from any action by Jones?

18.10 Shilling purchased a new car from Penny & Co. In the contract of sale was the clause: *'All conditions, warranties and liabilities implied by statute, common law or otherwise are hereby excluded'*.

In fact, the car delivered to Shilling was not new but a demonstration model, and now he wished to avoid the contract. Shilling argued that Penny had broken the contract by providing him with a demonstration model, while Penny & Co. relied on the exemption clause to exclude them from liability.

Who was correct in this case?

18.11 Mandrake was a magician who had been on tour together with an assistant. He left four trunks at the parcels office at Central station. The trunks contained various items used in an 'escape illusion'. Mandrake paid $2 for each trunk deposited and received a ticket for each one. He then left saying that he would send instructions for their dispatch. Some weeks after their deposit and before Mandrake had sent instructions for the dispatch of the trunks, Mandrake's assistant persuaded the clerk in the parcels office to let him open the trunks, though he was not in possession of the ticket. The assistant took several items and was later convicted of larceny. Mandrake then sued the railway company for damages for breach of contract, and the railway company pleaded the following term, which was contained in the ticket and which stated that the Railway Executive was 'not liable for loss, misdelivery or damage to any articles where the value was in excess of $10 unless at the time of the deposit of the article an extra charge was paid'. No such declaration or payment had been made.

Do you think that the railway company could successfully rely on the exemption clause to protect themselves from an action by Mandrake?

CRITICAL THINKING

18.1 Explain the operation of the *contra proferentum* rule. Is such a rule defensible today?

18.2 Has the statutory intervention of Commonwealth and state governments rectified the difficulties of the common law in the interpretation of exclusion clauses? Discuss.

CHAPTER 19

Rights of the Parties and Discharge

CHAPTER CONTENTS

PRIVITY OF CONTRACT

Acquiring rights

Incurring liabilities

ASSIGNMENT

Assignment of liabilities

Assignment of rights

DISCHARGE

By performance

By agreement

By frustration

By operation of law

By lapse of time at common law

By virtue of a term in the contract

By breach

CHAPTER OBJECTIVES

On completion of this chapter, you should be able to:

- explain the doctrine of privity of contract
- explain the circumstances that permit rights and obligations under a contract to be transferred
- recognise and explain the methods by which a contract is ended, including:
  - performance
  - agreement
  - frustration
  - operation of law
  - by lapse of time
  - breach
- explain the doctrine of frustration and outline its effects on a contract.

activebook

This icon is used throughout the following chapter to remind you to visit the *Business Law* online activebook for additional exercises, links to legal websites, and feedback. For a detailed explanation of what is in the activebook please refer to the inside cover of this textbook. The activebook is available through OneKey.

Where do I start?

Learning path: Use the activebook to complete a pre-chapter warm-up exercise.

There are many definitions of legal terms to assist with your understanding of the material.

KEY TERMS

An understanding of the following terms will help you to better understand the material in this chapter:

- **actual breach:** failure at the time required by the contract
- **anticipatory breach:** threatened failure to perform their contractual obligations at a time required by the contract by a party to the contract
- **assignment:** transfer
- **divisible contract:** a contract which is capable of being divided up into separate parts
- **frustration:** the discharge of a contract rendered impossible of performance because of the operation of external factors beyond the contemplation of the parties
- **privity:** (of contract) only those who are a party to the contract are affected by it
- ***quantum meruit*:** as much as a person has earned or as much as they deserve.

what if . . .

You decide to have a sailing holiday and hire a yacht to sail the Whitsundays in the Great Barrier Reef. Unknown to you or the owner of the yacht, a fire destroyed the yacht. Is there a contract in existence between you and the owner of the yacht? Will you still have to pay for the hire of the yacht?

In the previous chapters on contract law, the basic requirements for the formation of a valid and legally binding contract, and the extent of the obligations of the parties, were examined. Having created a contract, it can often happen in business that one or other of the parties may wish to assign their rights or obligations under the contract to a third party. Can this be done?

> This chapter considers, first, how third parties can acquire rights and incur liabilities under a contract and, second, the circumstances in which the obligations of the parties to a contract can be discharged or dissolved.

Hopefully, the parties to the contract will have performed their obligations exactly as they agreed to and discharged their duties. However, discharge can take place in a number of different ways apart from performance. A contract can be discharged by agreement, frustration, operation of law, by virtue of a term, lapse of time or breach. In the case of breach, one of the parties has not performed their duties under the contract. If that has happened, then the innocent party will be seeking a remedy for the breach and the damage that they have suffered and this is considered in the next chapter.

PRIVITY OF CONTRACT

IN BRIEF

Privity and assignment

As a general rule, only the persons who are parties to the contract can acquire rights and incur liabilities under it. The position of third parties is that obligations under a contract generally cannot be transferred unless all the parties consent (novation). Equity, and in limited cases the law, permits an assignment of rights.

Acquiring rights

As a general rule, only the persons who are parties to the contract can acquire rights and incur liabilities under it: *Dunlop Pneumatic Tyre Co. Ltd v. Selfridge & Co. Ltd* [1915] AC 847. Until the decision in *Trident General Insurance Limited v. McNiece Bros Pty Ltd* (1988) 165 CLR 107, a third party would not have been able to acquire any rights or incur any liabilities under the contract because they were not a party to it. However, while the third party, C, may not be able to sue A on their promise to B, B may be able to sue A for breach of contract.

Generally only the persons who are parties to the contract can acquire rights and incur liabilities under it

***BESWICK V. BESWICK* [1968] AC 58**

Beswick transferred his business to his nephew in return for an annual annuity during his lifetime and arranged that after his death, a smaller annuity would be paid to his wife. Following his death, the nephew made one payment and then failed to make any more. The widow brought an action against the nephew both in her personal capacity and as administratrix of her husband's estate.

ISSUE: As she was not a party to the contract, could she succeed in her claim against the nephew?

DECISION: The widow could not succeed in her personal capacity as she was not a party to the contract and so would be defeated by the doctrine of privity. However, she could succeed in her capacity as administratix of her husband's estate as she was his legal representative and in that capacity would be entitled to sue the nephew for breach of contract.

A number of situations exist in the common law, equity and statute where the doctrine of privity is not relevant, including:

- agency in relation to an undisclosed principal;
- novation;
- negotiable instruments as long as there has been a valid negotiation to the new parties;
- trusts of contractual rights, but it must be able to be proved that there is an intention to constitute a trust;
- trusts where the manager or trustee of a trust can enforce the equitable obligations in a trust deed;
- leases and restrictive covenants;
- property contracts where a third party obtains the benefit under the Property Law Acts in Queensland and Western Australia; and
- under consumer law, the consumer in a consumer–retailer contract can sue a third party manufacturer;
- under the *Insurance Contracts Act 1984* (Cth).

***TRIDENT GENERAL INSURANCE CO. LTD V. MCNIECE BROS PTY LTD* (1988) 165 CLR 107**

The owner of a quarry obtained indemnity insurance cover against liability for injuries suffered by the public and people working on the site. The policy defined the insured (the person taking out the policy) as the owner of the site, subsidiary companies, contractors, sub-contractors and suppliers. A sub-contractor successfully recovered damages when he was injured because of the negligence of a principal contractor. The principal contractor in turn claimed indemnity (protection) as one of the insured under the site owner's policy. The insurance company refused to pay.

ISSUE: Under the rule of privity of contract, were the sub-contractor, and principal contractor, a party to the contract between the insurance company and the site owner?

DECISION: The High Court held that the privity doctrine was in conflict with the 'legitimate expectations' and the expressed intentions of all the parties to the insurance contract. The insurer had to pay.

COMMENT: The decision reflects the current statutory position (see s. 48, *Insurance Contracts Act 1984* (Cth)). However, while the decision relates to insurance contracts, the decision is important in its potential application to other contracts because a majority of the judges were critical of the general operation of the doctrine of privity. Whether Australian courts will continue to adhere strictly to the doctrine of privity remains to be determined.

Incurring liabilities

A third party who knowingly and intentionally induces breach of contract may commit a tort

While no right of action in contract exists against a person who is not a party to a contract, a third party who induces a breach of contract may find that they have committed a **tort** if it can be proved that the breach was knowingly and intentionally obtained.

LUMLEY V. GYE [1843–60] ALL ER REP 208

Wagner entered into an agreement with Lumley to perform exclusively at a theatre in London for three months. Gye persuaded her to break her contract with Lumley and to sing at another theatre. Lumley successfully obtained an injunction to stop Wagner singing elsewhere and also attempted to sue Gye for damages.

ISSUES: As Gye was not a party to the contract, could damages be recovered against him in contract?

DECISION: No right of action in contract generally exists against a person who is not a party to a contract. However, as Gye had intentionally and without justification induced Wagner to breach her contract with Lumley, he could be sued in tort for damages for inducing breach of contract.

ASSIGNMENT

Assignment of liabilities

Assignment of liabilities generally can only be transferred by way of novation

As a general rule, a party who has contracted to perform obligations (liabilities) under a contract **cannot transfer those obligations to another**. The promisee cannot be forced to accept performance or a promise of performance from any person other than the promisor unless the liability that is transferred is one which involves no particular skill and is not connected with the character, credit or any other personal qualities of the promisor.

ROBSON AND SHARPE V. DRUMMOND (1831) 2 B & AD 303

Drummond had leased a carriage from Sharpe for five years. Sharpe was to paint the carriage every year and keep it in good condition. Sharpe was in partnership with Robson at the time of the contract with Drummond, but the contract was between Drummond and Sharpe. After three years, Sharpe retired from the business and Robson told Drummond that he should now be paid the lease. Drummond refused and returned the carriage. Sharpe sued for breach of contract.

ISSUE: Was the undertaking a personal one?

DECISION: Drummond was entitled to return the carriage because the contract between himself and Sharpe was a personal one. The undertaking on the part of Sharpe to repair and paint the carriage involved the use of Sharpe's own taste and discrimination.

If **all** the **parties consent**, liability may be transferred by way of novation. This is a tripartite agreement where the original parties agree to rescind their contract in consideration of a new contract being entered into on the same terms between one of the original parties and a third party. This involves substituting one original party with the third party in what is a new agreement. For example, if a partner in a partnership dies, the old partnership is dissolved and replaced by a new one and if the creditors of the old partnership continue to deal with the new partnership, they are considered to have accepted the new partner as their debtor.

Assignment of rights

Equitable assignment

Assignment of rights is permitted under equity

At common law, assignment of rights is not possible. **Equity, however, permits the assignment of contractual rights**, including debts, provided that the following matters are complied with:

- While the assignment may be oral or in writing, the intention to assign must be clear.
- Between the assignor (the creditor under the original contract, seeking to transfer the benefit) and the assignee (a stranger to the contract), an assignment of a *chose in action* (interest or right in an intangible item such as a debt) requires consideration if the new holder is to have enforceable contractual rights.
- The debtor is not bound until they receive notice, although it is enforceable between the assignor and assignee. If the right involves a debt and the debtor is unaware of the assignment and pays the original creditor, it is a discharge for that payment and the assignee will only have rights against the assignor, not the debtor.
- The assignor cannot give a better title than they themselves have. For example, if the creditor assigns a debt to a third party and the creditor also owes the debtor, the debtor may not set-off one debt against the other (called a set-off) to the disadvantage of the third party.

By statute

Property law legislation in all states permits assignment of rights

Property law statutes of the states and territories allow rights to be assigned and for the assignee to sue in their own name as long as:

- the assignment is absolute;
- the assignment is in writing and signed by the assignor; and
- notice is given in writing to the debtor or person liable under the contract.

The assignee cannot obtain a better title than that of the assignor because they take their rights 'subject to equities'. That is, they cannot obtain a better title than the transferor.

By operation of law

Assignment of rights can occur by operation of law

In certain cases, assignment of rights can take place by operation of law—for example:

- the executor of a will can enforce the rights that a deceased person had in contracts at the time of their death;
- the estate of the bankrupt vests in the Official Receiver in Bankruptcy or the appointed trustee; and
- under consumer law, the consumer in a consumer/retailer contract can sue the third party manufacturer, e.g., Part V, Div. 2A of the *Trade Practices Act 1974* (Cth).

A contract requiring the performance of a personal service is not assignable, such as a particular artist painting a portrait.

DISCHARGE

A party's duty under a contract is to discharge their obligations. Once they have done this, they are excused from further performance under that contract.

A party may be discharged because they have performed their obligations, or their promises, in full. If they have, the contract is fully executed. But total performance is not the only way in which a party, or even both parties, may be discharged from their obligations.

IN BRIEF

Methods of discharge

Method	Description
Performance	The parties to the contract carry out exactly the terms (the promises) of the contract. In limited cases substantial performance, acceptance of part performance and obstruction by the other party may discharge the contract.
Agreement	As the contract was created by agreement, so it can be changed by agreement. This could be by a mutual discharge, a release or waiver by one of the parties, a substituted agreement, or accord and satisfaction.
Frustration	The contract could be discharged as a result of impossibility of performance due to an event unforeseen by either party, such as destruction of the subject matter, change in the law, non-occurrence of a basic event, physical impossibility under a contract of personal service, or a radical change in a state of affairs.
Operation of law	The contract may be discharged independently of the wishes of the parties by operation of law, e.g., bankruptcy, material alteration, merger, death of either party or expiry of time.
Lapse of time	Where no time has been specified, a reasonable time has elapsed.
By virtue of a term	Where a term has been incorporated into the contract bringing it to an end, i.e. a condition subsequent, or there is a term preventing an agreement becoming a contract, i.e. a condition precedent.
Breach	By one party failing to perform their obligations as agreed.

By performance

When the promises made by the parties under an agreement have been properly performed by the parties, the contract is said to be concluded by performance (see Figure 19.1).

activebook

To help you to remember and understand the topics covered so far, and for links to legal websites, refer to your online activebook. Model answers provide feedback to problems and exercises.

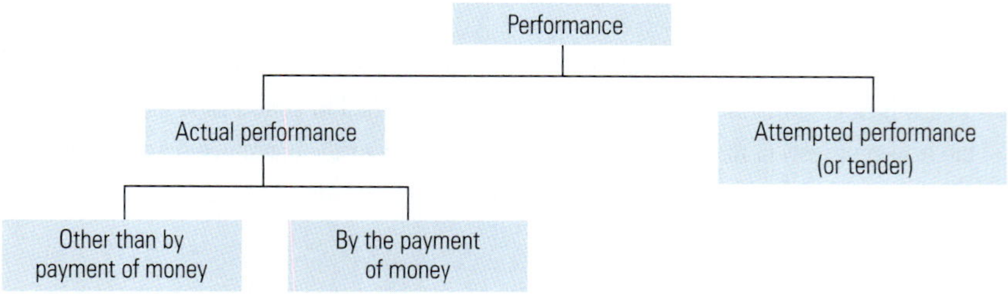

FIGURE 19.1 *Types of performance*

Actual performance

Variation from terms of the contract

The parties are discharged from any obligations, provided that the **performance corresponds** as closely as practicable with the terms of the contract. This rule is fairly strictly interpreted at common law.

***RE MOORE & CO. LTD AND LANDAUER & CO.* [1921] 2 KB 519**

An order was placed for tins of canned fruit to be delivered in cases of 30 tins per case. When the goods arrived, the correct quantity was delivered, but half the cases contained 24 tins.

ISSUE: Could the buyer reject the order because of a variation from the terms of the agreement?

DECISION: The buyer could reject all the goods if he so wished, as the method in which the fruit was packed was an essential part of the contract description. Performance had not been exactly as agreed.

COMMENT: While the decision to allow the buyer to reject the order may sound trivial, given that he received the right number of tins, it should be realised that storage costs may have been a significant factor in the buyer's decision. The cases containing 24 tins may have taken up more space than the 30-tin cases and if the profit margin is small, the extra storage space required could turn a profit into a loss.

If variation is only minimal or trivial, then generally the courts will not worry about it.

***SHIPTON, ANDERSON & CO. V. WEILL BROTHERS & CO.* [1912] 1 KB 574**

The seller agreed to supply 4950 tons of wheat to the buyer. Upon delivery the buyer discovered that they had only received 4895 tons and they refused to accept delivery.

ISSUE: Was the difference sufficiently serious to allow the buyer to reject the delivery?

DECISION: The buyer could not reject delivery because the shortfall was insignificant.

COMMENT: Unlike *Re Moore*'s case, space wouldn't be an issue given the size of the order.

Partial performance

IN BRIEF

Where there has been partial performance

Where there has been partial performance, payment does not automatically follow unless:

- the contract is divisible, i.e. can be divided up into its component parts—a question of construction;
- where there has been free and willing acceptance of partial performance by the party receiving the benefit;
- where substantial performance has taken place; or
- the actions by the non-performing party prevent performance.

Divisible or entire?

Contracts are either entire or divisible

Contracts can be classified as being either:

- **entire**—in this case the contract must be performed in full; or
- **divisible** or **severable**—this is a contract which is capable of being divided up into its component parts.

Whether a contract is entire or divisible is one of construction

It is not always easy to tell whether a contract is entire or divisible. It is a question of **construction**, taking into account what the parties said and did at the time of contracting. For example, imagine that you enter into a contract with a builder to build a house. The contract states that the builder is to be paid by stages, and that the first payment is due and payable when the site is cleared and prepared for the slab, and the last payment is due and payable at lock-up, with various stages identified in-between. If the builder is unable to finish the construction, it would not mean a loss of all rights for the builder because it is possible to identify what stage has been reached, and therefore what payment is due. In other words, the **contract is divisible. It would then be possible for the builder to seek payment for what has been completed** on the basis of a *quantum meruit*—'what he deserves'—for this is based on an implied promise to pay a reasonable sum for work actually done (see pp. 420–421).

With the house now at lock-up stage, imagine that you have entered into a contract with a painter which states that payment for painting the house is to be 'payable on completion'. In this situation, failure to complete the painting could have serious consequences for the painter because, unlike the case of the builder where the contract could be said to be divisible, the contract here appears to be entire, and entitlement to payment only comes upon completion of the task. The reason is that the consideration for the right to demand payment is the promise to complete the work. In this type of situation, where there is an express contract still in force to pay the full amount, the painter cannot even recover any money on the basis of *quantum meruit* because the **express promise takes precedence** over the implied promise.

CUTTER V. POWELL (1795) 101 ER 573

Powell agreed to pay Cutter 30 guineas if he would sail as second mate in a vessel from Jamaica to Liverpool. This was a higher rate than normal for such a voyage. He died at sea before the completion of the voyage. Cutter's widow attempted to recover a proportion of the agreed sum of 30 guineas.

ISSUE: Was the contract one that had to be performed in full or could it be divided up into parts?

DECISION: He had promised to serve as second mate for the whole of the voyage but had not done so. As the contract was not divisible (i.e. payment in full on completion of the whole voyage), and he did not perform his promise, there was no right for the widow to any part of the salary.

A number of exceptions to the principle that performance must be exact and complete before payment can be received can be identified and include:

- **Free and willing acceptance of partial performance by the party receiving the benefit**
  Here the parties are agreeing to abandon their original contract and substitute a new agreement based on the partial performance and the payment of a lesser amount than would have been due under the original contract.
  If the party accepting the changed circumstances has no option but to accept, then there is no free and willing agreement and therefore no acceptance of partial performance.
- **Substantial performance**
  If the breach is minor, so that the cost of rectification is small when compared with the contract price, the **doctrine of substantial performance** may still permit the defaulting party to obtain the contract price. However, it will generally be minus an amount (for rectification) that the innocent party needs to have the contract completed.

HOENIG V. ISAACS [1952] 2 ALL ER 176

FACTS: The plaintiff was employed to redecorate and furnish the defendant's flat for £750 to be paid 'as the work proceeds, and balance on completion'. Only £400 was paid. The work was poorly done and the cost of rectification was £60. The defendant refused to pay the balance.

ISSUE: Was the contract entire? If it was, because it hadn't been performed as agreed, should the plaintiff be able to recover?

DECISION: The plaintiff was entitled to recover the contract amount, less the cost of rectification because the contract had been substantially performed and the defects were easily rectifiable.

- **If one party is prevented from performing, the other party may regard the contract as at an end**
  The party being prevented from performing will be released from any further obligations and they can:
  - repudiate the contract;
  - claim for damages for breach of contract;
  - repudiate the contract and claim for damages; or
  - if performance had commenced but had not been completed, claim on a *quantum meruit*.

Quantum meruit

This is usually confined to those cases in which a person renders some service at the request of another and no remuneration is fixed. The party providing the service bases their claim on an implied term that they should be paid a reasonable amount for the work already done (see also pp. 420–421).

Performance and the delivery of goods

Buyers must take goods if they are ready for delivery

If one party to a contract offers to perform their obligations under the contract and the other party refuses to accept the offer, the person offering the service will be discharged from further performance, provided that the attempted performance was exactly in accordance with the terms of the contract. The contract will, in fact, be dissolved.

For example, if A delivers goods to B in accordance with the terms of the contract as to type, quality and quantity, and B rejects them, A has done all that is required under the contract and would therefore be discharged from any further liabilities under that contract. Furthermore, A would be entitled to sue B for non-acceptance of the goods, as B's refusal to accept the goods amounts to a breach of contract under state and territory sale of goods legislation.

Performance and the payment of money

- **Absolute discharge.** Where a contract is to be completed by the payment of money, it is necessary that the payment be made in the proper manner. That is, payment to the right person at the right place at the right time, and by legal tender—or bill of exchange, promissory note, cheque or payment order, as long as it is in absolute satisfaction of the debt.
- **Conditional discharge—payment by cheque.** Where payment is made by cheque, the debtor will not receive an absolute discharge unless the creditor has expressly asked for payment by cheque. A cheque is only a conditional payment. The bank has to honour the cheque before the creditor can get the money. If the creditor did not ask for payment by cheque and the cheque is subsequently dishonoured by the bank, then the parties revert to their former positions, but now the creditor is able to sue on the contract or the cheque.

Doing business

Take care where there is payment by cheque

If the creditor has expressly asked for payment by cheque, the contract is discharged as paid. If the cheque is then dishonoured, the creditor can only sue the debtor or drawer of the cheque. The creditor cannot sue on the contract, since this has been discharged in the manner requested by the creditor—that is, by cheque. If the creditor did not ask for payment by cheque, then the creditor can sue on either the cheque or the contract. ■

Place of payment

The payment must be made at the creditor's normal place of business within normal business hours, unless there has been some indication or agreement that payment is to take place somewhere else. The onus is on the debtor to find and pay the creditor. It is not necessary for the creditor to go out and find the debtor unless this is what the parties have agreed to, or the debtor is in default.

If the debtor offers to pay and the creditor refuses to accept it, the debtor is not discharged from liability. Provided that payment was made in the legal manner, in any subsequent action to recover payment the creditor's costs will have to be met by the creditor. The debtor pays the amount involved into court as soon as the action is commenced.

Payment by post

> **!** CAUTION NOTE
>
> *Determine at whose request payment by post was made because it is then possible to ascertain whether the post office was the agent of the creditor or the debtor.*

Payment by post can occur by way of request by the creditor or on the initiative of the debtor. Whichever way occurs, the consequences will differ:

- **Requested by the creditor**

  If the creditor requires payment to be made by post, the normal rules of contracts by post apply. Where the letter containing the money is lodged at the post office, this is considered as a discharge from liability if the letter is lost in transit, for the post office is the agent of the creditor. The debt itself is discharged when the claim connected with it is made on the debtor's bankers.

  If no claim is made because the cheque is lost, the debtor is not discharged and will be required to send another cheque. In such cases, the money should be sent in accordance with normal business practice.

- **Debtor pays by post**

  If the creditor has not expressly indicated that payment must be by post—for example, if the account reads 'Payment within 7 days' rather than 'Payment within 7 days by post'—loss of the letter and its contents is borne by the debtor, irrespective of what past practice has been, unless payment is in another city or a great distance away.

Doing business

Using money wisely—debtor owes more than one debt to creditor

If the debtor owes more than one debt to the creditor, the debtor has the option at the time of payment of nominating which of the debts is to be discharged. Different debts may carry different interest rates. If the debtor does not exercise this option at the time of payment, the creditor can appropriate the sum to the account of their choice. ■

By agreement

What can be done by the parties with one agreement can be undone by them with another. The new agreement must satisfy all the essential elements as to the formation of a contract.

IN BRIEF

Types of cancellation of the original agreement

Type	Description
Mutual discharge	Both parties abandon their original agreement while it is still executory.
Release	One party has performed their obligations and chooses to release the other before they have performed their contractual obligations.
Waiver	One party leads the other to reasonably believe that strict performance will not be insisted upon.
Substituted agreement	A new agreement is substituted for the old by the parties—novation.
Accord and satisfaction	One party has performed their obligations and agrees to relieve the other party of its obligations in return for doing something different.

Mutual discharge

The parties abandon their original agreement while there is still something to be done by both sides. The contract is still **executory** (yet to be performed).

***Mutual discharge*—both parties abandon executory agreement**

Both parties surrender their rights under the original contract, and it is this mutual abandonment that constitutes the consideration for the discharge of the contract. What you have is A and B saying to each other, 'I will not sue you for failing to perform your obligation if you promise not to sue me for my failure to perform'. These mutual promises constitute sufficient consideration to support the new agreement. This is called a **bilateral discharge** and should be contrasted with the unilateral discharge of release, below.

Release

This is similar to waiver (see below), but here one party has performed their obligations under the contract and the other has not. The contract is not executory. Such a release amounts to a **unilateral discharge**, and will not be effective unless it is:

***Release*—one party has abandoned their obligations**

- under seal; or
- supported by further consideration by the party still under the obligation; or
- subject to the principle of *promissory estoppel*.

For example, A owes B $50 under a contract. B says to A, 'I will accept $25 as a full satisfaction of the debt on the due date'. While it may appear that B has released A from any further obligations under the contract, the release would be invalid because of a lack of consideration. The release is unilateral, and to be effective must be under seal, supported by consideration (see, for example, *Foakes v. Beer*, p. 293), or subject to *promissory estoppel*.

If a **third party** offers a payment of a smaller sum in discharge of the whole debt, and the creditor accepts it, the creditor cannot then maintain an action against the debtor for the balance (see, for example, *Hirachand Punamchand v. Temple*, p. 294).

Waiver

***Waiver*—one party leads the other to believe that strict performance will not be insisted upon**

This occurs where one party leads the other party to reasonably believe that while strict performance can still technically be demanded, it will not be strictly insisted upon. It is usually done to suit the convenience and benefit of one party and may be inferred from the conduct of the parties.

Once given, the party granting the waiver must honour that agreement. They are *estopped* from going back on their word unless they give reasonable notice of its withdrawal. The most common example of waiver occurs where a buyer or seller of goods agrees to defer the delivery date at the request of the other party.

Substituted agreement

***Substituted agreement*—parties wish to continue but on different terms**

This applies where the parties wish to continue with a contractual relationship, but on different terms from those in the original agreement. An example is novation where a new contract is substituted for the old one.

The new contract need not be in the same form as the old one. A written contract, including a deed, can be discharged or varied orally, provided that the intention to rescind is clear.

Accord and satisfaction

***Accord and satisfaction*—defaulting party does something different**

When one party has performed their obligations under a contract and the other has not, if the defaulting party is relieved of their obligations in return for doing something different from what they were bound to do originally, the prior contract is discharged by accord and satisfaction. The '**accord**' refers to the **new agreement**, and the '**satisfaction**' to the **consideration** for it.

We saw above under 'release' that if A owes B $50 and offers B $25 'as full satisfaction of the debt', at common law A is already contractually obligated to pay the full amount. Equity may allow the debtor relief through the doctrine of promissory estoppel (see pp. 296–298). If A, however, arranges with B to pay the $25 at an earlier time or in a different kind or place, and B accepts this as full satisfaction of B's rights, the contract is then said to be discharged by accord and satisfaction.

By frustration

IN BRIEF

Applications of the doctrine of frustration

If a party promises to carry out a particular act, the law will hold them to their promise—the doctrine of absolute liability. Exceptions to this rule include:

- physical impossibility because of destruction of subject matter;
- physical impossibility under contract of personal service;
- change in the law rendering performance impossible;
- impossibility due to non-occurrence of event basic to contract;
- where the particular state of affairs ceases to exist; and
- in Victoria (1959), New South Wales (1978) and South Australia (1988), application of the *Frustrated Contracts Acts*.

If a party promises to carry out a particular act, the law will hold them to their promise. This principle is commonly known as the **doctrine of absolute liability**.

***Frustration*—performance is impossible owing to something beyond the control of either party**

The harshness of this doctrine was demonstrated in *Cutter v. Powell* (see p. 390). The **doctrine of frustration** puts forward a number of important exceptions to the general principle. For example, it would be unreasonable to hold A to a promise to sell B a house if, unknown to either party, the house had burnt to the ground. This contract would be impossible to perform—it is frustrated because its object is no longer attainable owing to something beyond the control of either party. A similar provision can be found in the sale of goods legislation of the various states.

Circumstances where frustration is not available

It is not possible to plead frustration where:

- the parties have made specific provision in the contract for what might otherwise have been a frustrating event;
- it should have been foreseen, but for some reason or another was not;
- the frustrating event was self-induced by the party making the plea;
- hardship;
- inconvenience; or
- expense in performance.

> **!** CAUTION NOTE
> *Frustration can only arise where there is an* ***unforeseen and radical change*** *in surrounding circumstances.*

Necessary ingredients of frustration

Frustration can only arise where:

- an unforeseen event outside the control of the contracting parties (a supervening event) has significantly or radically changed the obligations of the parties from their original intentions;
- neither party caused the supervening event;
- neither contemplated the supervening event, so there was no provision in the contract for it; and
- the new circumstances would make it unjust to hold the parties to their original contract.

NATIONAL CARRIERS V. PANALPINA (NORTHERN) LTD **[1981] 1 ALL ER 161**

Panalpina entered into a 10-year lease of a warehouse from National Carriers in 1974. In 1979 the local authority closed the only street access to the warehouse because of a dangerous building. The street was to be re-opened after the dangerous building was demolished in 1981.

ISSUE: Could Panalpina refuse to pay rent and have the contract set aside on the basis of frustration?

DECISION: Closure of the warehouse for two of the 10 years of the lease did not amount to frustration. The interruption was only temporary and the lease was unconditional. Thus, it did not destroy the identity of the arrangement and make it unjust to hold the parties to their original contract.

Applications of the doctrine of frustration

Cases involving the doctrine of frustration include:

Physical impossibility because of destruction of subject matter

Where the subject matter of a contract, whether for goods or services, is dependent upon the existence of a particular person or thing, the non-existence of that person or thing is sufficient to frustrate the contract.

TAYLOR V. CALDWELL **(1863) 122 ER 309**

A building had been hired to Taylor, who wished to hold a concert there. Before the date of the concert, the hall was destroyed by fire. The hirer claimed damages against the owner for his failure to complete his part of the bargain.

ISSUE: Was the contract frustrated by the destruction of the subject matter of the contract?

DECISION: The contract was frustrated because there was a reasonable expectation that the contract was based on the continued existence of the music hall.

COMMENT: The hall was burnt down after the contract had been entered into. If the hall had been burnt down without the knowledge of the parties while they were still negotiating and they subsequently entered into a contract, it would be void *ab initio* for common mistake. That is, both parties at the time of entering into the contract believed that the hall existed.

Physical impossibility under contract of personal service

If the contract is one for personal service and the promisor dies, becomes sick or incapacitated, is interned or called up for military service, then performance is rendered impossible and the contract is frustrated.

Change in the law rendering performance impossible

A change in the law or other interference by a government, such as the declaration of war, can cause a contract to become frustrated.

***HORLOCK V. BEAL* [1916] AC 486**

Horlock was a seaman on one of Beal's ships, which was detained in a German port at the outbreak of war. Horlock's wife sued Beal for the wages due to her husband under the two-year contract.

ISSUE: Was Horlock's contract frustrated by the outbreak of war and the detention of his ship?

DECISION: The wife's claim failed as the capture and holding of the ship by the Germans amounted to a frustration of the contract, which made performance impossible.

COMMENT: If the intervening events make the performance of the contract less convenient or more costly, the courts will not be prepared to allow a plea of frustration to succeed because the contract will still be possible.

Impossibility owing to non-occurrence of event basic to contract

If the entire basis of a contract is the happening of some event that does not occur, the contract may be discharged.

***KRELL V. HENRY* [1903] 2 KB 740**

Henry hired a room from Krell for the purpose of watching the coronation procession of King Edward VII. The procession was postponed because of the illness of the King, but Krell claimed the rent of the room.

ISSUE: Was the contract frustrated by the non-occurrence of the coronation procession?

DECISION: As it was no longer possible to achieve the substantial purpose of the contract, that is, to watch the procession from the room, the contract was frustrated by the non-occurrence of the event.

CASE REFLECTION: Since the owner was hiring out a room, what difference did it make whether or not there was a coronation procession?

However, if a contract has two objectives, one of which becomes non-attainable as a result of a frustrating event, the contract is not discharged.

***HEARNE BAY STEAM BOAT CO. V. HUTTON* [1903] 2 KB 683**

A steamboat was hired for the purposes of viewing a naval regatta and for a cruise around the bay. The regatta was cancelled, but the cruise around the bay was still possible.

ISSUE: Where the contract has more than one objective, and only one becomes non-attainable, is the contract frustrated?

DECISION: The contract could not be said to be frustrated. Part of it, the cruise around the bay, was still capable of performance.

Where the particular state of affairs ceases to exist

If the circumstances upon which the contract was based have ceased to exist or substantially changed without the fault of either party, so that performance has become radically different from that originally contemplated by the parties, a plea of frustration will succeed.

CODELFA CONSTRUCTION PTY LTD V. STATE RAIL AUTHORITY (NSW)
(1982) 149 CLR 337

Codelfa entered into a contract with the NSW State Rail Authority to excavate an underground railway tunnel within 130 weeks of the signing of the contract. To achieve this result, both parties were aware that Codelfa would need to work 24 hours a day, seven days a week. However, the noise and vibrations caused by the excavation were so great that local residents obtained an interim injunction restricting the amount of noise at night and reducing the working week to six days. This caused Codelfa additional costs and therefore a loss of profit.

ISSUE: Did the granting of the injunction frustrate the contract, entitling them to recover on a *quantum meruit* for the work done rather than the originally agreed price?

DECISION: The contract should be treated as terminated by frustration when there has been a fundamental or radical change in the surrounding circumstances and in the significance of the obligations undertaken. Because of the injunction, the change in shift operation and the actual mode of performance which were forced upon Codelfa, a radically different situation was produced from the one that had been envisaged in the contract. As a result, the contract had been frustrated and Codelfa was entitled to a claim for a payment on a *quantum meruit*.

COMMENT: Frustration will not occur where:

- the contract specifically provides for the change in circumstances;
- the change in circumstances was reasonably foreseeable; or
- the change in circumstances was self-induced.

Effect of frustration

The effect of a frustrating event is to discharge a contract immediately, but only as to the **future** (see Figure 19.2). The contract is not void *ab initio*, but only void from the time of the frustrating event.

For the period that the contract is valid, any obligations that arise must be fulfilled. Money paid under the terms of the contract—for example, by way of a deposit—before the frustrating event occurs cannot be recovered, because at the time the money was paid the contract was valid. You would need to establish a total failure of consideration to be able to recover the money.

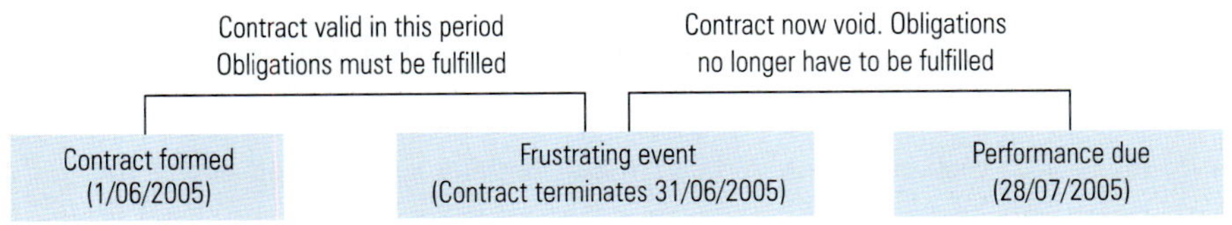

FIGURE 19.2 *The effect of frustration*

***FIBROSA SPOLKA AKCYJNA V. FAIRBAIRN LAWSON COMBE BARBOUR LTD* [1943] AC 32**

An English firm agreed to sell and deliver machinery to a Polish company, who paid a considerable sum of money in advance. Because of the outbreak of war and the German occupation of Poland, the contract was frustrated. The question of frustration was not in issue; the Polish company claimed the right to recover the deposit they had paid prior to the frustrating event.

ISSUE: Was there a total failure of consideration? Did Fibrosa get anything for the money it paid?

DECISION: As the machinery had not been delivered, there was a total failure of consideration; accordingly, the Polish company was entitled to its deposit back.

The position where there has been a part failure of consideration rather than a total failure has been remedied, at least in Victoria (1959), New South Wales (1978) and South Australia (1988) by the Frustrated Contracts Acts.

Application of the *Frustrated Contracts Act 1959* (Vic.)

Victoria—expenses incurred before frustration are recoverable

Money paid under a contract that is subsequently frustrated is recoverable, but if the payee has incurred some expense in carrying out their obligations under the contract they are entitled to recover expenses for the work performed before the occurrence of the frustrating event. This adopts the effects of the *Fibrosa* case, and includes situations in which there has not been a complete failure of consideration.

For example, if A agrees to erect a factory for B for $100 000 payable on the date of completion, and just prior to completion the factory is completely destroyed by fire, under the old common law rules A would not recover anything because the obligation to pay fell due after the frustrating event. However, in Victoria, A would receive some satisfaction under the *Frustrated Contracts Act* because it would be possible to recover expenses for work performed.

Act has no application if parties have anticipated frustrating event

The Act has no application if the parties have anticipated a frustrating event and introduced a term into their contract as to what will happen if such an event does occur, as in the common law position. The Act applies only where the parties do not expect the occurrence of a frustrating event in their contracts.

Application of the *Frustrated Contracts Act 1978* (NSW)

NSW—adjusts rights of parties where a contract has been frustrated

The New South Wales Act also **adjusts the rights** of the parties where a contract has been frustrated. Any monies paid before frustration must be repaid, as must any benefits a party receives from the actions of another party under the contract. Promises due but not performed because of the frustrating event are discharged (except where necessary to support a damages claim).

The Act provides a detailed schedule for adjustment on frustration in Part III to ensure that the parties to the contract share equally the costs that result from the contract's frustration.

Application of the *Frustrated Contracts Act 1988* (SA)

SA—equitable approach to try and ensure fairness

The South Australian Act attempts to ensure that no party is unfairly advantaged or disadvantaged as the result of a frustrating event, and to this end the court has been given wide powers to assure an equitable adjustment is achieved between the parties. It combines the value of contractual benefits received and the value of contractual performance up to the date of frustration, subtracting the latter from the former and then notionally dividing the remainder between the parties equally. However, the Act is subject to any provision in the contract itself as to the consequences of frustration.

By operation of law

Operation of law—contract discharged without either party wishing it

Situations where a contract can be discharged without either party wishing it through operation of law include:

- **Bankruptcy**
  If a person liable under a contract becomes bankrupt, they are statutorily released from all debts and liabilities (see Chapter 32).
- **Material alteration**
  Where a material alteration is made to a written contract without the consent of the other party, the contract becomes unenforceable for the party making the alteration.
- **Merger**
  The merger of a simple contract into a formal contract (a deed) discharges the simple contract.
- **Death of either party**
  A contract for personal services will be discharged by the death of either party.
- **Limitations legislation**
  Lapse of time under the Statute of Limitations legislation of the states and territories will discharge a contract.

By lapse of time at common law

***Lapse of time*—offer remains open for a reasonable time**

In addition to the Statute of Limitations legislation of the states and territories, an offer does not remain open for acceptance for an indefinite length of time at common law. It may cease to exist by lapse of time. However, the length of time depends on the nature of the contract. The courts will look at each case on its merits and decide what is reasonable (e.g., whether the goods are perishable, subject to market fluctuations, demand and supply, etc.).

BALLAS V. THEOPHILOS (NO. 2) (1957) 98 CLR 193

A partnership deed gave the surviving partner an option to purchase the deceased partner's share. The deed did not specify a time limit for the exercise of the option and the surviving partner did not exercise it until some 16 months had elapsed.

ISSUE: What is a reasonable length of time for an offer to remain open?

DECISION: The High Court held that the offer had lapsed by the 'passage of time'. It was not reasonable for the surviving partner to wait 16 months before exercising his option.

By virtue of a term in the contract

Terms may be included in the contract which will have the effect of either preventing the contract from coming into force (condition precedent), or which can bring the contract to an end on the occurrence of a certain event (condition subsequent). These terms were discussed in Chapter 18 on pages 366–367.

By breach

Breach—failure to perform terms as agreed

Where a party **fails to perform their obligations as agreed**, they are in breach of contract. A breach can occur in a number of ways including:

- failure to comply with a term of the contract;
- by a party announcing to the other party that they are no longer interested in carrying out their obligations prior to the time for performance **(anticipatory breach)**; and
- delay in the performance where time is of the essence in the contract.

Actual breach

***Actual breach*— failure to perform at the time required by the contract**

Where one of the parties to the contract fails to perform their promised obligations under the contract in the time that is required by the contract, this will amount to an **actual breach** of the contract. The seriousness of the breach will depend on whether the party in breach breaks a more important term (a condition and a total breach) or a less important term (warranty and a **partial breach**) of the contract. In the case of the former, the innocent party can rescind the contract and/or sue for damages. In the case of the latter, the innocent party must still meet their contractual obligations but may sue for damages.

Anticipatory breach

***Anticipatory breach*— threatened failure to perform at the time required by the contract**

Anticipatory breach can occur expressly or by implication. The threatened failure to perform, the 'anticipation' of the breach, entitles the innocent party to repudiate the contract and sue for breach. Alternatively, the innocent party can elect to affirm, wait until performance is to take place which gives the defaulting party time to complete the contract, or take advantage of any intervening circumstances which would allow them to decline, and then sue for breach.

***FORAN V. WIGHT* (1989) 168 CLR 385**

A contract for the sale of land included a 'time is of the essence' clause. Two days before the settlement date, the vendor's solicitor advised that settlement would have to be postponed. On the due date settlement as specified in the contract did not take place. The purchaser signed a notice of rescission on the settlement date (rather than on the anticipatory breach two days earlier). The purchasers were unable to obtain finance and did not tender performance of their side of the contract on settlement date.

ISSUE: Could the seller sue the purchasers for breach of contract?

DECISION: The High Court held that even though the purchasers were not able to complete on the due date, the notice given by the seller two days earlier of non-performance of an essential term amounted to an anticipatory breach and entitled the purchasers to rescind.

COMMENT: The purchasers were also able to recover their deposit as consideration had wholly failed.

Doing business

Beware of the effects of anticipatory breach

Allowing the innocent party to anticipate a breach has the benefit of allowing them to mitigate or minimise their loss by making alternative arrangements, which reduces the damages that the guilty party may have to pay for breach. By electing to wait until performance is due, the risk is that the party in breach may have an excuse for not performing, e.g., because a supervening event frustrates the contract, thereby depriving the innocent party of a remedy. ■

Effect of breach

Effect of breach depends on the importance of the term that is broken, i.e. condition or warranty

If one party fails to perform their obligations under the contract (a total breach) or breaches a condition, the innocent party is entitled to treat the contract as ended from the time of the terminating event and may be able to recover damages. The contract is not treated as void *ab initio*. Any rights and obligations that have already arisen from the partial performance of the contract will remain unaffected. The parties are only relieved of the obligation to perform after the date on which the contract was discharged.

If a party breaches a less important term (a warranty), then there is a partial breach and while the innocent party is still going to have to carry out their obligations under the contract, they may sue for damages.

If one party indicates that they will not be performing their part of the contract prior to the time for performance, the innocent party can immediately treat the contract as at an end and sue for breach. There is no need to wait until actual breach occurs.

Remedies for breach of contract are considered in the next chapter.

? REVIEW QUESTIONS

19.1 Indicate whether each of the following statements is true or false:

	TRUE	FALSE
▪ The parties are discharged from any obligations, provided that performance corresponds exactly with the terms of the contract	☐	☐
▪ A claim for *quantum meruit* can be made even where the contract is classified as entire	☐	☐
▪ If there has been substantial performance of the contract, the doctrine of substantial performance may permit the defaulting party to still obtain the contract price	☐	☐
▪ Where one party is prevented from performing, the other party may regard the contract as at an end	☐	☐
▪ Payment by cheque is considered to be an absolute discharge of the debt by the debtor	☐	☐
▪ If the debtor pays by post, the normal rules of contract by post apply and the loss of the letter and its contents is with the creditor	☐	☐
▪ Where one party has performed their obligations under the contract and the other has not, and the release of the party who is yet to perform is executed the release amounts to a bilateral discharge	☐	☐
▪ An example of novation is where the parties wish to continue their contract but on different terms from those in the original agreement	☐	☐
▪ If a party promises to carry out a particular act, the law will hold them to their promise	☐	☐
▪ An unanticipated event outside the control of the contracting parties is known as a supervening event	☐	☐
▪ If an event on which the contract was based does not occur, the contract is discharged by frustration	☐	☐
▪ Contracts for personal service will be frustrated if the performer dies	☐	☐
▪ Discharge by frustration applies only to future rights and obligations under the contract	☐	☐
▪ Money paid under a contract that becomes frustrated is recoverable	☐	☐
▪ A partial breach arises where one party breaches a less important term of a contract	☐	☐
▪ A party to a contract who indicates to the other party that they will not perform their contractual obligations prior to the time for performance commits an anticipatory breach of the contract	☐	☐

19.2 Explain the meaning of the following terms as they are used in contract law:

a novation

b *quantum meruit*

c legal tender

d waiver.

19.3 How have the courts tried to avoid the rule in *Cutter v. Powell*?

19.4 Discuss the rules of payment by post.

activebook

Activebook resources include in-depth summaries with links to the relevant part of the book. For revision, add your own notes to the summaries provided by using the note-taking function.

19.5 Under what circumstances will the *quantum meruit* rule operate?

19.6 For frustration to be successfully raised for discharge of a contract, what conditions must be met?

19.7 List the categories of events that the courts in the past have considered to be frustrating events.

19.8 A fishing company owned four trawlers of a type only useful if fitted with an otter trawl. The company then chartered a similar trawler, which increased the fleet size to five. To fit this type of trawl required the permission of the Minister of Fisheries. The company applied for five licences, but was granted only four. The company fitted the four trawls to four of the boats it owned, and then claimed that the charter of the fifth boat was now impossible and that the contract was at an end.

Is the fishing company correct in its belief?

19.9 A ship was chartered to proceed 'with all convenient speed' from Liverpool, and one of the terms of the agreement read 'all and every danger and accident of the seas excepted'. The ship left Liverpool but ran on to rocks the following day, and it was over three months before it could be towed off. After this was done, it was found that months of work would be needed before the ship would be seaworthy again.

Was the contract frustrated despite the term in the contract regarding accidents at sea?

19.10 Kowaiski and Smith entered into a charter-party contract whereby Smith was to load wheat in a Russian port. War was declared between Russia and England prior to the performance of this contract, which meant that Smith would be involved in trading with an enemy nation should he try to carry out the terms of the contract. This would be an illegal act.

Advise the parties as to their contractual position.

19.11 How do the following terms in a contract differ?

a condition

b condition precedent

c condition subsequent.

19.12 Where an offer has no stated duration as to when it should be accepted, how do the courts determine when it lapses, or does it remain open indefinitely?

19.13 In April, Jackson engaged Tim as a courier. Tim was to commence work on 1 June. On 1 May Jackson wrote to Tim telling him that, despite their agreement, economic circumstances were such that he no longer required his services.

Can Tim sue Jackson?

CRITICAL THINKING

19.1 The privity of contract rule has been criticised by both the courts and academics for a number of years. In the *Trident Insurance* case the High Court recognised these critcisms. Read the case (it can be found at the Austlii site on the Web <http://www.austlii.edu.au> under Commonwealth and then High Court decisions) and discuss what those criticisms were and whether today you think they are still justified.

19.2 What are the consequences at common law of frustration of contract? How have the statutory reforms of New South Wales, Victoria and South Australia addressed some of the difficulties created by the operation of the doctrine? Discuss.

CHAPTER 20

Remedies for Breach of Contract

CHAPTER CONTENTS

RESCISSION

RESTITUTION

DAMAGES

Principles upon which damages are based

Types of damages

Liquidated and unliquidated damages

Penalty

EQUITABLE REMEDIES

Specific performance

Injunction

Anton Piller order

Quantum meruit

LOSS OF RIGHT TO SUE

Statutes of limitations

> **activebook**
>
> This icon is used throughout the following chapter to remind you to visit the *Business Law* online activebook for additional exercises, links to legal websites, and feedback. For a detailed explanation of what is in the activebook please refer to the inside cover of this textbook. The activebook is available through OneKey.
>
> **Where do I start?**
> **Learning path**: Use the activebook to complete a pre-chapter warm-up exercise.
> There are many definitions of legal terms to assist with your understanding of the material.

CHAPTER OBJECTIVES

On completion of this chapter, you should be able to:

- list the remedies for breach of contract
- explain the remedies available to an injured party at common law
- describe situations where an equitable remedy may be used
- explain the principles upon which damages are decided
- classify the types of damages.

KEY TERMS

An understanding of the following terms will help you to better understand the material in this chapter:

- **causation:** the connection between the breach and the loss suffered by the plaintiff
- **damages:** compensation in monetary form for the loss suffered by the plaintiff, which puts the plaintiff back in the position they would have been in had the breach not occurred

- **exemplary damages:** punitive damages
- **injunction:** a discretionary remedy in equity restraining a party from doing something
- **liquidated damages:** agreed sum based on a genuine pre-estimate of the actual loss suffered by the plaintiff in the event of breach of the contract
- **mitigation:** the steps taken by the plaintiff to minimise his or her loss
- **nominal damages:** where the plaintiff's rights have been infringed but he or she has suffered no actual loss
- **ordinary damages:** the amount awarded by the court on its assessment of the loss suffered by the plaintiff as a result of the breach
- ***quantum meruit*:** as much as a person has earned or as much as they deserve
- **remoteness:** the losses suffered by the plaintiff must be reasonably related to the contract
- **specific performance:** a discretionary remedy in equity compelling a defendant to carry out their promise to complete the transaction
- **unliquidated damages:** damages for a loss, but whose value cannot be accurately determined or exactly calculated.

what if . . .

You were buying a popular second-hand car from a car dealer and after lengthy negotiations you settled on a price of $16 500 and signed a contract. However, you had to go to the bank to get the cash from your savings account. When you returned half an hour later the dealer told you that he had made a mistake in his calculations and that you needed an extra $2000 to cover statutory charges and registration or he wouldn't sell you the car.

The method by which an injured party enforces a right or corrects a loss is by way of a 'remedy'. The remedies available to the injured party will depend on the nature of the breach and the results will differ between the parties. The usual remedy for a breach of contract is an award of damages, which is a common law remedy. However, if a monetary remedy is not satisfactory, the court may exercise its discretion and order any one of several equitable remedies including restitution, specific performance, an injunction, *quantum meruit* or an Anton Piller order. It should be remembered from Chapter 1 that equitable remedies are based on the concept of fairness (see p. 12).

This chapter considers the main remedies that are available for a breach of contract at common law and in equity, i.e. damages, and the major equitable remedies.

IN BRIEF

Remedies for breach

Type	Description
Rescission	An equitable remedy that entitles the injured party to set the contract aside and restores the injured party to their pre-contractual position.
Restitution	Means restoration and is based on the concept of unjust enrichment. D must obtain a benefit or enrichment at P's expense and it would be unjust to allow D to keep that benefit or enrichment.
Damages	The normal common law remedy for breach of a condition, warranty or intermediate term. The object is to compensate P for the loss suffered as a consequence of the breach by D and put the parties in the position they would have occupied if the contract had been performed.
Specific performance	An equitable remedy granted at the court's discretion, usually if damages are not an adequate remedy, directing a person to carry out their obligations under the contract. Not available in contracts of personal service.
Injunction	An equitable remedy granted at the court's discretion, usually if damages are not an adequate remedy, restraining a party from breaking their contract or from committing a wrongful act. Aims at enforcing a negative promise.
Anton Piller order	Used where it appears D has incriminating evidence in their possession which can assist P's case but which D may destroy before a court order can be obtained.
Quantum meruit	Only arises in cases of part-performance and requires the party taking the benefit to pay a reasonable amount for the portion given.

RESCISSION

Rescission is an equitable remedy

Rescission is an equitable remedy, which allows an innocent party to cancel the contract by rescinding or, if there has been misrepresentation by the other party, raising that misreprepresentation as a defence if sued for damages or specific performance by the other party. Its purpose is to reverse the contract and restore the parties as near as practicable to their original pre-contractual positions, relieving each party of their obligations and permitting recovery of any benefits conferred on each other. However, the remedy of rescission is narrower than damages for breach of contract as it will not cover damages which might flow naturally and reasonably from the injury.

Rescission may be granted because of mistake, misrepresentation, undue influence, duress, unconscionability or under s. 75A of the *Trade Practices Act 1974* (Cth). Section 75A provides that a consumer is entitled to rescind a contract for the supply of goods for breach of implied conditions as to title, correspondence with description, merchantable quality, fitness for purpose and sale by sample corresponding to those that are implied in contracts of sale under Sale of Goods legislation.

Substantial restoration must be possible or rescission is not available to the injured party.

The injured party's right to rescind is lost:

- if the parties cannot be reasonably closely restored to their original positions, for example, because the subject-matter of the contract has been substantially altered;
- if they elect to continue with the transaction;
- if their conduct is unconscionable;

- if they fail to act;
- through lapse of time; or
- where an innocent third party acquires an interest in the subject matter where they have acted in good faith and for valuable consideration, eg., where they have bought a car from a person who only has a voidable title as in the case of *Phillips v. Brooks* (p. 320) and *Lewis v. Averay* (p. 321).

RESTITUTION

Restitution—its basis is unjust enrichment and is based in quasi contract

Restitution (or restoration) is sometimes referred to as **quasi-contract**. It is not contractual and does not rely on the plaintiff suffering loss or damage. Its basis is **unjust enrichment** (i.e. those situations where it would be very unfair if the defendant was allowed to retain the money, or the goods or services, without payment), and on its own in Australia this is not a cause of action. To overcome this, the law has evolved the remedy of quasi-contract.

Four requirements must be satisfied for a plaintiff's claim to succeed:

- the defendant has received a benefit and enrichment, e.g., an increase in the defendant's wealth or the saving of an expense; **and**
- the benefit was at the plaintiff's expense; **and**
- it would be unjust to allow the defendant to retain the benefit; **and**
- the defendant has no defences available to them to rely upon, e.g., *estoppel*, purchaser in good faith.

The court can require the defendant to pay to the plaintiff a sum of money equal to the sum received from the plaintiff. This may arise where there has been money paid for goods or services received from the plaintiff:

- and there has been a total failure of consideration;
- under a mistake of fact;

COMMONWEALTH V. McCORMACK (1984) 155 CLR 273

An arbitrator ordered the Commonwealth government to pay the appellant lessee (McCormack) $215 000 for improvements he had made to the land before it was resumed by the Commonwealth under the terms of the lease. The Commonwealth government paid the lessee the $215 000 but did not deduct $75 000 which they had previously paid to the lessee as part of an advance payment against any sum that the arbitrator might find to be still due arising from the arbitration.

ISSUE: Was the overpayment of $75 000 by the Commonwealth recoverable on the basis of money paid under a fundamental mistake of fact?

DECISION: The High Court held that the full award payment of $215 000 had been paid under a fundamental mistake of fact and that as a result the Commonwealth government was entitled to recover the $75 000.

- under a mistake of law;

DAVID SECURITIES PTY LTD V. COMMONWEALTH BANK (1992) 66 ALJR 768

David Securites Pty Ltd, a building company, borrowed almost $850 000 from the Commonwealth Bank. The loan was based on the foreign exchange value of the Swiss franc. During the 1980s, the value of the franc and the size of the interest payments increased substantially, placing the company in financial difficulty. They subsequently sought restitution from the Commonwealth Bank for money that they had paid the bank in the mistaken belief that they were required to do so under the *Income Tax Assessment Act 1936* (Cth).

ISSUE: Since this was a mistake in law, was restitution available?

DECISION: The High Court held that there should be no distinction between recovery as a result of mistake of fact and mistake of law where it could be shown that one party was becoming unjustly enriched at the expense of the mistaken party.

- under duress or compulsion.

Restitution makes use of the doctrine of *quantum meruit* where a person provides goods or services but has no right to contractual payment.

PAVEY & MATTHEWS PTY LTD V. PAUL (1987) 162 CLR 221

A builder did some work under an oral contract. The builder's licensing legislation required building contracts to be in writing and so technically the contract was unenforceable. The builder's client refused to pay for the work done. The builder could not sue under the agreement because it was unenforceable and instead sued under *quantum meruit* for work done and materials supplied.

ISSUE: Was this a case of unjust enrichment where to allow the defendants to escape payment because the contract was not in writing would be unjust or inequitable?

DECISION: The High Court held that the *quantum meruit* claim was based on unjust enrichment because of the client's acceptance of the benefits from the builder's performance of the unenforceable oral contract. To allow the defendants to escape payment because the contract was not in writing would be to confer an unjust enrichment upon them.

CASE REFLECTION: Could restitution apply to situations, such as any employee who is overpaid, or a customer of a bank who discovers a large amount of money has mysteriously been credited to their account? Why?

An action on a *quantum meruit* will also lie where the plaintiff has done work under a contract which the other party has broken in such a way as to entitle the plaintiff to treat it as discharged.

PLANCHE V. COLBURN (1831) 131 ER 305

A was employed by a company to write a book for them, which was to be published by instalments in their weekly magazine. After publishing a number of instalments, the company decided to stop publishing the magazine.

ISSUE: Was A entitled to be paid for the work he had done?

DECISION: It was held that A could recover on the basis of a *quantum meruit* for the work that he had done under the contract.

If the plaintiff only partially fulfils their obligations under the contract, and does not complete performance owing to default, then *quantum meruit* is not usually available to recover payment for what they had done.

***SUMPTER V. HEDGES* [1898] 1 QB 673**

The plaintiff, a builder, entered into a contract to build two houses on the defendant's land. After the plaintiff had done a little more than half the work he ran out of money and told the defendant that he could not complete the job. The defendant then completed the houses himself.

ISSUE: Could the plaintiff sue to recover payment for what he had done?

DECISION: The contract was entire, not divisible, and so the plaintiff could not recover under it. Furthermore, the fact that the plaintiff was unable to complete the job was not the fault of the defendant and so there was no entitlement to a *quantum meruit*. While the defendant obtained a benefit, it did not constitute acceptance of partial performance in this case.

CASE REFLECTION: Would the court have been likely to have refused the builder's claim for payment for the work done if the owner of the house had breached the contract? Why?

DAMAGES

Damages are a common law remedy and are awarded as of right

The main purpose of damages is to enable the innocent party to receive **monetary compensation** from the party responsible for the breach of contract. Damages are not awarded to punish a wrongdoer, but rather to put the injured party back in the position that they would have occupied if the contract had been performed as originally intended. Therefore, damages are calculated on the basis of looking at what the position should have been if the contract had been properly performed.

Principles upon which damages are based

There are five steps that must be taken in order to determine whether the injured party will recover damages (see Figure 20.1).

Step 1—Breach

Step 1—establish a breach

The injured party first has to establish that there has been a breach. That is, that the other party to the contract has failed to complete what has been agreed to in the contract. This may be a breach by the other party of:

- a condition
- a warranty
- an intermediate term.

Step 2—Causation

Step 2—causation: P must establish loss is connected to D's breach

The plaintiff must first prove that the loss or damage that they have suffered is a consequence of the defendant's breach. That is, **the loss or damage would not have been suffered 'but for' the defendant's breach**. This test is similar to that required to establish the third element in a negligence action—damage, which was examined in Chapter 7.

As with negligence, if there are multiple causes for the plaintiff's loss or damage, then the plaintiff may not be able to recover if an additional factor unconnected with the defendant's breach breaks the causal chain between the defendant's action and the plaintiff's loss or damage. In *Alexander v. Cambridge Credit Corporation (in rec.)* (1987) 9 NSWLR 310 (see p. 139 for the facts of the case), the causes of the plaintiff's loss were unfavourable economic

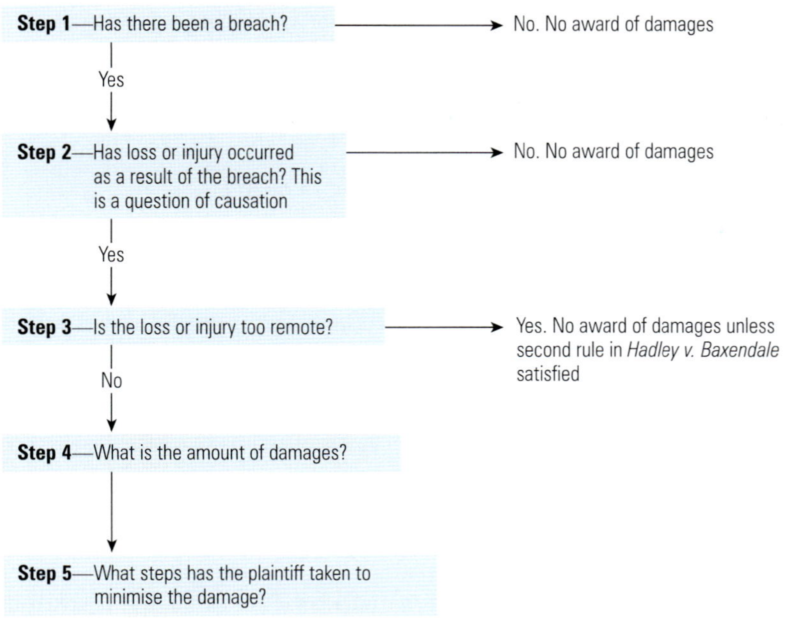

FIGURE 20.1 *Steps in determining an award of damages*

conditions causing a downturn in the property market, and the plaintiff's decision to expand in that market, rather than the defendant's breach of contract through their negligent audit. The question before the court was whether the loss would have occurred 'but for' the defendant's breach of contract and the New South Wales Court of Appeal held that there was no cause or connection between the breach and the loss.

Step 3—Remoteness of damage

> **!** CAUTION NOTE
>
> *Only losses which flow from the usual or normal course of things, and those losses which are special or exceptional and made known to D at the time of entering into the contract, are claimable.*

The court will only be interested in those losses reasonably related to the contract. Losses that are too far removed from the wrongful act are regarded as too remote from the breach and are irrecoverable.

Step 3—remoteness: losses *must* be reasonably related to contract

The court must consider whether the loss suffered by the injured party is a usual and reasonably direct consequence of the breach of contract, and this is a question of fact.

HADLEY V. BAXENDALE (1854) 9 EX 341

Hadley, a mill owner, had to stop work in the mill because of a broken crankshaft. The shaft had to be sent back to the manufacturer because a pattern had to be made for a new one. Baxendale, a carrier, promised

Hadley that the crankshaft would reach the manufacturer on the following day. His negligence, however, resulted in its delay and the mill was out of commission for longer than it should have been.

Hadley sued for damages for loss of profit caused by the delay. The carrier's defence was that he had no way of knowing that the delay in delivery of the shaft would cause the mill to be shut down.

ISSUE: Was the carrier liable for the loss of profits caused by the delay?

DECISION: The carrier was not liable for the loss of profits caused by the delay, as the loss did not flow directly from the breach of contract. It was too remote to have been foreseen by a reasonable person.

COMMENT: If the carrier had been made aware at the outset of entering into the contract that a delay could result in the mill having to be shut down, then he could have been liable for the loss of profits.

CASE REFLECTION: Does informing the other party of the reasons for urgency and/or any other special circumstances give that party a more complete idea of the importance of the contract and its consequences? Might the other party then think the risks are too high and choose not to enter into the contract?

The rule in *Hadley v. Baxendale* indicates that there are two types of loss for which an injured party can claim:

- loss occurring from the breach of contract in the usual or normal course of things; and
- loss arising from **special or exceptional circumstances where such loss was made known** to the offending party at the time the contract was entered into.

VICTORIA LAUNDRY LTD V. NEWMAN INDUSTRIES LTD [1949] 2 KB 528

Newman Industries contracted to deliver a boiler to the plaintiffs. They knew that the plaintiffs required the boiler urgently to enable them to take advantage of favourable trading conditions and to undertake expansion of their business. What the defendants didn't know was that the plaintiffs had successfully negotiated a lucrative government dyeing contract. The boiler was damaged in the course of delivery by Newman and was five months late in installation. The plaintiffs claimed:

- loss of the profit the laundry would have made had the boiler been delivered on time; and
- loss of profit from the dyeing contracts.

ISSUE: Were the loss of profits from the dyeing contracts recoverable under the rule in *Hadley v. Baxendale*?

DECISION: The laundry profits were recoverable, as the defendants must have contemplated that there would be a loss if there was a delay. However, the loss on the dyeing contracts was not recoverable. The defendants were not in a position to know of the highly profitable nature of such contracts for which the plaintiff was negotiating as they had not been told or put on notice of any special circumstances that might follow if there was a delay in delivery. As a result, this was reasonably beyond the contemplation of the defendants.

activebook

To help you to remember and understand the topics covered so far, and for links to legal websites, refer to your online activebook. Model answers provide feedback to problems and exercises.

A defendant is not liable for damages that could be considered to be abnormal or unforeseeable, because they are considered to be too remote. If a plaintiff wants to recover damages in this situation, they must put the defendant on notice of the special or exceptional circumstances that may apply.

Doing business

Put the other party in the know

P will only be able to **recover damages that are reasonably foreseeable** as likely to result from a breach. This depends on the **knowledge** possessed by the parties and may be actual or constructive. Actual knowledge means that D knew what the situation was. Constructive knowledge means that a reasonable person would have known what the situation was. To save litigation costs, tell D of any special or exceptional circumstances that may apply at the time of making the contract.

Step 4—Amount of damages

P must show some loss to recover ordinary damages

Once the court has decided that damages are payable to the injured party, what **amount of damages** should be awarded? The general principle is that an injured party should be put in a position they would have been in had the breach never occurred.

The injured party must be able to show that they have suffered some loss, if they are to recover ordinary damages. If this cannot be shown, then at best the injured party will only be entitled to recover nominal damages by proving that the other party did breach the contract. Thus, if A agrees to sell B a 1906 Rolls Royce for $50 000 and then refuses to go ahead with the sale, the only damage that B has suffered is the loss of the car. B is still to pay A. In this case, the measure of damages would be the difference between the original contract price and the price B has to pay to get another Rolls from someone else. If B has to pay $80 000, the amount of ordinary damages B would be entitled to claim would be $30 000. If B finds another Rolls for only $40 000, while there has been a breach of contract, B will be unable to show a loss because the cost of the second Rolls was $10 000 less than the first Rolls. As a result, B will only be entitled to nominal damages for proving that the contract was broken.

If, on the other hand, B refuses to accept delivery, A still has the Rolls, but no $50 000. In this case, the measure of damages would be the difference between the contract price and the price A could receive on the open market for the car. If A could sell the Rolls for $40 000, there is a shortfall of $10 000 to put A in the position that they would have been in had the breach never occurred. If buyers are plentiful and the Rolls can be easily resold, the buyer's default may be meaningless to the seller. In this case the seller would have to carefully consider whether it was worth bringing an action because only nominal damages would be awarded by the court. If buyers are hard to find, the seller would be entitled to compensation for the loss of profits.

Courts will generally not grant damages for anything other than provable or economic losses. However, in certain instances the courts will allow claims for damages for:

- **expectation losses** arise out of the plaintiff's expectation of prospective benefit arising out of or created by the contract, e.g., loss of a commercial opportunity and loss of profit arising from the loss of the defendant's performance;
- **reliance losses** arise out of expenditure incurred by the plaintiff relying on the defendant's promise:

COMMONWEALTH OF AUSTRALIA V. AMANN AVIATION PTY LTD **(1991) 104 ALR 1**

Amann agreed to provide the Commonwealth with aerial surveillance for Australia's northern coastline. Amann had to purchase and modify planes for the project. It was anticipated that this would take six months.

Before the six months had expired, it had become obvious that Amann would not be able to undertake its contractual obligations, so the Commonwealth terminated the contract on the basis of breach by Amann. However, the contract contained a clause that specified that in the event of a breach, the Commonwealth must serve a notice on the defaulting party to show cause why the contract should not be terminated. The Commonwealth had failed to do this.

By the time the matter reached the High Court, it was agreed that the Commonwealth had wrongfully terminated the contract and that the only question for the court was the assessment of damages.

ISSUE: Could damages be awarded for the wasted expenditure by Amann in buying and equipping the aircraft, i.e. could 'reliance damages' be recovered?

DECISION: The High Court held that in the circumstances, regard must be had for the expenditure incurred by Amann in purchasing and equipping the planes in anticipation of performing its duties under the contract. As a result, the court awarded Amann $6.6 million 'reliance damages', for its wasted expenditure in acquiring and equipping the aircraft for the contract.

COMMENT: On the question of remoteness, it was held that the damages claimable for the loss of chance of contract renewal by Amann were not too remote and fell within the second limb of the rule in *Hadley v. Baxendale*.

- **anxiety;**
- **inconvenience;**
- **disappointment and distress;**

JARVIS V. SWAN TOURS [1972] 3 WLR 954

Jarvis arranged a two-week holiday in Switzerland through Swan Tours' office as a result of information contained in one of its brochures. However, few of the statements contained in the brochure proved to be accurate.

ISSUE: Was Jarvis entitled to damages for disappointment caused by the breach?

DECISION: Jarvis was entitled to damages for disappointment caused by the breach. The holiday did not live up to the promises that were contained in the defendant's brochure.

- **frustration;**
- **discomfort;** and
- **mental distress**.

JACKSON V. HORIZON HOLIDAYS [1975] 1 WLR 1468

Mr Jackson booked a holiday to Sri Lanka for himself and his family through a travel agent, Horizon Holidays. He booked by providing the travel agent with specific directions on what he wanted for himself and his family after looking at a brochure. The hotel he had chosen was under construction, so the travel agent selected another hotel, which turned out to be grossly inferior to the one the travel agent had led the plaintiff to believe they would be staying in.

The travel agent admitted that there was a breach of contract, and the question for the court was only the question of assessing damage.

ISSUE: What could damages be awarded for? Were damages recoverable for disappointment, discomfort and mental distress? Were the wife and family entitled to recover damages as well?

DECISION: The wife and family were not parties to the contract. The contract was one entered into by Mr Jackson on behalf of his wife and family, so they were not parties to the contract. However, Mr Jackson could recover any expenses which they were entitled to recover and pay that over to them. This included damages for disappointment, discomfort and mental distress.

The courts seem to be prepared to allow recovery of damages by a plaintiff for injured feelings, anxiety, disappointment and distress in certain situations, for example, if there is breach of an express or implied term that the promisor would provide the innocent party with pleasure, enjoyment or personal protection, and the failure to do so has caused physical injury or inconvenience to the plaintiff.

BALTIC SHIPPING CO. LTD V. DILLON (1993) 111 ALR 289

Dillon was a passenger on board a ship that struck a shoal and sank eight days into the cruise. She was injured and, as a result, sued Baltic Shipping for damages.

ISSUE: Was she entitled to recover the full fare and damages for disappointment and distress?

DECISION: On appeal, the High Court said that where the object of a contract was to provide enjoyment and relaxation, if that object was not achieved then damages would be available for disappointment and distress. The damage claimed was a direct result of the breach and remoteness was not an issue.

COMMENT: On the issue of the recovery of the full fare, the respondent was unsuccessful since there had not been a total failure of consideration. She had enjoyed the benefits of the first eight days of sailing and to have allowed full restitution of the fare in addition to the damages awarded for breach of contract would have been excessive compensation.

It appears that damages for distress or disappointment will only be awarded by the courts where there has been a breach of an express or implied term that the promisor will provide the promisee with pleasure or enjoyment that can be typically derived from a holiday.

It can be difficult to determine the amount of damages to be recovered by the injured party for a breach. However, this is not a ground for disallowing a claim.

HOWE V. TEEFY (1927) 27 SR (NSW) 301

The defendant leased a racehorse to the plaintiff for three years. After six months, the defendant took the horse back. As part of his damages claim for breach of contract the plaintiff sued for loss of potential prize money and profits that he would have made from betting on the horse. The jury awarded the plaintiff damages and the defendant appealed.

ISSUE: Where damages, such as loss of potential prize money and winnings from bets are not calculable, is the plaintiff entitled to recover them?

DECISION: The plaintiff was entitled to recover damages for potential loss of prize money and profits he could have made.

COMMENT: The plaintiff had suffered a loss and the fact that it was difficult to calculate did not prevent the jury from trying to determine what would be an appropriate amount for the plaintiff to recover.

The courts examine all the material in order to arrive at what they believe is a reasonable approximation of the loss suffered by the injured party.

Step 5—Mitigation of damages

Doing business

Minimise the loss

Whether it be anticipatory or actual breach, the injured party should take immediate steps to minimise the loss or face the prospect of having the court reduce the amount of damages that can be recovered.

P must try to minimise damage

In addition to the questions of remoteness and measure, the law imposes **a duty upon the person claiming damages (the injured party) to take all reasonable steps to reduce or minimise (mitigate) their loss**. If they fail to take these steps, the amount of damages they can expect to recover will be reduced. If the plaintiff is able to avoid a loss, damages will not be recoverable for the potential loss that the plaintiff may have suffered.

PAYZU V. SAUNDERS **[1919] 2 KB 581**

Under a contract to deliver goods by instalments, payment to be made within one month of delivery, the buyers failed to make payment for the first delivery. The seller felt that he was entitled to treat the breach as sufficient to repudiate the entire agreement but offered to continue to make monthly deliveries if the buyers agreed to pay cash on delivery. The buyers rejected this offer. After the price of the goods rose, the buyers sued for breach of contract.

ISSUE: Was the seller liable for damages? Should the buyer have mitigated their loss by accepting the seller's offer?

DECISION: In the circumstances, the seller should not have treated the buyer's failure to pay the first instalment as a breach sufficient to entitle the seller to repudiate the entire contract. The seller was liable for damages but the buyer should have mitigated their loss by accepting the seller's new proposal for cash on supply. The damages were to be assessed on the loss they would have sustained if they had accepted the seller's cash on delivery proposal, not the difference between the contract price and the market price.

The burden of proof is on **the defendant** to show that the plaintiff failed to mitigate their losses and this is a **question of fact** in the particular circumstances. Thus, if a person is wrongfully dismissed from their job, they must take reasonable steps to find other employment. They will not be able to recover any part of the loss that is attributable to their failure to try to find another job.

***Mitigation* is a question of fact, with the burden of proof on D**

Types of damages

Once it has been established that the plaintiff is entitled to compensation, it will have to be determined what type of damages will be awarded (see Figure 20.2). This will be determined by the seriousness of the breach and whether the contract has specified the amount of damages to be paid in the event of a breach.

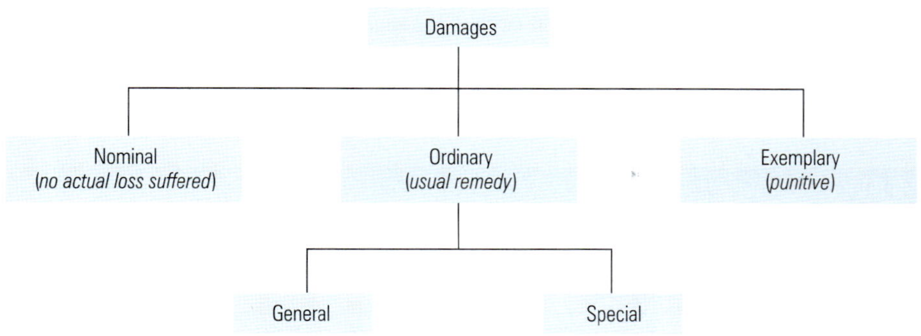

FIGURE 20.2 *Types of damages*

Nominal damages

These are awarded where the court feels that **the innocent party's legal rights have been infringed, but they have suffered no actual loss**.

***Nominal* damages—no actual loss is suffered by P**

***CHARTER V. SULLIVAN* [1957] 2 QB 117**

Sullivan entered into a contract with Charter to purchase a car. Sullivan subsequently refused to go ahead with the purchase, and Charter sued for breach of contract, seeking the profit he would have made if the sale had gone through. It was established that Charter would have had no difficulty in reselling the car at the same price, and that he could have sold every car of that make he could have obtained.

ISSUE: Was Charter entitled to damages? If so, what sort of damages should he get?

DECISION: While there was a breach of contract, Charter was not entitled to ordinary damages because he could not show any loss, but he was entitled to nominal damages for the breach (in this case £2).

In *Charter v. Sullivan* (above), the innocent party would need to consider whether it was worth bringing an action in the first place. The legal costs involved would outweigh the compensation received unless the innocent party was to be awarded costs, and there can be no guarantee that the court will do this.

Ordinary or 'real' damages

***Ordinary* damages—loss suffered by P as a result of the breach**

Ordinary damages are the usual remedy in contract law. **This is the amount awarded by the court on its assessment of the loss suffered by the innocent party as a result of the breach.** They are a means of compensation and can take two forms:

- **general damages**, which follow as a general consequence from the breach; and
- **special damages**, which, if they are to be claimed, have to be specially proved in court.

Exemplary damages

***Exemplary* damages—punitive and may be awarded for non-pecuniary loss**

These are generally not awarded unless the court feels that it should punish the party in default. However, where the breach of contract has resulted in inconvenience, disappointment or discomfort to the innocent party, the courts have been prepared to award what are termed 'aggravated damages for non-pecuniary loss'. Examples have included cases involving holiday packages where, for example, the facilities or accommodation have been misrepresented by the travel agent or the person they represent.

Liquidated and unliquidated damages

IN BRIEF

Liquidated and unliquidated damages and penalty

Type	Description
Liquidated	Fixed amount. Must be a genuine pre-estimate of actual loss flowing from the breach.
Unliquidated	Left to the court to determine. Not fixed in the contract.
Penalty	A clause intended to deter or penalise a party which is out of proportion with the loss that could be suffered from a breach.

A plaintiff can sue for either liquidated or unliquidated damages, or both, for breach of a contract.

Liquidated damages

***Liquidated* damages—agreed sum based on a genuine pre-estimate of actual loss suffered by P**

These are a **fixed amount** in the contract. The parties agree to what should be paid in the event of a breach, and the clause is known as an agreed damages clause. It must be a genuine or *bona fide* pre-estimate of actual loss that will flow from the breach. The defaulting party will then have to pay that amount without the innocent party even having to prove their actual damage, and without worrying whether it equates to the actual loss suffered. For example, building contracts will often specify an amount payable in the form of damages if a given building is not completed on time.

A problem with a liquidated damages clause is that it can be difficult to arrive at a satisfactory pre-estimate figure. If it is lower than the actual damage or loss suffered by the injured party, they would be held to this figure. On the other hand, if the figure is too high, the court may decide that the figure is in fact a 'penalty' rather than a genuine pre-estimated figure and assess the damage itself.

Unliquidated damages

***Unliquidated* damages—courts left to work out the sum**

These are awarded when a plaintiff is unable to assess precisely what should be the amount of recoverable damages, for example, for pain and suffering, and disappointment. In most cases no amount is mentioned in the contract and it is left to the court or the jury to determine the amount that should be awarded.

Penalty

Penalty—**threat and not enforceable**

In effect this is an amount agreed upon as a security to ensure that a contract will be performed. It is a **threat to ensure performance**, and is imposed on the weaker party by the stronger party. If the amount is quite disproportionate to the loss that could be suffered by an injured party, the courts will not enforce it.

The courts are often faced with the problem of deciding whether a sum is a penalty or liquidated damages. They do not attach great importance to what the parties may like to call 'the sum' in the contract.

The question in each case is whether the sum can be seen as a **genuine pre-estimate** of the damages that will result from a breach or a sum **intended to punish** the other party in the event of a breach.

***DUNLOP PNEUMATIC TYRE CO. V. NEW GARAGE AND MOTOR CO. LTD* [1915] AC 79**

Dunlop sold some tyres and other motor accessories to the defendants who agreed not to sell below the prices specified by Dunlop. The defendants also agreed that in the event they should breach the agreement they would pay £5 by way of liquidated damages for each breach. They subsequently sold a tyre in breach of the agreement.

ISSUE: Was the sum a penalty or a genuine pre-estimate of loss by Dunlop?

DECISION: The sum was recoverable as it was a genuine pre-estimate of loss flowing from the breach.

If the sum is clearly extravagant and totally out of proportion to the amount of loss suffered by the injured party, then it is probably a penalty and unenforceable. Only the actual loss sustained can be recovered.

The relevant time for determining whether a clause is a penalty or not is at the time of the contract. The onus is on the party alleging that the clause is a penalty to prove that it is.

Doing business

Penalty or liquidated damages?

A penalty is a liquidated amount that bears little relationship to the loss. Such a clause is not enforceable. To be enforceable the clause should be a genuine pre-estimate of loss in the event of breach but remember that it can be difficult to arrive at a satisfactory pre-estimate figure. If it is too low, you will be held to that figure. If it is too high, the court may decide that it is a 'penalty' rather than a genuine pre-estimated figure and assess the damage itself.

EQUITABLE REMEDIES

A court of equity may award damages for breach of contract in addition to the equitable remedies listed below.

IN BRIEF

Major types of equitable remedies

Type	Description
Specific performance	An equitable remedy which is discretionary, directing a person to carry out their obligations under the contract, and is only used in contract actions where damages are inadequate.
Injunction	An equitable remedy which is discretionary, restraining a person from breaking their contract or from committing a wrongful act, and will not be awarded if damages are available.
Quantum meruit	Arises only in cases of part performance where there is a contract for goods or services. The party taking the benefit of a breach must pay a reasonable amount for the work done.
Anton Piller orders	Available only where it can be shown that D has incriminating evidence, necessary to P's case, which may be destroyed before 'discovery' can be made.

Specific performance

***Specific performance*—discretionary equitable remedy compelling performance**

This is a discretionary order granted by the courts **directing a person to carry out their obligations** under the contract. It is not generally used in breach of contract actions unless damages prove to be inadequate. For example, with the purchase and sale of goods that are readily obtainable elsewhere, damages would be considered an adequate remedy.

In cases where common law damages are not an adequate remedy, particularly contracts of land and contracts where the subject matter is unique—for example, a rare artwork—specific performance may be granted by the court where it feels that damages would be inadequate compensation.

Not available in contracts of personal service

Where the court cannot supervise the implementation of a contract, it will not generally grant specific performance. Thus, contracts involving personal services create problems of supervision because the courts cannot determine whether the agreed promise is being properly performed. Nor will the courts grant specific performance where the contract would require constant supervision by the court.

***RYAN V. MUTUAL TONTINE WESTMINSTER CHAMBERS ASSOC.* [1893] 1 CH 116**

The lessor of a block of flats agreed to provide a porter who would be 'constantly in attendance' and would perform certain specified duties. The person appointed by the lessor also worked as a chef in a nearby club, and in his absence while he worked as a chef, other persons were employed to perform his duties.

ISSUE: Could a tenant seek an order for specific performance against the porter that he carry out his obligations?

DECISION: The court was not prepared to order specific performance because it would have had to constantly supervise the porter's attendance.

Injunction

This is also a **discretionary** court order. Unlike specific performance, this is a court order **restraining a party from breaking their contract or from committing a wrongful act** (an order prohibiting performance) and will not be awarded if damages are an adequate remedy.

***Injunction*—discretionary equitable remedy restraining a party from breaking their contract**

It may be:

- **prohibitory**, preventing the breach of a contract;
- **mandatory**, requiring a person to perform some contractual obligation; or
- **interlocutory**, where it freezes the *status quo* between the parties until the dispute can be heard by the court.

The applicant has to satisfy the court that they have a *prima facie* chance of success or it will not be granted. As an injunction aims at enforcing a **negative promise** in an agreement, it can be enforced even if the contract is one involving personal services and so it can be an indirect way of ensuring performance of a contract of personal services.

LUMLEY V. WAGNER (1852) 42 ER 687

Wagner contracted to sing at Lumley's theatre for a fixed period of time during which she was not to sing elsewhere. She broke this promise, and Lumley sought to restrain her from singing for another employer.

ISSUE: Was the injunction enforceable as it was an indirect way of ensuring performance?

DECISION: While it could not grant a decree of specific performance to compel Wagner to sing at Lumley's theatre, the court would enforce the negative promise 'not to sing elsewhere' by granting an injunction against Lumley. This prevented her from singing anywhere else during the term of the contract.

COMMENT: A similar result occurred in *Warner Bros Pictures Inc. v. Nelson* [1937] 1 KB 209, where Nelson had agreed not to work for a third party after entering into an exclusive work agreement for the plaintiff film producers. Subsequently she attempted to breach her contract. Similarly, in *Curro v. Beyond Productions Pty Ltd* (1993) 30 NSWLR 337 where Curro had entered into a contract with Beyond to appear in a television program *Beyond 2000*. She then entered into an agreement to act as a television reporter on another channel and attempted to repudiate her agreement with Beyond. In both cases the defendant was not being forced to work by the granting of an injunction. They could choose to work in some other profession than acting or television reporting which has nothing whatsoever to do with the business of the employer.

CASE REFLECTION: The courts will grant an injunction in regard to a contract of personal service but they will not grant specific performance in respect of the same contract. Why not?

However, compare those decisions with that of *Network Ten Pty Ltd v. Rowe* [2005] NSWSC 1356 and *Network Ten Pty Ltd v. Rowe* [2006] NSWCA 4, which illustrate well how difficult it can be to obtain injunctive relief where the terms of the contract between the parties are not clear-cut.

Mareva injunction

A *Mareva* injunction prevents the defendant removing or disposing of any assets in the jurisdiction **until the court makes a decision**. As a result of its potential to seriously interfere with the defendant's legal rights, a plaintiff must be able to establish that:

***Mareva* injunction—prevents D from removing assets from court's jurisdiction**

- the defendant has assets that are in the court's jurisdiction; **and**
- there is a real risk that the defendant will remove or get rid of any assets before judgement; **and**
- the plaintiff can establish a substantive cause of action such as a claim for damages.

***MAREVA COMPANIA NAVIERA SA V. INTERNATIONAL BULK CARRIERS SA, THE MAREVA* [1975] 1 ALL ER 213**

Ship owners hired out their ship, *Mareva*, to International Bulk Carriers. The hire of the ship was to be half-monthly in advance. After International Bulk Carriers were only able to meet the first two instalments, Mareva sued for damages and unpaid hire. They also sought an injunction to stop the hirers from removing from the court's jurisdiction any monies received from the voyage.

ISSUE: Was an injunction obtainable to prevent the removal of assets before judgement?

DECISION: The court granted them an injunction to continue until the dispute came to trial to prevent the defendants from disposing of any assets.

CASE REFLECTION: If a company that had breached a contract started to transfer assets to a related company, would a '*Mareva*' injunction be appropriate to stop this?

Anton Piller order

Anton Piller order—prevents D from disposing of any evidence before trial

An Anton Piller order may be made available in exceptional circumstances where it can be shown that the defendant has incriminating evidence in their possession, which is necessary to the plaintiff's case and which may well be destroyed before a court order for discovery can be made.

***ANTON PILLER KG V. MANUFACTURING PROCESSES LTD* [1976] CH 55**

The Anton Piller company was under the belief that one of its agents was supplying confidential information to one of its competitors. They believed that the agent had documentation in their possession that would prove their breach. However, they were concerned that a subpoena would give the agent advance warning of their intentions and that any relevant documents would then be destroyed.

ISSUE: Could the company obtain an order that would enable them to enter the agent's premises to inspect the documents and remove or copy the relevant ones?

DECISION: As there was a strong *prima facie* case of infringement which could cause damage to the applicant, and clear evidence that the defendants had incriminating material in their possession which they would destroy, the court granted them an order.

COMMENT: An Anton Piller order is not available for the purpose of a general search to find evidence.

CASE REFLECTION: Would an Anton Piller order be available as a matter of routine or only in special cases?

Quantum meruit

***Quantum meruit*—only arises in cases of part-performance**

Quantum meruit means 'as much as he has earned' and only arises in cases of **part-performance.** The contract may be discharged by breach, but where the contract is for goods or services, there is a **new implied contract** imposed by law on the party taking the benefit that they will pay a reasonable amount for the quantum or portion given. It is not available to the party in breach.

Quantum meruit can arise:

- where a defendant has prevented a plaintiff from carrying out the remainder of their contractual duties;
- where the parties cannot agree on payment; and
- where the parties agree on payment for the part-performance but not the actual amount.

The court can make an award on the basis of what is deserved. If the contract was entire and the plaintiff was not prevented from performing, or there was no free and willing acceptance of partial performance by the defendant, the defendant may take the benefit (see, for example, *Sumpter v. Hedges* on p. 408).

LOSS OF RIGHT TO SUE

Statutes of limitations

Statute of limitations—prevents actions remaining open indefinitely

An injured party can lose their right of action unless they act within a certain time period. This is generally referred to as extinction of remedies.

The Limitation of Actions Acts of the states and territories determine the time limits within which an injured party must act if they are to maintain an action (see Table 20.1). The aim of such legislation is to prevent the possibility of legal actions remaining open indefinitely.

If an action has not commenced within these time limits, and the contract involves a debt, the debt is still payable but its payment cannot be enforced by a court of law. The creditor is entitled to use any other means to obtain satisfaction of the debt. For example, if the goods come into the possession of the creditor, it may be possible for the creditor to exercise a lien over the debtor's goods and to enforce payment in spite of the fact that recovery of the debt is barred by statute.

Table 20.1 Statutes of limitation of the states and territories

State	*Statute*	*Simple contracts*	*Under seal*
Victoria	*Limitation of Actions Act 1958*	6 years	15 years
New South Wales	*Limitation Act 1969*	6 years	12 years
Queensland	*Limitation of Actions Act 1974*	6 years	12 years
South Australia	*Limitation of Actions Act 1936*	6 years	15 years
Western Australia	*Limitation Act 2005*	6 years	12 years
Tasmania	*Limitation Act 1974*	6 years	12 years
ACT	*Limitation Act 1985*	6 years	12 years
Northern Territory	*Limitation Act 1981*	3 years	12 years

? REVIEW QUESTIONS

20.1 Briefly explain the meaning of the following terms:

a damages

b remoteness of damage

c mitigation.

20.2 The rule in *Hadley v. Baxendale* indicates that there are two types of loss for which the party in breach may be liable. What are they?

20.3 Explain the difference between liquidated and unliquidated damages.

20.4 Under what circumstances will a clause assessing damages for breach in a contract be considered to be a penalty?

20.5 Joad Tyres sold car covers and other motor accessories to Casey under a contract which provided that Casey would not sell any of the items below certain listed prices. In the event of breach of the agreement, Casey agreed to pay $50 in liquidated damages for every item it sold below the listed price. Casey subsequently sold a tyre below the listed price, and was sued by Joad Tyres.

Would you classify the sum as a penalty or liquidated damages? Explain why.

activebook

Activebook resources include in-depth summaries with links to the relevant part of the book. For revision, add your own notes to the summaries provided by using the note-taking function.

20.6 A car dealer agreed in a contract with the Stellar Motor Company not to sell any of the cars or parts supplied by Stellar below the listed price. He also agreed that for each breach of the agreement, he would pay $3000 as 'the agreed damages which the manufacturer will sustain'.

In the light of your answer above, how would you classify the sum here? Ignore the operation of the *Trade Practices Act* and any other relevant state legislation.

20.7 Henrietta engaged a firm of solicitors to obtain an injunction to prevent a former male friend from visiting her and making a nuisance of himself. An unqualified litigation clerk was given the matter to handle, but his incompetence over an 11-month period created further embarrassment for Henrietta.

Has Henrietta any claim against the firm for 'mental distress and upset'?

20.8 Under what circumstances would a party seek an Anton Piller order? How is this different to a *Mareva* injunction? Discuss.

20.9 Joe, a well-known film actor, entered into a contract with Frère Bros for a period of five years, where he agreed to give his services exclusively to Frère Bros and not act in films for any other company during this period. During the first year of the agreement, Joe entered into a contract to star in a film being made by Pretty Pictures.

Do Frère Bros have any remedy?

20.10 Bird, a builder, entered into a contract to erect two houses and a stable on Geoff's land for $100 000. Bird did approximately two-thirds of the work and was paid about $26 000. Bird then told Geoff that he had no more money and could not finish the job. Geoff treated the contract as ended and finished the buildings himself using the materials left on site by Bird.

Can Bird recover the balance of the two-thirds of the price on *quantum meruit*?

20.11 Indicate whether each of the following statements is true or false:

	TRUE	FALSE
▪ Damages are an equitable remedy	☐	☐
▪ Nominal damages are the usual remedy in contract law	☐	☐
▪ Exemplary damages are awarded when the court feels that it needs to punish the party in default	☐	☐
▪ The main purpose of damages is to enable the innocent party to receive monetary compensation	☐	☐
▪ To recover special damages under the rule in *Hadley v. Baxendale*, the plaintiff must make known to the other party the special circumstances at the time the contract is entered into	☐	☐
▪ If the plaintiff can't show any loss, there is no action available under contract law	☐	☐
▪ Damages are not claimable for disappointment or anxiety	☐	☐
▪ Unliquidated damages are awarded where the plaintiff is unable to assess precisely what should be the amount of recoverable damages	☐	☐
▪ A penalty is a threat to ensure performance and is unenforceable	☐	☐
▪ Specific performance is an equitable remedy preventing a party from breaking their contract	☐	☐
▪ Specific performance is not available to enforce contracts of personal service	☐	☐
▪ *Quantum meruit* only arises in cases of part performance of the contract	☐	☐
▪ Restitution is based on unjust enrichment	☐	☐

20.12 Explain the purpose of rescission.

20.13 Explain the purpose of restitution.

20.14 For a claim in restitution to be successful, what does the innocent party have to establish? Discuss.

20.15 Under an agreement between Emtee Theatres and Mandrake, two theatres were to be leased to Mandrake and he in turn was to lease a third theatre back to Emtee. In the lease agreement with Emtee, it was agreed that they would have all the offices in the theatre. Mandrake in fact occupied an office in the third theatre for some months, and refused to move out even though he was repeatedly asked to do so by Emtee.

Can Emtee bring an action against Mandrake for specific performance of the agreement?

20.16 Explain why it is important to have an understanding of the *Limitation Act* or *Limitation of Actions Act* of your state or territory in relation to contracts.

CRITICAL THINKING

20.1 Should there be statutory limitation periods placed upon injured parties to limit the periods during which legal proceedings may be taken to enforce a right under a contract? Discuss.

20.2 Should the courts be able to award damages for anxiety, injured feelings, disappointment or distress as a result of breach of contract even though the parties cannot estimate subjective mental reactions to the breach? Discuss.

CONSUMER LAW

PART FIVE

CHAPTER 21 Sale of Goods

CHAPTER CONTENTS

activebook

This icon is used throughout the following chapter to remind you to visit the *Business Law* online activebook for additional exercises, links to legal websites, and feedback. For a detailed explanation of what is in the activebook please refer to the inside cover of this textbook. The activebook is available through OneKey.

Where do I start?
Learning path: Use the activebook to complete a pre-chapter warm-up exercise.
There are many definitions of legal terms to assist with your understanding of the material.

CHAPTER OBJECTIVES

On completion of this chapter, you should be able to:

- distinguish between a sale of goods and a contract for work done and materials supplied
- define and distinguish between specific and unascertained goods, agreements to sell, and contracts for work and materials
- explain the rules as to when ownership passes from the buyer to the seller and the reason for the importance of the rules
- recognise and apply the exceptions to the rule that a transferee has no better title than that which the transferor conveys
- list the rights of a buyer and seller.

KEY TERMS

An understanding of the following terms will help you to better understand the material in this chapter:

- **agreement to sell:** where the property in the goods is to be transferred at some later date, or where some condition has to be fulfilled, such as payment of the price
- **ascertained goods:** goods which, in a contract for the sale of unascertained goods, have become identified and agreed upon by the parties
- **chattels:** things which the law deems to be personal property
- **contract for the sale of goods:** defined in sale of goods legislation as a contract whereby the seller transfers, or agrees to transfer, the property in goods
- **existing goods:** goods owned or possessed by the seller at the time of the contract
- **future goods:** goods 'to be manufactured or acquired by the seller after the making of the contract for sale'
- **goods:** broadly defined, include all 'chattels personal other than things in action and money'. This generally only includes physical and movable things (ownership) sold to the buyer for a money consideration called the price
- ***nemo dat* rule:** when a person acquires goods (e.g., a buyer), they get only the same rights to the goods as the person from whom they took them (e.g., a seller)
- **possession of goods:** refers to the control or custody of goods
- **property in goods:** means the same thing as 'ownership' or 'title'
- **sale of goods:** where ownership (or property) transfers from the seller to the buyer at the time of the contract
- **specific goods:** goods identified and agreed upon at the time of the contract of sale
- **unascertained goods:** goods that are defined by description only. They are not identified when the contract is made and they may or may not be future goods.

what if . . .

You were buying a car and while you were in the office of the car yard finalising the deal, a large branch was broken from a tree by a very strong wind and fell on the car, crushing it. Who suffers the loss, you or the car yard?

This chapter considers both the formalities attached to the formation of a contract of sale of goods and the effect of transfer of the goods and ownership. There is a fundamental difference between 'property' in goods and 'possession' of goods which both consumers and businesses must be aware of because:

- 'risk' in goods passes with property; and
- for the sale of goods legislation to operate, property or ownership of the goods must pass to the buyer.

Must a seller have title at the time of sale or are there any exceptions? Under the *nemo dat quod non habet* rule ('one cannot give what one does not have'), a seller who does not have title cannot pass anything on to a buyer but there are exceptions to this rule that both consumers and businesses need to know.

This chapter considers the formation of the contract, the distinction between property and possession, the different classifications of goods, the rules to determine when property passes, the effect of transfer of title by a non-owner, the duties of the seller and buyer and the remedies for breach.

Finally, this chapter looks at the duties of the buyer and seller to complete a contract for the sale of goods and what remedies are available to the parties if there is a breach.

SALE OF GOODS

IN BRIEF

Application of the sale of goods legislation

The sale of goods legislation only applies to contracts involving the sale of goods. If the sale of goods legislation is to offer protection to a consumer, the main purpose of a contract involving goods must be transfer of ownership (see Figure 21.1). There is only limited statutory protection (Vic., SA, WA, NT, Cth) for a consumer in a contract for the supply of services.

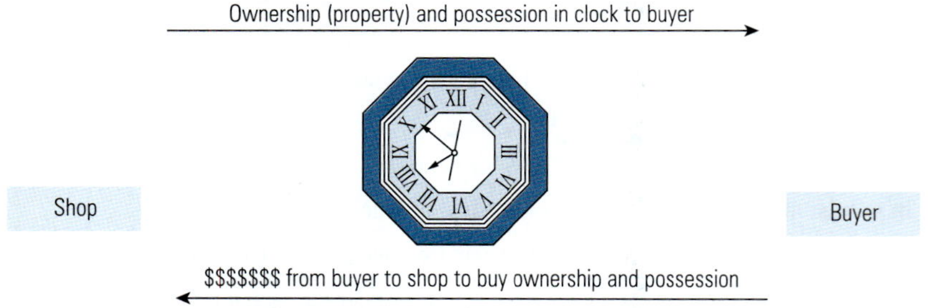

FIGURE 21.1 *A typical sale transaction*

The *Trade Practices Act* operates concurrently with the sale of goods legislation

These types of transaction are controlled by the sale of goods legislation of the various states and Part V of the *Trade Practices Act 1974* (Cth). Each Act is virtually identical in its wording, although the numbering of the sections varies considerably. Since the consolidation of the common law rules relating to sale of goods into the first *Sale of Goods Act* in 1893, there has been a great deal of legislative activity aimed at protecting the consumer in both Commonwealth, state and territory jurisdictions (see Table 21.1). Perhaps the best known legislative initiative in Australia was the passing by the federal Parliament of the *Trade Practices Act* in 1974.

The *Trade Practices Act 1974* is intended to operate concurrently (side by side) with state laws, and this is expressly provided for in s. 75. The effects of s. 75 are threefold:

- to widen the options available to a consumer, as rights or obligations now exist under both federal and state laws;
- to allow the states to continue to legislate in the area of consumer protection; and
- to restrict a conviction to either state or federal law, but not both.

In the event of any inconsistency between the *Trade Practices Act* and a state Act, Commonwealth law prevails.

Table 21.1 Legislation of the states, territories and Commonwealth dealing with sale of goods

State	*Legislation*
Commonwealth	*Trade Practices Act 1974*
Australian Capital Territory	*Sale of Goods Act 1954*
New South Wales	*Sale of Goods Act 1923*
Northern Territory	*Sale of Goods Act 1972*
Queensland	*Sale of Goods Act 1896*
South Australia	*Sale of Goods Act 1895*
Tasmania	*Sale of Goods Act 1896*
Victoria	*Goods Act 1958*
Western Australia	*Sale of Goods Act 1895*

FORMATION OF THE CONTRACT

ACT s. 6 : **NSW** s. 6 : **NT** s. 6 : **QLD** s. 4 : **SA** s. 1 : **TAS** s. 6 : **VIC** s. 6 : **WA** s. 1

Contracts of sale of goods

Sale of goods involves goods, price and transfer of property

A contract for the sale of goods is defined in sale of goods legislation as a contract whereby the seller transfers, or agrees to transfer, the property in goods (the ownership) to the buyer for a money consideration called the price. This means that there must be:

- goods;
- money consideration (called the price); and
- transfer of property.

What are 'goods'?

ACT s. 5 : **NSW** s. 5 : **NT** s. 5 : **QLD** s. 3 : **SA** s. 60 : **TAS** s. 3 : **VIC** s. 3(1) : **WA** s. 60

'Goods' includes tangible moveable property

Goods are broadly defined and include all '*chattels personal other than things in action and money*'. This generally only includes physical and movable things. It does not include:

- land or things attached to land (though it does include timber and growing crops which are to be harvested before sale or under the contract of sale);
- choses in action or rights, e.g., debts, negotiable instruments, shares or patents which can be sold but which are not goods; or
- services, such as work and labour, or repair.

The price paid for the goods

Price paid is money consideration

The price paid for the goods is the money consideration. If no money consideration is present, there can be no sale of goods contract; there is either a barter or exchange. The common transaction in which a used car is traded in as part-payment for a new one is considered to be a transaction that falls within the Act. The value of the car being traded in is considered the equivalent of a cash deposit on the new vehicle. Where the parties have not agreed on a price at the time of contracting, the price can be fixed by some other manner, such as valuation by a third party, or through the parties' previous dealings with each other. If still no price can be agreed upon, the buyer must pay a reasonable price and this is a question of fact in each case.

Transfer of ownership (or property)

There must be a transfer of ownership

There must be transfer of ownership (or property) in the goods if the transaction is to be caught by the sale of goods legislation. The importance of transfer of ownership is that risk of loss of the goods goes with the person who has the ownership in the goods.

The Trade Practices Act

In s. 4 the *Trade Practices Act* defines the terms 'goods', 'services' (which are not caught under the sale of goods legislation other than in Victoria) and 'supply' to cover as many activities as possible.

Who is a consumer?

Under *TPA*, goods and services must not exceed $40 000 in price

According to s. 4B(a), a person is taken to have acquired goods as a consumer if:

- the goods do not exceed $40 000 in price; or
- if the price exceeds $40 000, the goods are of a kind ordinarily acquired for personal, domestic or household use or consumption, or the goods consist of a commercial road vehicle;

and in both cases the goods were not acquired for re-supply or as inputs in the commercial production or repair of other goods or fixtures on land. While this section talks about 'acquired goods', s. 4(1) also catches the 'supply of goods' and includes both contracts of hire and hire-purchase.

In the case of services, a person is a consumer if:

- the price of services does not exceed $40 000; or
- if the price does exceed $40 000, the services are of a kind ordinarily acquired for personal, domestic or household use or consumption.

Is the contract a contract for sale of goods?

IN BRIEF

Is the transaction sale of goods or something else?

To work out whether a transaction falls under the sale of goods legislation, try to determine what the main purpose of the contract is. Is the main part of the agreement the skill and experience of one of the parties or the transfer of title to goods? Only the latter attracts the attention of the sale of goods legislation.

To determine whether a transaction falls under the sale of goods legislation, it is necessary to be able to decide whether a contract is for the sale of goods (where the sale of goods legislation will apply) or for work and materials or repair (where the Act will not apply and the buyer will have to rely on contract law).

Problems arise because a large number of contracts involve both an element of service and an element of goods (e.g., the supply and fitting of an oil heater, a washing machine, an air-conditioner, the service on a car, and so on).

The courts have to determine whether the main purpose of the agreement is to transfer ownership of goods. If it is, it is a contract for the sale of goods.

! CAUTION NOTE

Look to the main part of the contract and consider whether it is for the transfer of title of goods or skill and experience.

TOBY CONSTRUCTION PRODUCTS PTY LTD V. COMPUTER BAR SALES PTY LTD [1983] 2 NSWLR 48

The defendant agreed to sell a computer system containing three items of hardware and two items of software application to the plaintiff. Part of the agreement between the parties was that the defendant would install the equipment, train the plaintiff's staff on the use of the system and provide after sales service. After installation, the system failed to work properly.

ISSUE: Was the contract a contract for the sale of goods or a contract for the supply of labour and materials?

DECISION: *Rogers* J in the New South Wales Supreme Court held that the substance of the contract was the sale of a computer system and therefore was a contract for the sale of goods rather than a contract for the supply of labour and materials.

COMMENT: The question whether a contract for the sale of software is of itself a sale of goods within the meaning of the Act was left open.

CASE REFLECTION: If a person entered into a contract involving the supply of a mobile phone for $0 and a connection to a particular phone service with a compulsory minimum payment, does this contract involve a sale of goods (mobile phone)?

If the **main** part of the agreement is the **skill and experience** to be displayed by one of the parties in performance of the contract, and the transfer of title to the materials is of **secondary** importance, then it is a contract for work and labour and the supply of materials, and the Act will not apply.

ROBINSON V. GRAVES [1935] 1 KB 579

The plaintiff verbally agreed to paint the defendant's portrait for $500. In a dispute over payment, the defendant argued that it was a contract for the sale of goods and was unenforceable because it had not complied with a statutory procedural requirement.

ISSUE: Was the painting of the portrait one involving the supply of goods or skill and labour?

DECISION: The contract was not a contract for the sale of goods. The substance of the contract was the skill and labour of the artist in producing the portrait. It was only ancillary that some materials would pass from the artist to their client in addition to the skill involved in the production of the portrait.

CASE REFLECTION: If the contract is not a contract for the sale of goods, does that mean it is not a contract at all and therefore no rights are created?

Sale or agreement to sell?

ACT ss. 5, 6 : **NSW** ss. 5, 6, 62 : **NT** ss. 5, 6 : **QLD** ss. 3, 4 : **SA** ss. 1, 60 : **TAS** s. 6 : **VIC** ss. 3, 6(3), 84 : **WA** ss. 1, 60

The definition of a 'contract for the sale of goods' includes two types of contract:

- A **sale of goods** where ownership (or property) transfers from the seller to the buyer at the time of the contract, and hence is an executed contract.
- An **agreement to sell** where the property in the goods is to be transferred at some later date, or when some condition has to be fulfilled, such as payment of the price.

This type of contract is **executory**. Once the time elapses or the conditions are fulfilled, the agreement to sell will become a sale.

For example, if a person goes into a shop and buys some clothes from a rack, irrespective of whether it is a cash or a credit transaction, there is a contract of sale and ownership and **risk will pass immediately** to them. If, on the other hand, they order some clothes to be made according to their design, then there is an agreement to sell. The clothes are said to be unascertained goods at this stage because they are yet to be made, and ownership and risk will remain with the seller until they have been made. Once they have been made, and if there is nothing further to be done to them (e.g., delivery), the contract becomes a sale and the buyer assumes the risk.

The rights of the seller and buyer differ according to whether there has been a sale or an agreement. These are dealt with later in this chapter.

> **!** CAUTION NOTE
>
> *Property transfers in a sale at time of sale, while an agreement to sell it transfers at a later time, thus affecting the rights of the parties and who bears the risk if the goods are damaged.*

Formalities

In Victoria, New South Wales, Queensland, South Australia and the Australian Capital Territory there are no special formalities to be observed. The normal rules of contract law apply and the contract may be in any form—oral, written, partly oral and partly in writing, or implied from conduct.

Special formalities apply in Tasmania and WA

In Tasmania (s. 9) and Western Australia (s. 4) a contract for the sale of goods of the value of $20 or upwards is unenforceable unless:

- the buyer accepts part or all of the goods and has actually received them;
- the buyer has paid a deposit or given something in part-payment of the price (e.g., the trade-in of a car on another car);
- a written note or memorandum of the contract is signed by the defendant showing:
  - ames of the parties;
  - identity of the subject matter;
  - price and terms of payment if they have been agreed upon; and
  - the signature of the party to be charged or their authorised agent.

The note or memorandum need not be contained in one document, but may be contained in a series of documents, provided that they can be read together so as to satisfy the Act. Furthermore, they may be obtained later.

What are the terms of the contract?

Condition or warranty?

ACT ss. 4, 16 : **NSW** ss. 5, 16 : **NT** ss. 3, 15 : **QLD** ss. 15, 60 : **SA** ss. 14, 58 : **TAS** ss. 3, 16 : **VIC** ss. 3(1), 16 : **WA** ss. 11, 58

Where it is possible to discover, by inspection, the quality and condition of the goods and their fitness for a particular purpose, the buyer will generally lose any legal rights that may have existed against the seller if the goods are not satisfactory. Each party is negotiating on equal terms and so the maxim *caveat emptor*—'let the buyer beware'— prevails. Buyers have only themselves to blame if they fail to make a careful inspection of the goods before they purchase them.

However, while the idea of *caveat emptor* is to encourage buyers to take care, there are circumstances in which the application of the common law rule would prove unjust. Two examples would be:

- when there is no reasonable opportunity for inspection (e.g., goods packaged in containers or tins); and
- when the buyer has to rely on the special knowledge or expert judgement of the seller.

As a result, where the buyer is at a disadvantage, the legislation implies a number of terms into such contracts as either conditions or warranties. The distinction between conditions and warranties under the law of contract is preserved by the sale of goods legislation.

Whether a term is a condition or warranty depends on the construction of the contract

Whether or not a term in a contract is actually a condition or a warranty depends in each case on the construction of the contract. A term may actually be a condition, although it is referred to as a warranty in the contract by the parties. New South Wales incorporated s. 45(2) into the *Sale of Goods Act* in 1988 in recognition of the right to repudiate for a sufficiently serious breach of an innominate or intermediate term (see p. 365 for further discussion).

Where property has passed

ACT s. 39 : **NSW** s. 38 : **NT** s. 37 : **QLD** s. 37 : **SA** s. 35 : **TAS** s. 40 : **VIC** s. 42 : **WA** s. 35

The buyer can elect to treat a breach of condition as a breach of warranty and sue for damages, rather than treating the contract as at an end. However, where the buyer has accepted the goods and the property has passed to the buyer, breach of any condition to be fulfilled by the seller can only be treated as a breach of warranty. This is dealt with in more detail later in this chapter.

> **!** CAUTION NOTE
> *If property has passed, breach can only be treated as a branch of warranty.*

Rescission

Rescission is possible under the TPA and some state legislation

To ensure that all buyers have a reasonable opportunity to rescind, the Commonwealth and some states have introduced consumer protection legislation to overcome the difficulty of the buyer having to treat a breach of condition as a breach of warranty: s. 75A of the *Trade Practices Act 1974* (Cth), ss. 32P and 32PA of the *Fair Trading Act 1999* (Vic.), the omission of part of s. 16(3) of the *Sale of Goods Act 1923* (NSW), s. 11 of the *Misrepresentation Act 1972* (SA) and s. 16(4) of the *Sale of Goods Act 1954* (ACT).

Exclusion of implied conditions and warranties

Exclusion terms generally prevented by statute

The implied conditions and warranties may be excluded by the parties under the sale of goods legislation. However, to strengthen the position of the consumer, the Commonwealth and most states have passed other legislation to prevent the exclusion of the implied conditions. The implied conditions and the circumstances under which they may be excluded are dealt with in Chapter 22.

PROPERTY AND POSSESSION

Many people assume that if a person has possession of goods, they must also be the owner. This is a presumption based on appearance and one that can lead to serious problems for an unwary buyer because there is a vast difference between '**property in**' and '**possession of**' goods:

- **Property** means the same thing as '**ownership**' or '**title**'.
- **Possession** refers to the **control or custody of goods**.

For example, if you leave your car to be serviced at a garage, ownership or title of the car remains with you. The garage has possession. A change in possession has occurred without a change in ownership. But equally, a change in ownership may occur without a change in possession (e.g., where you sell your car to a leasing company and then lease it back from them).

> **!** CAUTION NOTE
>
> *Property and possession do not mean the same thing: property means ownership while possession means control.*

IN BRIEF

The importance of knowing when property passes

It is useful to know at what point property in the goods passes from the seller to the buyer because:

- Risk of loss or damage to goods is with the owner, assuming that the goods have not been lost or damaged because of the other party's fault.
- If property in the goods has passed to the buyer, generally the buyer is no longer able to reject the goods for breach of a condition; the seller's breach can only be treated as a breach of warranty.
- Once property in the goods has passed to the buyer, good title can be given to third parties, even though the buyer may not have paid for the goods.
- If the seller or buyer has gone bankrupt, it is necessary to determine whether property has passed for the purpose of determining whether the goods vest in the trustee.
- It is important to determine the rights of the parties in the event of a refusal to deliver by the seller or a refusal to accept delivery by the buyer.
- It determines whether a buyer can sue a carrier in tort if the goods are damaged in transit.

When does property pass?

ACT ss. 21–25, 32 : **NSW** ss. 21–25, 31 : **NT** ss. 21–25, 31 : **QLD** ss. 19–23, 30 : **SA** ss. 16–20, 28 : **TAS** ss. 21–25, 33 : **VIC** ss. 21–25, 35 : **WA** ss. 16–20, 28

Under state and territory sale of goods legislation, provision is made for determining when property in goods is transferred to the buyer in the absence of intention by the parties.

Risk passes with property

Unless the buyer has agreed to bear the risk, the general rule is that any damage or loss suffered to the goods before property passes to the buyer is borne by the seller. There are no problems where the goods are sold over a counter, but when delivery is to take place at a later date, and the goods are damaged before the delivery, it would often be difficult, in the absence of rules, to determine who should bear the loss. Even when the property has passed to the buyer, but possession remains with the seller, it does not necessarily follow that the seller must automatically deliver the goods to the buyer unless credit has been agreed between the parties. The seller is entitled to payment before delivery. However, the fact that the buyer has property usually means that the buyer also bears the risk. However, the seller may still be liable for lost or damaged goods as a result of negligence if they are acting as a bailee because they are bound to take reasonable care (see Bailment in Chapter 8).

Doing business

When does risk pass?

Unless the buyer has agreed to bear the risk, the general rule is that any **damage or loss** suffered to the goods **before** property passes to the buyer is borne by the **seller**. If problems are to arise, it is usually when delivery is to take place at a later date, and the goods are damaged before delivery—who has the risk? An appropriate clause should be inserted in the contract between the parties stating who is to bear the risk and appropriate insurance arranged by the party at risk. ■

CLASSIFICATION OF GOODS

ACT s. 5 : **NSW** s. 3 : **NT** s. 50 : **QLD** s. 3 : **SA** s. 60 : **TAS** s. 3 : **VIC** s. 3 : **WA** s. 60

activebook

To help you to remember and understand the topics covered so far, and for links to legal websites, refer to your online activebook. Model answers provide feedback to problems and exercises.

CAUTION NOTE

The classification of goods as existing, future, specific, unascertained or ascertained determines when property and risk pass.

Goods that are the subject of a contract of sale can be divided into a number of classifications under the sale of goods legislation:

- existing
- future
- specific
- unascertained or
- ascertained

though it will be apparent that there is an overlap. The distinction is important for the purpose of determining when the property, and hence risk, in the goods passes to the buyer.

Existing goods

Goods owned or possessed by the seller at the time of the contract (e.g., a dealer who has for sale and in stock a year 2007 new white Ford Falcon car).

Future goods

These are goods 'to be manufactured or acquired by the seller after the making of the contract for sale' (e.g., the purchase of a new Ford Falcon car which is yet to be manufactured by Ford).

Specific goods

These are goods identified and agreed upon at the time of the contract of sale (e.g., a year 2007 white Ford Falcon car). This overlaps with the classification of 'existing goods' above.

Unascertained goods

These are goods that are defined by description only. They are not identified when the contract is made and they may or may not be future goods. Until the goods are ascertained, it is merely an agreement to sell (e.g., a sale by a dealer of a new Ford Falcon car which is yet to be made. Until that particular car comes off the assembly line and is earmarked for you, the car is a future and unascertained good).

Ascertained goods

These are goods which, in a contract for the sale of unascertained goods, have become identified and agreed upon by the parties. For example, if A orders a new white Ford Falcon Forte car and the dealer has a number of that make, model and colour in stock, the goods are unascertained until a particular car from that dealer's stock is selected and identified (or ascertained) to A.

General rules regarding the passing of property

IN BRIEF

General rules regarding passing of property

Type of good	Description	Passing of property
Specific	Identified and agreed upon at time of sale/contract.	At a time agreed to by the parties.
Ascertained	Goods which, in a contract for the sale of unascertained goods, have become identified and agreed upon by the parties after the contract.	At a time agreed to by the parties.
Unascertained	Goods defined by description only.	When the goods are ascertained.
Future	Goods to be manufactured or acquired by the seller after the making of the contract for sale.	When the goods are ascertained.

Unascertained goods

ACT s. 21 : **NSW** s. 21 : **NT** s. 21 : **QLD** s. 19 : **TAS** s. 21 : **SA** s. 16 : **VIC** s. 21 : **WA** s. 16

Unascertained goods—property does not pass unless and until the goods are ascertained

Where there is a contract for the sale of unascertained or future goods, no property in the goods is transferred to the buyer unless and until the goods are ascertained. When the individuality or identification of goods depends on the need to weigh or test, measure or count them, they are treated as unascertained goods until the required act is done.

HEALY V. HOWLETT & SONS **[1917] 1 KB 337**

Healy, a fish exporter, agreed to sell Howlett & Sons 20 boxes of mackerel. He sent 190 boxes of mackerel by rail, and told railway officials to deliver 20 of these boxes to Howlett & Sons. The train was delayed and before 20 boxes could be set aside for Howlett & Sons, they began to go bad. Howlett & Sons refused to pay for the fish and was sued by Healy.

ISSUE: Had the boxes been sufficiently identified so that it could be said that the goods were ascertained and risk had passed?

DECISION: The boxes had not been 'earmarked' so the goods were still unascertained. Property and risk remained with the seller.

Ascertained goods

ACT s. 22 : **NSW** s. 22 : **NT** s. 22 : **QLD** s. 20 : **TAS** s. 22 : **SA** s. 17 : **VIC** s. 22 : **WA** s. 17

Where there is a contract for the sale of **specific goods**, the property in the goods is transferred to the buyer at a time agreed to between the parties. Goods are ascertained when they are identified as the goods agreed on after the contract has been made. Specific goods are goods identified at the time the contract is made.

Ascertained goods—property and risk pass when the parties intend it to pass

Specific rules determining the passing of property

IN BRIEF

Specific rules for determining when property passes

Rule	Type of goods	Passing of property
1	Unconditional contract—specific goods in a deliverable state.	At time of making of contract.
2	Conditional contract—specific goods not in a deliverable state.	When the seller has put the goods in a deliverable state.
3	Contract for specific goods that require pricing.	When the seller has done the act required to determine the price.
4	Contract for goods on approval.	When the buyer gives their approval or their actions indicate acceptance or they keep the goods beyond a reasonable time.
5(1)	Contract for unascertained goods or future goods.	When the described goods are in a deliverable state and unconditionally appropriated to the contract with the agreement of both parties.
5(2)	Delivery to the buyer or carrier without a right of disposal.	When the goods are delivered to the buyer or their agent if the seller has not set down any other conditions.

Intention

ACT s. 23 : **NSW** s. 23 : **NT** s. 23 : **QLD** s. 21 : **SA** s. 18 : **TAS** s. 23 : **VIC** s. 23 : **WA** s. 18

In ascertaining the intention of the parties as to when property is to pass, the court takes into account:

- the terms of the contract;
- the conduct of the parties; and
- the circumstances of the case.

If the intention of the parties is not clear, the following rules need to be looked at in order to determine the time at which the property in the goods is to pass to the buyer. Rules 1 to 4 deal with contracts for the sale of specific or ascertained goods, while Rule 5 applies to a contract for the sale of unascertained or future goods by description.

Rule 1: Unconditional contract for specific goods

Property passes to buyer in unconditional contract for sale of specific goods in a deliverable state

Property passes to the buyer if the following requirements are met:

- there is an unconditional contract;
- the contract is for the sale of specific goods;
- the goods are in a deliverable state.

The time of delivery or payment, or both, does not matter.

TARLING V. BAXTER **[1827] 6 B&C 360**

Baxter agreed to purchase a haystack that was to remain on the land of Tarling's brother until he had the opportunity to remove it. Before Baxter was able to take it away, it was destroyed by fire.

ISSUE: Did the loss fall on Baxter?

DECISION: Property and risk had passed to Baxter at the time of making the contract, and hence he was liable for the price; delivery being irrelevant.

Doing business

Take care where property, but not possession, has passed to the buyer

Where there is an unconditional contract for the sale of specific goods in a deliverable state, property and risk pass to the buyer when the contract is made and the time of delivery is immaterial. If the goods are not to be picked up immediately, the buyer should take steps to protect against damage to their goods while they are out of their possession, e.g., by insurance or a clause to the effect that they remain with the seller at the seller's risk. ■

Rule 2: Conditional contract for specific goods

ACT s. 5 : **NSW** s. 5 : **NT** s. 5 : **QLD** s. 3 : **SA** s. 60 : **TAS** s. 3 : **VIC** s. 3 : **WA** s. 60

Where the seller has to do something to the specific goods to put them into a deliverable state, property in the goods does not pass until it is done, and the buyer has had notice of it. For example, you buy a new car, but it has to be registered by the dealer. Goods are in a deliverable state when a buyer is bound to take delivery of them under the contract.

CAUTION NOTE

Property doesn't pass if seller has to do something to the goods.

Rule 3: Contract for specific goods that require pricing

Where there is a contract for the sale of specific goods ready to be delivered, but the seller must weigh, measure, test or do some other thing to the goods to work out the price, property does not pass until this has been done and the buyer notified. For example, where wheat is sold at a certain price per kilo, and the seller first has to weigh it to determine the price.

Rule 4: Contract for goods on approval

Where goods are delivered 'on approval' or 'on sale or return', property passes to the buyer:

- when they give their approval through words or conduct (e.g., using the goods);
- when they do any other act adopting the transaction (e.g., lending the goods to a third party); or
- if they retain the goods for more than the agreed time or beyond a reasonable time. This is a question of fact in each case. For example, if a buyer accepts goods under an agreement of sale or return within 14 days and keeps them longer than this, they would be considered to have adopted the agreement.

Rule 5(1): Contract for unascertained or future goods sold by description

Property in unascertained goods passes when the goods are unconditionally appropriated to the contract

Where there is a contract for the sale of unascertained or future goods by description, and goods of that description in a state ready for delivery are unconditionally appropriated (selected) to the contract by either party with the assent of the other, the property passes at once to the buyer.

Assent can be either express or implied. Once the seller notifies the buyer of an appropriation, unless the buyer objects within a reasonable time, the goods will be deemed to have passed to the buyer.

***PIGNATARO V. GILROY* [1919] 1 KB 459**

Pignataro purchased 140 bags of rice from Gilroy, which formed part of a large consignment in Gilroy's warehouse. As soon as Gilroy received Pignataro's cheque for the price, he sent him a delivery order and informed him where the rice was located. Some of the bags were at Gilroy's place of business, but Pignataro did not ask for the bags until four weeks later, when it was discovered they had been stolen. There was no fault on Gilroy's part.

ISSUE: Who had the property in the goods? This was necessary in order to determine who bore the loss.

DECISION: Pignataro had taken too long to object, and so had impliedly agreed to Gilroy's appropriation of the goods.

Rule 5(2): Delivery to the buyer or carrier without a right of disposal

Delivery to buyer or carrier where seller does not reserve right of disposal is an unconditional appropriation of goods

Where the seller has delivered the goods to the buyer or a carrier for the purpose of delivery to the buyer and the seller does not reserve the right of disposal, delivery is an unconditional appropriation of the goods to the contract.

***WARDAR'S (IMPORT AND EXPORT) CO. LTD V. W NORWOOD & SONS LTD* [1968] 2 QB 663**

A carrier was sent by the buyer, Wardar's (Import and Export), to pick up 600 cartons of kidneys that were being held by the seller, Norwood and Sons, in cold storage. The cartons were part of a larger consignment held in the cold store. When he arrived at 8.00 a.m. he discovered the cartons had been stacked on the pavement ready to be loaded. The carrier handed over the delivery note and started loading. The carrier did not turn on his truck's refrigeration unit until 10.00 a.m. By 11.00 a.m. some of the cartons had started to defrost. Loading was completed at noon. By 1.00 p.m. the refrigeration became effective. By the time the buyer received the cartons they were unfit for human consumption. He refused to pay for them, arguing that they were not of merchantable quality, and the seller counterclaimed for the price.

ISSUE: Had the goods become appropriated and if so, at what point in time had they become appropriated—before or after they had deteriorated?

DECISION: At the time of the contract the kidneys were unappropriated, and in good condition. Appropriation took place on receipt of the delivery note from the carrier. Deterioration occurred after loading had commenced and so property and risk had passed to the buyer. Accordingly, the buyer was held liable for the price.

CASE REFLECTION: What could a business do in regards to staff training and merchandise purchasing to avoid problems arising from the implied conditions as to quality?

RESERVATION OF RIGHT OF DISPOSAL

ACT s. 24 : **NSW** s. 24 : **NT** s. 24 : **QLD** s. 22 : **SA** s. 19 : **TAS** s. 24 : **VIC** s. 24 : **WA** s. 19

Doing business

Preserve ownership rights by a reservation of title clause

It is in the seller's interest to preserve their ownership rights where the buyer has possession but has not paid in full for the goods. If the buyer defaults, goes into receivership or liquidation, the seller may lose the goods if they have not used a 'reservation of title' or '*Romalpa*' clause to reserve title or legal ownership over the goods until the last payment is made. If the buyer defaults, the seller may be able to repossess the goods without finding themselves the subject of a police charge for theft. ■

If seller imposes a condition on right of disposal, appropriation is not unconditional

When the seller reserves the right to retake possession of the goods if certain conditions are not fulfilled (e.g., as to payment), the property in the goods will not pass until those conditions have been met. In such cases the appropriation is not unconditional. Under sale of goods legislation, there are two situations, both implied, where a seller is taken to have reserved a right of disposal:

- when the goods are shipped by sea, and the right of disposal is reserved by the bill of lading (a bill of lading is an indication of ownership); and
- where payment is by means of a bill of exchange or a cheque, together with a bill of lading. This often delays the passing of property until the bill of exchange or cheque has been honoured.

'*Romalpa*' clause reserves title to seller

In an attempt to **preserve the property** (or ownership) **rights** of the seller in the goods they have sold until they have been paid in full, sellers would often include a **reservation of title clause** in the contract of sale of goods. This created an equitable interest or charge in favour of the original seller. If the buyer failed to pay for the goods, went into receivership or became insolvent, it was argued that the seller could repossess the goods because they still had property and title in the goods. These clauses were often called '**Romalpa**' **clauses** after the decision in a United Kingdom case called *Aluminium Industrie Vaassen BV. v. Romalpa Aluminium Ltd* [1976] 1 WLR 676. In *Associated Alloys Pty Limited v. ACN 001 452 106 Pty Limited* [2000] HCA 25 (11 May 2000) the High Court considered that such clauses could not be used to defeat the priorities which the law enacts in cases of corporate insolvency under the Corporations Law, leaving the seller as an unsecured creditor. Effectively, the usefulness of such clauses for sellers hoping to be able to recover the goods in the event of non-payment by the buyer is now severely limited.

PASSING OF RISK

ACT ss. 11, 12 : **NSW** ss. 11, 12 : **NT** ss. 11, 12 : **QLD** ss. 9, 10 : **SA** ss. 6, 7 : **TAS** ss. 11, 12 : **VIC** ss. 11, 12 : **WA** ss. 6, 7

Where specific goods have perished before the agreement is entered into, the contract is void

Where there is a **sale of specific goods**, and without the knowledge of the seller they have been **destroyed** before or at the time the parties enter into the agreement, the loss falls upon the seller and the contract is void.

If there is an agreement to sell specific goods and the goods subsequently perish without any fault on the part of either party and before the risk has passed to the buyer, the agreement is voided. In both cases the contract has become impossible to perform.

If the contract had dealt with the sale of unascertained goods, the contract has not become impossible to perform as the seller has the opportunity to find other goods to satisfy performance.

General rule

ACT s. 25 : **NSW** s. 25 : **NT** s. 25 : **QLD** s. 23 : **SA** s. 20 : **TAS** s. 25 : **VIC** s. 25 : **WA** s. 20

The general rule, unless otherwise agreed between the parties, is that if goods are lost, damaged, destroyed or have deteriorated risk *prima facie* passes with property. However:

- if the property has not passed, the goods are at the seller's risk; but
- when the property is transferred, the goods are at the buyer's risk, whether delivery has been made or not.

Two limitations should be noted:

- where delivery has been delayed through the fault of a party, the goods are at the risk of the party at fault; and
- where the goods are in the possession of one party but at the risk of the other—a bailment situation—the party with possession must exercise reasonable care.

> **!** CAUTION NOTE
>
> *As a general rule, if property has not passed, the goods are at the seller's risk.*

what if . . .

You purchase a car believing that you were buying from the owner but in fact the car had been stolen. The police trace the car to you. You convince them that you bought it innocently and paid market value for it. Will you be able to keep the car?

TRANSFER OF TITLE BY NON-OWNER

ACT ss. 26–27 (no market overt) : **NSW** ss. 26–27 (no market overt) : **NT** ss. 26–27 (no market overt) : **QLD** ss. 24–25 (no market overt) : **SA** ss. 21–23 : **TAS** ss. 26–28 : **VIC** ss. 27–29 : **WA** ss. 21–23

Buyer normally gets same title as seller

As a general rule, when a person takes goods (e.g., a buyer), they get only the same rights to the goods as the person from whom they took them (e.g., a seller). This rule is expressed in the Latin maxim *nemo dat quod non habet* (i.e., one cannot give what one does not possess).

The rightful owner of goods is entitled to recover their goods from those who have no title to them. Thus, if A has their computer stolen by B, B has possession of the computer but no title to it. If B sells the computer to C, C will get possession of the computer and the title that B had (i.e. no title, because B had no title). If A can trace the computer to C, A will be able to repossess it because C has no right of ownership. C would be able to sue B for damages (if B could be found).

Exceptions

A number of exceptions exist to the *nemo dat quod non habet* rule where good title may be given by persons who are not the owners.

IN BRIEF

Exceptions to the *nemo dat* rule

Exception	Description
Special powers of sale	Persons with statutory or common law powers, e.g., sheriffs, innkeepers.
Estoppel	Owner gives the impression seller has authority to sell. Buyer must purchase in good faith and for value from seller to get good title.
Market overt	Goods must be purchased in a public market by buyer in good faith and without any knowledge of seller's lack of title.
Sale under a voidable title	Contract must not have been rescinded at time of sale and buyer must have purchased in good faith and without notice of seller's lack of title.
Seller in possession	A seller who continues in possession of goods or retains title documents may give good title to a third party who buys them in good faith and without notice of their previous sale.
Buyer in possession	A buyer in lawful possession of goods or documents of title, which are still subject to a lien or charge in the seller's favour, may give good title to a third party who buys them in good faith and without notice of a defect in title.
Factor or mercantile agent	If agent is entrusted with possession of goods or documents of title from a principal for consignment or sale, they will be regarded as the true owner and may give good title to a third party who buys in good faith and is unaware of the limitation of authority.

Special powers of sale

Certain kinds of person possess special powers of sale under the sale of goods legislation, e.g., sheriffs or bailiffs by court order, and innkeepers.

Estoppel

ACT s. 26 : **NSW** s. 26 : **NT** s. 26 : **QLD** s. 24 : **SA** s. 21 : **TAS** s. 26 : **VIC** s. 27 : **WA** s. 21

Owner may be estopped from denying seller's right to sell by words or conduct

In some cases the conduct of the owner may be such that the owner is estopped (or prevented) from denying the authority of the seller to sell the goods. The owner of the goods, by their words or conduct, must make a third party believe that another person has the right to sell the goods, for example, a sale by a car dealer of a car, where the car is in fact owned by a finance company.

Market overt

VIC s. 28 : **SA** s. 22 : **WA** s. 22 : **TAS** s. 27 : **NSW, QLD, ACT, NT**: no market overt

Market overt is an open public and legally constituted market

Market overt means an open, public and legally constituted market regulated by the rules framed under a local government Act or some other Act. Usually these markets are controlled by municipal councils. Where goods are purchased in market overt, a buyer acquires a good title provided that the goods are on open display, bought during market hours in good faith, and without any knowledge of the lack of title of the seller.

Sale under a voidable title

ACT s. 27 : **NSW** s. 27 : **NT** s. 27 : **QLD** s. 25 : **SA** s. 23 : **TAS** s. 28 : **VIC** s. 29 : **WA** s. 23

Sale under a voidable title may give a buyer good title

If a seller has a voidable title (i.e. a title which is valid and binding until and unless it is repudiated) at the time of sale, the buyer acquires a good title:

- provided that the goods were bought in good faith; and
- without notice of the seller's defective title.

The most common situation of this kind is one where the seller has been induced to enter into an agreement by a misrepresentation, innocent or fraudulent, by the buyer. For example, see *Phillips v. Brooks* [1919] 2 KB 243 and *Lewis v. Averay* [1972] 1 QB 198 on page 320.

Seller in possession

ACT s. 29(1) : **NSW** s. 28(1) : **NT** s. 28(1) : **QLD** s. 27(1) : **SA** s. 25(1) : **TAS** s. 30(1) : **VIC** s. 30 : **WA** s. 25(1)

A seller who continues in possession or holds title documents may give title to a third party

If a seller continues in possession of the goods or holds documents of title after a sale, and then they (or a mercantile agent acting for them) transfer the goods or the documents of title to a third party, who buys them in good faith and without knowledge of their previous sale, the second sale is considered as good. It is assumed that the owner had authorised it.

***PACIFIC MOTOR AUCTIONS PTY LTD V. MOTOR CREDITS (HIRE FINANCE) LTD* (1965) 112 CLR 192**

A car dealer entered into a display agreement with Motor Credits. Under the agreement, cars bought by the dealer were sold to the finance company for 90 per cent of their purchase price. The car dealer retained possession for display purposes.

When the dealer got into financial difficulty, the finance company cancelled its agreement with him. The same day as its authority was withdrawn, the dealer sold all his stock to Pacific Motor Auctions. Pacific Motor Auctions was unaware of the withdrawal of the car dealer's authority and the car dealer signed a declaration stating that all of its stock was unencumbered and was its sole property.

ISSUE: Can the finance company successfully sue Pacific Motor Auctions for the return of the cars?

DECISION: The High Court held that Pacific Motor Auctions had title to the cars as they had bought them in good faith and without notice of the sale from a seller who had continued in possession of the goods after the sale.

COMMENT: The remedy for the first buyer in such a case is to sue the seller for damages. It was not possible for the auctioneers to rely on the exception of estoppel because the sale was not in the ordinary course of business.

CASE REFLECTION: A customer buys and pays for a bulky electrical item like a VCR, then asks the sales person to hold the VCR while the customer buys other items in another department in the store. In the meantime, a second salesperson who is unaware of the earlier sale sells the same VCR to another customer, who takes it away. Who owns the VCR, customer 1, customer 2 or the store?

Buyer in possession

ACT s. 29(2) : **NSW** s. 28(2) : **NT** s. 28(2) : **QLD** s. 27(2) : **SA** s. 25(2) : **TAS** s. 30(1)(2) : **VIC** s. 31 : **WA** s. 25(2)

Buyer in lawful possession can give good title to third party

Where a buyer, with the seller's consent, is in lawful possession after sale of either the goods themselves or the documents of title to the goods which are still subject to some lien or charge in favour of the seller, the buyer can give a good title to a third person who receives the goods or documents of title in good faith and without notice of the rights of the seller. This section applies primarily to agreements to sell.

Factor or mercantile agents

NSW *Factors (Mercantile Agents) Act 1923* : **QLD** *Factors Act 1892* : **SA** *Mercantile Law Act 1936* : **TAS** *Factors Act 1891* : **VIC** ss. 65–72 : **WA** *Imperial Acts Adoption Act 1844* and *Factors Act 1878* (see s. 1)

Factor or mercantile agent with goods or documents of title regarded as true owner

Where a factor or mercantile agent is entrusted with the possession of goods or documents of title to any goods from a principal for consignment or sale, they will be **regarded as the true owner** for the purpose of any sale, pledge, lien or other disposition of the goods they make in the ordinary course of their business, provided that:

- the consignees act in **good faith**; and
- are **unaware of the limitation** placed on the agent.

FOLKES V. KING **[1923] 1 KB 282**

Folkes left his car with a mercantile agent and told him not to sell it below a certain price. The agent sold the car for less than the minimum price to King, who purchased the car in good faith and for valuable consideration, without any notice of any fraud. The agent then disappeared with the money. Folkes sued to recover his car from King.

ISSUE: Did the purchaser receive good title?

DECISION: As the mercantile agent was in possession of the car with the consent of the owner for the purpose of sale, and as the sale had been in the ordinary course of the agent's business, the purchaser received good title. Folkes therefore could not recover the car.

CASE REFLECTION: If the mercantile agent does not follow instructions, why should the seller suffer the loss and the buyer get good title? Would the seller have any rights against the agent?

PERFORMANCE OF THE CONTRACT

ACT s. 31 : **NSW** s. 30 : **NT** s. 30 : **QLD** s. 29 : **SA** s. 27 : **TAS** s. 32 : **VIC** s. 34 : **WA** s. 27

To complete a contract, obligations of parties must be concurrent

To complete a contract for the sale of goods:

- the seller must be ready to deliver or give possession of the goods; and
- the buyer must be ready to accept and pay for them in accordance with the terms of the contract.

Delivery takes place when there is a voluntary transfer of possession from the seller to the buyer. This need not be the physical act of handing over; it may be symbolic, as in the delivery of a key to the warehouse where the goods are stored, or in handing a document of title over, such as a bill of lading.

The duty of the seller in respect of delivery

ACT ss. 33–37 : **NSW** ss. 32–35 : **NT** ss. 32–36 : **QLD** ss. 31–35 : **SA** ss. 29–35 : **TAS** ss. 34–38 : **VIC** ss. 36–40 : **WA** ss. 29–35

In the absence of agreement, there are a number of duties imposed on the seller in respect of delivery

The sale of goods legislation sets out a number of general rules as to delivery. These will apply if the contract between the parties doesn't say anything about delivery:

Expenses

The expense of putting the goods into a deliverable state lies on the seller.

Place

This is usually the seller's place of business. However, in the case of specific goods which the parties know are in another place at the time of contract, that place is the place of delivery.

Third parties

If the goods at the time of sale are in the hands of a third party, there is no effective delivery until the third party acknowledges to the buyer that the goods are held on the buyer's behalf.

Time

If no time is fixed for delivery, the seller is bound to send the goods within a reasonable time. What is a reasonable time is a question of fact in each case. Thus, it would be expected that perishable goods would be delivered more quickly than non-perishable goods.

Quantity

It is the duty of the seller to deliver the exact quantity of goods ordered by the buyer. However, a trifling difference does not give the buyer the right to reject the goods, though this is subject to trade usage, special agreement, and the course of dealing between the parties.

SHIPTON, ANDERSON V. WEILL BROS & CO. **[1912] 1 KB 574**

The seller agreed to supply 4950 tons of wheat to the buyer. Upon delivery the buyer discovered that they had only received 4895 tons and they refused to accept delivery.

ISSUE: Was the difference sufficiently serious to allow the buyer to reject the delivery?

DECISION: The buyer could not reject delivery because the shortfall was insignificant.

Instalments

A buyer is not bound to accept delivery of goods by instalments, unless the parties have agreed to this. If the agreement is that the instalments are to be paid for separately, and the seller makes defective deliveries, the seriousness of the breach and the likelihood of it being repeated must be considered in the context of the contract as a whole when it comes to rescission.

HAMMER & BARROW V. COCA-COLA **[1962] NZLR 723**

Coca-Cola purchased 200 000 yo-yos, to be delivered in instalments. They were to be used in conjunction with an advertising program by Coca-Cola. Of the first 85 000 yo-yos delivered, 65 000 were returned as defective. Coca-Cola attempted to rescind the contract.

ISSUE: Was the breach sufficiently serious to permit Coca-Cola to rescind the agreement?

DECISION: The breach affected some 80 per cent of delivered yo-yos, and considering the cost of the promotion, which could be ruined by defective yo-yos, Coca-Cola were justified in rescinding the contract.

The buyer, when requested by the seller to take delivery of the goods, may be responsible for any loss occasioned by refusal or unreasonable delay.

Delivery to a carrier

Unless otherwise authorised by the buyer, any contract a seller makes with a carrier for a buyer must be in the buyer's interest. If the seller does not do this, and the goods are lost or damaged in transit, the buyer may:

- decline to treat the delivery to the carrier as a delivery to the buyer; or
- hold the seller liable for damages.

If the carrier is the agent of the seller, effective delivery occurs when the goods have been delivered to the buyer. However if delivery is to a distant place, for example, another state, the risk of deterioration of the goods is with the buyer.

The duty of the buyer to accept and pay for the goods

Once the seller has delivered the goods, the duty of the buyer is to accept and pay for them in accordance with the terms of the contract.

When does acceptance occur?

ACT ss. 38–40 : **NSW** ss. 37–39 : **NT** ss. 37–39 : **QLD** ss. 36–38 :
SA ss. 34–36 : **TAS** ss. 39–41 : **VIC** ss. 41–43 : **WA** ss. 34–36

Acceptance refers to performance and transfer of ownership

'Acceptance' in contracts of sale of goods refers to performance of the contract and transfer of ownership.

A buyer will be deemed to have accepted the goods when they:

- **inform** the seller that the goods have been accepted.
  In Victoria, New South Wales, South Australia and the Australian Capital Territory, this is subject to the buyer's right to examine the goods to ascertain whether they are in conformity with the contract;
- **perform** any act which is inconsistent with the ownership of the seller when the goods have been delivered (e.g., the resale of goods by the buyer, or use or consumption of the goods); or
- still have the goods after a reasonable time, without telling the seller that the goods have been rejected. What is considered a 'reasonable time' is a question of fact, but problems can arise where the defect is latent and considerable time passes before it is discovered.

Rejection of the goods

ACT s. 40 : **NSW** s. 39 : **NT** s. 39 : **QLD** s. 38 : **SA** s. 36 : **TAS** s. 41 : **VIC** s. 43 : **WA** s. 36

Unless the parties have agreed otherwise, the buyer is not bound to return goods that were not accepted in the first place. The buyer only needs to inform the seller of the refusal to accept them.

The buyer is not bound to return goods that they did not accept

Where there has been no agreement at all for the sale of goods, a person is not bound to inform the seller of rejection of the goods (e.g., a book sent to the buyer through the post on the chance that the buyer may buy it).

A buyer who accepts part of the goods cannot refuse to accept further deliveries which conform with the contract. Wrongful refusal or neglect of acceptance of delivery makes the buyer liable to the seller for any loss or expense as a result.

The buyer's duty to pay the price

ACT s. 32 : **NSW** s. 31 : **NT** s. 31 : **QLD** s. 30 : **SA** s. 28 : **TAS** s. 33 : **VIC** s. 35 : **WA** s. 28

It is the buyer's duty to pay the price fixed by the seller. If no price is stated, the buyer must pay a reasonable or customary price for the goods. If no arrangement has been made as to subsequent payment, the buyer must be ready and willing to pay for the goods on delivery.

It is the buyer's duty to pay the price

REMEDIES OF THE PARTIES FOR BREACH OF CONTRACT

Seller's remedies

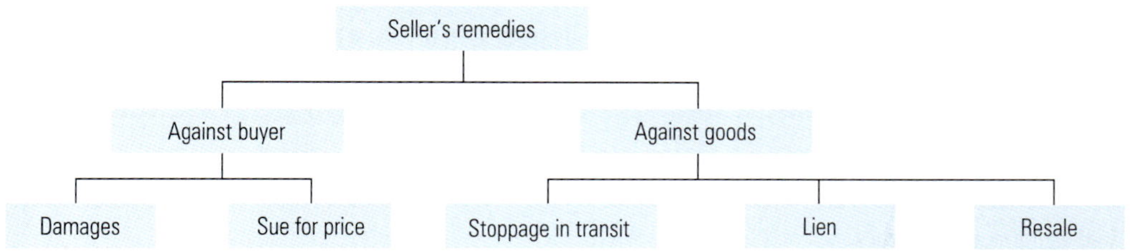

FIGURE 21.2 *Seller's remedies against the buyer*

Against the goods

ACT s. 42 : **NSW** s. 41 : **NT** s. 41 : **QLD** s. 40 : **SA** s. 38 : **TAS** s. 43 : **VIC** s. 45 : **WA** s. 38

Who is an unpaid seller?

The 'unpaid seller' may exercise certain rights against the goods even though property in the goods has already passed to the buyer. These rights may be preferable to the rights against the buyer where, for example, the buyer is insolvent.

An unpaid seller includes any person who is in the position of the seller, such as an agent for the seller, and who:

- has not been paid the full price; or
- has been paid with a bill of exchange or cheque as conditional payment, but which cheque or bill of exchange has been dishonoured.

An unpaid seller is someone who has not been paid the full price

Unpaid seller's rights

ACT ss. 44–49, 51 : **NSW** ss. 43–48, 50 : **NT** ss. 43–48, 51 : **QLD** ss. 42–47, 49 : **SA** ss. 40–45 : **TAS** ss. 45–50, 52 : **VIC** ss. 47–52, 54 : **WA** ss. 40–45, 47

Unpaid seller's rights depend on whether property and/or possession have passed

The unpaid seller's rights depend on whether or not the property and/or possession of the goods has passed to the buyer:

- Where property and possession have passed to the buyer, the unpaid seller has rights only against the buyer personally (see below).
- Where the unpaid seller has possession of the goods or they are still in transit to the buyer, the seller may:
  - exercise a lien on the goods for the price. That is, the right to retain possession until the price is paid;
  - in the case of insolvency, exercise the right of stopping the goods in transit, notwithstanding that the goods are no longer in the possession of the seller; and
  - have a right of resale (see Figure 21.2).
- Where property in the goods has not passed to the buyer, the unpaid seller has, in addition to the other remedies, the right to withhold or stop delivery of the goods.
- Where the seller has property and possession, the goods may be resold without the seller committing a breach of contract.

Against the buyer

The unpaid seller also has certain rights against the buyer for the price of the goods, or at least damages for non-acceptance of the goods (see Figure 21.2).

Where the buyer refuses to take delivery

ACT s. 41 : **NSW** s. 40 : **NT** s. 40 : **QLD** s. 39 : **SA** s. 37 : **TAS** s. 42 : **VIC** s. 44 : **WA** s. 37

A seller can sue for loss where a buyer refuses or neglects to take delivery

When the seller is ready and willing to deliver the goods and asks the buyer to take delivery, if the buyer does not act within a reasonable time the seller will be able to sue for any loss occasioned by their refusal or neglect to take delivery, as well as for storage charges.

Price

ACT s. 52 : **NSW** s. 51 : **NT** s. 52 : **QLD** s. 50 : **SA** s. 48 : **TAS** s. 53 : **VIC** s. 55 : **WA** s. 48

If property has passed, the seller can sue for the price

The seller may sue the buyer for the price of the goods if the property in the goods has passed and the buyer wrongfully neglects or refuses to pay for the goods according to the terms of the contract.

The seller may also sue for the price, even if the property has not passed, if the terms of the contract stipulate that the payment is to occur before the passing of the property and this has not occurred.

Damages for non-acceptance

ACT s. 42 : **NSW** s. 52 : **NT** s. 41 : **QLD** s. 51 : **SA** s. 49 : **TAS** s. 43 : **VIC** s. 56 : **WA** s. 49

The seller may sue the buyer for damages arising from non-acceptance where the property has not passed. This is reasonable, since the seller still has the ownership of the goods and may resell them. Of course, if the seller has actually resold the goods, the measure of damages will be the difference between the contract price and the market price at which the goods were sold. The seller is in no position to sue the buyer for the price because delivery is no longer possible.

Seller may sue the buyer for damages for non-acceptance

Buyer's remedies

ACT ss. 54–56 : **NSW** ss. 53–55 : **NT** ss. 53–54, 56 : **QLD** ss. 52–54 : **SA** ss. 50–52 : **TAS** ss. 55–57 : **VIC** ss. 57–59 : **WA** ss. 50–52

The buyer's remedies against the seller depend on whether the goods have been delivered or not (see Figure 21.3):

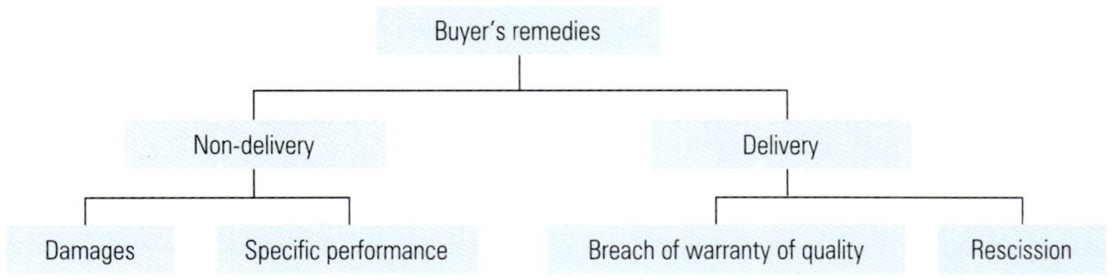

FIGURE 21.3 *Buyer's remedies for non-performance*

Damages for non-delivery

Where the seller wrongfully neglects or refuses to deliver the goods to the buyer, the buyer may sue the seller for damages for non-delivery. This is the equivalent of the seller's remedy in the previous section. The general measure of damages will be based on the loss that directly and naturally results from the seller's default, usually being the difference between the contract price and the current market price. Thus, if the market price is the lower, no damages can result. The onus is on the buyer to minimise their loss.

Buyer may sue a seller for damages for non-delivery

Specific performance

Where the seller fails to deliver the specific goods and they are of a rare kind or quality where damages would not be an adequate remedy, the court has a discretion to award a decree of specific performance.

Specific performance available if damages are not an adequate remedy

Breach of warranty of quality

Where there has been a breach of warranty by the seller, or where the buyer has elected (or has been compelled under the sale of goods legislation) to treat a breach of condition as a breach of warranty, the buyer may either:

- set up against the seller the breach of warranty as a ground for the reduction or extinction of the price asked by the seller; or
- bring an action for damages.

The damages that the buyer can recover are the difference between the value of the goods at the time of delivery to the buyer and the value they would have had if they had answered the warranty.

For the purpose of determining the measure of damages, a distinction is maintained between the situation where:

- the seller's breach caused economic loss; in which case the test is whether at the time of contract the seller could reasonably have contemplated the loss as a serious possibility in the event of a breach; and
- it caused physical injury to the person or property of the buyer; in which case it is whether the loss could be reasonably foreseen at the date of breach as a possible consequence of the breach.

Rescission

Rescission available where breach of condition exists

The buyer is entitled to rescind the contract and reject the goods where there is a breach of condition. If this amounts to a total failure of consideration, the buyer can recover the full purchase price they may have paid (e.g., as occurred in *Rowland v. Divall* in Chapter 22 see p. 455–456).

The right of repudiation can be lost in the following situations:

- where the buyer elects to treat the breach of condition as a breach of warranty, or elects to waive the breach entirely;
- where the contract of sale is not severable;
- where there has been a breach of a condition under s. 75A of the *Trade Practices Act 1974* (Cth);
- in Queensland, Western Australia, Tasmania and the Northern Territory where the contract is for specific goods and the property has passed to the buyer; and
- in South Australia the right to rescind is lost if the buyer doesn't exercise their right within seven days after delivery of the goods (*Consumer Transactions Act 1972*, s. 15).

THE VIENNA SALES CONVENTION

The United Nations Convention on Contracts for the International Sale of Goods 1980, known as the Vienna Sales Convention, came into force internationally on 1 January 1988. The states had passed uniform legislation between 1986 and 1987, called the Sale of Goods (Vienna Convention) Acts, enabling implementation of the Convention to take effect on 1 April 1989.

The Convention regulates contracts for the sale of goods between signatory countries

The Convention regulates contracts for the sale of goods entered into between parties whose places of business are in the signatory countries. The Convention provides a code regulating the international sale of goods including formation of the contract, rights and duties of the buyer and seller, and the remedies available for breach. Contracting parties can exclude or vary the operation of the Convention.

WEB RESOURCES

Consumer Affairs/Fair Trading Agency Web Links: A general gateway to the various consumer affairs and fair trading agency sites in Australia: **http://www.consumer.gov.au/copy/govlinks.html**

United Nations Convention on Contracts for the International Sale of Goods 1980: The full text site for the Vienna Sales Convention: **http://www.jus.uio.no/lm/un.contracts.international.sale.of.goods.convention.1980/index.html**

REVIEW QUESTIONS ?

21.1 Explain why it is important under the sale of goods legislation to distinguish between a sale and an agreement to sell.

21.2 Explain why it is necessary to be able to distinguish between a contract of sale of goods and a contract for work and materials or repair for the purposes of sale of goods legislation. Explain the test that the courts use.

21.3 Explain when a breach of condition will not enable the injured party the right of rescission.

21.4 Consider the following transactions and explain whether they fall under the sale of goods legislation or not:

a the manufacturing of a set of false teeth
b an agreement for the supply and installation of a lift in a particular building
c a contract for the supply and fitting of seats specially designed for a lecture theatre
d the exchange of a two-door fridge-freezer for a single-door refrigerator
e electrical work done by an electrician wiring a house for electricity
f the tune-up of a car where new spark plugs and points are included in the sale price
g the supply and fitting of a washing machine
h the purchase of a $15 000 boat for a cash price of $5000 plus a trade-in of an existing boat.

21.5 Indicate whether each of the following statements is true or false:

	TRUE	FALSE
▪ The terms 'property' and 'possession' mean one and the same thing in law	☐	☐
▪ One of the reasons why it is important to know when property passes is because risk of loss or damage is with the owner	☐	☐

▪ The general rule under sale of goods legislation is that any damage or loss to the goods before property passes to the buyer is carried by the seller	☐	☐
▪ Future goods are goods identified and agreed upon at the time of the contract of sale	☐	☐
▪ Unascertained goods are goods that are defined by description only	☐	☐
▪ In a contract of sale for specific goods, property is transferred to the buyer when the parties intend it to pass	☐	☐
▪ In a contract for specific goods that require pricing, property does not pass until the goods are priced and the buyer has notice of this fact	☐	☐
▪ Where the seller has delivered goods to a carrier for delivery to a buyer and does not reserve the right of disposal, delivery is an unconditional appropriation of the goods to the contract	☐	☐
▪ Risk and ownership are linked together under a contract of sale of goods	☐	☐
▪ When a buyer purchases goods, they get the same rights to the goods as the seller	☐	☐
▪ If the owner is prevented from denying the authority of the seller to sell the goods, this is known as an estoppel	☐	☐
▪ Market overt means a market	☐	☐
▪ A factor or mercantile agent who has either possession of the goods or their document of title with the authority of the principal, can be regarded as the true owner and pass on good title to a third party who buys in good faith and is unaware of any limitations on the agent	☐	☐
▪ It is the duty of the seller to deliver the exact quantity	☐	☐
▪ Any expenses in putting goods into a deliverable state are borne by the seller	☐	☐
▪ A buyer will be deemed to have accepted the goods if they retain them for any length of time	☐	☐
▪ A seller's right to a lien over the goods exists even where the buyer has both property and possession	☐	☐
▪ A seller always has a right of stoppage in transit whether the buyer has possession or not	☐	☐
▪ Where a seller fails to deliver specific goods that are of a kind which are rare and damages would not be an adequate remedy, the court may grant an injunction	☐	☐

activebook

Activebook resources include in-depth summaries with links to the relevant part of the book. For revision, add your own notes to the summaries provided by using the note-taking function.

21.6 Explain the meaning of the following terms, giving an example in each case:

a specific goods

b future goods

c unascertained goods.

21.7 Into which classification would the following goods be placed?

a 10 kilos of sugar out of a 100 kilo bag of sugar

b a Sanyo stereo unit on display in a music shop

c a second-hand blue Holden Barina car, registration number FJC 423.

21.8 Planter left his car on assignment with Baskerville Car Sales to sell it for not less than $10 000; any amount they received above this amount they could keep. After a month Planter asked for the return of his car within three days, or payment of $10 000. The car was returned a week later but it was badly damaged after a collision while being used by employees of Baskerville without permission. Planter refused to accept the car, and demanded $10 000. Will Planter succeed in his claim?

21.9 George took some jewels from Sam's Jewellery on 'sale or return' and immediately after leaving the shop he disposed of the goods to a pawnbroker.

Can the jewellers recover the jewels from the pawnbrokers, or does their only action lie against George?

21.10 Explain the purpose of a *Romalpa* clause in a sale of goods contract.

21.11 If a buyer purchases goods from a seller who has a voidable title, what sort of title will the buyer have? Explain.

21.12 There are three ways in which a buyer may 'accept the goods'. Describe each.

21.13 Anthony Office Supplies agreed to deliver a new photocopier to the premises of Brad's Light Fittings. When their driver arrived at the premises he found a person who he thought was an employee waiting in the loading bay. The person was wearing a Brad's Light Fittings shirt and appeared to know what he was doing. He signed a delivery receipt for the photocopier with the driver. The person was in fact a thief and after the driver had left, he loaded the photocopier into a truck and disappeared. Does the loss fall on the seller or the buyer? Explain your reasoning.

21.14 Chattis, a furniture manufacturer, supplied Ferry Road Home Furnishings with furniture on the following terms:

Ownership in such goods is retained by Chattis until payment is made for the goods and for all other goods supplied by Chattis. If such goods are sold by the customer prior to payment, and if they become constituents of other goods, then the proceeds of sale thereof shall be the property of Chattis.

Owing to financial difficulties Ferry Road Home Furnishings failed to pay for a delivery of furniture that they received. Eventually they were wound up, but the liquidator for Ferry Road Home Furnishings refused to return the furniture.

Advise Chattis. What defence would the liquidator put forward for the non-return of the furniture?

21.15 List the classes of rights that an unpaid seller has against a buyer and briefly discuss each.

21.16 Who is an unpaid seller? Briefly explain.

21.17 Where an unpaid seller exercises a lien over goods, what is the seller doing? Under what circumstances can such a lien be exercised?

21.18 Discuss whether the unpaid seller has a right of resale of goods under a contract for the sale of goods.

21.19 While the seller has remedies against the buyer, does the buyer have any remedies against the seller for breach of the contract for the sale of goods?

CRITICAL THINKING

21.1 Bodilingo were suppliers of office furniture and equipment. They entered into a contract with Webb Developers for the sale of office furniture and computers to the value of $500 000. The agreement between the parties was that Webb Developers would pay a deposit of $20 000 and the balance of $480 000 over two years at the rate of $20 000 per month. After 12 months Webb Developers went into liquidation. Bodilingo received no further repayments.

Can Bodilingo recover the office equipment and computers that they supplied to Webb Developers?

21.2 Wentworth represented to Brisbane Jewellers, who were retail jewellers, that he had the opportunity of selling jewellery to well-known actors who were moving to the Gold Coast to be near the film studios. He had told the jewellers that he was well-known on the Gold Coast as a successful letting agent by the movie studios and that he was always being contacted by them to find accommodation for their film stars.

On the basis of what they were told, Brisbane Jewellers gave Wentworth a number of jewellery items to sell. In respect of each item, Wentworth signed a note as debtor for the price of the item that was marked upon it, and the note was marked 'appro' or 'on appro' (i.e. on approval). It was agreed between the parties that Wentworth should be entitled to retain the difference between the sum for which he sold the item and the price marked on the appro note.

Wentworth never intended to sell the jewellery to actors. When he obtained the jewellery he intended to pledge it and retain the proceeds. He did this by using a number of women accomplices, who would take the various pieces of jewellery he had obtained to various pawnbrokers who took the jewellery in good faith.

Wentworth was subsequently arrested by the police and charged with larceny as a bailee. Can Brisbane Jewellers recover the jewellery from the pawnbrokers? What sort of action would they bring? Discuss.

CHAPTER 22

Terms Implied into Contracts—Consumer Protection

CHAPTER CONTENTS

CHAPTER OBJECTIVES

On completion of this chapter, you should be able to:

- explain the meaning of the implied conditions as to title, description, fitness for purpose, merchantable quality and sale by sample in both Commonwealth and state legislation
- explain the statutory initiatives to prevent exclusion of the seller's liability.

activebook

This icon is used throughout the following chapter to remind you to visit the *Business Law* online activebook for additional exercises, links to legal websites, and feedback. For a detailed explanation of what is in the activebook please refer to the inside cover of this textbook. The activebook is available through OneKey.

Where do I start?

Learning path: Use the activebook to complete a pre-chapter warm-up exercise.

There are many definitions of legal terms to assist with your understanding of the material.

KEY TERMS

An understanding of the following terms will help you to better understand the material in this chapter:

- **fit for purpose:** where the buyer expressly or by implication makes known to the seller the particular purpose for which the goods/services are required, which shows that there is a reliance upon the judgement and skill of the seller that the goods must be reasonably fit for that purpose
- **free from encumbrances:** there is an implied warranty that the goods are free from any charge (mortgage) in favour of a third party who is unknown to the buyer
- **merchantable quality:** the goods/services must be of a quality which makes them fit for sale for their usual purpose
- **quiet possession:** the buyer shall have and enjoy quiet (or undisturbed) possession of the goods. This assumes that a third party will not come and claim to be the true owner or that they have a right in the goods after the sale has taken place
- **sale by description:** where goods are sold by description, there is an implied condition that the goods will correspond with the description
- **sale by sample:** the bulk of the goods must correspond with the sample
- **title (right to sell the goods):** there is an implied condition that the seller has the right to sell the goods.

what if . . .

You buy an expensive boxed set of CDs by a famous group and the discs are defective. You return them to the store and they refuse to replace them. Do you have any legal rights to insist that they replace them or give you a refund? If you do have legal rights, where do you get them from?

To assist consumers in their dealings with traders, the Commonwealth, state and territory governments introduced consumer protection legislation which inserts certain specified terms into contracts for the sale of goods and, in some instances, services. These terms are therefore implied by statute into every contract for the sale of goods. However, the legal position varies from state to state. While most states extend the protection to services and prohibit the parties from contracting out of the implied terms, this is not consistent across all jurisdictions. The legislation is aimed at consumer protection.

This chapter considers the statutory terms that are implied into a sale of goods and services and the exclusion of seller's liability.

TERMS IMPLIED INTO EVERY CONTRACT FOR THE SALE OF GOODS

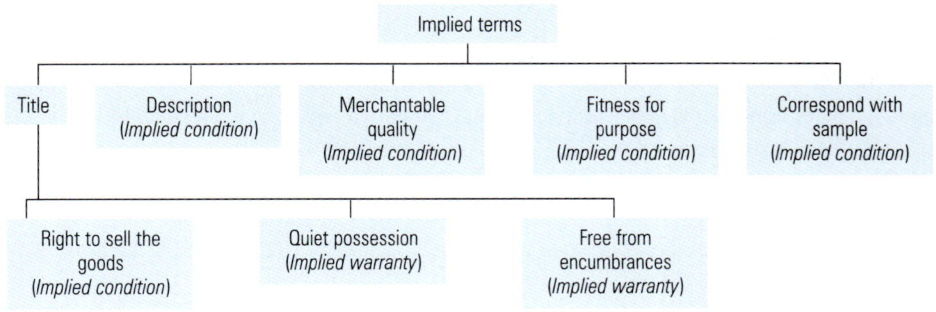

FIGURE 22.1 *Implied terms under sale of goods legislation*

Title

Jurisdiction	***Non-consumer***	***Consumer***
Commonwealth	*Trade Practices Act 1974*, s. 69	*Trade Practices Act 1974*, s. 69
ACT	*Sale of Goods Act 1954*, s. 17	*Sale of Goods Act 1954*, s. 17
NSW	*Sale of Goods Act 1923*, s. 17	*Fair Trading Act 1987*, s. 40
NT	*Sale of Goods Act 1980*, s. 17	*Consumer Affairs & Fair Trading Act 1990*, s. 62
QLD	*Sale of Goods Act 1896*, s. 15	*Sale of Goods Act 1896*, s. 16
SA	*Sale of Goods Act 1895*, s. 17	*Consumer Transactions Act 1972*, s. 6
TAS	*Sale of Goods Act 1896*, s. 17	*Sale of Goods Act 1896*, s. 17
VIC	*Goods Act 1958*, s. 17	*Fair Trading Act 1999*, s. 32G
WA	*Sale of Goods Act 1958*, s. 12	*Fair Trading Act 1987*, s. 36

Right to sell the goods

There is an **implied condition** that the seller:

- has the right to sell the goods in the case of a **sale**; or
- in the case of **an agreement to sell**, will have the right to sell the goods when the time comes for the buyer to become the owner (i.e. by the time property is to pass).

This condition amounts to a **guarantee**. The main purpose of a contract for the sale of goods is to transfer ownership to the buyer. If the seller does not have title (or ownership), then there has been a total failure of consideration.

***ROWLAND V. DIVALL* [1923] 2 KB 500**

Rowland bought a car from Divall and used it for four months before discovering it had been stolen. Rowland then had to hand over the car to the true owner.

ISSUE: Could Rowland recover the full amount he had paid from Divall even though he had used the car for four months?

DECISION: Although Rowland had had the use of the car for some time, he was entitled to recover the full price he had paid because Divall had no right to sell him the car because it was stolen. Rowland had failed to get the property (title) in the car, so there was a total failure of consideration.

COMMENT: It is interesting to note that there was never a claim from the true owner of the car against the buyer. The buyer learnt that the seller had no title and that the car had to be returned to the true owner. Should the buyer in such a case be allowed to recover the full amount?

! CAUTION NOTE

Implied condition that seller has right to transfer ownership at the time property is to pass or else there will be a total failure of consideration.

The section also catches intangible items such as trademarks.

***NIBLETT LTD V. CONFECTIONERS' MATERIALS CO. LTD* [1921] 3 KB 387**

An American firm sold a quantity of tins of 'Nissly brand' condensed milk to an English buyer. The order was stopped by English Customs officers on the basis that the labels infringed the Nestlé trade mark. The only way the buyer could get the goods was by removing the offending labels, which they did. As a result, the buyer could only sell the unlabelled goods at a loss. The buyer then sued the seller to recover his loss.

ISSUE: Did the American firm have the right to 'sell the goods'?

DECISION: The infringement of the registered trademark by the American firm meant that they had no right to 'sell the goods'.

If a seller subsequently obtains property (title) in the goods before the buyer has a chance to repudiate the agreement, title will pass to the buyer. Under s. 69(1) of the *Trade Practices Act*, title cannot be excluded.

Quiet possession

There is an **implied warranty** that the buyer shall have and enjoy quiet (or undisturbed) possession of the goods. This assumes that a third party will not come and claim to be the true owner or that they have a right in the goods after the sale has taken place.

Free from encumbrances

There is an **implied warranty** that the goods are free from any charge in favour of a third party who is unknown to the buyer, for example, storage charges which have to be paid before the goods can be collected.

Trade Practices Act

Under s. 69 of the *Trade Practices Act* where the seller breaches any of these implied terms the buyer is required to give the seller notice and a reasonable opportunity to clear the title to the goods.

Other relevant state legislation

Section 36 of the *Fair Trading Act 1987* (WA), s. 17 of the *Consumer Affairs and Fair Trading Act 1990* (NT) and Part 2A, Division 3 of the *Fair Trading Act 1999* (Vic.) have similar provisions. Note that in Victoria the Act implies a condition rather than a warranty in relation to freedom from charges or encumbrances.

IN BRIEF

Summary of title

Area	Term	Application
Title	Implied condition	The seller must have title in the goods at the time of sale, or there will be a total failure of consideration.
Quiet possession	Implied warranty	The buyer will enjoy undisturbed possession of the goods.
Free from encumbrances	Implied warranty	The goods will be free from any charges to a third party.

Description

Jurisdiction	*Non-consumer*	*Consumer*
Commonwealth	*Trade Practices Act 1974*, ss. 70 & 74C	*Trade Practices Act 1974*, ss. 70 & 74C
ACT	*Sale of Goods Act 1954*, s. 18	*Sale of Goods Act 1954*, s. 18
NSW	*Sale of Goods Act 1923*, s. 18	*Fair Trading Act 1987*, s. 40P
NT	*Sale of Goods Act 1980*, s. 18	*Consumer Affairs & Fair Trading Act 1990*, s. 63
QLD	*Sale of Goods Act 1896*, s. 16	*Sale of Goods Act 1896*, s. 16
SA	*Sale of Goods Act 1895*, s. 13	*Consumer Transactions Act 1972*, s. 6
TAS	*Sale of Goods Act 1896*, s. 18	*Sale of Goods Act 1896*, s. 18
VIC	*Goods Act 1958*, s. 18	*Fair Trading Act 1999*, s. 32H
WA	*Sale of Goods Act 1958*, s. 13	*Fair Trading Act 1987*, s. 37

Implied condition that the goods will correspond with description or sample and description

Where goods are sold by description, there are implied conditions:

- that the goods shall correspond with the description. This section applies where the buyer has not seen the goods and is relying on the seller's description.

***VARLEY V. WHIPP* [1900] 1 QB 513**

The buyer, without ever having seen it, purchased a second-hand reaping machine, which the seller described as new the previous year and used to cut only 50 or 60 acres. In fact, the machine was very old.

ISSUE: Was this a sale by description?

DECISION: This was a sale by description, and since the machine did not correspond to its description, the seller was in breach of this section.

The section also applies where the buyer has actually seen and examined the goods but the goods have been bought as corresponding to a description.

BEALE V. TAYLOR [1967] 3 ALL ER 253

The defendant advertised his car for sale as a 'Herald convertible, white, 1961' and the car was bought by the plaintiff after he had examined it in the belief that it was a 1961 model. It was later discovered that the car was made up of two cars welded together, the rear being a 1961 model and the front from an earlier model.

ISSUE: Could the buyer rely on description, even though an inspection had taken place?

DECISION: Although the buyer had examined the car, he had relied on the description in the advertisement stating the type of car he was buying. As a result, the sale was a sale by description and as the car did not correspond with description, he was entitled to damages assessed at the purchase price less scrap value.

- If the sale is by sample as well as description, the bulk of the goods must correspond with both sample and description.

A sale by description arises where the consumer selects goods on the basis of the description of the goods, or the consumer agrees to buy goods to be made to their specifications. Thus, the consumer who selects a DVD player described as being an 'infra-red remote control', and which does not perform the function described, has rights against either the manufacturer or the seller.

Unlike the next section, **these implied conditions apply whether or not the seller is someone who normally deals in goods of the given description**.

All sales of unascertained goods are sales by description

All sales of unascertained goods are sales by description, and many sales of specific goods can also be included in this category, particularly where the buyer has not seen the goods. So long as the goods have been bought on the basis of a description and they fail to correspond to that description, then this section is breached.

This section is concerned with descriptions that relate to the identity rather than the quality of the goods. If the goods are not of the expected quality but conform to the contract description, there is no remedy under this section.

ASHINGTON PIGGERIES LTD V. CHRISTOPHER HILL LTD [1972] AC 441

Mink food was sold to a mink farmer by a company that prepared animal foodstuffs. One of the ingredients used was herring meal which was supplied by a Norwegian firm. Unknown to any of the parties, the herring meal had become contaminated and this in turn contaminated the mink food. When it was fed to the minks, a lot of them died. The mink farmer then sued the company that he bought the food from.

ISSUE: Was there a breach of description on the part of the seller?

DECISION: The mink food did conform to description. The section was concerned with identity or description, not quality or fitness, and even though it was contaminated, it was still mink food as described. Therefore there was no breach of this section.

CASE REFLECTION: Although the goods literally complied with the description, would they have been of merchantable quality, that is, reasonable for the purpose described?

! CAUTION NOTE

Description is about identity, not quality of the goods.

Once it is decided what the description is, this section operates to treat all words of description as conditions precedent which the seller must strictly comply with (see, for example, *Re Moore & Co. Ltd and Landauer & Co.* [1921] 2 KB 519 on p. 389).

Sample and description

Goods sold by sample and description must correspond with both

Where goods are sold by reference to a sample as well as description, the goods must correspond with both the sample and the description. For example, if a seller offers carpet for sale by reference to a sample, and the manufacturer's advertising material states that the carpet is wool, if the carpet is not all wool then it is not in accordance with the description, even though the bulk of the goods may correspond with the description.

Trade Practices Act

***TPA* imposes obligations on both seller and manufacturer**

Sections 70 and 74C of the *Trade Practices Act 1974* apply to sales by description and impose obligations on both the seller (s. 70) and the manufacturer (s. 74C) that make sales in the course of a business. A manufacturer can escape responsibility if the failure to correspond with description occurs:

- after the goods have left the manufacturer's control; or
- without the manufacturer's express or implied consent.

Other relevant state legislation

The South Australian (*Sale of Goods Act 1895*, ss. 13 and 15), Western Australian (*Fair Trading Act 1987*, s. 37), Northern Territory (*Consumer Affairs and Fair Trading Act 1990*, ss. 63, 74), Victorian (*Fair Trading Act 1999*, s. 32H and 32HA) and Commonwealth (*Trade Practices Act 1974*, s. 70(1)) Acts are similar. The legislation of the states differs from s. 70 of the *Trade Practices Act* insofar as it applies even if a sale is not in the course of a seller's business. New South Wales has no direct equivalent to s. 70 of the *Trade Practices Act*, although s. 64(1) of the *Sale of Goods Act* (NSW) prevents s. 18 (which deals with sales by description) being excluded from consumer sales and so the end result is basically the same.

IN BRIEF

Summary for description to apply

Three questions must be satisfied for this section to apply:

- Is the contract for a sale of goods by description?
  There can still be a sale by description, even where the buyer can see and examine the goods. This section is concerned with descriptions which relate to the identity of the goods.
- Have words of description been used?
  The courts use an objective standard based on what reasonable persons in the position of the parties would have understood the meaning of the words to be.
- Do the goods comply with the description?

Fitness for a particular purpose

Jurisdiction	*Non-consumer*	*Consumer*
Commonwealth	*Trade Practices Act 1974*, ss. 71(2) & 74B	*Trade Practices Act 1974*, ss. 71(2) & 74B
ACT	*Sale of Goods Act 1954*, s. 19	*Sale of Goods Act 1954*, s. 19
NSW	*Sale of Goods Act 1923*, s. 19	*Fair Trading Act 1987*, s. 40Q
NT	*Sale of Goods Act 1980*, s. 18	*Consumer Affairs & Fair Trading Act 1990*, s. 64
QLD	*Sale of Goods Act 1896*, s. 17	*Sale of Goods Act 1896*, s. 17
SA	*Sale of Goods Act 1895*, s. 14	*Consumer Transactions Act 1972*, s. 6
TAS	*Sale of Goods Act 1896*, s. 19	*Sale of Goods Act 1896*, s. 19
VIC	*Goods Act 1958*, s. 19A	*Fair Trading Act 1999*, s. 32IA
WA	*Sale of Goods Act 1958*, s. 14	*Fair Trading Act 1987*, s. 38

There is an implied condition that where the buyer expressly or by implication makes known to the seller the particular purpose for which the goods are required, and shows that there is a reliance upon the judgement and skill of the seller, the goods must be reasonably fit for that purpose.

The following conditions need to be satisfied:

- The buyer must expressly or by implication make known to the seller the **particular purpose** for which the goods are required.

  Where the goods have only one purpose, the description of the goods is enough to indicate their purpose.

GRANT V. AUSTRALIAN KNITTING MILLS [1936] AC 85

Grant bought cellophane-packaged, woollen underwear from a shop that specialised in selling goods of that description. After wearing the garments for a short time he developed severe dermatitis because the garments contained chemicals left over from processing the wool.

ISSUE: Was there reliance on the retailer's choice of a quality product such that there was a breach of the implied condition of fitness for purpose?

DECISION: The High Court held that the goods were not reasonably fit for their only proper use. The plaintiff relied on the retailer's choice of a quality product that could be worn without being washed first and as this was not the case, there was a breach of the implied condition of fitness for purpose.

COMMENT: As the goods were unfit to be worn next to the skin, they were also of unmerchantable quality.

activebook

To help you to remember and understand the topics covered so far, and for links to legal websites, refer to your online activebook. Model answers provide feedback to problems and exercises.

If the goods are required for a special purpose, that purpose must be made clear to the seller. If the consumer suffers from any relevant peculiarities that the seller should be aware of, disclosure is required or the right to recovery is lost.

GRIFFITHS V. PETER CONWAY LTD [1939] 1 ALL ER 685

A woman with abnormally sensitive skin bought a coat without telling the salesman that she had sensitive skin. She subsequently contracted dermatitis from wearing the coat.

ISSUE: Had the buyer made known to the seller that she had abnormally sensitive skin?

DECISION: She was unable to recover for breach of fitness for purpose because there was nothing in the cloth that would have affected the skin of a normal person; she had failed to disclose that she suffered from skin problems.

CASE REFLECTION: Could a seller have reasonably been able to be aware of the buyer's abnormally sensitive skin if the buyer did not disclose that fact? Could it have possibly been implied by the circumstances?

- The buyer must show that there is at least **some reliance** upon the judgement and skill of the seller. It must be clear to the seller, either expressly or impliedly, at or before the contract is made, that the buyer is relying on the seller's skill and judgement, though this only need amount to a partial reliance.

! CAUTION NOTE

Implied condition that the goods will be fit for a particular purpose where this is made known to the seller, but must show reliance on the seller's skill and judgement.

Where the buyer has goods made to their own specifications, the seller will not be liable if the goods conform to those specifications but are not fit for the buyer's particular purpose. However, if the seller has a discretion in certain aspects of the production process, and in respect of those aspects the goods fail to suit the purpose for which they were required, the seller could be liable.

***CAMMELL LAIRD & CO. LTD V. MANGANESE BRONZE & BRASS CO. LTD* [1934] AC 402**

A firm of shipbuilders ordered two ship's propellers from MB to the firm's own design and specifications. The thickness of the propellers was left to the manufacturers. One of the propellers, after fitting, was noisy due to the thickness of the blade.

ISSUE: Will the fact that the buyer's reliance on the seller's skill and judgement is only partial prevent a successful claim under fitness for purpose?

DECISION: The manufacturers were in breach of an implied condition of fitness for a particular purpose because part of the manufacturing process was in the control of the blade manufacturers, and the ship-owners were relying on the manufacturer's skill to determine the correct thickness of the blades.

- The goods must be of a description which the seller normally sells.
- The buyer must not specifically request the goods under their patent or trade name. If they do, then there is no reliance on the seller's skill and judgement.

Trade Practices Act

TPA places obligations on the manufacturer as well as the seller

Sections 71(2) and 74B of the *Trade Practices Act* extend to place obligations on the manufacturer as well as the seller. Where a manufacturer or seller in the course of business supplies goods to a consumer, there is an **implied condition** that the goods shall be reasonably fit for any purpose for which the goods are being used, whether or not that is the purpose for which goods of that nature are commonly supplied. There is no such obligation where the consumer does not rely on, or it is unreasonable to rely on, the skill or judgement of the seller or manufacturer.

A manufacturer is not liable if the goods are rendered unsuitable for a particular purpose owing to something that has happened after they have left their control. Where no degree of special skill and judgement is claimed by the seller or expected by the consumer, the manufacturer's promotional material or packaging may determine whether this section operates in favour of the consumer.

Other relevant state legislation

The Western Australian (*Fair Trading Act 1987*, s. 38(2)), Victorian (*Goods Act 1958*, s. 90), New South Wales (*Fair Trading Act 1987*, Part 4, Div. 7), Northern Territory (*Consumer Affairs and Fair Trading Act 1990*, ss. 64(2) and 73) and the Commonwealth (s. 71(2) *Trade Practices Act 1974*) Acts are all similar.

IN BRIEF

Summary for fitness to apply

Four conditions **must** be satisfied:

- Has the buyer made known either expressly or impliedly the particular purpose for which the goods are required?
- Has the buyer relied on the seller's skill and judgement?
- Are the goods of a description which it is in the course of the seller's business to supply?
- Has the buyer ordered goods under their patent or trade name so that it is clear there is no reliance on the skill and judgement of the seller?

Merchantable quality

Jurisdiction	***Non-consumer***	***Consumer***
Commonwealth	*Trade Practices Act 1974*, ss. 64(1) & (2), 71(1), 74D	*Trade Practices Act 1974*, ss. 64(1) & (2), 71(1), 74D
ACT	*Sale of Goods Act 1954*, s. 19	*Sale of Goods Act 1954*, s. 19
NSW	*Sale of Goods Act 1923*, s. 19	*Fair Trading Act 1987*, s. 40Q
NT	*Sale of Goods Act 1980*, s. 19	*Consumer Affairs & Fair Trading Act* 1990, s. 64
QLD	*Sale of Goods Act 1896*, s. 17	*Sale of Goods Act 1896*, s. 17
SA	*Sale of Goods Act 1895*, s. 14	*Consumer Transactions Act 1972*, s. 6
TAS	*Sale of Goods Act 1896*, s. 19	*Sale of Goods Act 1896*, s. 19
VIC	*Goods Act 1958*, s. 19	*Fair Trading Act 1999*, ss. 32I
WA	*Sale of Goods Act 1958*, s. 14	*Fair Trading Act 1987*, s. 38

In the case of merchantable quality there are two **implied conditions**:

- that which deals with goods bought by description (this requirement does not apply to the Trade Practices Act); and
- that which deals with sale by sample (which will be dealt with in the next section).

Goods bought by description must be of merchantable quality

Where goods are bought by description from a seller who deals in goods of that description, whether the seller is the manufacturer or not, there is an implied condition that the goods will be of merchantable quality, unless the buyer has had the opportunity to examine the goods.

This section, as in the case of fitness for purpose, only applies where the sale is by description from a dealer in goods of that description, and the rules discussed in relation to the operation of correspondence with description will apply here as well. Thus, it is quite possible for the buyer to purchase goods by description, even where the goods have been seen and examined, provided that the buyer bought them as corresponding to a description.

> ! CAUTION NOTE
> *There must be a sale by description from a trader who deals in goods of that description.*

DAVID JONES LTD V. WILLIS (1934) 52 CLR 110

Willis went to the shoe department of David Jones and told the saleswoman that she wanted a comfortable pair of walking shoes because she had a bunion on her foot. After trying on a number of pairs she bought a pair that was recommended by the saleswoman. The third time that she wore the shoes the heel broke off one of them, causing her to fall and break her leg. The evidence showed that the shoes were not well made and that the heels had not been properly attached to the shoes.

ISSUE: Do goods sold by description over the counter have to be of merchantable quality? Should trying the shoes on have revealed the defect? Were the shoes fit for their intended purpose—walking on?

DECISION: The High Court held that as the shoes had been bought by description, there had been a breach of the implied condition of merchantable quality.

CASE REFLECTION: What could a business do in regards to staff training and merchandise purchasing, to avoid problems arising from the implied conditions as to quality?

Merchantable quality means reasonable for the purpose described

There is no need for the buyer to make known to the seller the purpose for which the goods are required. 'Merchantable quality' has been taken to mean that they must be reasonable for the purpose described. This requirement must be satisfied even where the article is sold under its trade or patent name.

Factors taken into account in determining 'merchantability' include:

- price (you get what you pay for);
- the description applied to the goods;
- whether the purpose for the goods had been made known to the seller; and
- any other circumstances relevant to the sale.

The duration of merchantability depends on the nature and purpose of the goods. However, it is clear that goods must remain merchantable for a reasonable time after sale. However, to a large extent what is reasonable depends on how much you paid for the goods, because you get what you paid for.

> **CAUTION NOTE**
>
> *If the goods are fit for several purposes but unfit for one, there is no breach.*

It should be noted that if the description in the contract is so general that goods sold under it can normally be used for several purposes, then goods would be merchantable under that description if they were fit for any one of those purposes.

HENRY KENDALL & SONS V. WILLIAM LILLICO & SONS LTD [1968] 2 ALL ER 444

Brazilian ground nut extract was sold to manufacturers of cattle and poultry foods all over England. The ultimate buyers of a large quantity of meal containing the extract lost a large number of young poultry. It was discovered that this was due to a high concentration of a poisonous substance in the extract which, while suitable for cattle and older poultry, was deadly to young poultry. The suppliers had known from their previous dealings with the manufacturers of the meal in question that they only made poultry foods, and for this purpose the extract was obviously unsuitable.

ISSUE: As the extract had a number of purposes for which it was suitable, but which did not include poultry, was the extract in this case of merchantable quality?

DECISION: As the extract was suitable for compounding into meal for cattle and older poultry, there was no breach of an implied condition of merchantable quality.

COMMENT: While there was no breach of merchantable quality, the suppliers were in breach of an implied condition of fitness for purpose.

However, if the description is so limited that the goods sold under the contract could only be used for one purpose, then the goods would be unmerchantable if they were of no use for that purpose.

***WREN V. HOLT* [1903] 1 KB 610**

Wren went into a hotel and asked for a beer. The beer contained arsenic as a result of the keg not being properly washed out, and as a result of drinking it he became ill.

ISSUE: As the beer had only one purpose, drinking, was it unmerchantable if it was not fit for that purpose?

DECISION: There was an implied condition that the beer would be of 'merchantable quality'. That is, that it would be fit to drink.

COMMENT: Because the beer had been drunk, it could only be treated as a breach of warranty because Wren could not return the goods in the manner in which he had received them.

Sometimes there can be a breach of both of the conditions of fitness for purpose and merchantable quality on the same set of facts. This occurred in *Grant v. Australian Knitting Mills* above (p. 460), but note also:

***MCWILLIAMS WINES LTD V. LIAWEENA (NSW) PTY LTD* [1988] ASC ¶55-695**

In 1983 McWilliams bought 500 000 corks from Liaweena. It was subsequently discovered that a large number of bottles sealed using these corks had been contaminated and were not fit for sale.

ISSUE: Were Liaweena in breach of the implied promises of fitness for purpose and merchantable quality in supplying corks that had no use?

DECISION: Liaweena were liable for breach of an implied condition of fitness for purpose. They had dealt with McWilliams for a number of years and it had been established that McWilliams relied on them to deliver corks that were not in any way contaminated and would cause the wine to become unsaleable. It was further held that the corks were not of merchantable quality as the only purpose for which they could be used was to seal bottles and prevent contamination of the contents, which they failed to do.

Trade Practices Act

Under both Part V, Div. 2A and Part VA of the *Trade Practices Act*, unlike the sale of goods legislation, the manufacturer can also have obligations, and these may extend beyond the original consumer who first acquired the goods from the seller to persons who subsequently derive title to them through a consumer—for example, by way of a gift or a second-hand purchase.

Other relevant state legislation

New South Wales (*Fair Trading Act 1987*, s. 40Q, Western Australia (*Fair Trading Act 1987*, ss. 38(1) and 39(c)), Victoria (*Fair Trading Act 1999* ss. 32I and 32IA) and the Northern Territory (*Consumer Affairs and Fair Trading Act 1990*, ss. 64(1), 65(c) and 75) have similar provisions and definitions of merchantability to s. 71(1) of the *Trade Practices Act*.

IN BRIEF

Merchantable quality

Four conditions must be satisfied:

- Has there been a sale by description?
- Have the goods been bought from a seller who deals in goods of that description?
- Has the buyer examined the goods? Would a reasonable examination have revealed the defects? This is a question of fact in each case.
- Do the goods have one purpose or several?

If the goods have more than one purpose and are only unfit for one, then the goods are of merchantable quality.

Sale by sample

Jurisdiction	***Non-consumer***	***Consumer***
Commonwealth	*Trade Practices Act 1974*, ss. 72 & 74E	*Trade Practices Act 1974*, ss. 72 & 74E
ACT	*Sale of Goods Act 1954*, s. 20	*Sale of Goods Act 1954*, s. 20
NSW	*Sale of Goods Act 1923*, s. 20	*Fair Trading Act 1987*, s. 40
NT	*Sale of Goods Act 1980*, s. 20	*Consumer Affairs & Fair Trading Act 1990*, s. 65
QLD	*Sale of Goods Act 1896*, s. 18	*Sale of Goods Act 1896*, s. 18
SA	*Sale of Goods Act 1895*, s. 15	*Consumer Transactions Act 1972*, s. 6
TAS	*Sale of Goods Act 1896*, s. 20	*Sale of Goods Act 1896*, s. 20
VIC	*Goods Act 1958*, s. 20	*Fair Trading Act 1999*, s. 32HA
WA	*Sale of Goods Act 1958*, s. 15	*Fair Trading Act 1987*, s. 39

Whether a sale is a sale by sample is a question of law

A contract is a **contract of sale by sample** where there is an express or implied term to that effect in the contract. Unlike the three preceding sections, **the test of a sale by sample is a question of law**. If the contract of sale is in writing, the court generally will not go beyond the written agreement if a dispute arises between the parties over the goods.

In addition to the earlier implied condition that the sale is by sample as well as description (i.e. that the bulk of the goods must correspond with both sample and description), there are three implied conditions in contracts of sale by sample:

- The bulk shall **correspond** with the sample in quality.
  If the differences are only of a minor nature and the quality of the goods is still the same, this condition will not be breached.
- The buyer shall have a **reasonable opportunity** of comparing the bulk with the sample.
  The buyer has a reasonable time to compare the bulk with the sample. Once this has been done, acceptance is deemed to have taken place. The right to reject the goods is then lost, although the buyer may still sue for damages for breach of warranty if the bulk does not correspond with the sample.
- The goods must be **free from any defect** which would not be apparent on a reasonable examination of the sample.

DRUMMOND V. VAN INGEN (1887) 12 APP CAS 284

A manufacturing firm submitted a sample of material to cloth merchants, and an order was subsequently given for a quantity of material of a weight and quality equal to the sample. It was later discovered that the cloth, when made up into garments by tailors who were customers of the cloth merchants, split at the seams and was therefore unsuitable for the purpose for which it was intended, though it was equal to the sample.

ISSUE: As the cloth was equal to the sample, was there a breach of an implied condition by the manufacturers of sale by sample?

DECISION: While the cloth was equal to the sample, this did not protect the manufacturer where the defect could not have been discovered by a reasonable examination, and so the purchaser was not bound to accept the material.

The goods must not only correspond with the sample, but also be of merchantable quality and this is therefore the second aspect of merchantability referred to above. **The three conditions are independent of each other.** This means that if any one of them is broken, the buyer may be able to reject the goods and treat the contract as ended.

There is no liability for the manufacturer under this section if they do not supply the sample or do not agree to a sample being offered. Nor is a manufacturer liable for goods that do not correspond with the sample because of something that happened after the goods have left their control and which could not reasonably have been foreseen to happen.

> **!** CAUTION NOTE
>
> *Each condition under sale by sample is independent of the others, so breach of any one will result in liability of the* ***trader****.*

Trade Practices Act

Sections 72 and 74E of the *Trade Practices Act* extend to place obligations on both the seller and the manufacturer.

Other relevant state legislation

The South Australian (*Sale of Goods Act 1895*, s. 15), Western Australian (*Fair Trading Act 1987*, s. 39), Victorian (*Fair Trading Act 1999* s. 32HA) and Northern Territory (*Consumer Affairs and Fair Trading Act 1990*, ss. 65 and 76) Acts have similar provisions.

IN BRIEF

Sale by sample

Any one of the following three conditions can be breached, as they **each operate independently**:

- Does the bulk correspond with the sample in quality?
  The test is one of whether a reasonable examination would have revealed the defects. Where minor variations in quality can be expected, substantial correspondence as to quality will suffice.
- Has the buyer had a reasonable opportunity of comparing the bulk with the sample?
  Inspection is normally carried out at the point of dispatch, but if this is impractical, then it will be at the point of receipt. In either case, the buyer will not be considered to have accepted the goods until there has been an opportunity to examine the goods.
- Are the goods free from any defects that would render them unmerchantable, which would not be apparent on reasonable examination of the sample?

The test of reasonable examination will vary from case to case.

SERVICES

Jurisdiction	*Non-consumer*
Commonwealth	*Trade Practices Act*, s. 74
NSW	*Fair Trading Act 1987*, s. 40S
NT	*Consumer Affairs & Fair Trading Act 1990*, s. 66
SA	*Consumer Transactions Act 1972*, s. 7
VIC	*Fair Trading Act 1999*, ss. 32J–32KA, 32N
WA	*Fair Trading Act 1987*, s. 40

Section 74 of the *Trade Practices Act 1974* (Cth) places an obligation upon the seller only. There is an **implied warranty** on the seller in a contract for the supply of services that:

- the services will be rendered with due care and skill; **and**
- any materials supplied in connection with these services will be reasonably fit for the purpose for which they are supplied. The manufacturer may also have obligations in respect of the goods supplied to the seller: s. 74(1).

> **!** CAUTION NOTE
> *Where the contract is for the supply of services, there is only an implied warranty.*

Where the consumer makes known to the seller the particular purpose for which the services are required or the result desired from the services, whether expressly or impliedly, there is an implied warranty that the services and materials supplied will be reasonably fit for that purpose unless the circumstances show the consumer did not rely on the seller's skill or judgement: s. 74(2). Section 68 of the *Trade Practices Act 1974* (Cth) does not allow the providers of goods and services to contract out of the statutory warranties established by the Act, in particular the requirement to provide services with due care and skill (s. 74).

In response to the increase in public liability insurance premiums the *Trade Practices Amendment (Liability for Recreational Services) Act 2002* amended the *Trade Practices Act* to permit self-assumption of risk by individuals who choose to participate in recreational activities which are inherently risky. The Act allows them to waive their rights under the *Trade Practices Act* to sue the business providing the activity if they suffer personal injury as a result of the service provider's failure to supply the service with due care and skill.

The Act defines recreational activities as services that consist of participation in:

(a) a sporting activity or a similar leisure time pursuit or
(b) any activity that:
  (i) involves a significant degree of physical exertion or physical risk; and
  (ii) is undertaken for the purposes of recreation, enjoyment or leisure.

'Services' are defined in very wide terms in s. 4(1) of the *Trade Practices Act 1974* (Cth). It includes transport, banking, finance, insurance, entertainment, recreation industries and the professions.

The Victorian *Fair Trading Act 1999*, Part 2A, Div. 3 treats **services as conditions**. There is a condition that where a buyer is induced by a demonstration by a seller to buy a service, the service will correspond in nature and quality with the services shown in the demonstration. There is also an implied condition that the services will be free from any defect rendering them unfit for the purpose for which they are commonly used.

IN BRIEF

Application to services

Where the legislation extends to services, the remedy for a dissatisfied consumer is limited to a claim for a breach of an implied warranty that the services were not rendered with due care and skill or that the materials supplied in connection with those services were not reasonably fit for their purpose.

CONSUMER

Jurisdiction	*Non-consumer*	*Consumer*
Commonwealth	*Trade Practices Act 1974*, s. 4B	*Trade Practices Act 1974*, s. 4B
NSW	*Sale of Goods Act 1923*	*Fair Trading Act 1987*, s. 5
NT	*Sale of Goods Act 1980*	*Consumer Affairs & Fair Trading Act 1990*, Pt V, Div. 2
SA	*Sale of Goods Act 1895*	*Consumer Transactions Act 1972*, ss. 7–10
Tas	*Sale of Goods Act*	*Fair trading Act 1990* s. 5
VIC	*Goods Act 1958*	*Fair Trading Act 1999*, s. 3
WA	*Sale of Goods Act 1958*	*Fair Trading Act 1987*, s. 6

In the context of terms implied into contracts for the sale of goods or services, the following is a summary of the meaning of the term 'consumer'. The concept of 'consumer' is important because the respective Acts prohibit the exclusion of the statutory implied terms where a consumer is involved. It will be noted that some jurisdictions allow the implied terms to be excluded.

Commonwealth (*Trade Practices Act 1974*, s. 4B)

Section 4B provides that a person will be a consumer if they acquire goods or services which do not exceed $40 000 in price, regardless of whether the goods or services are for personal/domestic use or for business use. If goods exceed $40 000 the person will still be a consumer if the goods are of a type ordinarily used in personal/domestic use and they are not used in business or resold or transformed in the course of a process of manufacture or production. The person will also be a consumer if the goods are a commercial road vehicle, which is a vehicle or trailer used in the transport of goods on public roads.

New South Wales (*Fair Trading Act 1987*, s. 5)

A consumer is a person who acquires goods or services from a supplier and the goods or services do not include goods or services acquired, or held out as being acquired, for re-supply or, in the case of goods, in the course of a business, other than a farming undertaking, for the purpose of consuming or transforming them by a process of manufacture or production, or using them for the repair or treatment of other goods or of fixtures on land.

A consumer also includes a person who acquires an interest in land, other than land used, or intended to be used, for industrial or commercial purposes.

Northern Territory (*Fair Trading Act 1992*, s. 6)

A consumer is a person who acquires goods or services from a supplier; however, a person is not a consumer if in the course of a business he or she acquires, or holds himself or herself out as acquiring, goods or services from a supplier for the purpose of:

- resupplying them;
- using them up or transforming them in, or in connection with, a process of manufacture or production; or
- repairing or treating other goods or fixtures on land.

South Australia (*Consumer Transactions Act 1972, s. 2*)

The expression 'consumer' means a person (other than a body corporate) who enters into a consumer contract with a view to purchasing, or acquiring the use or benefit of, goods or services, and includes a person to whom rights, interests or liabilities under the consumer contract are assigned.

A 'consumer contract' is a contract or agreement under which a person (other than a body corporate) purchases goods or services, or takes goods on hire or acquires by other means the use or benefit of goods or services, and the consideration to be paid by the consumer does not exceed $40 000, but does not include:

- a sale by auction; or
- a contract or agreement for the sale, bailment, or disposition of goods to a person who trades in goods of that description; or
- a contract or agreement that includes a provision conferring a right or licence to occupy land; or
- a contract or agreement of a kind declared by regulation not to be a consumer contract for the purposes of this Act.

Tasmania (*Fair Trading Act 1990, s. 5*)

Consumer is defined in similar terms to the definition in the *Trade Practices Act 1974*, however, it relates to unfair practices such as misleading and deceptive conduct, not to implied terms.

Victoria (*Fair Trading Act 1999, s.3*)

The Act refers to Consumer Sale which is defined as an agreement, whether or not in writing and whether of specific or general use, to supply goods or services of a kind ordinarily acquired for personal, domestic or household use or consumption, for the purposes of the ordinary personal, domestic or household use or consumption of those goods or services.

Western Australia (*Fair Trading Act 1987, s. 6*)

The Act defines a consumer in similar terms to the *Trade Practices Act 1974* (Cth) with an extension to include a person who acquires an interest in land which is not used, or intended to be used, for industrial or commercial purposes.

EXCLUSION OF SELLER'S LIABILITY

Non-exclusion of implied terms

Jurisdiction	*Non-consumer*	*Consumer*
Commonwealth	*Trade Practices Act 1974*, s. 68	*Trade Practices Act*, s. 68
NSW	*Sale of Goods Act 1923*, s. 57	*Fair Trading Act 1987*, s. 40M
NT	*Sale of Goods Act 1980*, s. 20	*Consumer Affairs & Fair Trading Act 1990*, s. 68
SA	*Sale of Goods Act 1895*	*Consumer Transactions Act 1972*, s. 8
TAS	*Sale of Goods Act 1896*	*Fair Trading Act 1990*, s. 51
VIC	*Goods Act 1958*	*Fair Trading Act 1999*, s. 32L

The sale of goods legislation of the states expressly permits the buyer and seller to exclude, in part or in whole, the operation of such legislation by express agreement.

A typical exclusion clause found in a standard form contract could contain wording such as:

> *All conditions, warranties and liabilities whether express or implied by statute, common law or otherwise, are hereby excluded.*

However, the use of such clauses in standard form agreements between a seller and a buyer, and the inequality of bargaining power that often existed between the parties, led to the Commonwealth, the states and the territories enacting legislation designed to protect consumers not only in relation to quality of goods supplied, but also for services and other unfair trading practices.

Australian Capital Territory

The *Fair Trading Act 1992* provides parallel consumer protection legislation with Part V of the *Trade Practices Act 1974*.

New South Wales

The *Fair Trading Act 1987* s. 40M prohibits the exclusion of the implied conditions as to merchantable quality, fitness for purpose, description and sample where the contract is a consumer sale. This means that the implied conditions are a part of the contract even if the parties expressly agree otherwise. However, they can be excluded when the contract does not involve a consumer sale, that is, where the goods are for use in a business.

Northern Territory

Part V, Division 2 of the *Consumer Affairs and Fair Trading Act 1990* mirrors the *Trade Practices Act* provisions found in Part V. The conditions and warranties are only implied in contracts with consumers. A consumer is defined in much the same terms as in the *Trade Practices Act*, s. 5(1). It is not possible to contract out of the implied conditions and warranties provisions of the Act: s. 68. However, it is permissible to provide for the limitation of liability for breach of the implied warranties and conditions under s. 69, except for the implied undertakings as to title, encumbrances and quiet possession found in s. 62.

Queensland

The *Fair Trading Act 1989* provides parallel consumer protection legislation with Part V of the *Trade Practices Act 1974*. Under s. 40(k), false representations as to conditions, warranties, guarantees, rights or remedies are prohibited and cannot be excluded: s. 107.

South Australia

The *Consumer Transactions Act 1972* is wide ranging in its coverage of consumer interests. Part II, ss. 7–24, entitled 'Consumer Transactions' and Division 1, ss. 7–19, headed 'Consumer Contracts Generally' are of primary concern to consumers who purchase goods or services up to the value of $40000. Section 8 implies into every 'consumer contract' for the sale or supply of goods conditions similar to those discussed above. This section will also catch hiring or leasing contracts. Section 10 prohibits exclusion clauses between the parties, while s. 11 catches co-suppliers who can also be jointly and severally liable to the consumer.

The *Fair Trading Act 1987* also contains provisions prohibiting false representations as to conditions, warranties, guarantees, rights or remedies and cannot be excluded: s. 96.

Tasmania

The *Fair Trading Act 1990* parallels Part V of the *Trade Practices Act*. Under s. 16(k), false representations as to conditions, warranties, guarantees, rights or remedies are prohibited and cannot be excluded: s. 51.

Victoria

Where a contract of sale falls within the scope of Part 2A of the *Fair Trading Act 1999*, the implied conditions and warranties as to title, description, fitness for purpose, merchantable quality and sale by sample discussed above no longer apply. They are replaced by the non-excludable implied terms contained in Division 3 (ss. 32G–32RA), which deals with sales of goods and services.

Western Australia

The *Fair Trading Act 1987* in Part III, ss. 34–39 introduced parallel legislation to the *Trade Practices Act 1974*.

Part III has implied conditions and warranties in contracts with consumers if the price does not exceed $40 000 or, if it does, when the goods were of a kind ordinarily acquired for personal or domestic use as to title, description, fitness for purpose and merchantable quality in consumer contracts for the supply of goods and services in a similar fashion to the *Trade Practices Act*. However, unlike the *Trade Practices Act*, these provisions are not limited to the supply of goods bought from corporations, but will apply to all suppliers of goods and services to consumers.

Contracting out is prohibited by s. 34. However, it is permissible to provide for the limitation of liability for breach of the implied warranties and conditions under s. 35, except with respect to the implied undertakings as to title, encumbrances and quiet possession of s. 36.

Doing business

Businesses must also know their rights

Under the consumer protection legislation of the Commonwealth and the states and territories, it is becoming increasingly difficult for businesses to exclude themselves from liability for faulty goods through the use of an exclusion clause or a 'No Refund' notice or policy. A consumer is entitled to a full refund if:

- the item is faulty;
- the item does not work as advertised;
- the item has a false description; or
- the item is different from that which the consumer agreed to buy.

However, a customer may not be entitled to a refund if they did not follow the manufacturer's instructions. Similarly, a customer will not be entitled to a refund without proof of purchase, for example, in the form of a receipt. ■

WEB RESOURCES

Commonwealth: For information on the ACCC and the *Trade Practices Act* see:
http://www.accc.gov.au/

Consumer Affairs/Fair Trading Agency Web Links: A general gateway to the various consumer affairs and fair trading agency sites in Australia:
http://www.consumer.gov.au/copy/govlinks.html

REVIEW QUESTIONS

22.1 How does a claim under a breach of an implied condition in a sale of goods by sample differ from that of other breaches of implied conditions?

22.2 What arguments can a seller put forward for limiting the scope of the section on merchantable quality found in sale of goods legislation?

22.3 Hui bought a second-hand computer from Ashmore Office Equipment for $500 and spent a further $95 having it overhauled. After using the computer for some three months, the police arrived at his home one day and asked to examine the computer. They discovered it had been stolen and seized it from him. It was eventually returned to its true owner.

Advise Hui of his rights, if any, under the sale of goods legislation against Ashmore Office Equipment.

22.4 Early in 2006, Loretta bought a car from Sally. After six months, Loretta decided to go overseas and sold the car to Irene. Unknown to any of the parties, there was tax owing on the car from a previous owner. Under the relevant legislation, the government had the right to seize the car and sell it to recover the tax owing. The car was duly seized.

Advise Irene.

22.5 Richard went to a fish and chip shop and asked for two fresh crayfish for dinner. The fish shop owner explained that he had no live crayfish, but that he had some boiled ones, which he sold to Richard. The crayfish were not fresh and Richard, after eating them, became seriously ill.

Advise Richard whether he has any action open to him under sale of goods legislation.

22.6 Citybus entered into a written contract with ABC Motor Company, manufacturers of buses and trucks, for a bus. Citybus explained that the bus was required to operate in a very hilly district and they were assured that an ABC bus would be more than suitable for such operating conditions. After taking delivery, Citybus found that the bus would not operate at all in hilly conditions, and was not even very satisfactory operating on their city routes.

Advise Citybus on the options open to them, if any, under the sale of goods legislation.

22.7 The plaintiff was given a blood transfusion during the course of an operation at a hospital. It was subsequently discovered that the blood carried an HIV virus and the plaintiff, as a result, contracted AIDS.

Can the plaintiff recover under s. 71 of the *Trade Practices Act 1974* (Cth)?

What argument/s will the hospital raise in its defence?

activebook

Activebook resources include in-depth summaries with links to the relevant part of the book. For revision, add your own notes to the summaries provided by using the note-taking function.

22.8 The *Trade Practices Act* implies certain warranties in contracts for the provision of services under s. 74. Discuss what is meant by the term 'services' and explain why they are treated as 'warranties' rather than 'conditions'.

22.9 Indicate whether each of the following statements is true or false:

	TRUE	FALSE
▪ There is an implied condition in every sale of goods that the seller has the right to sell the goods	☐	☐
▪ If a seller has not got title in the goods at the time of transfer, then there is a total failure of consideration	☐	☐
▪ Where goods are sold by description, there is an implied warranty that the goods shall correspond with the description	☐	☐
▪ Where goods are sold by description, description goes to both identity and quality of the goods	☐	☐
▪ In a contract involving a sale by sample, the test used by the courts is a question of law	☐	☐
▪ Where the goods in a contract for the sale of goods are not fit for their intended purpose, there is a breach of an implied warranty	☐	☐
▪ Where there is a contract for the sale of goods by sample, even if the difference between the bulk and sample is only of a minor nature, the condition will still be breached	☐	☐
▪ For the *Trade Practices Act 1974* (Cth) to operate, the goods must not exceed $40 000 in price, unless the goods are of a kind ordinarily acquired for personal, domestic or household use or consumption	☐	☐

CRITICAL THINKING

22.1 Jarvis was establishing a small stud hobby farm. To stock the farm he attended a sale of stud cattle held by Murrays Pty Ltd.

A salesman handed Jarvis a catalogue headed 'Murrays' Best Breeding Stock'. Jarvis's attention was drawn to a bull listed in the catalogue as 'Plentiful' with a price of $50 000. Jarvis said to the salesman, 'I want a good breeding bull. I believe your Murray Greys are very good breeding stock. I'll buy "Plentiful".' The salesman simply replied, 'Write out your cheque and I'll give you a receipt.'

After three months, Jarvis discovered that 'Plentiful', although a healthy Murray Grey, was useless as a stud bull.

Advise Jarvis whether he has any remedies against Murrays, and if so, what they are and why.

22.2 Brown purchased a pair of woollen underpants from Underwear Galore in Adelaide. As a result of wearing the underpants without first washing them, he contracted dermatitis as the underpants contained bisulphite of soda, which it was found had been left in the underpants during the manufacturing process. The underpants had been packaged in a clear cellophane wrap but the bisulphite of soda could not be seen on a reasonable inspection by either the retailer or the buyer.

Has Brown any remedy/ies available to him against the retailer, Underwear Galore, under the sale of goods legislation? Explain what Brown has to establish in order to succeed in an action and whether, in your opinion, he would be successful.

CHAPTER

Consumer Protection Legislation

CHAPTER CONTENTS

activebook

This icon is used throughout the following chapter to remind you to visit the *Business Law* online activebook for additional exercises, links to legal websites, and feedback. For a detailed explanation of what is in the activebook please refer to the inside cover of this textbook. The activebook is available through OneKey.

Where do I start?
Learning path: Use the activebook to complete a pre-chapter warm-up exercise.

There are many definitions of legal terms to assist with your understanding of the material.

CHAPTER OBJECTIVES

On completion of this chapter, you should be able to:

- recognise the significance of the *Trade Practices Act* as a major source of consumer protection law
- explain the constitutional limitations of the *Trade Practices Act 1974* (Cth) and the reason for the enactment of the state Fair Trading Acts
- explain and list unfair practices
- discuss the operation of the consumer protection provisions
- explain the remedies available to a consumer and the penalties that can be imposed under the Act against a trader in breach of Part V provisions of the *Trade Practices Act*
- explain the rights against manufacturers and importers under the *Trade Practices Act*
- list the functions of consumer claims tribunals and courts, and identify who constitutes a consumer under relevant consumer protection legislation
- differentiate between state departments of consumer affairs and the Australian Competition Tribunal.

KEY TERMS

An understanding of the following terms will help you to better understand the material in this chapter:

- **consumer:** a person who purchases goods or services priced under $40 000, or of a kind ordinarily acquired for personal, domestic or household use or consumption (s. 4B). Small businesses purchasing goods for less than $40 000 are treated as 'consumers' for the purposes of the TPA
- **corporation:** includes a foreign, financial or trading corporation, as well as a territorial corporation (s. 4(1)). A foreign corporation is a corporation incorporated outside Australia; a financial corporation is a corporation that engages in the conduct of dealing in finance; a trading corporation is a corporation that does, or will, engage in trading activities (providing goods and services for reward) of a not insignificant scale. Most corporations will be trading corporations. A territorial corporation is a corporation incorporated in the Australian Capital Territory or the Northern Territory
- **in trade or commerce:** conduct that is an aspect or element of activities or transactions which, of their nature, bear a trading or commercial character.

what if . . .

A company that provides finance for the purchase of new cars advertised its '10/10 deal' under which new car finance is available on $10 deposit and $10 per week. The advertisement did not state that the finance was only short term and that after three months the customer would have to convert to long term finance under which the repayments would rise to $500 per week.

Apart from the sale of goods legislation examined in Chapters 21 and 22, up until the late 1960s the only other remedies available to a dissatisfied consumer were to be found in the common law. Unfortunately the common law was unable to provide either adequate protection or redress for consumers against unfair or restrictive trading practices of suppliers or manufacturers. Shortcomings in common law rules that operated against the interests of the consumer included:

- difficulty for the consumer to prove misrepresentation;
- the unconscionable conduct of unscrupulous traders;
- maintenance of the principles of freedom to contract, for example, carefully worded exclusion clauses operated against consumers;

- price fixing;
- resale price maintenance; and
- lack of remedies to force the recall of faulty goods or fine unscrupulous traders.

This chapter is in part concerned with the relevant consumer protection provisions contained in Part V, Division 1 (headed 'Consumer Protection'), dealing with certain unfair trading practices. After examining the consumer protection provisions of the *Trade Practices Act*, consideration will be given to the more significant state consumer protection laws. Chapter 30 deals with the Act's regulation of restrictive trade practices under Part IV.

SCOPE OF THE *TRADE PRACTICES ACT 1974* (CTH)

The *Trade Practices Act* is principally concerned with:

- **regulating restrictive trade practices** with the aim of preventing monopolistic and anti-competitive activities among traders to produce greater competition and efficiency in the market (Part IV of the Act); and
- regulations aimed at **protecting the interests of consumers** of goods, services and land against unfair practices of traders (Part V, Division 1), supported by adequate remedies to protect the consumer in the event of a breach of the Act.

IN BRIEF

Major functions of the *Trade Practices Act*

Consumer protection	Restrictive trade practices
Protects interests of consumers against: – unfair practices of traders (things traders do to consumers) – unconscionable conduct of traders – misleading or deceptive conduct – specific false representations – unfair practices Provides safety and information standards Establishes manufacturer's liability Establishes product liability	Prevents monopolistic and anti-competitive activities among traders (things traders do to each other)

Constitutional basis

Commonwealth relies on specific constitutional power to regulate trade practices at interstate level

The legislative inactivity of the states in matters of consumer protection led to the enactment of the *Trade Practices Act* in 1974 by the Commonwealth government.

The Commonwealth government has no constitutional power as such to regulate trade practices. To avoid the Act being struck down by the High Court as being unconstitutional, the Commonwealth government based it on a number of specific constitutional heads, the main one being the **corporations power** (s. 51(xx) of the Constitution). However, the Act does extend to individuals engaged in interstate or overseas trade and commerce.

Because of the limitations imposed by the Constitution on the Commonwealth government's ability to pass uniform national consumer legislation, the states and territories have all now passed uniform provisions mirroring the consumer protection provisions of the *Trade Practices Act* in the form of the Fair Trading Acts. The state Acts contain similar civil and criminal sanctions for non-compliance as the *Trade Practices Act*.

Fair Trading legislation: **ACT** 1992 : **NSW, WA** and **SA** 1987 : **NT** *Consumer Affairs and Fair Trading Act* 1990 : **QLD** 1989 : **TAS** 1991 : **VIC** 1999

The state Fair Trading Acts catch intra-state activities

The purpose of the state legislation is to catch intra-state activities not caught under the *Trade Practices Act*, and to provide blanket protection for the consumer.

Part V, Division 1 is no longer limited in its application only to dealings between a consumer and a corporation because it is now possible through the application of the states' Fair Trading Acts to also catch intra-state dealings. In the event of a conflict arising between a state or territory law and the *Trade Practices Act*, s. 109 of the Constitution provides that the Commonwealth law shall prevail. Section 75 of the *Trade Practices Act* also expressly preserves the concurrent operation of state or territory law.

Who may be caught under the Act?

***TPA* prohibits restrictive trade practices and protects consumer interests**

The Act generally prohibits restrictive trading practices and provides protection for consumers against the activities of corporations. As a result, most of the provisions of the *Trade Practices Act* are specifically directed towards conduct engaged in by corporations or on behalf of a corporation by a director, agent or employee: s. 84(2).

Anyone (including persons, sole traders, partnerships and unincorporated bodies) may be caught by the Act if they are caught under one of the following constitutional heads of power:

- engaged in overseas trade and commerce: s. 51(i);
- engaged in business that requires the use of postal, telegraphic, telephone services, radio or television for the sale or supply of goods or services: s. 51(v);
- engaged in misleading conduct under s. 55 to which the Paris Convention for the Protection of Industrial Property applies: s. 51(xxix);
- involved in dealings by way of supply of goods and services to the Commonwealth government or any of its instrumentalities: s. 52; or
- involved in trade or commerce within a territory, between territories or between a state and a territory: s. 122.

Who is a 'consumer'?

Some implied rights against suppliers and manufacturers only apply to consumers

Some rights, particularly those implied against suppliers and manufacturers, only apply to consumers. Under the Act, a person is a consumer if:

- they acquire **goods or services** of less than $40 000;
- they acquire goods or services of a kind ordinarily acquired for personal, domestic or household use (of any value);
- they acquire a commercial road vehicle (of any value); or
- the goods were not acquired for resupply, or for use or transformation in trade or commerce.

The onus is upon the supplier to show that a person is not a consumer or that a sale was not a consumer sale: s. 4B(3).

Division 1 of Part V of the TPA prohibits both misleading and deceptive conduct

Division 1 of Part V of the *Trade Practices Act* prohibits both misleading and deceptive conduct generally under s. 52 and a range of specific types of misleading conduct in the remainder. The Act first prohibits general unfair practices under s. 52, and as it is not necessary to show that the conduct was deliberate, the section does not attract criminal sanctions when it is breached (see Figure 23.1). The Act then goes on to prohibit quite specific unfair trade practices (see summary at Table 23.1). Conduct here requires proof of deliberate intent as breaches of these sections carry both criminal penalties and civil remedies.

It is not uncommon to find that proceedings under the Act involving allegations of a breach of a specific section will also involve a breach of the more general s. 52. However, there will also be cases where there will be a breach of s. 52 without necessarily involving a breach of the more specific sections.

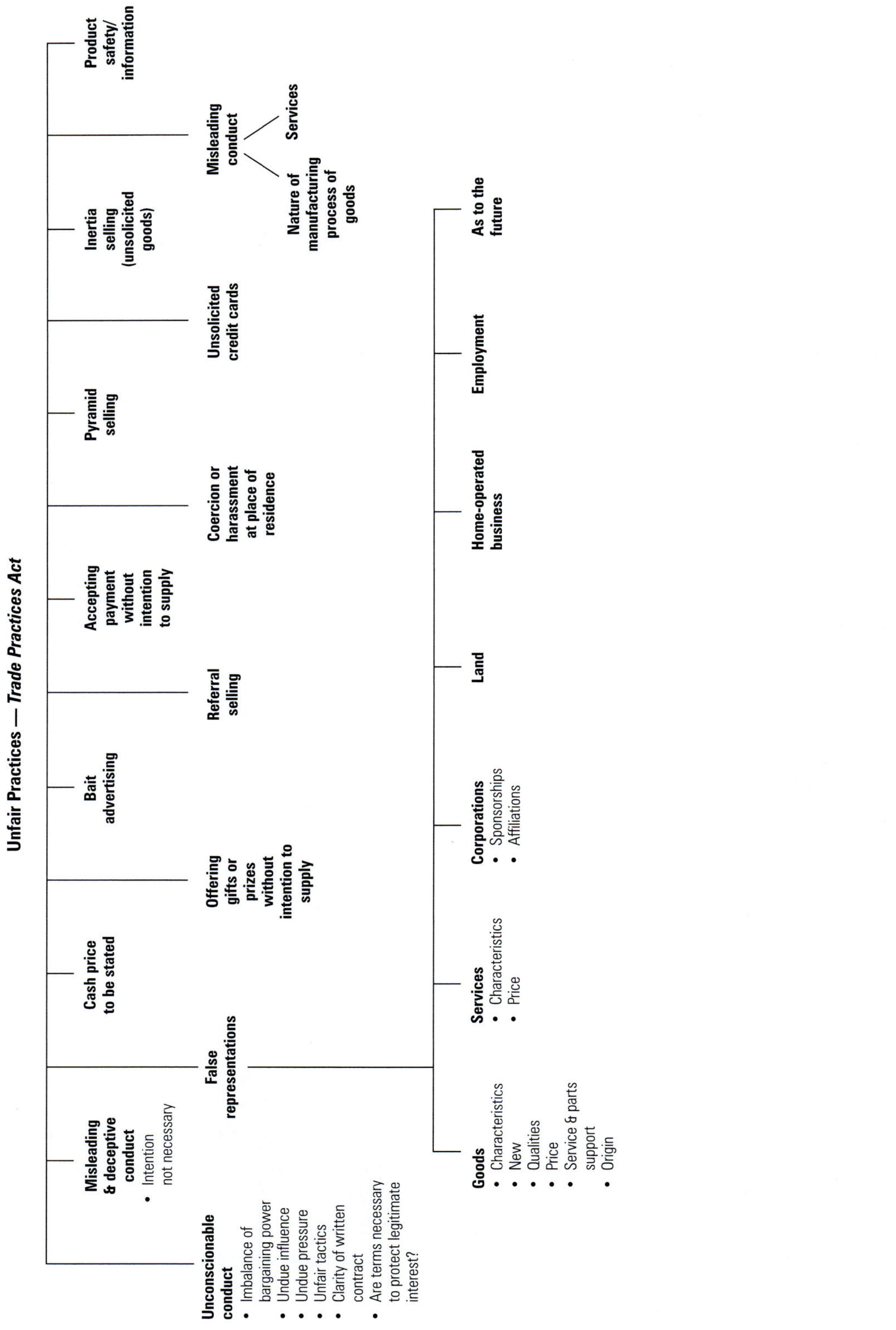

FIGURE 23.1 *Unfair practices*

Table 23.1 Summary of unfair practices

Practice	*Section of* Trade Practices Act
Unconscionable conduct	51AA, 51AB, 51AC
Misleading and deceptive conduct	52
False representations as to goods (various specific examples)	53, 53A, 53B, 59
False representations as to services	53(aa)
False representations as to sponsorships/affiliations of corporations	53(c)
False representations as to land	53A
Misleading statements about home-operated businesses	59
False representations as to employment	53B
Cash price to be stated (cannot advertise part only of the consideration)	53C
Offering gifts or prizes without intending to supply	54
Misleading conduct to which industrial property convention applies	55
Misleading conduct regarding services	55A
Bait advertising	56
Referral selling	57
Accepting payment without intending to supply	58
Coercion or harassment at place of residence	60
Pyramid selling	65AAA to 65AAE
Unsolicited credit cards	63A
Inertia selling (unsolicited goods)	64, 65
Product safety and product information	65B–65T

! CAUTION NOTE

Allegations of a breach of a specific section will often involve a breach of the general s. 52 (Part IVA, ss. 51AA, 51AB, 51AC).

PROHIBITION OF UNCONSCIONABLE CONDUCT (PART IVA, SS. 51AA, 51AB, 51AC)

IN BRIEF

Summary of unconscionability legislation—ss. 51AA-AD

The prohibition of unconscionable conduct is found in ss. 51AA, 51AB and 51AC of Part IVA, while s. 51AD is found in Part IVB and sets out Codes of Conduct:

- Section 51AA defines unconscionability in general terms and applies the common law principles that are derived from the *Amadio* case (see p. 334).
- Section 51AB is a more specific provision and prohibits corporations from engaging in unconscionable conduct when supplying goods or services to consumers. It is aimed at redressing the imbalance in bargaining power between sellers and buyers and sets out a number of guidelines on what constitutes unconscionable conduct.
- Section 51AC mirrors s. 51AB but only deals with commercial transactions which do not exceed $3 million. It has an almost identical checklist, with some extra business relevant tests added, to that found in s. 51AB.
- Section 51AD provides that all traders must obey any industry codes that are relevant to their industry.

Section 51AA provides:

> *(1) A corporation must not, in trade or commerce, engage in conduct that is unconscionable within the meaning of the unwritten law, from time to time, of the States and Territories.*

Fair Trading legislation: **ACT** s. 13 : **NSW** s. 43 : **NT** s. 43 : **QLD** s. 39 : **SA** s. 57 : **TAS** s. 15 : **VIC** ss. 7–8 : **WA** s. 11

The section extends the remedies available under the Act to conduct regarded as unconscionable by the courts in accordance with common law or equitable principles derived from *Amadio*'s case (see p. 334).

Aims to redress the imbalance in bargaining power between buyers and sellers

Section 51AB is more specific than s. 51AA, as it prohibits corporations from engaging in unconscionable conduct when supplying goods or services to consumers. It is aimed at redressing the imbalance in bargaining power between sellers and buyers and so the section is limited to goods or services of a kind ordinarily acquired for personal, domestic or household use or consumption: s. 51AB(5).

The term 'unconscionable' is not defined in the Act, but s. 51AB(2) sets out a number of guidelines in relation to unconscionable conduct along similar lines to s. 9 of the *Contracts Review Act 1980* (NSW) for the benefit of the court and the parties including:

- the bargaining positions of the corporation and the consumer;
- whether it would it be reasonably difficult to comply with any terms in the contract;
- whether the terms are reasonably necessary to protect legitimate interests of the corporation;
- establishing whether the form and wording of the contract was clear;
- determining whether any undue influence, pressure or unfair tactics were used; and
- the cost of purchasing, and the circumstances under which the consumer could have purchased identical or equivalent goods or services elsewhere.

Unconscionable conduct in business transactions

> **!** CAUTION NOTE
>
> *Section 51AC—provides protection to small businesses against unfair conduct by large businesses where the transactions are less than $3 million.*

Section 51AC of the *Trade Practices Act* provides protection to small businesses against unfair conduct by large businesses where the transactions are less than $3 million. It is similar to s. 51AB and the rights available to consumers. A 'business consumer' includes a company but not a publicly listed one.

Section 51AC(3) sets out a checklist to assist the court in deciding whether conduct is unconscionable. Sections 51AC(3)(a)–(e) are virtually the same as those under s. 51AB(2). However, s. 51AC(3) adds extra tests of unconscionability that are relevant to small business to assist the court to decide whether:

- there was consistency of the supplier's conduct towards the business consumer: s. 51AC(3)(f);
- the supplier failed to satisfy the requirements of any applicable industry code: s. 51AC(3)(g),(h);
- there was non-disclosure by the supplier of anything that it intended to do that could affect the interests of the business consumer or add to the risks of the business consumer: s. 51AC(3)(i);
- the supplier was prepared to negotiate terms and conditions with the business consumer and the extent to which the business consumer was able to understand the documentation involved: s. 51AC(3)(j); and
- the parties acted towards each other in good faith: s. 51AC(3)(k).

The consumer has two years within which to commence proceedings: s. 87(1)(c).

If the consumer is successful, and the Federal Court can take into account the conduct of the parties since the contravention (s. 87), remedies include:

- declaring the whole or any part of the contract void;
- refusing to enforce any or all of the provisions in the contract;
- varying a contract;
- directing a refund of money or return of property;
- paying the amount of loss or damage suffered;
- ordering the repair of the goods; and
- varying or terminating an instrument creating or transferring an interest in land.

While this chapter is primarily concerned with the application of the *Trade Practices Act*, situations may arise where the Constitutional limitations of the *Trade Practices Act* prevent it being applied. In those cases the state legislation, normally the *Fair Trading Act,* will be utilised by the state authorities. This occurred in Queensland where an individual (and therefore normally outside the scope of the *Trade Practices Act*) engaged in unconscionable conduct:

MILLER V. GUNTHER AND OTHERS **[2005] QSC 90**

Gunther was a real estate agent and pastor of a church with a large number of Samoans in the congregation. Gunther took advantage of the trust and confidence his Samoan clients put in church pastors. Gunther approached new arrivals to Australia, exploiting their commercial inexperience and simplicity and their comparative lack of education and English language skills to induce them to enter disadvantageous contracts.

He purchased cheap homes through his companies, then sold the properties to his clients, who were members of his congregation, for prices well above market rates. The bank funding the purchases was unaware of the arrangements and approved loans for amounts less than the full purchase price. Gunther obtained second mortgages over the properties in favour of his companies to secure the shortfall. As a result, the purchasers owed more than their houses were worth.

ISSUE: Can a person's role as pastor of a church contribute to unconscionable conduct in regard to commercial dealings?

DECISION: The Supreme Court of Queensland held that Gunther had engaged in unconscionable conduct in regard to the transactions.

Enforcement of industry codes

Part IVB of *TPA* makes provision for industry codes to give business efficacy to the law relating to their particular industry

Part IVB of the *Trade Practices Act* makes provision for industry codes. An 'industry code' is a code regulating the conduct of participants in an industry towards other participants in the industry or towards consumers who use the industry: s. 51ACA.

Section 51AD of the *Trade Practices Act* provides that all traders must obey any industry codes that are relevant to their industry. The idea behind an industry code is to give business efficacy to the law relating to the particular industry. That is to give it greater effect and efficiency. For example, the franchise industry must follow the Franchising Code of Conduct while the consumer credit industry must follow the Privacy Code with respect to privacy matters.

Section 51AE stipulates which codes or parts of codes will apply to an industry and provides that regulations:

- prescribe an industry code, or specified provisions of an industry code; and
- declare the industry code to be a mandatory industry code or a voluntary industry code.

PROHIBITION OF MISLEADING OR DECEPTIVE CONDUCT (S. 52)

IN BRIEF

Summary of misleading or deceptive conduct—s. 52

Three major elements must be established before there is a contravention of s. 52(1):

- conduct is given a wide meaning so that it catches not only positive statements but a wide range of statements, predictions, promises, inactions, puffs and the like;
- the activity of trade or commerce, even though the words have been given a wide meaning; must have some 'trading or commercial character' about them and be associated with the advertising and selling of goods, services or land; and
- misleading or deceptive conduct, or conduct likely to mislead or deceive. This is determined by an objective test of whether a reasonable person would be misled or deceived.

Section 52 is a catch-all provision and does not require that the conduct be deliberate, so there are no criminal penalties. A person who has suffered damage as a result of a breach of s. 52 may bring a civil action.

Misleading or deceptive conduct

Fair Trading legislation: **ACT** s. 12 : **NSW** s. 42 : **NT** s. 42 : **QLD** s. 38 : **SA** s. 56 : **TAS** s. 14 : **VIC** ss. 9–11 : **WA** s. 10

activebook

To help you to remember and understand the topics covered so far, and for links to legal websites, refer to your online activebook. Model answers provide feedback to problems and exercises.

Section 52 is a catch-all provision that provides that a corporation shall not engage in conduct that is misleading or deceptive or is likely to mislead or deceive. Because of the difficulty in satisfactorily defining conduct that is misleading or deceptive, the section has a wide application. As a result it has become the most litigated section of the Act. Section 52 is made up of three elements:

- conduct by a corporation or person (who is caught by s. 6);
- the activity of trade or commerce; and
- misleading or deceptive conduct, or conduct likely to mislead or deceive.

If these three elements are satisfied, any person or business can bring an action against a corporation involved in conduct that is misleading or deceptive or likely to mislead or deceive.

While Part V is headed 'Consumer Protection', s. 52 should not be restricted in its usage to consumers. It can equally be enforced by competitors or suppliers against other competitors or suppliers across a wide range of activities. For example: for misrepresentations on leases and purchase of franchises; protection of images, such as a face, character or name; in banking; in share issues and trading, prospectuses and takeovers; in cases involving comparative advertising or 'knocking copy' (where a rival's product is downgraded in an advertisement).

EVEREADY AUSTRALIA PTY LTD V. GILLETTE AUSTRALIA PTY LTD [2000] ATPR ¶41-751

Gillette ran a series of comparative television and billboard advertising promotions for its range of Duracell batteries. All three television advertisements featured a team of bunnies playing soccer and suggested that Duracell batteries outlasted the other team which was powered by other unidentified batteries. In each advertisement there was a representation that Duracell batteries would 'last four times longer' or 'up to four times longer' than the opposition. The subtext stated 'ordinary batteries = zinc carbon batteries'. The billboard advertisement showed a picture of a battery with the word 'Duracell' in capitals and in smaller print the words 'alkaline battery'. Below the battery in prominent black print were the words 'four times longer'. On the left-hand side of the billboard was the image of a bunny character. In smaller print appeared the statement that alkaline batteries 'last up to four times longer than ordinary zinc carbon batteries'. Had Gillette engaged in misleading or deceptive conduct in contravention of s. 52 of the *Trade Practices Act* in its advertising campaign?

ISSUE: Would Duracell's advertising lead consumers to think that the comparison being made was between Duracell's alkaline batteries and all the batteries (i.e. zinc carbon and alkaline) of other manufacturers?

DECISION: *Lindgren* J in the Federal Court held that the advertising campaign amounted to a misleading comparison between zinc carbon and alkaline batteries. There was the minimal reference to the comparison being between alkaline batteries and zinc carbon batteries and the words 'lasts up to four times longer' hold out to the viewer that Duracell batteries do offer a meaningful advantage over competing brands. The specificity of those words is inconsistent with the nature of advertising puff.

What is meant by 'conduct'?

'Conduct'—doing or refusing to do any act—has been given a wide meaning to catch statements

'Conduct' is defined under the *Trade Practices Act* as 'doing or refusing to do any act' and has been given a wide meaning under the Act. It not only catches positive statements by sellers of goods or services but it can also catch:

- **statements of opinion** that imply false representations of fact or are not reasonably held;
- **puffs**, for example, exaggerated advertisements, if they are likely to mislead or deceive;
- **silence**, if it is likely to mislead or deceive;

***HENJO INVESTMENTS PTY LTD & ORS V. COLLINS MARRICKVILLE PTY LTD* (1988) 79 ALR 83**

Henjo owned a restaurant business. The local council had granted approval for the seating of 84 people. The liquor licensing authority prohibited seating or service in the bar area. After opening the restaurant, the seating was increased significantly and the bar area was used as a service area, all without approval. Collins entered into negotiations to purchase the business and was told of the number of seats being used and shown the seating arrangements. Collins did not become aware of the lack of approval for the seating arrangements until after completion of the purchase. Collins brought proceedings under the *Trade Practices Act*.

ISSUE: Should the officially approved seating arrangements have been disclosed when disclosing the actual seating arrangements?

DECISION: The Full Court of the Federal Court held that silence can constitute misleading and deceptive conduct when the circumstances give rise to disclosing relevant facts. This duty to disclose is not negated merely because inquiries that would have disclosed the true position could have been made.

CASE REFLECTION: When supplying information to a customer, should a business consider not only the accuracy of the information, but also how it might be interpreted?

- **broken promises** and false predictions;
- **statements that are literally true** but which create a false impression; and
- **pre-contractual statements**, leading up to the entering into a contract, which were false.

***CLARK EQUIPMENT AUSTRALIA LTD V. COVCAT PTY LTD* (1987) 71 ALR 367**

The appellants had both orally and in a brochure represented that a tree-cutting machine was capable of felling a certain number of trees per day in a natural forest. On the basis of the information contained in the brochures and the statements of the appellants, the respondents entered into a leasing agreement for the machine.

The machine fell far short of expectations and was unsuitable for the work the respondents had described to the appellants.

ISSUE: Can pre-contractual verbal or unwritten representations constitute misleading and deceptive conduct?

DECISION: The Full Court of the Australian Federal Court held that both the oral representations and the statements in the brochure by the appellants about the capabilities of the machine were such that they had contravened s. 52.

By giving a warranty that is false, a corporation may engage in misleading and deceptive conduct even if it did not intend to mislead or deceive, and even if it has not engaged in any other false representations.

***ACCOUNTING SYSTEMS 2000 V. CCH AUSTRALIA LIMITED* (1993) 42 FCR 470**

Accounting Systems 2000 obtained a right to use the copyright in a computer program owned by another company (computer program A). It did not obtain any ownership rights to the computer program. Using this program it developed a computer program of its own (computer program B). This new program relied so heavily on the original program (computer program A) that it was an infringement of the copyright in that program. Accounting Systems 2000 then entered into a contract with CCH in which it warranted it had the right to assign the copyright in its own computer program (Program B).

ISSUE: Does the false warranty in the contract amount to misleading and deceptive conduct?

DECISION: The Full Court of the Federal Court held that a corporation, by making a contract containing warranties that are false may, by that conduct alone, be held to have engaged in misleading and deceptive conduct, without the need to show that the corporation made any separate false representations before making the contract.

CASE REFLECTION: How can a business make sure its sales representatives know what they are selling and the validity of the claims they make about the product?

What is 'trade or commerce'?

Conduct complained of must have trading or commercial character

The conduct complained of must have some trading or commercial character about it.

***PACIFIC DUNLOP LTD V. HOGAN* (1989) 23 FCR 553**

Hogan was a well-known television personality and performed the title role in the film *Crocodile Dundee*. Pacific Dunlop produced a television commercial for a brand of shoes it manufactured. The advertisement was an obvious parody of a notable scene from the film.

ISSUE: Did the advertisement amount to a misrepresentation that Hogan had entered into a commercial arrangement involving permission to use his character?

DECISION: The Full Court of the Federal Court held that a significant section of viewers could be misled into believing that a commercial arrangement had been entered into between Hogan and Pacific Dunlop. This amounted to both misleading and deceptive conduct under the *Trade Practices Act* and passing off.

CASE REFLECTION: Is the merchandising associated with sports, pop stars, movies, etc., based solely on the goods sold or is it largely dependent on the desire to participate in the image created by that sport, pop star or movie?

Section 52 is used as an alternative to an action of passing off not only by consumers but also by trade rivals

While it will catch statements made by a corporation to members of the public, the High Court has held that the expression 'any other person' in s. 80(1) can include business against business and competitor against competitor. The result is that s. 52 has not only been used extensively by consumers against sellers and suppliers but also by trade rivals. Thus, it has been used as an alternative to the action of passing off over:

- misleading or disparaging representations in advertising;
- the publishing of tests and surveys, which may not have been carried out or only partially carried out;
- claims in relation to the country of origin of goods; and
- the use of similar names.

The basis for the extended meaning of the expression 'any other person' can be found in the object of s. 52, which is to protect the public interest. A side benefit of an action by trade rivals is the benefit to their business interests, and in all probability the protection of their interests is their primary concern. However, the courts view such an application as one ultimately designed to protect the consuming public from being misled or misinformed.

Because of the potential width of s. 52(1), it is possible for the publication of statements made in the ordinary course of news through the media (i.e. newspapers, magazines, radio and television) to amount to conduct that could be misleading or deceptive. Section 65A exempts information providers from Part V, Division 1 in relation to the publication of news, but the section does not extend to advertising statements.

What type of conduct is misleading or deceptive?

Whether conduct is misleading or deceptive is determined by an objective test

Whether particular conduct is misleading or deceptive, or is likely to mislead or deceive, is ultimately a matter for the court to decide and the test is an objective one. The guidelines for deciding if conduct is misleading or deceptive were set down by the Federal Court in *Taco Company of Australia Inc. v. Taco Bell Pty Ltd* (1982).

TACO COMPANY OF AUSTRALIA INC. V. TACO BELL PTY LTD (1982) ATPR ¶40-303

A restaurant had been operating under the name Taco Bell for several years when an American fast food chain opened restaurants with the same name.

ISSUE: What type of conduct constitutes misleading and deceptive conduct?

DECISION: The Federal Court found in favour of the Australian company Taco Bell Pty Ltd.

CASE REFLECTION: The decision sets guidelines for determining what conduct is misleading and deceptive including:

- Identify the relevant section (or sections) of the public (which may be the public at large) targeted by the conduct of the defendant.
- Determine the effect of the defendant's conduct on the relevant section or sections of the public 'including

the astute and the gullible, the intelligent and the not-so-intelligent, the well-educated as well as the poorly educated, men and women of various ages pursuing a variety of vocations'. Only a small percentage of the relevant section of the public needs to be affected.

- Decide whether the conduct was capable of being misleading or deceptive or likely to mislead or deceive the relevant section or sections of the public. The Court must determine that question for itself. The test is objective.
- Decide whether the conduct of the defendant caused the misconception.

Mere confusion does not amount to conduct that is misleading or deceptive.

MCWILLIAMS WINES PTY LTD V. MCDONALD'S SYSTEM OF AUSTRALIA PTY LTD (1980) ATPR ¶40-188

McDonald's, a fast food chain, had extensively advertised one of its hamburger products as a 'Big Mac'. McWilliams Wines, in an advertising campaign for its new two litre bottles of wine, described them as a 'Big Mac'. McDonald's claimed that the conduct of McWilliams Wines was misleading or deceptive and therefore in breach of s. 52(1) and so they sought an injunction to stop the advertising campaign.

ISSUE: Does conduct that could confuse amount to misleading and deceptive conduct?

DECISION: The Full Court of the Federal Court held that the use of the words 'Big Mac' by McWilliams Wines might cause confusion in the minds of some consumers as to whether there was a connection between the two companies; however, such a person would not be misled by the advertisement into believing that there was such a connection. Thus, there was no breach of s. 52(1).

CASE REFLECTION: Even if confusing conduct is not misleading and deceptive, in some instances, could it still have an impact on the sales of a business?

Even if a product has a close resemblance to the product of another manufacturer to the point where a consumer would be likely to be misled, if the product is properly labelled with the name of its own manufacturer, there generally will not be a breach of s. 52(1).

PARKDALE CUSTOM BUILT FURNITURE PTY LTD V. PUXU PTY LTD (1982) 149 CLR 191

Puxu Pty Ltd manufactured and sold a variety of furniture under the name Contour, including lounge suites and chairs in a range it called 'Post & Rail'. Parkdale Custom Built Furniture also manufactured and sold a variety of furniture, including lounge suites and chairs called the 'Rawhide Range'. They were almost identical to the furniture manufactured by Puxu, although on close inspection various differences could be seen. Both manufacturers labelled their furniture, with Parkdale attaching a 25 centimetre square label to the bottom of the upholstery of the chairs clearly stating that they were manufactured by Parkdale. The labels could be easily hidden from sight or easily removed.

ISSUE: Has there been misleading and deceptive conduct if almost identical goods from different manufacturers are properly labelled?

DECISION: *Elliot* J in the Federal Court held that the conduct of Parkdale did not infringe s. 52(1) merely because it caused consumers to wonder whether both products were made by the same manufacturer. The goods were properly labelled.

Comparative advertising and s. 52

Comparative advertising is used to promote the attributes of the advertiser's product by comparing their goods or services with that of a competitor, generally using some form of 'evidence' such as statistics or 'expert' witnesses, to support their claims.

Special care must be taken by the advertiser to ensure the accuracy of the advertising. Consider, for example, the comments of *Fisher* J in *State Government Insurance Commission v. JM Insurance Pty Ltd* (1984) ATPR ¶40-465 on p. 45 362 (a case involving comparative price advertising of insurance policies) where he said:

> *In this sophisticated and highly technical area of motor vehicle insurance [the respondent] has decided to engage in comparative advertising. There is in my opinion a heavy responsibility on it to ensure that its comparisons are accurate for inaccurate comparisons are inherently likely to mislead the public.*

The problem for the advertiser is that the potential to mislead is far greater when using comparative advertising. Consumers place greater reliance on the accuracy of statements in comparative advertising than statements made in ordinary advertisements which people tend to regard as mere 'puffs'. For the advertiser, this means that:

- comparisons must be accurate and like must be compared with like;
- all relevant information must be disclosed so comparisons do not create a false impression;

HOOVER (AUST.) PTY LTD V. EMAIL LTD (1991) ATPR ¶41-149

Email made a video for wholesalers and retailers comparing a Hoover washing machine with an Email model. The video was meant to show the relative stability of the Email machine and showed a sack which was supposed to be equivalent of a 'two kilogram load' which was equal to a normal wash. The Hoover moved noticeably during the test. The sack in fact contained lead shot and with a normal load the Hoover did not move noticeably.

ISSUE: Was the comparison fair?

DECISION: *Gummow* J in the Federal Court held that the advertisement was misleading because it omitted material that would be necessary for the viewer to be able to make an informed decision about the comparative merits of each machine. In this case, how the machines would have compared if 'real' washing had been used.

CAUTION NOTE

Advertisers must take special care when using comparative advertising to ensure accuracy and independence of the statements made in the advertisement.

- tests that show up differences between products and suggest that one may be inferior to the other must be conducted by qualified independent researchers; and
- claims that lack real truth or substance should be avoided.

***COLGATE–PALMOLIVE PTY LTD V. REXONA PTY LTD* (1981) ATPR ¶40-242**

In introducing a new toothpaste, Rexona claimed that it was 50–90 per cent more effective than Australia's best known toothpastes in slowing down the growth of plaque between brushing. Colgate–Palmolive, Rexona's major competitor, claimed the advertisement breached s. 52.

ISSUE: Was Rexona able to establish that its claims were accurate so that the information contained in the advertisement could not be said to be misleading or deceptive and caught by s. 52?

DECISION: *Fisher* J in the Federal Court held that the tests relied upon by Rexona to support its claims were largely unpublished and had not been independently assessed by the dental profession. Section 52 was therefore breached and the company was ordered to withdraw its advertisements.

Character advertisements

Character advertising, that is, the association of a product with a well-known character or personality, can be an effective way of advertising a product. For example, in recent times there has been a significant increase in advertisers capitalising on the popularity of sporting personalities for product promotion. But care needs to be taken by advertisers to ensure that:

- approval has been obtained to use a character. See, for example, *Pacific Dunlop Ltd v. Hogan* (1989) 23 FCR 553 (the advertisement suggested that a product had some association with Hogan's character, Crocodile Dundee, which it didn't) where approval hadn't been obtained and the court held that the advertisement was misleading and breached s. 52; and
- approval has been given by a personality. See, for example, *Talmax Pty Ltd v. Telstra Corporation Ltd* (1996) ATPR ¶41-484 (Telstra featured the swimmer Kieren Perkins in its advertising without his approval and it was argued that there was an association between the two which did not exist) where, in this instance, the claim was unsuccessful but even so it still resulted in court action because permission had not been obtained from the swimmer to use his image.

! CAUTION NOTE

When using character advertising, ensure permission has been gained from the personality or character.

Doing business

Minimising the problem of association

The problem associated with character advertising can be reduced through the use of an express disclaimer repudiating any suggestion of a link between the character and the product or service being advertised. ■

Doing business

Exclusion clauses ineffective

It is not possible to rely on an exclusion or exemption clause to avoid the operation of s. 52. A clause to the effect that the consumer has not been induced to enter into the agreement as a result of any representations or warranties will not defeat s. 52. However, where a party acknowledges that there has been no reliance on representations by the seller (an acknowledgment clause), such a clause may be effective. ■

Conduct in bad taste

Section 52 does not catch conduct that is undesirable, in bad taste or involves obvious exaggeration unless it is misleading or likely to mislead and has caused the consumer to think wrongly.

REPRESENTATIONS AS TO THE FUTURE

Fair Trading legislation: **CTH** *Trade Practices Act 1974*, s. 51A : **ACT** s. 13 : **NSW** s. 43 : **NT** s. 43 : **QLD** s. 39 : **SA** s. 57 : **TAS** s. 15 : **VIC** ss. 7–8 : **WA** s. 11

It widens the operation of 'misleading' in s. 52 by providing that where a person makes a representation with respect to any future matter without reasonable grounds for making the representation, the representation shall be taken to be misleading. It also reverses the onus of proof by requiring the person who made the representation to show that they had reasonable grounds for doing so.

SPECIFIC FALSE REPRESENTATIONS (SS. 53, 53A, 53B, 59)

Each of these sections is narrowly defined and it is necessary to establish that the conduct was deliberate, because the sections provide criminal penalties as well as civil remedies.

IN BRIEF

Summary of specific false representations

Practice	Section
There are 14 types of specific false representations regarding goods or services relating to:	
• Standard, quality, value, grade, composition, style, model, history or previous use of goods	53(a)
• Standard, quality, value or grade of services	53(aa)
• Whether goods are new	53(b)
• Ordering of goods or services that haven't been ordered	53(bb)
• Sponsorship, approval, performance characteristics, accessories, uses or benefits of goods or services	53(c)
• Sponsorship, approval or affiliation of a corporation it does not have	53(d)
• Price of goods or services	53(e)
• Facilities for repair or availability of spare parts	53(ea)
• The place of origin of goods	53(eb)
• A buyer's need for goods or services	53(f)
• Limits on consumer's rights and remedies	53(g)
• Land sales	53A
• Employment advertisements	53B
• Misleading statements about home-operated business	59

False representations: s. 53

Fair Trading legislation: **ACT** s. 14 : **NSW** s. 44 : **NT** s. 44 : **QLD** s. 40 : **SA** s. 58 : **TAS** s. 16 : **VIC** s. 12 : **WA** s. 12

! CAUTION NOTE
Section 53—false representations narrowly defined, breach of which can result in civil and criminal liability.

While s. 52 is broadly defined, s. 53 is narrowly defined. Unlike s. 52, a breach of s. 53 can lead to fines of up to $1.1 million for companies and $220 000 for individuals under s. 79. A person suffering damage as a result of a breach may be able to recover civil damages (s. 82), or gain an injunction or other remedies under s. 87.

The section provides that a corporation shall not make false representations or false and misleading statements in relation to the supply or possible supply of goods or services in the following 11 subsections:

1 Section 53(a) applies to representations or statements that goods are of a particular:
- **standard** (refers to a basis for comparison);

HARTNELL V. SHARP CORPORATION OF AUSTRALIA PTY LTD (1975) 5 ALR 493

Sharp advertised in a number of national magazines that 'Every Sharp microwave oven is tested and approved by the Standards Association of Australia'. Similar claims were also made in advertising brochures, accompanied by a facsimile of the registered trade mark of the Standards Association of Australia together with certain Standards' certificate numbers. The statements were completely false.

ISSUE: Does an untrue statement that goods have been tested and approved by an independent organisation constitute a false representation that the goods are of a particular standard?

DECISION: The Full Court of the Australian Industrial Court held that the company had falsely represented that the goods were of a particular standard when they were not and so were in breach of s. 53(a).

- **quality** (refers to attributes of the goods. See *Australian Competition and Consumer Commission v. Golden Australia Paper Manufacturers Pty Ltd* (1995) ATPR ¶41-375 (an importer of facial tissues advertised the tissues as 100% cotton when tests showed this was not true—fined $7000));
- **value** (can mean market price);
- **grade** (for example, first grade wheat when in fact it is third grade—it can also mean quality);
- **composition** (catches deceptive labelling);
- **style** (covers another aspect of 'quality');
- **model** (for example, a 2003 model television with surround sound when in fact it was a 2002 model. See also *ACCC v. Nissan Motor Co. (Aust.) Pty Ltd* (1996) ATPR ¶41-660 (Nissan displayed the wrong model vehicle in advertisements as well as advertising a vehicle at an end of year price which was a price that the vehicle had been able to be purchased at for some time—fined $13 000));
- **history** (for example, claiming a 'one owner car' or 'low kilometres' when the speedo has been wound back, would be caught under this section, as well as under s. 53(b); or
- **previous use** (for example, claiming a car to be ex-GMH would be caught both under this section and the previous one, when this is not the case.

The types of representation are intended to cover all the attributes of the goods in question. They should be looked at individually when examining the attributes of the goods.

2 Section 53(aa) applies to services that are claimed to be of a particular:
- standard
- quality
- value or
- grade

when they are not.

Kiley v. Lysfar Pty Ltd (1985) ATPR ¶40-610 (promoters advertised a tennis tournament stating that two well-known tennis players, Lendl and McEnroe would be playing nightly at 7.30. They would only play each other once). The terms 'standard', 'quality', etc. carry the same meaning as that in s. 53(a) above. Section 4 of the Act defines 'services' broadly to include rights, benefits and privileges conferred under a contract.

3 Section 53(b) applies to representations or statements that goods are new, when they **are not.** What is 'new' will depend on the circumstances in each case. For example, in relation to a car it could mean that it has not been previously sold by a retailer, that it is not a superseded model, that it is not excessively used, that the vehicle is of recent origin.

4 Section 53(bb) prohibits false representations that goods or services have been ordered when they have not.

5 Section 53(c) prohibits representations that goods or services have:
- **sponsorship** (if goods or services are said to be sponsored, it must be literally true);
- **approval** (if goods or services are said to have been tested or approved by a person or an independent organisation, it must literally be true. The *Sharp* case (above) was also caught under this section);
- **performance characteristics** (covers advertising claims relating to things such as 'durability', 'speed' and 'fully automatic');
- **accessories** (catches representations or statements that a product has accessories when it does not or that extras are included in the price, when they are not. See *Eva v. Mazda Motors (Sales) Pty Ltd* (1977) ATPR ¶40-020 (Mazda car company published advertisements which incorrectly stated that certain Mazda cars had servo-assisted brakes—breach of s. 53(c)));
- **uses** (the item is either 'fit for its use' or is not); or
- **benefits** (an advantage, for example, that goods are maintenance-free when they are not, would be caught under this section);

that they do not have. Each representation is an independent offence.

6 Section 53(d) prohibits representations that a corporation has:
- sponsorship
- approval or
- affiliation

it does not have.

This subsection is aimed at the business structure itself and not at goods. For example, if a corporation was to state that it was affiliated with a well-known corporation when in fact it was not, it would be caught under this section.

7 Section 53(e) prohibits a corporation from making a false or misleading statement about the price of goods or services.

'Price' includes a charge of any description: s. 4(1). For example, not only would a claim that goods were $550 and are now $360, when no such reduction had been made, be caught, but also a claim that a vehicle would cost only $1590 plus on road costs when it needed other repairs at additional cost to be carried out. *Australian Competition and Consumer Commission v. Advance Bank Australia Ltd* (1993) ATPR ¶41-229 (advertisements for mortgage protection insurance stated that for $2 per week mortgagors with the bank could arrange cover for redundancy, retrenchment and illness. However, for the $2 per week, only the first two covers were offered; the bank and the insurance company were each fined $20 000).

8 Section 53(ea) prohibits false or misleading representations as to facilities for **repair or spare parts**. This section is intended to assist farmers and truck-owners who have experienced problems with promises made about obtaining spare parts for costly machinery.

9 Section 53(eb) prohibits false or misleading representations concerning the origin of **goods** (e.g., claiming goods are 'Made in Australia' when the goods are in fact made overseas). Since 12 August 1998, a label stating that goods were made in a particular country, for example, 'Made in Australia', can only be used if:
- more than 50 per cent of the cost of their production was incurred in Australia; and
- the goods have been substantially transformed in Australia in regard to their purpose, appearance or how they operate.

Goods can only be labelled as, for example, 'Product of Australia' where:
- all their major components or ingredients come from Australia; and
- all or the majority of the production process occurred in Australia.

For example, *Netcomm (Aust.) Pty Ltd v. Dataplex Pty Ltd* (1988) 81 ALR 101—a manufacturer that advertised modems as made in Australia when the circuit board was made overseas and the units were assembled in Australia—this constituted a breach.

10 Section 53(f) prohibits a corporation from making false or misleading statements concerning the **need** for any goods or services. For example, a statement that certain goods or services are needed to comply with local government regulations when this is not the case, or that certain parts or repairs are needed for a car when this is not the case, would infringe this section.

For example, *Keehn v. Medical Benefits Fund of Australia Ltd* (1977) 14 ALR 77—a medical benefits fund that issued a series of pamphlets following the introduction of Medibank suggesting that contributors should contribute to a particular benefits table in order to ensure that they could be treated by the doctor of their choice. Contribution to the particular table was in fact unnecessary.

11 Section 53(g) prohibits a corporation from making false or misleading representations concerning the:
- existence
- exclusion or
- effect

of any condition, warranty, guarantee, right or remedy.

This section applies to any statement that attempts to limit a consumer's redress in respect of unsatisfactory goods or services.

A statement such as 'no refund or exchange' would contravene this section, since other sections of the Act give consumers non-excludable rights (the consumer contracts provisions) and remedies (s. 75A—to return the goods and seek a refund). Also caught would be the unqualified money-back guarantees, such as 'satisfaction or your money back', where conditions are in fact attached. False representations as to the effect of a warranty are also caught.

Nationwide News Pty Ltd v. ACCC (1997) ATPR ¶41-543 (an advertisement stated, 'Free mobile phone for every reader. *Conditions apply. Don't miss Monday's *Telegraph Mirror*.' The conditions were in smaller print to the rest of the advertisement and required people taking up the offer to enter into a service contract with a service provider at a substantial cost. The court held that the advertisement was likely to be understood as an offer to obtain a free phone without having to undertake or outlay any money and as this was not correct, there was a breach of s. 53(g)).

False representations in relation to land: s. 53A

Fair Trading legislation: **ACT** s. 15 : **NSW** s. 45 : **NT** s. 46 : **QLD** s. 41 : **SA** s. 60 : **TAS** s. 18 : **VIC** s. 13 : **WA** s. 14

Section 53A prohibits false advertising in relation to land. For example, a representation that a house has ocean views when in fact it has not would be caught by this section. There does not have to be a sale to amount to a contravention of s. 53A. A brochure containing the misrepresentation that was available to the public would be enough.

False representations in relation to employment: s. 53B

Fair Trading legislation: **ACT** s. 16 : **NSW** s. 46 : **NT** s. 46 : **QLD** s. 41 : **SA** s. 60 : **TAS** s. 18 : **VIC** s. 13 : **WA** s. 14

Section 53B prohibits a corporation from publishing an advertisement seeking people for employment for jobs that do not exist or for self-improvement courses that are of little or no benefit to the job-seeker. The ACCC now requires that agencies marketing self-improvement courses be able to substantiate their claims.

Misleading statements about home-operated business: s. 59

Fair Trading legislation: **ACT** s. 25 : **NSW** s. 54 : **NT** s. 49 : **QLD** s. 49 : **SA** s. 68 : **TAS** s. 25 : **VIC** s. 20 : **WA** s. 22

Section 59 prohibits a corporation from making a statement that is false or misleading in a material particular (important aspect) concerning the profitability or risk of business activities that can, or can to a considerable extent, be carried on at a person's home—for example, anticipated income from home assembly of electronic components or other cottage industries. Advertisers should disclose:

- what the average person could earn in normal circumstances;
- profit estimates based on reasonable predictions;
- reasonable risks;
- where investment of money is required:
  - the minimum amount of capital required
  - expenses
  - the amount of time that needs to be devoted to the business for it to be successful
  - the market
  - licensing requirements (if any); and
- where supplies can be obtained.

The scope of this section has been expanded by s. 51A dealing with false representations as to the future, as discussed earlier in this chapter at page 489.

PROHIBITION OF OTHER 'UNFAIR PRACTICES' (SS. 53C, 54, 55, 55A, 56, 57, 58, 60, 61, 63, 64)

Again, as with specific false representations, each of these sections is narrowly defined and it is necessary to establish that the conduct was deliberate because they carry criminal penalties (s. 55 is penal only) as well as civil remedies.

IN BRIEF

Summary of other 'unfair practices'

Practice	Section
There are 11 types of other 'unfair practices' regarding goods or services that are prohibited:	
▪ Cash price to be stated	53C
▪ Offering gifts or prizes without intention to supply	54
▪ Misleading conduct as to the nature, manufacturing process, characteristics, suitability for purpose, or quantity of any goods or services	55
▪ Misleading conduct regarding services	55A
▪ Bait advertising	56
▪ Referral selling	57
▪ Accepting payment without intending to supply	58
▪ Coercion or harassment in relation to the supply of goods and services at place of residence	60
▪ Pyramid selling	65AAA–65AAE
▪ Unsolicited credit cards	63A
▪ Unsolicited goods and services (inertia selling)	64, 65

Cash price to be stated: s. 53C

Fair Trading legislation: **ACT** s. 17 : **NSW** s. 47 : **NT** s. 50 : **QLD** s. 42 : **SA** s. 61 : **TAS** s. 31A : **VIC** s. 15 : **WA** s. 15

Section 53C prohibits a corporation advertising only part of the consideration without disclosing the total price payable for the goods or services.

Offering gifts or prizes: s. 54

Fair Trading legislation: **ACT** s. 18 : **NSW** s. 48 : **NT** s. 51 : **QLD** s. 43 : **SA** s. 62 : **TAS** s. 19 : **VIC** s. 16 : **WA** s. 16

Section 54 prohibits a corporation from offering gifts, prizes or other free items when it doesn't intend to provide them. The section does not prohibit the use of gifts or prizes as a promotional method, but attempts to stop advertisers from making offers that are likely to mislead or deceive. For example, an offer of two for the price of one for $30, when in fact two such items could be purchased elsewhere for $15 each.

Proof of intention not to supply the goods or not to supply them as offered at the time of the offer is essential in order to succeed under this section.

Misleading conduct as to the nature or manufacturing process of goods: s. 55

Fair Trading legislation: **ACT** s. 19 : **NSW** s. 49 : **NT** s. 47 : **QLD** s. 44 : **SA** s. 63 : **TAS** s. 20 : **VIC** s. 10 : **WA** s. 17

Section 55 prohibits a person from engaging in conduct that is likely to mislead the public about the:

- nature
- manufacturing process
- characteristics
- quantity or
- suitability for their purpose

of any goods (not services) and thus appears to cover much the same ground as ss. 52 and 53, but applies specifically in relation to a person. However, the consequences for breach are only penal.

Calsil Ltd v. TVW Enterprises Ltd (1984) ATPR ¶40-451 (the Western Australian Claybrick Manufacturers Association ran a series of advertisements which suggested that the applicant's bricks lacked strength which was not true—breach of s. 55, injunction granted).

Misleading conduct regarding services: s. 55A

Fair Trading legislation: **ACT** s. 20 : **NSW** s. 50 : **NT** s. 48 : **QLD** s. 45 : **SA** s. 64 : **TAS** s. 21 : **VIC** s. 11 : **WA** s. 18

Section 55A provides that a corporation shall not engage in conduct that is liable to mislead the public as to the:

- nature
- characteristics
- suitability for their purpose or
- quality

of any services. This is a reinforcing section and should be read with ss. 53(aa), 53(c), 53(e) and 53(f) and 74.

Doherty v. Traveland Pty Ltd (1982) 4 ATPR ¶40-323 (a travel agent kept a brochure advertising a 13-day trip to Bali and Singapore after the tour had been changed to 11 days—breach of s. 55A, fined $2200).

Bait advertising: s. 56

Fair Trading legislation: **ACT** s. 21 : **NSW** s. 51 : **NT** s. 52 : **QLD** s. 46 : **SA** s. 66 : **TAS** s. 22 : **VIC** s. 17 : **WA** s. 19

Section 56 prohibits a corporation from 'bait advertising'—that is, advertising a product or service at special prices, only to tell the consumer that the product has been sold out, or the service is no longer available at that price, but that another better product or service is still available at a higher price. The section deals with the subject in two ways:

- It prohibits the advertising of goods or services at a special price where the advertiser does not intend to offer those goods or services for a reasonable period and in a reasonable amount: s. 56(1).
  - *Wallace v. Walplan Pty Ltd* (1985) 8 FCR 14 (a secondhand car dealer advertised motor vehicles below the market price for them and refused to sell them to customers).
  - *Reardon v. Morley Ford Pty Ltd* (1980) 49 FLR 101 (a motor car trader advertised vehicles at a special price for a limited time. Within that time, people who tried to purchase a car were unable to do so as no vehicles were available).
- It casts a positive obligation on corporations that advertise goods or services at a special price to supply those goods or services at that price for a reasonable period and in a reasonable amount: s. 56(2).

The term 'special price' is defined in s. 4(1) to mean a price that is represented in the advertisement to be a 'special or bargain price by reference to ordinary price'. For example, 'below cost sale', 'greatly reduced' or 'clearance sale' could all be representations of a special price. Having advertised the goods at a special price, the corporation must ensure that it has reasonable quantities for a reasonable time to meet what a reasonable person would consider would be needed to comply with the advertisement.

> **!** CAUTION NOTE
> *'Special price' suggests a price less than the normal price—to avoid breach sufficient quantities should be available at that price.*

The terms 'a reasonable period' and 'reasonable quantities' are not defined in the Act. Thus, the types of goods or services that are being offered, as well as the way that they are normally marketed, will vary from case to case.

Doing business

Defence to bait advertising

A defence for the advertiser for non-availability of the goods or services is to have a 'rain check' policy or offer to supply equivalent goods or services to the consumer at the advertised price: s. 56(3). ■

Referral selling: s. 57

Fair Trading legislation: **ACT** s. 23 : **NSW** s. 52 : **NT** s. 53 : **QLD** s. 47 : **SA** s. 66 : **TAS** s. 26A : **VIC** s. 18 : **WA** s. 20

Referral selling is the practice of allowing the purchaser of a product to become an 'agent' for the seller and to collect a commission for introducing new customers to the seller.

This section provides that a corporation shall not induce a consumer to acquire goods or services by representing that the consumer will, after the contract is made, receive a rebate, commission or other benefit in return for giving the corporation the names of prospective customers or otherwise assisting the corporation to supply goods or services to other customers, if receipt of the rebate, commission or other benefit is contingent on an event occurring after that contract is made.

The key words here are 'after the contract is made', because any benefit is dependent on an event occurring after the sale; consumers having paid the 'full price' often never hear from the supplier again. If the contract is completed and the supplier then makes representations as to rebates, commissions or other inducements to the consumer, the supplier will not be caught under this section because this amounts to a 'spotter's fee' and is a legitimate business practice.

Accepting payment without intending to supply: s. 58

Fair Trading legislation: **ACT** s. 24 : **NSW** s. 53 : **NT** s. 54 : **QLD** s. 48 : **SA** s. 67 : **TAS** s. 24 : **VIC** s. 19 : **WA** s. 21

Section 58 prohibits a corporation from accepting payment or other consideration for goods or services where at the time of acceptance it:

- does not intend to supply the goods or services; or
- intends to supply goods or services materially different from those ordered.

This section was intended to catch mail order advertising and selling. To succeed under this section it has to be established that, at the time payment is made, the corporation either intends not to supply the goods or services or to supply something different. This may be difficult to prove.

This section also applies where a corporation accepts payment for goods or services, but where there are reasonable grounds to believe that the corporation will be unable to supply the goods or services within the time set down by the contract, or within a reasonable time if no time is specified.

***DAWSON V. WORLD TRAVEL HEADQUARTERS PTY LTD* (1981) 53 FLR 455**

World Travel accepted bookings for a tour advertised as including two days in Singapore. However, before the tour was sold to a particular customer, the tour was changed to one day plus an overnight stopover in Singapore. The customer was not informed of this change.

ISSUE: What constitutes 'services in respect of which payment is accepted'?

DECISION: *Lockhart* J in the Federal Court held that 'services in respect of which payment is accepted' refers to services that the consumer reasonably expected to receive, NOT to services that the defendant subjectively proposed to supply.

COMMENT: The company was prosecuted under ss. 53, 55A and 58 of the *Trade Practices Act* and convicted under all three sections.

Coercion or harassment at place of residence: s. 60

Fair Trading legislation: **ACT** s. 26 : **NSW** s. 55 : **NT** s. 55 : **QLD** s. 50 : **SA** s. 69 : **TAS** s. 26 : **VIC** s. 21 : **WA** s. 23, s. 145 Consumer Credit Code

A corporation shall not cause or permit a servant or agent of the corporation to use, at a place of residence or a premises other than trade premises:

- physical force
- undue harassment or
- coercion

in connection with the supply or possible supply of goods or services to a consumer, or the payment for goods or services by a consumer. This is similar to duress under common law.

'A place of residence' is not limited to the consumer's own residence but extends to homes of friends and neighbours. It does not apply to the consumer's place of work or a public place.

The coercion, undue harassment or physical force need not be directed at the consumer who is the prospective customer or who owes money. It seems that this section will operate wherever coercion, harassment or physical force, which could force the consumer to act against their will, is used—for example, harassment of a consumer's children.

All the states have door-to-door sales legislation similar to this section and s. 60 should be read in conjunction with this legislation.

Pyramid selling: s. 65AAA–65AAE

Fair Trading legislation: **ACT** s. 27 : **NSW** s. 56 : **NT** s. 56 : **QLD** *Pyramid Selling Schemes (Elimination) Act 1973* : **SA** s. 70 : **TAS** s. 26B : **VIC** s. 22 : **WA** s. 24

Pyramid selling is a trading scheme in which a promoter offers to sell to a participant both:

- the right to sell a particular product or service; and
- the right to introduce others into the scheme in the same way.

Those at the top of the pyramid obtain their money from selling positions in the pyramid to others, not from selling the goods or services involved. Because the scheme works on the basis of participants recouping their outlay by introducing new participants, it is not long before a market for the goods or services is saturated and the chain tends to collapse, leaving those who have not had an opportunity to recoup their investment out of pocket. Examples of pyramid selling schemes include chain letters and money-making clubs. This section catches both the promoters and those participants who are attempting to enlist others in the scheme.

The Internet has become a major vehicle for the promotion of schemes like pyramid selling. The promoters have access to targets throughout the whole world plus they can hide behind national boundaries as a means of avoiding prosecution. However, the courts are showing a willingness to apply the *Trade Practices Act* wherever possible even if an Australian company which is a party to the scheme and other parties are located in other countries.

WORLDPLAY SERVICES PTY LTD V. ACCC [2005] FCAFC 70

World Games Inc. operated an international pyramid scheme using a website. People became members of the scheme hoping that they would receive rewards when they signed others into the scheme. The scheme was fragmented, with a company in the British Virgin Isles having overall control and service companies in Britain, The Netherlands and Australia contributing to the scheme.

Worldplay Services Pty Ltd, an Australian company, provided administrative and IT support to the scheme. WorldPlay Pty Ltd argued that the scheme was being run overseas and therefore outside the jurisdiction of Australian law.

ISSUE: Does the *Trade Practices Act* apply to Australian companies connected with an international organisation?

DECISION: The Full Federal Court of Australia rejected Worldplay's argument that the scheme was run overseas saying, 'the appellant's approach would allow an Australian corporation taking part in a pyramid scheme to avoid the imposition of a penalty or injunctions by ensuring that the scheme is put into effect elsewhere'.

Franchising involving the genuine sale of a product or service will not generally breach ss. 65AAA–65AAE. Nor will multi-level selling schemes, such as Amway, because here members are buying into a distribution scheme, which involves the selling of goods and/or services.

Unsolicited credit cards: s. 63A

Fair Trading legislation: **ACT** s. 28 : **NSW** s. 57 : **NT** s. 57 : **SA** s. 71 : **TAS** s. 27 : **VIC** s. 23 : **WA** s. 28

Section 63A was aimed at prohibiting the dispatch of unsolicited credit cards unless requested in writing or as a renewal, replacement or substitute. Credit cards include any token, card or document that can be used to obtain cash, goods or services on credit.

Inertia selling: ss. 64, 65

Fair Trading legislation: **ACT** ss. 29–30 : **NSW** ss. 58–59 : **NT** ss. 58–59 : **QLD** ss. 52–53 : **SA** ss. 72–73 : **TAS** *Unordered Goods and Services Act 1973* : **VIC** ss. 24–27 : **WA** ss. 29–30

Section 64 provides that a corporation shall not assert a right to payment from a person for unsolicited goods or services, that is, goods or services sent to a person without any request on their behalf. The section also catches directory entries. However, if the corporation has reasonable cause to believe that there is a right to payment or the consumer uses the goods or services in the course of their profession, business, trade or occupation, then s. 64 will not apply. A directory does not include a newspaper but includes any publication of a similar nature to a business directory.

Section 65 provides that a person who receives unsolicited goods is not liable for any payment, or for any loss or damage caused to them other than what may be caused by the consumer's own wilful or unlawful acts. If the goods are not collected from the recipient by the seller after either:

- one month from the date the sender is notified; or
- three months from receipt of the goods (when no notice is given to the seller),

then the goods will become the recipient's property.

There will be no transfer of ownership:

- if the recipient hinders the sender in their attempt to collect the goods; or
- if the recipient keeps the goods knowing, or the recipient ought reasonably be expected to know, that the goods were intended for someone else.

> **!** CAUTION NOTE
>
> *A person who receives unsolicited goods does not have to pay for them and is only liable for damage caused by wilful or unlawful acts to those goods.*

PRODUCT SAFETY AND PRODUCT INFORMATION

Division 1A of Part V, ss. 65B–65T, has established product safety and information standards to protect the consumer public.

Product safety standards

Product safety standards set out requirements as to:

- performance, composition, contents, methods of manufacture or processing, design, construction, finish or packaging of the goods;
- testing of the goods during, or after the completion of, manufacture or processing; and
- the form and content of markings, warnings or instructions to accompany the goods as are reasonably necessary to prevent or reduce the risk of injury to any person: s. 65C(2).

A corporation must not supply goods to consumers if the goods do not comply with a prescribed standard or they have been declared unsafe by notice, or are subject to a permanent ban by notice: s. 65C(1).

Product information standards

These include:

- the disclosure of information relating to the performance, composition, contents, methods of manufacture or processing, design, construction, finish or packaging of the goods; and

- the form and manner in which that information is to be disclosed on or with the goods, as are reasonably necessary to give persons using the goods information as to the quantity, quality, nature or value of the goods: s. 65D(2).

Enforcement of these provisions is by the Federal Bureau of Consumer Affairs.

Supply of unsafe or banned goods, or goods that do not comply with a standard, may result in a fine

If a corporation supplies goods that have been declared unsafe or have been banned, and voluntary recall measures have failed to be satisfactory, s. 65F allows the Minister to order a mandatory recall of the goods or to disclose to the public the nature of the defect and the methods for disposing of the goods.

State legislation

Fair Trading legislation: **ACT** s. 28 *Fair Trading (Consumer Affairs) Act 1973* : **NSW** ss. 26(2), 38(2) : **NT** ss. 25(2), 38 : **QLD** ss. 81(2), 83(2) : **SA** *Trade Standards Act 1979* : **VIC** ss. 43, 47 : **WA** ss. 50(2), 51, 59(2)

The Fair Trading Acts of Victoria, New South Wales, Queensland, Western Australia, the *Consumer Affairs and Fair Trading Act 1990* of the Northern Territory and the *Trade Standards Act Amendment Act 1988* of South Australia all contain provisions for prescribing product safety and information standards, prohibiting the supply of dangerous goods and providing for the recall of defective goods similar to those discussed above.

The Fair Trading Acts in Victoria, New South Wales, Western Australia, Tasmania and the *Consumer Affairs and Fair Trading Act* of the Northern Territory also make provision for the statutory recognition of standards of practice in particular industries. The codes of practice are prepared by working parties consisting of representatives from the particular industry, consumers and the government. The recommendations of the working parties are then approved by the Minister as a code and prescribed by regulation. Failure to comply with the code will not be a criminal offence; however, Victoria, New South Wales, Western Australia and the Northern Territory provide for court enforcement provisions. Western Australia and the Northern Territory also provide for fines for a trader who continues to breach an undertaking or order.

DEFENCES, ENFORCEMENT AND REMEDIES

Defences

Under s. 85 of the *Trade Practices Act*, there are several defences that a defendant can raise in relation to breaches of Part V, including:

- reasonable mistake;
- that the breach was caused by relying on information provided by a third party;
- that the breach was caused by a third party, an accident or some other cause over which the defendant had no control; and
- that in each case the defendant took reasonable precautions and exercised due care to avoid the breach.

Table 23.2 Summary of offences relating to unfair practices

Practice	*Section of* Trade Practices Act
False representations as to goods (various specific examples)	75AZC
False representations as to services	75AZC
False representations as to land	75AZD
Misleading statements about home-operated businesses	75AZM
False representations as to employment	75AZE

Cash price to be stated (cannot advertise part only of the consideration)	75AZF
Offering gifts or prizes without intending to supply	75AZG
Misleading conduct to which industrial property convention applies	75AZH
Misleading conduct regarding services	75AZI
Bait advertising	75AZJ
Referral selling	75AZK
Accepting payment without intending to supply	75AZL
Coercion or harassment at place of residence	75AZN
Pyramid selling	75AZO
Unsolicited credit cards	75AZP
Inertia selling (unsolicited goods)	75AZQ
Product safety and product information	75AZS, 75AZT, 75AZU

Enforcement and remedies

IN BRIEF

Enforcement and remedies for contravention

Remedy	Section
Fine	79
Injunction	80
Damages	82
Ancillary orders	87

If it is established that the defendant has no defence/s, then contravention of Part V may result in:

- a fine (s. 79), other than for a breach of s. 52, of up to $1.1 million in the case of a corporation and $220 000 in the case of an individual (s. 6). The penalty may be based on volume of business and overall conduct.

MILLER V. FIONA'S CLOTHES HORSE OF CENTREPOINT PTY LTD (1989) ATPR ¶40-963

Fiona's Clothes Horse were manufacturers and retailers of clothes. They pleaded guilty to 19 charges relating to breaches of s. 53 involving the sale of clothing with missing or incorrect labelling information, and falsely representing that consumers were not entitled to a refund of their purchase money on return of defective clothing.

ISSUE: When fixing a penalty, should regard be had to the fact that:

- the offence was not committed deliberately;
- steps had been taken to comply with the law;
- they had cooperated with the Trade Practices Commission (as it was then called); and
- that their business had suffered because of the adverse publicity?

DECISION: *von Doussa* J in the Federal Court held that in fixing a penalty it was relevant to have regard to the volume of the defendant's business and the conduct of the defendant overall. The matters pleaded in mitigation were relevant but were overridden by the circumstances of the case. In fining the store a total of $15 000, the court emphasised that penalties for contravention of consumer protection legislation should be a deterrent to the defendant and to others.

Prosecutions can be instituted by the Australian Competition and Consumer Commission (ACCC), or with the written consent of the Minister:

- An injunction restraining a person from engaging in conduct, or threatening to engage in conduct, that contravenes the Act: s. 80. The Commission, the Minister or any other person (including trade competitors) may apply to the Federal Court for an injunction.
- Disclosure of information or corrective advertising (s. 80A), which may be granted by the Federal Court only on the application of the Minister or the ACCC where they are satisfied that the conduct of the defendant contravenes the provisions of Part V of the Act.
- Damages, which are available by way of a private right of action where a person (including trade competitors) has suffered loss or damage through the contravention of Part V of the Act by a corporation or another person. In an action for damages, proceedings must commence within three years after the date on which the cause of action accrued: s. 82(2).

Section 82 is not available for a breach of Part IVA. Recourse must be made to s. 87 set out below:

- ancillary orders (s. 87), which are available to the court where it feels that any of the above remedies are not adequate to compensate, prevent or reduce the loss or damage suffered by a person as a result of another's contravention of Part V. These orders include:
  - declaring the whole or part of the contract void;
  - varying the terms of the contract;
  - refusing to enforce any or all of the terms in the contract;
  - directing a refund of any money paid or property transferred;
  - directing the person who was in contravention to repair or provide parts for goods supplied at their own expense, or to provide specific services, to the person who suffered the loss or damage;

or

- the variation or termination of a transaction involving land.

MANUFACTURER'S LIABILITY

Until 1974 it was very difficult for a consumer to have a remedy against anyone but the immediate supplier (e.g., the retailer) of defective goods. There was no remedy available to the consumer against third parties (e.g., a distributor or manufacturer) under contract law because no contractual relationship existed between them and the consumer. If the consumer suffered personal injury or property damage, then an action may have been available in negligence against a third party.

GRANT V. AUSTRALIAN KNITTING MILLS (1935) 54 CLR 49

Grant suffered dermatitis as a result of wearing a pair of woollen underpants that he had bought at a retail store in Adelaide. The underpants had contained bisulfite of soda, which it was found had been left in them owing to lack of care by the manufacturer. The manufacturer produced evidence that they had manufactured nearly five million pairs of underpants without a complaint.

ISSUE: Does a manufacturer owe a duty of care to the ultimate consumer of the manufacturer's products?

DECISION: The High Court held that a manufacturer does owe a duty of care. The manufacturer was negligent in leaving the excess bisulfite of soda in the underpants during the manufacturing process.

COMMENT: Grant was also entitled to damages from the retailer under the *Sale of Goods Act 1895* (SA). Implied into the contract of sale with the retailer were conditions relating to fitness for purpose and merchantable quality.

The difficulty in bringing an action in negligence against a manufacturer is basically twofold:

- Proof of fault has to be established, which raises factual and evidentiary problems.
- It is doubtful whether pure economic loss can be recovered for the purchase of a defective product.

New South Wales (by the addition of ss. 62–64 to the *Sale of Goods Act 1923*), South Australia (*Manufacturers Warranties Act 1974*) and the Australian Capital Territory (*Law Reform (Manufacturers Warranties) Act 1977*) all passed legislation providing for redress against a manufacturer of defective goods in the case of a defective sale. In 1978 the *Trade Practices Act* was also amended with the introduction of Part V, Division 2A entitled 'Actions against Manufacturers and Importers of Goods' (ss. 74A–74L). However, in the remaining states and territory, the consumer has to rely on common law remedies in negligence and contract, and statutory remedies available under states and territory sale of goods legislation and the Commonwealth *Trade Practices Act*.

The obligations of the manufacturer to the consumer were strengthened further in 1992 with the introduction of a new Part VA to the *Trade Practices Act* entitled 'Liability of Manufacturers and Importers of Defective Goods' (ss. 75AA–75AS). This had the effect of removing the need for the consumer to prove negligence against the manufacturer (s. 75AA). Unlike a traditional action in negligence, the plaintiff does not have to prove fault. If the defective goods damaged the person or property of the consumer, the manufacturer is strictly liable (see Figure 23.2).

Manufacturer's and importer's obligations under Part V, Division 2A

IN BRIEF

Manufacturer's and importer's obligations under Part V, Div. 2A

Division 2A of Part V of the *Trade Practices Act* allows consumers to sue the manufacturer, and, in limited cases, importers of goods if:

- the goods are defective, i.e. they breach the implied conditions of fitness for purpose, description, merchantable quality or sale by sample; and
- the goods have been supplied through sale, exchange, lease, hire or hire-purchase. Liability does not depend on the consumer having entered into a contract with the manufacturer.

Conditions that must be satisfied for manufacturer's liability

While the effect of Part V, Division 2A is to make manufacturers concurrently liable with the immediate supplier of the goods against the consumer, there are several conditions that must first be satisfied:

- **Goods** (s. 74A(2)(a))—must be of a kind ordinarily acquired for personal, domestic or household use or consumption, and this is a question of fact in each case.
- **Manufactured**—to be the manufacturer of goods, a corporation must either:
  - manufacture the goods;
  - hold itself out to the public as the manufacturer of the goods;
  - cause or permit its business or brand name to be applied to the goods;
  - cause or permit another to hold it out to the public as the manufacturer of the goods; or
  - import the goods from a manufacturer who does not have a place of business in Australia. The importer is then liable as though it was the actual manufacturer of the goods: s. 75A(3), (4).
- **Supply** (ss. 4(1), 74A(8)—in relation to goods, supply includes by way of sale, exchange, lease, hire or hire-purchase (s. 4(1)) and this has been extended by s. 74A(8) to include goods affixed to land or premises at the time of supply.
- **Consumer** (s. 4B)—this is a person (including a corporation) who has taken goods where:
  - the price of the goods does not exceed $40 000;
  - the price exceeds $40 000 but the goods were of a kind ordinarily acquired for personal, domestic or household use or consumption; or

- the goods consisted of a commercial road vehicle, provided the goods were not acquired for resupply, or to be used in some further manufacturing process, or to be used for repairing other goods or fixtures on land. 'Consumer' in Part VA has a wide meaning, including persons who acquire goods from the original consumer by purchase or to whom the goods are given as a gift.
- **Auction**—if the goods are bought at auction, the statutory obligations imposed on manufacturers will not apply.

Rights of action against manufacturers

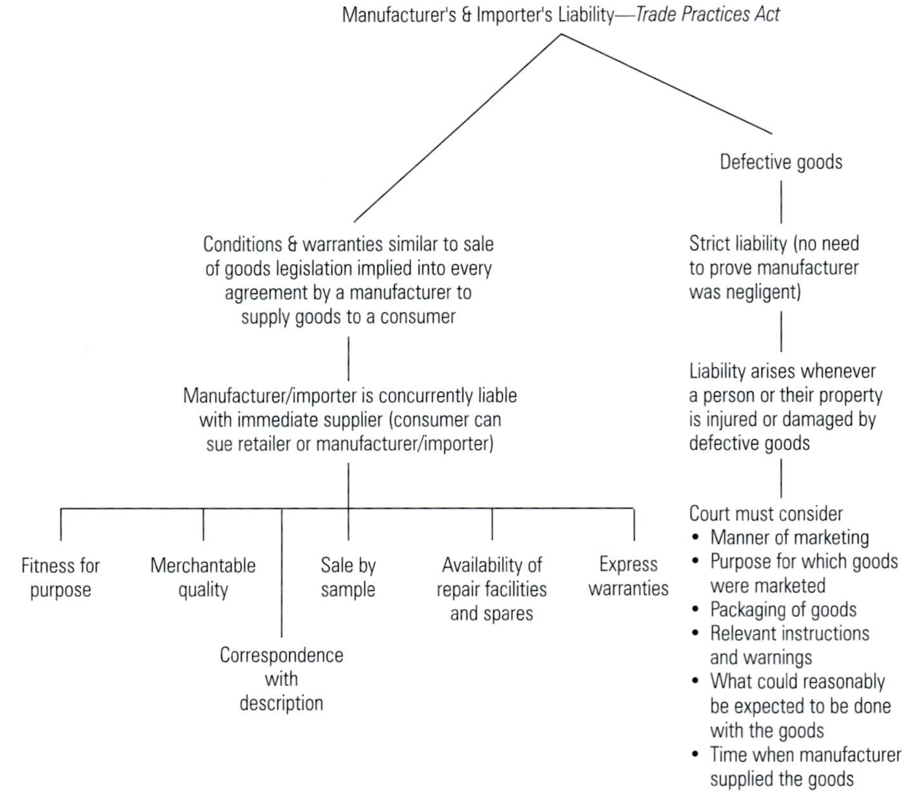

FIGURE 23.2 *Manufacturer's and importer's liability*

If pre-conditions are satisfied, then conditions similar to the sale of goods legislation will apply

Assuming that all of the above pre-conditions are satisfied, Part V, Division 2A imposes conditions equal to the sale of goods legislation, examined in Chapter 21, into every agreement by a manufacturer to supply goods to a consumer. Note these conditions can't be excluded (s. 74K):

- **Fitness for purposes** (s. 74B). Liability will not arise if the manufacturer can show that the lack of fitness for purpose was the result of:
  - an act or default of someone else;
  - causes outside human control after the goods had left the manufacturer; or
  - circumstances showing that the consumer did not rely, or that it was unreasonable for the consumer to rely, on the skill or judgement of the manufacturer.
- **Correspondence with description** (s. 74C).
- **Merchantable quality** (s. 74D). Note that the liability of a manufacturer under this section extends beyond the original consumer. The manufacturer may be able to avoid liability under this section if it can be shown that:

  - the unmerchantability was not caused by the manufacturer;
  - the defects were specifically drawn to the consumer's notice before the contract; or
  - the consumer examined the goods before the contract and should have noticed any defects.
- **Sale by sample** (s. 74E).

Availability of repair facilities and spare parts

A manufacturer must ensure that there is a reasonable availability of repair facilities and spare parts, or notify the consumer before entering into the contract that they are not available.

Where the repair facilities or spare parts are not available, the court will look at all the circumstances of the case and try to determine if, at the relevant time, they were not available due to circumstances beyond the control of the manufacturer.

Express warranties

Under s. 74G of the Act, a manufacturer is liable to compensate a consumer, or a person who acquires the goods from a consumer, for any loss or damage they suffer as a result of the manufacturer's failure to comply with an express warranty made about the goods. An express warranty is defined in s. 74A(1) as an undertaking, assertion or representation in relation to:

- quality, performance or characteristics;
- the provision of services;
- the supply of parts; and
- the future availability of identical goods, or of goods forming part of a set, which have formed part of a promotion of the goods and which would induce persons to acquire the goods.

Who to sue?

The consumer may elect to sue:

- their immediate supplier (e.g., the retailer); or
- the manufacturer directly.

If the consumer elects to sue the immediate supplier, then the supplier may seek an indemnity from the manufacturer in respect of their liability to the consumer.

> **!** CAUTION NOTE
>
> *The consumer can choose to sue the manufacturer or supplier. If the consumers sues the supplier, the supplier may seek an indemnity from the manufacturer.*

PRODUCT LIABILITY UNDER PART VA

Product liability

Part VA imposes strict liability on manufacturers and importers of defective goods that cause personal injury or property damage. There is no need to show negligence. The *Trade Practices Legislation Amendment Act 1992* added a new Part VA (ss. 75AA–75AS) dealing with the liability of manufacturers and importers for defective goods. The new provisions only apply to goods supplied by a manufacturer after that date.

Under Part VA, liability is strict as there is no need to prove negligence on the part of the manufacturer. If the goods have a defect and an individual or their property (including goods and land, buildings or fixtures) is injured or damaged because of the defect, the corporation is liable to compensate the person suffering the loss: s. 75AD. In other words, liability generally applies whenever a person or their property is injured or damaged by defective goods.

In determining the extent of safety of the goods, the court must take into account all the relevant circumstances including:

- the manner in, and purposes, for which the goods have been marketed;
- the packaging of the goods;
- the use of any mark in relation to them;
- any relevant instructions or warnings;
- what could reasonably be expected to be done with the goods; and
- the time when the manufacturer supplied the goods: s. 75AC(2).

The meaning of 'manufacturer' is the same as that in Part V, Division 2A and includes component parts manufacturers, importers and assemblers. Manufactured includes grown, extracted, produced, processed and assembled goods: s. 75AA.

> **!** CAUTION NOTE
>
> *Part VA—product liability: liability is strict and there is no need to prove negligence on the part of the manufacturer.*

Who can be compensated?

The manufacturer may be liable to compensate:

- an individual who is injured (s. 75AD);
- an injured third party, such as a bystander (s. 75AE);
- a person for damage to personal, domestic or household goods (s. 75AF); and
- a person for damage to land, buildings or fixtures (s. 75AG).

> **!** CAUTION NOTE
>
> *The liability of the manufacturer extends beyond the injured party who bought the goods.*

How long can a manufacturer remain liable?

Manufacturer's liability can extend up to 10 years

The duration of a manufacturer's liability is such that the consumer has a right to bring an action at any time within three years after the day on which the cause accrued, with an absolute limit of 10 years from the date of the first supply of the goods.

Defences of manufacturers and suppliers

Section 75AK sets out a number of defences including:

- the defect did not exist at the time the goods left the manufacturer, but occurred elsewhere in the distribution chain;
- the goods had the defect only because they complied with a mandatory standard;
- the defect could not have been discovered at the time of supply because the state of scientific or technical knowledge was not capable of detecting that type of defect; and
- the goods formed part of other goods and the defect is only attributable to the design of the finished goods. If a defective part is incorporated into finished goods, making the finished goods defective, both the component manufacturer and the finished goods manufacturer will be liable to pay any compensation for any loss that may occur.

Equivalent state legislation

Australian Capital Territory

The Australian Capital Territory introduced legislation in 1977 *(Law Reform (Manufacturers Warranties) Act)* imposing liability on a manufacturer for breach of statutory warranties as to correspondence with description, merchantable quality, fitness for purpose, correspondence with sample, and the availability of service facilities and spare parts in consumer sales of manufactured goods: s. 4.

New South Wales

Part VIII, entitled 'Consumer Sales' (ss. 62–64) was added to the *Sale of Goods Act 1923* in 1974, which created a right of action against the manufacturer or importer of defective goods where the contract is a consumer sale. This type of action is not available where the goods are second-hand. However, a manufacturer can be added to the proceedings by the court where it appears to the court that the goods were not of merchantable quality at the time of their delivery to the buyer.

South Australia

South Australia passed legislation in 1974 (*Manufacturers Warranties Act*) providing a consumer with rights against a manufacturer of defective goods. Where goods are sold retail, or are delivered upon being sold retail, the manufacturer warrants that the goods are of merchantable quality: s. 4.

Goods are of merchantable quality if they are fit for the purpose, or purposes, for which goods of the kind are ordinarily purchased, having regard to:

- any description that the manufacturer may apply to the goods;
- the price; and
- any other relevant factors.

Spare parts must be available for a reasonable time after the date of purchase (s. 4(1)(d)) unless:

- the manufacturer took reasonable steps to notify consumers that this would not be the case; or
- the lack of availability of spare parts arose because of unforeseen circumstances.

Manufacturers' liability in Victoria, Queensland, Western Australia, Tasmania and the Northern Territory

There are no specific legislative enactments in Victoria, Queensland, Western Australia, Tasmania and the Northern Territory. Consumers must rely on remedies in negligence, contract and the *Trade Practices Act 1974* (Cth).

Consumer protection bodies developed to provide greater access to the law for consumers

STATE CONSUMER PROTECTION BODIES

To counter the high cost of litigation and the intimidation often felt by aggrieved consumers in a courtroom scene through factors such as:

- unfamiliarity of surroundings;
- complex rules of evidence;
- confusing language;
- adversarial approach;
- inflexibility;
- formality;
- the unequal bargaining position of the consumer; and
- high legal costs;

state and territory governments have responded by either creating specialist consumer tribunals or giving their inferior courts additional jurisdiction to hear small claims with flexibility and informality, and without regard to technicalities and legal form. What these tribunals/courts attempt to achieve is:

- removal of the emphasis on the rules of evidence;

- much less formalised procedures;
- speedier resolution of disputes; and
- reduced costs for the consumer.

In Victoria, New South Wales and Western Australia, the tribunal is presided over by a referee, who is usually a lawyer. In Queensland every magistrate is a referee, while in Tasmania the tribunal is presided over by a special commissioner. In South Australia and the territories, the Magistrate's Courts hear small claims.

Trader defined

The legislation of all states defines a trader as a person (including a company) who carries on the business of supplying goods or services for any person. In Queensland, Western Australia and Tasmania a trader includes a lessor of a dwelling house. The expression does not include a private person (except in South Australia and Tasmania), so that the purchase of a second-hand item from a private person—for example, a stereo—will not be protected by a small claims tribunal.

> **!** CAUTION NOTE
>
> *Except in South Australia and Tasmania, small claims access is not available for private sales.*

Consumer defined

A 'consumer' means a person who buys or hires goods or for whom services are performed other than in the course of the consumer's business. New South Wales, Victoria and Queensland have extended the definition of consumer to include a business consumer such as a firm or a company.

> **!** CAUTION NOTE
>
> *'Consumer' is limited to a private person except in Vic., NSW and Qld.*

Jurisdiction

The jurisdiction of the tribunal/court in each state is extensive, particularly in Victoria (1998—the Victorian Civil and Administrative Tribunal) and New South Wales (2001—the Consumer, Trader and Tenancy Tribunal) where they have rationalised and reorganised various independent consumer tribunals under one umbrella organisation, and includes:

- actions for the payment of money up to a statutory maximum arising out of a contract involving a consumer and a trader: see Table 23.3;
- claims for the relief of payment;
- claims for the performance of work, including building work; and
- in some jurisdictions, claims between a landlord and tenant.

Table 23.3 Consumer protection tribunals and courts

State	*Act*	*Court/Tribunal*	*Max. claim*
Vic.	*Victorian Civil and Administrative Tribunal Act 1998*	Victorian Civil and Administrative Tribunal	$10 000
NSW	*Consumer, Trader and Tenancy Tribunal Act 2001*	Consumer, Trader and Tenancy Tribunal	$25 000
	Local Courts (Civil Claims) Act 1970	Small Claims Division of the Local Court	$3 000
Qld	*Small Claims Tribunals Act 1973*	Small Claims Tribunal	$5 000
SA	*Magistrates Court Act 1991* (minor civil actions)	Small Claims Division of the Magistrate's Court	$5 000

WA	*Small Claims Tribunals Act 1974*	Small Claims Tribunal	$6 000
Tas.	*Magistrates Court (Small Claims Division) Act 1989*	Small Claims Division of the Magistrate's Court	$2 000
ACT	*Small Claims Act 1974*	Small Claims Tribunal	$5 000
NT	*Small Claims Act 1974*	Small Claims Court	$10 000

Operation

The referee or magistrate's primary duty is to attempt to bring the parties in a dispute to an acceptable agreement, and if an agreement cannot be reached the referee or magistrate may make an order disposing of the dispute or dismissing the claim.

The tribunal has exclusive jurisdiction where no other proceedings in another court have been initiated. To initiate an action, a consumer must complete a claim form and lodge it with the registrar of the tribunal or a clerk of the court and payment of the appropriate filing fee. Upon receipt, the registrar notifies the trader and any interested parties of the lodging and arranges a time and place for an initial hearing by the tribunal in an attempt to find some basis for settlement.

Tribunal has exclusive jurisdiction if no other action has been commenced in another court first

Once a claim is submitted to a particular referee, only that referee can determine a result. The claim may be amended during the course of a dispute and adjournments may be sought. Other parties can be joined in the proceedings, provided that they are given notice or the registrar is convinced that they have sufficient interest in the resolution of the dispute. Each party is responsible for the conduct of their side of the case. South Australia is the only state where the parties may be represented by a lawyer so long as the parties and the referee agree.

As a general rule, proceedings are held in camera (in private), though in Victoria they are held in public unless the tribunal determines otherwise.

Evidence, while given on oath, may be oral or written. There are no technical limits on admissible evidence, so hearsay, opinions and all relevant information are admissible.

If one of the parties fails to appear and the dispute is resolved in their absence, a statutory period is set down in which to apply for a re-hearing, usually 14 days.

Once settlement or an order has been made, there is no appeal unless the tribunal has acted outside its jurisdiction or has denied natural justice to one of the parties. Costs cannot be awarded against the loser, although in South Australia, Western Australia and Tasmania, the court/tribunal is provided with a limited right to award costs. For further information on the Victorian and New South Wales tribunals, see Chapter 2.

There is usually no appeal once an order has been made unless there has been a denial of natural justice

What orders can a tribunal make?

A tribunal/court can make an order that:

- requires rectification of defects in goods or services;
- requires the defendant to pay money and/or perform work;
- dismisses the claim; and
- any other order that is fair and equitable for the parties.

Where an order to pay money is made, it is enforceable in the inferior courts.

REGULATION OF THE FINANCIAL SERVICES INDUSTRY

The *Financial Services Reform Act 2001* (Cth) regulates all sections of the financial services industry by inserting a new Chapter 7 into the *Corporations Act 2001* (Cth). Significant aspects of the Act are the requirements for licensing and product disclosure. A person who carries on a business dealing in financial products including the issuing, applying for or acquiring a financial product and/or the giving of advice about financial products must obtain an Australian Financial Services Licence.

The Act applies to all persons who provide financial services whether as principals, authorised representatives or financial intermediaries. Financial intermediaries include securities dealers, investment advisers, futures advisers, futures exchange dealers and brokers, including life insurance and general insurance brokers. The licence is issued by the Australian Securities and Investments Commission.

The provider of financial services must supply any information that might materially influence the decision of a reasonable client to acquire the product. In particular, when supplying personal advice to a retail client the financial services provider must prepare a statement of advice showing that the provider ascertained the client's objectives, needs and financial situation, investigated and considered options and based the advice on that investigation.

In addition to the particular obligations in regard to personal advice to a retail client, the financial services provider has a general obligation to provide a disclosure statement setting out:

- any significant risks associated with the product;
- significant characteristics of the product;
- significant tax implications;
- significant benefits that the holder of the product may be entitled to;
- all-inclusive cost of the product;
- particulars of the seller or issuer of the product;
- how further information may be obtained;
- dispute resolution procedures; and
- advice regarding the 14-day cooling-off period.

WEB RESOURCES

Australian Competition and Consumer Commission: the main site for the ACCC and useful for those interested in finding out what developments are taking place in the trade practices area:
http://www.accc.gov.au

Australian Department of the Treasury—Consumer Affairs Division: the Consumer Affairs Division is responsible for the implementation of service charters, consumer law, product safety, consumer policy and consumer information:
http://www.treasury.gov.au/consumer/consumer.asp

Australian Law Online: a useful site for finding current legal news in Australia on a wide range of topics including changes to the consumer protection law, accessed through the 'Topics' gateway index:
http://www.law.gov.au

Consumer Affairs/Fair Trading Agency Web Links: a general gateway to the various consumer affairs and fair trading agency sites in Australia:
http://www.consumer.gov.au

Lawlink NSW: a useful site for information on the NSW Consumer Trader & Tenancy Tribunal:
http://www.dft.nsw.gov.au/secondarymenus/cttt.html

REVIEW QUESTIONS

?

23.1 Discuss the main purposes of the *Trade Practices Act*.

23.2 Explain why most of the provisions of the *Trade Practices Act* are directed towards corporations.

23.3 For an action to succeed under Part V, Division 1 of the *Trade Practices Act*, what conditions must first be satisfied? Why do these conditions need to be satisfied first?

23.4 Who is a consumer under the *Trade Practices Act*?

23.5 When the founding fathers drafted the Commonwealth Constitution in the 1890s, they were careful to preserve their existing colonial powers. As a result, the Commonwealth's powers to legislate are those set out in the Constitution. There is no power to regulate trade practices as such. How has the federal government overcome the constitutional validity problem associated with the *Trade Practices Act*?

23.6 Indicate whether each of the following statements is true or false:

	TRUE	FALSE
▪ Conduct by a corporation or person in trade or commerce that is misleading or deceptive may result in unconscionable conduct	□	□
▪ Where a corporation or person in trade or commerce claims a right to payment from another person for unsolicited goods or services, this is known as inertia selling	□	□
▪ Advertising a product at special prices only to tell the consumer the product is no longer available or is available but at a higher price is known as bait advertising	□	□

activebook

Activebook resources include in-depth summaries with links to the relevant part of the book. For revision, add your own notes to the summaries provided by using the note-taking function.

23.7 In *Grant v. Australian Knitting Mills*, was Grant entitled to sue the retailer or the manufacturer or both? Were the legal grounds for suing, breach of contract or negligence? Were the same grounds applicable to both the retailer and the manufacturer and if not, why not?

23.8 What conditions are included in every agreement by a manufacturer to supply goods to a consumer?

23.9 What are the defences available to a manufacturer regarding product liability under Part VA of the *Trade Practices Act*?

CRITICAL THINKING

23.1 In 1986 Murrandoo, a successful property developer, needed finance for a new property development on the Gold Coast. He approached his bank and was told by the branch manager of the bank that a loan could be arranged in a foreign currency at a low rate of interest if he was interested. At a later meeting, another bank officer spoke about the advantages of such a loan in terms of it being good business for Murrandoo to borrow offshore: it was low risk, and it was not worth hedging such a loan against the Australian dollar, which was strong at that time.

As a result of these conversations, Murrandoo borrowed the equivalent of $1 million Australian in Japanese yen. At the time of the loan, the exchange rate for the Australian dollar against the yen was 1 : 130. Over the next few years, the value of the Australian dollar fell against the yen to 1 : 65, effectively doubling his debt to the bank.

Has Murrandoo any recourse against the bank under the *Trade Practices Act*?

23.2 Advertisements in a daily newspaper by Pioneering Homes Pty Ltd referred to land and house packages on payment of $1000 deposit and $120–$140 weekly repayments. The advertisement did not disclose that at some time between one and three years after the settlement date, long-term finance would be substituted for the temporary finance and that repayments could be expected to rise to just above $175 per week.

Do the advertisements contravene the *Trade Practices Act*? If they do, which section and why?

23.3 Since 1976 the 'Chile Con Carne' restaurant in Scarborough (in Perth) had been operated as a Mexican food restaurant by Chile Con Carne Pty Ltd. The restaurant had achieved an excellent reputation throughout Perth for its fine food. In 1981 'Chile Con Carne' of Australia Pty Ltd, a subsidiary of a US chain of Mexican restaurants, opened a Mexican food restaurant called Chile Con Carne in central Perth. Both companies complained of the use of the name of the other.

Has there been any infringement of the *Trade Practices Act* and, if so, which section/s and by whom?

CHAPTER 24

Consumer Credit and Privacy

CHAPTER CONTENTS

activebook

This icon is used throughout the following chapter to remind you to visit the *Business Law* online activebook for additional exercises, links to legal websites, and feedback. For a detailed explanation of what is in the activebook please refer to the inside cover of this textbook. The activebook is available through OneKey.

Where do I start?

Learning path: Use the activebook to complete a pre-chapter warm-up exercise.

There are many definitions of legal terms to assist with your understanding of the material.

CHAPTER OBJECTIVES

On completion of this chapter, you should be able to:

- discuss the application of the Consumer Credit Code
- define other types of credit arrangements
  - credit provider
  - linked credit provider
  - tied loan contract
  - continuing credit contract
  - tied continuing credit contract
  - consumer leases
- explain the formalities required for a regulated transaction
- define the various types of regulated security for credit
  - mortgages
  - guarantees
- discuss hardship and unjust transactions
- discuss the importance of the *Privacy Act 1988* (Cth) to consumer credit
- discuss the importance of the *Privacy Amendment (Private Sector) Act 2000*
- define hire-purchase.

KEY TERMS

An understanding of the following terms will help you to better understand the material in this chapter.

- **civil penalty:** a penalty imposed by the court for contravention by a credit provider of a 'key requirement' of the Code (s. 113A)
- **consumer lease:** a contract for the hire of goods by a natural person or a strata corporation under which the person or corporation does not have a right or obligation to purchase the goods (s. 147)
- **continuing credit contract:** a contract under which multiple advances of credit are contemplated and the amount of available credit usually increases as the loan is reduced (e.g., a credit card)
- **credit contract:** a contract in writing signed by the debtor and creditor under which credit is or may be provided and on which title does not pass until the instalments are paid (ss. 5, 12)
- **credit provider:** a person who provides credit in the course of a business of providing credit (e.g., bank, finance company, credit union, building society) or as part of, or incidental to, any other business of the credit provider (e.g., a retail store that provides credit to its customers (s. 6(1)(d))
- **debtor:** for the purposes of the Code, a natural person to whom credit has been supplied (s. (1)(a))
- **'key requirements':** specific disclosure requirements which must be complied with by the credit provider. Any contravention of the 'key requirements' by the credit provider may result in the court imposing a civil or criminal penalty (of up to $10 000) on the credit provider
- **linked credit provider:** a credit provider who has an arrangement with a supplier of goods or services (i.e., a dealer (s. 117(1))
- **related guarantee:** a third party to a contract between a credit provider and a debtor who promises to pay the full amount of the debt should the debtor default; must be in writing and signed by the mortgagor (debtor) to be enforceable (s. 51)
- **related mortgage:** a mortgage taken out by a credit provider to secure the debtor's obligations under a credit contract over goods and/or land which must be in writing and signed by the mortgagor (debtor) to be enforceable (s. 38)

- **tied continuing credit contract:** similar to a tied loan contract but involves a continuing credit contract under which a credit provider provides credit in respect of the payment by a debtor for goods or services supplied by a supplier in relation to whom the credit provider is linked (s. 117(2))
- **tied loan contract:** a credit contract entered into with a debtor to pay for goods or services from a supplier where the credit provider is a linked credit provider to the supplier of the goods or services, e.g., a finance company providing credit to a retailer's customers (s. 117(3)).

what if . . .

You go to a car yard and see a car you like but you need finance to buy it. The car salesperson gets you to sign a complicated and very long document and then says the car is yours, gives you the keys but does not give you a copy of the loan contract. What right do you have to demand a copy of the contract? What other rights do you have regarding such consumer credit?

The Australian economy is what could be called a credit economy. Consumers borrow money to make purchases, such as houses and cars, and use credit cards, for example, Bankcard, Visa, Mastercard, American Express to purchase goods and services at a variety of retail outlets and pay for them at a later time. Payment can be made in full when the account arrives or by instalments, with or without interest, and with or without the taking of security. In a credit transaction, the borrower is the **debtor** and the lender is the **creditor**.

Because of the opportunities for lenders to exploit consumers by the use of unfair or deceptive practices, uniform credit protection legislation was introduced into state and territory jurisdictions (except Western Australia) on 1 November 1996 when the Consumer Credit Code and Regulations came into effect. The Code is found in the consumer credit legislation of the states and territories (see Table 24.1).

Under the Uniform Credit Laws Agreement 1993, it was proposed that the uniform credit legislation would be passed by one state (Queensland). The other states and territories (except for Western Australia) would enact application of laws legislation to enable the Queensland legislation to apply in those other individual states and territories. Any amendments to the Queensland legislation would automatically apply to the legislation of the other states.

This chapter considers the operation and application of the Consumer Credit Code, the types of credit covered by the Code, security for the credit, the rules relating to harsh and unjust transactions, the role of the *Privacy Act 1988* (Cth) and the Credit Reporting Code of Conduct, penalties for breaching the Code and hire-purchase.

Table 24.1 Credit Acts in Australian states and territories

State	*Statute*
ACT	*Consumer Credit Act 1995*
NSW	*Consumer Credit (New South Wales) Act 1995*
NT	*Consumer Credit (Northern Territory) Act 1995*
Qld	*Consumer Credit (Queensland) Act 1994*
SA	*Consumer Credit (South Australia) Act 1994*
Tas.	*Consumer Credit (Tasmania) Act 1996*
Vic.	*Consumer Credit (Victoria) Act 1995*
WA	*Consumer Credit (Western Australia) Act 1996*

OPERATIONAL AREAS OF THE CODE

The major operational areas of the Code are:

- **precontract disclosure**, in particular the true cost of the credit;
- **rights and obligations** of the parties in the event of enforcement; and
- **relief for hardship** and reopening of unjust transactions.

The Code applies to virtually all personal or non-business credit including simple loans of money, purchase of goods on credit, credit cards and housing loans whether the credit was provided by a bank, credit union, building society, finance company, shop or other credit provider. It applies to all consumer credit contracts regardless of the amount or interest rate.

The Credit Code applies to virtually all personal or non-business credit

Application of the Code

Section 5 of the Code provides that a credit contract is a contract under which credit is or may be provided. The Code will apply if:

- credit is provided under a contract;
- the debtor is a natural person or a strata corporation;
- the credit is provided for personal, domestic or household purposes;
- a charge is imposed; or
- the provision of credit is part of the ordinary business of the credit provider.

The Code applies when credit is provided under a contract

> **!** CAUTION NOTE
>
> *If the debtor declares the credit is for business or investment purposes, the Code does not apply.*

For the purposes of the Code, if the debtor declares the credit to be provided is for business or investment purposes, the Code will not apply (s. 11(2)). Investment by the debtor is not for a personal, domestic or household purpose (s. 6(4)). Other exceptions to the application of the Code are:

- short-term credit (62 days or less). This exemption gave scope for a form of credit referred to as 'pay day loans'. Pay day loans are small amounts of money advanced for a fee until the borrower's next pay day. They are often secured by a direct debit authority over the borrower's bank account. Pay day loans are very expensive, a typical loan of $200 for two weeks for a fee of $40 is in effect an interest rate of 520% per annum. Such loans were not covered by the Consumer Credit Code because they were for a period of less than 62 days and the Code expressly excluded such short-term loans. This loophole in the Code has now been closed.
  Now the Code will not apply only if:
  - the loan period does not exceed 62 days; and
  - the maximum amount of credit fees and charges does not exceed 5% of the amount borrowed; and
  - the maximum amount of interest does not exceed 24% per annum;
- provision of credit without prior agreement;
- continuing credit contracts where the only charge is a periodic or fixed flat charge not exceeding the maximum prescribed by the regulations;
- a bill facility (bill of exchange);
- payment of insurance premiums by instalments;
- credit by a pawnbroker;
- credit in the form of an advance to a beneficiary by the trustee of an estate of a deceased person; and
- loans by employers to employees.

IN BRIEF

Application of the Consumer Credit Code

The Code will apply if:

- credit is provided under a contract;
- the debtor is a natural person or a strata corporation;
- the credit is for personal, domestic or household purposes;
- a charge is imposed; and
- providing credit is part of the ordinary business of the credit provider.

TYPES OF CREDIT ARRANGEMENTS AND PARTIES

Credit provider

Credit provider provides credit

A person who provides credit.

Linked credit provider

A linked credit provider has a link with supplier for referral of custom

A linked credit provider (see Figure 24.1) is a credit provider who has an arrangement with a supplier of goods or services whereby:

- any prospective purchasers who require credit to finance the purchase are regularly referred to the credit provider by the supplier; or
- the supplier supplies the credit provider's credit application forms to purchasers; or
- the supplier has purchasers sign contracts or credit applications at the supplier's premises.

Liability of a linked credit provider

A linked credit provider is liable for any representation, warranty or statement made by the supplier to the borrower in relation to a tied loan contract. The linked credit provider may also be liable for any loss or damage suffered because of the defective nature of the goods or services.

The linked credit provider's liability is limited to:

- the amount of credit under the tied loan contract;
- the amount of interest; and
- the amount of costs awarded by the court.

Defences available to the linked credit provider are:

- The credit was provided as a result of an approach made to the credit provider by the borrower and was not induced by the supplier.
- Before becoming a linked credit provider of the supplier, enquiries were made into the supplier's financial standing and business reputation which indicated it was good.

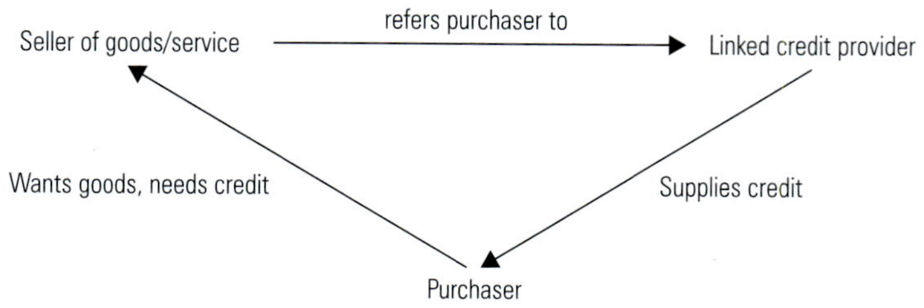

FIGURE 24.1 *Linked credit provider*

- After becoming the linked credit provider there was no reason to suspect a borrower might suffer loss or damage due to:
  - misrepresentation;
  - breach of contract; or
  - failure of consideration;

  or to suspect that the supplier may be insolvent.
- In respect to a tied continuing credit contract, the linked credit provider had no cause to suspect a person might be entitled to claim damages against the supplier for misrepresentation, breach of contract or failure of consideration.

Doing business

Liability of a linked credit provider to a purchaser

A linked credit provider may be liable to the purchaser of goods and services for:

- any representations or warranties given by the supplier of the goods or services; and
- any loss or damage suffered because of the defective nature of the goods supplied.

It is in the interests of linked credit providers to take steps to ensure the sound business practices of the suppliers of goods and services with whom they have arrangements to supply credit to consumers or else face the prospect of liability. ■

Tied loan contract

A credit contract entered into wholly or partly to pay for goods or services and where the credit provider is a linked credit provider of the supplier of the goods or services; for example, a finance company providing credit for a retailer's customers.

Continuing credit contract

This is a credit contract under which multiple advances of credit are contemplated and the amount of available credit usually increases as the loan is reduced. The common credit card is an example of this form of credit.

Continuing credit contract is one in which the amount of available credit increases as the loan is reduced

Tied continuing credit contract

Similar to a tied loan contract but relating to a continuing credit contract.

Consumer leases

A contract for the hire of goods by a natural person or strata corporation under which the person or corporation does not have a right or obligation to purchase the goods.

Section 73 of the *Trade Practices Act 1974* (Cth) extends the provisions of the Credit Code in respect to linked credit providers. If the consumer suffers a loss or damages as a result of misrepresentation, breach of contract, failure of consideration or as a breach of a condition or warranty implied in the contract by the *Trade Practices Act*, the supplier and the credit provider are joint and severally liable to the consumer for the amount of the loss or damage. Sections 73, 73A and 73B define credit provider, linked credit provider, tied continuing credit contract, tied loan contract, continuing credit contract and loan contract, in terms very similar to the definitions in the Consumer Credit Code.

FORMALITIES

Precontractual requirements

Before the contract is entered into, the credit provider must give the borrower:

- a precontractual statement—sets out the financial details, it may be a copy of the proposed contract document; and
- an information statement—sets out the debtor's statutory rights and obligations.

Form and contents of credit contract

The credit contract must be in writing

The credit contract **must** be in writing signed by the borrower and the credit provider. It may be a written offer of credit signed by the credit provider and accepted by the borrower drawing on the funds.

IN BRIEF

Disclosure requirements

Section 15 of the Code requires disclosure of the following matters:

- credit provider's name;
- **amount of credit***;
- **annual percentage rate***;
- **calculation of the interest charges***;
- **total amount of the interest charges payable***;
- repayments;
- details of credit fees and charges payable;
- **changes affecting interest and credit fees***;
- frequency with which statement of account will be provided;
- **default rate***;
- enforcement expenses;
- mortgage or guarantee to be taken, if any;
- commission paid by or to credit provider for introducing the credit business;
- particulars of any credit-related insurance contract which is financed under the credit contract including any commission paid for the introduction of the insurance business; and
- any other information or warnings required by the regulations.

*Items indicated above in bold type are referred to by the Code as '**key requirements**'.

activebook

To help you to remember and understand the topics covered so far, and for links to legal websites, refer to your online activebook. Model answers provide feedback to problems and exercises.

Any contravention of the key requirements by the credit provider may result in the court imposing a civil or criminal penalty (of up to $10 000) on the credit provider. The credit provider must give the borrower a copy of the credit contract within 14 days of the contract being made. However, this is not necessary if, at the time the credit provider gives the borrower a contract document to sign and return, the borrower is given a copy to keep, signed by the credit provider. After entering into a credit contract, but before obtaining the credit, the borrower may terminate the credit contract by written notice to the credit provider.

IN BRIEF

Formalities that a credit provider must comply with

A credit provider **must** give the borrower:

- a pre-contract statement (financial details);
- an information statement (setting out the borrower's rights and obligations);
- a credit contract in writing, signed by the credit provider and the debtor;
- prescribed information; and
- a copy of the credit contract within 14 days.

After entering into a credit contract and before receiving the credit, the borrower can terminate the contract by written notice.

Civil penalty

If the credit provider contravenes a 'key requirement', the court may make an order requiring the credit provider to pay an amount of money as a civil penalty.

A **civil penalty** may be applied for by:

- the debtor
- the credit provider
- a guarantor
- a government consumer agency.

Where a civil penalty is imposed as a result of an application by the credit provider or a government consumer agency, the maximum civil penalty for all contraventions of the particular 'key requirement' throughout Australia is not to exceed $500 000 in total. The money is to be paid into a fund to provide financial advisory and counselling services to credit consumers.

Credit provider in breach of a 'key requirement' may self-impose a penalty

If a credit provider becomes aware that it has contravened a particular key requirement in respect of a large number of credit contracts it may apply for a civil penalty upon itself. It may do this in order to place a limit on its liability and to prevent individual borrowers applying for individual civil penalties, thereby keeping the legal proceedings restricted to one court action.

Where a civil penalty is imposed as a result of an application by a borrower or a guarantor under a credit contract, the maximum civil penalty shall not exceed an amount equal to all the interest charges payable under the contract. The amount of the civil penalty may be set off against any amount due to the credit provider under the credit contract.

If a credit provider or government consumer agency has applied for a civil penalty in respect of a particular contravention, a borrower or guarantor may not make an application for a civil penalty in respect of the same contravention.

SECURITY FOR THE CREDIT—MORTGAGES AND GUARANTEES

Related mortgage

A mortgage arises where the borrower gives the lender rights to the borrower's assets as security for the loan

A mortgage arises when a borrower gives the lender rights to assets owned by the borrower as security for the repayment of the loan. If the borrower defaults, the lender may sell the assets to recover money owed. A mortgage may be over land or goods or both.

If the mortgage is to secure repayment under a credit contract, it is a related mortgage under the Code. A related mortgage is subject to similar disclosure requirements to those for the credit contract. The mortgagor must be a borrower or guarantor under a credit contract. The mortgage must be in writing signed by the mortgagor. It must identify the property covered by the mortgage or it will be void. Before disposing of property subject to a mortgage, the mortgagor must first obtain the consent of the credit provider or the court.

Taking possession of goods

If the amount owing under the credit contract does not exceed $10 000 or is less than 25 per cent of the amount of credit provided, whichever is the smaller amount, the credit provider may not take possession of the mortgaged goods without the consent of the court. Enforcement of a mortgage over land must comply with the relevant laws relating to real property (land).

These restrictions do not apply to a continuing credit contract (e.g., credit card—the amount outstanding may fluctuate from time to time), or if the credit provider has reasonable grounds to believe the mortgagor has or intends to remove or dispose of the goods.

A credit provider may not enter any part of residential premises in order to take possession of mortgaged goods without:

- **authorisation** from the court; or
- the **written consent** of the occupier.

Within 14 days after taking possession of goods, the credit provider must give the mortgagor a written notice stating:

- the estimated value of the goods;
- enforcement expenses;
- the mortgagor's rights:
  - that they can recover the goods by paying arrears and expenses or by paying out the credit contract within 21 days; and
- the mortgagor's obligations:
  - that failure to pay within 21 days may result in the goods being sold.

If the mortgagor does not exercise their rights within 21 days, the credit provider may sell the goods for the best price reasonably obtainable.

From the proceeds of the sale the credit provider may deduct:

- the amount currently secured by the contract;
- the amount required to discharge any other mortgages over the goods; and
- enforcement expenses.

The credit provider must give the mortgagor a written notice detailing:

- the amount realised on sale;
- the net proceeds of the sale;
- the net amount still due under the credit contract; and
- details of further recovery action to be taken against the borrower.

If the proceeds from the sale of the mortgaged goods do not fully discharge the debt, the borrower is still liable for the balance remaining under the loan contract.

IN BRIEF

Problems for the credit provider in taking possession of goods

If the amount owing does not exceed $10 000 or is less than 25 per cent of the amount of credit provided, goods cannot be repossessed unless the court gives approval.

A credit provider cannot enter residential premises to recover goods unless authorised by the court or the occupier has given written consent.

A credit provider must give the mortgagor (borrower) written notice of estimated value of the goods and enforcement expenses.

Mortgagor can recover goods by bringing payments, etc. up to date or by paying out the contract. If mortgagor fails to pay within 21 days, the credit provider may sell the goods.

Related guarantees

! CAUTION NOTE

A guarantor promises to repay the full amount of a loan in the event of default by the borrower.

If a credit provider considers that a person borrowing money does not have sufficient assets or income to ensure repayment of the debt, the credit provider may require the borrower to supply a guarantor. A guarantor promises to pay the full amount of the debt should the borrower default. The guarantor need not necessarily receive any personal financial benefit out of the arrangement.

As with the credit contract and a related mortgage, a related guarantee must be in writing and the guarantor must sign it. The credit provider must supply the guarantor with a copy of the credit contract and a statement explaining the rights and obligations of the guarantor.

Before enforcing a guarantee, a credit provider must obtain judgement against the borrower, and the judgement must remain unsatisfied for 30 days. Exceptions are where the credit provider has tried to locate the borrower but has been unable to do so, or if the court relieves the credit provider of obtaining judgement against the borrower.

HARDSHIP AND UNJUST TRANSACTIONS

Doing business

Can't meet your credit repayments?

If you can't meet your repayments under a credit contract due to illness, unemployment or other reasonable cause, you can ask the credit provider to extend the period of the contract, reduce the amount of the repayments or postpone repayment for a stated period. If they refuse, you may apply to the court for a variation and they may approve a variation. ■

Hardship

In the case of hardship, the borrower can request extension of repayment period

Where a borrower is unable to meet obligations under a credit contract owing to:

- illness
- unemployment or
- other reasonable cause

the borrower may request the credit provider to extend the period of the contract, reduce the amount of the repayments or postpone repayment for a stated period. If the credit provider does not agree to the proposed change, the borrower may apply to the court, which may approve or refuse the proposed change.

Reopening unjust transactions

Doing business

Make sure the credit transaction is not unconscionable

If the borrower can prove to the court that the credit contract, guarantee or mortgage that they entered into was unjust, harsh, oppressive or unconscionable, the court may reopen the transaction and adjust the rights and obligations of the parties to achieve a more equitable outcome. As a lender: disclose, disclose, disclose. ■

The court can reopen an unconscionable transaction and adjust the rights of the parties

If the court reopens a transaction on the grounds that it is unconscionable, it has the power to adjust the rights and obligations of the parties regardless of any settlement of accounts or any agreement closing previous dealings. The court may:

- reopen any account taken between the parties;
- relieve the debtor and guarantor from payment of any amount in excess of the amount the court considers to be reasonably payable;
- set aside, revise or alter an agreement or mortgage;
- order a mortgagee to discharge a mortgage;
- make an order of such amount as it thinks is justly due to a party;

- order the delivery of goods to which the contract, mortgage or guarantee relates; and
- make such other orders as may be necessary.

The court may also annul or reduce any interest or other charge it considers unconscionable.

In deciding whether a particular term in a credit contract, guarantee or mortgage is unjust, the court is to have regard to the public interest and to all the circumstances of the case.

IN BRIEF

Factors the court may take into account in deciding whether a term is unjust

Factors the court may take into account include:

- the consequences of compliance or non-compliance;
- the relative bargaining power of the parties;
- whether the provisions were the subject of negotiation;
- whether it was reasonably practicable for the applicant to negotiate an alteration of the provisions;
- whether any of the provisions are unreasonably difficult to comply with or not reasonably necessary for the protection of the legitimate interests of the party;
- age or physical or mental condition of the borrower or guarantor;
- the form of the contract and the intelligibility of the language used;
- whether independent legal or other expert advice was obtained;
- the extent to which the provisions and their practical effect were explained;
- any unfair pressure, undue influence or unfair tactics;
- steps taken to ensure borrower or guarantor understood the nature and implications of the transaction;
- whether the credit provider knew or could have ascertained by reasonable inquiry that the borrower could not pay or could not pay without substantial hardship;
- whether a particular term is justified in light of the risks undertaken by the credit provider;
- the terms of other comparable transactions involving other credit providers; and
- any other relevant factor.

PRIVACY ACT 1988 (CTH)

Amendments to the *Privacy Act 1988* by the *Privacy Amendment (Private Sector) Act 2000* mean that the *Privacy Act* now covers:

- Commonwealth agencies – Information privacy principles
- Credit providers/credit reporting agencies – Code of Conduct
- Private sector organisations – National Privacy Principles.

Credit information

The *Privacy Act* has applied to credit information in the private sector since 1990. Part IIIA of the *Privacy Act* places strict safeguards on the way the credit industry handles credit information of individuals.

The *Privacy Act 1988* (Cth) enables the Australian Privacy Commissioner to investigate complaints involving an interference with the privacy of an individual by a credit provider or a credit reporting agency.

Part IIIA of the *Privacy Act* sets out the safeguards for individuals regarding reporting on their credit worthiness.

Part IIIA of the *Privacy Act* sets out the safeguards for individuals regarding reporting on their credit worthiness

Aim of the *Privacy Act*

The aim of the *Privacy Act* is to ensure that the use of credit reports and other credit worthiness information about individuals is restricted to assessing applications for credit and other proper activities relating to the giving of credit.

Part IIIA of the Act sets out the safeguards for individuals regarding reporting on their credit worthiness. Major safeguards include restrictions on:

- the type of information that may be held on an individual's credit information file and how long the information may be retained;
- access to an individual's credit information file held by a credit reporting agency;
- the uses to which a credit provider can utilise a credit report obtained from a credit reporting agency; and
- the disclosure by credit providers of credit worthiness information about an individual.

The Privacy Commissioner has used powers granted by s. 18A of the Act to issue a Code of Conduct for credit reporting. In issuing the Code of Conduct, the Privacy Commissioner said:

> *Together, Part IIIA of the* Privacy Act *and the Credit Reporting Code of Conduct seek to apply information privacy to principles to the specialised area of consumer credit reporting.*
>
> *The information privacy principles aim to protect personal information by emphasising the need for information collectors to be open, fair and accountable in their use of information, to ensure that the individual is given a measure of control over the manner in which personal information about him or her is used and disseminated . . .*
>
> *The Code of Conduct supplements Part IIIA on matters of detail not addressed by the Act . . .*
>
> *Part IIIA and the Code of Conduct generally only apply to consumer credit. As such, commercial credit is generally unaffected other than in limited exceptional circumstances.*
>
> *Exceptions include where consumer credit information relating to an individual is disclosed in the context of a commercial credit application.*

A Credit Reporting Agency acquires information regarding the credit worthiness of a consumer and makes that information available to credit providers.

Major aspects of the Code of Conduct

Accuracy of information

A credit reporting agency must issue to credit providers and others supplying it with information, detailed instructions on the types of personal information permitted to be given to a credit reporting agency.

Section 18E of the *Privacy Act* permits the following information in a credit information file:

- information to identify the individual;
- a record of the enquiry made by a credit provider together with the amount of credit sought;
- a record of an enquiry made by a mortgage insurer in connection with an application for mortgage credit;
- a record of an enquiry made by a trade insurer regarding an application for commercial credit;
- a record of an enquiry made by a credit provider regarding a guarantor for a loan;
- the name of any current credit provider in relation to an individual;
- a record of credit more than 60 days overdue and for which steps have been taken for recovery;
- a record of a cheque for at least $100 which has been drawn by the individual and has been presented and dishonoured twice;
- court judgements and bankruptcies;
- the opinion of a credit provider that the individual has committed a serious credit infringement;
- a statement by an individual describing a correction, deletion or addition to personal information contained in the file;
- a record of disclosures made by a credit reporting agency for personal information in an individual's credit information file; and
- a note to the effect that the individual is no longer overdue in making payment.

Access by an individual

A credit reporting agency must ensure information is freely available to individuals and must explain the procedures by which access to the individual's credit information file may be obtained.

Similarly, a credit provider must ensure information is freely available to individuals, must explain the procedures by which access to credit reports held by the credit provider may be obtained, and ensure that adequate facilities are available for responding to requests for access to credit reports in its possession.

> ! CAUTION NOTE
>
> *Both a credit reporting agency and a credit provider must make credit information available to the consumer.*

Disclosure

A credit reporting agency should ensure that the person to whom information in a credit information file is disclosed has been notified of the requirements of the Act regarding the use and further disclosure of the personal information supplied. The credit reporting agency must make a note of the disclosure in the individual's file and must detail:

- the date of the disclosure;
- to whom the information was given; and
- particulars as to what part of the file was disclosed.

Similarly, before a credit provider obtains from another credit provider a report about an individual's credit worthiness, the credit provider obtaining the report must be satisfied that the individual has given specific written agreement to the disclosure.

The credit provider must make a note of the disclosure in the consumer's file and must detail:

- the date of the disclosure;
- to whom the information was given;
- particulars as to what part of the file was disclosed; and
- a note that the consumer's specific agreement to the disclosure has been furnished.

Dispute settling procedures

Credit reporting disputes must be dealt with in a timely, efficient and fair manner

Unresolved disputes may be heard by the Privacy Commissioner

The Code of Conduct requires credit reporting agencies and credit providers to process credit reporting disputes in a fair, efficient and timely manner. If a consumer is dissatisfied with the credit reporting process, the consumer should first discuss the matter with the credit provider and/or the credit reporting agency. The Privacy Commissioner is not required to investigate a complaint if the Commissioner considers the dispute should first be dealt with by the credit provider or the credit reporting agency.

If a credit reporting agency is unable to resolve a dispute it must inform the individual concerned that the individual may complain to the Privacy Commissioner. The Privacy Commissioner may decide not to deal with the complaint if the Commissioner considers that the dispute has been dealt with adequately by the credit reporting agency or the credit provider.

Legal consequences of the credit reporting Code of Conduct

It should be noted that the credit reporting Code of Conduct is a mandatory industry code and as such is covered by Part IVB of the *Trade Practices Act 1974* (Cth). An 'industry code' is a code regulating the conduct of participants in an industry towards other participants in the industry or towards consumers in the industry (s. 51ACA).

The idea behind an industry code is to give business efficacy to the law relating to the particular industry. That is, to give it greater effect and efficiency. With this in mind, s. 51AE of the *Trade Practices Act 1974* provides that regulations may:

- prescribe an industry code, or specified provisions of an industry code; and
- declare the industry code to be a mandatory industry code or a voluntary industry code.

Section 51AD *Trade Practices Act 1974* states that a corporation must not, in trade or commerce, contravene an applicable industry code.

Credit reporting disputes must be dealt with in a fair, efficient and timely manner. Unresolved disputes may be heard by the Privacy Commissioner.

THE *PRIVACY ACT 1988* (CTH), AS AMENDED BY THE *PRIVACY AMENDMENT (PRIVATE SECTOR) ACT 2000*

Application to the private sector

The Act establishes a framework for a national and consistent set of privacy standards for the private sector. The Act does this by implementing a set of National Privacy Principles (the NPPs) that outline minimum requirements in relation to how private sector organisations should collect, use, keep secure and disclose personal information. The principles also give individuals a right to know what information an organisation holds about them and a right to correct it if it is wrong.

The Act sets out a legislative framework in which organisations can obtain official recognition for codes of practice that they themselves develop and implement. Organisations covered by the Act that choose not to have a code, must handle personal information in accordance with the NPPs in the Act. Both the NPPs and approved codes are enforceable by law.

Who is bound by the Act?

The new privacy provisions will apply to businesses (including non-profit organisations) with an annual turnover of more than $3 million and health service providers regardless of their annual turnover.

Businesses with an annual turnover of $3 million or less are exempt from the new laws unless:

- it is related to another business (for example its holding company or a subsidiary) that has an annual turnover of more than $3 million;
- it provides a health service and holds health records;
- it discloses personal information for a benefit, service or advantage;
- it provides someone else with a benefit, service or advantage to collect personal information; or
- it is a contracted service provider for a Commonwealth contract.

If any of these circumstances apply to a business with an annual turnover of $3 million or less, it is covered by the new privacy legislation from 21 December 2002, unless it provides a health service in which case it must comply from 21 December 2001.

The *Privacy Act* also provides for exemptions from coverage in the following circumstances:

- the journalism activities of media organisations; and
- an act done by an organisation that is or was an employer of an individual in regard to an employee record held by the organisation relating to the individual.

The 10 National Privacy Principles

National Privacy Principles (NPPs) comprise 10 principles that form the basis for the protection of personal information. Personal information is information or an opinion about an individual whose identity is apparent, or can reasonably be ascertained, from the information or opinion (s. 6). Personal information relates to a natural living person.

Private sector organisations are bound by the NPPs unless they have a privacy code of their own and that privacy code has been approved by the Privacy Commissioner.

Section 6C defines 'organisation' as:

- an individual; or
- a body corporate; or
- a partnership; or
- any other unincorporated association; or
- a trust;

that is not a small business operator, a registered political party, an agency, a state or territory authority or a prescribed instrumentality of a state or territory.

1. Collection

An organisation collects personal information if it gathers, acquires or obtains personal information from any source and by any means. Collection includes personal information it has obtained by accident or has not asked for.

An organisation must not collect personal information unless the information is necessary for one or more of its functions or activities and the information is collected only by lawful and fair means and not in an unreasonably intrusive way.

If it is reasonable and practicable to do so, the personal information about an individual is to be collected only from that individual. If an organisation collects personal information about an individual from someone else, it must take reasonable steps to ensure that the individual is aware of matters, such as who collected the information, who holds the information, and why the information is being held.

2. Use and disclosure

An organisation must not use or disclose personal information about an individual for a purpose other than the primary purpose of collection unless the secondary purpose is related to the primary purpose of collection, and the individual would reasonably expect the organisation to use or disclose the information for the secondary purpose; or the individual has consented to the use or disclosure.

3. Data quality

Reasonable steps must be taken to make sure that the personal information is accurate, complete and up-to-date.

4. Data security

Reasonable steps must be taken to protect the personal information from misuse and loss and from unauthorised access, modification or disclosure. Reasonable steps must also be taken to destroy or permanently de-identify personal information if it is no longer needed for the purpose for which it was collected.

5. Openness

An organisation must set out its personal information management policies in writing. The policy is to be available to anyone who asks for it. Upon request, an organisation must, in general terms, inform the person who made the request, the type of personal information it holds, for what purposes it is held, and how it collects, holds, uses and discloses that information.

6. Access and correction

An organisation must on request by an individual, provide the individual with access to the information it holds on that individual. Note the NPPs sets out a number of exceptions to this requirement.

7. Identifiers

An identifier is simply a means of identifying an individual in respect of whom a record is kept. It includes a number assigned by an organisation to an individual to identify uniquely the individual for the purposes of the organisation's operations.

An organisation must not adopt as its own identifier of an individual, an identifier of the individual that has been assigned by a Commonwealth government agency.

For instance, the organisation must not use a tax file number as its means of identifying an individual. However, an individual's name or Australian Business Number may be used.

8. Anonymity

Wherever it is lawful and practicable, individuals must have the option of not identifying themselves when entering transactions with an organisation.

9. Trans-border data flows

While an organisation in Australia or an external territory may transfer personal information about an individual to someone who is in a foreign country there are several restrictions on such a transfer of personal information.

10. Sensitive information

An organisation must not collect sensitive information about an individual unless:

(a) the individual has consented; or

(b) the collection is required by law; or

(c) the collection is necessary to prevent or lessen a serious and imminent threat to the life or health of any individual.

Sensitive information means information or opinion about an individuals':

- racial or ethnic origin,
- political opinions,
- membership of a political association,
- religious beliefs or affiliations,
- philosophical beliefs,
- membership of a professional or trade association,
- membership of a trade union,
- sexual preferences or practices,
- criminal record; or
- health information.

Businesses may have their own codes

Any individual organisation, group of organisations or industry may make an application to the Commissioner to have a privacy code approved.

Section 18BB(2) requires the Privacy Commissioner to be satisfied that:

- obligations set out in the code are at least the equivalent of all the obligations in the NPPs;
- the code specifies which organisations are bound by it;
- the code must only bind organisations that have consented to be bound by it; and
- the members of the public are given an adequate opportunity to comment on the draft of the code.

Where the code proposes separate complaint handling procedures, s. 18BB(3) of the Act sets out additional matters that the Commissioner must be satisfied are met before a privacy code may be approved.

Health privacy

The *Privacy Act* now covers health records throughout Australia. The Act creates a general right of access for consumers to their own health records.

The Privacy Commissioner has issued guidelines specifically for health service providers.

HIRE-PURCHASE

A hire-purchase contract is an agreement whereby an owner agrees to hire out certain goods coupled with an **option** for the hirer **to purchase** the goods.

What is hire-purchase?

Hire-purchase is an agreement to hire, coupled with an option to purchase

It is a contract whereby the owner delivers goods to a hirer on the terms that the latter pays a fixed periodic rental as consideration under the contract, and in addition the hirer has the option of terminating the contract at any time by taking one of two alternatives:

- **purchasing** the goods by paying the total amount of the agreed hire at any time. The hirer is then entitled to ownership and thus becomes the new owner; or
- **returning** the goods to the owner before the stipulated period of hire has expired without further liability for the rental unaccrued.

The option to purchase the goods under hire-purchase forms the core of the hire-purchase agreement, because the majority of hirers who enter into this type of agreement have as their ultimate objective the purchase of the goods. The owner, on the other hand, can repossess the goods from the hirer should the hirer default on the repayments.

The uniform credit legislation has had the effect of reducing the importance of hire-purchase agreements in most states and territories in Australia.

The current position

Hire-purchase now considered sale by instalment under Consumer Credit Code

As a form of consumer credit, hire-purchase has virtually been abolished by the Consumer Credit Code. Section 10 of the Code provides that a contract for the hire of goods under which the hirer has the right or obligation to purchase the goods is to be regarded as a sale by instalments if the charge for the hiring of the goods exceeds the cash price of the goods.

Hire-purchase still exists as far as commercial credit is concerned. A brief explanation of hire-purchase is therefore relevant.

Characteristics

The modern hire-purchase agreement has four basic characteristics:

- Goods are hired at a **periodic rental**, which includes interest charges, equal to the total price payable by instalments.
- Property in the goods does not pass until the **last instalment** of hiring is **made**. This avoids the problem of documents amounting to a bill of sale and requiring registration for validity.
- The hirer has the **right to terminate** the agreement, either by returning the goods at any time or paying the remaining instalments. As the hirer does not agree to buy, this cannot be seen as an agreement to sell within the meaning of the sale of goods legislation.
- The owner has the right to **repossess** the goods if there is a breach of the agreement to hire.

> **!** CAUTION NOTE
> *Usually hire-purchase agreements are three party agreements involving three contracts.*

Formalities

As hire-purchase is a form of contract, it follows that there must be at least two parties to it—the owner and the hirer—though it generally happens that the transaction is financed by a third party, usually a finance company. Thus, the relationship between the parties will look as shown in Figure 24.2.

The finance company (Easy Touch Finance) purchases the goods from the seller (Rapide Car Sales) and then hires the goods to the customer (Plucker). The finance company is now the owner and the customer is the hirer. Usually the customer will make an offer through the first owner of the goods to the finance company to hire the goods from it.

Three contracts are usually involved:

- a **preliminary** contract between the dealer (Rapide Car Sales) and the customer (Plucker), which is particularly important where the customer provides a 'trade-in'—the price of which is retained as part-payment under the hire-purchase agreement;
- a contract for **sale of goods** between the seller (Rapide Car Sales) and a finance company (Easy Touch Finance); and
- a contract for **hire**, coupled with an option to purchase between the finance company and the hirer (Plucker).

In Figure 24.2, the 'owner' is the person who actually lets the goods on hire (Easy Touch Finance). The term 'dealer' refers to the person who initiates negotiations leading to the making of a hire-purchase agreement (Rapide Car Sales).

Where the hire-purchase agreement is only a two-party situation, the dealer, the seller and the owner would be one and the same person within the meaning of the legislation.

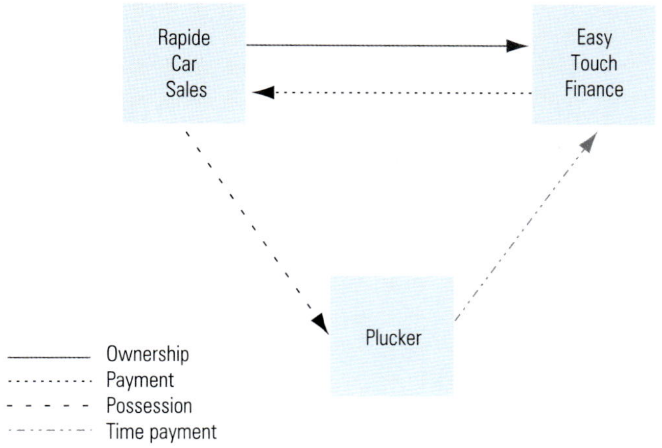

FIGURE 24.2 *Relationship between parties to hire-purchase*

WEB RESOURCE

Office of Federal Privacy Commissioner: A useful site for information on privacy issues: **http://www.privacy.gov.au**

REVIEW QUESTIONS

24.1 What is a linked credit provider?

24.2 What is a continuing credit contract?

24.3 What must be given to the borrower by the credit provider prior to entering into the credit contract?

24.4 What are the 'key requirements' for a credit contract and what are the results of not complying with any of them?

24.5 What is a civil penalty?

24.6 What is a related mortgage?

24.7 What are the circumstances under which the Consumer Credit Code prohibits a credit provider from taking possession of goods under a regulated mortgage?

24.8 What is a guarantor?

24.9 What is hire-purchase?

activebook

To help you to remember and understand the topics covered so far, and for links to legal websites, refer to your online activebook. Model answers provide feedback to problems and exercises.

CRITICAL THINKING

24.1 State, with reasons, whether or not any of the following contracts are regulated by the Credit Code. In each instance the contract includes a charge for interest and was entered into by consumers.

(a) A loan from an electrical goods retailer to purchase a refrigerator.

(b) A loan from a car dealer to an employee to purchase a vehicle on better credit terms than those offered to the public.

(c) A mortgage of $75 000 over a house and land as security for a loan from a bank to renovate the house.

(d) A loan requiring the debtor to repay the full credit amount within 28 days.

(e) A loan from a family friend to purchase bedroom furniture.

(f) A loan from a pawnbroker secured by pawning the family jewels.

CHAPTER 25 Electronic Commerce

CHAPTER CONTENTS

> **activebook**
>
> This icon is used throughout the following chapter to remind you to visit the *Business Law* online activebook for additional exercises, links to legal websites, and feedback. For a detailed explanation of what is in the activebook please refer to the inside cover of this textbook. The activebook is available through OneKey.
>
> **Where do I start?**
> **Learning path**: Use the activebook to complete a pre-chapter warm-up exercise.
> There are many definitions of legal terms to assist with your understanding of the material.

CHAPTER OBJECTIVES

On completion of this chapter, you should be able to:

- explain what an electronic communication is
- explain how to determine when an electronic communication is dispatched and received
- outline the requirements of the electronic transactions legislation in respect to the creation and maintenance of documentary records electronically
- explain how to determine the place from which an electronic communication is dispatched and received
- outline the requirements of the electronic transactions legislation in regard to signatures.

KEY TERMS

An understanding of the following terms will help you to better understand the material in this chapter:

- **Australian Business Number Digital Signature Certificates (ABN-DSC):** developed by the Commonwealth government to foster the use of digital certificates in Australia for identification in online transactions
- **cybercrime:** electronic criminal offences usually involving unauthorised access to a computer or alteration to computer records
- **cybersquatting:** registering, selling or using a domain name with the intent of profiting from the goodwill of someone else's trademark
- **digital signature:** a subset of the electronic signature which is attached to specific data
- **domain name:** an Internet address
- **electronic signature:** a method of authenticating an electronic transmission
- **encryption:** transforming data into a form that is unreadable without a key
- **spam (junk email):** electronic messages, usually of a commercial nature, sent without the consent of the recipient
- **typosquatting:** purchasing a domain name that is a variation on a popular domain name with the expectation that the site will get traffic from the original site due to users misspelling the name.

what if . . .

You decide to start your own business and operate it entirely from home using electronic communications such as the Internet and telephone. What are some of the legal issues which must be considered and how would you deal with them?

Business organisations and consumers are adapting new technology and are doing more and more business by electronic means rather than using traditional face-to-face methods and the exchange of paper-based documents. The use of cheques has declined from 49.6 per cent of all payments in 1994 to 19.2 per cent in 2002 (figures from the Australian Payments Clearing Association). This decline in the use of cheques has seen a rise in the use of credit cards and electronic payments such as Internet banking, Eftpos and ATMs. The *Electronic Transactions Act 1999* (Cth) provides a legal framework to support and encourage businesses and consumers using electronic commerce by providing that the law shall treat electronic and paper-based commerce equally. In May 1999, at a meeting of the Standing Committee of Attorneys-General, the states agreed to enact parallel legislation.

- Australian Capital Territory *Electronic Transactions Act 2001*;
- New South Wales *Electronic Transactions Act 2000*;
- Northern Territory *Electronic Transactions (Northern Territory) Act 2000*;
- Queensland *Electronic Transactions (Queensland) Act 2001*;
- South Australia *Electronic Transactions Act 2000*;
- Tasmania *Electronic Transactions Act 2000*;
- Victoria *Electronic Transactions (Victoria) Act 2000*; and
- Western Australia *Electronic Transactions Act 2003*.

The electronic transactions legislation uses media and technology neutral terms; that is, it does not specify particular forms of technology, to do so would mean that the legislation would need constant amendment to keep up with technological changes. The aim of the legislation is to identify particular legal requirements and to confirm that those legal requirements can be satisfied in an electronic form as an alternative to the more traditional methods, such as paper documents and the postal system.

The electronic transactions legislation does not impose an obligation to engage in transactions by means of electronic communications. The provisions of the legislation will only apply if a person has consented to engage in the transaction by using some element of electronic communication. The consent of the person may be either *express*, that is, they have indicated their consent orally or in writing, or it may be *implied* by other factors such as their conduct.

Electronic commerce is a new and expanding area of business. With rapidly changing technology it is difficult to keep up with the latest developments. Technology is developing far more rapidly than the law. This chapter is intended to identify some of the issues confronting this exciting area of business. Depending on your point of view the future is exciting or depressing; in five years' time the technology may have changed dramatically thereby necessitating a new approach to eCommerce.

ELECTRONIC TRANSACTIONS ACT 1999 (CTH)

The aim of the *Electronic Transactions Act* is to facilitate and encourage people to deal with government and private organisations electronically. The provisions of the Act are intended to clarify the legality of transactions or actions that might have previously been performed in writing on paper or verbally but which are now performed electronically.

Validity of electronic transactions

Transactions not invalid merely because they are completed electronically

A transaction is not invalid because it took place wholly or partly electronically: Cth: s. 8; ACT: s. 7; NSW: s. 7; NT: s. 7; QLD: s. 8; SA: s. 7; Vic: s. 7; WA: s. 7. This section does not unconditionally make the transaction valid, it must still comply with all existing contract requirements to be valid; however, it will not be invalid merely because of an electronic element.

An electronic communication is the communication of information in the form of data, text or images by electromagnetic energy. It includes communication in the form of speech where the speech is processed at its destination by an automated voice recognition system, that is, information forwarded by voice is recorded or reproduced in a written form. It does not make a telephone call an electronic communication—the distinction between oral and written communications is maintained.

A contract that has been negotiated and/or entered into wholly or partly by electronic means is to be treated in the same way as an equivalent contract entered into by more traditional means.

Electronic substitute for paper

Electronic form can substitute for paper

A legal requirement to provide information in writing can be satisfied if the person gives the information by means of an electronic communication, provided the information would be readily accessible and useable. The recipient must have consented to the information being given in an electronic communication: Cth: s. 9; ACT: s. 8; NSW: s. 8; NT: s. 8; QLD: s. 11; SA: s. 8; Vic: s. 8; WA: s. 8.

'Readily accessible and useable condition' means that the information contained in the electronic communication should be readable and capable of being interpreted. The section is concerned with the useability of the electronic communication and not with the mere receipt of it. It is quite possible to receive an electronic communication that cannot be converted into a form that can be read and/or otherwise used.

Electronic contracts

The Electronic Transactions legislation of the Commonwealth, states and territories clarifies the legal position of contracts negotiated and entered into by electronic means. The legislation sets out the legal position in regard to the matters set out below (for further information see Chapter 13 Law of Contracts—Agreement between the parties):

- offer and acceptance;
- time of dispatch of the communication;
- time of receipt of the communication;

- place of dispatch and receipt;
- evidence of the contract; and
- documentary records.

LEGAL ASPECTS OF MAINTAINING A BUSINESS WEBSITE

Domain names

A domain name is the method used to identify a particular Internet address. The assignment of domain names using the endings .com, .net and .org is controlled by an American company, Network Solutions Inc. With the rapidly expanding nature of the Internet, a new organisation, Internet Corporation for Assigned Names and Numbers (ICANN), was established to control the use of names and to authorise other organisations to allocate domain names subject to ICANN's standards. In Australia the authorised organisation is .AU Domain Administration. In Australia, domain names are allocated according to the following rules:

- To the first person or organisation to apply for the name.
- The applicant does not have to prove past use of the name.
- The name must be derived from a registered Australian business or company name controlled by the applicant.
- Ownership of a trade mark does not entitle the trade mark owner to incorporate that trade mark in a domain name.

In addition to being responsible for the domain name system management, ICANN also attempts to resolve domain name disputes under the Uniform Domain Name Dispute Resolution Policy. Under the policy, a complainant must prove that:

- the domain name complained of is identical or confusingly similar to a trade mark or service mark in which the complainant holds the rights;
- the holder of the domain name has no rights or legitimate interests in the domain name; and
- the domain has been registered and is being used in bad faith.

The ICANN Administrative Panel has ruled that it is not necessary for the complainant to be the registered trade mark or service mark holder and that individual names may have sufficient secondary association for 'common law trade mark right' purposes. For example, the panel allowed Jeanette Winterson to reclaim her name which had been registered as Jeanettewinterson.com (as well as '.org' and '.net'). The person who registered the sites claimed that he intended the sites to promote her works; however, he also asked for a 3 per cent share of her book profits from web sales. The panel found that the complainant had achieved international recognition for her works and as a result had established trade mark rights in her name for the purpose of the policy.

Domain names represent valuable assets for business. A domain name can infringe the assets of a business by, for example, cybersquatting or typosquatting. These infringements may be actionable under the *Trade Practices Act 1974* (Cth).

CSR LTD V. RESOURCE CAPITAL AUSTRALIA PTY LTD (2003) 128 FCR 408

'CSR' and 'CSR Sugar' were the registered trade marks of P. D registered the domain names 'csrsugar.com' and 'csrsugar.com.au' and then offered to sell the names to P. It was held that anyone seeing the domain names would assume that CSR was the real owner and that the act of registering both domain names was misleading and deceptive pursuant to s. 52 of the *Trade Practices Act* (and the equivalent *Fair Trading Act 1987* (NSW) provisions).

ISSUE: Did the registration of the domain name represent conduct which was likely to be misleading and deceptive?

DECISION: The Federal Court of Australia held that the registration and use of the names was in breach of the *Trade Practices Act* and ordered the transfer of the names to CSR.

***ACCC v. Chen* (2003) 132 FCR 309**

A US resident registered the domain name 'sydneyopera.org' and proceeded to falsely represent that it was affiliated with the Opera House and took credit bookings for events.

ISSUE: Did the registration and use of the domain name represent misleading and deceptive conduct and a misrepresentation as to an 'affiliation'?

DECISION: The Federal Court of Australia held that D's conduct was misleading or deceptive pursuant to s. 52, and a false representation as to an affiliation, ss. 53(c) and (d), of the *Trade Practices Act*.

***Architects (Australia) Pty Ltd v. Witty Consultants Pty Ltd* [2002] QSC 139**

P traded as Architects Australia. D registered the domain name 'architectsaustralia.com.au'.

ISSUE: Did the registration and use of the domain name represent misleading and deceptive conduct and a misrepresentation as to an 'affiliation'?

DECISION: The Queensland Supreme Court held that the words 'Architects Australia' were sufficiently distinctive to P's business for P to make out a case of passing off. Further, the use of the domain name by D could mislead or confuse the public, amounting to misrepresentation. The conduct of D also amounted to a representation of 'affiliation' and a breach of s. 53(d) of the *Trade Practices Act*.

Security

Security problems that have a great impact on commerce include protecting information and confirming the source of the information and the identity of the sender.

Protecting information

Once a computer is connected to the Internet it is possible for another computer to access it. The second computer may be controlled by either the organisation you have intentionally logged on to or a hacker. The second computer may then obtain information from the first computer and may even interfere with information on that computer without the owner knowing. In order to prevent, or at least minimise this unauthorised interaction, firewall technology can be used to protect the internal systems of the first computer from the second computer. Firewall technology is a combination of hardware and software and, as with virus protection software, it is constantly changing to meet new threats.

Secure Socket Layer (SSL) is used by browsers such as Microsoft Internet Explorer and Netscape Navigator to scramble personal information before it is sent over the Internet thereby protecting the information should the transmission be intercepted.

Confirming the source of the information and the identity of the sender

A requirement to provide a signature can be satisfied in relation to an electronic communication if a method is used which will identify the person and verify their approval of the information communicated. The method used needs to be as reliable as is appropriate for the purposes for which the information was communicated.

The electronic transactions legislation does not specify a particular method of electronic signature. This is in keeping with the aim of being technologically neutral. The legislation does, however, set certain standards for the signature method used. It must be:

Signature need not be in writing

- sufficient to identify the person;
- sufficient to indicate the person's approval of the information communicated; and
- as reliable as was appropriate for the purposes for which the information was communicated.

In deciding on an appropriate signature method, factors such as the following may need to be considered:

- The function of the signature in the particular transaction.
- The type of transaction.

Is it merely supplying information or is it going to create legally enforceable rights and obligations?

The more important the transaction, the more important the signature becomes

The signature does not necessarily have to be contained in the electronic communication itself. It must, however, be linked to the electronic communication in such a way as to indicate the person's approval of the electronic communication; for example, an email with an attachment. The email may merely operate as a covering letter, the real information being in the separate file which is attached. The electronic signature could be set out in the email only.

It must be noted that the purported originator of an electronic communication is bound by the communication only if it was sent by the purported originator or with the authority of the purported originator.

A person is not bound by an electronic communication unless the communication was sent by, or with the authority of, that person.

A digital form of identification can be obtained from independent certification organisations. An application for a digital identification can be made through the certification organisation's website. The certification organisation will verify the applicant's identity before issuing the digital identification. If necessary, the validity of a digitally signed message can be verified with the relevant certification organisation.

Public key technology

The digital identification is usually based on a 'private key', which is known only to the user, and a 'public key' which is made known to others. These keys are similar in concept to a password. Data that is encrypted (turned into a secret code) by one key, can only be opened by the other key. An advantage of this method is that if a dispute arises between the parties, the sender cannot validly deny sending the information because the sender is the only one with access to the private key that encrypted the message. This form of digital identification would be an appropriate method of providing a signature under the electronic transactions legislation.

The Commonwealth government has joined the ranks of certification organisations with the launching of a whole-of-government framework to validate Australian Business Number Digital Signature Certificates. The authentication framework has been developed by the Department of Employment, Workplace Relations and Small Business together with the Australian Taxation Office. The authorisation framework provides a service similar to the service that merchants use to verify credit cards. It will allow participating government agencies to validate a wide range of digital signatures for use in online transactions.

Website risk management

If a business entity maintains a website from which it transacts business, it should set out the terms and conditions that are to apply to the use of the website by others. The terms and conditions will vary depending on the risk of legal liability which might flow from such matters as:

- the content of the website;
- the nature of business transacted using the website;
- the nature of business facilitated by the website and therefore the possible liability for transactions indirectly transacted using the website;
- the nature of the transactions and the method of performing them; that is, are all the legal requirements to be performed electronically, and if so how? and

- are end users to be permitted to upload material to the website? in which case consideration would need to be given to:
  - the infringement of copyright
  - the publication of defamatory material
  - the publication of objectionable material.

Website terms and conditions

Terms and conditions, including any disclaimers of liability, must be set out in the website in such a way that the customer will be aware of them, or the customer will not be bound by them. See Chapter 18—Construction of the Contract, and in particular 'Exception, exemption or exclusion clauses or terms'.

Depending on the particular circumstances it may be advisable for the customer to acknowledge the terms and conditions. Common methods are a 'Clickwrap Agreement'. This procedure prevents the customer from proceeding until they have clicked on an acknowledgement button. The 'Clickwrap Agreement' technique is commonly encountered when installing new software onto a computer. Another method could be the digital signature or registered certification authority (Public Key Technology). These methods require the user to attach their unique digital signature or registration authority to signify their acceptance, otherwise they cannot proceed.

In the more traditional face-to-face methods of doing business a contract might be the result of an advertisement in a newspaper or on the television. In the event of a dispute as to the terms of the agreement the advertisement may be referred to, to support the particular argument. If the contract has been entered into over the Internet, problems can arise because of the frequent changes to material on websites and even the closing down of websites. A person transacting business via a website should therefore download all relevant information such as:

- the description of the goods and services;
- all the terms and conditions of supply; and
- particulars of the person or organisation responsible for the website, that is, name, street address, telephone number, and if appropriate, Australian Company Number or Australian Business Number and licence details (if applicable).

activebook

To help you to remember and understand the topics covered so far, and for links to legal websites, refer to your online activebook. Model answers provide feedback to problems and exercises.

ELECTRONIC COMMERCE CONSUMER PROTECTION

The Australian Competition and Consumer Commission has issued guidelines for the conduct of business by electronic commerce. The guidelines seek to establish:

- Fair business practices
- Fair advertising
- Identification of the business
- Information to be supplied prior to contracting
- Confirmation of contract
- Payment
- Dispute resolution process
- Applicable law and jurisdiction
- Privacy.

Doing business

An e-Commerce website should state:

- a real name, street address and telephone number;
- an Australian Company Number (ACN) or Australian Business Number (ABN);
- security when transferring detail; and
- a privacy policy. ■

JURISDICTION PROBLEMS

Jurisdictional problems with legal control over websites

Jurisdiction relates to legal rights and obligations and which legal system has power in respect to disputes and litigation that might arise regarding a particular website. With regard to contract law within Australia, the electronic transactions legislation makes provision for determining when and where communications are made and, as a result, what laws will apply. However, the Internet ignores state and national boundaries and operates on a global scale. This raises the obvious legal question—Is the website operator subject to the laws of the country the website is uploaded from, or to the laws of the country where the information is downloaded, or some combination of the two?

The issue was considered in France where the French subsidy of the well-known online portal Yahoo! Inc. was the means by which French citizens were able to access Nazi material from an American site. Under French law, providing access to material of that nature constitutes a public disturbance. The action was brought against the American parent company not the French subsidiary, because the subsidiary did not have sufficient assets against which a court order could be enforced. The French court made a ruling against Yahoo! Inc. and ordered that Yahoo! Inc. take all measures possible to restrict access by French users. The reason for this decision was that, although the site was based and hosted in the United States, the effects of the content were felt in France.

Yahoo! Inc. brought an action in the United States for a declaration preventing the enforcement of order of the French court in the United States. The United States court refused to enforce the order of the French court on the grounds that it would be in breach of the American constitutional right of freedom of speech. The United States court observed that civil matters on the Internet could be determined by French law but enforcement would depend on United States law. Therefore, the law of France may apply but the United States may choose not to enforce it.

While this case has no binding effect in Australia, it does demonstrate the difficulties in managing the Internet and the complexity of some of the issues that are emerging. Defamation via the Internet and the jurisdiction in which it can be litigated is currently the subject of litigation in Australia:

GUTNICK V. DOW JONES & CO. INC. [2001] VSC 305

Gutnick brought an action for defamation in regards to an article in *Barron*'s magazine, published by Dow Jones & Co. Inc. A version of the magazine is published online. Gutnick argued that publication took place in Victoria when the magazine was downloaded. Dow Jones argued that the online version was published in New Jersey in the United States, that is, the location of the web server on which the material was held pending downloading each time a copy was requested. Dow Jones argued that downloading was a separate independent action performed by the person using the site, and therefore an action for which they were not responsible. Gutnick argued that downloading was an intended consequence of the defendants' control of the entire publication process.

ISSUE: When and where did publication take place? At the location of the web server onto which the article was uploaded, or at the location of the computer monitor onto which it was downloaded?

DECISION: The Supreme Court of Victoria held that an actionable publication does not occur until a defamatory meaning is conveyed to a third party, in other words, when and where the subscriber downloads the article onto their computer monitor in Victoria.

Where an Australian company is part of an international organisation that is using the Internet to promote a scheme which is in breach of the consumer protection provisions of the *Trade Practices Act 1974* (Cth), the Australian courts will have jurisdiction to control the Australian company's actions.

WORLDPLAY SERVICES PTY LTD V. ACCC [2005] FCAFC 70

World Games Inc. operated an international pyramid selling scheme using a website. People became members of the scheme hoping that they would receive rewards when they signed others into the scheme. The scheme was fragmented, with a company in the British Virgin Isles having overall control, and service companies in Britain, The Netherlands and Australia contributing to the scheme.

Worldplay Services Pty Ltd, an Australian company, provided administrative and IT support to the scheme. WorldPlay Pty Ltd argued that the scheme was being run overseas and therefore outside the jurisdiction of Australian law.

ISSUE: Does Australian consumer protection legislation apply to Australian companies connected with an organisation which operates on an international basis?

DECISION: The Full Federal Court of Australia rejected Worldplay's argument that the scheme was run overseas saying, 'mechanisms have been put into place for international co-operation to protect consumers generally. It is well known that the Internet has facilitated conduct adversely affecting consumers in any number of countries.'

Tamberlin J, in his separate concurring judgement, said: 'the protection of consumers outside Australia from the acts of corporations participating in pyramid selling schemes within Australia can be perceived to promote the welfare of Australians by enhancing foreign confidence in Australia's ability to promote competition and fair trading outside Australia'.

PRIVACY

If the website utilises 'cookies', the business should inform the customers of the extent to which cookies are used and the privacy policy of the business regarding cookies. Cookies are a type of software tag that is saved onto the hard disk of a computer visiting the website. In the course of browsing the Internet, some sites that are visited will install cookies onto the computer of the visitor, often without the knowledge of the visitor. The cookie can then send detailed information back to the visited site from which the cookie came. The cookie can be programmed to perform such functions as track Internet browsing habits, gather information about the computer it is installed on, and collect personal information stored on the computer.

Need for a privacy policy

It should be noted that the *Privacy (Private Sector) Act 2001* (Cth) imposes obligations on certain businesses regarding the collection and use of personal information. Information provided by cookies could constitute such personal information. The Act sets out the National Privacy Principles (NPPs) which must be complied with by certain private organisations. The NPPs are dealt with more fully in Chapter 24 on Consumer Credit and Privacy at pages 525–527. In brief, the NPPs cover:

- collection of personal information;
- use and disclosure of personal information;
- data quality, accuracy and currency;
- data security;
- openness—disclosure of policy regarding collection and use of information;
- access and correction;
- identifiers—methods of identifying people;
- anonymity;

- transborder transfer of data; and
- sensitive personal information.

To assist private sector organisations to comply with the NPPs the Commonwealth Privacy Commissioner has issued guidelines on workplace email, web browsing and privacy. The Internet Industry Association has implemented its own privacy code in accordance with the *Privacy (Private Sector) Act 2001* (Cth).

CYBERCRIME

The development of computers and the Internet as intergral tools in our daily lives for both recreational and commercial purposes has seen an expansion in abuses of the Internet and the damaging of computers and information stored on computers. In response to these 'technology' crimes the Commonwealth and state governments have passed legislation to counter cybercrime.

The *Spam Act 2003* (Cth) and *Spam (Consequential Amendments) Act 2003* (Cth) make it illegal to send most types of commercial electronic messages to or from Australia without the recipient's consent. The legislation does not apply to non-commercial messages. While the Act is aimed primarily at emails, it will also apply to mobile text messages and faxes; however, voice messages are not covered by the Act.

Commercial messages are messages sent for a commercial purpose to an electronic address (s. 6). A message having the purpose of offering, advertising or promoting goods or services, land, a business or investment opportunity or a supplier of any of these things will be a commercial electronic message. It is also a commercial electronic message if it has the purpose of assisting or enabling a person, by deception, to dishonestly obtain property, a financial advantage or gain from another person.

Electronic messages that are exempted from the requirement of obtaining the recipient's consent are referred to by the Act as Designated Commercial Electronic Messages (Schedule 1). These are messages from government, political, religious, charitable or educational organisations and other organisations that:

- contain only factual information, the name, logo and contact details of the author and/or the organisation of the message;
- provide a functional unsubscribe facility; and
- would not have been a commercial electronic message if the name, logo, contact details and unsubscribe facility had not been provided, in other words it must not have a secondary purpose of offering, promoting or advertising goods or services.

It is not illegal to send the message if the recipient has consented to the message (s. 16). Consent may be expressed or implied.

The Act also makes it unlawful to supply, acquire or use software designed to collect electronic addresses from the Internet and to supply, acquire or use address lists generated by that software.

The Act imposes civil penalties of up to $1.1 million for contraventions (ss. 24–26). Other remedies are compensation (s. 28), recovery of financial benefit (s. 29) and injunctions (ss. 32–35).

The Australian Communications and Media Authority has registered a spam Code of Practice for Internet service providers and email service providers.

WEB RESOURCE

For more information on the Spam Code of Practice:
http://www.acma.gov.au

Electronic criminal offences

The *Cybercrime Act 2001* (Cth) amended the *Criminal Code Act 1995* (Cth) and now provides for several serious computer offences:

- Unauthorised access, modification or impairment with intent to commit a serious offence. An example of this offence would be hacking into a bank computer and accessing credit card details with the intention of using them to obtain money: s. 477.1.

- Unauthorised modification of data where the person is reckless as to whether the modification will impair data. An example of this offence would be hacking into a computer system and impairing the data even if the impairment of data was not the intention: s. 477.2.
- Unauthorised impairment of electronic communication. An example of this offence would be 'denial of service attacks', that is, where a website in inundated with a large volume of unwanted messages which result in an overloading and crashing of the computer system: s. 477.3.
- Unauthorised access to, or modification of, restricted data: s. 478.1.
- Unauthorised impairment of data held on a computer disk: s. 478.2.
- Possession or control of data with intent to commit a computer offence: s. 478.3.
- Producing, supplying or obtaining data with intent to commit a computer offence: s. 478.4.

activebook

Activebook resources include in-depth summaries with links to the relevant part of the book. For revision, add your own notes to the summaries provided by using the note-taking function.

Other offences relate to interference with telecommunications (Criminal Code 1995, Pt 10.6), including the Internet, computer services and computer systems. General provisions for stalking under the various Crimes Acts may be interpreted to apply to harassment by electronic means.

The *Internet Gambling Act 2001* (Cth) prohibits interactive gambling by customers who are physically present in Australia and prohibits Australian-based interactive gambling services from being provided in designated countries (ss. 9B, 15A).

An international treaty is being drafted on cybercrime and law enforcement to harmonise national legislation in this area.

WEB RESOURCES

Australian domain names:
http://www.ina.com.au

Commonwealth e-Commerce:
http://www.ecommerce.treasury.gov.html/ecommerce.htm

National Office for the Information Economy:
http://www.noie.gov.au

Office of Federal Privacy Commissioner:
http://www.privacy.gov.au

Online newsletter about copyright:
http://www.law.gov.au/copyright_enews

REVIEW QUESTIONS

25.1 Where a contract is entered into via a website, what methods might be used, by both the parties, to confirm the terms of the contract?

25.2 What is 'Public Key Technology?'

25.3 In the context of the electronic transactions legislation, what standards must the signature method meet?

25.4 If a person's signature is linked to an electronic communication, is the person bound by that electronic communication? Give reasons for your answer.

CRITICAL THINKING

25.1 You are the records manager of a large company. Prepare a procedure checklist for the preparation and maintenance of documentary records electronically.

25.2 In contract law, what is the significance of the case *Entores Ltd v. Miles Far East Corp.* [1955] 2 QB 327 (see p. 281) and how is the legal principle in that case affected by the *Electronic Transactions Act 1999* (Cth)?

BUSINESS ORGANISATIONS AND THE LAW

PART SIX

CHAPTER 26

Agency

CHAPTER CONTENTS

activebook

This icon is used throughout the following chapter to remind you to visit the *Business Law* online activebook for additional exercises, links to legal websites, and feedback. For a detailed explanation of what is in the activebook please refer to the inside cover of this textbook. The activebook is available through OneKey.

Where do I start?
Learning path: Use the activebook to complete a pre-chapter warm-up exercise.

There are many definitions of legal terms to assist with your understanding of the material.

CHAPTER OBJECTIVES

On completion of this chapter, you should be able to:

- explain the purpose of an agency
- explain how an agency relationship is created
- explain the authority of an agent
- explain the agent's duty to the principal
- explain the agent's rights against the principal
- outline the liabilities of principals and/or agents to third parties including breach of warranty of authority
- describe how an agency can be terminated
- recognise some specific types of agency relationships and their main features.

KEY TERMS

An understanding of the following terms will help you to better understand the material in this chapter:

- **agent:** a person employed to act on behalf of another
- **broker:** a mercantile agent who buys or sells goods for a principal (usually in their name), but who does not have possession or documents of title
- **'del credere' agent:** a person who guarantees payment by third parties to the principal in return for extra commission
- **employee:** a person employed under a contract of service and subject to the control of an employer regarding the manner in which their work is to be done
- **estoppel:** a rule of law which prevents a person from denying the truth of some statement formerly made by him or her, or the existence of facts which by his or her words or conduct has given the impression to others of its truthfulness
- **factor:** a mercantile agent who, in the usual course of their business, has possession of the goods, or the documents of title to the goods, of their principal and who can sell or pledge the goods whereby the principal is bound by such sale or pledge
- **independent contractor:** a person employed under a contract for services who undertakes to produce a given result for an agreed price
- **ratification:** the act of adopting a transaction by a person who was not bound by it originally
- **trust:** a fiduciary relationship where a person holds the title of property for the benefit of another person
- **trustee:** a person who holds property on trust for another.

what if . . .

You are a professional tennis player, you spend nearly all of your time training, playing, travelling or promoting your sponsors' products. You do not have time to concentrate on business matters such as negotiating sponsorships, or arranging travel and accommodation. You employ someone to do these things on your behalf. Can that person create contracts for you? How are the limits on that person's authority established?

Under the doctrine of privity of contract only those persons who were immediate parties to a contract could acquire rights and liabilities under it. However, because of the complexity of commercial dealings, today it is often necessary for an individual to deal through others, such as bankers, brokers, auctioneers, factors, commission agents, managers, partners, company secretaries or solicitors, to mention but a few. Where these persons negotiate on behalf of individuals with third parties, they will be their agents. **Agency** is thus an **exception** to the rule of the **doctrine of privity of contract**.

The law of agency, which is a mixture of contract and tort law, is considered in this chapter. Agency is distinguished from other relationships. Classification and creation of agents are discussed, as well as their authority, duties, rights and liabilities. Termination and remedies are also discussed along with some examples of specific types of agency.

INTRODUCTION TO AGENCY

The agency contract that has been created between the parties can be relied upon against, or by, third parties that have had dealings with the agent. In an agency contract there is an extension, or grant, of the contractual powers of the principal to their agent for those purposes authorised in prior agreement between them (see Figure 26.1).

Two points about agency in relation to the law of contract are:

Exercise of authority by A leads to creation of privity between P and TP

- There is an agreement between the principal and agent which creates the agency and provides the agent with authority. This is simply a contract like any other.
- There is an exercise of that authority by the agent, which leads to the creation of privity between the principal and third party. A contract made by the agent in the exercise of their authority with a third party is enforceable both by and against the principal.

By definition, the agency situation involves three parties:

1 the principal, who passes authority to act to
2 the agent, who in turn through this authority affects the legal relations of the principal *vis-à-vis*
3 the third party.

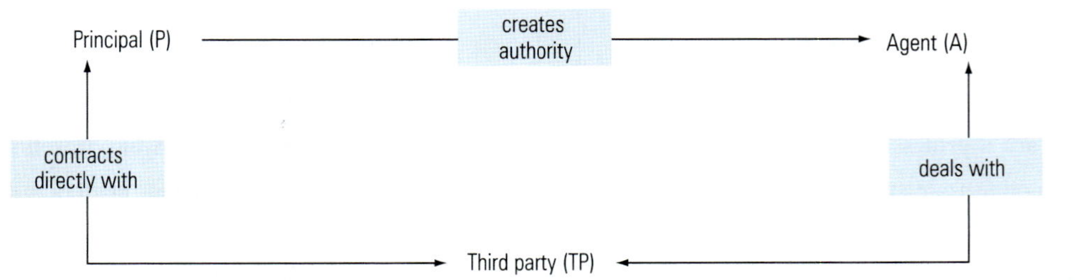

FIGURE 26.1 *Agency relationship*

DISTINGUISHED FROM OTHER RELATIONSHIPS

IN BRIEF

Kinds of employment relationships

Type of relationship	Description
Employer–employee	The employee is subject to the control and direction of the employer. An employee is often an agent for their employer.
Employer–independent contractor	The employer has no control over how the independent contractor will complete the task and so is usually not an agent of the employer.
Principal–agent	A has authority to act on behalf of P as authorised by P and implied from the agency.

Employer–employee

An employee is under the control and direction of the employer

An employee is expected to personally perform any directions that may be given to them by their employer. In the performance of these directions, **the employee is subject to the control and direction of the employer**.

As a general rule, an employee does not have the authority to affect an employer's legal relations with third parties because there is no direct involvement with them. However, if the employer expressly or impliedly directs the employee to affect the employer's legal relations with third parties, then an agency situation will arise. For example, a shop manager may be authorised to buy merchandise for the shop, or a commercial traveller is authorised to sell his or her employer's products. It is the essence of agency that it should be within the scope of employment that the employee brings the employer into a legal relationship with a third party (see Figure 26.2).

***DIRECTOR OF POSTS AND TELEGRAPHS V. ABBOTT* (1974) 2 ALR 625**

A clerk promised a customer that a telephone would be installed by a specified date.

ISSUE: Was the clerk an agent of the employer with power to bind the employer to the promise?

DECISION: The Full Court of South Australia found that there was no evidence of an intention on the part of the employer to give an employee in a clerical role the power to make contracts.

Employer–independent contractor

An independent contractor controls the manner, methods and materials for the task

Rather than use an employee to accomplish a desired end result, an employer may describe what they want and then contract with another party, called an independent **contractor**, to perform the agreed task for an agreed price (see

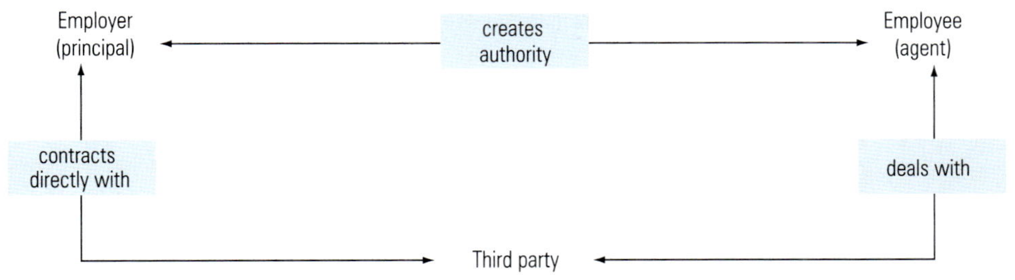

FIGURE 26.2 *Employer–employee relationship*

Figure 26.3). The finished task must meet certain requirements specified by the employer, but the contractor, and not the employer, controls the manner, methods and materials that are to be used to complete the task.

When a contractor deals with third parties it is usually as principal. However, an agent can be an independent contractor, as in the case of an auctioneer.

Doing business

The distinction between employees and independent contractors is important in cases of injury

Employers will not normally be liable for the tortious acts of independent contractors. In the case of employees acting as agents, the employer is liable to pay either damages at common law or compensation under the relevant state *Workers' Compensation Act* where the employee/agent is injured in the course of their employment. If the employee/agent injures a third party in the course of their employment, the employer may be vicariously liable for the employee's tortious act (see Chapter 8). ■

CLASSIFICATION OF AGENTS

IN BRIEF

Different classes of agents

Type of agent	Description
Special or limited	A can only make a particular type of contract or carry out a particular transaction on behalf of P.
General	A can make contracts of a class that are normal for this type of agency or do some act for P which is part of A's ordinary course of business.
Universal	A can do almost anything P can do.

The reason for the classifications is to determine the actual extent of an agent's authority.

Special or limited agents

Special or limited agent—authorised to only make a particular type of contract

Under a special or limited type of agency contract, the agent is **authorised by the principal** to make a particular type of contract or to represent the principal in a particular transaction.

If the agent acts beyond the principal's instructions, the principal is not bound. For example, if you ask a friend to bid up to $10 000 for you at a car auction and the friend bids $15 000, you are not bound. The friend has acted outside what they were instructed to do.

General agency

General agent—make contracts of a class normal for that type of agency

Under this type of agency, the agent is authorised:

- to make contracts of a certain class which are normal for such agents; or
- to do some act for a principal which forms part of the ordinary course of business for the agent. A manager of a company has an implied power to act as an agent of the business in all matters necessary for the running of the business.

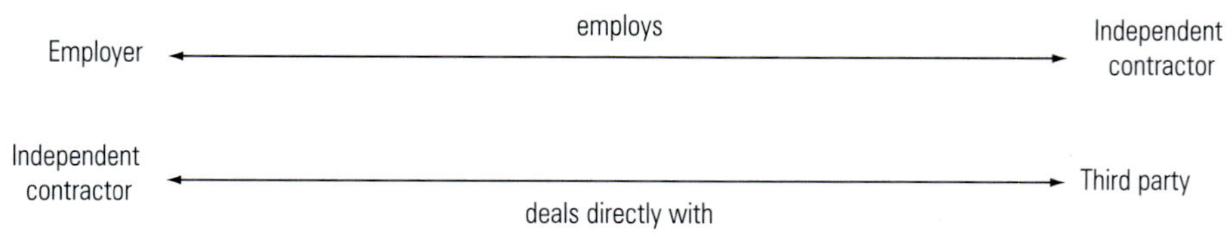

FIGURE 26.3 *Employer–independent contractor–third party relationship*

Universal agency

Universal agents have the power to do practically anything a principal can do. They are usually appointed under a power of attorney. Thus, a person going overseas for a long time could empower a close friend or their mother or father to act for them in their absence in any matters at all. They would be given this power through a power of attorney; they could pay debts, collect monies, enter into agreements and transact any business matters as though they were the principal.

Universal agent—power to do almost anything P can do

APPOINTMENT OF AGENTS

Express appointment

In an express agency there is a legal relationship created between the principal and the agent by agreement (see Figure 26.4). This agreement may be created:

Express appointment—agency created by agreement

Orally

Often an oral appointment is sufficient; however, a written appointment is the safest method as it creates a degree of certainty between the parties.

In writing

For reasons of security an appointment in writing is best. Statutes in each state require that many of the agency appointments be in writing. For example, if the agency is to last for more than one year, or it is concerned with a contract for the sale of land or an interest in land, or for the sale or purchase of a business.

By deed

The appointment of an agent under seal (or by deed) is necessary:

- where the principal can only carry out a particular transaction by deed; the agent's appointment for such a transaction must also be by deed;
- under a general power of attorney—for example, that given to a solicitor by a client can be under seal—but where such power involves signing a transfer of land, the power of attorney is required to be registered.

Implication or conduct

In the same way as any other contract may be implied from the conduct of the parties, the existence of a contractual relationship may be implied from the conduct of the principal and agent. Two examples of implied agency are cohabitation (see below) and partnership (see Chapter 28). The general rule is that an agreement may be implied where a reasonable person, examining the conduct and actions of the parties, would conclude that one party had authorised the other to act as agent and that both parties had assented to the arrangement.

Implication or conduct—implied from conduct of P and A

Operation of law

There are two situations where agency can arise which can be contrary to, or even against, the wishes of the parties.

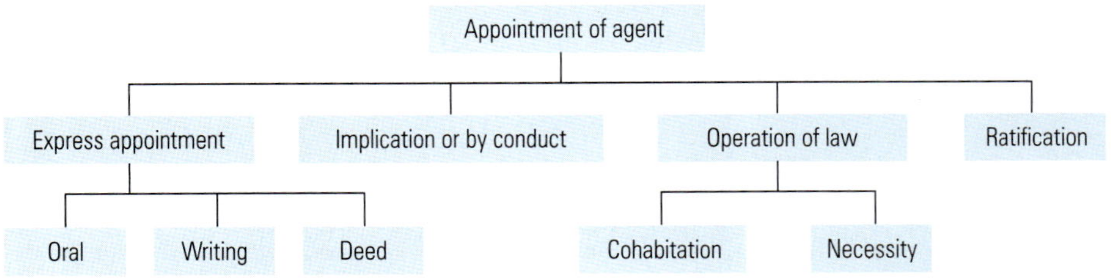

FIGURE 26.4 *Methods of appointment of agent*

Cohabitation

Cohabitation—presumption of agency

A spouse or de facto is presumed to have authority to pledge credit for necessaries suitable for their lifestyle. This presumption does not apply in the Northern Territory (*Married Persons (Equality of Status) Act 1989*, s. 5) or South Australia (*Law of Property Act 1936*, s. 104).

The onus of proof is on the supplier. If the supplier fails to show that the goods supplied to the spouse or de facto are necessaries, then the supplier is going to have to sue the spouse or de facto.

Necessity or emergency

Necessity—limited to genuine emergencies

An agent of necessity generally arises where a person who is entrusted with another's property finds it necessary to do something with it in order to preserve it. For example, a truck driver carrying perishable goods who finds that the freezer unit has broken down in the middle of nowhere could bind the employer if the only way to save the cargo is to have emergency repairs carried out on the freezer.

There are four conditions that must be satisfied before such an agency can arise:

- there must be a **genuine emergency**;
- it must be **impossible** or extremely difficult to get the principal's instructions;
- the person must be **entrusted** with another's property; and
- the agent must act *bona fide* in the principal's interests, and not merely for their own convenience.

GREAT NORTHERN RAILWAY V. SWAFFIELD (1874) LR 9 EXCH 132

A racehorse was consigned by rail to Swaffield at one of the plaintiff's railway stations. Swaffield was not at the station when the horse arrived. The railway did not have his address so there was no way they could get in touch with him to tell him it had arrived. As the horse could not be kept at the station, it was sent to a stable. The railway paid for its care until Swaffield arrived to pick it up. When they sought to recover the expenses for the upkeep of the horse Swaffield refused to pay.

ISSUE: Would the railway company have been in breach of their duty of care as a carrier, if they had failed to take care of the horse?

DECISION: The Court of Exchequer held that the railway company were agents of necessity. There was a genuine emergency, it was impossible to get in touch with the owner of the horse after being entrusted with his property and by feeding the horse the railway was acting *bona fide* in the best interests of Swaffield.

Agency by ratification

Agency by ratification—A has acted without P's authority but P subsequently ratifies A's actions

Where the agent has acted without the principal's authority, but nevertheless appeared to act on behalf of a principal, it is open to the principal to then ratify the transaction, thus assuming the benefits and burdens from the time the agent acted. **By ratification**, the **relationship of principal and agent is created retrospectively.** This situation usually arises when the agent has exceeded their authority.

BOLTON PARTNERS V. LAMBERT (1889) 41 CH D 295

On 1 August Lambert made an offer to buy land from A who in fact was manager and agent of the property on behalf of Bolton Partners. A had no authority to act for Bolton Partners, but on 2 August he accepted the offer on their behalf. On 6 August Lambert revoked the offer; on 8 August Bolton Partners ratified the acceptance of A.

ISSUE: Can the unauthorised actions of the agent be ratified by the principal?

DECISION: It was held that a contract existed as ratification related back to the moment when the contract between A and L was concluded—2 August. L's attempted revocation on August 6 was too late.

Acceptance by the agent on behalf of the principal must be complete and unconditional. If acceptance is conditional (e.g., 'accepted subject to the principal's ratification'), the acceptance would date from the date of ratification rather than the time of acceptance by the agent.

For ratification to be effective, the following conditions must all be satisfied or A will be personally liable:

- A must clearly be acting as an agent.
- A must have a known P in mind. It is not necessary that P be named; however, P should be capable of being ascertained at the time of making the contract.
- P must have contractual capacity at the time of making the contract.
- There should be an act capable of ratification. A contract that is void from its inception cannot be made good by ratification.
- P must have full knowledge of all the facts at the time of ratification.
- Ratification must occur within a reasonable time of the contract being entered into.
- Ratification may be express or implied by the conduct of P. The only time a special form is required is for the ratification of a deed.
- Ratification must apply to the whole contract.
- Ratification can only be retrospective.

The **effects of ratification** may be summarised as follows:

- It produces the rights and liabilities of principal and agent with regard to the act ratified.
- It relieves the agent from liability to a third party for breach of warranty of authority.
- As a general rule, ratification operates retrospectively, so that a third party (TP) can sue the principal on a contract, and vice versa, as though the agent's acts had been authorised.

IN BRIEF

Formation of agency relationships

Type of agency	Definition	Enforcement
Express	Authority is expressly given to A by P.	P and TP are bound to the contract.
Implied or conduct	Authority is implied from conduct of the parties based on an objective test of the reasonable person.	P and TP are bound to the contract.
Operation of law	Authority imposed on parties by law in cases of cohabitation and emergency.	P and TP are bound to the contract.
By ratification	Acts of A committed without P's authority but P subsequently ratifies A's actions.	P and TP are not bound to the contract unless P ratifies the contract.

AUTHORITY OF THE AGENT

IN BRIEF

Sources of authority of the agent

Type of authority	Description
Actual	Authority conferred by P either expressly or by action.
Implied	Authority is inferred from the conduct of the parties.
Apparent or ostensible	P creates the appearance of an agency by words or conduct when in reality it does not exist.

Actual authority

Actual authority—arises from express and implied powers, and from operation of law

The actual or express authority of the agent will be found in powers:

- expressly given by the principal to the agent;
- implied in the agency agreement; and
- which arise from operation of law (see p. 547).

Implied actual authority

An agent has authority to do anything that is incidental to or necessary for the carrying out of acts within their actual authority. For example, where a person acts as an agent of necessity (see p. 548).

***AUSTRALIA AND NEW ZEALAND BANK LTD V. ATELIERS DE CONSTRUCTIONS ELECTRIQUES DE CHARLEROI* [1967] 1 AC 86**

A Belgian manufacturer of electrical equipment appointed an Australian company as its agent to contract with the Snowy Mountains Hydro-Electric Authority. The contract stated that the price was to be paid in Australia in Australian currency payable to the Belgian company through its Australian agent by way of order cheques. The agent indorsed the cheques and paid them into its account with the bank. Some of the deposits were not forwarded to the Belgian company and, when the agent went bankrupt, the Belgian firm sued the bank.

ISSUE: Did the bank have implied authority to bank the order cheques into the agent's account?

DECISION: As the company had no bank account in Australia, the bank could rely on an implied actual authority that the Australian agent could indorse cheques payable to the Belgian company and bank the funds into its account.

COMMENT: The agent's authority to bank the cheques was both express (through the original agreement) and implied (on the basis of 'business efficacy') for the proper operation of the agency agreement.

Apparent or ostensible authority

Apparent or ostensible authority—P by words or conduct cannot deny agency

Apparent or ostensible authority arises where the principal, either by words or conduct, leads a third party to reasonably believe that an agent has authority to contract on their behalf when in fact this is not the case. If a third party mistakenly relies on the apparent authority of an agent, the principal is estopped or prevented from denying that such authority exists.

The impression of conferral created by the principal must be conveyed to the third party. A principal may be held liable on the basis of apparent authority if their conduct is such that it could reasonably lead a third party to believe that they could rely on that authority. Objective evidence could include:

- the words or conduct of the principal;
- custom or trade usage;
- those situations where the principal has appointed the agent to perform a task that implies a certain amount of authority; and
- whether the position creates an impression of authority.

TOOTH & CO. V. LAWS (1888) 9 LR (NSW) 154

Laws sold his hotel to a third party. After the sale, he allowed his name as licensee to continue to be displayed over the front door to the hotel. The persons who bought the business continued to purchase their liquor supplies, as Laws had done, from Tooth & Co. on credit. Tooth & Co. were not aware of the change of ownership. After several months of failing to pay their bills, Tooth & Co. sued Laws for the cost of the liquor supplied.

ISSUE: Did the actions of Laws, by his inaction in either notifying the supplier or removing his name from the sign saying he was the nominee, prevent him from denying an agency agreement existed?

DECISION: Laws was liable to pay for the liquor supplied because by allowing his name to remain over the front door of the hotel as licensee, he was representing to the public that he was still the owner. Thus, it was possible to infer that the new purchasers were his agent.

PANORAMA DEVELOPMENTS (GUILDFORD) LTD V. FIDELIS FURNISHINGS FABRICS [1971] 3 WLR 440

A company secretary hired cars for his own private use. He told the hire car company that he was hiring the cars for and on behalf of the company. When the company received the account for the car hire they refused to pay, arguing that there was no actual or implied authority for the secretary to enter into such contracts.

ISSUE: Is the position of company secretary such that a person in that position may be regarded as holding themselves out as having the necessary authority to do certain things, such as hire cars, on behalf of the company?

DECISION: The company had to pay because the secretary appeared to have authority to enter into the hiring arrangement, though he did not have actual or implied authority.

activebook

To help you to remember and understand the topics covered so far, and for links to legal websites, refer to your online activebook. Model answers provide feedback to problems and exercises.

DUTIES OF AGENT TO PRINCIPAL

IN BRIEF

Duties of A to P

Duty	Comment
A must follow P's instructions	Failure to follow P's instructions will leave A open to be sued for any losses P may incur.
A must act in person	Delegation is not possible where a personal confidence or skill is required unless P gives express consent.
A must exercise due care, skill and diligence	A gratuitous agent must exercise such care and skill as they would exercise in their own affairs. A non-gratuitous agent (paid) owes a degree of care and skill as is usual or necessary for an agent of that type.
A must act in P's interests	There must be no conflict of interest with duty.
A must maintain confidentiality of information	Information gained during employment should not be divulged.
A must keep separate and proper accounts	A must be able to account for all moneys.
A must not make a secret profit	A must give any profits to P.
A must not receive secret commissions	A is only entitled to the agreed or customary commission. All moneys or property received must be handed to P or it may amount to a secret commission and give rise to criminal penalties and civil remedies.

Duties of agent are based on contract

The duties of an agent are based in contract law and a fiduciary relationship is based on trust, which varies in degree according to the express terms of the agency agreement or the nature of the agency relationship. The following are the chief duties owed by an agent to their principal:

The agent must follow the principal's instructions

A must follow P's instructions

An agent must follow the lawful instructions of the principal. Failure to do so would result in the agent being in breach of contract (and quite possibly negligent), leaving the agent open to being sued for any losses that may arise.

The agent must act in person

A must act in person

Delegation is not possible where a personal confidence or skill is required by the agent.

***JOHN McCANN & CO. V. POW* [1973] 1 ALL ER 129**

Pow appointed a firm of real estate agents to sell his flat. Without Pow's knowledge or consent, the agents gave details to a sub-agent, who subsequently sold the property.

ISSUE: Were McCann & Co., who were instrumental in arranging the sale, entitled to commission?

DECISION: Personal skill and competence cannot be delegated. Thus, McCann & Co. were not entitled to commission.

However, there are a number of exceptions to this rule. They will render the delegate the agent, not of the principal, but of the original agent:

- where the delegation is sanctioned by the principal either expressly or impliedly—for instance, by trade usage, where an agent usually acts through other agents;
- where the delegation arises out of necessity; or
- where the agent's duties are purely administrative and do not involve the exercise of any discretion or skill on the part of the agent personally.

Where the agent has agreed to carry out the task and is to be paid for doing so, failure to follow the principal's instructions could result in the agent being sued for damages.

Where the instructions are vague or ambiguous, the agent will not be liable if their actions are reasonable, nor will any liability be incurred for failure to carry out an illegal contract.

The agent must exercise due care, skill and diligence

The standard of care expected of an agent will vary according to whether the agent is providing the skill gratuitously (for free) or for payment.

- **Gratuitous services**—where the agent provides their **services for free**, they are expected to exercise such care and skill as they actually possess and would exercise in their own affairs, unless they hold themselves out as having special expertise for the performance of a specific undertaking. Where the agent has a special expertise, a higher standard is expected, if the agent wishes to avoid being liable for negligence.
- **Paid services**—where the agent charges a fee for their services, they are expected to exercise such care, skill and diligence as is usual or necessary in the class of business undertaken by the agent. Usually, the higher the remuneration, the higher the standard of care, diligence and skill required of the agent.

MITOR INVESTMENTS PTY LTD V. GENERAL ACCIDENT FIRE & LIFE ASSURANCE CORP. [1984] WAR 365

A client instructed an insurance broker to obtain unqualified insurance cover against damage from storm or flood. The policy which the broker obtained did not cover flood caused by the sea. The client's property was subsequently damaged by flooding by the sea as a result of a cyclone.

ISSUE: Is the broker liable for the client's loss because he failed to check the risks covered?

DECISION: The broker was held liable by the Supreme Court of Western Australia for the loss suffered by the client because of the failure to exercise reasonable care and skill when carrying out the client's instructions.

! CAUTION NOTE

The care A must exercise will depend on whether they are providing their services for free or for payment.

The agent must act in the principal's interests (in good faith)

An agent is under a duty to act in the principal's interests. This duty arises from the fact that an agent stands in a fiduciary relationship to the principal. Therefore the agent must act in such a way that there will not be a conflict of interest with duty.

HEWSON V. SYDNEY STOCK EXCHANGE **(1967) 87 WN (NSW) 422**

Hewson, a stockbroker at the Sydney Stock Exchange, also carried on business as a share-trader. A question arose as to whether or not it was possible for a person to act as both a share-broker and share-trader without being in breach of their duty to act in good faith. Both Hewson and the stock exchange proceeded on the basis that there was no impropriety in such an arrangement.

ISSUE: Was there a conflict of interest?

DECISION: The New South Wales Supreme court was highly critical of such an arrangement because agency is a fiduciary relationship and one which imposes a heavy obligation on the agent not to promote personal interests in preference to those of the principal. In this type of situation the agent is put into a position where their interest and duty will be in conflict as they are entering the market and trading not for their clients but in competition with them.

Thus, if at any time the duty of the agent towards the principal clashes with any other duty, a proper disclosure of this conflict should be made.

The test of what should be disclosed is what a 'reasonable person' would consider material in the ordinary course of business. If circumstances arise where a disclosure should be made and it hasn't been, the transaction will be voidable at the principal's option. This will also be the situation, even after the contract has been performed, without the principal needing to establish fraud on the agent's part. However, this is not the case if the principal has elected to affirm the contract after learning the full extent of the agent's interest. The rule is that an agent must not become a principal as against their employer.

The agent must maintain confidentiality of information

If an agent gains access to confidential information while employed by a principal, this information should not be divulged to outsiders, nor used for the agent's personal gain, either during or after the termination of the agency relationship.

An agent must keep separate and proper accounts

An agent must be able to account for all property and money received on behalf of the principal.

An agent must not make secret profits

An agent must not make a secret profit—that is, a profit that should have gone to the principal. Where A has an interest in a contract, full disclosure should be made to P.

LUNGHI V. SINCLAIR **[1966] WAR 172**

Lunghi had a block of land that he wished to sell. He approached Sinclair, a real estate agent, to sell the land for him for a minimum price of $400. Sinclair informed Lunghi that his (Sinclair's) wife was an interested buyer and after some time, and little buyer interest, Lunghi eventually sold the land to her. Lunghi subsequently discovered that Sinclair's wife was a partner in the real estate agency and that no real attempt had been made to sell the land. It was, in fact, worth substantially more than he was told and Mrs Sinclair had resold the land for $1300.

ISSUE: Were the actions of Mrs Sinclair such that they could be said to amount to a secret profit?

DECISION: The Western Australia Supreme Court held that an agent who has a direct or indirect interest in a contract proposed by a principal should make full disclosure. It further held that Sinclair was under a duty to disclose the true value of the property and that the profit made by Mrs Sinclair was in fact a secret profit that should go to the principal (Lunghi).

An agent must not receive secret commissions

CAUTION NOTE

A secret commission is like a bribe and A may face both a criminal action and a civil penalty.

An agent is only entitled to the agreed or customary commission as payment for services that have been performed, and to nothing else. All monies and other property received by the agent must be handed over to the principal, less any expenses that may have been incurred and any commission or remuneration permitted by the contract. If the principal is aware of the agent being paid an additional commission by a third party and sanctions it, no offence arises. However, often the extra commission secretly earned by the agent is nothing less than a bribe, in which case the agent may face criminal law action by the police as well as civil action by the principal.

Under civil law, the principal may:

- claim the commission;
- claim the commission and cancel the agency agreement;
- cancel the agency agreement;
- recover damages for any loss suffered from the agent or the party that has paid the bribe; or
- recover the secret commission.

In addition to the civil remedies available to the principal, secret commissions are subject to both Commonwealth and state and territory legislation.

The *Secret Commissions Act 1905* (Cth) makes it an offence for any person who is acting as an agent to accept any gift or consideration as an inducement or reward without the full knowledge of the principal. The *Secret Commissions Act* is limited to transactions between the Commonwealth and the states, between the Commonwealth or states and other countries, among the states themselves, and between government departments and agencies. Conviction carries a fine of up to $2000 for a corporation and a fine of up to $1000 and/or a gaol sentence of up to one year for an individual.

Legislation between the states and the territories is reasonably uniform (see Table 26.1). All the legislation makes it an offence for an agent to corruptly receive or solicit from another person (or attempt to do so) any valuable consideration for their own benefit, or for the benefit of any other person other than their principal. Penalties on conviction for a corporation are a fine, while for an individual it is a fine and/or a gaol sentence. The fine and gaol sentence vary from state to state (e.g., NSW: up to seven years' gaol; Vic: up to 10 years' gaol).

Table 26.1 Secret commission legislation of the states, territories and Commonwealth

Source	*Statute*
Commonwealth	*Secret Commissions Act 1905*
Australian Capital Territory	*Agents Act 2003*
New South Wales	*Crimes Act 1900*
Northern Territory	*Criminal Code Act 1983*
Queensland	*Criminal Code Act 1899*
South Australia	*Criminal Law Consolidation Act 1935*
Tasmania	*Criminal Code 1924*
Victoria	*Crimes Act 1958*
	Estate Agents Act 1980
Western Australia	*Criminal Code Act Compilation Act 1913*

RIGHTS OF AGENT AGAINST PRINCIPAL

IN BRIEF

Rights of agent against principal

Rights of A	Obligation of P
Right to payment	Gratuitous agents are not entitled to remuneration. A non-gratuitous agent is entitled to payment fixed or implied by the agreement.
Right to indemnity and reimbursement	A is entitled to be indemnified against any liabilities, and reimbursed for any expenses while carrying out P's instructions.
Right of *lien*	A has a right to retain possession of goods of P until reimbursement of expenses and commission (if applicable) has been paid.
Right of stoppage in transit	If the goods are still in the carrier's possession, A may be able to resume possession.

Beside the responsibilities set out above, the agent has a number of rights against the principal:

Right to payment

The principal must pay the agent the remuneration (payment) fixed or implied by the agreement, plus any necessary expenses incurred by the agent in the course of carrying out the contract. Otherwise the agent is a gratuitous agent; though even gratuitous agents are entitled to reimbursement for any expenses.

If the terms of the agreement are express, the agent cannot claim more than what is laid down by those terms. If remuneration is implied, then it is determined according to the circumstances of each case.

If an agent's contract stipulates payment only on the performance of a particular transaction, a claim for payment does not arise until that transaction occurs and if the agent was instrumental in it.

Where the agent is to find a purchaser or introduce a prospective purchaser, no commission is payable unless the person is:

- ready and willing to purchase on the principal's price and terms;
- able to purchase; and
- in fact purchases by entering into a binding contract on these terms.

Right to indemnity and reimbursement

In general, an agent is entitled to be indemnified against any liabilities, and to be reimbursed for any expenses incurred in the course of carrying out the principal's instructions. However, the agent loses the right to indemnity and reimbursement where:

- the agent's acts are not authorised or ratified by the principal;
- the agent is in breach of a duty to the principal; or
- the loss is due to the unlawful or negligent acts of the agent.

Right of *lien*

An agent is entitled to retain the goods of the principal until reimbursement of expenses and commission has been received. The goods must not have been obtained through the agent's misrepresentation, and must have been acquired by the agent in respect of the particular transaction for which payment has not been made.

A *lien* is lost if the agent voluntarily parts with possession or if the principal tenders the sum due.

Right of stoppage in transit

Where an agent is personally responsible for the price of goods bought on the principal's behalf, the agent may be placed in the position of an unpaid seller if the principal were to become insolvent. In such a case, the agent may be able to exercise the seller's right of stoppage in transit if the goods are still in the possession of a carrier as provided for in the various sale of goods legislation of the states and territories. Once the agent has recovered possession of the goods, the right of *lien* can then be exercised.

LIABILITY OF AGENTS AND PRINCIPALS TO THIRD PARTIES

IN BRIEF

Liability of P and A

As a general rule A cannot sue or be sued on a contract between P and TP where:

- A discloses the agency relationship and names P; or
- A discloses the agency relationship but does not name P.

If A does not disclose the agency relationship or name P, A will be personally liable on the contract. Similarly, A will be liable for breach of warranty of authority if they exceed the authority, express or implied, given to them by P.

Agency has two different contractual aspects:

- the contract between the principal and the agent; and
- the contract formed, by the agent, between the principal and a third party.

The general rule in the latter case is that an agent cannot sue or be sued on a contract between the principal and a third party. However, the position with regard to a third party varies according to the circumstances:

Disclosure of an agency relationship and naming of the principal

Where A contracts for named P, A is discharged from agreement between P and TP

As a general rule, where the agent contracts for a named principal, the agent is completely discharged from the agreement and cannot incur either rights or liabilities. Privity of contract exists between the principal and the third party. However, an agent will incur liability where:

- they have executed a deed in their own name;
- usage or custom makes them liable;
- the principal is nonexistent;
- they agree to be liable; or
- they are in breach of warranty of authority by acting beyond the scope of their actual or apparent authority.

Disclosure of an agency relationship but unnamed principal

> **!** CAUTION NOTE
>
> *A must disclose agency relationship to avoid liability.*

If an agent makes a contract without naming the principal, to avoid being personally liable, the agent must expressly disclose to the third party that an agency relationship exists. If the third party is then prepared to accept an unknown principal as the other party to the contract, the agent is discharged. If the agent does not make it clear that they are only acting as an agent, they may find that the third party treats them as the principal and a party to the contract.

Where the agent does not disclose the existence of a principal

If the agent contracts in their own name and conceals the existence of the agency relationship, the third party will not know of the existence of the principal because the contract will only have the agent's name on it. If a dispute arises, the third party has the option of suing either the agent or, if they discover the principal's identity, the principal (this is called the doctrine of undisclosed principal). However, the third party cannot later sue the other unless given permission by the court, because to do so would be to allow two judgements for the one debt.

If the agent undertakes personal liability to the third party in the course of acting for the principal, the agent will be liable for any contractual undertaking that has been made (e.g., auctioneers who warrant that they have authority to sell on behalf of vendors).

The principal, when discovered, may sue and be sued by the third party as long as the authority of the agent existed at the time of the contract and the contract did not prevent the possibility of agency.

Breach of warranty

> **!** CAUTION NOTE
>
> *Only a TP can sue A for damages where there is a breach of warranty of authority.*

If an agent expressly or impliedly represents that they acted with the authority of the principal, and a third party acts on the basis of that representation, the agent is taken to warrant that the representation is true. If it is untrue, the agent has committed a breach of warranty of authority. The third party can then sue the agent for damages to the extent of the actual loss suffered. This action is only open to the third party.

The agent is liable whether the act was done fraudulently or innocently, and even if the authority had been terminated without the knowledge of the agent.

The doctrine of undisclosed principal

Where P undisclosed, P may disclose agency agreement and enforce contract with TP if A acting within agreement

Where the agent has contracted with a third party without disclosing they are acting as an agent, the principal may still disclose the existence of the agency agreement to the third party and enforce the contract in their own name but only if the agent had contracted within their authority.

***KEIGHLEY, MAXSTEAD & CO. V. DURANT* [1901] AC 240**

Roberts (A), a corn merchant, was authorised by Keighley, Maxstead & Co. (P) to buy wheat for himself and the company at a named price on a joint account. Roberts failed to buy the wheat at the agreed price and subsequently bought wheat without authority at a higher price from Durant (TP). He contracted in his own name and made no mention to Durant of his intention to contract for himself and his partner. Keighley, Maxstead & Co. approved the purchase the following day but Roberts and Keighley, Maxstead & Co. then failed to take delivery.

ISSUE: Can Durant enforce the contract against Keighley, Maxstead & Co.? Was the action of Keighley, Maxstead & Co. in approving the purchase of the wheat by Roberts ratification of the contract?

DECISION: As Roberts made the contract with Durant without authority and he did not disclose the existence of an agency relationship, the action of Keighley, Maxstead & Co. did not amount to ratification and so they could not be sued by Durant.

LIABILITY OF PRINCIPAL AND AGENT IN TORT

Doing business

Avoiding liability as an agent

An agent must ensure that they act within the scope of their actual or apparent authority if they want to avoid liability:

- for breach of warranty of authority; or
- any torts that they commit. ■

P liable for tortious acts of A committed in course of employment

The principal will be liable to third parties for any tort committed by the agent **if the agent has acted within the scope of their actual or apparent authority or employment**, whether or not the tort was committed for the benefit of the principal.

***LLOYD V. GRACE, SMITH & CO.* [1912] AC 716**

Grace, Smith & Co., a firm of solicitors, employed a managing clerk to conduct the conveyancing business of the firm. He fraudulently induced a client to sign some documents that she was told were necessary for the completion of a transaction but were a conveyance of the client's property to himself.

ISSUE: Was the firm liable for the unauthorised actions of their clerk?

DECISION: The court held the firm was liable for the fraud of their managing clerk as the fraud was committed within the scope of his apparent authority.

If the agent was engaged in a private venture outside the scope of the agency relationship when the tort was committed, or the agent commits a tort wholly outside the scope of their employment, the principal is relieved of any liability.

***DEATONS PTY LTD V. FLEW* (1949) 79 CLR 370**

Deatons operated a hotel. Flew, a customer at the hotel, acted offensively to one of their employees, a barmaid, who asked him to go away. An argument developed and the barmaid threw a glass of beer and then the glass into Flew's face. The customer brought an action against her employer for damages.

ISSUE: Was the barmaid acting within the course of her employment at the time of the incident?

DECISION: The High Court held that the barmaid's actions were outside the scope of her employment, which was to serve drinks to customers. Deatons was not liable to Flew for damages.

TERMINATION OF AGENCY

Doing business

Steps to take to avoid liability on termination of the agreement

If the agency is terminated by agreement, P is under a duty to notify those TPs with whom A may do business. The notice can be from P or some other recognised source, for example, A.

The termination of the agency agreement extinguishes A's actual authority to act on P's behalf. However, if P fails to give proper notice of the termination to a TP, A still has apparent authority to bind P to a contract with a TP who is not aware of the termination. The contract would be enforceable against P and P's only recourse then is to sue A for damages caused by the unauthorised contract.

To avoid problems arising in the first place, the following steps should be taken:

- **Parties who deal with A**: direct notice of termination should be given by P, preferably in writing.
- **Parties who have knowledge of the agency**: P must give direct or constructive notice to any TP who has knowledge of the agreement but with whom A has not dealt. Constructive notice would be satisfied by a notice in the Public Notices section of the local newspaper. It is irrelevant whether TP sees it or not.
- **Parties who have no knowledge of the agency agreement**: generally P is not liable to strangers. However, if there is written authority of an agency relationship, to avoid problems arising with TP subsequently relying on this, P should give constructive notice of termination of the agency to avoid liability. ■

Agency may be terminated by acts of the parties

The acts of the parties

An agency agreement may be terminated by the parties by:

Mutual agreement

While the agreement between the principal and agent is still in force, they may mutually agree to its termination.

Revocation of the agent's authority

Revocation can be done at any time by the principal without the agent's consent, even though the work of the agent may not be completed. This could lead to breach of contract and the agent bringing an action for wrongful dismissal.

Where the principal does revoke an agent's authority, third parties should be notified by the principal to avoid any problems arising from an apparent agency. For example, partners who retire from a firm should ensure that they notify the firm's customers of their retirement or they will be bound (or estopped) by the actions of the other partners in the normal course of business (see pp. 599–600).

The agent may withdraw from the agreement

This may be done at any time, provided that the agent makes good any loss that the principal may suffer, but the agent is not liable for any loss where the agency is a gratuitous one.

Secret commission

An agency may be terminated by the principal where the agent has accepted a secret commission (see p. 555).

Completion of a specific purpose or act agency

Where the agent is appointed for a specific purpose or act and that purpose or act has been completed, the agency agreement will be terminated by performance—for example, the sale of a house by a real estate agent.

Time limit

If there is a time limit involved in the agency agreement—for example, with respect to the sale of a house within 30 days—and the sale is not achieved within that time limit, the agency agreement would be terminated.

Operation of law

Agency may be terminated by operation of law

An agency may be legally terminated by:

Performance

The authority of the agent only continues up until the task has been completed.

Lapse of time

Where the agent has been appointed for a specific time, then the authority of the agent will cease when that time period expires.

Death

Legislation in all states provides that where the agent is acting in good faith under the scope of a power of attorney, any acts done after the death of the principal, but before notice of the death reaches the agent, are valid and the agent will not be held liable (see Table 26.2).

Table 26.2 Legislation regulating transactions where principal has died

Source	*Statute*
Australian Capital Territory	*Powers of Attorney Act 1956*
New South Wales	*Conveyancing Act 1919*
Northern Territory	*Powers of Attorney Act 1980*
Queensland	*Property Law Act 1974*
South Australia	*Powers of Attorney and Agency Act 1984*
Tasmania	*Powers of Attorney Act 1934*
Victoria	*Instruments Act 1958*
Western Australia	*Property Law Act 1969*

Insanity

Insanity of either the principal or the agent terminates the agency agreement.

Bankruptcy

In certain cases, bankruptcy of either the principal or the agent under the provisions of the *Bankruptcy Act 1966* (Cth) will terminate the agency agreement.

Frustration

Where it becomes impossible for the agent to carry out their obligations owing to the destruction of the subject matter, or by any event which makes the agency illegal or impossible of performance, the agency agreement ceases. On termination, whether through the act of a party or by the operation of law, rights vested before the terminating event, such as agent's rights to commission or indemnity, are not affected.

REMEDIES OF A PRINCIPAL

P's remedies include rescission, not paying commission, damages, or recovery of secret commission

The major remedies of a principal for breach by an agent include:

- rescission;
- refusing to pay a commission;
- suing for damages; or
- suing the agent for recovery of a secret commission.

SOME SPECIFIC TYPES OF AGENCY

Auctioneers

! CAUTION NOTE

Auctioneer is A of vendor but after fall of hammer becomes A for purchaser.

An auctioneer is the authorised selling agent of a property (land/or goods) owner. The fall of the auctioneer's hammer signifies acceptance of the highest bid and the auctioneer becomes the agent of the purchaser for the purpose of making a written memorandum of the sale, if such evidence is required by statute. The auctioneer is accountable to the principal for the collection of the purchase price. As a result, the auctioneer can sue for it in the auctioneer's own name. A *lien* may be exercised over any property of the principal that is legally in the possession of the auctioneer until remuneration and proper expenses are paid by the principal.

If the auctioneer makes no mention about a reserve price (the minimum price below which the seller is not prepared to sell), the law is unclear whether the auctioneer has to accept the highest bid or not. The bidder cannot sue on the contract of sale because there has been no acceptance, but there may be a personal action against the auctioneer. 'Without reserve' indicates that the goods or property may be sold to the highest *bona fide* bidder.

***WARLOW V. HARRISON* (1859) 120 ER 925**

The defendant auctioneer advertised an auction of horses as being 'without reserve'. This meant that the highest *bona fide* bidder should have been the successful bidder, whatever the price bid. At the auction the owner of a mare submitted a final bid that the auctioneer accepted. The plaintiff then sued the auctioneer, alleging a breach of the auctioneer's contractual obligation to sell the horse to the highest *bona fide* bidder.

ISSUE: Was the auctioneer entitled to accept a bid from the owner where the auction was 'without reserve'?

DECISION: By wrongfully accepting a bid from the owner, the auctioneer was in breach of his contractual undertaking to sell to the highest *bona fide* bidder. By advertising the auction as 'without reserve', he had undertaken to sell to the highest *bona fide* bidder, the plaintiff in this case.

Where a reserve price is published, the auctioneer's authority is limited and so 'acceptance' of a lower price than the reserve will not bind the principal.

Mercantile agents

A factor or mercantile agent (as they are strictly called) is an agent who is employed to buy, sell or otherwise deal with goods or merchandise on behalf of a principal (see Figure 26.5). They have possession or control of the goods, and so can sell them in their own name.

Factor or mercantile A has control or possession of goods

Remuneration is usually by way of a commission, and sometimes to secure payment it may be necessary to exercise a *lien* over the principal's property in the agent's possession.

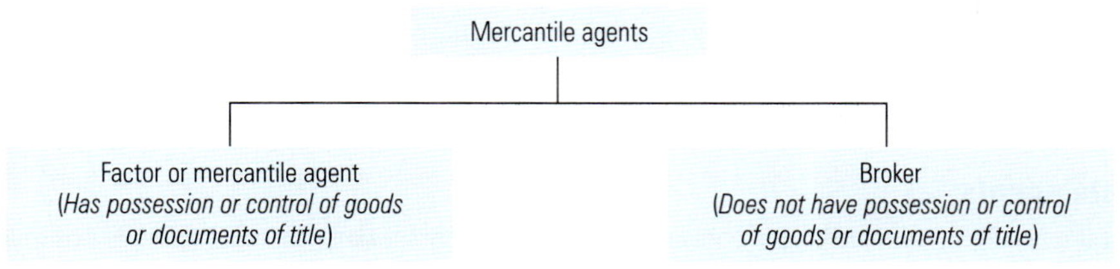

FIGURE 26.5 *Classes of mercantile agent*

All states and ACT have special statutory provisions dealing with factors (see Table 26.3). If a factor has possession or documents of title to goods, with the consent of the owner, any sale, pledge or other disposition of the goods made in the ordinary course of business is binding on the principal, with or without the principal's authority. This does not apply if the third party was aware of the factor's lack of authority. Where the factor's authority is revoked by the principal, revocation should be made public. Any third party who obtains either the goods or the documents of title from a factor, without knowledge of the withdrawal of authority, would get a good title.

Table 26.3 Statutory provisions dealing with factors

State	*Statute*
Australian Capital Territory	*Mercantile Law Act 1962*
New South Wales	*Factors (Mercantile Agents) Act 1923*
Northern Territory	*Sale of Goods Act 1972*, s. 28
Queensland	*Factors Act 1892*
South Australia	*Mercantile Law Act 1936*
Tasmania	*Factors Act 1891*
Victoria	*Goods Act 1958*, ss. 65–72
Western Australia	*Factors Act 1878*

Brokers

A broker is a general agent who buys and sells on behalf of a principal but does not have either possession or control of the goods, or their documents of title. Acting on behalf of both the buyer and the seller, a broker may be said to have two principals.

Brokers have neither possession nor control

Remuneration is called 'brokerage' and is usually fixed on a percentage basis. Brokers cannot sell, or sue, in their own name and have no authority to receive monies. Because they do not handle the goods or have any property in them, they cannot exercise a *lien* over the goods.

The most familiar type of broker is the stockbroker.

Del credere agents

***Del credere:* A guarantees both sale and payment to P**

A *del credere* agent ensures not only that goods will be sold but, for an additional commission, guarantees that they will be paid for, if not by the purchaser then by the agent. The transaction is something akin to a contract of guarantee.

The advantage to a principal of using a *del credere* agent is that while buyers might disappear or go bankrupt, the agent, by guaranteeing payment, is being more careful of any dealings with buyers. The risk borne by the agent is compensated for by the higher commission.

Partners

Partners are agents of co-partners

Partners are the agents of their co-partners. They have authority to make contracts binding on all the partners in a firm within the scope of that firm's business, unless public notification of a limitation of authority is made or a limitation on the partner's ability to contract is known to third parties. See Chapter 28 for a fuller treatment of this topic.

Real estate agents

Real estate agents—not strictly agents but stakeholders

The term 'real estate agent' is something of a misnomer because strictly speaking the relationship is **not** truly that of principal and agent. As a general rule, the real estate agent is merely authorised to find a purchaser and is not given authority, either actual or apparent, to enter into a binding contract on behalf of the vendor. All that the real estate agent can do is to bring the parties together. They are probably better described as **stakeholders**.

An agent acting on behalf of a vendor for the sale of a property who finds a purchaser must obtain the signature of both parties to a sale note for a contract to come into existence.

Other classes

Other types of general agent include sub-agents, company directors, shipmasters, married women, commission agents, bankers and travel agents.

REVIEW QUESTIONS ?

26.1 Distinguish between a special agency, a general agent and a universal agent and explain the need for the distinction.

26.2 Under what circumstances can an agency by necessity arise?

26.3 An agent arranged fire insurance for his principal, Magic Cinemas. Shortly before the policy was due to expire, the agent arranged with the insurance company on behalf of Magic Cinemas, but without their authority, to renew their policy. Two days after the policy was due to have expired, the cinema was burnt to the ground and Magic Cinemas then announced ratification of the contract of insurance. Is the ratification valid? Discuss.

26.4 Indicate whether each of the following statements is true or false:

	TRUE	FALSE
▪ A contract must exist between the agent and the third party as well as the agent and the principal for agency law to apply	☑	☐
▪ An independent contractor can never create an agency relationship with their employer	☑	☐
▪ The reason for the classification of agents is to determine the actual extent of an agent's authority	☑	☐
▪ Universal agents have the power only to make particular types of contract	☐	☑
▪ Partnerships are an example of agency arising by implication or conduct	☑	☐
▪ Ratification by a principal of an unauthorised act by an agent can bind the third party retrospectively	☑	☐
▪ An agent must always act in person	☑	☐
▪ A gratuitous agent is entitled to reimbursement of expenses they may incur while acting on behalf of the principal	☑	☐
▪ An agent has a right to stoppage in transit if they are placed in the position of an unpaid seller, even if the goods are in the possession of the buyer	☐	☑

26.5 Under agency law, it is assumed that a person to whom authority has been given cannot delegate that authority to another. Explain why and whether there are any exceptions to that rule.

26.6 What degree of care and skill is required from a gratuitous agent?

26.7 Agents are not expected to use their position as a means of making a gain for themselves without the knowledge and consent of the principal. Discuss.

26.8 Jones agreed to buy two racehorses from Brown, provided that Jones' veterinary surgeon gave them a clean bill of health. After inspecting the horses, the veterinarian certified them as being sound, and Jones accordingly sent Brown a cheque for them. After the horses were delivered, Jones noticed that both were unsound. He returned the horses and stopped payment of his cheque. In the course of evidence it was revealed that Brown had bribed the veterinarian. Advise Jones in the light of this evidence.

26.9 A solicitor had control of a number of companies, including Consul Developments Pty Ltd, which purchased, renovated and then resold properties. The solicitor's clerk owned a company called DPC Estates, which was also involved in property purchases, renovations and resale.

A manager was appointed to manage the companies under the control of the solicitor. He often passed on information to the solicitor's clerk about properties Consul Developments was going to buy, which was in breach of his agreement with the solicitor. The solicitor's clerk then used that information for the benefit of his own company, DPC Estates, by purchasing those properties. Has the solicitor any remedy against either the manager or DPC Estates?

Discuss.

26.10 List the ways in which an agency agreement may be terminated.

26.11 Under what circumstances will an agent find themselves in a breach of warranty situation?

26.12 Does the liability of an agent to a third party differ in the case of a disclosed but unnamed principal from that of an undisclosed principal? Discuss.

26.13 Pete owned a late 1998 model Falcon and delivered it to Al, a mercantile agent, for sale at not less than $16 500. Al sold the car for $10 000 to Terry, who bought it in good faith and without notice of any limitation on the mercantile agent's powers. Al then disappeared with the $10 000.

Can Pete recover the car from Terry?

> **activebook**
>
> Activebook resources include in-depth summaries with links to the relevant part of the book. For revision, add your own notes to the summaries provided by using the note-taking function.

CRITICAL THINKING

26.1 Sue and Mike formed a company to acquire and develop certain land. The board of directors was made up of Sue, Mike and a nominee of each. The development of the land was left to Sue who, with the knowledge of the board of directors, acted as managing director although she had never been formally appointed to the position. Sue employed Freeman and Lockyer, a firm of architects, to draw up plans for the development of the land but when they presented their bill for payment the company refused to pay, arguing that it had not authorised Sue to employ them.

Advise Freeman and Lockyer on whether you think they have a case that they can put forward as to why they should be paid, and what that case is.

26.2 A broker was instructed by a hotel owner to sell her hotel. The hotel was duly listed by the broker, and an inquirer, Robinson, was sent a list of hotels for sale and authorities to inspect. Accompanying the list of hotels was a letter which said: 'If business is done, we shall act for you at the usual brokerage'. Robinson looked at the list and bought one of the hotels after direct negotiations with the owner. The hotel owner paid the broker a commission.

Can the broker claim a commission from Robinson, the purchaser of the hotel?

26.3 Estate agents wrote to a house owner, A, who was keen to sell his property, accepting an offer from him to become his agent. In the letter they sent to A, they pointed out that if they were able to find a 'willing and able' purchaser, they would be entitled to a commission at normal Real Estate Institute rates. The agents then introduced the owner to B, who said she was prepared to buy 'subject to contract' and 'subject to a surveyor's report'. Subsequently, A received a higher offer from another party and accepted it. When the agents claimed their commission, stating that they had introduced a willing and able purchaser, A refused to pay.

Is the owner correct in refusing to pay the agent's commission?

CHAPTER 27

Companies and Incorporated Associations

CHAPTER CONTENTS

activebook

This icon is used throughout the following chapter to remind you to visit the *Business Law* online activebook for additional exercises, links to legal websites, and feedback. For a detailed explanation of what is in the activebook please refer to the inside cover of this textbook. The activebook is available through OneKey.

Where do I start?

Learning path: Use the activebook to complete a pre-chapter warm-up exercise.

There are many definitions of legal terms to assist with your understanding of the material.

CHAPTER OBJECTIVES

On completion of this chapter, you should be able to:

- define the essential characteristics of a corporation
- outline the legal requirements for a corporation
- identify the extent of liability of the parties in a corporation
- define the essential characteristics of an incorporated association
- outline the legal requirements for an incorporated association
- identify the extent of liability of the parties in an incorporated association.

KEY TERMS

An understanding of the following terms will help you to better understand the material in this chapter.

- **company:** a distinct legal entity separate from its shareholders
- **debenture:** a document whereby a company acknowledges a debt; also represents the division of a company's profits among its shareholders
- **directors:** the persons responsible for the management of a company
- **floating charge:** a form of security for a debenture holder whereby the company grants security over all its assets; it stops 'floating' and attaches itself to the assets of the company at the time of default
- **liquidator:** the person appointed to carry out the winding up of a company
- **proprietary company (also known as a private company):** a company limited by shares, or unlimited by share capital, and with not more than 50 non-employee shareholders
- **prospectus:** a disclosure document setting out the nature and objects of an issue of shares or debentures created by a company and inviting the public to subscribe (buy) to them
- **public company:** a company which is able to invite the public to invest in its shares
- **receiver:** a person appointed by a creditor or the court who enters into the possession of the property of a company in accordance with the powers granted by the creditors or the court
- **replaceable rules:** basic rules relating to the internal management of a company
- **shares:** choses in action (intangible personal property) and the parts into which the capital of a company is divided
- ***ultra vires*:** beyond the power.

what if . . .

You and a friend are starting a new business and your accountant advises you both to use a company to operate the business because it will be safer. How might a company protect you should the business fail? Do directors of a company have any special duties and obligations?

While most small businesses are started with a basic structure such as that of a sole trader or a partnership, it is common for them to convert to a company to obtain taxation benefits, for protection from creditors and eventually to widen the scope for gaining additional capital.

This chapter provides an overview of the nature of a company as well as outlining some of the important aspects of company law and concludes with an examination of incorporated associations.

COMPANIES

Company—a legal entity separate from its members

The word 'company' or 'corporation' is applied to various kinds of association in which a number of persons finance a business enterprise or joint undertaking. It has a perpetual existence and is a **separate legal entity**. It is separate from the persons who operate or are employed by it, as well as its shareholders, and is incorporated under the *Corporations Act 2001* (Cth).

WEB RESOURCE

The government body which is responsible for the administration and policing of the law relating to companies is the **Australian Securities and Investments Commission, a Commonwealth government body: http://www,asic.gov.au**

***SALOMON V. SALOMON & CO. LTD* [1897] AC 22**

Salomon and his sons worked for the business. A company was incorporated to give them a share of the business. At that time, legislation required the company to have a minimum of seven members, so Salomon, his wife and five children each held one share as nominees. Salomon lent the company $2000 and received a debenture as security for the loan. He then borrowed $10 000 from a mortgagee and lent this to the company. As security for the loan, the lender received a debenture from the company. The loans were not enough to save the company and it went into receivership and subsequently, liquidation. The liquidator found that there were insufficient assets to pay all the firm's debts.

ISSUE: Could the liquidator pay the unsecured creditors ahead of the debenture holders—Salomon and the lender? Could he successfully argue that the debentures were invalid because of fraud? He argued that the loan from the mortgagee was to Salomon and not to the company, and regarding Salomon's debenture, that the company and Salomon were one and the same person.

DECISION: The company was a legal entity separate from its shareholders, so the debts of the company were not the debts of Salomon. A person could be both a shareholder and a creditor of a company and as a valid debenture holder he was entitled to be paid ahead of other creditors.

LIFTING THE VEIL OF INCORPORATION

The concept of Separate Legal Entity is often referred to as the 'veil of incorporation' that is, the shareholders and the directors are completely separate and distinct from the company as though a veil hides and separates them. In exceptional cases the Courts may lift this 'veil of incorporation' and give rights and obligations to parties who would not otherwise have those rights and obligations. An example is where the company has been created in order to facilitate a fraud.

***GILFORD MOTORS V. HORNE* (1933) CH 936**

The Managing Director of Gilford Motors had an employment agreement which provided that he would not solicit or entice customers away from Gilford Motors. He resigned and formed a new company which solicited customers of his former employers. Horne argued that the employment agreement was between himself and

Gilford Motors and that he was not approaching the customers of Gilford Motors, his new company was and it was not bound by the employment agreement.

ISSUE: Should a company structure be allowed to be used specifically to permit an individual to avoid existing legal obligations?

DECISION: The new company had been formed as a 'cloak or sham' and a 'device or stratagem' to enable breaches of the agreement between Horne and his former employer. The veil of incorporation should be lifted. Injunctions were granted against both Horne and his new company prohibiting them from approaching the clients of Gilford Motors.

The 'veil of incorporation' may also be raised where the company is a party to a relationship of Principal and Agent, however, the mere fact that a company is merely one entity in a group of companies does not in itself mean the courts will lift the 'veil of incorporation'.

PIONEER CONCRETE SERVICES LTD V. YELNAH P/L (1987) 5 ACLL 467

Hi Quality Concrete (Holdings) P/L was the holding company for a large group of companies including Hi Quality Concrete (NSW) P/L which was a wholly owned subsidiary.

The holding company and the subsidiary entered into a deed with the plaintiff wherein 'Hi Quality' was defined as Hi Quality Concrete (NSW) P/L that is, NOT Hi Quality Concrete (Holdings) P/L.

The holding company entered into transactions which were alleged to be in breach of the deed. The subsidiary denied any breach of the agreement on the basis that it was not a party to these subsequent transactions and the holding company was not a party to the deed with the plaintiff—the deed defined 'Hi Quality' as Hi Quality Concrete NSW.

ISSUE: Are companies in a 'group' separate from each other or are they agents for each other?

DECISION: The Supreme Court of New South Wales held that the specific provision in the deed defining 'Hi Quality' meant the holding company was specifically excluded from the provisions in the deed and therefore could not be in breach of the deed.

COMMENT: The court was unable to justify lifting the corporate veil because it could not infer an agency relationship or a sham or facade. The company had not been formed for the sole or dominant purpose of evading a contractual or fiduciary obligation. The court would not lift the corporate veil when it appeared that there was a good commercial purpose for having separate companies in the group performing different functions even though the ultimate controllers would refer to the whole group as one.

! CAUTION NOTE

Because companies are legal entities, they must operate through others who are agents, directors and managers and who will not incur personal liability.

NATURE OF COMPANIES

To incorporate or not to incorporate is a difficult question for many businesses (see Table 27.1). However, under the *Corporations Act*, with the notable exception of professional partnerships, firms are prohibited from carrying on business for gain once they grow beyond 20 persons unless they form themselves into a company.

A company must employ real people to carry out its activities. Buying, selling, engaging staff, paying debts and so on are tasks performed on behalf of a company by its agents, directors and managers. These persons (if authorised) can delegate authority to others to bind the company, but do not become personally liable for contracts made by themselves or those other persons unless a contracting party is unwilling to accept the company as a creditor. It is not unusual nowadays for financial bodies, traders and manufacturers dealing with companies (many are operating with paid-up capital of only $2) to insist that a director or other member of the company give a personal guarantee for payment of money owed, particularly loans.

Classification by liability—s. 115

Most companies are incorporated with limited liability

Most companies are incorporated with limited liability. This means that the liability of the members is limited to the extent determined by the type of company.

Companies limited by shares

Limited by shares—liability of members limited to amount unpaid on shares

This is a company formed on the principle that the **liability** of its members (shareholders) is **limited** to the amount (if any) unpaid on the face value of their shareholding at the time funds are required to meet the company commitments (see Figure 27.1).

Such companies may be:

- **public** companies which are able to invite the public to invest in shares; or
- **proprietary** companies most of which are small businesses. These are the most common form of company in Australia today.

As the members of a company limited by shares have limited liability, creditors of such a company **do not** have access to the personal property of the members if the company fails. This is why a company must have 'Limited' or 'Ltd' after its name. It is a warning to creditors about the extent of liability of the members of the company.

Table 27.1 Advantages and disadvantages of a company

	Advantages	*Disadvantages*
1	A separate legal entity from the shareholders or members as well as those who control its operations	Cost of establishment and ongoing fees are expensive
2	Limited liability	Onerous administrative requirements required by law
3	Perpetual succession	Limited management role for shareholders
4	The company can sue and be sued	Possible loss of control of the company to shareholders
5	Transferability of shares	Onerous legal responsibilities imposed on company officers and directors
6	Taxation benefits	Can be onerous reporting requirements

Companies limited by guarantee

The liability of the members is limited to the amount which each undertakes to pay to the company in the event that the company is wound up, not upon their acquisition of membership. These types of companies are often formed by non-profit associations such as sporting clubs or other associations which use any profits they make for the advancement of the given association's objectives. An alternative to this type of company is incorporation under the association's incorporation legislation of the relevant state (see pp. 582–583).

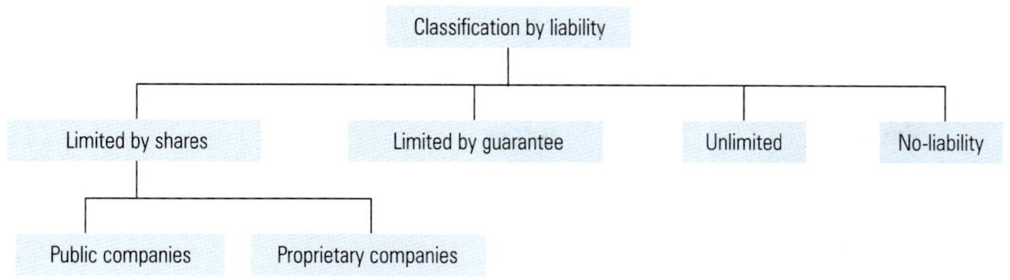

FIGURE 27.1 *Classification of companies by liability*

Unlimited liability companies

In this type of company the members have no limit on their liability to contribute to the assets of the company in order to discharge the company's liabilities. Legal firms often use this type of company because professional association rules give the members some of the advantages of incorporation.

No-liability companies

Members do not incur a liability to pay calls on the unpaid portion of any shares that they hold. Only mining companies can use this structure and part of their name must include the words 'No liability' or 'NL'.

Effect of incorporation on shareholders

A shareholder in any company should be aware of their personal liability. Limited liability is an important result of incorporation. Not only are shareholders made aware of their own personal liability in regard to their shareholding, but the principle also allows the transfer of a shareholder's interest in the company. The person who takes a transfer of shares does so subject to the same rights and liabilities as the person from whom the shares are purchased.

> **!** CAUTION NOTE
> *Limited liability is an important reason for incorporation as it offers a shareholder protection from liability.*

What are the functions of a modern company?

Today, from a functional point of view, there are five distinct types of company:

- Companies formed for reasons **other than the profits of their members**. For example, for social, charitable or quasi-charitable purposes.
- Companies which enable a **single trader or a small body of partners** to carry on a business. Incorporation is a device for obtaining legal personality for the business and divorcing its liability from that of its members, despite the fact that the members retain control and share the profits. The 'one-person' company is a frequent source of danger to creditors and is formed mainly for taxation purposes.
- Companies formed to enable the **investing public to share in the profits** of the enterprise without actually taking part in its management. These are economically the most important registered companies.
- Companies **established by statute**. These companies carry out administrative duties as required by particular Acts of Parliament. Examples include local municipal councils and electricity commissions or boards. They are entitled to sue and be sued. Where they are state bodies acting in the interests of the public in general, their funding is guaranteed by the state.
- **Subsidiaries of public companies**.

> activebook
> To help you to remember and understand the topics covered so far, and for links to legal websites, refer to your online activebook. Model answers provide feedback to problems and exercises.

Public or proprietary companies?

Companies can be classified according to membership into:

- **proprietary company**; and
- **public company** which may or may not be listed on the stock exchange.

This form of classification is done to separate those companies in which the public has invested money from those which it has not (see Figure 27.2). Proprietary companies are relieved of many of the statutory duties and obligations that confront public companies.

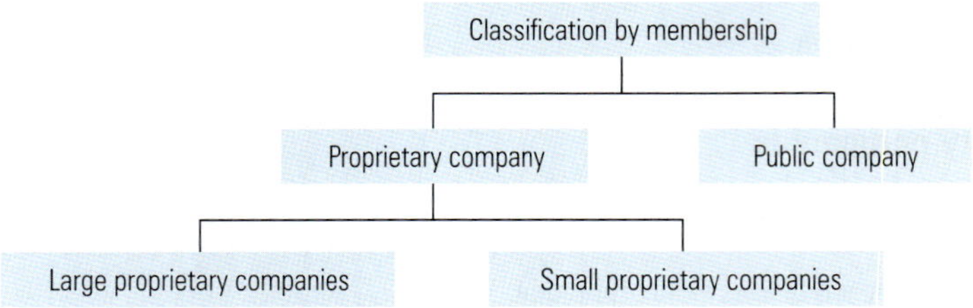

FIGURE 27.2 *Classification of companies by membership*

Proprietary companies

The vast majority of registered companies are proprietary companies. They are generally relatively small in size—well-suited for small to medium-sized businesses, although some are subsidiaries of large public companies, controlling sizeable assets.

There is now a distinction between large and small proprietary companies for reporting purposes

The *Corporations Act 2001*, s. 45A, draws a distinction between large and small proprietary companies for reporting purposes. A large proprietary company is one that satisfies any two of the following three tests:

- gross operating revenue of more than $10 million for the financial year;
- gross assets of more than $5 million at the end of the financial year; or
- 50 or more full-time employees (or their part-time equivalent) at the end of the financial year.

Large proprietary companies have to prepare and lodge audited accounts with the Australian Securities and Investment Commission (ASIC) annually. **Whether a company is considered to be small or large can change from year to year.**

Public companies

Public companies are any companies other than proprietary companies

A public company is any company other than a proprietary company. **A public company may or may not be listed.** Where it is listed on a stock exchange, the **marketability** of its shares will normally be better because of the information that a company must provide before listing will be allowed. Listing also facilitates valuation of that security and determination of its value for stock option and debt financing purposes.

Incorporation

The *Company Law Review Act 1997* provides a new one-step procedure for registering a company. Directors, secretaries and members listed with their consent on the application form are automatically appointed upon the company's registration. Upon lodgement of the application, which can now be done electronically via the ASIC site, ASIC is empowered to register the company and issue a certificate of incorporation.

> **!** CAUTION NOTE
>
> *Memorandum and articles have been replaced by a constitution or 'replaceable rules'.*

The old rules governing the operation of the company in the form of a memorandum and articles of association are no longer required. As a result of the *Company Law Review Act*, the *Corporations Act* contains numerous 'replaceable rules' which now govern the internal management of the company. A company can adopt a constitution, displacing some or all of these rules. Existing companies will continue to have their memorandum and articles as their constitution unless they repeal them, but as from 1 July 1998, the 80 000 new companies registered each year now operate under the new rules. New companies will continue to be allocated a unique nine digit Australian Company Number which must appear on every 'public document' and which may be used also as the company name. Alternatively, a new company may choose and register a name with ASIC. It should be noted that if a company carries on business under a name that is different from its company name, it will have to register the business name in the states or territories in which it wishes to trade under the relevant business names legislation (see Chapter 29). The requirement of a common seal is now optional.

Fund raising

Prospectus—invites members of the public to subscribe capital to the company

A disclosure document, such as a prospectus, is an invitation to members of the public to subscribe for shares or debentures in a company. It can be issued once a company has been incorporated. A proprietary company does not issue a prospectus, because its shares are not offered to the public.

The fund-raising provisions of the *Corporations Act*, s. 710, set out certain minimum requirements which must be contained in a prospectus. This ensures that prospective investors are fully and accurately informed about the company and its prospects. They will then be in a better position to make a decision whether or not to invest.

A prospectus must first be lodged with ASIC and if it is not accurate, ASIC will issue a Stop Order

The *Corporations Act*, s. 706, provides that a disclosure document must be lodged with ASIC before it is issued to potential investors. This enables ASIC to check that all legislative requirements have been met and that there are no misleading statements or omissions that could mislead investors. Some disclosure documents are required to be registered by ASIC.

If a disclosure document is lodged or registered and it appears to ASIC that:

- it contains misleading or deceptive information; or
- it contains a material misrepresentation;

a Stop Order can be issued.

Company capital

A company obtains its capital from two sources (see Figure 27.3):

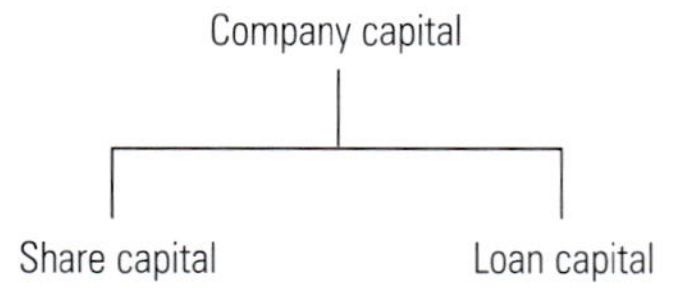

FIGURE 27.3 *Company capital*

Share capital

Shares are the stated proportions into which the capital of a company is divided. They are the interest of the shareholder in a company measured in monetary terms. As such, they are *choses in action* because they are personal property of an intangible nature. This means that the owner of the shares has certain recognisable rights that are enforceable by law (e.g., to buy, sell and bequeath the shares).

The owner of a share is entitled to:

- receive the stated proportion of the profits of the company, as dividend, when and if declared; and

- take part in the management of the company and receive a proportionate return of capital on its winding-up.

Shares no longer have a par value, but a company will be required to have authorised share capital.

Allotment

When a company wishes to raise capital by the issue of shares or other securities, the normal rules of contract apply. The 'offer' by the company is only an invitation to treat, and so it is the applicant who makes the offer upon sending in the completed application form plus payment to the company. Acceptance takes place when the directors decide to allot shares and the applicant is sent a notice of allotment. A person generally becomes a member of a company when their name is entered in the register of members that the *Corporations Act* requires all companies to keep.

> **!** CAUTION NOTE
> *Shareholders enter into a contractual relationship with the company when they purchase its shares.*

Sometimes a company may issue different classes of shares, each of which may have different rights attached to them, such as:

- different voting rights;
- preference in payment of dividends;
- dividends at a fixed rate; and
- priority in return of capital or distribution of surplus assets on winding-up.

There was an underlying principle in company law that companies must maintain their share capital. This was called the rule in *Trevor v. Whitworth* (1887) 12 App Cas 409, which referred to the issued capital of a company and generally prohibited a company from returning capital to its members without court confirmation. However, the *Corporations Act* now allows a company to reduce its share capital by buying its shares back from its members:

- if it is fair and reasonable to the company's shareholders as a whole;
- if it does not materially prejudice the company's ability to pay its creditors; and
- if it is approved by shareholders by an appropriate resolution.

Transfer of shares

Shares are a *chose in action* and can be transferred when the shareholder wishes

Because shares are *choses in action* or intangible personal property, shareholders can usually deal with them in any way they wish, subject to the *Corporations Act* and the constitution of the company. Shareholders are presumed to have the right to transfer their shares when they wish. This is done by the transferor (seller) signing an instrument of transfer and handing over their share certificate to the transferee (buyer) who also signs the instrument of transfer and lodges it together with the share certificate with the company. The company then removes the transferor's name from the register of members, places the transferee's name on it and sends out a share certificate in the transferee's name, stating the number of shares held. Many small companies restrict the right of members to transfer their shares. This is often because the other members only want new members of whom they approve. All **proprietary companies** must restrict the right to transfer shares through their **constitution**.

An alternative to share issues—loan capital

A company can also raise capital by borrowing. This is know as **loan capital** or **loan finance**. Determining the financial needs of the company and how they are to be met is a management decision on the part of the board of directors. Generally a company can borrow money in much the same way as an individual. For example, it can borrow from a financial institution, a moneylender, or it can obtain credit from a trade creditor. In addition, companies can also issue debentures. A **debenture** is a document whereby **a company acknowledges a debt**.

A debenture holder is a creditor of the company

A **debenture holder** is a **creditor** of the company, and the **debenture certificate** always contains an acknowledgement of the company's indebtedness. The relationship of a debenture holder to the company is that of a moneylender; the money is lent at a fixed rate of interest for a stated term. As a result, the debenture holder is not:

- a member of the company;
- entitled to participate in the affairs of the company; nor
- entitled to vote at general meetings.

The purpose of issuing debentures is to raise ready money for the use of the company without increasing its nominal capital. Most people willing to lend money wish to have some form of security for the loan. This may be either:

Fixed charge—attaches to specific assets

- **A fixed charge**
  This is a charge **attached to specific assets** such as land and buildings.
- **A floating charge**
  Here a company grants **security over all its assets**, including trading stock, which 'floats' above the assets of the company and which may be sold and replaced by new trading stock. In the event of the company defaulting under the debenture, the charge stops 'floating' and attaches itself to the assets of the company at that time. This is called **crystallisation**.
  The **holder** of a floating charge has no **legal or equitable interest** in the specific assets of the company while the charge is floating. It is for this reason that a borrowing company can freely deal with its assets, subject of course to the charge, in the ordinary course of business.
  Where a company has granted a floating charge over assets and later grants a fixed charge over the same assets (this is viewed as still being in the ordinary course of the company's business), the **fixed charge has priority** in the event of a winding up except where the floating charge had crystallised **before** the fixed charge was attached.

Registration of charges: s. 262

In order to ensure the company pays a debt or complies with some other type of obligation the company may provide one or more of its assets as security. This type of transaction is referred to as a charge. A charge is the right to have a particular item of property sold in order to raise money, that is, security for the loan.

A company that has transferred rights in property to another person but has retained possession can give a false appearance of absolute ownership. This false appearance could enable it to obtain credit it would not have been given, had the truth been known. It is for this reason the Act requires the company to make sure the charge is registered within 45 days: s. 263.

Registration of the following charges is required by s. 262:

- Floating charge
- Uncalled share capital
- Personal chattels
- Goodwill
- Book debt.

The obligation to register does not apply to a charge involving a lien, a pledge, or land.

Under s. 266 a registrable charge is void as a security against the liquidator or official manager unless:

1 notice is lodged within the commission within 45 days; or
2 not later than 6 months before the commencement of winding up/official management.

Section 280 sets out the following priorities of charges:

1 Registered charge has priority over:
   (a) all unregistered charges created after it;
   (b) all registered charges registered after it; and
   (c) all unregistered charges created before it unless the holder of the registered charge knew of the unregistered charge.
2 Unregistered charges have priority in the order in which they are created.

It can be seen that there is a very definite advantage for the creditor to register the charge quickly. As a result, although

s. 263 imposes the obligation on the company to ensure the charge is registered it is usual practice for the creditor who is granted the charge to register it.

> **!** CAUTION NOTE
> *Floating charge—does not attach to company assets until the company defaults, so until that time lender has no legal or equitable interest in the assets.*

Special rights of a debenture holder

Debenture holders have special rights over and above shareholders

Debenture holders have the following rights:

- They may sue the company if at any time payment of either interest or principal is not made in accordance with the loan agreement.
- They may appoint a receiver whose job it is to seize the secured property from which the debenture holder's debt is paid.
- The *Corporations Act* provides that they may present a petition to have the company wound up.
- They are entitled to prove their debt. Their claims rank before those of the shareholders.
- An application may be made to appoint a liquidator on behalf of debenture holders of a company which is being wound up by the court.

Management

Directors' duties arise from the nature of their fiduciary relationship with the company

The constitution invariably provides that the power of management vests in the board of directors. This gives the board of directors some flexibility in how the company will be managed, assuming that they comply with the *Corporations Act*, because the shareholders only have limited control over the board through the election of directors. Because the board of directors is empowered to manage the company's business, the law imposes certain duties on directors. These duties arise from the fiduciary nature of the relationship between directors and their company. This means that directors are under a **duty to act in good faith** for the **benefit** of the company. Thus, directors must avoid placing themselves in conflict of interest situations or exercising their powers for improper purposes.

Duties of a director

The role of the director of a company is to oversee the management of the company on behalf of its members. The director is responsible for ensuring that the company maximises its value for members and in doing so they are responsible for ensuring that the company meets its contractual and other legal obligations in a prompt and timely manner.

The precise role of directors is dependent on the constitution of the company. In large public companies, directors are unlikely to have involvement in the day-to-day management of the company. They will more than likely be non-executive directors whose function is to bring an independent view to, and a broader outlook on, the company's decision-making processes. In small and medium-sized proprietary companies, the directors may have a more hands-on role where they will be involved in the day-to-day management of the company.

The *Corporations Act* does not make any distinctions between the types of director or the extent of their involvement in the management of the company. It establishes a number of general principles that, along with the constitution of the company, the common law and other legislation, establish the range of duties and obligations of directors.

> **!** CAUTION NOTE
> *Directors are responsible for the management of the company on behalf of the members although their precise role is dependent on the constitution.*

Common law duties

Common law duties of directors are:

- contractual
- equitable
- tortious.

Contractual duties

Executive directors are employed under contracts of service which will have both express and implied terms relating to their duties, including a duty of care in the performance of the contract (see *Lister v. Romford Ice and Cold Storage Co. Ltd* on p. 223).

Equitable duties

In equity, a director's relationship with the company is regarded as fiduciary in nature. This means that directors owe a duty of loyalty and a duty to act with reasonable care, skill and diligence in performing their functions on behalf of the company. The duty of loyalty covers four specific areas:

- **Good faith**

  Directors are required to act in good faith for what they believe is for the benefit of the company as a whole. The court may intervene if an act is one that no reasonable director could regard as being in the interests of the company, or if the company is near insolvency and the interests of the creditors are not being considered.
- **Proper purpose**

  Directors of a company are **fiduciary agents**, and a power conferred upon them cannot be exercised in order to obtain some private advantage. Directors under this duty can be in breach even where they honestly believe their actions are in the best interests of the company.

***WHITEHOUSE V. CARLTON HOTEL PTY LTD* (1987) 5 ACLC 421**

New shares were to be issued by Mr Whitehouse, the permanent governing director who, under the constitution, had full powers normally vested in a board of directors. The purpose of the share issue was to defeat the voting power of existing shareholders by creating a new majority.

ISSUE: If there is more than one purpose for a directors action will the action be invalid if the shares would not have been allotted 'but for' an impermissible purpose?

DECISION: The High Court held that where there was more than one purpose of a decision to allot shares arrived at by directors it was not appropriate to look for the dominant or substantial purpose. '. . . The allotment will be invalidated if the impermissible purpose was causative in the sense that, but for its presence, "the power would not have been exercised" '. It was irrelevant that the director believed his action to be in the best interest of the company. The constitution of the company may determine the legitimate parameters of directors' behaviour.

- **Exercise discretion**

  As a general rule, directors cannot limit the exercise of their future discretions (e.g., to vote in a certain way in the future at board meetings).
- **Conflicts of interest**

  Because directors are **fiduciaries**, they must take care to avoid situations arising where their duties to the company and their personal duties are in conflict. This duty is strictly applied and it extends to a position whereby directors should not even **appear** to be acting in their own interests.

GREEN V. BESTOBELL INDUSTRIES PTY LTD [1982] WAR 1

Bestobell Industries Pty Ltd had obtained the contract for a major part of Stage 1 of a construction project. Green was a manager of Bestobell. Using a shelf company, Green submitted a tender for Stage 2 of the project, that tender was the lowest. The tender submitted by Bestobell for the same work was third lowest. Green's company obtained the contract and Bestobell Industries Pty Ltd sought to have Green and his company account for the profits made.

ISSUE: Should directors be able to acquire for themselves a business opportunity sought by the company?

DECISION: The Supreme Court of Western Australia held that Green had breached his fiduciary duty in attempting to acquire for himself a business opportunity which he knew would be sought by his employer, he was therefore liable to account to the respondent for the profit derived. Because Green's company had participated in his breach of duty it was also liable to account.

Degree of care and skill of a director is objective

Both executive and non-executive directors are subject to an equitable duty of care, skill and diligence. The degree of skill and care required of a director is that which may be reasonably expected of a person of their knowledge and experience and is an **objective standard**. Factors that could be considered relevant in determining if the director has fulfilled his duty include whether:

- the director has made enquiries regarding company affairs;
- the director has attended relevant company meetings; and
- reports, advice and opinions have been given by competent, honest staff.

ASC V. GALLAGHER (1993) 11 ACLC 286

Rothwells, a merchant bank, was experiencing a severe liquidity crisis and was also under investigation by Government authorities. The company subsequently failed.

One of the directors had written a number of reports outlining the problems the bank had with its loan portfolio. This information was not passed on to Gallagher, one of the other directors (a non-executive director).

Rothwells entered into negotiations to liquidate its loan portfolio and also mortgaged fees owed to it. Gallagher discussed these matters with the executive chairman of the company and expressed his concern over a number of board meetings that had been cancelled. Gallagher was on the board of the company to whom the fees were mortgaged and as such stood down from discussions on those matters.

The Australian Securities and Investments Commission subsequently commenced action against Gallagher for failing to exercise reasonable care and diligence in the discharge of his duty and that he failed to reasonably inform himself of the financial affairs of Rothwells.

The Australian Securities and Investments Commission alleged that Gallagher did not make sufficient enquiries into the financial position of the company. The case was dismissed by the magistrate and the ASIC appealed.

ISSUE: Are the duties of non-executive directors to inform themselves the same as those for executive directors?

DECISION: The Full Court of the Western Australian Supreme Court dismissed the appeal and made the following findings:

- Non-executive directors had a duty to inform themselves so that they could make independent judgements.
- Enquiries they were expected to make depended on the extent to which they were put on inquiry.
- To determine whether a director had performed their duties in a reasonable manner it was necessary to consider what an ordinary person with the knowledge and experience of the director might be expected to do if acting on their behalf.
- It was reasonable for Gallagher to rely on other directors providing him with important information.
- It was reasonable for Gallagher to rely on his communications with the chairman without the need to make further enquiries.

Tortious duties

Tortious duties—directors owe a duty of care and diligence to the company

Directors may be liable in negligence for breach of a duty of care and diligence to the company. A director has a duty to become familiar with the business of the company and how it is run. To achieve that end, a director must take whatever steps necessary to be satisfied that the company is being properly run.

Statutory duties

Corporations Act

Under the *Corporations Act*, a 'director' is any person who occupies or acts in the position of director, whatever they may want to call themselves, and whether validly appointed or not. Unless the contrary is stated in the company's constitution, the *Corporations Act* provides that directors are responsible for managing the business of the company and in doing so may exercise all the powers of the company. The *Corporations Act* has adopted the common law fiduciary duties of directors and requires them (and all company employees) to:

- act in good faith: s. 181;
- exercise reasonable care and diligence: s. 180;

ASIC v. Rich **[2003] NSWSC 85**

G was the non-executive Chair of One.Tel, he was also Chair of the Finance and Audit Committee. One.Tel failed and ASIC brought proceedings under s. 180(1)(b) of the *Corporations Act* against four of the company's six directors. G argued that as a non-executive director, he should have been treated in the same way as the other two non-executive directors against whom no action was taken. He also argued that the Chair of the Board of Directors had no greater responsibilities or duties under s. 180 than other directors.

ISSUE: Should the s. 180 duty of care and diligence be applied differently to different directors depending on their personal skills and experience as well as their roles and responsibilities within the company?

DECISION: The Supreme Court of New South Wales found that the responsibilities of a director would include any arrangements flowing from the experience and skills that the director brought to their office as well as any arrangements within the Board or between the director and the executive management regarding the work the director was expected to do.

- not make improper use of the company's information: s. 184; and
- not make improper use of their position as directors: s. 182.

CUMMINGS & ANOR V. CLAREMONT PETROLEUM NL (1993) 11 ACLC 125

Two directors of Claremont Petroleum NL used their dominant position in the company to appoint their private firms as consultants to the company. The consultancy agreements provided for their use of luxury cars and generous termination penalties. The directors took no steps to ensure an independent appraisal of the terms of their agreement with the company.

A new board was appointed to Claremont Petrolum NL and the private consultancy agreements were terminated. Under the consultancy agreements the directors were entitled to keep the luxury cars free of cost and were entitled to extremely generous termination penalties. One of the directors subsequently resigned, the other failed to get re-elected.

The company sought to recover the termination penalties and also alleged that the directors were in breach of the equivalent of s. 182 relating to the use of position for an improper advantage.

The directors argued that the benefits were reasonable.

ISSUE: Is the directors' opinion of what is reasonable and proper the correct test for improper use of position?

DECISION: The Full Court of the Federal Court held that the directors were in breach of the Act and that they were liable to repay the amounts to the company.

Whether the benefits due to the directors on termination were reasonable or not, was only one factor to consider in examining a breach of the directors' duties. Even if it were held that the benefits were reasonable, that alone would not stop the Court in deciding that they were in breach of their duties. The manner, the extent and level of the benefits were important factors to consider.

Sections 191 to 194 impose a duty on directors to disclose any personal interest they may have in a contract or other matter in which the company is or may become involved. For example, a director of a public company must not be present, or vote, at a board meeting in relation to a matter in which they may have a personal interest.

Business judgement rule

Section 180(1) imposes an obligation on directors to exercise care and diligence when exercising their decision-making responsibilities. This statutory obligation is the equivalent of the similar obligation at common law and equity. In order to clarify what is expected of a director when exercising care and diligence the Legislature set out the Business Judgement Rule.

Business judgement means any decision to take or not take action in respect of a matter relevant to the business operations of the corporation—s. 180(3).

A director or other officer of a corporation who makes a business judgement is taken to meet the care and diligence requirements of s. 180(1) and equivalent duties at common law and equity if they:

1. make the judgement in good faith for a proper purpose; **and**
2. do not have a material personal interest in the subject matter of the judgement; **and**
3. inform themselves about the subject matter; **and**
4. rationally believe that the judgement is in the best interests of the corporation.

The director or officers belief that the judgement is in the best interest of the corporation is a rational one unless the belief is one that no reasonable person in their position would hold.

Duty to prevent insolvent trading: s. 588G

Section 588G of the *Corporations Act* imposes a duty on the director of a company to prevent insolvent trading by the company. A director contravenes the section if, when the company incurs the debt, there are reasonable grounds **for suspecting** that the company is insolvent or would become insolvent. Defences are that:

- At the time when the debt was incurred, the director had reasonable grounds to expect, and did expect, that the company was solvent at that time.
- The director had reasonable grounds to rely on information provided by a competent and reliable person that the company was solvent.
- A director did not take part in the management of the company owing to illness or for some other good reason.
- The director took all reasonable steps to prevent the company from incurring the debt.

In *ASIC v. Plymin, Elliott and Harrison* [2003] VSC 123 the Victorian Supreme Court accepted the Australian Securities and Investments Commission's argument that in order to become aware of reasonable grounds for suspecting insolvency, the reasonable person referred to in s. 588G(2)(b) would obtain from management on a regular basis:

- a list of debtors and creditors with details of amount and age of debt;
- details of negotiations with creditors whose debts were outstanding beyond normal trading terms;
- a statement of financial performance (Profit and Loss Account); and
- cash flow statements.

It is not a defence for a director to remain entirely ignorant of the operations of the company. See *Morley v. Statewide Tobacco Service Ltd* (1992) 10 ACLC 1233—Chapter 32 on Insolvency.

It should be noted that the liability of a director for debts incurred while the company is insolvent is an exception to the concept of the separate legal entity of a company and limited liability.

Other legislation

The *Corporations Act* is not the only legislation to impose duties on directors. For example, the environmental protection legislation in a number of the states and territories imposes obligations on directors and companies.

Breach of duty

Where a director is in breach of their duty, as a general rule only the company can bring any action. An exception is where the company is being wound up, in which case the liquidator can **bring an action** in the name of the company. This occurs because the company is a legal entity in its own right, separate from its members.

The company's remedies will depend on the circumstances and it may seek any of the following:

- damages or compensation;
- account of profits;
- rescission of contract; or
- return of profit.

Civil penalty

Civil penalties apply to situations where an officer of the company has failed to comply with the Act relating to the management of the company. Civil penalties allow the court to prohibit the person from managing a company and/or impose a fine. Under s. 1317E, the following sections involve civil penalty provisions:

180, 181, 182, 183	Duty and liability of officers (act honestly, etc.)
209(2)	Related parties rules
242L(2), 256D(3), 259F(2), 260D(2)	Share capital transactions
344(1)	Requirements for financial reports
588G(2)	Insolvent trading
601FC(5), 601FD(3), 601FE(3), 601FG(3), 601JD(3)	Duties of members
674(2) or 675(2)	Continuous disclosure

1041A	Market manipulation
1041B(1)	False trading and market rigging
1041D	Dissemination of information about illegal transactions
1043A(1) and (2), Subclause 29(6) of Schedule 4	Insider trading

Under s. 1317G, if the court is satisfied that a person has contravened a civil penalty provision, the court is to declare that the person has contravened the provision and may also make an order of a pecuniary penalty up to $200 000. This pecuniary penalty will not apply unless contravention:

- materially prejudices the interests of the corporation or members; or
- materially prejudices the corporation's ability to pay its creditors; or
- is serious.

The penalty is a civil debt payable to the Australian Securities and Investments Commission.

The court may order a person to compensate a corporation for damages suffered; damages includes profits made by the person: ss. 1317H and 1317HA.

In hearing an application for a civil penalty order the court is to apply the rules of evidence and procedures used in civil matters: s. 1317L.

> **!** CAUTION NOTE
>
> *As a general rule only a company can sue a director for breach of duty.*

Disclosure of company accounts

The policy of the *Corporations Act* is to require companies to make a minimum degree of disclosure. Public companies and large proprietary companies must prepare a financial report and a director's report each financial year.

COMPANIES IN FINANCIAL DIFFICULTY

Companies in financial difficulties should be placed under administration

Companies which get into financial difficulties may be placed in administration, liquidation or receivership, for a brief overview of the impact and operation of these procedures refer to Chapter 32.

ASSOCIATIONS

There are two forms of association that can be readily identified by most people.

Common law unincorporated associations

Associations may be unincorporated or incorporated

Common law unincorporated associations are an association of two or more people organised for a common purpose and which may or may not include the carrying on of a business with a view to a profit, including sporting and social clubs. It has no independent legal existence as it has no existence apart from its members. Thus, if the association wishes to own property, this is usually done through trustees. If it wishes to sue, this will have to be done by the members on behalf of the association. On the other hand, it can't be sued, but the individual members of the association can be. The liability of the members is limited to the amount of their subscription as required under the rules of the association, unless the constitution or rules of the association say otherwise. However, the position of committee members is that they are personally liable to third parties in contract, though this may be able to be offset by the exercise of an equitable *lien* against the association's common fund.

> **!** CAUTION NOTE
> *Committee members of unincorporated associations may be sued personally although they may have an equitable* lien *against the common fund.*

Statutory incorporated associations

The only difference between the incorporated association and the unincorporated association is that here the members have chosen to incorporate under the associations incorporation legislation of the states or territories (see Table 27.2):

Table 27.2 Associations incorporation legislation of the states and territories

Source	*Statute*
Australian Capital Territory	*Associations Incorporation Act 1991*
New South Wales	*Associations Incorporation Act 1984*
Northern Territory	*Associations Act 2003*
Queensland	*Associations Incorporation Act 1981*
South Australia	*Associations Incorporation Act 1985*
Tasmania	*Associations Incorporation Act 1964*
Victoria	*Associations Incorporation Act 1981*
Western Australia	*Associations Incorporation Act 1987*

The only proviso for incorporation is that the association is not formed for trading purposes. If the association is formed for trading purposes, and the membership is less than 20 members then they are going to be a partnership. If there are more than 20 members, they must be incorporated under the *Corporations Act* unless they fall within one of the exceptions.

> **!** CAUTION NOTE
> *The association should not be formed for trading purposes or it will be subject to the* Corporations Act, *if membership exceeds 20.*

Advantages of incorporation for members, both general and committee, include:

- **Protection from liabilities**. These are enforceable against the association and not the members or the committee members personally. **Liability of members** generally only extends to any **unpaid membership dues**.
- The **right to sue** (and be sued) in the association's name.
- The **right to hold property** and enter into contracts in the association's name.
- It can **make a profit** (as long as it is not divided among the members).
- It can invest and deal in any surplus funds not immediately required, as well as raising or borrowing funds.
- It has a **continuous life** with a perpetual succession. The failure of members to renew their membership does not affect the continuity of the association. An unincorporated association, on the other hand, has no existence apart from that of its members.

All states require incorporated associations to call an annual general meeting and present the financial accounts for the previous year to the members at that meeting. Audit requirements of the financial statements, however, vary between the states. Committee members are in a fiduciary relationship with the association (as they are also in an unincorporated association) and must act in the best interests of members.

WEB RESOURCES

Australian Capital Territory:
http://www.dpa.act.gov.au/ag/rgo/rgo04.html

New South Wales: information is obtainable from the Department of Fair Trading. For information on Business Names, click on 'Your Business' and from there you will find information about incorporation of associations:
http://www.dft.nsw.gov.au/

Queensland:
Model rules:
http://www.consumer.qld.gov.au/forms/association/modelrules.pdf

Incorporation:
http://www.consumer.qld.gov.au/forms/association/incorporation-6.htm

South Australia:
http://www.ocba.sa.gov.au/licensing.htm

Tasmania:
http://www.justice.tas.gov.au/breg/contact_breg.htm

Victoria:
http://www.justice.vic.gov.au/dojsite.nsf/pages/OFTBABusiness?OpenDocument

Western Australia:
http://www.fairtrading.wa.gov.au/bizn_content.htm

Corporate affairs: A useful site for extensive information on the *Corporations Act*, including a full list of company and business names, is the Australian Securities and Investment Commission site:
http://www.asic.gov.au/

REVIEW QUESTIONS

27.1 Indicate whether each of the following statements is true or false:

Statement	TRUE	FALSE
Companies, unlike sole traders and partnerships, have a perpetual existence	☐	☐
A company has a separate legal existence to its shareholders and employees	☐	☐
Companies can now be established with only one member	☐	☐
A company limited by shares may be either a public or proprietary company	☐	☐
An important result of incorporation is limited liability	☐	☐
The shareholders of a company with a share capital are its members	☐	☐
A prospectus is an invitation to members of the public to subscribe to shares or debentures	☐	☐
Under a fixed charge, the debenture holder's security is attached to specific assets of the company	☐	☐
The duties imposed on directors arise from the fiduciary nature of the relationship between themselves and the company	☐	☐
Where a director is in breach of their duty to the company, as a general rule only a shareholder can bring an action	☐	☐
The only difference between an unincorporated and incorporated association is that the latter has taken steps to incorporate itself	☐	☐
An advantage of associations incorporation legislation is that it protects members from liability	☐	☐

27.2 You have been approached by some clients for advice on whether they should form a public or proprietary company for the purchase of a multi-million dollar petroleum distributorship. What factors would you take into account in offering them advice?

27.3 What do you understand the expression 'share capital' to mean?

27.4 What is the purpose of a prospectus?

27.5 How are debentures secured?

activebook

Activebook resources include in-depth summaries with links to the relevant part of the book. For revision, add your own notes to the summaries provided by using the note-taking function.

27.6 Explain the duties of a director.

27.7 A director has a duty to avoid a conflict of interest. Explain what a conflict of interest is and how it may arise in the case of a director.

27.8 Explain why, as a general rule, only a company can bring an action against a director who is in breach of their duty.

27.9 What sorts of bodies should consider incorporation under the associations incorporation legislation of the states and territories? What reasons can you put forward for a body to incorporate under this legislation?

CRITICAL THINKING

27.1 Wellington is the managing director of corporate finance in a merchant bank called Waterloo Limited. A clause in his service agreement states that he will not deal with customers of Waterloo Limited on leaving the employment of that company.

Wellington decides to resign from Waterloo Limited and joins a syndicate with 10 friends to take over and operate for themselves a small merchant bank. The takeover is successful and Wellington is appointed finance manager of the revamped company's corporate finance department. He then approaches the customers he formerly dealt with at Waterloo Limited.

Advise Waterloo Limited as to grounds on which it can take legal action to prevent Wellington's actions.

CHAPTER

Partnerships and Joint Ventures

CHAPTER CONTENTS

activebook

This icon is used throughout the following chapter to remind you to visit the *Business Law* online activebook for additional exercises, links to legal websites, and feedback. For a detailed explanation of what is in the activebook please refer to the inside cover of this textbook. The activebook is available through OneKey.

Where do I start?
Learning path: Use the activebook to complete a pre-chapter warm-up exercise.

There are many definitions of legal terms to assist with your understanding of the material.

CHAPTER OBJECTIVES

On completion of this chapter, you should be able to:

- explain the essential characteristics of a partnership
- discuss the elements/tests for determining the existence of a partnership
- distinguish between a partnership and a joint venture
- explain how a partnership is created
- discuss the rights and liabilities of the parties in a partnership to each other and outsiders
- list the circumstances by which a partnership is dissolved and explain how partnership assets are distributed
- explain what a limited-liability partnership is.

KEY TERMS

An understanding of the following terms will help you to better understand the material in this chapter:

- **joint venture:** two or more people entering into a one-off agreement for profit
- **limited partnership:** a partnership in which there is at least one general partner with unlimited liability and one or more partners whose liability for debts and obligations of the partnership is limited
- **partnership:** the relationship which exists between persons carrying on a business in common with a view of profit.

what if . . .

You are in business with a partner. You have a written partnership agreement that states you share profits and losses equally. The business fails and the outstanding creditors are demanding that you pay their debts in full. You refuse, saying that under the agreement with your partner you are only liable for half the losses and your partner is liable for the other half. Your creditors insist that you pay the full amount because your partner has run away and left the country.

The partnership legislation (see Table 28.1) is practically uniform, with only the numbering of sections varying between the jurisdictions. However, it is still necessary to consider:

- the **common law**, particularly those aspects concerning relationships between partners and third parties; and
- **equity**, with respect to relationships between the partners themselves.

Numerous businesses in Australia have multiple owners. Until the changes to the *Corporations Law* (as it then was) in 1998 such businesses could not operate as sole proprietorships. The owners had to choose to operate as a corporation or as one of several non-corporate forms of legal entity. These included general partnerships and limited partnerships, which form the basis of this chapter. This chapter discusses the concept of a partnership, which was originally a common law concept but which today has been largely codified by statute in all state and territory jurisdictions.

This chapter also considers the test for determining the existence of a partnership, distinguishing a partnership from other outwardly similar relationships, the ways in which a partnership can be created, the relationship between partners and outsiders, the liability of partners, the rights and duties of partners to each other, dissolution of partnership and limited liability partnerships.

Table 28.1 Partnership Acts of the states and territories

Australian Capital Territory	*Partnership Act 1963*
New South Wales	*Partnership Act 1892*
Northern Territory	*Partnership Act 1997*
Queensland	*Partnership Act 1891*
South Australia	*Partnership Act 1891*
Tasmania	*Partnership Act 1891*
Victoria	*Partnership Act 1958*
Western Australia	*Partnership Act 1895*

ESSENTIAL ELEMENTS OF A PARTNERSHIP

ACT s. 4 : **NSW** s. 45 : **NT** s. 5 : **QLD** s. 3 : **SA** s. 45 : **TAS** s. 4 : **VIC** s. 5 : **WA** s. 3

IN BRIEF

The three main elements that must be present

Element	Description
Carrying on a business	A 'business' is any trade, occupation or profession and it must be an active occupation or profession continuously carried on.
Carrying on a business in common	The business must be carried on by, or on behalf of, all the partners in an agency relationship.
Carrying on a business in common with a view to profit	The parties must intend to make a profit.

A partnership is defined as the relation that exists between persons carrying on business in common with a view to making a profit. This can be broken up into three elements and all must be present.

Carrying on a business

Carrying on business suggests an active occupation

A 'business' is defined as any trade, occupation or profession. The words 'carrying on business' suggest an active occupation or profession continuously carried on.

It can be difficult to determine whether an association of persons carrying on a business in common is a partnership, a joint venture or a syndicate. However, if it can be determined from the intention and actions of the parties that the venture is an **isolated transaction** or a **single venture**, then it will not constitute carrying on a business and will **not be treated as a partnership**.

SMITH V. ANDERSON **(1880) 15 CH D 247**

A trust was formed to purchase shares and debentures in a number of companies. Smith and more than 20 others were the holders of trust certificates. Each trust holder had the right to choose the trustees who had restricted powers of management. Smith applied to wind up the trust on the basis that it had more than 20 'partners', thus making it illegal under s. 4 of the *Companies Act 1862* (UK).

ISSUE: Was the business structure, which was called a 'trust', a partnership?

DECISION: The trust was not a partnership. There was no association for the purpose of 'carrying on a business' because there was no repetition of acts. The association was formed for the purpose of doing one particular act that was never to be repeated and therefore there was no infringement of the *Companies Act.*

COMMENT: An isolated act or undertaking, even where it is entered into with a view to making a profit, will not necessarily constitute carrying on a business, unless there is some intention of repeating the venture. It would more likely be a joint venture.

CAUTION NOTE

If the venture is a single venture or an isolated transaction, it is not carrying on a business and is not a partnership.

BALLANTYNE V. RAPHAEL **(1889) 15 VLR 538**

A syndicate containing more than 20 people was formed to buy a large tract of land. It was intended to subdivide the land and sell the individual blocks at a large profit.

ISSUE: Was the syndicate a partnership or a joint venture?

DECISION: The Victorian Supreme Court held that the syndicate was not a partnership as the venture was an isolated act.

Carrying on a business in common

Partners do not have to have active role in business

The business must be operated by, or on behalf of, all the partners. It is not necessary for all the partners to take an active part in the day-to-day running of a business. In fact, it is not unusual for only one partner, or even a hired manager, to play an active role in running the business.

There must be both an agency relationship and mutual rights or obligations between the parties on whose behalf the business is being carried on.

CAUTION NOTE

There must be an agency relationship and mutual rights or obligations.

KEITH SPICER LTD V. MANSELL **[1970] 1 WLR 333**

Mansell agreed to go into the restaurant business with another person by forming a company. Before incorporation, the other person ordered furniture for the new business from Spicer Ltd. When the furniture was not paid for, Spicer sought payment from Mansell.

ISSUE: At the pre-incorporation stage were the parties in a partnership relationship such that the furniture could be said to have been bought on behalf of both Mansell and the other party?

DECISION: At the time the furniture was ordered there was no evidence to suggest that there was a partnership since they had not been carrying on business in common with a view to profit. Rather, there was evidence that there had been preparations for carrying on business as a company. Thus, Mansell was not liable for the cost of the furniture.

With a view to profit

There must be a view to profit

Partnerships must be associations formed for making a profit. The legislation is really intended to exclude such organisations as social and sporting clubs and cultural societies from the concept of partnership.

Even though these organisations make profits, they are not shared among the members and the members are not liable for debts incurred by the committee in excess of their subscriptions. Nor are the members under any obligation to indemnify those persons engaged in the management of the club if they incur liabilities in the course of running the club.

WHEN DOES A PARTNERSHIP EXIST?

To determine whether a partnership exists, all the circumstances must be examined, that is:

- Was it the **intention** of the parties to form a partnership? It does not matter what the parties call themselves if all the facts indicate that they do not satisfy the definition of a partnership in the *Partnership Act*.
- Was there a **sharing** of profits and losses accompanied by a state of **agency**?
- Did **each** have a **voice** in the management of the business, so that it could be established whether agency has been created between the parties?

If the answers to these questions are 'yes', there is hardly any doubt that a partnership exists.

! CAUTION NOTE

Look at all the facts to determine if a partnership exists—intention, agency, management.

Statutory rules

ACT s. 7 : **NSW** s. 2 : **NT** s. 6 : **QLD** s. 6 : **SA** s. 2 : **TAS** s. 7 : **VIC** s. 6 : **WA** s. 8

In addition to these common law rules, the Partnership Acts also set out other rules, framed **negatively**, to assist the courts in deciding whether a partnership exists:

Rule 1: Common ownership of property

Co-owners are not agents for each other

This re-emphasises the essential ingredient of 'carrying on a business'. Common ownership of property, whether it be as joint tenants, tenants in common or part owners, does not necessarily mean that the common owners are in partnership (see below on p. 591). Co-owners are not agents for each other and do not usually share profits or losses.

Rule 2: Sharing of gross returns

Only net profits are important

Sharing of gross returns does not of itself indicate a partnership, though sharing of net profits would be another matter.

Rule 3: Sharing of profits

Sharing of profits suggests partnership but not conclusive

In any given case, the word 'profits' can mean what the parties want it to mean and, while it does create a strong presumption that a partnership exists, it is not conclusive evidence.

The stated intention of the parties is not important. If the parties enter into a contract and say, 'It is hereby agreed that there is no partnership between us', the court will take no notice of this. As the partnership relationship is fundamentally contractual, each case must be taken on its own facts. **This means that the courts will look not only at what the parties must be taken to have intended, but also at their conduct towards each other while carrying on the business**. Thus, a relationship can be declared a partnership even though this is contrary to the intentions of the parties.

Conversely, the parties may call themselves a partnership, but in the eyes of the law they may be something else—for example, a joint venture or a syndicate.

IN BRIEF

Limits on partnership numbers

The Partnership Application Orders set the maximum number of persons in a partnership as 20. However, Partnership Application Order No. 3 permits professional associations to have higher numbers:

- up to 1000 members for accountants;
- up to 400 members for solicitors;
- up to 100 members for architects, pharmaceutical chemists or veterinary surgeons; and
- up to 50 members for actuaries, medical practitioners, sharebrokers or stockbrokers.

RELATIONSHIPS THAT CAN LOOK LIKE PARTNERSHIPS

Various associations of people possess some of, but not all, the features of a partnership (see Figure 28.1).

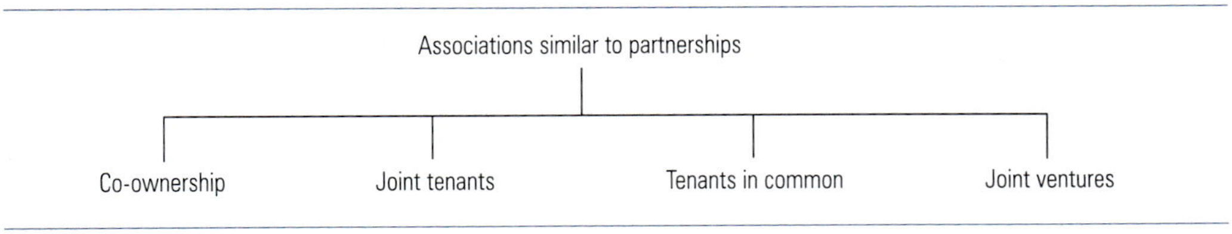

FIGURE 28.1 *Associations similar to partnerships*

Co-ownership

Co-ownership is not necessarily the result of agreement

Partnership and co-ownership are not the same thing. While partnership may include co-ownership, the reverse is not necessarily true. The main differences are:

- Partnership is the result of **agreement**, either express or implied, whereas co-ownership may not be. For example, co-ownership may be the result of a gift or an inheritance. If A by will leaves his business to his children, B and C, they are co-owners, they are not partners, even though they might share the income from the business; their relationship did not arise by way of agreement.
- A partner is the **agent of the co-partners**, while a co-owner is not the agent of the co-owners. In the example above, each can sell their share in their father's business without affecting the right of the other.
- A partner cannot transfer their share of the partnership without the consent of the other partners, but a co-owner can transfer their share without the permission of the other co-owners. This means that either B or C can sell their share of the business without needing to obtain the permission of the other.
- Partnership involves carrying on a business with a view to profit, whereas co-ownership does not.

Joint tenants

Joint tenants—separate rights between the parties but single owner against rest of world

Joint tenants have **separate rights between themselves**, but are in the position of a **single owner against the rest of the world**. The two principal features of a joint tenancy are:

- the **right of survivorship**, whereby on the death of one of the joint tenants any interest in property passes to the other joint tenants, and this process continues until there is only one survivor, who then holds the property as the sole owner; and
- the 'four unities' of **possession, interest, title and time**. That is, all joint tenants must be holders of an identical legal or equitable interest in property in equal parts that has been created at the same time, giving each joint tenant entitlement to possession of the whole property.

Tenants in common

Tenants in common—participate in co-ownership

Tenants in common have unity of possession, but not necessarily the other three unities of interest, title and time. The size of each tenant's share is fixed once and for all and is not affected by death, so that each can dispose of their undivided share by will as they wish. Such tenants also hold undivided shares, which means that they have quite separate interests but participate in co-ownership; the shares they hold in a single property have not yet been divided among them.

Joint ventures

Joint venture—a one-off commercial activity for profit

Another form of business organisation commonly encountered today is the 'joint venture', formed to undertake a commercial activity for joint profit. It can be found in such areas as mining, property development, manufacturing, publishing, entertainment and share farming.

The question often arises as to whether the relationship between the parties is a partnership, and thus whether partnership principles should apply, notwithstanding the wording that may be used by the parties, or a joint venture agreement. It can happen that a joint venture in respect of a single undertaking can still amount to a partnership where the participants are engaged in a commercial enterprise with a view to profit.

UNITED DOMINIONS CORP. LTD V. BRIAN PTY LTD **(1985) 157 CLR 1**

Three prospective participants had entered into a 'joint venture' for the development of land as a shopping centre. Prior to a formal joint venture agreement being signed between the three parties, the developer gave United Dominions three mortgages over the land for loans advanced by United Dominions for the project. Brian Pty Ltd was not aware that the mortgages contained a clause which provided that United Dominions were entitled to claim priority for repayment of all monies lent to the developer, not just for that joint venture project.

The shopping centre was subsequently sold for a large profit but Brian Pty Ltd received nothing. United Dominions claimed that the sale of the shopping centre triggered the clause in the mortgages, thus entitling them to take all the proceeds and reduce the debts owed by the developer in relation to two other projects with which Brian Pty Ltd had no association.

ISSUE: Was the agreement a joint venture or a partnership? If it was a partnership, were United Dominions entitled to take all the proceeds?

DECISION: The High Court held that the formal 'joint venture' agreement entered into between the parties was in reality a partnership, and furthermore the parties were in a fiduciary relationship even prior to this time. This placed all the parties under a fiduciary duty to refrain from obtaining any advantage without the knowledge and assent of the others. As Brian Pty Ltd was unaware of the clause in the mortgage agreements giving United Dominions the right to take all the monies from the sale of the shopping centre and offset them against other debts they had with the developer, the clause was unenforceable. As a result Brian Pty Ltd was entitled to a share of the profits.

Another example of a case where the High Court had to decide whether what was described as a 'joint venture' agreement between the parties was a partnership was *Canny Gabriel Castle Advertising Pty Ltd v. Volume Sales (Finance) Pty Ltd* (1974) 131 CLR 321. As in the United Dominions case above, the case was held on the particular facts that what the parties called 'the agreement', that is, a joint agreement, was in fact a partnership.

CANNY GABRIEL CASTLE ADVERTISING PTY LTD V. VOLUME SALES (FINANCE) PTY LTD (1974)131 CLR 321

Forth Media Management Pty Ltd had contracts with international pop stars for performances in Australia. Volume Sales (Finance) Pty Ltd agreed to finance those contracts and a written agreement was entered into in which Forth Media agreed to assign to Volume Sales a one-half interest in the contracts and to perform the contracts as a joint venture. The finance provided by Volume Sales was described as a loan to the joint venture. The profits were to be divided equally between the joint venturers after the loan had been repaid. All policy matters relating to the venture were to be agreed upon by the parties. Takings were to be paid into an account in the name of Volume Sales.

Forth Media granted Canny Gabriel Castle Advertising Pty Ltd an equitable charge over its interest in the enterprise, including Forth Media's right to takings. Forth Media defaulted and Canny Gabriel claimed a right over the takings as a secured creditor. Volume Sales disputed this right on the grounds that it was a partner with Forth Media and had a partner's equitable interest in the partnership assets (which would have priority over the later equitable charge).

ISSUE: Canny Gabriel argued that Volume Sales was a joint venturer and therefore did not have a partner's rights to the assets. In reality, was the arrangement a partnership?

DECISION: The High Court held that the arrangement was a partnership, notwithstanding that the parties had described it as a joint venture.

COMMENT: Merely calling an arrangement a joint venture or a partnership is not conclusive evidence that it is in fact a joint venture or partnership. A partnership is demonstrated by the way the parties relate to each other, rather than how they describe themselves. A partnership involves such things as joint liability for partnership contracts and torts, a principal and agent relationship between the parties and joint ownership of property.

! CAUTION NOTE

Look at what the parties do to determine if it is a partnership.

activebook

To help you to remember and understand the topics covered so far, and for links to legal websites, refer to your online activebook. Model answers provide feedback to problems and exercises.

The existence of a partnership is to be determined from what the parties do rather than what the parties call themselves. However, it may still be the case that the relationship between the parties is such that it constitutes a partnership, particularly where the parties are engaged in a commercial transaction with a view to profit.

There are **no formalities** that need to be satisfied to form a joint venture, other than those required by the business names legislation. Once it has been created, its existence will continue while the business for which it was created continues. However, the retirement of any of the parties may end the joint venture because it is not a separate legal entity.

IN BRIEF

Joint venture or partnership?

A joint venture can be distinguished from a partnership on the basis that:

- it is usually an *ad hoc* undertaking for a **specific time or task**;
- it is a **separate venture** for each of the parties;
- assets in the joint venture are usually held as **individual shares** by the parties on the basis of tenants in common;
- **liability is individual** rather than several;
- profits are received separately and invoices are usually issued separately and paid individually; and
- the parties can **dispose** of their interest in the joint venture without the need to **assign** as may be the case under the *Partnership Act*.

CREATION

A partnership is basically contractual in nature, with no set statutory form

Because a partnership is an agreement, it is basically contractual in nature. Therefore all the essential elements that must be present to create a valid contract must be present to create a valid partnership agreement.

While there is no set statutory form for the creation of a partnership, the parties contemplating such an action would be well advised to clearly and fully state the most important elements of the contract in written form. This is particularly important if the partners do not wish the provisions of the *Partnership Act* to apply.

The advantage of a carefully written document is that its terms allow (hopefully) no dispute. In Tasmania, where the partnership is to last for more than one year, or if it is to commence at a date later than one year after the making of the agreement, the agreement must be evidenced in writing if it is to be enforceable.

Doing business

Partnership agreements should be in writing

While a partnership may be formed either orally or from the conduct of the parties, either of these methods can create problems at some future date over the exact terms agreed to. It is better, where possible, to have a **written agreement**, because it provides certainty of terms. It should contain at least the following information:

1 **Details of partners**, including:
- full names and addresses; and
- the principal office of the partnership.

2 **Details of the partnership business**, including:
- the nature and purpose of the partnership;
- the firm's name, if different from the full names of the partners concerned; and
- how long the partnership is to last.

3 **Financial details**, including:
- the amount of capital to be contributed by each partner, if any;
- arrangements with respect to the withdrawal of partners from the partnership;
- whether interest is to be allowed on capital contributed;
- how profits and losses are to be shared;
- salaries payable to partners, if any;
- how the accounts are to be kept and audited; and
- how goodwill is to be calculated.

4 **Details of the authority and responsibilities of partners**, including:
- the share of management of the business to be exercised by each partner; and
- whether any limitation is to be placed upon the authority of each partner to act as an agent of the firm.

5 **Details on how changes in partners will be dealt with**, including:
- provision on admission and withdrawal of partners;
- terms, notices and conditions on retirement;
- continuance of the business on the death of a partner;
- provision with respect to the bankruptcy of a partner;
- settlement of the rights of the representative of a deceased partner; and
- prevention of competition from a retiring partner.

6 **Details on how the partnership may be dissolved.**

7 **How settlement of disputes will be dealt with.** ■

Can anyone be a partner?

Partnership is basically contractual in nature. While certain classes of persons have limited contractual capacity (see Chapter 15), the position of infants especially should be kept in mind. An infant can enter into a partnership agreement. However, they may avoid any liability or responsibility incurred in the ordinary course of the partnership agreement, thus leaving the co-partners personally liable to the firm's creditors without any right of contribution or indemnity from them. The infant would be liable as an ordinary partner if repudiation of the partnership agreement did not take place within a reasonable time of the coming of age.

The legal position of infants in New South Wales is different to that in other states because of the *Minors (Property and Contracts) Act 1970*. The Act provides that where a minor participates in a civil act (e.g., a contract), and their participation is for their benefit, they are bound unless they can show they lack the understanding necessary for such an involvement.

> ! CAUTION NOTE
> *Infants can enter into partnerships but remember there is a limitation on liability.*

RELATIONSHIP TO OUTSIDERS

ACT s. 9 : **NSW** s. 5 : **NT** s. 9 : **QLD** s. 8 : **SA** s. 5 : **TAS** s. 10 : **VIC** s. 9 : **WA** s. 26

Every partner is an **agent** of the firm and the other partners for the purpose of the business of the partnership. This means that any act of a partner done in the usual course of partnership business can bind the firm and their partners. An exception to this general principle arises where the partner has no authority to act for the firm in the particular matter and the other person knows this or has reason to believe they are not a partner.

Because the articles of a partnership agreement are not public property and open for inspection, it is very difficult for third parties to know the limitations placed on the authority of partners. This authority could be actual, ostensible or implied.

> ! CAUTION NOTE
> *Every partner is an agent for the firm and other partners so anything done in the course of the firm's business binds the firm and the other partners.*

Actual authority

If a partner has actual authority, the other partners are bound by the partner's acts. Every partner is an agent of the firm for the purposes of the partnership business because the partners operate a business in common.

Ostensible or apparent authority

Ostensible authority—arises where partner acts in scope of business in usual way

Ostensible or apparent authority only arises where the first limb—that is, the question of actual authority—is lacking. If a third party is to succeed against a firm, they must establish that:

- the particular partner was acting within the scope of the business of the kind carried on by the firm. This is a question of fact in each case;
- the transaction was carried out in the usual way. If the transaction is carried out in an unusual manner, that should alert the third party that perhaps the partner may not have the authority to bind the other members of the firm;
- they knew or reasonably believed that the partner was a partner; and
- they were not aware that the partner lacked authority to bind the firm.

If the third party knows the particular partner has no authority, or does not believe the person to be a partner, then no action will be able to be taken against the firm.

Implied authority

Provided that nothing is stated to the contrary in the partnership agreement, the powers of partners to bind the firm by their acts include:

- the selling of property and goods of the firm;
- purchasing goods usually used by the firm;
- employing suitable staff;
- receiving payments and giving receipts;
- entering into contracts on behalf of the firm; and
- in the case of trading partnerships only (engaged in buying and selling):
  - issuing, accepting and making negotiable instruments in the firm's name; and
  - borrowing money on the firm's credit and pledging the firm's assets.

LIABILITY OF PARTNERS

IN BRIEF

Personal liability of partners in contract and tort

Issue	Joint liability	Joint and several liability
Type of action	Contract.	Tort.
Who can be sued?	Plaintiff must sue all partners jointly. Those partners being sued can have remaining partners joined as co-defendants. Note, in NSW liability is joint and several.	Plaintiff can sue partners jointly or severally.
Can the plaintiff sue more than once?	No. Liability is joint except in NSW where it is joint and several.	Yes. It is possible to bring an action against each one of the partners until judgement is satisfied.

Who pays the damages if the plaintiff wins?	The partnership.	If suing severally, only the partner being sued. If jointly, all the partners.
Indemnity	If a partner pays the judgement, can recover proportion from others.	If a partner is sued severally, may be able to recover from others if tort committed in ordinary course of partnership business. If partners sued jointly, partnership pays.

Under contract law

ACT s. 13 : **NSW** s. 9 : **NT** s. 16 : **QLD** s. 12 : **SA** s. 9 : **TAS** s. 14 : **VIC** s. 13 : **WA** s. 16

> **!** CAUTION NOTE
>
> *Contract—partners are collectively liable (in NSW it is joint and several).*

Each partner is **liable jointly** (collectively) with the other partners for all debts and **contractual obligations** of the firm (in New South Wales, s. 97 of the *Supreme Court Act 1970* alters this to joint and several liability).

Where an action is brought against the firm, the partners are sued jointly and not individually. Where the partners are not joined in an action, those who are sued can have the remaining partners joined as co-defendants, or alternatively they may claim a proportionate share of the amount paid by them from the other partners.

Doing business

Better to sue in firm name

The Rules of Court in each jurisdiction in Australia allow a plaintiff to sue a partnership in the firm name, with judgement binding all partners. This is preferable to suing partners in their own names where there is a possibility of missing someone, for example, a silent partner. ■

Remember, as liability is joint, other partners cannot be sued later because they have been discharged from liability by the first action.

While each partner is liable for the whole of the debts of a firm, the creditor is only entitled to bring **one action** against the members of a firm, because their liability is joint. Thus, if A and B are equal partners and are jointly liable to C for a debt, C would normally apply under the Rules of Court (they are basically the same for each state) to sue in the name of the firm. This would catch all the partners, otherwise the partners are going to have to be named individually in any summons. If the firm's assets are insufficient to meet the debts, A and B will have to contribute equally from their private assets after first meeting their private debts, and if the assets of A, for example, were insufficient, B would have to make up the difference.

If C for some reason sues A alone, and A does not have B joined as a defendant, C cannot then sue B (unless the action is based in New South Wales) if A cannot meet the debt in full. C only has one right of action. If A had paid the debt in full, then A could recover 50 per cent from the firm and from B.

Under the law of torts

ACT ss. 14–17 : **NSW** ss. 10–13 : **NT** s. 16 : **QLD** ss. 13–16 : **SA** ss. 10–13 : **TAS** ss. 15–18 : **VIC** ss. 14–17 : **WA** ss. 17–20

Tort—act must be in the ordinary course of business

Under tort law, to establish liability of co-partners it must be shown that the act or omission was in the ordinary course of the business of the firm, or if the act or omission was not in the ordinary course of business, that it was with the authority of the co-partners.

POLKINGHORNE V. HOLLAND & WHITTINGTON **(1934) 51 CLR 143**

Holland Snr and Whittington were two of the three partners in a firm of solicitors. Holland had been advising Polkinghorne on questions of investment, and his advice had always been sound. Holland's son, the third partner, took over Polkinghorne's affairs and advised her to sell her stock and invest in a company he had registered for a friend. The company had no assets, no bank account and did no business. The friend, with the help of Holland's son, defrauded Polkinghorne. Polkinghorne sued Holland Snr and Whittington, arguing that the firm owed her a special duty of care, and that Holland's son had acted as a partner on behalf of the firm.

ISSUE: Was the giving of financial advice outside the ordinary business of a law firm, such that it could not be said that the partners would be jointly and severally liable?

DECISION: The High Court held that the firm was liable for the actions of the Holland's son. It could reasonably be regarded as part of a solicitor's business to give competent advice on the means of obtaining accurate information as to the desirability of investing money in a company in which he had an interest.

COMMENT: The partners also argued that the financial advice given by the junior partner lacked actual or apparent authority and that Mrs Polkinghorne should have realised this. However, the court rejected this argument and found that Mrs Polkinghorne had reasonable grounds for believing that the junior partner was acting with full authority.

Where money or property of a third person (including trust property) has been received or held in custody by the firm and then misapplied by a member of the firm, the partnership must make good any loss.

WALKER V. EUROPEAN ELECTRONICS PTY LTD (IN LIQUIDATION) **[1990] 23 NSWLR 1**

A partner in a firm of accountants was acting as receiver/manager of a company. Company funds received by the partner should have been paid into the partnership's trust account, but they were not because they had been misappropriated by the partner.

ISSUE: Was the partner acting in the ordinary course of the partnership's business or was the partner acting alone?

DECISION: The New South Wales Court of Appeal held that although the partner was the receiver/manager and as such acted alone, that activity formed part of the accounting firm's business. The fraudulent partner was therefore acting in the normal course of business and all of the partners were liable for the fraudulent actions.

Under tort law, partners are both jointly (or collectively) and severally (or individually) liable. If our earlier example of A, B and C had involved a tort action and A was unable to pay damages awarded to C by the court, B could be sued in full because the partners are jointly and severally liable. If the partners had been sued jointly, the innocent partners may be entitled to indemnity from the guilty partner if they were not involved in the tort.

> **!** CAUTION NOTE
> *Partners are collectively and individually liable in tort.*

BEING AN APPARENT PARTNER OR 'HOLDING OUT'

ACT s. 18 : **NSW** s. 14 : **NT** s. 18 : **QLD** s. 17 : **SA** s. 14 : **TAS** s. 19 : **VIC** s. 18 : **WA** s. 21

A person who obtains credit for a partnership, either by their words or conduct, can become liable as an 'apparent' partner. If, as a result of the actions of the 'apparent' partner the partnership is sued, the partnership can in turn sue the 'apparent' partner.

A person who holds themselves out as a partner may become liable as an 'apparent partner'

The partnership itself is not liable unless the partners accept the actions of the 'apparent' partner or in some other way acquiesce in this 'holding out' process.

LIABILITY ON CHANGE OF PARTNERS

ACT ss. 21, 41 : **NSW** ss. 17, 36 : **NT** s. 21 : **QLD** ss. 20, 39 : **SA** ss. 17, 36 : **TAS** ss. 22, 41 : **VIC** ss. 21, 40 : **WA** ss. 24, 47

Liability after retirement

In order to avoid incurring liability for debts that the partnership may incur after a partner has retired, the following steps should be taken:

Retiring partners remain liable for debts incurred before retirement

- specific notice of retirement should be given to all those persons who have had dealings with the firm;
- notices should be placed in the public notices section of the daily newspapers and in the Government *Gazette* to warn both existing and potential customers of the firm about the partner's retirement; and
- notice must be forwarded to the Corporate Affairs Commission or Registrar of Business Names, whichever the case may be, where the firm name has been registered.

If these steps are not taken, both former and new customers of the firm are entitled to hold the retired member responsible by conduct for the debts of the firm.

Retirement does not automatically relieve the retiring partner from liability for partnership debts contracted during their time with the partnership. However, it is not unusual for a retiring partner to be released from liability through agreement between the creditors and the existing partners.

Incoming partner

As a general rule, a new partner is not liable for any of the firm's debts incurred before they are admitted to the partnership. However, the new partner may agree to assume liability for any of the debts and obligations as a condition precedent to entering the partnership.

New partners only liable for future debts unless assuming liability for past debts

RELATIONSHIP BETWEEN PARTNERS

ACT s. 23 : **NSW** s. 19 : **NT** s. 23 : **QLD** s. 22 : **SA** s. 19 : **TAS** s. 24 : **VIC** s. 23 : **WA** s. 29

While a partnership agreement is not one of *uberrimae fidei* (of the utmost good faith), good faith is required between the partners and any matters affecting the partnership must be disclosed to all of them.

The mutual rights and duties of partners should be clearly set out in the partnership agreement. If nothing is said in the partnership agreement, then the *Partnership Act* outlines the rights that the partners will have.

> **!** CAUTION NOTE
> *Rights and duties of partners should be set out in partnership agreement.*

WHAT ARE THE RIGHTS OF EACH PARTNER?

ACT ss. 29–30 : **NSW** ss. 24–25 : **NT** ss. 28–29 : **QLD** ss. 27–28 : **SA** ss. 24–25 : **TAS** ss. 29–30 : **VIC** ss. 28–29 : **WA** ss. 34–35

Unless the parties say anything to the contrary, the *Partnership Act* sets out a number of rules as to partner's rights

Where no agreement is made by the parties, or subject to any agreement to the contrary, the *Partnership Act* sets out the following rules to determine the rights of the partners (see Figure 28.2):

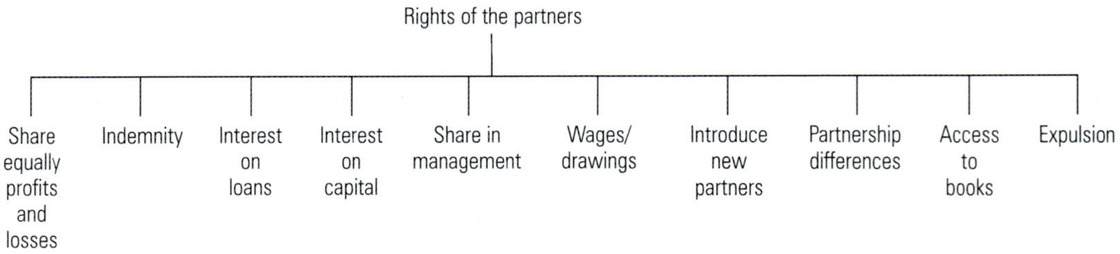

FIGURE 28.2 *Rights of the partners*

To share equally in profits and losses

Unless the partners have agreed to share profits and losses according to capital invested or in some other way, it is assumed they will be shared equally.

Indemnity

As each partner is an agent of the firm, any partner acting in the ordinary course of the business of the firm who incurs liabilities is entitled to an indemnity from their co-partners. All that a partner needs show is that what they did was necessarily done for the preservation of the businesses or property of the firm.

Interest on advances

A partner is entitled to interest on loans to the firm, but a maximum interest rate is set down in the *Partnership Act*.

Interest on capital

No partner is entitled to interest on their capital until net profit has been determined.

To share in the management of the business

Every partner may take part in the management of the partnership business if they want. However, partners often expressly agree to exclude the right of participation in management.

Wages/drawings

A partner cannot claim wages for what they are already bound to do to the best of their ability (unless this is varied by agreement between the partners). Partners receive drawings on their account rather than wages.

Introduction of new partners

The consent of all the existing partners is needed to introduce new partners. The basis of partnership is mutual trust and confidence and the introduction of an unreliable partner could cause problems for the existing partners. Where a partnership agreement states how a partner may nominate a new partner, the terms of the agreement must be followed precisely.

Differences over partnership business

A clear distinction is drawn between the day-to-day affairs of the partnership business and the fundamental nature of its business. Thus, where a proposed change, such as the addition of a new partner, would effect a change in the nature of the partnership business, a unanimous decision of all the partners would be required. In any other matters connected with the partnership, all that is required is a decision by the majority of the partners.

Access to the partnership books

The partnership books are to be kept at the place of business of the partnership (or the principal place if there is more than one) and every partner may then have access to inspect and copy any of them.

Expulsion of a partner

A majority of the partners *cannot* expel a partner unless the partnership agreement contains the power to expel, and even then it must be exercised in good faith and strictly in accordance with the terms of the agreement. Expulsion generally does not have the same effects as dissolution of partnership, for in the case of expulsion the remaining partners continue the business. In the case of dissolution, the business is usually wound up and the assets sold.

WHAT ARE THE DUTIES OF EACH PARTNER?

ACT ss. 33–35 : **NSW** ss. 28–30 : **NT** ss. 32–34 : **QLD** ss. 31–33 :
SA ss. 28–30 : **TAS** ss. 33–35 : **VIC** ss. 32–34 : **WA** ss. 39–41

Partners are under a fiduciary duty towards each other

The fiduciary duties of a partner are (see Figure 28.3):

To render true accounts

Every partner must keep an accurate account of all their dealings on behalf of the firm and supply full information to all the partners on anything that could affect the partnership.

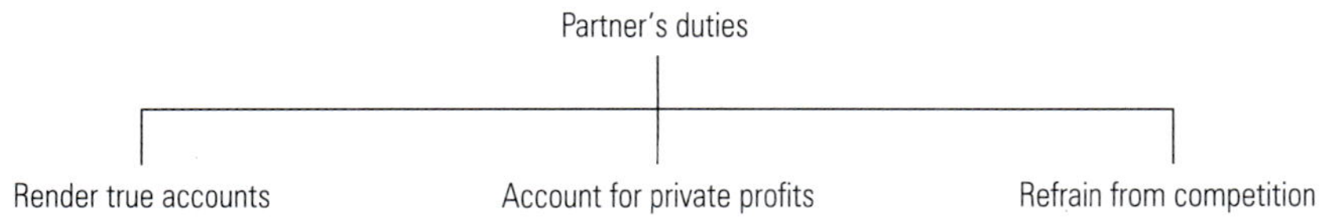

FIGURE 28.3 *Partner's duties*

To account for private profits

Partners must account to their co-partners for profits they make without their knowledge and consent or as a result of information gained during the course of the partnership.

To refrain from competition

Where a partner sets up a business in competition with the partnership firm, profits will have to be shared with the co-partners. However, if the business is of a totally different kind to that of the partnership, then the partner will only be accountable for any profits gained from the use of partnership property in the new business or for information gained from acting as a partner. A partner is not entitled to make a secret profit from their position as a partner.

WHAT HAPPENS TO PARTNERSHIP PROPERTY?

ACT ss. 24–25 : **NSW** ss. 20–21 : **NT** ss. 24–26 : **QLD** ss. 23–24 : **SA** ss. 20–21 : **TAS** ss. 25–26 : **VIC** ss. 24–25 : **WA** ss. 30–31

Whether property is partnership property is a question of fact in each case

Property used for the purpose of a partnership business will not necessarily become partnership property. It may remain the separate property of one or some of the partners, or even be owned, either jointly or in common, by all the partners as the private property of each of them. Whether the property used in a partnership has become the property of the partnership is a question of fact. This can be determined either by the express terms of the partnership agreement, or by inference from the way in which the parties have dealt with the property during the existence of the partnership.

DISSOLUTION

A partnership may be dissolved or terminated for any of several reasons (see Figure 28.4).

Action by the partners

ACT s. 37 : **NSW** s. 32 : **NT** s. 36 : **QLD** s. 35 : **SA** s. 32 : **TAS** s. 37 : **VIC** s. 36 : **WA** s. 43

Subject to any agreement between the partners, a partnership is dissolved:

- by the expiration of a fixed term. However, where the parties continue to carry on the partnership business after the expiry of the fixed term, other than as preparatory to winding it up, the partnership will continue as a partnership at will (ACT: s. 26; NSW: s. 26; QLD: s. 29; SA: s. 26; TAS: s. 31; VIC: s. 30; WA: s. 37);
- if entered into for a single undertaking, by the termination of that undertaking; or
- if entered into for an undefined time, by any partner giving notice.

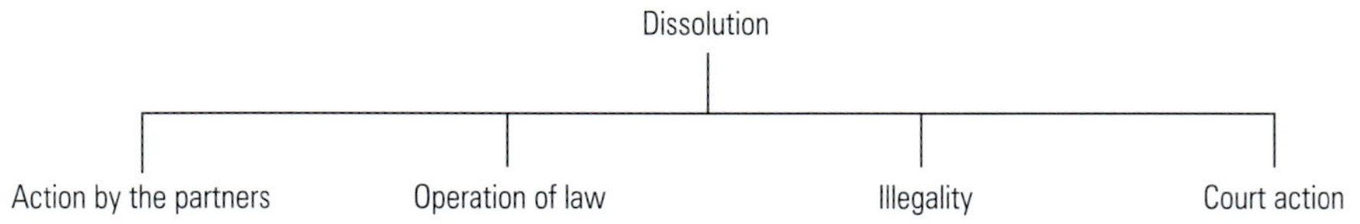

FIGURE 28.4 *Methods of dissolution*

Operation of law

ACT s. 33 : **NSW** s. 33 : **NT** s. 37 : **QLD** s. 36 : **SA** s. 33 : **TAS** s. 38 : **VIC** s. 37 : **WA** s. 44

A partnership may be dissolved at the option of the other partners on the death or bankruptcy (in Queensland, insolvency) of a partner.

Illegality

ACT s. 39 : **NSW** s. 34 : **NT** s. 38 : **QLD** s. 37 : **SA** s. 34 : **TAS** s. 39 : **VIC** s. 38 : **WA** s. 45

A partnership is automatically dissolved by the occurrence of an event that renders the purpose of the partnership illegal or against public policy.

By the court

ACT s. 40 : **NSW** s. 35 : **NT** s. 39 : **QLD** s. 38 : **SA** s. 35 : **TAS** s. 40 : **VIC** s. 39 : **WA** s. 46

The above grounds can be used as a basis for the automatic dissolution of a partnership without the aid of the court. In addition, a partner may apply to the court with the aim of having the partnership dissolved in the following circumstances:

- insanity;
- permanent incapacity. This is a question of fact in each case—for example paralysis as the result of a stroke;
- when a partner has been guilty of conduct that in the opinion of the court is detrimental to the interests of the business. The conduct in question does not have to be associated with the business. The fact that it could damage the partnership's reputation would be enough;
- where there is wilful or persistent breach of the partnership agreement—for example, where there is failure to keep the accounts;
- when the partnership can only be carried on at a loss. The loss must, of course, be of a permanent nature, not temporary because of special circumstances that may not occur again; and
- whenever in any case circumstances have arisen which in the opinion of the court render it just and equitable that the partnership be dissolved. For example, if partners are deadlocked and cannot agree as to management of the partnership, the court may exercise its discretion and decree that the partnership be dissolved.

Consequences of dissolution

ACT s. 13 : **NSW** s. 9 : **NT** s. 13 : **QLD** s. 12 : **SA** s. 9 : **TAS** s. 14 : **VIC** s. 13 : **WA** s. 16

Dissolution ends the partnership

Dissolution ends the relationship between the partners. They no longer have the power to act as agents for the firm. However, partners retain their authority for the purposes of winding up.

Distribution of assets on dissolution

ACT s. 45 : **NSW** s. 39 : **NT** s. 43 : **QLD** s. 42 : **SA** s. 39 : **TAS** s. 44 : **VIC** s. 43 : **WA** s. 50

Each partner is entitled to a proportionate return of their contribution to capital before distribution

All partners are entitled to have the partnership property applied in satisfaction of the firm's debts and, in the event of any surplus assets, to have them applied in payment of what may be due to them respectively, after deducting what may be due from them as partners to the firm.

Each partner is entitled to a proportionate return of their contribution to capital before distribution of the remaining assets, unless the partnership agreement contains an express term to the contrary. Where one partner has permitted their own separate estate to be used by the partnership, and that property has increased in value, it is obviously very important to decide whether it has become partnership property or not.

As a general rule, property used for the purposes of a partnership business is considered to have become partnership property. If the property has increased in value, the owner will only be entitled to receive an amount equal to the value of the property at the date of its introduction into the firm, together with the proportion of the share of the increased value. If, on the other hand, it has remained the partner's property and is unaffected by dissolution, the whole of its enhanced value will be received by the partner.

Dissolution because of death, bankruptcy or insolvency

Distinguish between partnership and private property to determine rights of different groups of creditors

If the partnership is being dissolved because of death, bankruptcy or insolvency, it is necessary to distinguish between partnership property and private property. This is because of the unlimited liability of the partners to a firm's creditors, which makes available to the firm's creditors both the partnership assets and the private property of each partner. The general rule is that business creditors must go first to the partnership property, and private creditors to the separate property. Business creditors cannot claim against the separate property until all private creditors have been paid in full. Similarly, private creditors cannot claim against the firm's assets until all business creditors have been paid in full.

Dissolution rules under partnership legislation

If partnership agreement is silent, *Partnership Act* applies

If the partnership agreement does not provide for the manner of disposition of the firm's assets on dissolution, the rules are laid down in the Act. They must be observed in the following order:

- Payment of the expenses of realisation.
- Payment of all debts of the firm to creditors (including employees) and other persons who are not partners in the firm. These obligations must be met first from profits not yet distributed to partners and then from the capital which has already been invested by the partners.
- Repayment to each partner of money they have lent the firm apart from ordinary contributions of capital made by them. If the remaining assets are insufficient, they will be paid in proportion to the amounts they advanced.
- Repayment to each partner of their capital to the firm. If the remaining assets are insufficient, the partners will be paid in proportion to their contributions to capital.
- Payment to the partners of any residue in the proportion in which they share profits.

In general, partners will share profits and losses on realisation in the same way as they would share normal profits and losses. However, where one partner becomes insolvent, the rule in *Garner v. Murray* [1904] 1 Ch. 57 applies in the case of dissolution and distribution of assets. Where there are:

- three or more partners who have contributed capital unequally but shared profits and losses equally, and
- one partner becomes insolvent on dissolution,

the solvent partners are required to contribute to the insolvent partner's deficiency in the proportion of their own capital at the start of the dissolution. The assets are then to be applied in paying to each partner rateably what is due from the firm in respect of capital.

Thus, if A, B and C have contributed $6000, $4000 and $1000 respectively to the partnership and on dissolution there is a loss of $6000 to be shared equally between them, A would receive $4000, B would receive $2000 and C would be deficient to the extent of $1000. This deficiency is shared by A and B in proportion to their original contributions of capital. Thus A's share of C's deficiency is six-tenths or $600, and B's share is four-tenths or $400.

The final return to A will be $3400 ($4000 less $600) and to B $1600 ($2000 less $400). All the creditors of the firm will be paid, as a result of A and B sharing C's liability. Therefore A and B would be entitled to claim these amounts from C at a subsequent date by claiming as normal creditors in the bankruptcy of C.

LIMITED PARTNERSHIPS

Limited partnerships are an alternative to limited liability companies

The concept of limited partnerships is to provide an alternative to running a business as a limited liability company. The formalities for the formation of a limited partnership are simple in comparison to the formalities required for the formation of a corporation and its day-to-day operational requirements under the *Corporations Act*. The states, but not the territories, have passed legislation for limited partnerships (see Table 28.2).

Where the limited partnership legislation does not apply, the rules under the relevant state or territory *Partnership Act* will apply.

Table 28.2 Limited partnership legislation

New South Wales	*Partnership (Limited Partnership) Amendment Act 1991* (amending the *Partnership Act 1892*)
Queensland	*Partnership (Limited Liability) Act 1988*
South Australia	*Partnership (Limited Partnerships) Amendment Act 1997*
Tasmania	*Limited Partnership Act 1908*
Victoria	*Partnership (Limited Partnerships) Act 1992* (amending the *Partnership Act 1958*)
Western Australia	*Limited Partnerships Act 1909*

Membership

While there are no limitations on the number of members in New South Wales, Victoria or Queensland, care must be taken to ensure that the number of general members must not result in the partnership becoming an outsize partnership for the purposes of the *Corporations Act*. In these states, a corporation may be either a general or a limited partner. In Western Australia and Tasmania the number of members is limited to 20 for trading partnerships and 10 for banking partnerships, while only a limited partner may be a corporation.

A limited partnership consists of at least one general partner, whose capital contribution on entering the firm will determine the extent of their liability for the debts of the firm. In New South Wales, Victoria and Queensland, there is no legislative requirement that limited partners make any contribution of capital at the time of formation of the partnership, while in Western Australia and Tasmania, liability is limited to the amount of capital a limited partner brings in. Limited partners are not liable for debts beyond their capital contribution.

Management

The role of general partners is to manage the limited partnership. As a result, they are **subject to the same rules as partners** under partnership law. That is, they face unlimited liability and are jointly and severally liable for all debts and obligations that the limited partnership may accrue. Limited partners, on the other hand, are similar to investors and do not normally participate in general management. However, if a limited partner takes part in the management of the business, he or she will be liable in the same way as a general partner.

A general partner can become a limited partner, though the effect on the limitation on liability only commences from the time of the transition to limited partnership status. Any debts that were incurred before the partner became a limited partner remain effective against the partner. It is also possible for a limited partner to become a general partner, thus incurring full liability. This may occur, for example, through their taking part in the management of the firm.

> **!** CAUTION NOTE
> *Membership must include at least one general partner who will have unlimited liability for all debts and obligations of the partnership.*

Registration

Registration is required in all states

Each state requires that the limited partnership be registered. Registration must contain details of:

- the firm's name;
- names and addresses of the limited partners;
- the address of the registered office;
- whether each partner is a general or limited partner; and
- in New South Wales, Victoria and Queensland, the extent of the limited partners' liability to contribute. In Western Australia and Tasmania this requirement is not required, and instead there must be a statement of the sum contributed by each limited partner and whether it was paid in cash or some other form. This information enables outsiders to determine who are members of the firm and the extent to which a particular limited partner will meet any liability of the firm.

Advantages

The **advantages** of a limited partnership are:

- simplicity;
- in New South Wales, Victoria and Queensland, the absence of a maximum number of limited partners; and
- achievement of limited liability of a limited partner without the need to form a limited liability company under the *Corporations Act*.

REVIEW QUESTIONS ?

28.1 What matters need to be taken into account when deciding whether or not a business is a partnership?

28.2 There are two important differences between joint tenants and tenants in common. Explain what they are.

28.3 What is a joint venture? What sorts of businesses should consider establishing themselves as joint ventures?

28.4 A father and his son carried on a business. They experienced financial difficulties owing to a slump in the market, and to avoid going into bankruptcy they executed a deed of arrangement with their creditors. The deed provided for five of the creditors to carry on the business as trustees for all the creditors, with the profits going to the creditors. One of the trustees did not act at all, and another resigned shortly after the deed was executed. The remaining trustees then carried on the business, purchasing goods and accepting bills of exchange from suppliers. Eventually the business had to close down.

Could the suppliers sue the trustees, claiming that they were liable as partners in the business?

28.5 Two parties agreed to stage a theatrical performance, and one agreed to receive 60 per cent of the takings and pay for the theatre, lighting and advertising and the other agreed to receive 40 per cent of the takings and pay for actors and scenery.

Was there a partnership in existence between the two parties?

28.6 Smith entered into an agreement with Cranitch and a third party to lend them $20 000 for the purposes of a business that Cranitch and another intended to carry on in partnership. The written agreement stated that the money was a loan by a creditor and it further expressly provided that the advance was not to be seen as constituting the lender as a partner. However, in addition, this tripartite agreement provided that Smith was to participate in the profits of the business in a fixed proportion; in certain circumstances, he was to have the option of dissolving the partnership and conducting the winding-up. It was further provided that the loan was only repayable in the event of dissolution. It also appeared that the $20 000 was the only capital of the partnership.

Is Smith a partner?

28.7 Indicate whether each of the following statements is true or false:

Statement	TRUE	FALSE
Conducting an isolated transaction suggests a joint venture	☑	☐
Partnerships must be associations formed with a view to profit	☑	☐
Tenants in common possess the four unities and the right of survivorship	☐	☑
The existence of a partnership is to be determined from what the parties do rather than what the parties call themselves	☑	☐
All partnerships can only have between two and 20 members	☐	☑
Sharing of profits and losses is complete proof of a partnership	☐	☑
Liability under contract law is joint and several	☐	☑
A person who obtains credit for a partnership may make themselves liable to the supplier by 'holding out'	☑	☐
An incoming partner is liable for all the firm's debts that were incurred before they were admitted to the partnership	☐	☑
Unequal contributions to capital raise a presumption that profits are to be shared unequally	☑	☐
A partner is automatically entitled to wages when working for the partnership	☐	☑
Only a majority of partners need to agree on the admission of a new partner but all partners need to agree for a partner to be expelled	☐	☑
Anyone, including an agent of a partner, may have access to the partnership books	☐	☑
If a partner sets up a business which is not in competition with the partnership firm, they do not have to share the profits with their co-partners	☑	☐
A partnership is automatically dissolved on insanity of a partner	☐	☑
Dissolution of the partnership ends the agency relationship between the partners	☑	☐
Partners share any residue on the dissolution of the partnership in the ratio of their contribution to capital	☑	☐
Limited partnerships are governed by the *Corporations Act 2001* (Cth) rather than the Partnership Acts of the states and territories	☐	☑

28.8 While it is not necessary for the creation of a partnership to reduce the agreement to writing, it is strongly advisable. Explain why.

28.9 Discuss the relationship of partners to outsiders.

28.10 Liability of a partner can be joint or several or joint and several. Discuss.

28.11 A and B formed a partnership to carry on the business of leasing out garages. The partnership agreement expressly provided that neither partner was to sell motor vehicles. A sold a motor vehicle, which he did not own, to C. A had previously sold a number of vehicles to C over the time of the partnership.

Could C sue the partnership for the cost of the vehicle?

28.12 Two partners carried on a business. One of them retired, but the partnership continued with a new partner, still using the name of the old firm. A customer, who had dealt with the firm over a number of years, supplied goods to the new firm, unaware of the change in the partnership. He was subsequently told of the change, and when the new partnership was unable to pay for the goods that he had supplied, he considered bringing an action against the retired partner for the partnership debts.

Advise the customer of his rights.

activebook

Activebook resources include in-depth summaries with links to the relevant part of the book. For revision, add your own notes to the summaries provided by using the note-taking function.

28.13 Three partners were engaged in the business of running laundrettes. The partnership agreement provided that no partner could pledge the credit of the firm without the consent of the other partners, unless this was done in the ordinary course of business. One of the partners borrowed money from a third party, explaining to the third party that it was to be used for further expansion of the laundrettes. In fact, it was always intended to be used by the borrower for his own personal use, and he subsequently disappeared with it.

Can the lender bring an action against either the firm or one of the partners for the recovery of the money?

28.14 A retail store partnership consisted of a large number of both active and sleeping partners. The active partners wished to purchase the interest of the sleeping partners in the business. Before agreeing to the sale, the sleeping partners wished to employ as their agent a business auctioneer and valuer to inspect the books of the partnership. The active partners refused the sleeping partners' request, claiming that only active partners could inspect the books.

Advise the sleeping partners.

28.15 The articles of a partnership gave each partner the right to nominate and introduce any other person into the partnership. Under this clause, A nominated his son, who was already employed in the business. A's co-partners refused to accept the son into the partnership.

Advise A.

28.16 Richard and Dinah were partners in a transport firm that dealt exclusively in the interstate transport of frozen foods. During a trip to Alice Springs, a freezer unit on the trailer broke down, and in order to prevent the loss of the frozen goods Richard was forced to purchase parts and have them flown out from Melbourne at a cost of $4200 to himself personally. When he produced the receipts and requested that the firm reimburse him, Dinah refused to have anything to do with them.

Advise Richard.

28.17 A partner in a firm of chemists was disabled by a stroke and his co-partner applied to the court for dissolution of the partnership on the ground that the stricken partner was incapable of carrying out his duties in the partnership business. Evidence was produced which showed that there was some slight improvement in the disabled partner's condition.

Would the application for the dissolution succeed?

CRITICAL THINKING

28.1 Steve and Pat wanted to establish a nursery business but to get the business started they needed $50 000 capital. Because of the nature of the business and the economic climate, they couldn't find a financial institution that was prepared to make them the necessary loan. However, Rod, a friend of Steve's, was prepared to put up the capital if the loan agreement expressly stated that there was neither expressly nor impliedly any intention to create a partnership agreement between them. The loan agreement further stated that Rod was to have a share of the profits and losses, access to the partnership financial records, and that the loan was not to be repayable until after the dissolution of the partnership.

Due to a lack of business acumen, Steve and Pat were eventually declared bankrupt. Rod then made a claim as a creditor which was rejected by the trustee in bankruptcy on the basis that Rod was a partner.

In your opinion, was the trustee in bankruptcy correct? Give reasons.

Choosing a Business Entity

CHAPTER

CHAPTER CONTENTS

activebook

This icon is used throughout the following chapter to remind you to visit the *Business Law* online activebook for additional exercises, links to legal websites, and feedback. For a detailed explanation of what is in the activebook please refer to the inside cover of this textbook. The activebook is available through OneKey.

Where do I start?
Learning path: Use the activebook to complete a pre-chapter warm-up exercise.
There are many definitions of legal terms to assist with your understanding of the material.

CHAPTER OBJECTIVES

On completion of this chapter, you should be able to:

- explain the essential characteristics and the advantages and disadvantages of a sole trader
- explain the essential characteristics and the advantages and disadvantages of a partnership
- explain the essential characteristics and the advantages and disadvantages of a corporation
- explain the essential characteristics and the advantages and disadvantages of a trading trust
- explain the essential characteristics and the advantages and disadvantages of a franchise
- explain the reasons for and importance of registering a business name
- discuss the legal restrictions imposed on the use of a business name.

KEY TERMS

An understanding of the following terms will help you to better understand the material in this chapter:

- **company:** a distinct legal entity separate from its shareholders
- **directors:** the persons responsible for the management of a company
- **franchise:** a contractual relationship between the franchisor and the franchisee in which the franchisor agrees to maintain a continuing interest in the business of the franchisee in such areas as technical knowledge; advertising and marketing; product control; and expertise and training. The franchisee agrees to operate under a common trade name, format and procedure owned and controlled by the franchisor
- **joint venture:** two or more people entering into a one-off agreement for profit
- **limited partnership:** a partnership in which there is at least one general partner with unlimited liability and one or more partners whose liability for debts and obligations of the partnership is limited
- **partnership:** the relationship that exists between persons carrying on a business in common with a view to profit
- **proprietary company (also known as a private company):** a company limited by shares, or unlimited by share capital, and with not more than 50 non-employee shareholders
- **public company:** a company that is able to invite the public to invest in its shares
- **trust:** when a person is given the possession and/or power over certain property to use that property for the benefit of some other person or object. The person who is given that possession or power is known as a **trustee**. He or she usually has legal ownership and control of the trust property but is under an **equitable obligation** to deal with property for the benefit of other persons (called **beneficiaries**) any of whom may enforce the obligation. The terms of the trust are usually set out in a trust deed.

what if . . .

You were about to start a new business with two of your friends. Why is it important to decide what type of business entity to use? Why would you choose one type instead of the others?

To a certain extent, the choice of business organisation (see Figure 29.1) is going to be dictated by the type of venture that the person is considering entering into. In Australia, small businesses make up approximately 95 per cent of all businesses. They often begin as a sole trader (one owner) or partnership (between two and 20 owners), and if they survive the first five years of operation (and 80 per cent do not), they may consider a different organisational structure for the purpose of gaining additional capital, taxation benefits or protection from creditors. A variety of business structures are available today for people to select from for business purposes. Partnerships and joint ventures are dealt with in more detail in the previous chapter.

This chapter considers the role of the sole trader, looks at what a partnership is and provides an overview of some of the important aspects of company law and trusts (see Table 29.5).

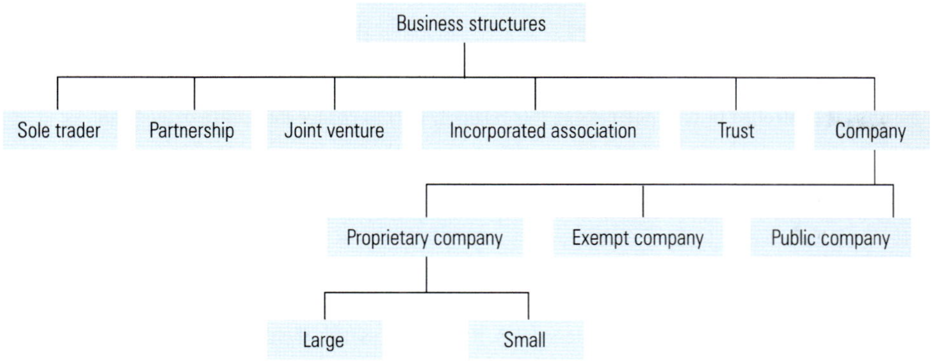

FIGURE 29.1 *Business structures*

SOLE TRADER

Sole trader—owns and controls their own business. It is the simplest form of business organisation

A sole trader owns and controls their own business or businesses. It is the simplest form of business organisation to establish because there are **no formal requirements** if the **name of the owner** is going to be used as the name of the business. If they are not going to use their own name, they will need to register a business name (see pp. 620–621).

In Australia, there are thousands of sole traders in every state who frequently assume the triple responsibilities of owner, manager and risk-taker—small shop-owners, builders, plumbers, electricians, tilers, lawn-mowing operators, doctors, dentists and solicitors, to mention a few. These are individual proprietorships and they vary from businesses where the owner does all the work to those in which many people are employed.

Anyone capable of entering into a contract can operate a business as a sole trader, subject to any statutory requirements that may be laid down by the relevant authorities for the given type of business. For example, a plumber or a builder will have had to complete an apprenticeship and be registered, while a dentist, doctor or lawyer will have studied and completed a course at university in dentistry, medicine or law to the satisfaction of the relevant state dental, medical or solicitors' registration board.

There are both advantages and disadvantages for a sole trader (see Table 29.1).

Advantages

Keeping all the profits

All the profits belong to the sole trader and form part of their income.

Ownership and control of the business

The sole trader can determine what the business will, and will not, do. Also the decision to close the business will be exclusively that of the sole trader. An exception to this rule is, of course, if the business is already in financial difficulty. In such a case, the sole trader may lose control of their destiny to their creditors.

Table 29.1 Advantages and disadvantages of a sole trader

Advantages	*Disadvantages*
1 Keep all the profits	Unlimited liability
2 Ownership and control of the business	The business and the sole trader are often synonymous
3 Lack of formalities and cheap to form	Degree of personal element
4 Nature of business can be easily changed	Lack of management skills or expertise
5 Maintenance of secrecy	Difficulty in raising large amounts of capital

Lack of formalities and cheap to form

There are no special requirements to start operating a business if the name of the sole trader is used.

Nature of business can be easily changed

As the business is controlled by only one person, it is relatively easy to change the nature of the business.

Maintenance of secrecy

Because there are no special statutory disclosure requirements, secrecy can be maintained by the sole trader.

Disadvantages

Unlimited liability

Sole traders are totally liable for all their business debts. If the business fails, their private assets may be used to satisfy any outstanding debts.

The business and the sole trader are often synonymous

The death of the sole trader can often mean the end of the business, if there is a large personal element of skill involved.

Degree of personal element

The degree of personal involvement in the business can make it difficult to sell, if the business exists only because of the personality of the sole trader.

Lack of management skills or expertise

Many small businesses are begun by people with little or no management skills or expertise. This is a major reason behind why 80 per cent of all small businesses fail within the first five years of their establishment.

Difficulty in raising large amounts of capital

Because sole traders often don't have an extensive asset base as security for loans, financial institutions are often reluctant to lend them capital to expand the business. Sole traders who require more capital may decide to take in a partner and thus form a partnership.

PARTNERSHIPS

Law relating to partnerships

Partnerships—a basic form of collective ownership

Partnerships are a common form of business ownership and are the most basic form of collective business organisation. A partnership is defined as 'the relation which subsists between persons carrying on business in common with a view to profit'.

They can be found in most sectors of the economy and are very popular in family enterprises. For example, an individual might enter into a partnership with their husband or wife and children in order to avoid incurring a heavier taxation burden associated with business activities as a sole trader. The services of doctors, accountants, architects, engineers and other professional groups are also admirably suited to the partnership type of business enterprise, for both legal and professional reasons. Advantages and disadvantages are shown in Table 29.2.

Table 29.2 Advantages and disadvantages of a partnership

Advantages	*Disadvantages*
Lack of formalities	Unlimited liability
Cheap to form	Numbers limited to 20 except in professional partnerships
The nature of the business can be easily changed by agreement between the partners	Lack of permanence
Tax advantages	Difficulty in selling one's interest
	Inability to contract with the firm

Maintenance of secrecy, except for details that are required to be disclosed under the Business Names Acts of the states and territories	Loss of control of management of business unlike a sole trader
Potential for partners to pool capital and experience, unlike a sole trader	

A joint venture, which has similar characteristics to a partnership, is distinguishable on the grounds that it is formed only for a specific time or task. There is not an ongoing relationship between the parties.

Partnerships and joint ventures are covered in more detail in the previous chapter.

COMPANIES

Companies—a legal entity separate from their members

A 'company' or 'corporation' is an association of persons who, having satisfied the requirements of the *Corporations Act 2001* (Cth) for registration, are given a **separate legal entity**. That is, the company is recognised by the law as a person and has rights and obligations separate and distinct from those of the shareholders, directors and other persons connected to its operation (see Table 29.3). For a more detailed examination of a company, see Chapter 27.

Table 29.3 Advantages and disadvantages of a company

Advantages	*Disadvantages*
A separate legal entity from the shareholders or members as well as those who control its operations	Cost of establishment and ongoing fees are expensive
Limited liability	Onerous administrative requirements required by law
Perpetual succession	Limited management role for shareholders
The company can sue and be sued	Possible loss of control of the company to shareholders
Transferability of shares	Onerous legal responsibilities imposed on company officers and directors
Taxation benefits	Can be onerous reporting requirements

TRUSTS AND TRUSTEES

A trust arises where property is held by a trustee for the benefit of another

A trust occurs when a person is given the possession and/or power over certain property to use that property for the benefit of some other person or object. The person who is given that possession or power is known as a **trustee**. He or she usually has legal ownership and control of the trust property but is under an **equitable obligation** to deal with property for the benefit of other persons (called **beneficiaries**), any of whom may enforce the obligation. The terms of the trust are usually set out in a trust deed. The trust is a concept derived from the principles of **equity**.

If the purpose of the trust is to carry on a business, it is a trading trust.

Trading trusts

In a **trading trust**, the goodwill and assets of a business are transferred to a trustee, either by will or by a business-person. The type of trust normally used is a discretionary trust. The business is conducted by the trustee.

Advantages

- Can give benefits to members of the family without losing control over those assets.
- Can protect assets against creditors.
- Can have limited liability if the trustee is a company.
- Can safeguard certain social security entitlements.
- Can be a means of passing wealth from one generation to another.
- Can be a tax effective structure.
- Maintains privacy.

Disadvantages

- Can be considerable cost to establish the trust.
- Can be considerable costs in maintaining the trust.

Who is a trustee?

Trustee—holds the legal title or exercises control over property

A **trustee** is an individual person or company that holds the **legal title** or exercises a control over the disposition of property for the purposes of applying it to the benefit of others. For example, if A, although registered as the legal owner of a property, is required by some trust document to hand over the profits and other income to B, who is said to have the equitable title, A is a trustee.

Types of trust

There are many different trusts (see Figure 29.2).

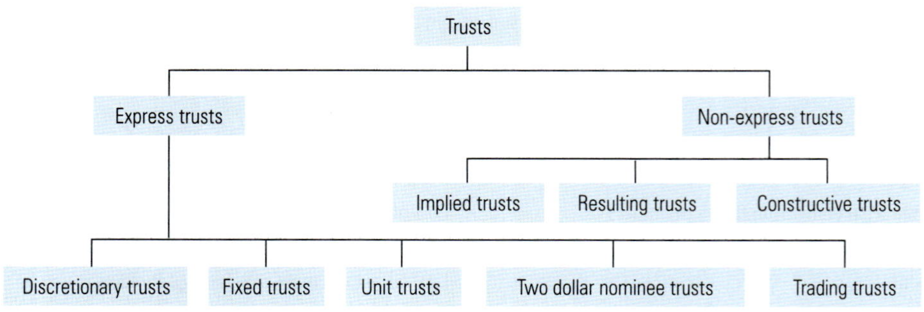

FIGURE 29.2 *Types of trust*

Express trusts

Express trusts are created by the intentional act of a person (a settlor) through a written instrument such as a will.

A 'settlement' rather than a 'declaration' is the common method of creating a trust *inter vivos*, as this refers to the documentary transfer of property by a 'settlor' to a 'trustee' to be held and dealt with in accordance with the purpose for which the trust was set up.

1 Discretionary trusts

A **discretionary trust** normally can be found in small to medium-sized family-owned businesses. The identity or interest of the beneficiary or beneficiaries is not determined at the creation of the trust. The trustee is able to exercise a discretion regarding the choice of beneficiary or beneficiaries and the amount, if any, each is to take from the trust fund or trust interest.

The discretionary trust is perhaps the most popular trust vehicle. The reasons for its popularity can be seen in its advantages:

- it is **flexible**;
- it is **simple** to operate;
- it is a **useful income-splitting device for tax purposes**, though the imputation system for taxing company dividends has taken away some of its attractiveness; and
- it plays an important role in **estate planning** to minimise the size of income-producing assets for income tax purposes.

2 Fixed trusts

In a fixed entitlement trust, the trustee has no discretion as to how to distribute income and property because each beneficiary has an equal share in the trust.

3 Unit trusts

A variation of the fixed entitlement trust is the unit trust where the number of units held by a person is evidence of that person's entitlement to profits and property distribution. Unit trusts are widely used to conduct business in the non-public company area and operate as trading trusts.

Advantages of a unit trust over a discretionary trust include:

- transferability of units;
- fixed annual entitlements to income; and
- fixed entitlements to capital.

A disadvantage of a unit trust is that the unit holders, who are the beneficiaries, could be personally and jointly liable to indemnify the trust if there is any shortfall in assets if the trust goes into liquidation, unless there is an indemnity clause in the trust deed.

activebook

To help you to remember and understand the topics covered so far, and for links to legal websites, refer to your online activebook. Model answers provide feedback to problems and exercises.

4 Two-dollar nominee trust

The trustee is often a $2 nominee proprietary limited company. The trustee's liability is limited to the company's share capital of $2, otherwise the company operates as if it were a natural person trustee.

5 Trading trust

The goodwill and assets of a business are transferred to a trustee.

Non-express trusts

1 Implied trusts

An implied trust arises where the intention is not expressed, but it is possible for the courts to imply or infer that there was an intention to create a trust.

2 Resulting trusts

This is an implied trust where property or an interest in property returns (or 'results') to the trust creator. The law presumes an intention on the part of the settlor to create a trust, even though intention may be unexpressed.

3 Constructive trusts

Constructive trusts are construed from the **circumstances or conduct** of dealing with property, for example, where two people both contribute to the purchase of property but it is only in the name of one of them, not because of any actual or implied intention on the part of the person holding the property or an interest in the property. They can be distinguished from implied and resulting trusts because they arise by operation of law. It would be inequitable for that person to hold the property or interest for themselves. A constructive trust will arise where a person makes a profit from a fiduciary relationship.

Creation

Statutory requirements for realty but none for personalty

Legislation in all states imposes **formal requirements** on the creation of **express trusts**. In the case of land or an interest in land, the trust agreement will be unenforceable unless it is **in writing and signed** by the trust creator. Where it is a declaration of trust over personal property, there is no statutory requirement for the arrangements to be evidenced in writing unless the property is an existing equitable interest.

Whether the trust is for land or personal property, if it is to be a valid express trust, there must be:

- certainty that a trust is intended;
- certainty of the identity of the trust property; and
- certainty as to the beneficiary under the trust.

It is not necessary that consideration be present, nor is it necessary for the beneficiaries to be parties to the agreement, or to even be aware of the existence of the trust.

Table 29. 5 Comparing partnerships, companies and trusts

Characteristic	*Partnership*	*Company*	*Trust*
Liability	Unlimited	Can be limited	Unlimited unless company is used to operate the business
Ownership of business assets	The partners	Owned by the company not members	Owned by trustee, beneficiaries only have equitable interest
Legal status	An accounting and economic entity but not a separate legal person	A separate legal entity	Not a separate legal entity
Agency	Each partner unless restricted as an agent of the partnership	A member is not an agent of the company	Beneficiaries are not agents for the trust
Legal action	Partners may sue or be sued personally	Can sue or be sued A member can sue their own company	Trustee may sue and be sued
Management	Each member	By the board of directors entitled to participate in management	By trustee
Alteration of constitution	By agreement	Must comply with *Corporations Act*	Subject to the Deed or by court order
Continuity of existence	Change of members means dissolution of existing firm	Perpetual succession	Limited by Rule against perpetuities
Taxation	Not a taxable entity	A taxable entity	Now similar to company
Capital gains tax	Partners liable	Company liable	Beneficiaries liable
Costs	Low	High	High
Raise capital from public	Not permitted	Allowed if public company	No—unless public company used

FRANCHISES

While a franchise is not a trading entity, it is a specialised method of trading which, on the one hand is particularly attractive to people who have little business experience and on the other hand is a means for the promoter of the franchise scheme to expand far more quickly than would otherwise be normally possible.

A franchise is a contractual relationship between the franchisor and the franchisee in which the franchisor agrees to maintain a continuing interest in the business of the franchisee in such areas as:

- technical knowledge;
- advertising and marketing;
- product control; and
- expertise and training.

The franchisee agrees to operate under a common trade name, format and procedure owned and controlled by the franchisor. It must be remembered that while the franchisee is self employed, the franchisor will retain considerable control to ensure the continued success of the franchise system.

The advantages of operating a franchise include:

1. virtually instant reputation/goodwill;
2. marketing;
3. financial expertise;
4. training and ongoing support;
5. proven operational system;
6. economies of scale;
7. expertise in site selection and shop fitting out; and
8. business risk is reduced.

Types of franchise

Franchise operations usually fall into one of the following categories, although a particular franchise system may fall into more than one category:

- manufacturing
- product
- system of operation
- group trading.

Possible conflicts with the *Trade Practices Act 1974* (Cth)

Part IV of the *Trade Practices Act 1974* (Cth) prohibits corporations from engaging in anti-competitive behaviour (see Chapter 30 on Restrictive Trade Practices). Most franchisors are companies and therefore the Act will apply to the operation of franchises. Examples of specific possible conflicts with the *Trade Practices Act* are as follows.

Exclusionary provisions: s. 45

- While most franchise agreements contain some aspects of exclusion provisions, the prohibition will not apply unless two or more parties to the agreement are in competition with each other.
- Most franchises are structured so that the parties to the franchise agreement are not in competition with each other.

Price fixing: ss. 45A, 45C

Arrangements involving price fixing are deemed to be likely to substantially lessen competition, irrespective of any actual effect they may have on competition.

Monopolisation: s. 46

This could occur with franchises if the franchise operation was large enough to substantially control the particular market.

Exclusive dealing: s. 47

This could arise in a franchise where the franchisor insists that the franchisee only acquire certain goods from a specific supplier nominated by the franchisor.

Resale price maintenance: s. 48

The price structure may be dictated by the franchisor. The prohibition on resale price maintenance could therefore have a considerable impact on the franchise scheme.

Franchising Code of Conduct

The rapid growth of franchising in recent times resulted in many cases of poorly organised systems and some cases of exploitation of unsuspecting franchisees. In order to protect against these problems the Franchising Code of Conduct was established in 1998. The code applies to all new franchises and to the renewal, extension or transfer of existing franchises on or after 1 October 1998. The aim of the code is to protect the rights of the franchisee and to detail obligations of the franchisor.

- The code has been prescribed under the *Trade Practices Act 1974* and has the force of law, the key sections being 51AC and 51AD.
- The Franchising Code of Conduct sets obligations on franchisors and in doing so establishes rights for franchisees. Key provisions are:

- Disclosure
  The disclosure document must provide particulars in respect to:
  - identity (particulars of the franchisor);
  - experience (summary of the business experience of the franchisor);
  - litigation (details of relevant legal proceedings against the franchisor);
  - payments to agents (in connection with the recruitment of the franchisor);
  - existing franchises;
  - intellectual property (use of trade marks, patents, copyright or designs);
  - franchise territory (whether the franchise is for an exclusive or non-exclusive territory or limited to a particular site);
  - supply of goods or services to a franchisee (any requirement to maintain an inventory level or acquire goods, any interest the franchisor has in a supplier of goods to the franchisee and any restrictions on the franchisee to acquire goods from other sources);
  - sites (policy of the franchisor in selecting a site for a franchise);
  - marketing and other cooperative funds (particulars of membership, financial contributions to the fund, management of the fund and types of expense permitted by the fund);
  - payments (particulars of any payment required prior to entering into the agreement, e.g., establishment costs);
  - financing (important conditions of any financing arrangement the franchisor offers the franchisee);
  - franchisor's obligations (summary of the franchisor's obligations under the agreement);
  - franchisee's obligations (summary of the franchisee's obligations under the agreement);
  - summary of other conditions of the franchise agreement;
  - obligation to sign related agreements (such as lease of premises, hire-purchase agreement, restraint of trade etc.);
  - earnings information (if given, earnings information for the franchise, must be based on reasonable grounds); and
  - financial details (statement as to the franchisor's solvency and copy of profit and loss statement and balance sheet);
- Cooling-off period
  A franchisee may terminate the agreement within seven days. The cooling-off provisions do not apply to the renewal, extension or transfer of an existing franchise.
- Copy of lease
- Association of franchisees (cannot be prohibited by franchisor)
- Prohibition on general release from liability
- Right to transfer franchise
- Termination
  - by the franchisor where there is a breach by the franchisee (the franchisee must be given reasonable time to remedy the breach);
  - by the franchisor where there is no breach by the franchisee (reasonable written notice must be given); or
  - in special circumstances.
- Resolving disputes
  A franchise agreement entered into on or after 1 October 1998 must provide for a complaint handling procedure.

Registration is required where owner/s don't use their own names

BUSINESS NAMES

The majority of businesses register a business name when they commence trading, rather than using the names of the owners. As a result, all states have enacted basically uniform business names legislation (see Table 29.6).

Table 29.6 Business names legislation of the states and territories

Northern Territory, Queensland, Tasmania, Victoria and Western Australia	*Business Names Act 1962*
Australian Capital Territory	*Business Names Act 1963*
South Australia	*Business Names Act 1996*
New South Wales	*Business Names Act 2002*

Where a business trades under a name other than, or more than, the one containing the owner's surname and initials, or in the case of corporate partners, their corporate names, then the Business Names Legislation requires that the business name be registered. If the business intends to trade in more than one state, it will need to register in each state in which it trades, because there is no automatic cross-registration across the whole of Australia.

Purposes of registration

Four purposes can be identified behind the registration of a business name. These are:

1. Although **no proprietary right** is gained by registration under the Act, the registering authority will generally refuse to register the same (or a similar) name, so registration virtually gives monopoly rights to the registered use of the name.
2. Registration is more in the realm of public interest because it compels persons who are not trading under their own names to provide a means whereby they can be **identified** and their whereabouts ascertained.
3. It also is meant to **prevent** the public from being confused or misled by people registering names that are identical or similar to established business names.
4. To provide a **public registry** where information concerning the registered business name is readily available to anyone interested.

Registration

Once registration requirements have been satisfied, a **Certificate of Registration of Business Name** is then issued and this must be displayed in a prominent place at the principal place of business. The registered business name must appear on all official business correspondence. Failure to comply with the legislation can result in a fine. In the case of a partnership, this will mean a fine for each individual partner.

On registration, a business is issued with a Certificate of Registration of Business Name

Changes to a firm's name, the membership of the firm or the firm's address must be registered.

The legislation of each state prohibits registration of a business name in certain circumstances—for example, if it is considered undesirable or if it has already been registered.

> **!** CAUTION NOTE
>
> *Registration does not give a proprietary right but it provides protection under the tort of passing off, trade marks law and the* Trade Practices Act.

Can you obtain protection for your business name?

While it is **not** possible to obtain a proprietary right through registration of a business name under the relevant state Business Names Legislation, businesses with registered names can obtain protection under the following areas:

The tort of passing off

If the plaintiff can establish that their business name is distinctive, and if it can be shown that the defendant's connection could mislead the public and cause a detriment to the public through, for example, lost sales, the plaintiff may have a cause of action through the tort of passing off. Remedies include damages, an account of profits and/or an injunction.

Trade marks law

There is limited protection under the *Trade Marks Act 1955* (Cth) where a registered trade mark forms part of the business name.

The *Trade Practices Act 1974* (Cth)

Sections 52 (misleading and deceptive conduct) and 53 (false representations) of the *Trade Practices Act 1974* (Cth) also provide a statutory remedy for business name infringement. Penalties include damages, injunctions, fines and corrective advertising.

Registration of a business name on the web

Businesses using the www should register an Internet Domain Name

For doing business on the web, thought should be given to registration of an Internet Domain Name. Because an Internet Domain Name only needs to be a derivation of a company name, business name or registered trademark, there are usually a few Australian businesses entitled to choose the same derivation, so it's a matter of getting in first. It is therefore possible for another company to register a derivation of a name similar to the one planned for registration, and end up with a derivation to which you think you have exclusive rights. Unless they are in the same trademark business category, there is no recourse because what they have done is legal.

WEB RESOURCES

Australian Capital Territory:
http://www.dpa.act.gov.au/ag/rgo/rgo04.html

New South Wales: information is obtainable from the Department of Fair Trading. For information on Business Names, click on 'Your Business' and from there you will find information about Business Names registration, the national Business Names Register:

http://www.dft.nsw.gov.au/

Northern Territory:
For business names registration information:
http://www.tbc.nt.gov.au/documents/dir49/doc504849.html

Queensland:
http://www.consumer.qld.gov.au/gbguide/names.htm

South Australia:
http://www.ocba.sa.gov.au/licensing.htm

Tasmania:
http://www.justice.tas.gov.au/breg/contact_breg.htm

Victoria:
http://www.justice.vic.gov.au/dojsite.nsf/pages/OFTBABusiness?OpenDocument

Western Australia:
http://www.fairtrading.wa.gov.au/bizn_content.htm

Corporate affairs: A useful site for extensive information on the *Corporations Act*, including a full list of company and business names, is the Australian Securities and Investment Commission site:
http://www.asic.gov.au/

REVIEW QUESTIONS ?

29.1 What is meant by a trust?

29.2 Who may become a trustee?

29.3 Name four ways in which a trustee may be appointed.

29.4 Name four duties of a trustee.

29.5 Indicate whether each of the following statements is true or false:

	TRUE	FALSE
▪ The shareholders of a company with share capital are its members	☐	☐
▪ A trustee is a person who benefits under a trust	☐	☐
▪ Under an express trust, the beneficiary is able to exercise a discretion as to whom should benefit and how much they should get	☐	☐

29.6 The registration of a business name protects that name from being used by someone else. Discuss.

CRITICAL THINKING

29.1 Juliet and Elroy want to go into business. Neither of them have any experience in business so they want to keep the administration as simple and as confidential as possible. They are confident they will be successful and will eventually need much more capital for expansion. They want to include their adult children as members of the business and, although they are prepared to share profits with the children, they do not want the children to have any control over the business operations.

(1) Briefly advise them as to the most suitable business entity for their situation. Refer to the concept of separate legal entity and some of the legal consequences that flow from being a separate legal entity.

(2) Is it possible to include their adult children in the manner they have suggested? If it can be done, outline how it can be done.

CHAPTER 30 Restrictive Trade Practices

CHAPTER CONTENTS

> **activebook**
>
> This icon is used throughout the following chapter to remind you to visit the *Business Law* online activebook for additional exercises, links to legal websites, and feedback. For a detailed explanation of what is in the activebook please refer to the inside cover of this textbook. The activebook is available through OneKey.
>
> **Where do I start?**
>
> **Learning path**: Use the activebook to complete a pre-chapter warm-up exercise.
>
> There are many definitions of legal terms to assist with your understanding of the material.

CHAPTER OBJECTIVES

On completion of this chapter, you should be able to:

- discuss the aims of the *Trade Practices Act*
- outline the constitutional limitation of the *Trade Practices Act*
- explain the national competition policy
- discuss and contrast the role of the Australian Competition and Consumer Commission, the Australian Competition Tribunal and the Federal Court
- define and discuss the terms 'market' and 'competition'
- list and describe the prohibited practices in Part IV
- describe the process of authorisation and notification
- outline the enforcement procedures and remedies under Part IV
- describe an industry code of conduct
- discuss the effectiveness of the legislation.

KEY TERMS

An understanding of the following terms will help you to better understand the material in this chapter:

- **authorisation:** a dispensation that the Australian Competition and Consumer Commission may grant for a restrictive trade practice which would otherwise be in breach of the Act
- **competition:** the process by which producers (or consumers) of goods within a market compete with one another
- **corporation:** includes a foreign, financial or trading corporation, as well as a territorial corporation (s. 4(1)). A foreign corporation is a corporation incorporated outside Australia; a financial corporation is a corporation that engages in the conduct of dealing in finance; a trading corporation is a corporation that does, or will, engage in trading activities (providing goods and services for reward) of a not insignificant scale. Most corporations are trading corporations. A territorial corporation is a corporation incorporated in the Australian Capital Territory or the Northern Territory
- **market:** all goods or services which compete with each other or which are generally substitutable for one another (s. 4E)
- **primary boycott:** two or more parties combine by refusing to supply goods or services to another party or refuse to acquire that other party's goods or services
- **secondary boycott:** the parties impose the boycott against a third party (with whom they usually have no dispute) in order to stop the third party from dealing with a fourth party, the real target.

what if . . .

You invest all your money in a new business and a week after you start your competitors approach you and tell you that you must only trade on the terms they dictate and if you refuse they will take combined action to force you out of business. What legal rights do you have to counter this intimidation?

The purpose of the trade practices legislation is to promote competition and to minimise the scope for market dominance and manipulation by corporations. The aim of the Act is to strengthen the competitiveness of private enterprise at the various levels of production and distribution of industrial and consumer goods and services to the benefit of the public as ultimate consumers and to the benefit of business in general. As a result of this aim, the *Trade Practices Act 1974* (Cth) has enormous importance for business.

As part of a national competition regime, the Commonwealth, states and territories have agreed to:

- the Conduct Code Agreement;
- the Competition Principles Agreement; and
- the Agreement to Implement the National Competition Policy and Related Reforms.

This chapter looks at the operation of the Act, the effect of the *Competition Policy Reform Act 1995* (Cth), the administration of the Act through the Australian Competition and Consumer Commission (ACCC) and the Australian Competition Tribunal. It then considers the concepts of 'competition' and 'market', Part IV of the Act, enforcement, authorisations and notifications, and industry codes of conduct.

OPERATION OF THE ACT

What is the constitutional basis for the Trade Practices Act?

No specific power under Constitution to regulate trade practices

In Chapter 23, it was pointed out that the *Trade Practices Act* provides protection for consumers by prohibiting such activities as misleading and deceptive conduct and false representations, and through manufacturer's liability. It was also pointed out that, under the Commonwealth Constitution, there is no specific power to regulate trade practices.

The Commonwealth government therefore based the legislation on a number of specific constitutional heads of power including:

- the corporations power—s. 51(xx)—which is the main power;
- overseas trade and commerce—s. 51(i); and
- trade or commerce within a territory, between territories or between a state and a territory—s. 122.

While the Commonwealth government has been able to use these specific powers collectively to indirectly obtain legislative power over activities not specifically provided for, they have limited the scope of the Act to situations primarily involving interstate trade and companies.

THE *COMPETITION POLICY REFORM ACT 1995* (CTH)

In adopting many of the proposals made by the 1993 Hilmer Report, the Council of Australian Government in April 1995 took three important steps towards a national competition policy which would overcome the constitutional limitations imposed upon the Commonwealth by the Constitution. The Commonwealth, states and territories signed:

- a **Conduct Code Agreement** with the purpose of ensuring that the competition provisions of the *Trade Practices Act* apply to all businesses in Australia, not just those within the constitutional reach of the Commonwealth;
- a **Competition Principles Agreement** for the establishment of a **National Competition Council**. The Agreement sets out the principles the state and territory governments would follow to ensure greater competition in markets that require access to essential services, such as electricity, gas, telecommunications and vocational education, which have previously been government-owned activities. As a result, there has been a wider range of choice of providers to consumers; and
- an **Agreement to Implement the National Competition Policy and Related Reforms**.

Extensive amendments were required to the competition provisions of the *Trade Practices Act* to implement these changes and this was done by the Commonwealth government passing the *Competition Policy Reform Act 1995*.

The changes were to take place in three stages:

- Stage 1 took effect in August 1995 and made a number of amendments to the restrictive trade practices provisions of Part IV of the *Trade Practices Act*. It also introduced a new Part XIA (ss. 150A–150K) which is essentially a modified version of the competition provisions of Part IV of the *Trade Practices Act* but applying to all persons, including corporations.
- Stage 2 took effect in November 1995. It merged the Trade Practices Commission and the Prices Surveillance Authority into the Australian Competition and Consumer Commission (see below) and renamed the Trade Practices Tribunal the Australian Competition Tribunal (see below). It also created a new advisory body, the National Competition Council (NCC) which was a joint creation between Commonwealth, state and territory governments to implement the national competition provisions found in Part IIIA (ss. 44B–44ZZO) of the *Trade Practices Act*. Its functions include:
  - assessing Part IIIA applications for access to essential service infrastructures;
  - making recommendations regarding access declarations; and
  - acting as a watchdog on prices charged by government businesses.
- Stage 3 came into effect in July 1996 with the addition of Part IIIA (ss. 44B–44ZZO) to the *Trade Practices Act*. This allows 'third party businesses' to gain access to those services that, for example, have previously been government-owned enterprises such as Telstra (which now no longer has sole control of the telecommunications

industry) and TAFE (which is no longer the sole provider of recognised vocational education). It was based on the belief that consumers would benefit through better service, a wider choice and a lower price. Access for new competitors can be voluntarily given by way of commercial agreements or by order of the NCC and the support of the appropriate government minister.

ADMINISTRATION OF THE ACT

The Act is administered by the ACCC and ACT

The *Trade Practices Act* is administered primarily by two organisations created specifically for the purpose (see Figure 30.1):

- the **Australian Competition and Consumer Commission** (ACCC) has general responsibility for the surveillance and enforcement of the Act (see below); and
- the **Australian Competition Tribunal** (ACT), which reviews decisions of the ACCC (see below).

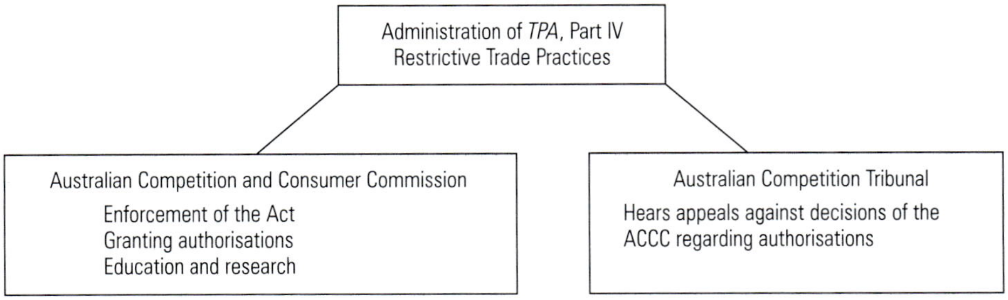

FIGURE 30.1 *Administration of the* Trade Practices Act

The Australian Competition and Consumer Commission (ACCC)

ACCC is responsible for granting authorisations, administration, enforcement, education and research

The ACCC is a Commonwealth statutory body with a full-time chairperson and a number of full-time members appointed by the Commonwealth government.

The main functions of the ACCC are:

- administration and enforcement of the Act;
- the granting of authorisations of certain restrictive trade practices that would ordinarily be prohibited but which give the public a benefit, that to the satisfaction of the Commission, outweighs the adverse effect on competition; and
- providing assistance to the public by engaging in research, education of the public and the business community and by providing consumer guidance. In performing its enforcement and authorisation functions, the ACCC can enter premises to obtain evidence and conduct public hearings. These hearings are conducted informally and are not subject to the rules of evidence, although evidence can be taken on oath. In circumstances where the Commission considers it appropriate, the hearings may be closed to the public. The Commission has the power to fine, order an injunction, or make an order directing the sale of shares or assets acquired by a corporation in an illegal manner.

WEB RESOURCE

More information on the Australian Competition and Consumer Commission may be obtained from:
http://www.accc.gov.au

The Australian Competition Tribunal (ACT)

ACT hears appeals from the ACCC on authorisations

The ACT consists of a president, deputy presidents who are judges of a Federal Court and several members who are economists and business people appointed by the Commonwealth government. A person who is dissatisfied with a decision of the ACCC in regard to an application for an authorisation or the revocation of an existing authorisation may apply to the ACT for a review, which is a re-hearing of the matter. The ACT must decide for itself if the ACCC's determination should be affirmed, varied or set aside: ss. 101(1) and 101(2). Proceedings before the ACT are similar to those before the ACCC in that they are informal and the rules of evidence do not apply.

The role of the Federal Court

The Federal Court has primary responsibility for hearing disputes involving the *Trade Practices Act*: s. 86. As a general rule, most cases will be heard before a single judge with appeals going to the Full Bench (three judges) and from there to the High Court. (See below under Enforcement Procedures and Remedies on p. 638.)

THE CONCEPTS OF 'MARKET' AND 'COMPETITION'

Two concepts that are essential to the effective operation of the legislation are 'competition' and 'market'. This is because most of the prohibited trade practices are only prohibited if there is a substantial reduction in competition. It is therefore essential to understand what competition is. Since competition takes place in a market, it is essential to understand what a market is.

'Competition' is a process that considers market structure

Section 4(1) of the Act defines competition as including competition from imported goods or from services rendered by persons not resident or carrying on business in Australia. As this definition merely defines competition as including certain specific types of competition, it is not particularly helpful in respect to the concept involved. It is therefore useful to examine what the former Trade Practices Tribunal said in *Re Queensland Co-Operative Milling Association v. Defiance Holdings Ltd* [1976] ATPR ¶40-012 on pages 17 245–17 246:

> *. . . we think of competition as a mechanism for discovery of market information and for enforcement of business decisions in the light of this information. It is a mechanism, first, for firms discovering the kinds of goods and services the community wants and the manner in which these may be supplied in the cheapest possible way. Competition is a process rather than a situation. Nevertheless, whether firms compete is very much a matter of the structure of the markets in which they operate. The elements of market structure that we would stress as needing to be scanned in any case are these:*
>
> *1 the number and size distribution of independent sellers, especially the degree of market concentration;*
> *2 the height of barriers to entry, that is the ease with which new firms may enter and secure a viable market;*
> *3 the extent to which the products of the industry are characterised by extreme product differentiation and sales promotion;*
> *4 the character of 'vertical relationships' with customers and with suppliers and the extent of vertical integration; and*
> *5 the nature of any formal, stable fundamental arrangements between firms which restrict their ability to function as independent entities.*

It can be seen that the tribunal's approach takes into account the broad economic idea of competition and the multitude of variables that this involves. Similarly, the concept of 'market' is defined in s. 4E of the Act:

Section 4E—'Market' area of competition between firms in Australia

> *For the purposes of this Act, 'market' means a market in Australia and, when used in relation to any goods or services, includes a market for those goods or services and other goods or services that are substitutable for, or otherwise competitive with, the first-mentioned goods or services.*

Again in *Re Queensland Co-Operative Milling Association/Defiance Holdings Ltd*, the Trade Practices Tribunal said:

> *A market is the area of close competition between firms, or putting it a little differently, the field of rivalry between them. (If there is no close competition there is of course a monopolistic market.) Within the bounds of a market there is substitution—substitution between one product and another, and between one source of supply and another, in response to changing prices. So a market is an area of actual and potential transactions between buyers and sellers, amongst whom there can be strong substitution, at least in the long run, if given a sufficient price incentive.*

It is the possibilities of such substitution which set the limits upon a firm's ability to 'give less and charge more'. Accordingly, in determining the outer boundaries of the market we ask a quite simple but fundamental question: If the firm were to 'give less and charge more' would there be, to put the matter colloquially, much of a reaction? And if so, from whom?

The Act demonstrates a recognition of the broad economic concept and is not adopting a purely legalistic approach. These concepts of competition and market are very important to the operation of the Act and the understanding of its application to the various specific restrictive trade practices and should be kept in mind at all times.

IN BRIEF

Meanings of 'competition' and 'market'

Competition

- A mechanism for the discovery of market information and for enforcement of business decisions in the light of that information.
- A mechanism for firms discovering the kinds of goods and services the community wants and the manner in which these may be supplied in the cheapest possible way.
- A process rather than a situation.

Market

A market is an area of actual or potential transactions between buyers and sellers, among whom there can be strong substitution if given a sufficient price incentive.

activebook

To help you to remember and understand the topics covered so far, and for links to legal websites, refer to your online activebook. Model answers provide feedback to problems and exercises.

RESTRICTIVE TRADE PRACTICES

Restrictive trade practices may be grouped into categories as shown in Table 30.1.

Table 30.1 Business practices caught by the *Trade Practices Act*

Conduct prohibited	*Section*
▪ price fixing:	s. 45A
– resale price maintenance	s. 48
▪ monopoly or market domination:	
– abuse of monopoly power in a market	s. 46
– mergers resulting in market dominance	s. 50
▪ exclusive dealing	s. 47
▪ third line forcing	s. 47(6)
▪ boycotts	s. 45D
▪ arrangements to substantially lessen competition:	
– contracts, arrangements and understandings	s. 45
– covenants	ss. 45B, 45C

Price (s. 45A)

IN BRIEF

Price fixing—any action by competitors in the market to fix, control or maintain prices. *Resale price maintenance*—a practice by which the supplier of goods and services tries to impose a minimum price below which the supplier's goods or services are not to be resold.

What is price fixing?

Price fixing: s. 45A—anti-competitive and is prohibited

Price competition is taken to be a major indicator of a viable market and any action by competitors in the market to fix, control or maintain prices is prohibited (s. 45A).

It is not necessary to inquire into the effect the action will have on the market. The ACCC is empowered to grant an authorisation for price fixing in certain limited circumstances under s. 88(1), if it can be shown that the benefit to the public outweighs the anti-competitive detriment to the public.

Section 45A provides that a provision of a contract, arrangement or understanding shall be deemed to have the purpose of substantially lessening competition, if the provision has the purpose of **fixing, controlling or maintaining the price** for goods or services and is prohibited outright (*per se*).

Horizontal price fixing agreements are agreements entered into between competing businesses at the same level of business activity, for example, retailer and retailer (see Figure 30.2). A wholesaler and retailer are not on the same level and so there could be no horizontal agreement here.

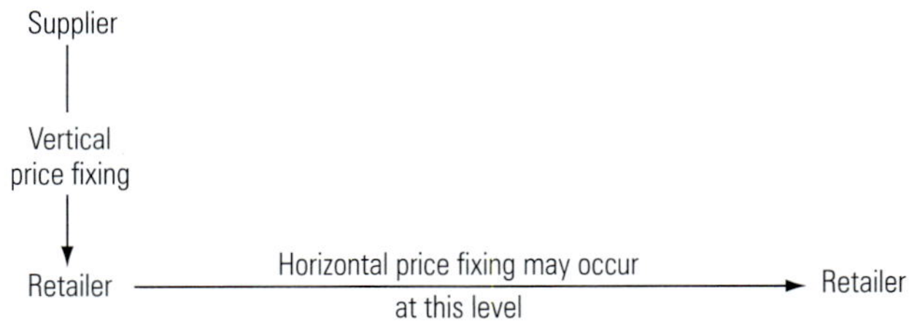

FIGURE 30.2 *Horizontal and vertical price fixing*

It can be seen that s. 45A deems price fixing to substantially lessen competition. Deeming means that price fixing is taken to be anti-competitive without the need to prove its effect on competition. When combined with s. 45, which prohibits a corporation entering into a contract or arrangement that has the purpose or effect of lessening competition, price fixing becomes prohibited conduct. It is, however, still necessary to prove the existence of a contract, arrangement or understanding to fix, control or maintain prices. Only a mere hope that something will be done is not price fixing.

TPC v. Email [1980] ATPR ¶40-172

Email and Warburton Franki were the only Australian manufacturers of certain electricity meters. Email held approximately 70 per cent of the market and was accepted as market leader. Both companies issued identical price lists, sent their respective price lists to each other and submitted identical tenders for contracts. The Trade Practices Commission brought an action alleging an arrangement or understanding in relation to prices that amounted to a breach of the s. 45A prohibition on price fixing.

ISSUE: The defendants argued that the parallel pricing was due to market forces and that because Warburton Franki could not survive a price cutting war with Email, Warburton Franki had to follow Email.

DECISION: *Lockhart* J of the Federal Court held that there was no price fixing agreement, *Lockhart* J saying: '[F]or there to be an arrangement or understanding there must be a meeting of the minds of those parties said to be parties to the arrangement or understanding . . . There must be a consensus as to what is to be done and not just a mere hope as to what might be done or happen.'

COMMENT: The parallel pricing of the products of the two companies could be explained by market forces rather than the result of the exchange of information about prices.

Section 45A(3) provides that if 50 or more persons who supply or acquire goods or services enter into an arrangement that recommends the price, discounts, allowances, rebates or credits in relation to the supply of goods or services, the arrangement is excluded from the deeming provisions of s. 45A(1). If the arrangement merely recommends a price and does not involve any enforcement of the recommendation—that is, the parties are free to accept the recommendation or reject it—the arrangement is not automatically prohibited. It would need to be examined to establish whether or not it had the purpose or effect of substantially lessening competition. It should be noted that any such recommendation would have a strong influence on prices and may therefore fail the test.

What is resale price maintenance?

Resale price maintenance: s. 48—anti-competitive because it involves a minimum price below which goods cannot be sold

Resale price maintenance is a practice by which the supplier of goods or services tries to impose a minimum price below which the supplier's goods or services are not to be resold (s. 48). In other words, the manufacturer or distributor tries to force the retailer to sell the goods or services for a price at least equal to a price set by the manufacturer or distributor.

The main reason for a supplier to engage in resale price maintenance is to promote the status of the product or service by ensuring it stays in the market price category the supplier is aiming at (as distinct from the category the retailer may be aiming at). Retailers will sometimes discount certain high-profile products or services as an advertising ploy. While this may be beneficial to the retailer, the supplier often considers it detrimental to their sales promotions and the market status of the product or service.

Resale price maintenance is deemed to be anti-competitive and is prohibited by s. 48. However, the ACCC may grant an authorisation where it is satisfied that the proposed conduct will benefit the public (s. 88(8)(A), (9)).

Certain actions are specified in s. 96 as constituting resale price maintenance. These actions include:

- threatening or actually refusing to supply goods or services unless the retailer agrees not to sell below the price specified by the supplier;
- inducing the retailer not to sell below a price specified by the supplier or some nominated third party; and
- agreement between supplier and retailer that the goods or services are not to be resold below a price nominated by the supplier.

Section 97 provides that a supplier will not be engaging in resale price maintenance if a price attached to the goods or services is preceded by the words 'recommended price', or if the supplier, in a written notification to the second person, states a price that the supplier recommends as appropriate, provided there is also a statement to the following effect: The 'price set out' or referred to herein is a recommended price only and there is no obligation to comply with the recommendation.

RON HODGSON (HOLDINGS) PTY LTD V. WESTCO MOTORS (DISTRIBUTORS) PTY LTD (1980) 5 TPC 704

The plaintiff had a franchise to sell Mazda vehicles. The defendant became aware that the plaintiff was selling vehicles below the list price. The defendant was also concerned with the plaintiff's financial position. As a result the defendant cancelled the plaintiff's franchise.

The plaintiff sought an injunction on the grounds that refusing to supply the vehicles for reasons such as discounting amounted to resale price maintenance. The defendant argued that there were sound commercial reasons for cancelling the franchise besides the defendant's price discounting.

ISSUE: Must price discounting be the sole reason for refusing to supply or will resale price maintenance exist if price discounting is only one of several reasons?

DECISION: *Franki* J of the Federal Court held that the defendant had sound commercial reasons for cancelling the franchise but the plaintiff was still granted an injunction. It was not necessary that the price discounting be the only reason for terminating the franchise. To establish resale price maintenance conduct, it was sufficient to show that the discounting practices were one of the reasons for the termination of the franchise.

Doing business

Resale price maintenance prohibited?

If a recommended resale price is enforced by some form of coercion or penalty, or the price is not preceded by the words 'recommended price', it becomes resale price maintenance and is prohibited under the *Trade Practices Act*. ■

MONOPOLY OR MARKET DOMINATION (SS. 46, 47, 50)

IN BRIEF

Monopoly or market domination

A corporation that has a substantial degree of market power is prohibited from using that power to:

- eliminate or substantially damage a competitor;
- prevent entry of a person into a market; or
- deter or prevent competitive conduct in a market.

Misuse of market power

Misuse of market power: s. 46—prohibits the abuse of market power

A corporation that has a substantial degree of market power is prohibited by s. 46 from using that power to:

- eliminate or substantially damage a competitor;
- prevent the entry of a person into a market; or
- deter or prevent competitive conduct in a market.

There is no provision for authorisation of misuse of market power.

Where a corporation has such a degree of market power, and uses it in one of the three ways mentioned in the last paragraph, a monopoly is usually said to exist. In Australia, there are many examples of a corporation having this substantial degree of market power, and Telstra is an obvious one. The Act does not prohibit the existence of this market power; it prohibits the abuse of the market power.

***QUEENSLAND WIRE INDUSTRIES P/L V. BHP* (1989) 63 ALJR 181**

BHP manufactured certain steel products, which it sold to its wholly-owned subsidiary and to overseas buyers. It would not otherwise sell the products, except at an excessively high price. Queensland Wire required the particular steel product in order to manufacture steel posts used in rural fencing.

ISSUE: Was the refusal of BHP to sell the product at other than an excessively high price an abuse of that company's dominance in the market?

DECISION: The High Court held that a market exists where there is a product for exchange, whether or not there had been an exchange or even if negotiations had taken place. In effectively refusing to supply the specific products to Queensland Wire by setting an excessively high price, BHP had taken advantage of its substantial market power by deterring or preventing a person from engaging in competitive conduct in a market. Setting an excessively high price was an abuse of market power.

However, if a business has been using a marketing system before it gained market dominance, the continued use of that marketing technique is not necessarily an abuse of market power.

***MELWAY PUBLISHING PTY LTD V. ROBERT HICKS PTY LTD* (2001) 205 CLR 1**

Melway published a street directory for Melbourne and held nearly 90 per cent of the market share. Melway's distribution system divided the market into segments and an exclusive distributor was appointed for each segment. Hicks was the distributor for the retail market segment served by auto parts suppliers. Melway terminated Hicks' distributorship and refused to supply directories to Hicks for distribution to his retail customers.

ISSUE: Did Melway's refusal to supply constitute taking advantage of market power to prevent competitive conduct?

DECISION: The High Court held that the segmented distribution system was created by Melway before it gained market dominance; the continued use of this system was not an abuse of market power.

Mergers

IN BRIEF

Mergers

A corporation is prohibited from acquiring any shares or assets of another corporation if the acquisition would be likely to place the first corporation in a position to dominate a market.

Mergers: s. 50—prohibits mergers of corporations that might lead to the creation of monopoly power

While s. 46 recognises the existence of monopolies and prohibits the abuse of power, s. 50 is aimed at prohibiting mergers of corporations that might lead to the creation of a monopoly which would substantially lessen competition in a market. The section prohibits a corporation from acquiring any shares or assets of another corporation if:

- the acquisition would be likely to place the first corporation in a position to dominate a market; or
- it would substantially strengthen the power of the first corporation to dominate the market.

In order to determine whether a merger may result in a corporation achieving a substantial degree of power in a market, the courts look at the corporation's total market power, taking into account related and associated companies. A corporation seeking to complete a merger can apply to the Commission for an authorisation. To evaluate the merger the Commission will use a five-stage process which addresses the following issues:

- Market definition, i.e. in which industry market is the merger occurring?
- Market shares, i.e. will the merger result in a substantial lessening of competition? If it won't, it probably won't be challenged.

- Is there strong import concentration? If there is, the merger will probably be approved.
- Are there low barriers to entry? If there are, it will probably not be challenged.
- Are there other structural and behavioural market features affecting competition that may prevent market domination?

This process incorporates the statutory factors set out in s. 50(3). The Commission will only grant an authorisation where the acquisition would result or would be likely to result in a benefit to the public. If a prohibited merger is completed, the Commission can seek an order to have the offending party dispose of shares or other assets.

Exclusive dealing

IN BRIEF

Exclusive dealing

Exclusive dealing arises where a corporation supplies goods and services on a condition that the person to whom the goods and services are supplied will not acquire goods from or supply goods and services to a competitor of the corporation.

Exclusive dealing: s. 47—supplying of goods or services on a condition

A corporation engages in exclusive dealing if the corporation supplies or offers to supply goods or services on a condition that the person to whom the goods or services are supplied:

- will not acquire goods or services directly from a competitor of the supplier; or
- will not re-supply goods acquired directly or indirectly from a competitor of the supplier (s. 47).

***TPC v. Legion Cabs (Trading) Co-operative Society Ltd* (1978) 35 FLR 372**

Legion Cabs, a cooperative society for taxi operators, had borrowed money from Shell Oil Co. for the purchase and installation of a new communications system. Members of the society were required to purchase products from Shell or be penalised. Shell had agreed to allow rebates to Legion where sufficient quantities of fuel were bought, the rebates being offset against the loan.

ISSUE: Did the agreement between Shell and Legion Cabs breach s. 47?

DECISION: The Federal Court held that Legion had engaged in exclusive dealing. The requirement to purchase a minimum amount of a third party's product or be penalised is exclusive dealing.

Exclusive dealing is only prohibited if it has the purpose or effect of substantially lessening competition in the market.

Parties that are engaged in exclusive dealing may notify the ACCC of their conduct under s. 93 and obtain protection from prosecution. That is, the parties may engage in the practice of exclusive dealing until the Commission determines the matter and makes a final decision on whether it may continue or it revokes its protection. Alternatively, the parties may apply for authorisation if the parties can show that in all the circumstances the conduct or practice would result in benefit to the public: s. 88(8).

Third line forcing: s. 47(6)—prohibited *per se* and arises where a supplier forces a buyer to obtain other goods and services from a third party

Third line forcing (s. 47(6))

Exclusive dealing will also exist if the supplier forces a person to acquire other goods or services from a third party with whom the supplier has a direct or indirect connection. This action is called third line forcing. An example is a finance company that supplies finance for the purchase of a car and then insists that the borrower insures the car with a particular insurance company. The loan becomes dependent on the insurance. This practice is prohibited by s. 47(6) (see, for example, *KAM Nominees Pty Ltd v. Australian Guarantee Corporation Ltd* [1994] ATPR ¶41-325).

It should be noted that the Act does not prevent the finance company from insisting that the car is insured or from specifying several insurance companies from which the buyer can choose. Third line forcing can be authorised if it can be shown that public benefit justifies it under authorisation 'test 2': s 93.

Boycotts (ss. 45, 45D)

IN BRIEF

Boycotts

Primary boycott—two or more parties combine by refusing to supply goods or services to another party or refuse to acquire that party's goods or services.

Secondary boycott—the parties who impose the boycott apply pressure against a third party, with whom they usually have no dispute, in order to stop that third party from dealing with a fourth party who is their real target.

Boycotts: ss. 45 & 45D—a systematic refusal to have dealings with another party

A boycott is a systematic refusal to have dealings with another party. For the purposes of the *Trade Practices Act*, boycotts can be divided into two classes:

- primary boycotts, which are prohibited outright; and
- secondary boycotts, which are permitted if the dominant purpose of the conduct relates to employment, environmental or consumer protection.

Primary boycott

Primary boycott—the parties take action directly against the party they are boycotting

Two or more parties combine by refusing to supply their goods or services to another party or refuse to acquire that other party's goods or services. It involves the parties taking action directly against the party they are boycotting—that is, their 'target'. Under s. 45, a catch-all section, a corporation is prohibited from making a contract or arrangement, or arriving at an understanding containing an exclusionary provision (sometimes referred to as a primary boycott) which has the purpose or effect of substantially lessening competition.

An exclusionary provision is a provision in a contract, arrangement or understanding that has the purpose of preventing, restricting or limiting the supply or the acquisition of goods or services to or from, particular persons. A corporation will engage in exclusive dealings if it refuses to supply services to a person because that person has acquired or refused not to acquire services of a competitor.

***MCCARTHY V. AUSTRALIAN ROUGH RIDERS ASSOCIATION INC.* [1988] ATPR ¶40-836**

McCarthy was a professional rough rider and a member of the Australian Rough Riders Association (ARRA). One of the rules of the ARRA prevented members from competing in rodeos conducted by organisations that were not associated with the ARRA.

To increase his income, McCarthy took part in rodeos conducted by organisations not associated with the ARRA.

The ARRA imposed a fine and a 12-month good behaviour bond on him and notified associated rodeo organisations that McCarthy was ineligible to compete until further notice. Biloela Rodeo indicated that in compliance with the notice from the ARRA, it would not permit McCarthy to compete in its rodeo.

ISSUE: Was the ARRA rule, that professional rough riders who chose to belong to the association could only ride in rodeos organised by the ARRA, an exclusionary provision contrary to s. 45?

DECISION: *Franki* J in the Federal Court held that Biloela Rodeo was a trading corporation that was a competitor in a market for the acquisition of services of rough riders, competing with other rodeo organisations. Biloela Rodeo was a party to an arrangement or understanding that contained an exclusionary provision and had given effect to that exclusionary provision.

Similarly in the 'Super League Case', *News Ltd v. Australian Rugby Football League Ltd* [1996] ATPR 41-521, the Full Federal Court ruled that agreements signed by the Australian Rugby League and 17 clubs which in effect prevented the 'Super League Clubs' from participating in a new competition until the end of 1999 were exclusionary and in breach of section 45.

The reference to 'contract' is a reference to the normal meaning of that word as an agreement enforceable by law. The expressions 'arrangement' and 'understanding' are not defined in the Act. However, it appears that they involve a meeting of the minds of the parties and the acceptance that each party will act in a particular way. Independently held beliefs or a hope that something might happen do not constitute a meeting of the minds. See *TPC v. Email Ltd* (1980) on page 630. Conduct prohibited by s. 45 may be authorised under s. 88(1) if the parties can show that the benefit to the public outweighs the anti-competitive detriment to the public.

Secondary boycott

Secondary boycott—the parties who impose the boycott apply pressure against a third party

In contrast with a primary boycott, under a secondary boycott, the parties who impose the boycott apply pressure against a third party, with whom they usually have no dispute, in order to stop that third party from dealing with a fourth party who is their real target. For example, for a secondary boycott to operate there must be concerted action between A and B to force C to stop supplying, acquiring or otherwise dealing with D.

The boycott by A and B is 'secondary', as their actions are not directed at C but at D. For the section to operate there must be a third person, C, who is prevented or hindered from supplying to or acquiring goods or services from D.

Originally the secondary boycott provisions of s. 45D were used by employers as a means of settling industrial disputes but this power was transferred to industrial relations legislation by the *Workplace Relations Act 1996* (Cth). The current s. 45D essentially applies to non-industrial or corporate boycotts. Conduct prohibited by s. 45D may be authorised by the Commission under s. 88(1) if the public benefit justifies authorisation.

Exceptions

Section 51 provides a number of exceptions to the prohibitions stated above and these include:

- conduct authorised by legislation;
- industrial agreements covering working conditions;
- non-competition provisions in contracts;
- contracts requiring compliance with prescribed standards;
- partnership agreements;
- consumer boycotts; and
- arrangements relating to copyright or patents.

Contracts, arrangements or understandings restricting or affecting competition (s. 45)

Section 45 could be described as a general 'catch all' provision which is intended to extend the prohibitions of the Act to situations which do not fall neatly into one or more of the more specific prohibitions. Because of its general nature it may be used in addition to other more specific prohibitions.

AUSTRALIAN COMPETITION AND CONSUMER COMMISSION V. LIQUORLAND (AUSTRALIA) PTY LTD (ACN 007512419) AND WOOLWORTHS LTD (ACN 000145675) [2005] FCA 683

Under the New South Wales *Liquor Act*, objections may be made to an application for the issue of a liquor licence for the supply of takeaway liquor. Liquorland had objected to several liquor licences; however, Liquorland proposed to withdraw its objections in return for a restrictive agreement in the form of a deed from the applicants for the takeaway liquor licence.

Liquorland admitted it had entered into agreements with five such liquor licence applicants in order to prevent them from competing with its own stores in the supply of takeaway liquor.

The restrictive agreements contained one or more conditions to the following effect:

- preventing liquor licence applicants from selling packaged takeaway liquor from their premises;
- preventing liquor licence applicants opening a dedicated bottle shop;
- restricting and preventing liquor licence applicants from establishing a separate drive-through bottle shop;
- restricting and preventing liquor licence applicants from advertising or conducting promotions for the sale of packaged takeaway liquor over the counter to consumers;
- preventing liquor licence applicants from being able to offer home delivery services for packaged takeaway liquor to consumers;
- preventing liquor licence applicants from expanding the size of their licensed premises to meet potential increased consumer demand; and
- limiting the amount of packaged takeaway liquor that liquor licence applicants can keep on their premises in order to meet consumer demand.

ISSUE: Can the statutory right to object to the issue of a business licence be a breach of the *Trade Practices Act 1974*?

DECISION: The Federal Court of Australia held that Liquorland was in breach of Section 45 and ordered it to pay pecuniary penalties of $950 000 for each of the five contraventions totalling $4.75 million.

AUTHORISATIONS AND NOTIFICATIONS (S. 88)

! CAUTION NOTE

To obtain an authorisation, public benefit must outweigh reduction in competition or the conduct must be of benefit to the public.

The ACCC, or on appeal the ACT, may grant a special exemption to a particular restrictive agreement or practice that would otherwise be prohibited (s. 88). The granting of an authorisation presupposes that the practice is contrary to the Act; however, the corporation and others involved in the conduct may proceed with immunity from any further action under the Act.

The ACCC may grant authorisations for types of conduct such as:

- anti-competitive contracts, arrangements or understandings;
- exclusive dealings;
- boycotts;

- mergers;
- resale price maintenance;
- price fixing arrangements for the supply of goods or services; and
- covenants in relation to land that have the purpose or effect of substantially lessening competition.

In order to obtain the authorisation, the corporation must apply to the ACCC or ACT and must satisfy it that either:

- the public benefit outweighs the reduction in competition (authorisation test 1); or
- the conduct will result in a benefit to the public (authorisation test 2).

Authorisation test 1 is applied to:

- anti-competitive contracts, arrangements, understandings or covenants running with the land which have the effect of substantially lessening competition (ss. 45(2)(a)(ii), 45(2)(b)(ii), 45B);
- price fixing of goods or services (s. 45A);
- covenants in relation to prices (s. 45C); and
- exclusive dealing (s. 47);

if it can be shown that in all the circumstances public benefit outweighs the anti-competitive disadvantages that flow from a lessening in competition.

Authorisation test 2 involves examination of public benefit because anti-competitive considerations are not part of the offence for these areas and includes:

- primary boycotts (ss. 45(2)(a)(i), 45(2)(b)(i));
- secondary boycotts (s. 45D);
- third line forcing (s. 47(6), (7));
- resale price maintenance (s. 48); and
- mergers (s. 50).

The ACCC cannot grant authorisation for:

- monopolisation; and
- price recommendation arrangements involving less than 50 persons.

ENFORCEMENT PROCEDURES AND REMEDIES

Enforcement is by way of an action in the Federal Court

Enforcement is by way of action in the General Division of the Federal Court of Australia. It can impose fines (s. 76) for breach of the restrictive practices provisions. In respect to a body corporate, the maximum penalty is $750 000 for breaches of ss. 45D or 45DB or ss. 45E or 45EA, and up to $10 million for breach of any other provision. Individuals can be fined up to $500 000: s. 76.

The Act also provides for injunctions (s. 80) restraining breach of the restrictive practices provisions. In respect to mergers, which are finalised in contravention of the Act, an order can be made for the divestiture of shares (s. 81). This means that the corporations that have become merged can be separated by forcing the disposal of shares.

Section 87 gives the court the power to make the following orders:

- an order declaring the whole or part of a contract void;
- an order varying a contract;
- an order refusing to enforce provisions of a contract;
- an order directing the refund of money or return of goods;
- an order directing payment of an amount of loss or damage;
- an order directing repairs or supply of parts for goods; and
- an order directing the supply of services.

An individual may recover damages for any losses in civil proceedings

A person who suffers loss or damage as a result of a contravention of the restrictive trade provisions may recover the amount of the loss or damages from the person who contravened the Act (s. 82). Proceedings brought for contraventions of the restrictive trade practices provisions are civil and the standard of proof is on the balance of probabilities.

INDUSTRY CODES OF CONDUCT

> **!** CAUTION NOTE
>
> *An 'industry code', which may be voluntary or mandatory, regulates the conduct of participants in an industry towards other participants or consumers.*

The *Trade Practices Amendment (Fair Trading) Act 1998* introduced a new Part IVB into the *Trade Practices Act* enabling industry codes of conduct to be prescribed and enforced under the Act by the ACCC. An 'industry code' is a code that will regulate the conduct of participants in an industry towards other participants or consumers.

A code may be voluntary or mandatory: s. 51AB. Where a code is mandatory, it will be compulsory for industry participants, for example, the Franchising Code of Conduct which came into effect on 1 July 1998. A corporation may agree to be bound by the provisions of a voluntary code. However, where the provisions of a code are binding, a corporation will have to comply with those provisions: s. 51AD.

Breach of a code can result in:

- the granting of an injunction: s. 80;
- damages: s. 82;
- corrective advertising: s. 80A; and
- such other orders as the court thinks appropriate in order to compensate for the loss or damage suffered: s. 87.

WEB RESOURCE

ACCC: home page provides a wealth of information on the operation of the *Trade Practices Act* in general, as well as the Australian Competition and Consumer Commission and the Australian Competition Tribunal:
http://www.accc.gov.au

? REVIEW QUESTIONS

30.1 In the context of the *Trade Practices Act*, what is the meaning and significance of the expressions 'market' and 'competition'?

30.2 What is the role of the Australian Competition and Consumer Commission? Do you think it performs that role well?

30.3 What is the constitutional basis for the *Trade Practices Act*?

30.4 What is the role of the Australian Competition Tribunal?

30.5 What is the central purpose of the *Competition Policy Reform Act 1995* (Cth)? Do you think it has achieved this purpose?

30.6 What is price fixing? Is it necessary to prove an adverse effect on competition?

30.7 What is resale price maintenance?

30.8 Indicate whether each of the following statements is true or false:

	TRUE	FALSE
▪ Only the ACT can make authorisations	☐	☐
▪ Decisions of the ACCC can only be appealed to the Federal Court	☐	☐
▪ Secondary boycotts are prohibited outright under s. 45D	☐	☐
▪ A financial institution who tells customers that they must take out insurance with a specified insurer is engaged in exclusive dealing, which is prohibited under s. 47(6)	☐	☐
▪ A supplier who supplies goods to a retailer is allowed to recommend a selling price for those goods	☐	☐

	TRUE	FALSE
▪ Agreements which have the effect of substantially lessening competition, such as market sharing agreements, are prohibited outright	☐	☐
▪ Where a seller supplies goods on condition that the buyer will not re-supply them on to a third party may amount to a situation of exclusive dealing under s. 47	☐	☐
▪ If there is strong import competition, a proposed merger is unlikely to be successfully challenged under s. 50	☐	☐
▪ Notification provides interim protection to parties engaged in exclusive dealing	☐	☐
▪ Only corporations can be liable for breaches of the *Trade Practices Act*	☐	☐

30.9 Explain the meaning of the following terms and provide an example of each:

- exclusive dealing
- monopolisation
- boycotts.

30.10 How does a corporation obtain authorisation and what authorisations can the Commission grant?

30.11 How do primary and secondary boycotts differ under the *Trade Practices Act*? Give an example of each in your answer.

CRITICAL THINKING

30.1 AustPower Ltd and Switchy Ltd both manufacture electricity fuse boxes. One company only trades in New South Wales and the other only trades in South Australia. They exchange price lists and both agree to set identical prices for each of the various items they manufacture. Does such an agreement breach the *Trade Practices Act*? Explain your answer.

30.2 A shipping company operating bulk coal carriers regularly loads coal for export at an Australian port. The ships are crewed by foreign workers who are paid much lower wages than Australian crews would be paid. The Australian Seamen's Union wants the shipping company to pay these workers the same rates as their Australian counterparts, but the company refuses.

The same union has members who operate the harbour tugboats, which must be used to dock the bulk coal carriers. These tugboats are owned by a different company.

The union brings pressure to bear on the tugboat owners not to dock the coal carriers. Is this a contravention of the *Trade Practices Act*? If so, what defences might be available?

30.3 Two large airline companies have for many years offered similar flight arrangements and services in a particular market. They also share airport terminal buildings, and at some airports share aircraft servicing facilities. A new company commences airline services in competition with the existing airlines. Neither of the existing airlines provides any assistance to or cooperation with the new airline. They also introduce large discounts on their prices (something they seldom did previously) and apply pressure on travel agents to promote their services and not to promote the services of the new airline.

Discuss.

activebook

Activebook resources include in-depth summaries with links to the relevant part of the book. For revision, add your own notes to the summaries provided by using the note-taking function.

FINANCIAL TRANSACTIONS

PART SEVEN

CHAPTER 31 Negotiable Instruments

CHAPTER CONTENTS

activebook

This icon is used throughout the following chapter to remind you to visit the *Business Law* online activebook for additional exercises, links to legal websites, and feedback. For a detailed explanation of what is in the activebook please refer to the inside cover of this textbook. The activebook is available through OneKey.

Where do I start?
Learning path: Use the activebook to complete a pre-chapter warm-up exercise.

There are many definitions of legal terms to assist with your understanding of the material.

CHAPTER OBJECTIVES

On completion of this chapter, you should be able to:

- define a bill of exchange and discuss its uses
- outline the rules for negotiation
- compare a cheque with a bill of exchange
- define a cheque
- state the liability of the parties to a bill in the event of dishonour
- distinguish between order and bearer cheques
- list the different types of crossings applicable to cheques
- contrast the duties of banks with those of their customers
- identify what protection is available for financial institutions
- distinguish between an ordinary cheque and a bank cheque
- describe other methods of money transfer
- discuss the objectives of the *Financial Transactions Reports Act*
- list the types of transactions required to be reported
- list the penalties for breaching the Act.

KEY TERMS

An understanding of the following terms will help you to better understand the material in this chapter:

- **bank cheque:** a cheque drawn by a bank on itself
- **bearer:** the person in possession of a cheque
- **bearer cheque:** an order to the drawee institution to pay the sum ordered to be paid by the cheque to the person in possession of the cheque, title being transferred on delivery
- **cheque:** an unconditional order in writing that is addressed by one person to another person, being a financial institution, and is signed by person giving it and requires the financial institution to pay on demand a certain sum of money
- **collecting financial institution:** the payee's financial institution (i.e. the financial institution where the cheque is deposited for 'cashing')
- **drawee:** the bank upon which the cheque is drawn (i.e. the drawer's bank and the paying institution)
- **drawer:** the person who gives the order and draws the cheque upon a bank and whose account will be charged with the value of the cheque
- **estoppel:** prevented
- **holder:** the person in possession of a cheque in the case of a bearer cheque, or the payee, or indorsee in the case of an order cheque
- **holder in due course:** a person who is a holder of a cheque, taking it as complete and regular on its face
- **inchoate instrument:** a cheque signed in blank by the drawer, to be subsequently completed by another person
- **indorsement:** the act of writing on a cheque the name of the person who is the transferor, indicating their intention to transfer the right to payment
- **not negotiable:** on a cheque, the phrase 'not negotiable' does not affect transferability but means that no one can claim to have a better title to the cheque than the previous holder

- **order cheque:** an order to the drawee institution to pay the sum ordered to or to the order of a person/s specified in the cheque as payee/s and must be indorsed by the payee/s before it can be cashed or negotiated unless paid into the account of the payee/s
- **payee:** the person entitled to payment
- **paying financial institution:** the financial institution upon which the cheque is drawn
- **stale cheque:** a cheque that has been in circulation more than 15 months from the date on the cheque.

what if . . .

You have sold your car and you agree to accept a cheque. The purchaser asks if you want an uncrossed bearer cheque or an order cheque crossed not negotiable and account payee only. What is the significance of the difference between the two cheques?

Negotiable instruments play an important role in the conduct of business and personal affairs. Without them, business could not function. Two common examples of negotiable instruments, which are the focus of this chapter, are bills of exchange and cheques.

To qualify as a negotiable instrument, the instrument must meet certain statutory requirements that establish what type of negotiable instrument it is. That is, is it a bill of exchange or promissory note under the *Bills of Exchange Act 1909* (Cth) or a cheque under the *Cheques Act 1986* (Cth)? And what of the holder of the instrument? What sort of title to the instrument will they have? If there is a defect in title, it will need to be determined whether the holder of the instrument is a holder in due course who takes the instrument free of many defences that can be raised against the original payee. In other words, who gets the money?

The concept of negotiation is an important component of the law of negotiable instruments. Negotiable instruments are used as a substitute for money and, as such, they must be freely transferable to subsequent parties. However, there is considerable confusion over the terms 'transferability' and 'negotiability'. All negotiable instruments are transferable by negotiation. However, only a cheque with two transverse parallel lines across its face and the words 'not negotiable' added between the lines is capable of rebutting the characteristics of a negotiable instrument so that the person taking such a cheque does so at their own risk.

The two most popular types of negotiable instrument, their creation and transfer, and the liability of the parties are the main focus of this chapter.

ORIGINS OF NEGOTIABLE INSTRUMENTS

Long before there was any Act of Parliament regulating their use, negotiable instruments were devised and used by merchants as a means of reducing the need to physically transfer cash in payment of their debts and thereby increase security. For example, A owes $100 to B and B owes $100 to C. If B gives A a written direction to pay the $100 to C, that single payment would satisfy both debts (see Figure 31.1).

Negotiable instruments have their history in the customs of merchants and it is these merchants' codes and customs (i.e. law merchant) that formed the original basis of this particular area of law. A large volume of case law involving negotiable instruments based on the law merchant was built up before the *Bills of Exchange Act 1882* (UK) brought together and codified the law merchant, the common law and a number of existing statutes which had some influence on negotiable instruments.

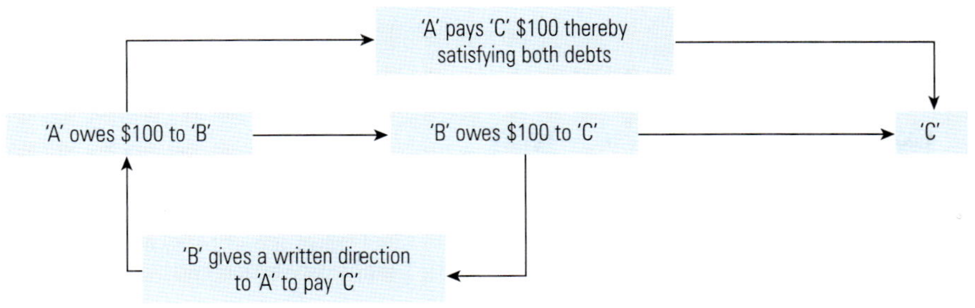

FIGURE 31.1 *How a negotiable instrument works*

The law governing negotiable instruments in Australia is found in:

- the *Bills of Exchange Act 1909* (Cth); and
- the *Cheques Act 1986* (Cth).

NEGOTIABILITY AS AN EXCEPTION TO THE *NEMO DAT* RULE

What is the distinction between negotiable and transferable?

In a legal context, the word 'instrument' refers to a formal legal document in writing. In many instances these formal documents mainly act as a record of what was agreed.

However, in the context of negotiable instruments, the word 'instrument' could be replaced by the word 'tool'; a tool being something we use to help us to physically perform a task, for example, a hammer.

A negotiable instrument is an instrument (document) which represents an amount of money, the property or rights in the instrument passing on delivery of the instrument. The document is the tool by which the rights are physically passed from one person to another.

***Nemo dat* rule—you cannot get a better title than you yourself have**

A negotiable instrument is an exception to the *nemo dat quod non habet* rule (called the *nemo dat* rule). The *nemo dat* rule means that no one can give a better title than they themselves have (see Figure 31.2). If A steals a car and sells it to B, A clearly has no right to the car. Although A can transfer possession of the car to B, A cannot give B any rights to the car. Therefore, when the true owner (the person from whom the car was stolen) discovers that B has possession of the car, the true owner can recover the car. B only has rights against A.

In contrast, if A stole money from a bank and used the money to buy a car, the money could not be recovered from the car dealer. The money is not only physically transferable, it is also negotiable. Being **negotiable** means that the **right to the money is also transferred**. The car dealer therefore obtains a better title than A had (see Figure 31.3).

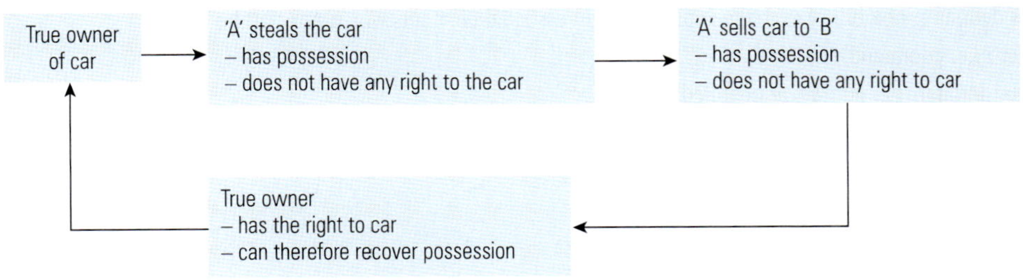

FIGURE 31.2 Nemo dat *rule—You cannot get a better title than that of the person you receive it from*

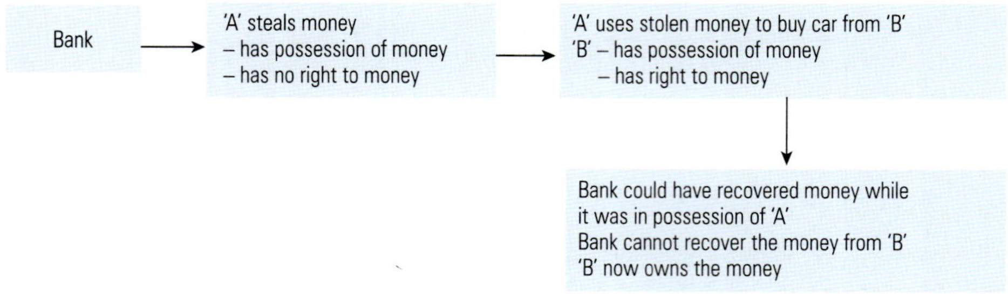

FIGURE 31.3 *Negotiable—Can get a better title than that of person it was received from*

BILLS OF EXCHANGE

IN BRIEF

Advantages of bills for debt settlement

Advantages	Reasons
Documentary proof of a debt	It enables the creditor to sue on the bill itself without necessarily referring back to the original contract that created the debt.
Bills can be transferred safely	The transfer of money involves book entries and not the handling of cash, so it can be transferred safely from place to place.
Negotiable instrument	It can be transferred by the holder in settlement of their own debts. Thus, one bill may be used to settle two or more debts.
Holder has rights	In the event of dishonour, a holder has rights against the prior parties to the bill.

Definition

A bill of exchange is defined in s. 8(1) of the *Bills of Exchange Act* as:

> *an unconditional order in writing addressed by one person to another signed by the person giving it, requiring the person to whom it is addressed to pay on demand, or at a fixed or determinable future time, a sum certain in money to or to the order of a specified person, or to bearer.*

! CAUTION NOTE

A bill of exchange must contain all eight essential elements to be valid.

This definition of a bill of exchange contains eight essential elements which must all be present:

- order (i.e. command);
- unconditional (i.e. entirely unqualified);
- in writing;
- addressed by one person to another;
- signed by the person giving it;
- a sum certain in money (i.e. capable of calculation);
- on demand or at a fixed or determinable future time; and
- payable to, or to order of, a specified person or bearer.

An instrument that does not comply with these conditions, or that orders any act to be done in addition to the payment of money, is not a bill of exchange. However, even if the document does not conform with the definition of a bill of exchange, it may still have independent validity in a contractual sense as between the parties. That is, there may still be a contract between the drawee (the party who must pay it) and the payee (the party named to receive payment).

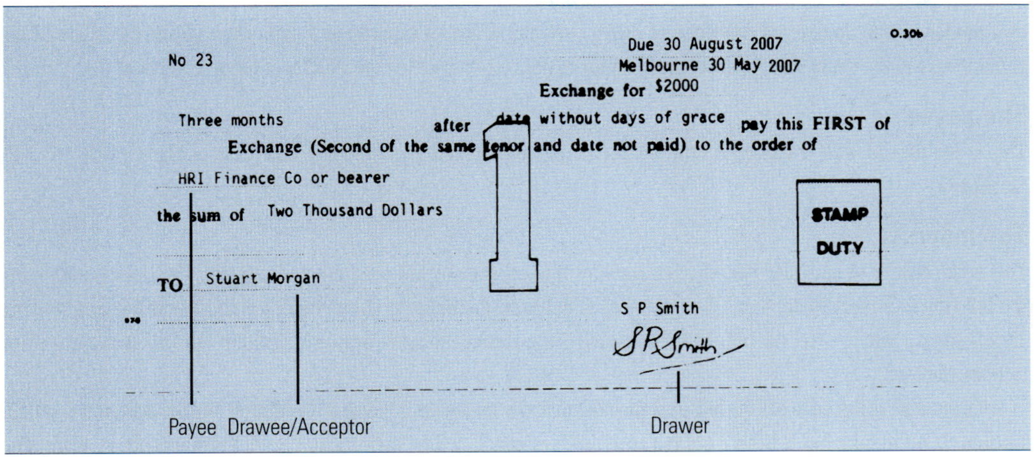
No 23

Due 30 August 2007
Melbourne 30 May 2007
Exchange for $2000

Three months after date without days of grace pay this FIRST of Exchange (Second of the same tenor and date not paid) to the order of

HRI Finance Co or bearer

the sum of Two Thousand Dollars

TO Stuart Morgan

STAMP DUTY

S P Smith

FIGURE 31.4 *A bill of exchange*

Rules for negotiation

Transferability should not be confused with negotiability. A bill of exchange or a cheque, being negotiable instruments, may be transferred from one person to another and, provided it is taken in good faith, the recipient will then acquire all the rights to it, regardless of any defect in title of the person from whom it was received.

The method of negotiation will depend on whether the bill or cheque is payable to bearer or order. Where the bill or cheque is payable to bearer, it is negotiated by delivery, that is by merely handing it over. Where the bill or cheque is payable to order, it is negotiated by indorsement and delivery, that is, it requires the holder's signature to be placed on it before it is delivered.

Parties

In order to understand the area of negotiable instruments, it is necessary to look briefly at the parties to a bill (see Figure 31.5).

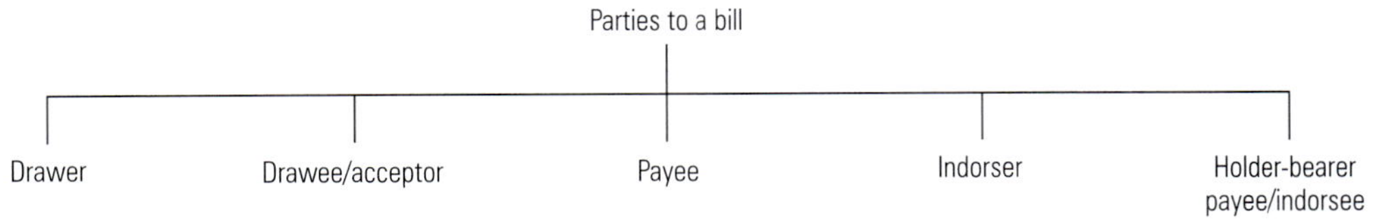

FIGURE 31.5 *Parties to a bill*

The drawer

This is the person who **gives the order** and is normally the **creditor** of the drawee. In Figure 31.4, this is S P Smith. The drawer is deemed to have promised that the bill will be paid by the acceptor upon presentment for payment: s. 60.

Drawer—person who gives the order

In the event of the acceptor not paying the bill, the drawer will be the next person liable, being obliged to indemnify the holder or any indorser who is obliged to pay it, provided that proper proceedings on dishonour are duly taken: s. 60(1)(a).

The drawee or acceptor

Drawee—person to whom the order is addressed

This is the person to whom the order is addressed and is usually the debtor of the drawer. In Figure 31.4 this is Stuart Morgan. When the drawee writes their acceptance on the bill they are called the acceptor and they become liable on the bill pursuant to s. 58.

As acceptor, they have an undertaking to pay the bill upon its presentation. The acceptor is prevented from denying to a holder in due course the existence of the drawer, the drawer's capacity and authority to draw the bill, and the genuineness of the drawer's signature. An acceptor is not responsible for the validity of indorsements: s. 59.

The payee

Payee—person entitled to payment

This is the person who is named on the bill as the person entitled to payment. In the case of Figure 31.4 it is HRI Finance Co.

The indorser

Indorser—holder of an order bill

This is the holder of an order bill who renegotiates it to another by indorsement and delivery. The person endorsing the bill (the indorser) to another (the indorsee) is liable on the bill to both the indorsee and to subsequent holders. To a holder in due course, the indorser's signature is a guarantee that the drawer's signature and all signatures prior to it are genuine.

If the indorser is forced to pay the bill, they are indemnified from the prior indorser, the drawer and the acceptor: s. 60(2).

There is no indorser of a bearer bill because they are negotiated by delivery and do not require indorsement. The bearer is the person in possession of the bill that is payable to the bearer.

The person who negotiates or transfers the bill is a 'transferor by delivery', and they are not liable on the bill since they are not required to put their signature on it. However, if the transferee is a holder for value (i.e. they have given consideration for the bill), the transferor by delivery warrants the validity of the bill to that transferee.

The holder–bearer, payee or indorsee

Holder—person who will receive payment from acceptor

This is the person who will **receive payment** from the acceptor, drawer or a prior indorser. In Figure 31.4 this is HRI Finance Co. The rights and powers of the holder are:

- the right to sue on the bill in their own name; and
- where the holder is a holder in due course, the right to hold the bill free from any defect of title of prior parties.

Where a holder's title is defective, s. 43(2) provides that if the bill is negotiated to a holder in due course (i.e. a *bona fide* purchaser for value without any notice of defect in the transferor's title), that holder obtains a good title to the bill and if payment of the bill is obtained, the person who pays the holder in due course obtains a valid discharge.

Must a bill comply with a particular format?

No particular form of words is required

No particular form of words is required by the Act, and the bill in Figure 31.6 may be taken as an example of the usual business document.

Note the features of the bill in Figure 31.6. It contains the eight essential elements required by s. 8(1) (see p. 646):

- it is an order;
- it is unconditional;
- it is in writing;
- it is addressed to a particular person;
- it is signed by the person giving the order;
- the amount payable is certain;
- the time of payment is certain; and
- it is expressed in money terms.

The bill also contains other items:

- a number—those businesses that commonly use bills find it to their advantage to have them printed and numbered to facilitate referencing and recording; and

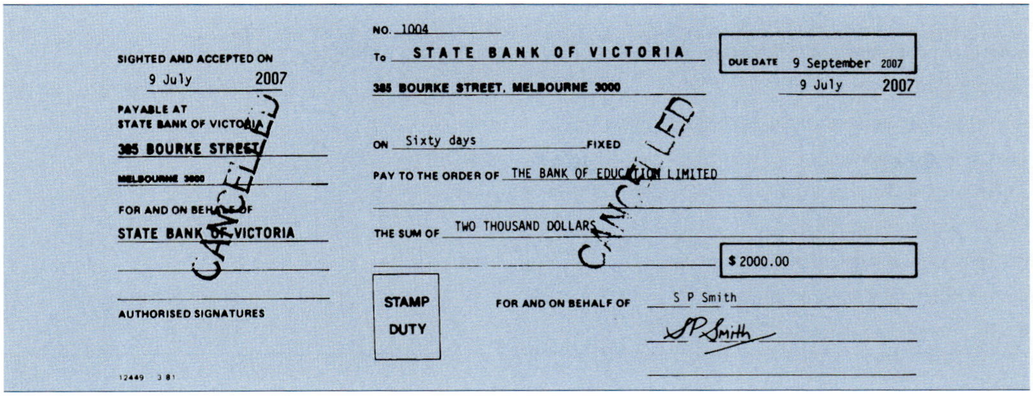
NO. 1004

SIGHTED AND ACCEPTED ON 9 July 2007

PAYABLE AT STATE BANK OF VICTORIA 385 BOURKE STREET MELBOURNE 3000

FOR AND ON BEHALF OF STATE BANK OF VICTORIA

AUTHORISED SIGNATURES

12449 3 81

To STATE BANK OF VICTORIA 385 BOURKE STREET, MELBOURNE 3000

DUE DATE 9 September 2007

9 July 2007

ON Sixty days FIXED

PAY TO THE ORDER OF THE BANK OF EDUCATION LIMITED

THE SUM OF TWO THOUSAND DOLLARS

$ 2000.00

STAMP DUTY

FOR AND ON BEHALF OF S P Smith

SPSmith

CANCELLED

CANCELLED

FIGURE 31.6 *Another bill of exchange*

- stamp duty—this is not an essential feature of the bill itself, though most states have made this a statutory requirement (e.g., in the form of the *Stamp Duty Act*).

CHEQUES

Background

A cheque is a specific type of negotiable instrument

The 20th century saw a dramatic change in the importance of bills of exchange and cheques. The use of cheques increased enormously, while the use of bills of exchange declined both domestically and internationally. The 21st century has already seen a dramatic decline in the use of cheques from 49.6 per cent of all payments in 1994 to 19.2 per cent in 2002 (figures from the Australian Payments Clearing Association). This decline in the use of cheques has seen a rise in the use of credit cards and electronic payments such as Internet banking, Eftpos and ATMs. While private use of cheques has diminished cheques are still in sufficiently wide use in business for managers to be aware of the legal consequences of the simple action of 'writing a cheque'.

Because a cheque is a **specific type of negotiable instrument** it is closely related to a bill of exchange. This is particularly so in regard to:

- the concept of negotiability;
- classes of holder; and
- the liability of parties to the instrument.

The *Cheques Act 1986* (Cth) created a new negotiable instrument called a payment order. The only significant difference between a cheque and a payment order is that the payment order is drawn on a non-bank financial institution such as a credit union or a building society. Non-bank financial institutions now have the power to issue cheques. This is to increase direct competition between banking and non-banking institutions.

Unless otherwise stated in this chapter, a reference to a cheque is also a reference to a payment order, and a reference to a financial institution is a reference to a bank or a non-bank financial institution such as a credit union.

> **!** CAUTION NOTE
>
> *The only significant difference between a cheque and a payment order is that the payment order is drawn on a non-bank financial institution.*

Cheques compared with bills of exchange

Under the *Bills of Exchange Act 1909* (Cth) a cheque was, by definition, a bill of exchange (s. 78) and the provisions of the *Bills of Exchange Act*, which are applicable to a bill of exchange, were equally applicable to a cheque. Yet there were at least the following differences (see Table 31.1):

Table 31.1 Summary of differences between a bill of exchange and a cheque

Characteristic	*Cheque*	*Bill of exchange*
Rules relating to presentment and acceptance apply	no	yes
Rules as to crossings apply	yes	no
Can be crossed 'Not Negotiable'	yes	no
Must be paid on demand	yes	not necessarily
May be payable at a determinable future time	no	yes
Must be drawn on a financial institution	yes	not necessarily
May be drawn on anyone other than the drawer	no	yes

- The rules relating to presentment and acceptance are inapplicable to cheques. This was not because a cheque could not be accepted, but because financial institutions would not accept it.
- The rules as to crossings apply to cheques but not bills.
- The relationship between the customer and the bank may not be the same as that between the drawer and the drawee of other bills. There are certain recognised duties and obligations between the customer and the bank.
- A crossed 'not negotiable' cheque remains transferable under s. 55 of the *Cheques Act*, but cannot be transferred free from equities. That is, you get no better title to the cheque than that which the person from whom you took it had. If the cheque was stolen, you would get no title even though you were an innocent purchaser for value.
- A cheque must be payable on demand, whereas other bills may be payable on demand or at a fixed or determinable future time.
- A cheque must be drawn on a financial institution; other bills may be drawn on anyone other than the drawer.
- A cheque must be presented for payment within a reasonable time, while a bill payable on demand is deemed to be a continuing security.

NOTE: a cheque that has been in circulation for more than 15 months is considered 'stale' and need not be paid by the financial institution on which the cheque is drawn.

activebook

To help you to remember and understand the topics covered so far, and for links to legal websites, refer to your online activebook. Model answers provide feedback to problems and exercises.

Definition

The definition of a cheque has been amended so that non-banking financial institutions may be the drawee of the cheque. Section 10 of the *Cheques Act* now defines a cheque as:

(1) *A cheque is an unconditional order in writing that:*
   (a) *is addressed by a person to another person, being a financial institution; and*
   (b) *is signed by the person giving it; and*
   (c) *requires the financial institution to pay on demand a sum certain in money.*

(2) *An instrument that does not comply with subsection (1), or that orders any act to be done in addition to the payment of money, is not a cheque.*

Section 3 defines a financial institution as:

(a) *the Reserve Bank of Australia; or*
(b) *a bank within the meaning of the* Banking Act 1959*; or*
(c) *an FIC institution*; or*
(d) *a person who carries on State banking within the meaning of paragraph 51 (xiii) of the Constitution; or*
(e) *a person (other than a person referred to in paragraph (a), (b) , (c) or (d)) who carries on the business of banking outside Australia.*

* An FIC institution is a building society; or a credit union; or a special services provider within the Financial Institutions Code of any of the States.

Although non-banking financial institutions may now issue cheques in their own right, the Act still allows them to issue 'agency cheques'. An agency cheque is one which is drawn on a bank by an issuing institution and the issuing institution has an agreement with its customer authorising its customer to fill up and sign the cheque. The cheque facilities that credit unions and building societies have been offering their customers have usually been on an agency cheque basis.

Non-banking financial institutions may now issue cheques in their own right or 'agency cheques'

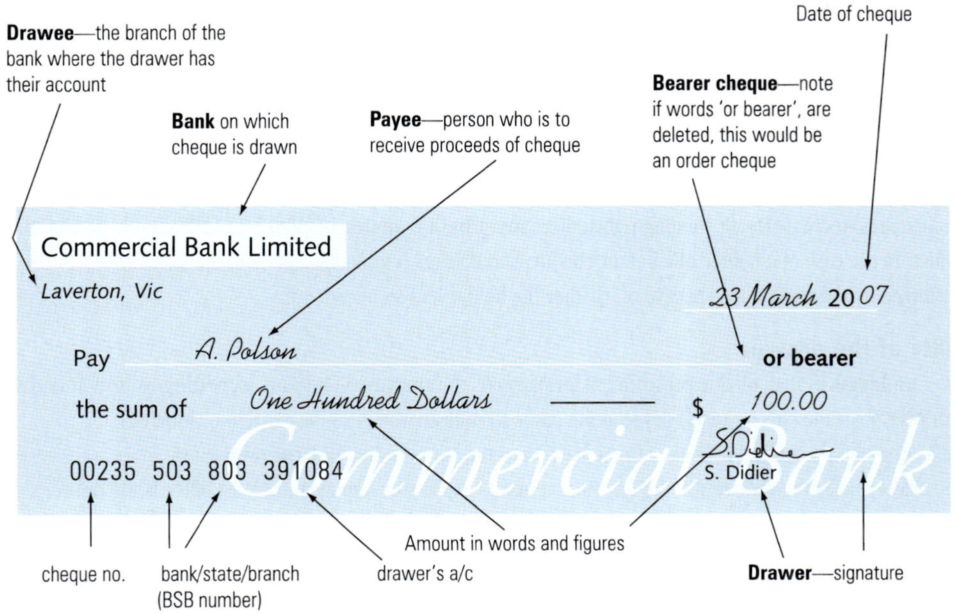

FIGURE 31.7 *A cheque*

Parties

There must be three parties involved in every cheque (see Figure 31.8):

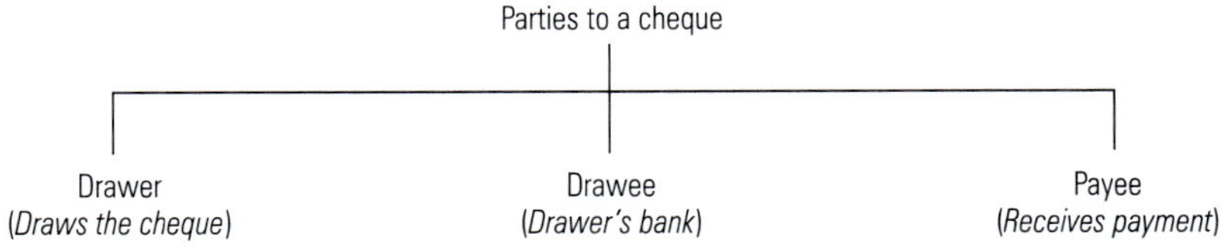

FIGURE 31.8 *Parties to a cheque*

Drawer

In Figure 31.7 this is S. Didier. The person who gives the order and draws the cheque (drawn upon a banker) and whose account will be charged with the value of the cheque.

Drawee

In Figure 31.7 this is the Laverton branch of the Commercial Bank, the bank upon which the cheque is drawn. In the case of a cheque, this is the drawer's bank. A cheque is not an assignment of money in the hands of a banker, and the payee or holder has no right of action against them if the cheque is dishonoured.

Payee

In Figure 31.7 this is A. Polson—the person or organisation named to receive payment of the cheque.

> **CAUTION NOTE**
>
> *Drawer gives the order and draws the cheque, drawee is the financial institution upon whom the cheque is drawn and the payee receives payment.*

Liability of the parties

Drawer undertakes that on presentment the cheque will be paid

A person who has the legal capacity to contract has the legal capacity to incur liability on a cheque. However, two essential requirements must first be satisfied:

- A person is **not liable** as the drawer or indorser of a cheque **unless they sign** the cheque as the drawer or indorser. This includes signing in a business name, or some other name than their own.
- If a cheque is to create legally binding rights, there **must be a transfer of possession** from one person to another. In the case of a holder of a bearer cheque who delivers it to another person, the instrument will be transferred by negotiation irrespective of whether the holder had so intended it.

Liability of the drawer

Indorser—similar liabilities to the drawer

A drawer **undertakes** that, on due presentment for payment, the cheque will be paid **according to how it is drawn**. If the drawer posts the cheque to the payee at the payee's request (whether it be express or implied):

- a delivery to the post office is delivery to the payee and the payee is then the true owner; or
- if the drawer posts the cheque without any such request (express or implied), the post office is the drawer's agent and the drawer remains the true owner until delivery is made to the payee.

It should be noted that if the cheque has come into the hands of the payee, the drawer is also protected from being called on to pay twice. If the cheque is dishonoured, the drawer undertakes to compensate the holder or an indorser who is compelled to pay the cheque. A person who is the drawer or indorser of a cheque that has been dishonoured is liable on the cheque.

The drawer cannot limit or negate liability on the cheque by writing 'without recourse' or 'sans recours' as an indorser could.

Liability of the indorser

In effect, an indorser is saying: 'This cheque is good. If the other signatories do not pay, I will'. The indorser and drawer are jointly and severally liable to the holder that the cheque will be honoured.

While the indorser has similar liabilities to the drawer as a result of signing, by adding the words 'without recourse' or 'sans recours' to the cheque the responsibilities of the indorser are then limited. Where these words have not been added, the indorser and drawer are jointly and severally liable to the holder that the cheque will be honoured.

Doing business

Take care if indorsing a cheque or you may be liable

Where a person signs a cheque other than as a drawer or indorser, and intends to become liable on it, the Act treats that person as an indorser. For example, if a cheque is drawn by a company and backed by a director personally signing it, then they would be liable as an indorser. To limit their liability, they should add the words 'without recourse' to the cheque. ■

Holder

A holder includes the payee, the indorsee or bearer:

- **Bearer cheque**—a 'holder' is the bearer.
- **Order cheque**—a holder is the person who is in possession of the cheque as payee or indorsee.

A **holder need not have given 'value' to be a holder**. Thus, a person who finds a cheque would still be a 'holder'. To take title to the cheque, they would also have to be a holder in due course.

> **!** CAUTION NOTE
> *A holder is the person who is in possession of the cheque, irrespective of how they came by it.*

Holder for value

Holder for value—consideration has been given for the cheque

Where value or consideration has at any time been given for a cheque, the holder shall be presumed to be a holder for value. The cheque can only be enforced by the holder for value, but this is 'subject to equities'. Where there is a prior defective title, the importance of being a 'holder in due course' becomes apparent.

Holder in due course

> **!** CAUTION NOTE
> *A holder in due course can obtain a better title than the transferor.*

Holder in due course—a holder who received the cheque in good faith and for value without any notice of defect

Unless the contrary is proved, the holder of a cheque is presumed to be a holder in due course. A holder in due course is capable of obtaining a better title to the cheque than the transferor, since a holder in due course will generally take the instrument free of equities (i.e. free from prior defects in title): s. 49.

The holder of a cheque is a holder in due course if the cheque was transferred by negotiation to the holder and, at the time when the holder took the cheque, the cheque:

- was complete and regular on the face of it;
- was not a stale cheque;
- had not been crossed 'not negotiable'; and
- the holder took the cheque:
  - in good faith;
  - for value; and
  - without notice of any defect in the title of the person who transferred it or that the person had no title to it.

If the holder has not taken the cheque in good faith or has taken it under circumstances amounting to fraud, the holder is not deemed to be a holder in due course.

It should be noted that a holder cannot be a holder in due course if they are:

- **The named payee**. In Figure 31.7 Polson is a holder, but not a holder in due course because the cheque was 'issued' by Didier to Polson, not negotiated from Didier to Polson.
- **The holder of a 'stale' or crossed 'not negotiable' cheque**. In the case of the latter, the holder (the transferee) takes the cheque subject to the defects of the transferor. The 'not negotiable' crossing gives notice of defects.

> **!** CAUTION NOTE
> *A person may be a holder but cannot be a holder in due course if they are the payee or they receive a stale or crossed not negotiable cheque.*

Distinguishing bearer and order cheques

Bearer cheque—order to financial institution to pay any bearer, title being transferred on delivery

All cheques are payable either to bearer or to order (see Figure 31.9). The Act defines cheques that are regarded as payable to order as those where the cheque specifies a person or indorsee. The Act regards all other cheques as payable to bearer.

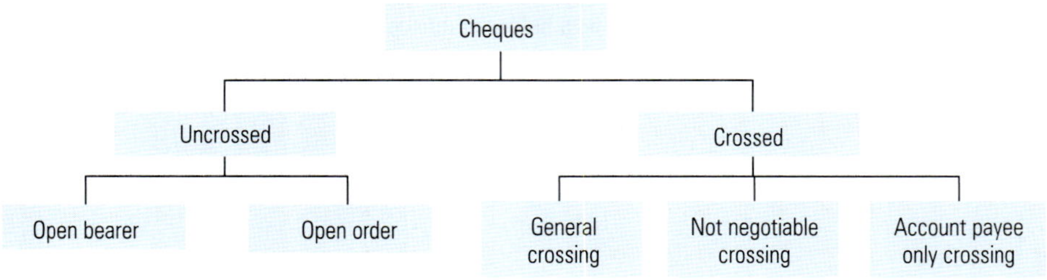

FIGURE 31.9 *Types of cheques*

Open bearer cheques

An open cheque is a cheque that does not have any 'crossing' on it (see Figure 31.10).

FIGURE 31.10 *An open bearer cheque*

Doing business

The unsafest form of cheque: a bearer cheque

An open bearer cheque is simply an order to a bank to pay to any bearer. It may be cashed over the counter at the branch of the bank at which it is drawn. Title is transferred merely by delivery from one person to another, with good title being obtained by the holder taking the cheque in good faith and for value. ■

If the holder is to **take the instrument in good faith**, they must not know that it may have been stolen or fraudulently obtained. They must also give value for it, that is, provide consideration. For example, if the cheque is drawn for $20, give $20 cash for it or $20 worth of goods.

Order cheque—drawn payable to order with words 'or bearer' crossed out

Open order cheques

For a cheque to be considered an open order cheque (see Figure 31.11) it can be:

- payable to a particular person, e.g., Pay D. Gee-Clough;

- payable to a particular person or order, e.g., Pay D. Gee-Clough or order; or
- payable to a named payee with the words 'or bearer' crossed out (see Figure 31.11).

Open order cheque must be indorsed by payee

The cheque must be **indorsed by the payee** before it can be cashed or negotiated, unless paid into the account of the payee. 'Pay D. Gee-Clough or order' means pay D. Gee-Clough or someone named by her, though the cheque does not have to be indorsed by subsequent holders unless the payee signed it and added 'Pay X or order'.

Indorsement requires that the payee writes their name on the cheque, usually on the back. If the person who indorses the cheque does not name someone as indorsee, the cheque has been indorsed 'in blank'. An indorsement in blank converts the order cheque into a bearer cheque.

Where the drawer signs a cheque in the belief that the named payee exists and that they will receive payment when in fact this is not the case—for example, because of an employee's fraudulent conduct—the payee will be treated as a non-existent person and the cheque will be treated as payable to bearer.

FIGURE 31.11 *An open order cheque*

Crossed cheques

Crossing hampers or prevents negotiation by unauthorised person

A cheque may also be crossed. The significance of the crossing on a cheque, however, is lost on most people. **Crossing a cheque does not affect its transferability by negotiation. Negotiability means that subsequent holders after the named payee who take the cheque in good faith and for value qualify as holders in due course** (s. 50) and get good title free of any defects in title that the transferor may have had.

Doing business

The effect of a crossing offers only limited protection

Two parallel lines drawn across the face of the cheque are a direction to the drawee financial institution that the instrument must be paid to a collecting institution and not as cash over the counter. The crossing offers some protection if the cheque is stolen, since payment may be stopped before the cheque is paid. ■

If the financial institution on which the cheque is drawn pays it as cash over the counter, they will become liable if the true owner suffers loss. The effect of the crossing is to offer protection to the person entitled to the cheque.

Crossed cheques have the addition of two parallel lines drawn across their face (see Figure 31.12). The *Cheques Act* provides for two categories of crossings:

- **general** crossings; and
- **not negotiable** crossings.

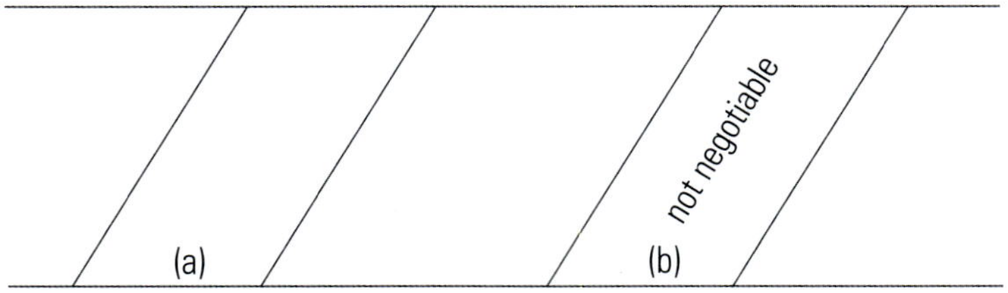

FIGURE 31.12 *Examples of two crossings—(a) General crossing, and (b) Not negotiable crossing*

If, in addition to the two parallel transverse lines, the words 'not negotiable' are added between, or substantially between, the lines, then you have a not negotiable crossing. The words on their own are ineffective.

Nothing else on the face of a cheque is as effective as a crossing. However, the Act does not prohibit the use of other words, such as Account Payee Only. The effect of using crossings not recognised by the Act is that they can only be seen as an instruction by the drawer to the financial institution, the paying institution, to ensure that they are paid only to a bank.

General crossing

General crossing tells the paying financial institution that the cheque must be paid into an account

Two parallel lines drawn across the face of the cheque are a direction to the drawee bank (in the examples given in Figure 31.13 this is the Commercial Bank Ltd) that the instrument must be paid to a financial institution and not as cash over the counter.

FIGURE 31.13 *A cheque with a general crossing*

NOTE:

- **the financial institution in which the cheque is deposited is the collecting financial institution**; while
- the **drawee financial institution** is the **paying financial institution**.

It is possible for the same financial institution to be both the paying and collecting financial institution in relation to a particular cheque. The crossing will not affect the negotiability of the cheque. Provided that a third party takes the cheque in good faith and for value, they will get good title, even though the person who gives it to them has a defective title. For example, A steals a cheque bearing a general crossing and worth $1000 from B. A takes it to C and, pretending to be B, buys a stereo. As C has taken the cheque in good faith and for value, then C will get good title to it ahead of B even though A stole the instrument.

CAUTION NOTE

A crossing does not affect negotiability, so a third party who takes the cheque in good faith, and for value, gets good title unless the cheque is also 'not negotiable'.

Duty relating to general crossings

If instead of paying the cheque to another financial institution the drawer, or paying financial institution, pays the cheque over the counter to someone who is not entitled to it, the bank is liable to the true owner of the cheque. 'True owner' is not defined by the Act and it is not necessarily the financial institution's customer who is the true owner of the cheque.

Not negotiable crossing

Doing business

'Not negotiable' and crossing the safest form of cheque

The use of the words 'not negotiable' on or near a crossing on a cheque offers the drawer and holder the best protection as no one can have a better title than the previous holder. A person who takes a crossed 'not negotiable' cheque does so at their own risk. Note that transferability is not affected. ■

The addition of the words '**not negotiable**' to a general crossing does not affect its transferability (see Figure 31.14). Cheques drawn in this way do circulate freely. The words 'not negotiable' on or near a crossing mean that **no one can claim to have a better title than the previous holder**.

The object of the 'not negotiable crossing' is to give the drawer or holder of a cheque who wants to transmit it to another person as much protection as can be reasonably given against dishonesty or accidental loss in transit. It rebuts the characteristic of negotiable instruments so a person who deals with a crossed 'not negotiable' cheque does so at their own risk. That is, the risk of the person from whom they took it having a defective title (e.g., having stolen it) is transmitted with the cheque. The true owner is the person immediately above the defect. For example, A draws a cheque in favour of B, crossing it and marking it 'not negotiable'. B gives the cheque to C to discharge a debt, and D steals it from C and gives it to E. The true owner is the person immediately above the defect, C. This is because C is the last person to have good title to the cheque. The true owner is the person who can support an action in conversion or a similar action against whoever receives the proceeds of the cheque. In the example above, that will be C.

The words 'not negotiable' are meant to be a clear signal to the person taking a cheque that they have not got and cannot give a better title to it than that of a person from whom they took it.

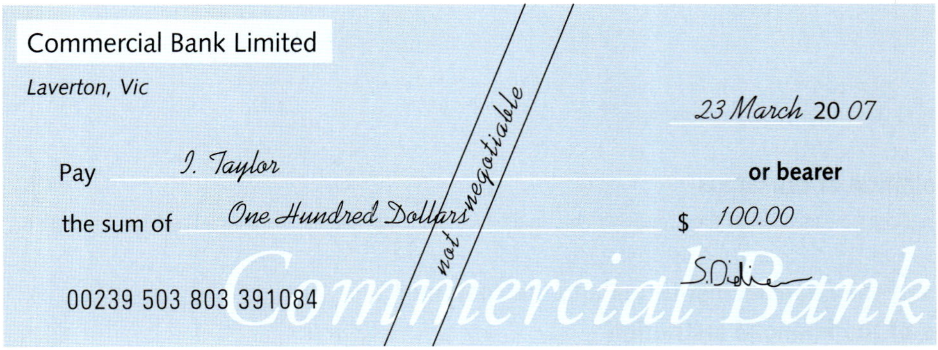

FIGURE 31.14 *A 'not negotiable' crossing*

> **CAUTION NOTE**
> *Person who takes a crossed 'not negotiable' cheque does so at their own risk.*

An open cheque may be crossed, or a crossing may be strengthened by any holder with the addition of the words 'not negotiable', and it is usual business practice to add the words 'not negotiable' to all cheques received.

The 'not negotiable' crossing is not a direction to either the paying or collecting bank, and it will not put either bank on inquiry even where the cheque is presented for payment by someone other than the payee.

> **CAUTION NOTE**
> *'Not negotiable' means that a third party only gets the title of the previous holder.*

Account payee only crossing

The words 'account payee only' have nothing to do with the drawee financial institution (see Figure 31.15). It will treat it as a general crossing and pay it to another financial institution. However, it does operate as a **direction to the collecting financial institution**, instructing them that when the proceeds are collected they are to be applied to the credit of the payee.

'Account payee only' is a warning to the collecting financial institution to apply funds to credit of payee

The words operate as a warning to the collecting financial institution to make reasonable inquiries if a person other than the payee collects the cheque. Failure to make such inquiries may amount to negligence. If the collecting financial institution pays the proceeds to a person not entitled to them, the collecting financial institution may lose the financial institution's statutory protection. The cheque can still be legally transferred by the payee to a third party and the negotiable or transferable characteristics of the cheque are not destroyed by the words 'account payee only'.

FIGURE 31.15 *An account payee only crossing*

Cancellation of crossings

A crossing can be cancelled by the drawer writing on the face of the cheque the words 'pay cash' and signing it.

Duties of the financial institution and the customer

Duties of the financial institution

Financial institution's duty is to honour its customers' cheques

The duty of a financial institution is to **honour its customers' cheques** to the extent of their credit, or to the extent of any overdrafts arranged. Failure to pay the cheques of a customer without good reason would render the financial institution liable in damages to the customer, not the presenter, as there is no 'privity' between the holder and drawee financial institution.

It is the financial institution's duty to obey the customer's mandate. The financial institution must pay according to its customer's directions, and if it pays to anyone other than the person entitled to receive payment, it cannot debit its customer's account unless:

- it has the benefit of statutory protection; or
- the customer is estopped from denying that the cheque is authentic and represents their direction: s. 32(2)(a) or (b). This estoppel will arise as a result of the customer's conduct.

Estoppel is a rule of evidence. If a person, by their conduct, has caused another person to believe in a certain state of affairs, and that second person relies on that mistaken belief and acts to their detriment, the first person will be estopped (prevented) from denying the truth of the false belief they created. In other words they have to accept liability for their conduct.

***GREENWOOD V. MARTINS BANK* [1933] AC 51**

Greenwood discovered that his wife had forged his signature on a number of cheques and operated on his account. When he discovered the forgeries, his wife promised to stop doing it. As a result, he did not tell the bank at that point. However, his wife continued to secretly forge his signature. When he discovered this, he confronted her, and she subsequently committed suicide. He then sued the bank for payment on the forgeries.

ISSUE: Does knowledge of forgeries impose a duty on the customer to tell the bank?

DECISION: The customer was estopped (prevented) from denying that the cheques were authentic. The error had been contributed to by the customer's failure to draw the cheques properly.

When can a financial institution refuse payment?

IN BRIEF

Situations where a financial institution can refuse payment are limited

A financial institution can refuse to honour a customer's cheques where:

- the cheque is stale (more than 15 months old);
- there is a countermand of payment;
- the cheque is postdated;
- there is notice of the customer's death;
- bankruptcy;
- customer's insanity; or
- there is a garnishee order.

Circumstances recognised by statute or custom where a financial institution can refuse payment on a cheque include:

Stale cheque: s. 3(5)

This is a cheque that has been in circulation for more than 15 months and which, in the absence of any agreement between the financial institution and the drawer, does not have to be paid by a financial institution. The 15 months commences from the date on the cheque.

Stale cheque—been in circulation more than 15 months

Where a cheque becomes stale, the duty and the authority of the financial institution to pay the cheque is terminated. Under each state's Statute of Limitations the drawer will remain liable on the cheque for six years from the date of issue, though there could be a reduction in the amount of the drawer's liability.

Countermand of payment—notice given by drawer to their financial institution to stop payment

Countermand of payment (stop payment)

The duty and authority of a financial institution to pay a cheque drawn on it by its customer can be stopped by countermand of payment. Countermand of payment (also referred to as 'stop payment') is notice given by the drawer of the cheque to the drawee financial institution requiring payment to be stopped.

Doing business

Only the drawer can stop payment on their cheque

Where a cheque is lost or stolen, only the drawer can stop payment. They must notify their financial institution as soon as practicable of the countermand of payment, identifying the particular cheque in writing. If the financial institution then fails to follow the drawer's instructions, they may be liable for the actual loss suffered which is not necessarily the same amount as that for which the cheque was drawn. ■

If instructions countermanding payment of the cheque are sent by telegram or telephone, the customer's written confirmation should be obtained as soon as possible, since the financial institution may incur liability by refusing to pay. If the customer's countermand fails to be effective owing to the negligence or default of the financial institution, the financial institution will then be liable to the customer for any actual loss that is suffered by the customer. This will not necessarily be for the amount of the cheque. In the case of a joint account, usually the signature of one party is sufficient to countermand payment.

It should be noted that the stop payment does not extinguish the drawer's liability and the drawer of the cheque may still be liable to the holder in due course.

Postdated cheques

Antedated and postdated cheques are not invalid

A cheque is **not invalid** because it is:

- **antedated**—one that bears a date before the date of issue; or
- **postdated**—one that bears a date after the date of issue.

However, a financial institution can refuse payment on a postdated cheque until the date stated. It is a direction to a financial institution to pay the cheque on the date it bears.

Notice of the customer's death

The duty and authority of a financial institution to pay a cheque drawn on it by its customer ends with the notice of the customer's death. Cheques paid after the death of the drawer but before the financial institution becomes aware of the death can be debited to their account.

Bankruptcy

A bankrupt is a person 'whose estate is vested in a trustee or assignee under the law for the time being in force relating to bankruptcy or insolvency'.

The *Bankruptcy Act 1966* (Cth) requires that once a financial institution has knowledge of a customer's bankruptcy, it must notify the trustee in bankruptcy of the account and pay no further cheques, except by court order.

Customer's insanity

Where the financial institution has notice of the disability of the customer, it automatically terminates the bank–customer relationship. Legally, the notice terminates only the authority to pay. The debt will remain owing until paid.

Garnishee orders

Garnishee order prevents customer from drawing funds

A garnishee order is a court order obtained by a creditor who has a judgement against a debtor (the financial institution's customer) attaching debts owing by such debtor. The purpose of the order is to stop the debtor withdrawing the money from their financial institution in an effort to prevent the judgement creditor being paid.

Financial institution's duty to honour cheques

IN BRIEF

Financial institution's duty to honour cheques

A financial institution must:

- pay on its customer's orders;
- pay the amount for which the cheque is drawn; and
- pay the true holder.

Customer's account can only be debited on customer's orders

A financial institution's duty can be broken down into three categories:

- The financial institution is entitled to debit its customer's account **only if it pays on its customer's orders**. If someone forges the customer's signature to a cheque and the financial institution pays it, they are not entitled to debit the customer's account, no matter how skilful the forgery, or how careful the bank has been. In such a case, the financial institution has no order to pay the cheque from the customer's account. However, there are exceptions. For example, a person may be estopped from denying the validity of their signature or indorsement (*Greenwood v. Martins Bank*, see p. 659); the relevant person may subsequently ratify their signature; or there may be statutory protection for the paying or collecting bank.

Financial institution's mandate is to pay the correct amount

- The financial institution's mandate (authority) is to **pay the amount for which the cheque is drawn**. Therefore, if after the customer has issued the cheque, the amount is fraudulently increased and the financial institution pays the increased amount, the financial institution is not entitled to debit the customer's account for the increased amount, but only to the extent of the original amount.

***VARKER V. COMMERCIAL BANKING CO. OF SYDNEY LTD* [1972] 2 NSWLR 967**

Varker was badly injured in a car crash and received a large compensation payout. He spoke with the manager of his local bank about handling his finances and the use of a cheque account. Because of his difficulty in writing and his previous inexperience, the manager explained the need for care and how to write a cheque. When Varker drew a cheque involving four figures, he always wrote the sum 'thousand' in describing the amount. On this occasion he drew a cheque for $140 cash which he gave to an acquaintance. The cheque was complete when signed but gaps where the amount was written enabled the cheque to be altered to a greater amount.

ISSUE: If the amount of the cheque is fraudulently increased, what amount should the bank pay?

DECISION: The Supreme Court of New South Wales held that the original amount constituted the customer's direction and the bank was therefore liable for the excess.

However, in *London Joint Stock Bank Ltd v. Macmillan and Arthur* [1918] AC 777, it was held that in the case of a cheque that does not have the amount written in words, that is, which was incomplete at the time of signature, a **customer does owe a duty to a bank to exercise reasonable care in drawing a cheque**, so as not to facilitate a fraudulent increase.

Doing business

Cheques must be drawn carefully

Failure on the part of a drawer to draw their cheque carefully can result in the drawer being unable to recover any money back from the bank if the cheque is fraudulently altered. Thus, giving an employee a blank signed cheque for petty cash is not good business practice because if the employee decides to withdraw substantially more than is needed for petty cash, the negligent drawing of the cheque by the business will prevent them recovering against the bank. ■

Customer owes a duty of care to their financial institution to draw their cheques carefully

Clearly the **customer owes the financial institution a duty of care** in the writing of their cheques to draw them carefully.

***COMMONWEALTH TRADING BANK OF AUSTRALIA V. SYDNEY WIDE STORES PTY LTD* (1981) 148 CLR 304**

A cheque was drawn payable to 'CAS'. After it had been signed, an employee of the company added an H, converting the payee to CASH. The employee then proceeded to collect the funds.

ISSUE: How careful should the drawer be when drawing the cheque?

DECISION: The High Court held that the drawer has a responsibility to draw the cheque in a manner that does not facilitate the alteration of the cheque.

COMMENT: The customer will be held to have committed a breach of this duty where the fraud or loss complained of is a natural and direct consequence of their negligence in drawing the cheque in question. Nor can the customer escape liability by asserting that the task had been delegated or entrusted to another person, whether they were an employee or someone in whom the customer had complete confidence.

The financial institution's duty is to pay the true holder

- The financial institution's duty is to **pay the true holder**. If it pays someone other than the holder, it has not fulfilled its mandate and may not debit the customer's account. This could cause hardship for the financial institution; if, for example, the payee's indorsement is forged on an instrument, no title is conferred on someone who subsequently comes into possession of the cheque, and the bank has not paid the holder if it then pays that person.

  As noted earlier, if the customer discovers that their cheques have been forged, they are under a duty to immediately tell their financial institution of this fact.

Protection for financial institutions

It will be rare for a financial institution to be liable in conversion. In deciding whether the customer's mandate has been properly fulfilled, two distinct steps are involved:

- Has payment been made to the proper person?
- If not, is the financial institution protected?

With respect to the second step, you must determine whether you are concerned with a paying financial institution or collecting financial institution, as the protection under the Act varies according to each.

Paying financial institution is financial institution upon which cheque is drawn

Paying and collecting financial institution

The **paying financial institution is the drawer's financial institution** (in the examples given in the figures in this chapter it is the Commercial Bank Ltd). When the cheque is presented to the paying financial institution by the holder or the holder's financial institution (the collecting financial institution) for collection, it is paid by the paying financial institution (see Figure 31.16).

Collecting financial institution is the payee's financial institution

The **collecting financial institution is the holder's financial institution**. It is the financial institution where the cheque is deposited for 'cashing'. The collecting financial institution collects payment on its customer's behalf from the paying financial institution.

As was noted previously, it is quite possible for a financial institution to be both a paying and collecting financial institution. For example, where a drawer writes out a cheque payable to cash and takes it to their financial institution to be cashed, the financial institution will be both the paying and collecting institution.

Liability of collecting financial institution for wrongful payment is to true owner

In *Commissioners of the State Savings Bank of Victoria v. Permewan Wright and Co. Ltd* (1914) 19 CLR 457, *Isaacs* J in the High Court pointed out that the liability of the collecting banker for wrongful payment is to the true owner of the cheque, whoever that may be. The term 'true owner' is not defined in the Act. It does not necessarily follow that the person who has possession of a cheque is the true owner, because the cheque may be stolen. It would seem that the true owner is the person who has (or is entitled to have) the **property in the cheque**, and is therefore entitled to possession.

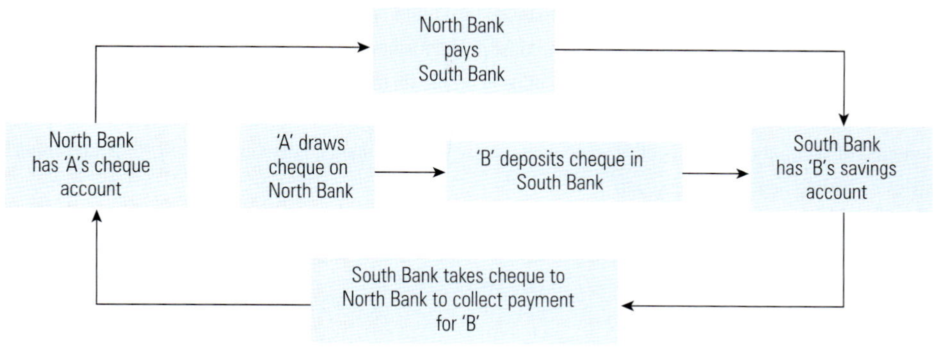

FIGURE 31.16 *Role of paying and collecting financial institutions*

Paying financial institution

Payment of cheque to another financial institution in good faith and without negligence relieves paying financial institution of liability to true owner

Where the paying financial institution pays a crossed cheque in **good faith and without negligence** to another financial institution in accordance with the customer's mandate (direction), it will not be liable to the true owner if payment is not received. The reason for this is because the paying financial institution is in no position to ascertain whether the person presenting the cheque is the true owner or not.

If the cheque is stolen or lost after it has come into the payee's possession and is subsequently paid, the drawer of the cheque is not liable to make out a further cheque. The drawer can claim that the debt to the payee has been discharged.

Where a paying financial institution fails to pay a crossed cheque to another financial institution—that is, pays the cheque across the counter—the paying financial institution will be liable for any loss that the true owner suffers.

Protection available to the paying financial institution outside the scope of the Act is limited to estoppel and the customer's negligence. If the customer's negligence has led to the financial institution making a wrongful payment of a cheque, the drawer (customer) may be estopped from denying liability. For example, because of a failure to draw the cheque carefully or failure to notify the financial institution promptly on discovery of their signature being forged.

Collecting financial institution

Collecting financial institution protected where it receives payment for a customer in good faith and without negligence

Where a collecting financial institution, in **good faith and without negligence**:

- receives payment of a cheque for a customer; or

- receives payment of a cheque and, before or after receiving payment, credits a customer's account with the sum ordered to be paid by the instrument; and
- the customer has no title or defective title,

the financial institution does not incur liability to the true owner in either conversion or negligence.

The collecting financial institution should not be treated as being negligent by failing to check irregular indorsements, provided that the name appearing on the cheque is that of the payee, and:

- is the same as the name or trade name of the customer; or
- is the same as a business name or trade name of the customer; or
- is so similar to the name of the customer that it is reasonable for the bank to assume it was the same person.

If a collecting financial institution is to be protected it must receive payment:

- for a customer;
- in good faith; and
- without negligence.

Generally the financial institution has no difficulty in establishing a financial institution–customer relationship. All that is required is that a person has an account at the financial institution (when the account was opened is not important), or that the financial institution acted in good faith. Most problems have arisen when looking at whether the financial institution has acted without negligence—and the onus is on the financial institution to prove that it has.

For convenience, these problems have been contained to two main areas:

- the opening of accounts for prospective customers, where it is the financial institution's duty to make proper inquiries regarding new customers; and
- the financial institution's carelessness in the collection of a cheque. For example, a cheque payable to a partnership being paid into the private account of one of the partners should make the financial institution's employees suspicious.

'Without negligence'

Banker's test for 'without negligence' is the ordinary practice of bankers

The protection afforded by the Act to paying and collecting financial institutions is all-embracing and will cover nearly every situation in which a claim is made against a financial institution.

Whether a financial institution in any given case has acted 'without negligence' is a question of fact and the test that is applied is the 'ordinary practice of bankers' test. This test was laid down by the Privy Council in *Commissioners of Taxation v. English Scottish and Australian Bank Ltd* [1920] AC 683.

The test of negligence is whether the transaction of paying in any given cheque, coupled with the circumstances antecedent and present, was so out of the ordinary course that it ought to have aroused doubts in the bankers' minds, and caused them to make inquiries.

Negligence would arise where the financial institution fails to make inquiries in circumstances where an ordinary prudent financial institution would be suspicious. In such a case, the financial institution would not be acting in the interests of the true owner and would therefore be unable to rely on the statutory protection afforded by the Act.

CARY V. RURAL BANK (1967) 2 DCR (NSW) 49

Cary drew a cheque payable to Ray Taylor P/L and mailed it to the company. The cheque went astray and fell into the hands of someone else who used it to open an account with the Rural Bank in the name of Ray Taylor, with the intention of collecting payment of the cheque. The bank did not take appropriate steps to confirm the identity of the customer and collected the funds and paid them to the customer. Cary, who was the true owner of the cheque, sued the bank.

ISSUE: Can negligence in opening an account be negligence in collecting payment of a cheque?

DECISION: The Supreme Court of New South Wales held that the bank was negligent in failing to properly identify the customer and for failing to make other inquiries which the circumstances suggested.

COMMENT: Other examples where negligence may be proved would include:

- an employee depositing cheques payable to their employer into their own account;
- the collection of a cheque for a customer marked 'Not Negotiable—Account Payee Only' when the customer is not the named payee; or
- the opening of an account for a customer without making proper inquiries.

It should be noted that there were no legislative guidelines for identification until the *Financial Transaction Reports Act 1988* (Cth), which requires a high standard of identification for the opening of a bank account.

BANK CHEQUES

Bank cheques (as well as payment orders) are drawn by a bank (or a non-bank financial institution) on itself and are considered by many to be almost as good as cash. However, it should be kept in mind that unlike cash, **bank cheques or payment orders can be dishonoured** by the bank or non-bank financial institution upon which they are drawn where:

- there has been a forged or unauthorised signature: s. 32;
- there has been a material alteration;
- the cheque has been lost or stolen;
- there has been a court order restraining payment; or
- there has been a failure of consideration by the holder.

Doing business

Bank cheques not equivalent to cash

Even where a bank cheque is used, proper safety precautions should still be taken. The payee, indorser or drawer should obtain special clearance or at least take steps to verify the validity of the cheque with the bank.

If the cheque is drawn as a bearer cheque, it should be changed to an order cheque as this places an onus on the collecting bank to take care where the collecting party is not named as the payee. ■

There is no duty on a bank to warn traders (*Johns Period Furniture Pty Ltd v. Commonwealth Savings Bank of Australia* (1980) 24 SASR 224) or the public (*Johnson Matthey Ltd v. Australia and New Zealand Banking Group Ltd* (1989) Aust. Torts Reports ¶80-256) of stolen bank cheques.

> **!** CAUTION NOTE
> *Bank cheques—drawn by a financial institution upon itself and can be dishonoured.*

OTHER METHODS OF MONEY TRANSFER

Electronic banking (see also Chapter 25)

EFTS is a method of transferring funds without the use of paper

Electronic Funds Transfer Systems (EFTS) is a method of transferring funds without the use of paper. It includes both Internet banking and banking transactions using an electronic terminal such as an ATM or EFTPOS. It is not regulated by either the *Bills of Exchange Act* or the *Cheques Act* but is subject to the following areas of law:

- **contract law** between the customer and the bank;
- **Code of Banking Practice, the Building Society Code of Practice, and the EFT Code of Conduct**;
- the *Trade Practices Act 1974* (Cth) and state consumer protection legislation;
- **Sale of Goods Acts** if the card is used to purchase goods; and
- **law of torts**, in particular negligence as a duty of care can exist to protect customers or banks from financial loss.

Cheques subject to an Electronic Funds Transfer Code of Conduct since 1989

As there is no specific legislation dealing with EFTS, the Commonwealth government through the Minister for Consumer Affairs issued an Electronic Funds Transfer Code of Conduct in 1989. The operation of the code is principally the responsibility of the Australian Payments System Council.

The code covers transactions by an individual through an electronic terminal by means of an EFT card and a PIN (personal identification number) and includes:

- availability and disclosure of terms and conditions of use in plain English;
- 30 days written notice of any changes to terms and conditions of use;
- paper receipts of any EFT transactions;
- no cardholder liability for unauthorised transactions unless the cardholder has contributed to the losses;
- technical malfunctions to be borne by the card issuer unless the cardholder should have been aware of the problem;
- deposits at terminals are the responsibility of the bank;
- networking arrangements are the responsibility of the banks;
- audit trails must be kept by the banks;
- the cardholders' financial privacy is to be maintained; and
- complaint investigation and resolution procedures are provided. Unresolved disputes must first be taken to senior management of the bank concerned. If the dispute is still unresolved, the cardholder may seek resolution through the relevant state Consumer Affairs or Fair Trading Bureau, Small Claims Tribunals or the Banking Ombudsman.

Cards

Types of credit card—'charge cards' and 'credit cards'

Two types of card can be identified:

- 'charge cards', such as American Express and Diners Club which require the amount owed each month to be paid in full within one calendar month of receiving the bill; and
- 'credit cards', such as Bankcard and Visa where the cardholder can defer full payment of the principal from one month to the next by paying a monthly minimum payment which covers the interest charges, government taxes and a small part of the principal.

A typical credit card transaction will involve three parties (the cardholder, the merchant and the bank) and four contracts (the cardholder and the bank, the merchant and their bank, the agreement between the cardholder and the merchant, and a reimbursement agreement between the cardholder's bank and the merchant's bank).

Typically, a cardholder has a choice on payment. They may pay the full amount within a specified period after receiving their account or defer full payment and pay by instalments.

Doing business

Higher rates of interest charged on interest free periods

Cards offering interest free periods on credit purchases are usually charged at a higher rate of interest if the amount is not paid in full by the cardholder on the due date. Also, cash advances accrue interest from the date of debiting the transaction. ■

The cardholder's liabilities and rights are contained in a written contract provided by the bank and, if the card is a credit card, it will be regulated by the Consumer Credit Code.

! CAUTION NOTE

A term of the agreement with the financial institution is to notify them immediately of loss, or be liable for any losses from unauthorised use of the card.

If a card is lost or stolen, the cardholder must notify the bank or issuer 'immediately' or 'as soon as is practicable' if they are to escape liability for any losses that may result from unauthorised usage. If the losses have arisen because of the cardholder's failure to observe basic security precautions, then most issuers provide for increased liability for the cardholder.

If the goods purchased by the cardholder are defective, the merchant may face an action under the *Trade Practices Act*, the *Sale of Goods Act* of the relevant state or territory or an action in contract or tort.

THE CODE OF BANKING PRACTICE

The Code of Banking Practice (1993), which was adopted on 1 November 1996 when the Consumer Credit Code began operation, is a self-regulatory code that sets out standards of disclosure and conduct which subscribing banks agree to observe when dealing with their customers. The standards cover matters such as terms and conditions of bank accounts, disclosure of fees and charges, privacy, confidentiality and how to resolve disputes (see the paragraph on the banking industry ombudsman below). It does not apply to non-consumers, for example, small independent businesses.

The code has been reviewed and now:

- contains a principle that banks will act fairly and reasonably toward their customers;
- extends to cover small business;
- monitors banks' compliance with the code and accountability for code breaches;
- contains provision for a sympathetic consideration for customers suffering financial difficulties;
- provides better information for prospective guarantors about the debt they're guaranteeing;
- provides details of accounts most suited to low income and disadvantaged persons; and
- provides an internal process for handling complaints.

Information on the new code and its progress can be viewed at **<http://www.bankers.asn.au>**.

THE BANKING INDUSTRY OMBUDSMAN

The Banking Ombudsman Scheme was set up in 1989 to help individual bank customers sort out their unresolved complaints with their banks. It requires the banks to provide personal customers with a free, external and independent process for resolving disputes, and since 1998 has been extended to small businesses. A small business is described as one that has 15 full-time equivalent employees or fewer; has an annual turnover of $1 million or less, and is independently owned and managed.

The types of matters that the ombudsman deals with includes complaints about a specific banking service that the bank has provided to a consumer, for example, credit card disputes or maladministration in lending matters up to $150 000. They do not consider disputes that relate purely to a bank's commercial judgement in decisions about lending or security and that do not involve maladministration.

More information on the Banking Industry Ombudsman can be obtained at:
http://www.abio.org.au

WEB RESOURCE

FINANCIAL TRANSACTION REPORTS ACT

The *Financial Transaction Reports Act 1988* (Cth) was formerly known as the *Cash Transaction Reports Act 1988* (Cth). Its principal object, as stated in s. 4, is to assist the administration and enforcement of taxation laws.

Its secondary objects are to assist the administration of non-taxation laws of the Commonwealth and territories and to make available to state authorities information that might assist the administration and enforcement of state laws.

The Australian Transaction Reports and Analysis Centre (AUSTRAC)

The *Financial Transaction Reports Act 1988* established the Australian Transaction Reports and Analysis Centre (AUSTRAC). The purpose of the Centre is to **collect, analyse and distribute information regarding cash transactions**, as well as to work closely with the Commissioner of Taxation and other government agencies involved in detecting criminal activities and money laundering.

WEB RESOURCE

More information on AUSTRAC can be obtained at:
http://www.austrac.gov.au

Where a cash dealer is a party to a significant cash transaction, the dealer shall report the transaction to the Director of AUSTRAC unless the transaction is an exempt transaction.

What is a 'cash dealer'?

The definition of a 'cash dealer' in s. 3 is very wide and includes:

- financial institutions (i.e. banks, building societies and credit unions);
- insurance companies;
- securities dealers and futures brokers;
- managers and trustees of unit trusts;
- currency and bullion dealers;
- casinos and gambling houses; and
- bookmakers, TABs and on-course totes.

Obligations imposed by the Act

The following obligations are imposed on cash dealers, and the public generally:

- To report **significant cash transactions** of $10 000 or more: s. 7. Currency is cash and it is defined by the Act as coin and paper money of Australia or of a foreign country.
- To report on cash transfers of $10 000 or more into or out of Australia, whether it be local or foreign currency by **anybody**: s. 15.
- To report transactions where the cash dealer has reasonable grounds to suspect they may involve tax evasion or some other breach of the law: s. 16.
- To establish the identity of any person or entity who opens and operates an account of $1000 or more with a cash dealer or becomes a signatory on such an account.

What is a suspect transaction?

In addition to reporting significant cash transactions, s. 16 of the *Financial Transaction Reports Act 1988* requires cash dealers to report a transaction in which there are reasonable grounds for the cash dealer to suspect that information they have received in regards to the transaction may be:

- relevant to a tax evasion investigation;
- relevant to an investigation of an offence against a law of the Commonwealth or a territory;
- of assistance in the enforcement of the *Proceeds of Crime Act 1987*; or
- relevant to an investigation of an offence under the *Corporations Act 2001*.

A transaction may be any business dealing between a cash dealer and a customer, including any negotiations or discussions that may not result in an actual dealing. A transaction does not include mere enquiries. In deciding whether a transaction is suspicious, the cash dealer must consider all the circumstances of the transaction. While the factors will obviously vary from case to case, examples of relevant factors are:

- Any unusual circumstances surrounding the transaction.
- The known business background of the person.
- The use of seemingly false identification.
- Admissions or statements of tax evasion or other criminal activity.
- Regular or unusual transactions involving countries that are a known source of narcotics or through which narcotics are known to pass.
- The behaviour, such as excessive nervousness, of the person conducting the transaction.

While the requirement to report significant cash transactions only relates to cash, suspect transactions are not limited to cash. They include telegraphic transfers, purchase of bank drafts or travellers' cheques. There is no monetary threshold for suspect transactions as there is for significant cash transactions.

Enforcement of the Act

In the event of a dealer failing to report a transaction that is subsequently investigated, the dealer has to be able to establish to the satisfaction of the authorities that there were no reasonable grounds for believing the transaction to be suspicious. Failure to establish reasonable grounds results in an offence under the Act (ss. 28–30). The Act imposes fines and/or prison terms for various types of non-compliance. Examples are:

- **Section 28: Failure to provide information**—a natural person: $13 200 and/or two years' gaol; corporation: $66 000;
- **Section 29: False or misleading information**—a natural person: $33 000 and/or five years' gaol; corporation: $165 000;
- **Section 24: Opening a bank account in a false name**—a natural person: $13 200 and/or two years' gaol; corporation $66 000.

In addition to these penalties, the court may grant an injunction where it is satisfied a person has engaged in, or is proposing to engage in, conduct in contravention of the Act: s. 32.

Any person who leaves Australia can be requested to make a declaration regarding the taking of currency out of Australia. The person may also be searched and any luggage or other goods examined. Any currency found may be seized and the person fined $6000 and/or given 12 months' imprisonment. A person suspected of an offence under the Act may be arrested without a warrant: s. 33.

WEB RESOURCES

Australian Bankers Association: Provides a useful list of organisations operating in the Australian Banking and Finance industry with websites:
http://www.bankers.asn.au

Australian Banking Industry Ombudsman: For extensive information about the role of the banking industry ombudsman, relevant legislation, the Banking Code of Conduct and industry self-regulation:
http://www.abio.org.au

Australian Transaction Reports and Analysis Centre (AUSTRAC):
http://www.austrac.gov.au

Comparative Banking Ombudsman systems: The Banking Ombudsman is not unique to Australia. A site worth looking at for comparative purposes is:
http://www.obo.org.uk/ (a UK site)

The Finance and Treasury Association: You can find most Australian bank websites from this page plus some major overseas banks:
http://www.fta.asn.au

Reserve Bank of Australia: This site provides extensive information on monetary policy and the maintenance of financial stability. It provides links to other central banks around the world, the Australian Payments Clearing House
http://www.apca.com.au/

and various other government departments concerned with monetary policy:
http://www.rba.gov.au

REVIEW QUESTIONS

31.1 What is the significance of something being negotiable?

31.2 State the parties to a bill of exchange and briefly describe each.

31.3 Discuss the main distinctions between a cheque and a bill of exchange.

31.4 Name the parties involved in a cheque and briefly describe each.

31.5 Under what circumstances can a bank refuse to honour a customer's cheque?

31.6 What are the consequences to a bank if it pays a cheque contrary to its crossing?

31.7 What is the effect on a holder of a cheque crossed 'not negotiable' and a cheque crossed only with two parallel lines, or is there no difference?

31.8 Indicate whether each of the following statements is true or false:

	TRUE	FALSE
▪ A person who has taken a cheque after value has been given but who did not themselves give value is called a holder for value	☐	☐
▪ A person who takes a cheque complete and regular on the face of it without notice of any defect and in good faith and for value is called a holder in due course	☐	☐
▪ A stale cheque is one that has been in circulation for more than six months	☐	☐
▪ Where a drawer discovers that their signature is being forged, failure to notify the bank as soon as possible of the discovery will result in the drawer being estopped from recovering any money	☐	☐
▪ The basic duty of a collecting bank is to credit the drawer's account	☐	☐
▪ The drawee is the person upon whom the cheque is drawn	☐	☐
▪ A holder for value is a person who has taken the cheque in good faith, for value and without notice of any defect in the title of the previous holder	☐	☐
▪ A cheque with two transverse lines drawn across it must be paid into a bank account and is not transferable	☐	☐
▪ Both a cheque and a bill of exchange can be drawn on a bank account	☐	☐
▪ A cheque payable to order can be transferred by delivery	☐	☐
▪ A cardholder who has a charge card can defer full payment of principal from one month to the next	☐	☐

activebook

Activebook resources include in-depth summaries with links to the relevant part of the book. For revision, add your own notes to the summaries provided by using the note-taking function.

CRITICAL THINKING

31.1 Wilma drew a cheque payable to 'Anna or order' for $100 in payment of goods purchased from Anna. Maria steals the cheque and forges Anna's indorsement on it and negotiates it to Gina in payment for goods. Gina indorses it and cashes it with her friend Saffron at the local supermarket.

Saffron banks the cheque but it is not paid because a stop payment order had been placed on it by Wilma.

Discuss.

31.2 On 1 November Anne signed a crossed 'not negotiable', cheque payable to George or bearer and drawn on the Australia Bank. The date written on the cheque was 24 November. The cheque was stolen from George by Bill, who cashed it with Sam, a grocer, on 15 November. On 18 November George notified Anne that the cheque had been stolen from him and Anne immediately notified the bank in writing to stop payment on the cheque. Sam cashed the cheque at the Common Bank on 21 November and two days later the Australia Bank debited Anne's account with the amount of the cheque.

(i) Explain, giving reasons, the positions of:
- Sam
- Anne
- George
- Australia Bank
- Common Bank
- Bill.

(ii) Would your answers in (i) above be any different if the cheque had been an open bearer cheque which Bill had found and cashed with Sam? Give reasons for your answer.

DEBT RECOVERY

PART EIGHT

CHAPTER 32

Insolvency and Debt Recovery

CHAPTER CONTENTS

activebook

This icon is used throughout the following chapter to remind you to visit the *Business Law* online activebook for additional exercises, links to legal websites, and feedback. For a detailed explanation of what is in the activebook please refer to the inside cover of this textbook. The activebook is available through OneKey.

Where do I start?
Learning path: Use the activebook to complete a pre-chapter warm-up exercise.

There are many definitions of legal terms to assist with your understanding of the material.

CHAPTER OBJECTIVES

On completion of this chapter, you should be able to:

- outline the procedures to recover a debt
- outline the steps required to obtain a sequestration order
- contrast bankruptcy with a Part X arrangement
- list the property available to the trustee
- list the order of payment of debts
- discuss the procedure for discharge from bankruptcy.

KEY TERMS

An understanding of the following terms will help you to better understand the material in this chapter:

- **act of bankruptcy:** a public indication of insolvency must be committed before a creditor's petition for sequestration order can be made
- **after acquired property:** any property a bankrupt receives after bankruptcy starts
- **available property:** property owned by a bankrupt when bankruptcy began
- **bankruptcy:** a legal state (or status) in which a person has their property and financial affairs controlled by a trustee under order of the court; arises because person is insolvent
- **bankruptcy notice:** a notice issued by the Official Receiver upon application by a creditor who has obtained a final judgement or order for the amount owing to the creditor by the debtor which directs the debtor to pay the judgement debt (normally within 28 days), failure to comply amounting to an act of bankruptcy
- **Consumer Price Index (CPI):** the index which measures quarterly changes in the price of a 'basket' of goods and services purchased by metropolitan households and provides the official measure of inflation in Australia
- **creditor's petition:** application to court by a creditor requesting a particular debtor be made bankrupt
- **debtor's petition:** application by debtor to be made bankrupt
- **Deed of Assignment:** debtor assigns (transfers) all of their property for the benefit of their creditors
- **deferred claims:** debts which are postponed until all other creditors have been paid in full, including claims by companies controlled by the bankrupt
- **Doctrine of Relation Back:** the bankruptcy is DEEMED to commence with the earliest act of bankruptcy within the six months immediately preceding the presentation of creditors' petition. NOTE: The application of the Doctrine of Relation Back can vary with the particular circumstances
- **fraudulent transactions:** a transaction at any time made with the intention to defeat or delay creditors and not for valuable consideration
- **insolvent:** unable to pay debts as and when they fall due out of debtor's own funds (this is a financial situation not legal status)
- **Official Receiver:** the person appointed for each bankruptcy district to act for and on behalf of the Official Trustee (s. 15)
- **Official Trustee in Bankruptcy:** the person (a body corporate: s. 18(1)) in whom a bankrupt's property vests for administrative purposes
- **Part X (part 10) arrangement:** arrangement where debtor agrees to have financial affairs controlled and thereby avoid bankruptcy

- **registered trustee:** usually a public or chartered accountant who is a representative of the creditors and in whom the bankrupt person's property vests, which the registered trustee will then administer in the creditor's interests (s. 156A)
- **sequestration order:** order of the court whereby all of a person's assets are taken from them and given to the trustee in bankruptcy for the benefit of all of their creditors
- **voidable preference:** where debtor is insolvent and within six months prior to filing creditors' petition debtor gives a preference priority or advantage to a particular creditor.

what if . . .

You were in business and a customer who owed you a very large amount of money went into liquidation and was unable to pay you. You have trade creditors to whom, in total, you owe a large amount of money. The financial failure of your customer could put your business in serious financial difficulties. What could be the legal consequences to your business and to you personally?

Credit management is a very important aspect of any business. It is not unusual for very viable, profitable businesses to be placed under extreme financial strain due largely to cash flow problems arising from debtors of the business not paying their accounts promptly. There have been some extreme cases where businesses have failed because of the non-receipt of money owed to them.

While the legal process of recovering overdue debts appears to be comparatively straightforward, this appearance can be deceptive. Debt recovery can be a drawn-out, highly frustrating process, and unfortunately the most difficult debts to recover are usually the ones a business needs to recover—that is, the large debts.

When making credit available to a customer, a good businessperson will not base decisions on the knowledge that they can take the debtor to court to make the debtor pay. They will base their decisions on a well-reasoned credit policy that will enable them to compete with the opposition and still be confident that they have minimised the level of potential bad debts. Legal action is the last resort and prevention is the best cure because, while the process seems simple and straightforward, it can in fact be very drawn out and frustrating.

This chapter will provide a brief overview of the recovery of debts through the inferior courts as well as examining bankruptcy proceedings. It will also explain the legal procedures applicable to companies that are insolvent or are having severe financial difficulties.

SHOULD LEGAL PROCEEDINGS BE COMMENCED?

! CAUTION NOTE

Before commencing legal recovery, the creditor should look at the 'cost–benefit' involved.

Before commencing legal proceedings, the creditor should consider the economic aspects. If the creditor is using a solicitor, the solicitor will be entitled to fees and expenses regardless of whether the action is successful. If successful, the full amount of legal costs may not be recoverable from the debtor because the amount may exceed the amount allowed to be recovered under the court rules.

The debtor may defend the action, so the creditor will need to produce evidence to the court with an associated consumption of time, effort and additional expense.

Having obtained judgement, the creditor may have to take further steps to enforce the judgement and make the debtor pay. All this effort and expense could be wasted if the debtor has no income or assets from which the debt can be paid. The debt may be virtually irrecoverable. The creditor should therefore base the decision to proceed on commercial considerations as much as legal ones.

In respect of the legal considerations, the creditor must establish the basic cause of action, that is, what happened and how can it be proved? In this regard the creditor must:

- establish the existence of a contract; how and when it came into existence; whether it was express or implied; and whether it was verbal or written;
- ascertain details of the breach: how has the debtor failed to comply with the contract?; and
- determine what loss has been suffered and how is it calculated.

THE DEBT RECOVERY PROCESS

The following procedures for the recovery of a debt are based on the Local Court of New South Wales. Although the rules of the courts in the other states differ in detail, the basic methods and principles are the same in all courts (see Figure 32.1).

Obtaining judgement

Judgement is the order of the court stating that the debt is in fact owed. It is necessary to obtain judgement prior to taking other recovery action such as a writ of execution or a garnishee order.

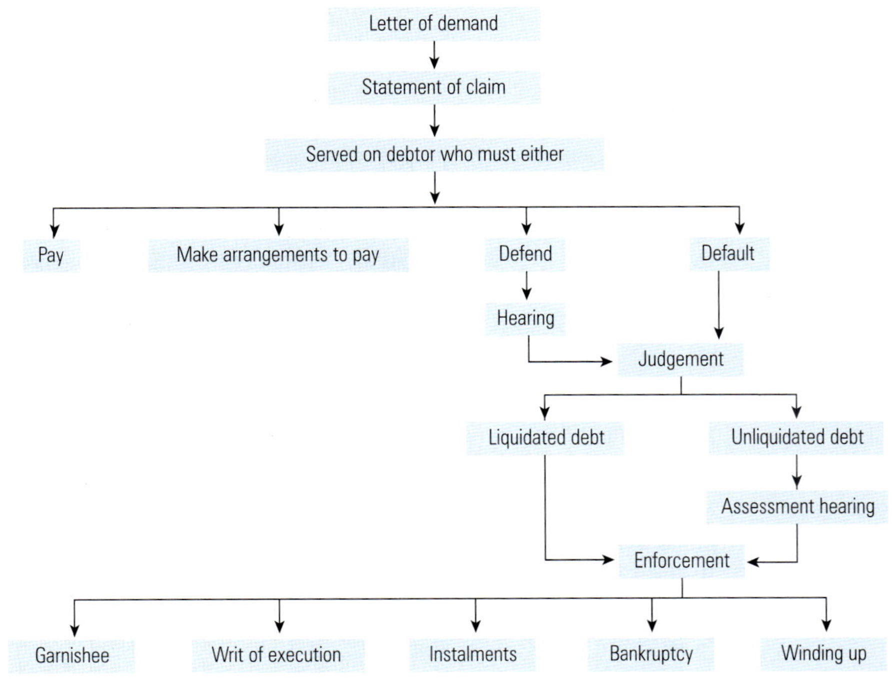

FIGURE 32.1 *Outline of debt recovery process*

The usual steps in obtaining judgement are:

- Letter of demand—demands payment within a specified time or legal proceedings will be commenced.
- Serve a statement of claim on the debtor to officially commence legal proceedings (see Table 32.1).
  - A copy is filed with the court.
  - A copy must be served on the debtor.
- The defendant has 28 days to do one of the following:
  - Pay the debt.
  - Make arrangements to pay or secure the debt.
  - File a defence.

If the defendant does none of these things the defendant is in default. Once the defendant has defaulted the plaintiff may file an application for default judgement.

If the defendant files a defence to the action the plaintiff will not be able to obtain a default judgement. The matter will proceed to a hearing.

Enforcement of judgement

If the judgement debtor still fails to pay the judgement amount the judgement creditor will have to apply to the court for further orders to make the debtor pay. Such orders are:

- **Writ of execution** authorises court officer to seize the goods of the debtor and sell them.
- **Garnishee order** directs a person who owes money to the debtor to pay the money into the court in satisfaction of the judgement. Usually served on the employer of the debtor in regard to wages. It may also be served on other people who owe money to the debtor.
- **Instalment order** directs the debtor to pay the judgement debt in specified amounts on specified dates.
- **Bankruptcy** may be commenced where the judgement debtor is a natural person.
- **Winding up or liquidation** where the debtor is a company. For further details see 'Corporate Insolvency', below.

Table 32.1 Terms used to describe documents commencing court process

State	*Court*	*Liquidated*	*Unliquidated*
Australian Capital Territory	Magistrate's Court	Special claim	Ordinary claim
New South Wales	Local Court	Liquidated statement of claim	Ordinary statement of claim
	District Court	Liquidated statement of claim	Ordinary statement of claim
Northern Territory	Local Court	Statement of claim	Statement of claim
Queensland	Magistrate's Court	Special summons	Ordinary summons
	District Court	Plaints	Plaints
South Australia	Magistrate's Court	Ordinary summons	Ordinary summons
	District Court	Ordinary summons	Ordinary summons
Tasmania	Magistrate's Court	Plaint	Plaint
Victoria	Magistrate's Court	Complaint	Complaint
	County Court	Complaint	Complaint
Western Australia	Magistrate's Court	Writ of summons	Writ of summons
	District Court	Writ of summons	Writ of summons

OVERVIEW OF BANKRUPTCY PROCEEDINGS

In common with much of our statute and common law, Australian legislation relating to bankruptcy and bankruptcy proceedings has its origins in English law. The earliest English bankruptcy legislation appeared in 1542. Evidence of English influence is found in our Acts of 1924 and 1966. Both are statutes enacted by the Commonwealth Parliament in exercise of powers conferred upon it by s. 52(xviii) of the Commonwealth Constitution. By virtue of the Constitution, the *Bankruptcy Act 1966* superseded the provisions of state Acts on bankruptcy. The situation now is that the *Bankruptcy Act 1966* governs all matters pertaining to bankruptcy throughout Australia.

Bankruptcy legislation is intended to provide a means by which a person acting *bona fide*, but in a hopeless financial position, is able to have their assets taken and distributed among their creditors equitably; eventually the bankrupt is discharged from further liability for any part of their debts still outstanding.

The aim of bankruptcy proceedings is to:

- Ensure all the creditors are treated fairly and there is an equitable distribution of the bankrupt's assets.
- Give the debtor the chance to have a new start.

It should be noted that it is not the aim of the legislation to punish the bankrupt.

A **bankrupt** is defined as **a debtor whose estate is vested in a trustee for division among their creditors**, pursuant to an order of a court having federal jurisdiction in bankruptcy. It should be distinguished from a company winding up, which is based on similar principles but is regulated by the Corporations Law. An outline of bankruptcy proceedings and the options available is set out in Figure 32.2.

A debtor in this situation is a person who is unable to pay their debts out of their own money as they become due. In such a situation, the debtor may become bankrupt voluntarily by requesting the Registrar in Bankruptcy to accept their petition, or one or more creditors of the debtor may approach the court by way of a petition for a sequestration

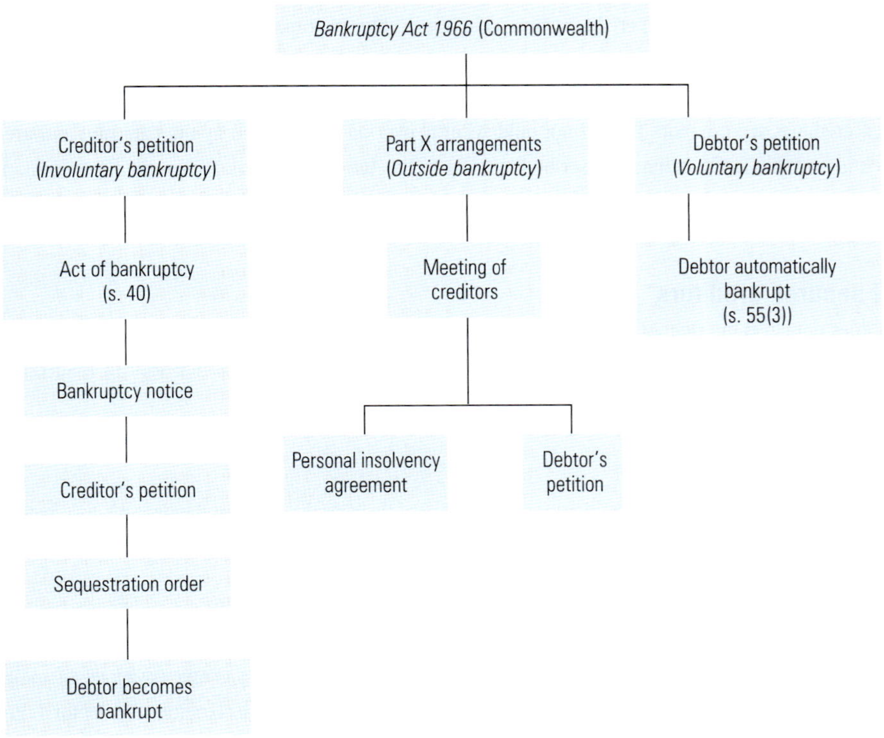

FIGURE 32.2 *Options under the* Bankruptcy Act 1966 *(Cth)*

Sequestration order—order made by the court on the petition of the creditor making the debtor bankrupt

order. The word sequestration is derived from the Latin *sequestrare*, which means 'to take away'. A sequestration order is an order the court may make on the petition of a creditor. If such a petition is granted, the debtor becomes a bankrupt and any assets, with minor exceptions, are vested in the Official Receiver in Bankruptcy or a registered Trustee in Bankruptcy.

At the time a debtor files a petition, or after a **sequestration** order is made, the bankrupt must file a statement of affairs, which is to assist the trustee in administering the estate. The trustee will sell the assets of the bankrupt and distribute the proceeds among the creditors. The bankrupt may be publicly examined as to their financial affairs and, at the discretion of the court, may ultimately be discharged and released from any further obligations to their creditors. The Act, in s. 81, provides that the public examination of the debtor takes place at a time and place appointed by the Registrar.

Trustee will be the Official Receiver in Bankruptcy

The bankrupt will be discharged automatically and released from any further obligations to their creditors three years after the filing of their statement of affairs, unless an objection to their discharge has been lodged. If an objection is lodged, the bankrupt will be discharged after five or eight years, depending on the grounds of the objection. A bankrupt can apply to their trustee for early discharge at any time after the elapse of six months from the filing of their statement of affairs.

OTHER EFFECTS OF BANKRUPTCY

Rights of an undischarged bankrupt

An undischarged bankrupt cannot be a director of a company without leave of the Supreme Court of the relevant state. An undischarged bankrupt will also be guilty of an offence if credit is obtained to the extent of $3000 or more from a person without informing the creditor of the undischarged bankruptcy. The penalty for such an offence is three years' imprisonment: s. 269.

Rights of unsecured creditors

Once debtor is bankrupt, creditor can take no further action

After a debtor becomes a bankrupt, no creditor whose debt is provable (i.e. capable of being proved in the bankruptcy proceedings) is entitled to commence or take any fresh steps for the enforcement of any remedy against the debtor or their property.

Unsecured creditors are creditors that do not hold security over an asset owned by the bankrupt and are owed money which is provable in the manner prescribed by s. 84 of the Act. A proof of debt is in the form of an affidavit (a written statement made under oath) specifying the particulars of the debt, and it must be lodged with the trustee (see Figure 32.3).

Rights of secured creditors

Bankruptcy does not affect rights of secured creditor

Bankruptcy does not affect the right of a secured creditor to realise or deal with the security. Subject to the provision of s. 66(4), a secured creditor is not entitled to vote in respect of a secured debt unless the security is surrendered.

KEY ASPECTS OF BANKRUPTCY

The petition for bankruptcy

A debtor may be made bankrupt on the petition of one or more of their creditors or on the debtor's own petition.

Debtor's petition (voluntary bankruptcy)

A debtor can present to the Registrar in Bankruptcy a declaration of intention to present a debtor's petition (see Figure 32.4).

This provides a procedure for a debtor who is contemplating voluntary bankruptcy to take advantage of an optional seven-day pre-bankruptcy moratorium period. If the Official Receiver accepts the declaration, the debtor's creditors are stayed (stopped) from enforcement action for seven days and the debtor is able to consider possible alternatives to bankruptcy.

Proof of Debt

I (*full name, address and occupation of person lodging proof of debt*) lodge the following proof of debt:

1. (*full name of bankrupt*) was at the date on which he became a bankrupt, namely (*date of bankruptcy*) and still is, justly and truly indebted to (*name of creditor/me*) in the sum of $................, in accordance with the particulars specified in the statement of account annexed hereto.
2. Security is not held by (*name of creditor/me*) or by any person on *his/my* behalf for the payment of the whole or any part of the sum specified in paragraph 1.
3. The following security is held by (*name of creditor/me*) for the payment of *part/the whole* of the sums specified in paragraph 1.
4. The vouchers by which the debt can be substantiated are specified in the statement of account.

Dated this day of 20

(*Signature of person lodging proof of debt*)

Statement of Account

Date of transaction	Consideration or nature of debt	Amount	Vouchers (if any)
	Insert details of judgement (if obtained)		
	Date obtained: Judgement no: Court: Judgement debt and costs on Judgement:		

FIGURE 32.3 *Example of a proof of debt*

If a debtor petitions for bankruptcy, a verified statement of the debtor's financial affairs must be filed with the Official Receiver. An Official Receiver may reject the debtor's petition if the statement of affairs is not properly completed or if it appears that if the debtor did not become bankrupt, the debtor would be likely to be able to pay the debts within a reasonable time. This discretion may only be exercised if it is evident to the Official Receiver that the debtor is petitioning because of an unwillingness (rather than an inability) to pay or the debtor has been bankrupt on his or her own petition at least three times or at least once in the last five years. Once the Official Receiver has accepted the debtor's petition, the debtor is bankrupt.

Creditor's petition (involuntary bankruptcy)

Creditor's petition may result in sequestration order against debtor

The court may, on a **petition presented by a creditor**, make **a sequestration order** against the debtor's estate if a debtor has committed an act of bankruptcy while personally resident in Australia or while they were carrying on business in Australia either personally or by means of an agent or manager.

Declaration of Intention to Present a Debtor's Petition

To: the Registrar

I, (*full name, address and occupation of debtor*), declare under s. 54A of the *Bankruptcy Act 1966* (Cth) my intention to present a debtor's petition.

I am not disqualified by the Act from presenting this declaration or a petition against myself.

Date ....20 ....

....

(*Signature of debtor*)

Signed by the debtor
in the presence of ....

(*Signature, address and occupation of witness*)

FIGURE 32.4 *Debtor's petition*

> ! CAUTION NOTE
> *Amount owing by debtor must be $2000 or more which can be the sum of two or more debts.*

A creditor's petition must be in accordance with the prescribed form and has to be verified by the affidavit of a person who has knowledge of the facts (see Figure 32.5). It must also be served (delivered to the debtor) as prescribed by law. Except by leave of the court, a creditor's petition cannot be withdrawn after presentation; the creditor is deemed to be taking the proceedings for the benefit of all creditors, not just the petitioning creditor. There is authority that requires evidence of solvency of a debtor to be given before a petition can be withdrawn.

A creditor's petition may not be presented against a debtor unless the amount owing is a **minimum of $2000**. This may be the sum of two or more debts owed to two or more creditors: s. 44.

Once a petition has been presented by a creditor, an application can be made to the court for the appointment of an interim receiver of the debtor's estate. Orders are usually only made when the creditor can prove that there is strong likelihood that a debtor will dispose of assets or put the assets beyond the reach of the creditors.

Assets of debtor are vested in the Official Receiver or Trustee in Bankruptcy

If, after considering the creditor's petition, the court makes a sequestration order, the debtor becomes bankrupt and any assets are vested in the Official Receiver or the Trustee in Bankruptcy with some minor exceptions. See p. 693 for specific examples of property not available to the trustee.

> ! CAUTION NOTE
> *If a composition is accepted, the bankruptcy is annulled.*

The Act, in ss. 73–76, provides that after a sequestration order has been made or a bankruptcy has occurred as the result of a debtor's petition, a bankrupt may make a proposal to their creditors for a composition in satisfaction of their debts or a scheme of arrangement of their affairs. If a meeting of the creditors, by special resolution, accepts the proposal, the bankruptcy is annulled. Upon annulment, the bankrupt's property is still vested in the Official Receiver or in any person the court appoints.

Creditor's Petition

I, (*full name and address and occupation of petitioning creditor*) petition the Court for a sequestration order against the estate of (*full name of debtor*) who resides at (*address of debtor*) (and carries on business at [*business address of debtor*]) and whose occupation is ...., hereinafter referred to as 'the debtor'.

1. The debtor was at the date of the commission of the act of bankruptcy specified in paragraph 4 personally present in Australia (or ordinarily resident in Australia, *or as the case may be*).
2. The debtor is justly and truly indebted to me in the sum of $.............. for (*consideration for debt to be shown*).
3. I do not, nor does any person on my behalf, hold any security over the property of the debtor or any part of it for the payment of the amount specified in paragraph 2.

or

3. I hold security over the property (or part of the property) of the debtor, being (*specify particulars of the security*), but the security is valued at $.............., leaving an unsecured balance owing to me of $..............

or

3. I hold security over the property (or part of the property) of the debtor for payment of the amount specified in paragraph 2, being (*specify particulars of the security*), but I am willing to surrender the security for the benefit of the creditors generally in the event of a sequestration order being made against the estate of the debtor.
4. The debtor, within 6 months before the presentation of this petition, committed the following act (or acts) of bankruptcy (*set out nature and date or dates of the act or acts of bankruptcy that are being relied upon*).

Dated this .... day of ...., 20......

....
(*Signature of petitioner*)

Signed by the petitioner
in the presence of ....
(*Signature, address and occupation of witness*)

This petition is filed by ....on behalf of ....
whose address for service is ....

FIGURE 32.5 *Creditor's petition*

Multiple debtors

A creditor of a partnership may present a petition against the partnership if they are entitled to present a petition against any one of the members of the partnership in **respect to a partnership debt**. The creditor may present the petition against any one of the partners without including the other partnership members: s. 45.

A debtor's petition may be presented against a partnership by all of the partners or by a majority of the partners who reside in Australia.

A creditor may also present a petition against two or more joint debtors whether or not they are partners. Where the petition is against joint debtors, the court may make a sequestration order against one or more of the joint debtors and dismiss the petition insofar as it relates to the other named joint debtors: s. 46.

Where a sequestration order is made against joint debtors, whether partners or not, the joint estate (jointly held assets) shall be applied to satisfy all the joint debts. If the joint estate is insufficient to satisfy all the joint debts, the individual estate of each joint debtor shall then be applied to his or her separate debts (non-joint debts). If there is any surplus in any of the separate estates after payment of all the debtor's separate debts, that surplus will then be allocated to any unpaid part of the joint estate.

activebook

To help you to remember and understand the topics covered so far, and for links to legal websites, refer to your online activebook. Model answers provide feedback to problems and exercises.

Should there be a surplus in the joint estate after satisfying all joint estate claims, that surplus shall be allocated to the respective separate estates in proportion to the right and interest of each joint debtor in the joint estate: s. 110.

Example

If 'A' and 'B' jointly decide to restore an old car, they may incur considerable debts in respect to replacement parts for the car, special tools and specialised services as part of the restoration process. They may be so obsessed with the restoration that they lose track of the costs and debts they are incurring. If they default, a creditor who supplied specialised services may successfully petition for the bankruptcy of both 'A' and 'B'.

The car and any tools, spare parts or other goods purchased for the restoration venture would be sold to pay all the outstanding debts of the restoration venture. If the sale of this joint property was insufficient to satisfy all the restoration venture debts, the personal assets of 'A' and 'B' would then be sold to pay all their personal (non-restoration venture) debts. If their personal assets exceed their personal debts, that surplus is then applied to the outstanding balance of the restoration venture debts.

On the other hand, if the proceeds from the sale of the car and other goods purchased for the restoration venture exceed the outstanding debts for that venture, the surplus is paid to 'A' and 'B' in proportion to their share in the restoration venture.

Acts of bankruptcy

An act of bankruptcy is in effect a public demonstration of insolvency committed by the debtor in the previous six months—that is, the inability to pay debts as and when they are due within the last six months. A creditor must be able to prove that a debtor has committed an act of bankruptcy, otherwise the court will reject the creditor's petition for a sequestration order.

Among the acts of bankruptcy listed in s. 40 of the Act are the following:

- If, in Australia or elsewhere, the debtor makes a conveyance or assignment of property, creates a charge on their property, makes a payment or incurs an obligation that would, if they became a bankrupt, be void as against the trustee—for example:
  - voidable preferences;
  - fraudulent transactions; or
  - certain settlements of property (see property available to Trustee in Bankruptcy for distribution amongst creditors).
- It is an act of bankruptcy for a debtor to change residential or business addresses with the intent of defeating or delaying the debtor's creditors.

***BARTON V. DEPUTY COMMISSIONER OF TAXATION* (1974) 131 CLR 370**

Shortly before the issue of an assessment notice for a large amount of income tax, Barton left Australia suddenly and without explanation or a forwarding address. At the time of his departure he declared he was only leaving for a short time. In fact, he went to South America by an indirect route and remained there indefinitely. The Deputy Commissioner of Taxation submitted a creditor's petition for a sequestration order on the act of bankruptcy involving departing or remaining out of Australia with intent to defeat or delay his creditors.

ISSUE: What constitutes an intention to defeat or delay creditors?

DECISION: The Hight Court, in granting the sequestration order held:

- There can be an intention to defeat future creditors.
- Intent relating to only one existing or future creditor is sufficient.
- Intent to defeat or delay creditors need only be one of several reasons for leaving Australia.

- Two or more intentions need not be mutually exclusive.
- The absence of an honest reason for remaining overseas is relevant.

- Where a debtor's property has been sold pursuant to an order of the court, or an execution issued against the debtor under court process has been returned unsatisfied, the debtor has committed acts of bankruptcy.
- If, at a meeting of creditors, the debtor consents to present a debtor's petition and does not do so within seven days, or if the debtor consents to sign an authority to call a meeting of the creditors and does not do so within seven days, an act of bankruptcy is committed.
- If a debtor admits insolvency to the creditors, and has been requested by a majority of the creditors to bring their affairs under the provisions of the Act, either through a debtor's petition or through taking steps to make one of the private arrangements provided for in the Act, the debtor has committed acts of bankruptcy.
- A debtor commits an act of bankruptcy when notice is given to any of the creditors that payment of the debtor's debts has been suspended or is about to be suspended, and signs an authority under s. 188. There is a similar situation if a debtor fails to attend a meeting of the creditors or to carry out the requirements of a special resolution from such a meeting, or if any private arrangement under Part X of the Act executed by the debtor is set aside by the court.
- The debtor fails to comply with a bankruptcy notice issued by the Registrar in Bankruptcy on the application of a creditor who has obtained a judgement against the debtor. This is by far the most prevalent act of bankruptcy.

Failure to comply with a bankruptcy notice

Failure to comply with a bankruptcy notice can amount to an act of bankruptcy

A judgement creditor can also issue a bankruptcy notice (see Figure 32.6). This requires the debtor to pay the debt, or arrive at some arrangement with the creditor, generally within 28 days of receiving the notice. Failure to comply with the notice will amount to an act of bankruptcy by the debtor unless he or she has filed a cross-claim or set-off for the amount owed.

EFFECT OF A SEQUESTRATION ORDER

Sequestration order forces debtor to give all relevant documents to the trustee

The effect of the making of a sequestration order by the court is to make the debtor bankrupt. He or she must give to the trustee all books, documents, papers and writings relating to their trade dealings, property or affairs, and a passport if they have one. The debtor must be prepared to file a statement of their financial affairs with the Registrar providing any information concerning their conduct, trade dealings, property and affairs to the trustee within 14 days of notification of the sequestration order as required. In s. 77, the Act stipulates that the debtor must execute such documents in relation to their property as are necessary for its realisation, and do the utmost in their power to administer their estate for the benefit of the creditors. If a bankrupt dies before discharge, the proceedings, subject to a court direction, continue as though the debtor were still alive: s. 63.

ALTERNATIVES TO BANKRUPTCY

The *Bankruptcy Act* provides two methods whereby a debtor who is in severe financial difficulties may make arrangements in respect to his or her debts and avoid bankruptcy.

Debtor arrangements

Under Part X of the Act, a debtor may make arrangements direct with their creditors (see pp. 688–689). Although the Act defines the nature of the agreements and sets out certain procedures for and consequences flowing from the agreements, they are private arrangements made with the creditors as a whole without intervention of the court or other government body. **This lack of any impartial official involvement or scrutiny is often cited as a serious defect in the satisfactory operation of Part X arrangements.**

Bankruptcy Notice

To: (*name, address and occupation of judgement debtor*)

WHEREAS (*name and address of judgement creditor*) (hereinafter referred to as 'the judgement creditor') has claimed that the sum of $.............. is due by you to him under a final judgement (*or* order) obtained by him against you in the (*name of court*) on the .... day of ...., 20........, being a judgement (*or* an order) the execution of which has not been stayed:

THEREFORE TAKE NOTICE that within ....days after service of this notice on you, excluding the day on which this notice is served on you, you are required –

(a) to pay the sum of $.............. so claimed by the judgement creditor to (*here insert* 'the judgement creditor' or, *if the judgement or order requires payment to be made to a court or person other than the judgement creditor, the name and address of the court or the other person to whom payment is required to be made*);

(b) to secure the payment of the sum referred to in paragraph (a) to the satisfaction of the (*name of the Court*) or the judgement creditor (or his agent whose name and address are) or compound the sum so specified to the satisfaction of the judgement creditor (or his agent):

AND FURTHER TAKE NOTICE that if, within the period set out above, you fail either to comply with either of the above mentioned requirements of this notice or to satisfy the (*insert the name of the Court*) that you have a counter-claim, set-off or cross-demand equal to or exceeding the sum specified in paragraph (a), being a counter-claim, set-off, or cross-demand that you could not have set-up in the action (*or proceeding*) in which the judgement (*or order*) was obtained, you will have committed an act of bankruptcy on which bankruptcy proceedings may be taken against you.

Dated this .... day of.................. , 20.........

Registrar

NOTE: if you have a counter-claim, set-off or cross-demand equal to or exceeding the sum specified in paragraph (a) being a counter-claim, set-off or cross-demand that you could not have set up in the action (*or proceeding*) in which the judgment (*or order*) was obtained, you may, under s. 41(7) of the *Bankruptcy Act 1966* (Cth), within the period set out above, file an affidavit to that effect giving details of the counter-claim, set-off or cross-demand, as the case requires, and the reasons why you were unable to set up the counter-claim, set-off or cross-demand, and, if you do so, the time for complying with the requirements of this notice shall be deemed to have been extended until the Court determines whether it is satisfied that you have such a counter-claim, set-off or cross-demand.

This notice was issued on the application of (*name of the solicitor for the judgement creditor or the name of the judgement creditor, as the case may be*) whose address for service is

....

....

....

FIGURE 32.6 *Bankruptcy notice*

Part IX arrangements must involve the Official Trustee

Part IX of the Act enables the debtor to enter into a debt agreement with the creditors as a whole. However, unlike a Part X arrangement, the debt agreement procedures must involve the Official Trustee. Debt agreements are aimed at debtors with comparatively small estates and who do not have a history of serious financial difficulties.

What is involved with a Part IX debt agreement?

Debt agreement proposal

A debtor may give the Official Trustee a written proposal for a debt agreement identifying the debtor's property which is to be dealt with under the agreement and specifying how the property is to be dealt with. A debt agreement proposal may provide for any matter relating to the debtor's financial affairs: s. 185C. A statement of the debtor's affairs must be submitted with the debt agreement proposal: s. 185D.

A debt agreement proposal identifies and specifies how the property is to be dealt with

The Official Trustee must not accept a debt agreement proposal for processing if the creditor's interests would be better served by not accepting the proposal for processing: s.185E.

Under s. 185C a debtor cannot submit a debt agreement proposal, if at the time of the proposal:

- the debtor has, in the 10 years immediately before the proposal, been a bankrupt, been a party to a debt agreement or given an authority under s. 188 (Part X arrangement); or
- the debtor's unsecured debts total more than the threshold amount (calculated by applying a formula to certain social security benefits—the amount is therefore subject to frequent change); or
- the value of the debtor's property that would be divisible among creditors if the debtor were bankrupt is more than the threshold amount; or
- the debtor's after tax income is likely to exceed half the threshold amount.

After a debt agreement proposal has been accepted for processing and recorded in the National Personal Insolvency Index:

- a creditor cannot apply for enforcement of a remedy against the debtor's property in respect to a frozen debt (a frozen debt is a debt owed by the debtor that would have been provable in bankruptcy if the debtor had become bankrupt when the Official Trustee accepted the debt agreement proposal for processing);
- the sheriff must not take action to seize or sell property under a court order (writ of execution) issued against the debtor's property; and
- a person who is entitled to retain or deduct money from money owed or payable to the debtor must not retain or deduct money (garnishee order).

The restrictions set out above apply until any of the following events occur:

- The deadline arrives (the end of the 25th working day after the Official Trustee accepted the proposal for processing).
- The proposal is rejected by the creditors at a meeting.
- The proposal lapses.

The proposal will lapse if:

- it is accepted for processing and a meeting of creditors is called but the creditors do not pass a special resolution accepting the proposal; or
- the Official Trustee writes to the creditors but no replies are received by the deadline; or
- the debtor dies before a debt agreement is made.

The debt agreement

When the creditors accept a debt agreement proposal, a debt agreement is made in accordance with the terms of the debt agreement proposal: s. 185H. The parties to the debt agreement are the debtor, and all the creditors to whom the debtor owed debts immediately before the debt agreement was made.

A debt agreement is made when the creditors accept a debt agreement proposal

Following the making of the debt agreement, the agreement is entered in the National Personal Insolvency Index. Upon the agreement being entered in that index, the debtor is released from all provable debts the debtor would have been released from had the debtor been discharged from bankruptcy immediately after the details were entered in the index: s. 185J.

The release does not:

- release anyone else from a debt they owe jointly with the debtor;
- release a guarantor from a guarantee given for the debtor's debt; or
- prevent a secured creditor from dealing with a security to obtain payment of a secured debt: s. 185J.

Section 185K provides that while a debt agreement is in force and details of it are entered on the National Personal Insolvency Index, a creditor cannot:

- present a creditor's petition against the debtor;
- proceed further with an existing creditor's petition; or
- enforce a remedy against the debtor or start or take a fresh step in legal proceedings in respect to a provable debt.

If the property subject to the debt agreement is insufficient to pay in full, or to the extent provided by the agreement, all the debtor's provable debts, the property must be distributed among the creditors in proportion to the provable debts: s. 185L.

The debtor, or a creditor who is a party to the debt agreement, may give the Official Trustee a written proposal to vary the agreement. If the proposal for variation is accepted, the agreement is varied accordingly: s. 185M. The procedure for acceptance of a variation is the same as that for acceptance of the original debt agreement proposal.

Ending a debt agreement

A debt agreement ends when the obligations created under it have been discharged or terminated

A debt agreement ends when all the obligations that it created have been discharged or if it is terminated prior to performance. The debtor is entitled to any property that was subject to the agreement but was not required by the agreement to be distributed to creditors: s. 185N.

A debt agreement may be terminated by the acceptance of a proposal for termination by the debtor or a creditor who is a party to it: s. 185P. The agreement may also be terminated by order of the court on the application by the debtor, a creditor or the Official Trustee. A creditor may include an application for a sequestration order in the application for an order terminating the debt agreement: s. 185Q.

The court may make an order terminating a debt agreement, if it is satisfied that:

- the debtor has failed to carry out a term of the agreement and it is in the interest of the creditors to terminate the agreement;
- carrying out the agreement would cause injustice or undue delay to the creditors or the debtor; or
- for any other reason and that it is in the creditors' interest to do so.

The debt agreement will be terminated if the debtor becomes bankrupt. Although a debt agreement normally avoids the bankruptcy of the debtor, the court still has power to permit a petition for bankruptcy.

Part X: Personal insolvency agreements

Part X of the Act provides for personal insolvency agreements. They are an alternative procedure to bankruptcy. A debtor who is unable to pay his or her debts may avoid bankruptcy, but may nevertheless obtain a release from their liabilities to their creditors.

If a debtor wishes his or her affairs to be dealt with under Part X of the Act, the debtor must sign an authority naming and authorising a solicitor, a registered trustee or the Official Trustee to call a meeting of creditors and to take control of the debtor's property: s. 188. A registered trustee is someone registered with the Registrar in Bankruptcy and qualified to act as such. Once an authority has been given, and it cannot be revoked by the debtor, the trustee is known as the controlling trustee: s 188.

At the meeting of creditors, the debtor must submit a statement of affairs in writing, specifying all the debtor's assets and liabilities: s. 194A. Unless prevented by illness or other sufficient cause, the debtor must attend the meeting and must, to the best of his or her knowledge and ability, help the person presiding over the meeting: s. 195. If, without sufficient cause, the debtor fails to attend the creditors' meeting, the court may, if it thinks fit, make a sequestration order against the estate of the debtor: s. 221. The creditors may, by special resolution, require the debtor to execute a personal insolvency agreement or require the debtor to present a debtor's petition for bankruptcy within seven days: s. 204.

Section 188A states that a personal insolvency statement is a deed that is expressed to be entered into under Part X and which:

- identifies the debtor's property and income that is to be available to pay creditors' claims and which specifies how that property and income is to be dealt with;
- specifies the extent to which the debtor is to be released from his or her debts;
- specifies the circumstnaces in which the agreement terminates;
- specifies the order in which income and the proceeds from sale of property are to be distributed among creditors;
- specifies whether or not the antecendent transactions provisions of the Act apply to the debtor;
- makes provision for a person to be trustee of the agreement; and
- provides that the debtor will execute documents and do anything necessary to give effect to the agreement.

If the personal insolvency agreement provides for a debtor to be released from a provable debt, the debtor is released from that debt unless the agreement is set aside or terminated: s. 230. The personal insolvency agreement is binding on all creditors of the debtor: s. 229.

PROPERTY AVAILABLE FOR PAYMENT OF DEBTS

Commencement of the bankruptcy

> **!** CAUTION NOTE
>
> *The date of the commencement of bankruptcy is not the date of the sequestration order but rather the earliest act of bankruptcy.*

All property that belonged to or was vested in the bankrupt at the commencement of the bankruptcy is divisible among the creditors: s. 116. However, the date of the commencement of the bankruptcy is not the date of the sequestration order.

The bankruptcy of a person who becomes a bankrupt on a creditor's petition is deemed to have relation back to and to have commenced at the time of the earliest act of bankruptcy committed by the debtor in the six months immediately preceding the date of the creditor's petition: s. 115. This is known as the 'Doctrine of Relation Back' (see Figure 32.7).

Debtor's petition and the Doctrine of Relation Back

The bankruptcy of a person who becomes bankrupt owing to a debtor's petition is also subject to the Doctrine of Relation Back. However, the method of calculation of the period varies with the circumstances.

A person who becomes bankrupt owing to a debtor's petition is also subject to the Doctrine of Relation Back

Direction of court

If the debtor's petition is accepted by the Official Receiver under a direction of the court, the commencement of the bankruptcy is the time specified by the court as the date for commencement of the bankruptcy.

Creditor's petition pending

If the debtor's petition was presented at a time when at least one creditor's petition was pending against the debtor, and the debtor's petition was accepted by the Official Receiver without a direction from the court, the bankruptcy is deemed to have commenced at the time of the earliest act of bankruptcy on which any of the creditor's petitions was based.

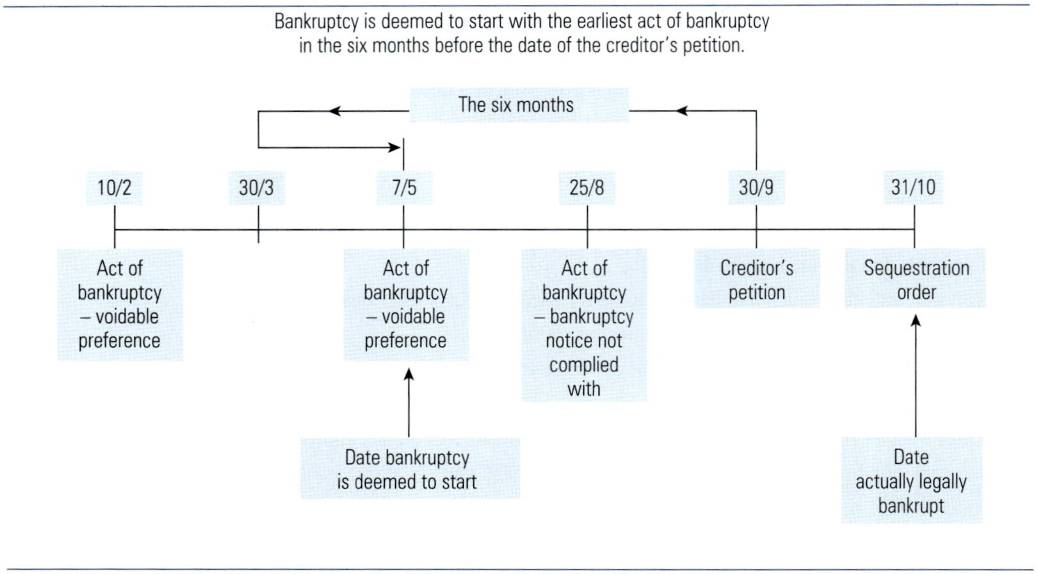

FIGURE 32.7 *Doctrine of Relation Back*

No creditor's petition pending but act of bankruptcy committed

If the debtor's petition was presented when no creditor's petition was pending but the debtor had committed at least one act of bankruptcy in the past six months, and the debtor's petition is accepted by the Official Receiver without a direction from the court, **the bankruptcy is deemed to start with the earliest act of bankruptcy within the six months before the debtor's petition was presented**.

No creditor's petition pending and no act of bankruptcy

If the debtor's petition is presented at a time when there are no creditor's petitions pending and the debtor had not committed an act of bankruptcy in the past six months, and the debtor's petition is accepted by the Official Receiver without direction by the court, **the bankruptcy commences at the time of presentation of the petition**.

It can be seen that, although the debtor is not legally a bankrupt until the sequestration order, the bankruptcy is in effect backdated. Therefore, any dealings a person has with a debtor in the six months prior to the presentation of a creditor's petition could be called into question by the trustee and possibly set aside. Since it can be difficult to predict what might happen in six months' time, the potential problems to creditors are obvious.

> **!** CAUTION NOTE
>
> *Although the debtor is not legally a bankrupt until the sequestration order, the bankruptcy is in effect backdated.*

Protection against the Doctrine of Relation Back: s. 123

The following transactions are protected against the Doctrine of Relation Back: s. 123:

- a payment to a creditor;
- a conveyance for market value;
- a contract, dealing or other transaction for market value;
- any transaction to the extent of a present advance made by an existing creditor;

if

- the transaction took place before the day on which the debtor became bankrupt;
- the person did not, at the time of the transaction, have notice of the presentation of a petition against the debtor; and
- the transaction was in good faith and in the ordinary course of business.

Knowledge at the time of the transaction that the debtor had committed an act of bankruptcy, does not mean the transaction was not in good faith and in the ordinary course of business.

Property available for distribution to creditors

The property available is therefore:

All property owned by the bankrupt

At the time of the commencement of the bankruptcy, as discussed above: s. 116.

All property acquired by the bankrupt

After the commencement of the bankruptcy (that is, after applying the Doctrine of Relation Back) and before the date of bankruptcy, usually the date of the sequestration order: s. 116.

All property acquired after the date of bankruptcy and before discharge

This is called after acquired property and could include such things as property left to the bankrupt under a will: s. 116.

The bankrupt's income

Even though a person has accumulated considerable debt, the person may still work in an occupation that commands a high salary.

The trustee is to make an assessment of the income of the bankrupt during the contribution assessment period. Where the income is above a specified threshold amount, the bankrupt will be required to contribute half the excess to the estate. The contribution assessment period starts on the date of commencement of the bankruptcy—that is, after applying the Doctrine of Relation Back—and lasts for each subsequent 12-month period until the bankrupt is discharged: s. 139S. The income that is likely to be received is reduced by any amount that the bankrupt is liable to pay in tax.

The threshold amount is the amount of income above which the bankrupt must contribute to his or her estate. In the case of a bankrupt who has no dependants, the threshold amount is equivalent to the social security pension multiplied by 3.5 (s. 139K). The threshold amount increases as the bankrupt's number of dependants increases.

At the time of writing the base income thresholds for the purposes of section 139K were:

Bankrupt with no dependents	$36 190.70
Bankrupt with one dependent	$42 705.03
Bankrupt with two dependents	$45 962.19
Bankrupt with three dependents	$47 771.72
Bankrupt with four dependents	$48 495.54
Bankrupt with more than four dependents	$49 219.35

In addition to this, a bankrupt's dependant is entitled to earn $2611.00.

Property seized under a writ of execution against a debtor who becomes bankrupt

Where a creditor receives money as a result of a writ of execution levied on a debtor and the debtor becomes bankrupt within six months, the creditor must refund the money to the trustee for distribution among all the creditors (s. 118).

Transactions void against the trustee

In addition to property which the debtor owned at the time of the commencement of the bankruptcy, certain transactions that the debtor entered into may be void against the trustee:

Undervalued transactions: s. 120

A transfer of property by a person who later becomes a bankrupt is void against the trustee in the transferor's bankruptcy if:

(a) the transfer took place in the period beginning five years before the commencement of the bankruptcy; and

(b) the transferee gave no consideration, or gave consideration of less value than the market value of the property.

A transfer is not void against the trustee if it took place more than two years before the commencement of the bankruptcy and the transferee proves that at the time of the transfer, the transferee was solvent. The rights of a third party who acquired the property from the transferee in good faith and for consideration which was at least as valuable as the market value of the property are not affected, they retain title to the property.

Transfer to defeat creditors: s. 121

A transfer of property is void against the trustee in the transferor's bankruptcy if:

(a) the property would probably have become part of the transferor's estate; and

(b) the transferor's main purpose in making the transfer was to prevent the property from becoming divisible among the transferor's creditors or to hinder or delay making the property available for division among the transferor's creditors.

A transfer is not void against the trustee if:

(a) the consideration given by the transferee was at least as valuable as the market value of the property; and

(b) the transferee did not know the transferor's main purpose in making the transfer; and

(c) the transferee could not reasonably have inferred that the transferor was, or was about to become, insolvent.

Inadequate consideration may indicate intention to defeat creditors.

RE BARNES EX PARTE STAPLETON **(1961) 19 ABC 126**

A debtor, realising he could be made bankrupt, sold his boat to his mother and then leased it back from her so that effectively he still had full use of the boat. The consideration in both transactions was inadequate. When the trustee attempted to seize the boat, the bankrupt claimed he was not the legal owner, his mother was, and therefore it did not form part of his estate.

ISSUE: Does a transaction with an inadequate consideration indicate an intention to defeat or delay creditors?

DECISION: The High Court held that the transaction was made with the intention to defeat or delay the creditors.

Avoidance of preferences: s. 122

A transfer of property by a debtor who is insolvent, in favour of a creditor, is void against the trustee in the debtor's bankruptcy if the transfer:

(a) had the effect of giving the creditor a preference, priority or advantage over other creditors; and

(b) was made in the period beginning six months before the presentation of the creditor's or debtor's petition, or if the bankruptcy was based on a debtor's petition which was presented when at least one creditor's petition was pending against the petitioning debtor, the preference was given in the period beginning on the commencement of the debtor's bankruptcy in accordance with the Doctrine of Relation Back.

A transaction is not void against the trustee if:

(a) it was in the ordinary course of business and the purchaser, payee or encumbrancer acted in good faith and gave consideration at least as valuable as the market value of the property;

(b) a third party making title through a creditor of the debtor, acted in good faith and gave consideration at least as valuable as the market value of the property;

(c) the transaction related to a maintenance order; or

(d) the transfer of property was under a debt agreement.

Property not available to creditors

Property that is not available to the trustee for distribution among the creditors includes:

- property held in trust by the bankrupt for the benefit of another person: s. 116 (2)(a);
- necessary clothes and household equipment as the creditors determine by resolution; and
- tools of trade (to a value of $3000), plant and equipment, reference books and a means of transport (to a value of $5900).

These items have maximum monetary limits that vary from time to time:

- damages or compensation for personal injury or wrong;
- certain types of life insurance policies, particularly:
  - policies of life or endowment, but not pure endowment, which have been in force for at least two years before the commencement of the bankruptcy and where the proceeds are received after the date of bankruptcy or not more than one year before that date; and
  - policies of pure endowment which have been in force for at least five years before the date of commencement of the bankruptcy.

  Life policies are payable on the death of the person, while endowment policies are payable on death or on reaching a specified age. It can be seen that, but for this provision, the debtor could anticipate the bankruptcy and convert all their assets into endowment policies and place them outside the bankruptcy. On the other hand, where a person makes provision for their long-term future, or that of their dependants, and not in anticipation of bankruptcy, the transaction is treated in a way similar to settlements of property referred to above;
- property used to secure a debt—for example, the bankrupt's home, which would normally be mortgaged to a bank; and
- a motor vehicle worth $5900 or less. (Note this amount is adjusted with changes in the Consumer Price Index.)

WHAT POWER DOES A TRUSTEE HAVE TO AVOID ANTECEDENT TRANSACTIONS?

Antecedent transactions—transactions entered into before the date of bankruptcy

Antecedent transactions are transactions entered into before the date of the bankruptcy—that is, before the sequestration order. As previously stated, the Doctrine of Relation Back deems the commencement of the bankruptcy to be the date of the earliest act of bankruptcy within the six months immediately preceding the creditor's petition.

Since all property owned by the bankrupt at the commencement of the bankruptcy is available for payment of the bankrupt's debts, it can be seen that anyone who dealt with the bankrupt (at the time merely a debtor) during those six months is at risk of having the transaction overturned and the property taken from them by the trustee.

This could result in considerable hardship where the transactions were in good faith, and particularly so where property has been transferred to third parties.

Section 123 moderates the potential severity of the Doctrine of Relation Back by providing that a payment to creditors or a transfer of property for valuable consideration, or any other contract or transaction for valuable consideration, shall not be invalid if:

Transactions in good faith and for valuable consideration may not be void against the trustee

- the transaction took place on or before the date the debtor became bankrupt;
- the other party did not have notice of the presentation of a petition against the debtor; or
- the transaction was in good faith and for valuable consideration in the ordinary course of business—that is, the transaction was of a type that a debtor and creditor might enter into without bankruptcy in mind.

In relation to voidable preferences, in addition to establishing that the transaction took place in good faith and for valuable consideration in the ordinary course of business, the creditor must also prove there was no preference.

Non-payment of a debt or the dishonouring of a cheque might be due to insolvency or it might be due to other unrelated factors. To warrant the creditor suspecting the debtor is insolvent requires more substantial indicators. In all these situations, the onus of proof is on the party who claims that the transaction is valid.

***QUEENSLAND BACON PTY LTD V. REES* (1966) 115 CLR 266**

The liquidator of a company sought to recover payments made to several suppliers before the commencement of the liquidation, as void preferences. The payments were made by cheques that in some cases were dishonoured several times before payment was finally received.

ISSUE: Does the dishonouring of cheques mean the drawer of the cheque is insolvent?

DECISION: The High Court held that a creditor must know or suspect that a debtor is insolvent. The dishonouring of cheques is not in itself sufficient to establish a suspicion of insolvency. All but two of the payments made to the suppliers were held to be valid.

COLLECTION OF MONEY OR PROPERTY FROM THIRD PARTIES

There have often been considerable practical and legal difficulties for the trustee recovering property from third parties; however, recent amendments to the Act have attempted to make the task easier.

The Official Receiver may on their own initiative or on the application of the trustee give a notice similar to a garnishee order to a person:

- from whom any money is due, or may become due, to the bankrupt;
- who holds money for or on account of a bankrupt;
- who holds money on account of some other person for payment to the bankrupt;
- who has authority from some other person to pay money to the bankrupt; and
- who is liable to pay money or transfer property, or who has received money or property in respect of consideration for personal services supplied by the bankrupt after the commencement of the bankruptcy.

These powers to recover from third parties continue to exist even after the bankrupt has been discharged. Failure to comply with a notice is punishable by six months' imprisonment. In addition, the court may also order the person to pay to the trustee an amount equivalent to the amount that should have been paid under the notice.

It should be noted that Parliament has before it the *Bankruptcy Legislation Amendment (Anti-avoidance) Bill 2005* which, if passed, will amend the *Bankruptcy Act 1966* to considerably strengthen anti-avoidance provisions by giving the trustee wider powers to recover property disposed of prior to the bankruptcy or owned by a third party but acquired by that person using the bankrupt's resources. At the time of writing there was no indication as to when the Bill might be passed by Parliament.

WHAT IS THE ORDER OF PAYMENT OF DEBTS?

The bankrupt's debts are payable in the order listed below. All amounts owing to creditors in each category must be paid in full before anything is paid to creditors in the next category. If there is more than one creditor in a particular category and there are insufficient funds to satisfy all the debts in full, the various creditors in that category are paid an amount that is proportional to their debt.

- Administration costs (including trustee's fees and the costs incurred by the petitioning creditor in making the debtor bankrupt).

- Child Support Payments: s. 50 *Child Support (Registration and Collection) Act 1988*.
- Costs of administration of a Part X scheme.
- Funeral expenses of a deceased debtor whose estate is being administered under the *Bankruptcy Act*.
- Employees' wages up to $3500 per employee.
- Workers' compensation payments.
- Employees' long service, annual and sick leave payments.
- Priorities given by special resolution of creditors. The bankrupt may have been operating a business that is dependent on a particular creditor for raw materials or other essential goods. If the business could be sold as a going concern, it may raise far more than it would if the assets were simply sold off. It could therefore be very beneficial for the creditors to allow a priority to the creditor who supplies the raw materials to ensure the maximum price for the business.
- Unsecured creditors.
- Deferred creditors:
  - the bankrupt's spouse regarding money lent to the bankrupt;
  - claims for interest exceeding the statutory rate;
  - claims for interest on interest-bearing deposits for a period after the date of bankruptcy; and
  - claims by persons under transactions 'void' against the trustee (e.g., voidable preferences).

It must be noted that the payment of the bankrupt's debts may be affected by proceedings under the *Family Law Act*. The *Bankruptcy and Family Law Legislation Act 2005* amended both the *Bankruptcy Act 1966* and the *Family Law Act 1975* to clarify the interaction between family law property and maintenance proceedings and bankruptcy proceedings generally. The amendments were particularly concerned with the rights of the non-bankrupt spouse and the interests of creditors. The *Family Law Act* (s. 72(2)) now provides that the liability of a bankrupt party to a marriage to maintain the other party may be satisfied by a transfer of bankruptcy property which has vested in the Trustee in Bankruptcy under the *Bankruptcy Act*. Section 79 of the *Family Law Act* now provides that the court may make a Family Law property settlement order in respect of bankruptcy property vested in the Trustee in Bankruptcy.

DISCHARGE AND ANNULMENT OF BANKRUPTCY

The Bankruptcy Amendment Act 1991, which came into operation on 1 July 1992, contains provisions affecting annulment and discharge.

Automatic discharge

The *Bankruptcy Act* provides that a bankrupt will be discharged automatically three years from the date the bankrupt's statement of affairs was lodged, providing there is no objection from the trustee or Official Receiver. Creditors cannot object.

Automatic discharge after three years if there is no objection

Extension of bankruptcy

> **!** CAUTION NOTE
>
> *Bankruptcy may be extended beyond three years to five or eight years if there is an objection.*

If an objection to automatic discharge is made on any of the following grounds, the bankruptcy may be extended to five years from the date of lodgement of the statement of affairs (i.e. an extra two years):

- the bankrupt failed to disclose a liability that existed at date of bankruptcy;
- the bankrupt failed to inform the trustee of any change in name, address or daytime telephone number;
- the bankrupt refused to sign a document after being lawfully required to do so by the trustee;

- the bankrupt failed to attend a creditors' meeting;
- the bankrupt failed to attend an interview or examination; or
- the bankrupt failed to disclose beneficial interest in property.

The bankruptcy may be extended to eight years from the date of the statement of affairs if the automatic discharge is objected to on any of the following grounds:

- the bankrupt continued to manage a company without court approval;
- the bankrupt engaged in misleading conduct regarding amounts exceeding $3000;
- the bankrupt failed to provide details of property and income;
- there was a failure to pay the contribution from the bankrupt's income as required; or
- the bankrupt failed to properly account for property disposed of or money spent during bankruptcy or during the five years before the bankruptcy.

Where the bankrupt leaves Australia, the bankruptcy may be extended for eight years from the date the bankrupt returns to Australia. This extension would arise out of either of the following objections to an automatic discharge:

- the bankrupt left Australia and has not returned; or
- the bankrupt has been requested to return to Australia by a particular time and has failed to do so.

Annulment of bankruptcy

A bankruptcy may be annulled (or cancelled) in any of the following three ways:

- **By order of the court**—the only grounds for such an order are that the sequestration order should not have been made or the debtor's petition should not have been accepted.
- **Automatically on payment in full**—where all the bankrupt's debts (that is, debts that have been proved in the bankruptcy) have been paid, the bankruptcy is automatically annulled by operation of law.
- **Automatically on acceptance of a composition or arrangement**—where a meeting of creditors passes a special resolution accepting a composition or scheme of arrangement, the bankruptcy is automatically annulled. The scheme may be annulled by the court and a sequestration order made if there is a default under the scheme, the creditors' approval was obtained by misrepresentation, or the scheme cannot proceed without undue delay.

Effects of a discharge

Effect of discharge is to release bankrupt from all debts

Generally, a discharge releases a bankrupt from all debts provable in the bankruptcy. However, they will still be liable for debts on recognisance, debts incurred through fraud and maintenance order debts. A discharge does not release a bankrupt from liability incurred to a secured creditor who has not chosen to surrender their security: s. 153. A discharged bankrupt 'shall give such assistance as the trustee reasonably requires in the realisation and distribution of such of his property as is vested in the trustee': s.152.

Duties and powers of a trustee

When a sequestration order is made, as pointed out earlier, the property of the bankrupt becomes vested in the trustee, whether they are the Official Receiver or registered trustee. The duties of the trustee include:

- to take possession of the bankrupt's property: s. 129; and
- to declare and distribute dividends among the creditors, having first published and served notice of their intention to do so—the trustee cannot pay a creditor a dividend of less than 50 cents: s. 140.

The powers of a trustee include:

- by implication, to do all things necessarily incidental to carrying out their duties;
- to disclaim onerous property (i.e. unprofitable contracts); and
- power to sell any of the bankrupt's property:
  - to carry on the bankrupt's business; and
  - to compromise any debt claimed to be due to the bankrupt.

Offences under the Act

The Act contains a number of provisions establishing offences and prescribing penalties for them.

Offences by bankrupts

The Act, in s. 263, deals with fraudulent concealment of property with the intent to defraud creditors. The prescribed penalty is imprisonment for three years. This section also provides that it is an offence punishable by imprisonment for one year where 'a person disposes of, removes, retains or conceals property that has been seized as part of the property of a bankrupt, knowing it to have been so seized or with intent to defeat the seizure of such property'.

Sections 265, 266, 269 and 271 of the Act concern irregular conduct by the bankrupt in respect of their assets and dealings. For example, a bankrupt must:

- disclose all their property to the trustee;
- disclose any disposition of property made within the two years immediately preceding the date of bankruptcy;
- comply with all directions of the trustee;
- if aware that a person has lodged a false proof of debt, inform the trustee about it; and
- provide a proper explanation of any loss or depreciation of any assets that has occurred within the previous two-year period.

The penalty for non-compliance is imprisonment for one year. However, a three-year gaol penalty is prescribed for a bankrupt who deceives or defrauds creditors in order to gain their consent on any matter connected with the bankrupt's trade dealing, property or business affairs. Sections 265, 268, 270 and 272 provide penalties ranging from one to three years' imprisonment for a debtor and/or bankrupt who seeks to evade or delay creditors by fraudulent actions or who leaves Australia without the consent in writing of the trustee.

Acts designed to delay realisation

A bankrupt who attempts to delay the realisation of their estate commits an offence

The Act provides that a bankrupt who commits any act designed to delay the realisation of their estate, to conceal or remove any of their property with a view to avoiding payment of debts, or to prevent or delay the trustee obtaining possession of their property, may be arrested by order of the court and committed to gaol: s. 78.

The court may, on the application of the trustee or a creditor, summon the bankrupt or an examinable person in relation to the bankrupt. An examinable person may include someone associated with the bankrupt, or who possesses property of the bankrupt, or who is indebted to the bankrupt. The examinee may be asked questions about the bankrupt and their dealings and affairs: s. 81.

CORPORATE INSOLVENCY

Bankruptcy proceedings are only brought against individuals, not against companies. If a company gets into financial difficulties the usual procedure would be to appoint an administrator, commence proceedings to have the company wound up (placed into liquidation) or to appoint a receiver.

Administration

If a company gets into severe financial difficulties an administrator may be appointed to take control of the company. The purpose of an administration is to provide for the business, property and affairs of an insolvent company to be administered in a way that:

- maximises the chances of the company continuing in existence;
- results in a better return to creditors and members in a winding up.

An administrator can be appointed by the company, if the board has resolved that the company is insolvent and an administrator should be appointed. This is likely if the directors believe the company is about to become insolvent. Under s. 588G of the *Corporations Act 2001*, directors may be personally liable for debts incurred by a company while it is insolvent. An administrator may also be appointed by the liquidator or a person entitled to enforce a charge (security) over all or substantially all the company's assets.

The role of the administrator is to control the company's business, property and affairs. In doing so the administrator may carry on the business and manage its affairs, terminate or dispose of all or part of the business or other property of the company and perform any function or power of the company or its officers.

Winding up (liquidation)

A company may be wound up or liquidated voluntarily, that is, by its own choice, or compulsorily, that is, against its will.

Voluntary

A company may have served its purpose and the members may have decided to terminate it. The members would hold a meeting and resolve to wind the company up.

The winding up will take place under the control of members of the company if solvent and under control of creditors if insolvent.

When the voluntary winding up is proposed, the directors must examine the company's financial position. If directors expect the company to pay all its debts within 12 months, they may issue a written declaration of solvency. It is then a members' voluntary winding up.

If there is no declaration of solvency, the winding up is called a creditors' voluntary winding up. A meeting of creditors is called for the same day or day after the members' winding up. The winding up will then be under the control of the creditors.

Compulsory, by court order

Winding up due to insolvency

Where the company owes a person one or more amounts that total at least the statutory minimum ($2000) and the debt(s) are due and payable the person may serve a statutory demand on the company. The statutory demand must:

- specify the amount or total amounts of the debt(s);
- require the company to pay, secure or compound the debt(s) to the creditor's reasonable satisfaction within 21 days;
- be in writing;
- be in the prescribed form;
- be signed by or on behalf of the creditor; and
- unless the debt is a judgement debt, be accompanied by an affidavit verifying that the debt is due and payable.

Non-compliance with the statutory demand is taken to indicate that the company is insolvent. The creditor may then apply to the court to have the company wound up due to insolvency.

Director's personal liability for debts

Section 588G of the *Corporations Act 2001* provides that a director may be held personally liable for debts incurred by a company while the company is insolvent.

A director contravenes s. 588G if, when the company incurs a debt, there are reasonable grounds **for suspecting** that the company is insolvent or would become insolvent. Contravention of s. 588G can give rise to both civil and criminal liability. Section 588G is included in the civil penalty provisions of the Act.

A director's defences to an action under s. 588G are:

- that at the time when the debt was incurred, the person had reasonable grounds to expect, and did expect, that the company was solvent at that time;
- that the director had reasonable grounds to rely on information provided by a competent and reliable person that the company was solvent;
- that a director did not take part in the management of the company for illness or some other good reason; or
- that the director took all reasonable steps to prevent the company from incurring the debt.

It is not a defence for a director to remain entirely ignorant of the operations of the company.

MORLEY V. STATEWIDE TOBACCO SERVICE LTD (1992) 10 ACLC 1233

The two directors of the company were a mother and her son. The son was responsible for the everyday running of the business and the mother knew very little of the actual financial details of the business nor did she have direct involvement with creditors. At first instance *Ormiston* J in the Victorian Supreme Court decided that a director's liability for the company's debts is determined by what the director ought to have known about the company's debts rather than what the director actually knew. Ignorance is no excuse. Mrs Morley appealed that decision.

ISSUE: Is a director's liability for the company's debts determined by what the director **ought** to have known about the company's debts, rather than what the director **actually** knew?

DECISION: The Appeal Division of the Supreme Court of Victoria unanimously dismissed an appeal. The court made two important points:

1. The director had given the necessary implied authority. This followed from the fact that she had asked her son to run the business and knew that her son was incurring such debts in the ordinary course of his duties.
2. An objective test was to apply to the application of the section, thus a director could not argue from a state of total ignorance that he or she had no reasonable cause to expect that the company would be unable to pay its debts. The director would have known of the company position if she had carried out her duties as a director.

Proceedings against a director

The company's liquidator may recover from the director an amount equal to the loss or damage resulting from incurring the debt. The amount recovered is a debt due to the company not the creditor: s. 588M(2).

Under s. 588M(3), a creditor may commence proceedings to recover the amount of loss or damage, but only after obtaining the liquidator's written approval (s. 588R).

If the liquidator fails to approve the creditor's request, the creditor may commence proceedings with the permission of the court.

Receivers

A receiver is appointed to safeguard property given to investors such as debenture holders or to creditors as security for the repayment of money loaned to the company. The receiver will collect (receive) income produced by the property or collect the proceeds from the sale of the property. The money will then be applied to the discharge of the secured debts. Unlike the administrator and the liquidator who in effect act on behalf of the company and the creditors generally, the receiver usually only acts on behalf of the particular creditor who was given security over the particular asset.

WEB RESOURCES

Financial & Consumer Rights Council: An informative site for those seeking further information on bankruptcy and debts of bankruptcy:
http://home.vicnet.net.au/~fcrc/bankrupt.htm

Law Society of NSW: For an interesting article by Steven McMillan on whether to issue a bankruptcy notice see:
http://www.lawsocnsw.asn.au/resources/lsj/archive/dec1995/36_1.htm

Part IV Proceedings. For a summary of the *Bankruptcy Act 1966* (Cth) dealing with Part IV see:
http://lexsun.law.uts.edu.au/~peteru/law/f4381.htm

Part VI Proceedings: For a summary of administration of property under the *Bankruptcy Act 1966* (Cth) see:
http://lexsun.law.uts.edu.au/~peteru/legislation/f7351.htm

REVIEW QUESTIONS

32.1 What is the purpose of bankruptcy law?

32.2 When does a debtor commit an act of bankruptcy?

32.3 Who may petition the court seeking a sequestration order?

32.4 Explain the meaning of the following terms:

a sequestration order

b creditor's petition

c insolvency

d bankruptcy.

activebook

Activebook resources include in-depth summaries with links to the relevant part of the book. For revision, add your own notes to the summaries provided by using the note-taking function.

32.5 What is the purpose of the Doctrine of Relation Back?

32.6 Explain how the Doctrine of Relation Back operates under the *Bankruptcy Act*.

32.7 In what ways can a person become bankrupt?

32.8 Explain the requirements for a creditor's petition.

32.9 Outline the arrangements that a person in financial difficulties may make with creditors under Part X of the *Bankruptcy Act* in relation to payment of debts.

32.10 Is all the property of a bankrupt available to the trustee for distribution to creditors or is there property that is not available? Discuss.

32.11 Explain the difference between secured and unsecured creditors for the purposes of the order of payment of debts under the *Bankruptcy Act*.

32.12 Indicate whether each of the following statements is true or false:

Statement	TRUE	FALSE
The court will reject the creditor's petition to have the debtor made bankrupt unless the creditor can prove that in the preceding six months the debtor committed an act of sequestration	☐	☑
The court will reject the creditor's petition for a sequestration order unless the creditor can prove the debtor owes a minimum of $2000	☑	☐
A deed under Part X transferring all the debtor's property for the benefit of creditors is called a deed of gift	☐	☑
A bankrupt will be discharged automatically and released from any further obligations to their creditors after three years	☑	☑

CRITICAL THINKING

32.1 On 30 June Tom went overseas. Although he was not in financial difficulties at the time he left, it had been necessary for him to notify his creditors on 20 February that he was temporarily suspending payment of his debts. At the time of his departure Tom knew he would be unable to pay his income tax when it was issued. He left no forwarding address.

On 15 July a creditor petitioned to have Tom declared bankrupt. The sequestration order was made on 30 July.

An investigation of Tom's affairs has revealed that he had disposed of property. He had:

- given his house to his mother on 8 April of the previous year;
- given his expensive golf clubs to his daughter on 30 January of the previous year; and
- sold his luxury cabin cruiser to his brother for $2000 on 5 March.

Consider the following questions, making sure that you give reasons for your answers:

(i) When will Tom's bankruptcy be taken to have commenced?

(ii) Can any of the property disposed of be recovered for the benefit of the creditors?

32.2 On 1 May Nicole was declared bankrupt. She has the following assets:

Money in the bank	$10 000
Life assurance policy taken out on 1 January six years ago	$6 000
Car	$4 000
Land	$30 000

Nicole has the following debts:

Money owing to her husband	$20 000
Wages owing to Julie	$1 000
Long service leave owing to Sandy	$2 000
Holiday pay owing to Peter	$1 000
Money owing to Acme Finance Ltd	$30 000
Money owing to Zenith Finance Ltd	$50 000

(i) What assets are available for distribution among the creditors?

(ii) What is the order of payment of the creditors and how much will each creditor receive?

PART NINE

TYPES OF PROPERTY

CHAPTER 33 Property and Mortgages

CHAPTER CONTENTS

activebook

This icon is used throughout the following chapter to remind you to visit the *Business Law* online activebook for additional exercises, links to legal websites, and feedback. For a detailed explanation of what is in the activebook please refer to the inside cover of this textbook. The activebook is available through OneKey.

Where do I start?
Learning path: Use the activebook to complete a pre-chapter warm-up exercise.

There are many definitions of legal terms to assist with your understanding of the material.

CHAPTER OBJECTIVES

On completion of this chapter you should be able to:

- distinguish between real and personal property
- distinguish between ownership and possession of property
- distinguish between a mortgage of Old System land and a mortgage of Torrens Title land
- define a mortgage and name the parties to a mortgage
- state a mortgagor's right to deal with the property
- outline the remedies available to a mortgagee
- outline the rules relating to a mortgagee's power of foreclosure and power of sale
- compare a lease of real property with a licence
- define a lease and identify the elements necessary for a lease
- list and define the usual covenants contained in a lease
- outline the ways a lease may be terminated
- outline the operation of residential tenancy legislation
- outline the operation of retail tenancy legislation.

KEY TERMS

An understanding of the following terms will help you to better understand the material in this chapter:

- **co-ownership:** joint ownership of property
- **fee simple:** the most extensive interest in land; referred to colloquially as 'ownership' of land. There are no restrictions on the ways in which the holder of the fee simple may deal with the land
- **joint tenancy:** a form of co-ownership where separate, equal and undivided rights exist between the parties but they appear as a single owner as against the rest of the world, with the distinguishing elements of a joint tenancy being the 'four unities' and the right of survivorship
- **lease:** a contract granting exclusive possession of property to a person other than the owner for a certain period of time (referred to as the 'term') in return for payment of money (referred to as 'rent'). A lease is to be contrasted to a licence, which generally does not grant exclusive possession of the subject property and is determinable at any time by either party
- **mortgage:** a contract transferring an interest in property as security for the repayment of a debt. On default, a mortgagee typically has recourse to the property and the right to re-take possession, sell the property and apply the proceeds against the debt. Various legislation affects the rights and obligations of mortgagors and mortgagees (e.g., the Consumer Credit Code)
- **personalty:** personal property; all property other than realty and real property (i.e. land and anything fixed to it)
- **possession:** the right to occupy land, or control and use goods. The right to the lawful possession of property need not be held by the lawful owner of that property, but may be granted to another
- **tenancy in common:** a form of co-ownership where two or more persons own distinct shares in the same piece of land but not necessarily with the other three unities of interest, title and time. They can leave their interest to whomsoever they wish.

what if . . .

You buy a factory unit as an investment and then lease it to a manufacturer. Is the buying, owning and leasing this type of property the same as other types of property such as a motor vehicle? If it is different, in what ways is it different and why?

It is important to have an understanding of the meaning of the term 'property' in business as it often has two meanings: to a layperson it means a **piece of land** (e.g., 'my property at 39 Mara Court, Brentville'); to a lawyer it also means the **rights or ownership in an object** (see Chapter 21, which dealt with sale of goods legislation and the passing of property, and hence risk, to the buyer).

In this chapter, the term 'property' is applied to ownership (title) or the rights pertaining to ownership in land. It can be absolute, where one party has complete ownership of an object, or it can be broken up into a number of parts, where more than one party is involved. For example, in the lease of land, there is a lessor (who may own the fee simple) and a lessee (who owns a leasehold interest), both of whom will have some form of property rights. The lessor may have the freehold rights while the lessee has a leasehold interest, but both rights can be sold like any other property.

This chapter begins by considering the distinction between property and possession, and then moves on to the distinction between personalty and realty (real property), what is the extent of land, interests in land, the methods by which land ownership is established and what a mortgage is, and concludes with an examination of the remedies of the mortgagee.

PROPERTY VERSUS POSSESSION

Possessory ownership is a form of ownership

In a legal sense, ownership of property must be contrasted with possession of property. Possession in law primarily means physical control, but it can also mean the right to occupation or to the enjoyment of rents and profits.

In the case of possessory ownership of property, a person in possession is deemed to have ownership against everyone else, except those who can prove a better title to it. That is, the mere possession of the land or goods will amount to a form of property or ownership in the land or goods. The rightful owner, the only person who can defeat the claim of the holder of the land or goods (except in the case of a statutory passing of time), will be the person who can establish a better title by evidence of a conveyance in the case of land or a receipt in the case of goods.

Land

Possessory ownership of land can lead to doctrine of adverse possession

The position with respect to land is that, in certain limited cases, mere possession can give title under the doctrine of adverse possession against all but the true owner.

PERRY V. CLISSOLD **[1907] AC 73**

Land was being resumed (reclaimed) by a public authority under legislation that required compensation to be paid to the owner of the land. The actual owner was unknown but the person in possession (originally as a trespasser) had entered into possession some 10 years earlier, had made improvements to the land, received rent, and appeared in the council's rate books as a rateable person and paid rates. During the 10 years of occupation they had held continuous exclusive possession and there had been no notice of adverse claims.

ISSUE: Can continuous long-term, undisputed possession constitute a possessory title?

DECISION: The occupier was not a mere trespasser but had a possessory title that gave the occupant a valid claim against everyone but the true owner.

Goods

Where goods are found, mere possession may establish a property in goods against everyone except the true owner, hence the expression 'possession is nine-tenths of the law'. That is, 'possession' by the finder is a form of 'property' in the goods that is generally superior to all but the claim of the true owner, being based on physical control and a clear intention to exclude all others.

Where goods are found, possession is good against all but the 'true owner'

ARMORY V. DELAMIRIE (1722) 1 STRANGE 505

A boy working for a chimney sweeper found a jewel in a flue that he was cleaning. He gave it to a goldsmith for valuation and when he returned he was given an imitation of the original jewel. The goldsmith refused to return the jewel on the grounds that the boy was not the true owner but only a finder. As such, he had no property in the jewel or title to sue.

ISSUE: Can possession be evidence of ownership?

DECISION: Possession is some evidence of ownership and will prevail over the claims of everyone in the world except the true owner. As the goldsmith had derived title through the boy, he could not prove he had better title and so he failed.

Where a person finds something in the course of their employment, they find that item for their employer. The employment is seen as an effective cause of the finding of the item. However, where the employment is incidental to the finding of the item—and it is often difficult to determine when the employment relationship begins and ends—the employee is entitled to the goods and not the employer. This distinction can be very fine in some circumstances.

BYRNE V. HOARE [1965] QdR 135

The plaintiff was a policeman with the Queensland police force. He was performing special duty at a drive-in theatre, supervising traffic leaving the drive-in. While walking to his post, he found a small ingot of gold, which was claimed by the Crown.

ISSUE: Was the finding of the item in the course of (or directly due to) the employment or was it merely incidental to (or indirectly connected with) the employment?

DECISION: The Queensland Supreme Court held that the time the policeman found the ingot he had not commenced his employment. He was in the same position as any finder, and the performance of his duties was not the real or effective cause of him finding the ingot. He was therefore entitled to possession against everyone in the world except the true owner.

Goods found on private property—question of intention to exercise control to determine possessory ownership

In the case of goods being found on or under the land of another, or in or on a building, the question of possessory ownership will be determined by whether the owner or occupier can demonstrate a clear intention to exercise control over everything on or under the land, or in or on the building. Thus, money found in the public mall of a shopping centre will generally belong to the finder. The same result will probably occur with money found on a shop floor. However, money found in a display would probably belong to the shopkeeper. Money found in a private home or on private land will generally belong to the owner of the house or land.

SOUTH STAFFORDSHIRE WATER CO. V. SHARMAN [1896] 2 QB 44

The plaintiffs owned land containing a pool. They employed the defendant, with a number of others, to clean the pool. During the course of cleaning the pool, the defendant found two gold rings which he gave to the police. The police were unable to find the owners and subsequently handed the rings back to the defendant. The plaintiffs sued to recover the rings.

ISSUE: Is the owner of land entitled to possessory title to the rings found in the pool due to control over the land and pool?

DECISION: As the plaintiffs owned the land containing the pool, and clearly intended to exercise control over it and whatever was found on it, they were entitled to the rings.

RANGER V. GRIFFIN (1967) 87 WN 531

The purchaser of land decided to renovate the house. The renovations involved the demolition of part of the house. One of the labourers found a box containing a large sum of money. Claims were made by the labourer because he found it, by the contractor because they employed the labourer, by the former owner of the land, and by the current owner of the land.

ISSUE: Is the owner of land entitled to possessory title to the money found in the house due to control over the house and land?

DECISION: In the absence of evidence that any of the claimants knew of the box prior to the discovery, the current owner was entitled to ownership.

The term 'property' is also used to describe every possible interest a person can acquire, and it covers both tangible and intangible interests. All property is divided into two main categories: real property and personal property (see Figure 33.1). Property is the highest right a person can have in a thing, whether that thing is land (real property or realty) or chattels (personal property, also known as personalty).

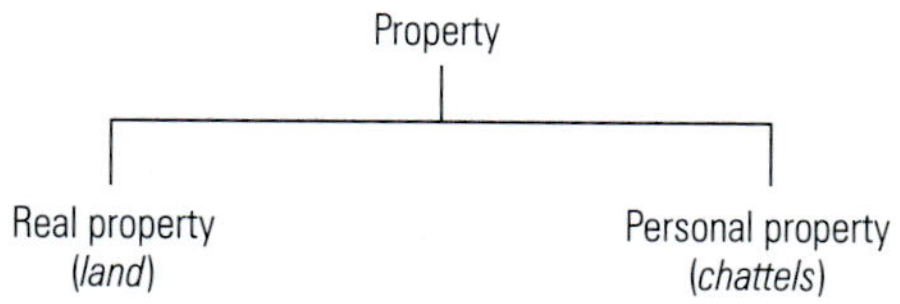

FIGURE 33.1 *Types of property*

WHAT IS PERSONAL PROPERTY?

Personal property (see Figure 33.2) can be divided into:

- **chattels real**—meaning leases of land that are considered to be personal rights in relation to real property; and
- **chattels personal**—these can be further divided into:
  - **choses in possession**; and
  - **choses in action**.

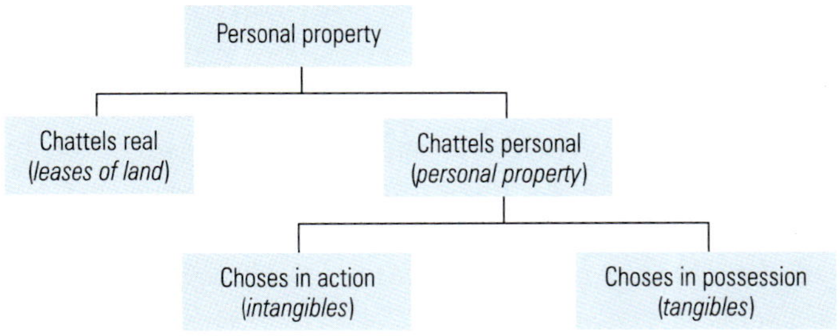

FIGURE 33.2 *Types of personal property*

The word 'chose' comes from the French language and means 'thing'. Therefore these categories could be referred to as 'things in possession' and 'things in action'.

***Chose in possession*—item a person has in their possession**

A *chose in possession* is an item that a person has in their possession—for example, an expensive watch. If someone else came up to them and said, 'That is my watch. Give it to me,' the person in possession of the watch would no doubt refuse. They would not commence any legal action to prove they own it; they would merely maintain their possession. They are maintaining their rights by maintaining possession.

***Chose in action*—intangible item of property**

In contrast, a *chose in action* is an intangible item of property. Since it is intangible, the owner cannot maintain their rights by possession; they can only enforce their rights by action in the courts. A trade mark is an example of a chose in action.

A company might have a registered trade mark that it uses in conjunction with its business and another person might use the same trade mark in association with their business. The company could only enforce its exclusive right to use the trade mark by taking action in the courts through an injunction to stop the other person from using the same trade mark.

WHAT IS REAL PROPERTY?

Historically, land has held a very important position in law because it is a great store of wealth and therefore power. Consequently, if a person was wrongfully deprived of possession of their land they could, as a right, bring a real action to specifically recover the property. It was therefore called real property. Objects that were not recoverable as a right gave rise to a personal action against the wrongdoer for damages. Such items were therefore called personal property.

Fixture—anything fixed to land

Real property is land and anything fixed to it (fixtures). Fixtures are chattels that were once moveable but have subsequently become attached to the land in a way that makes them part of the land. It is important to determine whether or not a particular item is a fixture or a chattel because, when the land is sold or otherwise disposed of, the fixtures are transferred as part of the land. However, the parties can agree to the contrary.

AUSTRALIAN PROVINCIAL ASSURANCE ASSOCIATION LTD V. CORONEO
(1938) 38 SR (NSW) 700

A building used as a theatre was sold and the vendor took a telephone switchboard, a large film projector (which was bolted to the floor) and a number of chairs.

ISSUE: Was it intended that the chattels remain there permanently?

DECISION: The judgement of *Jordon* CJ in the New South Wales Court of Appeal gives a good insight into the court's approach:

> *The question whether a chattel has become a fixture depends upon whether it has been fixed to land, and if so for what purpose. If a chattel is actually fixed to land to any extent, by any means other than its own weight, then* prima facie *it is a fixture and the burden of proof is upon anyone who asserts that it is not . . . The test of whether a chattel which has been to some extent fixed to land is a fixture is whether it had been fixed with the intention that it shall remain in position permanently or for an indefinite or substantial period . . . or whether it has been fixed with the intent that it shall remain in position only for some temporary purpose . . . In the former case, it is a fixture, whether it has been fixed for the better enjoyment of the land or building, or fixed merely to steady the thing itself, for the better use or enjoyment of the thing fixed . . . If it is proved to have been fixed merely for a temporary purpose it is not a fixture . . . The intention of the person fixing it must be gathered from the purpose for which and the time during which use in the fixed position is contemplated . . . If a thing has been securely fixed, and in particular if it has been so fixed that it cannot be detached without substantial injury to the thing itself or to that to which it is attached, this supplies strong but not necessarily conclusive evidence that a permanent fixing was intended . . . On the other hand, the fact that the fixing is very slight helps to support an inference that it was not intended to be permanent. But each case depends on its own facts.*

COMMENT: This judgement could be summarised as follows:

- Basic presumption—if a chattel is actually attached to land by means other than its own weight, it is *prima facie* a fixture and the burden of proof is on anyone who says otherwise.
- Where the basic presumption is disputed, the court will:
  - look at the intention of the person who places the thing in position; and then
  - examine the degree of annexation, that is, the extent to which the thing has become part of whatever it is attached to. In assessing the degree of annexation, the court will consider the ease of removal and whether or not substantial damage will be done if it is removed.

Obviously a house would be a fixture. Similarly, a ducted air-conditioning unit installed in the house after its completion would also be a fixture because it is attached to the house in a manner that makes it part of the house. By contrast, an air-conditioning unit that could be installed in a window of the house and moved from room to room as needed would not be a fixture because it is not part of the house. While these examples may be obvious, there will often be situations where the distinction is less clear.

Doing business

Fixture or chattel?

In order to avoid any disputes that might arise over whether or not certain items are fixtures or chattels it is advisable to expressly state in the written agreement a list of those items that might cause confusion and are to be included or excluded from the sale. ■

Tenant's fixtures

> **!** CAUTION NOTE
> *Subject to the terms of the lease, tenant's fixtures can become the property of the lessor.*

Subject to the terms of the lease, any fixtures affixed by the tenant, subject to three exceptions, become the property of the lessor. These exceptions are:

- trade fixtures
- ornamental fixtures
- domestic fixtures.

These fixtures can only be removed during the term of a fixed lease or within a reasonable time of its termination with respect to a periodic tenancy. All other fixtures are the lessor's property immediately they become fixtures.

Emblements are crops

Related to tenant's fixtures is the question of emblements. Crops are fixtures and become the property of the lessor on termination of the lease. Emblements are crops yielding a present annual profit and are categorised as goods rather than land. The right of the tenant to the crop is confined to those situations where the lease is for an uncertain period (e.g., a tenancy at will or a periodic tenancy). In these cases the tenant does not know when the tenancy will end.

IN BRIEF

What is a fixture?

Whether an item is likely to be considered a fixture or not requires consideration of the following factors:

- whether it has become attached to the land in a way that makes it part of the land;
- if the chattel is attached to the land by means other than its own weight, it is presumed to be a fixture; and
- if the presumption is disputed, the court will consider:
  - the intention of the person who placed the chattel in position;
  - the degree of annexation including:
    ease of removal; and
    whether or not substantial damage will be done if it is removed.

WHAT IS THE EXTENT OF LAND?

In ascertaining the extent of land, we must examine three aspects:

Surface

Surface—an extent of land

The extent of land in respect to its surface area is determined by surveyors who can scientifically determine the boundaries of the land and indicate where they are by pegging these out.

Substratum (subsoil)

Substratum—subsoil

Since the landowner derives ownership from the Crown, that ownership is subject to any conditions or reservations set out in the Crown Grant. A landowner therefore has no claim to minerals reserved to the Crown in the Crown Grant. Sometimes this reservation is general and sometimes it will refer to specific minerals or to minerals below a certain distance from the surface.

Airspace

Airspace—area above the land

The owner of land can only lay claim to the airspace above their property as far as is necessary for the ordinary use and enjoyment of their land and the structure erected upon it.

***BERNSTEIN V. SKYVIEWS AND GENERAL LTD* [1978] QB 479**

Skyviews were in the business of taking aerial photographs of people's land and selling them to the owners. Bernstein was offered photographs of his property and objected to the company taking them, arguing that the company had trespassed on his airspace above his property and had invaded his right to privacy. He sued in trespass.

ISSUE: Does ownership of airspace above the land extend to an unlimited height?

DECISION: A landowner's ownership of the airspace above the land is restricted to the height necessary for the owner to use and enjoy the land and its structures.

CASE REFLECTION: Could the amount of airspace owned by a landowner vary from location to location? What might be some reasons for such variation?

Right to airspace will therefore vary considerably from one location to another and from one form of land use to another.

The fact that land includes airspace above the surface has been recognised by all states and underlies the concept of the 'strata title'.

INTERESTS IN LAND

In the context of property law, an interest is any right, title or estate in any real or personal property (as shown in Figure 33.3).

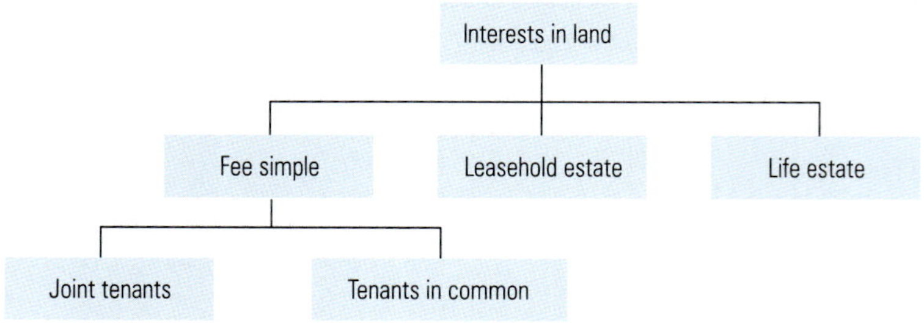

FIGURE 33.3 *Interests in land*

Fee simple

This is the greatest right to land a person can hold. To all intents and purposes, the person is the owner of the land; however, in the legal sense, the person only holds the land of the Crown. This conditional ownership gives the Crown the legal right to resume or take back the land should that action be necessary for Crown purposes.

> **!** CAUTION NOTE
>
> *Fee simple—ownership of land subject to right of Crown to resumption.*

Leasehold estate—exclusive possession of property

Leasehold estate

A contract by which one party has granted to another exclusive possession of property for a limited time.

Life estate

Life estate—right of possession of land during a stated time

Usually created by deed or will and gives the 'holder' or 'life tenant' rights to the land for a limited period. The period of the life estate is determined by the duration of the person's life—that is, the life tenant, or the life of some other specified person.

The life tenant has the right of possession of the land during the stated time, but cannot sell, destroy or materially alter the property. At the expiration of the life estate, the property and all rights will usually pass to some other person designated in the deed or will that created the life estate.

Easements and restrictive covenants

Easements

Easements—a right attached to a particular piece of land

An easement is a right attached to one particular piece of land, entitling its owner to use the land of another person in a particular manner or to restrict its use by the other person to some specified extent. Common forms of easement include right of ways and drainage easements.

Restrictive covenants

Restrictive covenant—restriction upon the use of a particular piece of land

A restrictive covenant is a term often found in a contract for the sale of land. It is a restriction upon the use of the land, agreed to by the purchaser of the land for the benefit of land retained by the vendor. An example would be a fencing covenant in which the vendor is released from liability to contribute towards the cost of a dividing fence while the vendor still owns the adjoining land. Other restrictions can include the size of future buildings and the materials they are constructed from and these are often included in the terms of a subdivision. They then become restrictions on the use of the land by future owners.

Joint ownership

Where two or more persons own the same property, they will usually own it as joint tenants or tenants in common. In this context, the word 'tenant' does not have the same meaning as it does in the expression 'landlord and tenant'. The word 'tenant' is derived from the French language and means 'holder'; it therefore can have a much wider meaning than just a person who rents property.

Joint tenancy

Under joint tenancy, the co-owners hold an equal and undivided interest in the property. **Joint tenancy is characterised by the 'four unities' and survivorship** (see Figure 33.4).

> **!** CAUTION NOTE
>
> *Joint tenancy characterised by the 'four unities' and survivorship.*

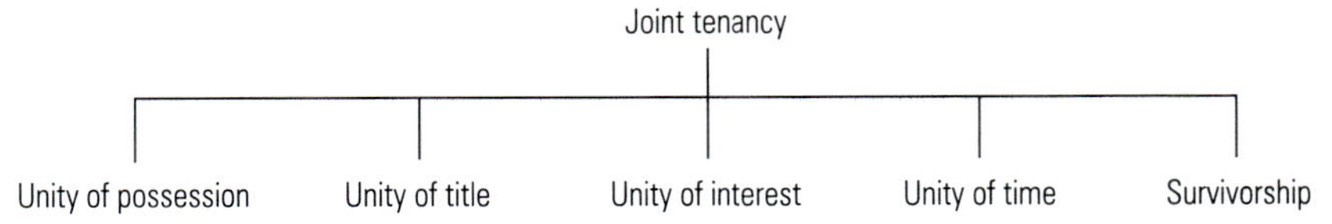

FIGURE 33.4 *Elements necessary for a joint tenancy*

Unity of possession

This means that all the co-owners have the same right to possession of the whole of the property, although they may make their own agreement regarding who exclusively occupies what parts.

Unity of title

All the co-owners derive their title from the same source. In the case of land, one set of deeds or Certificate of Title provides the evidence of title for all of them.

Unity of interest

All the co-owners hold the same interest or rights in the property.

Unity of time

All the co-owners became co-owners at the same time. It can be seen that the co-owners are unified or as one.

Survivorship means that if one of the parties dies, the interest of that person is automatically transferred to the surviving joint tenants, regardless of any provision to the contrary that the person may have made in their will.

It should be noted that legislation such as the *Family Provisions Act 1982* of New South Wales permits the court to override the principle of survivorship in situations where the court is of the opinion that the deceased person did not make adequate provision for their family.

Tenants in common

As tenants in common, the co-owners have an undivided (though not necessarily equal) share in the property (see Figure 33.5). In a case where the co-owners have contributed unequally to the purchase of the property, it is possible for them to hold the property in shares that recognise the proportion of their contribution to the property's purchase.

While unity of possession and unity of interest will apply, unity of title and unity of time may apply, although they are not necessary. **Survivorship does not apply to tenants in common**, therefore the usual rules relating to deceased estates apply and the joint owners can dispose of their interest in the property in their will.

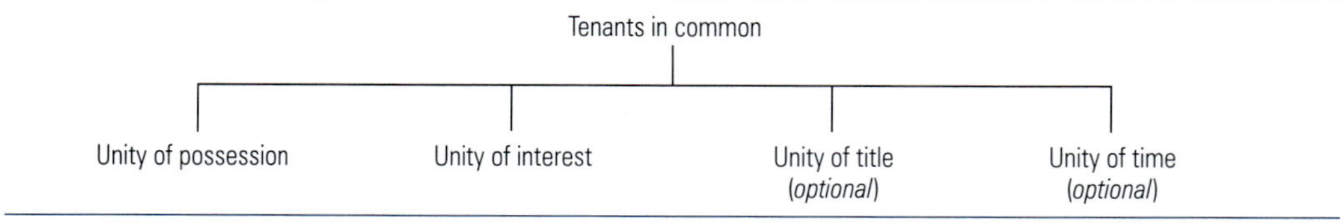

FIGURE 33.5 *Elements necessary for a tenancy in common*

METHODS BY WHICH LAND OWNERSHIP IS ESTABLISHED

Several different methods for establishing rights in relation to land exist in Australia

The *Native Title Act 1993* (Cth) and its impact are outside the scope of this book. However, given its importance in property law, we begin with an overview of native title and then we consider the two major systems that apply throughout all of Australia in a fairly uniform manner:

- The common law or general law system—as the name implies, this is derived from the common law.
- Torrens system—the second system is usually referred to as 'Torrens Title', in honour of the person who devised it in the mid-1800s. Officially, Torrens Title land is referred to by the name of the statute that created it (see Table 33.3 on p. 721).

Because the Torrens Title system is a relatively new development and was established to overcome deficiencies in the long-established common law or general law system, the common law system is referred to in some states as the old system title or general title.

Native title rights

In 1992 the High Court decision in *Mabo v. Queensland (No. 2)* (1992) 175 CLR 1 (see pp. 14–15) pronouncing the existence of native title added a third system to the two existing systems that the law had previously recognised: the general law system and the Torrens system. In response to the *Mabo* decision, the Commonwealth government passed the *Native Title Act 1993* (Cth). It gave legislative support to the concept of native title, although it did not define it, and attempted to clarify the uncertainty as to its extent and the rights it created.

Table 33.1 Complementary state native title legislation

State	*Statute*
Australian Capital Territory	*Native Title Act 1994*
New South Wales	*Native Title (New South Wales) Act 1994*
Northern Territory	*Validation of Titles and Actions Act 1994*
Queensland	*Native Title (Queensland) Act 1993*
South Australia	*Native Title (South Australia) Act 1994*
Tasmania	*Native Title (Tasmania) Act 1993*
Victoria	*Land Titles Validation Act 1994*
Western Australia	*Titles Validation Act 1995*

While the High Court ruled that state parliaments had the power to extinguish title, for example by grants of freehold or leasehold title, questions about the status of native title on pastoral leases remained. Pastoral leases apply to Crown (or government) land and are let to people for specific purposes for specific periods of time, such as farming and mining. In Australia vast areas of land, almost 42 per cent of the country, are held under pastoral lease.

The Commonwealth response to the *Mabo* decision was the passage of the *Native Title Act 1993*. It was created to recognise and protect Indigenous peoples' title rights and interests and provides a process by which application can be made for a determination of a native title claim to the Federal Court. It established a National Native Title Tribunal to which applications will be referred by the Federal Court to determine the validity of land rights claims and the payment for compensation to native titleholders who lost their land. Claims can only be determined on a case-by-case basis through reference to traditional laws and custom and evidence of a continuous link with the claimed land.

In *The Wik People v. The State of Queensland and Others* (1996) 187 CLR 1 the High Court had another opportunity to consider the rights of Indigenous people to the land when the Wik and Thayorre people made a claim in the Federal Court for title to native land which included two pastoral leases. Justice *Drummond* held that the claim could not succeed because the land was subject to pastoral leases that extinguished native title. The Wik people appealed to the High Court where by a four-to-three majority it was held that the Wik people could continue with their land claim. The grant of a lease did not automatically extinguish native title rights because:

- the statutes creating pastoral leases in Queensland did not reveal an intention to extinguish native title;
- pastoral leases did not give exclusive possession to pastoralists; and
- native title rights could continue at the same time the land was subject to a pastoral lease.

Pastoral leases and native title rights could co-exist on the same land where there was no inconsistency between them. However, in the event of a conflict between the two rights, the pastoral leaseholder would succeed.

What is native title?

Native title is defined in s. 223(1) *The Native Title Act 1993* (Cth) as 'the communal, group or individual rights and interests of Aboriginal peoples or Torres Strait Islanders in relation to land or waters where:

- the rights and interests are possessed under the traditional laws acknowledged, and the traditional customs observed, by the Aboriginal people or Torres Strait Islanders; and
- the Aboriginal people or Torres Strait Islanders, by those laws and customs, have a connection with the land and waters; and
- the rights and interests are recognised by the common law of Australia.'

Native title is not a new form of title. The High Court in *Mabo* recognised property rights which Aboriginal and Torres Strait Islander people have always possessed.

Australia's recognition of native title in common law since 1992 is consistent with the recognition given to indigenous peoples such as the Maoris in New Zealand, and the Native Americans in Canada and the United States.

Where does native title exist?

The High Court did not say which parts of Australia were subject to native title, or even who holds native title over any particular area/s. However, the High Court decision in *Mabo* suggests that native title may still exist on:

- vacant Crown land;
- state forests;
- national parks;
- public reserves;
- beaches and foreshores;
- land held by government agencies; and
- land held in trust for Aboriginal communities.

In addition, native title may also exist in:

- oceans, reefs and seas; and
- lakes, rivers, creeks and swamps

where those waters are not privately owned. For example, the Federal Court confirmed in *Mary Yarmirr v. Northern Territory* [1998] 156 ALR 370 that native title holders could have limited rights over offshore waters.

Native title and land rights

Native title and land rights are not one and the same thing. Land rights are grants created by government while native title is a pre-existing right derived from traditional law and customs that evolved in Australia long before white settlement occurred. Native title is not a grant or right created by governments.

Extinguishment of native title

The *Native Title Amendment Act 1997* (Cth) extinguishes native title over land that was subject to an act of exclusive possession before 1 January 1994. Acts which qualify for exclusive possession include grants of land for freehold, residential or commercial land and grants to use land for public works.

The High Court held in *Fejo v. Northern Territory of Australia* [1998] 195 CLR 96 that once land had been subject to freehold title, native title rights were then lost and could not be 'revived' if the land was subsequently taken back by the Crown. The High Court also indicated that legislative intention was not essential to effect an extinguishment of native title. If the act of the executive, for example, by way of a Crown grant, exhibited a clear and plain intention to extinguish native title, that would suffice.

Rights of pastoral leaseholders

Under the *Native Title Amendment Act 1997* (Cth), native title is extinguished where pastoral leaseholders have been granted exclusive possession by a government for primary production purposes, including farmstay tourism.

Governments also have the power to upgrade pastoral leases to primary production leases and thereby extinguish native title. However, where native title has been proved, compensation will have to be paid for the loss of rights.

Native title holders have the right to be notified of any proposed exploration for minerals and to negotiate an Indigenous Land Use Agreement with miners.

Native title rights versus miners' rights

The *Native Title Act 1993* (Cth) gave registered native title claimants an automatic right to negotiate with mining companies that wished to explore or mine the land being claimed. However, under the new Native Title Act the right of negotiation will be replaced by the right to be consulted under the new state systems. While miners must notify claimants about relevant matters, the claimants cannot prevent mining from occurring. In the event of a dispute arising, mediation must be first tried and if that fails, the dispute will then be settled by a mining warden or another appointed official. If the state feels that the determination is not in the 'state's interest', the state Mining Minister can override it.

Role of the Federal Court and the National Native Title Tribunal

Applications for native title have to be lodged with the Federal Court. Applications that comply with Federal Court requirements will then be referred to the tribunal for consideration for registration.

The role of the National Native Title Tribunal, which is a Commonwealth body, is to provide administrative processes to deal with native title applications. It does not have the power to decide whether native title exists or not. It will mediate native title applications that are referred to it by the Federal Court for mediation and also act as an arbitral body to determine disputes over proposed mining, mineral exploration or compulsory acquisition of land by governments for transfer to third parties.

The tribunal registered its first Indigenous Land Use Agreement on 21 June 1999. The agreement was reached between the New South Wales Aboriginal Land Council, representatives of the Walgalu and Wiradjuri people in the Tumut and Adelong areas of New South Wales and Adelong Consolidated Mines NL, giving the mine owners the right to mine for at least 20 years without going through the right to negotiate.

activebook

To help you to remember and understand the topics covered so far, and for links to legal websites, refer to your online activebook. Model answers provide feedback to problems and exercises.

The registration test

Claimants must first pass the registration test. The conditions are set out in ss. 190B and 190C of the *Native Title Act 1993* (Cth), that is, prove a physical connection with the land (this can be established by a person whose parent was forcibly removed or denied access to the land being claimed).

The conditions contained in s. 190B are termed '**merits**' conditions, while those contained in s. 190C are termed '**procedural and other**' conditions. The Registrar of the Federal Court must be satisfied that each of these conditions is met and this is the responsibility of a case manager. The recommendations made by the case manager will be provided to the registrar in two documents: a 'Registration Test Minute' and a 'Reasons for Recommendations' and will consititute the substance of the statement of reasons for the decision if the Registrar agrees with them. Once the Registrar has considered the application and relevant information, he or she will make the registration test decision.

Conditions of the registration test against which each application must be considered include:

- Has the claimant identified the area subject to native title with reasonable certainty: s. 190B(2)?
- Does the application identify the native title claim groups: s. 190B(3)?
- Are the native title rights and interests claimed by the applicant able to be readily identified: s. 190B(4)? For example, through use, occupation, possession or enjoyment.
- Is the factual basis on which it is asserted that the native title rights and interests claimed exist sufficient to support the assertion: s. 190B(5)? This condition of the registration test requires proof of three matters:
  - does the factual basis support the assertion that the native title claim group, and their predecessors, had an association with the area; and
  - that there exist tribal laws acknowledged by, and traditional customs observed by, the native title claim group that give rise to the claim to native title rights and interests; and
  - that the native title claim group has continued to hold native title in accordance with those traditional laws and customs.
- Is the Registrar satisfied that at least some of the native title rights and interests claimed in the application can be established: s. 190B(6)?
- Is the Registrar satisfied that at least one member of the native title claim group currently has or previously had a traditional physical connection with the land or waters covered by the application: s. 190B(7)?
- Is the area for which the application is being made subject to a previously approved native title determination, or a previous exclusive or non-exclusive possession act which because of s. 61A should not have been made: s. 190B(8)?
- Has there been an extinguishment of claimed native title by the Crown, a state or territory where ownership relates to minerals, petroleum or gas, to waters in an offshore place or otherwise extinguished: s. 190(9)(a), (b), (c)?
- Is the Registrar satisfied that the application contains all the details and information required by ss. 61 and 62: s. 190(C)(2)?

- Does the current claim overlap with any previous claims in whole or in part which have already passed the registration test: s. 190(C)(3)?
- Has the application been certified by the relevant representative Body or Bodies or is the applicant a member of the native title claim group and authorised to make the application?

Once the conditions of the registration test have been satisfied, a claimant will be able to:

- access the right to negotiate;
- oppose non-claimant applications over the same area;
- confirm pastoral lease access rights where those rights existed at the date of the Wik decision (i.e. 23 December 1996); and
- gain the benefit of certain procedural rights such as the right to enter into a registered Indigenous Land Use Agreement.

Common law title

Common law title established by deeds

The common law system establishes an individual's title to land by a series of deeds. When the Crown first granted a parcel of land to an individual, the person would have been given a document called a Deed of Crown Grant. This Crown Grant would have described the land in a manner that would enable it to be identified. It also specified any special conditions under which the grant was made, together with any restrictions. For instance, the land may have been granted to a particular individual or organisation for a particular purpose, and at the same time the Crown may have retained the rights to any minerals in the ground.

When a person sold or mortgaged the property, they would do so by another deed, indicating the rights that were being transferred. They would then hand over to the purchaser or mortgagee the new deed, setting out the details of the transfer together with the earlier deeds. As a result, the deeds would collectively create a chain of title that could be traced back from the current owner to the original Crown Grant.

It can be seen that loss of, or any errors in a document may affect the title. The loss of a document breaks the chain and casts doubts on the authenticity of any documents that come after it. Likewise, if the land was not described correctly in a document, that fact would adversely affect subsequent holders. As a result of problems such as these, the government gives no guarantee as to a person's title to common law title land. A purchaser must be very thorough with their enquiries.

> **!** CAUTION NOTE
>
> *The weakness in the common law system is the chain of title that needs to be established.*

As time went on, it became difficult to always be able to produce all the relevant deeds back to the Crown Grant. Legislation was then introduced to require the vendor to be able to provide documentary proof of title for a length of time sufficient to establish themselves as owners and to effectively exclude other claims.

Registration is optional

While the various states have provision for the registration of deeds, under the common law system registration is optional and does not of itself give the owner rights. The title to common law land therefore passes on delivery of the deed or conveyance, irrespective of whether or not the deed is registered with the relevant land title authority.

Under common law title the mortgage of the land involves the transfer of the land to the lender on the basis that it will be transferred back to the borrower on repayment of the loan. The lender becomes the owner of the land and the borrower is left with rights called the equity of redemption—that is, the equitable right to redeem the property on performance of their obligations under the mortgage.

As a result of this conditional transfer of the title, there can be only one legal mortgage—that is, a mortgage recognised by both common law and equity. Any second or subsequent mortgages are only mortgages of the mortgagor's equity of redemption and therefore recognised by equity only. In the event of default, a legal mortgage takes priority over an equitable mortgage.

Disadvantages of the common law system

Some of the disadvantages of this system are:

- **Uncertainty of title**—because of the need to have possession of every document involving the particular block of land before the owner can conclusively prove that they are the true owner, any lost or forged document may allow a break in the chain of ownership, which could deprive the present owner of a good title.
- **Cost**—because of the complexity of a conveyance involving common law title transfer, solicitors for both vendor and purchaser examine the title independently each time the land changes hands. This is time-consuming and costly.
- **Complexity**—special skill and knowledge is required to deal with the deeds relating to land.
- **Certification**—there is no state Certificate of Title.
- **Plan**—there may not be a separate plan for every block.

Features of the Torrens system

Torrens Title is based on registration

Robert Torrens, when a member of the South Australian Parliament in 1857, introduced a Bill embodying a scheme that he had founded on principles contained in merchant shipping legislation relating to the title of ships. This system is now operating in every state in Australia, as well as many other countries. Purchasers may transfer land under the general or common law system to the Torrens system and all grants from the Crown subsequent to the passing of the new legislation are registered under the Torrens system.

Torrens Title is a system of title based on registration. Each of the state governments has a Land Titles Office that maintains a central registry of all land in the state covered by the Torrens system. Instead of using deeds to provide documentary proof of ownership, the central register provides this proof. The owner, referred to as the 'registered proprietor', is issued with a Certificate of Title that is a duplicate of the entry in the central register (see Figure 33.6).

While title to land under the general law is transferred by deed, title to Torrens system land is transferred by entry in a public register (see Table 33.2). Everything revolves around the register and registration. Where the registered proprietor has mortgaged the land, it is usual for the registered proprietor's Certificate of Title to be given to the mortgagee until the loan is repaid. This makes it very difficult for the registered proprietor to deal with the property in a manner that may be to the mortgagee's detriment, since the registered proprietor would usually be called upon to produce the duplicate Certificate of Title to confirm their right to deal with the land.

Table 33.2 Comparison of systems of title

Common law (Old System)	*Torrens Title*
1 Title by a series of deeds	1 Title by registration
2 Loss of a document or any errors may affect title	2 Registered proprietor holds subject to interests recorded in register but free from all others
3 No state guarantee	3 State guarantees that the person registered as owner is owner
4 Title passes on delivery of deed of conveyance	4 Title passes on registration of the notice of transfer
5 Caveat system does not apply	5 Caveat system enables a person to record their interest in the land
6 Mortgage involves a transfer of land to lender on basis that it will be transferred back when loan repaid	6 Mortgage is by registration not by the transfer of the land

LT 11/101

Issued pursuant to the Real Property Act, 1900, and certified overleaf

No. 28

Search certified to:
Date 15. 5.1992 Time 8.00AM

TORRENS TITLE	
FOLIO IDENTIFIER	
113/31406	
EDITION No. & DATE OF CURRENT CERTIFICATE OF TITLE	
-	-

VOL 8195 FOL 144 IS THE CURRENT CERTIFICATE OF TITLE FOR THIS COMPUTER FOLIO AND SHOULD BE LODGED WITH THE NEXT DEALING

LAND

LOT 113 IN DEPOSITED PLAN 31406
MUNICIPALITY OF CAMDEN
PARISH OF CAMDEN COUNTY OF CAMDEN
TITLE DIAGRAM: DP31406

FIRST SCHEDULE

BRADLEY LEETON AND KYLIE LEETON

AS JOINT TENANTS (T S32135)

SECOND SCHEDULE
----

1. RESERVATIONS AND CONDITIONS IN THE CROWN GRANT(S)
2. H567822 LAND EXCLUDES MINERALS AND IS SUBJECT TO RIGHTS TO MINE
3. H567822 COVENANT
4. DP31406 EASEMENT AFFECTING THE LAND 6 FEET WIDE SHOWN IN DP31406
5. J472708 COVENANT
6. S32136 MORTGAGE TO THE ILLAWARRA MUTUAL BUILDING SOCIETY
* 7. W932352 CAVEAT BY GIFC LIMITED

NOTATIONS

UNREGISTERED DEALINGS: NIL

FIGURE 33.6 *Certificate of Title*

The register

The register contains a certificate or folio for each parcel of land subject to the Torrens system. Originally, the certificates or folios were similar to pages in a big book; however, these manual titles will eventually be converted to computer records with only the registered proprietor holding a 'hard copy' of the certificate or folio (see relevant legislation in Table 33.3).

The register records:

- the boundaries of the land;
- the registered proprietor; and
- the nature and extent of all registered encumbrances such as mortgages and covenants.

It should be noted that it is possible for differences to exist between the register and the Certificate of Title held by the registered proprietor in respect to registered encumbrances. For example, it is not necessary for the registered proprietor's Certificate of Title to be lodged with the Land Titles Office for a caveat to be recorded on the title. An intending purchaser should always check the Land Titles Office register and not rely on the registered proprietor's copy of the Certificate of Title.

Although encumbrances are recorded on the register, full details are not supplied. It is therefore necessary for an intending purchaser to examine the actual document which created the encumbrance. A copy of this document will be held by the Land Titles Office. An intending purchaser should also examine the plan of subdivision that created the particular lot as it may provide information regarding further encumbrances.

Table 33.3 State and territory Torrens registration legislation

State	*Statute*
Australian Capital Territory	*Real Property Act 1925*
New South Wales	*Real Property Act 1900*
Northern Territory	*Real Property Act 1886*
Queensland	*Land Title Act 1994*
South Australia	*Real Property Act 1886*
Tasmania	*Land Titles Act 1980*
Victoria	*Transfer of Land Act 1958*
Western Australia	*Transfer of Land Act 1893*

Doing business

Registering land

Always examine the register when dealing with Torrens Title land because differences can arise between the register and the Certificate of Title. ■

Indefeasibility of title

Indefeasibility of title—guarantees ownership to registered proprietor

Under the Torrens system there are very strict rules regarding the description of the land and identification of the parties. It is therefore much more accurate than the common law system. As a result of this greater accuracy and the emphasis placed on registration, the registered proprietor holds the land subject to interests, or other rights, recorded in the register, but free from all other interests. This is called indefeasibility of title.

A person who wished to purchase a particular parcel of land would examine the register kept by the state Land Titles Office and might find no record of any interests other than those of the registered proprietors. The purchaser might then complete the purchase and a short time later an unregistered mortgagee might come forward claiming rights to the land. The new owner will hold the land free of that mortgage or any other unregistered interest. The new owner has relied on the register and acted without any fraud on his or her part.

The new owner therefore has a title that cannot be defeated by any unregistered interests. This concept of indefeasibility of title is supported by the state, in that the state guarantees that the person who is registered as the owner is in fact the owner. Such a guarantee is not available for common law title land. Interests, such as a transfer of ownership, mortgage or lease, as well as rights of way and easements, can all be registered.

> **!** CAUTION NOTE
>
> *An unregistered interest cannot defeat a registered interest.*

There are many other situations where interests might arise but there is no specific provision for their registration. Examples of such situations include a marriage breakdown where one of the parties might want to protect their interest in the land in a property settlement, or where the land is mortgaged and the registered proprietor obtains another loan from a finance company; in this case, the finance company might require the borrower to give them an interest in the land as a form of security.

Exceptions to indefeasibility of title

Fraud

If the registered proprietor or their agent was a party to fraud, the registered interest will be defeasible on the grounds of that fraud. Fraud committed by the person from whom the registered proprietor obtained title does not make the registered proprietor's title defeasible, unless the registered proprietor or their agent was a party to the fraud or knew of it.

Unregistered interests

Not all interests are required to be registered. The registered proprietor will therefore hold title subject to these interests regardless of the fact that they are not registered.

While the exact nature of the non-registrable interests varies from state to state, they include such interests as:

- the interests of adverse possessors of the land;
- the interests of tenants in possession of land (it is common for leases for terms of less than three years to be non-registrable);
- rates and taxes which are a charge on the land; and
- rights reserved by the Crown Grant.

Rights *in personam*

In *Fraser v. Walker* (1967) 126 CLR 376, it was stated by the court that the principle of indefeasibility 'in no way denies the rights of a plaintiff to bring against a registered proprietor a claim *in personam*, founded in law or equity'.

Rights *in personam* include those:

- arising out of a contract;
- arising out of a trust created or accepted by the registered proprietor; and
- arising out of some other fiduciary relationship.

IN BRIEF

What does indefeasibility of title mean?

- Indefeasibility of title means that the registered proprietor (owner) holds the land subject to interests or other rights recorded in the register, but free from all other interests.
- An unregistered interest cannot defeat a registered interest.
- Indefeasibility of title guarantees title to the registered proprietor.

Bringing land under Torrens Title

As previously stated, Robert Torrens introduced a Bill implementing the scheme into the South Australian Parliament in 1857. The Torrens system was subsequently adopted by all the other colonies (now states). Any land granted in fee simple by the Crown after the commencement of the Torrens system in that colony/state was subject to Torrens Title. However, land grants prior to the commencement of the Torrens Title system were subject to the General Law (or Old System) of title.

Land subject to General Law or Old System title can be brought under the Torrens system by:

Primary application

A primary application must be supported by evidence and documents of title sufficient to establish the applicant's claim. If the application is granted, the land is brought under Torrens Title by the creation of a folio in the register.

Qualified title

A qualified title comes into existence upon creation of a 'qualified folio' in the register. The land is treated as Torrens Title in respect to all interests recorded in the register at the time of creation and any interests created thereafter. However, there may have been interests existing prior to the creation of the folio and not recorded on the folio in the register. The title will still be subject to those interests. In other words, qualified title is in effect a combination of Torrens and the Old System of title: Torrens in respect to interests recorded at the time of creation and any interests created thereafter, and Old System in respect to interests created prior to the creation of the folio and not recorded on the folio.

A caution to this effect is recorded on the title to ward off subsisting interests under the general law (Old System). This caution will lapse on the occurrence of certain events. In New South Wales, it will lapse after six years or upon a person becoming registered proprietor for value and without fraud, whichever is the later.

A qualified title may be granted:

- Where the applicant under a primary application withdraws the application and requests the issue of a qualified title. Primary applications can be quicker but they are also more expensive.
- Upon registration of a plan of subdivision of non-Torrens Title land.
- If a deed which adequately defines the boundaries of the land is lodged for registration the Land Titles Office will often issue a qualified title automatically.
- If the Land Titles Office receives appropriate information relating to the land together with an adequate description of the boundaries.

Limited title

This method is applied to Old System land, the boundaries of which are insufficiently defined to satisfy the creation of an ordinary or qualified folio in the register. The folio will be created as a qualified folio (as described above) but with a limitation recorded indicating that the description of the land has not been investigated and verified.

Caveats

Caveat—an interest recorded on the title

Under the Torrens system, a person who claims to have an interest can protect themselves by lodging a caveat on the title. The caveat is recorded on the title and acts as an injunction preventing the Registrar General from registering any dealing that is in conflict with the caveat. Because it is recorded on the register, a side effect of the caveat is that it gives notice of the interest to anyone who may be contemplating dealing with the registered proprietor.

Mortgages

Mortgage—a registrable interest

As previously stated, a mortgage of land covered by the common law system of title involves the conditional transfer of the land to the lender, subject to the borrower's right to redeem the land on repayment of the loan. The Torrens system involves a completely different approach. Under the Torrens system, the land is not transferred to the mortgagee. Instead the mortgagee is granted an interest in the land and that interest can be protected by the mortgagee registering it on the title. This is done by lodging the Memorandum of Mortgage accompanied by the Certificate of Title with the state Land Titles Office. The borrower remains the registered proprietor at all times.

Because there is no transfer of the land to the mortgagee, it is legally possible for the registered proprietor to grant more than one mortgage and for them all to be registered. It is therefore possible to have more than one legal mortgage of land under the Torrens system.

It can be seen from this brief comparison of the two systems of title that registration goes to the core of the Torrens system. It is often referred to as 'title by registration'. In keeping with this emphasis on registration, title does not pass from the vendor to the purchaser until registration of a notice of transfer accompanied by the Certificate of Title, both of which are lodged with the state Land Titles Office. This is in contrast with the common law system where title passes on delivery of the deed of conveyance, registration being optional.

> **!** CAUTION NOTE
>
> *Title by registration is the core of Torrens system.*

Doing business

Why use Torrens?

Three obvious reasons for using Torrens are:

- it is simpler and cheaper in regard to legal fees;
- it gives certainty of title; and
- if a building is going to be strata divided, it must be erected on Torrens Title. ■

Advantages of the Torrens system

The main advantage of the Torrens system is that it allows the parties to quickly and easily establish proof of title, which was the basic aim of the system. However, more specifically, the advantages of holding land under the Torrens system are the opposite of the disadvantages of the general law system. They are:

- **Certainty of title**—the registered owner is the true owner. There is no need to examine every document as the certificate is the paramount document.
- **Cost**—the Torrens system is simpler and therefore less costly.
- **Simplicity**—it is a simple matter for anyone to obtain a copy of the title from the state Land Titles Office for examination.
- **Certification**—the state guarantees the title of the person named on the certificate held at the Land Titles Office.
- **Plan of the land**—every Certificate of Title contains a plan of the land specified.

Strata Title

Strata title is concerned with the horizontal subdivision of land or airspace

Strata Title came about as an extension of Torrens Title. Where Torrens Title was concerned with land subdivided across the surface of the land, Strata Title was concerned with the horizontal subdivision of land and/or airspace into strata or layers (see relevant legislation in Table 33.4).

In recent times the concept has been further extended to 'town houses' and 'villas' as well as community and neighbourhood schemes. A strata (building unit) plan can only be registered in respect to Torrens Title land. If a developer wanted to erect a high rise on general law (Old System) title land it would be necessary to convert to Torrens Title prior to strata subdivision. Such a conversion would usually be done by primary application (discussed above) since time is important and delays cost money.

CAUTION NOTE

A strata plan can only be registered in respect to Torrens Title land.

Using a strata subdivided building as a typical example, the building is subdivided into lots which are usually referred to in normal conversation as units.

- A separate folio is created for each lot and a Certificate of Title is issued to each registered proprietor.
- When the building is subdivided there will be portions that are not included in the lots. This residue is referred to as 'common property'.
- Common property includes such things as hallways, stairwells, elevators, gardens, vehicle access and sometimes vehicle parking areas.
- The common property is vested in the owners' corporation.
- The owners' corporation is comprised of all the registered proprietors of the lots in the strata (or building unit) plan.
- The owners' corporation is responsible for the management, control and administration, as well as the maintenance and repair of the common property.
- To cover any costs incurred with its obligations, the owners' corporation will levy the registered proprietors to raise the funds. The registered proprietors will contribute to these levies in proportion to their unit entitlement.
- The unit entitlement is a number set out in a schedule in the strata (or building unit) plan which is supposed to reflect the value of that lot in relation to all the other lots.

Table 33.4 Strata Title legislation

Australian Capital Territory	*Land Titles (Unit Titles) Act 1970*
New South Wales	*Strata Schemes Management Act 1996*
Northern Territory	*Unit Titles Act 1975*
Queensland	*Building Units & Group Titles Act 1980*
	Body Corporate & Community Management Act 1997
South Australia	*Strata Titles Act 1988*
Tasmania	*Strata Titles Act 1998*
Victoria	*Building Units & Group Titles Act 1980*
Western Australia	*Strata Titles Act 1985*

WHAT IS A MORTGAGE?

A mortgage is a transaction in which an interest in land is given as security for the repayment of money lent. If the borrower defaults, the lender has rights against the land, the main right being the right to sell the land and recover the outstanding balance of the loan from the proceeds of sale.

Mortgages can be classified as legal mortgages or equitable mortgages (see Figure 33.7).

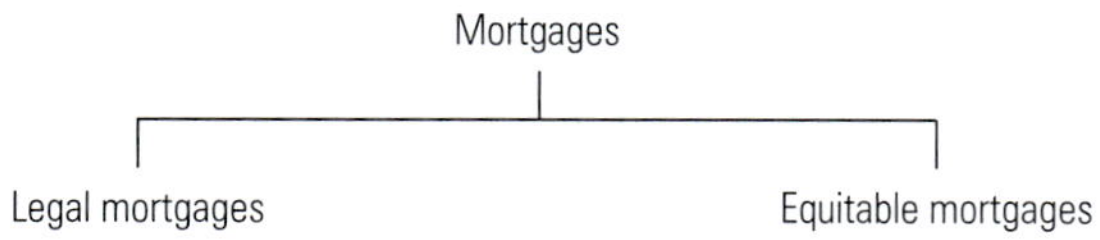

FIGURE 33.7 *Types of mortgage*

Legal mortgages

Legal mortgage is registered

A mortgage recognised by both common law and equity. It achieves this status because the parties have satisfied all the formalities and other requirements of both common law and equity. In the case of a mortgage under common law title, this means executing a deed of mortgage conveying the land to the mortgagee. In the case of land under the Torrens system, it means registration of the mortgage.

Equitable mortgages

Equitable mortgages give the lender an interest recognised by equity, but not by common law. They arise because the parties have not complied with the requirements of the common law but have nonetheless done something that affects rights to the land.

Equitable mortgage—unregistered interest in land

With respect to Torrens Title, all registered mortgages are legal mortgages, but an unregistered mortgage is only equitable because the fundamental requirement of registration has not been complied with. With respect to common law title, only the first mortgage is a legal mortgage; all others are equitable only. This is because the land can only be transferred to one mortgagee at a time. If the borrower wishes to use the land for security with other lenders, the borrower can only mortgage the equitable right to redeem the property from the first mortgagee.

In the event that there are several mortgages over the one parcel of land and the borrower defaults on them, there will be several mortgagees competing to exercise their rights over the land. The basic rule is that a legal mortgage takes priority over an equitable mortgage and equitable mortgages take priority in order of creation.

J AND H JUST (HOLDINGS) PTY LTD V. BANK OF NEW SOUTH WALES (1971) 125 CLR 546

The registered proprietor of land under the Torrens system executed a Memorandum of Mortgage in favour of the bank and deposited the duplicate Certificate of Title with the bank. The bank did not register the mortgage. Instead it decided to rely on the receipt of the memorandum of mortgage and the duplicate Certificate of Title. Money was subsequently lent to the registered proprietor by another lender and the registered proprietor executed a second memorandum of mortgage over the same land.

The registered proprietor told the second lender that the Certificate of Title was lodged with the bank for safe keeping only. The second lender did not require production of the duplicate Certificate of Title. The second lender lodged a caveat on the title and some time later the bank lodged the first memorandum of mortgage for registration together with the duplicate Certificate of Title. The second lender sought a declaration from the court that the second mortgage had priority over the first mortgage because it had lodged a caveat prior to the bank lodging any documentation.

ISSUE: Did the lodging of a caveat give the second equitable mortgage priority over the earlier equitable (unregistered) mortgage?

DECISION: The High Court held that the priority of the bank's equitable interest had not been lost by the failure to lodge a caveat or register the mortgage. The bank was entitled to rely on its possession of the duplicate Certificate of Title and on the practice of the Registrar-General of refusing to accept a memorandum of mortgage for registration without production of the duplicate Certificate of Title.

! CAUTION NOTE

Legal mortgage takes priority over equitable mortgage.

MORTGAGOR'S RIGHT TO DEAL WITH THE PROPERTY

The purpose of the mortgage is that the land should be security for repayment of a loan and nothing more. Accordingly, the mortgagee is not permitted to take the fee simple outright or to impose conditions or restrictions that make the mortgage materially harder to redeem. Lord *MacNaughten* in the House of Lords in *Noakes and Co. Ltd v. Rice* [1902] AC 24 said:

> *Redemption is of the very nature and essence of a mortgage . . . Equity will not permit any device or contrivance designed or calculated to prevent or impede redemption.*

The right to possession of the mortgaged property depends on whether it is common law system or Torrens system. The common law system mortgage takes effect as a conveyance of the land to the mortgagee of all of the mortgagor's interest. This means the mortgagor has also given up the right to possession. While this is the strict result of the granting of the mortgage, it is usual for the deed of mortgage to give the right of possession to the mortgagor until default.

Under the Torrens system, the registered proprietor remains the owner and merely gives the mortgagee an interest that entitles the mortgagee to possession in the event of default only.

If the mortgagor is in possession, they have the right to receive any rents or profits from the land. The right to lease the land may be subject to the mortgagee's consent.

REMEDIES OF THE MORTGAGEE

Right to sue on personal covenants

A covenant is a clause in an agreement—in this case the mortgage—whereby the party binds themself to give something to another person to do, or not do some act. The mortgagor's obligation to pay the principal and interest is a covenant.

Covenant—clause in an agreement obligating a party to do or not do some act

If the mortgagor defaults in payment of the principal or interest under the mortgage, the mortgagee is entitled to take action against the mortgagor for breach of the covenant. This right is based on the mortgagor's contractual obligations, not on the mortgagee's security interest. The right to sue on the personal covenant may be exercised in conjunction with any other remedies of the mortgagee.

Right to appoint a receiver

A receiver is a person who is usually appointed by the court on the request of the mortgagee to receive the rents and profits of the property and to account for them to the court.

Receiver—appointed by the court on request of the mortgagee on mortgagor's default

Legislation in all states provides that a mortgagee has an implied right to appoint a receiver. This applies to land under common law title and Torrens Title. However, the power to appoint a receiver is not exercisable until default has been made.

Foreclosure

Foreclosure is the forfeiture by the mortgagor of the equity of redemption as a result of default in payment. As a result of the foreclosure, the mortgagee acquires the fee simple of the land free from any right of the mortgagor to ever recover it.

Foreclosure—mortgagee acquires fee simple

With respect to land under common law title, proceedings are brought in the Equity Division of the Supreme Court. The court certifies the amount due and if the amount is not paid within the time specified, the mortgagor's interest is foreclosed.

Under the Torrens system, the mortgagee must first put the land up for sale by public auction. If no appropriate offer is received, an order for foreclosure may be made.

Power of sale

The power of sale is the usual remedy exercised by a mortgagee against a defaulting mortgagor. The effect of the exercise of the power of sale is to convey the fee simple to the purchaser free of the mortgagor's right of redemption. If the proceeds of sale are insufficient to clear the outstanding balance, the mortgagee may still sue the mortgagor for the balance.

Power of sale—usual remedy of mortgagee

In exercising a power of sale, the mortgagor will obviously be concerned with clearing the debt owed. Since the exercise of that power will extinguish the mortgagee's equity of redemption, the mortgagee must have some regard to the mortgagor's interests and those of subsequent encumbrances. The question is whether the mortgagee must merely act in good faith or whether they are bound to take reasonable care to obtain a better price.

In Queensland, the *Property Law Act 1974* states that the mortgagee has a duty to take reasonable care to ensure that the property is sold at market value. In *Commercial and General Acceptance Ltd v. Nixon* (1981) 38 ALR 225, the High Court considered the application of the Queensland legislation and the power of sale generally. *Aickin* J said:

> *The power of sale is an essential part of the mortgagee's security but it is not to be exercised exclusively in his own interest without regard to the interests of the mortgagor by directing attention exclusively to the recovery of the mortgage debt, interest and expenses rather than obtaining the market value of the property at the time of sale.*

The mortgagee must advertise the proposed sale adequately so that the property and its potential are brought to the notice of persons likely to be interested.

CUCKMERE BRICK CO. LTD V. MUTUAL FINANCE LTD [1971] CH 949

The plaintiffs had obtained planning permission to build either 100 flats or 35 houses on land they had mortgaged. The plaintiffs defaulted under the mortgage and the mortgagees advertised the land for sale by auction. The advertisement mentioned planning permission for 35 houses, no reference was made to the alternative approval for 100 flats. The omission was brought to the attention of the mortgagees but they refused to postpone the auction. The land was sold for much less than the mortgagor's estimate of its value.

ISSUE: Is the mortgagee under an obligation to attempt to obtain the true market value of the property?

DECISION: Once the power of sale has accrued, the mortgagee is entitled to exercise it for their own purposes whenever they choose to do so. However, a mortgagee in exercising their power of sale does owe a duty to take reasonable precautions to obtain the true market value of the mortgaged property at the date on which they decide to sell it.

A mortgagee must take reasonably adequate steps to get a fair price.

NATIONAL COMMERCIAL BANKING CORP. V. SOLANOWSKI (1984) (NSW) CONV. R ¶55-194

Solanowski granted a mortgage over land to the Commercial Banking Corp. of Sydney Ltd. Solanowski subsequently defaulted. The bank obtained estimates of the market value from two local real estate agents, one of whom ultimately acted on the sale. The estimated market value was stated to be $14 000 to $15 000. Some time later, the bank instructed one of the agents to sell the property. The agent placed an advertisement in a local newspaper and the *Sydney Morning Herald*, describing the property as unattractive, subject to flooding and filthy. The agent received an offer for $8000. Contracts were exchanged at that price.

Solanowski refused to vacate the property and sought an injunction restraining completion of the contract. Solanowski argued that the fair market value was not less than $20 000 and that the bank had acted in conscious and wilful disregard of, or with reckless indifference to, his interests when it contracted to sell at a gross undervalue.

ISSUE: What constitutes reasonably adequate steps to get a fair price?

DECISION: The New South Wales Supreme Court held that a fair market value of the land was $14 000–$15 000. The court also held that mere errors of judgement do not constitute a breach of a mortgagee's duty to the mortgagor. However, a failure to take reasonably adequate steps to ensure a fair price will constitute a breach of that duty. The bank was accordingly found to be in breach of its duty.

The mortgagee's duty to the mortgagor may also arise where the property is sold to an associate of the mortagee. A mortgagee who wishes to acquire the mortgaged property must demonstrate steps taken to protect the interest of the borrower.

Acquiring possession of property, as distinct from ownership, through leasing is common for both business and residential purposes. It makes sense then to have an understanding of the basic principles that are involved with leasing, because most people at some time in their lives are going to be involved in leasing a property, either to live in or work from.

***TSE KWONG LAM V. WONG CHIT SEN* [1983] 1 WLR 1349**

A mortgagee decided to exercise power of sale at a public auction. The mortgagee and his wife decided that the wife should bid for the property, on behalf of their family company, up to a price of $1.2 million. The mortgagee instructed the auctioneer that the reserve price was $1.2 million. Although there were 30 to 40 people present, the mortgagee's wife was the only bidder. The property was sold to the company for $1.2 million. The mortgagee then commenced proceedings against the mortgagor for the balance of the loan outstanding after deduction of the proceeds of sale.

ISSUE: Must a mortgagee who wishes to acquire the mortgaged property demonstrate steps taken to protect interest of borrower?

DECISION: A mortgagee who wishes to secure the mortgaged property for a company in which he or she is interested ought to show that he or she protected the interest of the borrower by taking expert advice as to the method of sale, the steps to be taken to make the sale a success, and the reserve price.

At common law, a lease was a contract by which one party granted to another exclusive possession of property for a limited time. The grantor usually received consideration in the form of rent or some other type of income, though the receipt of rent was not essential. Under common law, the lessee (tenant) had no estate in the land, but only a right of entry. The landlord and tenant relationship was not fully established until the lessee actually entered the premises. However, this doctrine no longer prevails, and a lease may take effect without the need for actual entry by the lessee.

LEASE AND A LICENCE DISTINGUISHED

It is necessary to distinguish between a lease and a licence in relation to land. A tenancy agreement creates an estate or an interest in land.

Licence

A licence has been defined as an **authority** to do something that would otherwise be illegal or wrongful—for example, to enter on to land in circumstances which, without a licence to do so, would constitute an act of trespass.

Licence—an authority to do something

The granting of a licence **does not** confer an estate or interest in the land; it is only a permission to use the property in a certain way. A gratuitous licence may be revoked by notice of either party and is not assignable—that is, the rights cannot be transferred to another person.

Doing business

Purchaser with possession before final settlement—lessee or licensee?

A purchaser of a house who obtains possession before final settlement usually enters into possession under licence, not under a lease. ■

Lease

A lease is defined as a **conveyance or grant of the possession of property** to last the life of a person, or for a term of years or other fixed period, usually with the payment of rent. The contract must specify the period for which the lease is to endure, as well as the beginning and ending of the term. The parties to a lease are:

Lease—grant of exclusive possession of property

- the **lessor**—the person granting the lease; and
- the **lessee**—the person to whom it is granted.

Leaseholder's right inferior to a freeholder's right

A leaseholder's right to possession has always been held to be inferior to that of the freeholder's right of seisin, the right to be paid rent for the land. The term of a lease is immaterial in considering the relative importance of the two interests in land, freehold or leasehold.

Leases may be seen as falling into two categories:

- those for periods of **fixed** or periodic duration; and
- tenancies **at will** and at sufferance.

IN BRIEF

What is a licence?

A licence is an authority to do something that would otherwise be illegal or wrongful. It is only permission to use the land in a certain way and it does not give the person any interest in the land.

CLASSIFICATION ACCORDING TO DURATION

Leases of fixed duration

Leases can be of fixed duration but may be further subdivided as follows:

- leases for a term of years;
- leases from year to year; and
- leases for lesser periods.

Leases for a term of years

A tenancy for a term of years is created where an agreement provides for a term of more than one year. Fixed term leases of Torrens Title land for periods longer than three years must be registered to be valid.

Leases from year to year

These are tenancies that last for a year and, if not terminated at the end of the first year, will continue for at least another year, and so on from year to year until terminated. A year-to-year tenancy is terminated when either party gives notice.

Periodic tenancies

These may be from quarter to quarter, month to month or week to week. The rent is normally payable for each period and notice of termination required is for the full period. For example, in the case of a monthly tenancy, a month's notice is required.

Tenancies at will

A tenancy at will exists whenever a tenant, with the consent of the owner, occupies land as a tenant on the terms that either may terminate the tenancy at any time. A tenant still in possession at the end of their lease cannot be termed a trespasser, as they occupy the land with the consent of the owner. Of course, on payment and acceptance of rent, the tenancy at will may be converted to a periodic tenancy.

! CAUTION NOTE

Tenancy at will may be terminated at any time, though termination will not make the tenant a trespasser.

Tenancy at sufferance

A tenancy at sufferance is not a true tenancy. It arises where a tenant has entered into possession under a lawful title—for example, a leasing agreement—and, after the designated period has expired, has remained in possession without either the consent or dissent of the landlord.

Such a tenant differs from a trespasser only in that their original entry was not wrongful. The landlord must re-enter before an action in trespass can be commenced.

TERMS OF AGREEMENT FOR LEASE

The terms of an agreement for a lease may be established where a formal document is not executed, by way of part-performance and a memorandum in writing. The memorandum must contain, either expressly or by reference to other documents or events, the following:

- a description of the parties sufficient for positive identification;
- identification of the property;
- details of the consideration;
- details of commencement, which will be from the date of possession, and duration of the lease; and
- any special conditions that have been agreed upon.

Parol evidence can be given where the memorandum does not contain the actual terms of the agreement. The memorandum may comprise more than one document.

TERMS OF A LEASING CONTRACT

The terms of a leasing contract are either express or implied. The former provides, by express stipulation, the covenants binding the parties—a covenant being a clause in an agreement whereby a party is bound to give something to another or to do or not to do something for another. The implied terms include:

- a covenant by the lessor to provide the tenant with **quiet possession**;
- a covenant by the lessor of a furnished house that the premises are **fit for habitation**; and
- a covenant by the tenant to use the premises in a 'tenant-like' manner—that is, to **take proper care** of the property by doing such things as cleaning the windows, mowing the lawn and not damaging the house.

Doctrine of waste—keep property in good repair

Generally, tenants are required by express provision to keep the leased property in repair. This liability, in the absence of express qualification, depends on the doctrine of waste, which can be either voluntary or permissive.

A tenant may be expressly released from any obligation to repair relating to fair wear and tear. However, they are bound to carry out such repairs as would be necessary where there is damage that ordinary wear and tear would not produce.

In *Haskell v. Marlow* [1928] 2 KB 45 at 50, it was stated that:

> *For example, if a tile falls off the roof, the tenant is not liable for the immediate consequences, but if he does nothing and as a result more and more water gets in, the roof and walls decay and ultimately the top floor, or the whole house becomes uninhabitable, he cannot say that this is due to fair wear and tear, and that therefore he is not liable under his obligation to keep the house in good repair and condition. In such a case, the want of repair is not in truth caused by fair wear and tear. Far the greater part of it is caused by the failure of the tenant to prevent what was originally caused by wear and tear from producing results altogether beyond what was so caused.*

Can a lease be assigned (transferred)?

Liabilities may be assigned to create a tripartite agreement

The general rule is that liabilities under a contract cannot be assigned. However, they may be assigned with the consent of the other party to the original contract (the party who is not the assignor). If consent is given, the assignment becomes a **tripartite agreement**; the contract between the original two parties is rescinded in consideration of a new contract being entered into on the same terms and between one of the original parties and the third party.

In the case of assigning a lease, the effect is to release the assignor from their obligations under the original contract and to impose them on the new party, the assignee.

Assignment must be distinguished from subletting

Assignment must be distinguished from subletting. If a tenant transfers the whole of their interest under a leasing agreement, the result amounts to an assignment. But if the intention is to create a subletting, some reversion of the term of the original lease, even for only a day, must be reserved by the original lessee.

TERMINATION OF LEASES AND TENANCIES

Leases and tenancies may be terminated in a number of ways:

Termination by time

The period of notice may be decided by the parties to the tenancy agreement, subject to statutory requirements, if any.

At common law, in the absence of express agreement to the contrary, the period of notice required is (with the exception of yearly tenancies) the period that corresponds to the recurring period of the tenancy—for example, a monthly tenancy would require notice of a month. Also at common law, the notice to quit to determine a periodic tenancy must expire at the end of the given recurring period.

By an option

The parties to the tenancy agreement may have decided to incorporate an option in the tenancy agreement whereby one or other of the parties may terminate the agreement on the exercise of the option.

Termination by surrender

Surrender of a lease can arise from an agreement between the parties that the lease will terminate through surrender at law.

Where an act done by one party and assented to by the other is consistent with discontinuing the lease—for example, if the tenant gives up possession of the premises, or another person is granted a lease and takes possession with the consent of the original lessee—the old tenancy is surrendered. The nature of the new tenancy or lease is immaterial in such cases.

Where the premises are re-let, this is not in itself an acceptance of the tenant's surrender.

Forfeiture

If, within the leasing agreement, there is no provision for re-entry on breach of a covenant, the lessor may only use the penalty of forfeiture if it can be established that the provision breached was not a mere covenant but a condition. It has been held that payment of rent is to be considered a condition rather than a mere covenant. For example, s. 146 of the *Property Law Act 1958* (Vic.) and s. 129 of the *Conveyancing Act 1919* (NSW) provide that a right of re-entry stipulated in a lease cannot be enforced unless and until the lessor serves the lessee a notice:

- specifying the particular breach complained of;
- if the breach is capable of remedy, requiring the lessee to remedy the breach; and
- in any case, requiring the lessee to make monetary compensation for the breach.

If the lessee fails within 14 days, or a period specified in the lease, to remedy the breach and make adequate compensation, the lessor may re-enter, forfeiting the lease. The effect of forfeiture is to deprive the lessee of any rights under the lease.

Notice to quit

A notice to quit may be given to the tenant by the landlord or lessor personally. A notice given by the lessee to the landlord or lessor is called a notice of **intention to quit**. It may also be served by the agent of either party, provided that the necessary authority exists. In a situation where the lessor is a company that wishes to give notice to quit to a lessee, it is advisable that such notice be sealed by the company in accordance with its articles of association. A notice to quit, at common law, may be given by an agent provided the agent has the authority to serve such notices.

CAN THE LANDLORD RECOVER POSSESSION OF THE PREMISES?

A landlord can retake possession where tenancy has ended

It has been held that where a tenancy has been ended, the landlord is entitled to take physical possession of the premises and to evict the tenant and their goods. If the tenant refuses to depart, the landlord may use such force as is necessary to expel the tenant without becoming liable to an action for damages for trespass or assault. However, there are obvious dangers in a landlord seeking to exercise such rights. In most cases where there is even the slightest possibility of any kind of resistance on the part of the tenant, the landlord should:

- make application to a Magistrate's Court for an order of possession;
- bring an action in the County or District Court where the case falls within that jurisdiction; or
- commence an action in the Supreme Court by issuing a writ of summons for recovery of possession of land.

RESIDENTIAL TENANCIES LEGISLATION

What is the purpose of residential tenancies legislation?

Landlord and tenant legislation, or residential tenancies legislation as it is now usually referred to, was one of the earliest forms of consumer protection legislation (see Table 33.5).

Queensland has passed the *Property Agents and Motor Dealers Act 2000* which replaces the *Auctioneers and Agents Act 1971* and became law on 1 July 2001. It gives more protection for consumers who buy or rent from licensed agents and dealers. It affects motor dealers, real estate agents, auctioneers, restricted letting agents, property developers, commercial agents and pastoral houses.

Residential tenancies legislation is intended to protect and improve the lot of tenants of residential property. To achieve this objective, the legislation establishes new rules to control landlord and tenant relationships involving residential property.

The legislation usually allows a Residential Tenancies Tribunal or a Consumer Affairs Tribunal to provide advice and assistance to parties to a residential tenancy agreement and to assist in dispute settlements where possible. Any decision made by the tribunal will be final and binding on both parties (subject to an appeal to a superior court on grounds of natural justice or the tribunal acting outside its jurisdiction).

The following agreements are usually excluded from its operation, and these agreements continue to be regulated by the old law:

- premises let for the tenant's trade, profession or business;
- lodging and boarding arrangements;
- farm letting;
- a tenancy agreement arising from the sale of a house or flat between the buyer and seller;
- where the premises are situated in a hotel, motel, hostel, nursing home, convalescent home, rehabilitation home, home for the aged, educational institution or hospital;
- holiday homes; and
- prescribed tenancy agreements and prescribed premises.

Table 33.5 Residential tenancies legislation of the states and territories

State	*Statute*
Australian Capital Territory	*Residential Tenancies Act 1997*
New South Wales	*Landlord and Tenant Acts 1899*
	Landlord and Tenant (Rental Bonds) Act 1977
	Residential Tenancies Act 1987
Northern Territory	*Residential Tenancies Act 2004*
Queensland	*Residential Tenancies Act 1994*
	Property Agents & Motor Dealers Act 2000
South Australia	*Residential Tenancies Act 1995*
Tasmania	*Residential Tenancies Act 1997*
Victoria	*Residential Tenancies Act 1997*
Western Australia	*Residential Tenancies Act 1987*

So long as the purpose of the letting arrangement is to let the property for residential use, the residential tenancies legislation will apply. This will be the case even though the premises may be used partly for business purposes.

Tenancy documents

The legislation usually requires the following documents to be given to a tenant at the start of the agreement:

- **receipts**—these must be provided for all monies paid;
- **copy of the agreement/lease**—the regulations to the legislation may prescribe a standard form tenancy agreement or specify certain covenants that must be included;
- **condition report**—the landlord may be required to provide the tenant with a copy of a report on the condition of the premises. If the tenant disagrees with anything in the report, a comment on the report should be made to indicate what the tenant does not agree with; and
- **statement of rights**—a standard statutory statement of the tenant's rights and duties may also be required to be given to the tenant (usually in the form of the prescribed statement of rights and duties), together with the landlord's name and address and the full name, address and telephone number of the estate agent (if applicable).

Common requirements imposed on the landlord

Common requirements imposed on the landlord by residential tenancies legislation are:

- **Rental increases**—not to increase the rent unless the tenant is given at least 60 days' notice in writing. If the tenant pays an increase following an invalid notice (or no notice at all), application may be made to the tribunal for a refund of the excess amount on the ground that the increase was illegal.
- **Vacant and clean premises**—to ensure that on the agreed date for occupation the premises are vacant and in a reasonably clean condition.
- **Keep premises in good order**—to ensure that the premises are in good repair at the commencement of the tenancy agreement and to keep them in good repair during the term of the agreement.
- **Quiet enjoyment**—to take all reasonable steps to ensure that the tenant has quiet enjoyment of the premises.
- **Security**—to provide locks to secure all external doors and windows.
- **Right of entry**—to ensure that the tenants' goods are not damaged when entering the rented premises in respect to the landlord's right of entry. When the landlord does enter, time spent on the premises cannot be any longer than is reasonably necessary.
- **Assignment and subletting**—assignment and subletting of the whole or any part of the rented premises requires the consent of the landlord. However, the landlord cannot unreasonably withhold his or her consent because the tenant may make an application to the tribunal for a determination that the consent of the landlord is not required. If the tribunal determines that the landlord's consent is required, then the assignment or subletting without the landlord's consent is void.

What are the duties of the tenant?

The duties of the tenant to a large extent reflect the rights of the landlord. The main duties of the tenant are:

- **To carry out necessary repairs**—to advise the landlord of necessary repairs. In the case of urgent or emergency repairs—the tenant can either do the work personally or pay a tradesperson and then get the landlord to recompense the tenant, provided that reasonable steps have been taken to get in touch with the landlord or agent.
- **To avoid damaging the premises**—either by their actions or those of an invitee. Where damage has been incurred, the landlord may require the tenant to do the repairs or undertake to have the repairs done.
- **Not to permit the premises to be used illegally**—whether at common law or by statute. The offence must be incidental to the use of the premises and the tenant must have some knowledge of the illegal activities—for example, running a gaming house.
- **Not to create a nuisance**—not to use the premises, or permit the premises to be used, in such a manner as to cause a nuisance—for example, loud and excessive noise from a stereo or television.

- **To keep the premises reasonably clean**—this does not mean a spotless condition, nor does it apply to untidiness. Failure to keep the premises clean may result in an order that the tenant clean the premises, that the tenant forfeit part or all of their security deposit, or that the tenant vacate the premises.
- **Not to make renovations or alterations**—without the landlord's consent. Where the tenant installs fixtures or renovates or alters the premises without consent, the tribunal may order the fixtures to be removed or the premises restored back to their original condition. The tenant may be required to pay compensation to the landlord, or the landlord may terminate the lease.
- **Pay the rent**—to pay the rent as it falls due.

How can tenancy agreements be terminated?

Tenancy agreements for a fixed period can, as a general rule, only be terminated in accordance with the agreement. However, there are special cases where the tenant or the landlord may terminate other than as provided for in the agreement, such as where the premises are destroyed by fire or the premises become unfit for human habitation. The tenancy agreement may be terminated upon the breach of a covenant by the tenant or for other reasons specified in the legislation, such as the landlord requiring the premises for their own purposes.

The landlord can recover possession by serving notice on the tenant to vacate the premises. A landlord usually cannot evict a tenant personally, or by having their agent enter the premises and physically taking possession.

The landlord usually needs the approval of the tribunal or court. The landlord is not allowed to seize the tenant's furniture or other goods to compensate for rent owing.

Dispute settlement

Dispute settlement may be through a tribunal

Residential tenancies legislation usually provides that either party to a tenancy agreement—the landlord or the tenant—may make application to the Residential Tenancies Tribunal where it is claimed that a dispute has arisen or a breach has occurred under the tenancy agreement or under the provisions of the Act. The tribunal was established as a low-cost and quick way to settle day-to-day tenancy disputes.

The tribunal hearing is an informal one and is heard and determined by one member of the tribunal. Evidence before the tribunal may be given on oath or by affirmation or declaration. The parties are generally expected to present their own case, but a party may be represented by a duly qualified legal practitioner in some instances. In New South Wales it is the Consumer, Trader and Tenancy Tribunal.

RETAIL TENANCIES LEGISLATION

Retail tenancies legislation protects small traders

The states and the Northern Territory have introduced retail tenancies legislation and regulations to protect tenants in small commercial premises (see Table 33.6).

Table 33.6 Retail premises legislation

State	*Statute*
Australian Capital Territory	*Leases (Commercial and Retail) Act 2001*
New South Wales	*Retail Leases Act 1994*
Northern Territory	*Business Tenancies (Fair Dealings) Act 2004*
Queensland	*Retail Shop Leases Act 1994*
South Australia	*Retail and Commercial Leases Act 1995*
Tasmania	*Fair Trading Act 1990* Part 4 (Fair Trading (Code of Practice for Retail Tenancies) Regulation 1998)
Victoria	*Retail Leases Act 2003*
Western Australia	*Commercial Tenancy (Retail Shops) Agreements Act 1985*

Retail premises are primarily those premises that are used wholly or predominantly for the carrying on of a business involving the hire or sale of goods or services.

A **retail shopping centre** means a cluster of premises of which five or more are retail premises and all of which have, or if leased would have, a common head lessor. It does not include a building with more than one storey unless each storey contains five or more retail premises.

Typical provisions of retail tenancies legislation

Retail tenancy legislation is aimed at protecting small commercial tenants, and generally provides that:

- the tenant must be given a copy of the retail premises lease or the lease can be terminated;
- a landlord can no longer demand key money or goodwill. An exception to the goodwill rule is retail premises in retail shopping centres;
- assignment and subletting require the consent of the landlord and must be in writing. If the landlord fails to respond, consent to the assignment or sublease is deemed to be given;
- the landlord will have to compensate the tenant if there is a failure to rectify a breakdown of plant or equipment or a failure to comply with any requirement of any authority;
- minimum tenancy periods may apply (though not in Queensland), and any renewal clause must set out the general conditions applicable to the exercise of any option for renewal;
- the landlord must inform the tenant, at least three months before the lease expires, as to whether the lease will be renewed, and the terms for renewal; and
- disputes between the parties, except in the case of rent, are to be settled by way of arbitration.

Commercial tenancies not covered by special legislation

Commercial tenancies in those states that do not have retail tenancies legislation, or where the particular commercial tenancy is outside the scope of the retail tenancies legislation, are regulated by the clauses of the lease agreement, the common law and sometimes legislation that may imply conditions into a lease. They are usually open to far greater freedom of agreement. They can be distinguished from residential tenancies by the following features:

- Rates, taxes and other outgoings are normally paid by the tenant.
- There is an option to renew at the tenant's discretion when the lease expires.
- They usually allow for regular rent increases based on the Consumer Price Index or a specified percentage per annum.
- The procedure for recovery of possession (eviction) is specified by the agreement.

WEB RESOURCES

Australian Capital Territory: This site has information about residential tenancies:

http://www.fairtrading.act.gov.au/pubs/Other/Rent_Book_Sept_2002.pdf/

New South Wales: For information on the Rental Bond Board and the Consumer, Trader and Tenancy Tribunal, see the general gateway located at:

http://www.fairtrading.nsw.gov.au

Northern Territory: For general information on renting, through the brochures site there is an information sheet on renting in the Northern Territory:

http://www.territoryhousing.nt.gov.au/dcdsca/web.nsf

Queensland: Residential but a gateway to other sites:

http://www.rta.qld.gov.au/

South Australia: This site is a gateway to information on both retail and residential tenancies:

http://www.ocba.sa.gov.au/landlords.htm

Tasmania:

http://www.justice.tas.gov.au

Victoria: A gateway to information on Victorian residential tenancies legislation can be found at:

http://www.justice.vic.gov.au

Western Australia: A gateway for information on retail leases and rentals:

http://www.docep.wa.gov.au

REVIEW QUESTIONS

33.1 Distinguish personal property from real property.

33.2 What is possessory ownership?

33.3 What is a fixture?

33.4 From a legal point of view, is a fixture part of or separate from land?

33.5 State the basic presumption regarding fixtures and give some tests of intention in relation to fixtures.

33.6 Distinguish joint tenancy from tenancy in common.

33.7 In the context of joint ownership, what is meant by 'survivorship'?

33.8 Indefeasibility of title is usually considered the most important feature of Torrens Title. What is meant by indefeasibility of title?

33.9 What is a mortgage?

33.10 What is the distinction between a legal mortgage and an equitable mortgage?

33.11 Indicate whether each of the following statements is true or false:

	TRUE	FALSE
▪ A transaction in which an interest in land is given as security for the repayment of money lent is called a caveat	☐	☑
▪ Chattels that were once moveable but have subsequently become attached to the land in a way that makes them part of the land are called real chattels	☐	☑
▪ The doctrine whereby the registered proprietor under Torrens Title holds the land subject to interests or rights recorded in the register but free from all others, is called indefeasibility of title	☑	☐
▪ Co-owners who hold an equal and undivided interest in property that is characterised by the four unities and survivorship are called joint tenants	☑	☐
▪ Under the Torrens Title system, title is based on registration	☑	☐
▪ The doctrine whereby if one co-owner dies the interest of that person is automatically transferred to the remaining joint tenants regardless of the deceased person's will, is called survivorship.	☑	☐

33.12 What is the difference between 'foreclosure' and 'the power of sale'?

33.13 When exercising a power of sale, is the mortgagee required to consider the interests of the mortgagor?

33.14 What is a covenant?

33.15 What is the difference between a lease and a licence?

33.16 What categories may leases of fixed duration be divided into? How is each distinguishable?

33.17 Briefly describe what the doctrine of waste is.

33.18 What types of document are required to be given to a tenant under the residential tenancies legislation? Briefly describe the operation of each.

33.19 What is the purpose of the residential tenancies legislation? Do you think that it has achieved its purpose?

33.20 What are typical duties of the landlord under the residential tenancies legislation?

33.21 What are typical duties of the tenant under the residential tenancies legislation?

activebook

Activebook resources include in-depth summaries with links to the relevant part of the book. For revision, add your own notes to the summaries provided by using the note-taking function.

CRITICAL THINKING

33.1 Don Greenthumb is a landscape gardener who has been contracted to install a fishpond and waterfall and five garden statues at Lot 10 Smith Street. He drives down the street and sees a house displaying the number 10 and although no one is home he proceeds to commence work. He excavates a hole to install the fishpond and waterfall and connects them both to the existing water supply and drainage. The pond and waterfall are both concreted into place. The cement statues are artistically arranged around the pond and waterfall but are not concreted into place.

Several days later Don receives a telephone call from a very distressed owner of Lot 10 Smith Street demanding to know when he is going to carry out the work. Don then discovers that he has carried out the work at house number 10 Smith Street and not Lot 10. Don approaches the owner of house number 10 requesting permission to remove the pond, waterfall and statues, but the owner refuses.

Advise Don.

33.2 Wang owned a caravan park at a beachside resort. The caravan park was mortgaged to the Ajax Finance Company. Wang defaulted in the repayment of the loan and the mortgagee decided to exercise the power of sale.

The mortgagee engaged a firm of real estate agents to sell the property by public auction. The agents inserted several advertisements in the local newspaper. Two days before the date of the auction, they inserted an advertisement in one of the major newspapers in the city. However, it was not the edition that regularly features real estate auctions. The auction was conducted and the property sold to the highest bidder.

Wang was dissatisfied with the price obtained at the auction, claiming it was well below the true market value and that if the auction had been better and more widely advertised there would have been a greater likelihood of obtaining the true market value. Wang wants to bring an action against the mortgagee claiming compensation because the power of sale had been exercised without due regard for his rights and interests.

The mortgagee claimed that by selling the property at auction they had satisfied any obligation they owed to Wang and that if the auction did not result in the best possible price being obtained, that was the fault of the agents and not them.

Discuss.

33.3 Bella rented a house from Mica. During a storm one of the roof tiles was blown off the roof. Although some rain entered the house, the water damage was only minor. Bella knew that the tile had been blown off the roof but did not attempt to fix it because she was afraid of climbing onto the roof. As only a small amount of water had entered the house she decided to do nothing further about it. About a month later during a very severe rainstorm a large amount of water entered the house and considerable damage was done to the plaster ceiling and walls.

Bella has contacted the agent for the landlord insisting that the damage be repaired at the landlord's expense. Discuss.

33.4 Gai received permission from a local farmer to keep her horse in a paddock that the farmer owned but was not using. In return she paid him $20 per week. On weekends Gai would groom the horse and exercise it in the paddock. On a particular weekend when she went to the paddock to attend to her horse, Gai found a bull and two other horses in the paddock. Gai was most upset and immediately went to the farmer, demanding that the new animals be removed from the paddock. The farmer said he was allowing a friend to leave the animals in the paddock for a month or two. Gai said he had no right to do that as she rented the paddock and therefore had the exclusive right to possession of the paddock.

Discuss.

34

CHAPTER

Intellectual Property

CHAPTER CONTENTS

activebook

This icon is used throughout the following chapter to remind you to visit the *Business Law* online activebook for additional exercises, links to legal websites, and feedback. For a detailed explanation of what is in the activebook please refer to the inside cover of this textbook. The activebook is available through OneKey.

Where do I start?

Learning path: Use the activebook to complete a pre-chapter warm-up exercise.

There are many definitions of legal terms to assist with your understanding of the material.

34

CHAPTER OBJECTIVES

On completion of this chapter, you should be able to:

- explain the concept behind the protection of intellectual property
- outline the kinds of works and statutory rules relating to copyright
- outline the kinds of works and statutory rules relating to designs
- define a patent and outline the requirements for patentability
- outline the registration process for patents
- define trade marks and outline the operation of the trade marks register
- contrast the actions for passing off, infringement of trade marks and breach of s. 52 of the *Trade Practices Act 1974* (Cth)
- discuss the common law action of breach of confidence
- state the obligation of employees regarding confidential information obtained from their employers.

KEY TERMS

An understanding of the following terms will help you to better understand the material in this chapter:

- **copy:** in the law of copyright refers to the literal copying of a work
- **copyright:** protects works that owe their origin to the expressive efforts of a writer, composer, artist or other creative individual. It gives the individual the exclusive right to copy a particular form of expression of literary, dramatic, musical and artistic work; sound recordings; films; television or radio broadcasts; published editions of works; or computer programs
- **design:** the overall appearance of the **product** resulting from one or more visual features of the product
- **inventive step:** closely associated with the concept of novelty in that it must be something new but need not be totally new. It can consist of taking a known invention and adapting it for a similar but nonetheless different use
- **made:** a literary, dramatic, musical or artistic work is considered to be made when the work is first reduced to writing or some other material form. The Act gives no protection to unpublished works not made
- **passing off:** arises where a person attempts to 'pass off' or pretend that their goods are those of another person. It is part of the law of torts
- **patentable invention:** an invention which is a manner of manufacture, novel and involving an inventive step; is useful and was not secretly used in Australia before the priority date, by or with the authority of the patentee or his or her predecessor in title
- **product:** a thing that is manufactured or hand made or a component part of a complex product may be a product for the purposes of the *Designs Act* if it is made separately from the product
- **published:** a literary, dramatic, musical or artistic work will be published only if copies of the work have been supplied to the public
- **trade mark:** a sign used or intended to be used to distinguish goods or services dealt with or provided in the course of the trade by one person from goods or services so dealt with or provided by another person.

what if . . .

You wrote and recorded a new song, or invented a better computer or designed an eye-catching trade mark, in what way are your efforts of real value to you? Is the value in the actual physical item or is it in some other rights? If it is in some other rights, what are those rights and how can you protect them?

What is the distinction between intellectual property and other forms of property? A carpenter might go to a timber yard and purchase some timber. The timber would be the carpenter's personal property and, because it can be touched, it is tangible property.

The carpenter could then take the timber and, using manual skills, turn it into something completely different—for example, a table and chairs. The carpenter still has the same personal property rights; however, they exist in a different and more useful form. If someone tried to interfere with the carpenter's rights to the table and chairs—for instance, by stealing them—the law provides a means for the carpenter to protect those rights.

The law relating to intellectual property is a recognition that, just as in the above example of turning raw timber into a table and chairs, intellectual or mental processes can produce something that is both valuable and useful. However, unlike the example of the carpenter there is no tangible raw material, and the property produced is therefore intangible.

Although this intangible property will be recorded in some physical, tangible form, the law of intellectual property recognises the distinction between the right to exploit this intangible property and the rights relating to the item which give the intellectual property its physical form.

For example, an author writes a novel and has it printed and published as a book, copies of which are sold to the public. The person who buys a copy of the book buys the physical item and the right to deal with that copy of the book, more or less as they feel fit. However, the purchaser does not buy the intangible property: the right to exploit the intellectual processes by making copies of the book. **This right to copy—copyright—belongs to the author.** Similarly, the law provides protection for the intellectual processes that result in the invention of a new product, an industrial design and a trade mark.

This area of law is also known as the **law of industrial property**. Patents, trade marks and industrial designs were once considered distinct from copyright because they all have a clear and direct connection with trade and commerce. In contrast, copyright relates to such things as literary, musical and artistic works, which may not necessarily relate to trade and commerce. It is usual to refer to this whole area of property rights as intellectual property (see Figure 34.1).

This chapter looks at the main areas of intellectual property—copyright, designs, patents and trade marks and the defences available to those who hold registered intellectual/industrial property rights.

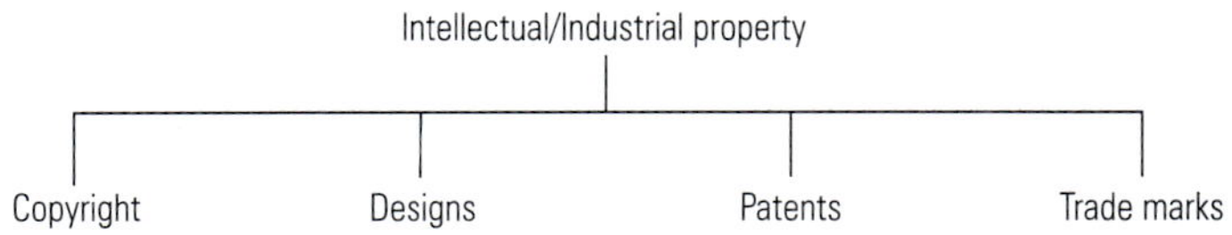

FIGURE 34.1 *Types of intellectual/industrial property*

COPYRIGHT

What is copyright?

Copyright protects works that owe their origin to the expressive efforts of a writer, composer, artist or other creative individual. It gives the individual **the exclusive right to copy** a particular form of expression of:

- literary
- dramatic
- musical or
- artistic work.

It has been extended by virtue of the *Copyright Act 1968* (Cth) to cover:

- sound recordings
- films
- television
- radio broadcasts
- published editions of works
- computer programs.

Section 31 of the *Copyright Act* defines the nature of copyright in original works as the exclusive right:

> *(a) in the case of a literary, dramatic or musical work, to do all or any of the following acts:*
> *(i) to reproduce the work in a material form;*
> *(ii) to publish the work;*
> *(iii) to perform the work in public;*
> *(iv) to broadcast the work;*
> *(v) to cause the work to be transmitted to subscribers to a diffusion service;*
> *(vi) to make an adaptation of the work.*

Section 31 gives similar rights in respect to an artistic work, with the exception of the right to perform the work in public and the right to make an adaptation of the work, neither of which are appropriate to an artistic work.

As far as the *Copyright Act* is concerned, 'literary work' is not confined to a work of literature such as a novel or a poem. It includes a table or compilation, expressed in words, figures or symbols (whether or not in a visible form), and computer programs and the compilation of them.

Literary works must be in a material form that can be perceived by the senses and this involves some form of writing, regardless of the literary quality and/or style.

> **CAUTION NOTE**
> *Literary works involve some form of writing but can include computer programs and their compilation.*

***COMPUTER EDGE PTY LTD V. APPLE COMPUTER INC.* (1986) 161 CLR 171**

Computer Edge imported a computer to compete with the Apple II computer. Apple Computer claimed that copies of its programs were used in the chips of the imported computer and brought an action against Computer Edge for breach of copyright.

ISSUE: What constitutes 'material form'?

DECISION: The High Court held that the object codes in the silicon chips were not literary works because the electrical impulses or circuits in the chips were not in a material form which could be perceived by the senses. However, the written source codes were original literary works and could be protected by copyright.

COMMENT: The *Copyright Act* was subsequently amended to give copyright protection to computer programs. This case is still relevant to the concept of 'material form'.

Other types of copyright

Digital agenda

The *Copyright Amendment (Digital Agenda) Act 2000* is aimed at new electronic technology, particularly the Internet, which enables material to be manipulated and distributed in ways not previously covered by legislation. The Act creates a right to communicate a work which means to make available or electronically transmit a work or other material.

Circuits layout

Circuits layout protected by *Circuits Layout Act 1989* (Cth)

A development of this area of law is the *Circuits Layout Act 1989* (Cth), which gives protection similar to copyright and patent rights in respect to original circuit layouts for integrated circuits. These rights are **Electronic Layout (EL) rights**.

The person who first makes an eligible layout is the owner unless he or she did so as an employee, in which case the owner is the employer. The owner of EL rights has the exclusive right to copy, manufacture or to exploit the layout commercially in Australia. EL rights have a duration of 10 years from the year the layout was made or, if commercially exploited within that 10 years, 10 years from the year it was first commercially exploited.

Dramatic works

Dramatic work involves a performance which need not necessarily be dramatic acting. The *Copyright Act* extends the definition to include a choreographic show (dancing) as well as the scenario or script for a film.

Musical works

Although musical work is not defined by the Act, it covers the lyrics of songs as well as the music.

The Act also provides for a compulsory licence for the production of recordings of musical works. This means that once a composer has agreed to the recording of their musical work, the composer is deemed to have consented to anyone else making a recording of the same musical work.

While the composer owns the rights to the work, the composer cannot prevent another performer recording their own performance of the work, or prevent a cover version. Although the composer is forced to consent to these cover versions, the composer is still entitled to royalties on the cover versions.

Artistic works

These include:

- a painting
- a sculpture
- a drawing
- an engraving
- a photograph
- a building or model of a building
- any other work of artistic craftsmanship.

Although the definition is of artistic work, the section specifically excludes artistic quality as a requirement. It does not have to be 'good' art.

What is originality?

Copyright exists in original works

Copyright exists in **original** works. If the work is the result of the author's own efforts and is not copied from someone else, it will be original as far as the Act is concerned. The literary or artistic merit of the work is not taken into consideration, and quality is irrelevant. It need not be unique in concept.

It can therefore be seen that two or more authors may come up with the same idea at the same time. As long as none of them copied from any of the others, each author will have copyright in their own work and none will infringe the copyright of the others.

Copyright applies to the expression of an idea

Copyright applies to the **expression** of an idea, not the idea itself and belongs to the person who gives form to the idea.

DONOGHUE V. ALLIED NEWSPAPERS [1938] CH 106

A newspaper reporter interviewed a well-known jockey regarding his racing experiences and subsequently published articles in his newspaper with the jockey's consent. Several years later the journalist wanted to publish an abridged version of the articles in another publication.

The jockey objected and sought an injunction on the basis that he owned the story.

ISSUE: Is the copyright in the idea or the finished work?

DECISION: In the course of his judgement *Farwell* J said:

> *A person may have a brilliant idea for a story, or for a picture, or for a play, and one that appears to him to be original. However, if that idea is told to an author or an artist who produces a work based on that idea the copyright belongs to the author or artist who converted the idea into a finished work. The owner of the idea has no rights in the finished work.*

The word 'copy' in the law of copyright refers to the literal copying of a work. As a result, altered versions of an original are not infringements of copyright so information set out in a different way is not a breach of copyright.

JOHN FAIRFAX AND SONS PTY LTD V. CONSOLIDATED PRESS LTD [1960] SR (NSW) 413

The *Sydney Morning Herald* published birth and death notices and was a noted source for this type of information. The *Daily Telegraph*, another Sydney morning newspaper, wanted to expand into this area and obtained the early editions of the *SMH* and published copies of their birth and death notices in its (the *Telegraph*'s) subsequent editions.

The *SMH* obtained an injunction preventing the *Daily Telegraph* from copying these notices. The *Daily Telegraph* continued to publish notices based on the information published in the *SMH*, however, they were set out in a different way and were no longer direct copies of the *SMH* notices.

ISSUE: Is the copyright in the information or the way it is presented?

DECISION: The NSW Supreme Court held the *SMH* held the copyright in the form or arrangement in which the notices appeared in the newspaper but it did not have any copyright in the information contained in the notices. There was no breach of the injunction.

What is publication?

There is no requirement under the *Copyright Act* to register copyright. It comes into existence upon publication of the work.

A literary, dramatic, musical or artistic work will be published only if copies of the work have been **supplied to the public**.

Copyright exists in a published original if the **first publication** of the work (made available to the public) was **in Australia** or if the author was an Australian citizen, protected person or resident (a qualified person).

Copyright will also exist in unpublished works if the author was a 'qualified person' at the time the work was made.

> **!** CAUTION NOTE
> *Copyright can exist in both published and unpublished works.*

When is a 'work' made?

A literary, dramatic, musical or artistic work is considered to be made when the work is first reduced to writing or some other material form. The Act gives no protection to unpublished works not made.

Copyright in things other than works

Copyright extends beyond literary works

In addition to granting copyright to the author of literary, dramatic, artistic and musical works, the *Copyright Act* also creates copyright in sound recordings, cinematographic films, television and sound broadcasts, and published editions of works (as distinct from the copyright in the work itself).

IN BRIEF

Some key points on copyright

- Copyright belongs to the person who converts an idea into a finished work.
- The same information set out in a different way is not a breach of copyright.
- Literary, dramatic, musical or artistic works are made when they are first reduced to writing or some material form.

Who is the owner?

Owner of copyright is the author unless the work is produced in the course of employment

Section 35 of the *Copyright Act* provides that the author of a literary, dramatic, musical or artistic work is the owner of any copyright in the work. Where the work is made in the course of the author's employment by a newspaper, magazine or similar publication, the owner of the publication owns the copyright in respect of the publication in any newspaper, magazine or similar periodical and the broadcasting of the work. However, the author retains the copyright in all other respects, such as the publication of the work as a book.

Where a person makes an agreement for valuable consideration to take a photograph, paint or draw a portrait, or make an engraving for another person, the person for whom the photograph, painting or engraving is made is the owner of the work. If the work was made for a specific purpose, the person for whom the work was made has the copyright for the specific purpose, but the person who made the work has the copyright for all other purposes. Similar provisions apply to the ownership of the copyright in sound recordings and films.

With respect to television and sound broadcasts, the owner of the copyright is the person who holds the licence or permit under the *Broadcasting Act 1942* (Cth) under which the broadcast was made. The Australian Broadcasting Corporation and the Special Broadcasting Service Corporation own the copyright in any television or sound broadcast made by them.

HOW LONG DOES THE COPYRIGHT LAST?

Copyright in artistic works lasts for 70 years after the year in which the work was made

Copyright in literary, dramatic and musical works lasts for 70 years after the calendar year in which the author died. However, if the work has not been published, performed in public or offered for sale to the public before the author dies, the copyright will continue to last for 70 years after the end of the calendar year in which it was first published.

Where there are two or more authors and the duration of the copyright is dependent on the life of the authors, the copyright will last for 70 years after the death of the last surviving author.

In the case of artistic works, copyright lasts for 70 years after the end of the calendar year in which the work is made, regardless of publication. Similarly, the copyright in sound recordings, cinematographic films, television and sound recordings, and published editions of works lasts for 70 years.

What constitutes an infringement?

Infringement: reproduction of work that is subject to copyright without owner's permission

An infringement of copyright occurs if a person **reproduces** in a material form, the whole (or even part) of a literary, dramatic, musical or artistic work that is subject to copyright, **without the consent of the owner**: s. 36(1).

In respect to musical works that have been reduced to writing or some other material form, such as a demonstration tape, any unauthorised reproduction would be an infringement. This would include a performance of the work in a sound recording by another performer.

Where music is performed without authorisation on a public sound system, such as background music at a shopping mall or a jukebox, the occupier of the premises may be liable for an infringement of the copyright by authorising the performance of the work in public.

When doesn't an unauthorised reproduction constitute an infringement?

There is no infringement if it is authorised by the copyright owner or is in the public interest

A reproduction that might ordinarily constitute an infringement of copyright may not in fact do so if it is authorised by the copyright owner or is in the public interest. The reproduction may also not be an infringement if it involves:

- a small part of the copyright work;
- fair dealing for research and study, or criticism and review;
- public readings of a reasonable length of a published literary or dramatic work where acknowledgment of the copyright is made;
- performance of literary, dramatic or musical works by radio or recording at residential premises for the benefit of residents and their guests;
- copying by libraries and archives for users of the library or archive for the users' research or study or where the copying is for the preservation of the work;
- copying of one or more insignificant portions of literary or dramatic works by educational institutions if the copy is made on the premises for the use of students or staff for the purposes of a course conducted by the institution. The amount copied must not exceed two pages or one per cent of the total number of pages of the work, whichever is the greater;
- drawings or photographs made of sculptures or other works of artistic craftsmanship, including buildings, which are permanently displayed in public; or
- the filming or recording of broadcasts for the private use of the person who made the recording and the recording of a sound or television broadcast for educational purposes by a non-profit educational institution.

It can be seen from the examples listed above that generally reproduction for private use will not breach copyright. However, what constitutes private use and what constitutes public use is a matter to be decided on the particular circumstances and does not relate to a particular number of people. 'Public' includes a portion of the public, no matter how small.

RANK FILM PRODUCTIONS LTD V. COLIN DODDS (TRADING AS TOWN AND COUNTRY MOTEL) **[1983] 2 NSWLR 553**

The *Copyright Act 1968* (Cth) provides that copyright in relation to a cinematographic film is the exclusive right to cause the film to be seen in public. Dodds operated a motel in which guests were able to watch movies in their rooms by means of television sets connected to a central video cassette recorder. Rank Film Productions sued for breach of copyright.

ISSUE: What constitutes 'public'?

DECISION: *Rath* J in the New South Wales Supreme Court held that 'public' includes a portion of the public however small. The court also held that a guest of a motel who pays for accommodation and other benefits, including the viewing of films in the privacy of their motel room, is a member of the copyright owner's public. The copyright had therefore been infringed.

A copy of an audio compact disc will be a non-infringing copy of a sound recording if:

- the recording is of a work that is protected by copyright in Australia;
- the work has been protected by copyright in the country in which the copy is made; and
- no infringement of the foreign copyright has occurred in making the copy.

This means that an Australian retailer could import audio compact discs from a cheaper legitimate source overseas rather than buying from the regular Australian distributor.

The countries in which these legitimate copies may be made are restricted to those countries that are members of the Berne Convention or the World Trade Organisation and have laws on ownership, duration and reproduction of copyright works that are in keeping with the Agreement on Trade Related Aspects of Intellectual Property Rights.

What constitutes fair dealing?

Where the literary, dramatic, musical or artistic work constitutes an article in a periodical publication—that is, an article in a magazine—a dealing with the whole or a part of that work will be a fair dealing for research and study by an individual. In any other case—for instance, a whole book—a fair dealing will involve no more than a reasonable portion of the work.

Fair dealing involves no more than a reasonable portion of the work

NICHOLS ADVANCED VEHICLE SYSTEMS INC. V. REES **[1979] RPC 127**

The plaintiff designed, constructed and raced racing cars. Several of the plaintiff's staff left to work with the defendant. One of these people took with him copies of some plans for the plaintiff's new car. By using these plans the defendant was able to design and manufacture a new car before the plaintiff could, and thereby obtain a competitive advantage.

ISSUE: Can copying part of a copyrighted work constitute a breach of the copyright?

DECISION: Although the plans were not for the plaintiff's complete car, there was a substantial and flagrant infringement of the plaintiff's copyright. The court ordered the defendant to deliver the infringing copies of the plans to the plaintiff together with those parts of the car made in breach of the copyright drawings. The defendant was also prohibited from driving the car.

A 'reasonable portion' of a work contained in an edition that exceeds 10 pages should not exceed in total 10 per cent of the number of pages in that edition. However, where the work is divided into chapters, the total number of pages may exceed 10 per cent of the total number of pages, providing they cover only the whole or part of a single chapter.

Moral rights

The *Copyright Amendment (Moral Rights) Act 2000* (Cth) gives authors of literary, dramatic, musical or artistic works, and directors and producers of films, rights of attribution and integrity which are referred to as 'moral rights' and are intended to protect the reputation of the authors and the creative integrity of their work.

Attribution

- the right of the author to be identified with their work; and
- the right to prevent others claiming authorship of their work.

Integrity

The right of the author to protect their work from derogatory treatment. Derogatory treatment involves doing anything that is a material alteration, mutilation or distortion of the work, or doing anything else to the work that is prejudicial to the honour and reputation of the author.

Remedies for breach of copyright

The civil remedies for infringement of copyright are as follows:

- **Injunction**

  This restrains the infringement or threatened infringement of the copyright.
- **Damages or an account of profits**

  Damages will be the amount of money that will compensate the author for the loss suffered as a result of the infringement. That is, the fees lost in the unauthorised performance of a musical work or the loss of sales of a book.

The *Copyright Act* deems the copyright owner to be the owner of any infringing copies or of the plates used for their production. That is, the copyright owner owns the intangible property in the copyright work and also the tangible results of the unauthorised infringement of those rights.

Where the court considers there has been a blatant infringement or there are other appropriate circumstances, it may make an order for exemplary damages.

Anton Piller orders

Infringing copies of copyright works and the materials used to manufacture them can be fairly easily destroyed or hidden by the defendant and thereby defeat or delay the owner's action for infringement of the copyright. The courts will therefore make an order permitting the plaintiff's representatives to enter premises to search for and remove copies of the work or other material or documents relating to them (see p. 420). In Australia, Anton Piller orders are also used against defendants who are persistent in their breach.

***ANTON PILLER KG V. MANUFACTURING PROCESSES LTD* [1976] CH 55**

The plaintiff was a German company that manufactured computer equipment. The defendant was the plaintiff's agent for the distribution of its products in the United Kingdom. The plaintiff claimed the defendant was supplying confidential information about the plaintiff's products to the plaintiff's rivals in Germany.

The plaintiff applied for an injunction prohibiting infringement of copyright and an order permitting the plaintiff to enter the defendant's premises to look for and inspect all infringing documents and to remove them into the custody of the plaintiff's solicitors.

ISSUE: Can the court order entry to premises and seizure of copyright infringing material?

DECISION: Where the plaintiff had a very strong *prima facie* case and there was a likelihood of serious damage to it and there was clear evidence the defendant possessed material that might be destroyed or disposed of, the court could order the defendant to permit the plaintiff to enter the defendant's premises and remove relevant material.

DESIGNS

What are designs?

Design relates to the appearance of an article

In order to understand what a 'design' is under the *Designs Act 2003* (Cth) it is necessary to examine the meaning of three expressions used in the Act: 'Design', 'Product' and 'Visual feature'.

Section 5 defines **design**, in relation to a product, as meaning the **overall appearance of the product** resulting from one or more **visual features** of the product.

Section 6 defines a **product**:

1 As a thing that is manufactured or hand made.
2 A component part of a complex product may be a product for the purposes of this Act, if it is made separately from the product.
3 A thing that has one or more indefinite dimensions is only a product for the purposes of this Act if any one or more of the following applies to the thing:
   (a) a cross-section taken across any indefinite dimension is fixed or varies according to a regular pattern;
   (b) all the dimensions remain in proportion;
   (c) the cross-sectional shape remains the same throughout, whether or not the dimensions of that shape vary according to a ratio or series of ratios;
   (d) it has a pattern or ornamentation that repeats itself.
4 A kit which, when assembled, is a particular product is taken to be that product (the unassembled kit is taken to be the assembled item).

Section 7 defines a **visual feature** as:

1 Including the shape, configuration, pattern and ornamentation of the product.
2 A visual feature may, but need not, serve a functional purpose.
3 The following are not visual features of a product:
   (a) the feel of the product;
   (b) the materials used in the product;
   (c) in the case of a product that has one or more indefinite dimensions:
      (i) the indefinite dimension; and
      (ii) if the product also has a pattern that repeats itself—more than one repeat of the pattern.

'Design' therefore relates to the appearance of the article and not to the article itself.

A product is an object of manufacture

A 'product' is an object of manufacture and includes any part of that object if manufactured separately. A product can therefore be the body of a car, which would be an object of manufacture, and could also be the door handle or radiator grille for the same car body, if made separately. The design of the car body or radiator grille is not the body or grille itself but the intangible artistic concept which makes it different from other car bodies or grilles.

Designs are also known as industrial designs because they are used for some industrial purpose, usually to make a particular manufacturer's products identifiable with that manufacturer and readily distinguishable from those of its competitors.

Conflicts between copyright and designs

The artistic nature of some designs enables them to be protected under both the *Designs Act* and the *Copyright Act*. An example of such a design could be the cover of a music CD. It could be registered under the *Designs Act* due to its pattern or ornamentation and the industrial purpose to which it will be put, and could also be protected by the *Copyright Act* due to its nature as an artistic work.

Since design relates to a shape, pattern or ornamentation as applied to an article and not the article itself, it is quite possible that there could be situations where an artistic work protected by the *Copyright Act* could also be applied to an article so as to become a design for the purposes of the *Designs Act*. A sculptor might create an abstract artistic work in the form of a wheel-like cylinder. A manufacturer might then use that artistic work as the basis for a new line of alloy car wheels. Designs could be said to be artistic works given an industrial application.

In such situations, problems will arise because the *Copyright Act* and the *Designs Act* create different rights and protect them in different ways:

> **!** CAUTION NOTE
> *Artistic nature of some designs enables them to be protected under both the* Designs *and* Copyright Acts.

IN BRIEF

Comparison of infringements under *Copyright* and *Designs Acts*

Copyright Act	*Designs Act*
There is an infringement of the Act if a person: ▪ reproduces the work in a material way; ▪ publishes the work; ▪ includes the work in a television broadcast; or ▪ causes a television program that includes the work to be transmitted to subscribers to a diffusion service.	An infringement occurs if a person without authority: ▪ applies the design to any article in respect of which the design applies; ▪ imports for sale an article to which the design has been applied; or ▪ sells or hires any article to which the design has been applied without authority.

The *Copyright Act* gives protection for the duration of the author's life plus 50 years and does not require registration of the artistic work. The *Designs Act* gives protection for a maximum of 10 years from the date of filing for registration. Registration is obviously essential in obtaining protection.

This conflict is resolved by the provisions of the *Coyprigbt Act* relating to 'corresponding designs'. Section 74 provides that a corresponding design is a design that is a particular shape, pattern or ornamentation which, when applied to an article, results in a reproduction of an artistic work.

Corresponding designs are three-dimensional items only

Section 75 specifically excludes a design consisting of a two-dimensional (length and breadth) pattern or ornament applicable to the surface of an article. Corresponding designs are concerned with three-dimensional items only (length, breadth and depth). It can therefore be seen that a painting that was reproduced on a CD cover would not fall within the definition of a corresponding design and would therefore be protected by the *Copyright Act*. In contrast, the above sculpture of the wheel-like cylinder, when applied to an alloy car wheel, would be a corresponding design. Where copyright exists in an artistic work and a corresponding design is registered under the *Designs Act*, it is not an infringement of copyright to apply the corresponding design to an article. It can therefore be seen that registration of a design under the *Designs Act* takes priority over the *Copyright Act* rights given to the same design as an artistic work.

With respect to a corresponding design that has been registered under the *Designs Act* by someone who is not the true owner of the design, and that registration was without the knowledge of the copyright owner, the design shall be deemed never to have been registered. The *Copyright Act* would then apply, making the person who registered the design liable for infringement of copyright.

activebook

To help you to remember and understand the topics covered so far, and for links to legal websites, refer to your online activebook. Model answers provide feedback to problems and exercises.

How is registration obtained?

Every application will be checked to ensure compliance with the statutory formalities, however, detailed examination will only be undertaken when requested. It is expected that such a request would come from a person who challenges the validity of the registration. This new procedure of not conducting an examination of the design should make the registration process quicker and less expensive.

To be registered the design will have to be 'new' and 'distinctive'. 'New' means not identical to designs previously used in public in Australia or previously published in Australia or anywhere else in the world. 'Distinctive' means not substantially similar in overall impression to a design previously used in Australia or published in Australia or anywhere else in the world.

Duration of protection

The maximum period for registration protection is 10 years from the date of filing for registration.

Who is entitled to be registered as the owner of a design?

Section 13 provides that the following persons may be registered as the owner of a design that has not yet been registered:

(a) the person who created the design (the *designer*);
(b) if the designer created the design in the course of employment, or under a contract, with another person—the other person, unless the designer and the other person have agreed to the contrary;
(c) a person who derives title to the design from a person mentioned in paragraph (a) or (b), or by devolution by will or by operation of law;
(d) a person who would, on registration of the design, be entitled to have the exclusive rights in the design assigned to the person; or
(e) the legal personal representative of a deceased person mentioned in paragraph (a), (b), (c) or (d).

Exclusive rights of registered owners

Section 10 provides that the registered owner of a registered design has the exclusive right, during the term of registration of the design:

(a) to make or offer to make a product, in relation to which the design is registered, which embodies the design; and
(b) to import such a product into Australia for sale, or for use for the purposes of any trade or business; and
(c) to sell, hire or otherwise dispose of, or offer to sell, hire or otherwise dispose of, such a product; and
(d) to use such a product in any way for the purposes of any trade or business; and
(e) to keep such a product for the purpose of doing any of the things mentioned in paragraph (c) or (d); and
(f) to authorise another person to do any of the things mentioned in paragraph (a), (b), (c), (d) or (e).

These exclusive rights are personal property and are capable of assignment and of devolution by will or by operation of law.

Infringement

A registered design will be infringed if the 'infringing' design is substantially similar in **overall impression** to the registered design. In determining whether or not a design is infringed, regard will be had to the **similarities** between the designs rather than the **differences**. The courts will also be required to look at the design through the eyes of those people who ordinarily deal with such products.

After market spare parts—s. 72

Component parts of a complex product, for example, a muffler on a car, may be registered as a design and the parts will not be able to be manufactured by a third party (someone who acts without the authorisation of the registered owner), for incorporation in a new product (the new car in the example given). However, the third party may manufacture the component part for spare parts to repair existing machinery (for example, to repair an existing car). Manufacturing a registered design as a spare part is not an infringement of the registered design.

PATENTS

What are patents?

Inventions can be patented

Inventions can be protected under the *Patents Act 1990* (Cth). A patentable invention is an invention which:

- is a manner of manufacture;
- is novel and involves an inventive step;
- is useful; and
- was not secretly used in Australia before the priority date, by or with the authority of the patentee or his or her predecessor in title.

'Manner of manufacture' covers both a new product or substance, or a machine or process that can be used for making something. It is essential that it be used or is capable of being used in commerce or trade. As a result, not every useful invention will be a patentable invention.

What is meant by 'novel'?

'Novel'—something that has not been used previously or known publicly

'Novel' means that the invention must be something that has not been used previously or known publicly. The Act refers to this pool of existing technical information as the prior art base.

For the purposes of patentability, the prior art base consists of any disclosures made publicly available in documentary or some other recorded form anywhere in the world. However, where the invention is disclosed orally or by the doing of an act, the disclosure will only form part of the prior art base if it took place in Australia.

What is meant by 'inventive step'?

> **!** CAUTION NOTE
>
> *Inventive step—something new, not merely an improvement.*

'Inventive step' is closely associated with the concept of novelty in that it must be something new but need not be totally new. It can consist of taking a known invention and adapting it to a similar but nonetheless different use—for example, the use of the telephone and its basic technology in the facsimile machine.

It could also mean taking an existing invention and applying it in a completely different field—for example, the use of a laser beam in communications and the use of a laser beam in medicine for surgery.

An invention will not involve an inventive step if it would have been obvious to a person skilled in the particular field after they had considered the common general knowledge existing before the priority date of the claim for a new patent. It can therefore be seen that the inventive step must involve the use of a person's inventive intellectual abilities.

What is meant by 'useful'?

'Useful' means it must be capable of being used in a practical way and must be marketable as such. As a result, mere ideas and theories are not patentable.

An invention sold prior to applying for a patent is not patentable

What is meant by 'not secretly used'?

If an inventor manufactures and sells the invention prior to applying for a patent, the invention will have become part of the prior art base and therefore it will not be patentable.

IN BRIEF

Key points to note about patents

- A patentable invention is:
  - a new product or substance; or
  - a machine or process that can be used for making something.
- It must be capable of being used in commerce or trade.
- It must be new.
- It must involve an inventive step.
- It must be useful.
- It must not be 'secretly' used.

Innovation patent

Innovation patent—simple and quick process

The *Patents Act 1990* (Cth) has been amended to create a new patent right called an innovation patent. The innovation patent replaces the petty patent. The aim of the innovation patent is to provide a quick and relatively inexpensive means to protect lower level inventions.

To be eligible for protection as an innovation patent, the innovation must be new, that is, it must not have been publicly disclosed by the applicant or form part of the prior art base. The prior art base is any disclosures made publicly available in documentary or other recorded form anywhere in the world, in other words it is the technological, scientific and methodology pool upon which existing patentable inventions are based.

Previously, an applicant for a patent was required to show an **inventive step**, that is, the invention must involve something new and not merely be an improvement. While this requirement must still be satisfied for a standard patent, an innovation patent merely requires an **innovative step**. For the invention to represent an innovative step it must involve new knowledge and that new knowledge must represent a substantial contribution to the working of the invention. The concept of substantial contribution represents a much lower degree of inventiveness than is the case with a standard patent where the invention must be new and not obvious to a person skilled in the relevant field.

While standard patents involve a detailed and lengthy examination process an innovation patent can be granted without examination. Because a thorough examination of the invention is very time consuming, the new procedure of granting an innovation patent without a detailed examination should make the process quick and comparatively cheap. However, it is also likely that many innovation patents may subsequently be found to be invalid and not enforceable. Although a person may hold an innovation patent they cannot commence infringement proceedings until the patent has been certified by the Australian Patent Office following an examination.

An innovation patent lasts eight years compared with 20 years for a standard patent, however, technology changes so rapidly eight years may in fact exceed the useful life of the new invention.

What is the method of obtaining a patent?

The applicant for a patent must file an application, details of which are published in the *Official Journal*. When submitting the application, particulars of the patent and its practical use are outlined. A search is then performed to check originality.

After a formal examination of the patent, it is accepted and the complete specification is requested. Acceptance is advertised in the *Australian Official Journal of Patents*, and if there is no opposition, the patent is granted (sealed) and entered in the register. The letters patent are sent to the patentee.

> **!** CAUTION NOTE
>
> *Patent applications are complicated and should be completed by a patent attorney.*

What are the remedies for infringement?

The owner of the patent may apply to the court for an injunction to restrain continued infringement of the patent and can also apply for damages or an account of profits. If the defendant can show that at the date of the infringement he or she was not aware of the existence of the patent, the court may refuse to award damages. However, if the patented product was sold or used to a substantial extent in Australia before the date of the infringement and the product was marked to indicate that it had been patented in Australia, the defendant will be deemed to have been aware of the existence of the patent unless the contrary is established.

International registration

The International Convention for the Protection of Industrial Property and the Patent Co-operation Treaty both attempt to provide certain priorities and protection among the countries that are parties to the convention.

While the convention does not attempt to control the patent law of the member countries, it does deal with procedural matters that assist in the process of obtaining the patent. The major feature of this cooperative procedure is provision for an application to have effect in as many countries as the applicant designates. It also provides for international publication of the application and search report.

Cooperation between member nations is primarily related to the registration process. Once the nature of the protection is granted, the question of who owns the rights and the protection of those rights is dependent on the patent laws of the individual country.

TRADE MARKS

Trade mark is a distinctive identification mark or symbol

A person carrying on business manufacturing or selling goods or providing services may want to show that there is a connection between themselves and the goods. The usual way of indicating this connection is the use of a distinctive identification mark or symbol. As the trader's reputation grows, the identifying mark becomes important in the establishment of the business goodwill. Every time a person sees the mark, they consciously or subconsciously make the connection between the product and the producer.

The common law recognised the worth of the identifying mark to the producer/supplier of goods and the potential damage to their reputation and goodwill if the mark was used without the particular producer's consent. The tortious action of passing off was developed. Passing off arises where a person attempts to 'pass off' or pretend that their goods are those of another person (see p. 757).

In Australia, the tort of passing off still exists; however, the *Trade Marks Act 1995* (Cth) provides statutory protection for the owners of trade marks.

The *Trade Marks Act 1995* (Cth) defines a trade mark as a sign used or intended to be used to distinguish goods or services dealt with or provided in the course of the trade by one person from goods or services so dealt with or provided by another person. The Act defines the term 'sign' as including the following or any combination of the following: letter, word, name, signature, numeral, device, brand, heading, label, ticket, aspect of packaging, shape, colour or scent.

The guidelines for registering a colour as a trade mark were considered in *BP p.l.c. v. Wooolworths Limited.*

BP P.L.C. V. WOOLWORTHS LIMITED [2004] FCA 1362,

BP made an application to trademark the colour green in relation to petrol sales, but was refused by the Registrar of Trade Marks. Woolworths opposed the registration, because it wanted to be able to use green as part of its own plans to sell petrol.

ISSUE: Can a colour be registered as a trade mark?

DECISION: *Finkelstein* J of the Federal Court of Australia held that:

> . . . for BP to succeed in its appeals it must establish two things: first, that it has used the particular shade of green as a trade mark and, second, that in the minds of the public the primary significance of that shade of green, when used in connection with the supply of petroleum products or the provision of petroleum services, identifies the source of those goods or the provider of those services as originating from a particular trader, though not necessarily from an identified trader.
>
> So far as BP is concerned, there is simply no doubt in my mind that its get up, with its predominant use of green, is a badge of origin. Not only do consumers know that a predominantly green (in a particular shade) service station signifies a source, for the most part they also know that source to be BP.

As a result of amendments to the World Intellectual Property Organisation's *Tradmark Law Treaty,* sounds and scents will also be able to be protected as trademarks.

How is the trade mark protected?

Registration is necessary for statutory protection

In order to obtain the statutory protection of the *Trade Marks Act*, the trade mark must be registered. If the trade mark is unregistered, the owner may still obtain protection, but it will be by virtue of the common law action of 'passing off'.

On 11 July 2001, Australia became a member of the Madrid Protocol with the result that international trade mark applications can now be filed with the Australian Trade Marks Office. An international trade mark application is a single application which seeks trade mark protection in Australia and other countries which are members of the Madrid Protocol.

Advantages are:

- single application therefore less paperwork;
- the application is in English; and
- the costs are reduced.

The procedure:

- The application must be based on an existing Australian trade mark.
- After receipt of the application the Australian Trade Marks Office forwards it to the International Bureau.
- The International Bureau forwards the application to the trade marks office in each member country in which registration is sought.
- The application is then processed according to the trade mark laws of that country.
- If the application is rejected by a member country it will not receive protection in that country. However, the rejection by one country does not invalidate it in other member countries.

Registration

The Act defines several distinct types of trade mark that may be registered.

- Trade marks generally
- Collective trade marks
- Certification trade marks
- Defensive trade marks.

General considerations

When submitting a trade mark for registration, the following matters must be considered:

- A mark must distinguish the goods or services of the applicant from the goods and services of others.
- An application for the registration of a trade mark must be rejected if the trade mark is not capable of distinguishing the applicant's goods or services from the goods or services of other persons.

- Trade marks that are not inherently able to distinguish goods or services usually consist wholly of a sign that is ordinarily used to indicate the:
  - kind
  - quality
  - quantity
  - intended purpose
  - value
  - geographical origin, or

  some other characteristic of the goods or services, or their time of production.
- A trade mark must be rejected if it contains scandalous matter or its use would be contrary to law, or if it is likely to deceive or cause confusion.
- As stated above, a mark cannot be registered as a trade mark, if it is a direct reference to a characteristic or quality.

***SAMUEL TAYLOR V. REGISTRAR OF TRADE MARKS* (1959) 102 CLR 650**

Samuel Taylor applied for the registration of a trade mark that incorporated the words 'Pressure Pak'. The Registrar of Trade Marks refused to register the application unless the applicant endorsed the application with a disclaimer that registration would not give them the exclusive right to use the words 'Pressure Pak'. The applicant refused and appealed.

ISSUE: Can a direct reference to some characteristic or quality be registered?

DECISION: The High Court held that the words 'Pressure Pak' indicated that the contents of the container were held under pressure and would be ejected when the valve was opened. This was a direct reference to some character or quality of the contents of the container and therefore could not be registered unless the applicant agreed to disclaim the exclusive right to use the words.

Collective trade marks

These apply to a sign used in relation to the goods or services of members of an association to distinguish those goods or services from those of persons who are not members of the association.

Certification trade marks

These apply to goods or services that are certified by a person or organisation with respect to quality, accuracy or another characteristic. The purpose of the mark is not to establish a connection between the product and the producer, but rather, between the product and some special quality (e.g., goods bearing the Australian Standards Association mark to indicate quality and accuracy).

Before registering a certification mark, the registrar must consider whether the applicant for registration is competent to certify the goods or services, whether the rules regarding the use of the mark are acceptable under the Act, and whether registration would be in the public interest.

Defensive trade marks

As previously stated, trade marks are registered for use in connection with the particular type of goods or services specified in the application for registration. The trade mark is not registered for any and every type of good or service. However, where a trade mark has been used so extensively that its use in relation to other goods or services could be taken as indicating a connection between the registered proprietor of the mark and the other goods or services, the registered proprietor of the mark may apply for a defensive trade mark in respect of the other goods or services, even if there is no intention to use it in relation to those other goods or services. To defend a well-established trade mark an injunction may be granted to prevent its use for other products.

***EASTMAN PHOTOGRAPHIC MATERIALS CO. LTD V. JOHN GRIFFITHS CYCLE CORP. LTD AND KODAK CYCLE CO. LTD, RE TRADE MARK NO. 207006* (1898) 15 RPC 105**

Eastman Photographic are the manufacturers of photographic equipment and the owners of the trade mark Kodak, which was registered with respect to photographic equipment. A bicycle manufacturer marketed its bicycles as 'Kodak Bicycles'.

ISSUE: To defend a well-established trade mark, can an injunction be granted to prevent its use for other products?

DECISION: Eastman Photographic were able to prevent the use of the name Kodak even though the registration did not extend to bicycles.

What constitutes an infringement?

It is an infringement of a registered trade mark when a mark, which is substantially identical or deceptively similar, is used without authorisation in the course of trade in goods or services in respect of which the mark is registered. In deciding whether a mark is deceptively similar to a registered trade mark, the test is the impression it would make on an ordinary member of the public.

The remedies available for an infringement are an injunction and either damages or an account of profits. With respect to the infringement of a certification trade mark, damages or an account of profits are not available.

WHAT IS PASSING OFF?

Common law tort of 'passing off'—deceptive conduct

Independently of the *Trade Marks Act*, protection can be obtained under common law by the tort of passing off, which is intended to protect the reputation of a business or its goodwill. It arises where one business represents its goods or services as those of another business in a way that is likely to injure the reputation or goodwill of that business. The plaintiff must establish that the business has acquired a relevant reputation or goodwill, otherwise there is nothing to protect. The remedy available will be an injunction and, where appropriate, damages. In order to establish the tort, the plaintiff must show that the representation creates a reasonable possibility of the public being misled.

***FRANCESCO CINZANO AND CIA (AUST.) PTY LTD V. RUGGIERO (NO. 2)* (1980) 25 SASR 341**

The plaintiff sold wines and spirits under the brand name 'Cinzano'. The defendant used the name Cinzano for his restaurant without the permission of the plaintiff. The plaintiff applied for an injunction.

ISSUE: Does simply using the brand name or mark of another trader constitute the tort of passing off or is something else required?

DECISION: The South Australian Supreme Court held that owing to the substantial difference in the nature of the two businesses there was no reasonable possibility of the public being deceived into thinking there was a connection between the two, so the injunction was refused.

In view of modern advertising and promotional techniques, slogans and visual images, which may be deceptive, can now be covered by the tort of passing off. However, these aspects of the product will only be protected if the court is satisfied that they are distinctive enough to be identified with the product of the plaintiff.

CADBURY SCHWEPPES P/L V. PUB SQUASH CO LTD **(1981) 32 ALR 387**

Pub Squash marketed a soft drink that was similar to Solo, which was produced by Cadbury Schweppes. Pub Squash used a can that had a label of similar colour and style to that used by Cadbury Schweppes for Solo. It also used similar ideas in advertising.

ISSUE: Are advertising and promotional techniques protected by the tort of passing off?

DECISION: The Privy Council held that the similarity between the promotion of the two products was not sufficient to confuse or mislead the consuming public.

TRADE PRACTICES ACT 1974 (CTH)—UNFAIR PRACTICES

The *Trade Practices Act* can also give protection for both registered and unregistered trade marks. Section 52 prohibits a company in trade or commerce from engaging in conduct that is misleading or deceptive or is likely to mislead or deceive. Again it is the impression the conduct will have on the public that is relevant (see p. 482).

Similarly, s. 53 (see pp. 489–493) provides that a corporation in trade or commerce, in connection with the supply of goods or services, should not:

- falsely represent that goods are of a particular standard, quality, value, grade, composition, style or model or have a particular history or previous use;
- falsely represent that services are of a particular standard, quality, value or grade; or
- falsely represent that goods or services have a sponsorship, approval, performance characteristics, accessories, uses or benefits they do not have.

Breach of these provisions can give rise to fines, damages and injunctions.

CONFIDENTIAL INFORMATION

Confidential information can be protected

Although not strictly intellectual property, in recent times the courts in their equitable jurisdiction have shown a readiness to protect confidential information on the basis of breach of confidence.

In *Coco v. AN Clarke (Engineers) Ltd* [1969] RPC 41 *Megarry* J said:

> *[T]his information . . . must have the necessary quality of confidence about it. Secondly, that information must have been imparted in circumstances importing an obligation of confidence. Thirdly, there must be an unauthorised use of that information to the detriment of the party communicating it.*

The courts have not satisfactorily defined what constitutes confidential information. However, it can be broadly categorised as:

- information having a commercial value, such as trade secrets, or commercial, industrial or scientific information that is confidential to a particular business; and
- information having no commercial value, such as personal secrets and public or government secrets, the disclosure of which could cause distress.

Confidential information is not required to be in any material form. Ideas can constitute confidential information.

! CAUTION NOTE

Businesses should take precautions to protect trade secrets by inserting an appropriate restraint clause in an employee's contract of employment.

FRASER V. THAMES TELEVISION LTD **[1983] 2 ALL ER 101**

The plaintiff's idea or concept for a television program was communicated to the defendant orally. There was no written or other documentary synopsis. The defendant argued that because the idea was communicated verbally and in a very general and disjointed form, it did not warrant protection.

ISSUE: Can ideas amount to confidential information?

DECISION: In rejecting the defendant's argument, *Hirst* J said:

> *. . . to succeed in his claim, the plaintiff must establish not only that the occasion of communication was confidential, but also that the content of the idea was clearly identifiable, original, of potential commercial attractiveness and capable of being realised in actuality.*

Contract

A contract may expressly create an obligation of confidence. The courts will also imply such a term in the same circumstances as the equitable obligation of confidence. Persons who stand in a fiduciary relationship to another person are by virtue of the fiduciary duty bound to maintain confidentiality.

Employees are under an obligation to maintain confidentiality

An employee is under an obligation to maintain confidentiality regarding any trade secrets obtained in the course of employment. If an employee removes information recorded in any material form, there is a presumption of breach of confidentiality. The same would be true if the employee memorised the information.

The presumption of breach of confidentiality would be greater if the information was not required by the employee for their particular job.

If the information acquired by the employee is due to the nature of the employee's employment coupled with their own natural skill and aptitude, and less to the special methods and operations of the employer, the information is less likely to be confidential.

In determining whether certain information constitutes confidential information for the purposes of a breach of confidentiality action, the courts would consider the uniqueness of the information, the cost to the employer in obtaining it and the measures the employer took to protect its secrecy.

Third parties

A third party who receives confidential information knowing that the disclosure is not authorised by the original source of the information is bound by the obligation to maintain confidentiality.

Remedies

The usual remedy will be an injunction, although once the information has been made public, an injunction will serve no practical purpose. Alternatively, or in addition to an injunction, the plaintiff may seek damages or an account of profits. The plaintiff may also seek an order for delivery up to the plaintiff or destruction by the court of the subject material.

WEB RESOURCES

For information on copyright in Australia, as well as other intellectual property sites, see:
http://www.ozemail.com.au/~pxc/iplocus/copyright.html

IP Australia see:
www.ipaustralia.gov.au

www.copyright.org.au

Intellectual Property Society of Australia and New Zealand:
www.ipsanz.com.au

REVIEW QUESTIONS

34.1 Define copyright in relation to literary, dramatic and musical works.

34.2 What is the significance of originality and copy in the context of copyright?

34.3 What is the significance of fair dealing with respect to the infringement of copyright?

34.4 Explain the meaning of design under the *Designs Act 1906* (Cth).

34.5 What are the remedies for an infringement of copyright?

34.6 What is a trade mark?

34.7 Define a patent.

34.8 Must a trade mark be registered before it can be used?

34.9 Distinguish between the tort of passing off and an infringement of a registered trade mark.

34.10 What constitutes confidential information?

34.11 Could any provisions of the *Trade Practices Act 1974* (Cth) apply to a situation involving the tort of passing off and/or an infringement of a registered trade mark? Give details.

34.12 Indicate whether each of the following statements is true or false:

	TRUE	FALSE
▪ The type of intellectual property that is not required to be registered for legal protection is copyright	☑	☐
▪ The type of patent most suitable for inventions such as household gadgets and small appliances that have a short commercial life is the petty patent	☐	☑
▪ In respect to published literary dramatic and musical works the copyright lasts for the author's life plus 10 years	☐	☑

CRITICAL THINKING

34.1 A town council commissions an artist to create a sculpture to commemorate the founding of the town. The sculpture, which is erected on permanent display in the town park, has become a major tourist attraction. The sculpture is depicted on postcards and thousands of photographs of the sculpture are taken by tourists each year.

The sculptor wants to prevent the taking of photographs and sale of postcards unless he is paid a royalty. Discuss.

34.2 Each night at 7.30 the Sleepy Haven Motel plays a video of one of the latest release movies. Guests in the motel rooms can view the video by turning on a switch at the back of the television set in their room. The film distribution company has become aware of this service to the motel guests and wishes to take action against the Sleepy Haven Motel.

Discuss.

34.3 Jay Author was holidaying at a quiet coastal fishing village. He became friendly with many of the locals and encouraged them to talk about their adventures of fishing and sailing. He made extensive notes of these stories and when he returned to his home he wrote a book of short stories called 'Tales of the Sea'. Following publication of the book, several of the residents of the village were amazed to see their stories included in the book. The residents request your advice regarding breach of copyright by Jay Author.

Advise the residents.

34.4 Coco had developed an idea for a completely new and novel television game show that would be cheap to produce and have great public appeal. Coco had a private meeting with a television producer and explained the idea in detail to the producer in the hope that the producer would assist Coco in making the idea a television reality. Coco had not put the idea in writing because she was concerned it might fall into the hands of people who would exploit the idea before she could, although she had discussed the idea with a trusted friend before approaching the producer.

Without further reference or credit to Coco the producer packaged the new game and sold it to a major television network. It became an international success.

Advise Coco.

activebook

Activebook resources include in-depth summaries with links to the relevant part of the book. For revision, add your own notes to the summaries provided by using the note-taking function.

EMPLOYMENT

PART TEN

CHAPTER 35 The Work Environment and the Employment Relationship

activebook

This icon is used throughout the following chapter to remind you to visit the *Business Law* online activebook for additional exercises, links to legal websites, and feedback. For a detailed explanation of what is in the activebook please refer to the inside cover of this textbook. The activebook is available through OneKey.

Where do I start?
Learning path: Use the activebook to complete a pre-chapter warm-up exercise.
There are many definitions of legal terms to assist with your understanding of the material.

CHAPTER CONTENTS

CHAPTER OBJECTIVES

On completion of this chapter, you should be able to:

- distinguish between an employee and an independent contractor and understand the reasons behind such a distinction
- explain how a contract of employment may be created
- identify the rights and responsibilities of employers and employees
- provide an overview of the Australian industrial relations system and industrial regulation
- consider human rights-based work regulations
- recognise the role of anti-discrimination legislation in the workplace
- recognise the role of occupational health and safety legislation in the workplace
- recognise the role of workers' compensation legislation in the workplace.

KEY TERMS

An understanding of the following terms will help you to better understand the material in this chapter:

- **Australian Workplace Agreement (AWA):** an agreement between an employer and employee/s of the employer regarding pay and conditions applicable to that particular workplace
- **award:** a binding order made by an industrial tribunal, setting out the rights and obligations of employers and employees who fall under the ambit of the award
- **employee:** works under a contract of employment and personally performs a task or tasks allocated by their employer, as well as being subject to the control and direction of the employer
- **enterprise agreement:** a collective agreement made between unions and employers or employees and employers, usually covering a single business (or a distinct operational or organisational unit within a single business) or a geographically distinct part of a business
- **independent contractor:** works under a contract for service and performs an agreed task for an agreed price and is only subject to limited control and direction of the employer.

what if . . .

You are starting a new business and from time to time you will need to obtain help from other people. What type of legal arrangements would you be likely to use to engage these people? How would you distinguish employees from contractors and what is the significance of the difference?

Australian business organisations provide the context for work and the employment relationship. Over the last 20 years business organisations in Australia have had to respond to many changes in the political, social and economic environments in which they operate. There has been a significant growth in human rights-based work regulations that goes to the very heart of the right of management to make decisions that affect the operation and survival of their organisations. There have also been enormous changes to factors in the work environment that influence the employment relationship. Since changes to industrial relations legislation in 1992, the focus of industrial tribunals and their decisions has moved away from the centralised, highly-regulated national and state coverage to a more decentralised focus on individual organisations and workplaces. We have seen changing workforce structures, changing occupational groups and changes in attitudes to work. These changes have not only been reflected in the internal organisational structure of business organisations, but also in legislation.

This chapter considers the difference between an employee and an independent contractor, how employment is created and the rights and duties that flow between the parties from that relationship, and how human rights-based legislation is impacting on the manager's right to manage and the employment relationship.

INTRODUCTION TO EMPLOYMENT LAW

The Australian industrial relations system, with its highly regulated system of industrial awards and agreements, is the most regulated and centralised system of labour regulation in the world.

There are essentially three tiers of regulation:

- **the common law**;
- **state legislation** (individual industrial relations Acts for each state and territory); and
- **federal legislation**.

As a result, inconsistencies abound. In accordance with s. 109 of the Constitution, Commonwealth law prevails over state legislation to the extent of any inconsistency. This means that a federal award or Certified Workplace Agreement made under the Commonwealth *Workplace Relations Act 1996* overrides any state legislation or award, and any common law rule or agreement that is inconsistent with it or whose terms are less favourable to an employee.

Where legislation is silent on an issue regulating industrial or employment matters, the common law will apply.

The legal rules that govern the employment relationship are numerous and complex, and are constantly changing in response to shifts in Australian values and prevailing political and economic conditions. The current thrust of new legislation, both federal and state, is to increase the ability of the system to cater for individual enterprise needs by emphasising flexibility through, for example, provisions for enterprise bargaining, resulting in certified workplace agreements that operate in a single enterprise or workplace.

Irrespective of ongoing changes, in general terms the employment relationship in Australia is regulated through three tiers of regulation represented by four different streams of rules, shown in Figure 35.1.

The employment contract

Employee or independent contractor?

Common law rules

It is necessary at the outset of any discussion of those involved in an employment relationship to know whether they are employees or independent contractors, or even in some other relationship where a person performs work for another, for example, under a partnership agreement, a bailment or even a tenancy agreement. Each relationship is recognised at law and has its own particular rights and duties, with the result that different consequences flow from the different relationships.

IN BRIEF

Differences between an employee and an independent contractor

Category of person	Description
Employee	Personally performs a task or tasks allocated to them by their employer. Is subject to the control and direction of the employer. **Works under a contract of services.**
Independent contractor	Performs an agreed task for an agreed price. Controls how the task is to be done, the manner it is to be done and the methods and materials used. Must meet the requirements set down by the employer for the completed task. **Works under a contract for service.**

It is not always easy to determine whether the relationship that exists between the parties is that of employer and employee or employer and independent contractor. To try to determine whether a contractual relationship is that of employer and employee, or employer and independent contractor, the courts have developed a number of tests, of which the best known is the control test. Here the courts ask: 'Was the person subject to the employer's orders and directions?' If the answer is 'Yes', the person may be an employee.

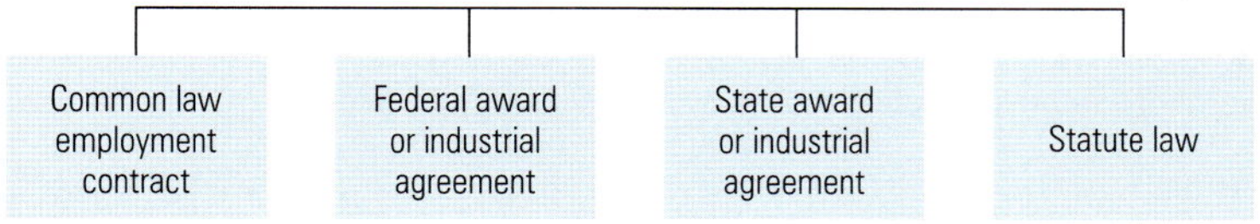

FIGURE 35.1 *Regulation of the employment relationship*

ZUIJS V. WIRTH BROS PTY LTD **(1955) 93 CLR 561**

A trapeze artist in a circus was injured in a fall while performing. The trapeze routine was devised by the injured performer and the other members of the team—the timing and method of performance of the routine was entirely at the discretion of the team of performers.

ISSUE: Does 'control' refer to physical control or the legal right to control?

DECISION: The High Court held that although the employer could not physically control the trapeze artist once the trapeze act had commenced, the employer still had the legal right to direct the trapeze artist. 'Control' refers to the legal right rather than the physical ability to control.

! CAUTION NOTE

There are limitations with the control test today because of the effect of technological change and the ability of the employer to control an employee.

However, the usefulness of this test today is limited because of technological change and the difficulty confronting employers in terms of their capacity to give detailed directions on how a person is to perform their job. In trying to determine whether a person is an employee or an independent contractor, the relationship must be examined in totality.

In 2001 the High Court held in *Hollis v. Vabu* that the proper approach for determining whether a relationship was one of employer and employee, or principal and independent contractor, was to apply what has been described as the 'multi-facet test'. The control test has now been incorporated into the multi-facet test, with control being but one of the relevant factors. The extent to which each factor is relevant will depend upon the particular facts and circumstances of each case but this test requires the court to consider the totality of the relationship between the parties.

STEVENS V. BRODRIBB SAWMILLING CO. PTY LTD (1986) 160 CLR 16

A truck driver who carried logs from a forest to a sawmill was injured due to negligence by the person loading the logs onto the truck. The truck driver claimed compensation for his injuries from the sawmill operator for whom the work was being carried out. The sawmill operator argued that both the truck driver and the person responsible for loading the truck were independent contractors, not employees.

ISSUE: Is 'control' the only factor in deciding whether a person is an employee?

DECISION: The High Court held that the truck driver and loader were independent contractors, the High Court suggested that the relationship between the parties should be examined in its totality. The right to control, rather than the level of actual control, was significant, but not the only relevant factor.

COMMENT: A number of factors are relevant to the existence of an employment relationship including:

- the nature of the task undertaken and the freedom of action given to the parties to perform it;
- who provides the equipment;
- whether the task is ongoing or 'one-off';
- the amount of remuneration, how it is to be paid and whether the employer is deducting income tax and superannuation guarantee;
- the hours of work and provision for holidays and sick leave;
- the method of termination; and, most importantly
- the nature and degree of detailed control the employer has.

HOLLIS V. VABU PTY LTD (2002) 207 CLR 21

While working, a bicycle courier knocked down and injured a member of the public. The injured person sued the courier company for whom the bicycle courier was working on the basis that the bicycle courier was an employee of the courier company and the courier company was vicariously liable for the actions of its employee.

The courier company argued that the bicycle courier was an independent contractor and not its employee and therefore it was not liable for the actions of the bicycle courier.

ISSUE: Was the bicycle courier an employee or an independent contractor?

DECISION: The High Court held that the bicycle courier was an employee.

COMMENT: The High Court examined the working relationship between the courier company and the bicycle courier and found that the bicycle courier:

- did not provide skilled labour or labour which required special qualifications;
- had made a capital outlay consisting of a bicycle and associated tools;
- was required to wear the courier company's uniform;
- was presented to the public as a representative of the courier company;
- had little control over the way in which work was performed:
  - set starting time
  - daily roster
  - could not refuse work;

- was subject to considerable control by the courier company:
  - courier company had control of the allocation and delivery of parcels; and
  - bicycle courier had to deliver parcels in the manner directed by the courier company.

Statutory rules

Over the last few years there has been an increase in legislative activity to extend the category of employee to workers that traditionally had not been considered employees at common law. This has often been done through extending the definition of 'employee' in the definitions section of legislation related to various aspects of the employment relationship.

Examples of legislation where the definition of 'employee' has been widened to catch independent contractors, or specific reference within the Act to incorporate independent contractors, includes, for example:

- **Income tax laws.** The Commonwealth government through the Taxation Office has tightened the rules on who can, and who can't, be treated as an independent contractor for PAYG (Pay-As-You-Go) purposes through changes to the definition of 'salary or wages' in the *Income Tax Assessment Act 1936* (Cth) in an attempt to boost the tax base.
- **Superannuation guarantee laws.** Again, the Commonwealth government has deemed it important that Australian workers have some self-financed financial support for their retirement, rather than relying on the government for a pension. To achieve that end they have deemed a person to be an employee under the *Superannuation Guarantee (Administration) Act 1992* (Cth) as any person whose labour exceeds 50 per cent of the value of the contract.
- **Occupational health and safety laws.** All jurisdictions require independent contractors, and often self-employed workers, to exercise statutory responsibilities in a similar manner to an employer.

IN BRIEF

Reasons for the distinction between employee and independent contractor

Category	Employee	Independent contractor
Workers' compensation	Employers in all jurisdictions must provide workers' compensation coverage for employees.	Expected to provide their own coverage through private insurance.
Torts	An employer is generally vicariously liable for the tortious acts of their employees who injure a third party while they are acting in the course of their employment.	Employers are generally not liable for the torts of an independent contractor.
Contract	May be able to bind an employer in contract, e.g., implied agency such as a shop manager.	Generally does not have the authority to bind an employer.
Tax	Employers liable for payroll tax, compulsory superannuation entitlements, FBT and must deduct income tax through PAYG.	Responsible for paying their own tax.
Leave entitlements	Entitled to statutory or award leave entitlements, e.g., annual leave plus loading, long service leave, statutory holidays, sick leave.	Self-employed so must make allowance for these leave loadings.
Awards	May be covered by an industrial award setting minimum terms and conditions of employment.	Not covered by awards.

Outsourcing

In an effort to cut overheads, it has become a common practice for business to 'downsize', that is, to reduce their workforce and to 'outsource' those jobs. Outsourcing involves the engagement of contract labour as and when needed rather than maintaining a large under-used workforce. This trend has led to the development of 'labour hire agencies'. The client business enters into a normal commercial contract relationship with the labour hire agency which then supplies its employees who work under the direction of the client business. At all times the worker is the employee of the labour hire agency not the client business. The labour hire agency has all the usual obligations to and liability for the employee under both common law and statute law. This obligation extends to obligations under the relevant occupational health and safety legislation, even though the labour hire agency is not in control of the workplace.

In *WorkCover Authority of NSW v. Labour Co-operative Ltd (No. 1)* [2001] NSWIR Comm 223 and *WorkCover Authority of NSW v. Labour Co-operative Ltd (No. 2)* [2002] NSWIR Comm 2, a labour hire agency employee was injured at the factory to which she was sent to work. Her injuries were the result of lack of training and supervision as well as general safety factors at the factory. The New South Wales Industrial Relations Commission fined the labour hire agency $90 000 and $10 000 costs and the owner of the factory was fined $150 000.

Formation of the contract of employment

Employment relationships are specialty contracts which must have all the elements of a contract present to be valid

In Part 3, the principles of contract law were discussed. The employment relationship is no more than a specialty contract dealing with employment, so the common law and statutory principles governing contract law will also apply to the formation of a contract of employment. The elements that are necessary to establish a valid contract, in the context of an employment relationship are as follows.

Intention to create legal relations (see Chapter 12)

Generally there are few problems with intention where contracts of employment are concerned. However, one exception is the voluntary employment agreement where the parties may not intend legal relations. In these types of cases the parties have entered into an agreement but it is clear from the surrounding circumstances that at the time of entering into the agreement, a contract was not intended. For example, because the person is volunteering their services for nominal or no payment: see *Teen Ranch Pty Ltd v. Brown* (1995) 38 AILR ¶5-036 on page 260.

Agreement (see Chapter 13)

If a position is advertised, then it will usually amount to an invitation to treat. However, because of the complexity of negotiations that are often associated with a contract of employment, it can be difficult to ascertain who is the offeror and who is the offeree. In practice, this may not be important unless the parties are negotiating in different states and a dispute arises between them. In that case, if the contract was silent on the point it would be necessary to determine who the offeror and offeree were in order to determine which state's law applied because industrial/workplace relations laws vary between Australian jurisdictions.

Consideration (see Chapter 14)

The employee's promise is the performance of a task while the employer's promise is to pay a wage for the performance of that task. Remember that promises of pay increases based on past performance are unenforceable because they are based on past consideration: see, for example, *Anderson v. Glass* (1869) 5 WW & A'B(L) 152 on page 287.

Capacity (see Chapter 15)

As a general rule, the only time that capacity is going to be an issue is where one of the contracting parties is an infant. A work arrangement with an infant can only be enforced if it is capable of being construed as either a contract for necessaries or a beneficial contract of service. New South Wales and South Australia have statutorily modified the position of the infant and in most states there is legislation regulating the minimum age at which a person can be employed during school hours.

Consent (see Chapter 16)

Like any other contract, the employment contract must be entered into on a voluntary basis. That is, there must be no mistake, misrepresentation, undue influence, duress or pressure that could be said to amount to unconscionable conduct and trigger the operation of Part V, Div. 2 of the *Trade Practices Act 1974* (Cth) or, in the case of New South Wales, the *Contracts Review Act 1980*.

> **!** CAUTION NOTE
>
> *Do the parties intend to create an employment contract or a voluntary agreement which does not create legal obligations?*

Legality (see Chapter 17)

The purpose of the contract of employment must be legal. Care must be taken in cases where an employee has the opportunity to 'structure' their salary package not to contravene income tax laws. Employers may also wish to include restraint of employment clauses in their employee's contract of employment, for example, in relation to confidential information, such as client lists or secret processes. These clauses are enforceable if they are reasonable and in the interests of the parties and the public. However, care still needs to be taken in drafting such clauses because the courts take the view that the parties are usually in an unequal bargaining position and they look at them very closely in determining their validity.

Doing business

Be careful that the job description and the job coincide

Employers should take care to ensure that the job that the employee thinks they are going to perform and the job description coincide. If they don't, the promise by the employer might amount to a misrepresentation and result in a costly breach of contract action for the employer. ■

IMPLIED DUTIES IN THE CONTRACT OF EMPLOYMENT

The employer

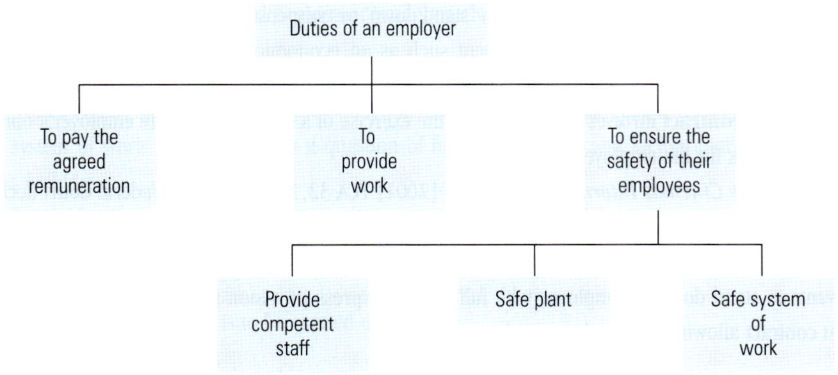

FIGURE 35.2 *Duties of an employer*

No matter how experienced the employee, if the system of work is defective the employer will be liable. However, if the employee in charge has established the system of work as part of their duties and they are injured as a result of the system being unsafe, there is a lower duty of care placed upon the employer.

In addition to the common law, the states and territories have also legislated to regulate working conditions and work processes, for example, all parts of dangerous machinery must be protected and adequately guarded.

The employee

IN BRIEF

Duties of an employee

Obligations during employment:

- a duty to work in a skilful and competent manner;
- a duty to obey the employer's lawful, reasonable and safe commands;
- a duty to maintain confidentiality;
- a duty to hand over inventions made during the course of employment;
- a duty to account for all money or property received in the course of the employment; and
- a duty to disclose information relevant to the employer.

Obligations after employment has ceased:

- a duty to maintain confidentiality; and
- a duty to hand over inventions made during the course of employment.

The major duties and responsibilities of employees can be divided up into two categories: obligations that must be fulfilled during employment and obligations that continue after the employment has ended.

Obligations during employment

A duty to work in a skilful and competent manner

Employee's obligations fall into two categories—during employment and post-employment

An employee owes their employer a duty to perform their work in a skilful and competent manner and to exercise reasonable care. Acceptance of employment in a job requiring a particular skill involves an implied warranty by the employee that they have the skill required and can carry out the task. Acceptance of employment also involves an implied promise to perform that work with reasonable care. See, for example, *Lister v. Romford Ice and Cold Storage Co. Ltd* [1957] AC 555 on page 170.

A duty to obey the employer's lawful, reasonable and safe commands

This supports the right of management (known as 'managerial prerogative') to make decisions about how the business will operate, what work will be carried out, by whom, when (i.e. attendance) and in what manner. The difficulty is in drawing the line between what is a 'fair and reasonable' request from an employer versus what is an industrial right.

Managerial prerogative is also restricted by the existence of industrial awards and agreements, and other special legislation such as anti-discrimination and occupational health and safety law. However, an employee is under a duty to obey all the employer's lawful and reasonable commands. Commands that expose an employee to risk of injury or damage to health can be disregarded.

OTTOMAN BANK LTD V. CHAKARIAN **(1930) AC 277**

An employee who was transferred to a branch in another country refused to go because he feared for his life in that country due to his ethnic heritage.

ISSUE: Are employees entitled to have regard to their own safety?

DECISION: An employee must obey reasonable commands but in the particular circumstances of this case the employee had good reason to fear for his safety.

A duty to maintain confidentiality

If employees become aware of confidential information that is peculiar to their employer or to the activities of their employer, they are under a duty not to disclose such information to business rivals of the employer nor to use the information for their own benefit if the release of that information would be injurious to the employer or of advantage to trade rivals.

A duty to account for all money or property received in the course of employment

An employee must account to their employer for any money or property that they receive (or find) in the discharge of their duties under their employment contract. One exception to the above rule is where it is customary for employees to be given tips—for example, porters or waiters—unless there is an express term in the employment contract to the contrary.

A duty to hand over inventions made during the course of employment

Where an employee makes an invention during the course of their employment, whether specifically as part of their employment or ancillary to it, the beneficial interest in the invention is the property of the employer, and the patents will normally be in the employer's name.

A duty to disclose information relevant to the employer

Three situations can be identified:

- **At prospective employee stage**—a prospective employee is under no obligation to volunteer information about their past employment history unless specifically asked.
- **On the employer's initiative**—if the employee is in a supervisory or management position, there is an implied duty to report any breach of another employee's employment contract to their employer.
- **On request by the employer**—an employer can question an employee where those questions are directly relevant to the employee's employment activities, and it would appear that the employee is bound to answer them.

Obligations after employment has ended

A duty to act confidentially

An employee will have continuing obligations to the employer in relation to confidential information, inventions and goodwill, even after the employment has ended. In the absence of any express clauses to the contrary from the contract of employment, these post-employment obligations are derived from the general law of property and confidence.

A duty to hand over inventions made during the course of employment

Where an employee is a trustee of an invention made during the course of the employment, the beneficial interest in the invention is the property of the employer, and remains the property of the employer even after the employment has ended.

activebook

To help you to remember and understand the topics covered so far, and for links to legal websites, refer to your online activebook. Model answers provide feedback to problems and exercises.

TERMINATION

> **!** CAUTION NOTE
> *An employment relationship is contractual and can be discharged in the same way as a normal contract.*

It only remains to say something about termination of the contract of employment. In addition to the ways in which a contract can be terminated at common law (see Chapter 19), termination of the contract of employment has also been modified and supplemented by industrial/workplace relations legislation, awards and agreements.

Methods by which a contract of employment could be terminated include the following:

Death

Because of the personal nature of the contract of employment, the death of either party will terminate the contract. Generally the employee, or their estate, will be able to recover any unpaid wages.

Where the business ceases to exist by bankruptcy or dissolution

The bankruptcy of a sole trader, the dissolution of a partnership, or the winding-up of a company will result in the termination of the contract of employment because in each case the employer ceases to exist. Legislation in all jurisdictions provides limited protection for an employee to claim for wages from the employer or from an industry fund.

Sale of the business

While employment contracts appear to attach to a business, the courts have consistently held that where that business is sold (as distinct from taken over or merged) to a new employer, all existing contracts of employment between the former owner and the employees are terminated. Those employees who stay on are employed under new contracts of employment with the new employer while the others only have recourse against the old employer. As a general rule, accumulated entitlements carry forward and this has been reinforced in legislative and award provisions across the country.

While an employee's accumulated entitlements generally carry forward on the sale of a business, the position has not been so clear when it comes to whether any awards or certified agreements binding on the former employer will also bind the new employer. However, the Federal Court in *Minister of State for Employment; Workplace Relations and Small Business v. CPSU, Community and Public Sector Union* [2001] FCA 316 held that the transmission of awards in a public sector context was possible under the *Workplace Relations Act 1996* (Cth) as long as it could be seen that the employees were performing essentially the same functions as they were in the former business. There seems to be no reason why the decision of the Federal Court cannot be extended to the private sector. If an employer intends to employ a substantial number of employees of a former business to perform essentially the same functions, this may be enough to suggest that a relationship exists between the former employer and the new employer for the purpose of s. 149(1)(d) of the *Workplace Relations Act*, that is, the award is binding on the new employer for the purpose of a succession, assignment or transmission of a business under the Act.

Frustration

In very limited circumstances a contract of employment can be terminated by frustration, for example, the employer's plant and equipment are destroyed by natural causes such as an earthquake or cyclone, or by fire. Most jurisdictions have passed legislation restricting the operation of frustration where an employee suffers a work-related illness or incapacity that makes it impossible for them to perform their duties under the contract of employment.

Termination by notice

The employee must terminate the contract in accordance with its terms or, if applicable, the relevant award or agreement. If the contract is of indefinite duration and no time is expressed, then the employee must give 'reasonable notice'. What is 'reasonable notice' will depend on whether the contract is subject to an award or agreement but where it isn't, the court will consider the nature and circumstances of the contract including the seniority of the position, tasks still to be performed, and pay periods.

Termination without notice

Where termination without notice occurs, the terminating party must be careful not to place themselves in a position of breach and thus be open to an action for damages. In the case of an employee terminating without notice, it is rarely worth the time or effort involved for the employer to pursue the matter. Where the employer terminates a contract without notice, this is known as 'summary dismissal'. Care must be taken to ensure that the conduct of the employee is sufficient to justify summary dismissal or the employer might face an action for unfair dismissal.

When terminating an employee's employment, employers must either give proper notice or be able to prove that the employee's actions were such that they justified summary dismissal. For an employer, getting it wrong can be quite expensive, as the decision of the Victorian Supreme Court in *Rankin v. Marine Power International Pty Ltd* [2001] VSC 150 illustrates. In this case the court awarded an employee whose contract of employment was ended without proper notice damages of over $170 000. Because of the seriousness of the act of termination and the effect of summary dismissal, justification by an employer is not an easy task. The employer will have to establish that:

- the acts (generally isolated conduct is not sufficient) of the employee amounted to misconduct, disobedience, incompetence or negligence; and
- they amounted to a breach of a serious nature; and
- they involved a repudiation by the employee of their contract of employment or their conduct was inconsistent with the relationship of employer and employee.

Failure to establish all three criteria will probably result in a finding of unfair dismissal.

Redundancy

Where redundancy is the reason for the termination of the contract of employment it is not fault-based but rather arises from external factors such as economic conditions. As a result, the employee's job no longer exists and the employee is retrenched. The employer must give notice in accordance with the terms of the contract, or if no notice is specified, then reasonable notice must be given.

All jurisdictions' industrial/workplace relations legislation make provision for notice or payment in lieu of notice requirements and severance payments, as do awards and agreements. The amount an employee will recover by way of severance payments usually depends on length of service.

Unfair dismissal

Incorrect termination of an employee can amount to unfair dismissal under Commonwealth and state industrial relations legislation

Where the contract is terminated by either party without complying with the terms for notice, then there is a breach of contract. Whether it amounts to an unlawful termination, or an unfair dismissal on the part of the employer, will depend on the type of breach and whether:

- it is an unlawful prohibited reason against dismissal. The *Workplace Relations Act* specifies several reasons for terminating employment which are unlawful. They include:
  - temporary absence from work due to sickness or injury;
  - membership or non-membership of a union;
  - acting as an employee's representative;
  - involvement in proceedings against an employer regarding a breach of a law;
  - race, colour, sexual preference, age, physical or mental ability, marital status, family responsibilities, pregnancy, religion, politics, nationality or social background; and
  - refusal to negotiate or sign an AWA.

The employer must prove that the termination was not for a prohibited reason, thus reversing the normal onus of proof; or

- the dismissal can be assessed as being 'harsh, unjust or unreasonable' based on an objective analysis of all the facts available to both the employer and the employee in the particular case. In assessing whether the reasons given for unfair dismissal are valid, industrial tribunals must take into account:
  - any valid reason such as the ability or conduct of the employee or workplace operational requirements;
  - any notification of reason given to employee;
  - opportunity given to the employee to respond to the employer's stated reason;
  - any warning given about unsatisfactory work performance; and
  - the operational requirements of the business.

If a breach is proved, a tribunal may make an order directing an employer to:

- re-employ or reinstate the employee in their original position or to an alternate position;
- order compensation if re-employment is not a viable option; or
- in the case of unlawful termination, impose a penalty on the employer.

Where there is an unfair dismissal, awards can only be made after arbitration of the claim and the arbitrator must have due regard to the specific impact of an order on the viability of the employer's business and the efforts the employee has made to mitigate their loss. For an employee under a federal award, this could be up to six months' pay while for employees not under federal awards, six months' pay or $34 000, whichever is the lesser amount. Similar remedies can be found in state jurisdictions: s. 170CH.

The *Workplace Relations Amendment (Termination of Employment) Act 2001* (Cth) introduced reforms to the federal unfair dismissal laws:

Qualifying period

Employees are prevented from making an unfair dismissal claim unless they have completed a qualifying period of three months unless some other period (or no period) is agreed to in writing.

Demotion

A demotion will not be deemed a termination of employment where:

- it does not involve a significant reduction in pay or duties; and
- the demoted person is still employed by the employer who effected the demotion.

Cost orders

Cost orders may be made against a party where:

- it should have been reasonably apparent to the applicant that the claim had no reasonable prospect of success; or
- a party has acted unreasonably in failing to discontinue an unfair dismissal claim.

Advisors

Penalties of up to $10 000 for a body corporate and $2000 for an individual may be imposed on advisors, such as advocates or lawyers engaged for a fee, or employees of unions who encourage the making or defence of claims which do not have reasonable prospects of success.

Remedies for breach

The remedies available to the injured party will depend upon whether the action is founded in a civil action or based on a statutory remedy, in which case availability depends upon the applicable Commonwealth or state law.

The *Work Choices Act 2005* (Cth) exempts businesses that employ up to and including 100 employees from the federal unfair dismissal laws.

For businesses with more than 100 employees, an employee must have been employed for six months before they can pursue an unfair dismissal claim.

Where the employment has been terminated because the employer genuinely no longer requires the job to be done, that is, where the employee's employment has been terminated because of operational requirements, the AIRC will be able to refuse any application for unfair dismissal.

IN BRIEF

Remedies for breach

Employer	Employee
Termination of the contract of employment	Resignation if the employer is guilty of repudiatory breach
Damages	Damages
In limited cases, an injunction	In very rare cases, an injunction prohibiting breach
In exceptional cases, intervention and an order by an industrial tribunal	Unlawful termination under statute Unfair dismissal under statute
Suspension if there is an express term in the contract of employment	Order by an industrial tribunal Statutory claims for sums due, e.g., unpaid wages
Stand down if it is authorised by statute or award	

The common law contract lays down the minimum obligations attached to an employment relationship in Australia. However, today much of the responsibility for determining wages and working conditions rests with legislation (e.g., annual leave, long service leave, sick leave, leave loading, hours per week). Some of this legislation is of a protective nature—that is, it establishes a code for the protection of employers and/or employees (e.g., workers' compensation, workplace health and safety).

The other type of legislation that has been developed, that is, industrial/workplace relations legislation, seeks to resolve industrial conflict in its vast variety of forms (e.g., strikes, lockouts, work bans). This is the primary focus of the industrial relations system, and accordingly, a system of quasi-judicial industrial tribunals has been established by legislation to act as an independent third party in conflict resolution.

THE IMPORTANCE OF THE AUSTRALIAN CONSTITUTION

Industrial relations was removed from the jurisdiction of the common law in 1901 by the Australian Constitution. In the 1890s, when the Constitution was being drafted, Australian society was suffering from devastating social and economic upheaval caused by economic depression and, initially at least, massive strikes across the country. As a direct result the new Constitution reflected the need for the Parliament to be able to legislate to establish an independent third party (the Conciliation and Arbitration Commission) to protect the public interest.

The Commonwealth's industrial powers come from s. 51(xxxv)

Section 51(xxxv) of the Constitution (the 'industrial power') allows the Commonwealth to enact laws with respect to 'conciliation and arbitration for the prevention and settlement of industrial disputes extending beyond the limits of any one state': s. 51(xxxv). The words 'industrial dispute' had been taken to refer to a dispute involving an 'industry' that is a productive activity and business carried on for profit.

This interpretation of industry eliminated those forms of personal service employment that did not 'produce' a product, for example, teachers and social work. In *Re Coldham, ex parte Australian Social Welfare Union* (1983) 57 ALJR 575, a dispute involving a social worker, the High Court held that an 'industrial' dispute between an employee and an employer was any dispute about work and conditions of employment.

Federal power is limited to settlement of disputes that extend over two or more states

Section 51(xxxv) only extends to settlement of disputes between two or more states. This permits the states to deal with wages and working conditions, and the resolution of industrial disputes within their own borders. Although the boundaries between state and federal jurisdictions are not always clear, a system of industrial relations has developed in which some parts tend to complement others. Over the years, the federal power has tended to grow, with decisions from the Australian Industrial Relations Commission and its predecessor becoming increasingly important.

In recent times the Commonwealth has extended its influence by using its power in respect to corporations (s. 51(xx))—since companies are the main employers of labour; and external affairs (s. 51(xxix))—to implement international treaties relating to employment and human rights matters. These other bases for constitutional power are very important to the current Commonwealth employment laws and have greatly extended its influence.

The Commonwealth and the states (but not Victoria as it gave its powers to the Commonwealth in 1996) all have the power to make industrial awards and agreements, which set out the wages and conditions of work in an industry, occupation or enterprise. Because Commonwealth law prevails over state legislation to the extent of any inconsistency (under s. 109 of the Constitution), it is therefore very important to distinguish between federal and state awards.

The fundamental difference is that every state award is a common rule award (unless it is specifically limited to named employers or to a specified district, as is the case of a state agreement, for example, Laminex Industries Gympie Certified Agreement).

Common rule award applies to all employees in particular industry

A common rule award applies to all employees in a particular industry or occupation, whether or not their employers are named as parties to the award. This means that the employer must pay all employees award rates and abide by award conditions, regardless of whether or not their employees are members of the union that is a party to the award. On the other hand, in *Australian Boot Trade Employees Federation v. Whybrow & Co.* (1910) 11 CLR 311, the High Court of Australia held that a federal award (except in the Northern Territory and the ACT, where it may be declared a common rule) is binding only on the employers and on the union/s named in it and their members.

If an employer is not cited as a party to a federal award, or the employer is not a member of an employer association bound by the award, or the employer's employees are not members of a union bound by the award, a state award will usually apply.

The role of awards and agreements

Industrial agreements and awards are the most important vehicle by which the majority of Australians are entitled to pay and conditions. They afford minimum protection to approximately 80 per cent of all employees in Australia.

An award is a legally binding order made by an industrial tribunal (either federal or state), which specifically sets out the rights and obligations of employers and employees, and the minimum rates and conditions of employment for employees covered by that award.

Any amount above the minimum set down in the award is by agreement and is often in the form of an over-award payment. It is important to recognise that awards and agreements are legally binding documents. If employers provide below the minimum, they may be prosecuted.

Award simplification

The *Workplace Relations Act 1996* (Cth) changed the emphasis from the traditional industry-based award to enterprise agreements—Certified Agreements and Australian Workplace Agreements—which were intended to be more flexible and better suited to the requirements. Matters that could be covered by federal award before the reforms of the *Work Choices Act* were:

- wages and salaries
- piecework rates
- hours of work
- shiftwork systems
- overtime rates
- allowances
- leave entitlements—annual, sick, etc.
- dispute settlement procedures
- mixed duties allowances

- classification of employees and skill-based career paths
- penalty rates
- redundancy pay
- pay and conditions for out-workers
- *jury service*
- *superannuation*
- *notice of termination*
- *long service leave*.

The *Work Choices Act* provides for the creation of an Award Review Taskforce to further simplify award classifications. The Act specifically refers to the matters above in italics, namely, jury service, superannuation, notice of termination and long service leave, as matters which would be removed from awards under the new system.

MAJOR REFORMS UNDER THE *WORK CHOICES ACT 2005* (CTH)

The main reforms the government hopes to implement by means of the *Work Choices Act* are:

- to simplify the complexity of six workplace relations jurisdictions by creating a national workplace relations system;
- to establish an independent body called the Australian Fair Pay Commission to set and adjust:
  - minimum and award classification wages;
  - minimum wages for juniors, trainees/apprentices and employees with disabilities;
  - minimum wages for piece workers; and
  - casual loadings;
- to enhance compliance with the *Workplace Relations Act*;
- to establish in law minimum conditions of employment regarding:
  - annual leave;
  - personal/carers leave (including sick leave);
  - parental leave (including maternity leave); and
  - maximum ordinary hours of work;

  all of which, along with the wages set by the Australian Fair Pay Commission, will be called the Australian Fair Pay and Conditions Standard (the Standard) and will apply to all employees in the national system;
- to place a greater emphasis on direct bargaining between employers and employees by replacing the certification and approval process for making agreements with a simpler streamlined lodgement-only process;
- to improve regulation of industrial action while protecting the right to take lawful industrial action by:
  - requiring the Australian Industrial Relations Commission to determine an application for an order to stop or prevent unprotected industrial action within 48 hours;
  - requiring secret ballots before protected industrial action;
  - expanding the grounds on which the Australian Industrial Relations Commission can suspend or terminate a bargaining period; and
  - creating a new power for the Minister for Employment and Workplace Relations to suspend or terminate a bargaining period in particular circumstances, such as where industrial action threatens life or personal health and safety and adversely affects the employer and possibly other employees, or where it threatens significant damage to the Australian economy;
- to retain a system of awards that will be simplified;
- to provide that where employees move to a new employer on transmission, the industrial instruments under which they were employed will be transferred to a successor, assignee or transmittee employer;
- to protect in the agreement-making process certain award conditions (which can only be modified or removed by specific provisions in an agreement), such as:
  - rest breaks (including meal breaks);

  - incentive-based payments and bonuses;
  - annual leave loadings;
  - allowances;
  - penalty rates; and
  - shift/overtime loadings);
- to preserve specific award conditions (long service leave, superannuation, jury service and notice of termination) for all current and new award employees, and to permit other award conditions (annual leave, personal/carers leave, parental leave) to apply to current and new award employees if they are better than the conditions provided in the Standard;
- to encourage employers and employees to resolve their disputes without a third party by introducing a model dispute settlement procedure for all employers and employees using an award, as well as those who rely on the Standard, and also employers and employees covered by agreements that do not contain dispute-settling procedures;
- to extend the compliance provisions in the *Workplace Relations Act* to cover:
  - the Standard;
  - agreement making;
  - state award and agreement reliant employers; and
  - employees that are brought into the national system;
- to establish transitional arrangements for employers and employees entering the federal system and employers and employees currently in the federal award system who will not be covered by the new federal system.

Constitutional situation

The aim of the Act is to simplify the complexity of six workplace relations jurisdictions by creating a national workplace relations system. The *Commonwealth Constitution Act 1900* (Imp), s. 51(xxxv), gives the Commonwealth Parliament power to make laws with respect to conciliation and arbitration for the prevention and settlement of industrial disputes extending beyond the limits of any one state. Clearly this 'power' incorporates many restrictions. These restrictions have led to each of the states and the Commonwealth having separate yet connected roles to play in the establishment of a viable system of laws regarding the workplace.

The Commonwealth used the corporations power in s. 51(xx) (see pp. 779–780) as the basis for the *Workplace Relations Act*; however, that Act was not intended to 'cover the field' and take precedence over state legislation (s. 109 of the Commonwealth Constitution). In contrast, the *Work Choices Act* is intended to 'cover the field' and to establish the national scheme. The government appears to be relying on recent High Court cases in which judges have spoken strongly in favour of the Commonwealth's use of the corporations power in regard to industrial matters, in particular *Re Pacific Coal, Ex parte CFMEU* (2000) 203 CLR 346 in which *Gaudron* J expressed the view that the corporations power extends to laws prescribing industrial rights and obligations of corporations and their employees (see also the dissenting decision of *Kirby* J in *Electrolux Home Products Pty Ltd v. Australian Workers Union* (2004) HCA40.

It should be noted that when the states agreed to refer their corporations powers to the Commonwealth following the turmoil caused by *Re Wakim, ex parte McNally* (1999) 198 CLR 511 and *The Queen v. Hughes* (2000) 74 ALJR 802, they did so subject to the proviso that the referred powers were not to be used in regard to industrial matters. At the time of writing, several states are saying they will bring an action in the High Court regarding the *Work Choices Act*; however, the grounds for such an action have not been stated.

Australian Fair Pay Commission

Australian Fair Pay Commission

An Australian Fair Pay Commission will be established to set and adjust minimum and award classification wages, along with minimum wages for juniors, trainees, apprentices, and employees with a disability. The commission will also determine wages for piece workers and casual workers. The Australian Fair Pay Commission will adopt a consultative evidence-based approach rather than the existing adversarial and legalistic approach.

The new system will have as its primary objective the promotion of economic prosperity. This will involve an assessment of what is required to encourage the unemployed and low paid to enter and remain in employment.

The Australian Fair Pay Commission will decide the timing, implementation, frequency and size of future minimum and award classification wage increases. The minimum and award wages will be protected at the level set after the Australian Industrial Relations Commission's 2005 Safety Net Review. Minimum and award wages will not fall below this level.

Award Review Taskforce

Award Review Taskforce

An Award Review Taskforce will be established to simplify award classifications. Provisions such as jury leave, superannuation, notice of termination, and long service leave, which are already provided for in other legislative entitlements, will be removed from awards. However, where these conditions are in existing awards, they will continue to operate for both existing and new award covered employees.

New system of lodgement in place of certification of agreements

Employers must comply with the procedural requirements under the law and meet the Australian Fair Pay and Conditions Standard. These rules will govern the negotiation, lodgement and content of agreements.

The new system will allow for collective agreements and AWAs to be lodged with the Office of the Employment Advocate, together with a statutory declaration attesting that the agreement was made in accordance with the law. The agreements or AWAs will be valid immediately on lodgement.

The agreements must comply with the Australian Fair Pay and Conditions Standard (the Standard). To do this, agreements must reflect the minimum conditions of employment as set out in the Standard, which provides for protection of annual leave, personal or carers leave (including parental leave), parental leave (including maternity leave) and maximum ordinary hours of work. These, along with the minimum wage and award classifications to be determined by the Australian Fair Pay Commission, will constitute the Australian Fair Pay and Conditions Standard.

Other employment conditions will be protected through the agreement-making process, but can be the subject of bargaining between employers and employees.

Unless specifically dealt with in an agreement, rest and meal breaks, incentive-based payments, annual leave loadings, allowances, penalty rates and shift/overtime loadings contained in any award will continue to operate.

Types of workplace agreements

Types of workplace agreements

The *Work Choices Act* has introduced new types of workplace agreements. Previously there was the Australian Workplace Agreement (AWA) and the Certified Agreement. While the Australian Workplace Agreement remains, the Certified Agreement is being replaced by one of five different types of agreement. The new types of agreement are:

Australian Workplace Agreement (AWAs): s. 96

An Australian Workplace Agreement is an agreement in writing between the employer and a person whose employment will be subject to the agreement. An AWA may be made before commencement of the employment.

Employee Collective Agreement: s. 96A

This is an agreement in writing between an employer and persons employed in a single business (or part of a single business) of the employer whose employment will be subject to the agreement.

Union Collective Agreement: s. 96B

A Union Collective Agreement is an agreement in writing between an employer and one or more organisations of employees if, when the agreement is made, each organisation:

(a) has at least one member whose employment in a single business (or part of a single business) of the employer will be subject to the agreement; and

(b) is entitled to represent the industrial interests of the member in relation to work that will be subject to the agreement.

Union Greenfields Agreement: s. 96C

This is an agreement in writing between an employer and one or more organisations of employees if:

(a) the agreement relates to a new business that the employer proposes to establish, or is establishing, when the agreement is made; and

(b) the agreement is made before the employment of any of the persons:

  (i) who will be necessary for the normal operation of the business; and

  (ii) whose employment will be subject to the agreement.

When the agreement is made, each organisation must be entitled to represent the industrial interests of one or more of the persons whose employment is likely to be subject to the agreement in relation to work that will be subject to the agreement.

The expression 'Greenfields' refers to the fact that it is a new business situation and the agreement is to apply to a completely new workforce, not to existing employees.

Employer Greenfields Agreement: s. 96D

An employer may make an agreement in writing if:

(a) the agreement relates to a new business that the employer proposes to establish, or is establishing, when the agreement is made; and

(b) the agreement is made before the employment of any of the persons:

  (i) who will be necessary for the normal operation of the business; and

  (ii) whose employment will be subject to the agreement.

Multiplebusiness Agreement: s. 96E

A multiplebusiness agreement is an agreement that:

(a) relates to any combination or combinations of the following:

  (i) one or more single businesses; or

  (ii) one or more parts of single businesses, carried on by one or more employers; and

(b) would be a collective agreement of a type mentioned in s. 96A, 96B, 96C or 96D but for the matters referred to in paragraph (a).

Bargaining Agents—AWAs: s. 97A and Employee Collective Agreements: s. 97B

An employer or employee may appoint a person to be his or her bargaining agent in relation to the making, variation or termination of an AWA. An employee whose employment is or will be subject to an Employee Collective Agreement may request another person (the Bargaining Agent) to represent the employee in meeting and conferring with the employer about the making or variation of the agreement. The appointment must be made in writing.

Australian Industrial Relations Commission

Australian Industrial Relations Commission

The role of the Australian Industrial Relations Commission (AIRC) has been changed considerably. The AIRC will no longer exercise compulsory powers of conciliation and arbitration or wage setting. During the negotiating process and during the term of an agreement, the parties may use the AIRC to assist in the negotiation process.

Awards and agreements will contain a model Dispute Settling Procedure which will set in place a 'staged' process so that, wherever possible, disputes will be settled at the workplace level. If necessary, the AIRC will provide dispute resolution services as it has done previously; however, the parties will also have the opportunity to nominate a dispute resolution service other than the Australian Industrial Relations Commission.

Where industrial action is started, such as a strike by employees or a lockout by employers, application can be made to the Australian Industrial Relations Commission for an order prohibiting the action. Such an order cannot apply to protected action.

The industrial action will be protected if:

- it is due to a failure of one of the parties to effectively negotiate a certified agreement or AWA;
- one party initiated a bargaining period by serving written notice on the other party of the intention to try to reach an agreement;
- seven days have elapsed since giving notice of the bargaining period;
- the action does not involve a secondary boycott;
- existing agreements or awards have expired;
- negotiations preceded the industrial action; or
- the action was authorised.

The commission will be responsible for issuing a Workplace Determination where a bargaining period has been terminated on public interest grounds, such as for the purposes of preserving essential services or to prevent undue economic damage. It will also provide an initial conciliation service where an unlawful termination claim has been made.

The Australian Industrial Relations Commission will retain a role in respect of transitional awards.

The commission is to implement award rationalisation measures once the findings of the Award Review Taskforce have been considered by government.

The jurisdiction and role of the Australian Industrial Relations Commission with respect to unlawful termination will remain largely unchanged.

Unions and other registered organisations

It will remain possible for unions to be appointed as bargaining agents on behalf of employees negotiating either collective or individual agreements. Employees will continue to have the right to join, or not join, a union, and cannot be discriminated against. This right to freedom of association includes such things as refusing to vote for or agree to a Certified Agreement, participating in proceedings under industrial law, and being a union official.

The grounds upon which a registered body may be deregistered have been expanded to include, for instance, breaches of court orders in relation to freedom of association provisions, financial reporting obligations, or conduct which seeks to prevent registration of a new organisation.

Australian industrial registry

State registered organisations (unions and employer organisations) will be required to satisfy the Industrial Registrar that they are an existing state-registered organisation prior to being allowed transitional status as a registered body, and will be able to obtain full registration once they have fully complied with provisions of the *Workplace Relations Act* within three years. Bodies that are substantially or effectively part of a body which is already federally registered will be disallowed from obtaining full registration.

Functions of the Australian Industrial Registry will be expanded to include:

- approving right of entry notices;
- conducting 'fit and proper person' tests in relation to the issuing of a permit; and
- keeping records relating to secret ballots and publishing the results of ballots.

Unlawful termination

Current remedies for unlawful termination will remain and be strengthened under the legislation.

It will remain illegal to dismiss an employee based on:

- temporary absence from work due to illness or family responsibilities;
- trade union membership;
- objection to signing an AWA;
- pursuing a complaint against the employer; or
- race, colour, sex and sexual preference, age, disability, marital status, religion, political opinion, social origin, pregnancy and family responsibilities.

Employees seeking redress for unlawful dismissal may be able to claim from the government up to $4000 for independent legal advice if they are eligible applicants who have a meritorious case and have exhausted conciliation options.

Transitional arrangements

The government expects that the full transition will take five years and has provided for two separate transitional systems:

1 Constitutional corporations moving from the state to federal jurisdiction

Current wages and conditions under state awards or agreements will continue to apply for up to three years.

In the case of both state awards and agreements, the terms and conditions contained will remain in effect until they expire or are superseded by a new federal agreement. However, if award pay and conditions are inferior to the provisions of the new Fair Pay and Conditions Standard, the relevant provisions of the Standard will prevail. Parties will be free to negotiate a new federal agreement at any stage during the transitional period.

In the event that state agreements or awards transit to the Commonwealth system and a new agreement has not been made, applicable Commonwealth award provisions will apply.

2 Employer is not a constitutional corporation

A five-year transitional period will apply to current federal collective agreements, during which period employers may incorporate, in which case a new federal agreement will be made at the end of the transition period. In the case where employers do not wish to incorporate, and the transition period expires, they will transit to the state system.

In the case of awards, a similar transitional period will apply, and at the conclusion of that period, any employer remaining unincorporated will transit to a state system.

The Australian Industrial Relations Commission will retain a limited power to vary wage rates and other entitlements in awards being operated by unincorporated corporations during the transition period, but will be unable to bind new parties to the award.

HUMAN RIGHTS-BASED WORK REGULATIONS

Managerial prerogative constrained by statute

Managerial prerogative is the right of management to make decisions that affect the operation and survival of their organisation. Managerial prerogative is supported by the common law and is a fundamental principle underlying the industrial relations system. However, managerial prerogative is constrained by statute law (e.g., legislation relating to occupational health and safety and workers' compensation).

A major area of infringement of managerial prerogative is in human resource management. Anti-discrimination legislation backed by affirmative action legislation severely curbs management's unilateral right to hire, terminate and set working conditions.

Workplace discrimination

Discrimination occurs where an individual or group of people are excluded from a benefit or opportunity because of a characteristic unrelated to their ability to do the job.

Doing business

Employers should adopt proactive polices towards eliminating workplace discrimination or face the consequences

All Australian jurisdictions have enacted anti-discrimination and equal opportunity legislation and it is important that employers realise that the community is no longer prepared to put up with workplace discrimination. To minimise the risk of vicarious liability and to avoid heavy fines and damages claims, employers must have in place appropriate and up-to-date policies dealing with workplace discrimination and must have taken reasonable steps to inform employees about unacceptable and unlawful conduct. ■

! CAUTION NOTE

Anti-discrimination and affirmative action legislation has severely impacted on managerial prerogatives in hiring, firing and working conditions.

Principal grounds for discrimination

The grounds for discrimination vary between federal and state jurisdictions; however, they include race, sex, marital status, age, physical and intellectual impairment, sexual preference, sexual harassment and religious or political beliefs.

Principal aspects of employment covered

The principal aspects of employment vary between federal and state jurisdictions, and include recruitment, selection, conditions of employment, promotion, termination, transfer, training, dealings with employment agencies, trade union membership and job advertisements.

Principal grounds for exemption

The principal grounds for exemption also vary between federal and state jurisdictions. They include employment in a small private household, terms in industrial awards or agreements, impairment requiring provision of special facilities not reasonably available or rendering a person incapable of doing the work, and genuine occupational requirements.

Discrimination may take two forms:

Direct discrimination

Any action by an individual or organisation that excludes an individual or group of people from a benefit or opportunity at that place of employment (e.g., an employer refusing to employ people from non-English speaking backgrounds).

Indirect discrimination (or systemic discrimination)

The outcome of established formal and informal organisational practices and procedures that appear to treat people equally but in practice may affect one group more than others (e.g., upper age limits for apprenticeships are written into awards. The apprenticeship system therefore indirectly discriminates against women who may be temporarily absent from the workforce for child rearing, or migrants who cannot meet the younger age criteria). Similarly, an employee may be 'constructively dismissed' by being demoted, if it can be shown that the demotion is due to one of the prohibited forms of discrimination.

HOWE V. QANTAS AIRWAYS LIMITED [2004] FMCA 242

Ms Howe was a flight attendant with Qantas. She argued that pursuant to an enterprise agreement and the policy of Qantas in relation to pregnant 'long haul' flight attendants (flight attendants on international flights) she was required, after falling pregnant, either to take unpaid maternity leave or to seek a ground-based position. She claimed that she was offered ground duties at a substantial reduction in salary. She also claimed that she was refused access to accumulated sick leave. In addition, Ms Howe asserted that the denial, on her return to work, of part-time employment in her previous position was either a constructive dismissal on the basis of family responsibilities or indirect discrimination on the basis of her sex.

Qantas denied that the care of young children is an attribute or characteristic particularly appertaining to women and asserted that if there was any indirect discrimination within the meaning of s.5(2) of the *Sex Discrimination Act* this was a condition, requirement or practice that was reasonable in all the circumstances within the meaning of s.7B of the *Sex Discrimination Act*.

ISSUE: Can an employee be 'constructively dismissed' by being demoted and also denied access to accumulated sick leave due to her becoming pregnant?

DECISION: The court held that Qantas had unlawfully discriminated against Ms Howe by refusing her access to accumulated sick leave contrary to sections 7(1) and 14(2)(b) of the *Sex Discrimination Act 1984* (Cth).

Federal legislation

Federal legislation is supported by state legislation in all states and territories.

IN BRIEF

Federal legislation

Act	Description
Sex Discrimination Act 1984	The Act gives effect to provisions of the International Convention on the Elimination of all Forms of Discrimination Against Women. It prohibits direct or indirect discrimination in employment on the grounds of sex, marital status or pregnancy and is administered through the Human Rights and Equal Opportunity Commission.
Racial Discrimination Act 1975	Discrimination in employment is prohibited on the grounds of race, colour, descent or national or ethnic origin. It is administered through the Human Rights and Equal Opportunity Commission.
Human Rights and Equal Opportunity Commission Act 1986	This legislation established the commission and the basic machinery through which the *Racial Discrimination* and *Sex Discrimination Acts* are administered.
Affirmative Action (Equal Employment Opportunity for Women) Act 1986	All private-sector companies in Australia with more than 100 employees and all higher education institutions must implement affirmative action programs for the employment of women and submit annual reports on the progress of those programs.
Equal Employment Opportunity (Commonwealth Authorities) Act 1987	Extends coverage of affirmative action programs to Commonwealth statutory authorities, targetting groups such as Aboriginals and Torres Strait Islanders, people with disabilities, and people from non-English speaking backgrounds.
Disability Discrimination Act 1992	Identifies disabled (including physically, sensorily, intellectually and psychiatrically) people, as well as those who carry organisms causing disease (such as HIV).
Workplace Relations Act 1996	Directs the commission to take into account the above legislation.

State legislation

- *Anti-Discrimination Act 1977* (NSW) Grounds for complaint include race, sex, marital status, physical and intellectual impairment, homosexuality and compulsory retirement.
- *Equal Opportunity Act 1995* (Vic.) Grounds for complaint include sexual harassment, sex, marital status, parental status, race, physical and mental impairment, religious or political beliefs, sexual activity. An employer can also be liable for harassment by employees, who, in the course of their employment, work 'off-site'. Victoria

also passed new legislation on racial and religious tolerance in 2001. The *Racial and Religious Tolerance Act 2001* prohibits racial and religious vilification.

- *Public Authorities (Equal Employment Opportunity) Act 1987* (Vic.).
- *Equal Opportunity Act 1984* (SA) Grounds for complaint are sex, marital status, pregnancy, sexuality, physical and intellectual impairment, race, sexual harassment and age.
- *Equal Opportunity Act 1984* (WA) Grounds for complaint include sex, marital status, pregnancy, family responsibility or family status, race, religious or political conviction, sexual harassment, racial harassment, physical and intellectual impairment and age.
- *Anti-Discrimination Act 1991* (Qld) Grounds for complaint include sex, marital status, pregnancy, parental status, age (compulsory retirement after 1 July 1994), race, impairment, religion, political belief or activity, lawful sexual activity, association with or relation to a person identified by any of the above attributes, and sexual harassment. Queensland's *Anti-Discrimination Act 1991* has been amended by the *Anti-Discrimination Amendment Act 2001.* The amendments repeal existing racial/religious vilification provisions and introduce new civil and criminal racial and vilification laws which bring Queensland into line with legislation in other jurisdictions.

  The amendments make it clear that the *Anti-Discrimination Act* applies to discrimination in work arrangements and prohibits work-related discrimination in relation to such matters as access to opportunities and promotion, the arrangements for offering work, in dismissal or by treating a worker unfavourably in any way.
- *Equal Opportunity and Public Employment Act 1991* (Qld).
- *Discrimination Act 1991* (ACT) Grounds for complaint include sex, sexuality, transsexuality, marital status, status as a parent or carer, pregnancy, race, religious or political conviction, membership or non-membership of organisation of employers or employees, association with a person identified by one of the above attributes and sexual harassment.
- *Anti-Discrimination Act 1992* (NT) Grounds for complaint include race, sex, sexuality, age, marital status, pregnancy, parenthood, breastfeeding, impairment, trade union or employer association activity, religious belief or activity, political opinion, affiliation or activity, irrelevant medical record, irrelevant criminal record or association with a person who has or is believed to have one of the above attributes.
- *Anti-Discrimination Act 1998* (Tas.) Grounds for complaint include gender, marital status, pregnancy, parental status, family responsibilities, sexual harassment, race, age, industrial activity, political and religious beliefs.

It should be noted that in certain cases an employer may be vicariously liable for the conduct of employees who breach the Act. If a person, in the course of their employment, engages in conduct which incites hatred against, serious contempt for, or revulsion or severe ridicule of a person due to their race or religion, both the person and the employer may be in breach of the Act and face criminal and/or civil liability. The employer will not be vicariously liable if they can prove that, on the balance of probabilities, they took reasonable precautions to prevent the employee breaching the Act. The only jurisdiction without racial vilification provisions is the Northern Territory.

Equal opportunity of employment

EEO—merit principle in employment

Equal opportunity is the positive alternative to discrimination. When discrimination does not occur, equal opportunity does occur. Equal opportunity is not defined in Australian legislation. The legislation approaches the issue by defining discrimination and by making certain acts of discrimination unlawful.

Equal employment opportunity (EEO) can be defined as the genuine application of the merit principle in employment. It aims to ensure that all individuals are judged according to their personal skills and merit without regard to stereotyped assumptions based on social prejudice. Its focus is on the personnel function to ensure that no unjustified discrimination occurs at any stage of the selection, promotion, transfer or training processes, or in the application of any other condition of service.

Affirmative action

EEO's principle of merit has little practical value without affirmative action's principle of equity (the notion of redress or catch-up for those groups that have been subject to long-term systemic discrimination). An affirmative action program is a set of positive and practical steps aimed at achieving real and measurable progress towards equal employment opportunity for groups that historically have had institutional barriers to exclude them from employment benefits or opportunities.

The systematic identification and elimination of those barriers enables target group members to compete on their merits. Without an affirmative action program, EEO policies would be unable to be converted into practice. EEO is therefore the end result of a successful affirmative action program.

Target groups for affirmative action programs include women, Aboriginal people and Torres Strait Islanders, and people from non-English speaking backgrounds.

> **!** CAUTION NOTE
>
> *EEO presupposes affirmative action for disadvantaged groups so that they can eventually compete on merit.*

Sexual harassment

Sexual harassment is unlawful discrimination

Under the *Sex Discrimination Act 1984* (Cth), and equivalent state legislation, sexual harassment is a form of unlawful discrimination.

Sexual harassment is defined as an unwelcome sexual advance or request for sexual favours, or unwelcome conduct or language of a sexual nature. It is unlawful if there are reasonable grounds for believing that the complainant's objections will endanger their application for a position, their current job or their future at work. It is also unlawful if, after their objection to sexual harassment, they are then unfairly treated by denial of a job or promotion, demoted or dismissed.

IN BRIEF

Types of behaviour which can amount to sexual harassment

Personally offensive verbal comments

Stares and leers

Offensive hand or body gestures, or physical contact such as patting or pinching

Provocative posters with sexual connotations

Sexual assault and rape

Sexual jokes, offensive telephone calls, photographs, reading matter or objects

Sexual propositions or continual requests for dates

Under the *Sex Discrimination Act 1984* (Cth) management has a duty to prevent sexual harassment and the employer may be responsible if it occurs in the workplace unless all reasonable steps have been taken to prevent it.

***HILL V. WATER RESOURCES COMMISSION* (1985) EOC ¶92-127**

Ms Hill was employed by the NSW Water Resources Commission. Several male co-workers made sexist remarks, displayed material of a sexually offensive nature in her work area and refused to recognise her authority. She also received offensive telephone calls and threats. Ms Hill reported this conduct to her supervisors but they failed to take any action.

ISSUE: Is an employer liable for failing to take steps to prevent discriminatory conduct by employees?

DECISION: The NSW Equal Opportunities Tribunal found that sexual harassment existed and was sufficiently severe as to produce a hostile workplace. The NSW Water Resources Commission was held in breach of the *Anti-Discrimination Act* because it knew of the conduct and failed to prevent it.

COMMENT: As soon as an employer becomes aware of an allegation of harassment, it should take positive steps to address the situation including:
- conducting an inquiry into the alleged harassment in accordance with established guidelines;
- providing the alleged harasser with an opportunity to respond to the allegations against them;
- if the harassment is, as a matter of fact, found to have occurred, directing the harasser to stop;
- informing the harasser of the consequences if they fail to stop; and
- if practicable, transferring the harasser to a different department or work site.

Non-discriminatory language

Non-discriminatory language breaks down barriers

The language we use is the cultural tool through which we come to understand what is 'normal' and what is not in our society. Non-discriminatory language practices seek to use this tool in a more constructive way—to break down long-standing prejudice and create images that see all people as equal.

If we actively seek to discard the prejudiced sexist, racist language that is a part of our society, a new view of what is 'normal' will emerge. From this new awareness may come a change in behaviour that will lead to more equitable outcomes for all minority groups.

Non-discriminatory language and presentation use terms and images that do not demean or categorise individuals because of a range of unrelated personal characteristics. They seek to treat individuals equally, irrespective of their gender, age, physical appearance, ethnicity, race, religion, political or ideological beliefs. For example:
- tradespeople not tradesmen;
- supervisor not foreman; and
- manager not manageress.

OCCUPATIONAL HEALTH AND SAFETY AND WORKERS' COMPENSATION

The two areas of occupational health and safety and workers' compensation are interrelated (see Figure 35.3). The former aims at reducing the risk of injury to workers while the latter focuses on compensating and rehabilitating an employee when they are injured, or if they contract a disease, at work.

Occupational health and safety

While workers' compensation legislation is intended to compensate employees for injuries sustained at work, the aim of occupational health and safety legislation is to prevent the injury in the first place. Occupational health and safety is intended to protect all persons in a workplace whether they are or are not employees. It also places a responsibility on more parties than just employers. Failure to comply with occupational health and safety procedures can result in substantial fines. As an example, a woman employed by a labour hire firm was severely injured when she was trapped between a machine and an unloading truck at a factory to which she had been hired out. The woman had no experience or training in using the machinery involved in the accident and she was not supervised at the time of the accident. For breaches of the *Occupational Health and Safety Act 1983* (NSW), the labour hire firm was fined $90 000 and $10 000 costs and the owner of the factory was fined $150 000. (*WorkCover Authority of NSW v. Labour Co-operative Ltd (No. 1)* [2001] NSWIR Comm 223 and *WorkCover Authority of NSW v. Labour Co-operative Ltd (No. 2)* [2002] NSWIR Comm 2.)

To reduce the number of workplace injuries and disease, their severity and cost

The cost of work-related injury and disease in Australia has been estimated at between $16 and $40 billion each year. This cost includes such things as compensation, fines, lost production, higher insurance premiums, industrial unrest and low morale.

Laws about occupational health and safety are the responsibility of state and territory governments and therefore differ from state to state. The National Occupational Health and Safety Commission (NOHSC) was established to encourage consistency between states and territories by developing national standards and codes of practice which can be used by governments when making laws.

The general approach of modern standards and codes developed by the National Occupational Health and Safety Commission is to:

- define what is a safe outcome:
  – safe workplace; and
  – safe level of exposure to noise, radiation or a chemical, etc.;
- define the duties of all parties involved in producing this outcome—employers, employees, suppliers, manufacturers, etc.;
- define a systematic process for achieving and continuing to achieve:
  – hazard identification;
  – risk assessment; and
  – risk control and review;
- identify any particular requirements that apply to the area.

The legislation creates a higher standard than the standard of reasonable care imposed by the common law. In most states the legislation imposes an absolute duty on employers to ensure health and safety at a place of work. Place of work means premises or any other place where persons work. This has been held to cover such diverse situations as the obvious—factories, offices and building sites—to the less obvious: scaffolding on a footpath and the back of a garbage truck.

The *Occupational Health and Safety Act 2000* (NSW) introduced significant changes to occupational health and safety law in New South Wales, in particular:

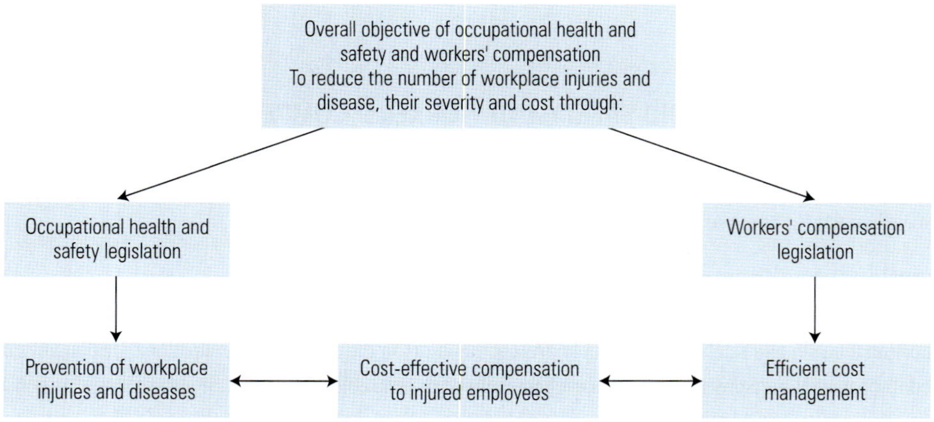

FIGURE 35.3 *Aims of occupational health and safety and workers' compensation*

Duty to consult

Employers must consult with employees regarding matters affecting the employee's health, safety and welfare. Employers must consult with employees whenever concluding a risk assessment and when changes that may affect occupational health and safety are proposed.

Risk assessment

There is now a specific obligation to implement risk management procedures that will:

- identify hazards;
- assess the risk involved; and
- introduce control measures.

This duty is imposed on:

- employers;
- persons in control of premises used as a place of work; and
- manufacturers and suppliers of plant.

The successful prosecution of Esso for breaches of the *Occupational Health and Safety Act 1995* (Vic.) following the death of two workers and the injury of eight others in September 1998 illustrates a change in attitude towards workplace safety and the need for strict regulation and punishment of offenders. For example, the *Occupational Health and Safety (Major Hazard Facilities) Regulations 2000* (Vic.), introduced as a result of the Esso plant's gas explosion at Longford in Victoria, imposes strict obligations on operators of major hazard facilities, punishing negligent employers with criminal penalties. The Commonwealth has also amended its *Occupational Health and Safety (Commonwealth Employment) Act 1991* with the passage of the *Occupational Health and Safety Amendment Act 2000 (No. 2)* which has significantly increased civil and criminal penalties for breach of an employer's duty of care.

In Victoria, the Crimes (Workplace Death and Serious Injuries) Bill allows owners and company directors to be prosecuted for gross negligence that has contributed to the death or serious injury of an employee. The Act also substantially increases penalties for breaches of the occupational health and safety legislation.

The legislation (see Table 35.1) imposes positive duties on employers, employees, self-employed persons, manufacturers, suppliers and designers. The following are generalised examples of the duties imposed under the various occupational health and safety statutes of the states and territories.

Occupational health and safety legislation imposes a higher duty on employers than the common law

Table 35.1 Occupational health and safety legislation

Jurisdiction	*Act*
Commonwealth	*Occupational Health and Safety (Commonwealth Employment) Act 1991*
Australian Capital Territory	*Occupational Health and Safety Act 1989*
New South Wales	*Occupational Health and Safety Act 2000*
Northern Territory	*Work Health Act 1986*
Queensland	*Workplace Health and Safety Act 1995*
South Australia	*Occupational Health, Safety and Welfare Act 1986*
Tasmania	*Workplace Health and Safety Act 1995*
Victoria	*Occupational Health and Safety Act 1985*
Western Australia	*Occupational Safety and Health Act 1984*

Employers

Employers must ensure health, safety and welfare of employees by providing:

- safe equipment and a safe system of work;
- for the safe use, handling, storage and transport of equipment and substances;

- information, instruction, training and supervision;
- for the maintenance of the workplace in a safe condition; and
- information about substances used at place of work.

Employers and self-employed persons

Ensure health and safety of people visiting place of work.

Employees

Employees must take reasonable care of health and safety of others.

Manufacturers and suppliers of plant and substances

Manufacturers and suppliers must:

- carry out necessary research testing and examinations; and
- supply information regarding research, tests and conditions for safe use.

General prohibition

No person is to interfere with or misuse things provided for the health, safety and welfare of persons.

In addition to claims for compensation for loss or injury, a breach of occupational health and safety legislation may result in fines and/or imprisonment.

Examples of the penalties are:

Commonwealth		
▪ Corporation		$242 000
▪ Individual		$9 000
New South Wales		
▪ Corporation	First offence	$550 000
	Second or subsequent offence	$825 000
▪ Individual	First offence	$55 000
	Second or subsequent offence	$82 500 and/or 2 years
South Australia		
▪ Corporation		$200 000
▪ Individual		$100 000
▪ An employee		$10 000
Tasmania		
▪ Corporation		$150 000
▪ Individual		$50 000
Western Australia		
▪ Corporation		$100 000
▪ Where breach results in death or serious harm		$200 000
▪ An employee		$10 000
Victoria		
▪ Corporation		$900 000
▪ Individual		$180 000
▪ Where the breach involves the reckless endangering of persons an individual may be imprisoned for up to five years in addition to a fine of up to		$180 000

Workers' compensation

Employee injured in course of employment is entitled to compensation

An employee who is injured (injury includes disease) while in the course of their employment, or where the employment is a contributing factor, will generally be eligible for payment under the relevant state or territory workers' compensation legislation (see Table 35.2). The Act does not cover independent contractors.

Workers' compensation legislation is a no-fault scheme

The workers' compensation schemes are no-fault systems of liability. This means that the injured employee is almost always guaranteed compensation for a work-related injury. To lose their right to compensation it would have to be shown that the employee's conduct deliberately or intentionally led to the injury.

The injury to the employee must be personal and can include aggravation, acceleration, exacerbation or deterioration of an existing or pre-existing injury. The schemes do not extend to cover damage to real or personal property.

The following matters are important in determining if an injury is covered by workers' compensation legislation.

Table 35.2 Workers' compensation legislation

Jurisdiction	*Act*
Commonwealth	*Safety, Rehabilitation and Compensation Act 1988*
Australian Capital Territory	*Workers Compensation Act 1951*
New South Wales	*Workers Compensation Act 1987*
	Workplace Injury Management and Workers' Compensation Act 1998
Northern Territory	*Work Health Act 1986*
Queensland	*Workers' Compensation and Rehabilitation Act 2003*
South Australia	*Workers Rehabilitation and Compensation Act 1986*
Tasmania	*Workers Rehabilitation and Compensation Act 1988*
Victoria	*Accident Compensation Act 1985*
Western Australia	*Workers' Compensation and Rehabilitation Act 1981*

Arising out of the employment

For an employee to succeed in a workers' compensation claim they must be able to show a connection between the employment and the injury. 'Arising out of employment' means arising out of the work the person is employed to do and which is incidental to it. It is possible for an incident to arise out of work, but not be incidental to it.

Acts outside the course of employment

Employees who are injured during activities that are outside the scope of their employment contract are usually unable to recover workers' compensation. Similarly, an employee may not be covered where they have deviated from their usual path of travel for a purpose not exclusively connected with their employment. Whether the employee is covered or not is usually a matter of degree.

Injury at the place of employment

'Place of employment' is widely defined and includes premises, works, plant or place for the time being occupied by or under the control of or management of the employer, by whom the worker concerned is employed and on, at, or in connection with which the worker was employed at the time of injury.

Injuries during lunch or other recess

As a general rule, lunch taken by an employee at the place of work, as long as it is taken within any guidelines set down by the employer, is covered by compensation if they are injured. This is considered to be an adjunct to employment and being in 'the course of employment'.

If an employee, during a lunch break or a recess, is injured while doing something not connected with their employment (often referred to as a 'frolic of their own'), they would not be covered because the injury could not be said to have arisen during the course of their employment. Thus, if during an employee's lunch hour the employee decides to drive to the bank, which is some distance away from the place of employment, and they are injured on the way there or back, they may well be outside the scope of their employment contract if it wasn't for business purposes.

Protected journeys

Certain journeys are considered to be incidental to the employment relationship. During these journeys the employee is considered to be covered by the Act. These include:

- journeys to and from the worker's home and the place of employment, provided that they are daily or periodic;
- journeys from trade, technical or other training school at which attendance is required by the terms of employment;
- journeys to or from medical attention;
- journeys to or from any medical consultation or examination;
- journeys between any camp or place of pick-up; and
- journeys between the worker's place or abode and place of employment when the journey is made for the purpose of receiving payment of wages or other money due under the terms of employment.

WEB RESOURCES

National Occupational Health and Safety Commission: This is a useful site for students looking for information on occupational health and safety:
http://www.nohsc.gov.au/

For information on the Australian Industrial Relations Commission and awards generally:
http://www.airc.gov.au/

For information on the *Work Choices Act* and Federal Industrial Relations:
http://www.workplace.gov.au

For information on workers' compensation and OHS, see:
http://www.workplaceinfo.com.au

and click on 'OHS & Workers comp' under 'Reference'.

A good gateway to a large number of Australian and overseas government departments' sites dealing with employee relations:
http://www.dpc.vic.gov.au/

A good site for OHS information:
http://www.nohsc.gov.au

REVIEW QUESTIONS

?

35.1 A duty of an employee is to work in a competent manner. What is meant by the expression 'work in a competent manner'? Provide examples of where an employee may not be working in a competent manner.

35.2 What are the problems that face the courts today in using the control test to determine whether the relationship of employer and employee exists?

35.3 What is the legal basis of the employer–employee relationship in Australia today?

35.4 What are the common law rights and responsibilities of both the employer and the employee?

35.5 A federal award overrides any state Act or award, and any common law rule or agreement that is inconsistent with it. Discuss.

35.6 Do you see a role for trade unions in the future? What is the role of trade unions in the industrial relations system?

35.7 Indicate whether each of the following statements is true or false:

	TRUE	FALSE
▪ A person working under a contract for service is known as an independent contractor	☐	☐
▪ Where there is no continuity of employment between the employer and the employee, the contract is a casual contract	☐	☐

- There is no difference between unlawful termination and unfair dismissal ☐ ☐
- A remedy available to an employer for breach by an employee is specific performance ☐ ☐
- The dissolution of a partnership terminates the contract of employment ☐ ☐
- Even in the case of casual contracts, there is a duty on the employer to provide work ☐ ☐
- A job advertisement in a newspaper is an offer ☐ ☐
- The right of management to make decisions that affect the operation and survival of their organisation is known as managerial prerogative ☐ ☐
- When discrimination does not occur, equal opportunity does occur ☐ ☐
- An agreement with a single employee or a group of employees in a particular incorporated business is known as a certified agreement ☐ ☐
- An agreement covering employees of a single business is called an Australian Workplace Agreement ☐ ☐

activebook

Activebook resources include in-depth summaries with links to the relevant part of the book. For revision, add your own notes to the summaries provided by using the note-taking function.

35.8 Are equal opportunity and affirmative action programs independent or interdependent? What do they hope to achieve? Discuss.

35.9 What is the purpose of Occupational Health and Safety legislation and what methods are used to ensure it is complied with?

35.10 What is the purpose of workers compensation? Is it the same as the purpose of Occupational Health and Safety legislation?

CRITICAL THINKING

35.1 An unincorporated surf life-saving club, through its secretary, accepted an invitation to provide security services at a boat show. These services were to be paid for and the proceeds were to go to the club. The club called for volunteers from within the club. Steve was one of a number of people who volunteered their services. He was rostered for duty and was subsequently injured while performing security services at the boat show.

Is there an employment contract in existence between Steve and the surf life-saving club or Steve and the boat show organisers with whom the club secretary had arranged the security service? (See *Unicomb v. Jimmy Cole Caravans Pty Ltd* [1979] WCR 65.)

35.2 Metka, an employee of ACI Pty Ltd, regularly used a pathway to gain access to a public street. The path was not in good repair and was unlit at night. It was never clear who owned the path, though it was clear that it was not owned by the employer. After leaving work late one night, Metka fell and broke her leg after tripping in a hole in the path.

Is the employer liable?

35.3 You are the Human Resource Manager for a medium-sized company. The Board of directors wants to introduce several significant changes to the work practices that have become entrenched in the company. The award is about to expire and the board of directors has asked you to report as to whether a Certified Agreement or an Australian Workplace Agreement under the *Workplace Relations Act 1996* (Cth) would be best suited for the company's workforce.

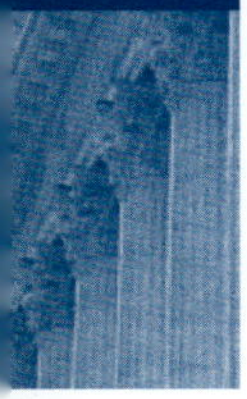

GLOSSARY

Glossary of legal terms

abatement: the proportionate reduction in value of a legacy or devise because the estate is insufficient to pay all debts, devises and legacies in full.

abrogate: to cancel or revoke.

act of bankruptcy: a public indication of insolvency must be committed before a creditors' petition for sequestration order can be made.

act of God: a natural event or occurrence that cannot be foreseen and which happens independently of human intervention, such as an earthquake or storm.

action: a civil proceeding commenced by writ or summons or in such other manner as may be allowed by the rules of the court. It usually refers to proceedings in which the common law remedy of damages is sought. It does not include a criminal proceeding by the Crown.

actual breach: failure at the time required by the contract.

actus reas: a guilty act, and in combination with *mens rea*, produces criminal liability.

affidavit: a written statement, made on oath in front of a person duly authorised to administer the oath, that the contents of the statement are a true and accurate record.

affirm: to uphold a judgement, or to declare without taking an oath that the evidence one is giving is the truth, or elect to abide by a voidable contract.

after acquired property: any property a bankrupt receives after bankruptcy starts.

agent: a person employed to act on behalf of another.

agreement to sell: where the property in the goods is to be transferred at some later date, or where some condition has to be fulfilled, such as payment of the price.

annuity: a yearly payment of a certain sum of money.

ante: before.

anticipatory breach: threatened failure to perform their contractual obligations at a time required by the contract by a party to the contract.

appeal: any proceeding taken by a litigant from a lower court to a higher court.

appellant: the party appealing a decision. They may be either the plaintiff or the defendant from when the case went to trial the first time.

arrears: debts unpaid at the due date.

arrest: the taking into custody of a person by the police.

ascertained goods: goods which, in a contract for the sale of unascertained goods, have become identified and agreed upon by the parties.

assault: direct interference with the person (the body) of the plaintiff and actionable *per se* (without proof of damage).

assign: to transfer.

assignee: one to whom an assignment is made.

assignment: transfer.

assignor: one who assigns, or transfers.

assurance: a term used interchangeably with insurance. Refers to contracts where the event or risk covered is a certainty, for example, death.

Australian Business Number Digital Signature Certificates (ABN-DSC): developed by the Commonwealth government to foster the use of digital certificates in Australia for identification in online transactions.

Australian Workplace Agreement (AWA): an agreement between an employer and employee/s of the employer regarding pay and conditions applicable to that particular workplace.

authorisation: a dispensation which the Australian Competition and Consumer Commission may grant for a restrictive trade practice which would otherwise be in breach of the Act.

available property: property owned by a bankrupt when bankruptcy began.

avoid: to set aside or to make void.

award: a binding order made by an industrial tribunal, setting out the rights and obligations of employers and employees who fall under the ambit of the award.

bail: the procedure by which an accused person charged with a criminal offence is released from police custody on the understanding that they will return to court at a future date.

bailee: the person to whom goods are delivered by the owner (the bailor) for safekeeping, but without the intention of transferring ownership.

bailiff: a court officer employed to serve writs, make arrests and executions on the property of judgement debtors.

bailment: where possession of goods passes from the hands of one person to another.

bailor: the owner of goods who entrusts them to another (the bailee).

bank cheque: a cheque drawn by a bank on itself.

bankrupt: a person who is unable to meet their debts when they fall due.

bankruptcy: a legal state (or status) in which a person has their property and financial affairs controlled by a trustee under order of the Court; arises because person is insolvent.

bankruptcy notice: a notice issued by the Official Receiver upon application by a creditor who has obtained a final judgement or order for the amount owing to the creditor by the debtor which directs the debtor to pay the judgement debt (normally within 28 days), failure to comply amounting to an act of bankruptcy.

Bar Council: the controlling body for barristers on the etiquette and practice of the Bar in each state or territory.

barrister: a legally qualified person who practises before the Bar, generally in intermediate and superior courts.

battery: the striking of another.

bearer: the person in possession of a cheque.

bearer cheque: an order to the drawee institution to pay the sum ordered to be paid by the cheque to the person in possession of the cheque, title being transferred on delivery.

bilateral contract: a promise for a promise.

Bill: a draft of proposed legislation which has yet to receive the Royal Assent.

bill of exchange: an unconditional order in writing, addressed by one person to another, signed by the person giving it, requiring the person to whom it is addressed to pay on demand, or at a fixed or determinable future time, a sum certain in money to, or to the order of, a specified person, or to bearer: *Bills of Exchange Act 1909* (Cth): s. 8(1).

bill of sale: a document that transfers property but not possession to the lender.

blank endorsement: the signing of one's name to a commercial paper.

bona fide: in good faith.

brief: a written statement of a party's case, usually prepared by a barrister.

broker: a mercantile agent for the purchase and sale of goods, stocks and shares, insurance policies, etc., but who does not have possession of the goods or documents of title.

brokerage: the commission payable to a broker.

call: a demand upon shareholders to pay up the whole or a specified portion unpaid on their shares by the company; or, if the company is in liquidation, by the liquidator.

canon law: part of Roman ecclesiastical law; today means the law of the Greek, Roman and Anglican churches.

categorical imperative: a standard of morality—'imperative', because it establishes principles; 'categorical', because the principles are unconditional with no exceptions.

causation: the connection between the breach and the loss suffered by the plaintiff.

cause of action: the right to bring a legal action.

caveat emptor: let the buyer beware.

certiorari: a writ directed to an inferior court or administrative body by a superior court that an order, record or proceedings was not proceeded with correctly and should be submitted to it for re-hearing.

***cestui que* trust**: a person who is the beneficial owner, or beneficiary, of property held in trust.

chattels: any property other than freehold land; articles which the law deems to be personal property.

cheque: a bill of exchange drawn on a banker and payable on demand; an unconditional order in writing that is addressed by one person to another person, being a financial institution, and is signed by the person giving it requiring the financial institution to pay on demand a certain sum of money (s. 10, *Cheques Act 1986* (Cth)).

chose: a thing.

chose in action: right of action to recover a debt or possession. It is often used to refer to intangible things such as book debts, contractual rights, cheques, etc.

chose in possession: moveable, tangible objects of personal property capable of physical possession, for example, jewellery, books.

CIF: cost, insurance, freight. A price quoted by a seller of goods which includes the cost of the goods, their insurance and freight from pick-up to delivery at the port or place of destination.

civil penalty: a penalty imposed by the court for contravention by a credit provider of a 'key requirement' of the Code (s. 113A).

civil rights: private rights, protected by law, of members of society.

class action: an action brought by one or a few on behalf of a larger group who have a common cause.

clause: a term in a contract.

collecting financial institution: the payee's financial institution (i.e. the financial institution where the cheque is deposited for 'cashing').

commission: the sum paid to an agent, usually expressed as a percentage of the price or premium or the sum insured.

common law: that part of the law of England which developed from the common custom of the country as administered by the common law courts. It can also mean judge-made law as distinct from statute law.

company: a person or body of persons formed for the purpose of trade or business by either Royal Charter, special Act of Parliament or registration under the *Corporations Law;* a distinct legal entity separate from its shareholders.

competition: the process by which producers (or consumers) of goods within a market compete with one another.

complainant: the plaintiff in a legal or equitable pleading.

composition: an arrangement with creditors whereby they accept payment of their debts by instalments or less than the full amount of their debts in full satisfaction of the entire debt.

condition: a provision that some right will depend on the happening of some event. In contract law it is a stipulation going to the root of the contract which allows the injured party the right to rescind and/or seek damages. *See also* warranty.

condition precedent: delays the vesting of the right until the happening of the event.

condition subsequent: destroys the right upon the happening of an event.

consequentialism: concerned with the consequences. It is an approach to morals that evaluates behaviour according to the consequences of that behaviour.

consideration: consideration may consist either in some right, interest, profit or benefit accruing to the one party, or some forbearance, detriment, loss or responsibility given, suffered or undertaken by the other (the benefit/detriment definition by *Lush* J in *Currie v. Misa* (1875) LR 10 Ex 153) or an act or forbearance of one party, or the promise thereof, which is the price for which the promise of the other is bought, and the promise thus given for value is enforceable (the price paid definition suggested by Sir Frederick Pollock and adopted by the House of Lords in *Dunlop Pneumatic Tyre Co. Ltd v. Selfridge and Co. Ltd* [1915] AC 847).

consumer: a person who purchases goods or services priced under $40 000, or of a kind ordinarily acquired for personal, domestic or household use or consumption (s. 4B, *Trade Practices Act 1974* (Cth) ('TPA')). Small businesses purchasing goods for less than $40 000 are treated as 'consumers' for the purposes of the TPA.

consumer lease: a contract for the hire of goods by a natural person or a strata corporation under which the person or corporation does not have a right or obligation to purchase the goods (s. 147).

Consumer Price Index (CPI): the index which measures quarterly changes in the price of a 'basket' of goods and services purchased by metropolitan households and provides the official measure of inflation in Australia.

continuing credit contract: a contract under which multiple advances of credit are contemplated and the amount of available credit usually increases as the loan is reduced (e.g., a credit card).

contra proferentum: the doctrine that the construction least favourable to the party putting forward an argument or document should be used against him or her.

contract: an agreement that gives rise to legal rights and obligations between the parties to it and which will be enforced by the courts.

contract for the sale of goods: defined in sale of goods legislation as a contract whereby the seller transfers, or agrees to transfer, the property (ownership) in goods.

contributory negligence: a defence to an action in negligence for damages for injuries arising from the plaintiff's own negligence which directly caused or contributed to their own injuries.

conversion: that tort which is committed by a person who retains another's property without permission and with the intention of depriving them of the use and possession of it.

co-ownership: joint ownership of property.

copy: in the law of copyright refers to the literal copying of a work.

copyright: protects works that owe their origin to the expressive efforts of a writer, composer, artist or other creative individual. It gives the individual the exclusive right to copy a particular form of expression of literary, dramatic, musical and artistic work; sound recordings; films; television or radio broadcasts; published editions of works; or computer programs.

corporation (also known as a 'company'): a legal entity (or legal person) created by the *Corporations Act 2001* (Cth).

covenant: a promise under seal which may be either positive, such as a promise to perform some act or to pay some money; or negative (restrictive), such as a promise not to carry out some act.

cover note: an interim contract of insurance pending the acceptance or decline of a full contract of insurance.

credit contract: a contract in writing signed by the debtor and creditor under which credit is or may be provided and on which title does not pass until the instalments are paid (ss. 5, 12).

credit provider: a person who provides credit in the course of a business of providing credit (e.g., bank, finance company, credit union, building society) or as part of, or incidental to, any other business of the credit provider (e.g., a retail store that provides credit to its customers (s. 6(1)(d)).

creditor: a person who is owed money.

creditor's petition: application to court by a creditor requesting a particular debtor be made bankrupt.

cybercrime: electronic criminal offences usually involving unauthorised access to a computer or alteration to computer records.

cybersquatting: registering, selling or using a domain name with the intent of profiting from the goodwill of someone else's trademark.

Damage: in tort: the loss or damage suffered by the plaintiff as a result of the defendant's breach of their duty of care and for which damages are payable.

damages: compensation in monetary form for the loss suffered by the plaintiff owing to a breach of contract or tort which puts the plaintiff back in the position they would have been in had the breach not occurred.

debenture: a document whereby a company acknowledges a debt; also represents the division of a company's profits among its shareholders.

debt: a sum of money owed by one person to another.

debtor: a person who owes money; for the purposes of the Consumer Credit Code, a natural person to whom credit has been supplied (s. (1)(a), *Consumer Credit Code*).

debtor's petition: application by debtor to be made bankrupt.

deed: an instrument that has been signed, sealed and delivered and which does not require consideration to be valid; for the purposes of the Code, a natural person to whom credit has been supplied (s. (1)(a)).

Deed of Arrangement: supervision and control of debtor's affairs is given to creditors with a view to eventual payment in whole (or in part) of debts.

Deed of Assignment: debtor assigns (transfers) all of their property for the benefit of their creditors.

defamation: a tortious action encompassing both words spoken (slander) or recorded (libel) that tend to injure a person's reputation.

defendant: the person against whom a civil action is being brought; the person being sued.

deferred claims: debts that are postponed until all other creditors have been paid in full, including claims by companies controlled by the bankrupt.

***del credere* agent**: an agent for the sale of goods who guarantees the payment of the price of all goods sold by the agent in return for a higher commission than is usually given to an agent.

delegated legislation: regulations and by-laws passed by a subordinate authority, such as a municipal council or a government undertaking like the railways, in reliance of some regulation-making powers conferred by an Act of Parliament upon it.

deontological ethics: requires a person to do the right thing regardless of the consequences.

design: the overall appearance of the **product** resulting from one or more visual features of the product.

detinue: the common law action available to a person claiming the specific return of goods wrongfully retained by another or their value.

devise: a disposal of real property by will.

digital signature: a subset of the electronic signature which is attached to specific data.

directors: the persons employed as officers of a company and responsible for its management.

disclaimer: a renunciation, refusal or denial.

dividend: the interest payable on the public funds; or the payment made out of profits to shareholders in a company; or the amount payable on each dollar of a bankrupt's liabilities.

divisible contract (also known as a 'severable contract'): a contract that is capable of being divided up into separate parts, strict performance of all the terms not being required before a claim for payment can be made.

Doctrine of Relation Back: the bankruptcy is DEEMED to commence with the earliest act of bankruptcy within the six months immediately preceding the presentation of creditors' petition. NOTE: The application of the Doctrine of Relation Back can vary with the particular circumstances.

domain name: an Internet address.

domestic agreements: ones made between family members and relatives.

domicile or **domicil**: the place in which a person is, or is presumed to be, permanently resident.

donee: the person who receives a gift.

donor: the person who gives a gift.

drawee: the person to whom a bill of exchange, cheque or payment order is addressed and who is requested to pay the sum of money named therein.

drawer: the person drawing a bill of exchange, cheque or payment order and addressing it to the drawee; the person who gives the order and draws the cheque upon a bank and whose account will be charged with the value of the cheque.

duress: threats of, or use of, force that deprives the innocent party of exercising their free will.

easement: a right enjoyed by the owner of the land over the lands of another, such as a right of way.

ejectment: an action to determine the title to certain land.

ejusdem generis: of the same kind of nature. In cases of statutory interpretation where particular words are followed by general words, then the general words will be limited to the same kind as the particular words.

electronic signature: a method of authenticating an electronic transmission.

emblements: the profits of a crop that is the result of farming, such as vegetables, wheat, corn, etc.

employee: a person employed under a contract of service and subject to the control of an employer regarding the manner in which their work is to be done.

encryption: transforming data into a form that is unreadable without a key.

encumbrance: a claim or *lien* that affects title to real property.

endorsement: a writing on the back of an instrument such as a bill of exchange, cheque, promissory note or bill of lading the name of the person who is the transferor, indicating their intention to transfer the right to payment.

enterprise agreement: a collective agreement made between unions and employers or employees and employers, usually covering a single business (or a distinct operational or organisational unit within a single business) or a geographically distinct part of a business.

equitable: that which is fair.

equity: fairness and justice. Originally operated alongside the common law and intended as a supplement to it, but now incorporated into a single system.

escrow: a written agreement is held by an independent party on the understanding that it will not be delivered as a deed (and therefore become operative) until the fulfilment of some condition.

estate: an interest in land.

estoppel: a rule of law which precludes a person from denying the truth of some statement formerly made by them or the existence of facts which by his or her words or conduct has given the impression to others of its truthfulness.

ethical considerations: involve going beyond self-interest in reaching a decision.

ethical investing: investment in companies that operate ethically, provide social benefits and are sensitive to the environment.

ethical judgement: one that can be seen to apply to everyone in similar circumstances and not only to a particular individual.

ethical opinions: concerned with behaviour and with establishing ways in which people should behave.

ethics relates to morals, the treatment of moral questions and acting in a morally correct, honourable way.

ex parte: an application in a judicial proceeding by one side only.

exclusion clause (also known as exemption or exception clauses): a contractual term that attempts to limit or exclude the liability of the person inserting it into a contract.

executed: completed or fully carried out.

executed contract: a contract completed or fully carried out by both parties.

executory: not completed, still to be performed.

executory contract: where one or both parties agree to perform their contractual obligations in the future.

exemplary damages (also known as 'punitive damages'): damages awarded in addition to general damages and are in excess of the amount needed to compensate the plaintiff for injury. They are awarded to punish the defendant for wilful or malicious conduct. Rarely awarded for breach of contract.

existing goods: goods owned or possessed by the seller at the time of the contract.

factor: a commercial agent who, in the usual course of their business, has possession of the goods, or the documents of title to the goods, of a principal with authority to sell, pledge or raise money on them. Contrast with a broker who has neither control or possession.

fee simple: a freehold estate and the most extensive interest in land; referred to colloquially as 'ownership' of land. There are no restrictions on the ways in which the holder of the fee simple may deal with the land.

felony: serious crime and an indictable offence (e.g. murder), in contrast to misdemeanour.

fit for purpose: where the buyer expressly or by implication makes known to the seller the particular purpose for which the goods/services are required, which shows that there is a reliance upon the judgement and skill of the seller that the goods must be reasonably fit for that purpose.

fixtures: anything annexed to the freehold, the property in it immediately vesting with the owner of the soil.

floating charge: a form of security for a debenture holder whereby the company grants security over all its assets; it stops 'floating' and attaches ('crystallises') itself to the assets of the company at the time of default.

FOB: free on board; a price quoted for goods by a seller which includes the cost of placing them on board ship. Risk and property pass to the buyer once the goods are on board so the buyer must be notified by the seller when this occurs so that he or she may insure the goods.

form: in the sense that it is used in contract law, those statutory procedural requirements that need to be satisfied for some contracts to be enforceable.

formal contract: a contract which is signed, sealed and delivered and which does not require consideration to be valid.

franchise: a contractual right given to a franchisee to sell goods or services under a franchisor's trademark or business name in a geographically defined area with no competition from the franchisor's other franchisees. The franchisee agrees to operate under a common trade name, format and procedure owned and controlled by the franchisor.

franchisee: the holder of a franchise.

franchisor: the person selling a franchise or the supplier of the goods or services.

fraud: an intentionally dishonest act or omission done with the design of gaining material advantage over another.

fraudulent transactions: a transaction at any time made with the intention to defeat or delay creditors and not for valuable consideration.

free from encumbrances: there is an implied warranty that the goods are free from any charge (mortgage) in favour of a third party who is unknown to the buyer.

frustration: the discharge of a contract rendered impossible of performance because of the operation of external factors beyond the contemplation of the parties.

future goods: goods 'to be manufactured or acquired by the seller after the making of the contract for sale'.

gift: the gratuitous (free) passing of property (ownership) in a thing from one person to another without consideration.

goods: all 'chattels personal, other than things in action and money'. These generally only include physical and moveable things (ownership) sold to the buyer for a money consideration called the price.

goodwill: an intangible asset of a business which represents the benefit or advantage a business has in its connection with its customers.

guarantee: a collateral promise to answer for the debt, default or miscarriage of another.

guarantor: a person who promises by guarantee to answer for the debt, default or miscarriage of another.

habeas corpus: a prerogative writ directed to a person who holds another in custody and commands them to produce or have the body of that person brought before the court, so that the propriety of the detention can be determined.

hire purchase: an agreement to hire coupled with an option to purchase, the buyer having possession, the seller or lender having property.

holder: the payee or endorsee of a bill or note who is in possession of it, or the bearer thereof (s. 4, *Bills of Exchange Act 1909* (Cth); s.3, *Cheques Act 1986* (Cth)). A holder includes the payee, the endorsee or bearer.

holder for value: a holder who has given value for a bill. A holder may also be deemed to be a holder for value when (a) they are a holder of a bill on which value has at some time been given; or (b) they are a holder who has a *lien* on the bill (s. 32, *Bills of Exchange Act 1909* (Cth); ss. 3, 35, *Cheques Act 1986* (Cth)).

holder in due course: a holder who takes a bill which is complete and regular on the face of it, before it is overdue and without notice of previous dishonour, in good faith and for value, without any notice in defect in the title of the transferor (s. 34, *Bills of Exchange Act 1909* (Cth); s. 50, *Cheques Act 1986* (Cth)).

ignorantia juris non excusat: ignorance of the law is no excuse.

imputation: meaning.

in camera: the hearing of a case in private; for example, in court (such as the Children's Court and the Family Court), the public being excluded.

inchoate instrument: a cheque signed in blank by the drawer, to be subsequently completed by another person.

indemnity: protection against loss, usually provided by way of contract of insurance.

independent contractor: a person employed under a contract for services who undertakes to produce a given result for an agreed price.

indictable offence: an offence that can be prosecuted on indictment. It is a more serious offence and generally tried by judge and jury.

indictment: a written document containing the charge against the defendant.

infant: a person under the age of 18 years and also known as a minor.

information: a pleading; the first stage in certain criminal and civil proceedings.

indorsement: a writing on the back of an instrument such as a bill of exchange, cheque, promissory note or bill of lading the name of the person who is the transferor, indicating their intention to transfer the right to payment.

injunction: a discretionary order or decree issued by a court in its equitable jurisdiction by which a party to an action is required to do, or refrain from doing, a particular thing. Injunctions are either restrictive (preventive) or mandatory (compulsory) and interlocutory (interim) or perpetual.

innominate term (also known as an intermediate term): a contractual term, the remedy for the breach of which depends on the seriousness of the breach rather than upon the classification of the term as a condition or a warranty.

insolvent: a person who is unable to pay their debts as and when they fall due out of debtor's own funds (this is a financial situation not legal status).

insurable interest: the pecuniary interest that the insured has in the subject matter of the insurance. It signifies the benefit the insured will gain from the preservation of the subject matter insured or the detriment they will suffer from its loss.

insurance: a contract whereby a person called the insurer agrees in consideration of money paid to them (the premium) by another person called the assured, to indemnify the latter against loss resulting on the occurrence of a specified event. It refers to terms based upon a risk or contingency.

insured: the person covered by an insurance policy.

insurer: the person who contracts, for a premium, to indemnify another against losses. Also called an assurer.

interstate: transactions or dealings between states and territories. Contrast with intra-state dealings

intra-state: transactions or dealings confined totally within the borders of a state or territory. Contrast with interstate.

in trade or commerce: conduct that is an aspect or element of activities or transactions which, of their nature, bear a trading or commercial character.

inventive step: closely associated with the concept of novelty in that it must be something new but need not be totally new. It can consist of taking a known invention and adapting it for a similar but nonetheless different use.

joint tenancy: the ownership of land held in common by several persons where on the death of one joint owner the land as a whole vests in the survivors, and can only be disposed of by will by the last survivor. For a joint tenancy to exist, the four unities of possession, interest, title and time must be present as well as the right of survivorship, or it will be a tenancy in common.

joint venture: two or more people entering into a one-off agreement for mutual profit.

judgement: the final order of a court entered upon the completion of an action.

jurisdiction: the power and authority conferred upon a court, either by statute or constitutionally.

jurisprudence: the science or theory of law.

jury: a body of sworn men and women summoned to decide questions of fact in a court of law.

'key requirements': specific disclosure requirements that must be complied with by the credit provider. Any contravention of the 'key requirements' by the credit provider may result in the court imposing a civil or criminal penalty (of up to $10 000) on the credit provider.

law merchant: that part of the common law relating to mercantile matters.

lay-by: a form of credit where property and possession remain with the seller or lender until the last instalment is paid.

lease: a contract granting exclusive possession of property to a person other than the owner for a certain period of time (referred to as the 'term') in return for payment of money (referred to as 'rent'). A lease is to be contrasted to a licence, which generally does not grant exclusive possession of the subject property and is determinable at any time by either party.

leasehold: land held under a lease for a number of years, known as chattels real.

legal tender: payment in a form which a creditor is obliged to accept. That is, notes for any amount, silver coins up to $5.

lessee: one to whom a lease is made.

lessor: one who grants a lease.

libel: defamation in some permanent form such as writing or film and actionable without proof of special damages.

licence: an authority or permission to do something which would otherwise be wrongful or illegal, for example, to go on to another's land, which would otherwise be a trespass.

licensee: one to whom a licence is given.

lien: the right to hold the property of another as security for the performance of an obligation, usually the payment of a debt.

limited partnership: a partnership in which there is at least one general partner with unlimited liability and one or more partners whose liability for debts and obligations of the partnership is limited.

linked credit provider: a credit provider who has an arrangement with a supplier of goods or services (i.e. a dealer (s. 117(1)).

liquidated damages: damages that must be paid, in the amount stipulated by a contract, in the event of a breach of the contract.

liquidator: the person appointed to carry out the winding up of a company.

lunatic: a person of unsound mind.

made: a literary, dramatic, musical or artistic work is considered to be made when the work is first reduced to writing or some other material form. The *Copyright Act 1968* (Cth) gives no protection to unpublished works not made.

mandamus: a prerogative writ which is an order from a superior court to an inferior court or administrative body that it shall act in the way that the law requires it.

market: all goods or services which compete with each other or which are generally substitutable for one another (s. 4E *Trade Practices Act 1974* (Cth)).

market overt: open market or recognised market. They are not recognised in either Queensland or New South Wales.

mens rea: guilty mind. The state of mind of a person required to do a particular crime and an essential ingredient in every criminal offence.

mercantile law: that branch of the law dealing with commercial transactions. It usually encompasses partnership, companies, agency, bills of exchange, sale of goods, insurance, carriers and bankruptcy.

merchantable quality: the goods/services must be of a quality which makes them fit for sale for their usual purpose.

minor: a person under the age of 18 years and also known as an infant.

misdemeanour: less serious crime and generally a summary offence.

misrepresentation: a false statement of fact, which may be intentionally or unintentionally made.

mitigation: the steps taken by the plaintiff to minimise his or her loss in contract or tort. The expression can also be used in criminal law by an accused where he or she produces facts to reduce the punishment they might be about to receive from the court for the offence they committed.

morals: concerned with the distinction between right and wrong.

mortgage: a contract transferring an interest in property as security for the repayment of a debt. On default, a mortgagee has recourse to the property and the right to re-take possession, sell the property and apply the proceeds against the debt.

mortgagee: the person to whom the property is mortgaged—the lender.

mortgagor: the person who mortgages his or her property as security for the debt—the borrower.

moveables: personal property, for example, goods.

negligence: a tort, actionable at the suit of a person suffering damage as the result of the defendant's breach of duty to take care to refrain from doing those acts which a reasonable person could reasonably foresee as being likely to injure them.

nemo dat quod non habet: no one can pass a better title to a person than the one they have.

***nemo dat* rule**: when a person acquires goods (e.g., a buyer), they get only the same rights to the goods as the person from whom they took them (e.g., a seller).

nominal damages: where the plaintiff's rights have been infringed, generally in contract or tort, but he or she has suffered no actual loss.

non est factum: it is not my deed. A defence in contract by a person who has signed a document that they should no longer be bound by its terms because they did not understand its terms.

noscitur a sociis: the meaning of a word can be gathered from the context.

not negotiable: on a cheque, the phrase 'not negotiable' does not affect transferability but means that no one can claim to have a better title to the cheque than the previous holder.

novation: a three-party agreement whereby a contract between two parties is rescinded and a new contract on the same terms is entered into between one of the parties and a third party.

nuisance: a tortious action encompassing both those actions that interfere with the enjoyment of a right that all members of the community are entitled to (public nuisance), and those actions that result in a wrongful disturbance or interference with a person's use or enjoyment of land (private nuisance).

obiter dictum: a saying by the way. An observation by a judge on a matter of law which is not essential to the decision before them, and which is therefore not part of the binding precedent established by the case.

objective test: would the words or conduct of the parties lead a reasonable person to believe, on the balance of probabilities, that legal relations were intended, i.e. they intended to create a contract?

offeree: the one to whom an offer is made.

offeror: the one who makes the offer.

Official Receiver: the person appointed for each bankruptcy district to act for and on behalf of the Official Trustee (s. 15).

Official Trustee in Bankruptcy: the person (a body corporate: s. 18(1)) in whom a bankrupt's property vests for administrative purposes.

option: a right of choice.

order cheque: an order to the drawee institution to pay the sum ordered to or to the order of a person/s specified in the cheque as payee and must be endorsed by the payee/s before it can be cashed or negotiated unless paid into the account of the payee/s.

ordinary damages: the amount awarded by the court on its assessment of the loss suffered by the plaintiff as a result of the breach.

organisational integrity: based on the self-regulation of an organisation in accordance with a formal set of guiding principles.

ostensible agency: an implied agency that exists when a supposed principal by their conduct induces another to believe that a third person is their agent, although the principal never actually employed the third person.

ostensible partner: a partner whose name is publicly made known (as distinguished from a silent partner).

ownership (also known as property): the right to exclusive enjoyment of property (real or personal) against all persons, including the right to possession and the right to any proceeds from its sale.

parol: oral, spoken.

***parol* evidence rule**: the rule of evidence which states that additional oral evidence is not considered by the courts to either contradict, vary, add to or subtract from its terms when a contract is complete on its face.

Part X (part 10) arrangement: arrangement where debtor agrees to have financial affairs controlled and thereby avoid bankruptcy under the *Bankruptcy Act 1966* (Cth).

partnership: the relationship which exists between persons carrying on a business in common with a view to profit.

passing off: arises where a person attempts to 'pass off' or pretend that their goods are those of another person. It is part of the law of torts.

patentable invention: an invention which is a manner of manufacture, novel and involving an inventive step; is useful and was not secretly used in Australia before the priority date, by or with the authority of the patentee or his or her predecessor in title.

pawn: a bailment of goods to a creditor as security for a debt; a pledge.

payee: the person to whom a bill of exchange or cheque is payable (s. 12, *Bills of Exchange Act 1909* (Cth); s. 19 *Cheques Act 1986* (Cth)).

paying financial institution: the financial institution upon which the cheque is drawn.

per annum: yearly.

per se: by itself.

personal loan: a loan where property and possession of the goods pass to the buyer at the time of entering into the agreement with the lender.

performance: doing what is required by a contract or condition.

personalty: personal property; all property other than realty and real property (i.e. land and anything fixed to it).

plaintiff: the party commencing a civil action in a court of first instance.

pledge: the transfer of possession (but not ownership) of goods as security for the payment of a debt.

pledgee: one to whom goods are pledged.

pledgor: the party delivering the goods in a pledge.

pluvius: characterised by or due to the action of rain, for example, insurance against rain.

possession: the right to occupy land, or control and use goods and should be contrasted with 'property' or 'ownership' in land or goods. The right to the lawful possession of property need not be held by the lawful owner of that property, but may be granted to another.

possession of goods: refers to the control or custody of goods, and should be contrasted with ownership.
possessory *lien*: the right to retain property as security for a debt.
postdate: to record a date later than the date of execution of the instrument.
power of attorney: an authority, usually under seal, whereby one person empowers another to act on their behalf for certain purposes.
preamble: that part of a statute set out in the beginning giving the reasons for the Act.
precedent (also known as *stare decisis*): a judgement or decision of a court of law cited as an authority for deciding a similar set of facts in later cases. Precedent may be binding if it is from a court in the same hierarchy and on a higher level. Persuasive precedents are non-binding on courts if they are outside their court hierarchy or from a court on a lower level.
preference: the payment of money or the transfer of property to one creditor in priority to other creditors.
premium: the price payable for a contract of insurance.
prerogative writs: writs issued from a superior court to an inferior court or administrative body for the purpose of preventing them from exceeding the limits of their authority, or compelling them to exercise their functions in accordance with the law. These writs include: (1) *habeas corpus*; (2) *certiorari*; (3) *prohibition*; (4) *mandamus*.
prima facie: on the face of it.
primary boycott: two or more parties combine by refusing to supply goods or services to another party or refuse to acquire that other party's goods or services.
principal: a sum of money put out at interest; or a person who authorises another to act on his behalf, the latter known as the agent.
privity: (of contract) only those who are a party to the contract are affected by it.
product: a thing that is manufactured or hand made or a component part of a complex product may be a product for the purposes of the *Designs Act* if it is made separately from the product.
prohibition: a writ issued out of a superior court to restrain an inferior court from exceeding its powers.
promisee: the one to whom a promise is made.
promisor: the one who makes a promise.
promissory note: an unconditional promise in writing made by one person to another, signed by the maker, engaging to pay on demand or at a fixed or determinable future time a sum certain in money to or to the order of a specified person or to bearer: *Bills of Exchange Act 1909* (Cth) s. 89.
promoters: the organisers of a company.
property in goods: means the same thing as 'ownership' or 'title'.
pro rata: proportionately.
proprietary company (also known as a private company): a company limited by shares, or unlimited by share capital, and with not more than 50 non-employee shareholders.
prospectus: a disclosure document setting out the nature and objects of an issue of shares or debentures created by a company and inviting the public to subscribe to (buy) them.
proxy: a person deputed to vote for another.
public company: a company which is able to invite the public to invest in its shares.
published: a literary, dramatic, musical or artistic work will be published only if copies of the work have been supplied to the public.
puisne: a judge of the High Court.
punitive damages (also known as 'exemplary' damages): see exemplary damages.
QC: Queen's Counsel.
quantum meruit: as much as a person has earned or as much as they deserve.
quasi-contract: a contract implied in law.
quasi-judicial: the exercise of a discretion and the making of a decision in a judicial manner, such as that made by an administrative tribunal.

quid pro quo: something for something.

quiet possession: the buyer shall have and enjoy quiet (or undisturbed) possession of the goods. This assumes that a third party will not come and claim to be the true owner or that they have a right in the goods after the sale has taken place.

quorum: the minimum number of persons that constitutes a valid formal meeting.

R: stands for **Rex** or **Reg**, depending on whether there was a King or Queen on the throne in England at the time the matter came to court and means that the Crown was a party to the case (often found in criminal law cases).

ratification: the act of adopting a transaction by a person who was not bound by it originally.

ratio decidendi: the reason for a decision and which makes binding precedent for the future.

real property: a general term for land and everything attached to it.

realty: real property.

receiver: a person appointed by a creditor or the court who enters into the possession of the property of a company in accordance with the powers granted by the creditors or the court.

registered trustee: usually a public or chartered accountant who is a representative of the creditors and in whom the bankrupt person's property vests, which the registered trustee will then administer in the creditors' interests (s. 156A, *Bankruptcy Act 1966* (Cth)).

related guarantee: a third party to a contract between a credit provider and a debtor who promises to pay the full amount of the debt should the debtor default; must be in writing and signed by the mortgagor (debtor) to be enforceable (s. 51, *Consumer Credit Code*).

related mortgage: a mortgage taken out by a credit provider to secure the debtor's obligations under a credit contract over goods and/or land which must be in writing and signed by the mortgagor (debtor) to be enforceable (s. 38, *Consumer Credit Code*).

relativism: provides that moral values are relative to a particular environment.

remoteness: the losses suffered by the plaintiff must be reasonably related to the contract or tort.

replaceable rules: basic rules relating to the internal management of a company (s. 135, *Corporations Act 2001* (Cth)).

representation: a statement of fact.

rescission: termination of a contract by one or both parties; to annul.

res ipsa loquitor: the thing speaks for itself. This maxim describes the legal position where the circumstances of an accident are such that there is little doubt that the accident would have happened only because of the defendant's negligence, and that in the absence of further evidence the defendant would be held liable.

rescind: cancel.

respondent: a person against whom an appeal is brought. They may be either the plaintiff or the defendant from when the case went to trial the first time.

restitutio in integrum: restoration to the original position. An equitable remedy available in rescinding a contract whereby the parties will be restored to the position they were in before they entered into the transaction.

restraint of trade: an agreement in which a party agrees to restrict or restrain their activities in the future to carry on their trade, profession or business with other persons who are not a party to the contract.

sale by description: where goods are sold by description, there is an implied condition that the goods will correspond with the description.

sale by sample: where the sale is by a sample of goods, the bulk of the goods must correspond with the sample.

sale of goods: where ownership (or property) transfers from the seller to the buyer at the time of the contract.

sans recours: without recourse. Where an agent signs a bill of exchange *sans recours* they are not personally liable on it.

SC: Senior Counsel; this term replaces that of Queen's Counsel and is a term given to a barrister of eminence in the profession.

secondary boycott: the parties impose the boycott against a third party (with whom they usually have no dispute) in order to stop the third party from dealing with a fourth party, the real target.

secured credit: a loan where the borrower puts up security.

set-off: a counter-claim.

sequestration order: order of the court whereby all of a person's assets are taken from them and given to the trustee in bankruptcy for the benefit of all of their creditors. Its effect is to make the debtor bankrupt.

shares: choses in action (intangible personal property) and the parts into which the capital of a company is divided.

simple contract: a contract that is not special and requires consideration to be valid unlike contracts which are described as 'formal' or 'under seal'.

slander: defamation of a non-permanent form such as words and gestures. It is actionable only on proof of special damage.

social agreements: ones made between friends or acquaintances.

spam (junk email): electronic messages, usually of a commercial nature, sent without the consent of the recipient.

specialty contract: a contract under seal.

specific goods: goods identified and agreed upon at the time of the contract of sale.

specific performance: an equitable remedy compelling a person to carry out their contractual obligations where damages would be an inadequate remedy for the breach of an agreement. It is not obtainable for contracts of personal service.

stale cheque: a cheque that has been in circulation more than 15 months from the date on the cheque (s. 3(5), *Cheques Act 1986* (Cth)).

stare decisis: to stand by that which has been decided. A case decision serves as a legal precedent in the deciding of a subsequent similar case.

statute: an Act of Parliament; a law passed by the legislature.

strict liability: liability without fault.

sub judice: under judicial consideration.

subrogation: the substitution of one person or thing for another so that the same rights and duties which were possessed by the original person are transferred to the substituted one. For example, an insurer is generally subrogated to the rights of the insured on paying their claim.

sui juris: having full legal capacity.

summary offence: less serious (or minor) offence where questions of law and fact are dealt with 'summarily' by a magistrate (no jury).

summons: an order to appear voluntarily at a certain court at a particular time and place to either give evidence, produce documents or answer a charge, in contrast to arrest.

surety: *see* guarantor.

survivorship: the right of a surviving tenant (or tenants) to take the share (or shares) of a tenant who dies.

tenancy at sufferance: an illegal staying on by a tenant after a lease has expired.

tenancy at will: the possession of land for an indefinite period of time that may be terminated at any time by either party without notice being given.

tenancy in common: a form of co-ownership where the ownership of property is by two or more persons who own distinct shares in the same piece of land but not necessarily with the other three unities of interest, title and time as exist in a joint tenancy. Unlike a joint tenancy, they can leave their interest to whomsoever they wish.

tenant: one who holds land.

tender: an unconditional offer by a party who is able to complete an obligation.

theft (or larceny): stealing (i.e. taking without the consent of the owner).

tied continuing credit contract: similar to a tied loan contract but involves a continuing credit contract under which a credit provider provides credit in respect of the payment by a debtor for goods or services supplied by a supplier in relation to whom the credit provider is linked (s. 117(2), *Consumer Credit Code*).

tied loan contract: a credit contract entered into with a debtor to pay for goods or services from a supplier where the credit provider is a linked credit provider to the supplier of the goods or services, for example a finance company providing credit to a retailer's customers (s. 117(3), *Consumer Credit Code*).

title (right to sell the goods): there is an implied condition that the seller has the right to sell the goods.

tort: a civil wrong (as opposed to a criminal wrong).

tort feasor: one who commits a tort.

tortious: wrongful.

trade mark: a sign used or intended to be used to distinguish goods or services dealt with or provided in the course of the trade by one person from goods or services so dealt with or provided by another person (s. 17, *Trade Marks Act 1995* (Cth)).

trespass: a tort involving the wrongful interference with the person or property of another and including: (a) trespass to the person—assault, battery and false imprisonment; (b) trespass to land; and (c) trespass to goods.

trust: an equitable obligation involving the holding of the title of property by a person (called the 'trustee') for the benefit of other persons (called 'beneficiaries').

trustee: a person holding a legal title or exercising a control over the disposition of property for the benefit of others.

typosquatting: purchasing a domain name that is a variation on a popular domain name with the expectation that the site will get traffic from the original site due to users misspelling the name.

uberrimae fidei: in the utmost good faith.

ultra vires: beyond legal power; an act in excess of the authority conferred by law, and therefore invalid.

unascertained goods: goods that are defined by description only. They are not identified when the contract is made and they may or may not be future goods.

unconscionable contract: an unfair or unjust contract.

underwriter: insurer.

undue influence: improper use of power.

unenforceable contract: a contract which is not valid because of a technical fault, for example, non-compliance with a statutory requirement which requires that the contract be in writing to be enforceable.

unilateral contract: a contract consisting of an exchange of an act for a promise.

unliquidated damages: damages for a loss, but whose value cannot be accurately determined or exactly calculated.

unsecured credit: a loan where no security is provided to the lender by the borrower.

utilitarianism: a form of consequentialism ethics, which holds that an act is right as long as it produces the greatest good for the greatest number.

vicarious liability: where the actions of one person render another person liable. For example, the actions of an employee in the course of their employment may make their employer tortiously liable.

virtue ethics: stresses the type of moral qualities that put us in a position to act morally.

virtues: personal qualities that provide the basis for an individual to lead a good and noble life.

vitiate: to make legally defective, to invalidate.

void: of no legal effect.

voidable: an agreement that may be affirmed or rejected at the option of one of the parties.

voidable preference: where debtor is insolvent and within six months prior to filing creditors' petition debtor gives a preference priority or advantage to a particular creditor.

volenti non fit injuria: voluntary assumption of the risk or that to which a person consents cannot be considered an injury. A tortious defence applicable to intentional acts that would otherwise be tortious, such as boxing and running the risk of accidental harm that would otherwise be actionable as negligence, such as watching car racing.

voluntary agreements: where the parties may volunteer their services.

waiver: renounce, disclaim or abandon a benefit or a remedy.

warrant: an official court document issued by a justice of the peace or judge directing a police officer to arrest a named person and present them to the court to face the charge/s set out in the warrant.

warranty: a guarantee or assurance. In the case of a sale of goods, a warranty is defined as collateral to the main purpose of such contract, the breach of which gives rise to a claim for damages, but not to a right to reject the goods and treat the contract as repudiated. Contrast with a **condition**.

winding up: the putting into liquidation of a company or partnership for the purpose of realising the assets and discharging the liabilities of the business.

witness: an individual who testifies under oath in a legal action.

writ: a document in the name of the Queen issued by a court or an officer of the Crown commanding the person to whom it is addressed to do or stop doing a particular act.

writ of *certiorari*: an order from an appellate court to a lower court requesting the record of a case that is to be reviewed by the appellate court.

INDEX

Index